Lecture Notes in Computer Science　10658

Commenced Publication in 1973
Founding and Former Series Editors:
Gerhard Goos, Juris Hartmanis, and Jan van Leeuwen

More information about this series at http://www.springer.com/series/7409

Guojun Wang · Mohammed Atiquzzaman
Zheng Yan · Kim-Kwang Raymond Choo (Eds.)

Security, Privacy, and Anonymity in Computation, Communication, and Storage

SpaCCS 2017 International Workshops
Guangzhou, China, December 12–15, 2017
Proceedings

 Springer

Editors
Guojun Wang
Guangzhou University
Guangzhou
China

Mohammed Atiquzzaman
Edith Kinney Gaylord Presidential Professor
University of Oklahoma
Norman, OK
USA

Zheng Yan ⓘ
Aalto University
Espoo
Finland

Kim-Kwang Raymond Choo
University of Texas at San Antonio
San Antonio, TX
USA

ISSN 0302-9743   ISSN 1611-3349   (electronic)
Lecture Notes in Computer Science
ISBN 978-3-319-72394-5   ISBN 978-3-319-72395-2   (eBook)
https://doi.org/10.1007/978-3-319-72395-2

Library of Congress Control Number: 2017961795

LNCS Sublibrary: SL3 – Information Systems and Applications, incl. Internet/Web, and HCI

Printed on acid-free paper

This Springer imprint is published by Springer Nature
The registered company is Springer International Publishing AG
The registered company address is: Gewerbestrasse 11, 6330 Cham, Switzerland

Preface

We would like to welcome you to the proceedings of the 10th International Conference on Security, Privacy, and Anonymity in Computation, Communication, and Storage (SpaCCS 2017), held in Guangzhou, China, during December 12–15, 2017. SpaCCS is jointly organized by Guangzhou University and Central South University.

SpaCCS 2017 and its associated symposiums and workshops provided a forum for international and national scholars to gather and share their research findings, ideas, and emerging trends in information security research. Previous SpaCCS conferences were successfully held in Zhangjiajie, China (2016), Helsinki, Finland (2015), Beijing, China (2014), Melbourne, Australia (2013), Liverpool, UK (2012), and Changsha, China (2011).

The workshop program this year consisted of 11 symposiums and workshops covering a broad range of research topics on security, privacy, and anonymity in computation, communication, and storage:

(1) The 9th IEEE International Symposium on UbiSafe Computing (UbiSafe 2017)
(2) The 9th IEEE International Workshop on Security in e-Science and e-Research (ISSR 2017)
(3) The 8th International Workshop on Trust, Security, and Privacy for Big Data (TrustData 2017)
(4) The 7th International Symposium on Trust, Security, and Privacy for Emerging Applications (TSP 2017)
(5) The 6th International Symposium on Security and Privacy on Internet of Things (SPIoT 2017)
(6) The 5th International Workshop on Network Optimization and Performance Evaluation (NOPE 2017)
(7) The Third International Symposium on Dependability in Sensor, Cloud, and Big Data Systems and Applications (DependSys 2017)
(8) The Third International Symposium on Sensor-Cloud Systems (SCS 2017)
(9) The Second International Workshop on Cloud Storage Service and Computing (WCSSC 2017)
(10) The First International Symposium on Multimedia Security and Digital Forensics (MSDF 2017)
(11) The 2017 International Symposium on Big Data and Machine Learning in Information Security, Privacy, and Anonymity (SPBD 2017)

The SpaCCS 2017 symposiums and workshops attracted 190 submissions from different countries and institutions around the globe. All submissions received at least three reviews by renowned experts, resulting in 75 papers selected for oral presentation at the conference (i.e., acceptance rate of 39.5%).

In addition to the technical presentations, the workshop program included 12 keynote speeches by world-renowned researchers. We are very grateful to the following keynote speakers for their time and willingness to share their expertise with the conference attendees: Prof. Geoffrey Charles Fox, Prof. Lajos Hanzo, Prof. Azzedine Boukerche, Prof. Jie Wu, Prof. Robert Deng, Prof. Ljiljana Trajkovic, Prof. Kin K. Leung, Prof. Vijay Varadharajan, Prof. Hai Jin, Prof. Jianhua Ma, Prof. Jinjun Chen, and Prof. Xiaofeng Chen. A big thank you to all of them!

This event would not have been possible without the contributions of many experts who volunteered and devoted their time and expertise to make this happen. We would like to thank the symposium and workshop organizers for their hard work in soliciting high-quality submissions, assembling the Program Committee, managing the peer-review process, and planning the symposium and workshop agenda. We would also like to acknowledge the strong support of the Organizing Committee of SpaCCS 2017, and in particular the Steering Committee chairs, Prof. Guojun Wang and Prof. Gregorio Martinez, the general chairs, Prof. Robert Deng, Prof. Yang Xiang, and Prof. Jose M. Alcaraz Calero, and the program chairs, Prof. Mohammed Atiquzzaman, Prof. Zheng Yan, and Dr. Kim-Kwang Raymond Choo. We would also like to thank the workshop chairs, Prof. Georgios Kambourakis, Prof. Ryan Ko, and Prof. Sancheng Peng; without their support and guidance, this event would not have been possible. We are also grateful to the experts who volunteered their time to act as reviewers and session chairs. Finally, we thank the contributing authors and attendees.

We hope you enjoy reading the proceedings of SpaCCS 2017!

December 2017

Guojun Wang
Mohammed Atiquzzaman
Zheng Yan
Kim-Kwang Raymond Choo

Sponsors

Contents

The 6th International Symposium on Security and Privacy on Internet of Things (SPIoT 2017)

The 5th International Workshop on Network Optimization and Performance Evaluation (NOPE 2017)

The 3rd International Symposium on Dependability in Sensor, Cloud, and Big Data Systems and Applications (DependSys 2017)

**The 3rd International Symposium on Sensor-Cloud
Systems (SCS 2017)**

**The 2nd International Workshop on Cloud Storage Service
and Computing (WCSSC 2017)**

**The First International Symposium on Multimedia Security
and Digital Forensics (MSDF 2017)**

**The 2017 International Symposium on Big Data and Machine
Learning in Information Security, Privacy and Anonymity (SPBD 2017)**

The 9th IEEE International Symposium on UbiSafe Computing (UbiSafe 2017)

UbiSafe 2017 Organizing and Program Committees

1 General Chairs

Shuhong Chen	Guangzhou University, China
Xiaoyong Li	Beijing University of Posts and Telecommunications, China

2 Program Chairs

David W. Chadwick	University of Kent, UK
Xiaodong Lin	University of Ontario Institute of Technology, Canada
Aniello Castiglione	Salerno and University of Naples, Italy

3 Program Committee

Flora Amato	University of Naples, Italy
Arcangelo Castiglione	University of Salerno, Italy
Ruinan Chang	Qualcomm, USA
Francesco Colace	University of Salerno, Italy
Tianchuan Du	University of Delaware, USA
Pietro Ducange	eCampus University, Italy
Zhe Liu	University of Luxembourg, Luxembourg
Vincenzo Moscato	University of Naples, Italy
Peter Mueller	IBM Zurich Research Laboratory, Switzerland
Xilong Qu	Hunan University of Finance and Economics, China
Qi Wang	Google Inc., USA
Lijun Xia	Google Inc., USA

4 Steering Committee

Vipin Chaudhary	University at Buffalo, SUNY, USA
Jingde Cheng	Saitama University, Japan
Yuanshun Dai	University of Tennessee, USA
Thomas Grill	Johannes Kepler University Linz, Austria
Runhe Huang	Hosei University, Japan
Qun Jin	Waseda University, Japan
Ismail Khalil	Johannes Kepler University Linz, Austria

Xiaolin (Andy) Li	University of Florida, USA
Jianhua Ma	Hosei University, Japan
Guojun Wang	Guangzhou University, China
Laurence T. Yang	St. Francis Xavier University, Canada
Qiangfu Zhao	The University of Aizu, Japan

5 Publicity Chairs

| Joseph Liu | Monash University, Australia |
| Wei Chen | Interdigital Communications Inc., USA |

6 Web Chair

| Xi Wen | Central South University, China |

MTIV: A Trustworthiness Determination Approach for Threat Intelligence

Lei Li$^{(\boxtimes)}$, Xiaoyong Li, and Yali Gao

Key Laboratory of Trustworthy Distributed Computing
and Service of the Ministry of Education,
Beijing University of Posts and Telecommunications, Beijing 100876, China
lilei9341@gmail.com, lxyxjtu@163.com,
gaoyalibupt@163.com

Abstract. With the gradually sharing of threat intelligences, users concern more about their trustworthiness, which is difficult to be judged. Some threat intelligence sharing platforms choose to show the risk or credibility, and inform users the trustworthiness of the threat intelligence. Several researchers have proposed the requirements and techniques for threat intelligence trust assessment. However, they do not present any tool-based or model solutions. In this paper, we present a Trustworthiness Determination Approach for Threat Intelligence (MTIV) to make up these shortcomings. First, we propose a framework to excavate threat intelligence via multiple sharing platforms, and extract multidimensional trustful features of the threat intelligence. Based on these, contributions of dimensional trustful features to the trustworthiness determination can be derived. Then we introduce Deep Belief Network (DBN) to determine the trustworthiness of the threat intelligence. The experimental results verify that MTIV is more effective than traditional methods. Our work will be of benefit to build a more credible threat intelligence sharing platform, and enhance the capability of real-time detection and resisting the cyberspace attacks.

Keywords: Threat intelligence · Multiple dimension · Similarity
Deep Belief Network · Trustworthiness

1 Introduction

The sharing of intelligences regarding threats, vulnerabilities and incidents is very useful for organizations to protect against today's sophisticated cyberattacks [6, 10, 13]. Numerous sharing platforms like IBM X-Force and ThreatBook are exchanging threat intelligence. However, a lot of false, faulty and inaccurate threat intelligence may exist on these platforms. Threat sources are the main ways to obtain threat intelligence because of its relative safety and flexibility, but, due to the uncertainty and complexity of the threat environment, the trustworthiness of the threat intelligence is still unknown.

At present, it is very important for stakeholder group and end user of sharing platform to be informed the trustworthiness of the threat intelligence. Several researchers have proposed various trust evaluation techniques, including credibility requirements [10], quality dimension management [11]. However, there is still few research reports on tool-based or directly applicable solutions. Moreover, it is not feasible to apply the most existing trust methods in social media and web information directly to threat intelligence.

© Springer International Publishing AG 2017
G. Wang et al. (Eds.): SpaCCS 2017 Workshops, LNCS 10658, pp. 5–14, 2017.
https://doi.org/10.1007/978-3-319-72395-2_1

In this paper, our goal is to reveal the trustworthiness of real multi-platform threat intelligence through a relievable and applicable solution. Initially, the end users from sharing platform met suspicious threat intelligence sometimes and wanted to find its truthfulness on cyber space. There was no doubt that this was a complex and pain-staking process. Users needed to judge the description, check their consistency, aggregate relevant domain-knowledge to confirm their credibility and then made a final decision about any suspicion. Afterward, threat intelligences in multiple sharing platform were diverse and lacked of general standard and format, even though several efforts had been made to facilitate threat intelligence sharing in a standardized manner, like STIX [12]. So it is difficult to conduct a cross-platform trusting analysis of a threat intelligence.

To solve these problems above, we propose a generic research framework to definite and excavate the threat intelligence. In the framework, we first define a threat intelligence based on bag of words. Second, we recommend that the trustful features should be extracted from multiple dimension for identifying the threat intelligence, including timeliness, domain knowledge, and content verification. Considering the relationship between features, it is common to further extract more valuable features. And we believe there are latent high-level features that can tell us if threat intelligence is trustworthy [9]. Unfortunately, because of information loss, it is difficult to get accurate results through traditional feature-extraction methods, such as clustering. To solve this problem, we introduce a new approach based on deep learning. It extracts the high-level features of threat intelligence through DBN's unsupervised greedy layer-by-layer training, and combines with traditional information classification and credibility measurement technology to determine the trustworthiness.

The contributions and rest of this paper is organized as follows. Section 2 presents the preliminary concepts and the research framework. Section 3 describes how to determine the trustworthiness of a threat intelligence using MTIV. Experiments and analysis, which are shown in Sect. 4, show MTIV's effective and high accuracy. Finally, we summarize our conclusions in Sect. 5.

2 Preliminary and Research Framework

Before more detailed discussions about trustworthiness assessment, we need to explain what threat intelligence in our study is and how it is represented and modeled.

2.1 Threat Intelligence

In recent years, Threat Intelligence has become one of the most mentioned words in the information security community [15]. According to the Gartner definition [16], threat intelligence is evidence-based knowledge, including context, mechanisms, indicators, implications and actionable advice. Unlike threat information, it must be valuable information of advanced analysis and assisting in making decisions. The pyramid of threat intelligence [14], which is shown in Fig. 1, has a specific exposition of threat intelligence. It includes hash value, IP address, domain names, network/host artifacts, tools, and TTPs. The higher, the more valuable it is, but the more difficult to get, even for suppliers.

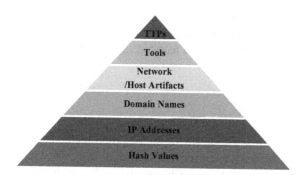

Fig. 1. The pyramid of threat intelligence.

In our research, threat intelligence is the basic threat information, which is recognized by main public sharing platform, like IBM, Cymon, Virustotal. It is a clue to network attack that is analyzed and discovered at a time. Generally, it can be described as a specific threat of an object or a situation, such as fishing URL, malware hash and botnet command IP. Furthermore, it is presented in a machine-readable formation on each sharing platform. Therefore, we represent each threat intelligence in a simple manner with the three atomic attributes listed below. In particular, 'description' is defined as bag of words which characteristically describe a threat intelligence.

Threat Intelligence = (source, time, description)

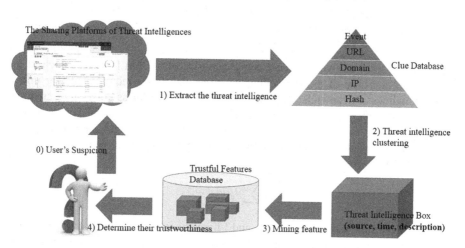

Fig. 2. The research framework: mining the multi-dimensional features, constructing trustful feature database and building trustworthiness evaluation model based on DBN.

2.2 Research Framework

Based on the formal representation, each threat intelligence is distilled and utilized by the processes in Fig. 2; (1) extracting the threat intelligence from online sharing platform, (2) clustering the threat clue by the pyramid, (3) mining and summarizing multi-dimensional trustful features, (4) evaluating the trustworthiness of each threat intelligence based on DBN and trustful features, (5) informing users the trustworthiness of threat intelligence.

3   Proposed Solution

In this section, we present the details of the proposed method, which has two steps. First, we extract multidimensional trustful features to describe a trustful threat intelligence. And the second step is to train DBN model so that the high-level latent features from multi-dimensional features can be captured, and we use the trained model to determine the trustworthiness of threat intelligence.

3.1   Multi-dimension Trustful Features

Lucassen thought user characteristic can motivate users to understand the characteristics of information itself and thus influence trust evaluation [4]. The credibility was divided into two categories: user characteristics and information characteristics. There were also several specific features in each category. For example, the user character included domain knowledge, information skills and experience. The character of information included semantic features, surface features and other features. Fundamentally, the trustworthiness of threat intelligence was the credibility problem of information quality [13]. So, combining the findings from reference [1, 4, 5, 13], we propose that trust of threat intelligence is mainly reflected in three areas, including the timeliness, domain knowledge, verifiable content.

Time Dimension Features. Table 1 shows the time-dimension features, which identify whether the time of threat intelligence meets the user's requirements for information timeliness. Meanwhile, they also correspond to timeliness criterion of credible evaluation. And they are described as follows: (1) T_p is the latest time of the threat intelligence, (2) T_f is the earliest published time, (3) I_{latest} is the time interval of T_p and it previous time, (4) F is the update frequency of n-times historical intelligence, which are calculated as:

$$F = \sum I_{ij} \Big/ (n-1) \tag{1}$$

where I_{ij} is the time interval of i-times and j-times historical intelligence, (5) D is the defense level of intelligence in response to network attack according to the interval of T_p and current time. And its value (1, 0.8, 0.6, 0.4, 0.2, 0) do correspond to the level (day, week, month, half year, one year, 2 years or more).

Domain-Knowledge Dimension Features. Untrustworthy threat intelligences often provide incomplete or irrelevant knowledge to confuse or even mislead users. In the Table 1, the domain-knowledge features are the evidences to determine whether the threat intelligences are complete and comprehensive. Then, they are calculated by the accumulation of the evidences, which include malware, DNS, IP, URL, and WHOIS.

Table 1. Multi-dimension trustful features: Time-based, Domain-based and Content-based.

Dimension	Feature	Symbol
Time-based	Published time	T_p
	First published time	T_f
	Latest update time interval	I_{latest}
	Update frequency	F
	Defense level	D
Domain-based	Number of malwares	N_{mal}
	Number of threat IPs	N_{ip}
	Number of threat DNSs	N_{dns}
	Number of threat URLs	N_{url}
	Length of WHOIS	L_{whois}
	Total length of domain knowledge	L_{domain}
Content-based	Authority of the threat feed	A_{auth}
	Number of the intelligence history	$N_{history}$
	Number of verifiable sources	N_{source}
	Rate of support sources	$R_{support}$
	Attitude of multiple source	A_{atti}

Content Dimension Features. The features of content dimension are used to identify whether there is a false behavior about the content of the threat intelligence. We consider extracting them by two ways: (1) verification of the source itself, (2) content consistency of multiple threat sources. So they are described as follows: (1) A_{auth} is the authority of the threat feed, its value (0, 0.2, 0.4, 0.6, 0.8, 1) is given respectively by (unknown, open, $r > 10^6$, $r \in [10^5, 10^6]$, organization, $r < 10^5$), where r is the Alex rank of threat feed; (2) $N_{history}$ and N_{source} are cumulative values of the intelligence history and verifiable sources respectively; (3) Given a target threat intelligence v_t and the verified intelligences $V = \{v_1, v_2, \ldots, v_i, \ldots, v_m\}$, we propose measuring the similarity of two threat intelligence v_t and v_i considering the different properties of each factor as follows:

$$S(v_t, v_i) = \theta_1 \times S_{time} + \theta_2 \times S_{source} + (1 - \theta_1 - \theta_2) \times S_{desc} \qquad (2)$$

$$S_{time} = 2|vt_t \cap vt_i| / (vt_t + vt_i) \qquad (3)$$

$$S_{desc} = vd_t \bullet vd_i / (\|vd_t\| \times \|vd_i\|) \qquad (4)$$

In the Eq. 2, the weights are currently ad-hoc values and will vary with the real scenarios put forward in our work. We compute the overlap rate to estimate the similarity S_{time} between two vt-time periods in the Eq. 3. Also, S_{source} is the ratio of v_t and v_i authority. Besides, in the Eq. 4, the similarity between two threat intelligences in the vd-description is compared by using the vector space model [7], which is usually employed to assess words similarity. We use R_{pos}, R_{neg} to denote the collections of positive, and negative verified intelligence respectively. With the help of κ, we get R_{pos} and R_{neg}. If $S(v_t, v_i) \geq \kappa$, $v_i \in R_{pos}$; if $S(v_t, v_i) < \kappa$, $v_i \in R_{neg}$. The optimal value of κ is evaluated by experiments. Then $R_{support} = \sum R_{pos}/m$, and if $\sum R_{pos} \geq \sum R_{neg}$, $A_{atti} = 1$; If not, $A_{atti} = 0$.

3.2   Trustworthiness Determination Method

As we discussed in Sect. 1, there are many possible high-level latent features of threat intelligence. Then, given a trust feature matrix X, how to represent the latent high-level feature underlying is our first problem. A common method to represent latent high-level features is using clustering techniques [3, 8]. But one limitation of clustering is that it usually forms a coarse-grained representation of potential features. To have a finer representation of more abstract and highly separable latent features for a threat intelligence, we propose to use Restricted Boltzmann Machine (RBM). The advantage of RBM is that it can discover a richer representation of the input data than clustering techniques.

Restricted Boltzmann Machine (RBM). RBM is a bipartite graph model, in which nodes of layer are independent and the joint probability distribution of the inter-node nodes satisfies the Boltzmann distribution. As shown in Fig. 3(a), the visible unit v in lower layer denote the observed data and the hidden unit h in upper layer denote the latent features description. There are symmetrically weighted connections W between each visible unit and each hidden unit. Inspired by the energy functional in statistics, RBM model introduces the energy function, which is calculated as:

$$E(v,h) = - \sum_{i \in visible} b_i v_i - \sum_{j \in hidden} a_j h_j - \sum_{i,j} v_i h_j w_{ij} \tag{5}$$

where a_i, b_j are biases for hidden and visible units and w_{ij} is the weight between them. The purpose of RBM is to find a configuration of (v; h) so that the energy function achieves its lowest level. Based on the partition function Z of RBM, namely $Z = \sum_{v,h} e^{-E(v,h)}$. The probability distribution of RBM is as follows:

$$p(v,h) = \frac{1}{Z} e^{-E(v,h)} \tag{6}$$

The individual activation probabilities of a hidden and a visible unit are given by

$$p(h_j = 1|v) = \delta(b_j + \sum_i v_i w_{ij}) \tag{7}$$

$$p(h_i = 1|v) = \delta(a_i + \sum_j v_i w_{ij}) \tag{8}$$

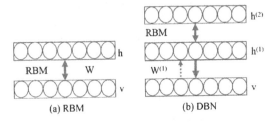

Fig. 3. A Restricted Boltzmann Machine and a 2-layer Deep Belief Network.

where δ denotes the logistic sigmoid function. For RBM, exact maximum likelihood learning is intractable. In practice, efficient learning is performed by using Contrastive Divergence (CD) [1].

```
DBN-based algorithm for multi-dimension trustful features
Input: train sample X₀, learning rate ε
Output: weight matrices of W, biases of a, b
Begin
1 Compute trusted feature vector X′ for each sample
2 randomly initialize v₀=x′₀; W, a, b
3 repeat
4    repeat
5    for all hidden units j and all visible unit i do
6       Compute P(h₀ⱼ=1|v₀)using Eq.8;Sample h₀ⱼ from P(h₀ⱼ|v₀)
7       Compute P(v₁ᵢ=1|h₀)using Eq.7;Sample v₁ᵢ from P(v₁ᵢ|h₀)
8       Compute P(h₁ⱼ=1|v₁)using Eq.8;Sample h₁ⱼ from P(h₁ⱼ|v₁)
9    W=W+ε(p(h₀=1|v₀)v₀ᵀ-p(h₁=1|v₁)v₁ᵀ)
10   a=a+ε(v₀-v₁); b=b+ε(p(h₀=1|v₀)-p(h₁=1|v₁))
11   until all parameters are converged; return W, a, b
End
```

Trustful-features-and-DBN-Based Determination Method. DBN is a neural network composed of multi-layer RBM in Fig. 3(b). It can be seen as a discriminate model. And its training process is using a greedy unsupervised pre-training by layer-by-layer to obtain weights. The training of DBN for multi-dimension trustful features is shown in Algorithm Program, where lines 6 to 10 prepares ingredients for CD [2]. Specifically, line 1 to 11 compute the activation probability of hidden units based on trustful features.

After the pre-training of DBN, the network parameters are trained to a set of appropriate initial values. Starting from this set, we can make the cost function reach a lower value [2]. According to the reconstruction error, we use the BP algorithm to make model converges to the local optimal point and the softmax classifier using for the top layer. Next, we put the test samples into the DBN model to get the Table 1's features of test samples, then enter the classifier previously trained, and get the results finally. The trustworthiness-determination process based on DBN is shown in Fig. 4.

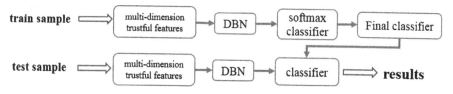

Fig. 4. The process of trustworthiness determination based on trust features and DBN.

4 Experiment Evaluation

4.1 Datasets

We simulate our methods on multiple sharing platforms of threat intelligence, which include ThreatBook, Cymon, Virustotal and IBM X-Force. According to the above framework and the website "SecRepo.com", we generate the dataset for our experiments, which is composed of 200 trustful threat intelligence and 200 untruthful ones. For each one, we collect its three atomic attributes as threat intelligence by platforms' API and web page parsing. 11 experienced users, who are security experts and graduate students, help to mark the threat intelligence.

4.2 Performance Evaluation

Performance Measures. To judge the performance of proposed method, several performance measures are proposed. Depending on the confusion matrix, which consists of true positive (TP), false negative (FN), false positive (FP), and true negative (TN), the measures are defined. Accuracy is the percentage of correctly identified fake and true threat intelligences (Eq. 9). Precision is the fraction of fake intelligences predictions that are correct (Eq. 10). Recall examines the fraction of fake intelligences being recognized (Eq. 11). F-score is the harmonic mean of precision and recall (Eq. 12).

$$Accuracy = (TP + FN)/(TP + FP + FN + TN) \tag{9}$$

$$Precision = TP/(TP + FP) \tag{10}$$

$$Recall = TP/(TP + TN) \tag{11}$$

$$F - score = 2 \times Precision \times Recall/(Precison + Recall) \tag{12}$$

Results Comparison. By the DBN model shown in Fig. 4, the accuracy of the results of two datasets is shown in Table 2. Among them, the less one is from IBM X-force and the more one is mainly from ThreatBook and Cymon. From the comparison results, the more training data they have, the more valuable information hidden in the threat intelligence the DBN-based model can dig. We tested the best results in 5-fold cross dataset, and the accuracy can reach up to 91.76%.

To test the classification performance of DBN-based networks, we also use KNN classifier, SVM and traditional BP neural network to do following experiments on the same dataset: (1) DBN is the 4-layer neural network of nodes is 1000-250-100-4, (2) BP neural network is a 3-layer neural network with nodes of 1000-250-4,

Table 2. Accuracy rate on two datasets.

Dataset	5-fold cross	Non-5-fold cross
100	85.29 ± 0.7	82.35 ± 0.4
300	**91.76 ± 1.0**	**88.24 ± 0.9**

(3) Both KNN and SVM use python's scikit-learn package. In the experiments, all these methods are tuned to choose best parameters, and a 5-fold cross validation is used. From the Table 3, the solution based on DBN and trustful features is superior to traditional shallow-network classifier in accuracy, precision, recall and F-score.

Table 3. Classification expreriments results.

Algorithm	Accuracy	Precision	Recall	F-score
KNN	82.05%	84.31%	76.99%	80.37%
BP	85.89%	93.75%	76.92%	84.51%
SVM	88.24%	88.89%	84.21%	86.49%
DBN	**92.31%**	**97.96%**	**85.71%**	**91.43%**

Furthermore, we experiment with the depth of DBN-based model. As is shown in Fig. 5, taking the dataset of non-5 fold cross as an example, the accuracy is gradually increasing after tier 1 to 4 layers. At these time the depth is useful. And the fifth layer has not increased significantly, which indicates that the depth of 4 is enough.

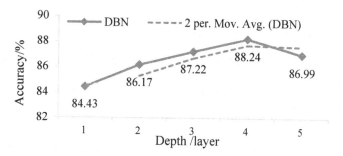

Fig. 5. Each layer performance of the proposed method.

To sum up, the essence of the DBN learning model is to build a machine learning model with a certain depth, to learn more valuable latent features, so as to improve the accuracy of the problem. At the same time, the complex original features of threat intelligence can effectively enhance the accuracy of the proposed method.

5   Conclusion

In this paper, we propose a new method MTIV to determine the trustworthiness of sharing threat intelligence. The results of experiments show that MTIV is effective and can be used for multiple open-sharing platforms. What's more, our work is beneficial to the sharing of trusted threat intelligence, which will strengthen the security of existing defense system indirectly. For the future work, we plan to take more dimensions into consideration, such as the feedback of users. Furthermore, we will develop a system to find trustful threat intelligences from multiple sharing platform and verify their trustworthiness based on the proposed MTIV method.

Acknowledgements. This work is supported by the National Key Research and Development Program of China (No. 2016QY03D0605), the National Nature Science Foundation of China (Nos. 61672111, 61370069), and Beijing Natural Science Foundation (No. 4162043).

References

1. Hinton, G.E.: Training products of experts by minimizing contrastive divergence. Neural Comput. **14**, 1771–1800 (2002)
2. Hinton, G.E., Salakhutdinov, R.R.: Reducing the dimensionality of data with neural networks. Science **313**(5786), 504–507 (2006)
3. Su, X., Khoshgoftaar, T.M.: A survey of collaborative filtering techniques. Adv. Artif. Intell. Article ID 421425, p. 19 (2009)
4. Lucassen, T., Muilwijk, R.: Topic familiarity and information skills in online credibility evaluation. J. Assoc. Inf. Sci. Technol. **64**(2), 254–264 (2013)
5. Ginsca, A.L., Popescu, A., Lupu, M.: Credibility in information retrieval. Found. Trends® Inf. Retr. **9**(5), 355–475 (2015)
6. Skopik, F., Settanni, G., Fiedler, R.: A problem shared is a problem halved: a survey on the dimensions of collective cyber defense through security information sharing. Comput. Secur. **60**, 154–176 (2016)
7. Gabrilovich, E., Markovitch, S.: Computing semantic relatedness using Wikipedia-based explicit semantic analysis. Morgan Kaufmann, San Francisco (2007)
8. Liu, J., Wang, C., Gao, J., Han, J.: Multi-view clustering via joint nonnegative matrix factorization. In: Proceedings of The 2013 SIAM International Conference on Data Mining. Society for Industrial and Applied Mathematics, pp. 252–260 (2013)
9. Ge, L., Gao, J., Li, X., Zhang, A.: Multi-source deep learning for information trustworthiness estimation. In: Proceedings of The 19th ACM SIGKDD International Conference on Knowledge Discovery and Data Mining (KDD 2013), pp. 766–774. ACM, New York (2013)
10. Dandurand, L., Serrano, O.S.: Towards improved cyber security information sharing. In: Proceedings of The 5th International Conference on Cyber Conflict, pp. 1–16, Tallinn (2013)
11. Umbrich, J., Neumaier, S., Polleres, A.: Quality assessment and evolution of open data portals. In: Proceedings of The 3rd International Conference on Future Internet of Things and Cloud, pp. 404–411 (2015)
12. Brown, S., Gommers, J., Serrano, O.: From cyber security information sharing to threat management. In: Proceedings of The 2nd ACM Work-shop on WISCS 2015, pp. 43–49. ACM, New York (2015)
13. Sillaber, C., Sauerwein, C., Mussmann, A., Breu, R.: Data quality challenges and future research directions in threat intelligence sharing practice. In: The ACM Proceedings on Workshop on Information Sharing and Collaborative Security, pp. 65–70. ACM, New York (2016)
14. Bianco, D.: The Pyramid of Pain. http://detect-respond.blogspot.jp/2013/03/the-pyramid-of-pain.html
15. Poision Ivy: Assessing Dam age and Extracting Intelligence. https://www.fireeye.com/content/dam/fireeye-www/global/en/current-threats/pdfs/rpt-poison-ivy.pdf
16. Definition: Threat Intelligence. https://www.gartner.com/doc/2487216/definition-threat-intelligence

Distributed Caching Based Memory Optimizing Technology for Stream Data of IoV

Xiaoli Hu[1], Chao Li[2], Huibing Zhang[1(✉)], Hongbo Zhang[1], and Ya Zhou[1]

[1] Guangxi Key Laboratory of Trusted Software,
Guilin University of Electronic Technology, Guilin 541004, China
352131667@qq.com
[2] Institute of Information Engineering, Chinese Academy of Sciences,
Beijing 100093, China

Abstract. With the expansion of the Internet of Vehicle's system size, traditional storage architecture has encountered performance bottleneck in terms of throughput and scalability. To address these issues, the essay builds a distributed caching system by using cache node, major node and query interface. To implement storage logic, vehicular terminal dynamically sends data, and the distributed business process of stream data is achieved by using cache system and compressed function in protocol server. Protocol server also assists database server in compression storage. Data from our IoV platform is adopted for testing, and experimental results show that memory optimizing system effectively improves throughput and scalability.

Keywords: IoV · Distributed storage · Cache · Throughput · Stream data

1 Introduction

Nowadays, the number of online vehicle in Internet of Vehicle (IoV) is soaring. Especially, with the rapid development of new energy vehicle, it is necessary to conduct real-time monitoring on all condition of vehicles. This requires collecting and sending over 200 status information to the database periodically, which regards the basic state, motor system, etc. The monitoring data has periodicity, large volume, and spatio-temporal correlation characteristics, which leads to some issues during the uploading and storage operations:

(a). Throughput bottleneck: For one vehicle, it takes about 3 s to collect and upload status data to the database. So if there are 100 thousand vehicles online at the meantime, 100 thousand status data must be written to database within 3 s. Otherwise, all the data would be out of memory, which would further lead to the denial of service of database server. To conclude, intensive disk writing makes throughput a possible bottleneck.

(b). Scalability issue: Since the number of vehicles in IoV is increasing, it requires the storage system dynamic scalability to cope with the increasing number of vehicles.

G. Wang et al. (Eds.): SpaCCS 2017 Workshops, LNCS 10658, pp. 15–24, 2017.
https://doi.org/10.1007/978-3-319-72395-2_2

Therefore, this essay puts forward a specific distributed caching system according to IoV's data characteristics, which effectively helps relieve I/O pressure, improves throughput and scalability by caching continuous streaming data into memory, and then compresses and writes data into disk database with a relatively lower speed.

2 Related Works

2.1 Distributed Caching Technology

Scholars have had deep insights into distributed caching technology. [1] designed a high-performance cache system based on memcached. [2] achieved a distributed storage middleware system, exHDFS, based on Hadoop. [3] proposed an encryption storage approach based on lightweight distributed caching. [4] proposed message-oriented middleware storage model based on distributed caching. To improve the performance of distributed caching, [5] designed a clustering distributed caching based on open-source framework ZooKeeper. [6] proposed HSDRA based on Elastic Distributed Scalability Approach, which can be applied into heterogeneous environment.

Meanwhile, various memory databases including Aerospike, Couchbase, Ehcache, GigaSpace, Hazelcast, Memcached, Redis have gotten better results in practical application [7–13], as shown in Table 1. However, all these databases are designed for all-purpose application scenarios, so they can't address the specific issues of IoV's data storage.

Table 1. Comparison of memory database

Memory database	Application of optimization	Support expansion or not	Intersection with internet of vehicle
Aerospike	Optimization aimed at flash storage medium	No	None
Couchbase	Optimization aimed at highly interactive application	No	Protocol server is interactive with vehicle terminal
Ehcache	Optimization aimed at Java storage improvement	Yes	None
GigaSpaces	Analytical application platform	Yes	Analysis of vehicle breakdown
Hazelcast	Distributed framework of JVM memory sharing	Yes	None
Memcached	Optimization aimed at web	Yes	Optimization of web server access
Redis	general key-value memory database	Yes	Provision of spatial indexes

2.2   Architecture of Traditional IoV

In recent years, several IoV real-time monitor platforms based on CAN bus have been applied in China, including Jinlong automobile G-BOS platform, Yutong coach and commercial vehicle platform, Shanxi Automobile internet of vehicle platform, ACTIA cloud platform and commercial vehicle platform. The structure of these platforms is shown in Fig. 1.

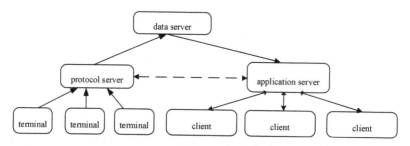

Fig. 1. Storage architecture of traditional internet of vehicle

Data is collected by vehicle terminal and sent to protocol server, and then it is sent to database server for storage after processed by protocol server. Clients send query requests to application server, which then queries database and sends related results back to clients. In addition, application server can send instruction to terminal via protocol server. Under the architecture, the pressure of protocol server and database server will go up with the increase of vehicles, which will eventually lead to throughput bottleneck and scalability issues.

3   Distributed Caching Based Architecture of IoV

To improve system's throughput and scalability, and to adapt to the rapid development of IoV, the paper introduces multiple modules into traditional structure, which includes cache node, major node, query interface, etc., as shown in Fig. 2.

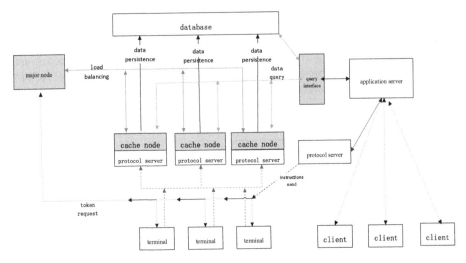

Fig. 2. Distributed caching based architecture of IoV

3.1   Optimization of Vehicular Terminal

Vehicular terminal essentially is an embedded system which contains processor and memory. The communication between vehicular terminal and protocol server follows 794 satellite data transmission format and protocol specification, and it is transmitted through GPRS/3G/4G standard network. The terminal has abundant free time and resource, so it is possible to deploy a 'distributed data transfer SDK' in the terminal, which will deal with the distributed logic, as shown in Fig. 3.

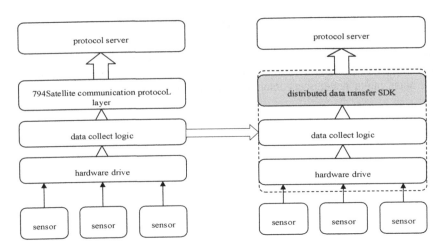

Fig. 3. Adding distributed data transfer SDK to vehicular terminal

Distributed data transfer SDK is responsible for integrating 794 satellite communication protocol and distributed data transfer logic, namely: for data collect module,
distributed data transfer SDK still plays the role of 794 satellite communication protocol layer; for protocol server, SDK needs to transfer static send mode to dynamic
send mode. This means vehicular terminal will send data packet to different protocol
servers rather than to a fixed one in the past.

3.2 Optimization of Protocol Server

Traditionally, protocol server receives protocol packet or gives response through terminal interface, and stores data to database server through database interface. Figure 4b
shows the architecture of protocol server after adding the function of distributed
caching, which contains 4 modules: cache node SDK (distributed data transfer SDK),
protocol server, caching system, and send interface of compressed data.

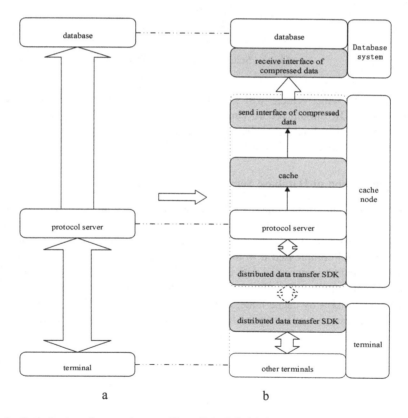

Fig. 4. Optimization of protocol server (**Note**: T the left side is the traditional data flow diagram,
and the right shadow part is the newly introduced function modules. The dashed arrow indicates
the short connection.)

Optimized cache node SDK works together with terminal SDK to complete distribute storage logic. It extracts protocol fields for distributed logic from received data package, and sends primitive 794 protocol package to protocol server. Especially, some 794 protocol package is context dependent: when terminal communicates with protocol server, the meaning of protocol package and whether it is effective depend on other packages. The dependence between different packages reflects the relationship of protocol server and terminal status. The state transition of terminal is shown in Fig. 5.

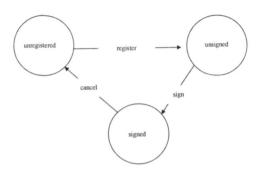

Fig. 5. State transition of terminal

Because the same vehicle will communicate with protocol servers at different storage node, SDK should record current context information of the terminal in its packet header, and it should check and then restore context information before sending 794 protocol packages to protocol server.

3.3 Optimization of Database Server

Currently, IoV system uses centralized database, and throughput bottleneck will occur when frequent writing happens. Also, there's no compression aimed specially at vehicle data: Data is firstly saved in distributed database, and then compressed program read this data and compressed it to memory. Afterwards, compressed data is stocked into database and uncompressed data is deleted. Receive interface of compressed data should be added in front of the database server to address this issue: it receives compressed data sent by cache node, deals with the differences of data format before and after compression, and is responsible for pushing into database, as shown in Fig. 6.

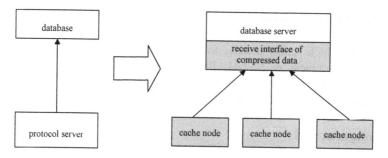

Fig. 6. Optimization of database server

3.4 Application Server

The main function of application server is communicating with database, querying data, or communicating with the protocol server. The relationship between application server and distributed caching is shown in Fig. 7. After the cache system is introduced, it will take some time to synchronize caching data to database. Therefore, distributed caching system needs to provide query interface for application server. Application server can query data from distributed caching and database at the same time, and then merge the returned data to users, as shown in Fig. 7a. Secondly, distributed caching only separates uplink data from previous architecture, terminal maintains long connection with protocol server when it is online, and receives instruction from protocol server (downlink data), as shown in Fig. 7b.

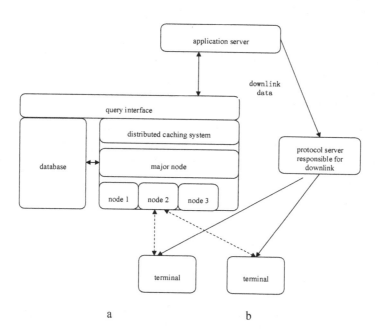

Fig. 7. Logical independence of uplink and downlink data

4 Performance Analysis

200 thousand vehicle status records from our IoV platform are adopted for test. Experiment environment is 2.3 GHz dual-core CPU, 8G memory, Ubuntu 14.04 operate system and 1T mechanical hard disk. Mysql database, caching system and data source are installed in one computer.

4.1 Throughput Test

Test data was sent to caching system and Mysql database separately, and was written into Mysql database with SQL approach. Customized mode was used by caching system to send data, and the data was sent concentrately to Mysql after compression. Results are shown in Table 2. It took more time to directly write uncompressed data into Mysql. By contrast, after adding cache system, the speed of putting data into memory was very fast. Because compress logic was simple, few cost occurred during compression, and the amount of data from memory to Mysql declined dramatically, writing was less time consuming and throughput was improved effectively.

Table 2. Comparison of throughput before and after adding cache system

	Directly write data into Mysql	Directly write data into cache	Write data from cache to database
Total amount of data items	200, 000 items	200,000 items	9, 467 items (after compression)
Time consumed	107, 085 ms	115 ms	5, 665 ms
Time consumed in total	107085 ms	5780 ms	
Throughput	1,867 items/second	34,602 items/second	

4.2 Scalability Testing

One, two, and three cache nodes (standalone process) were used respectively to test the time taken to write 200 thousand items of data. As Fig. 8 shows, three cache nodes only took one-third of time, which means that distributed caching could accept parallel extension and improves system performance.

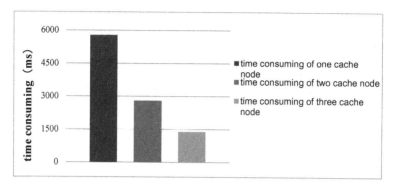

Fig. 8. Comparison of time consumed by using one, two, and three cache nodes

5 Conclusion

With the scale of IoV expanding, data uploading and storage mechanism's deficiency in extendibility and throughput is becoming increasingly serious. By introducing distributed caching system, the essay provides an optimized design for traditional technical architecture at multiple levels, including terminal, protocol server, database server and application server. Specific implementation is also introduced. Test results have shown that new cache system can well adapt to the need of massive scale of IoV.

Acknowledgments. This work was supported by the National Natural Science Foundation of China (61662013, U1501252, 61662015, 61562014, 61362021, 61363005, 61462017), Natural Science Foundation of Guangxi province (2014GXNSFDA118036, 2016GXNSFAA380149),the Key Laboratory of Cognitive Radio and Information Processing Ministry of Education (2011KF11), Guangxi Key Laboratory of Trusted Software (kx201511), Innovation Project of GUET Graduate Education (2016YJCXB02, 2017YJCX34).

References

1. Li, G.: Design and Implementation of Cache System based on Mmcached. Dalian University of Technology (2012)
2. Zhong, Y., Fang, J., Zhao, X.: A distributed storage scheme for big spatio-temporal data. Chin. High Technol. Lett. Chin High Technol. **23**(12), 1219–1229 (2013)
3. Guo, D., Wang, W., Zeng, G.-S.: An encrypted access for distributed cache in cloud computing. Microcomput. Appl. **35**(2), 1–3 (2016)
4. Li, W.-X., Yang, X.-H.: Storage model based on distributed cache for message oriented middleware. Comput. Eng. **36**(13), 93–95 (2010)
5. Li, R.-G., Zhao, J.: On design & realization of dispersed cache based on zookeeper. J. Mianyang Norm. Univ. **30**(11), 116–119 (2011)
6. Zhu, X., Qin, X., Wang, L.: Research on dynamic scaling of elastic distributed cache systems. J. Front. Comput. Sci. Technol. **06**(2), 97–108 (2012)
7. Wang, T.S.: Analysis of linear aerospike plume-induced X-33 base-heating environment. J. Spacecr. Rockets **36**(6), 777–783 (2012)

8. Vohra, D.: Using Couchbase Server. Pro Docker. Apress (2016)
9. Wind, D.: Instant Effective Caching with Ehcache. Packt Publishing, Birmingham (2013)
10. Nullable: GigaSpaces XAP Elastic Caching Edition (2015)
11. Johns, M.: Getting Started with Hazelcast. Packt Publishing, Birmingham (2015)
12. Fitzpatrick, B.: Distributed caching with memcached. Linux J. **2004**(124), 72–76 (2004)
13. Carlson, J.L., Sanfilippo, S.: Redis in Action. Manning, Shelter Island (2013)

Secure Transfer Protocol Between App and Device of Internet of Things

Zhaojie Xu[(✉)] and Xiaoyong Li

School of Cyberspace Security,
Beijing University of Posts and Telecommunications,
10 Xitucheng Rd, Haidian District, Beijing 100876, China
xuzj93@foxmail.com, lixiaoyong@bupt.edu.cn

Abstract. Communication security is one of the key component of Internet of Things. Now we can communicate with smart device, such as microwave oven, camera, and control it using App in our smart phone, but due to the poor computing power of smart device, it tends to be intractable to protect this communication from attack. By analyzing the security threats faced during the process of smart device and App authenticating each other's identity, this paper proposed a lightweight transfer protocol for smart device, and introduced "Authentication Center" to help with authentication for smart device and App. In consideration of poor computing power of smart device, the lightweight protocol achieves effective reduction of network resource usage. Acting as a hub, the Authentication Center does the heavy certification and authorization work as well as the management of smart device. This protocol can protect data confidentiality, data integrity against replay attack, man-in-the-middle attack by ensuring the identities of device and App with the help of Authentication Center.

Keywords: Network security · Security authentication protocol
Internet of Things

1 Introduction

1.1 The Present Situation of Internet of Things

By 2020, it is estimated that the number of connected devices is expected to grow exponentially to 50 billion. The main driver for this growth is not human population; rather, the fact that devices we use every day (e.g., refrigerators, cars, fans, lights) and operational technologies such as those found on the factory floor are becoming connected entities across the globe. This world of interconnected things - where the humans are interacting with the machines and machines are talking with other machines (M2M)—is here and it is here to stay. The Internet of Things (IoT) can be defined as "a pervasive and ubiquitous network which enables monitoring and control of the physical environment by collecting, processing, and analyzing the data generated by sensors or smart objects." Internet of things has developed quickly in the past few years, as well as the mobile Application related to it. Today we can control a smart device, like camera, fridge and microwave oven, with an App on our phone. At the same time, the enterprise can collect data from smart device through the Internet. Every

© Springer International Publishing AG 2017
G. Wang et al. (Eds.): SpaCCS 2017 Workshops, LNCS 10658, pp. 25–34, 2017.
https://doi.org/10.1007/978-3-319-72395-2_3

one of those smart device and App is sending data or receiving data through the Internet through some kinds of transport protocol. Often, it's very informative and very private data which can not be acquired by third parties. In normal circumstances, data packets transmitted over the Internet is not encrypted and signed, it is prone to eavesdropping, tampering, forgery and repudiation. Protecting data during network transit is very important, and any data traffic between a device and the server (including information transmitted via mobile apps) should be examined to make sure it is secured. Transport encryption such as the Secure Sockets Layer (SSL) or Transport Layer Security (TLS) methods can protect data—if employed in the correct manner. That usually starts with avoiding proprietary encryption protocols and sticking to commonly used and validated one.

1.2 Analysis of Existing Transfer Protocol

In most cases those smart devices in the domain of Internet of Things have poor storage and poor computing power, which make Secure Sockets Layer (SSL) or Transport Layer Security (TLS) inappropriate in the domain Internet of Things. A new transport protocol is needed to help those smart devices and Apps transfer data to each other and protect the security of data transmission in the domain of Internet of Things. The TCP/IP protocol did not emphatically consider the security mechanism at the beginning. Optional existing security solutions including PGP, IPSec, SSL/TLS are inappropriate in the domain of Internet of Things. The reasons are listed as follows.

(1) PGP (Pretty Good Privacy) not only provide privacy encryption and authentication functions, it is also often used to Email's signature, encryption/decryption to improve security. However, this program is only applicable to the application layer.
(2) SSL/TLS (Secure Socket Layer/Transport Layer Security) is a protocol used to ensure the communication exchanged data confidentiality and integrity. This standard does not provide security solution of the above transport layer, and it is not suitable for connectionless data communication.
(3) IPSec (Internet Protocol Security) is an encryption and authentication protocol used for IP packet in the data stream. This scheme is more complex, not flexible enough, and establishing a connection have to switch more packets than the solution in this paper.

This paper presents a protocol which realizes the networking data security transmission between smart device and Authentication Center. This protocol is lightweight for smart device while most of the heavy computing tasks are undertaken by Authentication Center. As this protocol finished, the Authentication Center authenticate those smart devices and maintain a list for them. Next, App could communicate with Authentication Center through https protocol, as well as establish s secure channel for data transmission with smart device with the help of Authentication Center. Authentication Center act as a broker during the process of authentication between App and smart device.

The Sect. 2 of this paper illustrates the present situation of security in Internet of Things. The Sect. 3 of this paper illustrates the overview of the overall framework. The

Sect. 4 describes the process of security protocol between smart device and Authentication Center, including key exchange and authentication. Then, the establishment of secure connection between App and smarts device with the help of Authentication Center is described in Sect. 5 in detail. Section 6 analyzes the establishment of secure connection between smart device and App, and shows the experimental analysis and conclusions finally.

2 Security in Internet of Things

As the applications of the IoT affect our daily lives, whether it is in the industrial control, transportation, SmartGrid or healthcare verticals, it becomes imperative to ensure a secure IoT system. With continued adoption of IP networks, IoT applications have already become a target for attacks that will continue to grow in both magnitude and sophistication. The scale and context of the IoT/M2M make it a compelling target for those who would do harm to companies, organizations, nations, and more importantly people. The targets are abundant and cover many different industry segments. The potential impact could span from minor irritant to grave and significant damage to the infrastructure and loss of life.

Although the threats in the IoT environment might be similar to those in the traditional IT environments, the overall impact could be significantly different. That is why there are several efforts in the community to focus on threat analysis and risk assessments to gauge the impact if a security incident or a breach occurs.

One of the fundamental elements in securing an IoT infrastructure is around device identity and mechanisms to authenticate it. As mentioned earlier, many IOT devices may not have the required compute power, memory or storage to support the current authentication protocols. Today's strong encryption and authentication schemes are based on cryptographic suites such as Advanced Encryption Suite (AES) for confidential data transport, Rivest-Shamir-Adleman (RSA) for digital signatures and key transport and Diffie-Hellman (DH) for key negotiations and management. While the protocols are robust, they require high compute power which may not exist in all IoT-attached devices. Consequently, authentication and authorization will require appropriate re-engineering to accommodate our new IoT connected world.

These authentication and authorization protocols also require a degree of user-intervention in terms of configuration and provisioning. However, many IoT devices will have limited access, thus requiring initial configuration to be protected from tampering, theft and other forms of compromise throughout its usable life, which in many cases could be years.

In order to overcome these issues, new authentication schemes that can be built using the experience of today's strong encryption/authentication algorithms are required. The communication and the data transport channels should be secured to allow devices to send and collect data to and from the agents and the data collection systems.

3   Overview of the Overall Framework

3.1   Infrastructure of the Transfer Protocol

Based on Transport Layer, this protocol consists of two parts: Light and Secure Transfer Protocol (LSTP), and Mediator Transfer Protocol (MTP). Light and Secure Transfer Protocol is designed for smart device to establish secure connection with Authentication Center, at the same time, Authentication Center maintains a list of all authenticated devices and their information.

A piece of data needs to be written into the ROM of each smart device, which contains ID, a random number and a key pair. The "ID" mentioned above is 32-bit long which can identify a unique smart device in the system. It is similar to MAC address in the Internet domain; The "random number" mentioned above is also 32-bit long. The "key pair" consists of one public key and one private key, which are used for asymmetric encryption during key negotiation with Authentication Center. It needs to be emphasized that the data inside ROM must not be exported or read from outside.

3.2   Overall Process of This Transfer Protocol

Before the key negotiation with App, smart device will get a SN-Key from Authentication Center. Likewise, before creating session with smart device, App tells Authentication Center which smart device it prepared to talk to, then Authentication Center responds with a SN-Token corresponding to the SN-Key mentioned above. App send the SN-Token to smart device to prove its identity, and smart device will use the SN-Key just received to validate the SN-Token. The result of the validation is sent to App to prove smart device's identity.

At this point, the communication connection has established successfully. Key point to the establishment of secure connection of App and smart device is SN-Key and SN-Token, and we will describe this process in detail in Sect. 4. The whole process of this key negotiation and validation is shown in Fig. 1.

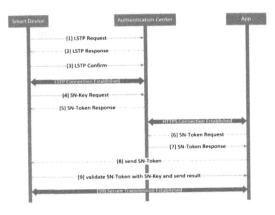

Fig. 1. The overall process of this protocol.

4   Light and Secure Transfer Protocol Between Smart Device and Authentication Center

Light and Secure Transfer Protocol, hereafter simply as LSTP, is specially designed for establishing secure connection between smart device and Authentication Center. Considering the poor storage and computing power of smart device, the goal for LSTP is to reduce the storage requirement and time consumption on smart device side as much as possible, and to simplify key negotiation between two side.

Establishing the connection aims at identity authentication and negotiation of various parameters, such as the encryption/decryption algorithm, identity and session key. The whole process needs to exchange three message, as shown in Fig. 2.

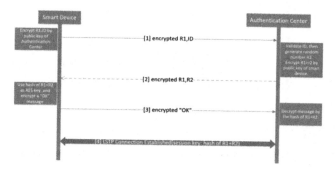

Fig. 2. The establishment of secure connection between device and authentication center.

(1)   The first message includes a random number R1, smart device ID. The R1 and ID is encrypted by the public key of Authentication Center.

(2)   The second message is the reply of the first message. The Authentication Center decrypts the first message by its private key and extract the R1 and smart device ID. Then Authentication Center query a database to validate this ID and its corresponding smart device's public key (The database stores each device's ID and public key before it leaves the factory). If the ID is legitimate then the Authentication Center generates a random number R2. Authentication Center encrypts R1 and R2 with the smart device's public key and send the result to the device.

(3)   The smart device decrypt the second message with its own private key and get the R1, R2. Then the smart device checks if the R1 is the one sent in the first message. After that, smart device will generate a AES key from R1 XOR R2, and use it as session key. Then it sends a message "OK" encrypted by the AES key to the Authentication Center.

(4)   If Authentication Center decrypt the encrypted "OK" successfully, then LSTP connection between smart device and Authentication Center is established and the session key is hash of R1 + R2.

5   Mediator Transfer Protocol Between Smart Device and App

Mediator Transfer Protocol, hereafter simply as MTP, aims at establishing secure connection between smart device and App. The Mediator here refer to Authentication Center. Before MTP begins, it need to make sure that the LSTP has established between smart device and Authentication Center so that their communication is secure. The whole process of the establishment of this protocol is shown in Fig. 3.

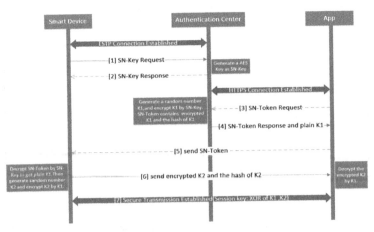

Fig. 3. The establishment of mediator transfer protocol between smart device and App.

(1) When App wants to establish a secure connection with a smart device, it sends a signal in clear text to this smart device. After receiving this signal, the smart device will send a SN-Key request to Authentication Center through LSTP which has been established before.

(2) To begin with, Authentication Center maintains a list which include ID of all registered and legitimate smart device. After receiving the SN-Key request from smart device through LSTP, Authentication Center extract the ID of this smart device from LSTP data packet, and verify the ID. If the verification is successful, then Authentication Center generate an AES key and send the AES key to smart device as SN-Key.

(3) Authentication Center generate a random number K1 and encrypt K1 with the SN-Key mentioned in step 2. Then encrypted K1 and the hash of K1 are packaged into SN-Token. Authentication Center will send SN-Token and plain K1 to App.

(4) App send the SN-Token just received from Authentication Center to smart device. After receiving SN-Token, smart device will decrypt the encrypted K1 to get plain K1 and use the hash of K1 to verify the plain K1. If verification is successful, then smart device generates a random number K2 and encrypt K2 with AES key which is generated from K1. Then smart device sends the encrypted K2 and the hash of K2 to the App.

(5) App decrypt the encrypted K2 in SN-Token by K1 received in step 3, then verify it using the hash of K2. If verification is successful, the key negotiation between smart device and App is completed, and the XOR of K1 and K2 will be the session key. At this point, MTP between smart device and App is established.

6   Experimental Analysis

6.1   Result Analysis

After realizing the above-mentioned protocol in Ubuntu 16.04, we take a time spent test on three connection mode between smart device and App (establish 1000 connections on each mode). The testing process of each mode is described in detailed as follows.

(1) Mode 1: Connect smart device and App through TCP (Transmission Control Protocol) directly;
(2) Mode 2: Firstly, smart device connects to Authentication Center through LSTP (Light and Secure Transfer Protocol); then smart device establishes a MTP (Mediator Transfer Protocol) secure connection with App.
(3) Mode 3: Connect smart device and App through SSL (Security Socket Layer).

Note: The symmetric encryption algorithm is Advanced Encryption Standard Algorithm (AES). The asymmetric encryption algorithm is RSA (256 bit). The hash algorithm is Secure Hash Algorithm (SHA-256).

The experimental result is shown in Figs. 4 and 5.

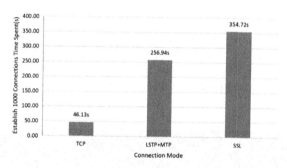

Fig. 4. Time cost on 1000 connections using different protocol.

As we can see from the Figs. 4 and 5 below, the connections through TCP (Transmission Control Protocol) directly are established in the shortest time and the transmission speed is fastest of three mode, which is to be expected. Establishing a connection through TCP cost 46 ms approximately. At the same time, the TCP transmission speed is 10.63 Mb/s approximately. Because TCP does not need encryption and decryption, its speed is faster than the other two modes. However, it is unsafe to establish connection between smart device and App through TCP, which transmits message in the clear and is prone to eavesdropping, tampering, forgery and repudiation.

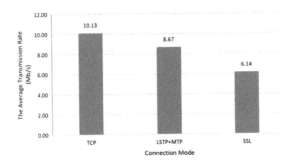

Fig. 5. The average transmission rate using different protocol (Mb/s).

As we can see from mode 2 in Fig. 4, establishing a secure connection between smart device and App through LSTP (Light and Secure Transfer Protocol) and MTP (Mediator Transfer Protocol) cost 256 ms approximately. As illustrated in the following Fig. 5, using the protocols in the paper affected the data transmission speed. Although the data transmission speed is lower than TCP mode, using LSTP and MTP make the transmission private and safe. In this test, we use Advanced Encryption Standard Algorithm (AES) as symmetric encryption algorithm, and RSA (256bit) as asymmetric encryption algorithm. Lower on the transmission speed than TCP is relatively large because of the need for a large number of calculations by AES and RSA.

We use PowerTutor to profile the energy consumption of devices in different scenarios. PowerTutor is an Android application performing an estimation of the actual energy consumption of the device, which has been used in many research papers as well as a basis for a new-wave of tools. We develop an application in Android phone to simulate smart devices of the Internet of Things and then use PowerTutor to estimate its energy consumption. During test, we blank the phone screen so the energy consumption estimated by PowerTutor is essentially equivalent to the actual energy consumption of simulated smart devices. As we can see from Fig. 6, establishing secure connection between smart device and App using LSTP and MTP cost lower CPU load than using

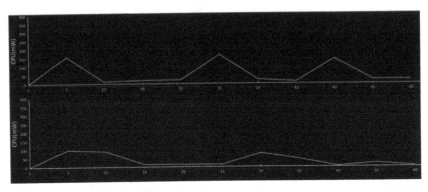

Fig. 6. Energy consumption (CPU) on 1000 connections using different protocol (measured by PowerTutor).

SSL. The energy consumption is mainly used for CPU load during key negotiation, so we can see that LSTP and MTP require lower calculation amount than SSL.

6.2 Conclusion

The LSTP and MTP in this article can ensure the security of data transmission of the smart device and App through white list, signatures, encryption and other measures. It can provide identity authentication in communication, data confidentiality protection, data integrity protection, protection against replay attack and non-repudiation protection function.

At the same time, the protocol composition, LSTP and MTP, is proven to be fast and efficient than SSL in the scenario where smart device has poor storage and computing power. In the Internet of Things, if we do not need secure transmission, we can just use TCP to transfer data. In the scenario of Internet of things where our data need to be protected from interception and attack, we could use the protocol composition, LSTP and MTP to establish secure transmission between smart device and App.

SSL protocol tends to require higher amount of calculation than LSTP+MTP during key negotiation, which increase the burden on smarts device. The protocol composition, LSTP and MTP, get rid of some inefficient part in key negotiation and transfer the calculation amount from smart device to Authentication Center and App. As a result, LSTP plus MTP is light for smart device, and make the key negotiation more simple. They behave more energy-saving and more efficient than SSL during the establishment of secure transmission of Internet of Things when smart device has poor storage and computing power.

Acknowledgments. This work is supported by the National Key Research and Development Program of China (No. 2016QY03D0605), the National Nature Science Foundation of China (Nos. 61672111, 61370069), and Beijing Natural Science Foundation (No. 4162043).

References

1. Stallings, W.: Cryptography and Network Security Principles and Practices, 4th edn. Prentice Hall, New Jersey (2005)
2. Saltzer, J., Schroder, M.: The protection of information in computer systems. Proc. IEEE **63** (9), 1278–1308 (1975)
3. Harn, L., Ren, J.: Design of fully deniable authentication service for e-mail applications. IEEE Commun. Lett. **12**(3), 219–221 (2008)
4. Feistel, H., Notz, W., Smith, J.: Cryptographic techniques for machine to machine data communications. Proc. IEEE **63**(11), 1545–1554 (1975)
5. Chou, W.: Inside SSL: accelerating secure transactions. IT Prof. **4**(5), 37–41 (2002)
6. Campbell, C.: Design and specification of cryptographic capabilities. In: Computer Security and the Data Encryption Standard, pp. 54–56. NBS Special Publication 500–27, February 1978
7. Oppliger, R.: Security at the internet layer. Computer **31**, 43–47 (1998)
8. Stewart, R.: Stream Control Transmission Protocol. RFC4960, September 2007

9. Ono, K., Schulzrine, H.: The impact of SCTP on SIP server scalability and performance. In: IEEE GLOBECOM, November 2008
10. Khalifa, T., Naik, K., Alsabaan, M., Nayak, A., Goel, N.: Transport protocol for smart grid infrastructure. In: IEEE UFN, June 2010
11. Braden, R.: Requirements for Internet Hosts - Communication Layers. RFC1122, October 1989
12. Bakken, D., Hauser, C., Gjermundrod, H.: Delivery Requirements and Implementation
13. Aboba, B.: Extesible Authentication Protocol (EAP) [S]. RFC3748, June 2004
14. Network Working Group. RFC2867 RADIUS Accounting Modifications for Tunnel Protocol Support, June 2000
15. Network Working Group. RFC2868 Attributes for Tunnel Protocol Support, June 2000
16. Network Working Group. RFC3575 IANA Consideration for RADIUS, July 2003
17. Zhang, L., Tiwana, B., Qian, Z., Wang, Z., Dick, R.P., Mao, Z.M., Yang, L.: Accurate online power estimation and automatic battery behavior based power model generation for smart phones. In: Proceedings of the Eighth IEEE/ACM/IFIP International Conference on Hardware/Software Codesign and System Synthesis, CODES/ISSS 2010, pp. 105–114. ACM, New York (2010). http://dx.doi.org/10.1145/1878961.1878982

Rogue Access Points Detection Based on Theory of Semi-Supervised Learning

Xiaoyan Li$^{(\boxtimes)}$ and Xiaoyong Li

School of Cyberspace Security, Beijing University of Posts and
Telecommunications, 10 Xitucheng Rd, Haidian District, Beijing 100876, China
xiaoyan_li_0912@qq.com, lixiaoyong@bupt.edu.cn

Abstract. It is very dangerous for wireless client to connect with rogue access point. Attackers could eavesdrop or modify client's information via rogue access point, therefore, rogue access point can be seen as the most serious threats in wireless local area network (WLAN). In this paper, we proposed a novel approach that can detect rogue access points (AP) quickly and accurately. We take advantage of Time-stamp field and signal field in the 802.11 beacon frame as the data in Gaussian distribution algorithm and Native Bayes Classify to generate the fingerprint of access point. The fingerprint is unique to each access point, which cannot be spoofed. In the detection process, we add sliding window and Semi-Supervised Learning, that give our method the ability to take dynamic self-adjustment. Experimental results indicated that the proposed approach could detect rogue access points more quickly and accurately compare with existing methods.

Keywords: Rogue access point · WLAN · Semi-Supervised learning
Beacon frames

1 Introduction

In recent years, wireless networks have developed at an unexpected rate. WLAN not only be used in public places such as stations, schools and companies, but also installed at home. As we all know, WLAN has many irreplaceable advantages, such as ease of deployment, low costs, mobility and so on. However, people often ignore that WLAN has more network security problems than the wired network. These security problems are often caused by WLAN's communicating protocol or its own characteristics such as the broadcast nature of the wireless medium [9].

IEEE 802.11 is the common standard for WLAN and it mainly works on the lowest two layers of the Open Systems Interconnection (OSI) protocol, defining the media access control layer (MAC layer) and the physical layer [7]. With the development of the 802.11, a series of security and encryption related technologies have been derived, such as Wired Equivalent Privacy (WEP), CTR with CBC-MAC Protocol (CCMP), Wi-Fi Protected Access (WPA) and so on. Cryptography enhances the security of WLAN, in a manner, but the following factors make wireless network still vulnerable.

The communication media of WLAN is open, malicious attackers can obtain users' communication data and decipher encryption. In existing wireless network, wireless's

© Springer International Publishing AG 2017
G. Wang et al. (Eds.): SpaCCS 2017 Workshops, LNCS 10658, pp. 35–44, 2017.
https://doi.org/10.1007/978-3-319-72395-2_4

clients use signal strength as the only criterion of selecting access point, which means that wireless clients can easily connect to rogue access points created by malicious attackers. What's more, in working and living, people use the basic service set identifier (SSID) to distinguish different Wi-Fi access points, but SSID is not unique, and anyone could get it and set the same SSID for any Wi-Fi access points.

Based on above reasons, we can find that one of the most common network security problems in WLAN is the Rogue access point. Rogue access points refer to any Wi-Fi access points that are installed by attackers to intrude or attack the wireless network without authorized of local administrator [1]. Wireless phishing access point attack and Man-in-the-Middle Attack (MITM) are the most common Rogue access point attacks. Wireless phishing access point attack is also known as "evil twin attack" because it creates some unauthorized Wi-Fi access points which have same characteristics with the authorized Wi-Fi access point, such as SSID, even mac address [6]. MITM is an attack where the attacker secretly relays and possibly alters the communication between wireless clients and authorized access point [Wi-Ki]. In WLAN, the MITM can be understood as some unauthorized access points built by malicious attackers between authorized access point and wireless clients, which forward the communication between them, and it can monitor or tamper with the communication contents [8]. These two Rogue access point attacks are shown in Fig. 1.

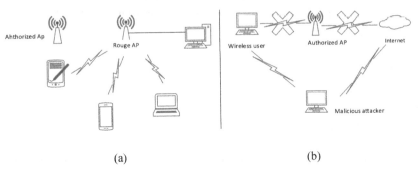

(a)   (b)

Fig. 1. The two principal rogue access points (a) Phishing access point attack (b) Man-in-the-Middle Attack

In this paper, we proposed a passive rogue access point detection method using the beacon frame without affecting the normal network communication. The innovation of the proposed method is using Semi-Supervised Learning combining with Gaussian distribution and Native Bayesian classification to update the device fingerprint dynamically, so that it can detect rogue access point quickly and accurately. The rest of paper is organized as follows. In the Sect. 2, we describe some of the related works. The proposed method is detailed described in the Sect. 3. The Sect. 4 gives the results and performance analysis of the proposed method. Finally, we sum up the paper and discuss future work.

2 Related Works

According to different standards, Rogue access point detection can be classified into different categories. The most common classification is according to the difference of source data, Rogue access point detection can be divided into two categories: Network-based detection and Host-based detection. Host-based methods often use operating system's event logs and management tool audit records as source data. Host-based approaches are associated with host system behavior, but they consume resources and rely on host system environments. The data source of the Network-based detection is the packet in the network, which can monitor the data traffic in the network and discover potential attacks behavior. Network-based detection is independent of any wireless client because it generally runs on an independent host and adopts a passive listening mode. In addition, some studies do not analysis any data but try to improve the wireless communication protocol to prevent users connecting with rogue access point.

Authors in [2–4] proposed a passive rogue access point detection method extract a fingerprint from beacon frames to identify access points. These methods usually use the Time-stamp of beacon frame that is used to synchronize the BSS in the STA and arrival time of the frame at the capture network card to get the fingerprint. Since these methods ignore the influence of channel loading on arrival time, they are more effective when the network is idle, but when the channel is busy, the accuracy of detection is reduced.

Kim and Park [11] used the Received Signal Strength Indicator to judge whether there is a rogue access point. A rogue access point is considered to being created when the Received Signal Strength Indicator (RSSI) exceeds a threshold. In this method, influence of environmental factors on RSSI is not considered. What's more, since the signal strength is bound up with the distance, as long as the distance is appropriate, the rogue access point can have the same signal strength with the authorized access point.

Yang and Song [12] developed two new algorithms: Trained Mean Matching (TMM) and Hop Differentiating Technique (HDT), both of them utilize the wireless IAR network statistic and consider the influence factors of RSSI and saturation, and employ Sequential Probability Ration Test (SPRT) technique to make the final detection [12]. However, method in this paper is only aimed at phishing access point detection and it is invalid to detect the intermediate attack of Rogue access point.

The work in [5], the IP addresses with the same SSID and MAC addresses are compared. If the IP address is not unique, the rouge access point will be considered being created in the network environment. But the detection method will not be valid when the authorized access point is not working because of malicious attack, and this method must get the data of Network lay to get IP address, which will cost the source of client-side.

Authors in [13–15] analyzed and studied the 802.11 standards or protocols and required the modification of the WLAN Communication Protocol, including the change of encryption algorithms and the access point selection methods. It is impossible to implement new WLAN communication protocols. Although 802.11 standards or protocols have many drawbacks, they have been widely used in actual production, and we cannot change frameworks and hardware equipment that are widely applied.

Our rogue access point detection is a passive method, which is based on Semi-Supervised Learning and extract access point's fingerprint from Beacon frames.

3 Proposed Method

Our work can be divided into four parts. Each part completes a different task, and the result of one part will serve the work of next part. The framework of rogue access point detection method is shown in Fig. 2. In this chapter, we will illustrate our work according to the framework.

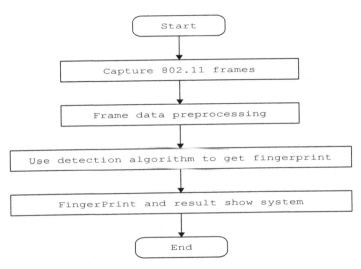

Fig. 2. The proposed framework of rogue access point

3.1 Capture 802.11 Frame Using Libpcap

Libpcap is a powerful network packet capture function library. We use Libpcap to capture 802.11 frame data under Linux System. Since the wireless network card cannot capture the data of the link layer on normal mode, it should be set on monitor mode.

3.2 Frame Data Preprocessing

According to the Mac layer frame's header, Mac layer frames can be divided into Management frames, control frames, and data frames. The management frames are responsible for joining or exiting the wireless networks as well as handling connection among access points. We could receive Beacon frame constantly which is one of the management frames so that we can find the wireless network. We can utilize these Beacon frames to check if there are rogue access points exist. The structure of the Beacon frame is shown in Fig. 3.

Fig. 3. Beacon frame structure

SSID can be considered as an alias for an access point, which is the name of the wireless network found around our cell phone. Time-stamp is made up of 64 bits, whose unit is microsecond (us), it is used to synchronize the BSS in the STA, which is started from the access point enabled and timed from 0. The Seqctl field can be divided into Sequence and Fragment. Sequence generated by the hardware represents the ordinal number of the Beacon frames, which is added one by one and cannot be changed by the software. Source Address (SA) can be seen as the MAC address of an access point, but it can be changed by software. In addition to the Beacon information, we can get the received time and the access point signal strength in the radio tap while grabbing the package.

Algorithm1: Beacon frame preprocessing

While true	//check if it is Beacon frame
If type=='00'&&subtype=='1000'	
SSID = getSSID(ssid_len);	//get SSID
If SSID.equals(targetSSID)	
MAC= getsrcMAC();	//get MAC of access point
sequence = getSequence();	//get Sequence
signal = getSegal();	//signal strength
timestamp = getTimestamp();	//get Timestamp
Insert(Beacon.Info) into beaconLlist;	//store beacon info
end if	
end if	
end while	

3.3   Fingerprint Calculate and Update

In first and second steps, we can obtain a variety of access point related attributes that could describe the features of access point. Using these properties reasonably we can distinguish rogue access point from authorized access point. Figure 4 illustrates the proposed method.

Firstly, we should identify MAC address spoofing by checking the MAC address. MAC address spoofing refers to a malicious attacker who modifies the MAC address of the rogue access point to the same as authorized access point. We can save the MAC address of the legal rogue access point in advance, and compare with the information of captured Beacon frames each time. If it is different, the rogue access point is indicated.

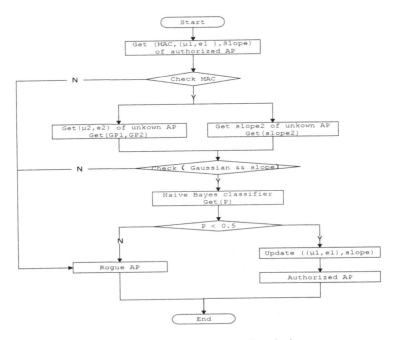

Fig. 4. Algorithm of proposed method

Signal strength is directly related with the distance, but the environmental factors such as temperature will also have slight impacts on it. Because the positions of access point and sniffer are immobile, the signal may vary slightly with environmental changes. In probability theory, the Gaussian distribution is a very common continuous probability distribution. Gaussian distributions are often used to represent real-valued random variables whose distributions are not known [Wi-Ki]. Using Gaussian Algorithm to deal with the strength of signal, we can find that signal strength is concentrated around a value. Gaussian distribution is represented by $N(\mu, \sigma)$.

$$\mu = \left(\sum_{i=1}^{n} signal_i\right) \bigg/ n \tag{1}$$

μ is the average. σ is variance, which can be calculated by follows:

$$\sigma^2 = \left(\sum_{i=1}^{n} (signal_i - u)^2\right) \bigg/ 2 \tag{2}$$

We use the Gaussian distribution to calculate the signal of beacon frames in sliding window. In the Gaussian algorithm, the $\delta 1$ represents the fluctuation degree of signal intensity, we use $2 * \delta 1$ as the threshold of detection. The new calculation results are compared with the authorized signal Gaussian distribution and updated according to the result. The processing method is shown as Algorithm 2.

Algorithm2:   Signal Algorithm

$(\mu1,\delta1)$ = Gaussian (authorized beacons) ;
while true
$(\mu2, \delta2)$ = Gaussian (unknown beacons);
if math.abs $(\mu2-\mu1) < 2*\delta1$ && $\delta2 < 2*\delta1$
$(\exp(-(|\mu1-\mu2|^2)/(2\delta1* \delta2))) = (\mu2, \delta2)$ //AP authorized
Continue;
else if $\delta2 > 5* \delta1$
return false;   //rogue access point exist;
else
GuasP = Similarity of $(\mu1,\delta1)$ and $(\mu2, \delta2)$
end if
end while

Thirdly, taking full advantage of Time-stamp could improve the detection accuracy effectively. Beacon frames are periodic frame, whose default period is 0.1 s. The Time-stamp is effective in synchronizing communication, which is generated by hardware before the emitted. Our proposed method uses the Least Square Fitting (LSF) to estimate the clock skew of an access point from its beacon frames sets. We assume t_i being receiving time in microsecond of the ith beacon frame and T_i being Time-stamp in it. Given a sets $(t_1, T_1), \ldots, (t_n, T_n)$, LSF finds a line $\alpha x + \beta$, where α is the slope of the line, β is the y-axis intercept, such that

$$\sum_{i-1}^{n} (T_i - (\alpha t_i - \beta)^2) \tag{3}$$

remains minimum. We also use sliding window and Semi-Supervised Learning to deal with the clock skew of Time-stamp. We defined $slopeP$ as:

$$slopeP = (\alpha_1 - \alpha_2) * 10 \tag{4}$$

where α_1 is the slope of last sliding window in which all beacons are from authorized access point, and α_2 is the slope of beacon frames that need to be detected.

Finally, we use the Native Bayes algorithm on the basis of second and third steps. The Naive Bayesian classifier algorithm has the characteristics of minor calculation and high velocity and the accuracy of it is very high when each feature is independent of each other. In the proposed experiment, the signal strength and Time-stamp are independent of each other, so the Native Bayes algorithm is a good classifier, which can divide the Beacon set into two categories: rogue access point and authorized access point. We can get:

$$P = (1 - GuasP) * slopeP \tag{5}$$

where $slopeP$ is the probability of rogue access point we can get from time-stamp and it has been defined. $GuasP$ is the similarity of Gaussian distribution. $GuasP$ can be defined as:

$$\text{GuasP} = \exp(-|\mu_1 - \mu_2|^2/(2\sigma_1 * \sigma_2)) \tag{6}$$

We can judge whether there is rouge access points on the basis of P. If P is greater than 0.5, there are rogue access points around. Otherwise, we need to update the fingerprint of access point in the light of Semi-Supervised Learning.

4   Experiment and Result Analysis

Our experiment requires at least one laptop and two blocks of wireless cards that can be set on Monitoring mode under the environment of ubuntu14.4. One of the network adapters is used as sniffer device to capture beacon data that we have described in Sect. 3. We use another network card and laptop as attacker to simulate rouge access point.

Dividing a series of beacons into different groups, slopes of different number of Beacon frames are shown in Fig. 5. The line chart on the left indicates that the slope is more stable when the size of sliding window is 10 or 20. At the same time, we can get that very large changes will take place in slope when there are rogue access points in the environment from the line chart on the right.

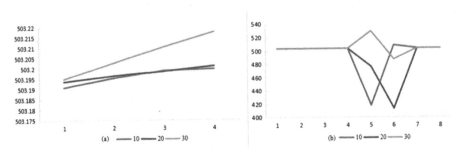

Fig. 5. Slopes of Beacon (a) Slope of authorized beacon (b) Slope of unknown beacon

We can get Gaussian distributions (μ, δ) of these groups, which are shown in Table 1. It can easily be find that signal strength fluctuates within a certain range and it will be more stable if the sliding window size is 20.

In the second paragraph, we have introduced a variety of existing methods of detection. Table 2 lists the comparison between our proposed method and some of similar existing techniques. We take four valuable factors into consideration including speed, accuracy and so on to analyze the performance of the existing techniques. At same time the influence of environmental factors on the accuracy should be considered. Therefore we conducted 100 Rogue AP detections at 8a.m., 2p.m. and 10p.m.. The advantage of Passive is that the method does not increase network load and affects normal communication. From Table 2 we can find that in addition to our technique, three methods are passive and not and add traffic to the WLAN. To a certain extent the

Table 1. The Gaussian distribution of beacons

Groups	Num		
	10	20	30
Authorized 1	−34.2/2.71	−35.5/2.95	−36.13/3.169
Authorized 2	−36.8/2.6	−37.1/2.93	−37.53/3.64
Authorized 3	−37.4/3.12	−36.9/3.26	−37.26/4.03
Authorized 4	−36.4/5.063	−37.3/2.99	−31.27/3.64
Unknown 1	−46.4/20.06	−56.9/17.68	−57/18.27
Unknown 2	−58.6/19.37	−52.5/20.63	−50/21.46

number of beacon frame (Bea Num) can represent the time of detection. Because of the use of sliding windows, proposed method can find the presence of illegal access points in 20 beacons, while Clock skew requires the number of beacon is at least 100, which indicates that our detection speed has been increased by 5 times. Although the number of beacon frame used in Signal Strength and Sequence number are very small, the accuracy of them are very low. What's more, our method used Semi-Supervised Learning to update the fingerprint in real-time, improving the accuracy of detection.

Table 2. Comparison with existing techniques

Technique	Passive	Bea Num	No Pr Mod	Accuracy
RTT [16]	✘	200 * 100 * 3	✔	33–66%
RSS [10]	✔	1 * 100 * 3	✔	20–50%
Clock skew [2]	✔	100 * 100 * 3	✔	90%
Sequence num [15]	✔	1 * 100 * 3	✔	60–80%
EAP SWAT [13]	NA	NA	✘	NA
Our method	✔	20 * 100 * 3	✔	95%

No Pr Mod: No protocol or standard revise is required.

In conclusion, we use efficient Gaussian distribution and Least Square Fitting to extract device fingerprint using multiple fields in beacon frame, and combine sliding window and Semi-Supervised Learning to improve detection speed and accuracy.

5   Conclusions and Future Work

In this paper, we explored the use of Semi-Supervised Learning to detect rouge access points in wireless local area networks. We proposed a methodology that benefits from signal strength and the clock skew of times-tamp. Our exploration results indicate that the use of Semi-Supervised method and sliding window appears to be and efficient and robust method for detecting rogue access points in WLAN. As part of future work, we plan to extend our work to positioning access point. We may apply the signal strength to the Trilateration positioning technique in the following.

Acknowledgments. This work is supported by the National Key Research and Development Program of China (No. 2016QY03D0605), the National Nature Science Foundation of China (No. 61672111, No. 61370069), and Beijing Natural Science Foundation (No. 4162043).

References

1. Alotaibi, B., Elleithy, K.: An empirical fingerprint framework to detect Rogue Access Points. In: 2015 Long Island Systems, Applications and Technology, Farmingdale, NY, pp. 1–7 (2015). https://doi.org/10.1109/LISAT.2015.7160206
2. Jana, S., Kasera, S.K.: On fast and accurate detection of unauthorized wireless access points using clock skews. IEEE Trans. Mob. Comput. **9**(3), 449–462 (2010)
3. Han, H., Sheng, B., Tan, C.C., Li, Q., Lu, S.: A timing-based scheme for rogue AP detection. IEEE Trans. Parallel Distrib. Syst. **22**(11), 1912–1925 (2011). https://doi.org/10.1109/TPDS.2011.125
4. Lanze, F., Panchenko, A., Braatz, B., et al.: Letting the puss in boots sweat: detecting fake access points using dependency of clock skews on temperature. In: Proceedings of the 9th ACM Symposium on Information, Computer and Communications Security, pp. 3–14. ACM (2014)
5. Nikbakhsh, S., Manaf, A., Zamani, M., Janbeglou, M.: A novel approach for rogue access point detection on the client side. In: International Conference on Advanced Information Networking and Applications Workshops (2012)
6. Vanjale, S., Mane, P.B.: A novel approach for elimination of rogue access point in wireless network. In: 2014 Annual IEEE India Conference (INDICON), pp. 1–4. IEEE (2014)
7. Kolias, C., Kambourakis, G., Stavrou, A., et al.: Intrusion detection in 802.11 networks: empirical evaluation of threats and a public dataset. IEEE Commun. Surv. Tutorials **18**(1), 184–208 (2016)
8. Dahiya, M., Gill, S.: Detection of rogue access point in WLAN using Hopfield neural network. Int. J. Electr. Comput. Eng. (IJECE) **7**(2), 1060–1070 (2017)
9. Amran, A.: Traffic characteristics mechanism for detecting rogue access point in local area network. Universiti Utara Malaysia (2015)
10. Kim, T., Park, H., Jung, H., Lee, H.: Online detection of fake access points using received signal strengths. In: 75th IEEE Vehicular Technology Conference (VTC Spring 2012) (2012)
11. Cross, T., Takahashi, T.: Secure open wireless access. In: Black Hat USA (2011)
12. Gonzales, H., Bauer, K., Lindqvist, J., et al.: Practical defenses for evil twin attacks in 802.11. In: 2010 IEEE Global Telecommunications Conference (GLOBECOM 2010), pp. 1–6. IEEE (2010)
13. Bauer, K., Gonzales, H., McCoy, D.: Mitigating evil twin attacks in 802.11. In: IEEE International Performance, Computing and Communications Conference, IPCCC 2008, pp. 513–516. IEEE (2008)
14. Alotaibi, B., Elleithy, K.: Rogue access point detection: taxonomy, challenges, and future directions. Wireless Pers. Commun. **90**(3), 1261–1290 (2016)
15. Bing, H., Yi, P.: Pseudo AP detection method based on beacon sequence. Electron. Measur. Technol. **40**(4), 123–126 (2017)
16. Watkins, L., Beyah, R., Corbett, C.: A passive approach to rogue access point detection. In: IEEE Global Telecommunications Conference, GLOBECOM 2007, pp. 355–360. IEEE (2007)

Phishing Detection Method Based on Borderline-Smote Deep Belief Network

Jiahua Zhang[✉] and Xiaoyong Li

The Key Laboratory of Trustworthy Distributed Computing and Service
Ministry of Education, Beijing University of Posts and Telecommunications,
Beijing 100876, China
jiahua_zhang@foxmail.com

Abstract. With the rapid development of Internet, phishing and other frauds are becoming more and more serious. Criminals posing as banks, electricity providers, social networking sites to send fraudulent information to induce users to log on, steal user information, so that the vast numbers of users and financial institutions suffered property and economic losses. How to accurately and effectively identify phishing related Internet risks has been a major concern of the Internet. This paper analyzes the development history of phishing prevention and control, and presents a Borderline-Smote (Synthetic Minority Over-sampling Technique) DBN (Deeping Belief Network) method to detect phishing. The method uses deep learning phishing detection method based on web documents content and other features to improve 1% on the recognition accuracy. Furthermore the paper uses Borderline-Smote to solve the imbalanced data problem in the training of phishing detection, and further improve 2% on the F-value and recall rate.

Keywords: Detection · Borderline-Smote · DBN · Imbalanced data

1 Introduction

Phishing is an attack that attempts to get recipient sensitive information by sending spam messages claiming to be from a bank or other well-known institution [1]. The most typical attack is to lure users into well-designed phishing sites that are very similar to target organizations to cheat personal information about users on this site.

In recent years, the number of phishing sites has been growing rapidly. According to the China Anti phishing website report, as of 2017.4, the Federation has identified and dealt with phishing sites 391747 [2]. According to statistics, from July 2011 to July 2012, including phishing attacks, malware and other cyber-attacks, leading to the global $111 billion loss.

There is a lot of research on anti-phishing, and many browsers provide phishing recognition function. However, these tools are basically based on black and white lists or simple URL rules to identify. Since the average time of phishing sites is only 4 days [3], the blacklist cannot be updated in a timely manner. The URL rules need to be fixed early and lack flexibility, all of which lead to limited recognition.

G. Wang et al. (Eds.): SpaCCS 2017 Workshops, LNCS 10658, pp. 45–53, 2017.
https://doi.org/10.1007/978-3-319-72395-2_5

Kang et al. [4] have calculated the URL similarity to judge the spoofing of DNS domain names; effectively preventing phishing attacks by confusing URL and modifying DNS mappings. However, the proportion of phishing is very small, which greatly limits the application of this method in practice.

Huang et al. [5] present a phishing detection method based on SVM (Support Vector Machine). Although relative to traditional methods, the recognition accuracy is improved, but this algorithm needs to extract features based on experience to train, and feature extraction doesn't analyze the page deeply. Feature selection directly determines the final effect, so if the feature extraction is not good sometimes, the experiment will be also poor. What's more, these studies also do not consider the data imbalance problem.

The contribution of this study is as follow: this paper spends a great deal of effort on the full extraction of page features. Introduce deep belief network into phishing detection; improve the accuracy of phishing detection by depth learning. In addition, the paper use Borderline-Smote to solve the problem of imbalanced data sets in phishing detection. Integrating Borderline-Smote and deep belief network, this paper presents a Borderline-Smote DBN model is proposed to identify phishing sites.

The remainder of the paper is organized as follows. Section 2 describes the Borderline-Smote DBN phishing detection method, including the deep learning method to phishing detection, discussion of the method of solving imbalanced data sets, and the method of solving imbalanced data sets in phishing detection. Section 3 presents the experiments and compares our methods with traditional method. Section 4 draws the conclusion.

2   Borderline-Smote DBN

This paper uses Deeping-learning model to detect phishing. Considering the problem in detects phishing that phishing example is too small. We use Borderline-Smote [6], a special Smote [7] method, to solve the imbalance data set problem in two classifications. Model training process is shown in Fig. 1.

When we get the training data, first use Borderline-Smote to rebalance the imbalanced training data set. Then process the previous step data through DBN. So we get the model that can help us judge, which is phishing site.

The whole phishing detection system is shown in Fig. 2: three-layer identification structure. First, detection through the black and white list layer, unidentified web data enter the second layer of the shallow machine-learning model, such as SVM. If it is still not recognized, continue to enter the third layer DBN for detection. The rest default judges as normal sites. In the shallow model layer, we set a relatively high precision threshold 95% through experiment, and only the very identified cannot be introduced into the lower layer. What's more, the detection sites are added to the black and white list Library finally. Through this three layers recognition system, we can greatly improve the accuracy of phishing sites.

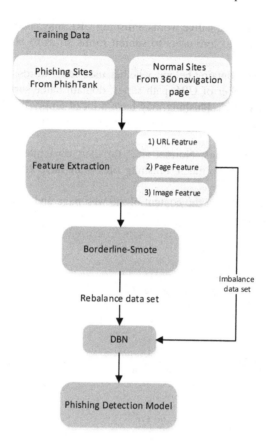

Fig. 1. Flow of borderline smote DBN phishing detection method.

2.1 Feature Extraction

The basis of phishing detection is to fully extract the features of the training web site. Many of the common features are mentioned in the study of applied machine learning to phishing detection [8]. The main features of web page are URL (Uniform Resource Locator) features, content features and web image features.

This paper summarizes the web features extraction of phishing detection research before, and further expands and perfect. Given the complexity of the experiment, web image is not handled here temporarily. The main features extracted are as follows:

- URL host is IP format. Phishing attackers use IP format URL host to hide their identity. However, normal websites tend to use URL, which is easy to remember and contains its own brand name, in order to increase their brand awareness.
- URL whether contains ports. Normal web site web services generally default is 80 ports, but some phishing are mounted on some very vulnerable ports of the server.

- URL whether contain sensitive words. Phishing URL may add sensitive words such as login and update to lure users to submit forms so as to obtain personal information of users.
- URL features also contains below: whether uses long words, whether URL path takes a dot, the number of URL path series, domain name survival time, etc.
- Number of empty links. Phishing may have a lot of empty links due to tampering with pages. Therefore, the number of empty links can also be used as a basis for judging phishing sites.
- Number of external links. Normal sites for their own interests, the numbers of external links are not too much. Phishing sites often have a lot of external links to confuse.
- Web content. Segmenting the content of the web page and using TF/IDF to do the content vectorization.

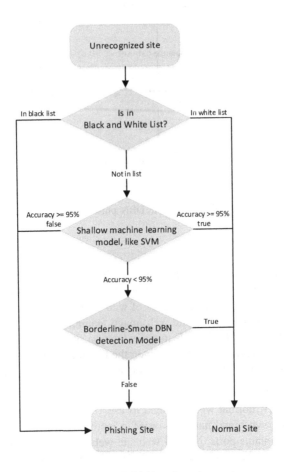

Fig. 2. Flow of phishing detection system.

2.2 Deep Belief Network

DBN (Deep Belief Network) [9] consists of many layers of RBM (Restricted Boltzmann Machines). RBM is a two-layer random neural network including the visible layer (V layer) and the hidden layer (H layer).

The neurons are two valued, and the weights between the visible layer and the hidden layer are represented by W. RBM is an energy-based model, and the energy function is:

$$E_\theta(v,h) = -\sum_{i=1}^{n_v} a_i v_i - \sum_{j=1}^{n_h} b_j h_j - \sum_{i=1}^{n_v}\sum_{j=1}^{n_h} h_j w_{j,i} v_i \tag{1}$$

So we can calculate the probability distribution of the visible layer or hidden layer through the edge distribution of the energy function, the edge distribution is the objective function of RBM, and its maximum likelihood estimation is then solved by contrastive divergence method. This is why we use DBN model that the multilayer neural network has good feature expression ability, so as to achieve better classification effect than the shallow model. However, the efficiency of this kind of learning algorithm is not high, and DBN can improve the learning efficiency by using RBM to generate the distribution of training data.

The specific training process is as follows:

(a) Train the first RBM fully.
(b) The weights and offsets of the first RBM are fixed, then the state of their hidden neurons is used as the input vector of the second RBM.
(c) After training the second RBM, stack the second RBM above the first RBM.
(d) Repeat the above three steps several times, you need to determine the exact number of times according to the experimental environment.

2.3 Imbalanced Data Set Problem

Because the phishing sites are only a small minority in phishing detection, the training of imbalanced data sets will hinder the recognition accuracy. This is the problem of imbalanced data sets in the two classifications. By convention, the class label of the minority is positive, and the class label of the majority class is negative. Table 1 illustrates a confusion matrix for a two-class problem having positive and negative class values.

Table 1. Table of confusion matrix.

	Predicted positive	Predicted negative
Positive	TP	FN
Negative	FP	TN

TP and TN denote the number of positive and negative examples that are classified correctly, while FN and FP denote the number of misclassified positive and negative examples respectively.

$$Accuracy = \frac{TP + TN}{TP + FN + FP + TN} \tag{2}$$

$$FP\_rate = \frac{FP}{TN + FP} \tag{3}$$

$$TP\_rate = Recall = \frac{TP}{TP + FN} \tag{4}$$

$$Precision = \frac{TP}{TP + FP} \tag{5}$$

$$F - value = \frac{(1 + \beta^2) * Recall * Precision}{\beta^2 * Recall + Precision} \tag{6}$$

The evaluation indicators of the most commonly used are accuracy, but accuracy is particularly suspicious performance measures when studying the effect of class distribution on learning since they are strongly biased to favor the majority class. For instance, it is straightforward to create a classifier having an accuracy of 99% (or an error rate of 1%) in a domain where the majority class proportion corresponds to 99% of the examples, by simply forecasting every new example as belonging to the majority class [10].

Here we use F-value (Eq. (6)) as evaluation metric for imbalance problem. We can see if β is 1, the F value is the harmonic mean of the correct rate and the recall rate. It is a kind of combination of recall (Eq. (4)) and precision (Eq. (5)), which are effective metrics for information retrieval community where the imbalance problem exists. F-value is high when both recall and precision are high, and can be adjusted through changing the value of β, where β corresponds to relative importance of precision vs. recall and it is usually set to 1.

There are two main ways to solve the imbalance training sets problem [11]:

(1) **Sampling**. The essence of sampling is to rebalance the imbalanced data set. There is over-sampling or under-sampling etc.
(2) **Improved algorithm**. Make algorithm is not hindered by imbalanced data sets.

The paper use Borderline-Smote, which is based on the theory that the examples on the borderline are more apt to be misclassified than the ones far from the borderline, and thus more important for classification. The specific steps of the Borderline-Smote method are as follows:

(a) Find out the border-line minority examples:
   Suppose the minority class is P and the majority class is N. Find the m nearest neighbors of P_i. The number of majority examples among the m nearest neighbors is denoted by m' $(0 < = m' < = m)$. If $m/2 < = m' < = m$, it will be regarded as Borderline example, then this minority one will put into DANGER.
(b) Find out the border-line minority examples.
   After find the Borderline Set, named DANGER, from minority class. Then we select s nearest neighbors of DANGER, which is also minority class. The distance between DANGER and its neighbors is denoted by $diff_i$ (i = 1, 2... s)

(c) Generate synthetic positive examples.

Make is a random number between 0 and 1. So the way to synthesize instances is like the following:

$$synthetic_i = P_i + r_i * diff_i \qquad (7)$$

3 Experiments

We use TP rate and F-value for the minority class to evaluate the results of our experiments. TP rate denotes the accuracy of the minority class. The value of β in F-value is set to 1 in this paper.

We will compare the experimental results of the three methods: SVM [8], DBN and Borderline Smote DBN. First of all, we compare the effect of SVM and DBN on phishing detection. At the same time, we don't consider the problem of whether the data is balanced. After that, the effect of training phishing detection model on normal DBN and Borderline Smote DBN in imbalanced data sets is compared. Because the experimental data of this paper is less and feature is more, the SVM model in this paper use the linear kernel.

In this paper, the training data is crawling from Internet using crawlers, there are 200 positive phishing examples from PhishTank website, and 2000 negative normal examples from 360 navigation page. Here, we make ratio of phishing sites to normal sites at 1:10 to simulate the unbalanced state of data in actual training.

We put a web document preprocessing into document feature vector $<F_1, F_2 \ldots F_n>$ for model training, e.g.: Judgment type fields use 0 or 1 represent false or true, use -1 to represent other case. Use $X(X > 0)$ to represent scalar type fields. According to the content of the article, by using TF-IDF to transform into vector $<C_1, C_2 \ldots C_n>$ after extraction. After that, the content vector is spliced into the document feature vector. This is the final model training vector.

In order to compare the results conveniently, the value of m in Borderline Smote is set in a way that, the number of the minority examples in DANGER is about half of the minority class. The value of k is set to 5 like SMOTE. For each method, the TP rates and F-values are obtained by 5-fold cross-validation. In order to reduce the randomness in Borderline Smote, the TP rates and F-values for these methods are the average results of three independent 5-fold cross-validation experiments.

Since the nature of imbalance problem is to improve the prediction performance of the minority class, we only present the results of the minority class. We compare the results of the data sets through TP rate and F-value of the minority class. TP rate reflects the performance of the learner on the minority class of the testing set, while F-value shows the performance of the learner on the whole testing set.

The Table 2 shows the effect of the SVM and DBN method on the two indicators, precision and recall, in phishing detection. We can see that the DBN method improves the precision and recall of phishing detection.

Table 2. Result compare SVM and DBN.

	Precision (%)	Recall (%)
SVM	95.2	90.3
DBN	96.5	90.7

Figure 3 shows the effect of DBN model on F-value and recall under the 400, 800, 1200, 1600 and 2000 synthetic positive examples used Borderline Smote method. We can see that with the ratio of the positive and negative examples close to 1, F-value and recall showed a rising trend.

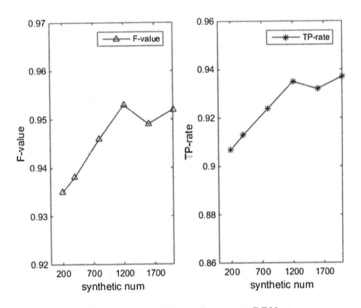

Fig. 3. Result of borderline smote DBN.

4   Conclusion

With the rise of deep learning, the paper presents a deep learning phishing detection method, aims to improve the phishing detection. Trying to solve the imbalance data set problem to further improve the accuracy of phishing detection. The result shows that deep learning has higher accuracy than shallow machine learning method, and more adapted to changing phishing detection. What's more, rebalance imbalance data set really works.

Acknowledgments. This work is supported by the National Key Research and Development Program of China (No. 2016QY03D0605), the National Nature Science Foundation of China (Nos. 61672111, 61370069), and Beijing Natural Science Foundation (No. 4162043).

References

1. Anti-Phishing Working Group [EB/OL]. http://www.antiphishing.org/
2. Anti-Phishing Alliance of China [EB/OL]. http://apac.cn/gzdt/qwfb/201705/P02017052 2548444760778.pdf
3. Anti-phishing Working Group. Phishing activity trends report [EB/OL] (2007). http://antiphishing.org/APWG_Report_March_2007.pdf
4. Kang, J.M., Lee D.H.: Advanced white list approach for preventing access to phishing sites. In: 2007 International Conference on Convergence Information Technology, pp. 491–496. IEEE (2007)
5. Huang, H., Qian, L., Wang, Y.: A SVM-based technique to detect phishing URLs. Inf. Technol. J. **11**(7), 921 (2012)
6. Han, H., Wang, W.Y., Mao, B.H.: Borderline-SMOTE: a new over-sampling method in imbalanced data sets learning. Adv. Intell. Comput. 878–887 (2005)
7. Chawla, N.V., Bowyer, K.W., Hall, L.O., et al.: SMOTE: synthetic minority over-sampling technique. J. Artif. Intell. Res. **16**, 321–357 (2002)
8. Lakshmi, S.V., Vijaya, M.S.: The SVM based interactive tool for predicting phishing websites. Int. J. Comput. Sci. Inf. Secur. **9**(10), 58 (2011)
9. Mohamed, A., Dahl, G., Hinton, G.: Deep belief networks for phone recognition. In: Nips Workshop on Deep Learning for Speech Recognition and Related Applications, vol. 1, no. 9, p. 39 (2009)
10. Batista, G.E., Prati, R.C., Monard, M.C.: A study of the behavior of several methods for balancing machine learning training data. ACM Sigkdd Explor. Newslett. **6**(1), 20–29 (2004)
11. Provost, F.: Machine learning from imbalanced data sets 101. In: Proceedings of the AAAI 2000 Workshop on Imbalanced Data Sets, pp. 1–3 (2000)

Research on Similarity Record Detection of Device Status Information Based on Multiple Encoding Field

Ziwen Liu[1,2], Liang Fang[1,3], Lihua Yin[1(✉)], Yunchuan Guo[1], and Fenghua Li[1,2]

[1] State Key Laboratory of Information Security, Institute of Information Engineering, Chinese Academy of Sciences, Beijing 100195, China
{liuziwen,lifenghua,yinlihua,guoyunchuan}@iie.ac.cn,
fangliang_iie@163.com
[2] School of Cyber Security, University of Chinese Academy of Sciences, Beijing 100049, China
[3] School of Cyberspace Security, Beijing University of Posts and Telecommunications, Beijing 100876, China

Abstract. Security management center needs to detect and delete many similar records of the device status information to reduce the data redundancy before analyzing the status of the supervised device. Most similarity record detection algorithms are based on the "sort-merge" model. Detection algorithms usually sort data set with keywords before detection of similar data. Existing methods of generating keywords tend to have the following problems: the keywords is not accurate, or multiple keywords are generated for sorting of multiple keywords. The paper proposes a method of synthesizing keywords by multiple encoding fields, and it is verified that this method can significantly optimize the performance of algorithm through experiment. We also compare the performance of each common detection algorithm through experiment.

Keywords: Similar records · Detection algorithms · Generate keywords
Device status information · Multiple encoding fields · Performance

1 Introduction

The security management center usually accumulates massive status information of cross-domain devices that is highly redundant, which is not conducive to state analysis, emergency response and other security management. Therefore, it is necessary to detect and delete similar data based on detection algorithms.

The purpose of similarity detection algorithm is to detect similar records [1]. Most Similar Record detection algorithms are based on the "sort-merge" model. The algorithms need to sort record set with keywords before calculating the similarity between records. Current methods of generating keywords have various problems, such as that the keywords are not accurate, or it may generate multiple keywords for sorting multiple keywords. Regarding the issue discussed above, the paper proposes a method of synthesizing keywords by multiple encoding fields based on the data characteristics

© Springer International Publishing AG 2017
G. Wang et al. (Eds.): SpaCCS 2017 Workshops, LNCS 10658, pp. 54–63, 2017.
https://doi.org/10.1007/978-3-319-72395-2_6

of device status information, and it is verified that this method can significantly optimizate the performance of algorithm through experiment. In order to choose an appropriate algorithm to detect the similarity of device status information, the paper also compares the detection performance of various common detection algorithms through experiment.

2 Similarity Record Detection Algorithms

The procedure of Similar Record detection algorithm consists of three steps: (1) Generate keywords; (2) Sort record sets based on keywords; (3) Detect similar records. Therefore, the similarity detection algorithms include two types: sorting algorithms and matching algorithms.

2.1 Similarity Record Sorting Algorithms

The most intuitive way to detect similar records is to match the pending record with the rest records one by one. Although this method can guarantee the accuracy of detection, it does not apply to the case involving massive data. The researchers have proposed various sorting algorithms to reduce the time of matching.

The purpose of sorting algorithm is to place potentially similar records in adjacent positions, and the pending record is only compared with adjacent records at a time. This algorithm can significantly reduce the number of comparisons and the time complexity. Common sorting algorithms include the Sorted-Neighborhood Method (SNM), Multi-Pass Sorted-Neighborhood Method (MPN) and Priority Queue Strategy (PQS).

(1) **Sorted-Neighborhood Method (SNM).** Hernandez et al. first proposed SNM algorithm [2, 3]. The algorithm sorts the record sets based on keywords, it has a slide window with fixed size for record sets that have been sorted, and the pending record is only compared with the rest records within the window. The SNM algorithm can reduce the number of comparisons and significantly improve the matching efficiency, but it heavily relies on the choice of keywords and window size.

(2) **Multi-Pass Sorted-Neighborhood Method (MPN).** In the SNM algorithm, it is difficult to use a single keyword to detect all similar records. To solve this problem, literature [4, 5] proposed MPN algorithm. MPN uses SNM independently on the sorted datasets for multiple times, different keywords are used for each sorting, and the results produced by SNM each time are integrated by calculating the transitive closure. MPN has the problem of mismatching because of calculating of the transitive closure.

(3) **Priority Queue Strategy (PQS).** Monge et al. proposed PQS algorithm [6, 7]. Instead of using slide window, PQS uses priority queue. Each of the priority queues represents a clustering of similar records. PQS also sorts datasets by keywords, and scans the sorted data set sequentially. The pending record is only compared with the records in priority queue, the pending record would be added

to the cluster when there is a record in the priority queue that matches it; otherwise, the pending record will be added to the priority queue as a new cluster, and the priority of the cluster will be set as highest. The greater the priority queue is, the greater the accuracy of the algorithm, but the longer the running time.

2.2   Similarity Record Matching Algorithms

The purpose of the matching algorithms is to calculate the similarity between records. Common matching algorithms include Field Matching Algorithm (FMA), Smith-Waterman Algorithm (SW) and Edit Distance Algorithm (EDA).

(1) **Field Matching Algorithm (FMA).** FMA divides the strings into several substrings [8], and the similarity is the result of the number of substrings that match two strings divided by the average number of all of their substrings.

(2) **Smith-Waterman Algorithm (SW).** Smith and Waterman proposed the Smith-Waterman algorithm [9]. The algorithm is a dynamic programming technique. It introduces the penalty and the gap through the score matrix to calculate the similarity between different records. The higher the value calculated by the score matrix is, the higher the similarity between the two strings.

(3) **Edit Distance Algorithm (EDA).** Levenshtein et al. proposed a similar record matching algorithm based on editing distance in [10]. The algorithm calculates the number of operations, such as insertion, deletion and substitution, that are required to change from a string to another string, and this number is called the "edit distance". The smaller the edit distance is, the higher the similarity between the two strings.

3   A Keyword Generation Method for Device Status Information

The sorting algorithm relies on keywords, and the selection of keywords has significant influence on the performance of algorithm. The keywords are required to represent the possibility of similarity between records, and how to select keywords depends on the data characteristics of the records.

The existing methods either select a field of the record to generate the keyword, or select multiple fields of the record to generate multiple keywords for sorting of multiple-keywords. The former method is simple, but it cannot guarantee the accuracy of the keyword; the latter can ensure the accuracy of the keyword, but it involves high time overhead. The paper proposes a method of synthesizing keywords with multiple encoding fields based on the data characteristics of device status information.

The device status information includes the device disk status, device network status, device memory status, and device process status. The device status information has the characteristic that the same device has highly similar data of status information during a certain period of time. According to this feature, we proposed a method to generate a keyword by using area encoding field, device encoding field and timestamp field.

The area field indicates the subnet area of device, the device field indicates the ID of device, and the timestamp field indicates the time when the record was generated.

In order to generate keywords easily, the area field and device field are simply encoded. The area field and the device field are encoded by a string of 0 and 1. The length of area field is related to the number of areas, and the length equals to the logarithm of the number of areas to base 2. The device field includes the area code and the device ID code, the value of the area code equals to area field, the length of device ID code equals to the logarithm of the number of devices to base 2, the area code is on the left side of the device ID code, and the whole length of device field equals to the sum of two lengths. The timestamp field is an integer number. Defining a timestamp field as an integer is for the convenience of synthesizing keywords; defining area field and device field as 01 string is intended to facilitate the dynamic expansion of the device while being easily converted to an integer. An example of area field, device field and timestamp field is as follows.

The example of area field, device field and timestamp field

```
char area[] = "101";
char deviceid[] = "10110";
int timestamp = 100;
```

The method of multiple encoding field synthesis keywords (MEFSK) treats the area field and device field as binary numbers, and changes them to decimal numbers to get two integers. Then, splice three integers in the order of the area encoding field, the device encoding field and the timestamp field to get a big integer, and this integer is the keyword. The pseudo code is as follows.

Pseudo code of generating keywords

```
begin
  char areabinary[] = getareafield();
  char deviceidbinary[] = getdeviceidfield();
  int time = gettimestamp();
  int area = binarytodecimal(areabinary);
  int deviceid = binarytodecimal(deviceidbinary);
  int keyword = splice(area, deviceid, time);
  return keyword;
end.
```

For example, generate keyword of the example above by MEFSK. Change the string "101" and "10110" to integer 5 and 22, then splice integer 5, 22 and 100 to get the big integer 522100, and the keyword is 522100.

While using the keyword generated by MEFSK to sort the record sets, it actually sorts records in the following order: sort by area field at first, and then sort by device ID field, and sort by timestamp field at last. This method can obtain the sorting results of multiple keywords based on only one keyword, reduce the time overhead of sorting, and place potentially similar records in adjacent positions to the highest extent.

4 Experimental Results and Analysis

The paper verifies that the method of synthesizing keywords by multiple encoding fields can significantly optimize the performance of algorithm through experiment. We also compared the performance of various common detection algorithms through experiment.

4.1 Environment of Experiment

(1) **Network Topology.** The experiment simulates the network environment of device cross domain, and the experimental topology is shown in Fig. 1.

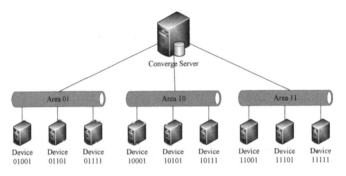

Fig. 1. The diagram of experimental topology. The experiment includes three network segments of area 01, area 10 and area 11, each network segment consists of three devices, and there are 9 devices in total.

The topology includes three network segments, and each network segment consists of three devices. In the experiment, we detected similar records of device status information created by the nine devices.

(2) **Hardware environment.** The system of converge server is Ubuntu. The system of device is either Windows or Ubuntu. The specific hardware environment is as shown below. All system were run in the virtual machine.

Hardware environment

```
Ubuntu System
  Version:14.04 x86
  RAM:1GB
  CPU:Intel(R) Core(TM) i7-6700 CPU @ 3.40GHz
  Disk:10GB
  Virtual Machine Version:VMware 10.0
Ubuntu System
Window System
  Version:Windows 7 x64
  RAM:1GB
  CPU:Intel(R) Core(TM) i7-6700 CPU @ 3.40GHz
  Disk:10GB
  Virtual Machine Version:VMware 10.0
Window System
```

(3) **Experimental Data Set.** In the experiment, 9000 similar records of device status information generated by nine devices in the topology were detected.

Each device generates device status information for two different time periods, and the data generated during the same time period are similar data. The device status information includes the device disk status, device network status, device memory status, and device process status.

4.2 Experimental Scheme

In the experiment, the Sorted-Neighborhood Method (SNM) and Priority Queue Strategy (PQS) were selected to sort the records and select Field Matching Algorithm (FMA), Smith-Waterman (SW) and Edit Distance Algorithm (EDA) to match the records. The experiment combines two sorting algorithms and three detection algorithms to obtain six different detection methods. The similarity threshold in the experiment was set at 0.9.

In terms of keywords, in the experiment, the following four different keywords were generated: (1) A keyword generated by MEFSK; (2) A keyword generated by using only area encoding field; (3) A keyword generated by using only device encoding field; (4) A keyword generated by using only timestamp field.

In the experiment, each detection method was used to sort records by four different keywords. Measures were taken to ensure that other conditions remain unchanged while only changing the sorting keyword for each detection method. Finally, the performance of algorithms was compared based on related statistics and analysis of detection results. The paper analyzes five performance indicators of detection algorithms: precision, recall, detection time, the number of matches and the score of performance.

The experiment consists of the following steps: (1) Select a method of detection; (2) Select one of the four keywords; (3) Sort record sets; (4) Match records; (5) Statistics and analysis of detect results.

4.3   Results and Analysis

The results are shown in line charts. In the charts, the horizontal axis indicates the detection method, and the vertical axis represents the relevant performance indicators. The horizontal axis consists of six fixed values that represent six detection methods. For example, SNM&FMA represents using the SNM sort records and FMA matching records. There are four different types of lines in charts: (1) The square point indicates that the keywords were generated by MEFSK; (2) The dots indicates that the keywords were generated by using timestamp field; (3) The positive triangle indicates that the keywords were generated by using area encoding field; (4) The inverted triangle indicates that the keywords were generated by using device encoding field.

Figure 2 shows the experimental results of precision and recall: the results of precision are shown on the left, and the results of recall are shown on the right.

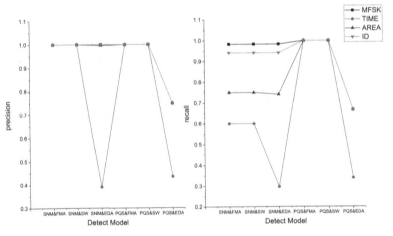

Fig. 2. The results of precision and recall. The results of precision are shown on the left, and the results of recall are shown on the right.

(1) **Precision.** Precision (precision $= tp/(tp + fp)$) represents the correct recognition rate for similar records, tp is the number of records that were recognized rightly, and fp is the number of records that were recognized incorrectly.

By observing the experimental results of the precision, we can see that FMA and SW have high accuracy close to 100% no matter what sorting algorithm or keywords are used. EDA has poor accuracy except at few points. When we use SNM algorithm to sort records, EDA has a high accuracy (except use keyword generated by timestamp). The reason is that SNM has a window, and it only matches the records within the window each time. When we use the right keywords to sort records, it can place the records that easily to match incorrectly on each side of window, do not match them and reduce the error rate.

From the chart, we can determine that EDA is not suitable for detecting similar records of device status information. For example, when judging whether the IP addresses "192.168.10.01" and "192.168.30.01" are similar, the results of the similarity are 0.75, 0.846 and 0.99 respectively by using the FMA, SW and EDA methods. When using the EDA method, the result is that they are highly similar; when using the FMA and SW methods, the results are that they are not similar. Although the two strings are highly similar, they represent two totally different IP addresses of two net segments.

(2) **Recall.** Recall (recall $= tp/(tp + fn)$) represents how many records of all similar records are matched. In which, tp is the number of records that recognized rightly, and fn is the number of unrecognized similar records.

According to the experimental results of recall, the recall of PQS is generally higher than that of SNM. The recall is poor when we use EDA to match the records, and the reason is that EDA has poor precision.

From the chart, we can see that when we use SNM to sort records, the recall is significantly different when we use different keywords. The recall obtained by using keyword generated by MEFSK is significantly higher than the recall of others.

Figure 3 shows the experimental results of detection time and the number of matches (nom). The results of time are shown on the left side of Fig. 3, the results of numbers are shown on the right.

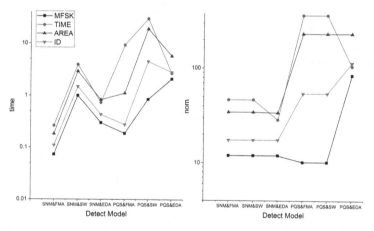

Fig. 3. The result of time and the number of matches. The results of time are on the left; the results of numbers (nom) are on the right.

(3) **Detection time.** Detection time refers to the whole time of detection from beginning to the end. The value of each point in Fig. 3 equals to the logarithm of real time to base 10, so that it can show them intuitively.

Based on the experimental results of time, we know that when we use the same matching algorithm, the time of PQS is generally longer than that of SNM. When we use the same sorting algorithm, the time of SW is the longest among all matching algorithms, and the time of FMA is the shortest. By observing the overall trend, we know that the time required by using keyword generated by MEFSK is significantly shorter than the time under other situation.

(4) **Number of matches(NOM).** NOM refers to the number of all matches during the detecting process. The value of each point in Fig. 3 equals to the actual number divided by 1000, and then logarithm it to base 10 to show them intuitively.

In accordance with the experimental results of NOM, we can see that when we use the same matching algorithm, the NOM obtained by using PQS is generally higher than that when the SNM method is used. We also know that when we use the same sorting algorithm, the NOM obtained by using keywords generated by MEFSK is significantly smaller than the NOM obtained by using other method. Figure 4 shows the experimental results of performance score.

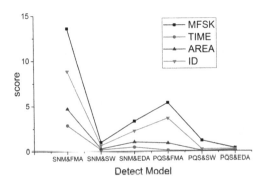

Fig. 4. The results of performance score. The score is calculated from Formula 2, and the higher the score is, the better the performance.

(5) **Performance score.** Literature [11] provides a method to measure the value of F. We introduce the value of S based on the value of F, and the value of S represents performance score.

We can get the value of F from formula 1.

$$F\_score = \frac{2 * precision * recall}{precision + recall} \tag{1}$$

We introduce the detection time to calculate the value of S based on formula 2, and we can obtain the value of S from Formula 2.

$$S = F\_score/rt \tag{2}$$

According to the experimental results of score, we can see that when we use the same matching algorithm, the score of SNM is generally higher than that of PQS. We also know that when we use the same sorting algorithm, the score of SW is the lowest among all matching algorithms. and the score of FMA is the highest. We can see from chart that the score obtained by using keyword generated by MEFSK is significantly higher than the score obtained by using other methods.

5 Conclusion

Through comprehensive analysis of all experimental results, we can draw the following conclusions: (1) EDA cannot detect similar records of device status information very well; (2) SW requires longer time for detection than FMA; (3) PQS has higher recall, and the SNM has better performance on the aspect of time; (4) By using keyword generated by MEFSK, it can significant optimize the performance of algorithm. For PQS, this method can significantly reduce the time overhead on the basis of high recall. For SNM, this method can significantly optimize the recall on the basis of short time overhead.

Acknowledgments. This work is supported by the National Key Research and Development Program of China (2016YFB0800303).

References

1. Dhivyabharathi, G.V., Kumaresan, S.: A survey on duplicate record detection in real world data. In: International Conference on Advanced Computing and Communication Systems, pp. 1–5 (2016)
2. Guo, W.: Improved SNM algorithm based on length filtering and effective weights. Comput. Eng. Appl. (2014)
3. Hernandez, M., Stolfo, S.: Real- world data is dirty: data cleansing and the merge/purge problem. Data Mining Knowl. Discov. **2**(1), 9–37 (1998)
4. Kolb, L., Thor, A., Rahm, E.: Multi-pass sorted neighborhood blocking with MapReduce. Comput. Sci. – Res. Dev. **27**(1), 45–63 (2012)
5. Hernandez, M., Stolfo, S.: The merge/purge problem for large databases. In: Proceedings of the ACM SIGMOD International Conference on Management of Data, San Jose, California, pp. 127–138 (1995)
6. Shankar V., Rao, C.V.G.: A density based priority queue strategy to evaluate iceberg queries efficiently using compressed bitmap indices. Int. J. Comput. Appl. **67**(21), 39–44 (2013)
7. Monge, A., Elkan, C.: An efficient domain independent algorithm for detecting approximately duplicate database records. In: Proceedings of the SIGMOD Workshop on Data Mining and Knowledge Discovery, Tucson, Arizona, pp. 23–29 (1997)
8. Minton, S.N., Nanjo, C., Knoblock, C.A., et al.: A heterogeneous field matching method for record linkage. In: Proceeding of the 5th IEEE International Conference on Data Mining, Houston, Texas, USA, pp. 314–321 (2005)
9. Smith, T.F., Waterman, M.S.: Identification of common molecular subsequences. J. Mol. Biol. **147**(1), 195–197 (1981)
10. Levenshtein, I.V.: Binary codes capable of correcting spurious insertions and deletions of ones. Probl. Inf. Trans. **1**, 8–17 (1965)
11. Rehman, M., Esichaikul, V.: Duplicate record detection for database cleansing. In: Proceedings of the 2nd International Conference on Machine Vision, Dubai, United Arab Emirates, pp. 333–338 (2009)

Security Review and Study of DoS Attack on DNS in the International Roaming EPC_LTE Network

Ya'nan Tian[(⊠)], Wen'an Zhou, and Wenlong Liu

School of Computer Science,
Beijing University of Posts and Telecommunications, Beijing 100000, China
tianyanan7080321@163.com, fans656@163.com,
zhouwa@bupt.edu.cn

Abstract. The communication standard Long Term Evolution (LTE) developed by 3GPP is becoming the mainstream technology of the next generation mobile communication, the new features meet the business needs and improve the user experience, but also bring some security threats. In this paper, we introduce the LTE roaming architecture, the attach procedure and the DNS resolution procedure. Then we analyze that MME initiate the DNS request before the authentication is completed based on the procedures and OpenAirInterface (OAI) code, which will lead to a large load on DNS server, this scheme is very vulnerable to DoS/DDoS attacks on DNS server. Finally, according to the characteristics of LTE, we propose a enhancement scheme in MME and analyze the feasibility.

Keywords: LTE · DNS · DoS/DDoS · OAI

1 Introduction

With more and more operators began to deploy LTE networks, LTE based international roaming is also being gradually promoted. According to China Mobile Communications Corporation (CMCC) news reports, by the end of April 2015, China Mobile and the United States, South Korea and other 73 countries and regions launched 4G roaming service, and has launched 4G network testing in many countries and regions, 4G roaming service in these countries and regions will be gradually opened with the completion of the test [1]. The GSMA developed IPX for operators to enable their subscribers to roam globally and to interconnect its full suite of voice and data services through a secure IPX connection. It defined standards to enable interoperability from technical and commercial perspectives.

LTE network has many features compared with UMTS, it uses more flat, all IP network architecture and has fewer network nodes, faster data transmission rate, more flexible bandwidth, lower transmission delay and seamless connection with other existing wireless communication system etc. These new features meet the business needs and improve the user experience but also bring some security threats.

© Springer International Publishing AG 2017
G. Wang et al. (Eds.): SpaCCS 2017 Workshops, LNCS 10658, pp. 64–73, 2017.
https://doi.org/10.1007/978-3-319-72395-2_7

LTE system is a mobile Internet system based on IP, which means that the LTE will face the challenge of traditional IP Internet security threats too. In the recent past, there have been many instances of flooding attacks on the Domain Name System (DNS) aimed at preventing clients from resolving resource records belonging to the zone under attack [2–4]. At the 2016 European black hat conference [5], researchers at NOKIA's Baer lab tested the simulation on a test network: an attack on an unnamed British mobile operator in Finland. The research team found that the Diameter framework can be used in different ways to interrupt the connection of specific users and nodes. The experiment proves that it can successfully launch Denial of Service (DoS) attacks.

The rest of this paper is organized as follows: Sect. 2 introduces the background knowledge. In Sect. 3, we analyze the security of DNS resolution procedures and describe the possibility of overload in the local DNS and the root DNS. In Sect. 4, a security enhancement scheme is designed, meanwhile we analyze the reliability of the new scheme. the last part is the conclusion part in Sect. 5.

2 Background Knowledge

DNS procedures take place in lots of mobile procedures [6–8]: attach procedure (the data session establishment procedure), inter-MME Tracking Area Update procedure, inter-MME S1-based Handover procedure. Because the first attachment request procedure includes the authentication procedure and the DNS resolution procedure, so this paper will describe the attach procedure in detail as an example. In addition, we will also describe LTE roaming architecture and the DNS resolution procedure.

2.1 LTE Roaming Architecture

Figure 1 represents the roaming with Home routed case. In addition, LTE roaming architecture consists of local breakout case with Application Function (AF) in the Home Network and in the Visited Network, due to space limitation, more information can be viewed in documentation [6].

Home Subscriber Server (HSS) stores subscription and profile information of every user registered in a Home Public Land Mobile Network (HPLMN). In the Visiting Public Land Mobile Network (VPLMN), each User Equipment (UE) connects with an evolved NodeB (eNB) through the Uu interface. eNB is the new enhanced Base Transceiver Station (BTS), provides the LTE air interface and implementation of radio resource management for the evolved access system. An eNB is connected with one or more Mobility Management Entities (MME) through the S1-MME interface. eNB connects Serving Gateway (SGW) through S1-U interface. The MME interacted with the HSS is the key control node for the LTE access network which is responsible for authenticating the user. For obtaining authentication data, the MME communicates with the HSS through the S6a interface. For obtaining the IP address of SGW/PGW, MME communicates with one or more Domain Name Server (DNS). SGW conveys user-plane traffic which connects PDN Gateway through S5/S8 interface, When the roaming network model is Home routed case, S8 interface is used.

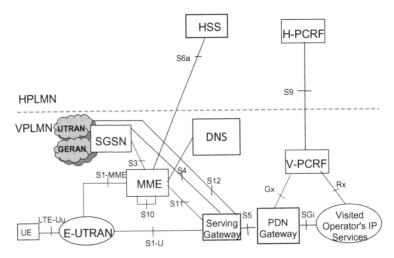

Fig. 1. LTE roaming architecture

2.2 The Attach Procedure

Figure 2 represents the attach procedure lunched by UE (For example, when the phone is turned on), this paper will introduce the key steps related to this topic in detail.

Step 1: The EPS Session Management (ESM) sub-layer of UE-NAS triggers the default PDN connection establishment process, sending the PDN connection request to the EPS Mobility Management (EMM) sub-layer of UE-NAS.

Step 2: The EMM sub-layer of UE triggers the attachment process after receiving the PDN connection request, and the EMM sub-layer of UE sends the Attach Request & PDN connection request to the UE-RRC layer.

Step 3: The RRC layer of UE trigger the RRC connection process after receiving the upper NAS message, send RRC connection request to eNB.

Step 4: eNB sends RRC connection setup response.

Step 5: The UE receives the RRC Connection Setup message, sent to the eNB RRC connection setup complete message which contains NAS information: Attach Request and PDN Connection Request.

Step 6: eNB receives the message, then selects a MME according to selected PLMN-Identity and Globally Unique MME Identifier (GUMMEI). The Initial UE message contain NAS message to MME: Attach Request and PDN Connection Request.

Step 7: After the EMM sub-layer of MME receives the message, the PDN Connection Request is passed to the ESM sub-layer of MME and the EMM of MME sub-layer handles only Attach Request, during the process of attaching the request, EMM of MME requests to the visited DNS for the IP of PGW. The detailed analysis of DNS is in the 2.3 part.

Step 8: EMM sub-layer of MME performs NAS authentication process.

Step 9: The ESM sub-layer of MME receives the PDN Connection Request message and sends the Diameter message to HSS: Location Update Acknowledge, HSS provide the data (PDN signing context, APN-AMBR) to MME.

Step 10: MME sends Create Session Request message to the SGW, which includes the GTP-C tunnel identifier for the down-link MME and the relevant information about the default bearer to be established.

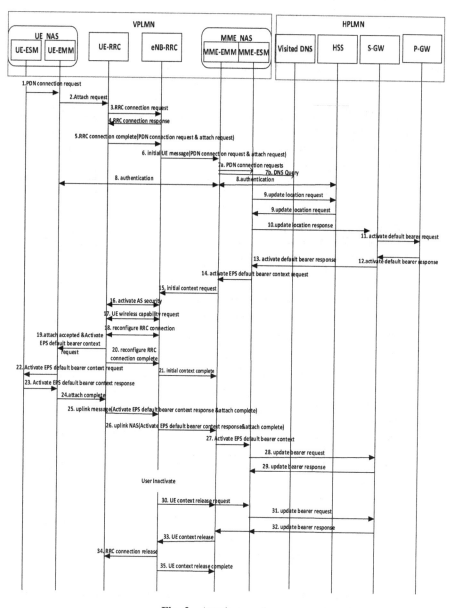

Fig. 2. Attach procedure

2.3 DNS Resolution Procedure

DNS is critical to such services as LTE roaming. The DNS call flow mechanism is based on the 3GPP standards defined in the following:

TS 23.401 [6], TS 23.060 [7] for node selection principles
TS 29.303 [8] for DNS procedures
TS 23.003 [9] for node identifiers

Figure 3 shows the typical call-flow for DNS interrogation on the IPX for one operator to resolve a domain name of another operator.

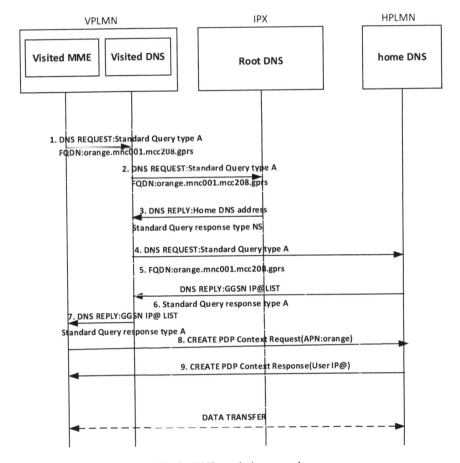

Fig. 3. DNS resolution procedure

Step 1: MME in VPLMN sends a query for the hostname for which it wants the IP address, to its Local Caching DNS server which is in VPLMN.
Step 2: The visited DNS server checks to see if it has the answer to the query in its cache. If it hit, it answers the visited MME immediately. If it does not hit, it

forwards the query on to the Root DNS server (in IPX). The addresses of the Root DNS server may be statically configured in the Local Caching DNS server.
Step 3: The Root DNS server (in IPX) returns a referral to the visited DNS server which is authoritative for the queried domain name of the host-name.
Step 4: The visited DNS server firstly caches the response for a specified amount of time and then re-sends the query to the Authoritative DNS server which is in HPLMN.
Step 5: The Authoritative DNS server responds to the query with the address of the host-name to the visited DNS server in the requesting network.
Step 6: The visited DNS server caches the response for a specified amount of time and forwards it on to MME.

3 Security Analysis

This paper analyzes the security of DNS server from two aspects: procedure and code of OAI.

3.1 Analysis the Attach Procedure

Some inter-relationship between the NAS and AS protocols is intentionally used to allow procedures to run simultaneously, rather than sequentially as in UMTS. For example, the bearer establishment procedure can be executed by the network without waiting for the completion of the security procedure [11].

So from the Fig. 2, we can see that step 7 and step 8 are respectively triggered by the EMM sub-layer of MME and the ESM sub-layer of MME. The two sub-layers have a parallel relationship. Step 9 is not obliged to wait for step 8, in other words the ESM sublayer of MME can launch a PDN connection request before the completion of the authentication request, this will lead to some malicious users or malicious software to launch a large number of continuous requests to the MME, resulting in excessive load on the local DNS server, this scheme is very vulnerable to DoS/DDoS attacks on the local DNS server. In addition if the local DNS server does not hit these requests, the local DNS server will send DNS requests to the root DNS server in IPX, which will cause excessive load on the root DNS server. In this scenario, the root DNS server in IPX is vulnerable to DoS/DDoS attack, which will exert a great influence on the international roaming service. The root server can serve a user that does not pass authentication, which is one of the weaknesses of IPX.

3.2 Analysis the Attach Code in OpenAirInterface (OAI)

(OpenAirInterface) OAI [10] is an open source software, and it can run in the traditional Linux system without extra configuration, more and more academic organizations, equipment manufacturers and operators are using and joining the design and development process of OAI open source software, it is gradually applied in the research work and production environment.

In addition to call-flow analysis, this paper also analyzes the security risks faced by DNS according to the OAI code.

Figure 4 is the _emm_attach_identify function which is in \openair-cn\SRC\NAS\ nas_itti_messaging.c, the function execute the attach procedure requested by the UE. It checks the IMSI firstly, then it sends authentication request to s6a_task.c.

```
static int
_emm_attach_identify (
  void *args)
{
  int                          rc = RETURNerror;
  emm_data_context_t           *emm_ctx = (emm_data_context_t *) (args);

  OAILOG_FUNC_IN (LOG_NAS_EMM);
  REQUIREMENT_3GPP_24_301(R10_5_5_1_2_3__1);
  OAILOG_INFO (LOG_NAS_EMM, "ue_id=" MME_UE_S1AP_ID_FMT " EMM-PROC   - Identify incoming UE using %s\n",
      emm_ctx->ue_id,
      IS_EMM_CTXT_VALID_IMSI(emm_ctx)   ? "IMSI" :
      IS_EMM_CTXT_PRESENT_GUTI(emm_ctx) ? "GUTI" :
      IS_EMM_CTXT_VALID_IMEI(emm_ctx)   ? "IMEI" : "none");

  /*
   * UE's identification
   * --------------------
   */
  if (IS_EMM_CTXT_PRESENT_IMSI(emm_ctx)) {
    // The UE identifies itself using an IMSI
    if (!IS_EMM_CTXT_PRESENT_AUTH_VECTORS(emm_ctx)) {
      // Ask upper layer to fetch new security context
      nas_itti_auth_info_req (emm_ctx->ue_id, emm_ctx->_imsi64, true, &emm_ctx->originating_tai.plmn, MAX_EPS_AUTH_VECTORS, NULL);
      rc = RETURNok;
    } else {
      ksi_t                        eksi = 0;
      int                          vindex = 0;

      if (emm_ctx->_security.eksi != KSI_NO_KEY_AVAILABLE) {
        REQUIREMENT_3GPP_24_301(R10_5_4_2_4__2);
        eksi = (emm_ctx->_security.eksi + 1) % (EKSI_MAX_VALUE + 1);
      }
      for (vindex = 0; vindex < MAX_EPS_AUTH_VECTORS; vindex++) {
        if (IS_EMM_CTXT_PRESENT_AUTH_VECTOR(emm_ctx, vindex)) {
          break;
        }
      }
    }
```

Fig. 4. Flow chart of _emm_cn_pdn_connectivity_res

Figure 5 presents another part of the _emm_attach_identify function which is in \openair-cn\SRC\NAS\ nas_itti_messaging.c. It checks the return value firstly, if the return value is not error, then it trigger the attachment request.

From the Fig. 4, we can see that the rc is directly assigned to RETURNok, which dose not wait for the result of the authentication and does not have any nothing with the authentication result, because rc is assigned to RETURNok, so the attachment request judgment can be directly executed, and did not have any relationship with the authentication result.

4   Security Enhancement Scheme and Reliability Analysis

The smart-phone is increasing gradually, Mobile phone virus is also growing. Mobile malware can create smart-phone botnets in which a large number of mobile devices conspire to perform malicious activities on the cellular network. Smart-phone botnets will be a major security threat faced by LTE networks, criminals can use its control of the botnets to launch a massive attack on DoS/DDoS mobile communication network. The authors in [12, 13] studied the feasibility of DoS attack and analyzes its impact on

```
/*
 * UE's authentication
 * -------------------
 */
if (rc != RETURNerror) {
    if (IS_EMM_CTXT_VALID_SECURITY(emm_ctx)) {
        /*
         * A security context exists for the UE in the network;
         * proceed with the attach procedure.
         */
        rc = _emm_attach (emm_ctx);
    } else if ((emm_ctx->is_emergency) && (_emm_data.conf.features & MME_API_UNAUTHENTICATED_IMSI)) {
        /*
         * 3GPP TS 24.301, section 5.5.1.2.3
         * 3GPP TS 24.401, Figure 5.3.2.1-1, point 5a
         * MME configured to support Emergency Attach for unauthenticated
         * IMSIs may choose to skip the authentication procedure even if
         * no EPS security context is available and proceed directly to the
         * execution of the security mode control procedure.
         */
        rc = _emm_attach_security (emm_ctx);
    }
}
```

Fig. 5. Code of emm_attach

QoS. Lain et al. in [14], in the roaming LTE network, realize a pulse DoS using the lack of coordination between local and remote components of the LTE network during the roaming authentication process.

Figure 6 shows the percentage of response of the DNS server with different configurations to the request packet. From the diagram, the percentage of the response will drop suddenly when the requested data reaches 1600.

In the Internet, although it is difficult to distinguish normal traffic and DoS attack traffic because the DoS attackers generally hide their true identities/origins, there have been many solutions for DoS/DDoS attack on DNS.

Ayyaz et al. in [15] proposed a security system which keeps track of every IP address of connecting device and provide services to each host based on the set threshold. by implementing a firewall in the network. Chiba et al. in [16] have proposed a new filtering scheme to mitigate the effect of DDoS attack by registering the correspondence DNS query and responsed to the ingress filtering rule of the firewall. The authors in [17, 18] monitor the traffic flow using the CUSUM algorithm. The authors in [19, 20] prevent DoS attacks by improving cache structure, according to the characteristics of TTL.

In this paper, we can set the cache in MME according to the characteristics of LTE. When there is a DNS query request, MME first query in its own cache, if the cache records this information, it is not necessary to initiate DNS request, only when records in the MME cache do not contain this information, it initiates the DNS request. This can reduce the load on the DNS server.

Because the hardware conditions can be easily upgraded, and the cost is lower and lower. If the MME cache hit, due to the omission of the DNS request, it can reduce the delay. If the MME cache does not hit, it can complete the local query in a very short time by adding fast cache in MME. For MME, because the cache is running very fast, the delay caused by it can not have a great impact on the overall efficiency, so on the whole, the quality of service (QoS) will not be reduced.

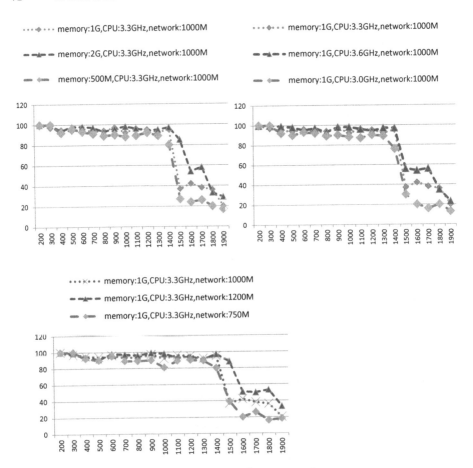

Fig. 6. Percentage of response packets

5 Conclusions

In this paper, we first introduced the LTE roaming architecture, the attach procedure and the DNS resolution procedure. By analyzing the procedure and OAI code, we reveal that MME initiated the DNS request before the authentication was completed, which will likely lead to DoS/DDoS attacks on DNS. Finally, according to the characteristics of LTE, we propose a enhancement scheme in MME and analyze the feasibility.

References

1. http://www.10086.cn/aboutus/news/GroupNews/201504/t20150429_58803.htm
2. Microsoft DDoS Attack, NetworkWorld, January 2001. http://www.networkworld.com/news/2001/0125mshacked.html

3. UltrDNS DDoS Attack, Washington Post, May 2005. http://blog.washingtonpost.com/securityfix/2006/05/blue_security_surrenders_but_s.html
4. http://it.sohu.com/20161025/n471217376.shtml
5. http://www.blackhat.com/eu-16
6. 3GPP TS 23.401: General Packet Radio Service (GPRS) enhancements for Evolved Universal Terrestrial Radio Access Network (E-UTRAN) access
7. 3GPP TS 23.060: General Packet Radio Service (GPRS) service description
8. 3GPP TS 29.303: Domain Name System Procedures
9. 3GPP TS 23.003: Numbering, addressing and identification
10. http://www.openairinterface.org/
11. Sesia, S., Toufik, I., Baker, M.: LTE-The UMTS Long Term Evolution from Theory to Practice. The People's Posts and Telecommunications Press (Posts & Telecom Press), Beijing (2009)
12. Jermyn, J., Sallesloustau, G., Zonouz, S.: An analysis of DoS attack strategies against the LTE RAN. J. Cyber Secur. 3(2), 159–180 (2014)
13. Henrydoss, J., Boult, T.: Critical security review and study of DDoS attacks on LTE mobile network. In: 2014 IEEE Asia Pacific Conference on Wireless and Mobile, pp. 194–200. IEEE (2014)
14. Ambrosin, M., Cecconello, S., Conti, M., Lain, D.: A roaming-based denial of service attack on LTE networks: poster. In: ACM Conference on Security and Privacy in Wireless and Mobile Networks, pp. 283–284. ACM (2017)
15. Ayyaz, S., Khan, M.A., Ahmad, J., et al.: A novel security system for preventing DoS attacks on 4G LTE networks. In: International Conference on Wireless Networks, ICWN (2016)
16. Chiba, T., Katoh, T., Bista, B.B., et al.: DoS packet filter using DNS information. In: 20th International Conference on Advanced Information Networking and Applications, pp. 1–6. IEEE (2006)
17. Wang, H., Zhang, D., Shin, K.G.: Change-point monitoring for detection of DoS attacks. IEEE Trans. Dependable Secure Comput. 1(4), 193–208 (2004)
18. Lee, P.P.C., Bu, T., Woo, T.: On the detection of signaling DoS attacks on 3G wireless networks. In: IEEE International Conference on Computer Communications, INFOCOM 2007, pp. 1289–1297. IEEE (2007)
19. Ballani, H., Francis, P.: A simple approach to DNS DoS mitigation. ACM Sigcomm Hotnets 12(34), 5536–5539 (2016)
20. Pappas, V., Zhang, B., Osterweil, E., Massey, D., Zhang, L.: Improving DNS Service Availability by Using Long TTLs. draft-pappas-dnsop-long-ttl-02. June 2006

A SYN Flood Detection Method Based on Self – similarity in Network Traffic

Daxiu Zhang, Xiaojuan Zhu[✉], and Lu Wang

School of Computer Science and Engineering,
Anhui University of Science and Technology, Huainan 232001, Anhui, China
1451358113@qq.com, 455729318@qq.com, xjzhu@aust.edu.cn

Abstract. Since the normal data fail to be transmitted under the SYN Flood attack, the paper proposes a detection method which can rapidly and accurately detect the SYN Flood attack. First, it takes a real - time intercept of network traffic, and selects network traffic to discrete. Second, the fitting function can be achieved by fitting the discrete network traffic repeatedly. Finally, the integral value of the fitting function is calculated, which is used to compare with the Hurst value. The SYN Flood attack can be effectively detected by comparing the integral value, which calculated by the fitting function curve, with the Hurst value of the network traffic.

Keywords: Curve fitting · Integral calculation · SYN Flood attack
Hurst value · Network self-similarity

1 Introduction

Network traffic can be monitored by software in real time or captured by some codes. What's more, in order to better reflect the characteristics of network traffic, many scholars use wavelet analysis, chaos theory, and support vector machines and other models [1] to analyze the network traffic. Howere, there are still congestion network traffic. The most traditional malicious attacks is denial of service attacks, which results in the host network congestion and makes the attack host fail to work. It occurs in Transmission Control Protocol (TCP) during data transmission process, producing a large number of SYN packets, thereby forming a SYN Flood attack. In order to detect SYN Flood attack, the network traffic of the self – similarity is monitored and intercepted in real time, and the intercepted network traffic is discreted to obtain corresponding discrete points. The discrete points is fitted by curve fitting, through comparing analysis of integral value with Hurst value, we can quickly and efficiently detected malicious attack.

2 Related Research

2.1 Network Self-similarity

Many scholars have found that network traffic has self - similarity characteristics. The concept of self - similarity was first proposed in the study of nonlinear problems. In

© Springer International Publishing AG 2017
G. Wang et al. (Eds.): SpaCCS 2017 Workshops, LNCS 10658, pp. 74–82, 2017.
https://doi.org/10.1007/978-3-319-72395-2_8

1994, Leland and others [2, 3] proposed that the network traffic exhibits the self - similarity phenomenon for the first time. Then by analyzing the LAN they found that the actual network traffic model had self - similarity. These models are simple and practical, and easy to control and better reflect self-similarity (at least one state has heavy - tailed distribution behavior) [4]. For detection methods of self - similarity networks, under ARMA (autoregressive moving average) model, [5] proposed EMD (Empirical Mode Decomposition) self - similarity sequence prediction method, which transformed the long - related network traffic problems into a short correlation problem.

TCP SYN Flood attack cause end users unable to use network resources normally. When client sends data to server, if client sends many requests to server, client need to accept SYN - ACK respond. But due to the IP addresses of these requests are forged and do not exist, server does not reply, which cause normal request cannot continue. Resources will be exhausted and unable to respond to normal data transmission. For the TCP/IP protocol to finish data traffic transmission from send requests to disconnection message, the specific process can be summarized as: "three - way handshake" and "four waving".

2.2   SYN Flood Attack Detection Method

At present, some attacks exploit some loopholes or erroneous software to attack in a short period of time [6], which makes server performance drop. Some attacks exhaust all available resource on the target, leading to server has no available resource. In [7] proposed a new defense mechanism, which uses edge router to connect hosts and the Internet storage devices to detect whether the outgoing SYN, ACK, or incoming SYN/ACK segment are valid. Milkovich [8] detects source of attack by monitoring output and input data flow and comparing them with the normal traffic model, it can find the behavior of attacks. [9] implemented a denial of service detection framework with TCP SYN Flood threshold and misuse detection, which include packet sniffer, feature extraction, attack detection and output modules. About this modules, [10] explains methods for preventing and mitigating of TCP SYN Flood Attacks. Many scholars use R/S analysis, variance time and wavelet analysis to calculate the Hurst value, and observe the changes in Hurst value to determine if the network traffic is being attacked. Base on the self - similarity, the Hurst exponential variance [11] is compared with the experimental data of MIT to judge whether it has been maliciously attacked. [12] proposed an improved detection method, WAIE, which uses the wavelet analysis method to detecte attacks. And others use information entropy to analyze IP address and calculate Hurst value to detect attacks. However, [13] implement Attack detection and defense algorithms in dual-stack firewall, and test the validity and performance.

Based on the self - similarity of network traffic, due to the defect of the semi - connection attack, the client sends SYN packets for data transmission. And each SYN packet must be handled as a server connection request, so server must use SYN - ACK to answer. In order to detect SYN Flood attacks, data packets are analyzed, not just packet headers. Monitoring packets can easily detect malicious attacks, so we can detect malicious attacks on the server by reducing the acknowledgement reply message to detect the forged IP address in the TCP packet.

3   Experimental Theoretical Analysis

The innovation of this paper is the nine - level fitting network traffic. Then the integral value of the fitting curve is calculated. Traditional SYN Flood attack detection is by calculating the Hurst value and observing the change. However, in this paper, the method is not the former ones, but to use the integral value of the fitting curve comparing with Hurst = 0.5.

Theoretical basis: For a given function f(x), the definite integral of f(x) in a range [a, b] is $\int_a^b f(x)dx$. We can understand that the fitting curve (x, f (x)), line x = a, x = b, and the area value of the curved trapezoid formed by the X axis. The formula is:

$$\int_a^b f(x)dx = \lim_{n \to \infty} \sum_{i=0}^{n} [a + f(t_i)\frac{b-a}{n}]$$

The Hurst index reflects the results of a long list of interconnected events. There are three forms:

1. If H = 0.5, the time series can be described by random walk;
2. If 0.5 < H < 1, it indicates that time series has long-term memory;
3. If $0 \le H < 0.5$, it indicates that the pink noise (anti - persistence) is the mean reverting processes. That is, as long as $H \ne 0.5$, the time series data can be described with a biased Brownian motion (fractal Brownian motion).

Hypothesis: the difference between normal network traffic and Hurst = 0.5 is within 0.5, and the difference (D) between attack network traffic and Hurst = 0.5 is D > 0.5. The main steps of proof are as follows:

Step 1. Obtain discrete points of network traffic: Capture network traffic using feature extraction to obtain feature point pixels.
Step 2. Function f(x) fit the discrete poin: Using the MATLAB platform, the obtained discrete points are fitted by function, and get the closest curve.
Step 3. The experimental proves the hypothesis: the relationship between the integral value of fitting curve and Hurst = 0.5 is proved by experimental result.

4   The Process of SYN Flood Attack Detection

4.1   Obtain the Discrete Points of Network Traffic

This paper use programs to capture the network traffic of local in real time. In the period of 18:00–20:00, other servers send TCP/IP data frequently to the machine, and artificially join attacks. The random intercept an attack packet traffic is shown in Fig. 1. And the local normal network traffic in Fig. 2 and parse it. The pixel points obtained by feature extraction are shown in Fig. 3 under scaling magnification.

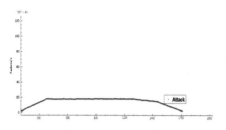

Fig. 1. Crawl added attack network traffic

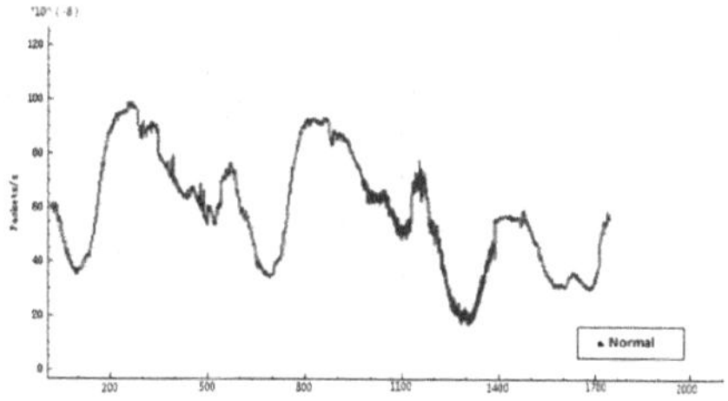

Fig. 2. The normal network traffic

4.2   Function Integral Fitting Discrete Points

This paper utilize curvilinear integral to analyze discrete points of network traffic after discretization. The fitting process is: given the time parameter, the new f(x) is obtained by changing the order and coefficients of the f(x) constantly. Then we set the relevant parameters by fitting constantly. Until we get the closest fitting curve to the network traffic, then calculate integral of the fitting curve. The parameters set as:

SSE : 8.258   R - square : 0.9786
Adjusted R - square : 0.9464   MSE : 0.4545

The function **CurveFit(){}** is used to fitting the discrete points. In the process of curve fitting, the individual coefficients of fitting polynomials are as follows:

$$p7 = -0.04914(-0.0675, -0.03077) \quad p8 = 0.5054(0.2945, 0.7145)$$
$$p9 = -1.321(-2.404, -0.239) \quad\quad p10 = 0.6859(-1.107, 2.479)$$

After multiple fitting, the difference between other levels fitting and the nine - levels fitting is shown in Fig. 4. The nine - levels fitting curve is closer to the network traffic of Fig. 3. Therefore, the nine-level fitting of network traffic can be more appropriate to show real-time data traffic diagram. Finally, the function f(x) fits to nine - levels.

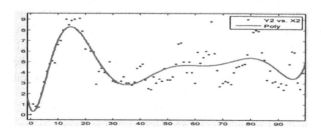

Fig. 3. Discrete points of network traffic

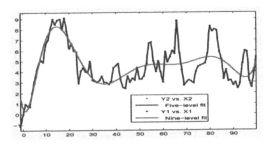

Fig. 4. Comparison chart of fitting curve

4.3   Comparative Analysis of Attack Detection

The normal network traffic is captured, and the integral calculation result of that network traffic is 0.4294. Through R/S analysis method, the calculation result is ans = 0.4804. Through these two methods, the comparison between the calculation of fitting integral and R/S analysis method for normal traffic is shown in Fig. 5.

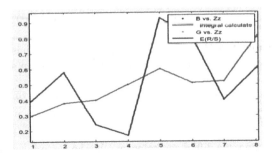

Fig. 5. The calculated values of integral fitting and R/S analysis

Compared with the R/S analysis method, the proposed method of fitting integral is not exactly equal, but there are obvious differences. Several times the normal network traffic data packets are captured to calculate integral value, and the difference between integral value and Hurst = 0.5 is shown in Fig. 6. It indicates that the threshold value of the integral difference between normal network traffic and Hurst = 0.5 is D < 0.5.

Also, we calculate the integral value of the network traffic that has been attacked, at 18:00–20:00, the integral value are obtained by scraping the network traffic data packet every 15 min, which is shown in Table 1.

At 18:00–20:00, the packet of attack is captured and calculated. The difference between the calculated integral value and Hurst = 0.5 is shown in Fig. 7. It indicates that the threshold value of the integral difference between the attack network traffic and Hurst = 0.5 is D > 0.5.

Based on the comparison between the integral value of network traffic and Hurst = 0.5, the hypothesis in this paper is correct. That is, when the difference is

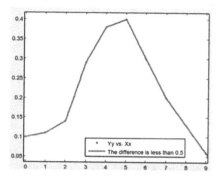

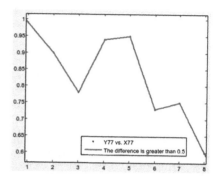

Fig. 6. The difference between the integral value of normal network traffic packets and Hurst = 0.5

Fig. 7. The difference between the integral value of abnormal network traffic packets and Hurst = 0.5

Table 1. The integral value of network traffic captured at 18:00–20:00 every 15 min

Grasping time	Calculated integral value
18:15	1.4845
18:30	1.4021
18:45	1.2328
19:00	1.4167
19:15	1.4217
19:30	1.2049
19:45	1.2108
20:00	1.1109

greater than 0.5 (the Hurst value is greater than 1), the network is attacked; And if the difference is less than 0.5, it indicates that the captured network traffic packet is normal.

This paper calculate integral value of the local lab network traffic packets by fitting integral value method in Fig. 8. Making a comparison between the integral value and Hurst = 0.5, it can directly detect whether the network traffic is attacked.

To detect SYN Flood attack, it makes a comparison between the function integral value of normal/abnormal network traffic and Hurst = 0.5 under normal condition. When we irregularly add the attack at 18:00–20:00, it is easy to see that the difference between the integral value of network traffic and Hurst = 0.5 is suddenly greater than 0.5. When the integral value of network traffic and Hurst = 0.5 is less than 0.5, that's normal network traffic. Since the Hurst value belongs to $0.5 < H < 1$, it shows that the time series have long-term memory, which conforms the self-similarity of the normal network. From the Fig. 8, we observe that the detection method can detect the attack accurately.

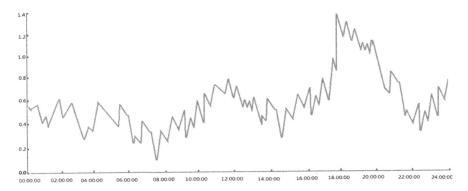

Fig. 8. The network traffic integral value of the local laboratory within a day

4.4 Time Complexity Analysis

It is the most important to calculate the integral value of fitting curve, which is simple to compute and easy to detect. For most other detection methods, such as the R/S analysis [16], it is simple and easy to use, but not effective. Generally thinking, the time complexity of R/S analysis is O (n^2); But the time complexity of calculating the integral value of the fitting curve is mainly obtained through the following algorithm.

Sum=0;//Initial value of area
for(i=1;i>N;i++)

{ Calculate the area of the ith small rectangle $s = \dfrac{b-a}{N} * f(N_i)$ }

Sum += s;
Compute the limit of Sum;

Using the segmentation method, the packet is divided into N parts, and each part is treated as a small rectangle. The area of N small rectangles for the loop calculation. Finally, the limit is added.

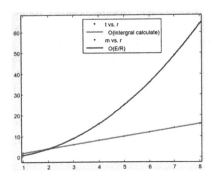

Fig. 9. Time complexity comparison chart

Therefore, in Fig. 9, it can be clearly found that, at the beginning of calculation, the time complexity of R/S analysis method is lower than integral value calculation method, but once the amount of calculation is much, the integral value calculation method is far less than the R/S analysis method. So this method is relatively efficient.

5 Conclusion

In the view of the self -similarity of network traffic, we calculate the integral value of the fitting curve for network traffic and compare it with Hurst = 0.5. It can detect whether the network has been attacked by SYN or not. By feature analysis, the network traffic is discretized. The discrete data points are fitted to curve by nine-levels, the corresponding f(x) function is obtained. In this paper, it is the key to discrete the local network traffic by feature analysis, then multiple fitting the discrete points to get the function of fitting. Furthermore, we use the integral value of fitting curve to compare with Hurst = 0.5. If it is beyond the reasonable range (Difference value $D \in (0.5, 1)$), the network traffic is to be considered as a malicious attack. The detection method of SYN Flood attack is applicable to a certain network size, which can simplify the detection process. The amount of calculation still needs further analysis and improvement.

Acknowledgments. This work is jointly supported by National Natural Science Foundation of China (Grant No. 51504010), and Key Projects of Anhui Province University Outstanding Youth Talent Support Program (Grant No. gxyqZD2016083).

References

1. Zhang, F., Zhao, Y., Wang, D., Wang, H.: Research on network traffic prediction based on traffic characteristics. Comput. Sci. **41**(04), 86–89+98 (2014)
2. Hui, W., Ji, Z., Zhu, S.: Self-similar network traffic model research. Intell. Comput. Appl. **3**(02), 34–41 (2013)
3. Dai, K., Hu, B., Wang, X.: Study on worm attack detection method based on network traffic self-similarity. Mod. Electron. Tech. **34**(04), 113–115 (2011)
4. Mei, X.: Research and Application of Network Traffic Model Based on Diffusion Wavelet. Beijing Jiaotong University, Beijing (2016)
5. Gao, B., Zhang, Q., Liang, Y.: Self-similar network traffic prediction based on EMD and ARMA. J. Commun. **32**(04), 47–56 (2011)
6. Kshirsagar, D., Sawant, S., Rathod, A.: CPU load analysis & minimization for TCP SYN flood detection. Procedia Comput. Sci. **85**, 626–633 (2016)
7. Wei, G., Gu, Y., Ling, Y.: An early stage detecting method against SYN flooding attack. In: International Symposium on Computer Science and its Applications 2008, pp. 263–268. IEEE Computer Society (2008)
8. Zhang, X., Xu, X., Zhu, S.: DDoS attack detection method based on Hurst exponential variance analysis. Comput. Eng. **14**, 149–151 (2008)
9. Kavisankar, L., Chellappan, C.: A mitigation model for TCP SYN flooding with IP spoofing. In: International Conference on Recent Trends in Information Technology 2011, ICRTIT, Chennai, Tamil Nadu, pp. 251–256 (2011)

10. Bogdanoski, M., Toshevski, A., Bogatinov, D.: A novel approach for mitigating the effects of the TCP SYN flood DDoS attacks. World J. Model. Simul. **12**(3), 217–230 (2016)
11. Wang, X., Zhang, J.: DDoS attack detection algorithm based on wavelet analysis and information entropy. J. Comput. Appl. Softw. **30**(06), 307–311 (2013)
12. Ren, Y., Liu, Y.: A DDoS attack detection method based on wavelet analysis. Comput. Eng. Appl. **48**(31), 82–88 (2012)
13. Ding, P., Tian, Z., Zhang, H.: Detection and defense of SYN flood attacks based on dual stack network firewall. In: IEEE International Conference on Data Science in Cyberspace 2017, pp. 526–531. IEEE (2017)
14. Haris, S.H.C., Ahmad, R.B., Ghani, M.A.H.A.: Detecting TCP SYN flood attack based on anomaly detection. In: IEEE International Conference 2010. IEEE (2010)
15. Bellaïche, M., Grégoire, J.C.: SYN flooding attack detection by TCP handshake anomalies. Secur. Commun. Netw. **5**(7), 709–724 (2012)
16. Deka, R.K., Bhattacharyya, D.K.: Self-similarity based DDoS attack detection using Hurst parameter. Secur. Commun. Netw. **5**(9), 4468–4481 (2016)

Annotating Network Service Fault Based on Temporal Interval Relations

Leonard Kok[1(✉)], Sook-Ling Chua[1], Chin-Kuan Ho[1], Lee Kien Foo[1], and Mohd Rizal Bin Mohd Ramly[2]

[1] Faculty of Computing and Informatics, Multimedia University,
63100 Cyberjaya, Malaysia
1122700374@student.mmu.edu.my, {slchua,ckho,lkfoo}@mmu.edu.my
[2] Telekom Malaysia, Menara TM, Jalan Pantai Baharu,
50672 Kuala Lumpur, Malaysia
mohdrizal.ramly@tm.com.my

Abstract. The internet has greatly revolutionized the communication and has undoubtedly affects our everyday life from work to entertainment. In order to uphold the quality of network service, Communication Service Providers (CSPs) are striving to keep network service faults to a minimum. To achieve this, they need to detect early of any potential network problems and resolve service incidents promptly before customers are impacted. However, to train a supervised learning algorithm to automatically detect service disruptions, the training data needs to be labeled. It is certainly costly and time consuming process to rely on domain experts to annotate the data. This paper addresses the data annotation problem based on temporal interval relations. We evaluated our method on real-world data and compared it with baseline method.

Keywords: Network service fault prediction
Temporal interval relations · Class labeling · Data annotation
Customer trouble tickets

1 Introduction

As pervasive computing and communications become more prevalent, guaranteeing the quality of service is becoming increasingly important and challenging. The telecommunication industry is currently trending toward enhancing customer service by ensuring that services offered over networks meet a service quality level. This, in turn, demands service faults be detected reliably and quickly for rapid fault alert. As the number of broadband users grows along with demand for faster connections, customers are certainly not pleased when they are not getting an ideal internet connection speed or facing an internet disconnection. This has put a strain on communication service providers (CSP) to keep service interruptions to a minimum.

In order to maintain a satisfactory service quality level, CSP can monitor service patterns and predict network service faults. If faults can be identified

© Springer International Publishing AG 2017
G. Wang et al. (Eds.): SpaCCS 2017 Workshops, LNCS 10658, pp. 83–92, 2017.
https://doi.org/10.1007/978-3-319-72395-2_9

and detected early, proactive action can be taken to resolve the issues before the customer even notices. However, CSP can only learn about service disruptions through customer complaints when they call the service center. A customer trouble ticket (CTT) is created to track reported customer complaints or issues and is closed when the problems are resolved.

Network service faults are likely under a reasonable assumption that faults occurred when a CTT is raised and remain as faulty until it is resolved (i.e., CTT closed). To identify faulty conditions, an experienced domain expert can manually go through the session logs and correlate with the corresponding CTT open and closed time. Session logs are recorded through customer premise equipment (CPE), which are installed in premise and contain information about session connections such as start and end time, total upload and download bytes and duration consumed in each session. Session instances are annotated as 'faulty' when it falls within the CTT open and closed time. However, manual hand-labeling is not feasible for most real-world applications, especially in telecommunication domain. It does not only rely heavily on domain expert but also a time-consuming process. A daily log could consist of hundreds of thousands of sessions and it is certainly not possible for human to label the entire log collection.

Some researches attempt to use unsupervised clustering approach to create class labels. However, specifying the true clustering on real-world data is difficult since firstly, prior knowledge is required determine the right number of clusters. Secondly, is the time-consuming validation process and feedback from domain experts.

This paper attempts to address the annotation problem by learning the temporal relations among time interval. We validate our approach with experiments on real-world data and compared with baseline method.

2 Related Work

Ho et al. [1] proposed a method for network anomaly detection based on thresholding. These thresholds are computed from historical transaction data. A one-dimensional time series analysis is used to separate out the different classes. Any incoming transaction that deviates from the threshold are considered as anomaly.

With limited labeled data, Glennan et al. [2] proposed a semi-supervised method based on fuzzy clustering to provide labels to the unknown cases. Within the same cluster, instances that exceeded a pre-defined threshold will be used to create labels for that cluster.

However, these network faults detection approaches relied on some labeled data. In real-world applications, some network data such as equipment generated session logs data do not contain labels.

The presence and correctness of data label are essential for supervised learning method since such method learns by inferring function from a labeled training data. However, in data mining, the process of class labeling is often neglected in favor of spending more time on feature engineering or optimizing the learning algorithm [3]. One of the reasons class labeling is often neglected is because of the cost involved in producing data labels. Data labels are usually produce by the domain experts. To scale down the data labeling cost, Hu et al. [4] proposed to use a grid-based labeling approach. Instead of scanning through all instances for labeling, this method selects a random instance that belongs to the desired class, and find other similar class instances by nearest-neighbor clustering. However, this approach assumed there is a clear boundary between classes, which is often not the case in real-world network data.

Erdmann et al. [5] proposed to improve the class labels by removing unnecessary noisy data. They first identified ambiguous semantics that would generate noise in their data and build a model from data based on labeled ambiguous titles. They then filtered the unrelated data by using the model to predict the relevancy of the data.

Similar to our work, Mostafazadeh et al. [6] attempt to label their collected semantic data by extracting event relations. This work emphasized on an automatically labeling process in semantic or natural language domain. In contrast, our work aims to label the data by determining the relations between events interval.

3   Proposed Methodology

Session logs (SL) capture the information about the behavior of users using the network, such as the time they connect/disconnect to/from the network, how long they have been on the network and how they relate to one another temporally. Whenever user disconnects from a connecting session, system will record the termination cause, total downloaded and uploaded volume of the disconnected session in the logs.

To predict network service faults, a binary classifier can be trained from users' session logs. However, session logs do not contain class labels indicating whether an instance belongs to a faulty class or non-faulty class. Customer trouble ticket (CTT) on the other hand, provides information about when network service faults occurred. CTT data were recorded by the telecommunication service customer supports for every users' reports with the information such as affected service, cause and solution for the fault. We can therefore make use of CTT data to label the session logs instances by correlating the CTT with session logs data.

To correlate between CTT data and session logs, we need to know the temporal ordering between them. Such ordering can be modeled in a qualitative form based on temporal relations. For example, *internet usage decreases before customer calls the service center*. Rather than expressing events in quantitative time points, events are expressed in terms of how they are related temporally. Extracting these relations are important to understand when service degradations occur. To do this, we need to first find a way to represent temporal relations and determine the nature of their relation, with each describing different temporal ordering.

Table 1. Allen's 7 basic temporal relations between two instances-$t1$ and $t2$

Relation	Schema	Definition
Equal	t_1 start ▬▬▬▬ t_1 end t_2 start ▪▪▪▪▪▪▪▪▪▪ t_2 end	$(t_1 start = t_2 start) \wedge$ $(t_1 end = t_2 end)$
Before	▬▬▬▬ ▪▪▪▪▪▪▪▪▪▪	$(t_1 end < t_2 start)$
Meets	▬▬▬▬▪▪▪▪▪▪▪▪▪▪	$(t_1 end = t_2 start)$
Overlap	▬▬▬▬▬ ▪▪▪▪▪▪▪▪▪▪	$(t_1 start < t_2 start) \wedge$ $(t_2 start < t_1 end) \wedge$ $(t_1 end < t_2 end)$
During	▬▬▬▬ ▪▪▪▪▪▪▪▪▪▪	$(t_2 start < t_1 start) \wedge$ $(t_1 end < t_2 end)$
Starts	▬▬▬▬ ▪▪▪▪▪▪▪▪▪▪	$(t_1 start = t_2 start) \wedge$ $(t_1 end < t_2 end)$
Finishes	▬▬▬▬ ▪▪▪▪▪▪▪▪▪▪	$(t_1 start > t_2 start) \wedge$ $(t_1 end = t_2 end)$

There are a number of widely known frameworks that provide formalisms for representing qualitative temporal data. Allen's interval algebra [7] is one of the well-known formalisms, which defined a set of 7 binary qualitative relations that may hold between two intervals. Table 1 shows Allen's 7 basic temporal relations. Each of the relation is defined by relating two intervals t_1 and t_2, with time running from left to right. For example, if an event t_1 ends at 10 am and another event t_2 starts at 11 am, then a "before" relation exists between the two events, t_1 and t_2.

It reveals that we can actually use Allen's temporal interval relations for class labeling; if a particular constraint is satisfied then we can annotate the session logs data as 'faulty'. Based on Allen's temporal interval relations, we have identified 3 possible service disruptions that may occur and refine the 7 temporal interval relations into 3 relations.

(a) **Before**

In the context of our work, "before" relation exists if any session logs instances occurred before the CTT is raised. This relation can well capture the pre-failure interval since some session logs instances may indicate service degradation before a final breakdown. However, there is an ambiguity in the granularity of the time intervals, i.e., how long before the CTT is raised?

To eliminate this ambiguity, we define 24 h as the boundary condition i.e., any session logs instances that fall within 24 h before the CTT is raised are annotated as 'faulty'. By setting this boundary condition, the "meet" relation becomes a sub-case of the "before" relation, as shown in Table 2(a).

Table 2. Proposed method based on 3 temporal relations: (a) *Before* relation with *meets* relation as a sub-case, (b) *Overlap* relation and (c) *During* relation with *equal*, *starts* and *finishes* relations as sub-cases of *during* relation. Solid line represents session logs instance and dashed line represents customer trouble ticket instance

Relation	Schema	Definition
Before		$(SL\ end \leq CTT\ start) \wedge$
Meets		$[(CTT\ start - SL\ end) \leq 1day]$

(a)

Relation	Schema	Definition
Overlap		$(SL\ start < CTT\ start) \wedge$ $(CTT\ start < SL\ end) \wedge$ $(SL\ end \leq CTT\ end)$

(b)

Relation	Schema	Definition
During		
Equal		$(CTT\ start \leq SL\ start) \wedge$ $(SL\ end \leq CTT\ end)$
Starts		
Finishes		

(c)

Session Logs instance	Customer Trouble Ticket
start ▬▬▬▬ end	start ▪▪▪▪▪▪▪▪▪▪ end

The temporal constraint for "before" relation as follows:

$$(SL_{end} \leq CTT_{start}) \wedge [(CTT_{start} - SL_{end}) \leq 1day] \tag{1}$$

(b) **Overlap**

If a CTT was raised by the user while he/she is still connecting to the network, then the relation between the session logs instances and CTT would be "overlap". We remain the same definition from Allen's interval algebra. Table 2(b) shows the "overlap" relation. The temporal constraint for "overlap" relation as follows:

$$(SL_{start} < CTT_{start}) \wedge (CTT_{start} < SL_{end}) \wedge (SL_{end} \leq CTT_{end}) \tag{2}$$

(c) **During**

Any session logs instances that fall between CTT created and closed time would be regarded as "during". For example, the user connected to the network after a CTT was raised and if the user is still connected to the network before the CTT closed, then any session logs instances occurred during that period would be labeled as 'faulty'. Since session logs instances with "equal", "starts" or "finishes" relation fall within the CTT's interval, we can therefore treat these relations as sub-cases of "during" relation, as shown in Table 2(c). The temporal constraint for "during" relation is thus:

$$(CTT_{start} \leq SL_{start}) \wedge (SL_{end} \leq CTT_{end}) \tag{3}$$

Algorithm 1. Class Annotation based on Temporal Interval Relations

---

Input: Session logs data, Customer Trouble Ticket data
Output: Labeled session logs data

1: **for each** SL **in** Session logs data **do**
2:    **for each** CTT **in** Customer Trouble Ticket data **do**
3:      **if** $SL_{login} == CTT_{login}$ **then**
4:        **if** $(SL_{end} \leq CTT_{start}) \wedge [(CTT_{start} - SL_{end}) \leq 1 \text{ day}]$ **then**
5:          $SL_{label} \leftarrow$ Faulty
6:        **else if** $(SL_{start} < CTT_{start}) \wedge (CTT_{start} < SL_{end}) \wedge (SL_{end} \leq CTT_{end})$ **then**
7:          $SL_{label} \leftarrow$ Faulty
8:        **else if** $(CTT_{start} \leq SL_{start}) \wedge (SL_{end} \leq CTT_{end})$ **then**
9:          $SL_{label} \leftarrow$ Faulty
10:       **else**
11:         $SL_{label} \leftarrow$ Non-faulty
12:       **end if**
13:     **end if**
14:   **end for**
15: **end for**

Algorithm 1 shows the process of class annotation for session logs data. The required inputs are the session logs data and CTT data. The algorithm correlates the session logs data and CTT data and flags as 'faulty' if any of the "before" (line 4), "overlaps" (line 6) and "during" (line 8) constraints are satisfied.

Line 3 compares each session logs data with CTT data. Variable *login* is used to ensure that the session logs data and CTT data belong to the same user. Session logs data that does not satisfy the constraint is annotated as *non-faulty*.

4   Experimental Setup

In this section, we describe the dataset and the evaluation method of our work (Table 3).

Table 3. Description of data instances

Number of users	Number of session logs	Number of CTT
112	22512	233

4.1   Dataset

We acquired real-world session logs and CTT data from a telecommunication company in Malaysia. The data contain information about home broadband subscribers from August, 2016 to September, 2016. From the acquired data, we selected 112 users with each of them has at least 50 instances of session logs and raised trouble ticket at least once. This is to make sure that we have adequate data to perform data mining on each user individually.

4.2   Evaluation Method

We used four measures for evaluation: accuracy, recall, precision and F1-score. Accuracy highlights the number of correct predictions made by the classifier. However, accuracy alone may not give a meaningful insight of the classifier's performance, especially when the data is imbalanced [8]. Therefore, we used 3 other performance measures: recall, precision, F1-score. Recall measures the number of faulty cases a classifier is able to predict correctly. Precision measures the number of predicted faulty cases correctly classified. F1-Score is the harmonic mean between recall and precision.

To evaluate the performance of our proposed method, we trained 3 different classifiers: C5.0, Naïve Bayes, and random forest with 10-fold cross validation. The purpose to train these classifiers is to validate the result of data annotation, and thus not comparing which classifier performs best.

5   Results and Discussion

5.1   Data Annotation

The data was annotated using two different approaches:

1. We first annotate the data following the assumption that fault occurred during CTT open and closed. This means that any session logs instances that fall within CTT open and closed are labeled as faulty. This annotated data served as the baseline.
2. The second approach is to annotate the data using our method (see Algorithm 1) on the same dataset. Figure 1 shows an example of data annotation for one of the users. Each horizontal bar represents a session logs instance interval. Session logs instances in darker horizontal bar are labeled as 'faulty'.

The results of annotation are shown in Table 4.

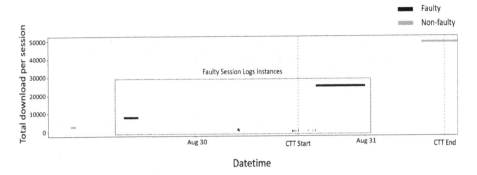

Fig. 1. Results of data annotation based on our proposed method from one of the users. Each horizontal bar represents a session logs instance interval. Dashed vertical lines represent CTT start and end. Session logs instances in darker horizontal bar are labeled as 'faulty'

Table 4. Number of faulty and non-faulty instances

Method	Non-faulty instances	Faulty instances
Baseline	17540	4972
Proposed	15087	7425

5.2 Classifiers Performance

After we have annotated the data, we compared the classification performances of both methods by training 3 different classifiers. Referring to Table 4, results from baseline method show that the number of non-faulty instances outnumbered the faulty instances with a ratio of 3.5(non-faulty):1(faulty). Although our proposed method has a ratio of 2(non-faulty):1(faulty), according to He and Ma [9], imbalanced data can hinder the learning algorithm performance even at the ratio of 2:1.

Therefore, to resolve the imbalance problem on the training data, we applied SMOTE [10] to resample the data, bringing the data to a 1(faulty):1(non-faulty) ratio. We then trained the classifiers on these balanced data. The test data is left as imbalanced so that we can test how are the methods perform in real-life scenario.

Table 5 shows the average accuracy, precision, recall and F1-score. Referring to Table 5, the baseline method has a slightly higher accuracy across all the classifiers. However, our method has a better recall, precision and F1-score, which shows that our method is able to identify the faulty cases and improve the prediction of faulty cases. As for accuracy, our method is comparable to the baseline method. It was observed that the overall performance of naïve Bayes classifier is lower across all the classifiers. This is expected since the naïve Bayes classifier has a strong independence assumption between features.

Table 5. Performance measures of C5.0, naïve Bayes, random forest between baseline and proposed method on accuracy, recall, precision and F1-score

Performance (%)	C5.0		Naïve Bayes		Random forest	
	Baseline Method	Proposed Method	Baseline Method	Proposed Method	Baseline Method	Proposed Method
Accuracy	73	72	64	63	77	74
Recall	50	66	43	54	51	63
Precision	36	49	23	34	40	52
F1-Score	39	53	26	38	43	55

Table 6. p-values of t-test

	C5.0	Naïve Bayes	Random forest
Accuracy	0.5463	0.6516	0.1488
Recall	0.0003	0.0334	0.0032
Precision	0.0010	0.0055	0.0025
F1-Score	0.0001	0.0022	0.0014

We have also conducted a significant test and the p-values of t-test is shown in Table 6. No significant difference in terms of accuracy in all classifiers. The one-sided t-test with alternative hypothesis $\mu_{proposed\_method} > \mu_{baseline\_method}$, showing significant improvement in recall, precision and F1-score for all these classifiers. This means that our method is able to efficiently identify the faulty cases.

Although our method has a higher precision, recall, and F1-score, the precision rate is slightly lower compared to recall. This was due to the number of overlapped classes between faulty and non-faulty cases. In future work, we plan to extend our work by discarding overlapped instances to improve the precision rate.

6   Conclusion

In this paper, we addressed the data annotation problem using Allen's temporal interval relations for predicting network service faults. Our method is able to capture pre-failure interval instances on session logs instances. We have evaluated our method on real-world customer trouble ticket and session logs data. Results show that our method significantly improved the predictive of network service faults compared to the baseline methods on three classifiers - C5.0, Naïve Bayes classifier and random forest.

Acknowledgments. This research is supported by Telekom Malaysia under the TM R&D Grant Scheme (No: MMUE/150061).

References

1. Ho, L.L., Cavuto, D.J., Hasan, M.Z., Feather, F.E., Papavassiliou, S., Zawadzki, A.G.: Adaptive network/service fault detection in transaction-oriented wide area networks. In: Proceedings of the Sixth IFIP/IEEE International Symposium on Integrated Network Management, 1999, Distributed Management for the Networked Millennium, pp. 761–775. IEEE (1999)
2. Glennan, T., Leckie, C., Erfani, S.M.: Improved classification of known and unknown network traffic flows using semi-supervised machine learning. In: Liu, J.K., Steinfeld, R. (eds.) ACISP 2016. LNCS, vol. 9723, pp. 493–501. Springer, Cham (2016). https://doi.org/10.1007/978-3-319-40367-0_33
3. Alonso, O.: Challenges with label quality for supervised learning. J. Data Inf. Qual. (JDIQ) 6(1), 2 (2015)
4. Hu, H., Kantardzic, M.M., Sethi, T.S.: Selecting samples for labeling in unbalanced streaming data environments. In: 2013 XXIV International Symposium on Information, Communication and Automation Technologies (ICAT), pp.1–7. IEEE (2013)
5. Erdmann, M., Ward, E., Ikeda, K., Hattori, G., Ono, C., Takishima, Y.: Automatic labeling of training data for collecting tweets for ambiguous tv program titles. In: 2013 International Conference on Social Computing (SocialCom), pp. 796–802. IEEE (2013)
6. Mostafazadeh, N., Grealish, A., Chambers, N., Allen, J., Vanderwende, L.: CaTeRs: causal and temporal relation scheme for semantic annotation of event structures. In: Proceedings of the 4th Workshop on Events: Definition, Detection, Coreference, and Representation, pp. 51–61 (2016)
7. Allen, J.F.: Towards a general theory of action and time. Artif. Intell. 23(2), 123–154 (1984)
8. López, V., Fernández, A., García, S., Palade, V., Herrera, F.: An insight into classification with imbalanced data: empirical results and current trends on using data intrinsic characteristics. Inf. Sci. 250, 113–141 (2013)
9. He, H., Ma, Y.: Imbalanced Learning: Foundations, Algorithms, and Applications. Wiley, Hoboken (2013)
10. Chawla, N.V., Bowyer, K.W., Hall, L.O., Kegelmeyer, W.P.: Smote: synthetic minority over-sampling technique. J. Artif. Intell. Res. 16, 321–357 (2002)

The 9th IEEE International Workshop on Security in e-Science and e-Research (ISSR 2017)

ISSR 2017 Organizing and Program Committees

1 General Chairs

Guojun Wang	Guangzhou University, China
Peter Mueller	IBM Zurich Research Laboratory, Switzerland

2 Program Chairs

Wanlei Zhou	Deakin University, Australia
Indrakshi Ray	Colorado State University, USA
Vasileios Vasilakis	University of York, UK

3 Program Committee

Imad Aad	Swisscom, Switzerland
Mohiuddin Ahmed	Canberra Institute of Technology, Australia
Marios Anagnostopoulos	Singapore University of Technology and Design, Singapore
Elena Apostol	University 'Politehnica' Bucharest, Romania
Junaid Arshad	University of West London, UK
Bruce Beckles	University of Cambridge Information Services, UK
Nik Bessis	Edge Hill University, UK
Andrea Bruno	University of Salerno, Italy
Arcangelo Castiglione	University of Salerno, Italy
Zesheng Chen	Indiana University - Purdue University Fort Wayne, USA
Dan Chen	China Wuhan University, China
Chang Choi	Chosun University, Korea
Dongmin Choi	Chosun University, Korea
Alessandra De Benedictis	University of Napoli Federico II, Italy
Geneiatakis Dimitris	DG Joint Research Centre, European Commission, Greece
Chao Gong	University of Mary Hardin-Baylor, USA
Ying Guo	Central South University, China
Guangjie Han	Hohai University, China
Wolfgang Hommel	University der Bundeswehr, Germany
Ing. Mauro Iacono	Universita degli Studi della Campania "Luigi Vanvitelli", Italy

Xiaoqi Jia	Institute of Information Engineering, CAS, China
Frank Jiang	University of Technology Sydney, Australia
Pankoo Kim	Chosun University, Korea
Shinsaku Kiyomoto	KDDI R&D Labs, Japan
Hoon Ko	Sungkyunkwan University, Korea
Juan Li	North Dakota State University, USA
Sofia Anna Menesidou	Democritus University of Thrace, Greece
Francesco Palmieri	University of Salerno, Italy
Dimitrios Papamartzivanos	University of the Aegean, Greece
Raffaele Pizzolante	University of Salerno, Italy
Peter Reiher	UCLA, USA
Yizhi Ren	Hangzhou Dianzi University, China
Roberto Rojas-Cessa	New Jersey Institute of Technology, USA
Haoxiang Wang	GoPerception, USA
Yupeng Wang	Shenyang Aerospace University, China
Sheng Wen	Deakin University, Australia
Carlos Westphall	UFSC, Brazil
Su Xin	Hohai University, China
Ming Xu	Hangzhou Dianzi University, China
Wencheng Yang	Edith Cowan University, Australia
Congxu Zhu	Central South University, China

4   Steering Committee Chairs

Guojun Wang	Guangzhou University, China
Wei Jie	University of West London, UK

5   Publicity Chairs

Christian Esposito	University of Salerno, Italy
Qin Liu	Hunan University, China

6   Web Chair

Qifan Wang	Central South University, China

An Anonymous Identity-Based Authentication Scheme in Vector Network

Jie Yu$^{(\boxtimes)}$ and Mangui Liang

Institute of Information Science, Beijing Jiaotong University,
Beijing 100044, China
{15120381,mgliang}@bjtu.edu.cn

Abstract. Vector Network is a new type of network, which is light connection and enables QoS. Vector Network provides two types of services: best effort and QoS guaranteed. The latter requires strict access authentication, which should be not only safe and convenient for use, but also able to protect the user's privacy, and prevent hackers from tracking. Therefore, this paper proposes an improved scheme for a hierarchical identity based on signature and authentication, which is used to meet the requirements of Vector Network authentication. At last we achieve the scheme in experiment and point out that it has advantages in terms of efficiency and security over traditional network.

Keywords: Vector network · Identity-based signature · Mutual authentication
Privacy · Security

1 Introduction

Nowadays, IP network has been mature and widely used in our work and daily life. However, the IP network runs into a stone wall of security and providing QoS services because of its characteristics of connectionless and shortest-path-routing. Thus people put forward a variety of connection oriented network technology, such as ATM, MPLS [1–3], etc. However, they have been applied only in some of the network backbone, rather than in the entire network, because of its complexity and high cost. So that a new type of light connection network, named vector network, is proposed in [4, 5], and put forward the basic concept of vector address and vector connection. Compared with IP network, the vector network is an information communication data network [4] which is light connection. What's more, the switching process of vector network does not need a routing table, which simplifies the data transmission. Due to this connection characteristic, the QoS can be guaranteed. From the perspective of authentication security, some traditional IP network authentication scheme have disadvantages such as single-tracking and high cost in key management. In the vector network, authentication objects can maintain connection by multi-path which is reliable, simple and low cost, especially in the variable wireless environment. The signalling data for authentication is much less than all communication data which makes it difficult for the attacker to capture user's information. Additionally, due to the particularity of vector address, it is impossible to get the sources of information even if a hacker intercepts vector packet of

© Springer International Publishing AG 2017
G. Wang et al. (Eds.): SpaCCS 2017 Workshops, LNCS 10658, pp. 97–104, 2017.
https://doi.org/10.1007/978-3-319-72395-2_10

authentication information, so as to prevent users from being cheated, and improve the safety of network further.

Hierarchical identity-based authentication technology has become mature and has been widely used at present. To satisfy the authentication requirement in the vector network authentication system, this paper proposes a kind of mutual authentication scheme based on hierarchical identification. The algorithm is proved to be full secure and effective through the dual system signature and we have achieved the scheme in experiment.

2 Related Work

In [6] proposed Vector Label Switching (VLS) architecture which supports high performance and low cost for the core Internet. In paper [7], it provides an innovative concept, Vector Address Switching (VAS) scheme, to support a high performance, energy-effective IP networks and/or Internet. It explains why vector network does not need a routing table for switching process, and how does it do the switching. In [8] it designs a reasonable and efficient accessing control scheme for the new Vector Network.

In 1984, Shamir [9] proposed an identity-based encryption method to simplify key management cost of certificate-based public key infrastructures. In order to protect user's identity and prevent from being traced, Kuzhalvaimozhi proposed a secure anonymous authentication method [10] which is based on group signature that users can get access to the cloud system without revealing their identities. Gentry [11] proposed an anonymous IBE scheme without random oracles. The scheme is based on a strong complexity assumption-augmented bilinear Diffie-Hellman exponent (ABDHE) assumption, though it is valid. Anonymous authentication [12–14] can also be applied in E-commerce, E-library, as well as some mobile agent applications and medical applications.

Chen [15] proposed and proved a secure HIBS scheme using composite order bilinear groups. In this paper, we apply and improve the algorithm.

3 Preliminaries

3.1 Composite Order Bilinear Groups

Let p1, p2, p3 be distinct primes, and set N = p1p2p3. For two multiplicative cyclic groups G and GT of order N, e: G × G → GT is a bilinear map. It satisfy the following properties:

(1) Bilinear: $\forall g, h \in G$, a, b $\in ZN$, $e(g^a, h^b) = e(g, h)^{ab}$;
(2) Non-degenerate: $\exists g \in G$, s.t. $e(g, g) \neq 1$;
(3) Computable: $\forall g, h \in G$, there is an efficient algorithm to compute e(g, h).

Group G is a composite order bilinear group. Gp1, Gp2, and Gp3 are subgroups of order p1, p2 and p3 in G respectively. Lewko and Waters have expounded that, when hi ∈ Gi, and hj ∈ Gj for i ≠ j, e(hi, hj) = 1 (identity element in GT) [16]. Such property is called as orthogonality property of Gp1, Gp2, Gp3.

3.2 Assumptions

According to [15], the algorithm is based on three assumptions.

(1) Gpipj is subgroup of order pipj in G and g, T2 are distinct random elements of Gp1. X3 is a random element of Gp3 and T1 is a random element of Gp1p2. Random T ∈ {T1, T2}, there is no probabilistic polynomial time algorithm A can determine T ∈ Gp1p2 or T ∈ Gp1 with negligible advantage.
(2) g, X1 are distinct random elements of Gp1 and X2, Y2 are distinct random elements of Gp2. X3, Y3 are distinct random elements of Gp3, T1 is a random element of G. T2 is a random element of Gp1p3. Random T ∈ {T1, T2}, there is no probabilistic polynomial time algorithm A can determine T ∈ G or T ∈ Gp1p3 with negligible advantage.
(3) Discrete Logarithm problem in multiplicative group is hard.

4   The Authentication Scheme and Hierarchical Identity-Based Signature Algorithm

4.1   Authentication Scheme and Process

Authentication consists of client, authentication server and trusted third party. The trusted third party is PKG. The authentication roles relationship is as follows Fig. 1:

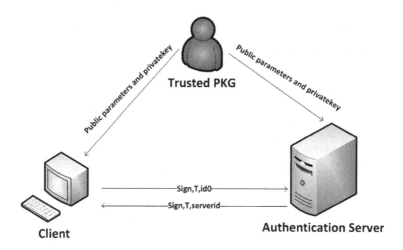

Fig. 1. The authentication roles relationship diagram

The PKG initializes the authentication system and generates all parameters as public parameters and send to the authentication server and client.

When user needs to use an application to enter the network, he must give his ID information to PKG. According to user's id, the PKG generates a new 'anonymous' id named id0 to protect user's privacy using a function and stores the 'id0', so that only the PKG can know the user's real information, hackers can't. Then the PKG generates private key based on id0. At last the PKG generates Timestamp T and sends (id0, private key, T) to the user.

The user uses the private key to sign the message and sends to the authentication server to authenticate. The authentication server checks the Timestamp T first, then the server takes id0 as public key to verify the user's signature. If it is success, the server sends its signature to client to mutual authentication using the same method, but authentication server don't need to generate 'anonymous' id. Only when mutual authentication successes, the user could use the network.

Before users' authentication to enter network, they must be anonymous and require private key through PKG each time to update user's id to prevent from being traced. The server is not required.

4.2   Overview of Hierarchical Identity-Based Authentication Algorithm

In this section, we describe the HIBS scheme and analyze the security and advantages of the algorithm which can protect user's privacy.

The HIBS scheme consists of the following algorithms and the authentication process is described in Sect. 4.1 which is as follows Fig. 2:

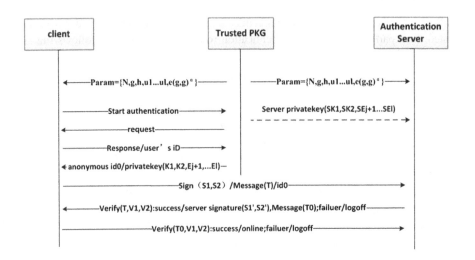

Fig. 2. The authentication process diagram

Setup: The PKG generates a bilinear group G of order $N = p1 * p2 * p3$. PKG chooses $g,h,u1...ul \in Gp1, \alpha \in Zn$ randomly, where α is the master key and l is the maximum depth of the scheme. The PKG publishes Param = {N, g, h, u1...ul, e(g, g)α} as public parameters.

Keygen: The PKG needs to hide the user's identity by function f. Actually, f is a function to generate fixed length string randomly. The new user's identity is $id0 = (I1, I2...Ij)(j \leq l)$ which represents the user's real id. The private-key-generate algorithm is that the PKG choose $r \in Zn$, $R3, R3', Rj + 1,...Rl \in Gp3$ and compute private key as output:

$$K1 = g^r R3 \tag{1}$$

$$K2 = g^\alpha (u1^{I1}...uj^{Ij}h)^r R3' \tag{2}$$

$$E_{j+1} = u_{j+1}^r R_{j+1} \tag{3}$$

$$E_l = u_l^r R_l \tag{4}$$

The private key is

$$(K1, K2, E_{j+1}...E_l) \tag{5}$$

Signing: let (T) be user's message M (T is timestamp based on the current time). The user signs the message with PKG public parameters by the private key. It picks $r' \in Zn$ and $R\_3, R\_3' \in Gp3$ randomly and computes

$$S1 = K1g^{r'} R\_3 \tag{6}$$

$$S2 = K2(u_1^{I1}...u_j^{Ij}h)^{r'} E_{j+1}^M u_{j+1}^{r'M} R\_3' \tag{7}$$

Then $\sigma = \{S1, S2\}$ is the signature.

Verification: The algorithm of verify user's signature is based on the user's $id0$ as public key and message M (it is timestamp T). First, the server sets time window t and gets the current time T1, then it checks if $T1 - T > Tmax$, it returns error information and ends the authentication. Else it sets

$$V1 = u_1^{I1}...u_j^{Ij} u_{j+1}^M h \tag{8}$$

and

$$V2 = g \tag{9}$$

and checks whether

$$e(S1,V1)e(g,g)^\alpha = e(S2,V2). \tag{10}$$

If the equation holds, the authentication is success.
Now, prove the verification.

$$S1 = K1g^{r'}R\_3 = g^{(r+r')}R3R3' \tag{11}$$

$$S2 = g^{\alpha}(u_1^{l1}\ldots u_j^{lj}u_{j+1}^M h)^{(r+r')}R3'R\_3'R_{j+1}^M \tag{12}$$

So,

$$
\begin{aligned}
&e(S1,V1)e(g,g)^{\alpha}\\
&= e(g^{(r+r')}R3R3', u_1^{l1}\ldots u_j^{lj}u_{j+1}^M h)e(g,g)^{\alpha}\\
&= e(g, (u_1^{l1}\ldots u_j^{lj}u_{j+1}^M h)^{(r+r')})e(g,g)^{\alpha}\\
&= e((u_1^{l1}\ldots u_j^{lj}u_{j+1}^M h)^{(r+r')}g^{\alpha},g)\\
&= e(S2,V2)
\end{aligned}
\tag{13}
$$

4.3 Security Analysis and the Application in Vector Network

According to the assumptions and the analysis of security using dual system signature in [15], this algorithm is security enough to meet the requirements of vector network access authentication for security. We achieve our improved authentication scheme based on java. Compared with the PKI method, the cost of public key management is greatly reduced, therefore it can save the resource and make the authentication become more convenient and efficient.

Base on the algorithm [15], this paper adds a time stamp, which is used to resist replay attack and Man-in-the-Middle Attack to enhance the network security. In order to achieve the protection of the user's personal information and prevent users from being traced and user's information leakage, we convert the user's personal information by a function.

1. Replay attack: Replay attack is that the attacker sends data repeatedly. The time stamp T updates each time in this protocol. And the T must be in the time window (T, Tmax). When the attacker intercepts the authentication data and sends it to server, the time stamp T exceed Tmax, thus the attacker cannot implement the attack.
2. Man-in-the-middle attack: The time T is also the signature message. If the attacker intercepts the authentication data and modifies the T, the verification using public key will be rejected by the authentication server because the attacker does not know the user's private key.
3. Privacy protected: The user's id is anonymous and will update each time when the user needs to authenticate. If the attacker intercepts the authentication data, he only know the random user's id, which cannot compute the real id. Even if the attacker intercepts authentication data more than once, he cannot calculate and trace user's information. So that, the authentication protocol can protect user's privacy information and prevent from being tracked. Though, the authentication server store all user's information which is secure for the system.

To sum up, the requirement of vector network access authentication is realized. So, the algorithm can be applied in vector network environment to ensure network security. When the user need to entry the network, he must certificate to the authentication server. Only when the user is legitimate can he entry the network which can clear user's responsibility attribution in the vector network. When there is misunderstanding between user and network operator, the authentication result can be proof to trace back the responsibility to protect the legitimate interests of users and network operators.

5 Conclusion

In this paper, we propose a mutual hierarchical identity-based authentication scheme which can protect users' privacy. We proved that the efficacy and safety of this scheme through the theoretical research and experiment. This scheme is suitable for vector network access authentication. It satisfies the requirement of vector network authentication system which is strict secure, convenience and privacy protection. Therefore, our authentication scheme can be applied to the vector network so that users can get convenient, safe and anonymous access to the network. And network operators can clearly specify every user' responsibility. When an objection starts to use the network, the users and operators can trace responsibility to safeguard the legitimate rights and interests of all parties which could purify the network security environment.

Acknowledgments. This research is supported by the National Natural Science Foundation of China (Grant No. U1636109). And the title is Scalability of Datacenter Network for Cloud Computing.

References

1. Yoon, H.S.: A large-scale ATM switch: analysis, simulation and implementation. In: 1st IEEE International Conference on ATM, ICATM 1998, pp. 459–464. IEEE (1998)
2. McDysan, D.: QoS and Traffic Management in IP and ATM Networks. McGraw-Hill Companies, Inc., New York City (2000)
3. Davie, B., Rekhter, Y.: MPLS Technology and Applications. Morgan Kaufmann Publishers, Burlington (2000)
4. Liang, M., Zhang, J., Wang, S.: A new network based on vector address. In: ICWMMN 2008 Proceedings (2008)
5. Liang, M.: Coding method of vector network address. US Patent No. 12/304,435, 27 Dec 2007
6. Wang, Z.W., Liang, M.G.: Vector label switching (VLS): a high-performance switching architecture for future internet. J. Internet Technol. **1**, 11–13 (2011)
7. Wang, Z.W., Liang, M.G.: Vector address switching: an energy-effective next-generation switching technology for internet. Tamkang J. Sci. Eng. **9**, 11–13 (2011)
8. Qi, G., Liang, M.: Research and design of layering accessing authentication based on RSA in vector network. In: Cross-Strait Conference on Information Science and Technology, Qinhuangdao, People's Republic of China, 9–11 July 2010, pp. 234–237 (2010)

9. Shamir, A.: Identity-based cryptosystems and signature schemes. In: Blakley, G.R., Chaum, D. (eds.) CRYPTO 1984. LNCS, vol. 196, pp. 47–53. Springer, Heidelberg (1985). https://doi.org/10.1007/3-540-39568-7_5

10. Kuzhalvaimozhi, S., Rao, G.R.: Privacy protection in cloud using identity based group signature. In: Applications of Digital Information and Web Technologies, pp. 75–80. IEEE (2014)

11. Gentry, C.: Practical identity-based encryption without random oracles. In: Vaudenay, S. (ed.) EUROCRYPT 2006. LNCS, vol. 4004, pp. 445–464. Springer, Heidelberg (2006). https://doi.org/10.1007/11761679_27

12. Boneh, D., Boyen, X., Shacham, H.: Short group signatures. In: Franklin, M. (ed.) CRYPTO 2004. LNCS, vol. 3152, pp. 41–55. Springer, Heidelberg (2004). https://doi.org/10.1007/978-3-540-28628-8_3

13. Nguyen, L., Safavi-Naini, R.: Efficient and provably secure trapdoor-free group signature schemes from bilinear pairings. In: Lee, P.J. (ed.) ASIACRYPT 2004. LNCS, vol. 3329, pp. 372–386. Springer, Heidelberg (2004). https://doi.org/10.1007/978-3-540-30539-2_26

14. Bellare, M., Shi, H., Zhang, C.: Foundations of group signatures: the case of dynamic groups. In: Menezes, A. (ed.) CT-RSA 2005. LNCS, vol. 3376, pp. 136–153. Springer, Heidelberg (2005). https://doi.org/10.1007/978-3-540-30574-3_11

15. Chen, P., et al.: An escrow-free hierarchical identity-based signature scheme from composite order bilinear groups. In: International Conference on Broadband and Wireless Computing, Communication and Applications, pp. 364–369. IEEE Computer Society (2015)

16. Lewko, A., Waters, B.: New techniques for dual system encryption and fully secure HIBE with short ciphertexts. In: Micciancio, D. (ed.) TCC 2010. LNCS, vol. 5978, pp. 455–479. Springer, Heidelberg (2010). https://doi.org/10.1007/978-3-642-11799-2_27

The 8th International Workshop on Trust, Security and Privacy for Big Data (TrustData 2017)

TrustData 2017 Organizing and Program Committees

1 General Chairs

Qin Liu   Hunan University, China
Arun Kumar Sangaiah   VIT University, India

2 Program Chairs

Jiankun Hu   University of New South Wales at the Australian,
                           Australia
Isaac Agudo   University of Malaga, Spain

3 Program Committee

Habtamu Abie	Norwegian Computing Center/Norsk Regnesentral, Norway
Salima Benbernou	Universite Paris Descartes, France
Christian Callegari	The University of Pisa, Italy
Wei Chang	Saint Joseph's University, USA
Anupam Chattopadhyay	Nanyang Technological University, Singapore
John A. Clark	University of York, UK
Alfredo Cuzzocrea	University of Trieste and ICAR-CNR, Italy
Sabrina De Capitani di Vimercati	Universita degli Studi di Milano, Italy
Yucong Duan	Hainan University, China
Sheikh M. Habib	Technical University of Darmstadt, Germany
Ching-Hsien Hsu	Chung Hua University, Taiwan
Hai Jiang	Arkansas State University, USA
Vana Kalogeraki	Athens University of Economics, Greece
Ryan Ko	University of Waikato, New Zealand
Ruggero Donida Labati	Universita degli Studi di Milano, Italy
Xin Liao	Hunan University, China
Giovanni Livraga	Universita degli Studi di Milano, Italy
Haibing Lu	Santa Clara University, USA
Joon S. Park	Syracuse University, USA
Roberto Di Pietro	Nokia Bell Labs, France
Vincenzo Piuri	Università degli Studi di Milano, Italy
Imed Romdhani	Edinburgh Napier University, UK
Bimal Roy	Indian Statistical Institute, India

Jun Shen	University of Wollongong, Australia
Dimitris E. Simos	SBA Research, Austria
Chao Song	University of Electronic Science and Technology of China, China
Chang-ai Sun	University of Science and Technology Beijing, China
Yuanyuan Sun	Huazhong University of Science and Technology, China
Luis Javier Garcia Villalba	Universidad Complutense de Madrid, Spain
Yunsheng Wang	Kettering University, USA
Mingzhong Wang	University of the Sunshine Coast, Australia
Yongdong Wu	Institute for Infocomm Research, Singapore
Hejun Wu	Sun Yat-Sen University, China
Muneer Masadeh Bani Yassein	Jordan University of Science and Technology, Jordan
Sherali Zeadally	University of Kentucky, USA

4 Steering Committee

Jemal H Abawajy	Deakin University, Australia
Isaac Agudo	University of Malaga, Spain
Jose M. Alcaraz Calero	University of the West of Scotland, UK
Jiannong Cao	Hong Kong Polytechnic University, Hong Kong
Raymond Choo	The University of Texas at San Antonio, USA
Minyi Guo	Shanghai Jiao Tong University, China
Jiankun Hu	University of New South Wales at the Australian, Australia
Konstantinos Lambrinoudakis	University of Piraeus, Greek
Jianhua Ma	Hosei University, Japan
Peter Mueller	IBM Zurich Research Laboratory, Switzerland
Indrakshi Ray	Colorado State University, USA
Bhavani Thuraisingham	The University of Texas at Dallas, USA
Guojun Wang	Guangzhou University, China
Jie Wu	Temple University, USA
Yang Xiang	Deakin University, Australia
Laurence T. Yang	Francis Xavier University, Canada
Kun Yang	University of Essex, UK
Wanlei Zhou	Deakin University, Australia

5 Publicity Chairs

Weiwei Chen   Hunan University, China
Bo Ou   Hunan University, China

6 Web Chair

Qifan Wang   Central South University, China

Two Improved Anonymous Authentication Methods for PCS

Chun-lin Jiang[1(⊠)], Shi-lan Wu[1], and Ke Gu[2]

[1] School of Mathematics and Computer Sciences,
Xinyu University, Xinyu 338004, China
38029747@qq.com
[2] School of Computer and Communication Engineering,
Changsha University of Science and Technology, Changsha 410004, China

Abstract. To avoid the weakness and also reduce the computation cost of Lee-Yeh's anonymous authentication protocol, an improved scheme has been proposed by Lee-Chang, but it still needs too much message rounds. A double delegation-based scheme has been proposed by Ou-Hwang to reduce the message rounds. Though it needs only four message rounds which are two rounds less than the previous one, it is still considered to be further improved. This paper exploits two improved methods, one of which reduces one message round by accurately combining message parameters, and the other achieves efficiency by decreasing public-key computation on MS. The comparison shows that, our improvements are efficient and practical.

Keywords: Anonymous authentication protocol
PCS (portable communication system) · Wireless roaming networks
Diffie-Hellman key exchange

1 Introduction

With the wide deployment of wireless roaming networks in Mainland China recently, security and privacy in PCS (portable communication system) are becoming more and more important. When a mobile station (MS) roams from its home network (HN) to visited network (VN), an authentication process is inevitable [1]. Too much authentication time will affect the quality of service (QoS), especially in real-time interpersonal communications. Besides, people often require anonymity when they roam among visited networks because the identity (ID) of MS is often valuable and should not be disclosed to others. Designing an anonymous authentication protocol is a good way to realize anonymity. At present, the computational capability of mobile terminals is limited, so the protocol should not be very complex in computation. Hence, an efficient and secure anonymous authentication protocol is always a prime concern.

Lots of such protocols have been proposed and analyzed, such as non-encryption based method [2], secret-key based method [3–5], and public-key based method [6–18]. Among these protocols delegation-based scheme is a hotspot [12–18]. This kind of scheme makes use of a proxy signature to achieve anonymity. In 2005, Lee-Yeh [12] first proposed an anonymous authentication protocol based on partial delegation to

© Springer International Publishing AG 2017
G. Wang et al. (Eds.): SpaCCS 2017 Workshops, LNCS 10658, pp. 109–118, 2017.
https://doi.org/10.1007/978-3-319-72395-2_11

achieve the security requirements. But in 2008, Tang-Wu [13] pointed out that their protocol has severe threat from an impersonation VN attack. In 2009, Lee-Chang [14] presented an improved protocol which avoided the weakness and also reduced the computation cost. In 2012, Lee et al. [15] demonstrated that Lee-Yeh's protocol has an instinctive design flaw, and then proposed a modification to improve it.

Based on the above work, many delegation-based protocols have been proposed. In 2013, Ou-Hwang [16] proposed a double delegation-based scheme which is two message rounds less than Lee-Chang's scheme. In 2014, Kumar et al. [17] proposed a robust authentication model utilizing the biometric to defend from popular attacks and frauds. In 2016, Gao et al. [18] proposed the proxy group signature scheme which is combined with proxy group signature and identity-based group signature, which not only simplifies the complex management of PKI but also guarantees anonymous authentication and owns high handover authentication efficiency.

In this paper, Lee-Chang's delegation-based anonymous authentication protocol [14] and Ou-Hwang's scheme [16] will be first introduced. Then two improved methods will be proposed and compared with them.

The rest of this paper is organized as follows: Sect. 2 reviews some relevant literatures and points out the scope for their improvements. Sections 3 and 4 give two improved schemes and provide their analyses including relevant discussion and comparison respectively. Section 5 provides security analysis. Finally, Sect. 6 presents the conclusion.

2   Review of the Literatures

In this section, two relevant literatures will be briefly reviewed. One of them is proposed by Lee-Chang [14], and the other is Ou-Hwang's improved method [16].

2.1   Review of Lee-Chang's Protocol

(a) Initialization:

Let Z_p^* be a group of large prime order p, g be a generator of it, and q be a prime factor of $p - 1$; K_{HV} be a shared key between HN and VN; (x, v) be a private/public key pair of HN, with x a random number and $v = g^x (\mathrm{mod}\, p)$; $[M]_K$ be the encryption of M using a symmetric key K; $h()$ be a one-way hash function; | be a concatenation operator.

(b) Delegation:

First HN generates a random number k and computes $\sigma = x + kK (\mathrm{mod}\, q)$ as MS's proxy signing key and $K = g^k (\mathrm{mod}\, p)$ as MS's pseudonym. Then HN stores (σ, K) in its database and gives them to MS simultaneously.

(c) Authentication:

Figure 1 is authentication process which is illustrated as follows:

Authentication process:

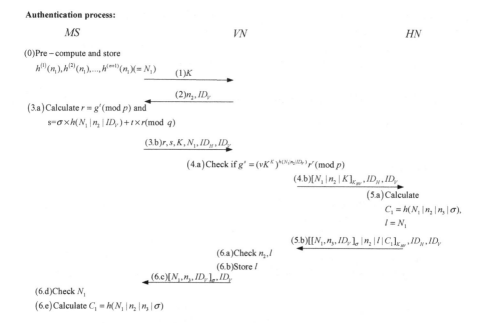

Fig. 1. The authentication process of Lee-Chang

1. MS selects a random number n_1, pre-computes $h^{(1)}(n_1), h^{(2)}(n_1), \ldots, h^{(n+1)}(n_1)$ with $h^{(1)}(n_1) = h(n_1)$ and $h^{(i+1)}(n_1) = h(h^{(i)}(n_1))$ for $i = 1, 2, \ldots, n$. It then sends K to VN.

2. VN selects a random number n_2 and sends (n_2, ID_V) to MS.

3. MS selects a random number t, sets $N_1 = h^{(n+1)}(n_1)$, and then computes $r = g^t(\bmod p)$ and $s = \sigma \times h(N_1|n_2|ID_V) + t \times r(\bmod q)$ as the proxy signature. It then sends $(r, s, K, N_1, ID_H, ID_V)$ to VN.

4. VN verifies the signature by checking $g^s = (vK^K)^{h(N_1|n_2|ID_V)}r^r(\bmod p)$. If the equation holds, VN sends $([N_1|n_2|K]_{K_{HV}}, ID_H, ID_V)$ to HLR. Otherwise, VN rejects the connection.

5. HN decrypts $[N_1|n_2|K]_{K_{HV}}$ and gets K. It then gets σ from its database and selects a random number n_3 to compute the session key $C_1 = h(N_1|n_2|n_3|\sigma)$ for VN and MS. Finally HN sets $l = N_1$ and sends $([[N_1, n_3, ID_V]_\sigma|n_2|l|C_1]_{K_{HV}}, ID_H, ID_V)$ to VN.

6. VN gets $[N_1, n_3, ID_V]_\sigma|n_2|l|C_1$, checks (n_2, l), and accepts C_1 as the session key. Then VN sends $([N_1, n_3, ID_V]_\sigma, ID_V)$ to MS.

7. MS decrypts $[N_1, n_3, ID_V]_\sigma$, checks N_1 and computes the session key C_1.

2.2   Analysis of the Protocol

Ou-Hwang [16] pointed out that the authentication phase of the scheme is relying on HN, so the main drawback of the scheme is that HLR is required to be active during the online authentication phase between VLR and MS. It is well known that the bandwidth of wireless networks is limited, and VN is often far from HN, so the real-time participation of HN often makes the communication time too long to bear.

To avoid such intervention of HN for the authentication phase, Ou-Hwang proposed a double delegation-based authentication protocol.

2.3   Review of Ou-Hwang's Protocol

Figure 2 is Ou-Hwang's protocol which is illustrated as follows:

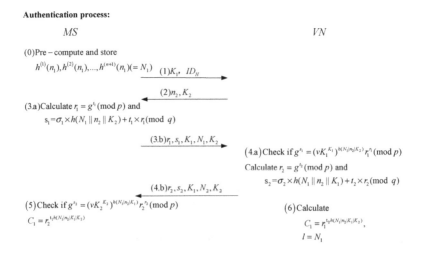

Fig. 2. Ou-Hwang's protocol

(a) Initialization:

Most of the symbols used are the same as the ones described in the previous protocol.

(b) Delegation:

HN generated two delegation key pairs (σ_1, K_1), (σ_2, K_2) for the MS and VN respectively.

(c) Authentication:

1. MS selects a random number n_1, pre-computes $h^{(1)}(n_1), h^{(2)}(n_1), \ldots, h^{(n+1)}(n_1)$ with $h^{(1)}(n_1) = h(n_1)$ and $h^{(i+1)}(n_1) = h(h^{(i)}(n_1))$ for $i = 1, 2, \ldots, n$. It then sends (K_1, ID_H) to VN.
2. VN selects a random number n_2 and sends $(n_2, K2)$ to MS.
3. MS selects a random number t_1, and then computes $r = g^t (\bmod p)$ and $s_1 = \sigma_1 \times h(N_1 || n_2 || K_2) + t_1 \times r_1 (\bmod q)$ as the proxy signature. It then sends $(r_1, s_1, K_1, N_1, K_2)$ to VN.

4. VN verifies the signature by checking $g^{s_1} = \left(vK_1^{K_1}\right)^{h(N_1|n_2|K_2)} r_1^{r_1} (\mathrm{mod}\, p)$. If the equation holds, VN computes $r_2 = g^{t_2} (\mathrm{mod}\, p)$ and $s_2 = \sigma_2 \times h(N_1||n_2||K_1) + t_2 \times r_2 (\mathrm{mod}\, q)$, and then sends $(r_2, s_2, K_1, N_2, K_2)$ to MS. Otherwise, VN rejects the connection.

5. MS verifies the signature by checking $g^{s_2} = \left(vK_2^{K_2}\right)^{h(N_1|n_2|K_1)} r_2^{r_2} (\mathrm{mod}\, p)$. If the equation holds, MS computes the session key $C_1 = r_2^{t_1 h(N_1|n_2|K_1|K_2)}$.

6. VN also computes $C_1 = r_1^{t_2 h(N_1|n_2|K_1|K_2)}$ as the session key, and sets $l = N_1$.

2.4 Analysis of Ou-Hwang's Protocol

Though Ou-Hwang's protocol needs only four message rounds which are two rounds less than Lee-Chang's protocol, it is still considered to be redundant and further improved. For example, symbols such as K_1 and K_2 have to be sent three times in the authentication phase. Actually only three rounds are needed if message parameters can be combined accurately.

3 Improved Protocol for Ou-Hwang

3.1 Description

Figure 3 is the improved protocol which is illustrated as follows:

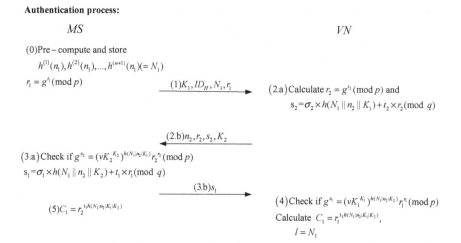

Fig. 3. Improved authentication phase for Ou-Hwang's protocol

(a) Initialization:

The symbols used are the same as the ones described in the previous protocol.

(b) Delegation:

HN generated two delegation key pairs (σ_1, K_1), (σ_2, K_2) for the MS and VN respectively, just like Ou-Hwang's protocol.

(c) Authentication:

1. MS selects a random number n_1, pre-computes $h^{(1)}(n_1), h^{(2)}(n_1), \ldots, h^{(n+1)}(n_1)$ with $h^{(1)}(n_1) = h(n_1)$ and $h^{(i+1)}(n_1) = h(h^{(i)}(n_1))$ for $i = 1, 2, \ldots, n$. It then computes $r_1 = g^{t_1}(\bmod p)$ and sends (K_1, ID_H, N_1, r_1) to VN.
2. VN selects a random number n_2, calculates $r_2 = g^{t_2}(\bmod p)$ and $s_2 = \sigma_2 \times h(N_1 \| n_2 \| K_1) + t_2 \times r_2(\bmod q)$, and then sends (n_2, r_2, s_2, K_2) to MS.
3. MS verifies the signature by checking $g^{s_2} = \left(vK_2^{K_2}\right)^{h(N_1|n_2|K_1)} r_2^{r_2}(\bmod p)$. If the equation holds, MS computes $s_1 = \sigma_1 \times h(N_1 \| n_2 \| K_2) + t_1 \times r_1(\bmod q)$ and sends it to VN. It then computes the session key $C_1 = r_2^{t_1 h(N_1|n_2|K_1|K_2)}$.
4. VN verifies the signature by checking $g^{s_1} = \left(vK_1^{K_1}\right)^{h(N_1|n_2|K_2)} r_1^{r_1}(\bmod p)$. If the equation holds, VN also computes $C_1 = r_1^{t_2 h(N_1|n_2|K_1|K_2)}$ as the session key, and then sets $l = N_1$. Otherwise, VN rejects the connection.

3.2 Analysis

Table 1 is the performance comparison between Lee-Chang's protocol, Ou-Hwang's protocol and our improved protocol. It shows that Lee-Chang's protocol involves three parties including MS, VN and HN in the authentication phase, and needs 6 message rounds which are the most among three protocols. Our improved protocol needs only three message rounds, so it is practical in bandwidth-limited networks. However, no matter in Ou-Hwang's protocol or ours, MS needs one more public-key computation than in Lee-Chang's protocol, and therefor has to bear more burdens.

Table 1. Performance comparison between three protocols

	Number of parties	Number of rounds	Public-key computation of MS
Lee-Chang's protocol	3	6	1
Ou-Hwang's protocol	2	4	2
Improved protocol for Ou-Hwang	2	3	2

4 Improved Protocol for Lee-Chang Without Double Delegation

In this section, we propose another improved protocol for Lee-Chang's protocol, without using double delegation to achieve efficiency.

4.1 Description

Figure 4 is the improved protocol which is illustrated as follows:

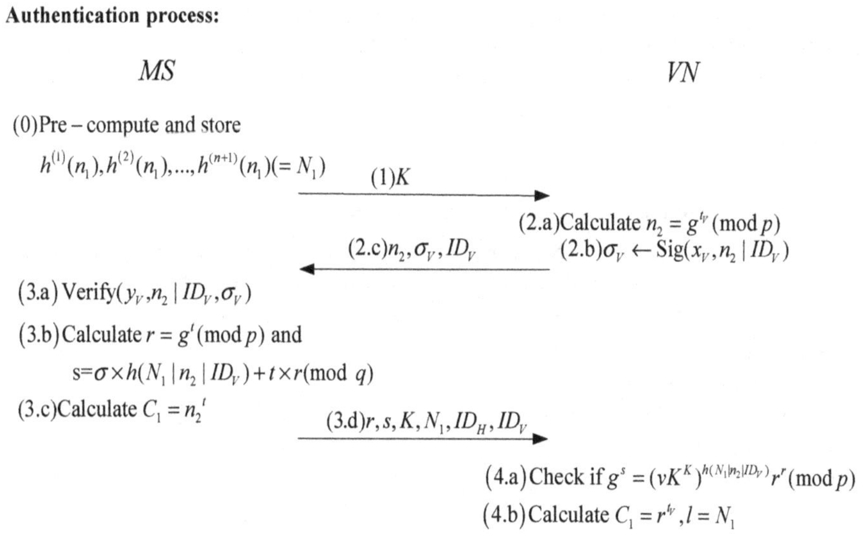

Authentication process:

$$MS \hspace{6cm} VN$$

(0)Pre − compute and store

$h^{(1)}(n_1), h^{(2)}(n_1),..., h^{(n+1)}(n_1)(= N_1)$ $\qquad$ (1)K $\longrightarrow$

$\qquad\qquad\qquad\qquad$ (2.a)Calculate $n_2 = g^{t_V} \pmod p$

$\qquad$ (2.c)n_2, σ_V, ID_V $\qquad$ (2.b)$\sigma_V \leftarrow \text{Sig}(x_V, n_2 \mid ID_V)$

$\longleftarrow$

(3.a) Verify($y_V, n_2 \mid ID_V, \sigma_V$)

(3.b) Calculate $r = g^t \pmod p$ and

$\qquad s = \sigma \times h(N_1 \mid n_2 \mid ID_V) + t \times r \pmod q$

(3.c) Calculate $C_1 = n_2^t$ $\qquad$ (3.d)r, s, K, N_1, ID_H, ID_V

$\longrightarrow$

$\qquad\qquad\qquad$ (4.a) Check if $g^s = (vK^K)^{h(N_1 \mid n_2 \mid ID_V)} r^r \pmod p$

$\qquad\qquad\qquad$ (4.b) Calculate $C_1 = r^{t_V}, l = N_1$

Fig. 4. Improved authentication phase for Lee-Chang's protocol

(a) Initialization:

The initialization phase is the same as Lee-Chang's protocol. Besides, VN has a key pair (x_V, y_V) of DSA.

(b) Delegation: The same as original protocol.

(c) Authentication:

1. MS selects a random number n_1, pre-computes $h^{(1)}(n_1), h^{(2)}(n_1), \ldots, h^{(n+1)}(n_1)$ with $h^{(1)}(n_1) = h(n_1)$ and $h^{(i+1)}(n_1) = h(h^{(i)}(n_1))$ for $i = 1, 2, \ldots, n$. It then sends K to VN.
2. VN selects a random number t_V and computes $n_2 = g^{t_V} \pmod p$. Then VN computes a DSA signature σ_V on $n_2 \mid ID_V$ and sends (n_2, σ_V, ID_V) to MS.
3. MS verifies σ_V, selects a random number t and sets $N_1 = h^{(n+1)}(n_1)$. It then computes $r = g^t \pmod p$ and $s = \sigma \times h(N_1 \mid n_2 \mid ID_V) + t \times r \pmod q$ as the proxy signature. Finally MS sends $(r, s, K, N_1, ID_H, ID_V)$ to VN and computes a session key $C_1 = n_2^t$.
4. VN verifies the signature by checking $g^s = (vK^K)^{h(N_1 \mid n_2 \mid ID_V)} r^r \pmod p$, if the equation holds, then VN computes $C_1 = r^{t_V}$ and $l = N_1$. Otherwise, VN rejects the connection.

4.2   Analysis

Table 2 is the performance comparison between Lee-Chang's protocol, Ou-Hwang's protocol and our two improved protocols. Our improved protocol for Lee-Chang has the same public-key computation of MS as Lee-Chang's protocol, but the message rounds are greatly reduced from six to three in the authentication process. Besides, VN and MS generate the session key based on Diffie-Hellman key exchange, which is secure under the decisional Diffie-Hellman (DDH) assumption. So our improved scheme for Lee-Chang is efficient and secure.

Table 2. Performance comparison between four protocols

	Number of parties	Number of rounds	Public-key computation of MS
Lee-Chang's protocol	3	6	1
Ou-Hwang's protocol	2	4	2
our improved protocol for Ou-Hwang	2	3	2
Our improved protocol for Lee-Chang	2	3	1

5   Security Analysis

We analyze our two improved schemes in terms of security.

(1) Server authentication
     In our two schemes, MS is sure of the ID of VN by verifying the signature of VN.
(2) Subscriber validation
     In our two schemes, MS signs a message on behalf of HN; VN verifies it to ensure that MS gets the delegation of HN and is a valid user.
(3) Key establishment
     In our two schemes, MS and VN establish a common session key by Diffie-Hellman (DH) key exchange, which cannot be derived by anyone else including HN.
(4) User Anonymity
     In our two schemes, besides the user and HN, anyone else even VN cannot tell the real identity of MS.
(5) Resistance to man-in-the-middle attack
     In our first improved scheme, an attacker cannot establish a fake Man-in-the-middle session key between MS and VN because it is impossible for the adversary to get knowledge of the secret key t_1 or t_2.

For the same reason, in our second scheme, an attacker cannot establish a fake Man-in-the-middle session key between MS and VN because it is impossible for the adversary to get knowledge of the secret key t_v or t.

Our two improved schemes therefore resist the man-in-the-middle attack.

6   Conclusion

In this paper we proposed two improved schemes which are not only more secure and efficient than Lee-Chang's protocol, but also more efficient than Ou-Hwang's protocol, especially the second one. Their high efficiency makes them more practical in power-limited and band-limited wireless roaming networks.

Acknowledgements. This work is supported by Science and Technology Project Founded by the Education Commission of Jiangxi Province (No. GJJ161195), Humanities and social science project of universities and colleges of Jiangxi Province (No. JC162001), Science and Technology Project Founded by the Xinyu science and Technology Bureau (No. 20163090862), and the National Nature Science Foundation of China (No. 61402055). The authors would like to thank the anonymous referees for their valuable suggestions.

References

1. Hwang, T., Gope, P.: Provably secure mutual authentication and key exchange scheme for expeditious mobile communication through synchronously one-time secrets. Wirel. Pers. Commun. **77**(1), 197–224 (2014)
2. Wu, K.Y., Tsai, K.Y., Wu, T.C., et al.: Provably secure anonymous authentication scheme for roaming service in global mobility networks. J. Inf. Sci. Eng. **31**(2), 727–742 (2015)
3. Zhu, H., Li, H., Su, W.L., et al.: ID-based wireless authentication scheme with anonymity. J. Commun. **30**(4), 130–136 (2009)
4. Khan, M.A., Kausar, F., Masood, A.: Modified anonymous authentication scheme with enhanced security for wireless communication. In: Bandyopadhyay, S.K., Adi, W., Kim, T., Xiao, Y. (eds.) ISA 2010. CCIS, vol. 76, pp. 198–208. Springer, Heidelberg (2010). https://doi.org/10.1007/978-3-642-13365-7_19
5. Kuo, W.C., Wei, H.J., Cheng, J.C.: Enhanced secure authentication scheme with anonymity for roaming in mobility networks. Inf. Technol. Control **43**(2), 151–156 (2014)
6. Kim, J.S., Jin, K.: Improved secure anonymous authentication scheme for roaming service in global mobility networks. Int. J. Secur. Appl. **6**(3), 45–53 (2012)
7. Mun, H., Han, K., Yan, S.L., et al.: Enhanced secure anonymous authentication scheme for roaming service in global mobility networks. Math. Comput. Model. **55**(1–2), 214–222 (2012)
8. Gope, P., Hwang, T.: Lightweight and energy-efficient mutual authentication and key agreement scheme with user anonymity for secure communication in global mobility networks. IEEE Syst. J. **10**, 1–10 (2016)
9. He, D., Zeadally, S., Kumar, N., et al.: Efficient and anonymous mobile user authentication protocol using self-certified public key cryptography for multi-server architectures. IEEE Trans. Inf. Forensics Secur. **11**(9), 2052–2064 (2016)
10. Alavalapati, G.R., Das, A.K., Yoon, E.J., et al.: A secure anonymous authentication protocol for mobile services on elliptic curve cryptography. IEEE Access **4**, 4394–4407 (2016)
11. He, D., Zeadally, S., Kumar, N., et al.: Efficient and anonymous mobile user authentication protocol using self-certified public key cryptography for multi-server architectures. IEEE Trans. Inf. Forensics Secur. **11**(9), 2052–2064 (2016)
12. Lee, W.B., Yeh, C.K.: A new delegation-based authentication protocol for use in portable communication systems. IEEE Trans. Wirel. Commun. **4**(1), 57–64 (2005)

13. Tang, C., Wu, D.O.: An efficient mobile authentication scheme for wireless networks. IEEE Trans. Wirel. Commun. **7**(4), 1408–1416 (2008)
14. Lee, T.F., Chang, S.H., Hwang, T., et al.: Enhanced delegation-based authentication protocol for PCSs. IEEE Trans. Wirel. Commun. **8**(5), 2166–2171 (2009)
15. Lee, C.C., Chang, R.X., Chen, T.Y., et al.: An improved delegation-based authentication protocol for PCSs. Inf. Technol. Control **41**(3), 258–267 (2012)
16. Ou, H.H., Hwang, M.S.: Double delegation-based authentication and key agreement protocol for PCSs. Wirel. Pers. Commun. **72**(1), 437–446 (2013)
17. Kumar, P., Gurtov, A., Iinatti, J., et al.: Delegation-based robust authentication model for wireless roaming using portable communication devices. IEEE Trans. Consum. Electron. **60** (4), 668–674 (2014)
18. Gao, T., Peng, F., Guo, N.: Anonymous authentication scheme based on identity-based proxy group signature for wireless mesh network. EURASIP J. Wirel. Commun. Netw. **2016** (1), 193 (2016)

Multi-match Segments Similarity Join Algorithm Based on MapReduce

Heng Xiao$^{(\boxtimes)}$ and Xianchun Zhou

Sanya University, Sanya 572022, Hainan, China
4383642@qq.com

Abstract. Similarity joint is applied in many fields. While the similarity joint algorithm is used to clean the massive data set, MapReduce can provide an effective framework of distributed computers. This paper mainly analyzes the similarity joint algorithm which is based on MapReduce, and proposes an improved strategy that introduces the implementation process base on the framework of MapReduce in detail after the improvement of PassJoin algorithm. The improved algorithm increases the filtering conditions to eliminate its own redundancy in the filtering phase and reduces the times of reading the original string. The time consumption is reduced considerably by experiments, which shows the effectiveness of the improved strategy.

Keywords: Massive data · Similar self-join · MapReduce · Filtering
Key-value pairs

1 Introduction

With the development of Internet technology and the deepened application of networks, applications on social network, interactive media, search engine and other ones' root in people's daily lives. MapReduce programming normal form proposed by Google provides a simple programming model that enables the efficient and flexible information mining on massive data. MapReduce has become the most popular parallel computing environment of big data dealing, for good scalability, serviceability and fault tolerance.

It is a research hotspot for the daily mass data information, how to store, manage, analyze, and find out the effective information from it. MapReduce provides a simple programming model that enables it to efficiently and efficiently mining the information from massive data. Now, MapReduce has become the most popular parallel computing environment for dealing with big data, with good scalability, usability, and fault tolerance.

Join operations play a very important role in data analysis and are widely used in data cleansing, similar text duplication checking, cluster analysis and so on. When there is a single data source, it is called self-joint. When there are 2 or more data sources, it is called multi-source joint. According to the parallelism, the similarity joint algorithm can be divided into the memory one and the parallel one. The memory algorithm runs on a standalone machine that allows the access to global information stored in memory during the connection process, such as index structures. Parallel algorithm runs on the cluster that is difficult to share information among nodes because

© Springer International Publishing AG 2017
G. Wang et al. (Eds.): SpaCCS 2017 Workshops, LNCS 10658, pp. 119–127, 2017.
https://doi.org/10.1007/978-3-319-72395-2_12

of parallel execution. Dealing with parallel joint operation based on MapReduce is the best choice in the current environment of big data, which can be widely used in the log analysis, online analysis, data analysis and so on.

MapReduce program runs on a multi-node computer cluster, which adopts the idea of ruling after division and abstracts the data processing tasks into 2 types of tasks that are Map and Reduce. IN the Map phase the data is filtered while in the Reduce phase it completes the data aggregation processing. A MapReduce task is divided into three phases: the map phase, the shuffle phase and the reduce phase, and the data in each phase is represented by key-value pairs (key, value). In the Map phase, complete the data filtering process, in the Reduce phase, complete the data aggregation processing. In this paper, the study of the algorithm also based on these three stages.

MapReduce-based similarity joint algorithm has also been the concern of many scholars, such as the algorithm adopting the prefix filtering technology proposed by the literature [4]. The algorithm in the map phase finds out the key with the token in the string prefix and uses the string itself as the value, while in the reduce phase it finds the strings that shares the same prefix token as the candidate pairs. In literature [2], a variety of similarity joint algorithms are proposed, and map load, load reduction and transmission consumption are also analyzed in detail. In literature [5], t it improved and upgraded the PassJoin algorithm proposed in literature [3], resulting in a similarity joint algorithm based on MapReduce. Literature [1] also puts forward a MassJoin algorithm through MapReduce based on PassJoin algorithm, which reduces the data transmission and maintains the ability of filtering by combining the same key-value pair. The algorithm in Literature [1] not only supports the string connection, but also has be extended to the collection joint.

In this paper, we will work on the current research related to the similarity joint algorithms based on MapReduce specifically, and try to improve the MassJoin algorithm. The algorithm is divided into three stages: filtering, verification 1 and verification 2, and each stage is done through MapReduce's map, shuffle and reduce operations. At last the performance of algorithms are analyzed and verified by experimental comparison.

2 MassJoin Algorithm

In the literature [1], Deng has improved the PassJoin algorithm based on MapReduce Framework, resulting in an improved algorithm called MassJoin. PassJoin [3] is such a similarity joint algorithm on strings in view of editing distance, which won the championship in the EDBT2013 international similarity joint competition. The algorithm, a memory algorithm, focuses on generating sub-strings of high quality during the filtering phase so that at least a sub-string can be shared by strings achieving the requirement. The algorithm gets rid of a large number of irrelevant strings by precisely selecting substrings.

The editing distance refers to minimal operations such as insert, delete, and replace to convert a string to another string. For example: ED ("Similarity", "Similar") = 3. Letting the edit distance threshold be τ, and if the editing distance between each pair of strings is less than or equal to τ, the pair are similar.

This algorithm is divided into three phases: the filtering phase, the verification phase 1, and the verification phase 2. When calculating the editing length, set the threshold to τ. The core idea is to divide the string into $\tau + 1$ segments. Due to the principle of pigeon nest, if the two strings are similar, then at least a segment in both must be matched. The implementation process is as follows.

(1) The filtering phase

Map process: The set of string of length l, S, is split into n blocks called s, where Si represents the set of the i-th block. Creating an inverted index Li for each Si, Li(ω) indicates that the i-th block is a set of substrings of ω. The initial state of Li is empty, then it generates the indexing substrings and the matching substrings for each segment.

A. First, a string S is split into $\tau + 1$ segments, and the length of the preceding segment is $\lfloor |s|/\tau + 1 \rfloor$, followed $|s| - \lfloor |s|/\tau + 1 \rfloor * (\tau + 1)$ segments length is $\lceil |s|/\tau + 1 \rceil$.

B. Each segment generates indexing substrings, which is pair (key, value). Use the length $|s|$, segment number i and the content of the index substring to compose the key, while get the value from the ID and type identifier (IIFlage) of the string s.

C. For each segment, a sub-string collection is generated respectively by the algorithm of substring selection, for example the substring set of the i-th segment is W (s, Li). The matching substring for each segment is pair (key, value). Also use the length $|s|$, segment number i and the content of the matching substring to compose the key, while get value from the string ID and type identification (SSFlage).

D. For each selected substring $\omega \in W(s, L_i)$, find Li(ω) in the index, and for each string $r \in Li(\omega)$, call the validation algorithm to verify that r and s matching.

E. After all the segments of the string s are processed, $\tau + 1$ segments are inserted into the corresponding index, for example, the i-th segment is inserted into L_i.

Continue to repeat the above steps until all the strings are processed.

Reduce process: Split the value list corresponding to each key, according to the IIlist and SSlist resulting from type of identification. Then verify each string pair <rid, sid> (rid $\in$ IILIS, sid $\in$ SSlist) to determine whether the editing distance between them meets the matching requirements

(2) Verification Phase 1

The main function of this phase is to get the set S. In the Map process, if the result of the filtering phase is read, <sid, list (rid)> is output as it is. If the S set is read, the string number and string contents <sid, s> are output. In Reduce process the content of the string s and the matching string list (rid) with the same sid are distinguished first. And the string number rid is replaced by the string content s, followed by the output <s, list (rid)>.

(3) Verification Phase 2

The main function of this phase is to read the set R and verify candidate pairs. In the Map process, if the result of the verification phase 1 is read, the list (rid) is split and the <rid, s> is output reversely. In the Reduce process, firstly distinguish the content of the string s and the matching string list (rid) with the same sid. Then for each <r, s> use the verification algorithm to testify and output string pairs that meets the similarity requirements and similarity degrees <<r, s>, sim (r, s)>.

The MassJoin algorithm supports both dual-source joint and self-joint. The algorithm solves the bottleneck of reading the original strings by two-step reading in the verification phase. However, the algorithm has several problems such as the problems of reading data sets repeatedly and self-connection redundancy when self-connection is made. For example, when self-joint is generating the indexing strings during the filtering phases, the set R is read once. And when generating the matching string, the set S is read once. Also in the validation phase 1 and the verification phase 2, the sets R and S are read once again separately, since the algorithm is self-connected and the set of R and S is exactly the same, which is equivalent to read the input set 4 times when performing self-connection so that much time is waste. And for that during the connection the algorithm cannot distinguish the same string in both the set R and set S to avoid the similarity calculation between themselves and their own, there are still their own redundant operations on self-connection.

3   Improved Multi-segment Matching Similar Self-join Algorithm

In this paper, It takes the similarity joint of strings as an example, makes full use of the advantages of Massjoin algorithm and improves the problems of self-connection to get a multi-segment matching similarity self-joint algorithm based on MapReduce. The algorithm is also divided into three phases: the filtering phase, the verification phase 1, and the verification phase 2. Each phase is a Map/Reduce process.

(1) The filtering phase

In the Map process the set of strings is segmented and the indexing substrings and the matching substrings are output in a long–short-matching way. In pair (Key, value), Key consists of length, block number and segment while value consists of string ID and type.

A. Reading the string set, the string set S is divided by the algorithm to obtain the string s with the length of length $(s) > \tau + k$. The algorithm runs several Map tasks and each Map task processes a string.

B. The string s is divided into $\tau + k$ segments and it generates the indexing substrings (type I). The length of substrings are set to $\lfloor |s|/\tau + k \rfloor$ and $\lceil |s|/(\tau + k) + 1 \rceil$. $|s|$ is length (s). In the outcome (key, value) pair, key consists of length, block number and block While value consists of string ID and type.

In long-short-substring-matching-control way, the number of the output matching substrings is reduced to cut down the load. If two strings, r and s, are similar, then s must have k substring matching a substring in r.

C. The substring selection algorithm of PassJoin is used to generate the matching substring (S type) for each segment. In the outcome (key, value) pair, the key is also composed of length, block number and block. The value is composed of string ID. Changing the upper limit of the length of the matching substring to the length of the substring can eliminate the redundant matching substring in the self-joint.

Shuffle process: Under the MapReduce framework, in the Shuffle process the records are confused and sorted by key values. Then the Shuffle results will be the input to the Reduce process.

Reduce process: There are multiple Reduce tasks during the runtime of the algorithm. Every time the Reduce process handles the key/value pairs in the Shuffle result, Reduce process reads the value of the (key, value) pair which use the ids of the indexing substrings and the matching substrings to form a list. The composition method of the list is:

A. It needs to split the list into the id list of indexing substrings and the id list of matching substrings.
B. If the two lists are not full, there are no matching pairs in the Reduce process.
C. When neither list is empty, the collection of the corresponding list elements will generate key/value pairs. Key selects the id value in the list of matching substrings while value only selects the id value of the indexing-substring list which is not equal to the id value of the key. So it will avoid the self-pairing for strings.

A simple example is showed in Fig. 1.

String	Map		Shuffle	Reduce
	Index	Match	sort	remove redundancy
1#ABBCDE	6&1#ABB, T1	5&1#AB, 1		
		6&1#ABB, 1		
	6&1#CDE, T1	5&1#CDE, 1	4&1#AB, (2)	
		6&1#CDE, 1	4&2#CD, (2)	
2#ABGCD	5&1#AB, T2	4&1#AB, 2	5&1#AB, (T2, 1, 2, 3)	⟨1, 2⟩
		5&1#AB, 2	5&1#CDE, (1, 3)	⟨2, 3⟩
	5&2#GCD, T2	4&2#CD, 2	5&2#GCD, (T2, 2)	⟨1, 3⟩
		5&2#GCD, 2	6&1#ABB, (T1, 1)	
3#ABFCDF	6&1#ABF, T3	5&1#AB, 3	6&1#CDE, (T1, 1, T3, 3)	
		6&1#ABF, 3	6&1#ABF, (T3, 3)	
	6&1#CDF, T3	5&1#CDF, 3		
		6&1#CDE, 3		

Fig. 1. The filtering phase

(2) Verification Phase 1

This phase has two sets of input data: the set of strings and the outcome of filtering phase. The main function of this phase is to extract the content of original strings and remove the duplicate candidate pairs.

Map process: In the Map, if the read string is in the string set, directly output the string id as the key and the content of string as value. If it reads the results of the filtering phase, then produce positive and negative candidate pairs. The purpose of the generation of the positive and negative candidate pairs is to facilitate the subsequent processing of matching the string ids and contents so as to avoid the re-read of the set of strings.

Shuffle process: In the Shuffle process, all the output key/value pairs from map are confused and sorted in accordance with the key and the pairs with the same ID are merged. For example the String "1#ABBCDE", "2#ABGCD" and "3#ABFCDE", their positive and negative pairs are <1, 2> <2, 1>, <3, 2>, <2, 3>, <1, 3> <3, 1> and the merged contents are <1, (1#ABBCDE, 2, 3)>, <2, (2#ABGCD, 2, 3)>, <3, (3#ABFCDE, 2, 3)>.

Reduce process: In the Reduce process, when dealing with an output key/value pair from Shuffle, the key is id of a certain string while value that contains both the contents of the string and the id list of the matching strings. Besides it will output new (key, value) pairs, in which the key is the contents of the string and the value is the id list after removing the duplicated value. Take the above Reduce process as an example, the results are: <1#ABBCDE, (2, 3)>, <2#ABGCD, (2, 3)>, <3#ABFCDE, (2, 3)>.

The process of Verifying Phase 1 is shown in Fig. 2.

Map	Shuffle	Reduce
pairs	sort	remove(sid)
⟨1, 2⟩ ⟨2, 1⟩	1, (1#ABBCDE, 2, 3)	1#ABBCDE, (2, 4)
⟨2, 3⟩ ⟨3, 2⟩	2, (2#ABGCD, 1, 3)	2#ABGCD, (1, 4)
⟨1, 3⟩ ⟨3, 1⟩	3, (3#ABFCDE, 1, 2)	3#ABFCDE, (1, 3)
1, 1#ABBCDE		
2, 2#ABGCD		
3, 3#ABFCDE		

Fig. 2. Verification phase 1

(3) Verification Phase 2

The input data of the verification phase 2 is the output of the verification phase 1. And the main function is to eliminate the redundancy and verify the candidate pairs in detail.

Map process: First to read the candidate pairs from the Verification phase 1. Then generate new key/value pairs. Combine the string id in the original key and the ids in the list to get the new group id as the key. During the combination sort the ids in ascending order. The purpose is to get an unique key/value pair for the same candidate pairs, that is not only to remove the positive and negative redundancy such as <id1, id2> and <id2, id1> but also to facilitate the matching of the content of strings.

Shuffle process: All output key/value pairs from the map are confused and sorted by key. The result is the input of Reduce. Each key/value pair are a candidate. Key is the id of the combination of two strings, and value is a list of the content of two strings.

Reduce process: Firstly, split the value to get the contents of the two strings. Then with the on-line algorithm calculate the editing distance between the two strings. We adopted the editing-distance-calculation method of PassJoin in literature [3]. If the editing distance meets the requirements, the matched pair is output.

The process of Verifying Phase 2 is shown in Fig. 3.

Map	Shuffle	Reduce
combination	sort	ED(s1,s3)<2
⟨1,2⟩,1#ABBCDE	⟨1,2⟩,(1#ABBCDE,2#ABGCD)	1,(1#ABBCDE,3#ABFCDE)
⟨1,3⟩,1#ABBCDE	⟨1,3⟩,(1#ABBCDE,3#ABFCDE)	
⟨1,2⟩,2#ABGCD	⟨2,3⟩,(2#ABGCD,3#ABFCDE)	
⟨2,3⟩,2#ABGCD		
⟨1,3⟩3#ABFCDE		
⟨2,3⟩3#ABFCDE		

Fig. 3. Verification phase 2

The algorithm is updated based on PassJoin and MassJion, the improvements as follows:

The string is split into multiple segments for matching. Reduce the work of data handling in the filtering phase by eliminating the self-joint redundancy, equally loaded. The selection algorithm of the matching substrings is improved during the filtering process to reduce the number of matched substrings.

Reduce the number of data set read. During the whole process it reads twice. One is during the filter phase and another is during the verification phase.

With the positive and negative candidate pairs and the method of combining ids, to achieve the id and string content matching. By combining ids further eliminate the duplication of the positive and negative pairs to reduce the running time of the algorithm for verification.

4 Experiments

Experimental environment: This experiment is carried out on the Hadoop platform. Real experiments are on the same Hadoop cluster. T There are 4 nodes in the cluster, 1 Namenode as Master, 3 Datanode as slaves. Hardware configuration for nodes: CPU i5 7500, memory 16 G, hard disk 1 TB. Software configuration for the Cluster: operating system Ubantu-16.04-desktop-amd64.iso, Hadoop 2.7.3, jdk1.8.0_131. Development Kit is Eclipse (Fig. 4).

Test data: Author+Title fields in DBLP (Digital Bibliography & Library Project) and the fields in query log of American Online (AOL). The experiment transforms the records into strings that contain only the author and the title which in the DBLP dataset (Fig. 5).

During the experiment, the larger the τ value is, the more obvious the time optimization of the algorithm. But with the growth of k, the time efficiency rises at first and then declines. When the value of k is 2 or 3, the algorithm is in the best state.

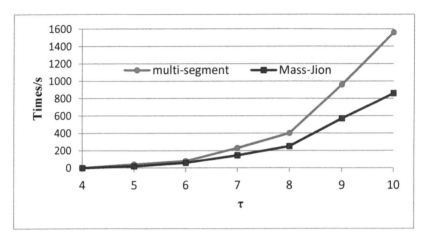

Fig. 4. The comparison of time between MassJion and multi-segment

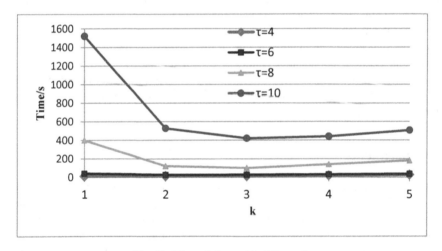

Fig. 5. Elapsed time with different k

5 Conclusions

This paper mainly studies the technology of similarity joint in data cleaning of big data set. Against the problems of string reading and self-redundancy existing in the current self-joint algorithm it analyzes an improved algorithm based on MapReduce. The string is split into $\tau + k$ segments and the comparison times are reduced by strict limits on verification conditions, which greatly improve the efficiency of the algorithm. This paper describes the operations of Map/Reduce in the process of self-join algorithm specifically and the way how to improve the algorithm. The improvement effectively reduces the times of reading the sets of strings, saves the filtering time and speeds up the joint process.

Acknowledgments. This paper is funded by the following project funds: the Natural Science Foundation of Hainan Province (No. 617182), Sanya City Institute of Science and Technology Cooperation Project (No. 2015YD11, No. 2015YD57).

References

1. Deng, D., Li, G.L., Hao, S., et al.: MassJoin: a MapReduce-based method for scalable string similarity joins. In: 2014 IEEE 30th International Conference on Data Engineering (2014)
2. Afrati, F.N., Sarma, A.D., Menestrina, D., et al.: Fuzzy joins using MapReduce. In: Proceedings of IEEE 28th International Conference on Data Engineering (2012)
3. Li, G., Deng, D., Wang, J., Feng, J.: Pass-Join: a partition-based method for similarity joins. Proc. VLDB Endow. **5**(3), 253–264 (2011)
4. Vernica, R., Carey, M.J., Li, C.: Efficient parallel set-similarity joins using MapReduce. In: Proceedings of the 2010 ACM SIGMOD International Conference on Management of Data, SIGMOD 2010 (2010)
5. Deng, D., Li, G.L., Hao, S., et al.: MassJoin: a MapReduce-based method for scalable string similarity joins. In: 2014 IEEE 30th International Conference on Data Engineering (2014)

GPU-Accelerated Histogram Generation on Smart-Phone and Webbrowser

Hai Jiang[1], Xianyi Zhu[1], Yi Xiao[1(✉)], Jiawei Luo[1], and Yan Zheng[2]

[1] College of Computer Science and Electronic Engineering, Hunan University,
Changsha 410082, People's Republic of China
yixiao_csee@hnu.edu.cn
[2] College of Electrical and Information Engineering, Hunan University,
Changsha 410082, People's Republic of China

Abstract. Histogram is a critical component of algorithms in image processing to count tonal percentage. The performance of generating histogram sequentially does not satisfy the demand of realtime applications on smart phone and webbrowser. This paper proposes a two-pixel voting scheme (2PVS) for histogram generation on GPU. Compared with previous methods, the scale of problem can be cut down by a half using 2PVS. Every two adjacent pixels are considered as one object to be voted into a bin of histogram, followed by a recursive texture reduction process. We implement this method with graphics interface, which is compatible with embedded device and webbrowser. Experiments show that our method runs 0.3 to 1.9 times faster than the baseline method on smartphone while 1.2 to 2.6 times faster on webbrowser.

Keywords: Histogram generation · GPU · Smartphone
Webbrowser · Two-pixel voting scheme

1 Introduction

In digital image processing, a basic representation of tonal distribution of one image is histogram. Histograms are widely used in image processing algorithms, such as thresholding methods [1–3], histogram equalization, histogram matching, tone mapping and mutual information-based image registration [4] etc. Even many realtime applications need to generate histogram, such as screen sharing [5], object detection [6], video abstraction [7,8] and volume rendering augmentation [9]. Moreover, with the development of applications in augmented reality and virtual reality on smart phone, there is a requirement to generate histograms as fast as possible for those realtime applications on smart phones.

With the fast development of graphics processing uints (GPUs), they are widely used for general purpose computing, including histogram calculation [10–12]. A basic idea of accelerating histogram generation on GPU is to reduce the access conflicts when multiple threads need to access the same bin simultaneously. When multiple threads update the same bin, the operation become sequential. To alleviate this problem, previous works [13] focus on mapping methods to make simultaneous running threads access different bins. However,

© Springer International Publishing AG 2017
G. Wang et al. (Eds.): SpaCCS 2017 Workshops, LNCS 10658, pp. 128–136, 2017.
https://doi.org/10.1007/978-3-319-72395-2_13

for a n pixels image, there are still n times of modification totally with any mapping methods, because one pixel is voted into a bin. Moreover, these algorithms rely on shared memory to deduce the bandwidth of the algorithm, which may be not available on some smart phones or webbrowsers.

As a novel route, we focus on how to decrease the entire times of modification. We propose a two-pixel voting scheme, in which two pixels are considered as one together to vote simultaneously, so that the number of modification becomes $\frac{n}{2}$. The scale of problem is cut down by a half. The method is quite simple, it can be efficiently implemented on GPUs which do not support CUDA [14] or OpenCL [15] or compute shader, but only support traditional graphics rendering pipeline. Therefore, our method is suitable for environments such as smart phones and webbrowsers, where shared memory is not available for users. We implemented our method with OpenGL ES and WebGL. In experiment, our method can run 190% faster than previous methods on smart phone and 260% faster on webbrowser in the best case.

Thus, our contribution contain two aspects:

1. The two-pixel voting scheme, which reduce the scale of problem for GPU-accelerated histogram generation;
2. The implementation with graphics interface, which is suitable for embedded devices and webbrowers.

2   Background and Previous Works

2.1   General Purpose on GPU

GPU owns serious computational abilities since each GPU device consists of hundreds or thousands of SIMD processors. Currently, there are two ways to accomplish general purpose GPU computing (GPGPU). One way is to use parallel programming environments such as CUDA [14] and OpenCL [15], which are powerful but not appropriate for applications on smart phones and webbrowsers. The other solution is to use graphics interface language such as OpenGL ES [16] for embedded device and WebGL [17] for webbrowser. Since our purpose is to provide fast histogram generating algorithm on smart phones or webbrowsers, we implement our method with graphics interface language.

Figure 1 shows a traditional graphics pipeline of GPU. It consists of two programmable shaders, the vertex shader unit and the fragment shader. Vertex shaders operate the transformations of vertices, and fragment shaders operate the color computation of pixels. Specially, fragment shaders can access and modify textures. To do GPGPU with graphics pipeline, the computing process should be fitted to the process of rendering 3D objects.

2.2   GPU-Accelerated Histogram Generation

In the actual, most GPU-accelerated methods [13] for histogram generation are implemented on CUDA or OpenCL. The effort of those works [10–12] is to reduce

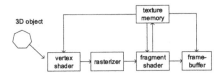

Fig. 1. A traditional graphics pineline of GPU

the position conflicts as less as possible, taking advantage of the *shared memory*. Unfortunately, since CUDA and OpenCL are rarely supported on embedded device and webbrowser, these algorithms are not suitable in these environments.

Our work focuses on algorithms suitable for environments where only traditional graphics interface is supported and shared memory is not available. In one work [18], the authors proposed to generate a number of small histograms in parallel, which are kept in texture memory. These small histograms are then merged into a final histogram in a gather step. In another work [19], a 1-pixel voting scheme (1PVS) is proposed, which use the scattering ability of vertex shader to locate the position for voting, and use the gathering ability of fragment shader to count the votes of each bin.

3   Two-Pixel Voting Scheme

In histogram generation, the normal way of voting is that one pixel at most can be voted into one bin of the histogram in a voting round (1PVS), as shown in Fig. 2(a). In other words, one vote involves only one pixel. With the scattering method of GPU [19], each pixel is treated as one single vertex primitive. If the number of pixels is large, the vote counting process will be serialized significantly. Because each counting step runs an atomic operation once. To decrease total atomic operations, we propose a 2-pixel voting scheme (2PVS).

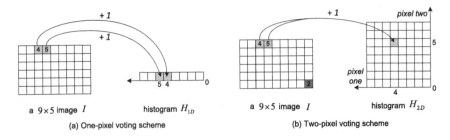

Fig. 2. Voting schemes of histogram generation

The main idea of 2PVS is shown in Fig. 2(b). The adjacent two pixels of a gray-scale image is packed into one single vertex. With this arrangement, the 1D histogram generation problem becomes a 2D one. The gray-scale values of

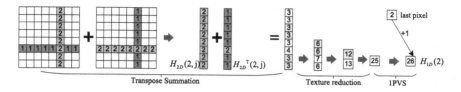

Fig. 3. An instance process from H_{2D} to H_{1D}, specified $H_{1D}(2)$, and n is odd

the first and second elements in the vertex decide the voting location of the bin in histogram H_{2D}. The first pixel determines the horizontal location while the second pixel determines the vertical location. In this way, the scale of this problem decreases to a half compared with 1PVS, and total atomic operations are also cut down by a half. After voting by all pair-wise pixels, a bin $H_{2D}(i,j)$ indicates the count of the pixel pairs whose intensity are (i,j). In other words, $H_{2D}(i,j)$ indicates a sub-part of count of the pixels that intensity are i or j. For a whole count of pixels of intensity i, summation over $H_{2D}(i,:)$ and $H_{2D}(:,i)$ is the answer. Therefore, histogram H_{1D} can be generated by summation on H_{2D}. A bin $H_{1D}(i)$ can be evaluated by following equation:

$$H_{1D}(i) = \sum_{j=0}^{b-1} H_{2D}(i,j) + \sum_{j=0}^{b-1} H_{2D}(j,i) \tag{1}$$

where b is the number of bins in one row. Equation (1) indicates that the ith bin of H_{1D} is the summation of the bins of H_{2D} on the ith row and the ith column. The summation can be completed efficiently by a recursive reducing process on GPU.

We only consider that the number of pixels is even in this section above. For a case that the number of pixels is odd, the last lonely pixel can be voted into H_{1D} directly using 1PVS after operations of reducing process on H_{2D}.

4   Implementation

Consider an image with n pixels, the implementation of our histogram generation consists of 5 steps described in Algorithm 1. In step (1), pixels are packed into a vertex buffer with a fixed format. In the steps followed, both 2PVS and 1PVS need to run two tasks: bin location selection and accumulation of bin contents. So we describe steps (2) and (5) in Sect. 4.1, while steps (3) and (4) in Sect. 4.2. Step (4) is rendered in $\lceil \log_2(b) \rceil$ passes, and other steps are rendered in three distinct passes respectively. Totally, our implementation needs $\lceil \log_2(b) \rceil + 3$ rendering passes.

4.1   Bin Location Selection and Accumulation

Those two tasks are performed in a same rendering pass. In this pass, we just draw $\lfloor \frac{n}{2} \rfloor$ vertices, each of which will generate one pixel in the framebuffer. The size of framebuffer is $b \times b$.

Algorithm 1. The framework of our histogram generation with 2PVS.

Input:
    An input image with n pixels;
    The histogram size b;
Output:
    A histogram H_{1D};
1: pack each two adjacent pixels to the first two component of a vertex, getting $\lfloor \frac{n}{2} \rfloor$ vertices;
2: perform the 2PVS by drawing the former $\lfloor \frac{n}{2} \rfloor$ vertices on H_{2D};
3: evaluate H_{2D}', the summation over H_{2D} and transposed H_{2D}^{T};
4: multiple times of texture reductions from H_{2D}' to H_{1D};
5: if n is odd, perform 1PVS on H_{1D} by drawing the last pixel as a single vertex.

Vertex shaders run the task, bin location selection. Figure 2(b) shows this process. Every two pixels are rendered as two attributes of one vertex primitive. Each vertex is transformed to a new coordinate. The $1st$ pixel p_1 determines the horizontal coordinate x while the $2nd$ pixel p_2 determines the vertical coordinate y in histogram H_{2D}. For a vertex containing p_1 and p_2 whose intensity levels are ℓ_1 and ℓ_2 respectively, its new coordinates (x, y) can be evaluated as the follow equation,

$$\begin{cases} x = (\frac{\ell_1}{\ell_{max}} + 0.5) \div b \times 2 - 1 \\ y = (\frac{\ell_2}{\ell_{max}} + 0.5) \div b \times 2 - 1 \end{cases} \tag{2}$$

where ℓ_{max} is the range of intensity level. The equation is obtained according to the definition of normalized window coordinate in OpenGL. Since we only draw 2D vertices here, the other component of the vertex are 0.

After the vertex shaders run over, the transformed vertices are automatically rasterized to pixels by the graphics pipeline. Each pixel is then processed by a fragment shader. The fragment shaders then run the task, accumulation of bin contents (votes counting). Before the task, all values of texture H_{2D} are initially assigned 0s. In the fragment shader, the output color of each pixel is set to 1, which means that a bin in the coordinate of fragment receives 1 vote. To do accumulation, the blend function in OpenGL ES and WebGL should be enabled with this parameter (GL_ONE, GL_ONE). After the running of fragment shader, the texture H_{2D} stores the 2D histogram.

4.2 Summation and Reduction

To compute each bin $H_{1D}(i)$, both the ith row and the ith column of H_{2D} should be reduced. According to Eq. (1), the ith row and the ith column should be reduced and then summed respectively. To decrease the times of reduction, we do summation firstly and then reduce. Before reduction, one pass rendering is necessary to add the transposed H_{2D}^{T} to H_{2D}. This process can be written as follow equation:

$$H_{2D}'(i, j) = H_{2D}(i, j) + H_{2D}^{T}(i, j) \tag{3}$$

where $H_{2D}{}^T(i,j) = H_{2D}(j,i)$. Then the $H_{1D}(i)$ can be computed after $\lceil \log_2(b) \rceil$ times reductions either on the ith row or the ith column of H_{2D}', namely as equation:

$$H_{1D}(i) = \sum_{j=0}^{b-1} H_{2D}'(i,j). \tag{4}$$

If n is odd, we will draw the last pixel using the 1PVS, after we get H_{1D} for other pixels. More specifically, Fig. 3 shows an instance for $H_{1D}(2)$ from steps (3) to (5).

5   Experiments and Discuss

To evaluate the performances of different methods, we tested methods of histogram generation with different images on smart phones and webbrowser. The methods are sequential method on CPU, scattering method with 1PVS on GPU [19] and our method with 2PVS on GPU.

5.1   On Smartphone

The configuration of tested smart phones is listed in Table 1. All methods are implemented in Java language. The two GPU-based methods, namely 1PVS [19] and 2PVS, are implemented with OpenGL ES packages of Android SDK. The version of OpenGL ES API is 3.0.

We did an experiment to generate histogram H_{1D} with sizes ranged from 64 to 256. Large size images are tested on Lenovo ZUK Z2, since Oppo A37m needs more time do perform those images. The runtimes of those methods are listed in Table 2. Both GPU-based methods are much faster than the CPU-based method.

And the runtime ratios between 1PVS and 2PVS are illustrated in Fig. 4, which shows that ratio grows up when image size increases for a same size histogram. On Oppo A37m, when the image size is 256×256, our method is about 50% faster than GPU-based scattering with 1PVS [19]. However, when the image size is 1024×1024, our method achieves the best performance, over 190% faster than the 1PVS method [19]. Similar situations happen on Lenovo ZUK Z2 when image size increases. Because if an image is large, the process of histogram generation will be sequential seriously on GPU. With our method, the being sequential problem can be relieved effectively. In a case that image size is 2560×1600, the parallel power of GPU is running out, so the runtime ratio does not increase at histogram size 256. From the tables, we can see that our method is very suitable for realtime applications on smart phones.

5.2   On Webbrowser

A similar experiment was performed on webbrowser. The configuration of our webbrowser is listed in Table 3. All methods are implemented in javascript language. The two GPU-based methods are implemented with the open source library Three.js [20]. The version of WebGL API is 2.0.

Table 1. The configuration of the two smartphones

Phone version	Oppo A37m	Lenovo ZUK Z2
OS	Android 5.1	Android 6.0.1
Chipset	Mediatek MT6750	Qualcomm Snapdragon 820 (MSM 8996)
CPU	Eight-core 1.5 GHz	Quad-core 2.15 GHz
RAM	2 GB LPDDR3	3 GB LPDDR4
GPU	ARM Mali-T860 MP2 (530 MHz)	Adreno 530 3D (624 MHz)

Table 2. The runtimes by different methods on smartphones (in ms)

Phone	Method		Sequential	1PVS [19]			2PVS (our)		
	Histogram size		64/128/256	64	128	256	64	128	256
Oppo A37m	Image size	256×256	224.4	4.87	4.75	4.56	3.62	3.51	3.37
		512×512	824.5	17.05	14.45	13.9	6.47	6.24	5.97
		1024×1024	3230.4	66.78	55.54	49.87	22.78	19.98	18.91
Lenovo ZUK Z2	Image size	1920×1200	6025.73	23.16	18.78	16.75	10.01	8.39	8.32
		1500×2000	7219.65	53.85	47.07	40.9	23.05	18.31	15.25
		2560×1600	11127.41	72.48	56.98	46.37	26.38	21.36	19.86

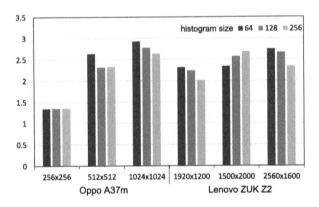

Fig. 4. The runtime ratio between 2PVS and 1PVS on phones

We did the experiment on webbrowser Chrome, generating histogram H_{1D} with different sizes from 256 to 1024. The runtimes of those methods are listed in Table 4. It shows that our method is faster than sequential method and 1VPS [19], to generate H_{1D} with same size. The speed of both GPU-based methods becomes faster when histogram size increases, since atomic operations

Table 3. The configuration of the webbrowser

Webbrowser version	Chrome 58.0.3029.110
OS	Windows 8.1
CPU	I7-4790K Quad-core 4.00 Gz
RAM	16 GB DDR3
GPU	GeForce GTX 960
GPU-RAM	4 GB DDR5

Table 4. The runtimes of different methods on Chrome (in ms)

Method		Sequential method	1VPS [19]			2VPS (our)		
Histogram size		64/256/1024	64	256	1024	64	256	1024
Image size	256 × 256	0.21	0.25	0.18	0.08	0.08	0.05	0.05
	512 × 512	0.57	1.16	0.85	0.37	0.41	0.28	0.23
	1024 × 1024	2.14	4.82	2.51	1.31	1.68	1.01	0.83
	1920 × 1200	5.12	5.81	3.93	2.67	2.51	1.56	1.42

of every bins decrease. Although with histogram size increasing, our method still runs faster than 1VPS [19]. Notice that image size is 256×256 and histogram size is 256, our method runs 2.6 times faster than 1VPS. In most situation, our method runs 1.2 times faster.

6   Conclusion

A GPU-accelerated method for histogram generation is proposed with a novel voting scheme, two-pixel voting scheme. With this scheme, the scale of problem can be decreased to be a half. Compared with the baseline method, our method reaches its best performance on smart phone, over 190% faster, when image size is large enough. On webbrowser, our method also runs 120% faster than the baseline method in general situation, and 260% faster at best.

Acknowledgement. This work is supported by NSFC (Project No.: 61502158) and HNSF (Project No.: 2017JJ3042) from PRC.

References

1. Otsu, N.: A threshold selection method from gray-level histograms. Automatica **11**(285–296), 23–27 (1975)
2. Kapur, J.N., Sahoo, P.K., Wong, A.K.: A new method for gray-level picture thresholding using the entropy of the histogram. Comput. Vis. Graph. Image Process. **29**(3), 273–285 (1985)

3. Sezgin, M., et al.: Survey over image thresholding techniques and quantitative performance evaluation. J. Electron. Imaging **13**(1), 146–168 (2004)

4. Shams, R., Sadeghi, P., Kennedy, R., Hartley, R.: Parallel computation of mutual information on the GPU with application to real-time registration of 3D medical images. Comput. Methods Programs Biomed. **99**(2), 133–146 (2010)

5. Sun, W., Lu, Y., Wu, F., Li, S.: Real-time screen image scaling and its GPU acceleration. In: 2009 16th IEEE International Conference on Image Processing (ICIP), pp. 3285–3288. IEEE (2009)

6. Messom, C., Barczak, A.: Stream processing of integral images for real-time object detection. In: 2008 Ninth International Conference on Parallel and Distributed Computing, Applications and Technologies, PDCAT 2008, pp. 405–412. IEEE (2008)

7. Zhao, H., Mao, X., Jin, X., Shen, J., Wei, F., Feng, J.: Real-time saliency-aware video abstraction. Vis. Comput. **25**(11), 973–984 (2009)

8. Zouaneb, I., Belarbi, M., Chouarfia, A.: Multi approach for real-time systems specification: case study of GPU parallel systems. Int. J. Big Data Intell. **3**(2), 122–141 (2016)

9. Jung, Y.H., Kim, J., Feng, D., Fulham, M.: Occlusion and slice-based volume rendering augmentation for PET-CT. IEEE J. Biomed. Health Inform. **21**(4), 1005–1014 (2017)

10. Gómez-Luna, J., González-Linares, J.M., Benavides, J.I., Guil, N.: An optimized approach to histogram computation on GPU. Mach. Vis. Appl. **24**(5), 899–908 (2013)

11. Podlozhnyuk, V.: Histogram calculation in CUDA. NVIDIA Corporation, White Paper (2007)

12. Shams, R., Barnes, N.: Speeding up mutual information computation using NVIDIA CUDA hardware. In: 9th Biennial Conference of the Australian Pattern Recognition Society on Digital Image Computing Techniques and Applications, pp. 555–560. IEEE (2007)

13. Eklund, A., Dufort, P., Forsberg, D., LaConte, S.M.: Medical image processing on the GPU-past, present and future. Med. Image Anal. **17**(8), 1073–1094 (2013)

14. NVIDIA: CUDA (2016). https://developer.nvidia.com/about-cuda

15. Khronos: Open Computing Language (2016). https://www.khronos.org/opencl/

16. Khronos: OpenGL ES (2016). https://www.khronos.org/opengles/

17. Khronos: WebGL (2016). https://www.khronos.org/webgl/

18. Fluck, O., Aharon, S., Cremers, D., Rousson, M.: GPU histogram computation. In: ACM SIGGRAPH 2006 Research Posters, p. 53. ACM (2006)

19. Scheuermann, T., Hensley, J.: Efficient histogram generation using scattering on GPUs. In: Proceedings of the 2007 Symposium on Interactive 3D Graphics and Games, pp. 33–37. ACM (2007)

20. Mr.doob: Three.js (2016). https://threejs.org/

An Efficient Message Routing Algorithm Using Overhearing in Community Opportunistic Networks

Junhai Zhou, Qin Liu, Siwang Zhou$^{(\boxtimes)}$, and Yapin Lin

College of Computer Science and Electronic Engineering, Hunan University,
Changsha 410082, China
Rj_zjh@hnu.edu.cn

Abstract. For the Opportunistic networks composed by mobile devices, which carried by people and have short-range wireless communication interface, its nodes movement reflects the characteristics of community. When nodes use wireless communication interface to broadcast information, other nodes within its sending range can overhear the sending information. The characteristic of broadcast is rarely used by the routing algorithms of the community opportunistic networks, so we present an efficient message routing algorithm using overhearing in community opportunistic networks. The algorithm divides the message routing into two phases: entering the destination community of message and reaching its destination node. The algorithm selects relay nodes for message based on the community attribute of nodes. At the same time, each node uses the overhearing information to advance the progress of message forwarding and clear redundant messages copies. Experiments result shows that it improves message delivery ratio effectively and reduce network overhead compared with some classic opportunistic networks routing algorithms.

Keywords: Opportunistic networks · Message routing · Community
Broadcast · Overhearing

1 Introduction

With the advent of a large number of mobile devices which having capabilities of short-range wireless communication, the opportunistic networks emerge [1, 2]. In the opportunistic networks, there is often no complete communication link between the source node and the destination node to transfer message. Nodes transfer messages in the way of storage-carrying-forwarding, and each node utilizes the encountering chance by means of the nodes movement to realize the transmission of messages [3, 4]. The networks composed by mobile devices, which carried by people and have capability of short distance wireless communication, are important application scenarios of the opportunistic networks. In this kind of opportunistic networks, because the social relations among people are relatively stable and have certain dependences, the nodes in the network often have aggregation phenomenon. Nodes form communities by means of self-organization. We call this kind of network as community opportunistic networks.

© Springer International Publishing AG 2017
G. Wang et al. (Eds.): SpaCCS 2017 Workshops, LNCS 10658, pp. 137–146, 2017.
https://doi.org/10.1007/978-3-319-72395-2_14

For opportunistic network is highly dynamic, the design of its routing algorithm is a very critical issue. According to the characteristics of opportunistic network, many routing algorithms have been put forward by researchers at home and abroad. Lindgren et al. proposed PROPHET [5] algorithm which is a benchmark forwarding algorithm [6] in opportunistic networks. The PROPHET algorithm uses history of encounters and transitivity to probabilistic routing messages to their destination nodes. But the POR-PHET algorithm is lack of effective control of the number of message copies which leads to greater network overhead, and it also does not consider the community nature of node movement and has lower message delivery ratio. Spyropoulos et al. proposed the classical Spray and Focus (SF) routing algorithm [7] for opportunistic networks which uses a finite number of message copies to achieve a balance between resource consumption and transmission success rates. But it does not take full advantage of the correlation of node movement in opportunistic networks and still has lower message delivery ratio.

When a node in opportunistic network broadcasts information via the wireless communication interface, the other nodes in the range of the transmission can overhear the information the node sends. So far, there is basically no routing algorithm using the overhearing of wireless broadcast for message delivery in community opportunistic networks. So we propose an efficient message routing algorithm using overhearing (EMRAUO) in community opportunistic networks. It uses the community nature of nodes movement to select the relay node, and each node uses the overhearing information to advance the progress of message forwarding and clear the redundant copy of the message, so as to effectively improve the message delivery ratio and reduce network overhead.

The rest part of this article is organized as follows: Sect. 2 introduces the message routing algorithm using overhearing in community opportunistic networks. Section 3 describes the experimental simulation and the experimental results analysis, Sect. 4 describes the conclusion.

2   EMRAUO Algorithm in Community Opportunistic Networks

The opportunistic networks, which composed of mobile devices carried by people, has the characteristics of the community. Nodes meeting often form communities by means of self-organization. The nodes of same community contact closely and the nodes of different communities have lower frequency of meeting. Some nodes only move in their local communities most of the time, and have less contact with nodes belonging to different communities. Some nodes are more active, have a wide mobile area, and have frequent contact with other community nodes, which enhances the inter-community relationship.

2.1   Detection of Community

In this paper, we use the sum of the length of contact time between nodes as the parameter of community detection, which refers to the Bubble algorithm [6], and adopt

Newman's weight network analysis algorithm [8] to make the partition of community. We use the relationship matrix, which consists of the contact duration time between nodes, as input and divide all nodes into different communities in the opportunistic network. In order to carry out community division, first 20% time of network operation is taken as the warm-up stage to collect the relevant meeting data and make community division. After the warm-up time, each node has known the community attribution of other nodes.

2.2 Message Routing by Overhearing in Community Opportunistic Networks

Definition 1: The destination community of message is the community which the destination node of the message belongs to.

Definition 2: The Destination Community Transmission Probability $DCTP_{iT}$ is the transmission probability of node i to the destination community T of message, which value is calculated by the following formula:

$$DCTP_{iT} = \frac{\sum\limits_{k=1}^{m} D_{Tk}}{TotalTime} \tag{1}$$

where $TotalTime$ is the total run time of the network up to now and D_{Tk} represents the duration time that node i encounters a node belonging to destination community T at the Kth time. The greater the $DCTP_{iT}$ value is, the more contact with the destination community node i has in per unit time.

Definition 3: The Destination Node Transmission Probability $DNTP_{id}$ is the transmission probability of node i to the destination node d, and node i belongs to the destination community T too. Its value is calculated by the following formula:

$$DNTP_{id} = \frac{\sum\limits_{k=1}^{n} d_{dk}}{TotalTime} \tag{2}$$

where d_{dk} is the duration of the Kth time that node i and node d meet in $TotalTime$ time. The greater the $DNTP_{id}$ value is, the more contact node i has with the destination node in per unit time.

Message Routing Based on Community. Based on the community character of node movement, the message routing of EMRAUO algorithm can be divided into two phase: entering the destination community of message, and then reaching the destination node in the destination community. In the first phase, the algorithm will generate forwarding tokens in the source node of message. Each token presents a permission to create one copy of the message and the L, which presents the value of token number, can be calculated by the following equation [7]:

$$(H_M^3 - 1.2)L^3 + (H_M^2 - \frac{\pi^2}{6})L^2 + (\alpha + \frac{2M-1}{M(M-1)})L = \frac{M}{M-1} \qquad (3)$$

Where $H_n^r = \sum_{i=1}^{n} \frac{1}{i^r}$ is the nth order and r rank harmony number, M is the total number of nodes in all communities. In the actual community opportunistic network simulation, the value of L is set to 1/4 to 1/3 of the value calculated by the above formula to obtain an average delay of up to @ times of the optimal time. And in the second phase, the algorithm sets token of message as one for nodes meet more frequently in same community.

In the above two stages, the searching for the destination community is the key to the successful transmission of the message. In the first stage, the EMRAUO algorithm chooses destination community active node j which has bigger $DCTP_{jT}$, as relay nodes as much as possible. The distribution of the number of message tokens is in proportion to the value of $DCTP$, and the nodes with larger $DCTP$ values have more tokens. If the encounter node j belongs to the destination community T, then node j receives the message and will broadcast a confirmation message to notify nodes, which not belonging to the destination community, to clear the copy of the message in time.

In the second stage, the EMRAUO algorithm chooses destination node active node j which has bigger $DNTP_{jd}$, as relay nodes as much as possible. And when message reaches its destination node d, it will also broadcast a confirmation message to notify all other nodes to clear the copies of the message in time.

Efficient Message Routing Using Overhearing. When a node sends a message over the wireless network, the other nodes within its transmission range can overhear the sent message.

When a node meets another node, they'll exchange their message summary vector and confirmation message list by broadcast in the EMRAUO algorithm, the other nodes within the range of node transmission can overhear and receive these management control messages. The messages in confirmation message list are compared with the messages they have buffered, messages which have already reach their destination node are cleared directly, and messages that have entered their destination community are also cleared if the node buffering the message doesn't belong to the destination community. Then it may reduce cache usage and unnecessary message delivery costs significantly.

The EMRAUO algorithm designs the packet header format of the data packet for message routing. Taking into account the message overhearing, there is a sequential list of outgoing messages in the packet header, so all nodes overhearing the list can make selective reception of the outgoing messages. The format of the packet header is shown in Table 1:

In Table 1, HdrLen and PayloadLen are the length of the packet header and the length of effective load, MsgListLen is the length of the sequence message list to be sent, MessageNum is the number of messages to be sent, MessageList is the list of messages description to be sent in the order, CheckSum is the check information of the header.

Table 1. Packet header format in EMRAUO algorithm

Ethernet Header		
Version	HdrLen	PayloadLen
MsgListLen	MessageNum	
MessageList		
CheckSum		
PayLoad		

The every item in the MessageList includes the information about the message ID, the destination node ID and corresponding transmission probability. After the node k overhears the MessageList, it determines which messages will be received: if node k is the destination node of a message, the message is received directly, if node k belongs to the destination community of the message and the message has not yet entered the destination community, node k will also receive the message directly and start the second transmission stage of the message as normal situation. Otherwise, if node k has the same kind of transmission probability as the sending node and its value is bigger, node k will receive the message and the message token is zero. If node k doesn't belong to the destination community, only when it meets nodes of destination community, it will send the overhearing message. Otherwise only when node k meets the destination node, it will send the overhearing message. If the buffer of node k overflows, such overhearing messages are priority discarded.

When two nodes meet, if messages need be sent have already been overheard by the other node, then only the token of these messages exchanged, the actual messages need not be delivered. Thereby it can reduce the delay and energy consumption of message delivery.

3   Experimental Simulation and Analysis

3.1   Experimental Dataset

This paper selects two datasets collected in two real environments to study the performance of the opportunistic network routing algorithms.

The datasets come from the Cambridge University project (Cambridge) [9] and the MIT Reality Mining project (Reality) [10], which are the typical opportunistic networks. The list of the characteristics of the two data sets is shown in Table 2:

Table 2. Correlation characteristics of two experimental datasets

Data set	Cambridge	Reality
Laboratory equipment	Imote	Smart Phone
Node number	54	97
Network style	Bluetooth	Bluetooth
Duration (day)	11	246
Scan granularity (second)	600	300
Contact times	10873	54667

3.2 Experimental Simulation and Analysis

This paper uses the ONE platform that is a well-known opportunistic network environment to verify the performance of EMRAUO algorithm, and compare its performance with that of some typical opportunistic network routing algorithms, just like PROPHET, Spray & Focus algorithm. In this paper, we import the real datasets of Cambridge and Reality project into the ONE platform, and make the actual model validation.

Comparison of Message Delivery Ratios at Different TTL Values. As shown in Figs. 1 and 2, the delivery ratio of the EMRAUO algorithm is higher than that of the SF and PROPHET algorithms in both datasets. And when the TTL value of message is less than 6 h, the delivery ratio of each algorithm is not much difference. With the TTL value increase, the delivery ratio of each algorithm increases gradually, and the delivery ratio of the EMRAUO algorithm increases fastest in both datasets.

It can be seen from Fig. 1 that the delivery ratio of EMRAUO algorithm is averagely 14.9% higher than that of SF algorithm and averagely 35.5% higher than that of the PROPHET algorithm in the Cambridge dataset.

It can be seen from Fig. 2 that the delivery ratio of the EMRAUO algorithm is at least 30.6% higher than that of the SF algorithm and at least 116.4% higher than that of the PROPHET algorithm in the Reality dataset.

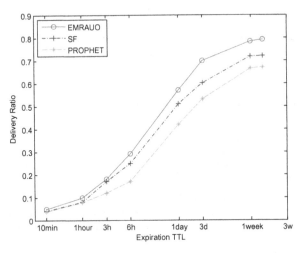

Fig. 1. Comparison of message delivery ratios at different TTL value in the Cambridge dataset

The EMRAUO algorithm takes full account of the community characteristics embodied in node movement, preferentially selects nodes with more contact with the destination community as relay nodes, and based on the characteristics of broadcasting, nodes can overhear and receive information. It may greatly reduce the transmission delay and increase the success probability of message delivery. Secondly, when a message enters its destination community or reaches its destination node, the

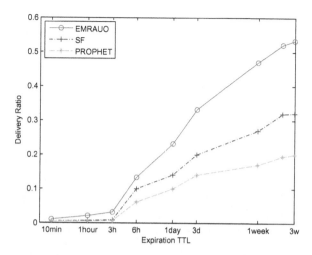

Fig. 2. Comparison of message delivery ratios at different TTL value in the Reality dataset

EMRAUO algorithm will both generate a confirmation message to clear the redundant copies of the message, which reduces the unnecessary message transmission and greatly improves the cache utilization of nodes, then may reduce the average delay of message transmission.

The SF algorithm divides the message routing into two stages of Spray and Focus, and produces multiple copies of the message in the Spray phase and uses the dichotomy method for fast message distribution so that its delivery ratio is higher than that of the PROPHET algorithm in the two data sets.

Comparison of Message Delivery Costs at Different TTL Values. As shown in Figs. 3 and 4, the delivery cost of each algorithm increases with the increase of the TTL value, in which the delivery cost of EMRAUO algorithm increases the most gently in both datasets.

It can be seen from Fig. 3 that when the TTL value of message is not Less than 3 h in the Cambridge dataset, the delivery cost of the EMRAUO algorithm is averagely 41.9% lower than that of the SF algorithm, and averagely 60.4% lower than that of the PROPHET algorithm.

It can be seen from Fig. 4 that when the TTL value of message is not less than 1 h in the Reality dataset, the delivery cost of the EMRAUO algorithm is averagely 65.3% lower than that of the SF algorithm, and averagely 75.6% lower than that of the PROPHET algorithm.

The EMRAUO algorithm and SF algorithm will both produce multiple copies of the message by means of tokens when a source node generates a message, so messages distribute faster in the initial phase, and the number of message delivery is relatively more. In the two real datasets, when the TTL value is less than 10 min, the EMRAUO and SF algorithm have higher message delivery costs than that of the PROPHET algorithm. With the increase of the TTL value, the PROPHET algorithm has a rapid increase in the number of copies of the message in the network. Since the PROPHET

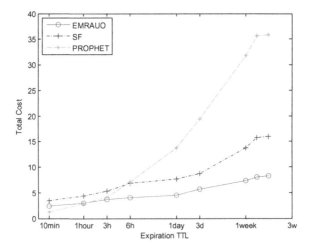

Fig. 3. Comparison of message delivery costs at different TTL value in the Cambridge dataset

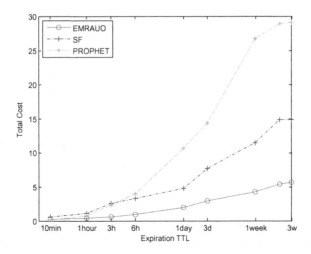

Fig. 4. Comparison of message delivery costs at different TTL value in the Reality dataset

algorithm does not provide effective means to control the number of messages, its message delivery cost gradually exceeds that of the EMRAUO algorithm and the SF algorithm.

The SF algorithm generates multiple copies of the message at the beginning of the message generation, so that the message can enter the destination community more quickly. In the destination community of the message, the nodes belong to the same community meet more frequently and the message can be delivered to the destination node as soon as possible. The SF algorithm limits the number of message copies, so the delivery cost of the SF algorithm is much lower than that of the PROPHET algorithm.

The EMRAUO algorithm uses the message overhearing to improve the message delivery ratio and reduce the message delivery delay, which will produce a small amount of redundant message copies. But when a message enters its destination community or reaches its destination node, it will produce a corresponding confirmation message to clear the redundant copies quickly by means of broadcasting and overhearing, and greatly avoids unnecessary message delivery. So with the increase of the TTL value of message, its message delivery cost increases most stably.

4 Conclusion

Nodes belong to same community meet often, and once message enters its destination community, it'll very likely reach its destination node. Based on the characteristics of node mobility in the community opportunistic network, the EMRAUO algorithm divides the message routing into two phases: entering the destination community of message and reaching the destination node of the message. According to the characteristic of wireless broadcasting, the EMRAUO algorithm uses messages overhearing among nodes to speed up the progress of the message entering its destination community and reaching its destination node. At the same time, by means of confirmation information overhearing, it can clear the redundant copies of the message as soon as possible. Thereby it can enhance the efficiency of message transmission in the community opportunistic network. In the community detection, the paper uses traditional node contact time to reflect the tightness between the nodes, and we'll consider more appropriate measure to carry out the community detection in the next step.

References

1. Yao, L., Man, Y., Huang, Z., Deng, J., Wang, X.: Secure routing based on social similarity in opportunistic networks. IEEE Trans. Wirel. Commun. 15(1), 594–605 (2016)
2. Zhu, X., Li, Y., Jin, D., Lu, J.: Contact-aware optimal resource allocation for mobile data offloading in opportunistic vehicular networks. IEEE Trans. Veh. Technol. 66(8), 7384–7399 (2017)
3. Alim, M.A., Li, X., Nguyen, N.P., Thai, M.T., Helal, A.: Structural vulnerability assessment of community-based routing in opportunistic networks. IEEE Trans. Mob. Comput. 15(12), 3156–3170 (2016)
4. Rahman, M.A., Lee, Y., Koo, I.: EECOR: an energy-efficient cooperative opportunistic routing protocol for underwater acoustic sensor networks. IEEE Access 5, 14119–14132 (2017)
5. Lindgren, A., Doria, A., Schelén, O.: Probabilistic routing in intermittently connected networks. ACM 7(3), 19–20 (2004)
6. Hui, P., Crowcroft, J., Yoneki, E.: BUBBLE rap: social-based forwarding in delay-tolerant networks. IEEE Trans. Mob. Comput. 10(11), 1576–1589 (2011)
7. Spyropoulos, T., Psounis, K., Raghavendra, C.S.: Spray and focus: efficient mobility-assisted routing for heterogeneous and correlated mobility. In: 5th Annual IEEE International Conference on Pervasive Computing and Communications Workshops, White Plains, NY, USA, pp. 79–85. IEEE (2007)

8. Newman, M.E.J.: Analysis of weighted networks. Phys. Rev. E: Stat. Nonlinear Soft Matter Phys. **70**(5 Pt 2), 1–9 (2004)
9. Haggle. http://www.haggleproject.org. Accessed 11 Oct 2016
10. Eagle, N., Pentland, A.: Reality mining: sensing complex social systems. Pers. Ubiquit. Comput. **10**(4), 255–268 (2006)

A Reversible Watermarking for 2D Vector Map Based on Triple Differences Expansion and Reversible Contrast Mapping

Fei Peng[1(✉)], Zhen-Jie Yan[1], and Min Long[2]

[1] College of Computer Science and Electronic Engineering, Hunan University, Changsha 410082, China
eepengf@gmail.com
[2] College of Computer and Communication Engineering, Changsha University of Science and Technology, Changsha 410014, China

Abstract. Aiming at the insufficient of the existed reversible watermarking for 2D vector map in capacity, imperceptibility and the requirement of high correlation in vector data, a reversible watermarking based on triple differences expansion and reversible contrast mapping is proposed in this paper. By establishing a new coordinates system, relative coordinates are constructed as cover data. The differences of every two adjacent relative coordinates are classified into 4 categories according to their values, and the watermark is embedded into the relative coordinates by using triple differences expansion and reversible contrast mapping. Experimental results and analysis indicate that the proposed watermarking significantly improves the capacity, imperceptibility, and it is robust against translation, rotation and scaling.

Keywords: Reversible watermarking · Digital watermarking
Triple differences expansion · 2D vector map · Reversible contrast mapping

1 Introduction

With the rapid development of geographic information system (GIS), it is widely used in resource planning, military and public security, post and telecommunications, and other fields. As a basic part of GIS, two-dimensional vector map is valuable and difficult to produce. Thus, the protection of 2D vector map is of great importance.

As an important protection means of digital data, digital watermarking has been attracted wide attention by researchers in recent years. Reversible watermarking is an important research branch of digital watermarking, and it can recover the original host after the watermark is extracted. It is well suited for 2D vector map, because high data precision is generally required in most of application situations. The first reversible watermarking for 2D vector map is proposed by Voigt [1]. After that, reversible watermarking for 2D vector map based on discrete wavelet transform (DWT) [2], lossless compression [3], differences expansion [4–11], virtual coordinates [12–15], quantization index modulation [12, 16–18], and other methods [19–21] are consequently put forward. Among them, difference expansion can achieve relatively high

© Springer International Publishing AG 2017
G. Wang et al. (Eds.): SpaCCS 2017 Workshops, LNCS 10658, pp. 147–158, 2017.
https://doi.org/10.1007/978-3-319-72395-2_15

capacity. However, it usually requires high correlation between the vertices. When the correlation is low, it may results in low embedding capability and large distortion.

To countermeasure the defects of the difference expansion, a novel reversible watermarking for 2D vector map is proposed in this paper. By expanding the differences between the adjacent coordinates with three times, the watermark in ternary is embedded, which can significantly improve the watermark capacity. Furthermore, for the vector map with low correlation, since it only modifies part of the coordinates, the invisibility and embedding capability are still maintained.

The rest of the paper is organized as follows: the related works are introduced in Sect. 2. Triple differences expansion and data preprocessing is presented in Sect. 3. The proposed reversible watermarking is described in Sect. 4. The experimental results and performance analyses are provided in Sect. 5. Finally, some conclusions are drawn in Sect. 6.

2 Related Works

Difference expansion is a typical technique used in image reversible watermarking. Recently, it has been widely used by reversible watermarking for vector graphics.

Wang *et al.* first applied difference expansion to reversible watermarking for 2D vector map [4]. The mean value of the adjacent coordinate is maintained, and the watermark embedding is carried out by expanding the difference and modifying the least significant bit of it. However, it needs to compress a location map, which introduces the high computational complexity and reduces watermark capacity. After that, Wang and Men proposed a fragile reversible watermarking for authenticating 2D vector map with localization [9]. According to unique handle value of each entity, a 2D vector map is partitioned into groups, and the authentication watermark is generated for each group by using its spatial and attribute information. The watermark is embedded using difference expansion. It can detect and locate attacks such as vertex addition/ deletion, entity addition/deletion, and vertex/entity modification. A reversible watermarking based on difference expansion and shifting is proposed for SVG graphics in [6, 7]. By shifting the coordinate pairs with large difference, space is put aside for watermark embedding. It needs not to compress the location map. Comparing with the aforementioned difference expansion based algorithms, the capacity is improved and the computational complexity is reduced. But it still requires the data has high correlation. An invariant sum value based reversible watermarking scheme is proposed by Geng *et al.* [11]. During watermark embedding, an integer transform is made for a pair of coordinate values to embed 1-bit watermark and makes the sum of the coordinate values unchanged. It is essentially a kind of deformation of difference expansion. As it does not need to compress and embed the location map, the computational complexity is low and the capacity is high. In [19], a reversible watermarking scheme base on reversible contrast mapping is proposed. The adjacent coordinates are transformed by reversible contrast mapping, and then the watermark is embedded by modifying the least significant bit of transformed data. The transformed coordinates can be lossless restored by using reverse reversible contrast transform. A nonlinear scrambling-based reversible watermarking for 2D vector maps is proposed in [20]. The relative position of feature points is first nonlinearly scrambled, and then both scrambled feature points and non-feature points are taken as cover data, the coordinates are modified to embed both watermark data and feature point identification data. Finally, combined with the scrambling secret key, the original vector data can be exactly recovered with watermark extraction. However, the imperceptibility is limited.

In a summary, to avoid large distortion, the aforementioned methods [4–7, 9, 11, 19, 20] all embed watermark into adjacent coordinates whose difference is mall. Thus the watermark embedding capability is heavily relied on the correlation of vector data, which limit their use in real application. To countermeasure this situation, a reversible watermarking scheme based on triple difference expansion and reversible contrast mapping is proposed in this paper.

3   Triple Difference Expansion and Data Preprocessing

3.1   Triple Difference Expansion Based on RCM

The basic idea of triple difference expansion is as follows: given two adjacent integer elements x_1 and x_2, which have high correlation, their difference is

$$d = x_1 - x_2 \tag{1}$$

This difference can expanded to its triple times by using RCM transform, which is define as

$$\begin{cases} x_1' = 2x_1 - x_2 \\ x_2' = 2x_2 - x_1 \end{cases} \tag{2}$$

According to Eqs. (1) (2), the difference between the transformed data x_1' and x_2' is triple of d, which is shown as

$$x_1' - x_2' = 3d \tag{3}$$

If both x_1' and x_2' are not changed, the original x_1 and x_2 can be lossless recovered by Eq. (4).

$$\begin{cases} x_1 = \dfrac{2 \times x_1' + x_2'}{3} \\ x_2 = \dfrac{x_1' + 2 \times x_2'}{3} \end{cases} \tag{4}$$

3.2   Data Preprocessing for 2D Vector Map

During watermark embedding, if watermark is embedded by directly modifying the original coordinates, it cannot resist against rotation and scaling. Furthermore, 2D vector map is composed of different entities, and the basic element of an entity is coordinate. Since the coordinates are generally in decimal. To make full use of the characteristics of 2D vector data and triple difference expansion, data preprocessing is performed to the original 2D vector data.

Calculation of relative coordinates. As 2D vector map is often undergone translation, rotation and scaling in practical application, relative coordinates are constructed as cover data to improve the robustness against these geometrical attacks. The calculation of relative coordinates is as follows.

Step 1. Traverse all vertices in a 2D vector map G and obtain all vertices. They are formed a set $V = \{v_1, v_2, \ldots, v_i, \ldots, v_n\}$ according to the reading order. With a secret key k, select two reference vertices $V_{f_1}(x_{f_1}, y_{f_1})$ and $V_{f_2}(x_{f_2}, y_{f_2})$, where the two endpoints of a line segment that is either parallel to the x-axis or y-axis are priority selection.

Step 2. V_{f_1} is used as the origin of the new coordinate system, and the straight line passing through V_{f_1} and V_{f_2} is regarded as the new x-axis. The unit vectors e_x and e_y in the new x-axis and y-axis can be respectively calculated via Eqs. (5) and (6).

$$e_x = (\frac{x_{f2} - x_{f1}}{d_L}, \frac{y_{f2} - y_{f1}}{d_L}) \tag{5}$$

$$e_y = (\frac{y_{f1} - y_{f2}}{d_L}, \frac{x_{f2} - x_{f1}}{d_L}) \tag{6}$$

where d_L is the Euler distance between V_{f_1} and V_{f_2}.

Step 3. For any vertex $v_i(x_i, y_i)$ in V (except V_{f_1} and V_{f_2}), its coordinate in the new coordinate system can be obtained as

$$[x_i^*, y_i^*] = [x_i - x_{f1}, y_i - y_{f1}]\left[e_x^T, e_y^T\right] \tag{7}$$

The reverse transform is

$$[x_i, y_i] = [x_i^*, y_i^*]\left[e_x^T, e_y^T\right]^{-1} + [x_{f1}, y_{f1}] \tag{8}$$

Integer transform for cover data. Since triple difference expansion needs the data to be integer, a preprocessing is done to the coordinates. Taking the x coordinates as example, given an embedding position P (the number of digits after the decimal point), the integer transform is described as follows:

Step 1. Traverse all vertices in G and obtain all x coordinates to form a set $X = \{x_1, x_2, \ldots, x_i, \ldots, x_N\}$ according to the reading order, where N represents the total number of vertices in G.

Step 2. Partition each adjacent coordinates into a group. Thus, $\lfloor N/2 \rfloor$ groups of adjacent coordinates (x_{i1}, x_{i2}) can be obtained from all coordinates, where $\lfloor \cdot \rfloor$ represents a floor function.

Step 3. For each group of adjacent coordinates (x_{i1}, x_{i2}), their decimal point are right moved p digits, and the integers are extracted according to Eq. (9).

$$\begin{cases} I(x_{i1}) = \lfloor x_{i1} \times 10^p \rfloor \\ I(x_{i2}) = \lfloor x_{i2} \times 10^p \rfloor \end{cases} (P > 0) \tag{9}$$

Data precision requirement. Given an error tolerance δ, the error between the original x coordinate and the x coordinate after RCM transform should satisfy Eq. (10).

$$\begin{cases} \Delta x_{i1} = (2I(x_{i1}) - I(x_{i2})) - I(x_{i1}) = I(x_{i1}) - I(x_{i2}) \leq \delta_0 \\ \Delta x_{i2} = (2I(x_{i2}) - I(x_{i1})) - I(x_{i2}) = I(x_{i2}) - I(x_{i1}) \leq \delta_0 \end{cases} \tag{10}$$

where $\delta_0 = \delta \times 10^P$.

According to Eq. (10), if the absolute value of difference $d \leq \delta_0$, the corresponding coordinates group is suitable for RCM transform.

For any coordinates group $(I(x_{i1}), I(x_{i2}))$, if $d < \delta_0/3$, the watermark bit can be embedded into this group, and it will be labeled as an element of a set E; if $\delta_0/3 \leq d < \delta_0$, no watermark bit is embedded, but RCM transform is still performed to them. It is labeled as an element in a set R; if $\delta_0 \leq d < 3\delta_0$, no RCM transform is done to them, but a slight modification is needed. It is labeled as an element of a set S; otherwise, they will be labeled as an element of a set O. It is represented in Eq. (11).

$$(I(x_{i1}), I(x_{i2})) \in \begin{cases} E & d < \frac{1}{3}\delta_0 \\ R & \frac{1}{3}\delta_0 \leq d \leq \delta_0 \\ S & \delta_0 < d \leq 3\delta_0 \\ O & d > 3\delta_0 \end{cases} \tag{11}$$

4 The Proposed Reversible Watermarking

It is composed of four parts: watermark generation, watermark embedding, watermark extraction and data recovery.

4.1 Generation of Watermark

Assuming the original watermark $W = \{w_1, w_2, \ldots, w_i, \ldots, w_n\}$ is a binary sequence, where $w_i \in \{0, 1\}$ and the length is n. The watermark is generated in the following.

Step 1. With a secret key t, it is used as the initial value of the Logistic map, and a chaotic sequence is generated. The length of the sequence is same as the length of the original watermark sequence. After binarization, a binary sequence H is obtained.

Step 2. A XOR operation is performed between W and H, then an encrypted watermark sequence W' is obtained, where $W' = \{w'_1, w'_2, \ldots, w'_i, \ldots, w'_n\}$.

Step 3. The encrypted binary sequence W' is converted to a ternary sequence, where $W'' = \{w_1'', w_2'', \ldots, w_i'', \ldots, w_l''\}$, $w_i'' \in \{0, 1, 2\}$. Here, W'' is the final watermark, which will be embedded into the 2D vector map.

4.2 Watermark Embedding

Taking x coordinates as example, the process of watermark embedding is as follows.

Step 1. For the 2D vector map G, two reference vertices V_{f_1} and V_{f_2} are selected by using a secret key k, and the Euler distance between two reference vertices is recorded as d_L. The distance d_L will be announced and used as an input parameter in the watermark extraction phase. After that, a relative vertices set $V^* = \{v_1^*, v_2^*, \ldots, v_M^*\}$ is obtained according to the method in Sect. 3.2, where $M = N - 2$, and N represents the total number of vertices in G.

Step 2. Traverse all vertices in V^*, extract the x of each vertex and obtain an x coordinate set $X^* = \{x_1^*, x_2^*, \ldots, x_M^*\}$.

Step 3. Each two adjacent x coordinates forms a group (x_{i1}^*, x_{i2}^*), and all elements in X^* can be partitioned into $\lfloor M/2 \rfloor$ groups. Then, $(I(x_{i1}^*), I(x_{i2}^*))$ is calculated according to the method in Sect. 3.2.

Step 4. Watermarking embedding. 4 situations are considered according Eq. (11).

(1) If $(I(x_{i1}^*), I(x_{i2}^*)) \in E$, transform $(I(x_{i1}^*), I(x_{i2}^*))$ to $(I'(x_{i1}^*), I'(x_{i2}^*))$ by using Eq. (2). Let max $= MAX(I(x_{i1}^*), I(x_{i2}^*))$ and set max $=$ max $+ w_j''$, where $MAX()$ represents a function that get the largest element from the input.

(2) If $(I(x_{i1}^*), I(x_{i2}^*)) \in R$, transform $(I(x_{i1}^*), I(x_{i2}^*))$ to $(I'(x_{i1}^*), I'(x_{i2}^*))$ by using Eq. (2).

(3) $(I(x_{i1}^*), I(x_{i2}^*)) \in S$, Let max $= MAX(I(x_{i1}^*), I(x_{i2}^*))$ and $d = \|I(x_{i1}^*) - I(x_{i2}^*)\|$. Here, tag information t_k is generated, and it will be used to form a secret t for watermark encryption.

   (a) If $d \bmod 3 = 0$, set max $=$ max $- 1$ and $t_k = 1$.
   (b) If $d \bmod 3 = 1$, no change is made to them.
   (c) If $d \bmod 3 = 2$, set $t_k = 0$.
(4) If $(I(x_{i1}^*), I(x_{i2}^*)) \in O$, no change is made to them.

Step 5. Modify the original coordinates according to the changes in the relative coordinates. In this way, the watermark can be embedded into the 2D vector map. Thus, a watermarked map G' is obtained.

In a same way, the watermark also can be embedded into y coordinates.

4.3 Watermark Extraction and Data Recovery

Watermark extraction. Given the watermarked 2D vector map G', the process of watermark extraction is as follows.

Step 1. With the secret key k, determine two reference vertices. Calculate the Euler distance d_L' and resize G' with a scale factor d_L/d_L'.

Step 2. Construct a new coordinate system. Get a relative vertices set $V^{*\prime} = \{v_1^{*\prime}, v_2^{*\prime}, \ldots, v_M^{*\prime}\}$ according to the method in Sect. 3.2 After that, traverse the x coordinates in set $V^{*\prime}$ and obtain an x coordinate set $X^{*\prime} = \{x_1^{*\prime}, x_2^{*\prime}, \ldots, x_M^{*\prime}\}$.

Step 3. Each two adjacent x coordinates forms a group $(x_{i1}^{*\prime}, x_{i2}^{*\prime})$, and all elements in $X^{*\prime}$ can be partitioned into $\lfloor M/2 \rfloor$ groups. Then, $(I(x_{i1}^{*\prime}), I(x_{i2}^{*\prime}))$ is calculated according to the method in Sect. 3.2

Step 4. Let $d' = \|I(x_{i1}^{*\prime}) - I(x_{i2}^{*\prime})\|$. When $d' < \delta_0$, it indicates that the corresponding coordinates group is in the set E. Extract the watermark bit $w_j'' = d' \bmod 3$.

Step 5. Repeat *Step* 4 until all watermark bits are extracted. After that, convert the extracted ternary sequence into a binary sequence and decrypt it through the secret key t. Thus, the watermark W'' is extracted.

Step 6. Transform W'' into a sequence in binary, and decryption is done to it, and obtain the extracted watermark $W^* = \{w_1^*, w_2^*, \ldots, w_i^*, \ldots, w_n^*\}$.

Data recovery. According to the difference d' and $d' \bmod 3$, the set that the coordinates groups are belonged to can be determined. The cover data can be recovered according to the following procedures.

(1) If $d' < \delta_0$, the coordinates group is in set E. let max $= MAX(I(x_{i1}^{*\prime}), I(x_{i2}^{*\prime}))$ and set max $=$ max $- d' \bmod 3$, then the cover data can be recover through Eq. (4).
(2) If $\delta_0 \leq d' < 3\delta_0$, the corresponding coordinates group is in set S or R, which depends on the value of $d' \bmod 3$.
   (a) If $d' \bmod 3 = 0$, the corresponding coordinates group is in set R, and the cover data can be recovered through Eq. (4).
   (b) If $d' \bmod 3 = 1$, the corresponding coordinates group is in set S, no operation is needed.
   (c) If $d' \bmod 3 = 2$, the corresponding coordinates group is in set S, let max $= MAX(I(x_{i1}^{*\prime}), I(x_{i2}^{*\prime}))$ and set max $=$ max $+ t_k$.
(3) If $d' \geq 3\delta_0$, the corresponding coordinates group is in set O, no operation is needed.

In this way, the original 2D vector map can be lossless recovered.

5   Experimental Results and Analysis

In the experiments, the watermark bits is a random binary sequence. Fifty different 2D vector maps are used for test. Five samples and the corresponding watermarked versions are shown in Fig. 1, and their basic properties are listed in Table 1, where P donates the embedding position.

As seen from Fig. 1, it is impossible to detect any visually difference between the watermarked vector maps and the original vector maps, which indicates the good performance of the proposed scheme.

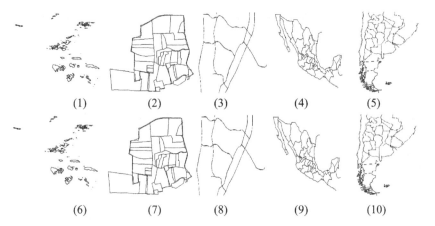

(1)   (2)   (3)   (4)   (5)

(6)   (7)   (8)   (9)   (10)

Fig. 1. Experimental results of some samples. (1)–(5) some samples of the original 2D vector maps, (6)–(10) the corresponded watermarked version of (1)–(5).

Table 1. Basic information of the samples

Map no.	P	Vertices number	Error tolerance (δ)
1	4	24214	9×10^{-4}
2	3	653	3×10^{-3}
3	3	540	3×10^{-3}
4	3	1973	3×10^{-3}
5	3	5060	3×10^{-3}

5.1   Analysis of Reversibility

The reversibility of the algorithm is evaluated by computing the root mean square error (RMSE) between the original 2D vector map and the recovered 2D vector map, and it is defined in Eq. (12).

$$RMSE = \left(\frac{1}{N} \sum_{i=0}^{N-1} (x_i - x_i')^2 \right)^{1/2} \tag{12}$$

where x_i and x_i' represent the corresponding x coordinate in the original 2D vector map and the recovered 2D vector map, respectively. Experiments are carried out with 50 2D vector maps, and it can be found that the RMSE are all 0, which demonstrates that the good reversibility of the proposed algorithm.

5.2   Analysis of Capacity

In the proposed scheme, the watermark sequence is in ternary. By converting binary bits into ternary bits, it can reduce the length and improve the capacity. Here, the capacity of the proposed scheme is compared with three methods in [9, 11, 19]. The results are listed in Table 2.

Table 2. Comparison of the capacity of difference schemes (bits/vertex)

Map no.	Wang [9]	Geng [11]	Peng [19]	Proposed scheme
1	0.8969	0.9908	0.9908	1.3946
2	-	0.2067	0.2067	0.3201
3	-	0.0741	0.0741	0.1111
4	-	0.1926	0.1926	0.2975
5	-	0.1826	0.1826	0.2150
Average of 50 maps	0.0861	0.1840	0.1840	0.2271

"-" represents the watermark cannot be embedded.

As seen from Table 2, the capacity of different 2D vector maps is varied, and it is heavily depended on data correlation of 2D vector graphics. Nevertheless, it can be found that the proposed scheme can achieve the largest capacity, which indicates the good capacity of the proposed reversible watermarking scheme.

5.3 Analysis of Imperceptibility

Here, RMSE is also used to evaluate the imperceptibility of the watermarked 2D vector map. In the experiments, watermark is embedded into the third digit after the decimal point for most of the 2D vector map. Since only part of data is modified in the 2D vector map, the RMSE is maintained between 10^{-4} and 10^{-3}, and the results are listed in Table 3.

Table 3. RSME of different schemes (10^{-4})

Map no.	Wang [9]	Geng [11]	Peng [19]	Proposed scheme
1	1.07	1.22	1.64	1.90
2	-	26.90	5.99	4.22
3	-	28.91	4.71	2.63
4	-	27.13	5.83	4.14
5	-	27.38	6.86	5.55

"-" represents the watermark cannot be embedded.

As seen from Table 3, the RMSE of the proposed scheme maintains the same level as the other three schemes when the correlation of coordinates is high. Nevertheless, the RMSE of the proposed scheme is obviously smaller comparing with the other three schemes when the correlation of coordinates is low. The results demonstrate the good imperceptibility of the proposed scheme.

5.4 Analysis of Robustness

Since the proposed watermarking is carried out by modifying the relative coordinates, it is unchanged after translation and rotation. Therefore, it has good robustness against translation and rotation. Meanwhile, during the construction of the new coordinate system, Euler distance of two reference vertices is recorded. If the watermarked 2D vector map is scaled, it can be restored according to the original distance between the reference vertices. Therefore, it is also robust against scaling. Here, the robustness is evaluated by NC, which is defined as

$$NC = \left(\sum_{i=1}^{n} w_i \odot w_i^* \right) / n \qquad (13)$$

where $\odot$ represents not exclusive or operation.

The experimental results are listed in Table 4.

Table 4. NC values after translation with different distance

Operation		Map no.					
		1	2	3	4	5	Average of 50 maps
Translation	(0.008, −0.009)	1.0	1.0	1.0	1.0	1.0	1.0
	(−0.06, 0.07)	1.0	1.0	1.0	1.0	1.0	1.0
	(0.35, −0.46)	1.0	1.0	1.0	1.0	1.0	1.0
	(−6.5, 7.8)	1.0	1.0	1.0	1.0	1.0	1.0
Rotation	30°	1.0	1.0	1.0	1.0	1.0	1.0
	60°	1.0	1.0	1.0	1.0	1.0	1.0
	120°	1.0	1.0	1.0	1.0	1.0	1.0
	150°	1.0	1.0	1.0	1.0	1.0	1.0
Scaling	0.8	1.0	1.0	1.0	1.0	1.0	1.0
	1.5	1.0	1.0	1.0	1.0	1.0	1.0
	2	1.0	1.0	1.0	1.0	1.0	1.0
	3	1.0	1.0	1.0	1.0	1.0	1.0

As seen from Table 4, the NCs of between the extracted watermark and the original watermark are all 1.0, which indicates that the proposed reversible watermarking is robust against translation, rotation and scaling.

6 Conclusions

In this paper, a reversible watermarking scheme based on triple difference expansion is proposed based on RCM. Different from the existed method, watermark in ternary is embedded, which improve the capacity. Meanwhile, relative coordinates are constructed as cover data, which is helpful for the improvement of the capability of resisting geometric attacks. Experimental results and analysis indicates that the proposed scheme has good reversibility, capacity, and imperceptibility compared with some existed methods, and it is robust against translation, rotation, and scaling. However, the proposed scheme still has some limitations in the robustness against some plausible attacks such as object addition/deletion, noise distortion and vertex recording. Our future work will be focused on the enhancement of the robustness against that plausible attacks.

Acknowledgments. This work was supported in part by project supported by National Natural Science Foundation of China (Grant Nos. 61572182, 61370225), project supported by Hunan Provincial Natural Science Foundation of China (Grant No. 15JJ2007).

References

1. Voigt, M., Yang, B., Busch, C.: Reversible watermarking of 2D-vector data. In: ACM International Workshop on Multimedia and Security, pp. 160–165. ACM, Magdeburg, Germany (2004)
2. Peng, F., Lei, Y.Z., Sun, X.: Reversible watermarking algorithm in wavelet domain for 2D CAD engineering graphics. J. Image Graph. **16**(7), 1134–1139 (2011)
3. Shao, C., Wang, X., Xu, X.: Security issues of vector maps and a reversible authentication scheme. In: Doctoral Forum of China, pp. 326–331, Nanjing, China (2005)
4. Wang, X.T., Shao, C.Y., Xu, X.G., et al.: Reversible data-hiding scheme for 2-D vector maps based on difference expansion. IEEE Trans. Inf. Forensics Secur. **2**(3), 311–320 (2007)
5. Shao, C.Y., Wang, X.T., Xu, X.G., et al.: Study on lossless data hiding algorithm for digital vector maps. J. Image Graph. **12**(2), 206–211 (2007)
6. Wu, D., Wang, G., Gao, X.: Reversible watermarking of SVG graphics. In: WRI International Conference on Communications and Mobile Computing, pp. 385–390. IEEE, Kunming, China (2009)
7. Ding, L., Qiu, Z.D., Zhang, C.: Reversible watermarking algorithm of SVG vector graph's high capacity. J. Netw. Comput. Secur. **5**, 24–26 (2010)
8. Li, L., Li, Q., Fang, X., et al.: Reversible watermarking algorithm based on difference expansion for 2D engineering drawings. J. Image Graph. **15**(2), 372–376 (2010)
9. Wang, N., Men, C.: Reversible fragile watermarking for 2-D vector map authentication with localization. Comput.-Aided Des. **44**(4), 320–330 (2012)
10. Peng, F., Lei, Y., Long, M., et al.: A reversible watermarking scheme for two-dimensional CAD engineering graphics based on improved difference expansion. Comput.-Aided Des. **43**(8), 1018–1024 (2011)
11. Geng, M., Yu, P., Han, H., et al.: Reversible watermarking based on invariant sum value for 2D vector maps. In: Network Infrastructure and Digital Content (IC-NIDC), pp. 521–525. IEEE International Conference on Network Infrastructure and Digital Content, Beijing, China (2012)
12. Wang, P.C., Wang, C.M.: Reversible data hiding for point-sampled geometry. J. Inf. Sci. Eng. **23**(6), 1889–1900 (2008)
13. Wang, N., Zhang, H., Men, C.: A high capacity reversible data hiding method for 2D vector maps based on virtual coordinates. Comput.-Aided Des. **47**, 108–117 (2014)
14. Wang, N., Zhao, X., Xie, C.: RST invariant reversible watermarking for 2D vector map. Int. J. Multimed. Ubiquit. Eng. **11**(2), 265–276 (2016)
15. Peng, F., Long, Q., Lin, Z.X., et al.: A reversible watermarking for authenticating 2D CAD engineering graphics based on iterative embedding and virtual coordinates. Multimed. Tools Appl. **76**, 1–21 (2017)

16. Peng, F., Lei, Y.Z.: An effective reversible watermarking for 2D CAD engineering graphics based on improved QIM. Int. J. Digital Crime Forensics **3**(1), 53–69 (2011)
17. Xiao, D., Hu, S., Zheng, H.: A high capacity combined reversible watermarking scheme for 2-D CAD engineering graphics. Multimed. Tools Appl. **74**(6), 2109–2126 (2015)
18. Wang, N.: Reversible watermarking for 2D vector maps based on normalized vertices. Multimed. Tools Appl. **76**, 1–19 (2016)
19. Peng, F., Chen, L., Long, M.: A reversible watermark scheme for 2D vector map based on reversible contrast mapping. Secur. Commun. Netw. **6**(9), 1117–1125 (2013)
20. Cao, L., Men, C., Ji, R.: Nonlinear scrambling-based reversible watermarking for 2D-vector maps. Vis. Comput. **29**(3), 231–237 (2013)
21. Cao, L., Men, C., Gao, Y.: A recursive embedding algorithm towards lossless 2D vector map watermarking. Digit. Signal Process. **23**(3), 912–918 (2013)

Image Encryption Based on Multi-scrolls Chaotic System and Logistic Map

Yaoqiang Xiao[(✉)], Zhiyi Wang, Jun Cao, and Jin Yuan

School of Information Science and Engineering,
Hunan University, Changsha 410082, China
yqxiao6@126.com

Abstract. The chaotic image encryption has been a hot research topic for years due to its remarkable functions. However, traditional chaotic systems exist some latent problems such as insecure key source, low key space, vulnerable to known-plaintext attacks and chosen-plaintext attacks. A novel encryption algorithm based on multi-scrolls chaotic system and Logistic map is proposed in the paper. The proposed algorithm uses multi-scrolls chaotic system and Logistic map to generate key sequences, and the cipher image is obtained by performing bit shuffling to the plain image according to key sequences, then double direction diffusion operations are applied to enhance the encryption performance. Multi-scrolls chaotic system has more complex dynamic characteristics and larger key space than single-scroll and traditional chaotic systems, which can obtain better encryption performance in image encryption. The experimental results show that our method has better encryption performance and higher security, which can be applied in other secure communication domain.

Keywords: Image encryption · Cryptography
Multi-scrolls Chaotic Attractor · Logistic map · Bit shuffling

1 Introduction

With the rapid development of multimedia and internet technology, the security and confidentiality of information are becoming more and more important. Digital images are widely used in communication because of their intuitive and large capacity, so the security of digital images is particularly significant. Many encryption algorithms have been proposed to protect the privacy of digital images transmitted over a public network. As the huge amount of data, redundancy, highly relevant adjacent pixels of image, traditional encryption algorithms, such as DES or AES, are insufficient to satisfy high security levels.

With the emergence of chaos [1], chaotic system has characteristics such as unpredictable, non-periodic, nonlinear, sensitivity to initial condition and parameters, which make chaos widely use in various fields and also in image encryption. The earliest chaotic cryptography scheme was proposed by Matthews [2]. In terms of chaos system, image encryption based on chaotic system can be generally classified into three categories: single chaotic system, multi-chaotic system, and hyper chaotic system.

© Springer International Publishing AG 2017
G. Wang et al. (Eds.): SpaCCS 2017 Workshops, LNCS 10658, pp. 159–167, 2017.
https://doi.org/10.1007/978-3-319-72395-2_16

For single chaotic system, Logistic map was used to encrypt images [3]. A hybrid domain selective image encryption technique was presented [4], which used Orthogonal Polynomial Transformation and spatial domain bit shuffling based Tent map. The hybrid domain combined frequency domain and spatial domain, and provided a good performance as well as less encryption and decryption time. But general chaos system has relatively small key space and non uniform distribution sequences which may bring the risk to encryption. Liu [5] proposed an encryption algorithm based on Logistic chaotic map with varying parameter. Parameter-varied Logistic map can cure the weakness of Logistic map and resist the phase space reconstruction attack.

Many researches show that encryption combined with multi-chaotic system is more security than only using single chaos system [6, 7]. Combination of Logistic map and Lozi map to generate key sequence was presented, and results achieved better image security and resistance to attacks than single Logistic or Lozi map [8]. Combination of Arnold cat map and Logistic map was proposed [6], original image firstly shuffled by Logistic map and then shuffled by iteratively using Arnold cat map operations to improve the security.

Hyper chaotic system has several characteristics such as at least two positive Lyapunov exponents, more randomness. Ye proposed encryption based time-delay and hyper chaotic system [9], integrated time-delay into hyper chaotic system, and presented a permutation function for shuffling the position index together with double direction diffusion operations. A scheme based on Cat map and hyper chaotic Lorenz system was proposed [10]. A hyper chaos system based on Hénon and Logistic maps was presented [11].

However, low dimensional systems, whether single or multi chaotic systems, are insecure key sources and small key space. To solve these problems, in this paper, key sequence for image encryption and decryption is generated based on $7 \times 5 \times 3$ multi-scrolls and Logistic map. The generation of multi-scrolls chaotic system is based on double-scrolls system. Common double-scrolls system is Jerk system [12] or Chua system [13]. Compared to traditional chaotic system, multi-scrolls chaotic system can generate multi direction hyper chaotic attractors, particularly, its dynamic trajectory can be extended to higher dimensional space and complex phase trajectory corresponds to more key parameters. We encrypt image with different hyper chaotic sequences to enhance encryption performance. In conclusion, our contribution in this paper can be summarized as follows: (1) we propose for the first time an image encryption algorithm based on multi chaotic system, including multi-scrolls chaotic system and Logistic map, to enhance the security of key source; (2) we propose an algorithm combined with permutation and diffusion to improve the robustness of the encrypted image.

The rest of this paper is organized as follows. In Sect. 2, multi-scrolls chaotic system is described. The proposed algorithm is discussed in Sect. 3. Experimental results are shown in Sect. 4. We conclude the work in Sect. 5.

2 Multi-scrolls Chaotic System

The high-order Chua's circuit with multi-directional and multi-scroll chaotic attractors was discussed [14, 15]. We use four-order grid multi-scrolls based on Chua system. This system is described as Eq. (1). Here, x_0, y_0, z_0, w_0 are four initial values. As stated [15], the function $f_m(x)$ is defined as Eq. (2), $f_m(y)$ and $f_m(w)$ are similar. Five control parameters are chosen as $a = 15$, $b = 2.5$, $c = 16$, $d = 2.5$, $e = 4$. A_m controls the width and height of $f_m(x)$ respectively, thus the relative positions between the equilibrium points and size of scrolls are controlled. M_m is for odd scroll and N_m is for even scroll in Eq. (2), hence it should be $(2M_1 + 1) \times (2M_2 + 1) \times (2M_3 + 1)$ for odd grid multi-scrolls. In order to generate multi-scroll chaotic attractors conveniently, typical parameters are selected. Therefore $A_1 = 0.5$, $M_1 = 3$ in $f_1(x)$, $A_2 = 0.25$, $M_2 = 2$ in $f_2(y)$, $A_3 = 0.25$, $M_3 = 1$ in $f_3(w)$ are chosen to generate $7 \times 5 \times 3$ grid multi-scrolls. Figure 1(a),(b) shows the phase diagram of grid multi-scroll chaotic attractors in x-y and x-w plane respectively.

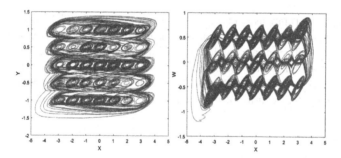

Fig. 1. $7 \times 5 \times 3$ grid multi-scrolls system in x-y plane (left) and x-w plane (right)

Detecting the presence of chaos in a dynamical system is an important problem that is solved by measuring the largest Lyapunov exponent. Lyapunov exponents quantify the exponential divergence of initially close state-space trajectories and estimate the amount of chaos in a system. We use the definition method to compute Lyapunov exponents of Eq. (1) and then obtain four Lyapunov exponents: $LE_1 = 8.1906$, $LE_2 = 1.4977$, $LE_3 = 0.2599$, $LE_4 = -12.3637$. According to the results, we can see that not only the sum of four exponents is negative, but also three of them are positive, which can demonstrate the high degree of chaos in the system.

$$\begin{cases} \dfrac{dx}{dt} = a(y - f_2(y)) - b(x - f_1(x) - (w - f_3(w))) \\ \dfrac{dy}{dt} = x - y + z \\ \dfrac{dz}{dt} = -c(y - f_2(y)) \\ \dfrac{dw}{dt} = d(x - f_1(x)) - e(w - f_3(w)) \end{cases} \tag{1}$$

$$f_m(x) = A_m \times \begin{cases} -sgn(x) + \sum_{i=1}^{N_m} sgn(x+2\,iA_m) + \sum_{i=1}^{N_m} sgn(x-2\,iA_m), N \geq 0 \\ \sum_{i=1}^{M_m} sgn(x+(2i-1)A_m) + \sum_{i=1}^{M_m} sgn(x-(2i-1)A_m), M \geq 1 \end{cases} \quad (2)$$

Here, $sgn(x)$ is defined as:

$$sgn(x) = \begin{cases} 1, x > 0 \\ 0, x = 0 \\ -1, x < 0 \end{cases} \quad (3)$$

3 Proposed Image Encryption Scheme

The proposed algorithm uses multi-scroll chaotic sequence and logistic map as key sequences. Then permutation operations to image are performed by key sequences, and double direction diffusions are employed to diffuse permuted image to obtain the cipher image. The proposed hybrid chaotic system not only enhances the security of key source but enlarges key space. Hence the two level encryption of permutation and diffusion improve the security of the algorithm.

3.1 Pretreatment

From Sect. 2, four chaotic sequences x, y, z, w are obtained. We make pretreatment to x, y, z, w to get new sequences $\dot{x}_i, \dot{y}_i, \dot{z}_i, \dot{w}_i$ by Eq. (4):

$$\dot{s}_i = mod\left(round\left(\left|s_i \times 10^{14} - round\left(s_i \times 10^{14}\right)\right| \times 255\right), 256\right) \quad (4)$$

where the function $round\,(s)$ rounds to the nearest integer, and $|s|$ obtains the absolute value of s while $mod(x, y)$ returns the remainder after division.

Then, we apply classical Logistic map to generate random number sequence h:

$$h_{i+1} = \mu h_i(1 - h_i), i = 1, 2, 3, \ldots, \mu \in (3.5699456, 4] \quad (5)$$

3.2 Encryption Algorithm

The process of image permutation algorithm is discussed step by step as follows:

1. Resize 2-D 8-bit gray scale image pixels of size $m \times n$ to 1-D image pixels $\{c_i\} = \{c_1, c_2, \ldots c_{m \times n}\}$.
2. Key sequence is obtained by following equation:

$$k_i = bitxor(\dot{x}_i + \dot{y}_i, h_i) \tag{6}$$

where $\dot{x}_i, \dot{y}_i$ are the sequences generated by Eq. (1) and pretreatment by Eq. (4), h_i is generated by Logistic system Eq. (5), and $bitxor(x, y)$ returns the result after bitwise XOR operation.

3. Permutated image pixels $\{p_i\} = \{p_1, p_2, \ldots p_{m \times n}\}$ are obtained by Eq. (7):

$$p_i = \mod(bitxor(c_i, k_i), 256) \tag{7}$$

4. Improved forward diffusion is performed as Eq. (8):

$$d_i = d_{i-2} + d_{i-1} + p_i + \lambda_1 \dot{z}_{i-1} + \theta_1 \dot{z}_i, i = 1, 2, 3, \ldots, m \times n \tag{8}$$

here, we let d_0 be a constant which is the first pixel of p_i and d_{-1} be the last pixel of p_i. $\dot{z}_i$ is the chaotic sequence generated by Eq. (1). λ_1, θ_1 are two additional control parameters.

5. Reverse diffusion is performed as Eq. (9) to enhance the encryption performance:

$$e_i = e_{i+1} + d_i + \lambda_2 \dot{w}_{i-1} + \theta_2 w_i, i = m \times n - 1, m \times n - 1, \ldots, 2, 1 \tag{9}$$

here, λ_2, θ_2 are control parameters, $\dot{w}_i$ is the chaotic sequence after inversion. Then, we resize e_i to 2-D, the encrypted image will be obtained.

3.3 Decryption

The decryption algorithm process is the inversion of encryption process. Back-diffusion process performs by Eqs. (10) and (11). After obtaining permuted image pixels p_i, reverse the permutation steps, the plain image pixels will be got.

$$d_i = e_i - e_{i+1} - \lambda_2 \dot{w}_{i-1} - \theta_2 w_i, i = m \times n - 1, m \times n - 1, \ldots, 2, 1 \tag{10}$$

$$p_i = d_i - d_{i-1} - d_{i-2} - \lambda_1 \dot{z}_{i-1} - \theta_1 \dot{z}_i, i = 1, 2, 3, \ldots, m \times n \tag{11}$$

4 Experimental Results and Analysis

The experiments are implemented by MATLAB R2016a on a computer equipped with AMD A6-3400 M, 1.40 GHz CPU, 6 GB RAM, windows 7 system. Initial conditions x_0, y_0, z_0, w_0 in Eq. (1) are randomly selected, and $\mu = 3.82, h_1 = 0.343$ in Eq. (5) and $\lambda_1 = 1, \theta_1 = 5, \lambda_2 = 2, \theta_2 = 4$ in Eqs. (8) and (9). Three 256×256 gray scale images of Lena, Cameraman, and Peppers respectively are chosen as test images. Then we use visual effect, histogram, information entropy, correlation, differential and key space for experimental analysis. We also compare our results to single Logistic map, single multi-scrolls, and other reference's methods. Figure 2 shows the visual effect of proposed scheme encrypting and decrypting image.

Fig. 2. (a) Lena image (b) Encrypted image (c) Decrypted image with correct key (d) Decrypted image with wrong key

4.1 Histogram Analysis

First of all, histograms of the plain image and encrypted image are analyzed. Histogram represents the number of times each gray level appears of image. Figure 3 shows histogram of plain image and cipher image. From the figure, we can see that the distribution of cipher image by our algorithm is relatively flat, so the proposed algorithm can effectively resist the statistical attacks.

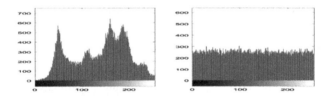

Fig. 3. Histogram of plain image (left) and cipher image (right)

4.2 Information Entropy Analysis

We analyze information entropy of encrypted image with our proposed algorithm in the second experiment. Information entropy is used to measure uncertainty, unpredictability of information. It is defined as Eq. (12):

$$H(x) = -\sum_{1}^{M} p(x_i) \log_2 p(x_i) \qquad (12)$$

here, for an image with 256 gray levels, $M = 256$, and $p(x_i)$ is the probability of symbol x_i. So, the ideal information entropy is 8.

Table 1 shows the entropy of different image by using our proposed method, single Logistic map, single multi-scrolls and other algorithms. The results demonstrate that our method is very close to the ideal value, which means that the encrypted image is high uncertainty and close to random source.

Table 1. Entropy values with different algorithm

Image	Lena	Cameraman	Peppers
Plain image	7.6934	7.4952	7.5327
Single logistic	7.9973	7.9971	7.9971
Single multi-scrolls	7.9979	7.9973	7.9973
Proposed algorithm	7.9991	7.9989	7.9986
Ref. [8]	7.9976	7.9973	7.9973
Ref. [16]	7.9970	7.9969	7.9972

4.3 Correlation Analysis

In the third experiment, we analyze the correlation of plain image and encrypted image. Correlation analysis is to measure the similarities between adjacent pixels. In original image, correlations of adjacent pixels usually very high, while encrypted image will be very low for an effective encryption scheme. The correlation coefficients are calculated by Eq. (13). In our experiments, 2048 pairs of adjacent pixels are randomly selected in horizontal, vertical and diagonal directions.

$$\rho_{xy} = \frac{\text{cov}(x, y)}{\sqrt{D(x)}\sqrt{D(y)}} \tag{13}$$

here, x_i, y_i represent the gray scale values of adjacent pixels of the image. $\text{cov}(x, y)$ is covariance of x, y, $D(x)$ is variance and $E(x)$ is expectation of x.

Table 2 shows the results of proposed scheme's correlation of adjacent pixels of plain image and cipher images with different algorithms. The results show that the correlation coefficients are closer to 0, which means that proposed algorithm effectively removes the correlation of adjacent pixels.

Table 2. Correlation coefficients with different algorithm

Direction	Horizontal	Vertical	Diagonal
Lena image	0.9739	0.9540	0.9682
Single logistic	0.0094	0.0081	0.0621
Single multi-scrolls	−0.0032	−0.0135	0.0424
Proposed algorithm	0.0072	0.0041	−0.0303
Ref. [4]	0.038	0.019	0.065
Ref. [8]	0.0321	0.0068	−0.0352
Ref. [9]	−0.0630	0.0509	−0.0986

4.4 Differential Analysis

In the fourth experiment, differential analysis is applied to test the performance of encrypted image to resist differential attacks. Differential analysis usually measured by the number of pixels change rate (NPCR) and the unified average changing intensity (UACI). NPCR and UACI are defined as follows:

$$NPCR = \frac{1}{m \times n} \sum_{ij} D(i,j) \tag{14}$$

$$UACI = \frac{1}{m \times n} \sum_{ij} \frac{|C_1(i,j) - C_2(i,j)|}{255} \tag{15}$$

here, $D(i,j) = 0$ if $C_1(i,j) = C_2(i,j)$, or $D(i,j) = 1$. The ideal value of NPCR and UACI is 0.9960940... and 0.3346350... for a gray image.

We randomly select 100 groups and each group of the original image only change 1 bit. Then we calculate NPCR and UACI of the cipher image respectively. Table 3 shows the result of the comparison with single Logistic, single multi-scrolls system, and reference [4, 16] in the same experimental conditions. According to the table, we know that proposed scheme has better performance than other algorithms and can effectively resist the known-plaintext attacks and chosen-plaintext attacks.

Table 3. NPCR and UACI using different original image

Lena image	NPCR	UACI
Single logistic	7.705e-04	7.429e-06
Single multi-scrolls	0.9959	0.3345
Proposed algorithm	0.9960	0.3347
Ref. [4]	0.9962	0.2738
Ref. [16]	0.9924	0.3649

4.5 Complexity and Key Space Analysis

Finally, we analyze the complexity and key space of proposed algorithm. As shown in Sect. 3, the total encryption calculating operations only have $2 \cdot m \cdot n$ bitwise XOR operations in Eqs. (6) and (7), $4 \cdot m \cdot n$ addition operations and $2 \cdot m \cdot n$ multiplication operations in Eq. (8), which are increasing linearly with image size. A large key space is essential to resist attacks. The key space of proposed scheme contains initial values x_0, y_0, z_0, w_0 in Eq. (1) and h_1 in Eq. (5). The parameters such as $a, b, c, d, e, \mu, \lambda_1, \theta_1, \lambda_2, \theta_2$ are not counted. We compute the initial values in the accuracy of 10^{-14}. Therefore, for five security keys x_0, y_0, z_0, w_0, h_1, the total key space is about $(10^{14})^5 = 10^{70}$, which has been larger enough to resist all kinds of brute-force attacks.

5 Conclusion

A novel encryption algorithm combined multi-scrolls chaotic system with logistic map is proposed. We employ $7 \times 5 \times 3$ grid multi-scrolls system and logistic chaotic system to generate key sequence, and shuffle the image according to the sequences. Then double direction diffusion is used to diffuse the permuted image. Experimental results show the performance of image encryption by proposed algorithm. The results demonstrate that our scheme is with high security which is safe to be used in encryption. For further work, we'll optimize the time efficiency of the method.

Acknowledgments. This work is partially supported by the Natural Science Foundation of Hunan Province (Grant No. 2017JJ2047), the Hunan province science and technology plan projects (Grant No. 2016GK2011), and young teachers program in Hunan University.

References

1. Lorenz, N.: Deterministic nonperiodic flow. J. Atmos. Sci. **20**, 130–141 (1962)
2. Matthews, R.: On the derivation of a chaotic encryption algorithm. Cryptologia **13**, 29–42 (1989)
3. Mandal, M.K., Banik, G.D., Chattopadhyay, D.: An image encryption process based on chaotic logistic map. IEEE Tech. Rev. **29**(5), 395–404 (2014)
4. Krishnamoorthi, R., Murali, P.: Chaos based image encryption with orthogonal polynomials model and bit shuffling. In: IEEE International Conference on Signal Processing and Integrated Networks (2014)
5. Liu, L., Miao, S.: A new image encryption algorithm based on logistic chaotic map with varying parameter. Springer Plus **5**, 289 (2016)
6. Huang, M.Y., Huang, Y.M., Wang, M.S.: Image encryption algorithm based on chaotic maps. In: IEEE Computer Symposium, pp. 154–158 (2010)
7. Zhou, Y., Bao, L., Chen, C.L.P.: Image encryption using a new parametric switching chaotic system. Signal Process. **93**(11), 3039–3052 (2013)
8. Rohith, S., Sujatha, B.K.: Image encryption and decryption using combined key sequence of Logistic map and Lozi map. IEEE Int. Conf. Commun. Signal Process. **1053–1058**, 2–4 (2015)
9. Ye, G., Wong, K.W.: An image encryption scheme based on time-delay and hyperchaotic system. Nonlinear Dyn. **71**(1–2), 259–267 (2012)
10. Zhang, J.: An image encryption scheme based on cat map and hyperchaotic lorenz system. In: IEEE International Conference on Computational Intelligence & Communication Technology, pp. 78–82 (2015)
11. Hassan, A.A.: Proposed hyperchaotic system for image encryption. Int. J. Adv. Comput. Sci. Appl. **7**(1), 37–40 (2016)
12. Liu, M.H., Yu, S.M.: Multi-scroll high-order general Jerk circuits. Acta Phys. Sin. **55**(11), 5707–5713 (2006)
13. Matsumoto, T., Chua, L.O., Komuro, M.: The double scroll. IEEE Trans. Circuits Syst. **32**(8), 797–818 (1985)
14. Yu, S., Tang, W.K.S.: Generation of n × m-scroll attractors in a two-port RCL network with hysteresis circuits. Chaos, Solitons Fractals **39**(2), 821–830 (2009)
15. Wang, C.H., Xu, H., Yu, F.: A novel approach for constructing high-order Chua's circuit with multi-directional multi-scroll chaotic attractors. Int. J. Bifurcat. Chaos Appl. Sci. Eng. **23**(2), 1350022_1–1350022_10 (2013)
16. Ye, R.: A novel chaos-based image encryption scheme with an efficient permutation-diffusion mechanism. Opt. Commun. **284**(22), 5290–5298 (2011)

A Novel Bivariate Entropy-Based Network Anomaly Detection System

Christian Callegari[1(✉)] and Michele Pagano[2]

[1] RaSS National Laboratory, CNIT, 56100 Pisa, Italy
christian.callegari@cnit.it
[2] Department of Information Engineering, University of Pisa, 56100 Pisa, Italy
michele.pagano@iet.unipi.it

Abstract. Detecting anomalous traffic with low false alarm rates is of primary interest in IP networks management. The complexity of the most recent network attacks, as well as the literature, seems to point out that observing a single traffic descriptor can be not enough to detect the wide range of network attacks, which are present in the Internet nowadays.

For such a reason, in this paper, we investigate a novel anomaly detection system that detects traffic anomalies by estimating the joint entropy of different traffic descriptors. The presented system is evaluated over the MawiLab traffic traces, a well-known data-set representing real traffic captured over a backbone network.

Keywords: Network security · Anomaly detection
Bivariate entropy · Information theory · Traffic analysis

1 Introduction

Network attacks are one of the main concerns in the evolution of the Internet since new attacks are frequently created by experienced hackers and a huge number of publicly–available tools can be used even without any specific technical knowledge. Anomaly-based intrusion detection permits to identify new attacks starting from the model of the normal behaviour of network traffic.

Among the many different systems proposed in the literature to detect anomalies, very promising performance are offered by those methods based on the estimation of the entropy associated to the network traffic. Nonetheless, the ever increasing number and the wide variety of new attacks that continuously appear in the Internet (together with some recent works in the literature, which will be discussed in Sect. 2) seem to point out that "standard" anomaly detection methods, which rely on the analysis of a single traffic descriptor , are not effective enough. For this reason, several research efforts have been focused on either combining together the alarms raised by several independent anomaly detection systems, or developing multi-dimensional methods, which analyse (either in a serial or parallel way) several traffic descriptors.

© Springer International Publishing AG 2017
G. Wang et al. (Eds.): SpaCCS 2017 Workshops, LNCS 10658, pp. 168–179, 2017.
https://doi.org/10.1007/978-3-319-72395-2_17

In this paper, we propose a novel anomaly detection systems that detects anomalous behaviours in the network traffic by evaluating the joint entropy associated to two different traffic features. The main contributions of the paper are:

- traffic aggregation is performed by means of sketches, suitably modified so as to allow the storage of bi-dimensionale histograms
- definition of *random* histograms to overcome the limitations of "standard" histograms (as discussed in Sect. 5)
- estimation of joint entropy of two distinct traffic descriptors (note that this is different from considering the two traffic descriptors sequentially or in parallel)

The proposed system has been evaluated over the MawiLab traffic traces, a publicly available traffic data-set widely used for testing anomaly detection systems. Experimental results show that, differently from expected, considering the joint entropy of two traffic features not always lead to performance improvements.

The remainder of this paper is organized as follows: Sect. 2 presents some relevant related works. Section 3 provides brief description of the theoretical background that can help the reader understanding the paper, while Sect. 4 details the architecture of the proposed IDS. Section 5 presents the experimental results. Finally, Sect. 6 concludes the paper with some final remarks.

2   Related Work

In the recent years several anomaly-based IDSs have been proposed in the literature, differing in terms of traffic descriptors and decision algorithms, as testified by the several surveys on the topic [1].

The idea to use some entropy measurements in anomaly detection is not new, but in most cases just the entropy of single random variables was taken into account. For instance, Shannon entropy has been applied in [2] to detect fast Internet worms taking into account the entropy contents (more precisely, the Kolmogorov complexity) of traffic parameters, such as IP addresses, and in [3] to detect anomalies in the network traffic running over TCP. In both works an upper bound of Shannon entropy has been estimated through the use of different state-of-the-art compressors. A different approach has been considered in [4], where Shannon entropy was used to "summarize" the distribution of specific traffic features to detect unusual traffic patterns. In [5] several information theoretic measures have been considered and their specific use is discussed defining a general formal framework for intrusion detection. The use of Tsallis entropy in intrusion detection has been proposed in [6], where it is also shown that the optimal value of the parameter q does not depend significantly on datasets and traffic patterns, while in [7] different values of q are considered, introducing the so-called Traffic Entropy Spectrum that permits to capture additional information on detected anomalies. Comparisons among Shannon, Tsallis and Réney

entropies are performed in [8] to identify the traffic features that are more relevant for detecting anomalies (but taking into account KDDCup99 dataset, which
is hardly representative of nowadays traffic and attacks), as well as in [9], where
the authors showed that it is possible to detect modern botnet-like malware
based on the entropy of anomalous patterns.

In general they act on monodimensional time series and, to consider different
traffic features, the same basic algorithm is sequentially repeated.

Nonetheless, the need for a detection mechanism that simultaneously analyse the behaviour of several traffic features has emerged as a key element for
improving the performance of such a kind of systems. In this field, [10] presents
an extensive comparison among several multidimensional approaches, mainly
based on the use of non-parametric CUSUM. In [11,12], the authors present two
bi-dimensional approaches: a parametric one and a non-parametric one, respectively. Nonetheless, these methods still rely on a sequential approach, taking into
consideration the second considered traffic descriptor iff a condition on the first
descriptor is satisfied.

As far as sketches are concerned, they can not be considered as a detection
method, nevertheless they can be used as a building block of several AD systems
(e.g., [13]). Indeed, the use of sketches corresponds to a random aggregation
that "efficiently" reduces the dimension of the data (wrt other deterministic
aggregations, such as according to input/output routers [14]); moreover, the use
of reversible sketches [15] permits to trace back the flows responsible for the
anomalies.

To the best of our knowledge, the combination of sketches and a detection
approach based on the estimation of a joint distribution of two traffic features
is a novel contribution of this paper.

3   Theoretical Background

In this section, after a brief description of the reversible sketches, we recall the
classical definition of Entropy and its extension to bi-dimensional distributions.

3.1   Reversible Sketches

A sketch is a probabilistic data structure (a bi-dimensional array) that can be
used to summarise a data stream, by exploiting the properties of the hash functions [16]. Sketches differ in how they update hash buckets and use hashed data
to derive estimates.

In more detail, a sketch is a bi-dimensional $D \times W$ array $T_{D \times W}$, where
each row d $(d = 0, \cdots, D - 1)$ is associated to a given hash function h_d. These
functions give an output in the interval $(0, \cdots, W - 1)$ and these outputs are
associated to the columns of the array. As an example, the element $T[d][w]$ is
associated to the output value w of the hash function h_d.

When a new item arrives, the following update procedure is carried out for
all the different hash functions:

$$T[d][h_d(i_t)] \leftarrow T[d][h_d(i_t)] + c_t \tag{1}$$

where i_t denotes the key (e.g., the IP destination address) and c_t the corresponding weight.

Given the use of the hash functions, such data structures are not reversible, which makes impossible to identify the IP addresses responsible of an anomaly, after the detection. To overcome such a limitation, in our system we have used an improved version of the sketch, that is the reversible sketch [15].

3.2 Shannon Entropy

The most basic concept in information theory is the entropy of a random variable (RV) X (or its distribution), often called Shannon entropy [17]. Roughly speaking, it is a measure of the uncertainty (or variability) associated with the RV.

In more detail, let $P = \{p_0, p_1, \ldots, p_{L-1}\}$ be the probability distribution of the discrete RV X, i.e.

$$0 \leq p_l \leq 1 \quad \text{and} \quad \sum_{l=0}^{L-1} p_l = 1$$

Then its Shannon entropy is defined as follows:

$$H(X) = -\sum_{l=0}^{L-1} p_l \log_2 p_l = \mathbb{E}\big[-\log_2 P(X)\big] \tag{2}$$

where $\mathbb{E}$ denotes the expectation operator, and is measured in bits (or shannon). Note that a change in the base of the logarithm just corresponds to a multiplication by a constant and a change in the unit of measure (nat for the natural logarithm and hartley (or ban) for the base 10 logarithm). In particular, when the natural algorithm is considered, (2) coincides with the well-known Boltzman–Gibbs entropy in statistical mechanics.

It is well-known that $0 \leq H(X) \leq \log_2 L$, where the infimum corresponds to the degenerate distribution (i.e., $p_l = \delta_{k-l}$ for some integer k with $0 \leq k \leq L-1$) and the supremum is attained in case of uniform distribution (i.e., $p_l = 1/L \ \forall l$).

3.3 Joint Entropy

The joint Shannon entropy (in bits) of two RVs X and Y is defined as

$$H(X,Y) = -\sum_x \sum_y \log_2[P(x,y)] \tag{3}$$

where x and y are particular values of X and Y respectively (in our case we will assume that both X and Y assume just L distinct values, but the definition applies to any countable set), and $P(x,y)$ denotes the joint probability of these values occurring together. Note that the joint entropy of a set of RVs is greater than or equal to all of the individual entropies, but less than or equal to their sum:

$$\max[H(X), H(Y)] \leq H(X,Y) \leq H(X) + H(Y)$$

4   System Architecture

The proposed IDS has a modular architecture and the functionalities of each system block are detailed in the following subsections.

4.1   System Input

The first block of the system is responsible for Data Formatting. In more detail, it reads the traffic data and parses them (e.g., by means of Flow-Tools [18] in case of NetFlow data [19]). The output of this module consists of one plain ASCII file for each time-bin, containing all the relevant information for further processing. Output data are organized according to the Turnstile Model [20], the most general way of representing data streaming: given an input stream $I = \sigma_1, \sigma_2, \ldots, \sigma_n$, each item $\sigma_t = (i_t, c_t)$ consists of a *key*, $i_t \in (1, \ldots, N)$, and a *weight* (in general a d-dimensional vector), c_t.

In our implementation we have considered pcap data as input and extracted the traffic going through a given router, collected over fifteen minutes time-bins. Thus, this module will output N distinct files (where N is the number of time-bins), each file containing a list of keys observed in the time-bin (in our case the list of destination IP addresses) and the associated weights (we focused on the number of bytes and flows received by that IP address).

Note that the modularity of the system and the generality of the data streaming model allow great flexibility, so that the system administrator can easily choose which traffic descriptors have to be used to better detect the different attacks.

4.2   Sketch Computation

Each file is passed as input to the module that builds the corresponding reversible sketch table [15].

Hash functions are used twice: the first time is for building random aggregates (as, for instance, in [14]) and then for the calculation of the entropy of the considered distribution. As far as the first step is concerned, we have used D distinct 4-universal hash functions [21] in order to aggregate the flows in D distinct ways. Then, for each bucket of the sketch we consider the histogram of the weights c_t. As discussed in Sect. 5, we considered L bins for each traffic descriptor and selected the bin associated to each key i_t as the hash of the corresponding weight c_t, realising a *random* histogram (the impact of using *random* histograms will be discussed in Sect. 5). Here the choice of the hash function is not critical and the same function $\tilde{h}$ has been used for all buckets. In the monodimensional (1D) case we simply considered a generic hash function $\hat{h}(x)$ with output in the interval $[0, L-1]$ and took

$$\tilde{h}(c_t) = \hat{h}(c_t)$$

while in the bi-dimensional (2D) case, i.e. $c_t = (c_t^1, c_t^2)$ we combine the two components as follows

$$\tilde{h}(c_t) = \hat{h}(c_t^1) * L + \hat{h}(c_t^2)$$

getting in this way L^2 possible output values (the 2D matrix $L \times L$ is mapped into a vector of size L^2).

Hence, instead of having a "standard" bi-dimensional array, in our system we have implemented a novel three-dimensional data structures $T[d][w][l]$, in which the third dimension is used to store histograms. In more detail, for each new data, the update procedure of the sketch is described by

$$T[d][h_d(i_t)][\tilde{h}(c_t)] \leftarrow T[d][h_d(i_t)][\tilde{h}(c_t)] + 1 \tag{4}$$

This results in N distinct sketches that are $\in \mathbb{N}_{D \times W \times L}$ (1D) or $\in \mathbb{N}_{D \times W \times L^2}$ (2D), where D, W, and L can be varied (in the experimental tests they have been set to $D = 16$, $W = 512$, as justified in [22], and $L = 64$).

It is important to point out that the hash functions h_d addresses two different issues. On one side, they improve the performance of the system due to the effectiveness of random aggregations, with respect to "classical" aggregations (e.g., according to network prefix) – as already discussed. On the other side, their use permit to cope with a drawback of entropy-based IDSs highlighted in [23]. Indeed, entropy does not always allow to discriminate two (also very different) histograms (as an example, scrambling time-bins does not change the sum due to the commutativity of addition). Hence, an attacker could realise a "mimicry" attack, so that the resulting histogram, although quite different from the reference one, has a very similar entropy value. In our case, given that the hashing scheme used to construct the sketches introduces some randomness (and it is in general unknown), such an attack is unfeasible.

4.3   Anomaly Detection

The anomaly detection block works on two distinct sketches: the reference sketch T^{ref}, i.e. the last observed non anomalous sketch, and the current sketch T^n. For each bucket $T^n[d][w][\cdot]$ of the latter, the entropy of the stored histogram is calculated according to (2) or (3) and compared with the entropy associated to the same bucket $T^{ref}[d][w][\cdot]$ in the reference sketch.

Thus the entropy difference is compared with a threshold ξ (by changing ξ it is possible to fix the desired trade-off between false alarm and detection rates) to decide if there is an anomaly or not in the considered bucket $T^n[d][w][\cdot]$. At each time-bin the output of this phase is a binary matrix $A \in \mathbb{N}^{D \times W}$, whose element $A[d][w]$ contains a "1" if the corresponding sketch bucket $T^n[d][w][\cdot]$ is detected as anomalous and "0" otherwise.

Since any flow will be checked D times to verify if it presents any anomaly (this is done because an anomalous flow could be masked in a given traffic aggregate, while being detectable in another one), a simple voting algorithm is applied to the matrix A. In more detail, the algorithm verifies if at least H rows (H is a tunable parameter, assumed equal to $D/2 + 1$ in our experiments) of A contain at least one bucket set to "1". If so, the system reveals an anomaly, otherwise updates $T^{ref}[d][w][\cdot]$ and analyses the next time-bin.

4.4   Identification

In case an anomaly is detected by the voting procedure in a given time-bin, the system applies the reversible sketch algorithm to the corresponding sketch table in order to identify the IP addresses responsible for the anomalies. Hence, for each time-bin the final output is given by the list of eventual anomalies and responsible flows.

5   Experimental Results

Our system has been extensively tested and evaluated using the traffic traces of the project MAWILab [24]. Taking into account the MAWI labels, we consider as "false positives" the flows that are not labeled as "anomalous" or "suspicious" in the MAWI archive, but that are anomalous according to the tested IDS. Instead, regarding the "false negative" definition, as discussed in [22], it depends on the actual interpretation of the MAWILAB labels, and can be defined in several ways:

- "all": the number of unrevealed flows labeled as "anomalous";
- "fn 2/3/4 detector": the number of unrevealed flows labeled as "anomalous" and detected at least by two/three/four of the four detectors used in MAWI classification;
- "fn attack": the number of unrevealed flows labeled as "anomalous" belonging to the "attack" category (known attacks);
- "fn attack special": the number of unrevealed flows labeled as "anomalous" belonging to the "attack" category or the "special" category (attacks involving well-known ports);
- "fn unknown": the number of unrevealed flows labeled as "anomalous" belonging to the "unknown" category (unknown anomalous activities);
- "fn unknown 4 detector": the number of unrevealed flows labeled as "anomalous" belonging to the "unknown" category and detected by all the four detectors used in MAWI classification.

It is important to highlight that, since we have focused on volume anomalies, we have taken into consideration, as traffic descriptors, the number of flows with the same destination IP address (indicated as Flow in the following) and the quantity of traffic received by each IP address expressed in bytes (indicated as Byte in the following).

5.1   Preliminary Analysis

Before discussing the achieved results in terms of false positives and false negative rates, some experimental tests have been carried out to evaluate the usage of the hashing scheme $\tilde{h}$ to realise the *random* histograms stored in each bucket of the sketch. Indeed, a more straightforward choice would be to realise "standard" histogram, simply dividing the samples of interest in L distinct bins (experimentally $L = 64$ offers the best trade-off between accuracy and memory occupation).

Nonetheless, simply realising the histograms in such a way we would obtain too dense histograms (in Fig. 1 (left part) we show as an example the histogram computed over the Byte feature contained in one of the MawiLab traces). This is due to the nature of the considered traffic features, whose main statistics are shown in Table 1.

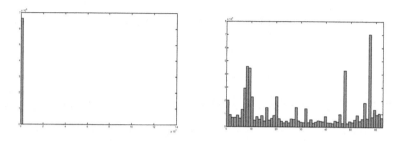

Fig. 1. "Standard" and random histogram (Byte, 64 bins)

Moreover, only statistics related to the training set may be available in advance, so even a non-uniform quantization does not solve the problem.

Instead, using the hashing scheme $\tilde{h}$ we obtain *random* histograms, which are much more sparse and hence more significant for our purpose (in Fig. 1 (right part) we show the *random* histogram computed over the same values used in Fig. 1 and the same number L of bins).

Table 1. Features statistics

Statistics	Byte	Flow
Min	46	1
Max	131524478	3941
50th percentile	122	1
75th percentile	382	2
95th percentile	2178	4
99th percentile	52474	18

5.2 Experimental Results

In this subsection we show the actual performance, in terms of detection probability and false alarm probability.

First of all, in Fig. 2 (left part) we present the performance when using Byte as traffic descriptor and varying the interpretation of the MAWILAB labels. The plots clearly show that the system performance are strongly influenced by the different definition of "false negative", going from unacceptable performance (e.g., "fn attack") to very good performance (e.g., "fn unknown 4 detector"). This variability, that is already known in the literature [22], can be justified by the very little number of flows belonging to some categories (e.g., "fn attack") compared with the total number of anomalies. In any case, the lack of effectiveness in detecting known attacks is not a major concern for the applicability of the anomaly detection systems. Indeed, anomaly-based IDSs are typically used in conjunction with misuse-based systems, which are effective in revealing known attacks, but are unable to find the unknown ones (for which the signatures are not present yet!). The latter are instead well detected by the proposed algorithms.

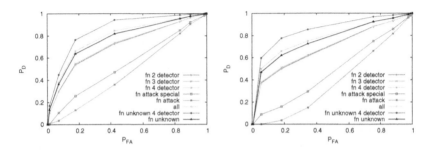

Fig. 2. ROC curves (Byte and Flow)

Figure 2 (right part) presents a similar analysis, when considering Flow as traffic descriptor. The considerations done in the previous case still hold.

Instead in Fig. 3 (left part), we present the performance achieved when taking into consideration the joint entropy (indicated as 2D). Differently from expected, we can see that the performance of the system are slightly worse then those achieved when considering the two metrics one at a time.

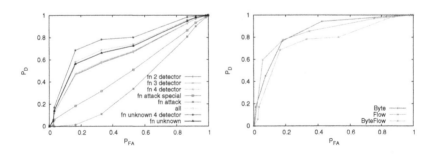

Fig. 3. ROC curves (2D and comparison)

Such an analysis is also confirmed in Fig. 3 (right part), where we present a comparison between Byte, Flow, and 2D in the "fn unknown 4 detector", and in Table 2, which shows the values of the Area-under-the-Curve (AuC) for all of the considered cases. It is worth noticing that in fact the use of the joint entropy does not always lead to worse the performance (e.g., in the "fn attack special" case, where 2D offers better performance than Flow).

Table 2. AuC

–	AuC (Flow)	AuC (Byte)	AuC (2D)
All	0.687534	0.709861	0.645492
fn 2 detector	0.690198	0.712274	0.648258
fn 3 detector	0.695619	0.717855	0.653673
fn 4 detector	0.778584	0.789252	0.713483
fn attack	0.38413	0.464528	0.370243
fn attack special	0.480757	0.537116	0.496618
fn unknown	0.763186	0.773084	0.699914
fn unknown 4 detector	0.84866	0.853584	0.770637

6   Conclusions

In this paper we have presented an anomaly detection system, based on the estimation of the entropy associated to *random* histograms of different traffic features. Differently from expected, the experimental results have shown that taking into consideration the joint entropy of different traffic descriptors does not improve the system performance.

As future work, the authors intend to further investigate such a result, verifying if it is also valid when taking into consideration other, different, traffic features and Entropy definitions (namely, Tsallis and Rényi entropies, which, thanks to their parametric nature, permits to weight in a different way all the histogram bins).

Acknowledgment. This work was partially supported by Multitech SeCurity system for intercOnnected space control groUnd staTions (SCOUT), a research project supported by the FP7 programme of the European Community.

References

1. Callegari, C., et al.: A methodological overview on anomaly detection. In: Biersack, E., Callegari, C., Matijasevic, M. (eds.) Data Traffic Monitoring and Analysis. LNCS, vol. 7754, pp. 148–183. Springer, Heidelberg (2013). https://doi.org/10.1007/978-3-642-36784-7_7
2. Wagner, A., Plattner, B.: Entropy based worm and anomaly detection in fast IP networks. In: 14th IEEE International Workshops on Enabling Technologies: Infrastructure for Collaborative Enterprise (WETICE 2005), pp. 172–177. June 2005

3. Callegari, C., Giordano, S., Pagano, M.: On the use of compression algorithms for network anomaly detection. In: 2009 IEEE International Conference on Communications, pp. 1–5. June 2009

4. Lakhina, A.: Diagnosing network-wide traffic anomalies. In: ACM SIGCOMM, pp. 219–230 (2004)

5. Lee, W., Xiang, D.: Information-theoretic measures for anomaly detection. In: Proceedings of the 2001 IEEE Symposium on Security and Privacy. SP 2001, pp. 130–143. IEEE Computer Society, Washington, DC (2001)

6. Ziviani, A., Gomes, A.T.A., Monsores, M.L., Rodrigues, P.S.S.: Network anomaly detection using nonextensive entropy. IEEE Commun. Lett. **11**(12), 1034–1036 (2007)

7. Tellenbach, B., Burkhart, M., Sornette, D., Maillart, T.: Beyond Shannon: characterizing internet traffic with generalized entropy metrics. In: Moon, S.B., Teixeira, R., Uhlig, S. (eds.) PAM 2009. LNCS, vol. 5448, pp. 239–248. Springer, Heidelberg (2009). https://doi.org/10.1007/978-3-642-00975-4_24

8. Lima, C.F.L., Assis, F.M., de Souza, C.P.: A comparative study of use of Shannon, Rényi and Tsallis entropy for attribute selecting in network intrusion detection. In: 2011 IEEE International Workshop on Measurements and Networking Proceedings (M&N), pp. 77–82. October 2011

9. Bereziński, P., Jasiul, B., Szpyrka, M.: An entropy-based network anomaly detection method. Entropy **17**(4), 2367 (2015)

10. Callegari, C., Casella, A., Giordano, S., Pagano, M., Pepe, T.: Sketch-based multidimensional ids: a new approach for network anomaly detection. In: 2013 IEEE Conference on Communications and Network Security (CNS), pp. 350–358. October 2013

11. Thatte, G., Mitra, U., Heidemann, J.: Parametric methods for anomaly detection in aggregate traffic. IEEE/ACM Trans. Netw. **19**(2), 512–525 (2011)

12. Callegari, C., Giordano, S., Pagano, M.: Bivariate non-parametric anomaly detection. In: 2014 IEEE International Conference on High Performance Computing and Communications, 2014 IEEE 6th International Symposium on Cyberspace Safety and Security, 2014 IEEE 11th International Conference on Embedded Software and System (HPCC, CSS, ICESS), pp. 810–813. August 2014

13. Lakhina, A., Crovella, M., Diot, C.: Mining anomalies using traffic feature. In: ACM SIGCOMM (2005)

14. Callegari, C., Gazzarrini, L., Giordano, S., Pagano, M., Pepe, T.: When randomness improves the anomaly detection performance. In: Proceedings of 3rd International Symposium on Applied Sciences in Biomedical and Communication Technologies (ISABEL) (2010)

15. Schweller, R., Gupta, A., Parsons, E., Chen, Y.: Reversible sketches for efficient and accurate change detection over network data streams. In: Proceedings of the 4th ACM SIGCOMM conference on Internet measurement. IMC 2004, pp. 207–212. ACM, New York (2004)

16. Cormode, G., Muthukrishnan, S.: An improved data stream summary: the count-min sketch and its applications. J. Algorithms **55**(1), 58–75 (2005)

17. Shannon, C.E., Weaver, W.: The Mathematical Theory of Communication. University of Illinois Press, Champaign (1949)

18. Flow-Tools Home Page. http://www.ietf.org/rfc/rfc3954.txt

19. Claise, B.: Cisco Systems Netflow Services Export Version 9. RFC 3954 (Informational). October 2004

20. Muthukrishnan, S.: Data streams: algorithms and applications. In: Proceedings of the Annual ACM-SIAM Symposium on Discrete Algorithms, p. 413. Society for Industrial and Applied Mathematics, Philadelphia (2003)
21. Thorup, M., Zhang, Y.: Tabulation based 4-universal hashing with applications to second moment estimation. In: SODA 2004: Proceedings of the Fifteenth Annual ACM-SIAM Symposium on Discrete Algorithms, pp. 615–624. Society for Industrial and Applied Mathematics, Philadelphia (2004)
22. Callegari, C., Casella, A., Giordano, S., Pagano, M., Pepe, T.: Sketch-based multidimensional IDS: A new approach for network anomaly detection. In: IEEE Conference on Communications and Network Security, CNS 2013, 14–16 October 2013, National Harbor, MD, USA, pp. 350–358 (2013)
23. Zhang, L., Veitch, D.: Learning entropy. In: Domingo-Pascual, J., Manzoni, P., Palazzo, S., Pont, A., Scoglio, C. (eds.) NETWORKING 2011. LNCS, vol. 6640, pp. 15–27. Springer, Heidelberg (2011). https://doi.org/10.1007/978-3-642-20757-0_2
24. MAWILab. http://www.fukuda-lab.org/mawilab/. Accessed Nov 2011

The Full Provenance Stack: Five Layers for Complete and Meaningful Provenance

Ryan K. L. Ko$^{(\boxtimes)}$ and Thye Way Phua

Cyber Security Lab – Department of Computer Science, University of Waikato,
Hamilton 3240, New Zealand
ryan.ko@waikato.ac.nz, twp7@students.waikato.ac.nz

Abstract. This paper distils three decades of provenance research, and we propose a layered framework, the Full Provenance Stack, for describing provenance completely and meaningfully – within and across machines. The provenance layers aim to proliferate layer protocols and approaches for appropriate data provenance levels of detail, and empower cross-platform features – enabling identifying, detecting, responding and recovering capabilities across all cyber security, digital forensics, and data privacy scenarios.

Keywords: Provenance · Data lineage · Logging · Cyber security
Digital forensics · Data privacy

1 Introduction

A plethora of data security, forensics and privacy issues stem from an inherent lack of capabilities to track and attribute data provenance. While there are 2.2 zettabytes of business information worldwide, and digital information dominating 49% of an organization's total value [1], few have studied the deeper implications and reasons of the inability to attribute and understand data provenance, data sources, and attribution. At best, we have logs and event management systems coupled with digital forensics tools but the attribution of information flow and sources across disparate environments remain a great challenge. This stems from the existing system-centric design, rather than a provenance centric design for all computing environments. At the time of writing, we cannot find a system in existing environments such as cloud computing, Internet of Things (IoT), and the Internet with complete and meaningful end-to-end provenance. This creates an opportunity for a layered framework to describe provenance across objectives, environments, and at different levels of abstraction – much like the layers in the OSI or TCP/IP network models.

The NIST Cybersecurity framework [2] provides a framework for cyber-attack response: Identify, Protect, Detect, Respond, Recover. However, it is not always the case where we are in position to execute some or all of these five actions. For instance, in cloud computing environments, the security of the cloud environment is dependent on how it was deployed and its infrastructure. End users typically have no data control or transparency, and several cloud service providers do not provide means of detecting

© Springer International Publishing AG 2017
G. Wang et al. (Eds.): SpaCCS 2017 Workshops, LNCS 10658, pp. 180–193, 2017.
https://doi.org/10.1007/978-3-319-72395-2_18

malicious activities. In our opinion, identifying, detecting, responding and recovering can be achieved through provenance.

Provenance is defined differently in different context or domain. Provenance originated from the arts, where it is defined as the history of ownership of a valued object or work of art or literature [3]. A provenance record in art can be in a form of signatures, receipts, stamps, pictures and more. In computer science, we define provenance as the derivation history of a digital object, such as files, emails or database records.

Although research in data provenance has been ongoing for about three decades with numerous of systems developed, we notice a lack of adoption in the general public at the time of writing. This is not without reason. The lack of adoption could be due to the lack of standardization and domain specific systems. Domain specific systems may fulfil a single person's or a small organization's needs but it is usually impractical in reality, as data that are deemed important by one may be completely irrelevant and meaningless to others and so on. A lack of global standardization defeats the purpose of having a vast amount of systems to choose from, as these systems will not be cross-compatible, either forcing everyone to be attached to a particular system, or to not use any system at all. Provenance details could also be lost through existing application programming interfaces (API) and data translations since there is no awareness of layers or levels of abstraction.

Due to the diversity in computing applications, we acknowledge that there will not be a silver bullet for capturing provenance, but neither is a domain specific system a solution. We represent provenance in an abstract way such that it can be appreciated by all by dividing them into distinct layers. In this paper, we present the different layers where provenance can and must be captured and the importance of each layer in ensuring complete and meaningful provenance data to be captured. We review previous work and existing technologies in capturing data provenance (Sect. 2). We then propose an abstract model for capturing provenance in multiple layers (Sect. 3). Subsequently, we identify the layers that are particularly important in capturing data provenance and how they differ with existing systems (Sect. 4).

2 Related Work

2.1 Provenance Systems

Work on provenance in digital information begun in 1986 [4]. Since then, active research on provenance grew – though most of the systems are domain specific. The initial research in provenance were largely focused on database systems [5, 6], targeting the e-science community. The importance of provenance in systems was then realized and triggered the research in data [7–12], files [13] and workflows [14].

PASSv2 [15] first proposed the concept of layering provenance. Muniswamy-Reddy et al. identified the importance of integrating provenance. In their system however, the layers are not formalized, in fact, the Disclosed Provenance API (DPAPI) was designed to support an arbitrary number of layers of provenance-aware applications, which may not necessarily be the case. As cloud computing gained momentum, [11] proposed with TrustCloud framework's System, Data, and Workflow layers for accountability based on provenance. In [16], Zhang et al. proposed provenance granularities for cloud computing data provenance via the Application, VM, PM, Cloud, and Internet layers.

2.2   File Metadata and Logs

The most obvious provenance-aware information found in systems are metadata and logs. However, information from metadata are often insufficient since they store limited data, and does not record or preserve the entire data history, as observed in Figs. 1 and 2. For example, if a file is updated a thousand times, only its first and last updates are recorded in metadata. Logs, on the other hand, preserve history and can be much more expressive than metadata. However, depending on the verbosity of the logs, this can be a double-edged sword, since increased verbosity in logs increases the so-called noise in log data, requiring pruning, labelling and sanitization of log data before they can be used meaningfully.

Fig. 1. Windows metadata

In our opinion, data provenance is beyond creation, modification and access. It is also critical to link provenance with the state of the system. For instance, an observation that a file was modified by the system is insufficient for understanding what was modified and why the file was modified in the larger scheme of things. Provenance from other aspects of the system is required in order to reason about certain behaviors and events that occurred in a system.

```
$ stat secret
  File: 'secret'
  Size: 7              Blocks: 8         IO Block: 4096   regular file
Device: ca01h/51713d   Inode: 256590     Links: 1
Access: (0664/-rw-rw-r--)  Uid: ( 1000/  ubuntu)   Gid: ( 1000/  ubuntu)
Access: 2017-08-22 13:29:16.624668022 +0000
Modify: 2017-08-22 14:01:27.647236412 +0000
Change: 2017-08-22 14:01:27.647236412 +0000
 Birth: -
```

Fig. 2. Linux inode metadata

3   The Full Provenance Stack

The fact that most system claim to capture 'data provenance' or 'provenance', but capture different scope raises a question: What *really* is data provenance? For example, in PASS [7] and FiPS [13], system calls are intercepted to capture provenance, capturing actions in the lower layers of the operating system, such as tracing Memory-mapped input/output (MMIO); while in Lineage File System (LFS) [9], only the process executable, command line arguments and files read by the process are recorded.

In this section, we seek to clarify what provenance is in computing systems. We present the full provenance stack (Figs. 3 and 4), an abstract model for classifying provenance into layers, similar to the concept of the Open System Interconnection model (OSI model) [17]. This model is aimed to be generic such that it applies to all computing, storage and networking devices, and their interconnections – to capture the provenance from a data-centric viewpoint.

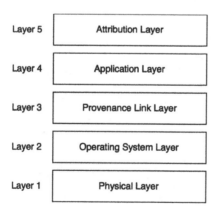

Layer 5	Attribution Layer
Layer 4	Application Layer
Layer 3	Provenance Link Layer
Layer 2	Operating System Layer
Layer 1	Physical Layer

Fig. 3. Full Provenance Stack

3.1   Advantages of a 5-Layered Provenance Stack

Awareness of Scope. With these five layers presented in Figs. 3 and 4, it is now obvious why past data provenance works were unable to fulfil complete provenance. For example, previous workflow provenance and database provenance works would fit

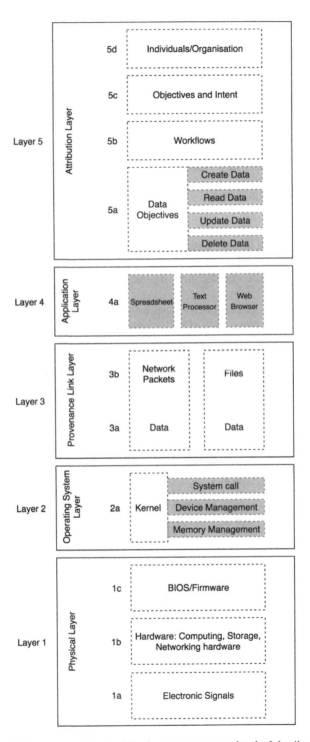

Fig. 4. Full Provenance Stack with relevant provenance level-of-detail examples

in Layer 5, and would need information from the stack's lower layers. System call and operating system-focused provenance work only satisfy Layers 2 and 3.

Levels of Detail. Our proposed provenance stack has also clarified the appropriate levels of detail for provenance information. For example, we can now understand that Layer 3 (Provenance Link Layer) presents a level of detail showing data flow and derivative history across hardware, while lower layers such as Layers 2 and 1 provide the needed information.

Attribution, Encapsulation and Ease of Abstraction. As one moves up from Layer 1 to Layer 5, one can observe an abstraction process similar to the digital forensics process in attributing criminal behavior and actions. In other words, the provenance data and intent becomes easier to understand as we move up from Layer 1 to Layer 5. For example, the electronic signals at the Physical Layer (Layer 1) can be abstracted as system calls at the Operating System Layer (Layer 2), which in turn show the data actions (e.g. open, write) within and across hardware through file actions and network packets at the Provenance Link Layer (Layer 3). Abstracting Layer 3 would then provide understanding of the actions performed at Application Layer (Layer 4) (e.g. an updating of a text document's names and contents). However, understanding the updates of the text document at this level would not provide full provenance, as the intent of the application usage is still unclear. The Layer 4 information leads us further up to the Attribution Layer (Layer 5), which encompasses the intent, and the workflows involved. For example, from Layer 5, we may see a cryptographic ransomware triggering the change of files which reflects the same updates to the just-mentioned Layer 4 text document example and so on.

3.2   Encapsulation and Provenance Layers Defined

Layer 5 encapsulates all layers below, Layer 4 encapsulates Layer 3 and below, and so on. We will now define each layer and their scope. The following layer definitions and scope refer to Figs. 4 and 5.

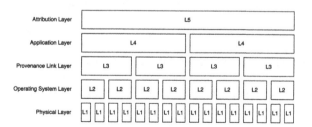

Fig. 5. Encapsulation

Layer 1: Physical Layer. Layer 1 describes the hardware-related electronic signals which occur after a provenance event. The individual signals by themselves are unable to provide deeper provenance understanding (e.g. a criminal intent), but contain portions of the full at atomic level and contributes to Layer 2. Layer 1 provenance is usually contained within the individual hardware. Layer 1 provenance may include:

1a Electronic Signals. Electronic signals are the lowest possible unit that can be captured as a provenance record.

1b Hardware related data. The Hardware Layer is comprised of removable and non-removable physical components of a computer, that may include the Central Processing Unit (CPU), Random-access Memory (RAM), Trusted Platform Module (TPM) and also sensors such as those found on IoT devices. The Hardware Layer tracks provenance of hardware present on the system and uniquely identifies them.

1c BIOS/Firmware related data. The purpose of the BIOS/Firmware Layer is to track provenance relating to the initialization of the hardware on the system to allow verification of integrity of the BIOS/Firmware and system hardware. Provenance relating to initialization of the hardware may include BIOS settings, power-on self-test (POST) results, BIOS/Firmware version and boot sequence.

Layer 2: Operating System Layer. Provenance information at the Operating System Layer consolidates Layer 1 provenance information into logical containers of atomic provenance data, such as individual files, network packets, and the system calls and processes relating to them. Provenance information at Layer 2 is still confined to the individual hardware. Some examples of Layer 2 information include:

2a. Kernel. The kernel is the basis of an operating system, it acts as a mediator/facilitator, the layer records provenance on allocations and management of physical resources (Layer 1) requested from Layer 4 and Layer 3.

Layer 3: Provenance Link Layer. Layer 3 focuses on data flow, and consolidates the logical containers from Layer 2 into provenance flows within and across hardware. This is the layer which starts to 'make more sense' from a human attribution point of view. The provenance flow at Layer 3 does not have to be strictly confined to provenance across traditional computer networks, but can also include other vectors such as the passing of USB sticks, light spectrum transmissions and so on. The focus is on the linking of Layer 2 provenance building blocks into Layer 3 flows. Some examples include

3a. Information flow through machines via sequences of network packets/files. As data is created, read, updated and deleted within machines and transmitted across hardware, we need to capture changes to files and packets including, but not limited to, access control and timestamps; properties of a network packet may include packet size, source and destination of the network packet.

Layer 4: Application Layer. The flows at Layer 3 are encapsulated into Layer 4 and it is at this level we can understand application specific, semantic rich provenance data. This layer provides applications the flexibility to specify and capture meaningful provenance that are specific to their needs.

Layer 5: Attribution Layer. The disparate Layer 4 information encapsulated into Layer 5 will empower attribution and an understanding of the objectives, intents, workflows and data objectives of a provenance event. A classic example is the understanding of cryptographic ransomware events at Layer 5, even though the individual provenance information captured at Layers 1 and 2 (e.g. system calls and changes to files) look relatively benign.

3.3 Properties of the Full Provenance Stack

$$\forall L1, L2, L3 \in S : (L1RL2 \wedge L2RL3) \Rightarrow L1RL3 \qquad (1)$$

Transitive relation. The Full Provenance Stack exhibits the transitive relation, that is when a layer N is related to layer N+1 and layer N+1 is related to layer N+2, then layer N is also related to layer N+2, this is the essence of how encapsulation can be achieved as described in Sect. 3.1.

Abstract. The Full Provenance Stack is an abstract model such that it only suggests the logic and relations of a complete provenance system, but does not dictate or prescribe implementation. This makes this model universal and futureproof, applicable to software and hardware implementations of the past, present and future systems.

Completeness. The Full Provenance Stack ensures that provenance is captured completely and meaningfully. The completeness comes from the layers and it is the relationships between the layers that provides meaningful provenance. A complete and meaningful provenance provides relevant use cases for all users, from a typical end user that tracks their data to law enforcements deducing a criminal intent.

3.4 Applications and Implications

The Full Provenance Stack looks beyond what is visible to a user, providing the depths that are important yet missing in existing provenance tracking systems. In existing systems, data provenance is confined to address the *Who, What, When, Where* questions but with limited capabilities in answering the *How* and *Why* questions. Each layer in the full provenance stack gives data provenance the additional support to make provenance more reliable, concise and conclusive, addressing the *How's* and *Why's* in greater detail.

Consider the case when a user copies a piece of data from file A and paste it in file B, in existing systems, the system only has the knowledge that the content of the file has changed, but have no knowledge of how was it changed, was it manually typed in, copied or did it come from the standard output stream? This information can be provided by other layers of the full provenance stack. For instance, if the data was copied, the operating system layer will be aware that RAM was allocated and the data from file A was stored on the RAM prior to pasting into file B.

The full provenance stack also enables systems to capture beyond data provenance. It expedites digital forensics needs since it allows us to narrow down the scope into specific parts of the system whereby we can leverage on provenance to scrutinize our systems, carry out debugging from any levels and identify sources of malicious activities. Table 1 shows a summary of how each layer can contribute in detecting common system attacks.

3.5   Where Are We Now?

Figure 6 illustrates how existing provenance system fits into the Full Provenance Stack. We observe that there is no current system that fits into a single layer of the stack perfectly as there is no clear distinction of boundaries. PASS [7], Flogger [12], S2Logger [10], Progger [8], Lineage File System [9], TrustCloud [11], FiPS [13] tracks data provenance (Layer 3) using techniques such as intercepting system calls or implementing a loadable kernel module (Layer 2). These systems track data and only data provenance, but the completeness can be questioned as they lack information from the rest of the layers. For example, a PASS system can only provide provenance for *What were the files involved in an event* but will not be able to provide provenance for *What were the contents of the file before and after an event.*

Table 1. Applications summary

Layer	Application
Attribution	Detecting criminal sequences (e.g. fraud)
Application	Detecting software keyloggers
	Detecting malware
Provenance link	Detecting unauthorized access
	Detecting data manipulation
	Detecting ransomware attacks
Operating system	Detecting row hammer attacks
	Detecting privilege escalation
Physical	Detecting BIOS rootkits
	Detecting hardware intrusion
	Detecting hardware keyloggers

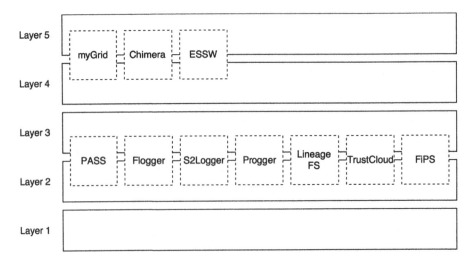

Fig. 6. How does existing systems fit?

Similarly, provenance tracking systems in e-science exhibit similar characteristics. myGrid [18], Chimera [19] and ESSW [20] are domain specific data-oriented or process-oriented provenance system. These systems track workflows and data objectives (Layer 5) and is enabled and provided by the application specific, semantic rich provenance in Layer 4.

4 Ransomware – an Example

In this section, we demonstrate the capabilities of the Full Provenance Stack in a catastrophic event such as a cryptographic ransomware attack. We begin by understanding how and why ransomware remains to be one of the most dangerous attacks [21] and how existing security systems fail in addressing them. We then employ the Full Provenance Stack to demonstrate how we can conceptualize and address these challenges.

4.1   How and Why Is It a Problem?

Cryptographic ransomware is an act of cybercrime where an attacker encrypts the victim's data, and then requires the victim to pay a ransom to retrieve the decryption key to decrypt their data. At the time of writing, ransomware is considered one of the most dangerous attack as it is valuable data at stake. For example, from the perspective of a large multinational company, it may be more feasible to pay the ransom as suffering a service interruption or bad reputation could potentially be costlier. We identify the shortcomings of existing security tools as follows:

Lack of detect and response capabilities. Anti-virus software vendors may claim that their software is capable of blocking and preventing ransomware attacks, but these claims are in our opinion not accurate, especially in a signature based anti-virus. Signature based anti-virus detects ransomware by matching them against signatures in their database, if it encounters a signature that is recognized as a ransomware it will then prevents it from executing. However, we need to realize that in order for a signature to be known as a ransomware attack, it signifies that at least one event of ransomware had occurred. Besides, these signatures are unique to a specific ransomware attack and not a generic one, thus a minor tweaking of a ransomware attack is sufficient to bypass the anti-virus detection.

Behavior based anti-virus comes into play in the rise of ransomware attack, files and directories are consistently monitored to detect malicious activities, in this case, the mass encryption of files. This method however strongly relies on confidence level as it may either trigger false alarms or not detecting a 'smart' ransomware that mimics the behavior of a user. These systems are not capable of providing a first-hand and accurate ransomware detection due to the lack of awareness of layers and working in a restricted scope in the system. For example, a behavior based detection functions only at Layer 3 equivalent of the Full Provenance Stack, and without the support from Layer 2 and Layer 4, an accurate detection of ransomware will never be possible.

Lack of recovery techniques. Ransomware uses encryption, the same technique used to protect our data, therefore it is designed to be unbreakable, or requires an impractical amount of time, effort and resource to break. In some smaller scale ransomware attacks, there are tools that exist to help in recovering files, these tools work on a case-by-case basis and mostly exist due to an implementation flaw in a specific ransomware. These, however, does not address recovering from ransomware as a whole. Recovery fails for a simple reason – a complete lack of provenance. A complete provenance allows for reenactment, providing ample information to recover or reverse an unintended or unauthorized action. We will further discuss this in the following section.

4.2   Detect, Identify, Respond and Recover

Figure 7 demonstrates the provenance in the event of a ransomware attack. The Full Provenance Stack allow us to Identify, Detect, Respond and Recover against ransomware, which is what we fail to do at the time of writing.

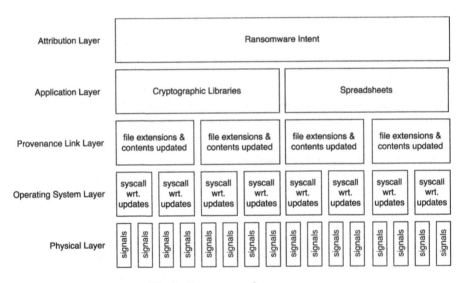

Fig. 7. Provenance of ransomware

Detect. Combating ransomware begins with the detection of malicious activities. A system can detect and be aware of possible malicious activities with the aid of Layer 2 of the Full Provenance Stack. For example, Layer 2 may notice a flood of system-calls that is traversing directories opening, updating and closing files.

Identify. Detecting a malicious activity in Layer 2 does not give away sufficient information to establish the type of attack. In order to identify the type of attack, we observe the effects on Layer 3, in which we will find that file extensions have been changed and the contents of the files are being updated. We can reassure our suspicion with the aid of Layer 4, to identify the malicious application that is triggering the actions in Layer 2 and Layer 3. From here, we can deduce the intent of this malicious activity – Ransomware.

Respond. Upon successful identification of a ransomware attack, we can identify the malicious application by tracing the provenance record upwards from Layer 2, identifying the application that triggered the provenance event, where it can be terminated and removed from the system.

Recover. Ransomware recovery is possible without breaking encryption or identifying an implementation flaw in the ransomware attack. However, we can leverage on the fact that the encryption was carried out on our own system to recover affected files. Provenance data from Layer 2 can provide exactly the information required to decrypt the affected files. Even if the encryption keys are deleted, using the provenance data from Layer 2, we can trace the memory address allocation and contents in the address space to recover the prime numbers used to regenerate the encryption keys.

5   Conclusion

We proposed the Full Provenance Stack, a 5 Layers of complete and meaningful provenance, comprised of the Physical, Operating System, Provenance Link, Application and Attribution layers. The Full Provenance Stack make aware the scope for complete provenance, and through abstraction and encapsulation, a complete and meaningful provenance can be achieved, addressing all system users. The Full Provenance Stack addresses the lack of usable provenance systems available to the general public despite the vast amount of research and provenance systems proposed over the last three decades and provides clear levels of detail. The Stack also addressed a lack of standardization and the current limitations of domain specific systems.

The Full Provenance Stack serves as a foundation for future research directions and development of provenance systems. Developing systems according to standards continue to allow multiple variation of systems to be proposed and exist but with the additional significance to allow systems to work coherently. Finally, we demonstrated a ransomware example on how a system that instruments the Full Provenance Stack can provide complete and meaningful provenance to detect, identify, respond and recover from ransomware attacks. Our work now paves the theoretical way for provenance layer related protocols and technology to be built for each of the five layers.

References

1. Symantec: State of Information Global Results (2012). https://www.symantec.com/content/dam/symantec/docs/security-center/white-papers/state-information-global-results-12-en.pdf
2. National Institute of Standards and Technology: Framework for Improving Critical Infrastructure Cybersecurity (2014)
3. Feigenbaum, G., Reist, I.J.: Provenance: An Alternate History of Art. Getty Research Institute, Los Angeles (2012)

4. Becker, R.A., Chambers, J.M.: Auditing of data analyses. In: Proceedings of the 3rd International Workshop on Statistical and Scientific Database Management, pp. 78–80. Lawrence Berkeley Laboratory (1986)
5. Buneman, P., Chapman, A., Cheney, J.: Provenance management in curated databases. In: Proceedings of the 2006 ACM SIGMOD International Conference on Management of Data, pp. 539–550. ACM, Chicago (2006)
6. Buneman, P., Cheney, J., Vansummeren, S.: On the expressiveness of implicit provenance in query and update languages. ACM Trans. Database Syst. **33**, 1–47 (2008)
7. Muniswamy-Reddy, K.-K., Holland, D.A., Braun, U., Seltzer, M.: Provenance-aware storage systems. In: Proceedings of the Annual Conference on USENIX 2006 Annual Technical Conference, p. 4. USENIX Association, Boston (2006)
8. Ko, R.K.L., Will, M.A.: Progger: an efficient, Tamper-evident Kernel-space logger for cloud data provenance tracking. In: Proceedings of the 2014 IEEE International Conference on Cloud Computing, pp. 881–889. IEEE Computer Society (2014)
9. Sar, C., Cao, P.: Lineage file system, pp. 411–414 (2005). http://crypto.stanford.edu/∼cao/lineage.html
10. Suen, C.H., Ko, R.K.L., Tan, Y.S., Jagadpramana, P., Lee, B.S.: S2Logger: end-to-end data tracking mechanism for cloud data provenance. In: Proceedings of the 2013 12th IEEE International Conference on Trust, Security and Privacy in Computing and Communications, pp. 594–602. IEEE Computer Society (2013)
11. Ko, R.K.L., Jagadpramana, P., Mowbray, M., Pearson, S., Kirchberg, M., Liang, Q., Lee, B.S.: TrustCloud: a framework for accountability and trust in cloud computing. In: Proceedings of the 2011 IEEE World Congress on Services, pp. 584–588. IEEE Computer Society (2011)
12. Ko, R.K.L., Jagadpramana, P., Lee, B.S.: Flogger: a file-centric logger for monitoring file access and transfers within cloud computing environments. In: Proceedings of the 2011 IEEE 10th International Conference on Trust, Security and Privacy in Computing and Communications, pp. 765–771. IEEE Computer Society (2011)
13. Sultana, S., Bertino, E.: A file provenance system. In: Proceedings of the Third ACM Conference on Data and Application Security and Privacy, pp. 153–156. ACM, San Antonio (2013)
14. Gil, Y., Deelman, E., Ellisman, M., Fahringer, T., Fox, G., Gannon, D., Goble, C., Livny, M., Moreau, L., Myers, J.: Examining the challenges of scientific workflows. Computer **40**, 24–32 (2007)
15. Muniswamy-Reddy, K.-K., Braun, U., Holland, D.A., Macko, P., Maclean, D., Margo, D., Seltzer, M., Smogor, R.: Layering in provenance systems. In: Proceedings of the 2009 Conference on USENIX Annual Technical Conference. USENIX Association, San Diego (2009)
16. Zhang, O.Q., Kirchberg, M., Ko, R.K., Lee, B.S.: How to track your data: the case for cloud computing provenance. In: 2011 IEEE Third International Conference on Cloud Computing Technology and Science (CloudCom), pp. 446–453. IEEE (2011)
17. Zimmermann, H.: OSI reference model–the ISO model of architecture for open systems interconnection. In: Partridge, C. (ed.) Innovations in Internetworking, pp. 2–9. Artech House, Inc. (1988)
18. Zhao, J., Wroe, C., Goble, C., Stevens, R., Quan, D., Greenwood, M.: Using semantic web technologies for representing E-science provenance. In: McIlraith, Sheila A., Plexousakis, D., van Harmelen, F. (eds.) ISWC 2004. LNCS, vol. 3298, pp. 92–106. Springer, Heidelberg (2004). https://doi.org/10.1007/978-3-540-30475-3_8

19. Foster, I.T., Vöckler, J., Wilde, M., Zhao, Y.: Chimera: a virtual data system for representing, querying, and automating data derivation. In: Proceedings of the 14th International Conference on Scientific and Statistical Database Management, pp. 37–46. IEEE Computer Society (2002)

20. Bose, R.K.: Composing and Conveying Lineage Metadata for Environmental Science Research Computing, p. 151. University of California, Santa Barbara (2004)

21. Symantec: Internet Security Threat Report (2017). https://www.symantec.com/content/dam/symantec/docs/reports/istr-22-2017-en.pdf

Neural Network Based Web Log Analysis for Web Intrusion Detection

Kai Ma[1,2(✉)], Rong Jiang[1,2], Mianxiong Dong[3], Yan Jia[1,2], and Aiping Li[1,2]

[1] College of Computer, National University of Defense Technology,
Changsha 410073, China
makai281@mail.ustc.edu.cn, jiangrong@nudt.edu.cn, jiayanjy@vip.sina.com,
13017395458@163.com
[2] State Key Laboratory of High Performance Computing,
National University of Defense Technology, Changsha 410073, China
[3] Department of Information and Electronic Engineering,
Muroran Insitute of Technology, Muroran, Japan
mx.dong@csse.muroran-it.ac.jp

Abstract. With the increased attacks of web servers and web applications, it is urgent to develop a system to detect web intrusions. Web log files are stream data recording users' clicks behavior during surfing the Internet. By carefully analyzing these log files, we can reveal some potential anomalies or attacks so as to reduce the loss of property. A method, that applies neural network method to web intrusion detection based on web server access logs, is proposed in this paper. Before feeding the raw log files into neural network algorithms, we need to preprocess these text files and make sure processed logs are of good quality with less noisy and errors. At the result part, our evaluations also demonstrate that the proposed method is superior to decision tree classifier, which shows neural network method can be transplant to web intrusion detection effectively.

Keywords: Web intrusion detection · Neural network
Web log analysis

1 Introduction

Rapid growth in web development provides an ease access to the internet, facilitating peoples life greatly. With the increase of web-based applications, more and more web-related vulnerabilities are exposed and therefore utilized by hackers. As a result, the web are easily get attacked. According to some authoritative reports [1], web-based attacks occupy most of the cyber security incidents. Luckily, web logs provide us a mean to detect these intrusions.

A web log file is usually a plain text file which records information every time a client user clicks a URL from a web site, which provide web administers with critical and meaningful information, usually containing information about IP address, time stamp (date and time), bytes transferred, status code, access request and user agent etc.

© Springer International Publishing AG 2017
G. Wang et al. (Eds.): SpaCCS 2017 Workshops, LNCS 10658, pp. 194–204, 2017.
https://doi.org/10.1007/978-3-319-72395-2_19

It is useful that web administers can recover or at least know the cause of the web server's failure. Besides, web logs can also be used as an auxiliary measure against hackers attacks such as cross site scripting (XSS), SQL injection, denial of service (DOS), session hijacking and so on [2]. By analyzing these log files, we can mine some potential patterns of web attacks.

To detect web-based attacks, many signature (misuse) based intrusion detection systems (IDS), for example snort[1], are equipped with lots of hand-craft signatures that support the detection of known attacks after carefully researching in the patterns of attacks and the vulnerabilities of systems and soft-wares. It performs effectively for the pre-known attacks, however, it suffers from the problem of not being able to detect newly emerging attacks and continuous discovered vulnerabilities, whose signatures are unavailable [1]. To overcome this deficiency, anomaly-based IDS is proposed as a supplementary tool, supporting the detection of attacks that have not been previously seen. Although it may suffer from high false positive rates, being able to detect previously unknown attacks has caused wide popularity.

Web server generates tremendous logs, usually ranging 1KB to 100 MB or even larger, which couldn't be analyzed manually. Web log files are stored in text format which is human-friendly oriented, usually containing unnecessary and noisy data which may affect the quality of intrusion detection process [3,4], so it is necessary to preprocess the raw log files.

There are three primary challenges while developing a neural network based web intrusion detection system. Firstly, the web logs used for training algorithm should collected from real network environment and may contain various common types of web based attacks. Secondly, for different kinds of web log formats, an appropriate field extraction and feature selections are very important. Because a proper feature selections determines upper bound performance of algorithms. Thirdly, there are few publicly available labeled datasets for web intrusion detection.

The remainder of this paper is organized as follows. In Sect. 2, we briefly review relate works about neural network and web intrusion detection. Then, in Sect. 3 we present our proposed model architecture, including web log data collecting, data preprocessing, building neural network based model for intrusion detection, followed by performance analysis in Sect. 4. Finally, we draw our conclusions and future work in Sect. 5.

2   Related Works

Many machine learning methods have been successfully applied in intrusion detection system, such as SVM, decision tree classifier and so on. But they are all built on traffic flow information. To the best of our knowledge, it is the first time to detect web attacks based on web log files exploiting neural network techniques. With its powerful representation learning and non-linear fitting architecture, neural network methods have dramatically pushed the state-of-the-art in

---

[1] https://www.snort.org/.

processing images [5], video [6], text [7] and speech [8]. And here, we choose multilayer perceptron (MLP) as our neural network structure.

According to the different detection mechanism, web intrusion detection systems are generally divided into two categories: (1) signature (misuse) based IDS; (2) anomaly based IDS. The former method extracts features from a number of known attacks and vulnerabilities, and then establish models. Any behaviors matching extracted features are considered as intrusion, while behaviors that do not match the characteristics of the model are treated as normal behavior. At present, the commonly used signature based detection methods are pattern matching [9], expert system [10], and so on. The latter method, anomaly based IDS, build models form a large number of normal access data. Any behavior that conflicts with the normal model is considered as an intrusion; otherwise, it is considered as a normal one. Cao [11] used Adaboost to detect web-based attacks, reducing loss of packets and false negatives. Das et al. [12] proposed clustering method, an unsupervised algorithm, to do anomaly detection without massive sets of pre-labeled training data. Zhang et al. [13] proposed a hybrid framework integrating both misuse based detection module and anomaly based module, which could complement each other to further improve system performance. But this work exploited SVM to perform anomaly based intrusion detection. Also there are some work using neural network to detect intrusions [14]. Although these works performed well, they were all based on traffic flow data.

There are some other works about web intrusion detection by analyzing web logs. Vasilev [15] used quantitative, qualitative and statistical methods to identify hackers attacks but this method only is suitable for relatively small volume of log files because it is totally done manually. Patil [3] mainly focused on preprocessing web logs for web intrusion detection and used Apriori algorithm to find frequent patterns assuming that attribute values have high co-occurrence in a specified type of attack.

3   Proposed Web Intrusion Detection System

The web intrusion detection system mainly consists of four basic components: web log data collecting, data preprocessing, building model and intrusion detection. The system architecture is depicted in Fig. 1.

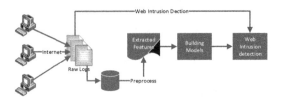

Fig. 1. Model architecture

3.1   Web Log Data Collecting

For most intrusion detection systems, they use the KDD 1999 Cup dataset[2] which is the only publicly available dataset for IDS, to build their systems. But the dataset is about TCP dump data from network traffic. In order to conduct our experiment, we crawled the web access log on a publicly available website[3]. These logs are generated by all people visiting this site, which guarantee that the web logs are collected from real networks. For this experiment, we use from January 2015 to June 2017 access log as our corpus for training and testing.

3.2   Data Preprocessing

Because there are almost no publicly available labeled web logs used for web based intrusion detection, we have to create a dataset by ourselves. Before doing that, let us firstly introduce something about web log formats.

There are various log file formats (NCSA, W3C, IIS) that have different configurations in the number of parameters and fields recorded. All of them have four types of web logs: access log, error log, agent log and referrer log.

No matter what kinds of log format are, the configuration of the common log format will look something like below:

> 68.180.230.181 - - [27/May/2017:03:16:36 -0700] "GET /self.logs/access.log.2016-02-16.gz HTTP/1.1" 200 7124 "-" "Mozilla/5.0 (compatible; Yahoo! Slurp; http://help.yahoo.com/help/us/ysearch/slurp)"

where,

- 68.180.230.181: The users IP address.
- [30/May/2017:02:17:19 -0700]: Timestamp when the request is made.
- GET /self.logs/error.log.2016-02-17.gz HTTP/1.1: The request sent from the client.
- 304: Status code sent by the server.
- 132: The size of the object returned to the client.
- -: Referred site.
- Mozilla/5.0 (compatible; Yahoo! Slurp; http://help.yahoo.com/help/us/ysearch/slurp): The agent information.

Now that we have a good understanding of web log formats, we can use a regular expression to match all of these fields and extract the wanted information from raw server log files.

> $regex = `([[(\d\.)]+) - -\[(.*?)[- | +](\d+)\]$ "$([A - Z]+)? (.+)$HTTP/$\d.\d$" (\d+) (.+) "(.*?)" "(.*?)"'$

---

[2] http://www.kdd.org/kdd-cup/view/kdd-cup-1999.
[3] http://www.secrepo.com/.

According to the need of our system, we choose six features as input: Timestamps, Method, Status code, URL length, Number of parameters in the query and Returned object size.

As [1] did, information about URL plays an important role during intrusion detection, such as number of parameters in the URL query and length of URL. Usually speaking, attacks, for example SQL injection and cross-site scripting, need to insert additional characters to URL, thereby increasing the length and number of parameters, so we make full use of these statistical information on URL. Besides, we also have a statistical analysis of the rest features as depicted in Figs. 2, 3 and 4.

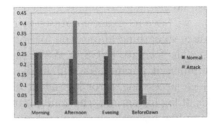

Fig. 2. The statistical information on time attribute

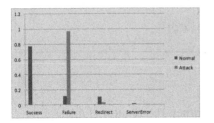

Fig. 3. The statistical information on status code

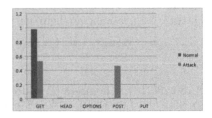

Fig. 4. The statistical information on method

From the above figures, we can conclude that the distributions of different values for the same feature are different between normal and attack behaviors. From the Fig. 2, we can see that hackers are generally more active in the afternoon and evening, while normal users don't show significant differences among these time periods. Figure 3 shows that abnormal activities causes much more failure than normal ones. And hackers tend to use POST method while GET method is frequently used for normal users in Fig. 4. So, we assume that the features we choose are reasonable.

After extracting fields, we can't directly feed them into our model but we have to do some data conversion because of nominal attributes. Nominal attributes are converted into discrete attributes using 1-to-n encoding, using only ones and zeros, also known as dummy code.

Table 1. Dummy code of timestamp

Time period	Description	Dummy code
08:00:00-11:59:59	Morning	1 0 0 0
12:00:00-18:59:59	Afternoon	0 1 0 0
19:00:00-23:59:59	Evening	0 0 1 0
00:00:00-07:59:59	BeforeDawn	0 0 0 1

Table 2. Dummy code of status code

Status code	Description	Dummy code
200 series	Success	1 0 0 0
300 series	Redirect	0 1 0 0
400 series	Failure	0 0 1 0
500 series	Service error	0 0 0 1

For timestamp, the day is divided into four time periods, expressed in 4 bits dummy code as shown in Table 1.

As the same with time attribute, status code is conveyed by dummy coding as shown in Table 2.

For method, there are in general six types including GET, POST, HEAD, PUT, PUSH, OPTIONS, but in this dataset we only find five of them, so method attribute is converted into 5-bit dummy code.

The rest of three attributes are numbers, so we don't have do data conversion. So the total number of attributes become 16 after performing aforementioned data conversion steps.

In this paper, we convert web attacks detection into classification problem which are supervised learning algorithms, meaning that they need to be trained with labeled data before using them to make prediction. Thus, training samples have to be labeled. Labeling should normally be done manually by experienced security experts. Because of lacking of manually labeled data, in this paper, labeling is done automatically using Apache-scalp, a log analyzer for the Apache web server that aims to look for specific patterns in each log and decides whether it is about an attack or not. Apache-scalp has pre-defined about 70 kinds of attack patterns and totally 9 types of web-based attack, such as Cross-site Scripting (xss), SQL Injection (ssli), Denial of Service (dos) and so on, and labeling is done through matching all of these patterns: if matched successfully then labeled as corresponding attack types; otherwise, we label it as a normal access activity.

After scanning the whole log file, we labeled 574465 lines of log and only detect three types of web attack and their statistical information is listed as shown in Table 3.

Table 3. Dummy code of status code

Cross-site scripting	Local file inclusion	Remote file execution	Normal	Total
19808	54	13	554590	574465

In summarization, data preprocessing consists of extracting the wanted features from raw log files and labeling it using corresponding labels. In our experiments, we exploit two labeling mechanism. One has only two labels: 1 to say that this log is considered as an attack and 0 for normal behaviors. The other has more fine-grained categories, here four labels. And we conduct different experiments for these two labeled training data.

3.3   Building Model

In this paper, we apply MLP to detect intrusions or suspicious activities in HTTP server logs. MLP, a class of machine learning algorithms, is composed of multiple cascading layers of linear and nonlinear processing units to learn representations of data and extracts features. Each successive layer takes the previous output as input. An MLP with a single hidden layer can be represented graphically in Fig. 5.

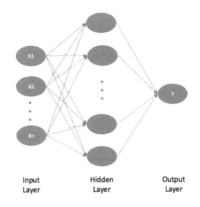

Fig. 5. Multilayer perceptron architecture

MLP is a supervised learning problem where we train the model through labeled training examples $(x^{(i)}, y^{(i)})$. During forward propagation

$$z^{l+1} = W^{(l)} a^{(l)} + b^{(l)}$$

$$a^{(l)} = f(z^{l+1}), for\ l = 0, 1, \ldots, n$$

where a^0 is the input; we write $W_{ij}^{(l)}$, initialized with random number in a range between 0.01 and -0.01, denoting the connection weight between unit j in layer l and unit i in layer $l + 1$. Also, $b_i^{(l)}$, initialize with zeros, is the bias for unit i in layer $l + 1$. $f(z)$ is the activation function, such as Rectified Linear Units (ReLU) [16] or tanh. In this paper, we find that ReLU performs the best in grid search process in the hidden layer.

$$f(z) = relu(z) = max(0, z)$$

We train our neural network using gradient descent. More formally, for a single training example x, y, the corresponding cost function is defined to be:

$$J(W, b; x, y) = \frac{1}{2} \parallel h_{w,b}(x) - y \parallel^2$$

Table 4. Distributions of two classes for training set and test set

	Training	Test	Total
Normal	522	128	650
Attack	571	146	717
Total	1093	274	1367

Table 5. Distributions of four classes for training set and test set

	Training	Test	Total
Normal	31	8	39
Xss attack	30	9	39
Rfe attack	11	2	13
Lfi attack	32	7	39
Total	104	26	130

During backpropagation process, we update the parameters W, b as follows:

$$W_{ij}^{(l)} = W_{ij}^{(l)} - \alpha \frac{\partial}{\partial W_{ij}^{(l)}} J(W, b)$$

$$b_i^{(l)} = b_i^{(l)} - \alpha \frac{\partial}{\partial b_i^{(l)}} J(W, b)$$

where α is the learning rate.

As descripted above, MLP takes as input extracted features and is trained through samples with corresponding labels. After training with large numbers of training samples, we can now predict the given inputs which have never been seen before. It is the very situation we face in the web attack detection and different from the misuse-based system.

4   Performance Evaluation

4.1   Experiment Settings

As discussed above, we preprocess the dataset before applying neural network based method on it. After data preprocessing, we have gotten 574465 lines of logs in total and about 554590 of them are labeled as normal and the remainder are all considered as abnormal. We split datasets into training and test two parts. The following two tables show the statistics of logs for these two parts. Tables 4 and 5 show the datasets with two types of web attacks and four types respectively. Given that there is a severely uneven distribution between the normal and the other three abnormal labels, we re-produce another smaller dataset using subsampling.

We use scikit-learn, a python machine learning package, to conduct all the processes of our experiment. Apart from implementing MLP for intrusion detection, we also implement decision tree classifier, widely used in mail spam detection systems [17], as our baseline. Decision tree is a non-parametric supervised learning method, so we don't have to fine-tune hyper-parameters. Instead, MLP is a parametric supervised learning method and choices of hyper-parameters determines greatly the performance. So in order to find the best set of parameters, we use grid search mechanism, which can exhaustively search over prespecified parameter values for an estimator. After that, we have found the best set of parameters.

In order to increase the ability of nonlinear fitting, good regularization is exploited. We use the L2 regularization [18] and the learned ratio for L2 regularization is 0.001. In order to speed up the training processing, we update the parameters in a mini-batch gradient that we process a small subset of the training set in each iteration. The mini-batch size is chosen to be 10. The parameters W, v are updated through SGD with gradually decreasing learning rate α at each time step t.

$$\alpha = \frac{0.001}{t^{0.5}}$$

4.2   Evaluation Result

In order to make a comparison, we evaluate the performance of two algorithms based on precision, recall and F1 score. Given a confusion matrix, True Positive (TP) is the number of intrusion records correctly classified; False Positive (FP) is the number of normal records which are incorrectly classified; False Negative (FN) is the number of attack records which however are incorrectly classified.

Precision: Precision is the proportion of the total predicted positive observations that are correct.

$$Precision = \frac{TP}{TP + FP} \times 100\%$$

Recall: Recall is the fraction of the all positive observations in actual class that are correctly predicted positive observations.

$$Recall = \frac{TP}{TP + FN} \times 100\%$$

F_1 score: Often, there is an inverse relationship between precision and recall, which means increasing one will reducing the other. F_1 Score is the harmonic mean of Precision and Recall, taking both false positives and false negatives into account.

$$F_1 = 2 \cdot \frac{Precision \cdot Recall}{Precision + Recall} \times 100\%$$

We implement our algorithms for two different labeled datasets: a) normal and anomaly (2-class), b) normal and three various web attack categories (4-class). The experimental results are shown in the Figs. 6 and 7.

From the result, we can see that for more grained labels, MLP is greatly better than decision tree in all metrics by 4%, 4% and 4% respectively, which is proved that neural network can be transplant to web intrusion detection effectively. However, for 2-class dataset, the two models is comparable, probably because of the highly uneven distribution of different types of labels and lacking of training

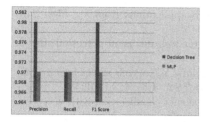

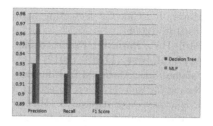

Fig. 6. Precision, recall, F-measure values using decision tree and MLP for 2-class

Fig. 7. Precision, recall, F-measure values using decision tree and MLP for 4-class

data. But further research needs to be done, such as user identification [19], time series mining etc. which guide our future work.

Unlike traditional misuse based detection system, our system are not dependent on experts knowledge and only learn learns potential attack patterns from big data and still performs well especially for previously unknown attacks.

5   Conclusions and Future Work

In order to overcome the disadvantage of misuse-based intrusion detection, a newly kind of intrusion techniques, anomaly-based intrusion detection tool, is proposed. This paper firstly describes the necessity of developing web-based IDS and then introduces the neural network method. But how to combine with these two areas is the purpose of this paper. Because of lacking of training data, we have to firstly to create dataset including data collecting and some preprocessing and then extracting features. From the result of experiment, neural network method exceeds the performance of traditional classifiers like decision tree.

Because web log files recording users' click stream always are time dependent. Especially, it holds true for hackers because their activities are carefully preplanned and hack step by step. For example, if a user that triggers a lot of errors in small period of time is suspicious to brute force attack. But this paper doesn't consider this kind of dependency and order. So one direction of future work is how to take this time order into consideration. Besides, training neural network algorithms need lots of correct and usually manually labeled training samples. Therefore, we have to employee more cyber security experts to label datasets.

Acknowledgments. This work is supported by the National Key Research, Development Program No. 2016YFB0800804 and No. 2016YFB0800303 and JSPS KAKENHI Grant Number JP16K00117, JP15K15976, and KDDI Foundation.

References

1. Kruegel, C., Vigna, G., Robertson, W.: A multi-model approach to the detection of web-based attacks. Comput. Netw. **48**(5), 717–738 (2005)

2. Meyer, R., Cid, C.: Detecting attacks on web applications from log files. Sans Institute (2008)
3. Patil, P.V., Patil, D.: Preprocessing web logs for web intrusion detection. Int. J. Appl. Inf. Syst. (IJAIS) (2012)
4. Salama, S.E., Marie, M.I., Elfangary, L.M., Helmy, Y.K.: Web server logs preprocessing for web intrusion detection. Comput. Inf. Sci. **4**(4), 123 (2011)
5. Krizhevsky, A., Sutskever, I., Hinton, G.E.: Imagenet classification with deep convolutional neural networks. In: International Conference on Neural Information Processing Systems, pp. 1097–1105 (2012)
6. Karpathy, A., Toderici, G., Shetty, S., Leung, T., Sukthankar, R., Li, F.F.: Large-scale video classification with convolutional neural networks. In: IEEE Conference on Computer Vision and Pattern Recognition, pp. 1725–1732 (2014)
7. Sundermeyer, M., Schlter, R., Ney, H.: LSTM neural networks for language modeling. In: INTERSPEECH, pp. 601–608 (2012)
8. Graves, A., Mohamed, A.R., Hinton, G.: Speech recognition with deep recurrent neural networks, vol. 38, no. 2003, pp. 6645–6649 (2013)
9. Kumar, S.: Classification and detection of computer intrusions (1996)
10. Sebring, M.M., Shellhouse, E., Hanna, M.F., Whitehurst, R.A.: Expert systems in intrusion detection: a case study. In: World Conference on Photovoltaic Energy Conversion, pp. 32–38 (1988)
11. Cao, L.C.: Detecting web-based attacks by machine learning. In: International Conference on Machine Learning and Cybernetics, pp. 2737–2742 (2006)
12. Das, D., Sharma, U., Bhattacharyya, D.K.: An intrusion detection mechanism based on feature based data clustering. In: International Conference on Emerging Technologies, pp. 172–175 (2009)
13. Zhang, M., Xu, B.Y., Xu, F.: Research on web intrusion detection module based on hybrid framework. Int. J. Netw. Secur. Appl. (9), 6–9 (2015)
14. Barapatre, P., Tarapore, N.Z., Pukale, S.G., Dhore, M.L.: Training MLP neural network to reduce false alerts in IDS. In: International Conference on Computing, Communication and Networking, pp. 1–7 (2008)
15. Vasilev, J.: Network security by analysis of log files of apache web server, no. 4, pp. 66–88 (2014)
16. Nair, V., Hinton, G.E.: Rectified linear units improve restricted boltzmann machines. In: Proceedings of the 27th International Conference on Machine Learning (ICML 2010), pp. 807–814 (2010)
17. Zhang, Y., Wang, S., Phillips, P., Ji, G.: Binary PSO with mutation operator for feature selection using decision tree applied to spam detection. Knowl.-Based Syst. **64**(1), 22–31 (2014)
18. Ng, A.Y.: Feature selection, L1 vs. L2 regularization, and rotational invariance, p. 78 (2004)
19. Orr, R.J., Abowd, G.D.: The smart floor: a mechanism for natural user identification and tracking. In: CHI 2000 Extended Abstracts on Human Factors in Computing Systems, pp. 275–276. ACM (2000)

The 7th International Symposium on Trust, Security and Privacy for Emerging Applications (TSP 2017)

TSP 2017 Organizing and Program Committees

1 General Chairs

Xiaodong Lin   University of Ontario Institute of Technology, Canada
Khalid Alharbi   Northern Border University, Saudi Arabia

2 Program Chairs

Imad Jawhar   United Arab Emirates University, UAE
Deqing Zou   Huazhong University of Science of Technology, China
Xiaohui Liang   University of Massachusetts at Boston, USA

3 Program Committee Members

Abdessamad Imine   Lorraine University, France
Chao Song   University of Electronic Science and Technology of China,
                      China
Chi Lin   Dalian University of Technology, China
Ed Fernandez   Florida Atlantic University, USA
Filipa Peleja   Yahoo Research Barcelona, Spain
Guangzhong Sun   University of Science and Technology of China, China
Haitao Lang   Dept. Physics & Electronics, China
Huan Zhou   China Three Gorges University, China
Lin Ye   Harbin Institute of Technology, China
Mingwu Zhang   Hubei University of Technology, China
Pouya Ostovari   Temple University, USA
Ricky J. Sethi   Fitchburg State University, USA
Toon De Pessemier   Ghent University, Belgium
Xiaofeng Ding   Huazhong University of Science and Technology, China
Xiaojun Hei   Huazhong University of Science and Technology, China
Xin Li   Nanjing University of Aeronautics and Astronautics, China
Xuanxia Yao   University of Science and Technology Beijing, China
Yanghua Xiao   Fudan University, China
Yaxiong Zhao   Google Inc., USA
Ying Dai   Temple University, USA
Youwen Zhu   Nanjing University of Aeronautics and Astronautics, China
Yunsheng Wang   Kettering University, USA

4 Steering Committee

Wenjun Jiang	Hunan University, China (Chair)
Laurence T. Yang	St. Francis Xavier University, Canada
Guojun Wang	Guangzhou University, China
Minyi Guo	Shanghai Jiao Tong University, China
Jie Li	University of Tsukuba, Japan
Jianhua Ma	Hosei University, Japan
Peter Mueller	IBM Zurich Research Laboratory, Switzerland
Indrakshi Ray	Colorado State University, USA
Kouichi Sakurai	Kyushu University, Japan
Bhavani Thuraisingham	The University of Texas at Dallas, USA
Jie Wu	Temple University, USA
Yang Xiang	Deakin University, Australia
Kun Yang	University of Essex, UK
Wanlei Zhou	Deakin University, Australia

5 Publicity Chairs

Can Wang	Griffith University, Australia
David Zheng	Frostburg State University, USA
Dawei Li	Montclair State University, USA
Wei Chen	Interdigital Communications Inc., USA

6 Web Chair

Tongshuai Cui	Central South University, China

Code Abstractions for Automatic Information Flow Control in a Model-Driven Approach

Kuzman Katkalov$^{(\boxtimes)}$, Kurt Stenzel, and Wolfgang Reif

Department of Software Engineering and Programming Languages,
University of Augsburg, Augsburg, Germany
{kuzman.katkalov,stenzel,reif}@informatik.uni-augsburg.de

Abstract. Automatic information flow control (IFC) can be used to guarantee the absence of information leaks in security-critical applications. However, IFC of real-world, complex, distributed systems is challenging. In this paper, we show how a model-driven approach for development of such applications consisting of mobile apps and web services can help solve those challenges using automatic code abstractions.

Keywords: Information flow · IFC · Model-driven development
Security by design · Privacy by design

1 Introduction

In our time of connected and ubiquitous mobile devices that aggregate and share our personal information, privacy seems hard to come by. Leaks of sensitive data such as personal photos or payment information due to insecure app implementations are abound [2]. Meanwhile, traditional security mechanisms such as the Android permission system are often not sufficient to prevent them [3].

Information flow control (IFC) is the preferable technique to guarantee that a system does not leak sensitive information. Our model-driven approach called *IFlow* leverages IFC to enable the development of information flow (IF)-secure, distributed applications consisting of mobile Android apps and Java web services (see Fig. 1) [7]. Using the new modeling language MODELFLOW based on UML, the developer can specify the structure, behavior, and IF properties of their application (1) [8]. From this abstract model, a code skeleton is generated automatically (2). It implements the IFlow formal application model based on abstract state machines (4) [15, 16] as a Java program, and serves as the basis for the final, distributed application (3). In addition, the code skeleton is used for automatic IFC with JOANA [5], a leading framework for flow-sensitive, context-sensitive, object-sensitive, and lock-sensitive information flow analysis of Java bytecode using program dependence graphs (PDGs).

However, static IFC of distributed, heterogeneous (w.r.t. the deployment platform), and complex applications is challenging. JOANA supports monolithic Java applications with limited size and complexity [6], whereas IFlow applications are distributed, and can consist of several mobile apps and services running on the Android and Java web service platforms.

© Springer International Publishing AG 2017
G. Wang et al. (Eds.): SpaCCS 2017 Workshops, LNCS 10658, pp. 209–218, 2017.
https://doi.org/10.1007/978-3-319-72395-2_20

Section 2 presents a solution to this challenge that leverages the unique advantages of a model-driven approach. It proposes a systems architecture that enables the IF analysis of complex, distributed applications, allowing for information flow-preserving extensions via manually implemented or automatically generated code. Section 3 outlines related work and concludes.

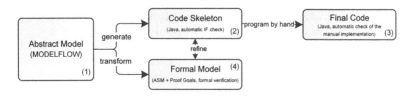

Fig. 1. The IFlow approach

2   Generating Java Code for Automatic IFC

Consider one of our case studies, a mobile travel planning application where the travel agency may not learn the user's credit card data. Using IFlow, it is modeled as a set of *application components* representing mobile apps and web services as MODELFLOW classes (see Fig. 2(a))[1]. In the automatically generated code skeleton, the components are implemented as individual Java classes, and interact with *application modules* as well as an additional Java library provided by IFlow (see Fig. 2(c)) which wraps Android and Java web service APIs to provide platform specific functionality. Application component behavior is modeled explicitly by the developer using sequence diagrams (see Fig. 2(b)), and is translated directly into simple, sequential Java code. MODELFLOW constructs such as variable declarations, assignments, or method calls are mapped to equivalent Java language statements that honor MODELFLOW's copy semantics, while message handling routines are implemented as Java methods.

Application components may interact with *application modules* such as:

- *manually implemented methods*, e.g., for accessing platform specific information sources or sinks such as the SD card of a mobile device,
- *manually implemented* and *predefined graphical user interfaces*, or
- *predefined operations* such as encryption routines.

Most application modules are underspecified and translated into abstract *code stubs* as part of the code skeleton. A stub implements an information flow over-approximating abstraction of the functional module implementation. This enables automatic IFC of the code skeleton as a simple, sequential, and monolithic Java console application. To this end, both the application components and the module stubs use a version of the IFlow Java library that emulates the information flows of platform specific APIs. The code skeleton can be extended

---

[1] See http://isse.de/iflow for models and code of our case studies.

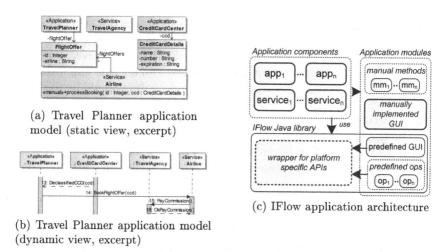

(a) Travel Planner application
model (static view, excerpt)

(b) Travel Planner application model
(dynamic view, excerpt)

(c) IFlow application architecture

Fig. 2. An IFlow application

to a final, runnable application by replacing the module stubs as well as the IFlow Java library with their functional, platform specific implementations.

However, in order to guarantee that the final application inherits the information flow properties of the code skeleton (i.e., it is an *IF preserving code refinement*), the module stubs must closely model their functional counterparts w.r.t. their information flows.

2.1 General Abstraction Techniques

Information dependencies between variables. One of the abstraction techniques used in IFlow is the emulation of information flow between several variables, e.g., from input to output parameters (or an optional persistent state) of a module. The goal is a PDG of the code skeleton where all fields of the output object(s) of the module depend on all fields of its input parameter(s). This can represent the worst-case information flow scenario for the module, if the final implementation only accesses a subset of such fields of an input parameter to calculate the output. Provided that the module does not access any further sources or sinks of information, this technique guarantees that its final implementation will never leak more information than its stub.

Our model-driven approach allows us to automatically implement such a dependency by generating the additional methods `extractIF` and `propagateIF` for every modeled MODELFLOW data type. `extractIF` recursively accesses every field of a MODELFLOW object, and returns an integer value that depends on the values of such fields. In turn, `propagateIF` propagates this value recursively to all fields of another MODELFLOW object.

In our pseudo code notation for module stub implementation, we write $out = (in_1...in_n)$ if all the fields of the object out depend on all fields of the objects $in_1...in_n$. The persistent state of a module is summarized as the variable sl.

Component communication. IFlow applications are distributed systems consisting of one or several Android apps and Java web services. Currently, JOANA does not support the analysis of such distributed systems. However, even if the code of the individual apps and services is merged into a single application and analyzed, the results of the static information flow analysis would be too imprecise.

The reason for this imprecision is the way such apps and web services handle incoming messages. Both implement a general message handling routine which checks the type of an incoming message before executing the appropriate, application-, and message-specific handling method. This presents a challenge for static code analyzers, since they cannot determine the type of the incoming message. Consider the pseudo code snippet in Listing 1.1 that depicts the simplified behavior of the application components from Fig. 2(b). Even though sensitive credit card information stored in `ccd` never flows to the public web service *TravelAgency*, the static analysis will not be able to differentiate between the branches in ll.9-10 and thus deem the application insecure.

Listing 1.1. Generic message handling methods as a challenge for static code analyzers

```
1   class TravelPlanner{
        void declassifiedCCD(var ccd){
3           msg.type = 1;
            msg.content = ccd;
5           Airline.handleIncomingMsg(msg); }}
    class Airline{
7       void handleIncomingMsg(var msg){
            if(msg.type==1) bookFlightOffer(msg);
9           else getFlightOffers(msg); }
        void bookFlightOffer(var msg){ TravelAgency.payCommision(); }
11      void getFlightOffers(var msg){ TravelAgency.retFlightOffers(msg); }}
```

Here, the model-driven approach offers another advantage: instead of using the generic message handling routines, the automatically generated application component code directly invokes the appropriate handling method for the modeled message, allowing for more precise information flow analysis (see Listing 1.2).

Listing 1.2. Component communication via specific message handling methods

```
1   class TravelPlanner{
        void declassifiedCCD(var ccd){
3           msg.type = 1;
            msg.content = ccd;
5           Airline.bookFlightOffer(msg); }}
```

In order to implement the modeled communication functionality in the final application, the code of the receiving component is replaced with an automatically generated proxy implementation (see Listing 1.3) which uses platform specific API to deliver the message as an Android intent or an HTTPS query.

Listing 1.3. Component communication via an automatically generated proxy

```
1   class Airline{
        void bookFlightOffer(var msg){ IFlowLib.sendMsg("Airline", msg); }
3       void getFlightOffers(var msg){ IFlowLib.sendMsg("Airline", msg); }}
```

User and attacker simulation. IFlow applications may request and receive user input, and execute different sequences of actions based on that input. In IFlow, we assume that the user's decision is arbitrary, and simulate it in the code skeleton using a pseudo random number generator. In cases where the execution is branched over the user's input, this approach guarantees that both branches are taken into account by the static information flow analysis. In our pseudo code notation, the user's input is summarized as the variable u.

In addition, an attacker may try to communicate directly with a modeled app or web service without adhering to the modeled application behavior in order to extract sensitive data. E.g., a malicious app could prompt the *Credit-CardCenter* app in Fig. 2(b) to disclose the user's credit card data via message *DeclassifiedCCD*. To prevent information leakage, IFlow apps may therefore only be invoked by other apps from the same modeled application that are cryptographically signed with the same private key. This is guaranteed by employing signature-level protection on Android permissions for IPC communication. In order to detect such information leakage due to direct queries of modeled web services, the code skeleton includes an additional component *Attacker* that is generated automatically from the application model.

Attacker implements a persistent state sl which it uses to assemble new messages and store web service responses. Let $ws_1(\texttt{var msg}) \ldots ws_n(\texttt{var msg})$ represent all message handling methods of modeled web service components, while $in_1(\texttt{var in}) \ldots in_n(\texttt{var in})$ handle their response messages. The code skeleton emulates a random number of web service queries by an attacker in a random order as shown in Listing 1.4 by interweaving them with actions of legitimate application users. Using this approach, IFlow can detect potential information leakage by annotating the internal state sl of *Attacker* as a public sink.

Listing 1.4. Simulating information flows due to an attacker

```
1  class Attacker {
       var sl;
3      void init (){
           while(u){
5              msg = (sl,u);
               if(u == 1)  ws1(msg);
7              . . .
               if(u == n)  wsn(msg);}}
9      void in1(var in){ sl = (sl,in); }
       . . .
11     void inn(var in){ sl = (sl,in); }
   }
```

2.2   Application Modules

This section describes application modules supported in IFlow, and defines the assumptions that are made about their functional implementations. Further, it shows their stub implementations based on those assumptions that allow for information flow analysis of an IFlow application with few false positives, and how those assumptions are guaranteed for the final implementation.

In the following, information flow dependencies within a module are expressed in the sense of the predecessor relation $\rightarrow^*$ in the PDG [5]. E.g., $in \rightarrow^* out$ for the parameters in and out of a method denotes that the value of out (and all of its fields) depends on the value of in (and all of its fields) due to paths existing in the PDG from all nodes representing in to all nodes representing out. M denotes all program locations which may hold information (such as variables or class attributes) that are accessed by the module, whereas C denotes all such locations accessed by the modeled application components. Q and S denote sets of platform specific sources and sinks (e.g., SMS), while the input and output parameters of a module are written as sets $\{in_1..in_n\}$ and $\{out_1..out_m\}$. The code generation of the application components guarantees that they interact with the modules only by writing their inputs and reading their outputs. Unless stated otherwise, we make the following default assumptions for every module:

- d_1: $M \cap C = \{in_1..in_n\} \cup \{out_1..out_m\}$
  The module interacts with the application components only by reading and writing its own input and output parameters
- d_2: $M \cap Q = \emptyset \wedge M \cap S = \emptyset$
  The module does not access any platform specific sources or sinks.
- d_3: The module is stateless

Manual methods. IFlow allows the modeler to specify and use methods which behavior is implemented manually using Java. This enables the developer to flexibly implement and reuse complex, possibly platform specific functionality that is not provided by the IFlow Java library. Using stub implementations of such methods for IFC reduces the complexity of the resulting PDG, allowing for more effective IF analysis. Using MODELFLOW annotations [8], the modeler specifies the sets $Q_e \subseteq Q$ and $S_e \subseteq S$ of platform specific sources and sinks that the manual implementation of the method may access.

The stub of a manual method mm with the input parameters $\{in_1...in_n\}$ and the return parameter out as shown in Listing 1.5 assumes the following:

- m_1: $M \cap Q = Q_e \wedge M \cap S = S_e$
  The module only accesses allowed, platform specific sources and sinks.
- m_2: $\forall_{x \in \{1..n\}} in_x \rightarrow^* out$
  All input method parameters interfere the output parameter.

Listing 1.5. Module stub of a manual method mm

```
  static var mm( var in₁ ,   .. ,   var inₙ ) {
2     return out = (in₁ ,.. ,inₙ) ;  }
```

Assumptions m_1, d_3, and d_3 are checked by statically analyzing the functional module implementation using the Soot framework [11], while M, C, Q_e and S_e are calculated automatically from the application model [8]. Q and S are provided by the SuSi tool [13] that calculates a list of Android sources and sinks using machine learning. Assumption m_2 denotes a worst case over-approximation of information flows between input and output parameters of the module, while the MODELFLOW copy semantics guarantee that the manual method implementation cannot introduce additional flows to objects passed to the method as input parameters. Further, the formalization of MODELFLOW information flow properties assumes the parameters of a manual method as platform specific sources and sinks if the method is allowed to access those [8].

Predefined operations. MODELFLOW provides a range of predefined operations that can be used by the modeled application, e.g., in order to access the GPS sensor data on a mobile device, or encrypt sensitive information. Most such operations are handled similarly to manual methods, both on the modeling level as well as w.r.t. their stub implementations. By providing such predefined functionality and stubs by default, we improve the precision of the IF analysis.

Cryptographic operations represent a special case of predefined operations, as they pose two challenges for static IFC: (1) their real, complex implementation results in larger PDGs, where (2) secret plaintext interferes public ciphertext. However, (2) does not capture the intuitive property of secure encryption: one cannot deduce the plaintext from the resulting ciphertext without knowing the secret encryption key. We therefore use a stub implementation of such operations as part of the information flow emulating version of the IFlow Java library as shown in Listing 1.6. Those stubs implement the *ideal* cryptographic functionality as proposed by Küsters in [9,10] (see also [4]).

Listing 1.6. Module stub of the predefined encryption functionality

```
   class Decryptor {
2     Map sl;
      var decrypt(var in_c){
4         if(sl.containsKey(in_c)) return out_p = sl.get(in_c);
          else return out_p = random(); }
6     Encryptor getEncryptor(){ return new Encryptor(sl); }
   }
8  class Encryptor {
      Map sl;
10    Encryptor(Map sl){ this.sl = sl; }
      var encrypt(var in_p){
12        var rand = random();
          sl.put(in_p, rand);
14        return out_c = rand; }
   }
```

This stub implementation of the module assumes the following:

- m_1: The module is stateful and has the persistent state $sl \in M$
- m_2: $in_p \to^* sl \land in_p \not\to^* out_c \land (in_c = out_c \implies sl \to^* out_p)$

The plaintext input of *encrypt* influences the internal state of the module, but *not* its ciphertext output. Further, the result of the decryption of this output is interfered by the internal state, and, transitively, by the original plaintext

The functional implementation of the predefined encryption module is provided by the platform specific versions of the IFlow Java library. It assures that the assumptions d_{1-2} and m_1 hold, while providing real encryption functionality as per [9,10] to establish cryptographic indistinguishability property for the application, which means i.a. that the private plaintext remains secret for a public observer of the corresponding ciphertext (assumption m_2).

Predefined and manual graphical user interfaces. MODELFLOW provides a predefined user interface (represented as the predefined component *User*) that allows the developer to model a number of predefined user interactions such as requesting user input or dialog confirmation. To implement a more complex or application specific user interface, the modeler can in addition use the GUI module (represented as a component with the «*GUI*» stereotype) which internal behavior is implemented manually using Java.

Graphical user interfaces present additional challenges to static IFC: (1) they employ callback methods that are triggered by the underlying platform, requiring its IF analysis, (2) on mobile devices, user interaction is not limited to GUI elements of the active app, and (3) modern mobile apps have sophisticated user interfaces that result in larger PDGs, making the IF analysis more expensive. IFlow therefore provides stub implementations of both predefined and manual user interfaces.

Listing 1.7 shows the stub of a predefined GUI, where every requested user interaction is represented as an automatically generated handling method in_x that presents the contents of its input parameter to the user. *showUI* implements a stub of the predefined IFlow Java library method for displaying the user interface on the screen. Based on user action, it explicitly triggers the callback method out_x which is the return message handling method of the caller app.

Listing 1.7. Module stub of the predefined user interface

```
1   class User {
        var in₁(var in₁){
3           var callback = (var out) -> out₁(outₙ);
            showUI(in₁, callback); }
5       ...
        var inₙ(var inₙ){
7           var callback = (var out) -> outₙ(outₙ);
            showUI(inₙ, callback); }
9       var showUI(var in, var callback){
            var out = (in, u);
11          if(u) callback(out); }
    }
```

The stub makes the following assumptions about the real implementation:

- m_1: $\forall_{x \in \{1...n\}} in_x \rightarrow^* out_x \wedge u \rightarrow^* out_x$
  The module output is interfered by the corresponding input request as well as the user input.
- m_2: The user may provide input to the interface, or cancel the input request, returning to the beginning of the modeled application sequence

In the functional implementation of the module, only the *showUI* method is replaced with its platform specific version that uses Android Fragments to display the user interface. Its predefined, stateless implementation is guaranteed to only access the provided module and user input to provide the module output via the out_x callback method (assumptions d_{1-3} and m_1). User interaction via the hardware navigation buttons on the mobile device is propagated to the invoking app, prompting it to reset the current behavior sequence (assumption m_2).

The stub of a manual GUI follows a similar structure as Listing 1.7. However, it also introduces a persistent state and additional flows between all inputs, outputs, and the module state, making the IF analysis less precise than for the predefined GUI. Its manual implementation is checked statically like that of a manual method, with $Q_e = S_e = \emptyset$.

3 Conclusion and Related Work

Information flow analysis can be used to guarantee that an application does not leak sensitive user information. However, static IFC of complex, distributed, real-world systems is challenging. There are several model-driven approaches for developing IF-secure applications such as [1,14], however, they do not use IFC on the code level to automatically guarantee IF properties. Code abstractions for IFC are used in JOANA for native methods in the Java standard library, while its Android specific version JoDroid [12] generates an entry method which simulates the Android framework by invoking all callbacks of the analyzed app. [4,9,10] propose how automatic IFC can be used to provide cryptographic privacy guarantees by employing ideal crypto functionality.

We propose a modular systems architecture that enables automatic IFC of real-world applications consisting of Android apps and Java web services using code abstractions. We show how such abstractions can be generated automatically in a model-driven development approach, and be securely expanded to obtain a final, deployable implementation of the modeled application. Using our approach, we are able to successfully provide IF guarantees for distributed applications such as the Travel Planner using automatic IFC.

Acknowledgments. This work is sponsored by the Priority Programme 1496 "Reliably Secure Software Systems - RS^3" of the Deutsche Forschungsgemeinschaft (DFG).

References

1. Ben Said, N., Abdellatif, T., Bensalem, S., Bozga, M.: Model-driven information flow security for component-based systems. In: Bensalem, S., Lakhneck, Y., Legay, A. (eds.) ETAPS 2014. LNCS, vol. 8415, pp. 1–20. Springer, Heidelberg (2014). https://doi.org/10.1007/978-3-642-54848-2_1
2. Enck, W., Octeau, D., McDaniel, P., Chaudhuri, S.: A study of android application security. In: Proceedings of the 20th USENIX Conference on Security, SEC 2011, p. 21. USENIX Association (2011)

3. Felt, A.P., Chin, E., Hanna, S., Song, D., Wagner, D.: Android permissions demystified. In: Proceedings of the 18th ACM Conference on Computer and Communications Security, CCS 2011, pp. 627–638. ACM (2011)
4. Graf, J., Hecker, M., Mohr, M., Snelting, G.: Checking applications using security APIs with JOANA. In: 8th International Workshop on Analysis of Security APIs, July 2015
5. Hammer, C.: Information Flow Control for Java - A Comprehensive Approach based on Path Conditions in Dependence Graphs. Ph.D. thesis, Universität Karlsruhe (TH), Fak. f. Informatik, July 2009. ISBN 978-3-86644-398-3
6. Hammer, C.: Experiences with PDG-based IFC. In: Massacci, F., Wallach, D., Zannone, N. (eds.) ESSoS 2010. LNCS, vol. 5965, pp. 44–60. Springer, Heidelberg (2010). https://doi.org/10.1007/978-3-642-11747-3_4
7. Katkalov, K., Stenzel, K., Borek, M., Reif, W.: Model-driven development of information flow-secure systems with IFlow. ASE Sci. J. 2(2), 65–82 (2013)
8. Katkalov, K., Stenzel, K., Borek, M., Reif, W.: Modeling information flow properties with UML. In: 2015 7th International Conference on New Technologies, Mobility and Security (NTMS). IEEE Conference Publications (2015). https://doi.org/10.1109/NTMS.2015.7266507
9. Küsters, R., Scapin, E., Truderung, T., Graf, J.: Extending and applying a framework for the cryptographic verification of Java programs. In: Abadi, M., Kremer, S. (eds.) POST 2014. LNCS, vol. 8414, pp. 220–239. Springer, Heidelberg (2014). https://doi.org/10.1007/978-3-642-54792-8_12
10. Küsters, R., Truderung, T., Graf, J.: A framework for the cryptographic verification of java-like programs. In: Proceedings of the 2012 IEEE 25th Computer Security Foundations Symposium, CSF 2012, pp. 198–212. IEEE Computer Society, Washington, DC (2012)
11. Lam, P., Bodden, E., Lhoták, O., Hendren, L.: The Soot framework for Java program analysis: a retrospective. In: Cetus Users and Compiler Infrastructure Workshop, Galveston Island, TX, October 2011
12. Mohr, M., Graf, J., Hecker, M.: JoDroid: adding android support to a static information flow control tool. In: Gemeinsamer Tagungsband der Workshops der Tagung Software Engineering 2015, Dresden, Germany, 17.–18. März 2015. CEUR Workshop Proceedings, vol. 1337, pp. 140–145. CEUR-WS.org (2015)
13. Rasthofer, S., Arzt, S., Bodden, E.: A machine-learning approach for classifying and categorizing android sources and sinks. In: NDSS (2014)
14. Seehusen, F.: Model-driven security: exemplified for information flow properties and policies. Ph.D. thesis, Faculty of Mathematics and Natural Sciences, University of Oslo, January 2009
15. Stenzel, K., Katkalov, K., Borek, M., Reif, W.: Formalizing information flow control in a model-driven approach. In: Linawati, Mahendra, M.S., Neuhold, E.J., Tjoa, A.M., You, I. (eds.) ICT-EurAsia 2014. LNCS, vol. 8407, pp. 456–461. Springer, Heidelberg (2014). https://doi.org/10.1007/978-3-642-55032-4_46
16. Stenzel, K., Katkalov, K., Borek, M., Reif, W.: Declassification of information with complex filter functions. In: Proceedings of the 2nd International Conference on Information Systems Security and Privacy, pp. 490–497 (2016)

WaybackVisor: Hypervisor-Based Scalable Live Forensic Architecture for Timeline Analysis

Manabu Hirano[1]([✉]), Takuma Tsuzuki[1], Seishiro Ikeda[1], Naoga Taka[1], Kenji Fujiwara[1], and Ryotaro Kobayashi[2]

[1] Department of Information and Computer Engineering,
National Institute of Technology, Toyota College, Toyota, Aichi 471-8525, Japan
hirano@toyota-ct.ac.jp
[2] Faculty of Informatics, Kogakuin University, Tokyo 163-8677, Japan
ryo.kobayashi@cc.kogakuin.ac.jp

Abstract. Current forensic investigations have to process a large amount of collected data in a limited time. Moreover, we need to ensure collected data are not compromised before seizing suspects' computers. For protecting evidences on important computers, this paper proposes a lightweight hypervisor that supports proactive collection and preservation of I/O logs. The proposed WaybackVisor automatically transfers all I/O logs of ATA drives to a Hadoop cluster. Our experiment showed the prototype implementation of WaybackVisor achieves write throughput of $79.7\,\mathrm{MB/s}$. This paper also demonstrates timeline analysis functions for the I/O logs on the Hadoop cluster. Finally, we compared the proposed WaybackVisor with similar lightweight hypervisors that support live forensics.

Keywords: Live forensics · Hypervisor · Timeline analysis
Parallel processing · Cluster computing · MapReduce

1 Introduction

1.1 Problems on Growing Size of Storage Devices

Current forensic investigations have to process a large amount of collected forensic data in a limited time [5]. The major bottleneck of analysis phase in forensic investigations is I/O speed. Richard and Roussev described that most investigative techniques like keyword search and file classification are I/O bound [16]. They proposed DELV (Distributed Environment for Large-scale Investigations) architecture. Their proposal showed that live regular expression search can be performed 18–89 times faster by using 8 machines [17]. Each machine loads the partial forensic files onto each machine's RAM. Then, the coordinator machine sends queries to each machine simultaneously and receives the results. The original DELV architecture is dependent on AccessData's Forensic Toolkit (FTK). Therefore, DELV can not be applied to other forensic applications.

© Springer International Publishing AG 2017
G. Wang et al. (Eds.): SpaCCS 2017 Workshops, LNCS 10658, pp. 219–230, 2017.
https://doi.org/10.1007/978-3-319-72395-2_21

We have to consider typical throughput of major I/O devices for efficient forensic investigations. For example, the theoretical transfer rate of SATA 3.0 drives is 600 MB/s, while the actual throughput of our laboratory's SATA 3.0 HDD was about 100 MB/s. Also, the actual throughput of our laboratory's SATA 3.0 SSD was about 400 MB/s. The theoretical throughput of DDR4 RAM on our Xeon E5-2630v3 machine is 59 GB/s, while the actual throughput of the same machine was 10 GB/s. Thus, transfer rate of our Xeon E5-2630v3 machine's DDR4 RAM was 25 times faster than our laboratory's SATA 3.0 SSD. If we need to scan all content from 10 TB SATA 3.0 SSD, we have to wait seven hours for reading all data from the SSD. Moreover, current affordable forensic workstations do not have enough memory to store all of the 10 TB data. If we have three machines that can process forensic data simultaneously, we can scan all of the 10 TB data from each machine's SSD in about 2.5 h.

For protecting evidences on important computers, this paper proposes a lightweight hypervisor that supports proactive collection and preservation of I/O logs. The proposed WaybackVisor automatically transfers all I/O logs of ATA drives to Hadoop distributed file system [19], so that we can process collected forensic data by using parallel distributed processing framework, MapReduce [1]. Our system aims to reduce the time of analysis phase for important computers' forensic investigations.

1.2 Problems on Anti-forensic Attacks and Timeline Analysis

The traditional forensic procedure consists of identification, preservation, collection, examination, analysis, presentation, and decision [14]. NIST SP800-86 describes the following four forensic phases: collection, examination, analysis, and reporting [10]. In the both framework, investigators obtain physical disk drives from a suspect's machine. After copying original drives' contents onto image files, the investigator analyzes the disk image by using forensic analysis software like EnCase and FTK. Typical analysis software can create timelines by using metadata information of file systems. For example, Microsoft's NTFS (New Technology File System) maintains timestamps of modification, access, change, and birth for files and directories. However, metadata of file systems can be manipulated by a suspect before seizing his or her disk drives. The creation time of an evidence file might be changed by a suspect. Timestamps of deleted or overwritten files in the past cannot be recovered when the metadata information were overwritten with new data. A suspect might delete or overwrite evidence files before seizing his or her drives. Thus, we need measures against this type of anti-forensic attacks [7].

This paper proposes a proactive forensic collection and preservation mechanism for all I/O logs of ATA drives. Our proposal can record all write operations on a remote cluster in real time. Therefore, we can analyze the exact past disk accesses on monitored ATA drives. Moreover, the proposed architecture can support reconstruction of a disk image at an arbitrary point in the past because our proposal records all past I/O logs.

2   Background

2.1   Thin Hypervisor Based on Parapass-Through Architecture

Shinagawa et al. proposed the lightweight security-purpose hypervisor called BitVisor [18] based on parapass-through architecture. BitVisor employs hardware-assisted virtualization on x86 platform, Intel VT-x [21] and AMD-V. BitVisor can monitor I/O accesses on hardware devices like ATA drives or network interface cards. BitVisor is designed to minimize the code size of hypervisor by allowing most of the I/O access from the guest operating system to pass-through the hypervisor [18]. Therefore, BitVisor can have efficient security functions with minimum performance overhead. We employ BitVisor as the fundamental component for our forensic collection and preservation function.

2.2   Live Forensics

Qi et al. proposed ForenVisor, a special purpose hypervisor for live forensics [15]. They employ parapass-through architecture with hardware-assisted virtualization that was proposed by Shinagawa et al. [18] for minimizing the size of its trusted computing base. ForenVisor supports evidence collection of process states, memory, keyboard, and network interface. ForenVisor collects evidences in hypervisor layer and stores them onto a local ATA drive. However, local saved evidences restrict the scalability of live forensics, especially in an environment that generates a large amount of I/O operations. In contrast, this paper shows a mechanism to transfer forensic evidence to a cluster that employs Hadoop distributed file system [19]. The proposed mechanism enables us to store a large amount of forensic evidence and to perform efficient analysis by using parallel distributed processing framework, MapReduce [1].

3   Design and Implementation

3.1   WaybackVisor for Proactive Forensic Data Collection and Preservation

Figure 1 shows the proposed hypervisor-based scalable live forensic architecture. In the proposed model, we assume that malicious users cannot bypass or compromise the hypervisor layer, for example, by using hardware-based trusted computing architecture [11]. The parapass-through ATA driver intercepts all write operations on ATA drives. The intercepted write operations are recorded as I/O logs shown in Fig. 2. Each I/O log consists of header and payload. Each header has UNIX timestamp (seconds and nano-seconds), Logical Block Address (LBA), size of its payload, and flag that differentiates contents of payload. If flag is 0×01 then its payload is a data sector written on ATA drives. Size of a payload is between 1 byte and 4096 byte (i.e. 4 KiB). If flag is 0×02 then it means read operation. The I/O log of read operation has no payload. If flag is 0×04 then its payload is metadata information about a monitored ATA drive.

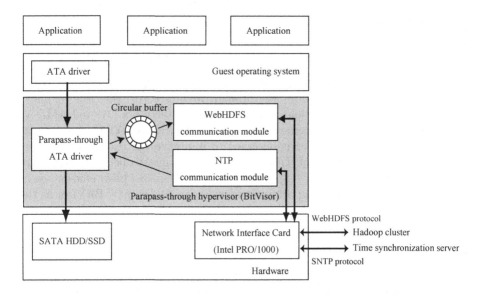

Fig. 1. The hypervisor-based scalable live forensic architecture

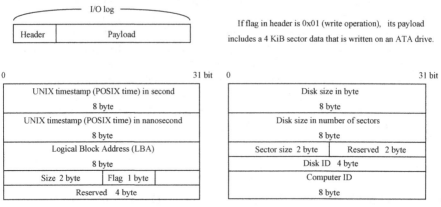

Fig. 2. The format of I/O logs

The I/O log of the metadata information is created once at boot time. All I/O logs are stored onto the circular buffer immediately after each I/O request. The size of the circular buffer in our prototype implementation is 64 MiB.

After buffering I/O logs in the circular buffer, WebHDFS communication module of WaybackVisor transfers the circular buffer's data to a remote Hadoop cluster periodically in background. WebHDFS module first connects with a NameNode of Hadoop distributed file system, then it transfers I/O logs to the DataNode that was specified by the NameNode. We implemented PUT method of WebHDFS REST API [20] in WaybackVisor. NTP communication module of WaybackVisor synchronizes precise time periodically by communicating with a remote time synchronization server. The obtained time is used for timestamps of each I/O log. WaybackVisor does not use guest OS's timestamp because the guest OS's timestamp might be compromised by malicious users. We implemented the essential part of simple network time protocol (SNTP) [13] in WaybackVisor. Both WebHDFS and NTP modules are implemented by using lightweight TCP/IP stack (lwip) [3] that is provided within the original BitVisor distribution.

3.2   Timeline Analyzer on Hadoop Cluster

Figure 3 shows the data flow of the proposed timeline analysis function on a Hadoop cluster that consists of three DataNodes. After receiving raw I/O logs from the client computer that runs WaybackVisor, the Hadoop cluster performs the following three steps for timeline analysis. Please note that our current prototype implementation shown in this paper supports an analysis function of I/O logs for write operations only. Step (1) converts raw I/O logs into key-value pairs of (header of I/O log, payload of I/O log) in SequenceFile format. Step (2) generates key-value pairs of (MD5 hash value of each written 4 KiB sector, its metadata information: timestamps, LBA, and size) by using MapReduce. If a sector was not 4 KiB sector then the remain of the sector is padded with zeros. Step (3) searches a file that is specified by our timeline analyzer web application, the GUI for cluster computation, from all past I/O logs. The file specified by the timeline analyzer web application is first split into 4 KiB sectors. Then, MD5 hashes of every 4 KiB sectors of the file are searched in the hash database that was created in previous step (2). Step(3) is executed by using MapReduce. Finally, the timeline analyzer web application shows the search results in two types of graphs, bar chart and heatmap. If no file was specified, the timeline analyzer web application displays all written sectors in graphs. We implemented

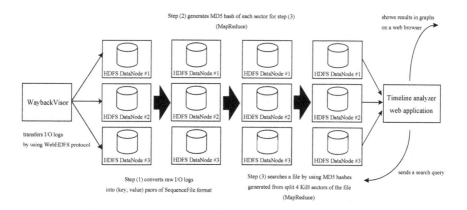

Fig. 3. The data flow of the timeline analysis function on a Hadoop cluster

the functions of the above three steps in Java with Hadoop MapReduce. We implemented the timeline analyzer web application by using Node.js and D3.js data visualization library.

4 Evaluation

4.1 Evaluation of Write Throughput on WaybackVisor

In our experimental setup, we employed the following machines. Table 1 shows specification of the client computer that runs WaybackVisor. We allocated 1 GiB of physical 8 GiB RAM for WaybackVisor. We used an Intel PRO/1000 Gigabit Ethernet card for WaybackVisor. WaybackVisor on the client computer intercepts all write operations on the SATA HDD. Our experiment used first 233 GB of the SATA HDD for Debian GNU/Linux as a guest OS. The logical sector size of the HDD is 512 byte and the physical sector size of the HDD is 4096 byte. In the experiment, we executed WaybackVisor by using Preboot eXecution Environment (PXE) before loading the guest OS's kernel located in the HDD. Table 2 shows specification of our Hadoop cluster that receives I/O logs from the client computer via a Gigabit Ethernet switch. The cluster consists of one master machine and three slave machines. Each machine of the cluster is inter-connected via a 10 GbE (10 Gigabit Ethernet) switch.

Table 1. Specification of the client computer that runs WaybackVisor

CPU	AMD Athlon II X2 245 2.9 GHz
RAM	DDR3 SDRAM 8 GiB
NIC	Intel PRO/1000 GT Desktop Adapter (for WaybackVisor)
	Broadcom NetLink Gigabit Ethernet (for guest OS)
Storage	TOSHIBA MQ03ABB300 3 TB HDD via SATA-300
Guest OS	Debian GNU/Linux 8 (amd64)
Hypervisor	WaybackVisor based on BitVisor that was cloned from BitBucket on 17 February 2016

We measured write throughput by using the following Linux command, `dd conv=fdatasync if=/dev/zero of=test.dat count=1 bs=512M`, on the guest OS. The size of the circular buffer of current implementation is 64 MiB. Therefore, writing data of 512 MB causes at least eight WebHDFS transactions. We measured write throughput in the following three cases: (1) OS only, (2) Guest OS and BitVisor with the standard parapass-through ATA driver [18], and (3) Guest OS and WaybackVisor. We calculated the average throughput of five tests in each case. Figure 4 shows the write throughput in the above three cases. The overhead of the proposed WaybackVisor was about 25% compared to the case (1).

Table 2. Specification of the Hadoop cluster

	Master	Slave
CPU	Xeon E5-2630v3 x2 (16 cores)	Core i7 5820K (6 cores)
RAM	DDR4 64 GiB	DDR4 64 GiB
NIC	Intel X540-T2 (10GbE)	Intel X540-T2 (10GbE)
Storage	RAID0 consists of 3 SATA SSDs (Crucial CT512, 512 GB)	RAID0 consists of 3 SATA SSDs (Crucial CT250, 250 GB)
OS	CentOS 6.8 (x86_64)	CentOS 6.8 (x86_64)
Hadoop	Version 2.7.1	Version 2.7.1
No. of machines	1	3

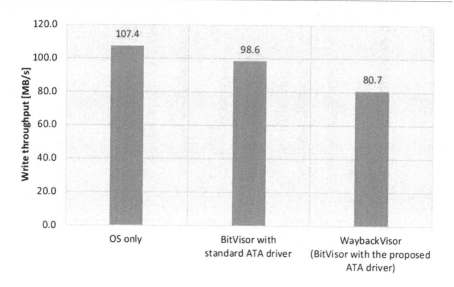

Fig. 4. Comparison of write throughput

4.2 Evaluation of Timeline Analysis Function on Hadoop Cluster

Next, we evaluated the timeline analysis function on our Hadoop cluster. We first created test I/O logs by writing 9,881 files from Govdoc dataset [2,4] on the guest OS of the client computer that runs WaybackVisor. The total size of written files was 4.52 GiB. We used the first 10 directories between 000/ and 009/ of Govdoc dataset [2]. In the experiment, we wrote files from each directory after waiting 60 s. All of the I/O logs were transferred to the Hadoop cluster. We measured the processing time for three steps that were described in Sect. 3.2. We needed 139 s for step (1), 69.9 s for step (2), and 0.138 s for step (3). In step (3), we searched the file 000281.doc (241 KiB) of Govdoc dataset from all the I/O logs.

Our timeline visualization function uses the above results to display the following two types of graphs. Figure 5 shows the bar chart that depicts the total size of write operations in each time interval. The x-axis shows time and the y-axis shows the total size of written sectors. Figure 5 includes all written sectors because we did not specify any file for the search function in this case. If a user searches a file then the graph displays the amount of detected sectors only. We can confirm 9 or 10 peaks of write operations in every 60 s. Investigators can grasp access patterns of the monitored ATA drives by using this bar chart.

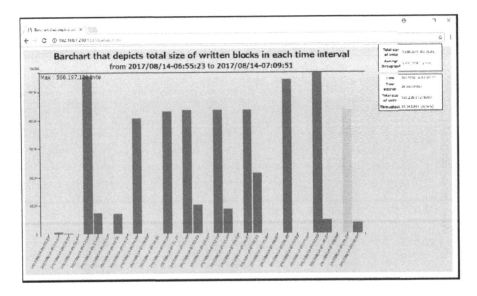

Fig. 5. Bar chart that depicts the total size of write operations

Figure 6 shows the heatmap that depicts frequency of write operations on each LBA area. The x-axis shows time and the y-axis shows each area of Logical Block Address (LBA) on the monitored ATA drive. Figure 6 includes all written sectors because we did not specify any file for the search function in this case. If a user searches a file then the graph displays detected sectors only. The first 2048 sectors of the monitored ATA drive were BIOS boot partition. The next 225.4 GB of the monitored ATA drive was Linux root partition that was formatted by ext4 file system. The following 7.5 GB of the monitored ATA drive is Linux swap partition. The sector size of the monitored ATA drive was 512 byte. We can confirm that the red or yellow area appeared in every 60 s. Investigators can use this heatmap to grasp access patterns on each LBA area and time.

5   Related Work

The idea that uses hypervisor as a live forensic tool has been widely explored in the literature. For example, Garfinkel et al. introduced the concept of virtual

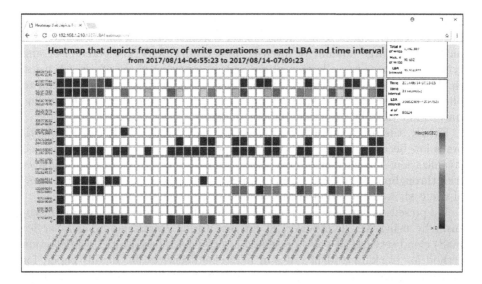

Fig. 6. Heatmap that depicts frequency of write operations on each LBA area (Color figure online)

machine introspection by using a modified version of VMware Workstation [6] in 2003. However, we focus on the comparison with live forensic systems that employ the latest hardware-assisted lightweight hypervisors.

We compare the proposed WaybackVisor with ForenVisor [15] and Hyper-Sleuth [12]. All of the three hypervisors employ hardware-assisted virtualization. Table 3 shows the comparison with the three hypervisor-based live forensic systems. WaybackVisor and ForenVisor employ parapass-through architecture [18] to reduce the code size of the trusted computing base. ForenVisor supports live forensics from many types of devices than WaybackVisor. However, WaybackVisor can support other devices by employing additional parapass-through drivers because the both hypervisors employ same architecture. ForenVisor and HyperSleuth support on-the-fly installation that enables users to insert hypervisor without rebooting the system. ForenVisor has limitation of the capacity

Table 3. Comparison with three hypervisors for live forensics

	WaybackVisor	ForenVisor	HyperSleuth
Live forensic supports	ATA drives	Process status, memory, NIC, and keyboard	Memory and system call
On-the-fly installation		✓	✓
Logging on cluster	✓		
Timeline analysis	✓		

of evidence data because it saves evidence data onto local drives. WaybackVisor transfers evidence data to a remote cluster automatically, so that our proposal can handle a large amount of forensic data than ForenVisor. ForenVisor and HyperSleuth focus on collection phase and preservation phase of live forensics. On the other hand, our WaybackVisor considers analysis phase in addition to collection phase and preservation phase. This paper demonstrated the timeline analysis functions by using our Hadoop cluster.

Finally, the overhead of live forensic functions of the above three hypervisors is low because they are lightweight hypervisors based on hardware-assisted virtualization. The current prototype implementation of WaybackVisor achieves write throughput of 80.7 MB/s, an extra 25% of overhead only. This experimental result showed our proposal can be used in practical environments.

We presented our previous proactive data collection and preservation mechanism by using Xen hypervisor [8] for monitoring Infrastructure-as-a-Service (IaaS) cloud services. We also presented a sector-hash based rapid file detection method for tracking evidence files in IaaS cloud services [9]. In this paper, for protecting forensic evidence of important client computers, we implemented the novel proactive I/O collection and preservation mechanism in the lightweight hypervisor instead of Xen hypervisor.

In future work, we need further cluster-based analysis functions that can interpret file system information. Moreover, the monitored I/O logs will be used in machine learning for anomaly detection, malware detection, or future prediction.

6   Conclusion

This paper described the problem on the increase of the size of storage devices and anti-forensic attacks on digital evidences. To solve these problems, we proposed WaybackVisor, a lightweight-hypervisor for live forensics that supports cluster-based analysis functions. The experimental results showed WaybackVisor has low performance overhead. This paper also showed two graphs for timeline visualization, bar chart and heatmap, for analyzing I/O accesses of the monitored ATA drives. Finally, we compared the proposed WaybackVisor with other similar lightweight hypervisors for live forensics.

Acknowledgments. The authors thank Dr. Suguru Yamaguchi for his longstanding support for this research project. The authors thank developers and contributors of BitVisor. The authors would like to thank the anonymous reviewers for their valuable comments and suggestions. This work was supported by JSPS KAKENHI Grant Number JP26330168 and JP17K00198.

References

1. Dean, J., Ghemawat, S.: MapReduce: simplified data processing on large clusters. Commun. ACM **51**(1), 107–113 (2008)
2. Digital Corpora: Govdocs1. http://digitalcorpora.org/corpora/govdocs. Accessed 1 Mar 2017
3. Dunkels, A.: Design and implementation of the lwIP TCP/IP stack. Swed. Inst. Comput. Sci. **2**, 77 (2001)
4. Garfinkel, S., Farrell, P., Roussev, V., Dinolt, G.: Bringing science to digital forensics with standardized forensic corpora. Digit. Invest. **6**, S2–S11 (2009)
5. Garfinkel, S.L.: Digital forensics research: the next 10 years. Digit. Invest. **7**, S64–S73 (2010)
6. Garfinkel, T., Rosenblum, M., et al.: A virtual machine introspection based architecture for intrusion detection. In: NDSS, vol. 3, pp. 191–206 (2003)
7. Harris, R.: Arriving at an anti-forensics consensus: examining how to define and control the anti-forensics problem. Digit. Invest. **3**, 44–49 (2006)
8. Hirano, M., Ogawa, H.: A log-structured block preservation and restoration system for proactive forensic data collection in the cloud. In: 2016 11th International Conference on Availability, Reliability and Security (ARES), pp. 355–364. IEEE (2016)
9. Hirano, M., Takase, H., Yoshida, K.: Evaluation of a sector-hash based rapid file detection method for monitoring infrastructure-as-a-service cloud platforms. In: 2015 10th International Conference on Availability, Reliability and Security (ARES), pp. 584–591. IEEE (2015)
10. Kent, K., Chevalier, S., Grance, T., Dang, H.: Guide to integrating forensic techniques into incident response. NIST Special Publication 10, 800–86 (2006)
11. Maene, P., Gotzfried, J., de Clercq, R., Muller, T., Freiling, F., Verbauwhede, I.: Hardware-based trusted computing architectures for isolation and attestation. IEEE Trans. Comput. **PP**(99), 1 (2017). https://doi.org/10.1109/TC.2017.2647955
12. Martignoni, L., Fattori, A., Paleari, R., Cavallaro, L.: Live and trustworthy forensic analysis of commodity production systems. In: Jha, S., Sommer, R., Kreibich, C. (eds.) RAID 2010. LNCS, vol. 6307, pp. 297–316. Springer, Heidelberg (2010). https://doi.org/10.1007/978-3-642-15512-3_16
13. Mills, D.L.: RFC4330: simple network time protocol (SNTP) version 4 for IPV4, IPV6 and OSI (2006)
14. Palmer, G., et al.: A road map for digital forensic research. In: First Digital Forensic Research Workshop, Utica, New York, pp. 27–30 (2001)
15. Qi, Z., Xiang, C., Ma, R., Li, J., Guan, H., Wei, D.S.L.: ForenVisor: a tool for acquiring and preserving reliable data in cloud live forensics. IEEE Trans. Cloud Comput. **5**(3), 443–456 (2017). https://doi.org/10.1109/TCC.2016.2535295
16. Richard III, G.G., Roussev, V.: Next-generation digital forensics. Commun. ACM **49**(2), 76–80 (2006)
17. Roussev, V., Richard III, G.G.: Breaking the performance wall: The case for distributed digital forensics. In: Proceedings of the 2004 Digital Forensics Research Workshop, vol. 94 (2004)
18. Shinagawa, T., Eiraku, H., Tanimoto, K., Omote, K., Hasegawa, S., Horie, T., Hirano, M., Kourai, K., Oyama, Y., Kawai, E., et al.: BitVisor: a thin hypervisor for enforcing I/O device security. In: Proceedings of the 2009 ACM SIGPLAN/SIGOPS International Conference on Virtual Execution Environments, pp. 121–130. ACM (2009)

19. Shvachko, K., Kuang, H., Radia, S., Chansler, R.: The hadoop distributed file system. In: 2010 IEEE 26th Symposium on Mass Storage Systems and Technologies (MSST), pp. 1–10. IEEE (2010)
20. The Apache Software Foundation: WebHDFS REST API. http://hadoop.apache.org/docs/current/hadoop-project-dist/hadoop-hdfs/WebHDFS.html. Accessed 15 Aug 2017
21. Uhlig, R., Neiger, G., Rodgers, D., Santoni, A.L., Martins, F.C., Anderson, A.V., Bennett, S.M., Kagi, A., Leung, F.H., Smith, L.: Intel virtualization technology. Computer **38**(5), 48–56 (2005)

Cloud Ownership and Reliability – Issues and Developments

Isaac Odun-Ayo[1]([✉]), Nicholas Omoregbe[1], Modupe Odusami[2],
and Olasupo Ajayi[3]

[1] Department of Computer and Information Sciences,
Covenant University, Ota, Nigeria
{isaac.odun-ayo,
nicholas.omoregbe}@covenantuniversity.edu.ng
[2] Department of Electrical and Information Engineering,
Covenant University, Ota, Nigeria
modupe.odusami@covenantuniversity.edu.ng
[3] Department of Computer Science, University of Lagos, Akoka, Lagos, Nigeria
olaajayi@unilag.edu.ng

Abstract. Cloud computing is a composite paradigm that provides crucial services to individuals and organisations over networked infrastructure at a cost. The Cloud provides custom built applications, made available by a CSP to customers. Several customers can access an instance of one application. The Cloud also affords an avenue for customers to build their own application in a language compatible with a CSP and subsequently deploy that application on the Cloud. In addition, massive scalable storage and computing devices are available on the Cloud. A customers expects optimum services whenever and wherever it is required. Hence, system failure on the part of a CSP must not affect the services being provided to the customer. This paper examines present trends in the area of Cloud ownership reliability and provides a guide for future research. The paper aims to answer the following question: what is the current trend and development in Cloud ownership reliability? In addition, analysis was done on existing work published in journals, conferences, white papers and those published in reputable magazines, to answer the question raised. The expected result is the identification of trends in Cloud ownership and reliability which will be of benefit to prospective Cloud users and service providers alike.

Keywords: Cloud computing · Reliability · Ownership · CSP · TCO
IaaS · SaaS · PaaS

1 Introduction

"Cloud computing is a model for enabling ubiquitous, convenient, on-demand network access to a shared pool of configurable computing resources (e.g., networks, servers, storage, applications, and services) that can be rapidly provisioned and released with minimal management effort or service provider interaction" [1]. Cloud computing is expanding on all fronts and mutually benefiting both Cloud providers and users alike. These benefits are either in the utilization of Cloud applications or migration of services

© Springer International Publishing AG 2017
G. Wang et al. (Eds.): SpaCCS 2017 Workshops, LNCS 10658, pp. 231–240, 2017.
https://doi.org/10.1007/978-3-319-72395-2_22

to the Cloud. Cloud computing has three primary services, Software-as-a-Service (SaaS), Platform-as-a-Service (PaaS) and Infrastructure-as-a-Service (IaaS). SaaS is used by Cloud service providers (CSP) to provide Cloud consumers with applications deployed over the Internet such application can be utilized by individuals or enterprises at a cost. User do not have to worry about installation and licenses. In PaaS, the CSP provides an environment for the Cloud user to create and deploy custom applications. However, the CSP has control over the application deployed. IaaS provides compute resource and storage to Cloud users at a metered rate. This is quite beneficial to both small business and large enterprises alike as they do not have to invest in computing infrastructure. The Cloud user has control over some resources such as storage and the operating system, while the CSP has control over the infrastructure. Cloud computing is offered in four deployment models viz. private, public, community and hybrid Cloud.

A private Cloud is completely owned by an organization and the users are staff of that organization. It can be hosted by a third party or on-premise and it is considered more secured. Public Cloud is owned by large CSP who have large infrastructure to offer services to the public on a pay-as-you-go basis. The services can spread across geographical region, but considered less secure than the private. Community Clouds are owned by several organization with shared or common interest with infrastructure shared by a community of users. Hybrid Clouds are a combination of either private, public or community Cloud. The organizations are unique entities utilizing the Cloud infrastructure which is managed by a single unit.

The issue of ownership and reliability is essential in Cloud computing, as one of the major deterring factors to individuals owning data centres is the huge Total Cost of Ownership (TCO) and associated operational cost. These are often responsible for customers choosing to buy service from CSPs rather than build their own data centres, as this eliminates the need to purchase, deploy and maintain IT assets [2]. A primary advantage of Cloud services is that the Cloud vendors take on the full infrastructure responsibility for running hosted applications.

The TCO is made up of cost of acquisition, deployment, operation and retirement of a product or piece of equipment. This cost can be very huge and often unnecessary particularly if the business objectives of the customer is not IT related. To this end, customers no longer see reasons to spend a lot of money to acquire large data centres (or server room) and spend even more on managing and running them. They would rather outsource this to a CSP, focus on their core competence and also cut down on unnecessary expenses.

Though seemingly attractive, there are also flip side to moving to the Cloud, versus running an in-house data centre. These disadvantages can broadly be classified into two groups: quantifiable and unquantifiable. The quantifiable are those which a direct cost implication can be obtain for, these include but are not limited to monthly or annual Cloud service fees, cost of reliable Internet access and cost of Cloud-compatible software (in the case of IAAS). While the unquantifiable include: security and privacy concerns, legal and ethical issues and data migration and vendor lock-in.

Reliability on the other hand implies being trusted to perform at expected level. The author in [3] considered reliability from a Cloud computing perspective and inferred it to mean avoiding situations whereby as a CSP combines too many Virtual Machines onto a physical server, which results in performance degradation problems due to CPU or I/O bottlenecks.

Considering these, the purpose of this paper is to examine ownership and reliability in Cloud computing. The paper will do a comparison of TCO on different services and highlight current trends in the industry. The rest of the paper is as follows. Section 2 examines related work. Section 3 discusses Cloud computing, TCO and highlights current industry trends. Section 4 concludes and suggests future work.

2 Related Work

In [3], Cloud computing Reliability, Availability and Serviceability (RAS): issues and challenges were presented. A number of RAS challenges were highlighted, though most bordered around security concerns, such as data leakage, privacy, Cloud attacks and data remnants. The author proposed possible ways of mitigating these challenges. In [4], the authors presented a way of improving Cloud reliability by using a model called Distributed De-duplication system. The authors showed though data de-duplication negatively affects reliability as the deletion of duplicates copies of data can result in single point of failure. The authors then introduced four secure de-duplication systems, which addressed de-duplication at the file and block levels. A secure tag-based system to ensure consistency and integrity with little network overhead. The work also presented an architecture for auditing files on the Cloud and notifying the data owner. In [5], a survey of Cloud monitoring systems was done. It was observed that the growing infrastructure on the Cloud makes monitoring important. Various issues relating to Cloud monitoring systems were extensively discussed, including challenges and future direction. In [6], ways of improving reliability in Cloud computing systems were presented. The main focus of the paper was in assuring reliability. It was noted that reliability was important in order to enhance user satisfaction. A reliability algorithm for mitigating Cloud disasters was shown. In [7], Reliability as it affects the Internet Cloud was presented. The paper viewed the Internet as being synonymous to the public utility telephone but instead of phones, a network of computing resources. It discusses reliability in the Cloud in terms of services and system failures. The author identified availability, consistency and accuracy of access as fundamental reliance criteria for Cloud data centres. They also proposed one-to-one redundancy for critical data centres and the replication of data across multiple data centres. The security and cost implications of these were however not considered. In [8], accountable proof of ownership for data using timing element in Cloud services was proposed. The author reported that a major challenge to proof of ownership is the fact that there is usually insufficient accountability in storage. The focus of the paper was to present a model to be used by service providers to account for user generated data. In [9], case studies of total costs of ownership in Cloud computing was presented. A survey of the Cloud services and service providers was conducted, with the main focus of the work being cost with respect to migration and services provided by Cloud providers. In [10], a comprehensive cost analysis of owning and operating an in-house data centre versus employing a CSP (AWS) was done. The authors claimed that employing AWS, customers could save up to 80% more money than when an in-house data centre was deployed. Numerous scenarios were shown and across all flexible payment scheme was a major advantage listed in favour of the Cloud option. In [11], the total cost of (non) ownership of a NoSQL database Cloud service was presented. The approach compared the cost of using non-relational database on the AWS Cloud versus a NoSQL database running on an on-premise data centre. [12], the total cost of ownership of Cloud and premise-based contact center systems was presented. The paper focused on a comparison between the TCO of Cloud data centres versus their on-premise counterpart. The authors gave various recommendations based on sizes of data centers. In [13], Reliability and energy efficiency in Cloud computing systems: Survey and taxonomy is proposed.

3   Cloud Computing and Total Cost of Ownership

In a bid to appreciate the issue of cost of ownership in Cloud computing, it is essential know what benefits the Cloud has to offer.

3.1   Characteristic of Cloud Computing

The following are the characteristics of Cloud computing as described in [14, 15].

On Demand Self-Service: Cloud services such as web applications, server time processing power, storage and network can be provisioned automatically and on needs basis by customers without the CSP's intervention.

Broad Network Access: Ubiquitous access to Cloud resources over the Internet via mobile, computers, and other smart devices or platforms.

Resource Pooling: Physical and virtual computing resources are pooled together and presented as a single entity to Cloud users. The location and actual size of these resources are abstracted from the user.

Rapid Elasticity and Scalability: Computing resources can be rapidly and elastically provisioned and released with respect to user demand. This gives an illusion of an infinite resource pool to the Cloud users. Cloud infrastructure are also scalable as CSPs can easily add new nodes and servers with minor modifications to the entire system.

Measured Service: Cloud resource and services are controlled and monitored by the CSP through a pay-per-use business model. Consumers utilize those rescues in a way similar to using utility such as electricity or gas.

Multi-tenancy and Customization: CSPs are able to host numerous users simultaneously by sharing physical hardware resources amongst them. The physical resources are configured in such a way that users get a sense of using dedicated resources (through virtualization). These virtual dedicated resources can be configured, customized and adjusted in tune with user demand.

Reliability: This is achieved by replicating user data across multiple redundant sites. High reliability makes the Cloud a perfect solution for disaster recovery and business critical tasks requiring high availability.

Economies of Scale: In order to take advantage of economies of scale, Clouds are implemented as large as possible. Other considerations are also taken to reduce cost such as locating the Cloud close to cheap power stations and in low cost real estate.

Cost Effectiveness: Customers are allowed to lease computing resources and purchase IT services that match their needs instead of investing in complex and expensive computing infrastructure and services. This lowers the cost of the IT services for organizations and individuals.

Efficient Resource Utilization: Delivering resources only for as long as they are needed allows for efficient utilization of resources.

Collaborating: PaaS allows for collaborative work among users within an organization or among different organizations.

Green Technology: Cloud computing shares resources between users and does not require large resources that consume power.

High performance: Cloud computing provides users with high performance computing environment due to extremely large storage and powerful computing resources of the Cloud infrastructure.

3.2 Challenges of Cloud Computing

Despite the appealing characteristics of Cloud computing, it has its challenges, some of which have been discussed in [3] and summarized as follows:

Though the Cloud provides seemingly unlimited resource pool to house data, the exact location of these data are unknown. This might pose a problem for sensitive data particularly those related to legal and governance.

Unfortunately, in multi-tenant environment (such as at the SaaS level where databases are shared), service fluctuations are common, and a user can suddenly experience a drop in performance as a result of growth in the resource utilization of neighbours' applications. This growth in utilization would inevitably takes resources away from other users. This phenomenon is sometimes called "Noisy-neighbor" effect [16] and usually affects computing resources especially processors, and memory. Cloud security policy are often times not transparent as CSPs are not mandated to share such information, this may create conflict with some organizations' information compliance requirement. There is also the issue of data ownership, whereby it is often believed that the CSP owns the data stored in their data centre. The users might need to pay to obtain the data stored with the CSP on expiration of service tenure. Similar to this is the case of Cloud consumer lock-in; wherein user are stuck with a particular vendor due to the use of proprietary technology. This results in a lot of effort and cost if and when the user chooses to migrate to another service provider.

3.3 Reliability in Cloud Computing

Reliability, Availability and Serviceability (RAS) are vital components of Cloud computing. Appropriate reliability standards will need to focus not just on availability but also on consistency and accuracy of access, with heighted requirements for data security and protection. RAS in Cloud can be in multiple dimensions. These dimensions are as follows: [3, 4, 6, 13]

Redundant Power Supply: Over time, data centres have evolved into rack-mounted systems where multiple CPUs share more reliable, efficient and redundant power supplies. These power are often sourced from multiple locations such as the main grid, backup generators and high capacity inverters. The failure of one power source would no longer mean loss of a server as active backups power supply would be in place.

Data Replication: Reliable access to data is further achieved by distributing copies of data across multiple data centres. These data centres are often located across continents, thereby increasing RAS. A limitation to this however is that changes made on data at a particular centre, may not be immediately reflected in other centre. Ensuring that two copies of data are consistent, while allowing users to access the same data at the same time might not be possible, as it is difficult to read and write to the data simultaneously. Many CSPs thus sacrifice consistency to enable high availability.

Hybrid Clouds: Hybrid Clouds is a Cloud architecture whereby a private Cloud is linked with a public Cloud often for the purpose of scaling up. Certain organizations might prefer to own and manage their own data centre, possible for security reasons however need to cater for occasional/seasonal spike in traffic. During these instances, the user can burst into the public Cloud to cater for these traffic spikes.

Multi-homing: This is a system of providing RAS, wherein users sign up to multiple Cloud providers. This ensures that data are always available yet avoiding vendor lock-in. Cost might however be a challenge, as the user would be paying twice or more. While it is expected that reliability should be managed via market forces, market forces may fail, and the range of potential failures is exacerbated by the increased distribution and decentralization of control and functionality across enterprises, end-user networks and equipment. CSPs often times do not have explicit agreements with each other that can help ensure reliability, hence the user is stuck with using these multiple CSPs as independent entities.

3.4   Comparison of TCO of Running Application in the Cloud and in Traditional Data Centres

Running Application on the Cloud gives many technical advantages and results in significant cost savings over running them on traditional servers based on analysis conducted in [9]. A comparative analysis of the TCO when running an instance of an application on the Cloud and in a traditional in-house server is shown in Table 1.

For this comparison, the Microsoft SQL Server 2016 Standard Edition is used; which has the following minimum system requirement according to [17]: 6 GB of storage for installation and an additional 100 GB for data, for a total of at least 106 GB; 4 GB of memory; 2.0 GHz processor; and Windows Server 2012 operating system.

For the Cloud deployment, Amazon's AWS is used. AWS offers two options for Microsoft SQL Server deployment – the Amazon's Elastic Cloud Computer (EC2) and the Relational Database Service (RDS). For the sake of direct comparison with the in-house server, we considered the EC2, specifically the M4 Large [18] with Windows Reserved option, as it had the closest match to the minimum system requirement for the version of Microsoft SQL Server being considered. For the traditional server, we considered the Dell PowerEdge T30 Mini Tower Server Desktop [19]. At least two of these would be needed for redundancy purposes. Prices were obtained from www. Amazon.com, aws.amazon.com, www.microsoft.com and www.ec2instances.info.

In Table 1, the following assumptions were made:

1. The server is under warrantee, as such maintenance is provided for free for the first one year.
2. The in-house server is deployed within the premises of the client, hence cost of rent is eliminated.
3. For network connectivity, figures used are based on the local Nigerian rates for an unlimited data plan.
4. Cost of personnel is extracted from [11], however rather than US$1,200 for six servers, we used US$400 for two servers. We also included a US$200 fee for the Cloud option, as an above average level of IT competence (AWS certified professional) is usually required to sign up and configure a fully functional enterprise level database system on AWS. Albeit this is a one-off payment, unlike the in-house which is recurrent.

A comparison was done using the Standard one year term for the Cloud deployment (with both the full upfront payment and On-Demand hourly payment options) and the traditional in-house server. Table 1 shows that using the Cloud model,

Table 1. A comparison of TCO of in-house servers versus cloud deployment

Description	Cost (USD)		
	In-house server	Cloud deployment	
	Always on	Always on	Business hours (8 am–5 pm)
Server acquisition cost	438.82 * 2 = 877.64	507	0
Server daily recurrent cost	0	0	0.672 (per hour) * 9 = 6.048
Microsoft Server 2016 Standard edition [20]	3,717 (Volume licensing, hosting)	0	0
Network/Connectivity (Daily)	0	0.91	0.91
Power and cooling [11]	172	0	0
Personnel [11]	400	200	200
One-off payments	877.64 + 3,717 = 4,594.64	5,517 + 200 = 5,717	200
Annual recurrent expenditure	572 * 12 = 6,864	0.91 * 12 = 10.92	6.958 * 365 = 2,539
TOC per annum	11,458.64	5,727.92	2,739.6
Annual cost savings		49.9%	76%

particular the on-demand option, users only pay 24% of the total amount they would have, if using the in-house option. This a savings of up to 76%. It is however important to note that using the on-demand option is only cheaper because the server is only used during business hours that is between 8am and 5pm daily. Should the customer require an always on option, then the on-demand becomes prohibitively expensive as shown in [11]. For such cases, the Cloud deployment with the Always-on option would be the best, as it gives the user about 50% savings versus the in-house option.

It is interesting to note that the software being deployed did not significantly contribute to the large difference in TCO of the in-house versus the Cloud. Table 2 shows that using an open-source option, such as MySQL and running on Linux operating system, then the difference in cost would similar, with a cost saving of about 45% on the average. An analysis of this is shown on Table 2, using the same in-house server but Amazon EC2 M4 Large instance with Linux as basis of comparison.

Table 2. A comparison of TCO of in-house servers versus cloud deployment for an open source software

Description	Cost (USD)		
	In-house server	Cloud deployment	
	Always on	Always on	Business hours (8am–5pm)
Server acquisition cost	438.82 * 2 = 877.64	507	0
Server daily recurrent cost	0	0	0.1 (per hour) * 9 = 0.9
MySQL standard edition [21]	5,000 (Annual subscription)	5,000 (Annual subscription)	5,000 (Annual subscription)
Network/Connectivity (Daily)	0	0.91	0.91
Power and cooling [11]	172	0	0
Personnel [11]	400	200	200
One-off payments	877.64 + 5,000 = 5,877.64	507 + 5000 = 5,507	200
Annual recurrent expenditure	572 * 12 = 6,864	0.91 * 12 = 10.92	0.9 * 365 = 328.5
TOC per annum	11,864.64	5,517.92	5,328.5
Annual cost savings		46.5%	44.9%

From both tables it can be inferred that the actual factors responsible for the large difference in TCO are the annual recurrent expenses spent on IT personnel, power and cooling of the data centre. With the Cloud deployment model, these elements are eliminated and transferred to the CSP and the user only pays an average of approximately US$10, thus highlighting the advantage of Cloud computing with respect to TCO.

4   Conclusion

Cloud computing is providing services that is facilitating growth and development in IT services. Cloud computing provide applications for customers on the Internet and also make available different kinds of resources to enhance organization IT operations. Ownership and reliability are vital aspect of could computing. Ownership is examined in terms of TCO which is used to estimate the cost of providing services. Such cost enable the Cloud consumer to determine either to subscribe to a Cloud service and utilize the resources being made available by the CSP or to setup a data centre and continue to do things the traditional way. Although, major CSP, such as AWS, Microsoft Azure and Google Platform offer good prices for services, it is still essential to determine if migrating to the Cloud aligns with the business objective of the customer and if such decision would be cost effective in the long run.

Acknowledgments. We acknowledge the support and sponsorship provided by Covenant University through the Centre for Research, Innovation and Discovery (CUCRID).

References

1. Peter, M., Grance, T.: The NIST Definition of Cloud Computing. NIST Special Publication 800-145 (2011)
2. Cloud Strategy: Understanding TCO cloud economics crunching the numbers in the cloud. Cloud Strategy Mag. **17** (2016). http://www.Cloudstrategymag.com/articles/86033-understanding-tco-Cloud-economics
3. Farzad, S.: Cloud computing reliability, availability and serviceability (RAS): issues and challenges. Int. J. Adv. ICT Emerg. Reg. **4**(2), 12–23 (2011)
4. Salma, S., Guntapalli, M., Sayeed, Y.: Improve reliability using secure distributed deduplication system in cloud. Int. J. Emerg. Technol. Comput. Sci. Electron. (IJETCSE) **23**(8) (2016). ISSN: 0976-1353
5. Giuseppe, A., Alessio, B., Walter, D., Antonio, P.: Cloud monitoring: a survey. Comput. Netw. (2013). https://doi.org/10.1016/j.comnet.2013.04.001
6. Suma, V., Chintureena, T.: Improving reliability in cloud computing systems. Int. J. Comput. Appl. (0975 – 8887) Advanced Computing and Communication Techniques for High Performance Applications (ICACCTHPA 2014) (2014)
7. William, L.: Reliability and the Internet Cloud. Massachusetts Institute of Technology (2012)
8. Mainul, M., Lutfor, R., Rasib, K., Munirul, H., Ragib H.: Accountable Proof of Ownership for Data using Timing Element in Cloud Services (2013). Accessed 24 May 2017
9. Han, Y.: Cloud computing: case studies and total costs of ownership. Inf. Technol. Libr. **30**(4), 198 (2011)
10. Jinesh, V.: The Total Cost of (Non) Ownership of Web Applications in the Cloud. Amazon Web Services (2012)
11. Jinesh, V., Jose, P.: The Total Cost of (Non) Ownership of a NoSQL Database Cloud Service. Amazon Web Services (2012)
12. Keith, D.: The Total Cost of Ownership of Cloud and Premise-Based Contact Center Systems. The Total Cost of Ownership of Cloud and Premise-Based Contact Center Systems (TE001-000551) (2013)

13. Yogesh, S., Bahman, J., Weisheng, S., Daniel, S.: Reliability and energy efficiency in cloud computing systems: survey and taxonomy. J. Netw. Comput. Appl. **74**, 66–85 (2016)
14. Ahmed, E.Y.: Exploring cloud computing services and applications. J. Emerg. Trends Comput. Inf. Sci. **3**(6), 838–847 (2012). ISSN 2079-8407
15. Sabahi, F.: Cloud computing reliability, availability and serviceability (RAS): issues and challenges. Int. J. Adv. ICT Emerg. Reg. **4**(2), 12–23 (2011)
16. Le-Quoc, F., Cabanilla, C.: The Top 5 AWS EC2 Performance Problems, Whitepaper. Datadog Inc. (2013)
17. Microsoft: Hardware and Software Requirements for Installation of SQL Server (2017). https://docs.microsoft.com/en-us/sql/sql-server/install/hardware-and-software-requirements-for-installing-sql-server
18. EC2Instances.info: Easy Amazon EC2 Instance Comparison (2017). http://www.ec2instances.info/?selected=m1.large
19. Dell: PowerEdge T30 Mini Tower Server (2017). http://www.dell.com/ng/business/p/poweredge-t30/pd
20. Microsoft: SQL Server Pricing (2017). https://www.microsoft.com/en-us/sql-server/sql-server-2017-pricing
21. AWS: Amazon RDS for MySQL Pricing (2017). https://aws.amazon.com/rds/mysql/pricing/

A Trust-Based Service Self-organizing Model for Cloud Market

Wenjuan Li[1,2(✉)], Jian Cao[1], Jiyi Wu[2], and Keyong Hu[2]

[1] Computer Science and Technology,
Shanghai Jiao Tong University, Shanghai 200240, China
Liellie@163.com, cao-jian@sjtu.edu.cn
[2] Key Lab of E-Business, Hangzhou Normal University,
Hangzhou 310036, China
CloudLab@aliyun.com, 438334589@qq.com

Abstract. In view of the incomplete cloud market model and related mechanisms, and also the poor performance of cloud against malicious and false service, combined with the theory of self-organization system, multi-agent technology and trust, this paper introduced a trust-enabled three-tier cloud market model. The theory of self-organization system can well describe the dynamic relationship between inter-entity in the cloud service market, because it ensures the autonomy and intelligence of the market entities, and relies on the autonomous cooperation between them to adapt to the continuous changing, uncertain and open cloud environment. The implementation of market behavior by intelligent agents instead of cloud entities, realizes the decentralization and parallelization of service processing. In addition, trust factor is introduced into the model construction process in order to improve the ability of cloud market against malicious behavior. Finally, simulation experiments show that the new model can accelerate the differentiation and balance of cloud service market and improve the success rate of transactions.

Keywords: Cloud market model · Trust mechanism
Multi-agent technology · Self-organization

1 Introduction

Cloud computing is an Internet based platform for sharing all kinds of resources at different levels [1]. The remarkable features of cloud include full virtualization, resource sharing, low-cost on-demand services, and anytime, anywhere fast access, etc.

As a commercial market providing services, cloud entities will form a variety of complex relationships because of service transactions. A fully functional cloud service model needs to be regulated by market mechanisms. Many researchers proposed market-oriented cloud computing services. Buyya et al. [2] proposed a three-tier cloud computing market framework. Song et al. [3] introduced the concept of cloud service market intermediaries. Do et al. [4] introduced the Nash equilibrium theory into the service selection process and helped the users find the most suitable service providers

© Springer International Publishing AG 2017
G. Wang et al. (Eds.): SpaCCS 2017 Workshops, LNCS 10658, pp. 241–250, 2017.
https://doi.org/10.1007/978-3-319-72395-2_23

through the two-stage price game between cloud users and service providers; Xiaolong et al. [5] proposed an auction and trust combined cloud resource allocation and pricing strategy.

The above mechanisms tried to enable cloud to operate in a market-oriented manner. But there are still many challenges in building an efficient cloud service market. According to the market theory, market is a self-organized system, and the interaction between market entities is a dynamic and self-adaptive process. Cloud markets are in a state of chaos in the beginning, and with the continuous market transactions, will ultimately achieve the stability and balance. However, the traditional cloud service strategies often overlook the autonomy and intelligence of the market subject, and adopt the centralized control mode.

This paper introduces the concept of self-organization system into cloud service market, which means decentralizing the process of services, give more independence and intelligence to cloud entities and rely on their own abilities to adapt to the continuous changing, uncertain and open cloud environment. In order to make cloud entities have the ability of autonomy, we use agent [6–10] in replace of them to implement market behaviors.

As a commercial business model, there are likely to be some unusual circumstances in cloud, such as some service providers don't provide services in accordance with the declared SLA, a very small amount of malicious nodes, for the interests of the group, conspiracy or to provide false recommendations. Thus users and providers should have the identify ability. So, the self-organizing cloud service market model still needs to solve the credibility problem.

This paper proposes a trust-enabled self-organizing cloud market model. Through the combination of self-organizing system and agent technology, cloud entities are given the ability of autonomy, sociality, reactivity, and initiative and realize the self-organization and dynamic evolution of cloud services. Trust mechanism helps cloud entities identify the unreliable services or resources while improving the success rate and customer satisfaction.

The rest of paper is organized as follows. Section 2 describes the related work. Trust-based self-organizing cloud market model is proposed and specified in Sect. 3. And the experiment and analysis are presented in Sect. 4. Finally, conclusions and future work are stated in Sect. 5.

2   Related Work

Trust is a mechanism to solve the reputation and reliability problems in the open environment. The significance of trust management is to provide a security decision framework which is suitable for web application system's open, distributed and dynamic characteristics. In recent years, researchers have made great achievements in the research of trust [11–17]. Trust has also been used in the cloud environment, such as trust-based cloud task scheduling algorithm and trust enabled service selection strategies [18–20].

Agent is generally considered as a computational model, a special software entity that can automatically represent its owner's behavior to achieve its owner's goals.

When multiple Agents are organized into application system of a specific areas according to a certain mechanism, we call it multi-Agent system (MAS). In the highly distributed autonomous cloud environment, all entities involved in the transactions are highly distributed and collaborative. Agents can be naturally applied to represent the entities of cloud market. Some scholars have integrated agent with cloud computing, for example, professor Sim [6, 7] from University of Kent proposed a multi-agent system for cloud resource management. In this paper, we define agent as a distributed software entity that can interact with cloud computing environments and with a certain intelligence and autonomous capabilities, play a specific role in the cloud transaction model (Fig. 1).

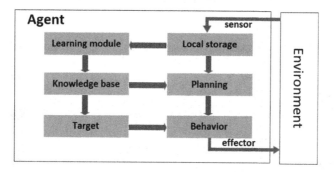

Fig. 1. Agent concept

3   A Trust-Based Self-organizing Model for Cloud Market

Despite the differences in the realization technology of cloud in different service providers, doubtlessly the techniques have become increasingly mature. However, as a kind of commercial solutions, the underlying business architectures of cloud computing is still not perfect especially due to the lack of built-in business management strategies.

Therefore, not surprisingly, the concept of market oriented cloud computing model has been proposed [2]. Under this concept, market mechanisms are designed and combined with service provisioning, service billing and virtual machine scheduling. Cloud is becoming a real market.

In order to model the cloud market and also provides system structure to support cloud market, our model is based on multi-agent framework in which each agent represents an entity in this market.

Like any real market, some service providers may exaggerate the effects of the service quality. Moreover, fraudulent behavior cannot be avoided with the development of cloud market. Trust is a simple and safe alternative of security strategy in the distributed network environment. Therefore, trust is also added to the framework.

3.1 System Framework

The framework consists of three main components, i.e., user agent, service provider agent and broker agent (See Fig. 2). User agents are on behalf of users to submit service requests according to their service requirements, select services, use services and evaluate service quality. Provider agents are on behalf of service providers, organize resources and provide services to users after receiving the service requests. Since there are large quantity of users and service providers in cloud market, which lead to low efficiency of service match-making. Broker agents play the role of intermediary and coordinator between users and service providers. Broker agents receive user agents' requests, calculate the credibility of provider agents and user agents, and recommend provider agents with high credibility to user agents.

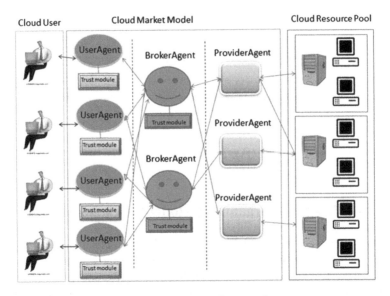

Fig. 2. The system framework

Furthermore, we add trust modules to user agents and broker agents. Trust mechanisms will be integrated into the market behaviors of the corresponding agents. The actions relating to trust mechanism in user agents include: (1) a user agent conducts a trust assessment of each transaction, and (2) records the credibility of transaction partners into the local database. Later, a user agent only sends service demands to those broker agents whose trust value exceeds the specific threshold. Accordingly, the actions relating of trust mechanism in broker agents includes: (1) a broker agent evaluates the trust value every time when it interacts with user agents or provider agents, and (2) it records the data in the local database. A broker agent only recommends the providers to user agent whose reputation values are higher than the threshold. Broker agents only want to maintain trading relationships with credible user agents and provider agents.

3.2 Agent Interaction Protocols

Initially, a user agent sends a service request for certain cloud services to its familiar broker agents. The broker agents then recommend providers from their provider agent lists. Then the user agent sends an "accept" message to the most suitable broker and "reject" to the others after selection. The broker agent who receives the "accept" message will forward the service request to the corresponding provider. If the provider agrees to provide the service, broker will reply a confirmation message to the user agent and thus a transaction channel is constructed between the user agent and the provider. After the service invocation, the user agent and the provider agent will send evaluation feedback to the broker (Fig. 3).

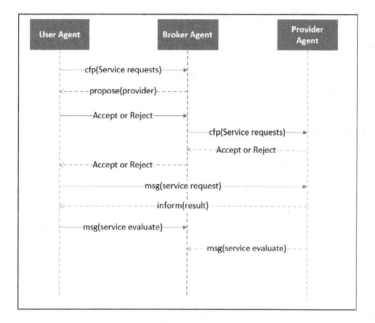

Fig. 3. Service matching process

3.3 Trust Management Strategy

Trust can be calculated by following equation:

$$T = \alpha T_d + \beta T_r \tag{1}$$

where T_d and T_r refer to the direct trust and the recommended trust respectively, α and β represent the weights of the above two kinds of trust.

In order to simplify the process of trust management, the calculation of direct trust in TSLAM is based on the weighted average of historical data. The following concepts are defined to support trust update:

- Transaction sliding window (*TSW*): it records the results of several recent transactions between entities. In the model, the size of the transaction sliding window is fixed, denoted as *TWLength*.
- Window refresh cycle (*WRC*): it means the update cycle of transaction window *TSW*. The sliding window will be periodically refreshed to delete expired transaction records, because the trading history too long ago has no reference value for the current trust decision.
- Trust attenuation function: it represents the trust value (or degree) attenuation over time.

With the lapse of time and the generation of the new transaction data, the credibility of history trust will continue to decay. According to evidence theory, the following Eq. (2) is used to express trust decay over time.

$$T_{ij} = T_{0j}e^{-\lambda \Delta t} \qquad (2)$$

where T_{ij} means the trust value entity i to entity j, T_{0j} means the initial trust, Δt means the time interval between the two moments, and $\Delta t = T_{ij} - T_{0j}$.

4 Experiments and Analysis

4.1 Experiment Design

The experiments were based on the famous Multi-Agent framework JADE [21] and deployed on the Ali-Cloud server ECS, configured with 4 core CPU, 16G memory and operating system Windows Server2012 64bit Chinese Edition.

There are many types of cloud services, such as cloud storage services, cloud virtual machine services, cloud database services, and so on, provided by different providers and have different performance attributes. The differentiation process of the cloud service market is a very complex multi-dimensional learning process. However, for the simulation system, different type of cloud service and the related attributes are only the different set of multi-dimensional vectors, meaning that the experimental principle and effect are the same despite of the service type. Therefore, for the sake of simplicity, the cloud database service is chosen as the experiment object, thus, other kinds of services can refer to the results.

We collected and sorted out the SLA in the cloud database services of Tencent Cloud and Ali Cloud. And the SLA of Tencent and Ali both include ten categories of properties: the durability of data storage, data destructibility, data mobility, data privacy, the right to know, data reviewability, business function, business availability, business resource allocation capabilities and fault recovery capabilities.In this paper, five attributes are chosen to describe the performance of cloud database services, including service prices(price), memory(ram), storage(space), service response time (rt) and reliability (reliable). In the experiments, each dimension attribute value came from the performance of cloud providers in the real platform and through normalization the range of each dimension attribute was limited within 1–100.

The initialization phase of the simulation experiment generated a series of user agents, broker agents and provider agents. Among them, each user agent had its own unique preference, therefore, its service requests were generated randomly on the basis of the preference. Each provider agent also had above five properties, in accordance with the performance differences which were randomly assigned values within 1 to 100. User agents at regular intervals (in this experiments per minute) produced a new service request, and they only told broker agent part of their demands, say, only three dimensions of the accurate demands, namely using semi open mode. However when the transactions were finished, the service satisfaction was evaluated according to the complete service demands. So as for broker agents, they did not know the exact user service preference, and had to sum up and learn in the long run after a number of services.

In order to verify the performance of the model, the experiments were conducted to test in the dual role of trust and broker, whether or not the success ratio and user satisfaction can be improved, also whether or not cloud market can evolve faster.

4.2 Results and Analysis

In the model, trust mechanism is mainly used to find the "bad" trading entities. Here, "bad" or "malicious" indicates such behaviors as providers do not provide services in accordance with the quality of declared, do not respond in a timely manner caused by congestion, and false recommendation, etc. Brokers gradually learn users' service preferences, determine the market positioning, and accelerate the market differentiation. In order to better analyze the efficiency, several models were compared below.

The performances of the following five strategies were compared: (1) the new proposed model in this paper (Proposed model), (2) the cloud trading model based on agent proposed in [8] (G&Sim model), and (3) the price priority cloud trading model based on Multi-Agent platform (Price model), (4) the performance priority cloud

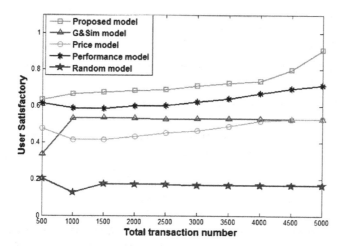

Fig. 4. Empirical result of user satisfactory under different strategies

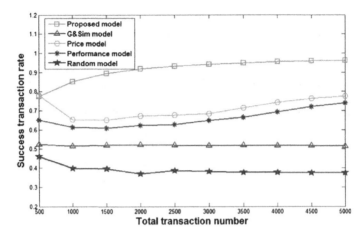

Fig. 5. Empirical result of transaction success rate under different strategies

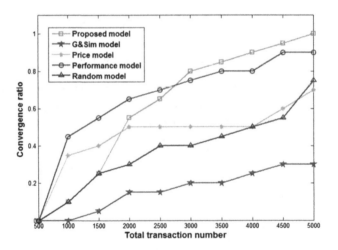

Fig. 6. Empirical result of convergence speed under different strategies

trading model based on Multi-Agent platform (Performance model) and (5) random trading model (Random model).

Figures 4, 5 and 6 show the experimental results of the five different strategies. The horizontal coordinate represents the total number of transactions. Figure 4 is a reflection of the change curve of user satisfaction, Fig. 5 reflects the variation of transaction success rate and Fig. 6 shows the change curve of market convergence ratio (the volatility stability of broker in a very small range). By processing, the results of the experimental data were limited within 0–1.

From the experimental results, we can see that the transaction success rate and the user satisfaction of the proposed model are higher than the other models. Among them, the random trade model has the worst effect, which indicates that the free market is chaotic and inefficient. In addition, although there is no trust and learning mechanisms in the other models, with the increasing number of transactions, the transaction success rate and customer satisfaction will gradually increase, despite the pace of ascension slower than the new model. It can be explained by the fact that learning mechanisms do exist in the fundamental layer of the traditional markets which are gained through the numerous direct exchanges and transactions between consumers and producers, although this process is very slow. Thus, the conclusion is obvious: trust-based self-organizing mechanism improves the efficiency of the cloud services market, and accelerates the market differentiation and evolution.

5 Conclusion

This paper presented a novel cloud market model based on multi-agent platform and trust mechanism. The new model used smart agents to replace the behaviors and targets of the different entities in cloud market, constructed a three-layered cloud trading structure, improved the efficiency of the market, accelerated the market differentiation. The introduction of trust mechanism helped cloud entity better identify the honest and dishonest candidates in the market, thus improved the probability of successful transactions. The simulation experiments based on JADE platform verified the validity of the model.

There are still a lot of further work need to do. For example how can brokers learn their customers' real service preferences and provide on-demand services; in the market competition, how do brokers differentiate; how much system management cost will be brought about by the trust mechanism, etc.

Acknowledgments. This work was supported by a grant from National Natural Science Foundation of China Nos. 61402144, 61472253 and 61702151", Zhejiang Provincial Natural Science Foundation No. LY17E070004 and the Research Project for Department of Education of Zhejiang Province No. Y201635438.

References

1. Liu, P.: Cloud Computing, 3rd edn. Electronic Industry, Beijing (2015)
2. Buyya, R., Yeo, C.S., Venugopal, S.: Market-oriented cloud computing: vision, hype, and reality for delivering it services as computing utilities. In: Proceedings of 10th IEEE International Conference on High Performance Computing and Communications, pp. 5–13 (2008)
3. Song, B., Hassan, M.M., Huh, E.N.: A novel cloud market infrastructure for trading service. In: Proceedings of International Conference on Computational Science and Its Applications, pp. 44–50 (2009)
4. Do, C.T., Tran, N.H., Tran, D.H., Pham, C., et al.: Toward service selection game in a heterogeneous market cloud computing. In: Proceedings of the 2015 IFIP/IEEE International Symposium on Integrated Network Management (IM2015), pp. 44–52 (2015)

5. Ma, X., Liu, L.: Research of multiple cloud computing resource allocation and pricing based on the combinatorial double auction and trust. Sci. Technol. Eng. **15**(1), 100–105 (2015)

6. Sim, K.M.: Agent-based cloud commerce. In: Proceedings of the IEEE International Conference on Industrial Engineering and Engineering Management, pp. 717–721 (2006)

7. Sim, K.M.: Towards complex negotiation for cloud economy. In: Bellavista, P., Chang, R.-S., Chao, H.-C., Lin, S.-F., Sloot, P.M.A. (eds.) GPC 2010. LNCS, vol. 6104, pp. 395–406. Springer, Heidelberg (2010). https://doi.org/10.1007/978-3-642-13067-0_42

8. Gutierrez-Garcia, J.O., Sim, K.M.: Agent-based cloud bag-of-tasks execution. J. Syst. Softw. **104**, 17–31 (2015)

9. Son, S., Sim, K.M.: Adaptive and similarity-based tradeoff algorithms in a price-timeslot-QoS negotiation system to establish cloud SLAs. Inf. Syst. Front. **17**(3), 565–589 (2015)

10. Sim, K.M.: Complex and concurrent negotiations for multiple interrelated e-markets. IEEE Trans. Cybern. **43**, 230–245 (2013)

11. Li, X., Gui, X.: Cognitive model of dynamic trust forecasting. J. Softw. **21**(1), 163–176 (2010)

12. Pan, J., Xu, F., Lv, J.: Reputation-based recommender discovery approach for service selection. J. Softw. **21**(2), 388–400 (2010)

13. Hu, J., Wu, Q., Zhou, B., Liu, J.: Robust feedback credibility-based distributed P2P trust model. J. Softw. **20**(10), 2885–2898 (2009)

14. Shouxin, W., Li, Z., Hesong, L.: Evaluation approach of subjective trust based on cloud model. J. Softw. **21**(6), 1341–1352 (2010)

15. Juan, D.: Simulation of algorithm for P2P network node trust path optimization. Comput. Simul. **31**(2), 362–365 (2014)

16. Qiao, L., Hui, H., Binxing, F., Hongli, Z., et al.: Awareness of network group Anomalous behaviors based on network trust. Chin. J. Comput. **37**(1), 1–14 (2014)

17. Xiaolan, X., Liang, L., Peng, Z.: Trust model based on double incentive and deception detection for cloud computing. J. Electron. Inf. Technol. **34**(4), 812–817 (2012)

18. Duan, K.R., Zhang, G.X.: Multi-objective immuse system algorithm for task scheduling in cloud computing. J. Comput. Appl. **36**(2), 324–329 (2016)

19. Ni, Z.W., Li, R.R., Fang, Q.H., Pang, S.S.: Optimization of cloud task scheduling based on discrete artificial bee colony algorithm. J. Comput. Appl. **36**(1), 107–112, 121 (2016)

20. Zhang, H.W., Wei, B., Wang, J.D., He, J.J.: Cloud resource scheduling method based on estimation of distribution shuffled frog leaping algorithm. Appl. Res. Comput. **31**(11), 3225–3233 (2014)

21. Jade Company: JADE Document (2017). http://jade.tilab.com/

A Reliable Resource Scheduling for Network Function Virtualization

Daoqiang Xu[1], Yefei Li[2], Ming Yin[3], Xin Li[4(✉)], Hao Li[5], and Zhuzhong Qian[5]

[1] State Grid Jiangsu Electric Power Company, Nanjing 210000, China
13851759165@139.com
[2] Jiang Su Frontier Electric Technology Co. Ltd., Nanjing 210000, China
imliyf@163.com
[3] State Grid Nanjing Power Supply Company, Nanjing 210000, China
13605146644@139.com
[4] Nanjing University of Aeronautics and Astronautics, Nanjing 211106, China
lics@nuaa.edu.cn
[5] State Key Laboratory for Novel Software Technology,
Nanjing University, Nanjing 210023, China
qzz@nju.edu.cn

Abstract. Network function virtualization (NFV) is designed to reduce high cost of the hardware deployment and maintenance, which will be of great importance in the future resource management. NFV makes it possible for general servers to realize fast deployment of network functions, namely virtual network function (VNF), to achieve on-demand requests. The service request is generally composed of a sequence of VNFs, which is defined as a service chain. Although one node (server) only run one VNF at a time, the VNF could be shared with several VNF chains. How to deploy VNF and share VNF to achieve high usage of both computing and bandwidth resource is a challenge. In this paper, we present the VNF request model and the formal definition of the VNF deployment problem. Then, we investigate the VNF reuse and deployment problem, and propose a greedy strategy to deploy VNFs, so that the system could effectively offer a reliable VNF service. Simulations show that this VNF deployment schema could effectively improve the resource usage compared with other classic algorithms.

Keywords: Network function virtualization · Resource management
VNF deployment · Reliable method · Virtual Network Embedding

1 Introduction

With the rapid development of Internet and the increase of network function, more and more middlebox will be deployed in the network out of technology requirement and function requirement. Middlebox which is playing a crucial role in current network can provide plentiful network functions from security aspects, such as Firewalls, collision detection and etc.; to service aspects, such as cache,

G. Wang et al. (Eds.): SpaCCS 2017 Workshops, LNCS 10658, pp. 251–260, 2017.
https://doi.org/10.1007/978-3-319-72395-2_24

server Proxy and etc., which make hardware and deployment cost much too high. It takes hardware that requires a lot of specialization and very complicated process to deploy network middlebox. This means that hardware-based middlebox may result in significant human resources and physical resources costs, meanwhile reducing the flexibility of the network system.

Network function virtualization (NFV) aims to separate the network function from the underlying proprietary hardware and make software function running in the more general hardware instead of function running in a specialized hardware. By separating network function from specialized hardware, the deployment of physical device will be quite flexible, while the cost of redeployment of network function will be reduced by changing and repairing software instead of changing hardware device. In NFV, virtual network function (VNF) offers the basic service instead of traditional middlebox.

Since the function of single VNF is limited, the user request is often composed of several VNFs and the dataflow goes through these VNFs in a certain order, which is named as service chain. When a new service chain request is submitted, the system need to allocate new nodes (servers) to deploy VNFs and reserve related bandwidth to construct a VNF path for the coming dataflow. Generally, one node could only run one VNF at a time, while the running VNF could be shared with several VNF service chains. That is, for a new coming service chain request, we may map the VNFs to some exist VNF nodes where run the same functions. However, although this resource sharing improves computing resource utilization, it may also increase the bandwidth cost. This is because the exist running VNFs for one service chain may located in different nodes that is far away. And there is also capacity limitation for VNF sharing, we could not overload the VNF nodes. Consequently, how to allocate resources to an incoming VNF service chain request to effectively offer a reliable VNF service, is a challenge problem.

In this paper, we firstly present the VNF service chain request model and formally define the reliable resource allocation for VNF service chain. We also deeply investigate the resource sharing mechanism and propose dynamic resource sharing schema to increase the resource sharing. And then, we propose the resource scheduling mechanism, which includes the VNF reuse and VNF deployment. The simulations show that this mechanism could effectively allocate resources and have a good performance compared with other classic algorithms.

The remainder of this paper is organized as follows. We introduce the related work in Sect. 2. The problem formulation and VNF scheduling mechanism are proposed in Sects. 3 and 4. Finally we conclude our paper in Sect. 5.

2   Related Work

Derived from *Virtual Network Embedding problem* (VNE) [5] that mapping *Virtual Network* (VN) to the *Substrate Network* (SN) with guaranteed *Quality of Service* (QoS) [7], the VNF deployment problem has been proposed to be a important research challenge [9]. A strategy calculating a new VN embedding solution efficiently when some nodes failed was proposed in Shahriar et al. [10], and Cankaya et al. [1] proposed a VNE algorithm for link protection.

There are some existing work about the VNF deployment problem. Wang et al. [11] proposed a strategy using preplanned VNF deployment solutions to minimize network communication cost. An algorithm consolidating adjacent VNFs to one server was proposed to reduce the resource cost in the network in Ye et al. [12]. Kuo et al. [8] designed a two-step VNF deployment strategy, and argued that taking both server resources and link resources into consideration leading to a better performance in VNF deployment. VNF deployment was divided into two NP-hard subproblems in Cohen et al. [2], and authors designed strategies related to the subproblems to solve the deployment problem. For reliable issue, Hmaity et al. [6] concluded 3 redundancy models of VNF deployment, while Fan et al. [4] minimized the total resources cost by consolidating VNF redundant backups. Besides, in response to dynamic traffic of NFV, [3,13] proposed some online VNF deployment to implement reconfigurations when request traffics change.

3   Background and Problem Statement

3.1   Network Function Virtualization

In NFV, hardware and software are separated, every network function is independent from the physical environment. A physical network can be modeled as an undirected graph $G^s = (V^s, E^s)$, where V^s is a set of nodes and E^s is a set of edges, while v^s represents a node and e^s represents an edge. $Rest(e^s)$, e^s is the rest bandwidth capacity of an edge e^s, $Rest(v^s)$, v^s is the residual computing power of a node v^s. If the rest bandwidth capacity of an edge is insufficient, no more data transmission could be through this link; and if the rest computing power of a node is insufficient, no more VNF could be deployed on it. Figure 1 shows a naive physical network with only six nodes, where the number in the node represents the residual computing power of a node, and the number on the edge represents the rest bandwidth capacity of an edge. An update will be done after a deployment of a new requirement to the network.

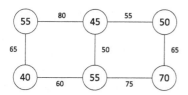

Fig. 1. Pyhsical network

SFC R1

Fig. 2. Service chains

A complete network function is often composed of several VNFs in a certain order, named service chain. Similar to the definition of physical network, a service chain is defined as $R_i = (r_1^i, r_2^i, r_3^i, r_n^i)$, where r_j^i represents the jth network function in the ith service chain. $|R_i|$ is the number of thevirtual network function in the service chain. A directed subgraph $G_{R_i}^t = (V_{R_i}^t, E_{R_i}^t)$, where $V_{R_i}^t = (v_{R_1^i}^t, v_{R_2^i}^t, v_{R_3^i}^t, ..., v_{R_j^i}^t)$ is a set of the nodes that service chain R_i passes, $E_{R_i}^t = (e_{R_1^i}^t, e_{R_2^i}^t, e_{R_3^i}^t, ..., e_{R_j^i}^t)$. In addition, every VNF has bandwidth requirement to transfer data as well as computing capacity. $Cp(r_j^i)$ is the required computing capacity of the jth network function in the ith service chain, bandwidth(r_j^i) is the requiring bandwidth between jth network function and $(j+1)$th network function in the ith service chain. Figure 2 shows that four function nodes in service chain $R1$ require a chain of computing capacity of $(40, 20, 15, 25)$ and bandwidth of $(40, 35, 25)$.

Since different VNF is deployed for different purposes (e.g. network address translate, firewall, etc.), different VNF requires different bandwidth resources and computing resources. For example, an NAT will not require much computing resources, while an IDS requires a lot. In this paper, we define π_{v,v_1} as the path between node v and node v_1, $|\pi_{v,v_1}|$ is the length of the path. Map$(R_{i,j})$ is the physical node mapped to the jth function in the R_i service chain, and obviously $Map(R_{i,j})/inV_{R_i}^t$.

3.2   Problem Statement

The request of VNF is represented as service chains, as defined above. For a service provider, finding an optimal deployment plan for multiple service chains is a challenge problem. When a VNF request arrives, system firstly find out whether it can be accepted by the rest resources. Generally, a node (i.e. sever) can be mapped to only one VNF function, but can be shared to multiple service chains if they have the same function request in the chain. The formal goal of the deploying is defined as followed.

$$maximize : N_R^s$$
$$minimize : Cost(G^s, R, M)$$

In this equation, N_R^s is the number of the requirement in R which can be accepted by network G^s, Cost(G^s, R, M) is the cost of R in the network G^s.

In this paper, we consider two aspects of problem, to reduce the cost of computing resources and to reduce the cost of bandwidth resources. the process is divided into two parts:

1. Deployment of functions: optimal nodes set will be selected to load all the required VNF because virtual functions of different nodes in the physical network are different. A better deployment plan will promote the network efficiency, and make the deployment easier.
2. Selection of path: after selection of nodes, a proper path between nodes is also needed to make one node corresponding with another and achieve a splendid working efficiency.

For an incoming VNF chain requests, we need to map all the VNFs of the service chain and construct a physical path to link all the nodes. Since we can

Table 1. Denotations

G^s	a physical network
V^s	a set of nodes
E^s	a set of edges
$Rest(e^s)$	the rest bandwidth capacity of an edge e^s
$G^t_{R_i}$	a directed subgraph
r^i_j	the requiring bandwidth between jth network function and (j+1)th network function in the ith service chain
$Map(R_{i,j})$	the physical node mapped to the jth function in the R_i service chain
$p^t h$	a threshold value
$p^{R_i}_{v_i}$	the floating possibility of the service chain R_i who requires the resources of node v_i
bandwidth(r^i_j)	the requiring bandwidth between jth network function and (j+1)th network function in the ith service chain
$Cp(r^i_j)$	the requiring computing capacity of the jth network function in the ith service chain

reuse VNFs that already deployed in the substrate network, we may have two choices for any VNF.

1. Select a new node where no VNF is deployed.
2. Select a rest-computing-power-enough node where a same VNF has already been deployed.

It is non-trivial to construct the mapping plan for all the VNFs in a service chain to have the best performance, since choosing new nodes to deploy VNFs cost computing resources while reusing VNFs may cost more bandwidth. For example, a service chain R_i includes 3 VNF A, B and C, Fig. 3 shows the substrate network, where a, b and c are 3 nodes without any VNFs, while d, e and f are deployed VNF A, B and C respectively. Thus, we can deploy A, B and C again to node a, b and c, and the link cost is bandwidth(a) + bandwidth(b). But if we reuse A, B and C from node d, e and f, the cost is bandwidth(a) * 2 + bandwidth(b) * 2.

Furthermore, the sharing node has the capacity constraints, we can not map all the VNF to one node which may cause performance decline. In previous works, the resource requirement of VNF is always fixed when the VNF request is submitted. In this paper, we divide the resource requirement into two parts: one is basic (fixed) resource requirement and one is dynamic part with the possibility p, which is defined as a three tuple. For a VNF r^i_k, the tuple(r^i_k) $<basic^k_i, variable^k_i, p^k_i>$ presents the resource requirement, where $basic^k_i$ is the basic resource and $variable^k_i$ is the resource with possibility p^k_i. In the Fig. 4, the basic requirement of $R_1.a$ is 8 and the dynamic requirement of a is 4 and the possibility is 0.3.

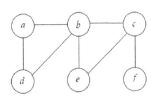

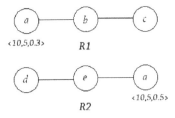

Fig. 3. A possible physical network model   **Fig. 4.** Two possible service chains

If two VNFs are mapping to one node (i.e. two VNF requests share one node), if $RestCp(v_i) \geq \sum_i^j basic_i^k + variable_i^k$, the second requirement is accepted. If the condition is not satisfied, the deployment will not be refused directly yet. $p_{v_i}^{R_i}$ is the floating possibility of the service chain R_i who requires the resources of node v_i, given a threshold value $p^t h$, if the possibility of two service chains requiring the resources at the same time below the threshold value, what is:

$$p_{v_i}^{R_i} * p_{v_j}^{R_j} < p^t h$$

As the figure shows, chain R_1 and R_2 have the same VNF a. so they can share the nodes. They want to be deployed in a virtual node whose computing power is 25. For the given tuple(r_1^1) <10, 5, 0.3> and tuple(r_2^2) <10, 5, 0.5>, and func(r_1^1)=func(r_2^2), suppose $p^t h = 0.2$ in this network. Since,

$$0.3 \times 0.5 = 0.15 \leq 0.2$$

The collision possibility is lower than threshold, so the VNF a in both R_1 and R_2 may map to this node and share the resource.

4   VNF Deployment Mechanism for Dynamic Requirements

Reuse VNF that has already been deployed could save computing resources, while deploying VNFs along with a shortest path will consume the least bandwidth resources. In this paper, we define VNF reuse factor x to represent the reused VNFs in a service chain and define $l(x)$ as the length of the edges when reusing x VNFs.

4.1   Finding the Reuse Factor x

For a certain service chain, it is difficult to find its optimal reuse factor. Assume that there are infinite same service chains R_i, find a x and $l(x)$ to maximum the number of the capacity of R_i. then it is considered to be a optimal plan, the aim is:

Definition 1 (Reuse Factor). *Given an infinite same service chains R_i, find a x and $l(x)$ such that the number of the capacity of R_i is maximized.*

$$\max \quad n$$

$$s.t. \quad x \in \{0, 1, 2, ...\bar{x}\}$$

$$nTrans_i l(x) \leq \sum_{e}^{e \in E} Res(e) \tag{1}$$

$$n(|S_i| - x) \leq \sum_{v}^{v \in V} Res(v)$$

The first constraint represents the range of x. Intuitively, $\bar{x}=|R_i|$,because the reuse nodes number is certainly lower than the function number of the chain. obviously, a lower $\bar{x}$ value can be accepted because not all VNFs in the chain can be reused if some VNF is not been deployed in the network or the VNF is already overloaded. R_i' is the subchain in R_i that has the possibility to reuse, thus, $\bar{x}=|R_i'|$. The second constraint is that for every link in the R_i, the requirement must be lower than the bandwidth resources. The third constraint is for the computing power. We may try all the possible x, and choose the one that gets the maximum n.

4.2 VNF Deployment Strategy Based on Greedy

The greedy search algorithm described in this section consider both bandwidth and computing resource. The basic steps of deployment is as follows.

1. Find the reused function x for an incoming VNF chain.
2. Divide a service chain into $(x+1)$ subchains.
3. Greedily find an optimal deployment for each subchain, and finally deploy the entire VNF service chain.

In this algorithm, line 1 sorts all the incoming requests and handles the service chains according to priority. Line 3 to 5 find the accessible physical nodes and Line 6 to 11 select the optimal physical nodes for every VNF with some greedy strategy, and select an optimal path p_j, and G is updated. Here, the greedy strategy is to find the nodes with the largest flow bandwidth and computing resource. The distance between possible reused node will be controlled and costs of links will be reduced as a result of sorting the service chains by VNF reused number. How to deal with the $(x+1)$ subchains where no VNFs could be reused. These subchains may fill in one of the 4 possible situations: no reuse VNF at all, both begin and end nodes are reused VNF, one of the end node is reused VNF node.

As shown in Fig. 5, function c and e have nodes A, B and C, D respectively. Thus, the chain is divided into three subchains, a-b-c, c-d-e, and e-f. For a-b-c, this is a subchain that has one reused VNF. The algorithm will first deal with function c and then deploy a and b. For c-d-e, this is a subchain with two reused VNF nodes, and a shortest path can be found by breadth first search algorithm. For e-f, it is similar to a-b-c.

Algorithm 1. Greedy Deployment Algorithm

Input:

   D:service chains which represent requirements set; G:physical network graph

Output:

   the deployment of D in G; or D refused by G.

 1: sorting(D)
 2: **for** d in D **do**
 3:    **for** each VNF in d **do**
 4:       find the exist VNF nodes in G;
 5:       return as V_i;
 6:    **for** each v in V_i except the last one **do**
 7:       findPath p_j from v_j to v_{j+1};
 8:    **if** p!= NULL **then**
 9:       Add p_j to P;
10:       Update(G);
11:    **else**
12:       return REJECT;
13: **return** P;

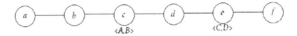

Fig. 5. A possible service chain

4.3   Simulation Results

A deployment model based on different feature networks and random requirements is designed to verify the robustness of the algorithm. Python networkX
is used in the experiment. We set two substrate network topology, one has 300
vertex and 0.1 edge link possibility, the other one has 300 vertex and 0.3 edge
link possibility, which is model randomly by setting the ER relationship is used
to simulate real network environment. Each node has the computing power
resources of 100 and every edge has the bandwidth of 100. 20 kinds of VNF
and its requirement is set here, and about 20 to 120 service function chains
whose length is between 2 and 6 are randomly combined. Bandwidth requirements between VNF functions in every chain are controlled between 20 and 50.
We get the following results by simulations.

   Figures 6 and 7 show that, two ways can not achieve the optimal result and
the network simulated here is a bandwidth-free network, so the effect of the
bandwidth greedy strategy is better than balanced deployment. Compare Fig. 6
with Fig. 7, when the link possibility improves, the result improves obviously. It is
assumed that for more linked network, the distinct between different deployment
algorithm is lower and the successful deployment is more. It is seen that the
success rate is significantly improved by using a resources strategy based on
dynamic requirements, which proves the effectiveness of the strategy to improve
the network efficiency.

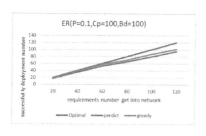

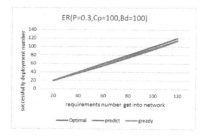

Fig. 6. ER(P=0.1, Cp=100, Bd=100)   **Fig. 7.** ER(P=0.3, Cp=100, Bd=100)

5   Conclusion

This paper investigates VNF service chain deployment problem. We firstly give the formal VNF request model and formalized the resource scheduling problem. And then, we present the VNF scheduling mechanism including finding VNF reuse factor and related resource scheduling algorithm based on greedy strategy. Simulations show that this mechanism works well and achieve better performance compared with other classic resource allocation algorithms.

References

1. Cankaya, H.C., Kim, I., Jue, J., Kong, J., Zhang, Q., Hong, S., Ikeuchi, T., Xie, W., Wang, X.: Availability-guaranteed virtual optical network mapping with selective path protection. In: Optical Fiber Communication Conference, p. W1B.4 (2016)
2. Cohen, R., Lewin-Eytan, L., Naor, J.S., Raz, D.: Near optimal placement of virtual network functions. In: 2015 IEEE Conference on Computer Communications (INFOCOM), pp. 1346–1354. IEEE (2015)
3. Eramo, V., Miucci, E., Ammar, M., Lavacca, F.G.: An approach for service function chain routing and virtual function network instance migration in network function virtualization architectures. IEEE/ACM Trans. Netw. **25**, 2008–2025 (2017)
4. Fan, J., Ye, Z., Guan, C., Gao, X., Ren, K., Qiao, C.: Grep: guaranteeing reliability with enhanced protection in NFV. In: Proceedings of the 2015 ACM SIGCOMM Workshop on Hot Topics in Middleboxes and Network Function Virtualization, pp. 13–18. ACM (2015)
5. Andreas, F., Botero, J.F., Beck, M.T., De Meer, H., Hesselbach, X.: Virtual network embedding: a survey. IEEE Commun. Surv. Tutor. **15**(4), 1888–1906 (2013)
6. Hmaity, A., Savi, M., Musumeci, F., Tornatore, M., Pattavina, A.: Virtual network function placement for resilient service chain provisioning. In: 2016 8th International Workshop on Resilient Networks Design and Modeling (RNDM), pp. 245–252. IEEE (2016)
7. Khan, M.M.A., Shahriar, N., Ahmed, R., Boutaba, R.: Simple: survivability in multi-path link embedding. In: International Conference on Network and Service Management, pp. 210–218 (2016)

8. Kuo, T.W., Liou, B.H., Lin, K.C.J., Tsai, M.J.: Deploying chains of virtual network functions: on the relation between link and server usage. In: The 35th Annual IEEE International Conference on Computer Communications. IEEE INFOCOM 2016, pp. 1–9. IEEE (2016)

9. Mijumbi, R., Serrat, J., Gorricho, J.L., Bouten, N., De Turck, F., Boutaba, R.: Network function virtualization: state-of-the-art and research challenges. IEEE Commun. Surv. Tutor. **18**(1), 236–262 (2015)

10. Shahriar, N., Ahmed, R., Chowdhury, S., Khan, A., Boutaba, R., Mitra, J.: Generalized recovery from node failure in virtual network embedding. IEEE Trans. Netw. Serv. Manag. **PP**(99), 1 (2017)

11. Wang, F., Ling, R., Zhu, J., Li, D.: Bandwidth guaranteed virtual network function placement and scaling in datacenter networks. In: 2015 IEEE 34th International Performance on Computing and Communications Conference (IPCCC), pp. 1–8. IEEE (2015)

12. Ye, Z., Cao, X., Wang, J., Hongfang, Y., Qiao, C.: Joint topology design and mapping of service function chains for efficient, scalable, and reliable network functions virtualization. IEEE Netw. **30**(3), 81–87 (2016)

13. Zhang, B., Hwang, J., Wood, T.: Toward online virtual network function placement in software defined networks. In: 2016 IEEE/ACM 24th International Symposium on Quality of Service (IWQoS), pp. 1–6. IEEE (2016)

On Global Resource Allocation in Clusters for Data Analytics

Daoqiang Xu[1], Yefei Li[2], Songyun Wang[2], Xin Li[3(✉)], and Zhuzhong Qian[4]

[1] State Grid Jiangsu Electric Power Company, Nanjing, China
13851759165@139.com
[2] Jiang Su Frontier Electric Technology Co. Ltd., Nanjing, China
imliyf@163.com, wsy_hi@163.com
[3] Nanjing University of Aeronautics and Astronautics, Nanjing, China
lics@nuaa.edu.cn
[4] State Key Laboratory for Novel Software Technology,
Nanjing University, Nanjing, China
qzz@nju.edu.cn

Abstract. Hadoop YARN is one of the most commonly used frameworks for implementing MapReduce distributed computing model. The current resource allocation modes in YARN are triggered by events, which are executed when every slave sent heartbeat message to the master. In another word, the resource allocation is based on the order of every slave node, rather than the global information. A global resource allocation can achieve a better outcome than the allocation method based on every single node. In reality, resource allocation is a complicated issue and many influencing factors need to be considered. Based on the YARNs existing cluster architecture and allocation mode, this paper designs the mechanism of resource allocation and carries out work schedules to optimize the running time of cluster mainly focuses on network bandwidth and node execution rate. We make an improvement on the basis of the existing algorithm, and propose an algorithm used strategy based on the greedy choice to make resource allocation. We designed an experimental simulation of the operation of the clusters. Compared to the existing resource allocation model, the result shows our algorithm has improved the performance and shortens the execution time for the whole cluster.

Keywords: Hadoop YARN · Data center · Resource allocation
Greedy Algorithm · Data analysis

1 Introduction

With the rapid development of information and technology, especially the mobile Internet and Internet of Thing, we are currently in a time full of information. At the same time after finding that the traditional serial computing method is more and more difficult to support the application problem of computing ability and requirement of computing speed, Parallel Distributed Computing Technology

© Springer International Publishing AG 2017
G. Wang et al. (Eds.): SpaCCS 2017 Workshops, LNCS 10658, pp. 261–270, 2017.
https://doi.org/10.1007/978-3-319-72395-2_25

appears. Parallel computing means a number of instructionsmultiple tasks or multiple data is processed at the same time, MapReduce is the most successful and easiest to use big data parallel processing technology.

YARN is a new Hadoop resource manager [4]. It has a major difference from old Hadoop framework and it is different from the old Hadoop frame. It separates resource management and task scheduling. They are ResourceManager RM and ApplicationMasterAM. The former manage the whole resource scheduling and the latter manages applications and monitor. This change reduce resource consumption. NodeManager is equal to the TaskTracker in old Hadoop. At the same time, YARN also assigns an abstract resource Container and NodeManager monitor it. When AM applies for resource from AM, the returned resource is container.

Cloud Computing is that user-terminal accesses to resources and computed by remote connection. The computing and data are stored in the cloud data center, and then are assigned away. Cloud Computing is able to improve the computing and acess speed. For example, time is necessary for some data. If the data is transported to the cloud, it will result in waste of data timeliness. Some data is on the contrary, so it is a lot of waste to transfer data to the cloud. It can be seen that data schedualing between different data centers is very important. So in recent years, Fog Computing and Edge computing [3,6] are on the basis of the Cloud Computing.

To shorten the entire cluster running time, the paper optimize the cluster resource proportion assigned by data center by the network bandwidth and the node execution rate. Based on the algorithm we know, we design a greedy alloation algorithm considering the former two questions. We make experiment to simulate the cluster running and get the result. From the result, the algorithm we designed optimizes the cluster running time. Conveniently narrativing stored-data units are called data center and we ignore the diferent type between data center.

2   Related Work

Some of the works that already exists are task-oriented resource-aware scheduling for MapReduce. In [7], the authors design and implement a resource-aware scheduler for Hadoop. It couples the progresses of MapTasks and ReduceTasks, utilizing Wait Scheduling for ReduceTasks and Random Peeking Scheduling for MapTasks to jointly optimize the task placement. They use the strong dependence between map tasks and reduce tasks to achieve jointly optimize. And the authors introduce a fine-grained resource-aware Map Reduce scheduler that divides tasks into phases, where each phase has a constant resource usage profile, and performs scheduling at the phase level in [8]. The scheduling can effectively utilize available resources to reduce job execution time even if tasks can have highly varying resource requirements during their lifetime. In [1], the authors present a resource-aware scheduling technique for MapReduce multi-job workloads that aims at improving resource utilization across machines while observing completion time goals.

Data locality and load balancing are two important factors to improve computation efficiency in MapReduce systems for data-intensive computations. In [9], the main objective is to minimize total flowtime of all jobs based on above two factors. The authors design a strict data locality tasks scheduling algorithm for map tasks on map machines and a load balance aware scheduling algorithm for reduce tasks on reduce machines.

As we all know, delay scheduling is a common way to achieve high data locality and system performance. In [5], the authors propose a deadline-enabled delay DLD scheduling algorithm that optimizes job delay decisions according to real-time resource availability and resource competition, while still meets job deadline constraints, system throughput and the original job priority constraints.

Besides, there are other works focus on network congestion. Network traffic is always a most important bottleneck in data-intensive computing and network latency decreases significant performance in data parallel systems. Network bottleneck is caused by network bandwidth and the network speed is much slower than disk data access. In [2], the authors present a locality-aware scheduling algorithm for Hadoop-MapReduce scheduler to solve the network congestion problem.

3 Resource Scheduling for MapReduce Framework

3.1 Problem Background

We consider that each data center is composed of a large Map node and a Reduce node. Each data center initially has a different number of input data and Map node execute the data. After each Map node implementing, the intermediate data is stored in the Map node local cache temporarily. Each Map node needs to transport the local data to all Reduce node. Its own data transimiss doesnt cost time. It is on the contrayIf it transport to non-local data center. It also costs time for each Reduce node to receive data. Each Map node has data uplink bandwidth, Reduce node also has data downlink bandwidth. One case if some nodes downlink bandwidth is small, it will be a long time to receive data. So we must minimize the Reduce task in the node. So we should transferred the data to other data enters during Shuffle stage. The other case, becase of low execution rate, some nodes need to be allocated less Reduce task.

We aim to optimize the total cluster processing time. If the number of input data is determination, so is the number of output data after Map. We can get task allocation proportion about Reduce node and use the proportion to transport data to minimize the total cluster processing time.

3.2 Research Example

The next example only consider the network bandwidth. Assume that there are three data center S_1, S_2 and S_3, and each one has a Map node and Reduce node. The amount of intermediate data and network bandwidth of the three is following (Table 1).

Table 1. Data sheet

	S_1	S_2	S_3
Intermediate data/MB	90	60	60
Uplink bandwidth/MB	10	10	10
Downlink bandwidth/MB	1	10	10

Three Reduce nodes each allocate 1/3 of the task and data. So the proportion is (0.33, 0.33, 0.33). Each node transport 2/3 of local intermediate data, and it receive each 1/3 data of other two nodes. Specific task scheduling and resource allocation is following (Fig. 1).

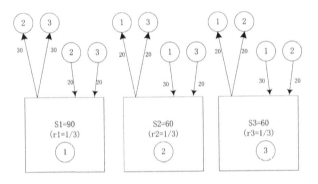

Fig. 1. Scheduling chart

From the above figure we can see that downlink bandwidth of S1 is low and it can be bottleneck node. S1 needs 40 s to receive data if the sum is 40 MB with 1 MB/S bandwidth.In summary, we need improve allocation strategy. From the result, if the proportion is (0.07, 0.465, 0.465), it only needs 6.3 s. So tranporting the bottleneck to other nodes can reduce the running time.

3.3   Problem Description

Given the initial amount of data, uplink bandwidth, downlink bandwidth and speed of processing,we can get different Reduce node task allocation proportion which can minimize the total cluster runing time.

First we should make some assumptions and simplification about the problem. (1) The Map phase doesnt reduce the size of the data. (2) Intermediate data is stored at local after Each Map node processes data. Then it will be transported to another data center from local cache. (3) Each Map node can transport data while it is processing data. (4) After each Reduce node receive all the intermediate data, it can process Reduce task. (5) Not considering that the Reduce node can not receive data when receiving data.

The whole problem can be considered from two stages, namely the Map phase and the Reduce phase. In the Map phase, Map can process data while it is transporting data. So the maximum amount of the two takes the total time spent as a single Map node. In Reduce phase, the Reduce node must wait until it receives all the intermediate data it needs before starting the Reduce task. Furthermore, Reduce node can receive data while Map node is transferring. So both of them can process at the same time. Because the Map node data transmission and Map node data processing are carried out at the same time, Map node data processing, Map node data transmission and Reduce node data reception are carried out at the same time. The maximum of the three and Reduce node data processing time are the total time. We work out the correct proportion to realize the minimum time.

3.4   Problem Formulation

We define some notations here.

S_i represents the amount of intermediate data after processing the data by each Map node.

S represents the sum of intermediate data by all nodes.

K_i represents the speed of each Map node processing.

P_i represents the speed of each Reduce node processing.

U_i represents the uplink bandwidth of Map.

D_i represents the downlink bandwidth of Reduce.

R_i represents the proportion of Reduce nodes data.

T_i represents the total time spent on each data center.

T represents the total time spent on total cluster. $(1 \leq i \leq N)$

Hence, we have: (1) The data processing time of the i-th Map node is $\frac{S_i}{K_i}$. (2) For i-th Map node, its intermediate data is S_i and the proportion is R_i. So the amount of transferring to other data center is $S_i (1-R_i)$. If the rate of uplink bandwidth is larger than the rate of Map node processing, Map node actual upload rate is useless. So the actual rate is min (U_i, K_i). In a summary, for i-th Map node, the transmission time is $\frac{S_i(1-R_i)}{min(U_i,K_i)}$. (3) For i-th Reduce node, the original intermediate data is S_i, so the others is $(S-S_i)$. This nodes proportion is R_i, The amount of transferring to this node is $(S-S_i)*R_i$, In a summary, for i-th Reduce node reception time is $\frac{(S-S_i)R_i}{D_i}$. (4) For i-th Reduce the processing time is $\frac{SR_i}{P_i}$. (5) For one data center, the time = max (Map node processing time , Map node transmission time, Reduce node reception time) + Reduce node processing time , so: $T_i = max(\frac{S_i}{K_i}, \frac{S_i(1-R_i)}{min(U_i,K_i)}, \frac{(S-S_i)R_i}{D_i}) + \frac{SR_i}{P_i}$ $T = maxT_i = max\{max(\frac{S_i}{K_i}, \frac{S_i(1-R_i)}{min(U_i,K_i)}, \frac{(S-S_i)R_i}{D_i}) + \frac{SR_i}{P_i}\}$ For each node, S_i, K_i, U_i, D_i, P_i are constant. Our aim is to find the proportion to make the cluster processing time minimum. It can simplified as:

$A_i = \frac{S_i}{K_i}$

$B_i = \frac{S_i}{min(U_i,K_i)}$

$$C_i = \frac{S - S_i}{D_i}$$
$$E_i = \frac{S}{P_i}$$
$$T = max\{max\,(A_i, B_i\,(1 - R_i),\, C_i R_i) + E_i R_i\}$$

Express in mathematical form:

$$minimize \quad T \tag{1}$$

$$s.t. \quad T = max\{max(A_i, B_i(1 - R_i), C_i R_i) + E_i R_i\}$$

$$\forall i : R_i \geq 0$$

$$\sum_i R_i = 1$$

The R_i for each node should be more than 0. The sum of each node is 1.

Algorithm 1. Greedy Allocation Algorithm

Input: Number of data centers: N; $S_i K_i P_i U_i D_i$ of each data center; Number of copies: K.

Output: Resource allocation ratio: R_i.

1: **for** $i = 0 \to N - 1$ **do**
2:     $R_i = 0$;
3: **for** $k \in K$ **do**
4:     **for** $i \in N$ **do**
5:         $T_i = max(\frac{S_i}{K_i}, \frac{S_i(1 - R_i - 0.01)}{min(U_i, K_i)}, \frac{(S - S_i)(R_i + 0.01)}{D_i}) + \frac{S(R_i + 0.01)}{P_i}$;
6:         Sort all the T_i from high to low;
7:         Choose the maximum T_x and the corresponding x;
8:         $R_x = R_x + 1/K$;
9: Return $(R_1, R_2, \ldots, R_n)$;

3.5 Resource Allocation Algorithm Based on Greedy Strategy

About T expression, it is not easy to make T minimum so we use greedy thoughts to design algorithms. The usual step is: Firstly, We can divide the problem into several sub-questions based on mathematical model. Secondly, work out the sub-question. Lastly, combine the all the local optimal solution. The following is the steps.

The condition is $\sum_i R_i = 1$.

We consider that the unit 1 is divided into many small copies, and the distribution for each of them is sub-question. For example, if we divide unit 1 into k copies, each size is 1/k. ALL the original R_i are 0. So K times after distribution, it satisfies the above expression. We try to distribute 1/k to each R_i. We will get N answers, then sort them and find the minimum. If T_x is the minmum, add 1/k to R_x.

For the above steps we try K times attempt. Each attempt is local optimal solution. We combine them and get the answer. The all steps are based on Greedy

Algorithm so it is named Greedy Allocation Algorithm. There are N data centers and k sub-questions so the algorithm complexity is N^2*k. The ablove algorithm spends a little for small cluster.

The pseudocode is shown in Algorithm 1.

For above pseudocode, we need input the number of data center N and S_i, K_i, P_i, U_i, D_i. It output the result R_i. For line 1–3 make R_i being zero. The next are K cycles. For line 5–10 it work out the minimum and add $1/k$ to R_x. For line 12 there is the result.

4   Experimental Design and Result Analysis

Firstly, we will introduce how to realize Simulation of YARN Clusters by programming. Then it is how do we design experiment. Lastly, we will show the algorithm promotion.

4.1   Programming Implementation

We use a program to simulate the process in which multiple machines are running, assign tasks to these machines, observe the effects of the simulation.

We use Java multithreading to simulate the operation of multiple data center of YARN. A thread is on behalf of the Map node or the Reduce node in the process of processing data or transferring/receiving data.

The nodes are defined as public class. Different nodes are different node class objects and the execution of different threads changes the data inside these objects. At the same time, We use Java thread communication to simulate the process of data transmission in different data centers. For example, a Map node thread processing makes Map node data less and Reduce node data is on the contrary.

We define a function to execute Greedy Allocation algorithm. After it receives some parameters, it can figure out the allocation proportion R_1, R_2, R_3, ..., R_n and it can transfer them to the port of each thread Runnable. Each thread execute in using each parameters. The all cluster work as it.

4.2   Simulation Setting

The experiment use three kinds of allocations to analyze the result. They are fair allocation, only consider the allocation of network bandwidth and Greedy Allocation Algorithm. The three types of allocation determine different R_i. At last there will be three T and we will get the result.

First we should understand some problem.

(1) By default we consider that a data center is made up of a big Map node and Reduce node. The number of Map node or Reduce node stands for the number of data center. The experiment we set three Map nodes and three Reduce nodes as three data centers.

(2) Set bottleneck node to highlight this problem. We can set a random data set.
(3) To simplify the problem, when a node cant execute at once we can consider the speed of processing for Reduce node too slow. Then set Reduce node slower speed than before.
(4) Actually when a data center dont have enough resource the data can be transferred to neighbor. We can consider that the cluster have one more data center. It has no effect to our experiment.

4.3 Experimental Results

For the case that there exist node(s) with the network transmission as the bottleneck. Our expectation is that the allocation that based on bandwidth and Greedy Allocation Algorithm cut down the processing time. The latter better than the former (Fig. 2).

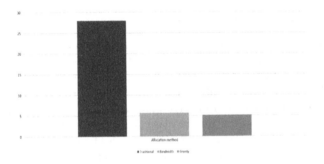

Fig. 2. Histogram of the transmission bandwidth bottleneck

From Table 2 we know that 1 is a bottleneck. Its processing time is long by traditional allocation. But from Table 3, the time is shorter than traditional allocation especially by Greedy Allocation Algorithm. The result meets our expectation.

For the case with ordinary data, the expectation is that the allocation based on bandwidth and the Greedy Allocation Algorithm has sight effect on the result.

Table 2. Experimental data containing bottlenecks in transmission bandwidth

	S_1	S_2	S_3
S_i/MB	20	30	50
U_i/MB	10	10	10
D_i/MB	1	10	10
K_i/MB	20	20	20
P_i/MB	20	20	20

Table 3. Experimental results of transmission bandwidth bottlenecks

	Traditional	Bandwidth	Greedy
Node allocation proportion	(0.33, 0.33, 0.33)	(0.03, 0.40, 0.57)	(0.06, 0.43, 0.51)
Cluster processing time/s	28.0	5.7	5.1

Table 4. Result(1)

	Traditional	Bandwidth	Greedy
Node allocation proportion	(0.33, 0.33, 0.33)	(0.12, 0.30, 0.58)	(0.46, 0.28, 0.26)
Cluster processing time/s	5.6	5.1	5.0

Table 5. Result(2)

	Traditional	Bandwidth	Greedy
Node allocation proportion	(0.33, 0.33, 0.33)	(0.15, 0.35, 0.50)	(0.25, 0.41, 0.34)
Cluster processing time/s	6.4	5.0	5.0

From Tables 4 and 5 the result meets our expectation. Because there are not any bottleneck nodes.

In summary, our Greedy Allocation Algorithm has effect on result whatever is the data set.

5 Conclusion

In this paper, we investigated resource allocation problem based on Hadoop YARN. We designed the mechanism of resource allocation and carried out work schedules to optimize the running time of cluster mainly focuses on network bandwidth and node execution rate. We made an improvement on the basis of the existing algorithm, and proposed an algorithm used strategy based on the greedy choice to make resource allocation. The simulation results showed that has effective impact on the reducing of execution time for the whole cloud cluster.

References

1. Castillo, C., Carrera, D., Becerra, Y., Whalley, I., Steinder, M., Torres, J.: Resource-aware adaptive scheduling for mapreduce clusters. In: International MIDDLEWARE Conference, pp. 180–199 (2011)
2. Chen, T.Y., Wei, H.W., Wei, M.F., Chen, Y.J., Hsu, T.S., Shih, W.K.: LaSA: a locality-aware scheduling algorithm for hadoop-mapreduce resource assignment. In: International Conference on Collaboration Technologies and Systems, pp. 342–346 (2013)

3. Chun, B.G., Ihm, S., Maniatis, P., Naik, M., Patti, A.: Clonecloud: elastic execution between mobile device and cloud. In: Conference on Computer Systems, pp. 301–314 (2011)
4. Vavilapalli, V.K., Murthy, A.C., Douglas, C., Agarwal, S., Konar, M., Evans, R., Graves, T., Lowe, J., Shah, H., Seth, S., Saha, B., Curino, C., O'Malley, O., Radia, S., Reed, B., Baldeschwieler, B.: Apache hadoop yarn: yet another resource negotiator. In: Symposium on Cloud Computing, p. 5 (2013)
5. Li, H., Wei, X., Qingwu, F., Luo, Y.: Mapreduce delay scheduling with deadline constraint. Concurr. Comput. Pract. Exp. **26**(3), 766–778 (2014)
6. Shi, W., Cao, J., Zhang, Q., Li, Y., Lanyu, X.: Edge computing: vision and challenges. IEEE Internet Things J. **3**(5), 637–646 (2016)
7. Tan, J., Meng, X., Zhang, L.: Coupling task progress for mapreduce resource-aware scheduling. In: 2013 Proceedings of IEEE INFOCOM, pp. 1618–1626 (2013)
8. Zhang, Q., Zhani, M.F., Yang, Y., Boutaba, R., Wong, B.: Prism: fine-grained resource-aware scheduling for mapreduce. IEEE Trans. Cloud Comput. **3**(2), 182–194 (2015)
9. Zhao, H., Yang, S., Fan, H., Chen, Z., Xu, J.: An efficiency-aware scheduling for data-intensive computations on mapreduce clusters. IEICE Trans. Inf. Syst. **E96.D**(12), 2654–2662 (2013)

An Automatic Generation Method for Condition Expressions of CPN Model Focus on Tested Behaviors

Tao Sun$^{(\boxtimes)}$, Linjing Zhang, and Huiping Ma

College of Computer Science, Inner Mongolia University,
Hohhot 010021, China
cssunt@imu.edu.cn

Abstract. Testing of the parallel software becomes more difficult because of the state space explosion. In theory, all possible input should be considered when testing. However, in actual, completely test is impossible, so we should carry on the targeted test rather than blindly choose test cases.

Colored Petri Net (CPN) is an excellent language to describe parallel system. But, testing based on this method couldn't complete efficiently when the state space is huge. A new automation algorithm which based on CPN is proposed in this paper. This method could generate the condition expressions automatically. The conditional expressions are a combination of the conditions on all feasible paths which from the initial place to the tested behaviors. First, all paths from current initial place to tested behaviors are found in this method. Second, all the pending arc expressions and guard expressions that obtained from these paths are extracted and processed, especially, the equivalence problem of the namesake variable of the key nodes would be resolved, and these key nodes mainly contain synchronous transition and synchronous concurrency transition. Besides, the substitution problem between different variables also is considered in this process. Finally, we obtain the conditional expressions by integrating all the pending expressions, these expressions are all about the initial position output variables. Test data that meet these conditions could reach the test target.

These expressions could guide tester to choose the appropriate test case and remove redundancy data from testing data set. It can also be used to implement boundary value analysis, equivalence class division, and system model analysis. At the end of the paper, we give the instance to show this method is reasonable and effective.

Keywords: Testing · Colored Petri Net · Condition expressions
Automatic generation algorithm

1 Introduction

Because of the state space explosion of parallel software, software testing becomes very difficult [4, 5]. As a formal modeling language, Colored Petri Nets (CPN) can directly and accurately depict the interaction and concurrent behaviors of parallel software, so CPN is more suitable for the modeling and analysis of parallel software.

© Springer International Publishing AG 2017
G. Wang et al. (Eds.): SpaCCS 2017 Workshops, LNCS 10658, pp. 271–285, 2017.
https://doi.org/10.1007/978-3-319-72395-2_26

The test method based on CPN is divided into two types: state space based and model based. The method based on state space always limited to the complexity of model [6, 7]. And the method based on model, to a great extent, also restricted by the model complexity. This article is precisely under such background, research on parallel software testing based on CPN model.

Traditional testing method could detect all errors in the program only when considering all possible input cases [8–10]. And, many testing efforts also indicate that many errors are found on the boundary of the input/output data set, rather than the inside of this data set. Therefore, it is very significant to obtain the boundary value of the test data set according to the tested behaviors, which could improve the quality of the software and the efficiency of software testing [11, 12]. Such a method is proposed in this paper, this method could generate the condition expressions about the initial value of the system automatically, and these expressions just could be used to determine whether the two test data subsets have intersection, then the test data sets could be classified by executing equivalence partition, so that we could obtain the test data which satisfy different test target combinations. Besides, tester also could use these conditions to analyze the model of the software system to be tested. Moreover, it also could be used to estimate whether the initial values of system data meet expectations.

A new concurrent coverage criterion was given in the literature [1], and proposed a random walk algorithm based on the state space searching method, which could generate a large number of test data automatically. However, these test data is still a large collection. Literature [2] proposed a new method that improved ant colony algorithm and researched the generation method of test sequence based on CPN model, but it still need manual method to analyze, that is to say, it is not fully realize the automation of test data generation. Literature [3] presented 18 test selection criteria based on the TIOSTS model, and also presented their detailed formalized definitions, including the transition coverage and data coverage and so on, but it is not given the specific methods of generation.

In this paper, we propose a method that could generate condition expressions automatically. First of all, we build software system model and record information of this model. The next, searching all paths which from the current place of the model to the tested behaviors. Then, consider the arc expressions and the guard expressions on these paths. Moreover, logical relation between different nodes on these paths also need take in consider. Then, extract condition expressions based on pending condition expressions, which contain the arc expressions and guard expressions. These Condition expressions could provide the range and boundary value of current initial place. These expressions integrate the variable of guard expressions and arc expressions on paths that from current place to the tested behaviors. And all of the variables of these expressions must be the output variable of the current place. Besides, the logical relation between nodes, the type of the pending condition expressions and the operator relationship also need be considered in this process.

The remainder of this paper is organized as follows. The second part gives the key definitions in this method. The Sect. 3 will introduce the algorithms for generate condition expressions. The Sect. 4 will show an instance to prove our approach. Sect. 5 summarizes this paper.

2 Related Definitions

This part proposes several key definitions about condition expressions generation method. The definition of CPN that we used in this paper is the standard definition. In the parallel software testing, the CPN model of the software is established according to the requirement specification of the software to be measured. For example, the model shown in Fig. 1 is a CPN model with concurrency behaviors.

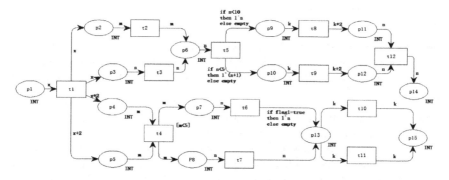

Fig. 1. An example of CPN model

2.1 Definition of Tested Target and Condition Expressions

Definition 1: Tested Target Place Set
Tested target is different for each test, so, we assume tested target places are denoted as TTPS. And it is the set of tested target places. Places set of system CPN model is denoted as P_SM. Then we have principles as follows:

1. TTPS is a finite set of tested target places.
2. P_SM is a finite set of places.
3. TTPS $\neq \emptyset$.
4. TTPS $\subseteq$ P_SM.

For example, we assume the tested target places is p_3 for one test, which in Fig. 1, then we can conclude that the TTPS = $\{p_3\}$. Similarly, assume the tested target places is p_3, p_7 and p_{12}, which in Fig. 1, then we can conclude that the TTPS = $\{p_3, p_7, p_{12}\}$.

Definition 2: Condition Expressions
Condition Expressions are the expressions that extracted and integrated all conditions on the all feasible paths, and all these paths could be executed from the current place to the tested target place. The variables in these condition expressions are all about the output variables of the current initial place. Then, if the token of current initial place meet the condition expressions, it can flow to the tested target.

2.2   Behavior Preparing for FullPath Search Operation

FullPath search mainly refers to the search with the specified target in the system for backtracking. The operation will be terminated when find the initial element. And then repeat the backtracking operation until you find all paths from the initial element to the target in the model. Simply speaking, it could find all paths from the initial element to the specified target.

Definition 3: Full Path set of TTPS
Assuming a set named FullPath denotes all paths which are reachable from initial element to the tested target.

Definition 4: Choose Pending Nodes Operation
The function of choose pending nodes operating is to choose a nodes randomly which in parameter set, called Pn. It could be define as: Choose_Pn (S) {(Pn) |Pn is a node in set S}.

Definition 5: Search Precursors Operation
The function of search precursors operating is to search current precursors for place which have been chosen. Assume a set named Pre to store the precursor nodes for tested target place. Then, define the operation for searching precursor nodes as: Search_Pre (Pn) = {(Pre)|, Pre is a precursor set for place Pn}. For example, assume the tested target place is p_{13}, which in Fig. 1. That is, Pn = p_{14}. Then, the results of Search_Pre (Pn) is Pre = $\{t_{10}, t_{11}\}$ under this assumption.

Definition 6: Link Operation
Link (Pre, Pn) is linking Pn with the nodes which in the sets of Pre. And take the results of this function as the sub path. For example, assume the pending node is p_{14}, which in Fig. 1. That is, Pn = p_{14}, And Pre = $\{t_{10}, t_{11}\}$, which obtained from search precursors operation. Then, the result of Link (Pre, Pn) is $\{\{t_{10}p_{14}\}, \{t_{11}p_{14}\}\}$.

Definition 7: Match Operation
Match Operation is an operation with respect to pending node and set of Full Path. The function of match operating is to judge whether there is a path starting with pending node in FullPath. If there have, return these paths, called Psubpath. Then, denotes match operations as Match (Pn, FullPath). For example, assume the pending node is t_{12}, which in Fig. 1. That is, Pn = t_{11}, And current FullPath is $\{\{t_{10}p_{14}\}, \{t_{11}p_{14}\}\}$. Then, the result of Match (Pn, FullPath) is Psubpath = $\{t_{11}p_{14}\}$.

Definition 8: × Operation
× Operation is an operation between different path sets. This function will combine the two sets above according multiplication cross. For example, assume there are two paths set: subpath1 = $\{\{p_{11}t_{12}\}, \{p_{12}t_{12}\}\}$ and subpath2 = $\{t_{12}p_{13}\}$ Then, the result of subpath1 × subpath2 is $\{\{p_{11}t_{12}p_{13}\}, \{p_{12}t_{12}p_{13}\}\}$.

2.3 Behavior Preparing for Pending Condition Expressions Analyze Operation

In this section, we mainly introduced some definition about the analyze operation. This operation mainly refers to fetch the minimum analysis module, substitute the variable between the expressions, and combine the expressions of the key transitions. During this process, we need consider the arc expression and the guard expression and the logical relation between different nodes on these paths also need take in consider. It's worth mentioning that we only consider the simple color sets such as integers, strings, or bools. The structured color sets is not on our radar.

Definition 9: Initial Place

If a place is the start for a path, then we named it as initial place, and denotes as p_{initial}. For example, in Fig. 2, the set of path can be denoted as $\{p_1t_1p_2\}$, and then the p_{initial} is p_1.

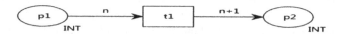

Fig. 2. An example to introduce operation

Definition 10: Ending Place

If a place is the end for a path, then we named it as ending place, and denoted as p_{end}. For example, p_2 is p_{end}, showed in Fig. 2.

Definition 11: Pending Condition Expression, Pending Condition Expression Set

Pending Condition Expression is an expression to control the flow of tokens, which is the integration for the arc expressions and guard expressions for the path. Assuming PCE denotes the pending condition expression for one path of TTPS. Assuming a set to denotes the pending condition expressions for full path, called PCES.

Definition 12: Input Expression

Assuming IE denotes the input expression for a transition. For example, in Fig. 2 the input expression for t_1 is n. That is, the IE for t_1 is n.

Definition 13: Pending Expression

Assuming Pe denotes the expressions, which need be further processed. For example, in Fig. 2 the pending expression is n + 1. That is, the Pe = (n + 1).

Definition 14: Subsequent Place

Assuming SP denotes the subsequent place for a place. For example, in Fig. 2 the subsequent place for p_1 is p_2.

Definition 15: Fetch Expression Operation

Fetch Expression Operation is an operation to fetch the information for a path. This information above includes the input expression, the pending expression, and the subsequent place. The Fetch operation could be define as Fetch (p_{initial}, Path). For example, Path = $\{p_1t_1p_2\}$ showed in Fig. 2, $p_{\text{initial}} = p_1$. Then, the results of Fetch (p_{initial}, Path) is IE = n, Pe = n + 1, SP = p_2.

Definition 16: Substitute Operation

Substitute Operation is an operation between different expressions. This function will use the latter expression substitute the variable in former expression. The function could be denoted as Substitute (exp1, exp2), where exp1 and exp2 represent two different expressions. For example, assume there are two paths expression: exp1 = (if m > 5 then 1`m else 1` (m * 2)) and exp2 = (n + 1) and Then, the results of Substitute (exp1, exp2) = (if (n + 1) > 5 then 1` (n + 1) else 1` ((n + 1) * 2)).

2.4   Behavior Preparing for Key Transitions Analyze Operation

Key Transition mainly refers to Synchronous Concurrency Transition (SCT) and Synchronous Transition (ST). ST or SCT could be fired only when the number of token for input place equals to the number of input arcs and the value of arc expressions are unanimous. That is to say the pending condition expressions should meet all of conditions in the branch instead of meet one of them, when the target is in SCT or ST branch. So, these kinds of situation need special treatment. Then, in this section, we mainly introduced some definition about the key transitions analyze operation. This operation mainly refers to fetch the key transitions, divide the input variable, and fetch the precursors which have same input variable. Then, get the key expressions.

Definition 17: Fetch Key Transitions Operation

Fetch key nodes operation mainly refers to fetch the key transitions for a path by traversing nodes. These key transitions include SCT and ST. Assume KTS denotes the sets to store ST and SCT. Then, define the fetch key transitions operation as Fetch_Key (Path). For example, assume the Path = $\{p_1t_1p_3t_3p_6t_5p_9t_9p_{12}t_{12}p_{13}\}$, which in Fig. 1. Then, the result of Fetch_Key (Path) is $\{t_{12}\}$ under this assumption.

Definition 18: Fetch Input Variable Operation

Fetch Input Variable Operation is an operation to fetch the input variable for the specified transition. This function will return a multiset, named IV, which include all input variable for current parameter. Then, define this operation as: Fetch_Input(t) = $\{(IV)|t \in T, IV \in V$, IV is a finite multiset for variable v$\}$. For example, assume the current parameter is t_1, which showed in Fig. 3. Then, the result of Fetch_Input(t_1) is IV = $\{n, n, m, n, m\}$.

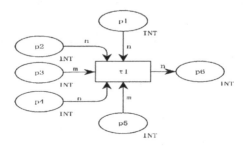

Fig. 3. An example to introduce key nodes

Definition 19: Divide Operation

Divide operation will return a set, named IVS, which contain many subsets. And that subset consists of the same variable. In other words, this operation could find the same variable in current parameter and put them to a subset, then return that subset. Denote this operation as Divide (V). For example, assume the current parameter is IV = {x, n, m, n, m}, IV $\in$ V. Then, the result of Divide (IV) is IVS = {{n, n, n}, {m, m}}.

Definition 20: Fetch Precursor Operation

Fetch Precursor Operation is an operation to fetch the precursor place for a transition according to the input variable. This operation is denoted as Fetch_Pre(IVS, t). It will return two parameters: NUM, IVP[NUM]. NUM is the number of the precursor place combination which have same input variable. And, IVP[NUM] is an array to store these precursor place combination. For example, assume the current transition is t_1, which showed in Fig. 3. And the result of Divide operation is IVS = {{n, n}, {m, m}}. Then, the results of Fetch_Pre(IVS, t) are NUM = 2, IVP[2] = {{p_1, p_2, p_4},{p_3, p_5}}.

Definition 21: Fetch Key Path Operation

Fetch Key Path Operation is an operation to fetch paths, which from the initial place to the specified place. All of these paths are stored in a set, named KeyPath. And, each element in this set is named as SubKeyPath. This operation could be defined as Fetch_KeyPath (FullPath, IVP[NUM]).

For example, there is a key transition t_5 which showed in Fig. 4. And we assume the TTPS = {p_6}. FullPath = {{$p_1t_1p_2t_2p_3t_3p_4t_5p_6$},{$p_1t_1p_2t_2p_3t_4p_5t_5p_6$}}, IVS = {{n, n}},NUM = 1, IVP[1] = {{p_4,p_5}. Then,{{$p_1t_1p_2t_2p_3t_3p_4$, $p_1t_1p_2t_2p_3t_3p_5$}} is the result of Fetch_KeyPath (FullPath, IVP[1]).

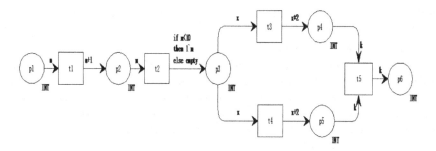

Fig. 4. An example to introduce fetches key path operation

Definition 22: Combine Operation

Combine Operation is an operation between different elements in set. This function will link these elements by "=". For example, assume there is a set KE = {{(if n < 10 then 1`n else empty) * 2)}, {(if n < 10 then 1`n else empty) + 2)}} Then, the results of Combine (KE) is {(if n < 10 then 1`n else empty) * 2) = (if n < 10 then 1`n else empty) + 2)}.

2.5   Behavior Preparing for Condition Expressions Extract Operation

In this section, we mainly introduced some definition about the condition expressions extract operation, which denote as CEE (PCE), this operation mainly refers to distinguish the different kinds of pending condition expressions, find the minimum sub expression, get the component of the minimum sub expression and replace current expression with the result of processing. During this process, we need consider the logical relation between different minimum sub expression and the composition within the expression.

Definition 23: MinSE
We define a minimum sub expression, called MinSE, and should only include three parts. We use IFC indicate the assumption, THC indicate the result when the condition is true, and ELC indicate the result when the condition is false. Besides, a MinSE can't have nesting assumption.

Definition 24: Invert Operation
We define a function to realize this operation, which denote as NOT(), this function flips the value of the parameter. For example, there is an IFC expression: $(n > 2)$. Then, the result of NOT(IFC) is $(n \leq 2)$.

Definition 25: Get Component Operation
Get Component Operation will return the component of the MinSE, namely, IFC, THC and ELC. Denote this operation as GC (MinSE). For example, there is a minimum sub expression: "if $(n > 2)$ then $1`(n + 1)$ else $(n + 2)$. Then, the IFC is $(n > 2)$, THC is $(n + 1)$ and ELC is $(n + 2)$".

Definition 26: Recognize Operation
Recognize (PCE) is an operation to judge whether the pending condition expression has logical expressions or not. And the result of this operation is a Boolean expression.

Definition 27: Locate Operation
Locate Operation is an operation to find and return the minimum sub expression of current pending condition expression. Denote this operation as Locate (PCE). For example, there is a pending condition expression (PCE): "if(if$(n > 2)$ then $1`(n + 1)$ else empty) < 5 then $1`($if$(n > 2)$ then $1`(n + 1)$ else empty) else (if$(n > 2)$ then $1`$ $(n + 1)$ else empty) + 2". Then, MinSE as the result of Locate (PCE) is: "if $(n > 2)$ then $1`(n + 1)$ else empty".

Definition 28: Replace Operation
Replace Operation can be denote as Replace(MinSE, Exp). The parameter Exp indicate a condition expression. It is an operation between the MinSE with the THC or ELC. This function will replace the MinSE of current pending condition expression (PCE) with the latter.

For example, there is a pending condition expression (PCE): "if(if$(n > 2)$ then $1`$ $(n + 1)$ else empty) < 5 then $1`($if$(n > 2)$ then $1`(n + 1)$ else empty) else (if$(n > 2)$ then $1`(n + 1)$ else empty) + 2". So, the MinSE of this PCE is: "if $(n > 2)$ then $1`(n + 1)$ else empty", the value of IFC is $(n > 2)$, the value of THC is $(n + 1)$ and the value of

ELC is (empty). Then, the results of Replace(MinSE, THC) is "if(n + 1) < 5 then 1` (n + 1) else (n + 1) + 2". And this result just the next pending expression.

2.6   Chapter Summary

In this chapter, we gave the definitions of tested target place set, behavior preparing for FullPath search operation, behavior preparing for pending condition expressions analyze operation, behavior preparing for key transitions analyze operation, and behavior preparing for condition expressions extract operation also be given, all of these definition are the basis of the algorithm.

3   Algorithms of the Method

This chapter mainly includes seven sections. Section 3.1 gives the sub algorithm which named as FullPath searching. Section 3.2 gives the pending condition expression analyzing algorithm. And, the key transitions analyzing algorithm will be given in Sect. 3.3. Pending condition expression distinguish algorithm also will be given in Sect. 3.4. Next, Sect. 3.5 gives the condition expressions generate algorithm. And, Sect. 3.6 gives the main algorithm. The last section will summarize this chapter.

3.1   FullPath Searching Algorithm

In this section we will introduce the algorithm of FullPath searching, which showed in Fig. 5. FullPath searching is the first step of our method. This algorithm would return all paths from the initial element to the specified target, it mainly refers to choose pending nodes, search precursors, match subpath, link subpath, and × operation. All of these operations have been introduced in Sect. 2.2.

```
Input: SM,TTPS                          if (Pn ∈ TTPS)
Return: FullPath                            FullPath=Fullpath + SubPath;
Searching(SM,TTPS)                      else
{                                       { Psubpath= Match (Pn, FullPath);
    RNS=TTPS;                             FullPath = FullPath +
    FullPath=∅ ;                           Psubpath × Subpath − Psubpath;
    while (RNS != ∅)                    }
    {                                     RNS=RNS + Pre - Pn;
        Pn=Choose_Pn(RNS);            }
        Pre=Search_Pre(Pn);           return FullPath;
        SubPath=Link(Pre, Pn);        }
```

Fig. 5. FullPath searching algorithm

RNS in this algorithm is standing for Reference Nodes Set, which is a set of nodes which are used to control the circulation of searching function. There have principles: First, RNS is a finite set of tested target places. Second, RNS ⊆ SM. Last, the initial value of RNS is TTPS. There are two parameters when the FullPath searching algorithm is executed. They are SM, TTPS. SubPath is a set to denote the results of link function.

For example, assume TTPS = $\{p_{13}\}$, showed in Fig. 1, then the result of Searching (SM, TTPS) is the FullPath: $\{\{p_1t_1p_2t_2p_6t_5p_9t_8p_{11}t_{12}p_{13}\}, \{p_1t_1p_3t_3p_6t_5p_9t_8p_{11}t_{12}p_{13}\}, \{p_1t_1p_2t_2p_6t_5p_9t_9p_{12}t_{12}p_{13}\}, \{p_1t_1p_3t_3p_6t_5p_9t_9p_{12}t_{12}p_{13}\}\}$.

3.2 Pending Condition Expressions Analyzing Algorithm

In this section we will introduce the algorithm for pending condition expression analyzing. The Fig. 6 shows algorithm of pending condition expression analyzing. It is an algorithm to handle the guard expressions of transition and expressions of arc. We will deal with conditions for all paths, which get from the FullPath searching operation. Thus, we could get the pending condition expression. This Operation mainly refers to fetch expression operation, substitute operation.

Input: a path FullPath
Return:
one pending condition expression, called PCE
Analyzing(path)
  {
    PCE=∅;
    while($p_{initial}$!= p_{end})
    {
      (IE, Pe, SP)=Fetch($p_{initial}$, path);
	if(PCE=∅)
	      PCE=Pe;
	  else
	  { IE=PCE;
	    PCE= Substitute(Pe, IE);
	  }
	    $p_{initial}$=SP;
	  }
	  return PCE;
	}

Fig. 6. Analyzing algorithm

The parameter is a path ∈ FullPath when the pending condition expression analyzing algorithm is executed. IE is a set to store the input expression for a transition. Pe is a set to store the pending expression. SP is a set to store the subsequent place. IE is a set to store the input expression for a transition. Pe is a set to store the pending expression. SP is a set to store the subsequent place.

For example, assume TTPS = $\{p_6\}$ showed in Fig. 1, the result of Searching (SM, TTPS) is $\{\{p_1t_1p_2t_2p_6\}, \{p_1t_1p_3t_3p_6\}\}$, then for a path ∈ FullPath, which is $\{\{p_1t_1p_2t_2p_6\}$, the result of Analyzing (path) is $\{(x + 1)\}$.

3.3 Key Transitions Analyzing Algorithm

In this section we will introduce the algorithm for key transition analyzing, showed in Fig. 7. It is an algorithm to handle key transitions for all paths, which get from the FullPath searching operation. Logical relation between different nodes on these paths would be solved in this process. KE is a set to store the key expression and Sub_KES is a set to store the result of the combine operation.

Input: FullPath
Return: key expressions set,
called KES.
KPH(FullPath)
{
  for each path ∈ FullPath
  { KTS=Fetch_Key(path);
    ke=∅;
  }
  for each t ∈ KTS
  { IV=Fetch_Input(t);
    IVS=Divide(IV);
    (NUM,IVP[NUM])=
       Fetch_Pre(IVS, t);
  }
	while(NUM != 0)
	{
	  KeyPath=
	   Fetch_KeyPath(FullPath,IVP[NUM]);
	  for each SubKeyPath ∈ KeyPath
	  {
	    SubKe= Analyzing(SubKeyPath);
	    KE=KE+ {SubKe};
	    Sub_KES= Combine(KE);
	  }
	  NUM--;
	}
	KES = KES + Sub_KES;
	return KES;
	}

Fig. 7. Key transitions analyzing algorithm

For example, assume TTPS = $\{p_{13}\}$ showed in Fig. 1, then the result of Searching (SM, TTPS) is the FullPath: $\{\{p_1t_1p_2t_2p_6t_5p_9t_8p_{11}t_{12}p_{13}\},\{p_1t_1p_3t_3p_6t_5p_9t_8p_{11}t_{12}p_{13}\},$ $\{p_1t_1p_2t_2p_6t_5\ p_9t_9p_{12}t_{12}p_{13}\},\{p_1t_1p_3t_3p_6t_5p_9t_9p_{12}t_{12}p_{13}\}\}$,then the result of this algorithm $\{((\text{if } (x + 1) < 10 \text{ then } 1`(x + 1) \text{ else empty}) * 2) = ((\text{if } (x + 1) < 10 \text{ then } 1`$ $(x + 1) \text{ else empty}) + 2)\}$.

3.4 Pending Condition Expression Distinguish Algorithm

The function of the distinguish algorithm, showed in Fig. 8, is to distinguish the type of the minimum condition expressions based on their logical relationship. SubDF is a set to store sub data field. NPE indicate next pending expressions. ANPE indicate the other pending expressions.

Input: MinSE SM, TTPS
Return: SubDF, NPE, ANPE
Distinguish(MinSE)
{
  (IFC, THC, ELC)=GC(MinSE);
  SubDF=∅;
  if(THC!="empty"&&ELC="empty")
    SubDF =SubDF + {IFC};
    NPE=Replace(MinSE, THC);
	if (THC="empty" && ELC!="empty")
	  UIFC=NOT(IFC);
	  SubDF= SubDF + {UIFC};
	  NPE= Replace(MinSE, ELC);
	if(THC!="empty" && ELC!="empty")
	  NPE=Replace(MinSE, THC);
	  ANPE=Replace(MinSE, ELC);
	  return SubDF, NPE,ANPE;
	}

Fig. 8. Distinguish algorithm

For example, there is a PCE: $\{((\text{if } (x + 1) < 10 \text{ then } 1`(x + 1) \text{ else empty}) * 2) = ((\text{if }$ $(x + 1) < 10 \text{ then } 1`(x + 1) \text{ else empty}) + 2)\}$. And current MinSE: if $(x + 1) < 10$ then $1`(x + 1)$ else empty, then the result of this algorithm is SubDF = $\{(x + 1) < 10\}$, NPE = $\{((x + 1) * 2) = ((x + 1) + 2)\}$.

3.5 Condition Expressions Extract Algorithm

In this section, we mainly introduce the condition expressions extract algorithm, showed in Fig. 9.

Input: PCE ∈ PCES
Return: Data Condition Field, called
DCF
CEE(PCE)
{ SubDF=PCE;
    while(Recognize(PCE))
  { DCF=∅;
    MinSE=Locate(PCE);
    (SubDF,NPE,ANPE)=
        Distinguish(MinSE);
	if("=" ∈ NPE && NPE ⊉ MinSE)
	    SubDF=SubDF + {NPE};
	if("=" ∈ ANPE && ANPE ⊉ MinSE)
	    SubDF =SubDF + {ANPE};
	DCF=DCF + {CEE(NPE)};
	DCF=DCF + {CEE(ANPE)};
	  }
	DCF= DCF + {SubDF};
	return DCF;
	}

Fig. 9. Condition expressions extract algorithm

The two if statements in algorithm above with the purpose of gain the key conditions. The key condition of key nodes (SCT, ST) need not contain and not equal to a MinSE. Besides, an important feature of this condition is it include "=". We can obtain the condition field for one PCE, which is denoted as DCF. For example, there is a PCE: $\{(((if\ (x + 1) < 10\ then\ 1`(x + 1)\ else\ empty) * 2) = ((if\ (x + 1) < 10\ then\ 1`(x + 1)\ else\ empty) + 2))\}$. Then the result of this algorithm is DCF: $\{(((x + 1) < 10), ((x + 1) * 2) = ((x + 1) + 2))\}$.

3.6 Condition Expressions Generate Algorithm

In this section, we mainly introduce the condition expressions generate algorithm, showed in Fig. 10. A condition expression includes three parts. We use IFC indicate the assumption, THC indicate the value when the condition is true, and ELC indicate the value when the condition is false. DCFS is a set to store the final result.

We give a simple example to introduce the execution of this algorithm. Assume there is a SM, showed in Fig. 1. And TTPS is $\{p_7\}$, the result is FullPath = $\{\{p_1t_1p_4t_4p_7\}, \{p_1t_1p_5t_4p_7\}\}$ according FullPath searching operation. There has a guard expression: $\{m < 5\}$. Then conclusion is PCES = $\{\{x * 2\}, \{x + 2\}, \{(x < 5)\}\}$ according the analyzing operation. And, t_4 is a key transitions in these path, the result of KPH is KES = $\{(x * 2) = (x + 2)\}$. Then, the result is PCES = $\{\{x * 2\}, \{x + 2\}, \{(x < 5)\}, \{(x * 2) = (x + 2)\}\}$. Then, execute condition expressions extract operation, the DCFS = $\{\{\varnothing\}, \{\varnothing\}, \{(x < 5)\}, \{(x * 2) = (x + 2)\}\}$.

| Input: SM,TTPS
Output: Data Condition Field Set,
called DCFS
CEG(SM,TTPS)
{
   FullPath=Searching (SM,TTPS);
   for each path ∈ FullPath
   {
      PCE=Analyzing(path); | PCES=PCES + {PCE};
KES=KPH(FullPath);
PCES = PCES + {KES};
DCFS=∅;
}
for each PCE ∈ PCES
    DCFS=DCFS +{ CEE(PCE)};
output DCFS;

} |

Fig. 10. Condition expressions generate algorithm

3.7 Chapter Summary

In this chapter, we mainly introduced the algorithms for our method. We can obtain the condition expressions by executing these algorithms, which can enhance the quality of software as well as efficiency of software testing. The conditional expressions generated by these algorithms are based on the tested target, for the token in the current initial place, if it satisfies these conditions expressions, then it can reach the tested target along all feasible paths.

4 Example of Algorithm and Analysis

The example in Fig. 1 is a CPN system model with the concurrent behavior. And this model can describe parallel software systems very accurately. It includes concurrency transition, synchronous transition, synchronous concurrency transition, and other special nodes.

Assume TTPS is $\{p_{13}, p_{14}\}$, and p_{13} have be chosen as the current pending target after execute choose pending nodes operation. That is to say, Pn = p_{13}. Then, the result is FullPath = $\{\{p_1t_1p_4t_4p_7t_6p_{13}\}, \{p_1t_1p_5t_4p_7t_6p_{13}\}, \{p_1t_1p_4t_4p_8t_7p_{13}\}, \{p_1t_1p_5t_4p_8t_7p_{13}\}\}$ according FullPath searching operation. The conclusion is PCE = {{if flag1 = true then 1`(x + 2) else empty}, {if flag1 = true then 1`(x * 2) else empty}, {x + 2}, {x * 2}, {x < 5}} according the analyzing operation. And, t_4 is a key transitions in these path, so the result of key transitions analyzing operation is KES = {(x * 2) = (x + 2)}. Then, execute condition expressions extract operation, the result is SubDF = {{(flag1 = true)}, {(x * 2) = (x + 2)}, {(x < 5)}}.

Similarly, assume Pn = p_{14}. There have a key transitions in the FullPath, which is t_{12}, the result of key transitions analyzing operation is KES = {((if x < 10 then 1`x else empty) * 2) = ((if x < 5 then 1`(x + 1) else empty) + 2)}. The result is SubDF = {{(x < 10)}, {(x < 5)}, {(x * 2) = (x + 1) + 2}}. Then, the final result of this algorithm is DCF = {{{(flag1 = true)},{(x * 2) = (x + 2)},{(x < 5)}},{{(x < 10)}, {(x < 5)}, {(x * 2) = (x + 1) + 2}}. Here, the algorithm was executed integrally at a time. Next, we analyze the result and remove redundant data, then we could conclude the test data set need to meet the conditions:{(flag1 = true), (x * 2) = (x + 2), (x < 10), (x < 5), (x * 2) = (x + 1) + 2}, if we want to reach the place p_{13} and place p_{14} at the same time.

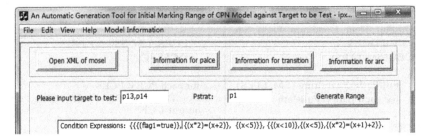

Fig. 11. Computational results

Table 1. Analysis result of other case

Pn	FullPath	KES	DCFS
P_7	$\{p_1t_1p_4t_4p_7\}, \{p_1t_1p_5t_4p_7\}$	$\{(x * 2) = (x + 2)\}$	$\{\{(x * 2) = (x + 2)\}, \{(x < 5)\}\}$
P_9	$\{p_1t_1p_2t_2p_6t_5p_9\},$ $\{p_1t_1p_3t_3p_6t_5p_9\}$	$\varnothing$	$\{(x < 10)\}$
P_{12}	$\{p_1t_1p_2t_2p_6t_5p_{10}t_9p_{12}\},$ $\{p_1t_1p_3t_3p_6t_5p_{10}t_9p_{12}\}$	$\varnothing$	$\{(x < 5)\}$
P_{13}	$\{p_1t_1p_4t_4p_7t_6p_{13}\},$ $\{p_1t_1p_5t_4p_7t_6p_{13}\},$ $\{p_1t_1p_4t_4p_8t_7p_{13}\},$ $\{p_1t_1p_5t_4p_8t_7p_{13}\},$	$\{(x * 2) = (x + 2)\}$	$\{\{(flag1 = true)\},$ $\{(x * 2) = (x + 2)\},$ $\{(x < 5)\}\}$
P_{14}	$\{p_1t_1p_2t_2p_6t_5p_9t_8p_{11}t_{12}p_{14}\},$ $\{p_1t_1p_3t_3p_6t_5p_9t_8p_{11}t_{12}p_{14}\},$ $\{p_1t_1p_2t_2p_6t_5p_{10}t_9p_{12}t_{12}p_{14}\},$ $\{p_1t_1p_3t_3p_6t_5p_{10}t_9p_{12}\ t_{12}p_{14}\}$	$\{((\text{if } x < 10 \text{ then } 1`x$ $\text{else empty}) * 2) = ((\text{if}$ $x < 5 \text{ then } 1`(x + 1) \text{ else}$ $\text{empty}) + 2)\}$	$\{(x < 10)\}, \{(x < 5)\},$ $\{(x * 2) = (x + 1) + 2\}\}$

The processing of other cases in the table is similar. The computational result shows in Fig. 11. And Table 1 shows the analysis result for other case.

Compared with other methods, our method is more effective. For example, the randomly generate algorithm in Literature [1]. The generated test data is still a huge collection. On the contrary, the range generated with our method is more proper.

5 Conclusion

A new method of test data set generation is proposed in this paper. This method could gain the condition expressions of the teste data set, which could be used to analyze system model whether meet the requirements. These conditional expressions also could be used to set or select more accurate test data, thus making the test more targeted. Moreover, we realize the tool which is generating condition expression automatically. In the further, we will consider the combination situation of the different conditions and how to cover more possible conditions with less data. Besides, we will also test more complicated CPN models to optimize the method.

Acknowledgments. This work was supported by the National Natural Science Foundation of China under Grant Nos. 61562064, 61462066, 61362011, and 61661041.

References

1. Farooq, U., Lam, C.P., Li, H.: Towards automated test sequence generation. In: Australian Conference on Software Engineering, pp. 441–450. IEEE Computer Society (2008)
2. Hu, N.: The Algorithm of Test Sequence Optimization Based on the Improved ant Colony Algorithm. Beijing Jiaotong University (2015)
3. Moraes, A., Andrade, W.L., Machado, P.D.L.: A family of test selection criteria for timed input-output symbolic transition system models. Sci. Comput. Prog. **126**, 52–72 (2016)
4. Sun, T.: Research on Testing Method for Parallel Software Based on Colored Petri Nets. Inner Mongolia University (2012)
5. Sun, T., Ye, X.: A test sequence selection method for parallel software systems. In: Processing of Forth International Symposium on Parallel Architectures, Architectures, Algorithms and Programming, pp. 163–167 (2011)
6. Gongzheng, C.: EFMS Model Based Optimal Generation and Instantiation of Test Cases. ShangHai University (2014)
7. Yan, J.: Survey of model-based software testing. Comput. Sci. **31**, 184–187 (2004)
8. Constant, C., Jéron, T., Marchand, H., Rusu, V.: Integrating formal verification and conformance testing for reactive sysems. IEEE Trans. Softw. Eng. **33**(8), 558–574 (2007)
9. Leye, S., Himmelspach, J., Uhrmacher, A.M.: A discussion on experimental model validation. In: Proceedings of the 11th International Conference on Computer Modeling and Simulation, pp. 161–167 (2009)
10. Rai, V., Siva Subramanian, S., Bhulai, S.: A multiphased approach for modeling and analysis of the BitTorrent protocol. In: Proceedings of the 27th International Conference on Distributed Computing Systems, pp. 1–10 (2007)
11. Stanley, J., Liao, H., Lafortune, S.: SAT-based control of concurrent software for deadlock avoidance. IEEE Trans. Autom. Control **60**, 3269–3274 (2015)
12. Rushby, J.: Automated test generation and verified software. In: Meyer, B., Woodcock, J. (eds.) VSTTE 2005. LNCS, vol. 4171, pp. 161–172. Springer, Heidelberg (2008). https://doi.org/10.1007/978-3-540-69149-5_18

The 6th International Symposium on Security and Privacy on Internet of Things (SPIoT 2017)

SPIoT 2017 Organizing and Program Committees

1 Steering Committee

Guojun Wang	Guangzhou University, China (Chair)
Gregorio Martinez	University of Murcia, Spain (Chair)
Mauro Conti	University of Padua, Italy
Hua Wang	Victoria University, Australia
Vasilis Katos	Bournemouth University, UK
Jaime Lloret Mauri	Polytechnic University of Valencia, Spain
Yongdong Wu	Institute for Infocomm Research, Singapore
Zhoujun Li	Beihang University, China

2 Program Chairs

Georgios Kambourakis	University of the Aegean, Greece
Constantinos Kolias	George Mason University, USA

3 Technical Papers Committee

Roger Piqueras Jover	Bloomberg Lp - Security Research Lab, USA
Marilia Curado	University of Coimbra, Portugal
Weizhi Meng	Technical University of Denmark, Denmark
Edmundo Monteiro	University of Coimbra, Portugal
Corrado Aaron Visaggio	University of Sannio, Italy
Vittoria Cozza	University of Padua, Italy
Fernando Pereniguez Garcia	University Centre of Defence, Spanish Air Force Academy, Spain
Dimitrios Damopoulos	Stevens Institute of Technology, USA
Yacine Challal	Universite de Technologie de Compiegne, France
A. Selcuk Uluagac	Florida International University, USA
Shahid Raza	SICS Swedish ICT, Sweden
Enrico Natalizio	Universite de Technologie de Compiegne, France
Dan Garcia-Carrillo	University of Murcia, Spain
Asaf Shabtai	Ben-Gurion University, Israel
Rodrigo Roman	University of Malaga, Spain
Sofia Anna Menesidou	Democritus University of Thrace, Greece
Marios Anagnostopoulos	Singapore University of Technology and Design, Singapore

Daisuke Mashima	Advanced Digital Sciences Center, Singapore
Dimitris Geneiatakis	JRC, Italy
Vin Hoa La	Telecom SudParis, France
Wissam Mallouli	Montimage, France
Georgios Karopoulos	University of Athens, Greece
Lanier A. Watkins	The Johns Hopkins University, USA
Konstantinos Fysarakis	Foundation of Research and Technology - Hellas (FORTH), Greece
Christoforos Ntantogian	University of Piraeus, Greece
Zeeshan Pervez	University of the West of Scotland, UK
Afrand Agah	West Chester University of Pennsylvania, USA
Renita Murimi	Oklahoma Baptist University, USA
Cataldo Basile	Politecnico di Torino, Italy
Mohamad Badra	Zayed University, UAE
Hsiang-Cheh Huang	National University of Kaohsiung, Taiwan
Altair Santin	Pontifical Catholic University of Parana, Brazil
Juan Pedro Muñoz-Gea	Technical University of Cartagena, Spain
Youssef Iraqi	Khalifa University of Science, Technology, and Research, UAE
Riccardo Lazzeretti	Sapienza University of Rome, Italy
Angelo Spognardi	Sapienza University of Rome, Italy
Corinna Schmitt	University of Zurich, Switzerland

Analysing the Resilience of the Internet of Things Against Physical and Proximity Attacks

He Xu[1,2], Daniele Sgandurra[3(✉)], Keith Mayes[3], Peng Li[1,2], and Ruchuan Wang[1,2]

[1] School of Computer Science, Nanjing University of Posts and Telecommunications, Nanjing 210023, China
{xuhe,lipeng,wangrc}@njupt.edu.cn
[2] Jiangsu High Technology Research Key Laboratory for Wireless Sensor Networks, Nanjing 210003, China
[3] Information Security Group, Royal Holloway, University of London, Surrey TW20 0EX, UK
{daniele.sgandurra,keith.mayes}@rhul.ac.uk

Abstract. The Internet of Things (IoT) technology is being widely integrated in many areas like smart-homes, smart-cities, healthcare, and critical infrastructures. As shown by some recent incidents, like the Mirai and BrickerBot botnets, security is a key issue for current and future IoT systems. In this paper, we examine the security of different categories of IoT devices to understand their resilience under different security conditions for attackers. In particular, we analyse IoT robustness against attacks performed under two threat models, namely (i) physical access of the attacker, (ii) close proximity of the attacker (i.e., RFID and WiFi ranges). We discuss the results of the tests we performed on different categories of IoT devices, namely IP cameras, OFo bike locks, RFID-based smart-locks, and smart-home WiFi routers. The results show that most of IoT devices do not address basic vulnerabilities, which can be exploitable under different threat models.

Keywords: IoT · Smart home · IoT attacks · Threat models

1 Introduction

The Internet of Things (IoT) is the interconnection of billions of "smart" devices to the Internet, from smart-lights, smart-door locks, smart-air conditioners, smart-cameras, to intelligent fridges, and even vehicles. These objects are typically networked devices that bridge the physical and virtual worlds. The growth of IoT in recent year is significant, as consumers, businesses, and governments recognize the benefit of interconnecting these devices together to provide additional features. By 2020, it is estimated that 24 billion IoT devices will be installed world-wide [2]. Furthermore, IoT market is set to increase from

© Springer International Publishing AG 2017
G. Wang et al. (Eds.): SpaCCS 2017 Workshops, LNCS 10658, pp. 291–301, 2017.
https://doi.org/10.1007/978-3-319-72395-2_27

$1.9 trillion in 2013 to $7.1 trillion by 2020 [1]. However, many IoT devices are manufactured with minimal security considerations, which render them an easily-exploitable target for attackers. As an example, on October 21st of 2016, the Mirai IoT botnet [15,16], a network composed by hundred of thousands of IoT devices controlled by an attacker, launched a distributed denial-of-service (DDoS) attack against DYN, a major DNS provider. The attack generated 1.2 terabits of malicious traffic forcing DYN off the Internet for hours. This botnet was largely formed by vulnerable IP cameras, digital video recorders, and routers. Some months later, an allegedly white hacker, named Janit0r, claims to have "bricked" more than 2 million IoT devices since January 2017 in an attempt to "protect" the devices before they could be enslaved by Mirai [3,23]. While the initial motivations of this attack (called Brickerbot) were to "teach" a lesson to the IoT industry to improve the security of IoT devices, it has actually achieved to permanently create a DoS on these devices. All of these attacks are just some examples of the security risks faced by current IoT devices, which are mainly due to a lack of proper security testing by several IoT manufacturers. The goal of this paper is to analyse the attack surface of some notable categories of IoT devices to understand their resiliency under different attack scenarios.

The rest of the paper is organised as follows. In Sect. 2 we will review some notables related works on IoT attacks. In Sect. 3, we examine the security of some representative classes of IoT devices and describe some possible attacks under two threat models: physical attack and proximity attack. Section 4 reports the details of our attacks under these threat models, which show that IoT devices contains vulnerabilities that can be easily exploited using different attackers' capabilities. Finally, Sect. 5 concludes the paper.

2   Related Works

In [10], the authors have analysed the security of Samsung's SmartThings platform and found several security vulnerabilities. Similarly, Ronen and Shamir [18] have performed functionality extension attacks on IoT devices using smart-lights as a covert LIFI communication system to exfiltrate data from a highly secure office building. The authors were able to read the leaked data from a distance of over 100 m using cheap equipment. The authors of [17] have designed a feature-distributed malware to perform various malicious activities, such as unlocking smart-locks and disarming security alarms. These results show that traditional web attack techniques, such as cookie stealing, can be turned into sophisticated attacks on IoT devices. Similarly, the authors of [12] examine the security of five commercial home smart-locks, and show that most of these devices suffer from poor design and implementation choices. In addition, the authors of [20] use an existing Apple app (called Loki), which is a survey app that integrates the authors' malware and approved by Apple Store, to infiltrate home networks. The results show that home routers are poorly protected against some attacks. Bertino and Islam analyse the IoT vulnerabilities [8] from insecure web/mobile/cloud interface, insufficient authentication/authorization, insecure network services, lack of transport encryption/integrity verification, privacy concerns, insufficient security configurability, insecure software/firmware, and poor physical security. However, none of these papers has analysed the risk of IoT vulnerabilities by including a detailed threat model, which instead is a required condition (i) to understand the privileges needed by an attacker to perform an attack [19], (ii) to enable manufacturers to address security methodically by using different security assumptions. This is the main goal of this paper.

3   Physical and Proximity Attacks for IoT

We describe two existing main threat models, which should be considered when designing and testing IoT devices for security. To illustrate these threat models, we will refer to Device-Cloud-Mobile (DCM) model shown in Fig. 1, as it is widely used today in commercial products. Here, the IoT devices (IP camera, smart-lock, and bike lock) need to connect to the back-end Cloud system, and support services by an user app running on mobile devices. In some case, the app connects directly with the IoT device using the device Wi-Fi hotspot capabilities, which either processes the requests directly or bridges it to the Cloud backend. We will refer to the legitimate owner of IoT devices as "Alice", and we will user the generic term "attacker" to refer to a generic attacker.

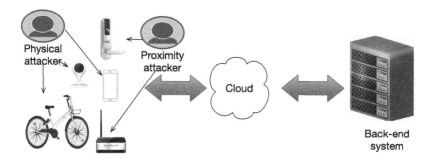

Fig. 1. Device-Cloud-Mobile IoT architectural model

Physical Attack. In this threat model, an attacker can physically interact with the IoT device without notification to Alice. For example, the attacker can access the hardware, and read and modify the default IoT device's settings, which may impact the privacy and authentication credentials of Alice. An example of such attacks is when an IoT device is left unattended for short or long period of time, or when it is publicly available (e.g., a sensor in an open field), which enables an attacker to achieve unguarded access to it.

Proximity Attack. Several IoT devices use wireless communication technology, such as Bluetooth, infrared, ZigBee, and RFID to communicate data to a central station or with other devices (e.g., a smart-phone or another node). Therefore, many of theses communications, if not properly protected, might be available for listening or modification in proximity areas. In this attack, an attacker can observe Alice's interactions with the IoT devices and can also interact with them by injecting data into the available channel. However, this type of attacker does not possess an authorized device and cannot physically alter its setting or firmware. For example, through the analysis of the wireless communication, an attacker can perform replay or clone attacks. In addition, several WiFi-based IoT devices can become a client of a botnet [8] because of their vulnerable OS, such as a vulnerable BusyBox-based Linux distribution (the preferred target of several IoT botnets). Therefore, the WiFi-based IoT device can be used to hide the botnet software, which may be exploited to remotely control the IoT device. This type of attacker does not possess the authorized device and cannot physically alter it. The two classes of adversaries are also shown in Fig. 1.

4   Performing Physical and Proximity Attacks on IoT

In the following, we describe eight attacks we have analysed and tested under the previous threat models. In detail, they are: physical attacks for IP camera and OFo bike lock, proximity attacks for RFID-based smart-locks, and proximity attacks for WiFi routers in smart-home environment. Table 1 details each IoT device we studied, their architecture, the analysed threat model and the attack we have performed.

Table 1. Details of the tested IoT devices

Type of devices	Device	Architecture	Threat model	Attacks
IP camera	360 camera	DCM	Physical attack	Default login Reset password
Smart lock	OFo bike lock	No direct Internet connection	Physical attack	Default login Reset password Malicious QR code
Smart lock	RFID lock	DCM	Proximity attack	Tag emulation Tag cloning
WiFi router	Fast FW150RM	DCM	Proximity attack	De-authentication

4.1   Physical Attacks: Attacks on IP Webcams and OFo Bikes

In this section, we describe the analysis of some commercial webcams against physical attacks. In particular, we describe how default login settings of IoT devices and the mobile phone number may be used by the attackers to access the device illicitly, or to reset the password. Note that these attacks also work on similar classes of IoT devices, such as OFo bikes app [4,6]. Here, we report the results of the analysis of the Qihoo 360 camera[1] (360Camera), which is designed by Qihoo 360 Technology Co. Ltd. in China. This camera is Qihoo's premier security camera, and includes several home security options, and is controlled by a mobile app. The camera offers real-time live streaming, including video recording. Text alerts can be set up when the camera detects movements, whereas the "Homewatch" function can send alerts to user's phone when the camera detects movements in a specific "anti-theft area" so the user is alerted, for instance, when doors and windows might be unprotected. Regarding its security, the camera app uses the mobile phone number as the username: hence, if the owner forgets the password, she can reset the password by requesting it on the website, and the mobile will receive a PIN so that the user is granted the right to reset the password. Note that the 360Camera app can support sharing the real-time and history videos with family people and other friends, which is a privacy-sensitive feature.

Initial Settings. The 360Camera mobile app is essential for camera setup and operation. This app is available for Android from Google Play, or for iOS from the Apple Store, which makes the whole process very easy and trusted for users. After the installation of this app on user's smartphone, the user uses the phone number as the username and sets a password for connecting to the web camera. The user sets the login process as default settings, so that it does not need to input the password and username again in the future.

Default Login Attack. In an example scenario, Alice loses her mobile phone or this has been left unattended for some time. The attacker's goal is to access the phone for a short amount of time to be able to modify the camera app setting to spy on Alice's privacy through the cam. In this scenario, after the attacker gets the mobile phone, he/she can login to the 360Camera app and share the camera's feeds with anyone he/she chooses. Note that this attack works only if the phone is unlocked, otherwise, as described in the "Reset Password Attack" (in the following), the attacker can remove the SIM card, insert it briefly into another phone to perform the reset password attack. Figure 2 shows the default login attack of 360Camera. The feed function is given by the Camera, as shown in Fig. 2 titled "Invite Family to View". If the feeds have been shared with others, there is a list shown as "1 invited", where the number "181*****586" is the phone number of the attacker. In addition, the camera can be set as a public camera, so that everyone in the list can see the video.

Reset Password Attack. If the mobile phone is lost or the attacker gets it (as described in the previous attack), the attacker can remove the SIM card and insert it into his or her phone[2]. Since the number of the SIM card can be easily obtained by dialling another number, this allows the attacker to get the web

---

[1] http://jia.360.cn/.

[2] We assume the SIM card is not locked, as over %60 people do not use the SIM lock functionality to restrict removing the SIM to another phone [14].

Fig. 2. Owner's APP: default login and inviting others to access the camera

camera's username, and he/she can obtain the PIN for resetting the password through the online reset password function. Then, the attacker obtains the access rights to access the camera's feed, and the attacker might even share it with others. In the tested environment, we have found that even if the legitimate owner has changed the login password, the shared users can still login to and get the real-time video of camera. In addition, the owner's app does not receive any notification that there is an app running in a third-party smartphone (that has been granted the sharing rights) that is accessing the camera. All the attacks on 360Camera have been reported to manufacturer, which believes there is little security risk while the phone number is used as a username to login the app. However, the manufacturer has produced an updated version that clearly displays the sharing function to the owner through a dynamic tab at the top left corner of app to show who has been granted access to the video feeds. The manufacturer is also considering the possibility of asking the owner to re-grant the same privileges to users when the password is reset.

We also have performed similar attacks on OFo bikes (China's "Uber for bikes")[3], similar to the one discussed previously on the 360Camera. In particular, if the mobile phone is lost or the attacker gets it, and if the phone has no default login setting, the attacker can remove the SIM card and insert it into his or her phone. When the attacker logs in to the OFo app, he/she can login successful if the phone is configured with the default login and gets the unlock code for entering the bike number. In addition, the attacker can re-obtain the verification code by using the phone number. To this end, OFo includes a QR code on the plate to allow users to retrieve the bike's number by scanning the code with a smartphone. However, an attacker can create a fake QR Code for this bike, and stick on top of the real QR code. Then, the user that will scan this QR Code with their mobiles phones will be redirected to a fake website that may request

---

[3] http://www.ofo.so/.

downloading a trojanized app that is similar to OFo app. Figure 3 shows this attack: here, we can see that an attacker can stick a transparent QR code to replace the bike's QR code, and when the user scans the code she will download a fake app update, which gives an attacker remote access to it [20].

Fig. 3. Malicious QR code attack

4.2   Proximity Attacks: Attacks on RFID-Based Smart Lock

RFID devices are widely used in smart-lock systems for security protection, and also because they are very convenient for users. When someone loses the RFID key, he/she just needs to elect a new RFID tags as the new key. RFID can also support access control very easily. However, RFID tags used in these systems are often vulnerable to various attacks, such as clone and relay attacks. Many researches have showed generic attacks for RFID systems, but little practical attacks for actual smart-lock system have been performed so far. In this section, our focus will be on attacks for gaining access to a restricted area by either cloning or emulating an access RFID tag. We will describe the following practical attacks on RFID smart-lock system: tag emulating, and tag cloning.

Tag Emulation. Because many RFID systems lack some security considerations, the default keys for each sector of tag often do not change, which can be used to get all of the data of the tag. Here, we describe how a default key attack is performed, and how all the tag data can be obtained. In this scenario, the tag can be emulated by a device that presents itself as a tag to the reader. A tag emulating device is implemented and can be bought online [7]. In our experiments, we have used the ACR 122U reader together with LIBNFC tools to emulate a tag. LIBNFC [22] is an open-source C library implementation for Near Field Communication (NFC) devices providing NFC Software Development Kit and Programmable API that can be used by RFID and NFC applications. Some of the important features of this library are: support for ISO 14443-A/B modulation, MIFARE Classic and Sony Felica protocol implementation, and ability to transform an USB-based NFC hardware device into a reader or tag. When the tag is emulated, we can use the ACR 122U reader to unlock the smart-lock.

Tag Cloning. The tag data can be maliciously read by some devices, such as PN532 [9] or ACR 122 [13] and Proxmark III [11], and dumped into a file. Then, the content of this dump file can be revised according to specific access requirements and could be written to a writeable UID tag. In detail, Proxmak III is used to sniff the communication information between the tag and the reader, and can produce the tag content to a dump file. ACR 122U reader can use specific software to write the dump file to a writeable tag. Then the cloned tag has the same information as the legal tag. An attacker can then use this cloned tag to unlock the smart-lock.

4.3   Proximity Attack: Attack on Smart-Home WiFi Router

Currently, several WiFi devices are used in smart-home environments and they need to connect to a WiFi router to access the Internet. In this section, we discuss how de-authentication (deauth) attack [5] for WiFi router can be used to disconnect smart-home IoT devices from the Internet. The 802.11 WiFi protocol contains deauthentication frame which is used to disconnect clients from a WiFi network. Attackers can send a deauthentication packet to the WiFi transmitter station at any time using the spoofed source address of the wireless AP. The attacker does not need to know the password to get into the WiFi network, as he/she needs just to be in the WiFi signal range. For this attack, we have used a Pocket 8266 NodeMCU, which is an open source hardware that can be revised as an attack device. The attack can be extended to external networks by using an Unmanned Aerial Vehicle (UAV) [21] to perform the attack when the attacker is out of the WiFi local network. Figure 4 depicts the steps of this attack. In detail, a mobile phone (Phone 2) is connected to NodeMCU, which we call a *proxy-attack-device*. Then, the UAV first brings this device into the WiFi area and then it leaves the WiFi area, so that the proxy-attack-device is left in the WiFi area. Note that the mobile phone (Phone 2) gives power supply to Node MCU, and the Node MCU is controlled by another (remote) mobile phone (Phone 1) via Phone 2. The attack is now performed by the proxy-attack-device controlled by Phone 1.

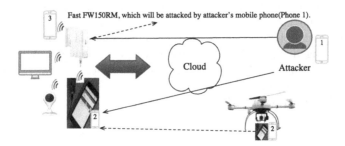

Fig. 4. WiFi attack

The steps to perform the attack are described in the following:

Initial Settings and Attack. In the experiment, the WiFi device (Fast FW150RM[4]) is configured to use the default settings of the manufacturer. Note that all the smart-home IoT devices are connected to this router. Then, the next steps are: (i) UAV brings the attack device, which includes a mobile phone (Phone 2) connected to Pocket 8266 NodeMCU, to the target WiFi network. The attacker uses another mobile phone (Phone 1) browser to connect to a web server running in NodeMCU. Therefore, the attacker can use it to control Pocket 8266 NodeMCU to attack the WiFi devices (see Fig. 5); (ii) the attacker scans the available WiFi hotspots, as shown in Fig. 5; he/she selects one WiFi hotspot, and then it scans which IoT devices are connected to the WiFi hotpot (Fig. 5 shows that five clients were found in this range during our experiments); finally, (iii) the attacker selects one client to start the attack, which is shown in Fig. 5. Then, the selected device is disconnected from the WiFi after it has been attacked.

Fig. 5. Attack on smart-home WiFi router

5   Conclusion

In this paper we have examined the security of commodity IoT devices by performing physical and proximity attacks. The attack scenarios and experimental results show that IoT devices attacks are practical and may seriously impact the safety and privacy of users. In our analyses, we have seen that many commodity

---

[4] http://www.fastcom.com.cn/.

IoT devices do not address basic vulnerabilities under different attackers capabilities. In detail, we have found that IP cameras may expose private feeds to third parties, smart-locks can be easily opened, and smart-home WiFi routers may be exploited in WiFi range, and in extended range with the help of UAVs. Many of the attacks presented in this paper highlight the need to improve the usability of IoT applications in order to improve their security. These attacks also clearly demonstrate that manufactures should design IoT security carefully by consider different threat models, such as physical and proximity attacks.

Acknowledgments. This work is financially supported by Jiangsu Government Scholarship for Overseas Studies, the National Natural Science Foundation of P. R. China (Nos. 61373017, 61572260, 61572261, 61672296, 61602261), the Natural Science Foundation of Jiangsu Province (Nos. BK20140886, BK20140888), Scientific and Technological Support Project of Jiangsu Province (Nos. BE2015702, BE2016185, BE2016777), China Postdoctoral Science Foundation (Nos. 2014M551636, 2014M561696), Jiangsu Planned Projects for Postdoctoral Research Funds (Nos.1302090B, 1401005B), Postgraduate Research and Practice Innovation Program of Jiangsu Province (KYCX17_0798).

References

1. The Internet of Things has started, April 2016. http://www.mycustomer.com/community/blogs/corelynx/the-internet-of-things-has-started-have-you-joined-the-iot-bandwagon
2. There will be 24 billion IoT devices installed on earth by 2020, June 2016. http://uk.businessinsider.com/there-will-be-34-billion-iot-devices-installed-on-earth-by-2020-2016-5?r=US&IR=T
3. BrickerBot, the permanent denial-of-service Botnet, is back with a vengeance, April 2017. https://arstechnica.com/security/2017/04/brickerbot-the-permanent-denial-of-service-botnet-is-back-with-a-vengeance/
4. Chinese bike-sharing start-up Ofo says it's now worth more than $2 billion, April 2017. http://www.cnbc.com/2017/04/17/ofo-chinese-bike-sharing-start-up-says-its-now-worth-more-than-2-billion.html
5. ESP8266_deauther, July 2017. https://github.com/spacehuhn/esp8266_deauther#supported-devices
6. Look out Cambridge: here comes Ofo - China's 'Uber for bikes', April 2017. http://www.wired.co.uk/article/chinese-bike-sharing-company-ofo-is-coming-to-cambridge-in-the-uk
7. RFID Emulator, July 2017. http://www.instructables.com/id/RFID-Emulator-How-to-Clone-RFID-Card-Tag-/
8. Bertino, E., Islam, N.: Botnets and internet of things security. Computer **50**(2), 76–79 (2017)
9. Coskun, V., Ozdenizci, B., Ok, K.: A survey on near field communication (NFC) technology. Wirel. Pers. Commun. **71**(3), 2259–2294 (2013)
10. Fernandes, E., Jung, J., Prakash, A.: Security analysis of emerging smart home applications. In: 2016 IEEE Symposium on Security and Privacy (SP), pp. 636–654, May 2016
11. Garcia, F.D., de Koning Gans, G., Verdult, R.: Tutorial: Proxmark, the swiss army knife for RFID security research. Technical report, Radboud University Nijmegen (2012)

12. Ho, G., Leung, D., Mishra, P., Hosseini, A., Song, D., Wagner, D.: Smart locks: lessons for securing commodity internet of things devices. In: Proceedings of the 11th ACM on Asia Conference on Computer and Communications Security, ASIA CCS 2016, pp. 461–472. ACM, New York, NY, USA, March 2016. http://doi.acm.org/10.1145/2897845.2897886

13. Huang, C.H., Chang, S.L.: Study on the feasibility of NFC P2P communication for nursing care daily work. J. Comput. **24**(2), 33–45 (2013)

14. Imgraben, J., Engelbrecht, A., Choo, K.K.R.: Always connected, but are smart mobile users getting more security savvy? A survey of smart mobile device users. Behav. Inf. Technol. **33**(12), 1347–1360 (2014)

15. Jerkins, J.A.: Motivating a market or regulatory solution to IoT insecurity with the Mirai botnet code. In: 2017 IEEE 7th Annual Computing and Communication Workshop and Conference (CCWC), pp. 1–5. IEEE, January 2017

16. Kolias, C., Kambourakis, G., Stavrou, A., Voas, J.: DDoS in the IoT: Mirai and other botnets. Computer **50**(7), 80–84 (2017)

17. Min, B., Varadharajan, V.: Design and evaluation of feature distributed malware attacks against the internet of things (IoT). In: 20th International Conference on Engineering of Complex Computer Systems (ICECCS), pp. 80–89. IEEE, December 2015

18. Ronen, E., Shamir, A.: Extended functionality attacks on IoT devices: the case of smart lights. In: IEEE European Symposium on Security and Privacy, pp. 3–12. IEEE, March 2016

19. Sgandurra, D., Lupu, E.: Evolution of attacks, threat models, and solutions for virtualized systems. ACM Comput. Surv. **48**(3), 46:1–46:38 (2016). http://doi.acm.org/10.1145/2856126

20. Sivaraman, V., Chan, D., Earl, D., Boreli, R.: Smart-phones attacking smart-homes. In: Proceedings of the 9th ACM Conference on Security & Privacy in Wireless and Mobile Networks, pp. 195–200. ACM, July 2016

21. Valavanis, K.P., Vachtsevanos, G.J. (eds.): Handbook of Unmanned Aerial Vehicles. Springer, Dordrecht (2015). https://doi.org/10.1007/978-90-481-9707-1

22. Verdult, R., de Koning Gans, G., Garcia, F.D.: A toolbox for RFID protocol analysis. In: Proceedings of the Fourth International EURASIP Workshop on RFID Technology (EURASIP RFID), pp. 27–34. IEEE, September 2012

23. BrickerBot: "The Doctor's" PDoS Attack Has Killed Over 2 Million Insecure Devices, April 2017. https://fossbytes.com/brickerbot-malware-pdos-attack-iot-device/

Ensuring IoT/M2M System Security Under the Limitation of Constrained Gateways

Kuan-Lin Chen and Fuchun Joseph Lin[(✉)]

Department of Computer Science,
National Chiao Tung University, Hsinchu 300, Taiwan
{efajk.cs05g, fjlin}@g2.nctu.edu.tw

Abstract. The Internet of Things (IoT)/Machine to Machine (M2M) service must provide security mechanisms to avoid illegal usage of the service. However, in some situation the gateways involved in the IoT/M2M systems are resource-constrained. Hence, the commonly used Transport Layer Security (TLS) protocol cannot be readily applicable to ensure the security of the IoT/M2M systems. Our research focuses on providing IoT/M2M system security under the limitation of constrained gateways. We design a security mechanism on top of the security framework defined in the oneM2M standard to address this problem. Furthermore, we implement this mechanism on the OM2M platform and evaluate it in terms of cost and performance.

Keywords: IoT · M2M · Security · Authentication
Resource-constrained · OneM2M

1 Introduction

Security is a very important issue for IoT/M2M systems because the data collected, such as those for e-Health, often is confidential and needs to be protected through encryption [1]. However, these systems are normally equipped with constrained devices and gateways without sufficient computing power for cryptographic computation required to achieve high confidentiality and reliability. This imposes a great challenge in how to establish the secure communications among devices, gateways and the server in an IoT/M2M system.

Transport Layer Security (TLS) is the most widely used cryptographic protocol that provides communications security over computer networks [2]. Another commonly used variation is Datagram Transport Layer Security (DTLS) based on the stream-oriented TLS protocol that provides equivalent security guarantees [3]. However, with the constrained devices/gateways these two protocols may not be readily applicable to IoT/M2M systems because of the computation required during the TLS/DTLS handshake [4–6].

In this research, we focus on enabling the security mechanisms recommended in the oneM2M standard between a constrained gateway and a server. With our approach the constrained gateway will be able to carry out full TLS/DTLS authentication procedures by delegating its cryptographic computation to a powerful proxy server. Via our

© Springer International Publishing AG 2017
G. Wang et al. (Eds.): SpaCCS 2017 Workshops, LNCS 10658, pp. 302–311, 2017.
https://doi.org/10.1007/978-3-319-72395-2_28

method, the constrained gateway can establish the secure communications with the server even with its limited resource.

The rest of this paper is organized as follows: Sect. 2 gives the background knowledge of oneM2M and its security framework. Section 3 explains our proposed design on top of the oneM2M security framework. Section 4 presents the implementation and evaluation results. Finally in Sect. 5, we provide our conclusion and future work.

2 Background

The oneM2M is the global standard for IoT/M2M platforms. Its purpose and goal is to develop technical specifications which address the need for a common M2M service layer that can be readily embedded within various hardware and software, and relied upon to connect numerous devices in the field with M2M application servers [7]. We will introduce both the functional architecture and the security framework of oneM2M below.

2.1 OneM2M Functional Architecture

The oneM2M functional architecture [8] comprises the following functions:

Application Entity (AE): Application Entity is an entity in the application layer that implements some M2M application service logic. Such application service logic can reside in a number of M2M nodes.

Common Service Entity (CSE): A Common Service Entity represents an instantiation of a set of "common service functions" of the M2M environment. Examples of service functions offered by CSE include Data Management, Device Management, M2M Service Subscription Management and Location Services.

Underlying Network Services Entity (NSE): A Network Services Entity provides services from the underlying network to the CSEs.

The possible configurations of inter-connecting the various entities supported within the oneM2M system are illustrated in Fig. 1. The oneM2M architecture enables the following types of nodes: Infrastructure Node, Middle Node, Application Service Node and Application Dedication Node. Each of them is explained below.

Infrastructure Node (IN): An IN is a node that contains one CSE and zero or more AEs. There is exactly one IN in the Infrastructure Domain per oneM2M Service Provider. A CSE in an IN may contain CSE functions not applicable to other node types.

Middle Node (MN): A MN is a node that contains one CSE and zero or more AEs. There may be zero or more MNs in the Field Domain of the oneM2M system. A MN normally resides in an M2M gateway.

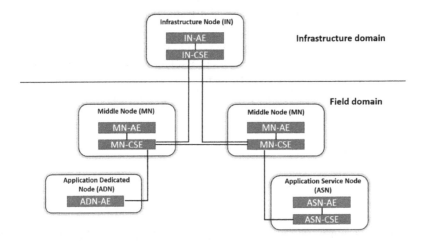

Fig. 1. Configurations supported by oneM2M architecture

Application Service Node (ASN): An ASN is a node that contains one CSE and at least one AE. There may be zero or more ASNs in the Field Domain of the oneM2M System. An ASN normally resides in an M2M Device.

Application Dedicated Node (ADN): An ADN is a Node that contains at least one AE without CSE. There may be zero or more ADNs in the Field Domain of the oneM2M System. An ADN normally resides in a constrained device.

2.2   OneM2M Security Frameworks

The OneM2M security framework consists of two phases: enrollment phase and operational phase.

Enrollment Phase: M2M devices typically require provisioning and configuration phases before being put in actual operation [9]. This can be performed by a pre-provisioning procedure that can be integrated in the manufacturing or product deployment phase, or by means of a security bootstrapping procedure (called remote security provisioning) that takes place before the device starts its actual operation.

Such a Remote Security Provisioning Framework (RSPF) needs the involvement of a special network entity called M2M Enrollment Function (MEF). OneM2M defines several types of remote security provisioning framework including:

- *Pre-Provisioned Symmetric Enrollee Key Remote Security Provisioning Framework:* In this framework, a symmetric key is pre-provisioned to the Enrollee and M2M Enrollment Function for the mutual authentication of those entities.
- *Certificate-Based Remote Security Provisioning Framework:* In this framework, both Enrollee and M2M Enrollment Function will do mutual authentication based on their private keys and certificates that contain their public keys.

Operational Phase: M2M services are offered by CSEs. To be able to use M2M services, the AEs/CSEs need to be mutually identified and authenticated with that CSE. This mutual authentication enables encryption and integrity protection during the message exchange. The oneM2M system supports the following authentication mechanisms for Security Association Establishment Framework (SAEF):

- *Provisioned Symmetric Key Security Association Establishment Framework:* The bootstrap credential for this framework is a long-term symmetric key that has been pre-provisioned into the Enrollee and M2M Enrollment Function during the enrollment phase. Then, the entities authenticate each other by verifying message authentication codes in the security handshake which were generated using the pre-provisioned symmetric key.
- *Certificate-Based Security Association Establishment Framework:* Security Association end-points (i.e. Enrollee, MEF) authenticate themselves using their private keys and certificates containing the corresponding public keys and establish the security association.

3 Proposed Security Design

As our focus is to enable the security framework between a constrained gateway and its remote server, we first introduce the security architecture with the proposed proxy server. Second, we describe the whitelist application procedure between the proxy server and the constrained gateway. Third, we describe the flows of Certificate-based RSPF. Fourth, we describe the flows of Provisioned Symmetric Key SAEF. Finally, we describe a key revocation procedure to deal with attack cases.

3.1 Security Architecture

As depicted in Fig. 2, in our previous work [10] we developed the M2M Enrollment Function (MEF) which is the security function used for authentication and authorization in Enrollment Phase. Moreover, we also developed the Certificate-based RSPF between MN and MEF and the Provisioned Symmetric Key SAEF between MN and IN. Now with the consideration of the constrained gateway, MN no longer is able to use the Certificate-based RSPF to carry out full authentication procedures with MEF due to heavy computation required by TLS handshakes.

Hence, we proposed to use a powerful proxy server to help establish the secure communication between the MEF and the constrained gateway. This powerful proxy server can be provided by a trusted third-party or the service provider and must be placed in a secure, local area. In our research, we assume the symmetric key used for the secure communication between the proxy server and constrained gateway has been pre-provisioned to each of them before starting authentication procedures.

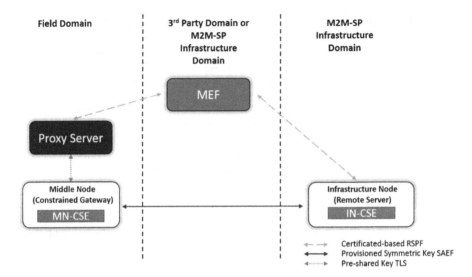

Fig. 2. Proposed security architecture

3.2 Whitelist Application Procedure

In our previous work, we put all the MAC addresses of the device in the expanded ID filed of its object identifier (OID)-based M2M device ID defined by oneM2M standards. Then, we put its OID-based M2M Device ID in the Certificate Signing Request (CSR) and send this CSR to CA to get the signed certificate. In this research, we use the same method to generate the gateway's certificate.

Figure 3 shows the flows of the Whitelist Application procedure as described below.

(1) First, the gateway will generate the OID-based M2M Device ID and store it in the secure storage as read-only data after being started.

(2) Then, the gateway will send a request to register to the proxy server. Both the gateway and the proxy server will select the corresponding pre-provisioned symmetric key which has been distributed to each of them before authentication procedures to perform TLS-PSK handshakes and establish secure communications.

(3) The proxy server will send a request to the gateway in order to fetch its certificate. After receiving the gateway's certificate, it will extract out OID-based M2M Device ID.

(4) Through Restful API the proxy server will also send a request to the gateway in order to fetch its OID-based M2M Device ID.

(5) Finally, the proxy server compares the OID-based M2M Device ID from received certificate with the one from the gateway's response. If they are matched, the OID-based M2M Device ID will be added into the whitelist. Otherwise, the request will be rejected.

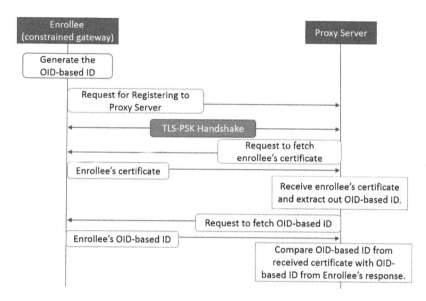

Fig. 3. Flows of whitelist application procedure

3.3 Remote Security Provisioning Framework

Figure 4 shows the flows of Certificate-based RSPF with Proxy Server as follows.

(1) ***Whitelist Verification:*** Fist, the gateway will generate the OID-based M2M Device ID and send a request for using proxy's service. After establishing the secure communication, Proxy Server sends a request to the gateway in order to fetch its OID-based M2M Device ID and compare it with the legal IDs in the whitelist.

(2) ***Bootstrap Enrollment Handshake:*** If gateway is legal, Proxy Server will send a request for registering to MEF with the gateway's OID-based M2M Device ID. Then, both of them will perform TLS handshakes by using their certificates.

(3) ***Enrollment Key Generation:*** In this stage, MEF will generate the symmetric enrollment key (Ke) and the corresponding enrollment key identifier (KeId) in order to share with the enrollee. The proxy server will send Ke and KeID to the gateway after receiving them from MEF.

(4) ***Use of Provisioned Credential:*** In this stage, Both the gateway and MEF will use Ke and KeId to generate the connection key, called provisioned credential for the M2M security association establishment (Kpsa), used in the Provisioned Symmetric Key SAEF later. First, the gateway would send the KeId to the remote server. If the remote server does not have the credentials associated with the KeID, it will send a request to MEF to retrieve the corresponding Kpsa. Finally, the gateway and the remote server would have the same symmetric key, Kpsa, for secure communications.

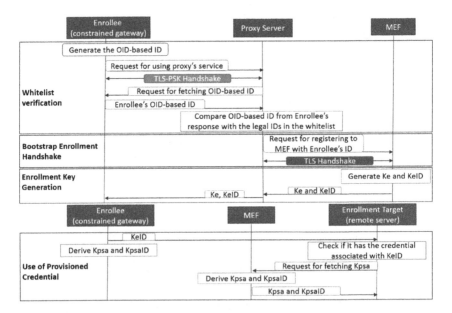

Fig. 4. Certificate-based RSPF with proxy server

3.4 Security Association Establishment Framework

Figure 5 shows the flows of Provisioned Symmetric Key SAEF as described below.

(1) *Credential Configuration:* After performing Certificated-based RSPF, the gateway and the remote server are provisioned with the same provisioned secure connection key (Kpsa).

(2) **Identity Configuration and Association Configuration:** In this stage, remote server shall know its identifier, and the gateway needs to configure with the remote server's identifier.

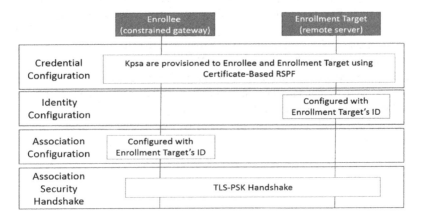

Fig. 5. Provisioned symmetric key SAEF

(3) *Association Security Handshake:* Identification, authentication and security context establishment between these two entities will be carried out in this stage. The gateway and the remote server will perform TLS-PSK handshakes by using provisioned secure connection key (Kpsa), and the data being transmitted will be encrypted finally.

3.5 Key Revocation Procedure

Because the gateway is resource-constrained, it cannot receive software updates frequently. Thus, its security vulnerabilities may be exposed and become the target of security attacks.

In order to solve this situation, a key revocation procedure is put in place. We assume the proxy server is equipped with the functionalities of a bastion host so it can detect the unusual traffic generated by the compromised gateway and start the key revocation procedure.

(1) Once the proxy server detects the unusual traffic generated by the compromised gateway, it would send a request with KeID to MEF in order to revoke the corresponding key.
(2) After MEF revokes the key associated with the KeID from the secure storage, it will also send a request to the remote server in order to revoke the corresponding key and abort the TLS session between the remote server and the compromised gateway.
(3) Finally, the proxy server adds the OID-based M2M Device ID of compromised gateway to the blacklist. If the gateway intends to register to the proxy server again, the proxy server will reject the request according to the blacklist.

4 Implementation and Evaluation

Next we will explain our system implementation and performance evaluation.

4.1 System Implementation

In our system, the M2M server, MEF and the proxy server are all developed in virtual machines. Each virtual machine runs Ubuntu Desktop 16.04 64 bit edition with two 2.80 GHz CPU cores and 2 GB RAM. We use Raspberry Pi 3 with four 1.2 GHz CPU cores and 1 GB RAM as our gateway.

We install OM2M [11] software in each virtual machine and Raspberry Pi 3 to set up our IoT/M2M platform. OM2M provides an open source IoT/M2M service platform based on the oneM2M standard. We implemented both MEF and the proxy server on top of OM2M in order to test the proposed security mechanism.

4.2 Performance Evaluation

In order to evaluate the performance of the gateway, VisualVM [12] is used to measure both memory and CPU usage. VisualVM is a visual tool integrating command line JDK tools and lightweight profiling capabilities. We measured the resource usage, authentication time and total execution time of the gateway developed on Raspberry Pi 3 under three different configurations: no security mechanism, security mechanism without Proxy Server, and security mechanism with Proxy Server.

Table 1 on the top shows the metrics comparison of the gateway under three different configurations. The base value in each compare item represents the cost of running the original OM2M platform without any security mechanisms. In terms of memory and CPU usage, our proposed mechanism with Proxy Server reduces the usage of memory and CPU down to 1/4 and 1/3, respectively, when comparing to the one without Proxy Server. The authentication time which starts from the Whitelist Verification stage to the Enrollment Key Generation stage also has better performance under our proposed mechanism due to the help of Proxy Server. Hence, the total execution time for the Certificated-based RSPF and the Provisioned Symmetric Key SAEF is also improved.

Table 1. Gateway comparison

Gateway	No security mechanism	Security mechanism without proxy server	Security mechanism with proxy server
Memory (MiB)	Base = 31	Base + 7.7 = 38.7	Base + 1.9 = 32.9
CPU (%)	Base = 36	Base + 8 = 44	Base + 2.6 = 38.6
Authentication time (sec.)	–	6.89	5.58
Execution time (sec.)	Base = 21.5	Base + 7.64 = 29.14	Base + 6.2 = 27.7

5   Conclusion and Future Work

In this research, we propose a mechanism to help the constrained gateway carry out full authentication procedures by delegating its cryptographic computation to a powerful proxy server. We design a Whitelist Application Procedure to protect the proxy server from the compromised gateways. The Certificated-based RSPF and the Provisioned Symmetric Key SAEF defined by oneM2M standard are re-designed in order to adapt the proxy server into our system. The proxy server can detect the unusual traffic and launch the Key Revocation Procedure to isolate the compromised gateway.

The experimental test proves that our proposed security mechanism can effectively improve the performance and the resource usage of the constrained gateway. Moreover, adding the proxy server into our system does not increase the total execution time. On the contrary, it can accelerate the authentication procedure between the gateway and MEF.

Our future effort is to investigate the possibility of applying the security design developed for the constrained gateway in oneM2M to the Fog/Mobile Edge Node in the emerging area of Fog/Mobile Edge Computing.

Acknowledgments. The research reported in this paper is funded by QNAP Systems. We would like to thank Amol Narkhede and Mohan S. P. of QNAP for their guidance and feedback during the process of research.

References

1. Al-Fuqaha, A., Guizani, M., Mohammadi, M., Aledhari, M., Ayyash, M.: Internet of Things: a survey on enabling technologies, protocols, and applications. IEEE Commun. Surv. Tutor. **17**(4), 2347–2376 (2015). https://doi.org/10.1109/COMST.2015.2444095
2. Network Working Group: The Transport Layer Security (TLS) Protocol, Version 1.2. (2008)
3. Network Working Group: Datagram Transport Layer Security, Version 1.2. (2012)
4. Hummen, R., Shafagh, H., Raza, S., Voig, T., Wehrle, K.: Delegation-based authentication and authorization for the IP-based Internet of Things. In: 2014 Eleventh Annual IEEE International Conference on Sensing, Communication, and Networking (SECON), pp. 284–292 (2014)
5. Apostolopoulos, G., Peris, V., Saha, D.: Transport layer security: how much does it really cost? In: Proceedings of the Eighteenth Annual Joint Conference of the IEEE Computer and Communications Societies, INFOCOM 1999, vol. 2, pp. 717–725. IEEE (1999)
6. Kuo, F.C., Tschofenig, H., Meyer, F., Fu, X.: Comparison studies between pre-shared key and public key exchange mechanisms for transport layer security (TLS). Institute for Informatics, University of Goettingen, Technical Report IFI-TB-2006-01 (2006)
7. oneM2M. http://www.onem2m.org/about-onem2m/why-onem2m
8. oneM2M, TS 0001 v2.10.0: Functional Architecture
9. oneM2M, TS 0003 v2.4.1: Security Solutions
10. Hsu, Y.-H., Lin, F.J.: Preventing misuse of duplicate certificates in IoT/M2M systems. In: The 7th International Workshop on Internet on Things: Privacy, Security and Trust (IoTPST), 31 July–3 August 2017, Vancouver, Canada (2017)
11. OM2M. https://wiki.eclipse.org/OM2M/one
12. VisualVM. https://visualvm.github.io/

Spatial Reconfigurable Physical Unclonable Functions for the Internet of Things

Armin Babaei and Gregor Schiele$^{(\boxtimes)}$

Embedded Systems, Faculty of Engineering, Duisburg Essen University,
Bismarck Str. 90, 47057 Duisburg, Germany
{armin.babaei,gregor.schiele}@uni-due.de

Abstract. Internet of Things (IoT) devices encounter security and resource constrains as two confronting challenges. In this paper we demonstrate a ring oscillator Physical Unclonable Function (PUF) that uses spatial reconfiguration on an FPGA to provide secure authentication for resource constrained IoT devices. We discuss our main design decisions and present an example implementation of our approach. Our experimental evaluations shows that our approach can increase the number of unique challenge response pairs by a factor of six without increasing the size of the PUF implementation takes on the FPGA. This confirms the applicability of our proposed solution.

Keywords: Hardware security · Physical Unclonable Function
Internet of Thing · Field Programmable Gate Array
Reconfigurable PUF

1 Introduction

The Internet of Things (IoT) will change our way of life. Physical objects are enhanced with embedded electronics to become identifiable, to sense their environment, and to connect to a global communication network. This will lead to a multitude of new solutions, e.g., in the fourth industrial revolution (Industry 4.0) [1]. However, to be usable in real world systems, IoT devices must face several tough challenges, such as low energy consumption [2,3], lack of computational resources, as well as the need to secure devices against cyber-attacks [4–7]. Unfortunately, energy footprint concerns as well as the scarcity of computational resources restrict which cryptographic methods can be implemented for these devices, making it difficult to implement traditional security mechanisms.

Recently, Physical Unclonable Functions (PUFs) have been proposed as a light-weight, ubiquities and low-cost solution to secure IoT devices [8–10]. They can act as a kind of fingerprint for IoT devices, allowing to identify them reliably. At the same time, IoT devices must be highly flexible, both in terms of software and hardware, to adapt to unforeseen application scenarios and security concerns [11]. To provide such flexibility, Field Programmable Gate Arrays (FPGAs) have been proposed for IoT devices [3]. FPGAs consist of Configurable

© Springer International Publishing AG 2017
G. Wang et al. (Eds.): SpaCCS 2017 Workshops, LNCS 10658, pp. 312–321, 2017.
https://doi.org/10.1007/978-3-319-72395-2_29

Logic Cells (CLBs) that can instantiate specialized hardware architectures at runtime. FPGAs thus allow to change a device's hardware dynamically. They are often used for chip prototyping and for System on Chip (SoC) design. A flexible IoT device can thus be implemented by placing its needed hardware modules on the FPGA, ranging from a small micro-controller, to special modules for signal processing or encryption. As an example, see Fig. 1. The depicted IoT device consists of four modules that are placed on the FPGA: Module X, Y, Z and PUF P. Since the energy consumption of the resulting IoT device depends on the size of the used FPGA, developers aim at using FPGAs with a small number of CLBs. In this paper, we assume XC7A35T FPGA (Artix family) by having 5200 CLBs and low power consumption as a small FPGA. As the FPGA hosts multiple modules, a PUF implementation can typically use only a fraction of these CLBs, e.g., 10–20%. The resulting PUF will therefore support only a small number of secure identifications that may not be sufficient for its lifetime.

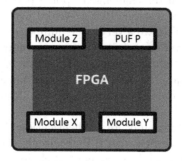

Fig. 1. The FPGA with PUF circuit

In this paper we propose a novel approach to increase the number of identifications that a PUF implemented on an FPGA can handle securely. Our approach does not increase the size of the used PUF, making it applicable for low energy, small scale IoT devices with long lifetimes. Our general idea is to change the placement of the PUF on the FPGA as shown in Fig. 2. By doing so, we can create new fingerprinting data sets that are unique and independent from each other. Our paper is structured as follows. Section 2 elaborates current PUF implementation challenges in IoT. Section 3 describes our solution and Sect. 4 validates our approach. We conclude our work in Sect. 5.

2 PUF Challenges in IoT

PUF circuits have been proposed as a new path towards IoT security [4,8,12]. However, hardware design challenges are mostly ignored. In this section we take a closer look at the problems regarding PUF utilization in IoT from a hardware design perspective.

PUF circuits are intrinsically created during a manufacturing process. They receive a sequence of bits; alleged challenges, as the input and generate a sequence

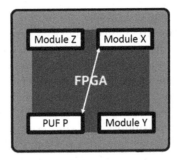

Fig. 2. Spatial exchange of PUF P and module X

of bits; so-called responses, as the output. No two chips generate identical responses for a particular challenge. The combination of a challenge and its correspond response is called a challenge response pair (CRP). PUF circuits can be categorized into weak and strong PUFs. Weak PUFs have a restricted number of CRPs [13]. Strong PUFs have a very large number of CRPs [14]. Using a PUF does not guarantee full system security. There are a number of known attacks on PUFs [14–16] as well as different proposed solutions to overcome them [13,17]. Our approach can integrate these solutions and by doing so, can be made secure against known PUF attacks. Therefore, we do not discuss such attacks further in this paper.

PUF circuits are used mainly for authentication [18]. In a simple scenario suppose we have an IoT device with a PUF circuit. The authentication works as follows: First the server sends a sequence of challenge bits to the IoT device. The IoT device then generates a sequence of response bits and sends it back to the server. If the response bits match the expected response bits (which are pre-stored on the server), then the IoT device is authenticated. For each authentication, at least one CRP must be used. Since IoT devices are often expected to be used for multiple years, they may need to authenticate themselves many times, using a large number of CRPs. To provide an adequate number of CRPs, we have two traditional approaches:

(i) First, we could reuse CRPs. This would allow us to work with a limited number of CRPs but requires the CRPs to remain secret. To realize this, traditional cryptographic methods are needed to protect them. This results in an increased resource utilization for the IoT device, which may require stronger hardware and higher energy consumption. In addition, the approach introduces new risks, e.g. replay attacks or breaking the encryption. Therefore, reusing CRPs is not a good option.

(ii) The second approach to provide enough CRPs for a larger number of authentications is to use a larger PUF which can generate more CRPs. However, embedded developers need to use small FPGAs to reduce power consumption in their IoT devices. Using a large PUF occupies a big slice of the resources on small FPGAs. As an example, in one of our ongoing IoT projects [3] only 15% of the FPGA resources are available to implement a PUF. With this, the used PUF generates 8128 CRPs.

Both these approaches require more computational resources and thus increase energy consumption to be implemented. This runs contrary to the original reason for using a PUF: to have a lightweight authentication solution that introduces little overhead. Therefore, we developed a novel approach to increase the number of supported CRPs on a PUF of fixed size, which we present in the next section.

3   Spatial Reconfigurable PUF

Our goal is to increase the number of CRPs supported by a PUF, without increasing the PUF circuit size. As discussed before our main idea is to place a PUF circuit at different regions on an FPGA (through online re-programming of the FPGA or using DPR technology) and increase the number of supported CRPs by this. To realize this, we have three major design questions: (i) what type of PUF to use, (ii) what size of PUF to use, and (iii) how to determine the different PUF circuit placements. In the following we discuss these.

3.1   PUF Selection for IoT

Selecting an appropriate PUF for IoT applications is not trivial. There is a variety of silicon-based PUFs. To make a selection, we derived three main requirements for a PUF used in IoT devices: (i) good statistical properties, (ii) simple implementation process on FPGA, and (iii) large number of CRPs. In terms of statistical properties, according to previous studies [14,19], the best options are SRAM and Ring Oscillator (RO) PUFs. SRAM PUFs have good statistical properties but fit better in ASICs rather than FPGAs [19]. In addition, SRAM PUFs are categorized as weak PUFs with restricted numbers of CRPs. Therefore, they do not meet our requirements.

With respect to strong PUFs, RO PUFs are one of the most flexible (in term of implementation on FPGA) and reliable PUFs. In addition, they also have good statistical properties [19]. Therefore, we chose to use an RO PUF in our design. An RO PUF circuit (see Fig. 3) is made of n identical Ring Oscillators(ROs) [20]. ROs oscillate with different frequencies ($f_a,...,f_n$). Each incoming challenge selects a pair of ROs with different frequencies, out of all n ring oscillators. Due to process variations, f_a and f_c tend to differ from each other. The comparison between the speeds of f_a and f_c determines the value of the response bit.

3.2   PUF Size

Our next design question is the size of the used RO PUF. The number of generated CRPs in a RO PUF circuit with size of k ROs can be given as [13]:

$$N_{CRP} = \frac{k(k-1)}{2} \tag{1}$$

By increasing the size of ROs, the number of CRPs will increase. Taking into account the size of an FPGA typically used in embedded systems (in this case an

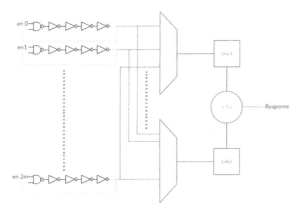

Fig. 3. RO PUF Architecture

XC7a35T FPGA) and the constraints of a real ongoing project [3], we restricted
our selection to between 128 and 256 RO pairs. RO PUFs of these sizes occupy
10% to 18% of the available resources respectively, and the rest of resources can
be used for other purposes, e.g., a general purpose computation core or digital
signal processing cores.

3.3   PUF Placement

After choosing PUF type and size, our goal is to increase the number of CRPs
by implementing the PUF circuit in different regions. For this purpose, first,
we need a better understanding of a region and its boundaries on an FPGA.
According to previous studies [12,19], we can assume that the regional clock
has a direct influence on the ROs oscillation frequencies. In our FPGA there
are six different clock regions (see Fig. 4). The border lines of the clock regions
are shown in this figure. We implemented an identical RO PUF architecture on
these regions as shown in Fig. 5. Orange dots are manually routed and placed
ROs. Conceptually, the RO architecture in all these regions is the same, but due
to some constrains (e.g. IO ports, responses uniformity and etc.) their placement
are horizontally, vertically or tightened.

4   Evaluations and Results

To evaluate our approach, we implemented the aforementioned RO PUF in each
of the six clock regions A to F of an XC7a35T FPGA. This FPGA is part of
the Artix 7 family by Xilinx and well suited for embedded applications. We then
switched between the resulting six different FPGA configurations and applied
identical sequences of challenges to each one of them. We extracted the produced
responses R1 to R6, measuring the quality of responses by using two performance
metrics: the uniformity and the uniqueness of responses.

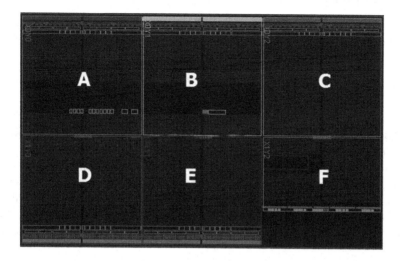

Fig. 4. XC7A35T FPGA floor plan with 6 different clock regions

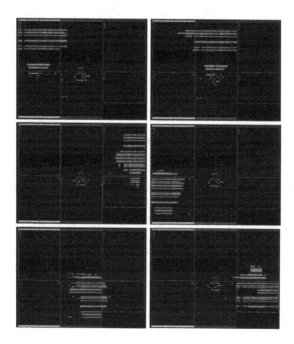

Fig. 5. Different RO architecture placement in 6 clock regions of XC7A35T FPGA (Color figure online)

4.1   Uniformity

To quantify the distribution of zeros and ones of the outputs, we computed the uniformity. The response uniformity at region i of the FPGA, can be determined as the mean value of all n response bits:

$$Uniformity = \frac{1}{n} \sum_{1}^{n} (r_{i,l}) * 100\% \qquad (2)$$

The optimum value is 50%. We computed the uniformity for all six regions. The obtained values are shown in Table 1. We tried to expand our design at each clock region to measure our assumption about the definition of regions on the FPGA. In some areas, this expansion had no influence on response bits. Nevertheless, in some areas this expansion influenced on the uniformity distribution rate of that region. To compensate this term, we modified the placement of ROs in these regions.

Table 1. Distribution of 0 and 1 in response bits at each region and their distance from optimal value

	Region A	Region B	Region C	Region D	Region E	Region F
Distance from opt. value	6%	4%	7.5%	7%	6%	8%
Placement modification	Unmodified	Modified	Unmodified	Unmodified	Modified	Unmodified

4.2   Uniqueness

To quantify the uniqueness of responses in different regions of the FPGA, i.e., how much the responses of the PUF implementations in the different regions differ from each other, we used the inter-device hamming distance measurement [14,19]. This measurement previously has been used to determine how good an individual FPGA can be distinguished in a whole population of FPGAs based on generated response bits. By using this estimation, we evaluated how well we can distinguish an individual region on the FPGA from other regions based on the generated responses. The optimum value for this measurement is 50%. We computed the inter hamming distance HD_{inter} between regions i and j as follows [19]:

$$HD_{inter} = \sum_{i=1}^{k-1} \sum_{j=i+1}^{k} \frac{HD(r_i, r_j)}{n} * 100 \qquad (3)$$

Factor k determines the number of regions which in our case is 6. The results of our measurements are shown in Table 2. This table shows the distance from HD_{inter} optimum value. The worst cases are HD_{inter} between regions D & B

Table 2. Distance from HD_{inter} optimum value between i and j regions of FPGA

	Region A	Region B	Region C	Region D	Region E
Region A					
Region B	1%				
Region C	0%	2%			
Region D	8%	8%	2%		
Region E	4%	3%	1%	6%	
Region F	1%	5%	1%	5%	3%

and regions D & A. The mean value of HD_{inter} between all 6 different regions on the FPGA is 49%., i.e., each region at the FPGA acts like an identifiable PUF and the generated responses are unique. This is a very important result for us, since it proves the usability of our general approach.

5   Conclusion

Using our approach we were able to increase the number of unique CRPs that are supported by a 128 RO PUF from 8,128 to 48,768 – six times more that the original PUF. To do so, we placed a PUF in each of the FPGA clock regions and switched between them at runtime. Our evaluation shows that each clock region acts like an identifiable PUF that is distinguishable from the other ones. At the same time, our solution didn't increase the required space on the used FPGA and occupies only 10% of the available resources on an XC7A35T FPGA. This makes it easy to integrate our approach into a SoC design. Large PUF circuits, due to the required resources, may not have this flexibility. If more space is available on an FPGA, then we can use our approach with larger size PUFs to generate even more CRPs. Note however, that the response bit uniqueness in large size PUFs is an open problem [20,21]. One drawback of our approach is the necessity to switch between FPGA configurations. Although this must only be done seldomly(thus energy consumption for this procedure can be neglected), after the current CRPs have been used up, in our future work, we plan to use Dynamic Partial Reconfiguration technology to reduce the switching overhead and possible downtime. In addition, we plan to do further experiments with additional placement strategies. By placing PUFs in overlapping clock regions we hope to gain more placements and to increase further the number of achievable CRPs. We will also look into combining our approach with reconfigurable PUFs [21]. This should increase the number of CRPs even more.

References

1. Shrouf, F., Ordieres, J., Miragliotta, G.: Smart factories in industry 4.0: a review of the concept and of energy management approached in production based on the internet of things paradigm. In: 2014 IEEE International Conference on Industrial Engineering and Engineering Management (IEEM), pp. 697–701. IEEE (2014)
2. Zhang, C., Ahn, W., Zhang, Y., Childers, B.R.: Live code update for IoT devices in energy harvesting environments. In: 2016 5th Non-Volatile Memory Systems and Applications Symposium (NVMSA), pp. 1–6. IEEE (2016)
3. Burger, A., Cichiwskyj, C., Schiele, G.: Elastic nodes for the internet of things: a middleware-based approach. In: 2017 IEEE International Conference on Autonomic Computing (ICAC), pp. 73–74. IEEE (2017)
4. Sicari, S., Rizzardi, A., Grieco, L.A., Coen-Porisini, A.: Security, privacy and trust in internet of things. Comput. Netw. **76**, 146–164 (2015)
5. Radomirovic, S.: Towards a model for security and privacy in the internet of things. In: Proceedings of the First Int'l Workshop on Security of the Internet of Things (2010)
6. Wurm, J., Hoang, K., Arias, O., Sadeghi, A.R., Jin, Y.: Security analysis on consumer and industrial IoT devices. In: 2016 21st Asia and South Pacific Design Automation Conference (ASP-DAC), pp. 519–524. IEEE (2016)
7. Bertino, E., Islam, N.: Botnets and internet of things security. Computer **50**(2), 76–79 (2017)
8. Johnson, A.P., Chakraborty, R.S., Mukhopadhyay, D.: A puf-enabled secure architecture for fpga-based IoT applications. IEEE Trans. Multi-Scale Comput. Syst. **1**(2), 110–122 (2015)
9. Huth, C., Aysu, A., Guajardo, J., Duplys, P., Güneysu, T.: Secure and private, yet lightweight, authentication for the IoT via PUF and CBKA. In: Hong, S., Park, J.H. (eds.) ICISC 2016. LNCS, vol. 10157, pp. 28–48. Springer, Cham (2017). https://doi.org/10.1007/978-3-319-53177-9_2
10. Krishna, M.B., Verma, A.: A framework of smart homes connected devices using internet of things. In: 2016 2nd International Conference on Contemporary Computing and Informatics (IC3I), pp. 810–815. IEEE (2016)
11. Wang, C., Zhou, J., Guruprasad, K., Liu, X., Weerasekera, R., Kim, T.T.: TSV-based PUF circuit for 3DIC sensor nodes in IoT applications. In: 2015 IEEE International Conference on Electron Devices and Solid-State Circuits (EDSSC), pp. 313–316. IEEE (2015)
12. Torğul, B., Şağbanşua, L., Balo, F.: Internet of things: a survey. Int. J. Appl. Math. Electron. Comput. **4**, 104–110 (2016)
13. Rührmair, U, Sehnke, F., Sölter, J., Dror, G., Devadas, S., Schmidhuber, J.: Modeling attacks on physical unclonable functions. In: Proceedings of the 17th ACM Conference on Computer and Communications Security, pp. 237–249. ACM (2010)
14. Maes, R.: Physically unclonable functions: constructions, properties and applications. Ph.D. thesis, Department of Electrical Engineering (ESAT), Katholieke Universiteit Leuven (KU Leuven) (2012)
15. Becker, G.T., Kumar, R., et al.: Active and passive side-channel attacks on delay based PUF designs. IACR Cryptol. ePrint Arch. **2014**, 287 (2014)
16. Mahmoud, A., Rührmair, U., Majzoobi, M., Koushanfar, F.: Combined modeling and side channel attacks on strong PUFs. IACR Cryptol. ePrint Arch. **2013**, 632 (2013)

17. Yu, M.-D.M., Hiller, M., Delvaux, J., Sowell, R., Devadas, S., Verbauwhede, I.: A lockdown technique to prevent machine learning on PUFs for lightweight authentication. IEEE Trans. Multi-Scale Comput. Syst. 2(3), 146–159 (2016)
18. Suh, G.E., Devadas, S.: Physical unclonable functions for device authentication and secret key generation. In: Proceedings of the 44th Annual Design Automation Conference, pp. 9–14. ACM (2007)
19. Merli, D.: Attacking and protecting ring oscillator physical unclonable functions and code-offset fuzzy extractors. Ph.D. thesis, Technical University Munich (2013)
20. Maiti, A., Schaumont, P.: Improved ring oscillator PUF: an FPGA-friendly secure primitive. J. Cryptol. 24(2), 375–397 (2011)
21. Maiti, A., Schaumont, P.: Improving the quality of a physical unclonable function using configurable ring oscillators. In: 2009 International Conference on Field Programmable Logic and Applications, FPL 2009, pp. 703–707. IEEE (2009)

Localizing Wireless Jamming Attacks with Minimal Network Resources

Jing Yang Koh[1] and Pengfei Zhang[2($\boxtimes$)]

[1] School of Computing, National University of Singapore,
Singapore 117417, Singapore
a0113481@nus.edu.sg
[2] Department of Engineering Science, University of Oxford,
Oxford OX1 1JP, UK
pengfei@robots.ox.ac.uk

Abstract. Wireless networks such as the wireless sensor networks (WSNs) are increasingly becoming ubiquitous in today's Internet of Things (IoT) environment. However, wireless networks are very vulnerable to jamming attacks which can be easily carried out by small concealable wireless transmitters. Thus, there is a need to quickly localize and remove the jammer node to prevent further disruptions to the network. In addition, an efficient jammer node localization algorithm should use minimal network resources, e.g., number of reporting nodes. Based on this idea, we propose a maximum likelihood estimator (MLE)-based localization method for the jammer node which allows each node that detected a jammed link to probabilistically transmit a jamming report. The node transmission probabilities are optimized using the cross-entropy (CE) method to ensure that the localization algorithm satisfies a pre-defined reliability threshold. Our simulation results show that the proposed scheme performs significantly better than the simple centroid-based localization methods while using lesser number of reporting nodes and traffic.

Keywords: Wireless jamming attacks · RSS-based localization
Maximum likelihood estimation · Optimization

1 Introduction

Wireless jamming attacks [1–3] are easy to execute and effective in disputing wireless communications. An easily available and low-cost off-the-shelf wireless sensor node can be easily reprogrammed to function as a jamming device without incurring additional hardware costs. The small wireless transmitters can then be used to emit radio frequency signals to intentionally corrupt legitimately transmitted packets or to keep the wireless channel busy. Without access to the wireless channel, the reliability of many wireless applications is put at risk. Hence, the wireless jamming attacks pose a significant threat, especially to emerging Internet of Things (IoT) applications that use wireless networks, e.g., the time-critical

© Springer International Publishing AG 2017
G. Wang et al. (Eds.): SpaCCS 2017 Workshops, LNCS 10658, pp. 322–334, 2017.
https://doi.org/10.1007/978-3-319-72395-2_30

smart grid [4] or the low-cost wireless sensor networks [5,6], or applications used in battlefield awareness and secure area monitoring [1].

In the event of a wireless jamming attack, a Denial of Service (DoS) occurs, and the affected wireless nodes will be unable to communicate with each other or to a backend fusion center. Thus, the wireless network needs to quickly localize the jamming device and remove it to prevent further disruption to the network. As the jamming attacks pose a significant threat to the wireless networks, many research works, e.g., [4–9] have focused on localizing the jammed region or the jammer node. However, few works have *statistically modeled* the jammer node localization problem and formulate a *cost-effective* solution. An efficient jammer node localization scheme which uses minimal network resources (subjected to a constraint on its accuracy) can reduce the degradation of network performance experienced by the unjammed nodes.

In this paper, we develop an effective and efficient localization algorithm to localize a jammer node using minimal network resources. We apply the *maximum likelihood estimator* (MLE) statistical modeling technique and incorporate the concept of *audibility* [10,11] to allow the backend fusion center to effectively localize the jamming device. In addition, we can reduce the amount of overheads incurred by the localization algorithm by reducing the expected number of reporting nodes. Specifically, we allow each node that detected a jammed link to probabilistically transmit its neighbors' link status information to the gateway. The probabilities are optimized offline via a Monte Carlo method which uses the *cross-entropy* (CE) optimization to ensure that the localization algorithm satisfies a pre-defined reliability threshold.

1.1 Our Contributions

Our main contribution is twofold.

1. We propose a novel way of estimating the jammer's location via the maximum likelihood estimator (MLE) method which only requires the audibility statuses of the wireless nodes as inputs.
2. We improve the efficiency of our localization algorithm by reducing the expected number of reporting nodes while ensuring that the localization algorithm satisfies a pre-defined reliability threshold. We allow each node to probabilistically report its neighbor's link status (audibility) information to the gateway and the probabilities are optimized using the cross-entropy (CE) method.

1.2 Related Work

We briefly review existing jamming detection techniques before moving to the jammer localization algorithms. In [5,6], Xu *et al.* introduced the notion of consistency checking where the packet delivery ratio (PDR) is used to classify the quality of a radio link, and a received signal strength (RSS) consistency check is used to determine if a poor link quality is due to jamming attacks from the various (constant, deceptive, reactive, random) types of jammers. The authors concluded that a node is jammed when the observed PDR is low or zero, but the RSS is high. A detailed survey on jamming attack detection strategies can be found in [1–3].

To localize the jammer node, the work in [7] considered a constant jammer and proposed that the jammed nodes temporarily violate their medium access control (MAC) protocols and broadcast a "jammed" message to its neighbors. This allows the boundary nodes to map the jammed regions. The works in [4,12] studied the impact of a reactive jammer in time-critical network applications and introduced a new metric, the message invalidation ratio, to quantify the impact of probabilistic jamming attacks. The work in [8] computed the convex hull of the set of jammed nodes at the border of the jammed region and estimates the jammer's location to be the centroid of the jammed region. The centroid-based localization technique was improved in [13] which then proposed the virtual force iterative localization method to estimate the jammer's location. The virtual force iterative method uses the estimated jammer's location (estimated by finding the centroid location of all jammed nodes) as a starting estimate and iteratively improves the jammer's location estimate. The iterations terminate when the estimated jammed region matches all the actual jammed nodes while all the boundary nodes are outside the jammed region. The work in [9] used a gradient descent algorithm to identify the node closest to the jammer node assuming that the packet delivery ratio (PDR) value decreases as we move closer to the jammer.

To the best of our knowledge, none of the current works attempted to minimize the amount of network resources needed to localize the jammer node, e.g., by reducing the number of reporting nodes. This action may lead to a faster detection period (albeit with lower accuracy) and more importantly, minimizes the degradation of network performance e.g., latency, throughput, or even mobile data charges experienced by the unjammed nodes.

2   Problem Formulation

We first list our system and adversary models before presenting our proposed maximum likelihood estimator and Monte Carlo method for minimizing the expected number of reporting nodes.

2.1   System Model and Assumptions

Our network model (see Fig. 1) is as follows.

1. *Nodes:* The wireless network consists of M wireless nodes and L gateway (GW) nodes placed at known locations $\mathbf{x}_{1,\dots,M}$ and $\mathbf{y}_{1,\dots,L}$ respectively. In addition, we assume that there is a single constant jammer node located at an unknown location $\boldsymbol{\Theta}_J$. Let $\mathcal{M}$ represent the set of M wireless nodes, and $\mathcal{L}$ represent the set of L gateways. All nodes (except for the jammer's) are

assumed to be using the IEEE 802.11 or 802.15 MAC protocols. We assume that the network is stationary and the gateways are connected to a fusion center which executes the jammer node localization algorithm.

2. *Connectivity:* We adopt the widely used log-normal propagation (path loss) model in Definition 1 and assume symmetric links. We also define *audibility* in Definition 2 and use the indicator variable $a_{A,B}$ to indicate if a node A is audible to B. Mainly, in order for two nodes A and B to communicate with each other, their transmitted signals should be audible to the each other [10,11]. Each wireless node i maintains a neighbor list $\mathcal{N}_i$, and periodically exchanges heartbeat (beacon) packets with its neighbors $j \in \mathcal{N}_i$ assuming that the heartbeats are time-synchronized and transmitted with known power P_{Tx}^j. Each node then compute the packet delivery ratio (PDR) for each of its neighbor's link [5]. We let $\text{PDR}^{A,B}$ denote the PDR between nodes A and B.

3. *Routing:* We let e represent an edge (link) between two neighboring nodes and c_e represent the cost of using the edge e. We set $c_e = \infty$, if the edge e is jammed, and $c_e > 0$, otherwise. Let $\mathcal{R}^{i,GW}$ be the set of routing paths r from the node i to the gateway. The cost of using a path r is given in Definition 3.

4. *Node Classification:* A wireless node i (including the gateway) can be classified into the following categories. Node i is a:
   (i) *fully jammed (or simply jammed) node* if
   $a_{i,j} = 0, \forall j \in \mathcal{N}_i$
   or $\nexists r \in \mathcal{R}^{i,GW}$ where $\sum_{e \in r} c_e < \infty$,
   (ii) *partially jammed (or boundary) node* if
   $\exists j \in \mathcal{N}_i : a_{i,j} = 1 \wedge \exists j \in \mathcal{N}_i : a_{i,j} = 0$,
   (iii) *unaffected node* if
   $a_{i,j} = 1, \forall j \in \mathcal{N}_i$.

5. *Jamming Detection:* We assume that the wireless nodes have a jamming detection algorithm that relies on the RSS and PDR values of its links (see Definition 4). We further assume that $\text{PDR}^{A,B} \leq \lambda_{\text{PDR}}$ is always satisfied when the jammer node is audible to either node A or B where λ_{PDR} is a pre-defined threshold. Each boundary node i that detects a jamming attack will send its neighbors' link (audibility) status list $\{\mathcal{N}_i, a_{i,j}\}_{\forall j \in \mathcal{N}_i}$ to its nearest gateway with probability α_i.

Definition 1 (Path loss model). *The received signal power (in dBm) by a node A located at $\mathbf{x}_A = [x_A, \ y_A]$ from a signal sent by node B which is located at $\mathbf{x}_B = [x_B, \ y_B]$ is given by*

$$P_{Rec}^A = P_{Tx}^B - 10\alpha \log \frac{d(\mathbf{x}_A, \mathbf{x}_B)}{d_0} + \epsilon_r,$$

where P_{Tx}^B is the received power from node B at a reference distance d_0 (typically 1m), α is the path-loss exponent, $d(\mathbf{x}_A, \mathbf{x}_B)$ is the Euclidean distance between nodes A and B, and $\epsilon_r \sim \mathcal{N}(0, \sigma_\epsilon^2)$ is the received power noise (due to the shadowing effect).

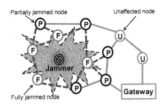

Fig. 1. Example network of wireless nodes with one gateway and one jammer node. The wireless links between the nodes are solid if it is not jammed and dotted if jammed. The wireless nodes (including the gateway) can be classified into the following three types: fully jammed (F), partially jammed (P), and unaffected nodes (U) and are colored in grey, black, and green respectively. (Color figure online)

Definition 2 (Audibility). *Node* B *is said to be audible to node* A *if* $P_{Rec}^{A} \geq \lambda_{audible}$, *where* $\lambda_{audible}$ *is a predefined threshold representing the receiver's sensitivity. Otherwise, node* B *is said to be inaudible to node* A.

Definition 3 (Cost of using a routing path). *We define the cost of using a routing path* r *to be* $\sum_{e \in r} c_e$, *where* $c_e > 0$ *if the link is not jammed and* $c_e = \infty$, *otherwise.*

$$
\begin{aligned}
\dot{\Theta}_J &= \arg\max_{\Theta_J} \prod_{i=1}^{\mathcal{M}} \{ p(P_{Rec}^{i}(J), P_{Rec}^{i}, S(i), \mathcal{N}_i, x_i | \Theta_J) \} \\
&= \arg\max_{\Theta_J} \prod_{i=1}^{\mathcal{M}} \{ \int p(P_{Rec}^{i}(J), P_{Rec}^{i}, S(i), \mathcal{N}_i, x_i | \Theta_J, P_{Tx}^{J}) p(P_{Tx}^{J}) dP_{Tx}^{J} \} \\
&= \arg\max_{\Theta_J} \prod_{i=1}^{\mathcal{M}} \Big\{ \int \Big(p(P_{Rec}^{i}(J) < \lambda_{\text{audible}}) \prod_{j=1}^{\mathcal{N}_i} (p(P_{Rec}^{J}(j) \geq \lambda_{\text{audible}}) \mathbb{1}(S(j) = F) \\
&\quad + p(P_{Rec}^{J}(j) < \lambda_{\text{audible}}) \mathbb{1}(S(j) \neq F)) \mathbb{1}(S(i) = P) \\
&\quad + (p(P_{Rec}^{J}(j) \geq \lambda_{\text{audible}}) \mathbb{1}(S(j) = F) \\
&\quad + p(P_{Rec}^{J}(j) < \lambda_{\text{audible}}) \mathbb{1}(S(j) \neq F)) \mathbb{1}(i \in \mathcal{N}_{S_p}) \Big) p(P_{Tx}^{J}) dP_{Tx}^{J} \Big\}.
\end{aligned}
\tag{1}
$$

2.2 Adversarial Model

We assume that the adversary uses a *constant jammer* node which continually emits a radio signal [1,5,6] with an unknown transmission power P_{Tx}^{J} from a known distribution. The (physical layer) jamming attack (see Definition 4) prevents legitimate nodes from using the channel due to their MAC protocol restrictions [6]. Hence, we assume that the received signal strength (RSS) at a partially jammed node A will contain either P_{Tx}^{J} or P_{Tx}^{B} but not both. We also assume that there is at least one node and one gateway that are not jammed. Otherwise, it is not possible to localize the jammer node when the fusion center does not receive any information.

Definition 4 (Jamming attack). *We use a simple thresholding mechanism based on the PDR and RSS values (based on [5,6]) to detect a jamming attack between two neighboring nodes A and B. Mainly, a jamming attack occurs at node A if*

$$PDR^{A,B} \leq \lambda_{PDR} \text{ ,and } P^A_{Rec} \geq \lambda_{RSS},$$

where $\lambda_{PDR}, \lambda_{RSS}$ are predefined thresholds.

2.3   Estimating the Jammer's Location

We apply the maximum likelihood estimator (MLE) method to estimate the location of the jammer node. The MLE is a commonly used statistical estimation method and can be used for RSS-based localization [14] for wireless nodes. However, our MLE formulation differs from [14] as we do not require the wireless nodes to report their RSS readings. Instead, we allow each boundary node i that detects a jammed link to probabilistically report its neighbors' link status (or *audibility*, see Definition 2) information $\{\mathcal{N}_i, a_{i,j}\}_{\forall j \in \mathcal{N}_i}$ (e.g., {neighbor 1, audible}, {neighbor 2, not audible}) to the gateway with probability α_i. The audibility concept allows us to extract information about the jammer's location even when the nodes are jammed and did not transit to the gateway while the probabilistic reporting allows us to reduce the expected number of reporting nodes.

Let $S(i) \in \{F, P, U\}$ denote the classification (fully jammed (F), partially jammed (P), and unaffected nodes (U)) of a node i. If each boundary node has probability α_i to transmit its neighbors' link status list $\{\mathcal{N}_i, a_{i,j}\}_{\forall j \in \mathcal{N}_i}$ to its nearest gateway, we have $p(S(i) = F|S(i) = P) = 1 - \alpha_i$. Thus, the estimated jammer node location $\hat{\Theta}_J$ is given obtained by solving the proposed MLE in (1). The MLE consists of the two summation terms where the first term considers the likelihood of boundary nodes which transmit back to GW and the second term considers the neighbors of the boundary nodes which transmitted to the GW.

2.4   Minimizing the Number of Reporting Nodes

Given that some of the links are jammed due to a jammer node located at Θ_J, each node needs to compute the minimum-cost path r (see Definition 3) to the nearest gateway (GW), i.e., $\arg\min_{r \in \mathcal{R}^{i,GW}} \sum_{e \in r} c_e$. If each node i reports its neighbors' link status list $\{\mathcal{N}_i, a_{i,j}\}_{\forall j \in \mathcal{N}_i}$ with probability α_i, the total expected overhead incurred by the network is $\sum_{i \in \mathcal{M}} \left(\alpha_i \min_{r \in \mathcal{R}^{i,GW}} \sum_{e \in r} c_e \right)$. Now, we have to decide how to assign the α_i values to the boundary nodes such that the total overhead incurred by the network is minimized while the estimated jammer localization accuracy for $\hat{\Theta}_J$ (using the proposed MLE for $\hat{\Theta}_J$ in (1)) is not worse than a threshold η from the optimal MLE estimate $\hat{\Theta}^*_J$ where $\alpha_i = 1$ for all boundary node i. As such, we formulate the overhead minimization problem as shown below:

$$\underset{\{\alpha_i\}_{i \in \mathcal{M}}}{\text{minimize}} \quad \sum_{i \in \mathcal{M}} \left(\alpha_i \min_{r \in \mathcal{R}^{i,GW}} \sum_{e \in r} c_e \right) \tag{2}$$

$$\text{subject to} \quad |\hat{\Theta}_J^* - \hat{\Theta}_J| \leq \eta.$$

Next, we elaborate on how we apply the cross-entropy (CE) method to solve Problem 2.

Cross-Entropy (CE) Method. In order to find the optimal α_i values for each boundary node i, we use a well-known optimization technique called the cross-entropy method. First, we show how the cross-entropy method [15] is applied to solve optimization problems. Suppose we wish to minimize a function $U(\mathbf{x})$ over some set $\mathcal{X}$. Let the minimum value of $U(\mathbf{x})$ be denoted by γ^*:

$$\gamma^* = \min_{\mathbf{x} \in \mathcal{X}} U(\mathbf{x}) \tag{3}$$

The CE method casts (3) into an estimation problem for rare-event probability and aims to locate an optimal parametric sampling distribution, i.e., a probability distribution on $\mathcal{X}$, rather than locating the optimal solution $\mathbf{x}$ directly. We define a collection of indicator functions $\{\mathbb{1}_{\{U(\mathbf{x}) \leq \gamma\}}\}$ on $\mathcal{X}$ for various $\gamma \in \mathbb{R}$. Hence, we associate (3) with the following problem of estimating the rare-event probability:

$$l(\gamma) = \mathbb{P}_u(U(X) \leq \gamma) = E_u[\{\mathbb{1}_{\{U(\mathbf{x}) \leq \gamma\}}\}], \tag{4}$$

where $\mathbb{P}_u$ is the probability measure under which the random state X has a discrete pdf $f(\cdot; u)$ and $\mathbb{E}_u$ denotes the corresponding expectation operator.

CE Method for Minimizing Number of Reporting Nodes. The CE method involves an iterative procedure where each iteration can be broken down into two phases: (i) generate a random data sample (trajectories, vectors, etc.) according to a specified mechanism, and (ii) update the parameters of the random mechanism based on the data to produce a "better" sample in the next iteration. We describe the generic algorithm for the cross-entropy method in Algorithm 1. The algorithm follows the procedure described in Sect. 2.4. In Step 1, random samples are generated from a Bernoulli distribution with $p = 0.5$. In Step 2, we evaluate the objective function for all the samples generated in Step 1. In Step 3, we set a fixed quantile β_t and update $\mathbf{P_t}$ using $E_u[\{\mathbb{1}_{\{U(\mathbf{x}) \leq \gamma\}}\}]$ in Step 4. Algorithm 1 uses three parameters ϕ, ρ, and K, where ϕ is a smoothing parameter that controls the speed of learning (a larger ϕ indicates a fast learning speed, i.e., $P_{t,j}$ is prone to changes),ρ is the quartile level used for selecting the samples (a large ρ indicates a small quartile β_t, thus a large number of samples), and K determines the number of samples generated in each iteration.

Algorithm 1. Cross-Entropy Generic Algorithm

Input: $\mathbf{x}_{1,\ldots,M}, \mathbf{y}_{1,\ldots,L}, \mathbf{c_e}, \phi, \rho, K, \eta, \hat{\mathbf{\Theta}}_J^*$
  Initialization: at iteration $t = 0$, set $\mathbf{P_0} = \{p_1, p_2 \cdots, p_N\}$ such that $p_j = 0.5$,
  $\forall j = \{1, 2 \cdots, N\}$.
  while stopping criterion **do**
    1. Generate K independent samples of the binary set $\mathbf{\Gamma_i} = \{\gamma_{i,1}, \gamma_{i,2} \cdots, \gamma_{i,N}\}$,
    where $\gamma_{i,j} \sim Ber(p_j)$ for $1 \leq i \leq K$.
    2. Evaluate $U(\mathbf{\Gamma})$ for all the K samples.
    3. Calculate $\beta_t = (1 - \rho)$ quartile.
    4. Update $\mathbf{P_t}$ as follows:

$$P_{t,j} = \phi \frac{\sum_{i=1}^{K} \mathbb{1}(U(\mathbf{\Gamma_i}) \leq \beta_t) \mathbb{1}(\mathbf{\Gamma_{i,j}} = 1)}{\sum_{i=1}^{K} \mathbb{1}(U(\mathbf{\Gamma_i}) \leq \beta_t)}$$
$$+ (1 - \phi) P_{t-1,j},$$

    where ϕ is a smoothing parameter.
    5. $t = t + 1$.
  end while
  Output: $\mathbf{P_t}$

To apply Algorithm 1 to our minimization problem in (2), we let $U'(\alpha_i) = \sum_{i \in \mathcal{M}} \left(\alpha_i \min_{r \in \mathcal{R}^{i,GW}} \sum_{e \in r} c_e \right)$, and let $C(\alpha_i) = 1$, if $|\hat{\mathbf{\Theta}}_J^* - \hat{\mathbf{\Theta}}_J| \leq \eta$, and $C(\alpha_i)$ equals some large constant, otherwise. The modified cross-entropy objective function, incorporating the constraints is given by $U(\alpha_i) = U'(\alpha_i) C(\alpha_i)$. Next, we can proceed with the minimization of $U(\alpha_i)$ (without modifying the algorithm), as the cases which fail to satisfy the constraint $C(\alpha_i)$ will return a large $U(\alpha_i)$ score that does not satisfy the indicator function $\mathbb{1}(U(\alpha_i) \leq \beta_t)$. The algorithm arranges the evaluated scores $U(\alpha_i)$ from the K samples in increasing order, and chooses the percentile value from the ordered K samples according to ρ. For instance, if $\rho = 0.5$ and the ordered samples are $\{10, 40, 70, 110, 130\}$, the percentile value selected is $\beta_t = 70$.

Finally, given a fixed wireless network with an unknown jammer location $\mathbf{\Theta}_J$ and unknown estimate $\hat{\mathbf{\Theta}}_J^*$, we use the Monte Carlo method in Algorithm 2 to obtain the node transmission probabilities $\alpha_1, \ldots, \alpha_M$. The algorithm is executed offline and the optimized $\alpha_1, \ldots, \alpha_M$ are then assigned into the wireless nodes. In an actual jamming scenario, the boundary nodes transmit according to their assigned α_i probabilities and the fusion center simply uses the proposed MLE for $\mathbf{\Theta}_J$ in (1) to estimate the jammer node location $\hat{\mathbf{\Theta}}_J$.

Algorithm 2. Optimization of Transmission Probabilities

Input: $\mathbf{x}_{1,\ldots,M}, \mathbf{y}_{1,\ldots,L}, \phi, \rho, K, \eta$

    1. Generate N random samples of jammer node location $\Theta_J^{(1)}, \ldots, \Theta_J^{(N)}$, and compute c_e for all edges e.

    foreach $\Theta_J^{(i)} \in \{\Theta_J^{(1)}, \ldots, \Theta_J^{(N)}\}$ **do**

        2.1 Solve for the optimal jammer node location estimate $\hat{\Theta}_J^*$ using (1), with all α values set to 1.

        2.2 Solve for $\alpha_1^{(i)}, \ldots, \alpha_M^{(i)}$ using Algorithm 1.

    end

    3. Set $\alpha_1, \ldots, \alpha_M$ to be the mean of all the respective $\alpha_1^{(i)}, \ldots, \alpha_M^{(i)}$ values.

Output: $\alpha_1, \ldots, \alpha_M$

---

3   Simulation Results and Discussion

3.1   Simulation Setup and Performance Metric

We compared our proposed CE (and MLE) method against the centroid-based localization schemes, similar to what was used in [8,13], and the optimal[1] MLE method where all boundary nodes send their reports to the fusion center, i.e., $\alpha_i = 1$ for all boundary nodes i. We used two variants of the centroid-based localization scheme: *Centroid 1*, which takes the centroid coordinates of all the boundary nodes, while *Centroid 2*, which takes the centroid coordinates of all the jammed nodes as used in [8,13]. An illustration of how our proposed MLE method (optimal) and the centroid schemes work is given in Fig. 2.

We examine the different schemes and compare the mean squared error (MSE) and traffic (total number of hops transmitted by the reporting nodes to the gateways) under different network configurations with 20 wireless nodes and 1–5 gateways (GWs). For each scenario, we ran our simulation for 100 different network topologies with an area of $100\,\mathrm{m} \times 100\,\mathrm{m}$. A smaller MSE or traffic value

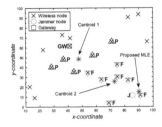

Fig. 2. Jammer estimates from the proposed MLE method against the two baseline centroid-based localization methods. The nodes labeled with **P** and **F** indicate that they are partially jammed and fully jammed respectively.

---

[1] Since the fusion center receives all the reports from the nodes, the localization algorithm should produce the lowest possible MSE values.

indicates a better localization scheme. Let $c_e = 1$ for all unjammed links e in the network. We use the following parameters for the wireless network: $P^i_{Tx} = 15$, $P^J_{Tx} = 30$, (but we only assume that the distribution of the jammer node's transmit power, i.e., $\mathcal{N}(30, 1)$ is known to the fusion center) $\lambda_{\text{audible}} = -85$, $\sigma^2_\epsilon = 1$, $\alpha = 3$, and the following parameters for Algorithm 1: $\phi = 0.6$, $\rho = 0.01$, $K = 50$, and the stopping criterion is when $t \geq 50$.

3.2 Results and Discussion

We study the MSE values for the schemes when the number of GWs vary from 1 to 5 and plot the average MSE values of 100 different network topologies for $\eta = 2$ in Fig. 3 where we used Algorithm 1 to assign the α values for each jammer node location. The results show that our proposed CE method is able to produce the MSE values close to that of the optimal MLE estimate $\hat{\Theta}^*_J$ where $\alpha_i = 1$ for all boundary nodes i. Both MLE estimates have a much lesser MSE value than the Centroid 1 (C1) and Centroid 2 (C2) schemes. Similarly, we plot the corresponding expected traffic values in Fig. 4 where the traffic values for the C1, C2, and optimal MLE methods are simply labeled as "Opt". The proposed CE method incurs less traffic compared to the optimal MLE method, and the traffic decreases when the number of GWs is increasing. In addition to using $\eta = 2$, we simulated the same network scenarios with $\eta = \{3, 4, 5, 8, 10\}$ and the same conclusion holds. Due to the length constraint, we present the results for $\eta = 10$ in Figs. 5 and 6, which contain the MSE and traffic values respectively.

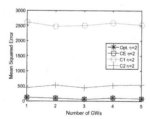

Fig. 3. Mean squared error (MSE) with respect to different number of GWs when $\eta = 2$.

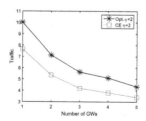

Fig. 4. Traffic incurred with respect to different number of GWs when $\eta = 2$.

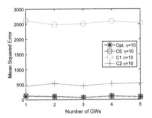

Fig. 5. Mean squared error (MSE) with respect to different number of GWs when $\eta = 10$.

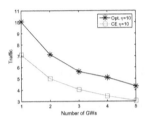

Fig. 6. Traffic incurred with respect to different number of GWs when $\eta = 10$.

Next, we used Algorithm 2 to assign the α values for each node and used $N = 100$ different jammer node locations as training data. In Figs. 7 and 8, we show the MSE and traffic values for an arbitrary network with one GW and $\eta = 2$. The results show that our CE method can achieve almost the same MSE values as the optimal MLE method but consumes lesser traffic. Lastly, we plot the MSE and traffic results in Figs. 9 and 10 for $\eta = 2$ when the optimized α values are used for all 100 different jammer node locations. Overall, the MSE values do not differ much with respect to the number of GWs but our CE method uses lesser traffic than the optimal MLE method. However, the incurred traffic is quite fluctuated due to some outliers. A higher η parameter will allow further traffic savings at the expense of an increase in the MSE.

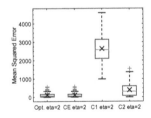

Fig. 7. Boxplot of the mean squared error (MSE) for an arbitrary network and $\eta = 2$ with 1 GW. The mean values are denoted by the cross markers.

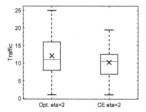

Fig. 8. Boxplot of the traffic incurred by an arbitrary network and $\eta = 2$ with 1 GW. The mean values are denoted by the cross markers.

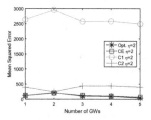

Fig. 9. Mean squared error (MSE) with respect to different number of GWs and $\eta = 2$.

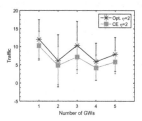

Fig. 10. Mean and standard deviation values for the traffic incurred in networks with different number of GWs and $\eta = 2$.

4 Conclusion

The jammer node localization problem is an important and widely studied problem in the wireless network literature. Ideally, the localization algorithm should not use more network resources than necessary to prevent the unjamming nodes from experiencing degradation in their own tasks too. Therefore, we propose a maximum likelihood estimator (MLE)-based localization method for the jammer node and minimize the expected number of reporting nodes by optimizing the node transmission probabilities using the cross-entropy method. Our simulation results indicate that our proposed scheme achieves much lesser mean squared error values compared with the centroid-based schemes and can achieve comparable estimation performances while incurring lesser traffic than the optimal MLE method. The future work will be to extend our localization algorithm to detect multiple jammer nodes.

References

1. Mpitziopoulos, A., Gavalas, D., Konstantopoulos, C., Pantziou, G.: A survey on jamming attacks and countermeasures in WSNs. IEEE Commun. Surv. Tutor. **11**(4), 42–56 (2009)
2. Pelechrinis, K., Iliofotou, M., Krishnamurthy, S.V.: Denial of service attacks in wireless networks: the case of jammers. IEEE Commun. Surv. Tutor. **13**(2), 245–257 (2011)
3. Grover, K., Lim, A., Yang, Q.: Jamming and anti-jamming techniques in wireless networks: a survey. Int. J. Ad Hoc Ubiquitous Comput. **17**(4), 197–215 (2014)
4. Lu, Z., Wang, W., Wang, C.: From jammer to gambler: modeling and detection of jamming attacks against time-critical traffic. In: Proceedings of the IEEE International Conference Computer Communications (INFOCOM), pp. 1871–1879, April 2011
5. Xu, W., Trappe, W., Zhang, Y., Wood, T.: The feasibility of launching and detecting jamming attacks in wireless networks. In: Proceedings of the ACM International Symposium on Mobile Ad Hoc Networking and Computing (MobiHoc), pp. 46–57 (2005)
6. Xu, W., Ma, K., Trappe, W., Zhang, Y.: Jamming sensor networks: attack and defense strategies. IEEE Netw. **20**(3), 41–47 (2006)
7. Wood, A.D., Stankovic, J.A., Son, S.H.: Jam: a jammed-area mapping service for sensor networks. In: IEEE Real-Time Systems Symposium (RTSS), pp. 286–297, December 2003
8. Sun, Y., Wang, X., Zhou, X.: Jammer localization for wireless sensor networks. Chin. J. Electron. **20**(4), 735–738 (2011)
9. Pelechrinis, K., Koutsopoulos, I., Broustis, I., Krishnamurthy, S.V.: Lightweight jammer localization in wireless networks: system design and implementation. In: IEEE Global Telecommunications Conference (GLOBECOM), pp. 1–6, November 2009
10. Koh, J.Y., Nevat, I., Leong, D., Wong, W.C.: Geo-spatial location spoofing detection for internet of things. IEEE Internet Things J. **PP**(99), 1–8 (2016)
11. Nevat, I., Peters, G.W., Avnit, K., Septier, F., Clavier, L.: Location of things: geospatial tagging for iot using time-of-arrival. IEEE Trans. Signal Inf. Process. Over Netw. **2**(2), 174–185 (2016)
12. Lu, Z., Wang, W., Wang, C.: Modeling, evaluation and detection of jamming attacks in time-critical wireless applications. IEEE Trans. Mobile Comput. **13**(8), 1746–1759 (2014)
13. Liu, H., Liu, Z., Chen, Y., Xu, W.: Determining the position of a jammer using a virtual-force iterative approach. Wirel. Netw. **17**(2), 531–547 (2011)
14. Patwari, N., Hero III, A., Perkins, M., Correal, N., O'Dea, R.: Relative location estimation in wireless sensor networks. IEEE Trans. Signal Process. **51**(8), 2137–2148 (2003)
15. Rubinstein, R.Y., Kroese, D.P.: The Cross-Entropy Method. A Unified Approach to Combinatorial Optimization, Monte-carlo Simulation and Machine Learning. Information Science and Statistics. Springer, New York (2004). https://doi.org/10.1007/978-1-4757-4321-0

The 5th International Workshop on Network Optimization and Performance Evaluation (NOPE 2017)

NOPE 2017 Organizing and Program Committees

1 General Chairs

Kim-Kwang Raymond Choo	University of Texas at San Antonio, USA
Guojun Wang	Guangzhou University, China

2 Program Chairs

Gaocai Wang	Guangxi University, China
Tao Peng	Guangzhou University, China

3 Program Committee Members

Pinial Khan Butt	Sindh Agriculture University, Pakistan
Dunqian Cao	Guangxi University for Nationalities, China
Hongbin Chen	Guilin University of Electronic Technology, China
Jinfu Chen	Jiangsu University, China
Shun Dai	National Astronomical Observatories, Chinese Academy of Sciences, China
Chengzhi Deng	Nanchang Institute of Technology, China
Xiaoheng Deng	Central South University, China
Yihui Deng	Jinan University, China
Dieter Fiems	Ghent University, Belgium
Shuqiang Huang	Jinan University, China
Shuai Kang	Zunyi Normal College, China
Daofeng Li	Guangxi University, China
Shijun Li	Hunan Institute of Engineering, China
Xiong Li	Hunan University of Science, China
Yan Li	Yunnan Minzu University, China
Junbin Liang	Hong Kong Polytechnic University, Hong Kong
Chi Lin	Dalian University of Technology, China
Xianfeng Liu	Hunan Normal University, China
Yunzheng Liu	Institute of Information Engineering, Chinese Academy of Sciences, China
Songfeng Lu	Huazhong University of Science and Technology, China
Entao Luo	Hunan University of Science and Engineering, China
Mingxing Luo	Southwest Jiaotong University, China

Gordhan Das Menghwar	Sindh Agriculture University, Pakistan
Yitian Peng	Southeast University, China
Juan F. Perez	Imperial College London, UK
Barkatullah Qureshi	Sindh Agriculture University, Pakistan
Jiankang Ren	Dalian University of Technology, China
Zhefu Shi	University of Missouri, USA
Mahendra Shukla	Indian Institute of Information Technology, India
Bin Sun	Beijing University of Posts and Telecommunications, China
Kun Tang	Central South University, China
Mingdong Tang	Guangdong University of Foreign Studies, China
Haoqian Wang	Tsinghua University, China
Zhiwei Wang	Nanjing University of Posts and Telecommunications, China
Chuyuan Wei	Beijing University of Civil Engineering and Architecture, China
Qianqian Xing	National University of Defense Technology, China
Canhui Xu	Qingdao University of Science and Technology, China
Hongyun Xu	South China University of Technology, China
Suneel Yadav	Indian Institute of Information Technology, India
Jin Ye	Guangxi University, China
Hao Zhang	Central South University, China
Lei Zhang	Beijing University of Civil Engineering and Architecture, China
Shaofeng Zhang	Tsinghua University, China
Yousheng Zhou	Chongqing University of Posts and Telecommunications, China

4 Steering Committee

Gaocai Wang	Guangxi University, China (Chair)
Guojun Wang	Guangzhou University, China (Chair)
Mohammed Atiquzzaman	University of Oklahoma, USA
Kim-Kwang Raymond Choo	University of Texas at San Antonio, USA
Keqin Li	State University of New York, USA
Keqiu Li	Dalian University of Technology, China
Taoshen Li	Guangxi University, China
Wei Li	Texas Southern University, USA

5 Publicity Chair

Md Zakirul Alam Bhuiyan	Fordham University, USA
Mir Sajjad Hussain Talpur	Sindh Agriculture University, Pakistan

6 Web Chair

Tongshuai Cui	Central South University, China

An Architecture of Urban Regional Health Information System and Its Data Conversion Algorithm

Jinfu Chen$^{(\boxtimes)}$, Lin Zhang, Ackah-Arthur Hilary,
Omari Michael, and Jiaxiang Xi

School of Computer Science and Communication Engineering,
Jiangsu University, Zhenjiang 212013, China
jinfuchen@ujs.edu.cn

Abstract. With the development of health information systems, people are placing increasing demand for better medical care. In order to improve the convenience and intelligence of medical service, many researchers have begun to study the regional health information system in recent years. In this paper, based on the existing integrated digital city information infrastructure, an architecture of urban regional health information system is proposed, and the application of this architecture within cities in China is also presented. To start with, the overall architecture of health information system is presented. In this architecture, we mainly focus on the application portal, the regional health information application platform, the business systems, and the application support platform. Additionally, a data conversion algorithm is proposed. Finally, the paper analyzes the application performance of the proposed architecture of urban regional health information system in China. The experimental results show that the architecture proposed in this paper is feasible and effective.

Keywords: Regional health information system · Electronic health record
Hospital information system · Data conversion · Unified application platform

1 Introduction

With the rapid development of the social economy, people are expecting to enjoy better health services, but current limited health resources cannot meet the expectations. As a powerful means to improve the quality and the efficiency of health services, health information technology has reached a consensus in the industry [1–3]. The construction of urban regional health information system is an inevitable requirement for developing health services, and it is a crucial part of the realization of the smart city [4–7]. However, in the process of accelerating the construction of medical information system, many existing problems must be tackled. These problems are mainly reflected in the lack of overall construction planning in the early stage of construction, leading to the inconsistence of business data and exchange standards [8, 9]. In this paper, the architecture of urban regional health information system is established based on the health business model. The architecture puts forward practical and comprehensive

© Springer International Publishing AG 2017
G. Wang et al. (Eds.): SpaCCS 2017 Workshops, LNCS 10658, pp. 339–349, 2017.
https://doi.org/10.1007/978-3-319-72395-2_31

planning and design on application portal, regional health information application platform, UAP/UAP-H application support platform, and business systems respectively.

We make the following contributions in this work:

(1) We present an architecture of urban regional health information system, focusing on basic information application portal, regional health information application platform, business systems, and application support platform;
(2) We propose a regional health information data conversion algorithm;
(3) We analyze the application of the proposed architecture.

The remainder of this paper is organized as follows: Related work is discussed in Sect. 2. The urban regional health information system is described in Sect. 3. The regional health information data conversion algorithm is detailed in Sect. 4. The analysis of system application is reported in Sect. 5, and the conclusion is presented in Sect. 6.

2 Related Work

In recent years, countries around the world have attached great importance to the construction of medical and health information [10–13]. In order to promote the construction of national regional health information in Canada, a non-profit company has been established, which is constructing reference architecture of the provincial electronic health record system. By 2020, the electronic health records of all the citizens in Canada will be established [14–16]. The residents in Zhabei District, Shanghai, are all distributed a health key. Residents can insert their personal health key to the computer and check their health through the network, which can help them to know their health status. Qingdao city has also built a basic health information system based on electronic health records [17, 18]. Results throughout domestic and international research indicate that, the regional health information construction has been recognized as the new trend in the development of the medical industry.

3 Urban Regional Health Information System

The architecture of urban regional health information system consists of eight layers: (1) application portal; (2) regional health information application platform; (3) application support platform; (4) data center; (5) data sharing and exchange service platform; (6) business systems; (7) specification standard system; and (8) information security system. The detailed explanations of application portal, regional health information application platform, business systems, and application support platform are presented as follows.

3.1   Application Portal

In a technical sense, the application portal is split into intranet portal and extranet portal for different users. Intranet portal has integrated antivirus applications. Extranet portal can be seen as the carrier for releasing information to the public and the major network channel for people to know about health issues.

3.2   Regional Health Information Application Platform

Applications can be divided into four categories, including: (1) Information sharing: It contains health card system, electronic medical records sharing system, and so on. (2) Business collaboration and linkage: In this category, functions include mutual recognition of examination results, the inspection commission, two-way referral, and making an appointment. (3) Health services for individuals: There are three modules in this part: health assessment, health education and health hut intelligent examination. (4) Management and decision-making: This category mainly contains community integrated management, disease management, medical management, etc.

3.3   Business Systems Based on Regional Health Information Platform

Business systems based on regional health information platform mainly includes: (1) Community health service system: It establishes a health service network by collecting community residents' health records information. (2) Hospital information system based on electronic medical record: It acquires and organizes hospital information and clinical information through the integrated platform, sends information to the regional health platform through the external interface, and transmits the current resident medical records information back to the hospital information system to help the diagnosis. (3) Hospital operation management system: It achieves the overall management of the transactions related to the hospital's business objectives. (4) Disease control management system: It mainly includes the slow disease management, infectious disease management, and so on. (5) Medical office automation system: It integrates personnel, processes and business operations, to promote the effective use of information and enhance the overall efficiency.

3.4   UAP/UAP-H Application Support Platform

UAP (Unified Application Platform) is a platform which provides the development, integration, management and other functions. UAP integration platform can assemble the various functional modules in the form of components, and then complete the corresponding development. UAP-H is a business support technology platform based on UAP integration platform, which provides the EHR sharing service, EHR browser, and so on. UAP-H application support platform can greatly shorten the development cycle in the construction of the application system, and improve the software quality and adaptability.

4 Regional Health Information Data Conversion Algorithm

The regional health information system needs to exchange and share data among the basic business information systems of health institutions, which involves the data conversion between the heterogeneous databases. The framework uses the data conversion between heterogeneous databases based on XML, which actually is the mapping between XML documents and relational databases, including the mapping from the database to XML documents and the mapping from XML documents to the database. Data conversion is required to complete the following steps: extract relational schema (Algorithm 1), transform XML schema and relational schema (Algorithm 2), extract data of relational databases to the XML documents (Algorithm 3) and import the XML data into relational databases (Algorithm 4).

ALGORITHM 1.   Algorithm for extracting relational schema

1: INPUT *database connection information* (**DCI**)
2: Read the type of the database and the type of connection from **DCI**;
3: Construct a connection string;
4: Establish a database connection;
5: Obtain the number (n) of the database table columns and table name *tempTableName*[n];
6: **while** $n \geqslant 0$ **do**
7:    Obtain the number (m) of the metadata fields in *tmpTableName*[n];
8:    Obtain the primary key *tmpTablePK*[n] of *tmpTableName*[n];
9:    **while** $m \geqslant 0$ **do**
10:      Get the field name and field type of *tmpTableName*[n];
11:      $m=m-1$;
12:    **end while**
13:    Save table information;
14:    $n=n-1$;
15: **end while**

Algorithm 1 shows the extraction process of relational schema. It aims at establishing the relationship model of the sharing database. The number of the database table columns is recorded as n, and the number of meta data fields of tmpTableName[n] is recorded as m, so the time complexity of Algorithm 1 is O (m * n).

ALGORITHM 2.   Algorithm for the transformation of XML schema and relational schema

1: INPUT *Relational database schema* (**RDS**)
2: Establish the XML Schema standard header and the correct namespace according to **RDS**;
3: Obtain the number (n) of the tables and the name (*tmpTableName*[n]) of the tables;
4: Obtain the number (m) of columns of *tempTableName*[n];
5: **while** $n \geqslant 0$ **do**
6:    **while** $m \geqslant 0$ **do**
7:      Create type elements of the table content;
8:      $m=m-1$;
9:    **end while**
10:    Create the table schema;
11:    $n=n-1$;
12: **end while**
13: Create type elements of the database;
14: **while** $n \geqslant 0$ **do**
15:    Create primary key type and the foreign key type of the table;
16:    $n=n-1$;
17: **end while**

Algorithm 2 gives the transformation process of the XML schema and relational schema. Then XML mapping files can be generated from XML schema according to the user's needs and XML definition files. In Algorithm 2, the number of tables is recorded as n, the number of columns is recorded as m, so the time complexity of the algorithm is O (n * m).

ALGORITHM 3. Algorithm for extracting data of relational database to the XML documents

1: INPUT *XML mapping files* (**XMF**)
2: Parse the root element of **XMF**.
3: Obtain the child elements *childElementofRoot* of the root element;
4: **for** each element *Relemt* in *childElementofRoot* **do**
5: **if** the type of *Relemt* is *attribute* **then**
6:    Obtain the value of *Relemt* according to the definition of XML mapping files.
7: **else if** the type of *Relemt* is *sqlRoot* **then**
8:    Obtain the child elements *childElementofSqlRoot* of *Relemt*.
9: **end if**
10: **if** *childElementofSqlRoot* is not null **then**
11:   **for** each element *SRelemt* in *childElementofSqlRoot* **do**
12:    **if** the type of *SRelemt* is *attribute* **then**
13:     Obtain the value of *SRelemt* according to the definition of XML mapping files.
14:    **else if** the type of *SRelemt* is *data* **then**
15:     Obtain the database information;
16:    **end if**
17:   **end if**
18: **end for**
19: **end if**
20: **end if**
21: **end for**
22: Generate the XML files containing the structure information of the database and the users' data;
23: Update the format of the XML files;
24: Generate the XML documents;

Algorithm 3 shows how to extract data from the relational database to the XML files. In the algorithm, the root element describes the root element in the XML documents; the sqlRoot element describes the child elements of the root element; the data element describes the corresponding database information. Assuming that the number of child elements for the root element is recorded as m, the number of *childElementofSqlRoot* is recorded as n, so the time complexity of this algorithm is O (m * n).

ALGORITHM 4.   Algorithm for importing the XML data into the relational database

---

1: INPUT *XML data* (**XD**)

2: Obtain the name of all the tables from **XD**，which is recorded as *atn*;

3: **while** *atn!=null* **do**

4:    Obtain a table, which is recorded as *tb*;

5:    Obtain the information (including the information of the source database, source tables, and source fields) of the primary tables for table *tb*;

6:    Obtain and parse the XML documents with the name of the source database for table *tb*;

7:    Navigate the record set *prs* of table *tb* in the XML documents;

8:    **while** *prs*!=null **do**

9:     Obtain a record;

10:     Write the SQL statements with values of all the source fields;

11:    **end while**

12:    Obtain the database information *dbInfo* (including the information of the source database, source table, and source fields) of all the non-primary tables for table *tb*;

13:    **while** *dbInfo*!=null **do**

14:     Obtain a non-primary table *ntb*;

15:     **if** the source database name of table *ntb* has been changed **then**

16:         Obtain and parse the XML documents with the name of the source database for table *ntb*;

17:       **else** Navigate the record set *nprs* of table *ntb* in the XML documents;

18:     **end if**

19:     **while** *nprs*!=null **do**

20:      Obtain a record;

21:        Obtain the values of the source fields from the non-primary table according to the relation of the primary table and non-primary table;

22:       Write the SQL statements with values of all the source fields;

23:     **end while**

24:    **end while**

25: **end while**

Algorithm 4 shows the process of importing XML data into the relational database. The XML documents indicate the data and table structure. They can be parsed by using SAX. With the support of the database engine, different SQL statements are implemented, and then the content of XML documents can be imported to the target database. Assuming that the number of the tables in XD is m, the number of the record set for table *tb* is recorded as n, the number of non-primary tables for table *tb* is recorded as p, and the number of record set for table *ntb* is recorded as q, so the time complexity of this algorithm is O (m * (n + p * q)).

5   System Application Analysis

The architecture of urban regional health information system has been applied preliminarily in a city of China. The system is mainly constructed for the application and the development of the basic medical, public health, two-way referral collaborative business of the 32 community centers and 2 specialized hospitals. Some key functions were tested and analyzed in the system to analyze the performance of urban regional health information system. We have tested three main functions: (1) community health analysis and decision- making; (2) outpatient and inpatient management; and (3) regional collaborative medical service. The testing results and analysis are presented as follows.

The hardware environment in the testing process is shown in Table 1. In addition, some software configurations of servers used in the testing are as follows. The operating system is Linux 2.6, the database system is Oracle 11 g, and the middleware is WebLogic 11 g. In the experiment, we use the ART (Average Transaction Response Time) as a metric. ART represents the average transaction response time from sending the requirement to receiving the response by client. The TPS (Transaction Per Second) is also used as a metric. TPS represents the number of transactions that are processed by the tested software per second.

Table 1. The testing hardware environment

No.	Type	Function	Main configuration
1	HP DL180	Oracle database server; Weblogic application server; Encryption machine middleware	CPU: 4 X5560; Memory: 4 GB; Disk: 2 × 300G with SAS 15000 RPM
2	Asus	LoadRunner client	CPU: Intel core 2350; Memory:2G; HD: 700G
3	HP	Application client	CPU: 2G; Memory: 8G; HD: 700G

(1) Community Health Analysis and Decision-making Subsystem

In order to evaluate the performance to concurrently process the community health data, lots of users are simulated and tested with the LoadRunner (HP, 2013); a flexible software testing tool for application performance. Some testing data have been generated in the database, and lots of terminals are simulated to vend the mobile phone cards in the testing process. Some testing scripts are generated and debugged in the LoadRunner.

Community health analysis and decision-making subsystem provides a lot of services, such as analysis of community diagnosis and treatment, analysis of community residents' health, and so on. In our experimental evaluation, the average number of records processed by each sub-module per day was 237.29. The analysis for community health analysis and decision subsystem is shown in Table 2. The Column "Num. of records" shows the number of records which are processed daily. The average transaction response time is shown in the Column "ART". The minimum response time is 0.67 s, and the maximum response time is 3.68 s. The average transaction response time is 1.95 s. The number of transactions per second is shown in the Column "TPS". The minimum value is 27, and the maximum value is 68. The average value is 43.43.

Table 2. The analysis for regional collaborative medical service

No.	Functions	Num. of records	ART	TPS
1	Analysis of community diagnosis and treatment	526	3.68	68
2	Diagnosis of community residents health	318	2.69	47
3	Community chronic disease analysis	85	0.89	29
4	Maternal and child health analysis	98	1.25	38
5	Analysis of epidemic situation of infectious diseases	210	1.67	42
6	Analysis of residents health status	368	2.78	53
7	Health supervision and law enforcement	56	0.67	27
AVE.		237.29	1.95	43.43

(2) Outpatient and Inpatient Management

In order to evaluate the performance to concurrently process the outpatient and inpatient management, lots of users are simulated and tested in the LoadRunner. Some testing data have been generated in the database, and lots of terminals are simulated to charge for electronic wallets in the testing process. Some testing scripts are generated and debugged in the LoadRunner.

Outpatient and inpatient management mainly includes outpatient registration, pharmacy charge, comprehensive charge, pharmacy store management, and so on. In our experimental evaluation, the average number of records processed by each sub-module per day was 679.44. The analysis for outpatient and inpatient management is shown in Table 3. The column "Num. of records" shows the number of records which are processed daily. The average transaction response time is shown in the column "ART". The minimum response time is 0.97 s, and the maximum response time is 5.73 s. The average transaction response time is 2.81 s. The number of transactions per second is shown in the Column "TPS". The minimum value is 18, and the maximum value is 83. The average value is 48.67.

Table 3. The analysis for outpatient and inpatient management

No.	Functions	Num. of records	ART	TPS
1	Outpatient registration	1327	4.51	79
2	Pharmacy charge	1518	5.73	83
3	Comprehensive charge	892	2.53	54
4	Pharmacy store management	398	2.24	41
5	Pharmacy management	412	2.93	49
6	Nursing station management	1041	3.32	65
7	Doctor station management	134	1.27	21
8	Inpatient management	286	1.75	28
9	Family medical management	107	0.97	18
AVE.		679.44	2.81	48.67

(3) Regional Collaborative Medical Service

Lots of users are simulated and tested in the LoadRunner to evaluate the performance to concurrently process regional collaborative medical service. Some testing data have been generated in the database, and lots of terminals are simulated to process regional collaborative medical service in the testing process. Some testing scripts are generated and debugged in the LoadRunner.

The main functions of regional collaborative medical service include: mutual recognition of examination results, the inspection commission, two-way referral, making an appointment, and so on. In our experimental evaluation, the average number of records processed by each sub-module per day was 404.80. The analysis for regional collaborative medical service is shown in Table 4.

Table 4. The analysis for regional collaborative medical service

No.	Functions	Num. of records	ART	TPS
1	Two-way referral	416	5.24	65
2	Electronic health record sharing	395	4.65	54
3	Network reservation system	754	3.16	37
4	Mutual recognition of examination results	296	2.97	48
5	Citizen-card sharing system	163	3.37	18
AVE.		404.80	3.88	44.40

Column "Num. of records" shows the number of records which are processed daily. The average transaction response time is shown in Column "ART". The minimum response time is 2.97 s, and the maximum response time is 5.24 s. The average transaction response time is 3.88 s. The number of transactions per second is shown in the Column "TPS". The minimum value is 18, and the maximum value is 65. The average value is 44.40.

6   Conclusion

The architecture of urban regional health information system, taking the EHR as its core component, integrates health data of different organizations into a complete information system. The system has been running successfully online and more than 50 sites have been accepted with good effect. In addition, with the help of "3 + X" team, quality and high-touch personal health services are provided for the general public. The system promotes the socialization of community health service management, and achieves the standardization and the institutionalization of community health service.

The system architecture proposed in this paper needs to be further improved and upgraded. We will continue to keep up with new technologies to optimize the proposed architecture in time.

References

1. DesRoches, C.M., Rosenbaum, S.J.: Meaningful use of health information technology in U.S. hospitals. N. Engl. J. Med. **362**(12), 1153–1155 (2010)
2. Schleicher, J.M., Vogler, M., Dustdar, S., Inzinger, C.: Enabling a smart city application ecosystem: requirements and architectural aspects. IEEE Internet Comput. **20**(2), 58–65 (2016)
3. Liu, P., Peng, Z.: Smart cities in China. Computer **47**(10), 1–10 (2013)
4. Li, H., Yang, C., et al.: The application and implementation research of smart city in China. In: Proceedings of the 2012 International Conference on System Science and Engineering ICSSE, Liaoning, China, pp. 288–292. IEEE Computer Society (2012)
5. Hussain, A., Silva, A.L.D., Nadher, M., Mudhish, M.: Health and emergency-care platform for the elderly and disabled people in the smart city. J. Syst. Softw. **110**(C), 253–263 (2015)
6. Zhang, X., Sheng, H., Rong, W.G., et al.: Cooper: intelligent transportation systems for smart cities: a progress review. Sci. China Inf. Sci. **55**(12), 9–19 (2012)
7. Khekare, G.S., Sakhare, A.V.: A smart city framework for intelligent traffic system using VANET. In: Proceedings of the 2013 International Multi-Conference on Automation, Computing, Communication, Control and Compressed Sensing, Kottayam, India, vol. 7903, pp. 302–305. IEEE Computer Society (2013)
8. Greco, I., Cresta, A.: A smart planning for smart city: the concept of smart city as an opportunity to re-think the planning models of the contemporary city. In: Gervasi, O., Murgante, B., Misra, S., Gavrilova, M.L., Rocha, A.M.A.C., Torre, C., Taniar, D., Apduhan, B.O. (eds.) ICCSA 2015. LNCS, vol. 9156, pp. 563–576. Springer, Cham (2015). https://doi.org/10.1007/978-3-319-21407-8_40
9. Zhang, Z., Hu, X., Dong, J., Yang, J., Jiang, T.: Research on regional health information platform construction based on cloud computing. In: Li, S., Jin, Q., Jiang, X., Park, J. (eds.) Frontier and Future Development of Information Technology in Medicine and Education. LNEE, vol. 269, pp. 2431–2435. Springer, Dordrecht (2014). https://doi.org/10.1007/978-94-007-7618-0_301
10. Mcloughlin, I.P., Garrety, K., Wilson, R., Yu, P., Dalley, A.: The Development of a National EHR in England: Electronic Records and the Disruption of Moral Orders. The Digitalization of Healthcare (2017)
11. Adler-Milstein, J., Desroches, C.M., Kralovec, P., Foster, G., Worzala, C., Charles, D., et al.: Electronic health record adoption in US hospitals: progress continues, but challenges persist. Health Aff. **34**(12), 2174 (2015)
12. Friedman, D.J., Parrish, R.G.: The population health record: concepts, definition, design, and implementation. J. Am. Med. Inform. Assoc. **17**(4), 359–366 (2010)
13. Xi, A., Qin B., Huang, C.: The regional medical business process optimization based on cloud computing medical resources sharing environment. Cybern. Inf. Technol. **13**(Special Issue), 18–29 (2013)
14. Pan, L., Fu, X., Cai, F., Meng, Y., Zhang, C.: Design a novel electronic medical record system for regional clinics and health centers in China. In: IEEE International Conference on Computer and Communications, pp. 38–41. IEEE (2017)
15. Morrison, Z., Robertson, A., Cresswell, K., Crowe, S., Sheikh, A.: Understanding contrasting approaches to nationwide implementations of electronic health record systems: England, the USA and Australia. J. Healthcare Eng. **2**(1), 25–42 (2015)
16. Hsiao, C.J., Hing, E.: Use and characteristics of electronic health record systems among office-based physician practices: United States, 2001–2013. NCHS Data Brief **143**(111), 1–8 (2017)

17. Hua-Ming, K., Yao, Q., Li, P.-F., Li, J.-S.: Design and implementation of the regional health information collaborative platform. In: Li, S., Jin, Q., Jiang, X., Park, J. (eds.) Frontier and Future Development of Information Technology in Medicine and Education. LNEE, vol. 269, pp. 669–677. Springer, Dordrecht (2014). https://doi.org/10.1007/978-94-007-7618-0_64

18. Zhang, Z.A., Zhang, J.J., Zhu, Y.L., Ren, J.: Planning and construction of regional medical and health information platform. Chin. J. Med. Libr. Inf. Sci. **22**(2), 68–70 (2013)

CCN Hotspot Cache Placement Strategy Based on Genetic Algorithm

Hongjia Wu[1,2(✉)], Nao Wang[1,2], and Gaocai Wang[1,2]

[1] School of Computer and Electronic Information,
Guangxi University, Nanning 533004, Guangxi, People's Republic of China
949644270@qq.com, 748227@qq.com, wanggcgx@163.com
[2] Guangxi Colleges and University Key Laboratory of Parallel and Distributed
Computing Technology, Nanning 530004, People's Republic of China

Abstract. Content-centric networks provide effective support for content services through a caching mechanism, so the caching of the placement strategy
has become a hot research. In this paper, the problem of content placement in
CCN is taken as the starting point, focusing on the allocation of caching
resources for district partitioning according to the number of users given the
content of predictable hotspots. When the hot topic breaks out, the first to the
user from the content of the nearest as the goal, from the user's point of view as
its characteristics, nested using improved genetic algorithms to select hotspot
cache placement points, and a CCN hotspot cache placement strategy based on
genetic algorithm is proposed. In the simulation experiment, the cache placement strategy proposed in this paper is compared with other traditional strategies
in network performance. The simulation results show that the strategy can
effectively reduce the access hops and average access latency, reduce the server
load and improve the user satisfaction.

Keywords: Content-centric networks · Hotspot · Delay
Cache placement strategy

1 Introduction

The traditional Internet, was born in the seventies of last century, mainly for the
transmission of messages between the hosts, in the past few decades has achieved great
success. Now based on the TCP/IP network architecture, because the dissemination of
content generated by the explosive, facing enormous challenges, has not yet effectively
solve the wireless equipment energy consumption, delay and other issues [1]. In order
to solve these network problems, a content-centric network (CCN) is proposed as a way
to promote the current host-centered Internet to novel content-centric network. Compared with TCP/IP CCN network architecture has many advantages, such as congestion
mitigation, redundancy elimination, content security, effective dissemination of information and so on [1]. While CCN has some advantages, there is room for improvement
when communicating information in specific situations. For example, when the hot
content outbreaks, CCN suitable for the use of the cache strategy has been rarely
studied, easily overlooked. This article considers the performance problem of the
network (the hotspots are out) when a large number of users need the same content

© Springer International Publishing AG 2017
G. Wang et al. (Eds.): SpaCCS 2017 Workshops, LNCS 10658, pp. 350–360, 2017.
https://doi.org/10.1007/978-3-319-72395-2_32

during the same time period. This situation will greatly increase the time required for users to obtain content and network load, especially for time-sensitive real-time business will cause a greater impact.

This article focuses on how to optimize content access latency, to reduce the amount of "hops" that users need to get content, thereby reducing the time it takes to access the content. This paper studies the content placement strategy that minimizes network latency and average hops in the event that user behavior is consistent. User behavior is consistent, referring to the same time the user access to the same content (that is, hot information).

In this paper, the content placement problem in the information center network is taken as the starting point, and the allocation of caching resources is divided according to the number of users in the case of known hotspot content. This strategy reduces the average number of hops required by users to get content, reduces latency, when a hotspot event breaks out, the average number of hops, latency, and server load required to get the content are reduced compared to the content-centric traditional network strategy. In the simulation experiment, the proposed cache placement strategy compared with the traditional cache placement strategy, the comparison results of the algorithm are given in terms of average hops and network average delay. The results of several experiments show that the proposed cache placement strategy has a good effect of reducing the average number of hops, so as to achieve the purpose of optimizing and reducing the delay.

2 Related Work

In the content-centric CCN network, the issue of caching has been a lot of researches, in which cache placement strategy is the core of content-centric network cache research. In a content-centric network, the full-cache (LCE) policy was used as the default policy, that was, all nodes in the network have to cache the received packets, although this method was simple and easy to deploy, but will cause more redundancy to the network [2]. In [3], a strategy was proposed to select the cache node based on the node and the storage data was stored in the node with the largest number of paths on the path, but the cache distribution was not balanced. In [4], the WAVE strategy was proposed to store the content items with higher content of heat as much as possible to the nodes that were closer to the user, it was not only can improve the cache hit rate, but also can reduce the number of cache replacement, but the implementation of the higher complexity. Literature [5] proposed the ProbCache strategy, not only considered the length of the transmission path also took into account the node's cache capability, but to calculate each node, resulting in a lot of overhead. In [6], a distributed cache placement strategy was proposed, as a random cache strategy, a single transmission process only in a single node in the data cache, although to avoid the cache resource redundancy, but ignored when multiple users need content at the same time, did not improve the cache utilization. Liu Tao et al. Proposed a content placement algorithm based on cooperative caching [7], this method defined the content activity to reflect the frequently requested rate, improved cache hits, but did not take into account when the number of users was increasing, the traffic increased the path of the congestion problem, but from the service point of view and not really from the user's point of view to place the cache. In [7], an adaptive routing node caching algorithm was proposed, but the algorithm needed to be parameterized and the computational complexity was increased. LCD (Leave Copy Down) [8, 9], only in the hit node directly downstream node cache content object, to avoid the same content object a lot of cache. But this meant that a certain access frequency was required to push a content object from the server to the edge of the network. In order to improve the lack of single-point cache, Syntila and Berger, who proposed a collaborative cache [10]. Collaborative cache to better meet the growing number of users in the network, but its algorithm was complex, to achieve a certain degree of difficulty. In [11], a random cache placement algorithm was proposed, which was improved on the basis of random selection of cache location to realize the equal probability selection method, this strategy was simple and easy to implement, but its effectiveness was not impressive.

In view of the current research situation of CCN cache strategy, some existing cache schemes have solved some cache problems in CCN, but there are still some shortcomings. Based on the traditional caching strategy, this paper proposes a CCN hotspot cache placement strategy based on genetic algorithm. This strategy reduces the average delay of the network by minimizing the average number of hops while the user's behavior is consistent.

3   Problem Description and Model Establishment

3.1   CCN Hotspot Cache Placement Strategy Based on Genetic Algorithm (HCS)

First, the first to the user from the content of the nearest as the goal, from the user's point of view as its characteristics, nested using improved genetic algorithms to select hotspot cache placement points. Random selection of a user, as the user as the center, according to the size of different distance for the radius to draw a different area, and then use each region as a collection, in each set of nested use of improved genetic algorithm, and then in each region to find an optimal cache placement point.

The detailed steps are as follows:

---

1. randomly select a user A, as the center, to the distance (by the number of hops, the initial minimum distance of 3) for the radius of 180 degrees arc, draw a region, recorded as U1;

2. The user in the area U1 as a collection, the use of genetic algorithm to find the first cache placement point M1;

3. Continue to use user A as the center, with a distance of 5 to draw a region, denoted as U2;

4. The user in the area U2 as a collection, the use of genetic algorithm to find the second cache placement point M2;

5. And so on, find the placement of the cache M1, M2, M3 ....;

3.2   CCN Optimization Model Establishment

The network can be abstracted into an arbitrary graph, with a directed graph G (V, E) representing a given network, where V and E represent the node set and the directional link set [12–14], respectively. Set the node set of node $i \in V$ to $V = \{e_{ij} \in E;$ $i, j \in V\}$.

$min\{d(vi, uj)\}$ represents the distance from user v_i to its nearest cache placement point, that is, the nearest cache point u_j is the service node of user v_i. If there are multiple distances from u_j to v_i, select the point with the smaller number of adjacent routes as the service node of v_i. If the service node of v_i not be selected on this basis, the cache placement point in the area containing the smaller number of users is selected as the service node of v_i. The distance between the node or user and the node is represented by the number of hops. There is a minimum hop distance between each user and the cache placement of its area. The maximum of all the minimum hops is:

$$h(o) = \max_{v_i \in V} \left\{ \min_{u_j \in U} \{ d(v_i, u_j) \} \right\} \tag{1}$$

where o is defined as the content cache placement scheme, $h(o)$ is the maximum distance of the cache placement scheme, also known as the maximum number of hops. The smaller the $h(o)$, the better the service of the placement scheme.

The main goal of this paper is to reduce the delay of users' content acquisition and improve the service satisfaction of users when the user's behavior is consistent (that is, when the hot information breaks out),we assume that the delay between each hop is T, the size of the delay is proportional to the number of hops, then the research goal of this paper can be transformed into the problem of finding a cache placement that minimizes $h(o)$. For the sake of convenience, we assume that the average spread of the content from one node to another is T, and one time is delayed by one node. Where K is defined as the number of hotspot places, assuming that the location where the cache is to be placed is K, the model is described as follows:

$$\begin{aligned} &\min h(o) \\ &s.t. |K| = k \end{aligned} \tag{2}$$

When solving, the model is designed and constrained for specific functions [13]. Let x_{ij} be a boolean variable.

$$Xij = \begin{cases} 1, & \text{indicates that node j is in the area where user i is located} \\ 0, & \text{indicates that node j is not in the area where user i is located} \end{cases}$$

The goal function is designed to minimize the average delay of the user's access to the content:

$$f(x) = \frac{\left(\sum_{j=1}^{n}\sum_{i=1}^{n} min(dijxij)\right) * T}{\sum_{i=1}^{n} i} \tag{3}$$

The satisfying constraints are:

(1) Each user only in a cache placement point to obtain content, $\sum_{j=1}^{n} xij = 1$.

(2) Set the k cache placement points in n network nodes, and $\max_{i=1...n}\left(x_{ij}\right) = 1$ means that the node j is set as the cache placement point, then the constraint condition $\sum_{j=1}^{n} \max_{i=1...n}\left(x_{ij}\right) = k$ is satisfied.

The model of the genetic algorithm is:

$$\begin{aligned} &\min f(x) \\ &s.t. \sum_{j=1}^{n} Xij = 1 \\ &\sum_{j=1}^{n} \max_{i=1...n}\left(X_{ij}\right) = k \end{aligned} \tag{4}$$

3.3   Model Solving

In order to improve the efficiency and accuracy, we reduce the problem of "premature convergence" and improve the local search ability. In order to improve the efficiency and accuracy of the model, we will use the genetic algorithm to solve the problem. In this paper, the use of nested genetic algorithm, while the use of elite retention strategy to achieve from the breadth and depth of the parallel iteration.

This article to find the three best cache placement as an example, detailed as follows:

We use an improved genetic algorithm [15] to solve the problem, first of all the fitness function is designed as:

$$F(x) = f(x) + r\left(\sum_{j=1}^{n} Xij + \sum_{j=1}^{n} \max_{i=1...n}\left(Xij\right)\right) \tag{5}$$

r is the penalty factor. According to Eq. (4), the number of individuals in this population is p, and the number of feasible points is $p1$, then the number of feasible points is

$p- p_1$, the feasible domain is denoted as U, and the standard deviation function is std, the penalty factor r is:

$$r = \begin{cases} \dfrac{\frac{1}{p_1}\sum\limits_{x\in U} f(x) - \frac{1}{p-p_1}\sum\limits_{x\in U} f(x)}{\frac{1}{p-p_1}\left(\sum\limits_{x\notin U}\sum\limits_{j=1}^{n} xij + \sum\limits_{j=1}^{n} \max\limits_{i=1...n}(xij)\right)}, p_1 > p*0.1 \\[3em] \dfrac{std\ (f(x))}{std\ (\sum\limits_{j=1}^{n} xij + \sum\limits_{j=1}^{n} \max\limits_{i=1...n}(xij))}, x\notin U, p_1 \le p*0.1 \end{cases} \tag{6}$$

First find out the optimal seed x' of the population, making

$$x' = min\, F(x_i) \tag{7}$$

The remaining population is divided into population *1* and population *2* according to the distance of seed to x'. The population is defined by the limit value $L_{k,}$ and the seed to A distance is less than or equal to L_k into the population 1, and the seed whose distance is greater than L_k enters the population 2. You can use two fitness functions to represent the seed selection, select the seed into the population *pop1* and *pop2* according to the fitness function *F1*, and sort the population according to the fitness function *F2*. Define norm for the Euclidean distance function, ε for the calculation accuracy, the *popsize, popsize1* and *popsize2* are the total population size, population *1* size, population *2* size, and k is the evolutionary algebra.

$$F_1 : \begin{cases} pop\ 1 = \{x|norm(x,x') \le L_k\}; L_k > \varepsilon \\ pop\ 2 = \{x|norm(x,x') > L_k\}; L_k > \varepsilon \\ pop\ 1 = \{x|norm(x,x') > L_k\}; L_k \le \varepsilon \\ pop\ 2 = 0; L_k \le \varepsilon \end{cases} \tag{8}$$

$$L_k = min(max(norm(x,x'))*0.5, \\ \xrightarrow[norm(x,x')]{}*(popsize*0.45)) \tag{9}$$

where $\xrightarrow[norm(x,x')]{}$ and $norm(x,x')$ are the ascending sequences of the array. After the two populations are sorted by the fitness function $F(x)$, they enters the mating pool according to the roulette method, and the roulette selection probability formula is:

$$Q(i) = \frac{q(1-q)^{i-1}}{1-(1-q)^{n}} \tag{10}$$

The mating pool size of population *1, 2* is *n1* and *n2* respectively, and the formula is:

$$\begin{cases} n_1 = popsize * 0.5; n_2 = popsize * 0.5; L_k > \varepsilon \\ n_1 = popsize * 0.5; n_2 = 0; L_k \leq \varepsilon \end{cases} \tag{11}$$

The step of using the genetic algorithm in each region can be expressed as follows:

Step1: determine population size P, initialize population.

Step2: according to the formula (6) to find the penalty factor; find the optimal feasible point for the current optimal seed, and calculate the other seeds to the current optimal seed Euclidean distance.

Step3: calculate Euclidean distance according to formula (8) and divide the population.

Step4: respectively, the population *1, 2* according to the formula (6) to calculate the penalty factor, the formation of new fitness.

Step 5: use the formula (11) to calculate the size of the mating pool and use the roulette method to generate seeds into *1* to *2* mating ponds; place the population *2* repeat seed at the rear of the mating pool and count the number of repeated seeds.

Step6: select one of the populations to cross and mutate.

Step7: test evolution end, otherwise the two populations will be mixed back to step2.

3.4 Algorithm Performance Analysis

The HCS algorithm proposed in this paper combines the centralized and distributed, taking into account the depth of the network search and the breadth of the network. Each user belongs to multiple regions according to the different number of users, and each user participates in the iterative solution of multiple genetic algorithms. This method is a good solution to the problem of insufficient local search ability of genetic algorithm. The time complexity of the HCS algorithm is linearly related to the number of cache point k and the number of iterations m of the genetic algorithm. The time complexity of the genetic algorithm used in this paper is $O\left((n - k)^2 * k * t\right)$, which shows that the time complexity of HCS is $O((n - k)^2 kt * m)$. Where n is the number of network nodes, k is the number of gateways deployed, and t is the number of iterations. At the same time, it is also shown that the algorithm has better network performance than other traditional cache placement strategies, and is more suitable for the optimal placement of hotspot cache.

4 Simulation Results and Analysis

The main performance indicators used in the experiment are the average number of hops, the average delay and the cache hit rate. In order to verify the validity of the CCN hotspot cache placement strategy proposed in the paper, the simulation experiment is carried out. The model of HCS strategy is numerically calculated by MATLAB, and LCE and Random are compared with HCS proposed in this paper. Where the LCE strategy caches all the contents of all nodes, the Random policy is characterized by the probability of selecting the cache node during the placement process [2, 11]. The network topology uses a fully binary tree with a depth of five, and the server is located at the root node. Each leaf node is connected to multiple users. In a traditional IP network, the content needs to be reached at the source server, and the number of hops required by each user to obtain the content is a fixed value. However, in the CCN network, as a result of the introduction of the cache, the user can get the content from the node closer to him, thus greatly reducing the average number of hops. In order to evaluate the cache performance of HCS policy, the number of network users is 30–350, and the cache capacity is 20 MB–100 MB. The performance of several cache place-ment strategies is studied. As can be seen from Fig. 1, in the case of the same number of users, HCS strategy allows users to get hot content when the minimum number of hops required, followed by Random and LCE. Due to the choice of Random proba-bility [11], while LCE and Random do not consider the cache placement problem from the user's point of view [2, 11], ignoring the centralized area of the user's distribution, so that the average number of hops is larger than the HCS strategy. With the increasing number of users in the case of the average number of hops is the slowest growth of HCS, LCE strategy and Random strategy similar. As the HCS strategy is from the user's point of view to select the hot spot cache placement point, so when the number of users is increasing, still able to maintain the ideal average number of hops.

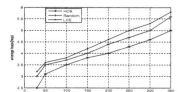

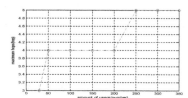

Fig. 1. Comparison of average hops for different caching strategies

Fig. 2. The impact of the number of users in the HCS strategy on the maximum hops

Figure 2 shows the maximum number of hops required by users to get content when using HCS policies in different numbers of users. As can be seen from Fig. 2, in the case of rapid growth in the number of users, HCS strategy can still allow users to access the content required to maintain the maximum number of hops in a good state.

As shown in Fig. 3, it is shown that the size of the user in the network has an effect on the average delay. It can be seen from the figure, the number of users from 30 to 350 changes in the process, the average delay of several different cache placement strategies has improved in different degrees. This is because, when the number of users more and more, the network traffic increases, the acquisition of hot content is also growing, resulting in path congestion, even in the edge of the user can not effectively use the cache resources, and then increase the number of hops, the average delay is also greatly increased, and finally reduce the user satisfaction with the service. In these three strategies (LCE, Random, HCS), with the increasing number of users, HCS strategy growth rate of the smallest and sometimes even gradually stabilize the level. Among them, Random slightly superior to LCE, indicating that the three cache placement strategy, especially HCS, the network size changes have a strong ability to adapt.

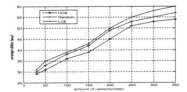 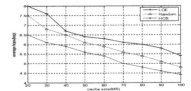

Fig. 3. Comparison of average delay for different caching strategies

Fig. 4. The impact of the cache size on the average number of hops in different caching strategies

Figure 4 shows the decreasing trend of the average number of hops for the three cache placement strategies as the cache capacity increases. In the case of random distribution, when the cache capacity of the cache placement point is set to 20 MB, the average hop count of the LCE policy is eight. This is because the cache space is small, frequent cache replacement, and this strategy ignores the hotspot cache priority features, so when the user behavior consistent circumstances, can not be timely access to the required hot content, but to reach the source server to get content. With the increase in cache capacity, due to the characteristics of the cache at the end of LCE, not only does not make the average hops have greatly improved, but the network cache redundancy more and more, reducing network performance [2]. For the Random strategy, the cache placement point capacity is very small when the network can not be a good solution to the hot content of a large number of needs. When the cache capacity increases, because of its equal probability to choose the placement point, so that the user at the edge is still unable to effectively get the service, so the average number of hops is relatively large. But after all, LCE strategy in the network has more cache, so the simulation of these two strategies is relatively close. As can be seen in Fig. 4, which HCS strategy with the increase in cache capacity, because of its user-centric, hotspot priority, the average number of hops is the largest reduction. Compared to the other two strategies, HCS is more suitable for user behavior consistent, hot information outbreak of the situation.

As shown in Fig. 5, the hit rate of the cache increases as the cache capacity increases, indicating that the hit rate of the network cache is related to the choice of cache placement, and is also related to the size of the cache. The use of the Random strategy is better than the LCE strategy, which verifies the improved validity of the method of random selection of the cache placement point on the basis of LCE [11]. However, because the two strategies ignore the issue from the user to consider the placement of the cache point, while the replacement method does not select the hot content priority and other factors, resulting in its cache hit rate compared with HCS hit rate is low, and with the increase in cache capacity, hit rate increase is not large. As can

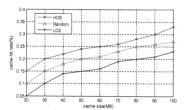
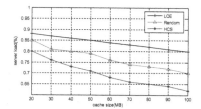

Fig. 5. The impact of cache size on cache hit rates in different caching strategies

Fig. 6. The impact of the cache size on the server load in the different cache policies

be seen from Fig. 5, the use of HCS strategy cache hit rate of the starting point is higher than the first two strategies, and when the cache capacity increases, hit rate increase is also relatively large.

Figure 6 shows the trend that the server load decreases as the size of the cache increases. In the cache placement point capacity is small, because of its frequent replacement, and retain the content is also less, so the LCE strategy almost forwards all interest packets to the source server. So its server is the most affordable, with the cache capacity increases, the reduction is also the smallest. Random load is slightly lower than LCE, where the load value of HCS is the smallest. This is because, from the analysis of Figs. 4 and 5 shows that with the increase in cache capacity, the average number of hops continue to decrease, the cache hit rate continues to increase, indicating that most users get the content is no longer need to reach the source server, but through the area where the hot cache place to get, so greatly reduce the load on the server.

5   Conclusions

In order to improve the effectiveness of hot content cache placement, the author proposes a CCN hotspot cache placement strategy based on genetic algorithm, and the relationship between the average hops, the maximum hops and the average delay is related to the number of users and the effect of cache size on cache hit rate, server load, and average hops are analyzed under this strategy. Unlike the traditional cache placement strategy, the HCS strategy takes the user as the center and takes the user's point of view to consider the hotspot placement problem. The simulation results show that, the HCS strategy can effectively reduce the average number of hops and average delay required by users to obtain content, and with the increase of cache capacity, the cache hit rate is improved and the server load is greatly reduced. Thus effectively optimizing the performance of the content-centric network, improve the user's satisfaction with network services.

Acknowledgments. This research is supported in part by the National Natural Science Foundation of China under Grant No. 61562006, in part by the Natural Science Foundation of Guangxi Province under Grant No. 2016GXNSFBA380181 and in part by the Key Laboratory of Guangxi University.

References

1. Xu, G.: Content center network cache placement strategy. Beijing University of Posts and Telecommunications (2015)
2. Li, Y., Lin, T., Tang, H., et al.: A chunk caching location and searching scheme in content centric networking, pp. 2655–2659. IEEE (2012)
3. Cui, X., Liu, J.: Code strategy in content center network based on node and replacement rate. J. Electron. Inf. Technol. **36**(01), 1–7 (2014)
4. Cho, K., Lee, M., Park, K., et al.: Wave: popularity-based and collaborative in-network caching for content-oriented networks. In: Proceedings of IEEE Conference on Computer Communications Workshops, pp. 316–321. IEEE (2012)
5. Psaras, I., Chai, W.K., Pavlou, G.: Probabilistic in-network caching for information - centric networks. In: Proceedings of the Second Edition of the ICN Workshop on Information-Centric Networking, pp. 55–60. ACM (2012)
6. Hu, Q., Wu, M.: A caching random placement strategy for content center networks. J. Xidian Univ. **41**(06), 131–136 + 187 (2014)
7. Liu, T.: Study on time-delay optimization technology of network access in content center. Information Engineering University, PLA (2013)
8. Laoutaris, N., Syntila, S., Stavrakakis, I.: Meta algorithms for hierarchical web caches. In: Proceedings of IEEE International Conference on Performance, Computing, and Communications, pp. 445–452. IEEE (2004)
9. Laoutaris, N., Che, H., Stavrakakis, I.: The LCD interconnection of LRU caches and its analysis. Perform. Eval. **63**(7), 609–634 (2006)
10. Guo, C., Hui, Y., Ming, Z.: Design and implementation of cooperative cache strategy for opportunity network node. Comput. Eng. **36**(18), 85–87 (2010)
11. Altmeyer, S., Cucu-Grosjean, L., Davis, R.I., et al.: Progress on Static Probabilistic Timing Analysis for Systems with Random Cache Replacement Policies (2013)
12. Shuqiang, H., Gaocai, W.: Study on optimization scheme of wireless network node deployment in smart city. J. Comput. Res. Dev. **51**(02), 278–289 (2014)
13. Xiandong, C., Jiang, L., et al.: Caching strategy of content center network based on node number and replacement rate. J. Electron. Inf. Technol. **36**(01), 1–7 (2014)
14. Shuqiang, H., Gaocai, W., et al.: A method of geometric k-center gateway deployment of wireless mesh networks. Chin. J. Comput. **36**(7), 1475–1484 (2013)
15. Ximing, L., Chan, Z., Donghuang, Y.: Novel genetic algorithm based on species selection for solving constrained nonlinear programming problem. Central South Univ.: Nat. Sci. Ed. **40**(1), 185–189 (2009)

The Impact of Routing Protocols
on the Performance of a Mobility Model
in Mobile Ad Hoc Network (MANET)

Martin Appiah[(⊠)] and Rita Cudjoe

Vaal University of Technology,
Andries, Potgieter, Vanderbijlpark 1911, South Africa
martina@vut.ac.za

Abstract. Mobile Ad Hoc Network (MANET) comprises a group of mobile or wireless nodes that are placed randomly and dynamically which causes the constant change between nodes. When considering a routing protocol to deploy in any given situation on MANET, factors such as the mobility model, mobility of nodes, the network size and packet size should be carefully considered because the routing protocols configured with the mobility model can highly affect the performance of MANET. This paper analysed the impact of two different routing protocols (i.e. Dynamic Source Routing (DSR) and Optimized Link State Routing (OLSR)) on the performance of Random WayPoint (RWP) mobility model. Three measures of performance metrics (i.e. average throughput, average delay and average traffic received) were used. In all three-performance metrics, the simulated results indicated that Random Way-Point (RWP) configured with OLSR protocol performed better than RWP configured with DSR protocol. This indicates that the choice of a routing protocol for a specific mobility model should be considered in a network design.

Keywords: MANET · Mobility model · Routing protocols
Pause time · Average delay · Average throughput · Average traffic received

1 Introduction

MANET consists of a group of mobile or wireless nodes that communicate together. This indicates that the mobiles nodes can communicate and share information without the help of any central device. On MANET, the network topology (i.e. the physical connectivity of communication in a network) changes frequently since nodes are mostly in motion [14, 16, 17]. The communication between active nodes is made possible through routing protocols. In other words, routing protocols determine the route(s) that packets need to follow from the source node to the destination node. The overall performance of MANET greatly depends on the communications and agreement between mobile nodes [1, 2, 7, 8].

The aim of a mobility model is to portray the movement pattern of mobile nodes in MANET under different network scenarios. Nodes can move in any direction and at any speed. During movement, mobile nodes can pause at regular intervals or may not stop at all. It is important to consider the movement patterns of the mobility models

© Springer International Publishing AG 2017
G. Wang et al. (Eds.): SpaCCS 2017 Workshops, LNCS 10658, pp. 361–368, 2017.
https://doi.org/10.1007/978-3-319-72395-2_33

when analysing the performance of MANET. In Random WayPoint (RWP), mobile nodes normally wait for a period (pause time) before it moves to its destination at a given speed. Mobile nodes in RWP normally travel near the centre of the simulation area [9, 12, 15].

In this paper, OLSR and DSR were used because OLSR is a proactive routing protocol whiles DSR is a reactive routing protocol. The difference is that, DSR determines proper route when a packet is required to be forwarded whereas with OLSR, all nodes study the network topology before a forward request comes in. In situations like this, mobility model's role is very crucial because a mobility model specifically depicts the pattern of mobility and the features of real mobile nodes for particular scenario, and as such, this will be the dimension for accurately examining the effectiveness of a protocol for a particular scenario [2].

The aim of the paper is to analyze the impact that routing protocols have on the performance of Random WayPoint (RWP) mobility model. The objective of this paper is to examine routing protocols and their impact on the performance of MANET.

This paper is arranged as follows: Sect. 2: methodology, Sect. 3: results, Sect. 4: conclusion and Sect. 5: future work.

2 Methodology

OPNET is used as the simulation environment because of its ability to offer a complete modeling environment for unique design, simulation and analysis of the performance of any network [3, 4]. It also has the capability to model or modify MANET mobility models and routing protocols [5, 6, 13, 18, 19]. Two routing protocols and one mobility model are used in analysing the same network sizes, same speeds, pause time and traffic loads. The network standard used was 802.11 g and all the nodes are mobile. Scenarios are used to compare the performance of two different routing protocols in MANET. The OPNET simulation was carried out in an area of 500 m × 500 m and all the scenarios have an equal node size of 500 mobile nodes. The objects available in the simulation environment are mobile nodes, mobility, application and profile. For the configuration of node speeds, Random Waypoint model with Vector trajectory was used. The node speed of 5–10 m/s is also used. The used pause time is 5 s. File Transfer Protocol (FTP) and Electronic mail (E-mail) are the data types that generate traffic. The data rate that Media Access Control (MAC) uses to transmit data frames through the physical layer is 24 Mbps. Each scenario was simulated six times (to get more consistent and accurate results) [19] in a 3600 s simulation time. The general simulation parameters and the parameters for the chosen routing protocols are shown in Tables 1, 2 and 3.

Two scenarios are configured using DSR and OLSR protocols. The mobility configuration object is used for the configuration of mobility model, node's speed and pause time. Explanation of the network scenarios can be seen in Table 4.

Throughput, end to end delay and routing traffic received are the performance metrics used to measure the performance of MANET. **Throughput** is the average rate

Table 1. General simulation parameters

Parameters	Value
Number of nodes	500
Network area	500 × 500 square meters
Mobility model	Random WayPoint
Routing protocol	Optimized link state routing; Dynamic source routing
Speed	5–10 meters/second (m/s)
Pause time	5 seconds (s)
Traffic/data type	FTP; E-mail
Data rate	24 Mbps
Simulation time	3600 s

Table 2. OLSR parameters

OLSR	
Parameters	Values
Willingness	Default
Hello interval (sec)	2.0
TC interval (sec)	5.0
Neighbour hold time (sec)	6.0
Topology hold time	15.0

Table 3. DSR parameters

DSR	
Route expiry time (route cache)	300
Request table size (nodes) (route discovery)	64
Max Request retransmission (route discovery)	16
Max request period (sec) route discovery	10
Max buffer size for route maintenance (packets)	50
Maintenance hold time (sec)	0.25
Max maintenance retransmission	2
Maintenance acknowledgement timer (sec)	0.5
Route replies using cached routes	Enabled
Packet salving	Enabled

of data packets received successfully over a communication path and is measured in bits per second (bits/sec) [7]. Mathematically, Throughput (S) can be represented as in Eq. 1:

$$S = Number\_deliveredpacket * Packet\_size * 8 / Total\_simulationtime \qquad (1)$$

Table 4. Network scenarios

Network scenarios	
Scenario	Description
1: Random WayPoint OLSR	• This network has 500 nodes • It implements the OLSR protocol • Mobility speed is 5–10 m/s • Pause time is 5 s
2: Random WayPoint DSR	• This network has 500 nodes • It implements the DSR protocol • Mobility speed is 5–10 m/s • Pause time is 5 s

Delay (end-end) is defined as the time taken to pass through from a source to a destination node and is measured in seconds (s). These delays are caused by processing, queuing, transmission and propagation [7]. Mathematically, Delay (D) can be represented as in Eq. (2):

$$D_{end-end} = N \, [D \, trans + D \, prop + D \, proc] \qquad (2)$$

where $D_{end\text{-}end}$ = End-End Delay, D_{trans} = Transmission Delay, D_{prop} = Propagation Delay, D_{proc} = Processing Delay and N = Number of Nodes.

Equations 1 and 2 will be implemented in Microsoft Excel to generate the correct results.

Routing Traffic Received is defined as the amount of routing traffic received in bits/sec in the entire network. For best effort traffic, throughput and end to end delay are the most essential metrics to take into consideration. Lower throughput and great delays may occur when there are large overheads. All the same, a short delay does not mean higher throughput because delay is only measured in data packets delivered successfully.

3   Results

The simulation results are grouped as follows: Random WayPoint (RWP) DSR versus Random WayPoint (RWP) OLSR.

Random WayPoint (RWP) DSR versus Random WayPoint (RWP) OLSR
Figure 1 shows that Random WayPoint configured with OLSR performed better in terms of average throughput by delivering 182321.0 bits/sec of data, which is 78% of the total data. Random WayPoint DSR had the lowest average throughput by delivering only 50455.9 bits/sec of data, which is 22%. The percentage value for RWP OLSR was calculated as follows:

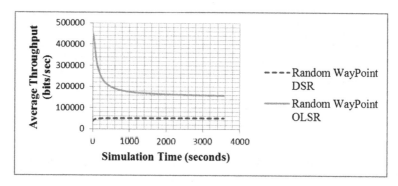

Fig. 1. Average throughput for RWP DSR & RWP OLSR

Average throughput of RWP OLSR $\div$ sum (RWP OLSR, RWP DSR average values) $\times$ 100

$$= 182321.0 \div (182321.0 + 50455.9) \times 100$$
$$= (182321.0/232776.9) \times 100$$
$$= 78.3\% \sim \mathbf{78\%}$$

This same formula was used to calculate the average percentages for all values in all scenarios.

Figure 2 shows that Random WayPoint OLSR recorded no delay at all. It had an average delay of 0.02 s. The highest average delay of 24.2 s was obtained by Random WayPoint DSR. This means that RWP OLSR had 0% delay while RWP DSR had 100% delay.

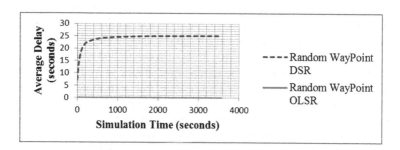

Fig. 2. Average delay for RWP OLSR & RWP OLSR

In Fig. 3, it could be seen that the average routing traffic received in Random WayPoint OLSR performed better in delivering 2110434.8 bits/sec of traffic or data, which is about 72% of total traffic. Random WayPoint DSR on the other hand delivered 812623.1 bits/sec of traffic, constituting only 28% of the entire traffic.

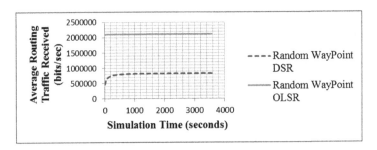

Fig. 3. Average routing traffic received for RWP OLSR & RWP OLSR

Analysis and Discussion of Results

This analysis and discussion was for the results obtained from Figs. 1, 2 and 3, which was, RWP DSR versus RWP OLSR. The pause time and speed for this scenario were 5 s and 5–10 m/s respectively. Once again, the analysis of different protocols with the same mobility model was made. RWP DSR obtained an average throughput of 50455.9 bits/sec whereas RWP OLSR delivered 182321.0 bits/sec. The average throughput in terms of percentage was 22% for RWP DSR and 78% for RWP OLSR. RWP DSR had an average delay of 24.2 s, which was 100% delay. RWP OLSR on the hand had 0.02 s and this was 0% delay. In routing traffic received, 812623.1 bits/sec of routing traffic was delivered by RWP DSR. This is equivalent to 28% of the total routing traffic delivered by the protocol. But RWP OLSR sent 72% of routing traffic, thus, delivering 2110434.8 bits/sec of traffic. The above analysis indicates that, RWP OLSR performed better than RWP DSR by providing 78% of throughput; no delay (0%) and 72% of routing traffic delivered.

The analysis showed that routing protocols can greatly affect the performance of MANET and the mobility model chosen. In all the performance metrics, that is throughput, delay and routing traffic received, RWP OLSR performed better than RWP DSR. This means that even when a network has the same mobility model and parameters, the routing protocol selected can have adverse influence on the network. The statistics showed that OLSR once again had 0% delay with RWP. OLSR use of the sensing of neighbouring nodes technique to set up a connection is the cause of its great performance. With this technique, it senses other nodes to verify their availability before sending a message that reduces packet drops and tends to increase performance. Throughput and routing traffic are also high in OLSR because it uses MPR nodes and these nodes works well in network where mobility speed is low, as it is in the case of this scenario, therefore, the possibility of OLSR maintaining a valid route is very high. DSR on the other hand, due to the availability of cache routes has high possibility of having expired routes and link failures. This is the reason why RWP DSR recorded 100% delay and fewer throughputs. With the reason given, the author could therefore say that RWP configured with OLSR improved MANET's performance than RWP configured with DSR. For this reason, the choice of a protocol for a specific mobility model should be considered in a network design [10–12].

Table 5 shows a summary of the performance results of the two routing protocol and mobility model discussed.

Table 5. Summary of performance results

Scenarios	Average throughput (bits/sec)	Average delay (sec)	Average routing traffic received (bits/sec)
RWP DSR	50455.9/22%	24.2/100%	812623.1/28%
RWP OLSR	182321.0/78%	0.02/0%	2110434.8/72%

4 Conclusion

In view of the simulated results shown above, it could be concluded that, OLSR protocol would perform better on MANET when used with RWP mobility model in an environment where the pause time is 5 s and mobility speed is 5–10 m/s. RWP OLSR had better performance than RWP DSR by providing 78% of throughput, no delay and 72% of routing traffic received. The simulation results prove that the choice of a protocol for a specific mobility model should be considered in a network design.

5 Future Work

In future, different mobility models, different routing protocols and different speed and pause time can be simulated to determine the performance of MANET. Future categories may include the following: MANET_Down_Left DSR versus MANET_Down_Left OLSR and MANET_Down_Left DSR versus Random WayPoint OLSR.

References

1. Corson, S., Macker, J.: Mobile Ad hoc Networking (MANET): Routing Protocol Performance Issues and Evaluation Considerations, RFC: 2501, January 1999. IEEE/IET Electronic Library. Accessed 29 July 2016
2. Soujanya, B., Sitamahalakshmi, T.: Study of routing protocols in mobile ad-hoc networks. Int. J. Eng. Sci. Technol. (IJEST) **3**(4), 2622–2631 (2011). IEEE/IET Electronic Library. Accessed 17 Aug 2016
3. Garrido, P.P., Manuel, P.M., Carlos, T.C.: NS-2 vs. OPNET: a comparative study of the IEEE 802.11e technology on MANET environments. Presented at the 1st International Conference on Simulation Tools and Techniques for Communications, Networks and Systems & Workshops, Marseille, France, pp. 1–10 (2008). IEEE/IET Electronic Library. Accessed 16 Aug 2016
4. Hogie, L., Bouvry, P., Guinand, F.: An overview of MANETs simulation. Electron. Notes Theor. Comput. Sci. **150**(1), 81–101 (2006). IEEE/IET Electronic Library. Accessed 16 Aug 2016
5. OPNET Modeler (2012). http://www.opnet.com. Accessed 17 Aug 2016

6. Chang, X.: Network simulations with OPNET. Presented at Simulation Conference Proceedings, pp. 307–314, Winter, 2010. IEEE/IET Electronic Library. Accessed 30 July 2016

7. Tie-yuan, L., Liang, C., Tian-long, G.: Analyzing the impact of entity mobility models on the performance of routing protocols in the MANET. In: 3rd International Conference on Genetic and Evolutionary Computing, WGEC 2009, [E-Journal], pp. 56–59 (2009). IEEE/IET Electronic Library. Accessed 16 Aug 2016

8. Hong, X., Gerla, M., Pei, G., Chiang, C.-C.: A group mobility model for ad hoc wireless networks. In: ACM/IEEE MSWiM, [E-Journal] (2010). IEEE/IET Electronic Library. Accessed 3 Sept 2016

9. Davies, V.: Evaluating mobility models with ad hoc network. Master's thesis, Colorado School of Mines (2000). IEEE/IET Electronic Library. Accessed 9 Sept 2016

10. Johnson, D., Maltz, D.: Dynamic source routing in ad hoc wireless network. In: Imielinski, T., Korth, H. (eds.) Mobile Computing, pp. 153–181. Kluwer Academic Publishers (1996). IEEE/IET Electronic Library. Accessed 9 Sept 2016

11. Ariyakhajorn, J., Wannawilai, P., Sathitwiriyawong, C.: A comparative study of random waypoint and gauss-markov mobility models in the performance evaluation of MANET. In: ISCIT 2006 (2006). IEEE/IET Electronic Library. Accessed 9 Sept 2016

12. Prabhakaran, P., Sankar, R.: Impact of realistic mobility models on wireless networks performance (2011). IEEE/IET Electronic Library. Accessed 3 Sept 2016

13. Kurkowski, S., Camp, T., Colagrosso, M.: MANET simulation scenarios: the incredibles. ACM Mob. Comput. Commun. Rev. (MC2R) 9(4), 50–61 (2005). IEEE/IET Electronic Library. Accessed 3 Sept 2016

14. Lenders, V., Wagner, J., May, M.: Analyzing the impact of mobility in ad hoc networks. In: ACM REALMAN, Florence, Italy, May 2006. IEEE/IET Electronic Library. Accessed 6 Sep 2016

15. Madsen, T.K., Fitzek, F.H.P., Prasad, R.: Impact of different mobility models on connectivity probability of a wireless ad hoc network. In: 2004 International Workshop on Wireless Ad-Hoc Networks, [E-Journal], pp. 120–124 (2004). IEEE/IET Electronic Library. Accessed 5 Sept 2016

16. Bhatt, M., Chokshi, R., Desai, S., Panichpapiboon, S., Wisitpongphan, N., Tonguz, O.K.: Impact of mobility on the performance of ad hoc wireless networks. In: 2003 IEEE 58th Vehicular Technology Conference, VTC 2003-Fall, [E-Journal], pp. 3025–3029 (2003). IEEE/IET Electronic Library. Accessed 5 Sept 2016

17. Li, X., Agrawal, D.P., Zeng, Q.-A.: Impact of mobility on the performance of mobile ad hoc networks. In: Wireless Telecommunications Symposium, [E-Journal], pp. 154–160 (2004). IEEE/IET Electronic Library. Accessed 5 Sept 2016

18. Sarkar, N.I., Halim, S.A.: Simulation of computer networks: simulators, methodologies and recommendations. Presented at the 5th International Conference on Information Technology and Application (ICITA 2008), Cairns, Australia, pp. 420–425 (2008). IEEE/IET Electronic Library. Accessed 3 Sept 2016

19. Cavin, D., Sasson, Y., Schiper, A.: On the accuracy of MANET simulators. Presented at the Second ACM International Workshop on Principles of Mobile Computing, Toulouse, France, pp. 38–43 (2002). IEEE/IET Electronic Library. Accessed 6 Sept 2016

A Comparative Study of Zynq-Based OpenFlow Switches in a Software/Hardware Co-design

Jian Kang[1], Xiaojun Hei[1(✉)], and Jianjian Song[2]

[1] Huazhong University of Science and Technology, Wuhan 430074, China
{kangjian,heixj}@hust.edu.cn
[2] Rose-Hulman Institute of Technology, Terre Haute, IN 47803, USA
song@rose-hulman.edu

Abstract. The end-to-end design principle has been re-examined over the years with the increasing number of middle-boxes on the Internet. The newly released Xilinx Zyqn-based chipsets have been reshaping popular embedded computing platforms, which provide cost-effective but all programmable approaches to enable intelligence at the network edge. In this paper, we design and implement a software defined networking (SDN) switch on ONetSwitch based on Zynq series chip. The previous switch implements the software-based switching functions running in the Linux kernel. We added the FPGA hardware structure to the software switch for accelerating packet processing and flow-table matching; therefore some functions of the SDN switch were transformed to FPGA. We constructed an SDN testbed using the re-constructed switch system, the Ryu controller and the client building software to evaluate the performance of the pure software switch and the new switch. We utilized network performance testing tools, such as iPerf and Ping, to evaluate the streaming performance including throughput, delay and delay jitter for these two SDN switches. The experiment results demonstrated the accelerating capability of hardware-based flow-table matching, indicating that the hardware and software co-design method is promising to provide a broad design and optimization space for network systems. As a case study, this switch project demonstrated the design process, verified the hardware platform and the software tool chain to accomplish a hardware/software co-design.

Keywords: Software defined networking
Software/Hardware co-design · OpenFlow switch · FPGA · ONetSwitch

1 Introduction

The traditional Internet is constructed based on the TCP/IP protocol suit. The nominal feature of the IP-based network is the distributed control architecture. Each switch or router determines the forwarding of data packets based on their own local routing tables. Whenever the network states change, network state information are exchanged between routers relying on various dynamic routing

© Springer International Publishing AG 2017
G. Wang et al. (Eds.): SpaCCS 2017 Workshops, LNCS 10658, pp. 369–378, 2017.
https://doi.org/10.1007/978-3-319-72395-2_34

protocols, and routers re-calculate the routing table. Due to the nature of the distributed control, in-complete or inaccurate network information often leads the network control to be sub-optimal. The rapid development of Internet applications have been driving the network to become more intelligent. The emergence of a large number of middle boxes demonstrates the feasibility of enabling network intelligent at the edge in an evolutionary approach. More and more edge devices need a unified network control and management. Edge devices are of potential to become the communication/information/storage/control center for the smart edge networking scenario, which requires strong control functions and traffic delivery capacity. The software-defined networking (SDN) proposes various features such as the centralized management, the separation of the control plane and the data plane. These features are advantageous to build a measurable, manageable, and controllable smart edge network.

OpenFlow is a representative south-bound protocol [1]. This protocol requires the SDN switches supporting the protocol-independent message handing. It requires the flexibility to define the field combination needed to match and the flexibility to define the operation for the implementation of the messages. This requires that the forwarding chip provides flexible programmable interfaces. Nevertheless, it is difficult to realize such flexibility for merchant silicon [1]. The cost of SDN switches remains high which may hinder a wide deployment of SDN networks. Till now, they have only been used for places such as data centers that are not sensitive to cost [2]. The emergence of Xilinx Zynq series of chips provides a cost-effective but all programmable approach to implement SDN switches in a software/hardware co-design. Previous studies have shown that it is possible to achieve a good design balance between the speed of hardware and the flexibility of software [3]. As a fast-developing technology, the cost of SDN switches may be dropping quickly low enough for wide applications in smart home. We are interested to redesign smart home networks with SDN [4]. We can connect all devices of our home to a SDN network through WiFi and control this network through SDN switches [5].

The rest of this paper is organized as follows: In Sect. 2, we present the hardware/software co-design method. We report the technical details of our SDN switch in hardware/software co-design as a case study in Sect. 3. The evaluation results are reported in Sect. 4. Finally, we conclude this paper and outline some future work in Sect. 5.

2   Software/Hardware Co-design

2.1   Design Method

The Zynq-series chips combine with processors and FPGA separately, called PS (Processing System) and PL (Programmble Logic). PL has ten of thousands of programmble logic cell. PS is two powerful ARM Contex-A9 processing core. These two parts are connected by the AXI bus. PS is the leading system of the whole system and it can control PL part through the AXI bus [6]. PL reflects to

PS part through address. This structure is different from the pure FPGA and the traditional SoC. We need to find a suitable method to develop the entire system.

The developing process can be divided into the hardware part and the software part. Xilinx provides a series of the tool chain to complete the whole process. We use Vivado to finish the hardware development and SDK to finish the software development.

The hardware development includes using Verilog to design custom digital logic circuits and set up the processing cores. The best way is encoding this digital logic into IP (Intellectual Property) cores and adding them into your project. Except for your custom IP cores. Xilinx and other third party organizations provide many ready-made IP cores to speed up the pace of development. Setting up the processing cores includes selecting clock source, peripheral interface configuration and so on. Xilinx packages two processing cores into one IP core. We can adjust parameters and connect it to other IP core in Vivado. After all IP cores connected, we need add the clock constrains and the pin constrains. Then, the synthesis and the implementation of the project will be complete by Vivado. We design software based on hardware. If the software is simple and we can develop the program directly on bare silicon. Or else we transplant a embedded operating system such as Linux on the hardware platform and develop the software in OS.

2.2 TCL Scripting

TCL stands for the tool command language. We use TCL scripts to control Vivado to complete the development of hardware part. In the past, TCL was often used in industry rather than academia. We use it in our program. TCL is an interpreter language with variables, procedures and control structures that can be used as interfaces for various design tools and design data. Similar to most EDA software suppliers, Xilinx uses TCL as the development language of the Vivado tool chain. TCL can provide commands to read and write the local file system, support engineers to dynamically create the project directory, start building FPGA projects, and add files in the project. After circuit design, TCL can control Vivado to complete the synthesis, implementation and simulation and bitstream generation of the design. In addition, we also use TCL to constrain time delay and circuit pin connection.

Vivado provides a good graphical interface. The motivation to use TCL scripts to complete the hardware design is multi-fold. First, a complete Vivado project is huge and need a suitable Vivado version to open the project. TCL scripts are stored in a text file and can be edited by any text editors. Second, we can use Github or other software for version control and multi-person collaborative design. When the design is finished, we run the TCL scripts in the Vivado and generate a bitstream file which defines the hardware structure.

3   Constructing an SDN Switch

In this section, we discuss how to construct this SDN switch in a hardware/software co-design. The whole project includes hardware and software. We complete the design on the ONetSwitch development board, which uses Zynq as its processing core. We separately implement switches in two ways. The hardware structure and software are different but the design method is similar.

3.1   Hardware Implementation

The structure of the ONetSwitch hardware platform is unchangable. This board was designed for networking applications. Hence, it is equipped with 5 RJ45 interfaces. They are connected to dedicated commercial chips. The commercial chip completes the physical layer function. It can perform interface protocols for the physical layer of 1000BASE-T, 100BASE-TX and 10BASE-T on the cabling of Category 5 unshielded twisted pair. The theoretical transmission speed can reach to 1 Gbps. One RJ45 interface is connected to the PS part of ZYNQ through one commercial chip and the other four RJ45 interfaces are connected to the PL part of ZYNQ through the other commercial chip.

The hardware can be divided into two parts. One is the circuit on the developing platform. It is unchangable. The other is our own custom digital logic in FPGA. Maybe calling it firmware is more accurate. We will report the implementation details of a SDN switch. The SDN switch works in the second layer of the standard ISO model. The dedicated chip on the hardware platform implements the functions of the physical layer. Hence, we are required to implement the MAC functions. We can integrate the IP core modules provided by the third parties. The IP core connects the physical layer chip through the RGMII or GMII interface.

Only one IP core cannot work. It needs to connect with the clock source. It is required to transfer data through the AXI-Streamer Interconnector and the processor visits the register of IP core through the AXI-LITE Interconnector for control. We can collect network data through these circuits. But how can we forward network package to the right place or right port. For switches based the software flow table, we just forward the data to the RAM through DMA; then, the software processes them. Then, they will be forwarded to the corresponding network port based on the flow tables. For switches based on hardware flow table, packets will be forwarded to our customized IP core. In this digital circuit, the data will be processed and match with the flow tables. Then, they will be sent to the right ports. The software will not process data. It only controls the whole procedure.

3.2   Software Implementation

The SDN switch need to exchange data with peripheral and storage. If we run the software on commodity computers, the software will be very complex. Hence, we first transplant the operating system on the platform; then, we install our switching software on the OS.

Transplanting the operating system includes three parts including the boot file, the kernel image and the file system. The embedded system does not have BIOS. After power-up, the codes that are solidified in the Boot ROM run first. These codes initialize the CPU and SD card peripherals, so that the CPU can read the codes above the storage medium. Then, the other peripherals will be initialized. A file named FSBL (First Stage Boot Loader) will complete this process. We can retrieve this file through SDK. We import the hardware project to SDK then we can retrieve this file automatically. For this project, we use a dedicated chip as an important clock source and add codes to FSBL to initialize this chip. Then, we set up FPGA to realize the digital logic we designed before. The bitstream file can complete this work. The bitstream file is generated by Vivado. After the hardware is initialized. We start the operating system. A software tool, Uboot, can support the guidance of many operating systems for many architectures. We did not change Uboot, which is provided by the third party. FSBL, bit file and Uboot are used to generate the boot file.

For an embedded system, just boot file is not enough. We need a file called the device tree to manage all peripherals and Interrupt source. This file can also be generated by SDK. A whole system also include kernel and file system. Xilinx may provide official Linux kernels for specific Zynq boards. But we need to do some minor changes to support using one chip to manage four RJ45 Interface. Then, we need to recompile the kernel source to retrieve the kernel image. After that, we need to download a file system on the Internet.

In this project, we boot the switch through the SD card. Hence, we place these files in a SD card. We need to divide the SD card into two partitions of FAT and EXT4. Then, we put the boot file, the device tree and the kernel to the FAT partition and the file system to the ext partition. For the switches based on the hardware flow table and the software flow table, the hardware structure is different. Hence, the bitstream file is different.

4   Performance Evaluation

We have discussed the design and implementation issues of our software defined network testbed. In this section, we conducted a number performance tests on different switches based on software flow table and hardware flow table. In order to examine the feasibility of the switch and evaluate the performance difference between the software flow table and the hardware flow table, we construct a small network. We used Ryu, which supported OpenFlow 1.3 protocol to deploy the flow table. We tested our switch qualitatively and quantitatively.

4.1   Video Delivery Prototype

First, we used three computers and one switch to deploy a simplest network as shown in Fig. 1. Host A and Host B are two computers with Linux. The controller is a computer installing the RYU controller software. We connected the hosts and the controller to the switch via the twisted cable. Then, we could test our switch.

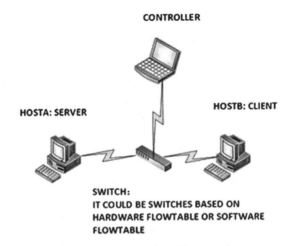

Fig. 1. A single-hop network topology.

The switch could not work when the power was on. When we implemented our switch as before, we just constructed the hardware and firmware configuration and transplanted the operating system and the switch software. Then, we start the network port and configure the switch software then the switch could connect to both hosts and the controller.

We connected a computer to our switch via a serial port. Then, we can interact with the Linux OS operating on our switch. We installed the SD card prepared before on the switch and started the switch. We can read the initial information on the hyper terminal. Then, we opened the network port and configured the MAC addresses and the IP addresses. We set a default gateway to the controller. Then, we start the switch software. We configure the data path between eth1 and eth4 which separately connected to Host A and Host B. Finally, we needed to create a secure channel connecting the switch with the controller.

Single-Hop Transmission. After the configuration of switch, we verify the feasibility of the switch. We installed a video software on both hosts. Host A generated video stream and transmitted it on the network. Host B received the stream and play back the video. The video was streamed smoothly with some time delay between the client and the server.

Multi-path Transmission. We constructed another test network as shown in Fig. 2(a). The controller runs the example switch program. This program selects an end-to-end route to transfer data. We use a server to generate the video stream and transmit to the network. The client receives the stream. When the video transmit smoothly, we disconnect one line as shown in Fig. 2(b). The video playback on the client will be suspended and then continue. During the pausing time, the controll program running in the controller selects a new path and deploys this new policy to the switches. Hence, the video can be streamed through another path.

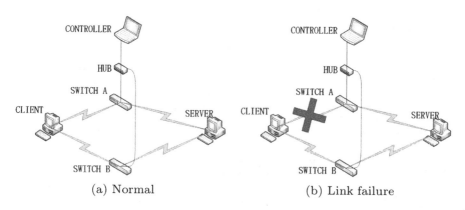

(a) Normal   (b) Link failure

Fig. 2. A multi-path network topology.

4.2   Data Forwarding

After the feasibility verification of tested. We needed to do a more accurate evaluation to our switch. We implemented the switch project on three different hardware platforms including ONetSwitch20, ONetSwitch30 and ONetSwitch45. We needed to know the what difference between the switches implemented on different hardware platforms and what difference between the switches implemented on the same hardware platform but based on hardware flow table and software flow table.

We used the same topology network in our experiments. We installed iPerf v2.0.5 both on two hosts. In our evaluation experiments, we mainly intend to achieve three objectives. First, we obtain the maximum throughput of the switch by measuring the receiving rate and the packet loss rate as the sending rate of sending side increasing in the UDP testing mode of iPerf. Second, We could measure the time delay jitter at different transmission rate of different switches. Finally, we could measure the time delay in the Ping test. We can compare the measurement results collecting from different switches for performance evaluation.

Maximum Throughput. Figures 3 and 4 are the performance result of the switches implementing on ONetSwitch20, ONetSwitch30 and ONetSwitch45. We find that the results show similar performance trends regardless the hardware platforms. Nevertheless, the performance gap is significant between the hardware flow table and the software flow table.

For the switches based on software flow table, the receiving rate will not increase when the sending rate reaches to 20 Mbps. The packet loss rate will also increase quickly and reach to 100%. We find the point where the packet loss rate begins to increase quickly. The sending rate where the point lies is also 20 Mbps. Hence, the maximum throughput of the switch based on software flow table is about 20 Mbps. Because the performance of switch based on software flow table is determined by the processor performance and three hardware platforms we used use the same processor core.

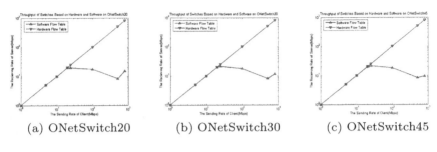

| (a) ONetSwitch20 | (b) ONetSwitch30 | (c) ONetSwitch45 |

Fig. 3. Throughput comparison

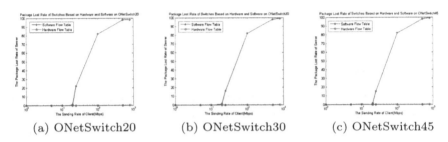

| (a) ONetSwitch20 | (b) ONetSwitch30 | (c) ONetSwitch45 |

Fig. 4. Packet loss comparison.

The performance of switch based on hardware flow table is quite different. The receiving rate increases as the sending rate increases. The packet lost rate is always keeping zero. We cannot observe the packet lost rate increases rapidly. Because the maximum sending rate of our hosts is only 800 Mbps and the switch based on hardware flow table has not reach its limit when the sending rate is 800 Mbps. So we estimate that the maximum throughput is more than 800 Mbps.

When we compare the maximum throughput of the switches based on software flow table and switches based on hardware flow table. We can find that the performance is significantly improved when we use FPGA for acceleration rather than the processing core to complete the network packet matching and processing. As we mentioned previously, from the speed of processing data, the hardware has an unparalleled advantage. The results of our experiments also validate this conjecture. The limit bandwidth of network interface we used on our switches is 1 Gbps. The final results of the switches based on hardware flow table approach the expected performance bound. The actual performance of the switches based on software flow table is quite far from the performance bound. Note that although hardware is faster than software, the software has better flexibility. We should consider the hardware and software co-design and balance the trade-off between speed and flexibility.

Delay Jitter. For quality of service of switches, there's a very important indicator called the delay jitter. The delay jitter is the absolute value of the difference between two delays. If the network is stable, the time delay of each packet passing is almost the same, when the user experience will be very good. We measure time delay jitter using iPerf. The measurement method is the same with the previous section. Taking ONetSwitch30 as an example, we separately measure time delay jitter of the switches based on the hardware flow table and the software flow table. The results are shown in Fig. 5.

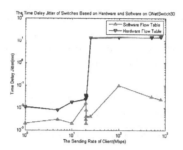

Fig. 5. The delay jitter of the switches based on hardware and software flow table

As the increasing of sending rate, the time delay jitter will increase whichever flow table is based. The delay jitter of the switches based on hardware flow table is always less than the one based on the hardware flow table when the sending rate is the same. When the sending rate is higher than 20 Mbps, the delay jitter of switch based on software flow table will increase rapidly. We analyze the reasons in the previous section that the limitation of the switch based software flow table is 20 Mbps. In terms of the quality-of-service, the switches based on hardware flow table can provide a more stable service.

5   Conclusion

In this paper, we applied the hardware/software co-design method, utilized the Zynq-based ONetSwitch board as the hardware platform, and reconstruct the Vivado switch hardware project using TCL scripts. We implemented the SDN switches based on software flow table using toolchain provided by Xilinx. Then, we implement the function of the flow table matching and forwarding to in FPGA so the software and hardware work together in the switches based on the hardware flow table. We conducted a series of performance evaluation experiments on an instrumented testbed. This testbed consists of various switches and hosts. Our experiments demonstrate the feasibility of constructing the SDN switches on Zynq-based embedded system in a hardware/software co-design. We reported the evaluation results of the maximum throughput, the delay jitter and the average delay of the switches based on hardware flow table and software flow table. The result comparison demonstrates the advantages of the software and hardware co-design. In the future, we plan to add the support of wireless communication on the Zynq-based switches and enhance the switches with additional

SDN features in a software/hardwared co-design approach to manage both the data forwarding and the MAC-layer parameters to implement a software defined WiFi network for performance evaluation [7]. We will design various experiments to study the impact of important MAC parameters on the WiFi network performance against the theoretical results predicted by the analytical models for single-BSS WiFi networks and multi-BSS WiFi networks [8,9].

Acknowledgments. The authors thank Yuteng Deng and Jian Liang for their contributions in the early stage of this research. This work was supported in part by the National Natural Science Foundation of China (No. 61370231), and in part by the Fundamental Research Funds for the Central Universities (No. HUST:2016YXMS303).

References

1. Nadeau, D.T., Gray, K.: SDN: Software Defined Networks. O'Reilly Media Inc., Sebastopol (2013)
2. Kalyaev, A.: FPGA-based approach for organization of SDN switch. In: 9th International Conference on Application of Information and Communication Technologies (2015)
3. Schaumont, P.R.: A Practical Introduction to Hardware/Software Codesign, 2nd edn. Springer, Heidelberg (2014). https://doi.org/10.1007/978-1-4614-3737-6
4. Zahid, T., Dar, F.Y., Hei, X., Cheng, W.: An empirical study of the design space of smart home routers. In: Chang, C.K., Chiari, L., Cao, Y., Jin, H., Mokhtari, M., Aloulou, H. (eds.) ICOST 2016. LNCS, vol. 9677, pp. 109–120. Springer, Cham (2016). https://doi.org/10.1007/978-3-319-39601-9_10
5. Zahid, T., Hei, X., Cheng, W.: Understanding the design space of a software defined WiFi network testbed. In: 14th International Conference on Frontiers of Information Technology (FIT) (2016)
6. Crockett, L.H., Elliot, R.A., Enderwitz, M.A., Stewart, R.W.: The Zynq Book: Embedded Processing with the ARM Cortex-A9 on the Xilinx Zynq-7000 All Programmable SoC. Strathclyde Academic Media, Glasgow (2014)
7. Chen, Z., Fu, D., Gao, Y., Hei, X.: Performance evaluation for WiFi DCF networks from theory to testbed. In: The 16th IEEE International Conference on Ubiquitous Computing and Communications (IUCC), December 2017
8. Gao, Y., Sun, X., Dai, L.: Throughput optimization of heterogeneous IEEE 802.11 DCF networks. IEEE Trans. Wireless Commun. **12**(1), 398–411 (2013)
9. Gao, Y., Dai, L., Hei, X.: Throughput optimization of multi-BSS IEEE 802.11 networks with universal frequency reuse. IEEE Trans. Commun. **65**(8), 3399–3414 (2017)

Design and Implementation of a Low-Cost Software Defined Wireless Network Testbed for Smart Home

Watipatsa W. Nsunza, Samuel Rutunda, and Xiaojun Hei$^{(\boxtimes)}$

School of Electronic Information and Communications,
Huazhong University of Science and Technology, Wuhan 430074, China
{nsunza,rutunda,heixj}@hust.edu.cn

Abstract. The evolvable nature of software defined wireless networking offers great opportunities toward the design and implementation of a low-cost network testbed for smart home. Programmability is an essential component on a network gateway to enable efficient management of energy and other network resources for secure, scalable, and cost-effective solutions. In this paper, we proposed a software defined edge-cloud network architecture for smart home. We studied the programmable features of several popular SoC and FPGA platforms and design a software defined wireless network testbed for smart home by integrating several open-source projects including OpenWrt, Lede, and OpenFlow, which may be extended for other application scenarios such as smart grid and Internet-of-Things. We implemented WiFi, BLE, and ZigBee networking features on our low-cost FPGA and SoC platforms and evaluated the TCP and UDP throughput on our testbed. We conducted a series of experiments on our testbed and examined optimization issues based on recent developments in SDN. Our testbed may provide experiment supports for advancing smart home research and development.

Keywords: Smart home · Network testbed · Home area networks
Internet-of-Things · Software defined networking
Wireless networking · OpenFlow

1 Introduction

Smart home applications have been penetrating into our daily life in recent years. Gartner has predicted that over 25 billion IoT devices will be connected by 2020. A smart home is a communications network linking key electrical appliances and services accessible and monitored remotely. Smart homes can be classified into 2 categories: autonomous houses based on sensor-driven activation, or intelligent houses which can learn without human intervention. Smart homes utilize recent development in different domains such as smart grid, wearable IoT and a variety of sensors utilizing different protocols. Smart homes can also be centralized or decentralized, however, most systems have adapted a centralized approach

© Springer International Publishing AG 2017
G. Wang et al. (Eds.): SpaCCS 2017 Workshops, LNCS 10658, pp. 379–388, 2017.
https://doi.org/10.1007/978-3-319-72395-2_35

where all devices are connected to a single gateway [1,2]. There are a few challenges in standardizing smart home protocols such as energy efficiency, security, and efficient management. In recent years, a huge number of WiFi networks have been deployed at homes as dominant broadband network access in an unplanned manner and compete for unlicensed bandwidth in same areas, which may lead to significant degradation of network performance [3,4]. The emerging software defined networking (SDN) has been proposed to support smart home research and development. As a new paradigm shift in networking, SDN separates the control plane from the data plane, offering network flexibility, introducing programmability and ease of management [5]. SDN is often combined with network function virtualization (NFV) to enable manageable and controllable networks. To meet the needs of smart home applications, SDN can unite different communication technologies, provide better security against external attacks, and offer better energy saving schemes [6].

In this paper, we design and implement a low-cost software defined wireless network testbed for smart homes based on multiple SoC development boards. The testbed platforms include the Digilent Zybo™ FPGA with a dual-core ARM®Cortex®-A9 processor, Intel®Galileo Gen 2 with an Intel®Quark™ SoC X1000 application processor, Raspberry Pi 1 Model B+ with the ARM11 CPU, and Raspberry Pi 3 Model B with a quad-core ARM®Cortex®-A53 CPU (see Table 1). These platforms have much higher processing speeds than conventional routers. We investigated the programmable features of these hardware platforms as a network testbed for smart home research to provide connectivity solutions for software defined IoT.

Table 1. Hardware specification

Platform[a]	Processor			Memory
	CPU	*Cores/Threads*	*Freq* (MHz)	*DRAM* (MB)
Galileo 2	Quark™ SoC X1000	1/1	400	256
Zybo	Cortex®-A9	2/2	650	512
RPi B+	ARM11	1/1	700	512
RPi 3B	Cortex®-A53	4/4	1200	1024

[a]The FPGA/SoC platforms augmented are priced roughly between 20 to 200 USD.

The remaining of this paper is organized as follows. First, we present a software-defined edge-cloud network architecture for smart home in Sect. 2. Next, we describe the design and implementation of our testbed to support the research of the proposed architecture in Sect. 3. In Sect. 4, we report the evaluation results of our testbed followed by discussing optimization issues. Then, in Sect. 5, we review some related work. Finally, we conclude this paper and outline some future work in Sect. 6.

2   A Software Defined Edge-Cloud Network Architecture

The essential components in building a software defined edge-cloud network architecture for smart home are depicted in Fig. 1. There are four key components in a smart home environment, including the network gateway, an SDN controller, and high bandwidth and low bandwidth communication channels to manage appliances with efficiency and security. The data paths to the communication interfaces between the gateway device and smart home network appliances or external networks are illustrated by grey arrows and wireless links to the the appliances and home devices are depicted by the bold dashed lines. The SDN control plane can receive status information from home appliances and send control messages to the appliances through the SmartWLAN and SmartWPAN access networks. The controller can also implement security schemes by extending the OpenFlow protocol to secure the data transmission.

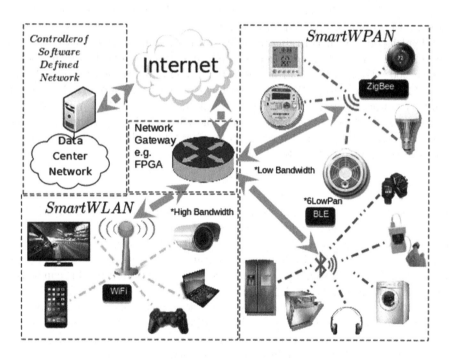

Fig. 1. A proposed software-defined edge-cloud network architecture.

2.1   Smart Home Gateway

We studied the programmable features of low-cost SoC platforms with both FPGA and non-FPGA architectures as network gateways for a smart home. The gateway device can be implemented on programmable SoC architectures with the latest Linux kernels. The proposed design does not incorporate wired links on the data path to home appliances though wired links are used for linking the gateway to the Internet. Wired communication links are much secure and provide high throughput; however, we consider the modern structure of smart homes and cabling costs of wired systems and integrated the latest wireless communication standards in this design. Wireless systems also have a low complexity during setup and configuration when compared with wired links which is preferred in Home Area Networking (HAN) scenarios. The proposed smart home gateway accommodates wireless communication networks much more easily by adapting wireless interfaces such as Bluetooth (IEEE 802.15), WiFi (IEEE 802.11) and BLE and ZigBee (IEEE 802.15.4).

2.2   SmartWLAN

WiFi has become the most dominant networking technology for implementing wireless local area networks "WLAN". WiFi technology is built on top of the IEEE 802.11 standard set of media access control (MAC) and physical (PHY) specifications that support applications in computers, smart phones, and other bandwidth sensitive networking devices. WiFi standards include IEEE 802.11a, 802.11b/g/n, and 802.11ac wireless communication standards which operate at the 900 MHz and 2.4, 3.6, 5, and 60 GHz communication frequency bands. "802.11ac" is the latest WiFi standard with dual band support. It supports multiple connections at once and operates at the 2.4 and 5 GHz WiFi frequency bands. 802.11ac is also backward compatible with 802.11b/g/n wireless devices and supports data bandwidth rates up to 1300 Mbps when operating at 5 GHz and 450 Mbps at a 2.4 GHz frequency.

2.3   SmartWPAN

BLE and ZigBee are designed for low data rate applications to efficiently conserve energy. This enables devices and sensors to operate for a number of years depending on the amount of activity and stability of the energy source. These low complexity wireless standards have specifications on both Layer 1 (PHY) and Layer 2 (MAC) and are highly adopted and anticipated solutions for connecting smart grid devices in IoT. The short range and restricted topology in BLE and ZigBee devices requires mesh and start networking protocols with multi-hop support to overcome the limitations. WiFi radios don't efficiently manage power. Using WiFi to manage appliances in the smart home network would exhaust battery powered home appliances much frequently. This has encouraged the development of power efficient home appliances with other wireless technologies. BLE and ZigBee provide sufficient throughput for smart home network communication in low bandwidth devices, which efficiently utilize energy to improve connectivity for smart home.

2.4   SDN Controller

As a new method for managing a smart home network, we propose a software defined edge-cloud architecture to efficiently manage network traffic from an extensible number of connected IoT devices. OpenFlow extends generic features of TCAM switches and routers and provides an open protocol for configuring different switches and flow tables on routers. While using OpenFlow to manage the network, researchers can distinguish between experimental streams and workflows to control their own experimental streams by selecting packets, routing lines, and handling received packets. This enables experimenting of routing protocols, security models, address scheduling, and select IP. The data path of the OpenFlow switch contains a flow table and an action corresponding to each flow entry. These operations are extensible to a subset of switches for a limited and useful set of operations. The OpenFlow switch matches each flow entry in the table to a corresponding operation with instructions on handling an incoming flow and provides a secure channel to link the switch to a remote controller and transmits control commands using the OpenFlow protocol.

3   Testbed

3.1   Overview

In this section, we describe the design and implementation of a network testbed to support the research of the proposed edge-cloud architecture. In our testbed, the gateway is instrumented using different platforms and deploys the Open-Flow protocol to manage communication channels via a few interfaces. All the platforms followed an overall similar development structure, with different levels of difficulty and procedures for building our system firmware. We developed an "OpenWrt" and "Lede" Linux system with supporting drivers for the on-board input and output interfaces (i.e. Ethernet, USB, PCI expansion, etc.) specific to the hardware requirements on each platform. We implemented a WiFi access point based on each platforms hardware and software requirements. Our "Zybo" and "RPi 3" platforms have been implemented with the latest supporting Linux kernel, and are therefore capable of supporting 802.11ac WiFi, while other platforms only support 802.11n. We installed packages to support the OpenFlow protocol as well as QoS routing schemes which are currently under test for all our systems.

3.2   Firmware

The Intel®Galileo Gen 2 (Fig. 2a) system firmware is built based on the "Linux kernel 3.8.13" OpenWrt "Trunk" source code. The wireless access point (WAP) on this platform is built on an Atheros AR9380 PCI Card. Linux has supports 6LowPan for Bluetooth Low Energy "BLE" on kernel version 3.17 and above. We're still investigating alternative solutions for implementing ZigBee and BLE support on this platform. Digilent Zybo (Fig. 2b) supports the latest OpenWrt trunk "Linux kernel 4.4.14". This firmware supports OpenFlow and QoS, BLE, ZigBee, and WiFi devices via USB. The challenges with this platform are due to

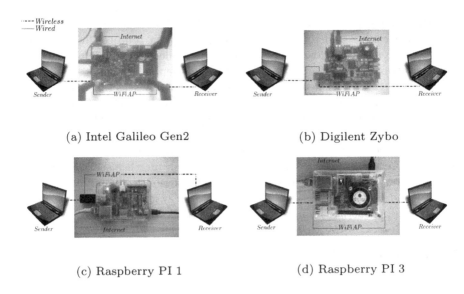

(a) Intel Galileo Gen2

(b) Digilent Zybo

(c) Raspberry PI 1

(d) Raspberry PI 3

Fig. 2. Testbed platforms.

the limited number of USB interfaces which limits the number of active connections to one communication technology at time based on our current implementation. To resolve this issue we have been looking into interfacing through other peripheral module inputs on the device. The Raspberry Pi 3 platform (Fig. 2d) offers an in-built 802.11n WiFi and Bluetooth 4.1 chipset. The Raspberry Pi 1 (Fig. 2c) however contains no built-in communication interfaces and requires a USB based dongle to support both Bluetooth and WiFi features. The firmware on the Raspberry Pi testbed has been developed on the OpenWrt Chaos Calmer source codes and the Raspbberry Pi 3 firmware is based on the Lede 17.01.0 source codes. All these firmwares also support the latest developments of Open-Flow, QoS, BLE, ZigBee, and WiFi.

4   Evaluation

We evaluated the testbeds under both TCP and UDP against the performance of a traditional TP-link router running on the vendor firmware using iPerf. With the datagram size set at 1470 bytes, a TCP window size of 416 Kbytes and the UDP buffer size at 208 Kbytes, we conducted 100+ experiments on each platform to summarize our measurement results. We observed that the Intel®Galileo Gen 2 achieved the highest TCP throughput when compared with other platforms, though this performance was still less than the average when compared to the TP-link router as shown in (Fig. 3a). The maximum TCP throughput for Galileo ranged at 13.6 Mbps while the TP-link router achieved a 25.7 Mbps TCP throughput. Our Digilent Zybo platform however achieved the highest throughput on UDP traffic even compared with the TP-link router, achieving a maximum throughput of 50 Mbps; a performance equivalent to the line rate (see Fig. 3b) and (Table 2). Zybo offers a decreased latency and also encountered the lowest UDP jitter ratio averaged at 0.224 ms on a minimum UDP buffer size, and caused by a single packet loss.

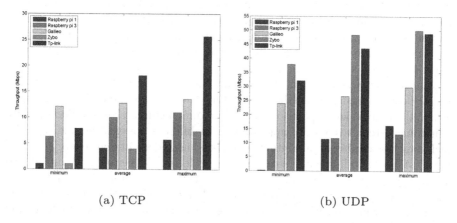

(a) TCP   (b) UDP

Fig. 3. Throughput performance.

Table 2. Performance summary

Platform	TCP max (Mbps)	UDP max (Mbps)	Latency avg. (ms)	Jitter avg. (ms)
Galileo 2	13.6	15.7	4.12	1.57
Zybo	7.34	50.0	0.04	0.22
RPi B+	5.77	16.2	6.82	1.63
RPi 3B	11.0	13.1	7.42	1272.2

Our measurement results show a very low performance of the software based packet switching module on our testbed. We conjecture that by utilizing the latest developments in SDN, we may optimize the TCP and UDP throughput. The performance tests for our testbed are still being analyzed as we continue the developments. The above tests demonstrate the most basic analysis. Due to the current progress, other parts of our testbed have yet to be evaluated. As an on-going research project, we have been conducting further experiments and analysis on our all the required parameters of our network testbed.

5   Related Work

Prior research on the smart home testbed has centered primarily on creating simulation environments for conducting experiments on energy saving. In [7], Perumal et al. reviewed machine-to-machine distributed home networks and describe the performance trade-offs which covers quality of service, energy efficiency, and security issues. In [8], Suh and Ko designed and implemented a multi-purpose smart house simulation system for designing and simulating all aspects of a smart house environment. This simulator provides the ability to design the house plan and different virtual sensors and appliances in a two dimensional model of a virtual house environment. This simulator can connect to any external smart house remote controlling system, extending the evaluation capabilities to the system. In [9], Louis proposed to improve the energy efficiency of smart buildings as an essential part of the smart grid system. The theoretical aspect of the paper introduced ideas for promoting energy efficiency in smart home while underlining that data safety and privacy are major concerns in the system. The practical aspect based on Matlab and Simulink modeled key aspects of a smart building including 10-year climate data, a lighting system, twenty-one appliances with different power rates, and variables including the number of inhabitants & bed-rooms and small-scale energy production systems including wind, solar, and fuel cell. In [10], Fensel et al. introduced a smart home system for energy efficiency. Their study emphasized that energy efficiency is an important element in smart home development due to the rising energy cost, which have created a growing need for energy saving systems and increased demands for energy saving solutions world-wide. Companies including Apple, Cisco, and Google have also introduced semantic energy saving solutions for homes on the market.

The energy-saving approach in [10] similar to one we're developing on our testbed demonstrated the efficiency of using non-semantic interface specific solutions such as a ZigBee communication interface approach for home controlling. Zigbee-like Bluetooth low energy devices are designed to be energy efficient. Integrating support interfaces for these technologies on our testbed promotes energy efficiency in our Smart Home. In [11], Gill et al. also presented a low-cost stand-alone ZigBee Smart Home automation system. The system adapted a low-complexity architecture to lower financial costs by eliminating complex and expensive hardware components. This architecture consisted of a home gateway for inter-operability between heterogeneous networks including ZigBee and WiFi for connecting to smart home devices from the Internet-enabled devices through serial and parallel interfaces on a Jennic JN5139 Micro-controller. The architecture was managed by a virtual environment responsible for administering security to the home automation system. This architecture however adapted traditional advanced encryption standard (AES) public/private key exchange methods in the virtual environment for securing the network devices. This may present intrusion threats to an IoT network including smart homes from reverse engineering with a microcontroller unit (MCU) debugger to obtain keys stored on the devices, which will affect all attached TCP/IP networks [12]. Once the session keys are compromised, security will be ineffective. Other testbeds in [8,13,14] also employed new routing schemes to optimize performance while maintaining traditional methodologies of managing the network devices and therefore face similar potential threats previously described. In [15] Tang et al. also proposed a simulation testbed for the Cyber-security experimentation on a smart home network based on traditional wireless network protocols.

In [1,2], Zahid et al. conducted a measurement-based empirical study on the design space of different OpenFlow switches in multiple scenarios of a smart home network. In that study, they focused on the throughput performance for different software-based OpenFlow switches based on ONetSwitch20, ONetSwitch45, and the NetGear WNDR3700v4. Their results demonstrated significant higher throughput with hardware-based switching than software-based switching. The design space was discussed for high-bandwidth WiFi devices while we are interested to investigate efficient schemes to manage energy and other network resources to increase the number of connected devices in smart home. Our study also covered several popular low-cost SoC architectures by extending our previous work [16].

6   Conclusion

In this paper, we proposed a software defined edge-cloud network architecture for smart home. We designed and implemented a network testbed based on popular SoC and FPGA platforms. We conducted comprehensive measurement experiments to evaluate the TCP and UDP throughput on our testbed. Our results demonstrate a very low performance of the software based packet switching module on our testbed. This has motivated us to conduct further experiments to track the performance bottleneck of our testbed. We plan to continue analyzing the performance of our switch implementation of the "WiFi", "BLE", and ZigBee modules. Our experiments will include energy consumption, network performance, bandwidth utilization and CPU load. We have been examining the prototype results with the emulation results and the theoretical results [17]. Such a comparison study may provide more insights into the design space of a software defined edge-cloud architecture for the emerging edge computing and networking applications. We also plan to instrument a representative SDN controller in a software/hardwared co-design approach [18] to manage both the data forwarding and the MAC-layer parameters to implement a software defined wireless network testbed for performance evaluation. The emerging software defined edge-cloud architecture is advantageous to achieve measurable, manageable and controllable high-density smart homes [19].

Acknowledgments. This work was supported in part by the National Natural Science Foundation of China (No. 61370231), and in part by the Fundamental Research Funds for the Central Universities (No. HUST:2016YXMS303).

References

1. Zahid, T., Dar, F.Y., Hei, X., Cheng, W.: An empirical study of the design space of smart home routers. In: Chang, C.K., Chiari, L., Cao, Y., Jin, H., Mokhtari, M., Aloulou, H. (eds.) ICOST 2016. LNCS, vol. 9677, pp. 109–120. Springer, Cham (2016). https://doi.org/10.1007/978-3-319-39601-9_10

2. Zahid, T., Hei, X., Cheng, W.: Understanding the design space of a software defined WiFi network testbed. In: International Conference on Frontiers of Information Technology (FIT), pp. 170–175, December 2016

3. Zhang, C., Qiu, D., Mao, S., Hei, X., Cheng, W.: Characterizing interference in a campus WiFi network via mobile crowd sensing. In: Guo, S., Liao, X., Liu, F., Zhu, Y. (eds.) CollaborateCom 2015. LNICST, vol. 163, pp. 173–182. Springer, Cham (2016). https://doi.org/10.1007/978-3-319-28910-6_16

4. Gao, Y., Dai, L., Hei, X.: Throughput optimization of multi-BSS IEEE 802.11 networks with universal frequency reuse. IEEE Trans. Commun. **65**(8), 3399–3414 (2017)

5. McKeown, N., Anderson, T., Balakrishnan, H., Parulkar, G., Peterson, L., Rexford, J., Shenker, S., Turner, J.: OpenFlow: enabling innovation in campus networks. SIGCOMM Comput. Commun. Rev. **8**(2), 69–74 (2008)

6. Shin, S., et al.: Enhancing network security through software defined networking (SDN). In: IEEE ICCCN (2016)

7. Perumal, T., Ramli, A.R., Leong, C.Y.: Interoperability framework for smart home systems. IEEE Trans. Consum. Electron. **57**(4) (2011)

8. Suh, C., Ko, Y.B.: Design and implementation of intelligent home control systems based on active sensor networks. IEEE Trans. Consum. Electron. **54**(3), 1177–1184 (2008)

9. Louis, J.N.: Smart buildings to improve energy efficiency in the residential sector. Ph.D. thesis, University of Oulu (2012)

10. Fensel, A., et al.: Sesame-S: Semantic smart home system for energy efficiency. Informatik-Spektrum **36**(1), 46–57 (2013)

11. Gill, K., Yang, S.H., Yao, F., Lu, X.: A ZigBee-based home automation system. IEEE Trans. Consum. Electron. **55**(2), 422–430 (2009)

12. Sood, K., Yu, S., Xiang, Y.: Software-defined wireless networking opportunities and challenges for Internet-of-Things: a review. IEEE Internet Things J. **3**(4), 453–463 (2016)

13. Han, D.M., Lim, J.H.: Design and implementation of smart home energy management systems based on ZigBee. IEEE Trans. Consum. Electron. **56**(3), 1417–1425 (2010)

14. Osiegbu, C., et al.: Design and implementation of an autonomous wireless sensor-based smart home. In: IEEE ICCCN (2015)

15. Tong, J., Sun, W., Wang, L.: A smart home network simulation testbed for cyber-security experimentation. In: Leung, V.C.M., Chen, M., Wan, J., Zhang, Y. (eds.) TridentCom 2014. LNICST, vol. 137, pp. 136–145. Springer, Cham (2014). https://doi.org/10.1007/978-3-319-13326-3_14

16. Nsunza, W.W., Hei, X.: Design and implementation of a smart home router based on Intel Galileo Gen 2. In: EAI TRIDENTCOM, December 2017

17. Chen, Z., Fu, D., Gao, Y., Hei, X.: Performance evaluation for WiFi DCF networks from theory to testbed. In: The 16th IEEE International Conference on Ubiquitous Computing and Communications (IUCC), December 2017

18. Kang, J., Hei, X., Song, J.: A comparative study of Zynq-based OpenFlow switches in a software/hardware co-design. In: International Workshop on Network Optimization and Performance Evaluation (NOPE), December 2017

19. Chen, Z., Manzoor, S., Gao, Y., Hei, X.: Achieving load balancing in high-density software defined WiFi networks. In: International Conference on Frontiers of Information Technology (FIT), December 2017

Energy-Efficiency Aware Cooperative Caching Strategy for Content-Centric Networks

Wenfei Han[✉], Gaocai Wang, and Peng Ying

School of Computer and Electronic Information, Guangxi University,
Nanning 530004, Guangxi, China
878770427@qq.com, gcwang@gxu.edu.cn, 623833@qq.com

Abstract. Content-Centric Networking (CCN) is a new network architecture approach that each content router in it has caching capability, it can shorten the distance of user requests and improve network content distribution efficiency through the content cache of the routing nodes. In-network caching is one of the key technologies of CCN, which is widely concerned recently. However, most of the current caching strategies mainly concern about the performance of CCN, without considering the problem of transmission cost when the network provides service for users, and the energy efficiency of CCN is largely ignored. In this paper, to overcome this problem, firstly, an energy consumption model for content distribution is built and a judging condition for energy efficiency optimization in caching is designed. And in combination with content popularity the node centrality, a method is presented to calculate the probability that the content is cached by the node. Use the probability to measure the Content cache priority, then consider the Content cache priority and the Energy Efficiency Decision Conditions together, on this basis, an energy-efficiency aware cooperative caching strategy for content-centric networks (EEACC) is proposed. Simulation results demonstrate that the proposed strategy can effectively reduce the overall energy consumption of the network while ensuring a high cache hit rate and a smaller average response hops.

Keywords: Content-Centric Network · Energy efficiency · Content popularity In-network caching · Cooperative Caching

1 Introduction

With the rapid development of Internet technology. The "content" and "personalization" of information services have become the main trend of the current network development [1], the traditional host-based Internet architecture has gradually been unable to adapt to the growing data requirements from the large number of users. As a potential solution, CCN architecture [2] has received great attention from relevant scholars. It adopts the name of content data to complete the identification, routing and acquisition of content, thus realizing the separation of content and physical location. In order to alleviate the severe pressure caused by the fast growth of network traffic, the ubiquitous In-network caching technology is widely used in CCN network architecture, through which can improve the performance when distribute content to the network.

© Springer International Publishing AG 2017
G. Wang et al. (Eds.): SpaCCS 2017 Workshops, LNCS 10658, pp. 389–398, 2017.
https://doi.org/10.1007/978-3-319-72395-2_36

However, it may generate excessive cache redundancy, resulting in reducing network resource utilization and energy efficiency. A collaboration caching mechanism based on the age of the content has been proposed in paper [3], it has reduced the content acquisition latency and network flow by setting a longer age to the contents which have high popularity and on the edge of the network. However, the article assumes that the popularity of the content and the network topology is known already, it is not easy to know these information. On the basis of homogeneity cache allocation, a cache space dynamic temporary transfer mechanism based on substitution has been proposed in paper [4]. According to the degree of the node's demand for cache resource, the mechanism dynamically allocate the spare cache to the more demanding nodes, which improves the network's caching performance effectively. In paper [5, 6], a selective content cache is realized by considering the cache capacity of each node in the path and the popularity of content.so as to alleviate the negative impact of short-term users' sudden visit to network performance.

However, the existing research work mainly focus on the optimization of network resource utilization to design CCN cache decision and replacement strategy, the focus on energy efficiency is limited. The current network energy consumption generates 10 percent of the world's energy consumption, and this proportion continues to grow rapidly [7]. Therefore, the energy consumption of the network has become an important issue in the study of CCN cache mechanism. The effects of different caching strategies on CCN performance are analyzed from the energy consumption point of view, and some open issues are discussed in paper [8]. In paper [9], the optimization of the efficiency of CCN cache is transformed into a problem that minimizes the number of average user response hops, and then proposes an energy efficiency caching mechanism APC based on the aging popularity. In paper [10], the problem of CCN cache content placement is formed into a non-cooperative game, this paper proposes a distributed cache mechanism based on energy efficiency, each node in the network make the decision by considering cache energy consumption and the transmission energy consumption of the content.

In this paper, we proposed a new distributed collaborative caching mechanism, various factors such as energy efficiency, content popularity and node importance are integrated to implement the content caching decision, so as to gain greater network performance achieving the reasonable balance between the efficiency of the network and the quality of the cache service while ensuring the smaller energy consumption.

2 System Model

2.1 Network Model

It is assumed that the topology of CCN network can be represented by undirected connected graph $G = (V, E)$, where $V = (v_1, v_2, \ldots v_n)$ is the collection of routing nodes in the network, $U \subseteq V$ is the collection of terminal nodes, and $E \subseteq V \times V$ is the set of links between nodes in the network. Let $O = (O_1, O_2, \ldots, O_m)$ be the collection of all content objects available in the network. All of the objects are initially distributed in the original content servers (OCS), OCS are distributed on the edge of the network directly connected to edge content routers. End nodes are responsible for collecting the interest packets for different content objects from their users and spreading them to the network along the selected routers. Each node $v_i \in V$ has a certain cache capacity so that the content forwarded by the node can be stored locally, which can store up to M_i content items.

2.2 Energy Consumption Model

In this section, we analyze the energy consumption of CCN network. The energy consumption of CCN network mainly comes from the cache and transmission of content. In this case, the total energy consumption of CCN network consists of two parts: the cache energy consumption E_c and the transmission energy consumption E_t, and the total of energy consumption $= E_c + E_t$. To make the presentation of the energy consumption model formula and calculation process easier to follow, we briefly summarize the notations of the key parameters used in the process of calculation and simulations in Table 1.

Table 1. Notations of the key parameters used in the simulations.

Symbols	Notations
M_i	Number of different network contents
t	Time duration
E_t	The transport energy consumption
q_i^k	Request rate for object O_k at node v_i
s_k	Size of the content object O_k
h_{ij}	Hop distance between content router v_i and j
w_r	Power density of a core router
w_l	Power density of a ROADM
w_c	Power efficiency of storage
E_c	The caching energy consumption
E_{tot}	The total of energy consumption
f_i^k	The request frequency for content O_k from node v_i

Using the energy consumption model in [5]. If node v_i caches content object O_k within an observed time interval t, the energy consumption of caching s_k is given in [5], the energy consumption for node v_i caching content O_k can be expressed as formula (1).

$$E_c = w_c s_k t \qquad (1)$$

The transmission energy consumption mainly consists of the energy consumption at routers and energy consumption along the links. To simplify our energy consumption model with optimal cache locations, we assume that a user acquires any one content from a single content router. Based on the mentioned parameters in Table 1, the transmission energy consumption by node v_j to transfer content object O_k from node can be expressed as formula (2).

$$E_t = q_i^k s_k \left[h_{ij}(w_r + w_l) + w_r \right] \tag{2}$$

So for node v_i to cache and transport O_k need the amount of energy consumption is E_{tot}.

$$E_{tôt} = w_c s_k t + q_i^k s_k \left[h_{ij} \left(w_r + w_l \right) + w_r \right] \tag{3}$$

3   Energy Efficiency Aware Cooperative Caching Strategy

3.1   Energy Efficiency Decision Conditions

CCN is actually reduces the user's distance to the content objects through content cache. From the view of energy consumption, at the expense of cache resource and energy consumption to lower users access to content of the required transmission energy consumption and delay. To make sure the intermediate node to caching content O_k to reduce the total energy consumption while through intermediate node to get content O_k, we need the energy consumption of getting content O_k from less than the same when user get the content from the OCS. According to the energy consumption model proposed above. We have the inequality (4).

$$w_c s_k t + q_i^k s_k \left[h_{ij}(w_r + w_l) + w_r \right] < q_i^k s_k \left[h_{sj}(w_r + w_l) + w_r \right] \tag{4}$$

After the reduction available, we get the inequality (5).

$$\frac{q_i^k}{t} > \frac{w_c}{(w_c + w_l)(h_{sj} - h_{ij})} \tag{5}$$

According to the physical meaning of each variable, the left side of inequality (6) is the request frequency for O_k at node v_i, which can be expressed by f_i^k, while on the right side of the inequality, according to the physical meaning of each variable.

$$f_i^k > \frac{w_c}{(w_c + w_l)h_{si}} \tag{6}$$

We increases a hop number segment hops in each content grouping head, when user's request hit at some node, this node generate a special content group, and value the hops segment as 0.as the content group transmit along the reverse path of user's request path, the segment hops INC each hop. In this way each node can get the value of the hops as the distance from the current node to OCS(h_{si}). So we confirm the above inequality as the Energy consumption decision condition, Before node v_i decide whether caching O_k or not, the node v_i statistics the request frequency of O_k from v_i and h_{si} as well, if the consequence meet the above inequality, then caching, otherwise don't caching O_k.

3.2   Cooperative Caching Strategy

From the content point of view, the higher the popularity of the content expressed the more interested users and the greater the chance of being accessed next time. Therefore, the content with higher popularity should be cached in the node. As a matter of fact, the degree of the user's interest in the content change over time. In this caching strategy, we refer to the method in the literature [9], the estimation method is as follows.

$$P_k = \sum_{j=1}^{n} \left(\frac{1}{2}\right)^{\lambda\left(t_{now} - t_j\right)} \tag{7}$$

P_k means the popularity estimates of the content O_k in current node, t_{now} means the current time, t_j means the arrival time of the JTH request for the content. λ is a adjust parameter which satisfy the formula $\lambda \in [0, 1]$ to weigh the access frequency of the contents. According to the analysis results of literature [12], we give λ the value of e^{-4}. The higher the value of popularity of the content in the current node is, the greater the probability of the content be cached in the current node will be.

From the point of view of the node itself, the nodes closer to the center in the network usually have a stronger ability to connect to other nodes, they have more chance to receive request from other different nodes. If we caching the content to these nodes, the cache hit rates will be increased, and the response speed faster as well. So we chose the centrality of the ego network as another basis of cache decision. The nodes with higher centrality will have a higher probability to caching contents. Then consider P_k and the centrality of node v_i together to calculate the probability for node v_i to caching content $O_i(P_c(k))$ the computing method as follows, and the centrality of node v_i together to calculate the probability for node v_i to caching content $O_i(P_c(k))$, the computing method as follows.

$$P_c(k) = \theta \frac{P_k}{P_{max}} + (1 - \theta) \frac{B_i}{B_{max}} \tag{8}$$

θ is weight coefficient used to adjust the influence by content popularity and centrality on $P_c(k)$. P_{max} is the maximum of content popularity for node caching all contents, B_i express the centrality values of node v_i, B_{max} express every node's maximum of centrality values during content O_k return path. In CCN, content grouping returns the client through the reverse of its request packet path, so we record B_{max} during the content request packet path. When a cache hit, the hit node write B_{max} in the corresponding content group. Thus every node at the content return path can get their corresponding B_{max} through their received content group.

3.3   Cache Decision Strategy Algorithm

The process of the energy of Energy-efficiency Aware Cooperative Caching Strategy algorithm execute as follow description:

Step 1:   When the content O_k get to node v_i, at first, the node get the hops(h_{si}) from OCS to current node centrality of from the content groups,

Step 2:   If the request frequency for content O_k from node v_i (f_i^k) satisfy the above-mentioned inequality of the energy efficiency decision condition, then proceed to step 3; otherwise the node don't caching content O_k, transmit forward to next hop.

Step 3:   Node v_i consider about the probability and the performance of collaborative cache to caching content O_k.

Step 4:   If become the new caching node of content O_k, then duplicate the content O_k to node, set the value of hops as 0; and set the received original content groups segment as 0. Then proceed to next hop.

4   Simulation Results and Analysis

In order to evaluate the performance of the above methods, we chose the leave cache everywhere (LCE) strategy [10] and the aging popularity-based in-network caching scheme (APC) [10] strategy as comparison, the algorithm is simulated and analyzed using the ndnSIM [8] simulator. This article considers an autonomous domain network where all the routers in the network form a mesh network and are connected to the content server through the Content Server Manager. The content server stores the required content objects, and when the content is not found in the content router's network cache, the required content can be obtained from the OCS by routing. At the same time, we assume that the arrival process of the user request obeys the poisson distribution. The main experimental parameters are shown in Table 2.

Table 2.   Experimental parameter.

Key parameter	Default values	MS-CG/DPD
Content quantity	2000	100–5000
Node cache(MB)	100	5–1000
Simulation time(s)	200	
w_c (W/bit)	1×10^{-9}	
w_r (J/bit)	2×10^{-8}	
w_r (J/bit)	1.5×10^{-9}	

During the simulation, we observed the influence of different parameters on network performance by changing the size of network parameters such as node cache capacity, contents of the network. The main performance indicators used in this paper include:

(1) Cache hit rate. (2) Average response hops. (3) Energy saving rate.

4.1   The Influence of the Cache Size

This section firstly studies the influence on the main network performance under different caching mechanisms when node cache size changes, Fig. 1(a) displays how the Cache hit ratio varies with cache size of the node. As the node cache space grows, the number of content that the node can cache increases and the cache replacement frequency decreases, the cache ratio of the three cache mechanisms increases as well. Among them, LCE has the lowest cache hit ratio because of its lack of reasonable selection of cache content and cache location. EEACC takes the content and various key factors related to the node into account, making the node's caching decision more reasonable, thus obtaining the highest cache hit rate. When the cache size is 5 MB, the cache hit rate of EEACC still reaches 22.4%, compare with that of LCE (3.4%) and APC(13.5%), respectively, about 558.82% and 65.93%.

Figure 1(b) displays how the Average response hops varies with cache size of the node. As the node cache space increase, the chance for the node to respond to user requests via the cache node, it had greatly reduced the numbers of hops when the user get the request content. Therefor the average hops of three kinds of cache mechanisms decreased with the increase of node cache. APC's consideration of content popularity and its timeliness improves the effectiveness of the cache decision making process, significantly reducing the average hops of content acquisition. Therefore, the average hops of APC is significantly lower than LCE. During the cache decision process, EEACC make use of the energy efficiency decision conditions limit content cache location near the side of the user node, combining with the content popularity and node centricity implements the probabilistic cache content at the same time, make the cached copy approach the client, and gain the lowest of the three average response, when

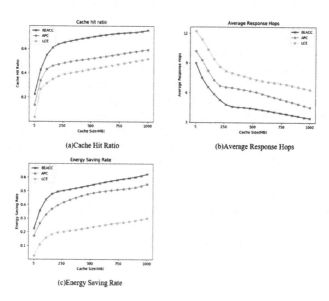

(a)Cache Hit Ratio   (b)Average Response Hops

(c)Energy Saving Rate

Fig. 1. The impact of cache size on network performance.

increasing the node cache from 5 MB to 1000 MB, the average response hops was nearly 14.54%lower than that of APC.

When the content cache is identical, the energy saving rate of the three cache mechanisms is shown in Fig. 1(c). As t cache size increases, the opportunity for user's requests get respond from a more recent cache node increases significantly, resulting in a significant reduction in the amount of energy consumption to find and return the requested content. Therefore, the energy saving rate of the 3 kinds of caching mechanism increases with the increase of cache size. LCE has the lowest energy saving rate because it caches every content to each of the node, too much redundant cache and content substitution, which will inevitably leads to additional energy costs. However, EEACC reduces the total energy consumption of content access through energy efficiency ruling, optimizes the efficiency of the decision-making process and thus obtains the highest energy saving rate. As shown in Fig. 1, when the cache size is 1000 MB, EEACC has an energy efficiency rate of 62.3%, compared with the APC (55.6%) and LCE (30.1%), respectively, increasing by about 12.1% and 107.0%.

4.2   The Influence of the Content Quantity

In the case of node cache, the number of content objects in the network is the reflection of the scarcity degree of network. As the number of content increases, the cache capacity of the nodes becomes more and more inadequate relative to the content cache requirements. Then, the cache replacement frequency increase, the content of the cache time is relatively short, resulting in content cache's role in reducing subsequent user requests the response of the distance and the overall energy consumption, improve the cache hit chance is waning. We can see from Fig. 2, when the content number increases from 100 to 5000, all the three kinds of caching mechanism of energy saving rate and the cache hit ratio curve are obviously declining, while the average response hops are growing. EEACC and APC of all the performance is much better than the LCE, for their selection of proper cache content and cache node, to avoid the LCE relatively radical caching policy cache redundancy. And because EEACC uses the arrival frequency and new inaccuracy of the user's request to estimate the content popularity more accurately, such as it can effectively place the popular content from the user's frequently request at the appropriate cache nodes, so that EEACC obtained the highest cache hit rate and the minimum average response hop. As displayed in Fig. 2(a) and Fig. 2(b), when the number of the content is 2000,the cache hit ratio of EEACC reached 57.8%, which was nearly 32.3% higher than that of APC (43.7%), and the average response hops were only 6.54, compared with the APC, which decreased by about 11.86%. According to the optimization of energy efficiency model, EEACC greatly reduces the overall energy consumption of the system. As shown in Fig. 2(c), the energy saving rate is significantly better than APC and LCE,In the case of 2000 content, EEACC obtained 43.6% energy saving rate, which is about 25.3% and 177.7% higher than APC and LCE, respectively.

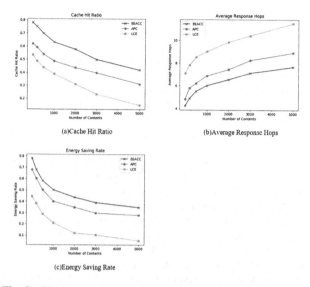

(a)Cache Hit Ratio   (b)Average Response Hops

(c)Energy Saving Rate

Fig. 2. The impact of content quantity on network performance.

5 Conclusions

In order to improve the energy efficiency of the CCN, and ensure the caching performance at the same time. In this paper, we proposed Energy-efficiency Aware Cooperative Caching Strategy. Through the analysis of CCN network energy consumption model, an energy efficiency judgment condition is set up to ensure that the strategy can reduce the overall energy consumption of the network, On the basis of energy efficiency we take into account the factors such as content popularity, node location and cache coordination of neighboring nodes, and coordinate these factors to calculate the probability priority of caching a content. Simulation results demonstrate that the proposed strategy can effectively reduce the overall energy consumption, with guaranteeing comparatively higher cache hit rate and smaller average response hops.

Acknowledgments. This research is supported in part by the National Natural Science Foundation of China under Grant No. 61562006, in part by the Natural Science Foundation of Guangxi Province under Grant No. 2016GXNSFBA380181 and in part by the Key Laboratory of Guangxi University.

References

1. Xylomenos, G., Ververidis, C.N., Siris, V.A., et al.: A survey of information-centric networking research. IEEE Commun. Surv. Tutor. **16**(2), 1024–1049 (2014)
2. Named Data Networking. https://named-data.net/project/archoverview/. Accessed 21 Nov 2016

3. Ming, Z., Xu, M., Wang, D.: Age-based cooperative caching in information-centric networks. In: International Conference on Computer Communication and Networks, pp. 1–8. IEEE (2012)

4. Ge, G.D., Guo, Y.F., Lan, J.L., et al.: Dynamic cache size transfer scheme based on replacement rate in content centric networking. J. Commun. **36**(5), 124–133 (2015)

5. Kim, D., Lee, S.W., Ko, Y.B., et al.: Cache capacity-aware content centric networking under flash crowds. J. Netw. Comput. Appl. **50**(C), 101–113 (2015)

6. Majd, N.E., Misra, S., Tourani, R.: Split-Cache: a holistic caching framework for improved network performance in wireless ad hoc networks. In: Global Communications Conference, pp. 137–142. IEEE (2015)

7. Chiaraviglio, L., Mellia, M., Neri, F.: Minimizing ISP network energy cost: formulation and solutions. IEEE/ACM Trans. Netw. **20**(2), 463–476 (2011)

8. Braun, T., Trinh, T.A.: Energy efficiency issues in information-centric networking. In: Pierson, J.-M., Da Costa, G., Dittmann, L. (eds.) EE-LSDS 2013. LNCS, vol. 8046, pp. 271–278. Springer, Heidelberg (2013). https://doi.org/10.1007/978-3-642-40517-4_22

9. Li, J., Liu, B., Wu, H.: Energy-efficient in-network caching for content-centric networks. IEEE Commun. Lett. **17**(4), 797–800 (2013)

10. Fang, C., Yu, F.R., Huang, T., et al.: An energy-efficient distributed in-network caching scheme for green content-centric networks. Comput. Netw. Int. J. Comput. Telecommun. Netw. **78**(C), 119–129 (2015)

The 3rd International Symposium on Dependability in Sensor, Cloud, and Big Data Systems and Applications (DependSys 2017)

DependSys 2017 Organizing and Program Committees

1 General Chairs

P. Vijayakumar	University College of Engineering Tindivanam, India
Habib M Amri	Norfolk State University, Norfolk, USA
Md Zakirul Alam Bhuiyan	Fordham University, USA

2 Program Chairs

Jian Shen	Nanjing University of Information Science & Technology, China
Houbing Song	West Virginia University, USA
Thaier Hayajneh	Fordham University, USA

3 Program Committee

A. B. M. Alim Al lIslam	Bangladesh University of Engineering and Technology, Bangladesh
Aniello Castiglione	University of Salerno, Italy
Bing Tang	Hunan University of Science and Technology, China
Charlie (Seungmin) Rho	Sungkyul University, Anyang
Chi Lin	Dalian University of Technology, China
Chi-Hua Chen	Chunghwa Telecom Co. Ltd., China
Farzana Rahman	James Madison University, USA
Gabriele Mencagli	University of Pisa, Italy
Geng Yang	Zheijiang University, China
Giancarlo Fortino	DIMES - University of Calabria, Italy
Guangjie Han	Hohai University, China
Guerroumi Mohamed	University of Sciences and Technology Houari Boumediene, Algeria
Houbing Song	West Virginia University, USA
Jinkyu Jeong	Sungkyunkwan University, Korea
Junggab Son	Kennesaw State University, USA
Kamruzzaman S. M.	Ryerson University, Toronto
Kaoru Ota	Muroran Institute of Technology, Japan
Karampelas Panagiotis	Hellenic Air Force Academy, Greece

Kenli Li	Hunan University, China
Laizhong Cui	Shenzhen University, China
Lien-Wu Chen	Feng Chia University, Taiwan
M. Thampi Sabu	Indian Institute of Information Technology and Management, India
Mahmuda Naznin	Bangladesh University of Engineering and Technology, Bangladesh
Mamoun Alazab	Australian National University, Australia
Manuel Mazzara	Innopolis University, Russia
Md Zakirul Alam Bhuiyan	Fordham University, USA
Md. Abdur Razzaque	University of Dhaka, Bangladesh
Md. Arafatur Rahman	University Malaysia Pahang, Malaysia
Md. Rafiul Hassan	King Fahd University of Petroleum and Minerals, Saudi Arabia
Mir Sajjad Hussain Talpur	Sindh Agriculture University, Pakistan
Mohamad Badra	Zayed University, UAE
Mohammad Asad Rehman Chaudhry	Department of Electrical & Computer Engineering University of Toronto, Canada
Mohammad Asadul Hoque	East Tennessee State University, USA
Mohammad Mehedi Hassan	King Saud University, KSA
Mohammad Shahriar Rahman	University of Asia Pacific, Bangladesh
Mubashir Husain Rehmani	COMSATS Institute of Information Technology, Pakistan
Muhammad Mostafa Monowar	King AbdulAziz University, Saudi Arabia
N. Musau Felix	Kenyatta University, Kenya
Naeem Shehzad Muhammad	COMSATS Institute of Information Technology, Pakistan
P. K. Paul	Raiganj University, Raiganj, India
Pandi Vijay Kumar	University College of Engineering, Tindivanam, India
Qingchen Zheng	St. Francis Xavier University, Canada
Ragib Hasan	University of Alabama at Birmingham, USA
Risat Mahmud Pathan	Chalmers University of Technology, Sweden
Rossi Kamal	Kyung Hee University, South Korea
Salvatore Distefano	Politecnico di Milano, Italy
Saqib Ali	Guangzhou University, China
Shahriar Hossain	Kennesaw State University, USA
Shan Lin	Stony Brook University, USA
Shawon Rahman	University of Hawaii-Hilo, USA
Sheng Wen	Deakin University, Australia
Shigeng Zhang	Central South University, China
Sk Md Mizanur Rahman	King Saud University, KSA
Subrota Mondal	Hong Kong University of Science and Technology, Hong Kong

Tanzima Hashem	Bangladesh University of Engineering and Technology, Bangladesh
Tarem Ahmed	BRAC University, Bangladesh
Tauhidur Rahman	The University of Alabama in Huntsville, USA
Tian Wang	Huaqiao University, China
Tzung-Shi Chen	National University of Tainan, Taiwan
Vaskar Raychoudhury	Indian Institute of Technology Roorkee, India
Wahid Khan	University of Saskatchewan, Canada
Weigang Li	University of Brasilia, Brazil
Weigang Wu	Sun Yat-sen University, China
William Liu	Auckland University of Technology, New Zealand
Xiong Li	University of Science and Technology, China
Yacine Djemaiel	Communication networks and Security, Res. Lab, Tunisia
Yifan Zhang	Binghamton University, USA
Yu Wang	Deakin University, Australia
Yuan-Fang Chen	University of Paris VI, France
Zhiwei Zhao	University of Electric Science and Technology of China, China

4 Steering Committee

Jie Wu	Temple University, USA (Chair)
Guojun Wang	Guangzhou University, China (Chair)
A. B. M Shawkat Ali	The University of Fiji, Fiji
Al-Sakib Khan Pathan	Southeast University, Bangladesh
Jiannong Cao	Hong Kong Polytechnic University, Hong Kong
Kamruzzaman Joarder	Federation University and Monash University, Australia
Kenli Li	Hunan University, China
Laurence T. Yang	St. Francis Xavier University, Canada
Mohammed Atiquzzaman	University of Oklahoma, USA
Shui Yu	Deakin University, Australia
Sy-Yen Kuo	National Taiwan University, Taiwan
Yang Xiang	Deakin University, Australia
WenZhan Song	Georgia State University, USA
Kim-Kwang Raymond Choo	The University of Texas at San Antonio, USA

5 Publicity Chairs

Md. Abdur Razzaque	Dhaka University, Bangladesh
Wenjia Li	NYIT, USA
Md. Arafatur Rahman	University Malaysia Pahang, Malaysia
Tian Wang	Huaqiao University, China
Yuan-Fang Chen	University of Paris VI, France

6 Web Chair

Xi Wen	Central South University, China

Password Recovery for ZIP Files Based on ARM-FPGA Cluster

Xu Bai[1,2], Lei Jiang[1,2(✉)], Jiajia Yang[1,2], Qiong Dai[1,2], and Md. Zakirul Alam Bhuiyan[3]

[1] Institute of Information Engineering,
Chinese Academy of Sciences, Beijing 100093, China
jianglei@iie.ac.cn
[2] School of Cyber Security, University of Chinese Academy of Sciences,
Beijing 100040, China
[3] Department of Computer and Information Sciences, Fordham University,
Bronx, NY 10458, USA

Abstract. Password recovery of ZIP encrypted files is an important problem in computer forensics. The encryption is based on standard cryptographic algorithms as SHA1, HMAC and AES. The traditional methods such as dictionary and brute-force require very large computing power and techniques of reducing the password space. In this paper, we have developed a distributed password recovery system based on Zynq (a heterogeneous chip combining ARM CPU and FPGA fabric) cluster. The FPGA provides hardware acceleration for cryptographic algorithms. And the ARM completes the decompression after decryption to check candidate passwords. To reduce the computation of unzip, we only decompress the header of the file compressed according to different headers of common document formats. We adopt a cluster-building methodology to improve parallelism and calculation power. Finally, the experimental results show that single node is as fast as a core of i7-3770 CPU and the 48-node cluster can check 50,000 passwords per second. It also achieves about 2× energy efficiency.

Keywords: Password recovery · ZIP-encrypted · Heterogeneous Zynq · Cluster

1 Introduction

Nowadays, computers and the Internet have become an indispensable part in people's life and they are playing a more important role in current information society. But the illegal and criminal activities with computers also emerge in an endless stream. As an attractive research area, through computer forensics [5] technology crackdown on Internet crime has become an important means of information security. And one of important methods is password recovery. Meanwhile, because of the popularity at home and abroad, ZIP encrypted files are often encountered in the process of computer forensics. So how to find out

© Springer International Publishing AG 2017
G. Wang et al. (Eds.): SpaCCS 2017 Workshops, LNCS 10658, pp. 405–414, 2017.
https://doi.org/10.1007/978-3-319-72395-2_37

the correct password of a ZIP-encrypted file quickly and efficiently is a problem in the information security area.

On the other hand, the most commonly encryption algorithms used in ZIP files is based on standard cryptographic algorithms (such as SHA1, HMAC and AES). For the sake of convenience, the secret key of AES is created by hash functions with user's password. It is strong and supported by new WinZip (9.0 or higher). The traditional cryptographic attacks including dictionary and brute-force need to try massive passwords. This requires powerful calculating ability and acceleration for cryptographic algorithms. So password recovery also has the academic significance.

Conventional password search speed is limited by too many mathematical calculations in the recovery process and low performance restriction of serial general-purpose CPU comparing with specific processing units for particular algorithms. In order to meet the requirement of computing capability, we choose FPGA, a kind of semi-custom circuit chip, to implement a password recovery system. Considering the high speed acceleration for specific algorithms and dynamic reconfigurability, FPGA is suitable for multiple cryptography scenarios. However, as user's passwords are becoming longer and more complex, single FPGA can't bear the calculating pressure alone. So we take advantage of cluster to achieve greater computational capacity. With the help of ARM, an FPGA cluster is built.

This paper uses Zynq SoC [2], consisting of an ARM processor and an FPGA fabric, to deploy a cluster for password recovery of ZIP-encrypted files. The process is divided into two parts: decryption and decompression for checking. We take full advantage of different features of ARM and FPGA to realize different function. The contribution is stated as follows:

(1) A password recovery application for ZIP-encrypted files is implemented on Zynq. FPGA is responsible for repetitive computational works such as standard cryptographic algorithms. And ARM takes flexible tasks including decompression and internal communication in the cluster.
(2) The hardware acceleration for PBKDF2 (based on HMAC and SHA1) algorithm is designed and optimized on FPGA. And multiple instances are implemented on single chip.
(3) Common formats, such as DOC, PDF, JPG and so on, have fixed header information. So we only extract the header of the file in ZIP for checking passwords to reduce decompression workload and the calculation of AES in most cases. And finally we decompress one full document in ZIP file in the cases with non-common formats.
(4) The experiment results that a single node can perform as fast as a core of i7-core and 3× than a core of GX36. The 48-node cluster process 50,000 passwords per second, which is 7.7× and 0.7× compared to a 8-core i7-3770 desktop and a 288-core server. It also achieves about 2× energy efficiency.

This paper is organized as follows: Sect. 2 lists the related work. Section 3 presents the background of Zynq-based cluster and ZIP-encrypted format.

Section 4 modifies the decryption algorithm of ZIP. Section 5 introduces partly decompression to check passwords. Section 6 proposes system implementation. Section 7 analyses the experiment results. And Sect. 8 makes a conclusion.

2 Related Work

Many researchers recently pay attentions to crack passwords with special hardwares. Kim [9] proposed a distributed password cracking protocol on multiple GPU nodes. They avoided passwords overlapping between working nodes and achieved 220,000 passwords per second for PDF cracking using FX-5600 mostly. Hranický et al. [7] developed a password recovery tool based on multi-core CPU and GPU processors. They estimated the execution time of multiple file formats cracking and it got a high speedup on GPUs. Lu et al. [10] implemented a parallelized system to crack passwords of WINZIP files based on GPU. With 8 ATI 6990 GPUs, they achieved a speed of 5,670 password/s for WINZIP-128. Apostal et al. [3] established a HPC framework with MPI based on GPUs and proposed the divided dictionary and password database algorithms. They got a speedup of 57× and 40× over a single processor using 8 GPUs across 4 compute nodes, respectively. Ge and Wang [6] proposed a parallel random search to scan the dictionary database. The experiment results showed its effectiveness. Hu et al. [8] processed the password recovery of RAR files with NVIDIA 9800 GTX+ GPU and they achieved tens-fold speedup compared to CPU.

At present, researchers have made great process in the acceleration of hardware-based cryptography algorithms. In this paper, we study how to crack passwords for ZIP files with multi-FPGA.

3 Background

In this section we introduce the Zynq-based cluster and the detail of ZIP format.

3.1 ARM-FPGA Cluster

We built a 48-node cluster based on Zynq SoC to achieve more computing power and scalability through the fully interconnected structure based on network [4]. Each node is a kind of board with Xilinx Zynq-7020 SoC composed a dual-core ARM Cortex-A9 CPU and an XC7Z020 FPGA. It also has a Gigabit Ethernet Interface for network communication. The ARM is responsible for communication and a few calculations, and the FPGA accelerates computation-intensive algorithms. The nodes in the cluster interconnect to one another through a 48-port switch to construct a local network. The data of computing tasks is distributed to every node through the switch, too.

3.2   ZIP Password Recovery Algorithm

The compressed header information of each file in a ZIP file is arranged in sequential order. Except for local file header and encrypted data, additional overhead data required for decryption is stored with them. The actual format of ZIP file is show as Fig. 1.

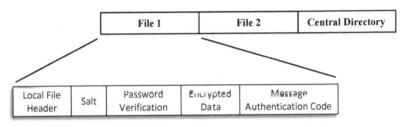

Fig. 1. ZIP format analysis

The specific meanings [1] of these value are described below:

- *Local File Header:* This field contains the file name, the compressed and uncompressed size and other information about the compressed file.
- *Salt:* This value is a random or pseudo-random sequence of bytes which is combined with the encryption password. It is used to create encryption and authentication keys through the function PBKDF2.
- *Password Verification (PV):* This 2-byte value is produced as part of the process that derives encryption and decryption keys with user's passwords. Before decrypting, a verification value can be generated with AES key together and be compared to the value stored in the file. But there is a 1 in 65,536 chance to match an incorrect password.
- *Encrypted Data:* The compressed file data is encrypted bit-by-bit with AES algorithm in CTR mode.
- *Message Authentication Code (MAC):* This is a super-CRC check on the data in the file after compression and encryption.

Based on the above analysis, we can conclude the process of password recovery as Fig. 2.

(1) Analysis the local file headers of the files in ZIP file and extract necessary information including file name, compressed size, salt value, PV and so on. Then we choose an appropriate file for further checking. This operation is executed just once.
(2) Through the hash function (PBKDF2), we use candidate password and salt value to compute the PV and AES key at the same time.
(3) Compare the PV to the value extracted from the ZIP file to first check. This step executes more than 90% of whole computation and is the performance bottleneck. It is implemented on FPGA.
(4) If the first checking is passed, the AES key will goes on to the second checking. The detail is referenced in Sect. 5. This step is implemented on ARM.

The password passing two checking is the correct one we want.

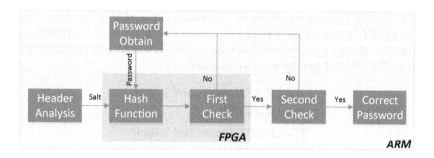

Fig. 2. The process of password recovery

4   Modify PBKDF2 Algorithm

The hash function is the bottleneck of password recovery process because of a large amount of iterations. PBKDF2 (Password-Based Key Derivation Function) is used to derive three keys with an iteration count of 1000. The first one is the AES key. The second one is used to compute the *MAC*. And the third one is the 2-byte *PV*. The sizes of the first two keys are the same and depend on the encryption strength of AES (128-AES or 256-AES) used in the encrypted ZIP file. The detail of this algorithm is shown in Algorithm 1.

Algorithm 1. PBKDF2 Algorithm

Input: $password, salt, loop$ (loop value is 2 or 4 for 128-AES or 256-AES)
Output: $keys$
 1: **function** PBKDF2($password, salt$)
 2:    **for** $i = 1 \rightarrow loop$ **do**
 3:       $L \leftarrow HMAC(password, salt \parallel i)$
 4:       $U \leftarrow L$
 5:       **for** $j = 1 \rightarrow 1000$ **do**
 6:          $L \leftarrow HMAC(password, L)$
 7:          $U \leftarrow U \oplus L$
 8:       **end for**
 9:       $keys \leftarrow keys \parallel U$
10:    **end for**
11:    **return** $keys$
12: **end function**
13:
14: **function** HMAC($key, message$)
15:    $opad \leftarrow 0x5c5c5c5c$, $ipad \leftarrow 0x36363636$
16:    $T \leftarrow HASH(key \oplus opad \parallel HASH(key \oplus ipad \parallel message))$
17:    **return** T
18: **end function**

The symbol $\|$ means stitching. In Algorithm 1, the *HASH* function is implemented by *SHA1* algorithm. SHA1 produces a message digest by 512-bit blocks and the size of user's passwords can't be longer than 512 bits normally. So the step 6 in Algorithm 1 can be rewrote as follows:

$$\begin{aligned}
X &\leftarrow HASH(password \oplus ipad) \\
Z &\leftarrow HASH(X \| L) \\
Y &\leftarrow HASH(password \oplus opad) \\
L &\leftarrow HASH(Y \| Z)
\end{aligned} \tag{1}$$

From the above we can know that X and Y are constant for one candidate password. So we can pre-calculate these two variables in advance. The algorithm is modified as Algorithm 2.

Algorithm 2. Modified PBKDF2 Algorithm

Input: *password, salt, loop* (loop value is 2 or 4 for 128-AES or 256-AES)
Output: *keys*
1: **function** PBKDF2(*password, salt*)
2:     *opad* $\leftarrow$ 0x5c5c5c5c , *ipad* $\leftarrow$ 0x36363636
3:     $X \leftarrow HASH(password \oplus ipad)$
4:     $Y \leftarrow HASH(password \oplus opad)$
5:     **for** $i = 1 \rightarrow loop$ **do**
6:         $L \leftarrow HASH(X \| (salt \| i))$
7:         $L \leftarrow HASH(Y \| L)$
8:         $U \leftarrow L$
9:         **for** $j = 1 \rightarrow 1000$ **do**
10:             $L \leftarrow HASH(X \| L)$
11:             $L \leftarrow HASH(Y \| L)$
12:             $U \leftarrow U \oplus L$
13:         **end for**
14:         $keys \leftarrow keys \| U$
15:     **end for**
16:     **return** *keys*
17: **end function**

In the innermost loop of Algorithm 2, the *HASH* number is reduced from 4 to 2. So we can expect a speed-up by a factor of 2 to original algorithm.

5   Partial Decompression

After passing the *PV* checking, the *MAC* should be computed using decrypted data to compare to the value stored in ZIP file. The AES CTR mode is used for encryption and decryption. In this mode, a counter is encrypted by AES, and the result will xor with a data block. Then the counter is incremented and the next data block is processed until the last one. So does decryption. Thus, the bigger a file is, the more computation of AES and decompression are required.

On the other hand, the main idea of compression and decompression is based on Huffman coding. The first few bytes of compressed data contain all necessary information to decode and following bytes will be decompressed bit by bit. So we can decrypt a small amount of data and extract the header of decompressed file. For common file formats, there are specific bytes in the header to identify file types, such as[1]

Format type	Header bytes
PDF	0x255044462D312E
DOCX	0x504b0304140006000800
JPG	0xFFD8FF
...	...

It means that if we know a extension of a file type, we can ensure the first few bytes of that file header. By comparison between the header of a known file type and the information of partial decompressed header, it could be known if the password is correct.

Hence we can extract the names of files from local file headers of a ZIP file to achieve filename extensions and search a known one. At the same time, smaller size of a file implies fewer bytes of necessary information to decode in the head of the compressed file. So we extract the compression size and choose the smallest one from the known type files to crack passwords. For the most part, AES only need to be calculated less than twice no matter how big a compressed file is.

6 System Implementation

In this Section, we propose the detail of the password recovery system based on ARM-FPGA cluster and Fig. 3 shows the overview. In this cluster, a computer, as a master node, is used to distribute tasks and receive results through the switch; 48 boards with Zynq SoC, as slave nodes, are ready to process the received data.

In this system, following two modes are used to generate candidate passwords:

- **Dictionary Password Generator:** This mode takes a given dictionary as a source of candidate passwords. The dictionary is averagely partitioned and distributed to all ready nodes in advance.
- **Brute Force Password Generator:** This mode enumerates every possible permutation of given characters including uppercase and lowercase letters, numbers and special symbols (as option). The enumeration is in order. So we can configure the range of password generation on each node by the sequence number of every possible permutation, in case of overlapping each other.

---

[1] http://www.filesignatures.net/.

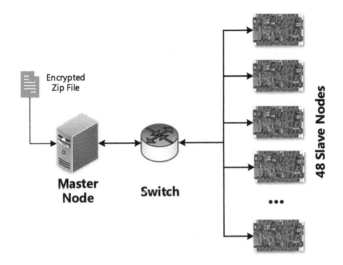

Fig. 3. Password recovery system based on ARM-FPGA cluster

When an encrypted ZIP file reaches the master node, the analysis work would begin to find out a small and known-file-type compressed file to crack passwords. Then the master node send the selected file data to every ready slave node. Next the ARM on each node extracts the salt and PV value and sends them to the FPGA for first checking. The passing passwords will be returned to the ARM for AES decryption and partial decompression to complete second checking. Finally, the master node will get the password passing two checking and decrypt the ZIP file with it. If success, the master node would announce the correct password and stop all working nodes.

For each slave node, we use Vivado HLS 2016.2 to compile the high-level C++ descriptions of PBKDF2 algorithm to FPGA logic. The resource utilization is 40.29% LUT and 15.54% FF. To improve performance, we realize a blocking pipelined SHA1 module and it completes one calculation in 96 clock cycles. Avoiding to a waste of resources, we implement 2 instances of PBKDF2 on one FPGA to execute first checking in parallel.

7   Experimental Results

In this Section, we conduct a series of experiments to test the performance of the password recovery system based on Zynq cluster.

7.1   Performance Analysis

Firstly we test and record the execution time of the software and hardware computing processors with single node. In order to compare the acceleration gained by Zynq-based cluster against traditional processors, we deploy the same environment and algorithm on two other platforms as follows.

- A desktop with an 8-core i7-3770 CPU @ 3.40 GHz.
- A server with eight 36-core Tilera GX36 Processors @ 1.20 GHz. There are 288 cores in total.

The result is tabulated in Table 1 and the execution time is measured in milliseconds (ms). The frequency is 667 MHz for ARM and 200 MHz for FPGA.

Table 1. Execution time (ms) of different platforms

	ARM	FPGA	i7-3770	GX36
AES128	6.58	1.92	1.01	3.30
AES256	12.74	3.92	2.01	6.37

From Table 1, it is clear that the execution time increases as the AES key size growing. This is because the strength of AES influences the loop of PBKDF2 algorithm. For traditional processors, frequency is the major factor affecting speed. The operations of SHA1 are simple and in serial, and the memory consumption is less. Such a calculation-sensitive algorithm is suitable for hardware implementation. Considering two instances implemented on one FPGA, the passwords cracking speed of a node is the same with a core of i7-3770 CPU. The detail is shown in Table 2. The *Single Speed* means the passwords cracking number per second on single node or thread. And the *Whole Speed* means working on multi-threaded mode for traditional processors. We choose 128-AES and brute force mode as an example.

Table 2. Cracking speed of different platforms

	Single speed	Whole speed	Power	Energy efficiency
Desktop	990/s	6,520/s	100 W	65.20
Server	303/s	70,270/s	680 W	103.34
Zynq cluster	1,042/s	50,000/s	280 W	178.57

In Table 2, since we also care about the overall energy efficiency, we define a metric of speed over power, which means *Performance per Watt*. It reflects how many passwords the platforms can check per unit time per unit energy consumption. The mathematical expression is as follows:

$$Energy\ Efficiency = \frac{Passwords\ per\ Second}{Energy\ Consumption} \qquad (2)$$

For Zynq-based cluster power, the Switch is included and single node is about 5 W. From above we can see that the cluster achieves 7.7× and 0.7× compared to 8-core desktop and 288-core server. It also offers 2.74× and 1.73× energy efficiency. Namely it can check more passwords under the same energy consumption.

8   Conclusion

In conclusion, this paper proposes a high scalability distributed structure based on Zynq SoC to implement a Password Recovery System for ZIP-encrypted files. We divide the process into two parts: computing type and flexible type. According to different features of ARM and FPGA we realize these two kind tasks on different processors. The experiment results demonstrate that the passwords checking speed of single node is about the same as a core of i7-3770 CPU. And the Zynq-based cluster achieves about 2 times energy efficiency.

Acknowledgments. This work is supported by the National Science and Technology Major Project under Grant No. 2017YFB0803003, and the National Science Foundation of China (NSFC) under grant No. 61402475.

References

1. Aes encryption information: Encryption specification ae-1 and ae-2. http://www.winzip.com/aes_info.htm
2. Xilinx inc. http://www.xilinx.com
3. Apostal, D., Foerster, K., Chatterjee, A., Desell, T.: Password recovery using MPI and CUDA. In: 2012 19th International Conference on High Performance Computing (HiPC), pp. 1–9. IEEE (2012)
4. Bai, X., Jiang, L., Dai, Q., Yang, J., Tan, J.: Acceleration of RSA processes based on hybrid ARM-FPGA cluster. In: ISCC (2017)
5. Garfinkel, S.L.: Digital forensics research: the next 10 years. Digit. Invest. **7**, S64–S73 (2010)
6. Ge, L., Wang, L.: Research of password recovery method for RAR based on parallel random search. In: Batten, L., Li, G., Niu, W., Warren, M. (eds.) ATIS 2014. CCIS, vol. 490, pp. 211–218. Springer, Heidelberg (2014). https://doi.org/10.1007/978-3-662-45670-5_20
7. Hranický, R., Matoušek, P., Ryšavý, O., Veselý, V.: Experimental evaluation of password recovery in encrypted documents. In: Proceedings of ICISSP 2016, pp. 299–306 (2016)
8. Hu, G., Ma, J., Huang, B.: Password recovery for RAR files using CUDA. In: Eighth IEEE International Conference on Dependable, Autonomic and Secure Computing, DASC 2009, pp. 486–490. IEEE (2009)
9. Kim, K.: Distributed password cracking on GPU nodes. In: 2012 7th International Conference on Computing and Convergence Technology (ICCCT), pp. 647–650. IEEE (2012)
10. Lu, K.C., Huang, A.F., Su, A.Y., Ding, T.J., Su, C.N.: Information password recovery with GPU. In: 2015 International Carnahan Conference on Security Technology (ICCST), pp. 1–5. IEEE (2015)

Comparison of Different Centrality Measures to Find Influential Nodes in Complex Networks

Fanpeng Meng⑩, Yijun Gu$^{(\boxtimes)}$⑩, Shunshun Fu⑩, Mengdi Wang, and Yuchen Guo

College of Information Technology and Network Security, People's Public Security University of China, Beijing 102600, China guyijun@ppsuc.edu.cn, mengfanpeng0202@126.com

Abstract. In this paper, we compare the performance of representative centrality measures, classical and up-to-date, on more real networks in various fields. With the aid of SIR information diffusion model to simulate the vertices' influence in real networks, we apply the kendall's tau correlation coefficient, distinguishability and robustness to test different centrality measures at the same level., to show the best application scenarios for certain measure.

Keywords: Influential nodes · Comparison of centrality measures Centrality methods · Complex networks · Social networks

1 Introduction

Studies have shown that influential nodes play an important role in all kinds of dynamic behavior in the complex network. Identifying influential nodes allow us to better control epidemic outbreaks, accelerate information propagation, conduct successful e-commerce advertisements, and so on. In this paper, we compare the performance of representative centrality measures, classical and up-to-date, on more real networks in various fields. With the aid of SIR information diffusion model to simulate the vertices' influence in real networks, we apply the kendall's tau correlation coefficient, distinguishability and robustness to test different centrality measures at the same level. All these work is aimed to provide a deep understanding of various characteristics and best application scenarios for certain measure.

The rest of the paper is organized as follows. In Sect. 2, we briefly overview of centrality measures mentioned above. In Sect. 3, we describe the dataset, the influence simulation model SIR model, and evaluation criteria. In Sect. 4, experiment results are illustrated to show the characteristics of centrality measures. Finally, some conclusions are presented in Sect. 5.

2 Review of Centralty Messures

Many centrality methods have been proposed to measure the estimated importance of nodes within the networks. In this paper, we divide these measures into four categories. They are local-based centrality measures, global-based centrality measures, semi-local-based centrality measures, and multi-centralities based measures.

© Springer International Publishing AG 2017
G. Wang et al. (Eds.): SpaCCS 2017 Workshops, LNCS 10658, pp. 415–423, 2017.
https://doi.org/10.1007/978-3-319-72395-2_38

2.1   Local-Based Centrality Measures

The local-based measures tend to capture the features of the node through the partial information around it in general, such as degree centrality (dc) and K-shell (ks) decomposition method [1].

2.2   Global-Based Centrality Measures

The global-based methods considering global information gives ranking results much better, such as betweenness centrality (bc) and closeness centrality (cc) and PageRank [2] (pg).

2.3   Semi-Local-Based Centrality Measures

Semi-local-based centralities are most widely studied nowadays which are tradeoff of the local structure and global structure, such as Local centrality (LC) [3], local structural centrality (LSC) [4], Local Weight (LW) [5], Sum of Edge Importance Coefficient (SEIC) [6], Local Triangle-based Centrality (LTC) [7], Coefficient of Local Centrality (CLC) [8], Two-Hop Connected Coreness Centrality (THCC) [9].

The vast majority of these semi-local-based centrality measures consider several hop of neighbors and have better performance both in computation complexity and effect than classical centrality measures, Multi-centralities-based Measures.

2.4   Multi-centralities-Based Measures

Some researchers think node importance is not affected by a single factor, but is affected by a number of factors. Hence a new evaluation method of node importance in social network is proposed, based on multi-centralities, i.e., dc, ks, bc, cc, pg, etc. The majority of the multi-centralities-based methods [10, 11, 12, 13] apply a multiple attribute decision making (MADM). However, some centrality measures in MADM are very time-consuming. Hence multi-centralities-based measures are out of discussion in this paper.

3   Data and Evaluation Criteria

3.1   Datasets

In this study, we focus on real social neworks and the datasets used in the paper are listed: Karate [16], Jazz [17], Netscience [18], Facebook [19], Email [20], Blogs [21], CA-HepPH [22], PGP [23], Twitter [24], Epinions [25], Slashdot [26].

From Table 1, we can observe the computational complexity of the centrality measures above. An outline of some of the basic properties of these networks is shown in Table 2. In this table, n is the number of nodes, m is the number of edges, $\bar{k}$ is the average degree in the network, $\bar{d}$ is the average distance between reachable pairs of nodes in networks, $\overline{cc}$ is the average clustering coefficient of nodes, β_{th} is the epidemic threshold calculated by $\frac{<k>}{<k^2>-<k>}$ [27, 28].

Table 1. Summary of the ranking methods mentioned in this paper

Algorithm	Complexity	References
Degree centrality (dc)	$O(n)$	[14]
k-shell decomposition (ks)	$O(m)$	[1]
PageRank (pg)	–	[2]
Closeness centrality (cc)	$O(n(n+m))$	[15]
Betweenness centrality (bc)	$O(nm)$	[14]
Local centrality index (LC)	$O\left(n(\bar{k})^2\right)$	[3]
Local structure centrality (LSC)	$O\left(n(\bar{k})^2\right)$	[4]
Local weight index (LW)	$O(n\bar{k})$	[5]
Sum of edges importance centrality (SEIC)	$O\left(n(\bar{k})^2\right)$	[6]
Local triangle centrality (LTC)	$O\left(n(\bar{k})^2\right)$	[7]
Local structure with a coefficient index (CLC)	$O\left(n(\bar{k})^2\right)$	[8]
Two-Hop connected coreness index (THCC)	$O\left(n(\bar{k})^2\right)$	[9]

Table 2. The basic topological properties of the real networks studied in this work

Network	n	m	$\bar{k}$	$\bar{d}$	$\overline{cc}$	β_{th}
Karate	34	78	4.59	2.34	0.571	0.148
Jazz	198	2742	27.70	2.21	0.095	0.027
Netscience	379	914	4.82	1.98	0.113	0.142
Email	1133	5451	9.62	3.60	0.220	0.057
Facebook	4039	88234	43.69	3.69	0.606	0.010
Blogs	3982	6803	3.42	6.25	0.284	0.078
CA-HePh	12008	118521	19.74	5.21	0.611	0.008
PGP	10680	24316	4.55	7.48	0.266	0.056
Twitter	30173	137811	9.13	11.12	0.047	0.057
Epinions	75879	508837	13.41	4.75	0.138	0.005
Slashdot	77360	828161	23.41	4.11	0.056	0.004

3.2 SIR Model Simulation

To simulate a realistic spreading process and obtain the true spreading influence of nodes, we adopted the susceptible-infected-recovered (SIR) model [29]. The spreading ability of the original node v, $S_\beta(v)$, is defined as the number of nodes that were infected by the end of the spreading process that originated from node v. We assigned a small value to infection probability β, which was approximately the epidemic threshold $\beta_{th} = \frac{<k>}{<k^2> - <k>}$ [27, 28], where $<k^i>$ is the ith moment of the degree distribution [30]. We set the number of simulations to be 1000. The spreading influence of a node is defined as the average spreading ability of node v, except for 'epinions' and 'slashdot' whose size is too big to simulate the influence on the whole range of β but just simulate on the β_{th}.

3.3   Evaluation Criteria

All experiments conducted in this paper are on the PC with 8G of memory and Intel(R) Core(TM) i7-6500U CPU 2.50 GHz. The CPU time of 12 measures on 11 real networks is shown in Table 3.

Table 3. The CPU time (in seconds) of 12 measures on 11 real networks

	pg	cc	bc	LC	LSC	LW	SEIC	LTC	CLC	THCC
Karate	0	0	0	0	0	0	0	0	0	0.0
Jazz	0	0	0	0	0.07	0	0.04	0.02	0	0.1
Netscience	0	0	0	0	0.02	0	0.01	0	0	0.0
Email	0.2	2.4	7.3	0.1	0.17	0.1	0.24	0.05	0.1	0.2
Facebook	3.3	94	198	2.4	6.64	3.2	13.78	2.56	6.4	6.3
Blogs	0.5	23.2	75.3	0.1	0.16	0.2	0.19	0.05	0.2	0.2
CA-HepPH	5	539	1675	4.7	11.82	5.1	33.5	5.7	11.0	11.3
PGP	1.4	205	739	0.2	0.72	0.3	0.97	0.2	0.6	0.9
Twitter	2.6	2046	8612	0.5	2.42	1.8	2.23	0.58	1.8	3.9
Epinions	8.4	8841	63883	8.8	39.66	16.2	175	7.94	16.8	29.3
Slashdot	12.8	26120	158430	22.8	69.25	36.2	1451	18.0	44.5	78.3

Kendall's Tau Correlation Coefficient [31]

Kendall's τ is defined as follows:

$$\tau(R_1, R_2) = \frac{N_c - N_d}{\frac{1}{2}N(N-1)} \tag{1}$$

where R_1 and R_2 are two ranked lists that contain N elements, respectively. N_c and N_d denote the amount of concordant and discordant pairs, respectively.

4   Experiments and Analyses

4.1   Computation Complexity

The CPU time of ten centrality measures on eleven networks is in Table 3. The CPU time of dc and ks is too little, all close to zero, so they are not included in the table.

4.2   Rank the Influence of Nodes

Rank the Influence of All Nodes

The kendall'a tau is to measure the consistency between the rank of nodes' values calculated by certain centrality measure and the rank of nodes' influence simulated by the SIR model.

We take the kendall's tau, a method of quantitative analysis, to show the performance of different centrality measures on networks. As mentioned in the previous paragraph, the better a centrality is, the more correlative the values under certain centrality to the real influence. The kendall's tau values results from the ranked values generated by twelve centrality measures and the ranked influence generated by SIR model on nine networks is show in Fig. 1.

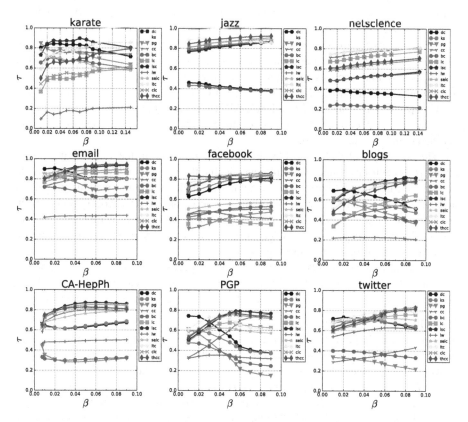

Fig. 1. Kendall's τ results from the ranked values generated by twelve centrality measures and the ranked influence generated by SIR model on nine networks.

The coefficient lines (hereafter called line) of local-based dc and ks usually have same trends, and perform mediocrely. Sometimes the coefficients of them are even below 0.5 (in jazz, netiscience and PGP).

In seven semi-local-based centrality measures, three of them (LW, LTC, THCC) consider the two-hop neighbors' local structure and four of them (LTC, CLC, SEIC and LSC) consider the three-hop neighbors' local structure. In eleven networks, only netscience's average distance is below 2, while others' larger than 2. That's why the semi-local-based centrality measures' line in netscience performs not well, except the LTC. LTC takes the number of mutual neighbors between node and its nearest neighbors to adjust the nearest neighbors' degree and sum up, which depend more on the nearest neighbors' degree. In this case, LTC is less sensitive to the average distance of network than other six semi-local-based measures.

The lines of LSC perform very well in eight of nine networks, having high coefficients and low volatility. Only in the netscience, LSC performs bad, in which the coefficients are most below 0.6. The reason is that the netscience's average distance is below 2 while LSC considers the second and third hop neighbors that nodes in netscience usually don't have. Hence the average distance of network should be checked greater than 2 before applying the LSC.

CLC performs well, also better than LC, in eight of nine networks. CLC is actually the adaption of LC. Compared with LC, CLC takes the node's clustering coefficient, which usually plays an negative impact on the information spreading, into consideration. Only in netscience, CLC is lower than LC.

Compared with LSC and CLC, LTC and THCC have more stable and close-to-best performance. In addition, LTC is less sensitive to the network's average distance and can be applied to more networks.

The core ideas of SEIC and LW are similar, summing up the weights of a node's edges as its centrality value. The difference is that the weights in LW is decided by the number of mutual neighbors of two neighboring nodes while the weights in SEIC is decided by the number of mutual two-hop neighbors of two neighboring nodes. SEIC considers the three-hop neighbors' structure, but its line performs mediocrely and even bad in facebook and blogs. LW performs even worse in most networks and the coefficients are all below 0.5 in these networks.

As global-based centrality measures, pg and bc perform almost the worst among all measures. The lines of pg and bc are usually under all other measures. To conclude, pg performs very well in hyperlink webpages, but is not practical in social networks.

Rank the Most Influential Nodes

In many practical applications, people are interested only in the most influential nodes in the networks. In this paper, we also focus on the performance of different centrality measures on the nodes whose influence ranks top 10% in the networks. The result is shown in Fig. 2. The topn_ratio list is [0.01, 0.02,...,0.09, 0.1].

Firstly, we analyze the large decrease of many measures in facebook when topn_ratio is larger than 0.5. We find that the average number of two-hop neighbors of the nodes, whose rank between topn_ratio[i] and topn_ratio[i + 1] of facebook, is [764.8, 756.25, 756.0, 756.65, 756.0, 941.601, 921.95, 946.37, 970.13, 965.95]. In this list, when topn_ratio is larger than 0.5, the number of two-hop neighbors of new nodes that taken into calculation grow abnormally. Thus centrality measures that have considered the impact of two-hop neighbors' structure give a high value to these new nodes, resulting in the decrease in the line.

THCC performs the best in general. Its lines are the highest in six of eight networks and rank third in epinions and slashdot. In addition, THCC has low volatility and more stable than other measures.

LTC perform stably too, but its coefficients are usually 5%–10% lower than THCC.

CLC performs better than LC in most networks, but the line of CLC in facebook and CA-HepPH have large rise and falls and the lowest coefficient is even below 0.

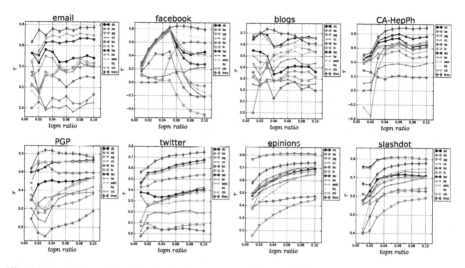

Fig. 2. Kendall's τ values for twelve measures on eight networks as topn_ratio varies from 0 to 10%

Although the local clustering coefficient usually plays a negative role during information spreading, but it may not be suitable to the all kind of networks. Combining the result in facebook and CA-HepPH and the experimental result in [8], we find when the average clustering coefficient of the network in above 0.5, the kendall's tau coefficient lines resulting from top 10% influential nodes' ranked list generated by SIR model and their ranked list generated by CLC perform bad and have relative high volatility.

SEIC and LW perform mediocrely in most networks. The lines of SEIC have high volatility and the lines of LW in six of eight networks are under 0.4, which is bad.

As shown in the Fig. 2, classical centrality measures (dc, ks, pg, cc and bc) are not practical in these networks, pg and bc perform the worst.

We further analyze the average simulation influence of nodes that rank in the top 100 under twelve centrality measures on eight networks. Here we add three points. (1) THCC and LTC's performance improve in epinions and slashdot, comparing favorably with LSC and even better in facebook and twitter. (2) Except facebook, CLC's performance in other networks improve as well. (3) ks and dc perform best among classical centrality measures in identifying the 100 most influential nodes.

5   Conclusion and Future Work

In this paper, we apply the five classical and seven up-to-date centrality measures on eleven widely used networks. Three criteria (kendall's tau correlation coefficient, distinguishability and robustness) have been taken into consideration to evaluate the performance of twelve measures. All these work is aimed to provide deeper understanding of various characteristics and best application scenarios of certain measure, and the conclusions.

For the purpose of influence maximization based on the influence ranking, we recommend to analyze the average degree, average distance and average clustering coefficient of networks before experiments. Combine the demands of efficiency and effectiveness, and determine the centrality measure suitable to you research.

For future work, we will simulate the influence of epinions and slashdot generated by SIR model on the whole range of epidemic probabilities and test the robustness of centrality measures on the epinions and slashdot networks. In future, we can test the measures on the diffusion data flows, the influence of which is based on the real information spreading instead of simulation by SIR. The application conditions of CLC and LSC in average clustering coefficient and average distance is based on the observation. For precise values more experiments need to conduct.

References

1. Kitsak, M., Gallos, L.K., Havlin, S., Liljeros, F., Muchnik, L., Stanley, H.E., Makse, H.A.: Identification of influential spreaders in complex networks. Nat. Phys. **6**(11), 888–893 (2010)
2. Brin, S., Page, L.: The anatomy of a largescale hypertextual web search engine. Int. Conf. World Wide Web **30**(17), 107–117 (1998)
3. Chen, D.B., Lü, L.Y., Shang, M.S., et al.: Identifying influential nodes in complex networks. Phys. A Stat. Mech. Appl. **391**(4), 1777–1787 (2012)
4. Gao, S., Ma, J., Chen, Z.M., et al.: Ranking the spreading ability of nodes in complex networks based on local structure. Phys. A Stat. Mech. Appl. **403**(6), 130–147 (2014)
5. Cheng, J.J., Zhang, Y.C., Zhou, X., et al.: Extracting influential nodes in social networks on local weight aspect. Int. J. Interdisc. Telecommun. Netw. **8**(2), 21–35 (2016)
6. Zhang, W., Xu, J., Li, Y.: A new method for identifying influential nodes and important edges in complex networks. Wuhan Univ. J. Nat. Sci. **21**(3), 267–276 (2016)
7. Han, Z., Chen, Y., Liu, W. et al.: Social network node influence measuring method based on triangle structures. CN 105719190 A (2016)
8. Zhao, X., Liu, F., Wang, J., Li, T.: Evaluating influential nodes in social networks by local centrality with a coefficient. ISPRS Int. J. Geo-Inf. **6**(2), 35 (2017)
9. Saxena, C., Doja, M.N., Ahmad, T.: Neighborhood topology to discover influential nodes in a complex Network. In: Satapathy, S.C., Bhateja, V., Udgata, Siba K., Pattnaik, P.K. (eds.) Proceedings of the 5th International Conference on Frontiers in Intelligent Computing: Theory and Applications. AISC, vol. 515, pp. 323–332. Springer, Singapore (2017). https://doi.org/10.1007/978-981-10-3153-3_32
10. Du, Y., et al.: A new method of identifying influential nodes in complex networks based on TOPSIS. Phys. A Stat. Mech. Appl. **399**(4), 57–69 (2014)
11. Hu, J., et al.: A modified weighted TOPSIS to identify influential nodes in complex networks. Phys. A Stat. Mech. Appl. **444**, 73–85 (2016)
12. Bian, T., Hu, J., Deng, Y.: Identifying influential nodes in complex networks based on AHP. Phys. A Stat. Mech. Appl. **479**(4), 422–436 (2017)
13. Yang, Y., Xie, G.: Efficient identification of node importance in social networks. Inf. Process. Manag. **52**(5), 911–922 (2016). Pergamon Press, Inc
14. Freeman, L.C.: A set of measures of centrality based upon betweenness. Sociometry **40**(1), 35–41 (1977)

15. Brandes, U.: A faster algorithm for betweenness centrality. J. Math. Sociol. **25**(2), 163–177 (2001)
16. Zachary, W.W.: An information flow model for conflict and fission in small groups. J. Anthropol. Res. **33**(4), 452–473 (1977)
17. Gleiser, P.M., Danon, L.: Community structure in jazz. Adv. Complex Syst. **06**(04), 565–573 (2003)
18. Newman, M.E.J.: Finding community structure in networks using the eigenvectors of matrices. Phys. Rev. E: Stat. Nonlin. Soft Matter Phys. **74**(3 pt 2), 036104 (2006)
19. Mcauley, J., Leskovec, J.: Learning to discover social circles in ego networks. In: Advances in Neural Information Processing Systems, pp. 539–547 (2012)
20. Guimerà, R., Danon, L., Díaz-Guilera, A.: Self-similar community structure in a network of human interactions. Phys. Rev. E: Stat. Nonlin. Soft Matter Phys. **68**(6 Pt 2), 065103 (2003)
21. Xie, N.: Social Network Analysis of Blogs. University of Bristol, Bristol (2006)
22. Leskovec, J., Kleinberg, J., Faloutsos, C.: Graph evolution: densification and shrinking diameters. ACM Trans. Knowl. Discov. Data **1**(1), 2 (2007)
23. Boguñá, M., et al.: Models of social networks based on social distance attachment. Phys. Rev. E: Stat. Nonlin. Soft Matter Phys. **70**(2), 056122 (2004)
24. Hopcroft, J., Lou, T., Tang, J.: Who will follow you back?: reciprocal relationship prediction. In: ACM Conference on Information and Knowledge Management, CIKM 2011, Glasgow, UK, pp. 1137–1146. ACM, October 2011
25. Richardson, M., Agrawal, R., Domingos, P.: Trust management for the semantic web. In: Fensel, D., Sycara, K., Mylopoulos, J. (eds.) ISWC 2003. LNCS, vol. 2870, pp. 351–368. Springer, Heidelberg (2003). https://doi.org/10.1007/978-3-540-39718-2_23
26. Leskovec, J., Lang, K.J., Dasgupta, A., et al.: Community structure in large networks: natural cluster sizes and the absence of large well-defined clusters. Internet Math. **6**(1), 29–123 (2009)
27. Shu, P., Wang, W., Tang, M., et al.: Numerical identification of epidemic thresholds for susceptible-infected-recovered model on finite-size networks. Chaos **25**(6) (2015)
28. Lü, L., et al.: The H-index of a network node and its relation to degree and coreness. Nat. Commun. **7**, 10168 (2016)
29. Dorogovtsev, S.N., Goltsev, A.V., Mendes, J.F.: Critical phenomena in complex networks. Rev. Mod. Phys. **80**(4), 1275–1335 (2007)
30. Newman, M.: Networks: An Introduction. OUP Oxford, Oxford (2010). vol. 327, no. 8, pp. 741–743
31. Kendall, M.G.: A new measure of rank correlation. Biometrika **30**(1/2), 81–93 (1938)

An FPGA-Based Algorithm to Accelerate Regular Expression Matching

Jiajia Yang[1,2], Lei Jiang[1,2]($\boxtimes$), Xu Bai[1,2], Qiong Dai[1,2], Majing Su[1,2], and Md Zakirul Alam Bhuiyan[3]

[1] Institute of Information Engineering, Chinese Academy of Sciences,
Beijing 100093, China
jianglei@iie.ac.cn
[2] School of Cyber Security, University of Chinese Academy of Sciences,
Beijing 100040, China
[3] Department of Computer and Information Sciences, Fordham University,
Bronx, NY 10458, USA

Abstract. State-of-the-art Network Intrusion Detection Systems (NIDSs) use regular expressions (REs) to detect attacks or vulnerabilities. In order to keep up with the ever-increasing speed, more and more NIDSs need to be implemented by dedicated hardware. A major bottleneck is that NIDSs scan incoming packets just byte by byte, which greatly limits their throughput. Besides, huge memory consumption limits it's practicability. In this paper, we propose an algorithm for regular expression matching that consumes multiple characters per time while maintaining memory efficiency. It includes 3 ideas: (1) top-k state extraction; (2) variable-stride acceleration; (3) DFA compression. We tested our algorithm on several real-life RE rulesets. The experimental results show that it achieves good performance on both memory efficiency and high throughput. It could achieve 14–22x efficiency ratio than the original DFA on Bro and Snort rulesets, and 2–7x efficiency ratio than the original DFA on l7_filter ruleset.

Keywords: Deep Packet Inspection · Regular expression matching · DFA · FPGA · NIDS

1 Introduction

In order to protect networking devices and computer systems from networking security attacks, signature-based Deep Packet Inspection (DPI) technologies have taken root as a dominant security mechanism to detect and neutralize potential threats by discarding malicious traffic. Most of the attacks are described by RE for its powerful and flexible expression ability [1]. REs are usually represented by Finite automata. It is known that REs, deterministic finite automatas (DFAs), and non-deterministic finite automatas (NFAs) are equivalent in terms of expressive power. Thus, REs are usually converted into NFAs or

© Springer International Publishing AG 2017
G. Wang et al. (Eds.): SpaCCS 2017 Workshops, LNCS 10658, pp. 424–434, 2017.
https://doi.org/10.1007/978-3-319-72395-2_39

DFAs to perform matching process. Given a RE, we can use Thompson's algorithm to construct an NFA that recognizes the same language as the given RE [2]. Then an NFA can be converted to a DFA by using the subset construction algorithm.

For a RE of length m, with an input string of length n, the time complexity of the DFA-based algorithm is $O(n)$. However, DFA's space complexity is $O(2^m)$, which is called "space explosion" problem. Moreover, matching network traffic against a DFA is inherently a serial activity, which results in limited throughput of DFA. These existing problems make DFA a challenge to be deployed practically on current network security devices. There have been a lot of recent work about RE matching for use in high-speed networking environment, particularly with representations based on DFA. However, as for practicality, how to balance throughput and memory consumption is still a difficult problem for DFA.

In this paper, we focus on improving the throughput of DFA while maintaining memory efficiency. We present a DFA accelerated algorithm based on three our proposed ideas: top-k state extraction, variable-stride acceleration, DFA compression. (1) the top-k state extraction is motivated by the fact that only a few high frequency states will be accessed at most time. (2) the variable-stride acceleration is a method to consume multiple input characters per time. (3) we use the classical compression algorithm D^2FA to compress the rest low frequency states to achieve memory efficiency.

Our algorithm is implemented on Field-Programmable Gate Array (FPGA). The experimental results show that it performs well on both memory efficiency and high throughput. It achieves a better efficiency ratio on most of the tested rulesets (except the l7_3 and l7_5 rulesets) than other algorithms. The efficiency ratio of our algorithm is 2–22x than the original DFA. We summarize our contributions as follows:

(1) We propose the ideas of the top-k extraction, variable-stride acceleration to accelerate DFA matching.
(2) We use the classical algorithm to compress the DFA transition table to achieve memory efficiency, while it has little effect on the throughput.
(3) Detailed descriptions is provided to evaluate the time complexity and space complexity. Theoretical analysis shows that we can speedup the DFA's matching by consuming only a little additional memory than original DFA.
(4) Detailed performance analysis wrt throughput, memory usage compared with other algorithms.

The rest of this paper is organized as follows. Section 2 presents the previous work related to RE. Section 3 describes the details of our proposed algorithm. Section 4 shows the performance evaluation. Finally, Sect. 5 concludes this paper.

2   Related Work

Many works about RE have been proposed, especially DFA algorithms' practical application in NIDS. These works can be divided into two aspects: (1) memory reduction; (2) acceleration of DFA.

As for memory reduction, many methods have been presented. Kumar et al. [3] observes that there are many similar next state transitions among states for a same input characters subset. According to this observation they propose a new algorithm called D^2FA to compress the transition matrix by introducing a default transition to eliminate these same transition between two states. However, D^2FA engine may lookup up memory multiple times per input character, leading to a higher memory band. The authors [4] present a multi-dimensional cub DFA algorithm (MDC-DFA) for anomaly feature matching. They achieve a logarithm-level compression to the number of states and the storage space while maintaining the time complexity. The paper [5] gives a novel solution, called DFA/EC. Experimental results show that this algorithm is over four orders of magnitude smaller in the best cases than conventional DFAs. But its construction algorithm and matching process are much more complexity. Liu et al. [6] give a RegexGrouper to grouping REs based on DFA size estimation. Their method can generate less states than prior works under the same RE rulesets.

Besides, some strategies focus on improving the performance of RE matching. For example, Brodie et al. [7] use multi-stride DFAs to increase the throughput. Specially, a stride-k DFA consumes k characters per state transition, thus yielding a k-fold performance increase. However, multi-stride DFAs lead to an exponentially increased memory requirement in the worst case. Bando et al. [8] present LaFA, an on-chip RegEx detection system that employs a novel lookahead technique to reorder the sequence of pattern detections. In order to achieve high throughput, the authors use parallel engines to accelerate RegEx. However, parallel engines may lead to a failure for RegEx matching when applied for multi-packet, multi-flow and multi-session application. Su et al. [9] show the best performance FPGA-based DPI prototype in 2016. It is able to provide up to 60Gbps full-text string matching throughput. However, it uses the 48 parallel engines to accelerate the matching. It can process packet-level data but not flow-level data. Liu et al. [10] parallel the consecutive state transitions on the frequently traversed states. A Match Unit is used to check whether a character is a Leaving Char. By this, they can achieve high performance on their datasets.

3   Our Algorithm

This section consists of 3 subsections. Subsect. 3.1 introduces the concept of DFA and the DFA's serial matching process. Subsect. 3.2 describes our idea. Subsect. 3.3 analyzes the throughput and memory consumption.

3.1   The Introduction of Original DFA

The left side of Fig. 1 shows a standard DFA defined on the alphabet a, b, c, d that recognizes the three patterns [3], $p1 = a^+$, $p2 = b^+c$, and $p3 = c^*d^+$. In this DFA, state 1 is the initial state, and states 2, 5 and 4 are match states for the three patterns $p1$, $p2$ and $p3$, respectively.

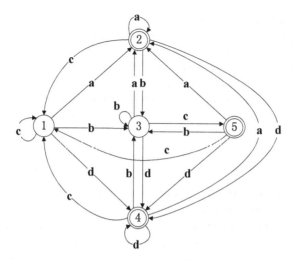

Fig. 1. Example of automata which recognizes the expression a^+, b^+c, and c^*d^+.

If given the *current state*, the *next state* can be calculated after consuming a character. For example, the *current state* is 1. If given a character 'a', then the *current state* jumps to the *next state*, which is 2. Because the state 2 is a match state, then this character is accepted by this DFA. We define a transition function δ: $S_{next} = \delta(S_{cur}, ch)$, where S_{next} denotes the *next state*, S_{cur} denotes the *current state*, ch denotes an input character. Now, suppose there is an input string T where $T[n]$ denotes the nth character, S_0 is the initial state. The process of original DFA matching can be shown as following.

$\delta(S_0, T) = \delta(S_0, T[0, 1, \ldots, n-1]) = \delta(S_1, T[1, 2, \ldots, n-1]) = \ldots = \delta(S_{n-1}, T[n-1]) = S_n$

For example, if the input string T = '*aaaabbbcd*', the traversal path is: 1 $\xrightarrow{a}$ 2 $\xrightarrow{a}$ 2 $\xrightarrow{a}$ 2 $\xrightarrow{a}$ 2 $\xrightarrow{b}$ 3 $\xrightarrow{b}$ 3 $\xrightarrow{b}$ 3 $\xrightarrow{c}$ 5 $\xrightarrow{d}$ 4. So the traversal states are 1222233354.

However, since original DFA matching is in serial, its throughput is limited. What's more, its memory consumption is large. So we need to find a method to improve the throughput of DFA while maintaining memory efficiency.

3.2 The Detail of Our Algorithm

(1) motivation
A lot of works show that a bulk of the DFA transitions are concentrated around a few DFA states [8,9] (We name them top-k states, which are the top k highest frequency states).

On the other hand, given an input string T = '*aaaabbbcd*', the traversal states are 1222233354. Before the state 2 turns to state 3, there're 4 consecutive identical states 2. If the *current state* is equal to 2, that means we can skip a stride of 4 characters before the *current state* turns to 3. Similarly, there are 3 identical states '333'. So the stride of characters is equal to 3, which means we skip 3 characters without needing to access the DFA transition table[1]. By this, we can achieve about 3× speedup. If we use the traditional DFA matching, it takes 10 steps to consume these characters. But our algorithm only takes 5 steps. If enlarging the length of stride, we take less steps.

In addition, only a few most frequency states would be accessed during the matching process, while the rest states may not be accessed at most time. So we use the classical algorithm D^2FA to compress these states to achieve memory efficiency.

(2) the detail of our algorithm

The process of our algorithm includes two stages. (1) the pre-processing stage; (2) the lookup process stage.

The pseudo-code of the pre-processing stage is shown in Algorithm 1. This algorithm is used to extract the top-k states by scanning a network traffic trace. Line 1 counts each state's frequency. Line 2 selects the most k frequency states.

Algorithm 1. Extract the top-k states

Input: A network traffic trace
Output: the top-k states
Procedures:
1: Use original DFA to match against the network traffic trace, and statistics each state's frequency
2: Select the most k frequency states

The lookup process is shown in Algorithm 2. Suppose DFA's *initial state* is given, then we set the *current state* equals to the *initial state* as line 1 described. Line 3–27 describe whether the input string T is accepted. Line 4–6 show that if T is accepted by the DFA, then the process halts. Line 7–26 show the main idea. If *current_state* is equal to the value of a top-k state, e.g. $S_0,...,S_6$, it will justify how large the stride can we skip. For example, if *current_state* $= S_0 = TOP[S_0][T[0]] = TOP[S_0][T[1]]$, but $TOP[S_0][T[2]] \mathrel{!=} S_0$, $TOP[S_0][T[3]] \mathrel{!=} S_0$, then i = i + 2^2, where $TOP[y][z]$ denotes the zth component of the yth top-k states. It means we can skip 2 characters. Otherwise, we execute the D^2FA compression algorithm [3] as line 14 described. There may be some states not in the range of the top-6 states. In this case, they execute the D^2FA compression algorithm as line 24 described. It must be noted that the value of top-k states can be larger or smaller as needed.

---

[1] Paper [10] focuses on whether a char is a Leaving Char. However, we focuses on whether a transition is a Leaving transition.
[2] 4'b110x, 4'b10xx, x denotes 0 or 1.

Algorithm 2. Lookup process

Input: an input string T
Output: whether T is accepted
Procedures:
1: *current state ← initial state*
2: i ← 0;
3: **while** (*T* is not accepted) **do**
4:   **if** (*current_state* is match) **then**
5:     *T* is accepted; return
6:   **end if**
7:   **switch** *current_state* **do**
8:     **case** S_0:
9:       casex(TOP[S_0][T[0]] == S_0,..., TOP[S_0][T[3]] == S_0)
10:        4'b1111: i ← i + 4;   break;
11:        4'b1110: i ← i + 3;   break;
12:        4'b110x: i ← i + 2;   break;
13:        4'b10xx: i ← i + 1;   break;
14:        default: { Get the *next_state* by applying the algorithm D^2FA;
15:                     *current_state ← next_state*; i ← i + 1;}
16:      endcasex
17:      break;
18:     **case** S_1:
19:      casex
20:       ...
21:      endcasex
22:      break;
23:     ...
24:     **otherwise:** { Get the *next_state* by applying the algorithm D^2FA;
25:                  *current_state ← next_state*; i ← i + 1;}
26:   **end switch**
27: **end while**

3.3   Analysis of the Throughput and Memory Consumption

Let S denotes the number of DFA states, k denotes the number of the top-k states, ρ denotes the compression ratio of the compression algorithm D^2FA applied on the DFA transition table. In addition, the number of ASCII characters is 256.

(1) The analysis of memory consumption
Our algorithm's memory consumption includes two parts: (a) the top-k states; (b) the rest low frequency states. Actually, we use the whole DFA transition table to replace these low frequency states.

The memory consumption of the top-k states is shown in Eq. (1)

$$Mem\_1 = k \times 256 \times \lceil log_2 S \rceil \qquad (1)$$

The memory consumption of the rest low frequency states (use the whole DFA transition table to replace) is shown in Eq. (2)

$$Mem\_2 = S \times 256 \times \lceil log_2 S \rceil \times \rho \tag{2}$$

So the total memory consumption of our algorithm is $Mem(total) = Mem\_1 + Mem\_2 = (k + S \times \rho) \times 256 \times \lceil log_2 S \rceil$. In most cases, the $k \ll S$, so the Mem(total) $\approx$ Mem_2. Assume that $k = 6$, $S = 10000$. If $\rho = 0.1$, then $Mem(total)$ is equal to 3.42 Mb.

(2) The analysis of throughput
The calculation of throughput is shown in Eq. (2), where 8 denotes 1 character equals 8 bits. Let *Stride* denotes the expectation of characters processed per time. So the throughput of our algorithm is shown in Eq. (3), where *freq* denotes the frequency.

$$Th = freq \times Stride \times 8 \tag{3}$$

4   Performance Evaluation

4.1   Test Bed and Data Sets

The evaluation tool is Vivado 2015.4. Hardware simulation is based on the Xilinx Virtex-7 FPGA chip (XC7VX1140t) with 1,139,200 logic cells (LCs) and 67,680Kb BlockRAM.

The RE real-life rulesets used in our test are all publicly available, listed in Table 1, including RE ruleset Snort [1], Bro [12] and l7-filter [13]. Since the rules are too complex to generate a composite DFA, the l7-filter ruleset is divided into 8 rule subsets from l7_1 to l7_8. We also use real-life network traffic traces

Table 1. Detail of different rulesets.

Rulesets	#of rules	#of states	#of length range
bro217	217	6475	3–211
snort24	24	8335	15–98
snort31	31	4864	15–263
snort34	34	9754	19–115
l7_1	67	3703	17–202
l7_2	7	1702	16–218
l7_3	12	2863	11–218
l7_4	5	3322	16–87
l7_5	6	3040	6–438
l7_6	5	8704	6–139
l7_7	5	5720	11–438
l7_8	1	308	147

obtained from MIT Lincoln lab for statistical performance evaluation [14]. For fair comparison, we implement other algorithms on our FPGA chip.

4.2   Experimental Results

(1) throughput and memory consumption
From Table 2, we know that our proposed algorithm is higher than the other algorithms in the aspect of throughput (except that the throughput of our algorithms is almost same as the Spec($N = 1$)). Specifically, the throughput of our algorithm is about 1.30–1.46x than that of the original DFA matching, and is about 2–3x than D^{2}FA or RICS-DFA's. From Tables 2 and 3, the memory consumption of ours is roughly same as the D^{2}FA's and the RICS-DFA's, while the throughput of our algorithm is much higher than these two algorithms.

Comparing Tables 2 and 3, we can draw the following conclusions: (1) we only consume a little additional memory than that of the D^{2}FA and the RICS-DFA, while we can achieve higher throughput than theirs. (2) compared with original DFA, our algorithm shows better performance on both throughput and memory consumption, which is consistent with the theoretical analysis.

Table 2. Throughput between different algorithms (Gbps)

Rulesets	DFA	D^{2}FA	RICS-DFA [15]	Spec($N = 2$) [16]	Ours
bro217	1.98	0.68	0.75	2.52	2.61
snort24	2.09	0.75	0.76	N/A	2.70
snort31	2.08	0.76	0.69	2.83	2.76
snort34	2.09	0.75	0.92	N/A	2.57
l7_1	2.00	0.72	0.71	2.76	2.86
l7_2	1.97	0.71	1.0	2.73	2.82
l7_3	2.03	0.69	0.79	2.80	2.92
l7_4	2.00	0.61	0.76	2.80	2.87
l7_5	2.01	0.73	0.73	2.77	2.85
l7_6	2.02	0.71	0.75	N/A	2.81
l7_7	2.02	0.68	0.71	2.79	2.93
l7_8	2.02	0.71	0.79	2.72	2.85

As for D^{2}FA and RICS-DFA, because they are compression algorithms, their throughput is low for processing a character needs to access the memory serval times. As for Spec, it's an accelerated algorithm. In theory, it can achieve 2× speedup of original DFA. However, as it speculates on just a highest frequency state, its speculative probability is low. This limitation leads to its speedup is less than 2× speedup. Similarly, our algorithm's accelerated effect is limited as the number of consecutive transitions is limited. Usually, the number is no more than 3 characters in average.

Table 3. Memory consumption between different algorithms (Mb)

Rulesets	DFA	D²FA	RICS-DFA	Spec(N = 2)	Ours
bro217	20.55	1.27	1.60	41.10	1.28
snort24	28.49	2.28	2.05	N/A	2.28
snort31	15.44	0.93	1.45	30.88	0.93
snort34	33.34	3.00	1.90	N/A	3.00
l7_1	10.85	3.14	3.45	21.70	3.14
l7_2	4.57	0.93	1.32	9.14	0.94
l7_3	8.39	6.20	1.11	16.78	6.21
l7_4	0.70	2.08	2.08	19.46	2.09
l7_5	8.91	4.52	0.92	17.81	4.53
l7_6	29.75	12.88	4.43	N/A	12.89
l7_7	18.15	12.16	3.18	36.31	12.18
l7_8	0.68	0.19	0.06	1.35	0.20

Table 4. Efficiency ratio (throughput/memory consumption)

Rulesets	DFA	D²FA	RICS-DFA	Spec(N = 2)	Ours
bro217	0.10	0.53	0.47	0.06	**2.05**
snort24	0.07	0.33	0.37	N/A	**1.18**
snort31	0.13	0.82	0.48	0.09	**2.98**
snort34	0.06	0.25	0.48	N/A	**0.86**
l7_1	0.18	0.23	0.21	0.13	**0.91**
l7_2	0.43	0.76	0.76	0.30	**3.01**
l7_3	0.24	0.11	**0.71**	0.17	0.47
l7_4	0.21	0.29	0.36	0.14	**1.38**
l7_5	0.23	0.16	**0.80**	0.16	0.63
l7_6	0.07	0.06	0.17	N/A	**0.22**
l7_7	0.11	0.06	0.22	0.08	**0.24**
l7_8	2.98	3.71	13.27	2.01	**14.45**

As for memory consumption, different algorithms have different memory consumptions. The D²FA and RICS-DFA are compression algorithms. So their memory consumption is relatively lower than the original DFA's. Since Spec algorithm is an accelerated algorithm, it memory consumption is large. In these compared algorithms, our algorithm is the most memory efficiency. Because it only needs to accelerate the top-k states.

(2) efficiency ratio

We define $\rho = throughput/memory\ consumption$. From Table 4, our algorithm shows the best efficiency ratio (except for the l7_3 and l7_5 rulesets). Compared with original DFA, we can inter that the efficiency ratio of our algorithm is about 14–22x than original DFA on the bro, snort rulesets, and is about 2–7x on the l7_filter ruleset. By this advantage, we can effectively implement our algorithm on modern limited resource devices.

5   Conclusion

We present a practical algorithm for regular expression matching. We apply the top-k state extraction, variable-stride acceleration and DFA compression to consume multiple characters per time while maintaining memory efficiency. Meanwhile, we take the full advantage of FPGA's parallelism to accelerate our algorithm. Experimental results show that it does well in many available publicly rulesets.

Acknowledgments. This work is supported by the National Science Foundation of China (NSFC) under grant No. 61402475, and the National Science and Technology Major Project under Grant No. 2017YFB0803003.

References

1. Roesch, M., et al.: Snort: lightweight intrusion detection for networks. In: LISA, vol. 99, no. 1, pp. 229–238 (1999)
2. Hopcroft, J.E.: Introduction to Automata Theory, Languages, and Computation. Pearson Education, India (1979)
3. Kumar, S., Dharmapurikar, S., Yu, F., Crowley, P., Turner, J.: Algorithms to accelerate multiple regular expressions matching for deep packet inspection. ACM SIGCOMM Comput. Commun. Rev. **36**(4), 339–350 (2006)
4. Li, Y., Luo, X., Shao, X., Wei, D.: MDC-DFA: a multi-dimensional cube deterministic finite automata-based feature matching algorithm. In: 2015 Fifth International Conference on Information and Communication Technology Convergence (ICTC), pp. 1119–1124. IEEE (2015)
5. Liu, C., Pan, Y., Chen, A., Wu, J.: A DFA with extended characterset for fast deep packet inspection. IEEE Trans. Comput. **63**(8), 1925–1937 (2014)
6. Liu, T., Liu, A.X., Shi, J., Sun, Y., Guo, L.: Towards fast and optimal grouping of regular expressions via DFA size estimation. IEEE/ACM J. Sel. Areas Commun. **32**(10), 1797–1809 (2014)
7. Brodie, B.C., Taylor, D.E., Cytron, R.K.: A scalable architecture for high-throughput regular-expression pattern matching. In: ACM SIGARCH Computer Architecture News, vol. 34, no. 2, pp. 191–202. IEEE Computer Society (2006)
8. Bando, M., Artan, N.S., Chao, H.J.: Scalable lookahead regular expression detection system for deep packet inspection. IEEE/ACM Trans. Netw. **20**(3), 699–714 (2012)
9. Su, J., Chen, S., Han, B., Xu, C., Wang, X.: A 60GBps DPI prototype based on memory-centric FPGA. In: Proceedings of the 2016 Conference on ACM SIGCOMM 2016 Conference, pp. 627–628. ACM (2016)

10. Liu, X., Shao, Z., Liu, X., Sum, N.: Fine-grained parallel regular expression matching for deep packet inspection. J. Comput. Res. Dev. **5**(51), 1061–1070 (2014)
11. Jiang, L., Dai, Q., Tang, Q., Tan, J., Fang, B.: A fast regular expression matching engine for NIDS applying prediction scheme. In: 2014 IEEE Symposium on Computers and Communication (ISCC), pp. 1–7. IEEE (2014)
12. The Bro Network Security Monitor. http://www.bro.org
13. Levandoski, J., Sommer, E., Strait, M., et al.: Application Layer Packet Classifier for Linux (2008)
14. DARPA Intrusion Detection Data Sets. https://www.ll.mit.edu/ideval/data/
15. Tang, Q., Jiang, L., Dai, Q., Su, M., Xie, H., Fang, B.: Rics-DFA: a space and time-efficient signature matching algorithm with reduced input character set. Concur. Comput.: Pract. Exp. (2016)
16. Luchaup, D., Smith, R., Estan, C., Jha, S.: Speculative parallel pattern matching IEEE Trans. Inf. Forensics Secur. **54**(2), 438–451 (2011)

A Collaborative Filtering Recommendation Algorithm Based on Score Classification

Jiachang Hao[1(✉)], Kun Niu[2], Zichao Meng[1], Shuo Huang[1], and Bing Ma[1]

[1] School of Computing, Beijing University of Posts and Telecommunications, Beijing 100876, China
{haojc,mzc,huangshuodcxx}@bupt.edu.cn,
echobingo@foxmail.com
[2] School of Software Engineering, Beijing University of Posts and Telecommunications, Beijing 100876, China
niukun@bupt.edu.cn

Abstract. Living in the "information society", we are bombarded with information whether or not we actively seek it, collaborative filtering technology on personalized recommendation are proposed as a solution in recent years. In order to improve the accuracy of the algorithm, this paper proposed a collaborative filtering recommendation algorithm based on score classification. In view of the behavioral habits that a user tends to give the items with extreme scores which he is interested in, every rating is classified according to the rating's extremality. In the similarity measurement, the extreme ratings are classified as high-level ratings which are assigned with higher weights, and the moderate ratings that users rate out of herd mentality are assigned with lower weights. Experiments on test dataset show that our algorithm performs better in predicting the user's ratings than traditional algorithms.

Keywords: Collaborative filter · Score classification · Similarity measurement
Rating's extremality · Personalized recommendation

1 Introduction

1.1 Background

With the development of big data, cloud computing and other new technologies, people can enjoy more and more services and resources. Living in the "information society", we are also affected by another phenomenon, "information overload", that too much information resulting in low efficiency to deal with and use. Therefore, it is quite important to find out useful information directly and accurately, and collaborative filtering appears as the keystone and hotspot in the personalized recommendation field which emerges as the times require.

Developed from information filtering, collaborative filtering was first proposed by Goldberg et al. [1]. Generally, it can be divided into two kinds: user-based collaborative filtering technology and item-based collaborative filtering technology [2]. Both use

© Springer International Publishing AG 2017
G. Wang et al. (Eds.): SpaCCS 2017 Workshops, LNCS 10658, pp. 435–445, 2017.
https://doi.org/10.1007/978-3-319-72395-2_40

users' scores to items in similarity calculating, however, the former makes recommendation based on users' similarity, and the latter based on items' similarity.

The advantage of collaborative filtering is that it doesn't need to take the attributes of users into account and it can find user's new interests in the meantime. However, it also has many challenges needed to be solved, such as cold start, data overload, data sparsity, recommendation accuracy, and so on [3]. How to solve these problems effectively has become a hot research spot in recent years.

1.2   Related Work

In the collaborative filtering recommendation technique, selecting an appropriate similarity method can improve the accuracy of recommendation effectively. Shi proposed a collaborative filtering recommendation algorithm based on item classification [4] to improve the accuracy of recommendation, which calculates the similarity of each item in each class based on the classification to increase the number of common user ratings. Sun proposed a Pear_After_SVD method [5], which is a feature increasing model, and a LCM_STI method which is conversion model for solving the problem of sparse data. To address the problem of collaborative filtering approach for big data application, [6] proposed a clustering-based collaborative filtering approach, which aims at recruiting similar services in the same clusters to recommend services collaboratively. [7] proposed a model that fully captures the bilateral role of user interactions within a social network and formulated collaborative filtering methods to enable people to people recommendation. [8] implemented a novel and improved method of recommending movies by combining the asymmetric method of calculating similarity with matrix factorization and typicality-based collaborative filtering.

In fact, compared to high and low ratings, the moderate ratings cannot effectively reflect the user's preferences. However, the existing algorithm pays equal attention to ratings when calculating the similarity, which inevitably obscures users' actual characteristics. To improve the above-mentioned problem, the paper proposes a new collaborative filtering recommendation algorithm based on score classification. The algorithm improves the similarity calculation formula to promote the accuracy of the recommendation, which adding the adjustment coefficient that assign a higher weight to the high or low ratings, a lower weight to the moderate ratings.

1.3   Our Contributions

In this paper, we improve the similarity measure function based on the traditional collaborative filtering algorithm, to improve the accuracy of recommendation. The contributions of our works are:

1. We improve the similarity measure function by adding the adjustment coefficient and propose a collaborative filtering recommendation algorithm based on score classification.
2. We proposed two algorithms, user-based and item-based. The optimized algorithms introduce weight for each rating in the similarity method and improve the accuracy of recommendation.

3. We use the authoritative data set movieLens to verify the superiority of the algorithm proposed in this paper compared to the algorithm before optimization.

2   A Collaborative Filtering Recommendation Algorithm Based on Score Classification

2.1   Statement of Problem

In both user-based collaborative filtering and item-based collaborative filtering, the similarity measures is the core of the algorithm, which greatly affects the accuracy of algorithm recommendation. There are three methods of traditional similarity measurement: Cosine, Correlation and Adjusted cosine [9]. Cosine similarity treats the user or item information as a vector in n-dimensional space, and measures the similarity by the cosine angle between vectors. Correlation similarity measures the similarity between users or items by the Pearson correlation coefficient. Adjusted cosine, on the basis of Cosine similarity, subtracts the average score of the user or item, taking into account the problem of the scoring scale of different users. These three similarity measures all share a common flaw: they do not take into account the association between the extremality of the ratings and the user's interest.

Because a user tends to rate the items he is interested in, not all of them [10], all ratings of a user provide an envelope covering all the user's interests. Among the envelop, the relevance between the extreme ratings and the user's interest is strongest, while the relevance between the moderate and the user's interest is weakest. As shown in Fig. 1, User 1's extreme ratings are more similar to those of User 2, which indicates that User 1 is more similar to User 2 in terms of interests and hobbies.

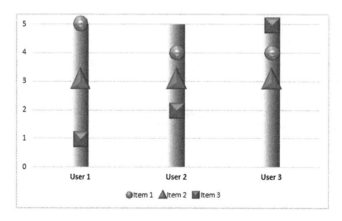

Fig. 1. Rating distribution of three users

One user's highest ratings and the user's interests have the strongest relevance, because the user's highest ratings tend to belong to the user's favorite, and in line with the user's taste. Similarly, one user's lowest ratings and the user's interests also have a strong relevance. In view of that users tend not to rate the item he isn't interested in, low ratings are out of user's dissatisfaction to the poor quality of items which type belong to user's favorite. The moderate ratings that users rate out of herd mentality have the lowest relevance with the user's interests.

The traditional similarity measures do not pay more attention to the extreme ratings, so it is much more possible to recommend something users aren't interested in to users. For example, given a user rates Transformers 5 points which is his highest rating, Gravity 1 point which is his lowest rating and Titanic 3 points, it can be inferred that the user is interested in sci-fi movies not romance movies and he prefers the sci-fi movies like Transformers, not Gravity. However, the traditional similarity measures would not pay more attention to the sci-fi movies, resulting in that it is possible to recommend romance movies to the user.

To compensate for these shortcomings, this paper proposes a collaborative filtering recommendation algorithm based on score classification. The core idea of the algorithm is to optimize the similarity methods by classifying each rating according to the extremality of the rating, in which the extreme ratings are assigned with higher weights and the moderate ratings are assigned with lower weights.

2.2 Optimization of Similarity Measure Function

In the collaborative filtering, user's ratings are stored in the form of two-dimensional matrix as shown in the following figure [11]. Let the user-item rating matrix $R(m, n)$ has m users $\{u_1, u_2, \ldots, u_m\}$ and n items $\{i_1, i_2, \ldots, i_n\}$, where R_{ij} is the rating by user i on item j and $R_{ij} > 0$.

$$\begin{pmatrix} R_{11} & \cdots & R_{1n} \\ \vdots & \ddots & \vdots \\ R_{m1} & \cdots & R_{mn} \end{pmatrix}$$

Calculated by the similarity method, $\text{sim}(u, v)$, presenting the similarity between two elements u, v, is the measure of the nearest neighbors and is also the important weight when predicting ratings [12].

In the algorithm proposed by this paper, weights are introduced for each rating, all of which construct a weight matrix $W(m, n)$ to be used in the similarity method.

$$W_{u,k} = \alpha + \beta |R_{u,k} - \overline{R}_u| \tag{1}$$

Here $R_{u,k}$ is the rating by user u on item k, R_u is the average rating of user u, $W_{u,k}$ presents the weight of $R_{u,k}$, and α, β are adjustable parameters.

Table 1 shows the difference in expression $\text{sim}(u, v)$ based on user between tradition and the optimized. Table 2 shows the difference in expression $\text{sim}(i, j)$ based on item between tradition and the optimized.

Table 1. The expression of $sim(u,v)$ based on user

The similarity measure	Traditional expression	Optimized expression
Cosine	$\dfrac{\sum_{k\in I_{uv}} R_{u,k}R_{v,k}}{\sqrt{\sum_{k\in I_u} R_{u,k}^2}\sqrt{\sum_{k\in I_v} R_{v,k}^2}}$	$\dfrac{\sum_{k\in I_{uv}} (W_{u,k}R_{u,k})(W_{v,k}R_{v,k})}{\sqrt{\sum_{k\in I_u} (W_{u,k}R_{u,k})^2}\sqrt{\sum_{k\in I_v} (W_{v,k}R_{v,k})^2}}$
Correlation	$\dfrac{\sum_{k=1}^{N} (R_{u,k}-\bar{R}_u)(R_{v,k}-\bar{R}_v)}{\sqrt{\sum_{k=1}^{N} (R_{u,k}-\bar{R}_u)^2}\sqrt{\sum_{k=1}^{N} (R_{v,k}-\bar{R}_v)^2}}$	$\dfrac{\sum_{k=1}^{N} (W_{u,k}(R_{u,k}-\bar{R}_u))(W_{v,k}(R_{v,k}-\bar{R}_v))}{\sqrt{\sum_{k=1}^{N} (W_{u,k}(R_{u,k}-\bar{R}_u))^2}\sqrt{\sum_{k=1}^{N} (W_{v,k}(R_{v,k}-\bar{R}_v))^2}}$
Adjusted Cosine	$\dfrac{\sum_{k\in I_{uv}} (R_{u,k}-\bar{R}_u)(R_{v,k}-\bar{R}_v)}{\sqrt{\sum_{k\in I_u} (R_{u,k}-\bar{R}_u)^2}\sqrt{\sum_{k\in I_v} (R_{v,k}-\bar{R}_v)^2}}$	$\dfrac{\sum_{k\in I_{uv}} (W_{u,k}(R_{u,k}-\bar{R}_u))(W_{v,k}(R_{v,k}-\bar{R}_v))}{\sqrt{\sum_{k\in I_u} (W_{u,k}(R_{u,k}-\bar{R}_u))^2}\sqrt{\sum_{k\in I_v} (W_{v,k}(R_{v,k}-\bar{R}_v))^2}}$

In Table 1, $sim(u,v)$ presents the similarity between two users u, v, $R_{u,k}$ is the rating by user u on item k, $W_{u,k}$ presents the weight of $R_{u,k}$, $\bar{R}_u$ is the average rating of user u, N is the total number of items rated by both user u and v, I_{uv} presents the set of items rated by both users u and v, I_u presents the set of items rated by user u.

Table 2. The expression of $sim(i,j)$ based on item

The similarity measure	Traditional expression	Optimized expression
Cosine	$\dfrac{\sum_{k\in U_{ij}} R_{k,i}R_{k,j}}{\sqrt{\sum_{k\in U_i} R_{k,i}^2}\sqrt{\sum_{k\in U_j} R_{k,j}^2}}$	$\dfrac{\sum_{k\in U_{ij}} (W_{k,i}R_{k,i})(W_{k,j}R_{k,j})}{\sqrt{\sum_{k\in U_i} (W_{k,i}R_{k,i})^2}\sqrt{\sum_{k\in j} (W_{k,j}R_{k,j})^2}}$
Correlation	$\dfrac{\sum_{k=1}^{N} (R_{k,i}-\bar{R}_i)(R_{k,j}-\bar{R}_J)}{\sqrt{\sum_{k=1}^{N} (R_{k,i}-\bar{R}_i)^2}\sqrt{\sum_{k=1}^{N} (R_{k,j}-\bar{R}_J)^2}}$	$\dfrac{\sum_{k=1}^{N} (W_{k,i}(R_{k,i}-\bar{R}_i))(W_{k,j}(R_{k,j}-\bar{R}_J))}{\sqrt{\sum_{k=1}^{N} (W_{k,i}(R_{k,i}-\bar{R}_i))^2}\sqrt{\sum_{k=1}^{N} (W_{k,j}(R_{k,j}-\bar{R}_J))^2}}$
Adjusted Cosine	$\dfrac{\sum_{k\in U_{ij}} (R_{k,i}-\bar{R}_k)(R_{k,j}-\bar{R}_k)}{\sqrt{\sum_{k\in U_i} (R_{k,i}-\bar{R}_k)^2}\sqrt{\sum_{k\in U_j} (R_{k,j}-\bar{R}_k)^2}}$	$\dfrac{\sum_{k\in U_{ij}} (W_{k,i}(R_{k,i}-\bar{R}_k))(W_{k,j}(R_{k,j}-\bar{R}_k))}{\sqrt{\sum_{k\in U_i} (W_{k,i}(R_{k,i}-\bar{R}_k))^2}\sqrt{\sum_{k\in U_j} (W_{k,j}(R_{k,j}-\bar{R}_k))^2}}$

In Table 2, $sim(i,j)$ presents the similarity between two items i, j, $R_{k,i}$ is the rating by user k on item i, $W_{k,j}$ presents the weight of $R_{k,j}$, $\bar{R}_i$ is the average rating of item i, $\bar{R}_k$ is the average rating of user k, N is the total number of users who rated on both items i and j, U_{ij} presents the set of users who rated on both items i and j, U_i presents the set of users who rated on item j.

Having calculated the similarity, we can predict the unknown ratings using one of the following formula where N is the set of the nearest neighbors. Formula 2 applies to the algorithm based on the user. Formula 3 applies to the algorithm based on the item.

$$P_{i,k} = \frac{\sum_{j\in N} |sim(i,j)| * R_{j,k}}{\sum_{j\in N} |sim(i,j)|} \tag{2}$$

$$P_{i,k} = \frac{\sum_{j\in N} |sim(k,j)| * R_{i,j}}{\sum_{j\in N} |sim(k,j)|} \tag{3}$$

In the user-based collaborative filtering, assigning the extreme ratings higher weights in the similarity measure can make the nearest neighbors more similar to the original user in interest and aesthetic taste.

In the item-based collaborative filtering, assigning the extreme ratings higher weights in the similarity measure can make the nearest neighbors more similar to the original item in classification and quality.

Table 3. A user-item rating matrix

	Item A	Item B	Item C	Item D	Item E	Item F
User 1	4	?(3)	5	2	1	3
User 2	1	3	2	–	5	3
User 3	3	2	3	2	1	–
User 4	3	1	–	5	3	2
User 5	–	5	3	1	3	5

For example, Table 3 shows a user-item rating matrix. We have known $R_{1,2} = 3$. Now we try to use collaborative filtering algorithm to predict its value by other known ratings, where the size of the nearest neighbors $S = 2$, $\alpha = 0$, $\beta = 1$.

Based on user, traditional algorithm will select User 3, whose similarity to User 1 is 0.952, and User 5, whose similarity to User 1 is 0.272, as the nearest neighbors of User 1 and get the predict result $P_{1,2}^1 = 3.200$, using formula 2. Optimized algorithm will select User 3 and User 5, whose similarities to User 1 are 0.907 and 0.159, as the nearest neighbors and get the predict result $P_{1,2}^2 = 3.068$. Evidently, $P_{1,2}^2$ is more closer to $R_{1,2}$ than $P_{1,2}^1$. We can see from the similarity changes of the two algorithms, the optimized algorithm pays more attention to User 3 who rated the same ratings as User 1 on Item A, C, E than to User 5, so that the predicted result is closer to the original rating.

Based on item, traditional algorithm will select Item F and Item E, whose similarity to Item B are 0.98 and 0.23, as the nearest neighbors of Item B, and get the predict result $P_{1,2}^1 = 2.243$. Optimized algorithm will select Item F and Item E, whose similarity to Item B are 0.93 and 0.03, as the nearest neighbors, and get the result $P_{1,2}^2 = 2.456$. We can see that the optimized algorithm pays more attention to Item F which is rated extreme ratings by User 4 and User 5 just like Item B so that optimized the accuracy of the result.

3   Algorithm Description

3.1   Process of Algorithm

- Algorithm based on user:

  1. Normalization. The user-item rating matrix $R(m, n)$ is normalized by the following min-max according to the row to obtain the normalized matrix $M(m, n)$. $min(j)$ is the minimum rating of User j, $max(j)$ is the maximum rating of User j,

$j \in U$, U is the user set which contains all users, $k \in I$, I is the item set which contains all items.

$$M_{j,k} = \frac{R_{j,k} - min(j)}{max(j) - min(j)} \tag{4}$$

2. Calculate all users' average rating $\bar{U}_j$, $j \in U$.
3. Calculate the weight matrix $W(m, n)$. Based on $M(m, n)$, calculate every rating's weight $W_{u,k}$ by formula 1 to obtain the weight matrix $W(m, n)$.
4. Measure the similarity. Select one expression in Table 1 to calculate the target user's similarities to other users.
5. Determine the nearest neighbor set. Select the top S users with the highest similarity to the target user i to form the nearest neighbor set of User i.
6. Predict ratings. Calculate all the ratings that the target user i didn't rate by Formula 5. $k \in I_n$, I_n is the item set that contains all items that User i didn't rate.

$$MP_{i,k} = \frac{\sum_{j=1}^{S} |sim(i,j)| * N_{j,k}}{\sum_{j=1}^{S} |sim(i,j)|} \tag{5}$$

7. Recommendation. De-normalized all the predictive rating $MP_{i,k}$, to obtain the final predictive rating $P_{i,k}$. Select the top N items with the highest predictive rating as the recommended result.

- Algorithm based on item:

  1. Normalization. Specific steps are same as step 1 based on user.
  2. Calculate all users' average rating $\bar{U}_j$ and all items' average rating $\bar{I}_k$. $k \in I$, $j \in U$.
  3. Calculate the weight matrix $W(m, n)$. Specific steps are same as step 3 based on user.
  4. Measure the similarity. Select one expression in Table 2 to calculate every unknown-rating item's similarity to other known-rating items.
  5. Determine the nearest neighbor sets. For every unknown-rating item k, select the top S items with the greatest similarity, to form the nearest neighbor set of item k.
  6. Predict ratings. Calculate every unknown rating of the target user i by the following formula. $k \in I_n$.

$$MP_{i,k} = \frac{\sum_{j=1}^{S} |sim(k,j)| * N_{i,j}}{\sum_{j=1}^{S} |sim(k,j)|} \tag{6}$$

  7. Recommendation. Specific steps are same as step 7 based on user.

3.2   Pseudo Code

See Table 4.

Table 4. Pseudo Code of CF based on Score Classification

```
Procedure Collabora-
tive_Filtering_Based_Score_Classification(Coefficient
A, Coefficient B, Method, Rating_Matrix)
{
  Nomalization(Rating_Matrix);
  /* Caculate the weight matrix */
  avg[i] = item i's average rate;
  for (each item i)
    for (each user u)
      Weight_Matrix[u][i] = A + B *
fabs(Rating_Matrix[u][i]-avg[i]);

  /* Caculate the similarity of items */
  Simirarity_Matrix =
Simirarity_Matrix_Calculation(Method, Weight_Matrix,
Rating_Matrix);

  /* Predict the rating and generate recommendation
*/
  Rating_Matrix = Rating_Prediction(Rating_Matrix);
  Recommendation_Grenerate();
}

Matrix Simirarity_Matrix_Calculation(Method,
Weight_Matrix, Rating_Matrix)
{
  if (Method = Cosine) {
  /* Calculate the similarities using the optimized
Cosine method */
  } else if (Method = Adjusted_Cosine) {
  /* Calculate the similarities using the optimized
Adjusted_Cosine method */
  } else if (Method = Person) {
  /* Calculate the similarities using the optimized
Person method */
  }
  return Simirarity_Matrix;
}
```

4 Experiments

4.1 Environments and Datasets

We program both the traditional collaborative filtering recommendation algorithm and the optimized in C++ on a notebook computer. All experiments are under the environment of Windows7@Home Premium 64 bit, Intel(R) Core(TM) i7-4710MQ CPU @ 2.50 GHz, 8 GB RAM@1600 MHz, 480 GB SSD hard disk. We also download the movieLens dataset (https://grouplens.org/datasets/movielens/), collected by GroupLens Research of UMN, as a testing dataset, which consists of 100,000 ratings form 943 users on 1682 movies, and each user rated at least 20 movies.

The experiment first tests out a pair of optimal α and β, and then compared with the traditional algorithm. S is the total number of the nearest neighbors. We use RMSE (Root Mean Square Error) as the evaluation criterion of two algorithms, and a lower value means a higher accuracy [13].

4.2 Experimental Results and Analysis

As shown in Figs. 2, 3, 4 and 5, the RMSE value of the optimization algorithm is generally lower than the traditional algorithm, which means our optimization algorithm is more accurate. As shown in Figs. 6 and 7, though the RMSE value of the optimization algorithm is higher when the number of nearest neighbors is small. With increasing of nearest neighbors, the RMSE value becomes lower, which proves the accuracy and the number of nearest neighbor is positive correlated in our optimized algorithm.

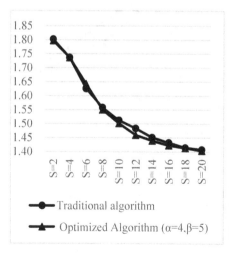

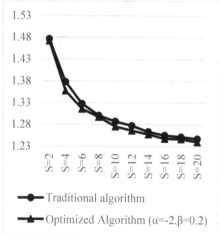

Fig. 2. RMSE of UserCF with cosine method vs its optimized version

Fig. 3. RMSE of ItemCF with cosine method vs its optimized version

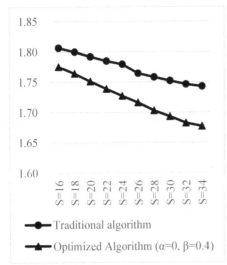

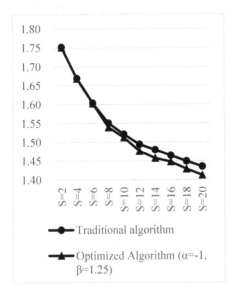

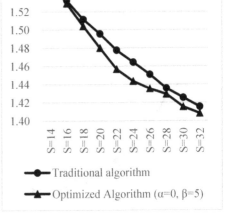

Fig. 4. RMSE of UserCF with correlation method vs its optimized version

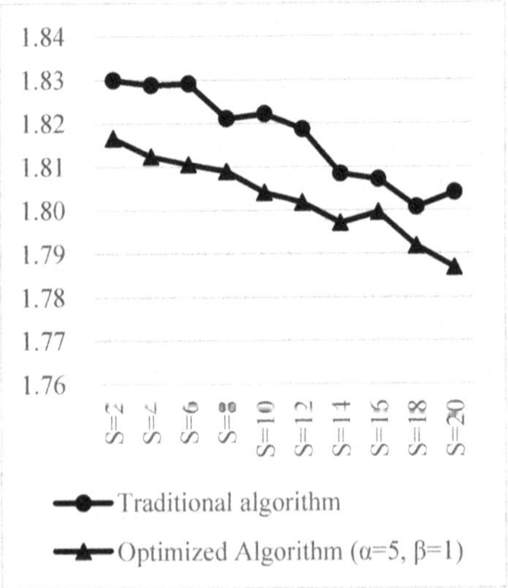

Fig. 5. RMSE of ItemCF with correlation method vs its optimized version

Fig. 6. RMSE of UserCF with adjusted cosine method vs its optimized version

Fig. 7. RMSE of ItemCF with adjusted cosine method vs its optimized version

5 Conclusion and Future Work

In this paper, we proposed a new collaborative filtering algorithm based on score classification. The algorithm first takes the correlation between the extreme rating and user's interests into account, and adds weights in the similarity method to get a more accurate recommendation. Besides, we give both implementations of user-based and item-based algorithms. Experiments on movieLens dataset shows that our algorithm performs better than traditional algorithms, get more accurate rating predictions and more appropriate recommended results. However, the algorithm cannot work well with the data sparseness and cold start situation. The future work will pay more attention to modifying the algorithm so that it can solve the problems above.

Acknowledgments. This work was supported by the Research Innovation Fund for College Students of Beijing University of Posts, Telecommunication and Special Found for Beijing Common Construction Project, the National Natural Science Foundation of China (Nos. 61272515, 61171102, 61671081), National Science and Technology Pillar Program (2015BAH03F02).

References

1. Goldberg, D., Nichols, D., Oki, B.M., Terry, D.: Using collaborative filtering to weave an information tapestry. Commun. ACM **35**(12), 61–70 (1992)
2. Langseth, H., Nielsen, T.D.: A latent model for collaborative filtering. Int. J. Approx. Reason. **53**(4), 447–466 (2012)
3. Ba, Q.: The recommendation technology research based on user attribute clustering and SVD algorithm. Beijing University of Posts and Telecommunications, Beijing (2013)
4. Shi, M.: Research of personalized internet advertising recommended system based RSS. Huazhong University of Science and Technology, Wuhan (2008)
5. Sun, X.: Research of sparsity and cold start problem in collaborative filtering. Zhejiang University, Hangzhou (2005)
6. Hu, R., Dou, W., Liu, J.: ClubCF: a clustering-based collaborative filtering approach for big data application. IEEE Trans. Emerg. Top. Comput. **2**(3), 302–313 (2014)
7. Shinde, R.U., Raut, S.D.: Typicality-based collaborative filtering recommendation system. Int. J. Innov. Res. Comput. Commun. Eng. (IJIRCCE) **4**(6), 12498–12504 (2016)
8. Katarya, R., Verma, O.P.: Effective collaborative movie recommender system using asymmetric user similarity and matrix factorization. In: The International Conference on Computing, Communication and Automation (ICCCA) (2016)
9. Leng, Y., Lu, Q., Liang, C.: Survey of recommendation based on collaborative filtering. PR AI **27**(8), 720–734 (2014)
10. Ren, K., Qian, X.: Research on user similarity measure method in collaborative filtering algorithm. Comput. Eng. **41**(8), 18–23 (2015)
11. Yan, D.M., Lu, C.H.: Optimized collaborative filtering recommendation based on user's interest degree and feature. Appl. Res. Comput. **29**(2), 497–501 (2012)
12. Xu, X., Wang, X.: Optimization method of similarity degree in collaborative filter algorithm. Comput. Eng. **36**(6), 52–54 (2010)
13. Su, Y.-Q.: Collaborative filtering algorithm improvement and research. Softw. Guide **14**(2), 74–78 (2015)

FluteDB: An Efficient and Dependable Time-Series Database Storage Engine

Chen Li$^{(\boxtimes)}$, Jianxin Li, Jinghui Si, and Yangyang Zhang

Department of Computer Science, Beihang University, Beijing, China
{lichen,lijx,sijh,zhangyy}@act.buaa.edu.cn

Abstract. Recently, with the widespread use of large-scale sensor network, time-series data is vastly generated and requires to be processed. Those traditional databases, however, show their limitations in storage when handling such a large stream data. Besides, the actual dependability of databases are also difficult to be guaranteed. In this paper, we present FluteDB, an efficient and dependable time-series database storage engine, which is composed of multiple time-series enhanced sub-modules. The validations of all sub-modules have demonstrated that our improved strategies significantly outperform the existing methods in real time-series environment. Meanwhile, the complete FluteDB utilizes various measures to guarantee its dependability and achieves a higher overall storage efficiency than the state-of-the-art time-series databases.

Keywords: Time-series · Database storage · Resource cost
Data compression · Dependability

1 Introduction

Since the multimedia data sampling devices are widely available nowadays, the scale of time-series data has thus expanded drastically [1, 2, 6, 7, 9, 10]. Meanwhile, with the increase in demand for real-time compute, the sampling interval of vast sensors, monitors and other devices has immensely shortened. Such situations directly lead to the vast growth in the scale of time-series data, and the traditional storage engine (SE) cannot meet the requirement for storing such large volume of data. Although the distributed databases are partially able to fulfil the data requirement, their storage and compute resources are still wasted due to the specific characteristics of time-series, such as high redundancy and large scale [1].

To solve these problems, this paper firstly designs and realizes a hybrid compression strategy integrated with different compression methods, which not only reduces the storage resources cost but also provides assistance for the follow-up machine learning task (e.g. cycle mining) [9]. Then, combined with the cache strategy, a flexible triggered batch-operations mechanism is proposed to ensure a high write ability for the entire SE under an acceptable query latency. In addition, we optimize the overall cache mechanism to promote the write ability of

G. Wang et al. (Eds.): SpaCCS 2017 Workshops, LNCS 10658, pp. 446–456, 2017.
https://doi.org/10.1007/978-3-319-72395-2_41

the complete SE based on the characteristics of time-series indirectly. Among them, we also establish a comprehensive fault-tolerant mechanism to ensure the dependability of the complete SE [1, 6, 7].

To sum up, the main contribution of our work is that FluteDB, an efficient and dependable time-series database SE has been proposed, and each time-series enhanced sub-module of it has been proven effective in independent tests. Furthermore, the overall experimental results show that FluteDB outperforms the state-of-the-art method in the real large-scale time-series application environment.

This paper is organized as follows. Section 2 introduces the existing databases and the improved methods for time-series. Section 3 gives the definition and specifies the characteristics of time-series data. Moreover, the key challenges for processing time-series data are briefly presented. Sections 4 and 5 present FluteDB and analyze its dependability and experimental results in detail. Section 6 concerns the conclusions of this work.

2 Related Work

Continuous interests in the management of time-series data have been observed in the field of the database for decades [1, 2, 6, 7, 9]. Due to its immense growth and valuable implicit knowledge, people have begun to pay much more attention to explore how to efficiently and steadily read and write time-series data at present.

The traditional Relational Database Management System (RDBMS) (e.g. PostgreSQL, MySQL) does not perform well while dealing with time-series data. Because its write efficiency is positively correlated with the data scale [3, 4]. Specifically, massive time-series data not only makes the unoptimized indexing to update much more frequently, but also leads the continuous files to be written in different locations of the disk resulting since the random write mechanism.

In response, some improved database services based on Not Only Structured Query Language (NoSQL) (e.g. MongoDB, Casandra) or specialized customized Time-Series Data Databases (TSDB) (e.g. OpenTSDB, InfluxDB) are presented in succession [1, 2]. Such databases' SE supports horizontal scalability, which has higher write ability and facilitates retrieval by using column-oriented or document-oriented indexing and storage mechanism. However, their high redundancy mechanism, simple compression strategy and other unoptimized modules make the entire database system occupy too many storage resources and even indirectly reduce their throughput capacity [6, 7].

In addition, some improved file systems such as HDFS can also be used to store time-series data, but the complexity of its retrieval, data backfill, too large immutable data blocks and other factors lead to its low efficiency in the practical application.

In this paper, we have focus on optimizing the overall SE by modifying relevant sub-modules based on time-series. Experiments conducted here has proved that FluteDB, with a high write ability, drastically reduces the storage resource cost and satisfies the follow-up special needs of data (e.g. machine learning, compressed sensing) and dependability requirements [9].

3   Time-Series Data and Key Challenges

Time-series data has extensive sources (such as the sensors on Internet of Thing, Smart City) and is valuable for further analyzing and extracting meaningful statistical characteristics from it. As a series of data points with fixed meaning in chronological order, time-series data can be represented as $C = (t_1, v_1), (t_2, v_2), \cdots, (t_n, v_n)$, where t_i denotes the sampling time and v_i are the corresponding observation values.

However, as illustrated in Table 1, to store time-series data efficiently will still face several key challenges. First, working steadily in a high write rate state[1] is an important guarantee for efficient large-scale SE [1,6]. However, how to meet such a high write rate requirement under limited conditions, needs to be considered carefully. Secondly, since time-series data is highly redundant and massive, its direct storage will cause the unnecessary waste of storage resources and lead to a long delay during write or read operations, which is particularly serious in large-scale, multi-copy storage systems [7]. Hence, the reduction of compute and storage resources cost is an indispensable work of the time-series data SE [10,11]. Thirdly, as a preparation for the corresponding downstream tasks, the time-series data SE needs to be flexible and dependable enough to be capable of adapting to different application scenarios. Meanwhile, due to its particularity, the dependability of the time-series data SE is distinct from that of general storage systems. How to balance the efficiency and the dependability legitimately is an major problem that cannot be neglected.

Table 1. Several real examples of time-series data.

Data source	Time stamp t_i	Observation values v_i
Temperature sensor	1401335396.997 s	+46.5 °C
	1401335397.998 s	+46.4 °C
	1401335399.002 s	+46.4 °C
	...	...
Smart grid	1363894780 s	(220.15 V, 50 Hz, 2.768×10^{-6} kW/h)
	1363894781 s	(219.95 V, 50 Hz, 2.883×10^{-6} kW/h)
	1363894782 s	(220.85 V, 49.4 Hz, 2.425×10^{-6} kW/h)
	...	...
Road monitor	2016-09-11T17:20:48.134Z	09204821c7c2.jpg
	2016-09-11T17:20:49.635Z	092049dc62ad.jpg
	2016-09-11T17:20:51.011Z	09205135e380.jpg
	...	...

---

[1] Write rate is a quantitative measurement of the storage ability.

4   Design of FluteDB

In this section, FluteDB and its architecture will be elaborated in detail. Figure 1 briefly shows the specific architecture of the FluteDB and demonstrates the data relationships between different sub-modules.

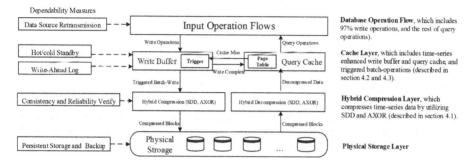

Fig. 1. The hierarchical structure and sub-module interaction of FluteDB.

4.1   Time-Series Compression

The main purpose of data compression is to reduce the resource cost, which is especially obvious in the large-scale database environment. Compared with the traditional data compression task, time-series data, on the one hand, has some special additional constraints for time-series compression owing to its special characteristics, but on the other, it is properly relaxed in other common constraints as well. To obtain the best compression efficiency, we respectively adopt the suited compression strategies to the corresponding object based on its numeric characteristics [6].

Time stamps compression. The time stamp $t_0, t_1, \cdots, t_n$ is a monotonically increasing sequence. And the delta between t_{i-1}, t_i is roughly fixed since the intervals of most sampling sources are fixed[2]. Hence, rather than storing the whole time stamp, only storing a delta of deltas is able to save a lot of resources and does not significantly increase the compression and decompression time.

Specifically, we encode the time stamp into blocks by utilizing an improved variable length encoding algorithm named Sliced Delta of Deltas (SDD). As described in Table 2, we pre-establish the delta between two continuous sampling points as $1000\,\mu s$, and the delta of deltas is much smaller than original delta obviously. In order to further minimize the compression rate, we store the true form of delta of deltas in fixed-size slices[3], which is able to reduce the use of the flag bits (if the slice is the last slice of a value, its first bit is set to bit '1',

---

[2] Though the interval of data sampling is not specified, it will be limited in a fixed range according its own streaming and large-scale characteristics.

[3] The size of slice is determined by the average size of delta of the deltas.

Table 2. An example for SDD.

Time stamp (µs)	Delta of Delta (µs)	SDD Code
1452202444 009 003	-	-
1452202444 010 028	25	0011 1001
1452202444 011 031	3	1011

otherwise the first bit is set to bit '0'). As shown in Table 2, we select four bit as the length of single slice. So we can directly encode the binary code of 25 as 011001 (the first bit is sign bit), and further divide it into two slices, 0011 and 1001.

The theoretical compression ratio as shown in Eq. 1, where $length(\cdot)$ denotes the number of bits of the corresponding numeric, $f(\cdot)$ is the function of SDD, $size\_of(\cdot)$ is the length of t_i (e.g. int, float and so on).

$$
\begin{aligned}
compression\_ratio_{SDD} &= \frac{size\_of(file_{compressed})}{size\_of(file)} \\
&= \frac{length(t_0) + length(\delta t) + \sum_{i=1}^{n} f(\delta\delta t_i, t_i, t_{i-1}, l_b)}{\sum_{i=0}^{n} size\_of(t_i)},
\end{aligned}
\tag{1}
$$

Observation values compression. In addition to the time stamp compression, we also compress the observation values. Apparently, as real data collected by sensors or other devices, observation values are still continuous like time stamp. However, the delta between two continuous sampling points is not stable, which means the variance of delta become much larger. Therefore, we present a novel algorithm AXOR by considering the data characteristics and calculation complexity to achieve efficient compression. Likewise, we still use variable length encoding to compress the observation values. Due to the type of observation values are mostly double, we felicitously and efficiently compresses the XOR values between continuous observation values.

As a real instance in Table 3, we will introduce AXOR step by step. In the compression process, we encode the input value into double representation, approximately set the trailing bits of its double representation to 0 (the number of variation bits is shown in Eq. 2), and ensure its approximate error to be limited at $1 \times 10^{-(n+2)}$,

$$
n_{omitted\_bits} = l_{decimals} - \lfloor \log_2 observation\_values \rfloor - \lceil \log_2 10^{n+2} \rceil,
\tag{2}
$$

where n denotes the precision of the initial input value, $l_{decimals}$ is the length of decimal part in double representation (default value is 52). Then, we calculate a simple XOR between the current and previous values, and break the XOR'd value into three parts, which includes the meaningful code's start position, length and specific content (meaningful part denotes the code between first '1' and last '1' in XOR binary value). Of course, there are three control bits to explain the

Table 3. An example for AXOR.

Original data	Approximate double representation	XOR with previous	Control bits	Start point	Length	Meaningful code
40.687612	0x40445803AB800000					
40.673564	0x4044563758400000	0x00000E34F3C00000	111	10101	010110	111000110100111001111
40.723569	0x40445C9DE8A00000	0x00000AAAB0E00000	101	-	010111	10101010101010110000111
40.583876	0x40444ABC72E00000	0x000016219A400000	100	-	-	1011000100001001101001
0.000000	-	-	000	-	-	-
40.892842	0x40447248A5800000	0x000038F4D7600000	101	-	011001	11100011101001101011011

following codes. The first bit indicates whether the XOR'd value is 0, the second bit denotes whether the meaningful bits start at the same position as previous bits, and the final bit means whether the length of the meaningful bits are same as the previous ones.

Both of SDD (lossless) and AXOR (approximate lossless) are compressed in an unit of database blocks, and the compressed information is stored in the block header of the data file. In addition, in order to ensure the dependability, consistency and completeness of the compressed data, we add the check code behind the tail of each block. Experimental results (in Sect. 5) show that SDD and AXOR can efficiently compress the time-series data. Besides, our compressed result can be easily converted into other compressed formats (e.g. PAA, APCA) for downstream tasks [12].

4.2 Triggered Batch-Operations

When database stores such large-scale time-series data, it has to run under a high write rate state, which requires SE to have higher data writing capability [1]. So we design a novel and flexible commit strategy to enhance the write rate sharply and promote the query performance to a certain extent, which is shown in Fig. 1. Specifically, we pre-process and put the input time-series data in the cache, then use a dynamic triggering mechanism to appropriately write the cached data into the database in batches. The trigger has three triggering conditions, read operation, time threshold and space threshold, which means that only too long time interval for cached data or too big cached size will trigger the follow-up batch-operations.

For sure, batch-write operations commit a continuous period of time-series data at once will greatly reduce the calculation complexity of the structural change of indexing tree[4] [10]. Meanwhile, since the query operations of time-series data generally focus on recent hot data, putting the hot data into write cache (will be described in Sect. 4.3) in batches is conducive to reduce the cache replacement ratio and disk read rate. At last, batch-operations facilitate the implementation of the time-series data compression method mentioned in

---

[4] Our method, which is a partial sequential operation strategy, is different from LSM Tree [8].

Sect. 4.1, and it is possible to ensure that the physical storage locations of consecutive time-series data blocks are adjacent to each other, when the data block is written to disk (the random write mechanism of the hard disk causes the sector to be replaced frequently when the range query of time-series data takes place) [1].

Finally, we need to consider the risk of data dependability brought by this batch-operations. Since we will temporarily store the input data in memory, the necessary measures for fault tolerance are also essential[5]. So we record the Write-Ahead Log (WAL) to ensure the data can be recovered based on persistent storage in the equipment from the vast majority of errors. Meanwhile, WAL can also ensure the consistency of data between cache and disk. Experiments (in Sect. 5) show that triggered batch-operations can significantly improve the write efficiency at the expense of partial read efficiency (read operations are only a small part of time-series operations).

4.3   Cache Mechanism

Data caching is one of the important measures to improve database performance. Particularly in the application environment of time-series, a suited cache mechanism can optimize the efficiency of data retrieval and write operation by reducing the number of times of operating disk. Specifically, the objects of time-series query operations are separated into hot and cold data very separately (the querying frequency of data is inversely proportional to its generated time), and the form of query operations is mainly limited to point query and region query. So we design a multiple cache structure in memory for realizing batch-operations described in Sect. 4.2 and adapting of the time-series characteristics (as shown in Fig. 1). This means that we firstly query in write cache when cache misses, and trigger its batch-write operations. If query is hit in write cache, the query response is returned directly, and the corresponding block will be loaded into the cache after the batch-write operations are completed. Otherwise, this operation will query in the indexing of physical storage. On this basis, we also improve the original cache replacement strategy by modifying the replace unit, which means that we no longer load a single block into cache, but a number of continuous data blocks. And we also replace the corresponding number of blocks of data (not necessarily continuous) each time in accordance with the improved original replacement algorithm.

Because our improved replacement strategy can load continuous hot data into cache at once, the hit rate, efficiency of read and write operations are significantly enhanced, despite the overall number of read and write operations do not change. In order to verify our design, we modify a number of existing replacement algorithms by using the same improvement. The experimental results (in Sect. 5) show that our method can significantly improve the hit rate and the overall efficiency, and the time-series enhanced Clock outperforms best among the several algorithms. Meanwhile, to guarantee the basic dependability of cache,

---

[5] An ability to respond the possible node or Information Data Center (IDC) failure.

we partially follow the original fault tolerance mechanism, which mainly includes the mentioned log mechanism and persistent operations. In fact, we found that time-series data has more advantages than normal data on storage dependability when we investigated it. Because most sensors have their own cache for responding the IDC's requests again.

5   Experiments

In this section, we will perform experiments with the algorithms presented above, including the independent experiments of each time-series enhanced sub-module and the overall performance and dependability of FluteDB. In addition, all of the experiments in this section run at a single point by default.

5.1   Independent Experiments

Compression algorithms. In order to test the compression ability of SDD and AXOR when they process real time-series data, we select the real-time information of taxis in New York as input time-series data. This dataset contains 100,000 pieces of data, and its time stamp is formatted in millisecond UNIX timestamps, the observation value denotes the taxi's real-time direction information.

In the compression, we set the default delta of SDD to average delta in single storage block, and the slice size is four bit. As the contrast algorithms, we choose four commonly used compression algorithms to compress the same time-series data. The experimental results as illustrated in Table 4, our method outperforms other compression algorithms in compression ratio. Moreover, the compression and decompression time is also acceptable and competitive.

Similarly, we also compress the time-series observation values, and the result is shown in the Table 5. Through observing the result, we are still optimal at the compression rate, and reach an acceptable standard of compression and decompression.

Triggered batch-operations. To check the efficiency of proposed strategy in Sect. 4.2, we selected several sequential operations from the operational log of

Table 4. Comparison of different compression methods for compressing 100,000 time stamps.

Compression method	Compression ratio	Compression time	Decompression time
RLE [13]	95.63%	0.6635 ms	**0.9754 ms**
LZ77 [12]	61.46%	1.7367 ms	2.9964 ms
Delta	35.06%	**0.4391 ms**	1.1078 ms
Original DD [6]	18.74%	0.5433 ms	1.2127 ms
SDD	**11.01%**	0.6468 ms	1.2931 ms

Table 5. Comparison of different compression methods for compressing 100,000 observation values.

Compression method	Compression ratio	Compression time	Decompression time
RLE [13]	98.84%	0.7362 ms	**0.9535 ms**
LZ77 [12]	68.43%	1.8453 ms	3.4363 ms
Delta	77.54%	**0.5884 ms**	1.0435 ms
XOR [6]	48.48%	0.8582 ms	1.5324 ms
AXOR	**43.98%**	0.7964 ms	1.3624 ms

the database (microblog) as dataset, which is composed of 96,384 write operations and 4,616 query operations. Most of the read operations in experimental dataset concentrated emergence from 60,000 to 80,000, which can be obviously found in experimental results (as shown in Figs. 2 and 3). That is to say, the efficiency of our method is inversely proportional to the sparse degree of the read operation to a certain extent. However, experimental results show that triggered batch-operations greatly improve the write efficiency (includes indexing insertion and write operation) of time-series data in general, and partial promote the performance for query operations.

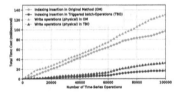

Fig. 2. Indexing insertion & write operation (physical)

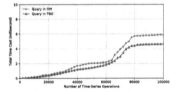

Fig. 3. Query operation

Cache mechanism. We selected some of commonly used cache page replacement algorithms to verify whether our design is valid. The experimental data still follow the dataset in the previous experiment. Moreover, we set the number of cache block to 400, the size of each replacement unit is four.

As shown in Figs. 4 and 5, we select LRU, OPT, CLOCK, LFU and LIRS five classic cache replacement algorithm and its corresponding time-series enhanced version (names as LRU-E and so on) as experimental objects [14]. The experimental results show that our design can greatly improve the hit rate and overall efficiency of read and write operations for each original algorithm for time-series data. And Clock-E is the most suited algorithm for time-series data.

5.2   Comprehensive Experiments

Our comprehensive experiment selects the real data from the Smart Grid as a time-series input, which contains 11,200,000 data in about 30 min. We hijack

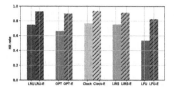

Fig. 4. Hit rate

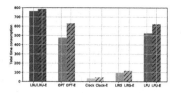

Fig. 5. Total time consumption

the original database services by adding our improvements to the PostgreSQL service as plug-ins and using Redis as a write cache, to achieve our improvements [4,5]. And then, we directly record the size of database file, the returning values of operation's *Timing* function and the times of calling replace function as the experimental data. The final comprehensive results as shown in the Table 6, our method outperforms the original database on most of indices in the real time-series data environment, where the average read time is also acceptable.

Table 6. The efficiency of the application of FluteDB in real single point time-series environment.

	Size of database file	Average time for write	Average time for querying	Cache hit rate
Original PostgreSQL	438.34 MB	0.043 ms	**0.564 ms**	85.38%
PostgreSQL (FluteDB)	**174.75 MB**	**0.019 ms**	0.614 ms	**92.47%**

At present, as a time-series data SE running on only a single node, we test the dependability of FluteDB by simulating some real faults (e.g. power outage, network failure). Due to the enhancement and modification of several functional sub-modules and the addition of appropriate dependability and consistency strategies, the cost of recovering data from redo log (WAL) and other persistent storage (hot/cold standby) is slightly increased, but acceptable.

6   Conclusion

As a popular research and analysis object, time-series data becomes much more valuable for further mining. Thus, this paper presents an efficient and dependable time-series SE designed for the characteristics of time-series. We modify several close sub-modules, which mainly includes hybrid compression algorithm, triggered batch-operations and improved cache mechanism, to achieve the overall promotion of the efficiency of SE. Especially, compared with the existing time-series data storage solutions, FluteDB is able to work with higher write rate, occupy less storage and compute resources, and have enough flexibility and dependability. Of course, the proposed strategies are only several important components of the time-series SE, so our future work will mainly focus on designing and implementing other optimizations (e.g. indexing mechanism) to improve the overall efficiency of the whole database system. Meanwhile, the storage and dependability strategy for time-series of distributed system are also worth further studying.

Acknowledgments. This work is supported by NSFC program (No. 61472022, 61421003), SKLSDE-2016ZX-11, and the Beijing Advanced Innovation Center for Big Data and Brain Computing.

References

1. TimescaleDB: SQL made scalable for time-series data. http://www.timescale.com/papers/timescaledb.pdf
2. Storage Engine of InfluxData. https://docs.influxdata.com/influxdb/v1.2/concepts/storage_engine/
3. The world's most popular open source database. https://www.mysql.com/
4. The world's most advanced open source database. https://www.postgresql.org/
5. An open source in-memory data structure store. https://redis.io/
6. Pelkonen, T., Franklin, S., Teller, J., Huang, Q., Cavallaro, P., Meza, J., Veeraraghavan, K.: Gorilla: a fast, scalable, in-memory time series database. PVLDB **8**(12), 1816–1827 (2015)
7. Rhea, S., Wang, E., Wong, E., Atkins, E., Storer, N.: LittleTable: a time-series database and its uses. In: Proceedings of SIGMOD, pp. 125–138. ACM Press, Chicago (2017)
8. Sears, R., Ramakrishnan, R.: bLSM: a general purpose log structured merge tree. In: Proceedings of SIGMOD, pp. 217–228. ACM Press, Scottsdale (2012)
9. Cai, Y., Tong, H., Fan, W., Ji, P., He, Q.: Facets: fast comprehensive mining of coevolving high-order time series. In: Proceedings of the 21th SIGKDD, pp. 79–88. ACM Press, Sydney (2015)
10. Papadopoulos, S., Datta, k., Madden, S., Mattson, T.: The TileDB array data storage manager. In: Proceedings of VLDB, pp. 349–360. Springer Press (2017)
11. Jermaine, C., Omiecinski, E., Yee, W.G.: The partitioned exponential file for database storage management. The VLDB J. **16**(4), 417–437 (2007)
12. Eamonn, J.K., Kaushik, C., Sharad, M., Michael, J.P.: Locally adaptive dimensionality reduction for indexing large time series databases. In: Proceedings of SIGMOD, pp. 151–162. ACM Press, California (2001)
13. Bassiouni, M.A.: Data compression in scientific and statistical databases. IEEE Trans. Softw. Eng. **SE–11**(10), 1047–1058 (2006)
14. Podlipnig, S., Böszörmenyi, L.: A survey of web cache replacement strategies. ACM Comput. Surv. **35**(4), 374–398 (2003)

Attacks on the Anti-collusion Data Sharing Scheme for Dynamic Groups in the Cloud

S. Milton Ganesh[1(✉)], Vijayakumar Pandi[1], L. Jegatha Deborah[1], and Md. Zakirul Alam Bhuiyan[2]

[1] University College of Engineering Tindivanam, Melpakkam,
Tindivanam 604001, Tamil Nadu, India
softengineermilton@gmail.com, vijibond2000@gmail.com,
blessedjeny@gmail.com
[2] Department of Computer and Information Sciences, Fordham University,
Bronx, NY 10458, USA
zakirulalam@gmail.com

Abstract. As the hype of the evolution of cloud computing has become a real possibility in the modern day outsourcing scenarios, users can benefit from cloud computing by uploading documents into the cloud servers for sharing it among a group of legitimate users. But, though cloud is a viable present day option for elastic storage facilities, its security is still a grave concern. Hence, in order to improve the secure communication among group members, Zhu and Jiang have proposed a protocol and claimed that key distribution to the group users can be done without any secure communication channels. They have claimed that their scheme is resistant to collusion attack and all the other attacks, thereby ensuring forward and backward secrecies as well. Firstly, in this research work, after extensive analysis, we have identified several issues in the protocol proposed by Zhu and Jiang which make it vulnerable to various attacks. Secondly, we have proved that an attacker can use the man-in-the-middle attack and break the protocol thereby getting the secret keys shared between the group manager and the group user. Thirdly, we have given enough proof that the scheme is vulnerable to message modification attack too. Finally, we claim that the earlier proposed protocol is not secure and a new protocol with improved security is the need of the hour.

Keywords: Security · Cloud storage · Mobile user · Key distribution
Man-in-the-middle attack

1 Introduction

Secure sharing of sensitive data across a group of users through Internet has become part and parcel of many applications [1]. Though this tradition of sharing data between multiple users has been in practice since a long time ago, this method has become indispensable with the advent of mobile phones and cloud computing [2]. For example, the manager of a software company wants to share a confidential document with the employees of the company. Since cloud supports elasticity for user access and storage provisions [3, 4], the manager stores the document in the cloud. Now, the manager is

© Springer International Publishing AG 2017
G. Wang et al. (Eds.): SpaCCS 2017 Workshops, LNCS 10658, pp. 457–467, 2017.
https://doi.org/10.1007/978-3-319-72395-2_42

responsible for protecting the document not only from intruders, but from the cloud service provider as well.

With the advent of cheap mobile phones with efficient android operating systems installed in high speed processors and primary memory, people preferring to access the applications stored in the cloud through mobile phones is not a surprise [5–7]. Nowadays, business houses often tend to move their business related documents to the cloud storage for efficient storage, retrieval and sharing the same with others [8].

Though the combination of mobile phones and cloud computing is a right mix, the vulnerability of cloud computing to attacks by hackers and intruders make the corporations to rethink their decisions to move their businesses to the cloud. The attacks on the cloud [9, 10] is very common and is still unsolved.

One of the most common attacks in cloud is that of a collusion attack, in which intruders and revoked users secretly cooperate with each other in order to break the system by exploiting its vulnerability in any possible way for acquiring the confidential data stealthily.

A collusion resistant data sharing among the members of a dynamic group in the public cloud was proposed recently by Zhu and Jiang [11]. They claim that, their scheme securely distributes the secret keys to the group members through insecure transmission channels.

But, as a consequence of the extensive analysis of the research work in [11], it has been identified that the scheme proposed by Zhu and Jiang is susceptible for Man-in-the-Middle (MITM) attack and the message modification attack. In this research work, we have presented our research findings and claim that the scheme proposed in [11] is not secure and hence further improvement in this direction is needed.

Ultimately, the objectives of this research paper can be summarized as follows:

1. To review the collusion attack resistant scheme for dynamic groups in the public cloud environments proposed by Zhu and Jiang [11],
2. To point out the issues in the scheme proposed by Zhu and Jiang [11],
3. To present an attack model and prove that the proposed scheme is insecure against MITM attack,
4. To design an attack strategy in order to prove that the scheme is vulnerable to Message Modification attack.

The rest of this research work is organized as follows. Section 2 reviews the works done relevant to sharing data among multiple users in untrusted environments in the recent past and points out their advantages and limitations. Section 3 presents a review of the existing protocol [11] proposed by Zhu and Jiang. Section 4 presents the issues in [11] and the proposed attack models to prove that the scheme is vulnerable to MITM and message modification attacks. Finally, Sect. 5 presents the conclusions and future research directions in this line of research.

2   Literature Survey

Many schemes have been proposed by authors in the recent past in order to provide secure group communication among the group members by averting attacks.

Kallahalla et al. [3] have proposed a secure storage technique in untrusted environments where dynamic join and leave operations happen frequently. The documents have been shared without any trust on the centralized server but involved server overhead due to the necessity to update file-block keys frequently.

Another work proposed by Goh et al. [12] efficiently distributed the keys with simple revocation procedure through out-of-band communications. Boneh et al. [13] had invented two schemes to protect the system against colluders. One of the schemes kept the ciphertext and the private keys of constant size while the other kept a trade-off between the two. The drawback of this scheme is that a new key needs to be computed for each join or leave operation.

Goyal et al. [14] had put forward a new mechanism which introduced Key-Policy Attribute-Based Encryption (KP-ABE) and Lu et al. [15] proposed a system based on secure provenance and the encryption techniques based on security policies.

Vijayakumar et al. [16] had proposed a key-star-based novel and secure multicast key distribution technique based on the Chinese Remainder Theorem by keeping the computational complexity at bare minimum of $O(1)$. But, a new group key has to be computed which can substantially drain the energy level of battery in mobile phone scenarios.

Liu et al. [17] introduced a successful scheme called Mona for secure sharing of document among group members and Zhou et al. [18] provided a role based access control scheme for the shared documents and the scheme introduced by Zou et al. [19] makes effective use of access control polynomials to efficiently distribute the secret keys among the users of the dynamic group.

Zhu and Jiang [11] have recently proposed a secure data sharing scheme for dynamic member based groups in the cloud and they have proved that secret keys for encryption and decryption can be sent securely through insecure communication channels. But, to their disappointment, the scheme can be broken using the MITM attack and the message modification attack.

Thus, compared to most of the protocols in the literature, the protocol recently proposed by Zhu and Jiang in 2016 seems to provide secure key distribution under insecure communication channels. The basic reason for selecting this protocol among other contemporary works is that, it is one of the novel works proposed to enhance the security of secure document storage and retrieval from the cloud servers. This work is also a sequel to their earlier work in 2013 which proposed a protocol called Mona which allows a user to anonymously share data in the cloud servers with other users. Firstly, an extensive review of their work is performed to analyze the issues in their protocol. An attempt to attack the system based on the MITM attack actually breaks the system and makes it vulnerable. Moreover, message modification attack can be used to break the security of the system. Hence, a thorough analysis of the existing system is done in this research manuscript along with the corresponding attack models so that a new version of the protocol can be reinvented in the future with more security provisions.

3   Review of the Existing Scheme

The scheme proposed by Zhu and Jiang [11] consists of six phases such as Initialization of the system, Group user registration phase, File upload phase by the mobile user, File download phase by the mobile user, registration phase for a new mobile user and user revocation phase.

3.1   Initialization of the System

The group manager takes responsibility for initializing the parameters of the bilinear system and distributing it in the public domain. It consists of the following steps:

1. The group manager proposes a bilinear map system which consists of $S = (q, G_1, G_2, e(., .))$ where G_1 and G_2 are additive cyclic groups based on the same prime order q and $e : G_1 \times G_2 \rightarrow G_2$.
2. The group manager randomly selects two points P and G from the additive cyclic group G_1 and also selects γ from Z_q^*.
3. Computes three parameters such that $W = \gamma.P$, $Y = \gamma.G$ and $Z = e(G, P)$.
4. The group manager publishes the parameters such as $S, P, W, Y, Z, f, f_1, Enc()$ where f is a hash function: $\{0, 1\}^* \rightarrow Z_q^*$, f_1 is also a hash function $\{0, 1\}^* \rightarrow G_1$ and $Enc()$ is a symmetric encryption algorithm.

The group manager keeps the parameters such as G and γ as secret parameters.

3.2   Group User Registration Phase

Both the group manager and an existing user participate in this phase. The group user requests for registration in the group. The group manager and the user perform the following steps for achieving this.

1. The user sends (ID_i, pk, v_1, ac) as a request to the group manager in which ID_i is the identity of the user, pk is the public key of the user, v_1 is a random number from the group Z_q^* and ac refers to the account number pertaining to the payment by the user to the cloud service provider.
2. After receiving the request from the user, the group manager chooses a random number r from Z_q^* and computes $R = e(P, P)^r$ and $U = (r + \gamma.v_1.f(pk\|ac\|ID_i)).P$ and sends the newly computed parameters U and R to the user who has sent the registration request.
3. The user verifies the received parameters U, R by ascertaining whether $R.e(v_1.f(pk\|ac\|ID_i).P, W)$ equals $e(U, P)$. By verifying this, the mobile user confirms that the parameters have come from the legitimate group manager. Now, the cloud user sends $ID_i, v_2, AENC_{sk}(ID_i, v_1, ac)$ where v_2 is a random number from Z_q^*, sk is the secret key to the corresponding public key of the user and $AENC()$ is an asymmetric encryption algorithm.
4. After receiving the above parameters, the group manager decrypts $AENC_{pk}(ID_i, v_1, ac)$ using the public key of the user received in the first step and

compares the ID_i with the one in the message and also with the ID_i received in the first step. Also, the group manager compares the decrypted v_1 with the v_1 received in the first step. On successful verification, the group manager randomly selects x_i from Z_q^* and computes $A_i = \frac{1}{\gamma + x_i}.P$, $B_i = \frac{x_i}{\gamma + x_i}.G$ and $V_i = f(B_i)$. Now, the group manager sends $AENC_{pk}(KEY, v_2)$ to the user where $KEY = (x_i, A_i, B_i)$. Moreover, the group manager stores (x_i, A_i, v_i, ID_i) in the local storage and adds (A_i, x_i) to the group user list which contains the identity of the group, corresponding to all the users in the group, timestamp to ascertain the freshness of the list and the group manager's signature. Also, the group manager sends the group user list to the cloud server.

5. The mobile user, after receiving the message $AENC_{pk}(KEY, v_2)$ from the group manager, decrypts it using the private key and stores (x_i, A_i, B_i) for encryption and decryption purposes.

6. The cloud server, on receiving the updated group user list from the group manager verifies the authenticity of the group manager by checking the equation $e(W, f_1(UL)) = e(P, sig(UL))$.

3.3   File Upload Phase

The steps for the file upload phase are as follows.

1. The group member selects an identity ID_{data} for the data file to be uploaded to the cloud server and also selects an random number k from Z_q^*. Then computes $C_1 = k.Y \in G_1, C_2 = k.P \in G_1, K = Z^k \in G_2$ and $C = Enc_K(M)$. Now, the group member sends $Enc_{B_i}(ID_{data}, C_1, C_2, C, t_{data})$ to the group manager where t_{data} is the timestamp.

2. The group manager now decrypts as $Dec_{B_i}(Enc_{B_i}(ID_{data}, C_1, C_2, C, t_{data}))$ using the B_i of the corresponding user. After that, the group manager constructs $\{W_0, \ldots W_m\} = \{G^{a_0}, \ldots G^{a_m}\}$ based on the polynomial function $f_p(x) = \prod_{j=1}^m (x - V_j) = \sum_{i=0}^m a_i x^i (mod\, q)$. Also, the group manager selects K_r from Z_q^* for re-encrypting the document received from the mobile group user and hides K_r as $EK = \{K_r.W_0, \ldots W_m\}$. Now, the group manager computes $CE = \{C_1, C_2, C\}_{K_r}$ and sends $DF = (ID_{group}, ID_{data}, CE, EK, t_{data}), \sigma_{DF}$ to the cloud server where $\sigma_{DF} = \gamma.f_1(DF)$ representing the signature of the group manager. Moreover, the group manager adds the current $ID_{data}, t_{data}, sig(DL), t_{DL}$ to the data list and sends the list to the cloud server. The cloud server verifies the identity by checking $e(W, f_1(DF)) = e(P, \sigma_{DF})$.

3.4   File Download Phase

The following steps achieve this scenario.

1. To download the document from the cloud server, the cloud user sends $ID_{group}, ID_i, Enc_{A_i}(ID_{data})$ to the cloud server.

2. The cloud server decrypts $Enc_{A_i}(ID_{data})$. If the A_i matches with the A_i in the list represented by ID_{group}, then it sends $DF = (ID_{group}, ID_{data}, CE, EK, t_{data}), \sigma_{DF}$ to the cloud user along with the data list DL.

3. Now, the cloud user verifies the authenticity of the cloud server by $e(W, f_1(DF)) = e(P, \sigma_{DF})$. The cloud user computes $V_i = f(B_i)$ and substitues V_i in the polynomial equation $K_r.W_0.\Pi_{j=1}^m (W_j)^{V_i^j} = K_r.G^{f_p(V_i)} = K_r$ constructed based on the parameters in EK which yields the re-encryption key K_r. Using K_r, the mobile cloud user decrypts CE to get C_1, C_2, C. Now, the cloud user finds the key K using the equation $K = e(C_1, A)e(C_2, B)$. Finally, the cloud user decrypts C such that $Dec_K[C] = M$, where M refers to the actual file uploaded by the data owner.

3.5   User Revocation Phase

To remove a user i with the identity ID_i, the group manager does the following:

1. First of all, the group manager removes the group user from the group user list in the local storage space. If there are m members in the list, the group manager constructs the polynomial equation based on the m members such that $f(p)'(x) = \Pi_{j \neq i j=1}^m (x - V_j) = \sum_{j=0}^{m-1} a_j x^j (mod \ q)$. A new random re-encryption key K_r' is selected and the exponential function becomes $\{K_r'.W_0, \ldots W_{m-1}\} = \{K_r'.G^{a_0}, \ldots G^{a_{m-1}}\}$.

2. The group manager downloads the cipher text from the cloud server and re-encrypts as $CE = \{C_1, C_2, C\}_{K_r'}$. Now, the new $DF = (ID_{group}, ID_{data}, CE, EK, t_{data}'), \sigma_{DF}$ is uploaded to the cloud server where t_{data}' is the new timestamp and σ_{DF} is the new signature.

3. Now, the cloud server verifies the signature by $e(W, f_1(DF)) = e(P, \sigma_{DF})$ and if successful, the new file is stored in the cloud replacing the existing one.

4. The group manager updates the data list for all the ID_{data} using the new time stamp.

The new user registration phase is more or less same as that of the existing user registration phase.

4   Issues and Attacks on the Existing Scheme

The proposed protocol in [11] has strong vulnerabilities which are listed below. For a valid representation of the vulnerability in the existing scheme, the following assumptions have been made based on the previous works.

Assumption 1: All the messages transmitted between the sender and receiver are sent through insecure channels. Hence, if there is vulnerability in the protocol, the attacker can easily make use of the loop hole.

Assumption 2: The attacker has access to the parameters such as P, R. So, if an attacker wants to successfully impersonate the group manager, he has to successfully compute $U = (r + \gamma.v_1.f(pk\|ac\|ID_i)).P$ for an unknown value of $\gamma \in Z_q^*$. But, it cannot be successful, since it contradicts the Decisional Diffie-Hellman Problem.

Assumption 3: The group user sends a random number $v_1 \in Z_q^*$ and also sends the same $v_1 \in Z_q^*$ encrypted using his private key as $ID_i, v_2, AENC_{sk}(ID_i, v_1, ac)$. The attacker has access to both v_1 and v_2.

Assumption 4: The group manager generates the key such that $KEY = (x_i, A_i, B_i)$. Then, he encrypts it using the public key of the mobile user as $AENC_{pk}(KEY, v_2)$ and sends the encrypted message to the group user. Since the private key is possessed only by the group user, there is no point of key being revealed to attackers and hackers.

4.1 Issues Identified in Protocol [11] Proposed by Zhu and Jiang

Based on the review provided above and after extensive analysis of the work proposed by Zhu and Jiang [11], we have identified the following issues.

Issue 1

In step 1 of the group user registration phase, a legitimate group user who wants to upload document sends (ID_i, pk, v_1, ac) without any encryption in the vulnerable transmission channels. Hence, an attacker either passive or active, may listen to this communication, can get hold of this information for the request for registration. Since the identity of the mobile user is publicly accessible, an attacker can easily come to know if a person with high confidential data is part of the group. If an attacker is interested in learning who is part of the data sharing process, he can easily listen to it.

Issue 2

During the first step of the registration process, the group manager receives the public key of the user. During the fourth step of the registration process, the group manager validates the genuineness of the user by decrypting $AENC_{sk}(ID_i, v_1, ac)$ using the public key of the user received from user in the first step and comparing the ID_i in the decrypted message with the one received in the first step. Also, after this verification, the public key pk becomes a valid and negotiated public key. In this case, if this is to be used as a negotiated public key, then divulging this is not recommended.

Issue 3

Since the registration request (ID_i, pk, v_1, ac) in the first step of the registration process is sent as plaintext, there is a chance that an attacker can replace his public key in place of pk and hence there exists a subtle chance for the MITM attack.

4.2 Attack 1

Let us assume that an adversary or an attacker replaces the public key present in (ID_i, pk, v_1, ac) with his own public key as (ID_i, pk_a, v_1, ac) where pk_a is the public key of the attacker. The group manager without checking the validity of the pk_a against the identity of the user, proceeds to the computation of U, R. This paves the way for the MITM attack.

Let us analyze the impact of this MITM attack in detail.

Impersonating a legitimate user in the registration process
An attacker may perform the following steps through impersonation to attack the system proposed by Zhu and Jiang [11].

1. In the first step of the registration process, a legitimate user sends the message (ID_i, pk, v_1, ac). Here, the attacker replaces pk by his public key pk_a and sends (ID_i, pk_a, v_1, ac) to the group manager.
2. The group manager computes $U = (r + \gamma.v_1.f(pk_a\|ac\|ID_i)).P$ and $R = e(P, P)^r$ as per the second step of the registration process and sends U, R to the legitimate user. But, the attacker who is present in between the legitimate user and the group manager, captures U and R.
3. The attacker knows that $U = (r + \gamma.v_1.f(pk_a\|ac\|ID_i)).P$ can be rewritten as $U = r.P + \gamma.P.v_1.f(pk_a\|ac\|ID_i)$. But, as per the third step of the initialization phase, $W = \gamma.P$ which yields $U = (r.P) + (W.v_1.f(pk_a\|ac\|ID_i))$.
4. The attacker has come to know the value of $f()$, W from the initialization phase. He knows the pk_a himself and has come to know the values of ac and ID_i from the first step of the registration phase. Hence, he can compute $T = W.v_1.f(pk_a\|ac\|ID_i)$ and let us assume that the inverse of T is T^{-1} and it can be computed from T easily in such a way that if (xp, yp) is a point, then its inverse is its reflection across the x-axis which is $(xp, -yp)$.
5. By adding $U = (r.P) + (w.v_1.f(pk_a\|ac\|ID_i))$ and $T^{-1} = (w.v_1.f_1(pk_a\|ac\|ID_i))^{-1}$, we can find $(r.P)$. The calculation of $(r.P)$ can be represented as follows:

$$U + T^{-1} = [(r.P) + (W.v_1.f(pk_a\|ac\|ID_i))] + \left[(W.v_1.f_1(pk_a\|ac\|ID_i)^{-1}\right]$$
$$= (r.P)$$

6. Now, the attacker computes $(W.v_1.f(pk\|ac\|ID_i))$, since he knows all the parameters needed to compute it.
7. Now, the attacker computes $U' = (r.P) + (W.v_1.f(pk\|ac\|ID_i))$.
8. The attacker discards U received from the group manager and sends U', R to the legitimate user who has sent the request for registration.
9. Now, the legitimate user verifies U', R as in third step of the registration process and sends $ID_i, v_2, AENC_{sk}(ID_i, v_1, ac)$ to the group manager. But, the attacker in the middle decrypts $AENC_{sk}(ID_i, v_1, ac)$ using the pk and sends $AENC_{sk_a}(ID_i, v_1, ac)$ to the group manager where sk_a is the private key of the attacker.
10. After receiving $ID_i, v_2, AENC_{sk_a}(ID_i, v_1, ac)$ from the attacker, the group manager will send $AENC_{pk_a}(KEY, v_2)$ to the legitimate user. But, the attacker catches this message and decrypts it using his private key sk_a. Finally, the attacker creates a new message $AENC_{pk}(KEY, v_2)$ and sends it to the legitimate user.
    Formal proof for the attacker and the legitimate user obtaining the private key value KEY is as follows:

    (i) The attacker decrypts $AENC_{pk_a}(ID_i, v_1, ac)$ using his private key: $ADEC_{sk_a}\left(AENC_{pk_a}(KEY, v_2)\right)$

   (ii) The attacker gets access to the KEY value.

  (iii) The attacker encrypts KEY and v_2 using the public key of the legitimate user: $AENC_{pk}(KEY, v_2)$

  (iv) The legitimate user decrypts the message and gets the KEY value using his private key $ADEC_{sk}(AENC_{pk}(KEY, v_2))$

11. As per the above step, both the attacker and the legitimate user have access to the private key $KEY = (x_i, A_i, B_i)$ generated by the group manager.

Impersonating a legitimate user in the document download process

1. Since the attacker posses the secret key value $KEY = (x_i, A_i, B_i)$, he can easily compute $ID_{group}, ID_i, Enc_{A_i}(ID_{data})$ and send it to the cloud server impersonating the user i.

2. Receiving this message from the attacker, the cloud server sends $DF = \left(ID_{group}, ID_{data}, CE, EK, t_{data}\right), \sigma_{DF}$. Following this, the attacker computes $V_i = f(B_i)$ and substitues V_i in the polynomial equation $K_r.W_0.\Pi_{j=1}^{m}\left(W_j\right)^{v_i^j} = K_r.G^{f_p(V_i)} = K_r$ and gets access to the group key K_r and hence decrypts CE to get C_1, C_2, C. Moreover, the attacker computes the secret key $K = e(C_1, A)e(C_2, B)$ and hence decrpts C to get the plaintext M.

Thus, the protocol proposed by Zhu and Jiang [11] is vulnerable to MITM attack and can be easily broken.

4.3   Attack 2

In the message modification attack, an intruder alters a message sent by the sender before it reaches the receiver. It is done without the knowledge of both the parties. Based on the observations from Sect. 4.2, the attacker has access to $KEY = (x_i, A_i, B_i)$. During the document upload phase as in the first step of Sect. 3.3 which is done by the group user, the intruder can decrypt $Enc_{B_i}(ID_{data}, C_1, C_2, C, t_{data})$ and modify the value of C. The group manager, without being aware that the document itself has been changed, will upload it by re-encrypting it using the group key. The group members, during the document download will receive an illegible document after decrypting it through K. Thus, the protocol proposed by Zhu and Zhang [11] is vulnerable to Message Modification Attack as well.

5   Conclusions and Future Works

In this research paper, we have put forward the fact that the scheme proposed by Zhu and Jiang is vulnerable to man-in-the-middle attack and message modification attack. Based on the formal proof for the attack scenario as provided in the Sect. 4, it has become clear that the proposed scheme is vulnerable and hence it is not secure against attacks. Moreover, forward and backward secrecies are under threat as well. Hence, we claim that, the proposed protocol is not suitable for implementation which ensures secure communication among group members using the cloud storage. It needs to be refined enough for ensuring the secure communication and to avert the main-in-the-middle attack and message modification attack and to ensure the forward and backward secrecies.

References

1. Boneh, D., Boyen, X., Goh, E.-J.: Hierarchical identity based encryption with constant size ciphertext. In: Cramer, R. (ed.) EUROCRYPT 2005. LNCS, vol. 3494, pp. 440–456. Springer, Heidelberg (2005). https://doi.org/10.1007/11426639_26
2. Alzahrani, A., Alalwan, N., Sarrab, M.: Mobile cloud computing: advantage, disadvantage and open challenge. In: Proceedings of the 7th International Conference on Euro American Association on Telematics and Information Systems (EATIS 2014) (2014). https://doi.org/10.1145/2590651.2590670
3. Kallahalla, M., Riedel, E., Swaminathan, R., Wang, Q., Fu, K.: Plutus: scalable secure file sharing on untrusted storage. In: Proceedings of USENIX Conference File and Storage Technologies, pp. 29–42 (2003)
4. Buyya, R., Ranjan, R., Calheiros, R.N.: InterCloud: utility-oriented federation of cloud computing environments for scaling of application services. In: Hsu, C.-H., Yang, L.T., Park, J.H., Yeo, S.-S. (eds.) ICA3PP 2010. LNCS, vol. 6081, pp. 13–31. Springer, Heidelberg (2010). https://doi.org/10.1007/978-3-642-13119-6_2
5. Zhang, X., Kunjithapatham, A., Jeong, S., Gibbs, S.: Towards an elastic application model for augmenting the computing capabilities of mobile devices with cloud computing. Mob. Netw. Appl. **16**(3), 270–284 (2011). https://doi.org/10.1007/s11036-011-0305-7
6. Giurgiu, I., Riva, O., Juric, D., Krivulev, I., Alonso, G.: Calling the cloud: enabling mobile phones as interfaces to cloud applications. In: Bacon, J.M., Cooper, B.F. (eds.) Middleware 2009. LNCS, vol. 5896, pp. 83–102. Springer, Heidelberg (2009). https://doi.org/10.1007/978-3-642-10445-9_5
7. Zhang, X., Jeong, S., Kunjithapatham, A., Gibbs, S.: Towards an elastic application model for augmenting computing capabilities of mobile platforms. In: Cai, Y., Magedanz, T., Li, M., Xia, J., Giannelli, C. (eds.) MOBILWARE 2010. LNICSSITE, vol. 48, pp. 161–174. Springer, Heidelberg (2010). https://doi.org/10.1007/978-3-642-17758-3_12
8. Rahimi, M.R., Ren, J., Liu, C.H., Vasilakos, A.V., Venkatasubramanian, N.: Mobile cloud computing: a survey, state of art and future direction **19**(2), 133–143 (2014). https://doi.org/10.1007/s11036-013-0477-4
9. Bakshi, A., Yogesh, B.: Securing cloud from DDoS attacks using intrusion detection system in virtual machine. In: Second International Conference on Communication Software and Networks, ICCSN 2010, pp. 260–264 (2010). https://doi.org/10.1109/ICCSN.2010.56
10. Jensen, M., Schwenk, J., Gruschka, N., Iacono, L.L.: On technical security issues in cloud computing. In: IEEE Conference on Cloud Computing, CLOUD 2009, pp. 109–116 (2006). https://doi.org/10.1109/CLOUD.2009.60
11. Zhu, Z., Jiang, R.: A secure anti-collusion data sharing scheme for dynamic groups in the public cloud. IEEE Trans. Parallel Distrib. Syst. **27**(1), 40–50 (2016). https://doi.org/10.1109/TPDS.2015.2388446
12. Goh, E., Shacham, H., Modadugu, N., Boneh, D.: Sirius: securing remote untrusted storage. In: Proceedings of Network and Distributed Systems Security Symposium (NDSS), pp. 131–145 (2003)

13. Boneh, D., Gentry, C., Waters, B.: Collusion resistant broadcast encryption with short ciphertexts and private keys. In: Shoup, V. (ed.) CRYPTO 2005. LNCS, vol. 3621, pp. 258–275. Springer, Heidelberg (2005). https://doi.org/10.1007/11535218_16
14. Goyal, V., Pandey, O., Sahai, A., Waters, B.: Attribute-based encryption for fine-grained access control of encrypted data. In: Proceedings of ACM Conference Computer and Communications Security (CCS), pp. 89–98 (2006). https://doi.org/10.1145/1180405.1180418
15. Lu, R., Lin, X., Liang, X., Shen, X.: Secure provenance: the essential of bread and butter of data forensics in cloud computing. In: Proceedings of ACM Symposium Information, Computer and Communication Security, pp. 282–292 (2010). https://doi.org/10.1145/1755688.1755723
16. Vijayakumar, P., Bose, S., Kannan, A.: Chinese remainder theorem based centralized group key management for secure multicast communication. J. IET Inf. Secur. 1–9 (2013). https://doi.org/10.1049/iet-ifs.2012.0352
17. Liu, X., Zhang, Y., Wang, B., Yan, J.: Mona: secure multi-owner data sharing for dynamic groups in the cloud. IEEE Trans. Parallel Distrib. Syst. 24(6), 1182–1191 (2013). https://doi.org/10.1109/TPDS.2012.331
18. Zhou, L., Varadharajan, V., Hitchens, M.: Achieving secure role-based access control on encrypted data in cloud storage. IEEE Trans. Inf. Forensics Secur. 8(12), 1947–1960 (2013). https://doi.org/10.1109/TIFS.2013.2286456
19. Zou, X., Dai, Y., Bertino, E.: A practical and flexible key management mechanism for trusted collaborative computing. In: The 27th IEEE Conference on Computer Communications, INFOCOM 2008, pp. 1211–1219 (2008). https://doi.org/10.1109/INFOCOM.2008.102

Research on Coupling Reliability Problem in Sensor-Cloud System

Yuzhu Liang[1], Tian Wang[1(✉)], Md Zakirul Alam Bhuiyan[2],
and Anfeng Liu[3]

[1] College of Computer Science and Technology, Huaqiao University,
Xiamen 361021, China
cs_tianwang@163.com
[2] Department of Computer and Information Science, Fordham University,
Bronx, NY 10458, USA
[3] School of Information Science and Engineering, Central South University,
Changsha 410083, Hunan, China

Abstract. With the integration of WSNs and cloud computing, sensor-cloud system becomes popular in many fields where the physical nodes can be shared with multiple users. However, when a physical sensor node receives multiple service commands simultaneously, there are some service collisions, namely, coupling problem. This coupling problem leads to the failure of services. It is necessary to solve this problem, thus the reliability of system can be improved. In this paper, we propose a fog-based model and extend the classical Hungarian algorithm. The fog layer acts as a buffer and controller between the wireless sensor networks layer and the cloud layer in this model, where we use the classical Hungarian algorithm in the first matching and then schedule idle resources to achieve optimal matching. Experimental results and theoretical analysis show that our method can efficiently solve the coupling problem and increase the resource utilization and resource reliability.

Keywords: Sensor-cloud · Coupling reliability problem · Cloud computing
Fog computing · Wireless sensor networks

1 Introduction

The Internet of Things (IoT) refers to the use of radio frequency identification (RFID), global positioning system (GPS), sensors, actuators and other intelligent devices [1]. It relies on the network for information exchange, and realizes the perception, identification, real-time control, precise management and scientific decision-making of the physical world [2]. More and more government departments, research institutions and enterprises concern the development of IoT [3].

As the underlying sensing technology of the IoT, wireless sensor networks can be applied to the wide range fields, including target location, smart home, environmental monitoring, medical monitor and so on [4]. However, the application fields are limited, because of the shortcoming of WSNs, such as small memory, lack of energy, weak communication capacity, and weak computing power [5, 6]. In recent years, with the

© Springer International Publishing AG 2017
G. Wang et al. (Eds.): SpaCCS 2017 Workshops, LNCS 10658, pp. 468–478, 2017.
https://doi.org/10.1007/978-3-319-72395-2_43

rapid development of cloud computing technology, WSNs is combined with cloud computing, which is the so-called sensor-cloud system [7]. Cloud computing provides superior computing power and near-unlimited storage capacity [8]. Combining the sensor network and cloud computing together, you can better play the advantages of both. For example, the physical nodes in the sensor-cloud system can be shared to provide services for multiple users. However, when a physical sensor node receives multiple service commands simultaneously, there are some service collisions, namely, coupling problem. This coupling problem leads to the failure of services.

Coupling problem has a negative impact on the user's use of sensor networks for related services. These problems can cause deadlocks and even be exploited by attackers to artificially create system conflicts. Coupling security problem has a huge impact on reliability of the cloud system. In this paper, we design a mechanism which is based on the fog computing model. The sensor-cloud system can avoid the coupling problem, and improve the utilization rate of resource.

The rest of this paper is organized as follows. In Sect. 2, the related work is reviewed. The new problem of coupling reliability is defined in Sect. 3. Algorithm design is described in Sect. 4. Section 5 is analysis and comparison of experimental results. We conclude in Sect. 6.

2   Related Work

In recent years, sensor-cloud system has caused wide concern, and it integrates the advantages of sensor networks and cloud computing. Physical nodes of sensor-cloud can be shared by multiple users [9, 10]. Previously, users needed to build a sensor network and constructed their own system to complete a service. In sensor-cloud system, users do not need to buy their own sensor to construct systems, instead of calling the service interface provided by the sensor of cloud. As the number of calling resources of the user is increased, it is necessary to provide a method to maximize the utilization of resources to better meet the needs of users.

Nowadays, the security of the sensor-cloud system has also attracted attention. Among them, the security of the service provider for third-party software is difficult to achieve full authentication. In order to prevent the influence of malicious code on the system, relevant scholars proposed to establish the corresponding third-party software credibility analysis [11]. Encrypting important data is still an important method of data security protection [12]. In addition, in order to prevent illegal objects from accessing protected network resources and unauthorized access of legitimate users to protected network resources, access control mechanism is proposed in [13].

It can be seen from the above that, for the security of the sensor-cloud, scholars mostly study the security privacy and sensor-cloud services of data. But there are few studies on the sensor cloud coupling problems. It is necessary for users to solve the coupling problem and it's also useful to improve the reliability of resources. In order to solve the problem of multiple distribution, the kuhn-munkres (k-m) algorithm is a classical method to deal with task assignment, and the authors improve k-m algorithm to propose solutions for m-m assignment problems [14]. In [15], Amponsah et al. propose a heuristic method based on Hungary algorithm [16], this method can reduce computing time, and easy to implement. In [17], Rodriguez and Buyya present infrastructure as a service (IaaS) cloud scientific workflow resource allocation and scheduling strategy. Bhoi and Ramanuj puts forward the improved Max - min task scheduling algorithm. The improved algorithm of the Max - min distributes tasks to resources to generate the maximum execution time of (maximum) minimum completion time (the slowest resources) [18]. In [19], Vizuete-Luciano et al. develops new assignment algorithms by using a wide range of aggregation operators in the Hungarian algorithm. The new process of using an ordered weighted mean distance (OWAD) operator and the induction of OWAD (IOWAD) operator is introduced. In [20], Kim and Dong designs an iterative technique, iterative Hungarian method (IHM). Numerical results show that the proposed technique can provide approximate optimal performance with polynomial complexity.

The above study is the allocation of resources in some improvements of classic algorithms, adopt different distribution strategy. Which is joining in classical allocation algorithm parameters and combining with heuristic algorithm for processing. However, in the case of sensor-cloud coupled security, the proposed scheme cannot effectively meet the optimal matching of users and resources in the case of satisfying the maximum matching. First of all, we don't have enough information to predict the real-time demand of users in the sensor network, and the combination of heuristic algorithms cannot solve this problem well. Second, if we first call a resource that takes the longest or shortest, it can lead to a system shutdown. And the longest or shortest resource is not necessarily the most urgent resource. Finally, the algorithm mentioned above is about 1 to 1 while there is the case that the matching of 1 to n is allowed in the security coupling problem.

To solve the problem of the above methods, this paper proposes an extended Hungarian algorithm. The core idea is to use the classical Hungarian algorithm to complete the initial matching, and determine whether the unmatched resources can continue to be scheduled. Then add it to the initial matching to achieve the optimal match. In addition, we design a mechanism based on the fog computing mode, and put the algorithm in the fog computing layer, which can further improve the utilization of resources.

3 Coupling Reliability Problem

The problem of couple reliability is defined in Sect. 3.1, and a specific example is illustrated in Sect. 3.2.

Definition 1: In the sensor-cloud system when the physical node at the same time received multiple commands, some commands will be conflicting with each other, which leads to failures of sensor cloud services, namely, couple reliability problem.

Here is an example of invocation situations using different methods when there is a coupling problem in sensor-cloud system.

As shown in Fig. 1, there are five different resources and seven users, assuming that the user calls a resource will take three time units. The relationship between user and resource is as follows: User 1 calls resources B and C; User 2 calls resources A and E;

User 3 calls resources B and D; User 4 calls resources A and E; User 5 calls resources B and D; User 6 calls resources A and C; User 7 calls resources D and E.

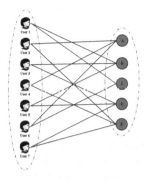

Fig. 1. An example of coupling security problems schematic diagram

The results of the different scheduling strategies are shown in Table 1 above. The FIFO needs 4 times to complete the scheduling, totaling 12 time units; HG takes 4 times to complete the scheduling, totaling 12 time units; and the optimal algorithm needs 3 times to complete the service, a total of 9 time units.

Table 1. Comparisons for different scheduling methods

	FIFO (First Input First Output)	HG (Hungarian algorithm)	Optimal algorithm
First time	1-BC 2-AE	4-A 5-B 1-C 3-D 2-E	4-A 5-B 1-C 3-D 2-E
Second time	3-BD 4-AE	2-A 1-B 6-C 5-D 4-E	2-A1-B 6-C 5-D 4-E
Third time	5-BD 6-AC	6-A 3-B 7-D	6-A 3-B 7-D 7-E
Fourth time	7-DE	7-E	Completed

4 Algorithm Design and Analysis

The detailed extension of Hungarian algorithm is introduced in Sect. 4.1 and analyses are discussed in Sect. 4.2.

4.1 Algorithm Design

This section describes the proposed algorithm. The Hungarian algorithm mainly solves the traditional problem of assignment or maximum matching. Our problem is that the user and the resource is not a 1-to-1 correspondence, but a many-to-many correspondence, and even in a match the user can still call multiple resources. So, we add a loop to the Hungarian algorithm. When the number of corresponding relationships is equal to the sum of all the matching numbers, the loop is finished. If there is free resources after the initial match, the user continues to call the resource. At the same time, we put the algorithm on the fog layer for processing. The three-tier architecture of the fog computing is shown below (Fig. 2):

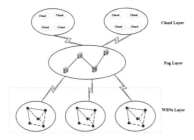

Fig. 2. Illustration of the three-tier architecture in fog computing framework

In fog computing framework, the fog node as the interface between upper and lower layers is playing the role of the intermediary: On the one hand, it can process order or data in the fog layer, to further reduce the scheduling time; on the other hand, fog node have better understanding of the underlying sensor node, and the security privacy of the resource will be better. In order to reduce the coupling degree, the control information should be reduced between the sensor and the cloud. The fog layer can reduce the control message transmission by making initial processing of the data.

Algorithm 1 gives detailed steps to extend the Hungarian algorithm. Firstly, the method input two types of node resources and users of the coupling problem, and the correspondence between them, then initialize the vertices and their matching. The bool function is used to find the possible augmenting path from each user vertex. If there is an augmenting path, the matching number is incremented by 1 and the corresponding vertex is recorded. At the same time, the augmenting path is negated to obtain the number of matches and the matching result. Finally, determining whether the unmatched resources can continue to be scheduled. Then add it to the initial matching to achieve the optimal match.

Algorithm 2 gives a detailed design of the bool function. The input of the function is the two types of vertices of the coupling problem, the correspondence between the two types of vertices and the given arbitrary user vertex. Traversing the corresponding relationship from the given user's vertex, if the corresponding vertex of the corresponding relation is resource j, and the resource j is not in the augmenting channel, add the resource j to the augmenting channel. If the corresponding user from resource j is present in the case of an augmenting path, exists augmenting path, and returns true; otherwise, returns false.

Algorithm 1. Extension of Hungarian algorithm

Input: correspondence between the two types of vertices and two kinds of vertices

Output: Match the results

1:   Initialize the bipartite graph and match;

2   for matching times $m = 1$ to n

3:       for matching vertex $k= 1$ to n

4:           find out from the k exists augmenting path;

5:           matching number plus 1;

6:           output the number of matching and initial matching results;

7:           if(unmatched resources can continue to be scheduled)

8:               add it to the initial matching;

9:           end if

10:      end for

11:   end for

Algorithm 2. Search of augmenting paths

Input: correspondence between the two types of vertices and two kinds of vertices
and one vertices such as k

Output: true or false

1:   Initialize the bipartite graph and match

2:   bool find the augmenting path from k

3:       while (Enumerates the vertices k can associate with j)

4:           if (j is not on the augmenting path)

5:               Add j to augmenting path;

6:               if (J is an uncovered vertices or has an augmenting path)

7:                   Modify the corresponding item of j to k;

8:                   return true; //Augmenting path existence

9:               end if

10:          end if

11:      end while

12:   return false; // Augmenting path is not existence

4.2   Theoretical Analysis

Theorem 1: Suppose M is a match of the bipartite graph. M being necessary and sufficient conditions for the maximum matching augmenting path does not exist.

Proof

Necessity: M is the maximum match $\rightarrow$ there is no augmenting path.

Assume that M is the largest match and there is an augmenting path. According to the definition of the maximum match we can see that the matching number is the most. And there is an augmenting path in the graph, there must be a new match than the original match 1. The original match is the biggest match. There is no augmenting path for maximum match.

Sufficiency: No Existence augmenting path$\rightarrow M$ is the maximum match

Suppose there is a greater match M' and $|M'| = k$, finding the augmenting path P of M'. P contains $2k + 1$ edge, where k belongs to M', $k + 1$ does not belong to M'. Modify M' for M' & P (M' and P symmetry difference operation) that $|M'| + 1$, there is augmenting path. The original proposition is evidence.

Theorem 2: Assuming that the user's resource usage time must be t time intervals, if there are M users (M_1, M_2, ..., M_m), N resources (N_1, N_2, ..., N_n), M users the number of using resources is $P(P_1, P_2,..., P_m)$, then takes $X = M \times t$ for the FIFO method. Using the extended Hungarian algorithm, the optimal time used is $Y = \Sigma(P_i) \div N \times t$ and $Y < X$.

For the scheduling situation, each time can only meet the needs of a user. The larger the number of users, the longer the scheduling time, and the total time required is the number of users $\times$ use time which is $M \times t$. Every time the resources can be used, the resource utilization rate will be largest, and natural time will be the shortest. The time it takes for the user to call all the sum of the resources $\div$ the number of resources $\times$ use time, which is $\Sigma(P_i) \div N \times t$. We know that $M \times N$ means that each user uses all the resources, obviously the value must be bigger than $\Sigma(P_i)$, that is, $\Sigma(P_i) \div N \times t < M \times t$. The original proposition $Y < X$ proved.

Time complexity analysis: We make the bipartite graph store in the adjacency matrix. The input scale of the algorithm is the correspondence between the two types of vertices and two kinds of vertices. The two types of vertices are n_1, n_2, where $n = max$ (n_1, n_2). The number of correspondence is m. The basic statement in the algorithm is the number of matches plus one. This basic statement is contained in a loop and a recursive lookup function. The loop is executed n times, the recursive function in the loop executes $m \times m$ times. So the basic statement is executed on the order of $n \times m^2$, the time complexity of the algorithm is $O(n \times m^2)$. The time complexity of the algorithm is polynomial time.

5   Simulation Experiment

In this section, extensive simulations are conducted using Visual C++6.0 and MATLAB R2012b to validate the performance of our proposed solutions. In the simulation scenario, the distribution of the initial network is shown in Table 2. In Sect. 5.2, we discuss the performance differences between the FIFO, HG and EHG (Extended Hungarian algorithm).

Table 2. Experiment parameters

Scene 1		Scene 2		Scene 3	
Parameter	Value	Parameter	Value	Parameter	Value
Users	7	Users	40	Users	80
Resources	5	Resources	30	Resources	60
Sum	14	Sum	220	Sum	1100

5.1   Experimental Environment Settings

This section describes the basic settings of the experimental environment. The experiment constructs three experimental scenarios, and we takes Scene 1 as an example to explain. In Scene 1, the number of users is 7, the number of resources is 5, and the sum of resources invoked by users is 14. Considering the complexity of the experimental scenario, this section describes the experimental environment no longer adding a legend. The legend can refer to the example in Sect. 3.

5.2   Analysis of Experimental Results

In order to compare the advantages of our proposed method. We compare it with HG and FIFO methods respectively. Among them, HG algorithm is the classic Hungarian algorithm, which is the most commonly used method to solve the maximum matching of bipartite graphs. FIFO is the method of user scheduling, that is, according to the principle of "first come, first served". In the graph, we propose the EHG (Extended Hungarian algorithm). The following calculations: The time unit = the number of round × user calls each resource time. Resource utilization = total number of resource calls ÷ (rounds × resource number); the unit number of resources = total number of resource calls ÷ times. The user calls each resource to take 3 time intervals.

Figure 3 shows the calling time of the three scenarios under the three algorithms. In the Scene 1, the EHG algorithm takes the calling time for 9 time intervals, while the HG and the FIFO are all 6 time intervals. In the Scene 2, the EHG algorithm takes the calling time for 24 time intervals, while the HG and the FIFO are 39 and 42 time intervals. In the Scene 3, the EHG algorithm takes the calling time for 60 time intervals, while the HG and the FIFO are 84 and 93 time intervals. Further analysis shows that the EHG time is shortened by 33.3% and 33.3% in Scene 1; reduced by 42.9% and 38.5% in Scene 2; shortened by 35.5% and 28.6% in Scene 3; compared to FIFO and HG.

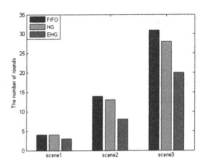

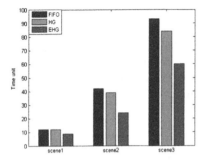

Fig. 3. Comparison of total scheduling times

Fig. 4. Comparison of rounds number

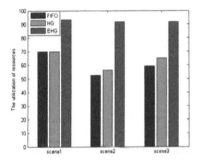

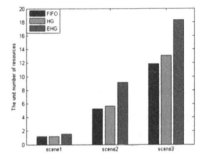

Fig. 5. Comparison of resources utilization

Fig. 6. Comparison of unit number of resources

Figure 4 shows the calling rounds of the three scenarios under the three algorithms. In the Scene 1, the EHG algorithm takes the call rounds for 3 times, while the HG and the FIFO are all 4 times. In the Scene 2, the EHG algorithm takes the call rounds for 8 times, while the HG and the FIFO are 13 and 14 times. In the Scene 3, the EHG algorithm takes the call rounds for 20 times, while the HG and the FIFO are 28 and 31 times. Further analysis shows that the EHG call rounds are shortened by 25% and 25% in Scene 1; reduced by 42.9% and 38.5% in Scene 2; shortened by 32.3% and 28.6% in Scene 3; compared to FIFO and HG.

Figure 5 shows the resource utilization of the three scenarios under the three algorithms. In the Scene 1, the EHG algorithm takes the resource utilization for 93.3%, while the HG and the FIFO are all 75%. In the Scene 2, the EHG algorithm takes the resource utilization for 91.7%, while the HG and the FIFO are 52.4% and 56.4%. In the Scene 3, the EHG algorithm takes the resource utilization for 91.7%, while the HG and the FIFO are 59.1% and 65.2%. Further analysis shows that the resource utilization of EHG is raised by 24.4% and 24.4% in Scene 1; enhanced by 75% and 62.6% in Scene 2; raised by 55.2% and 40.6% in Scene 3; compared to the FIFO and the HG.

Figure 6 shows the unit number of resource of the three scenarios under the three algorithms. In the Scene 1, the EHG algorithm takes the unit number of resource for 1.56, while the HG and the FIFO are all 1.17. In the Scene 2, the EHG algorithm takes the unit number of resource for 9.17, while the HG and the FIFO are 5.64 and 5.62. In the Scene 3, the EHG algorithm takes the unit number of resource for 18.33, while the HG and the FIFO are 13.09 and 11.83. Further analysis shows that the unit number of resource of EHG is raised by 33.3% and 33.3% in Scene 1; enhanced by 75% and 62.6% in Scene2; raised by 54.9% and 40% in Scene 3; compared to the FIFO and the HG.

These results show that the EHG takes the shortest calling time, the least calling round, and the largest resource utilization. The reason is that our method can combine the advantages of the classic HG and FIFO, which can maximize the utilization of resources.

6   Conclusion

With the developments of the Internet of things and cloud computing, sensor-cloud system is widely used in military, industry, agriculture, and many other fields. With the employment of cloud platform, the physical nodes in the sensor-cloud system can be shared with multiple users. However, there are still some technical problems that need to be solved. The coupling problem is the most urgent one among these problems because the coupling problem has terrible effects on system reliability. Based on fog computing and the classical Hungarian algorithm, we propose a new mechanism to achieve optimal resource scheduling. Theoretical analysis and experimental results show that our method efficiently reduces scheduling time and improves the utilization of resources. For the future work, we plan to solve the problem that the resources will be occupied with difference time for difference users.

Acknowledgments. Above work was supported in part by grants from the National Natural Science Foundation (NSF) of China under Grant Nos. 61772148 and 61672441 and the Foster Project for Graduate Student in Research and Innovation of Huaqiao University (No. 17013083005).

References

1. Li, S., Da Xu, L., Zhao, S.: The internet of things: a survey. Inf. Syst. Front. **17**(2), 243–259 (2015)
2. Wortmann, F., Flüchter, K.: Internet of things [J]. Business & Information Systems Engineering **57**(3), 221–224 (2015)
3. Zanella, A., Bui, N., Castellani, A., et al.: Internet of things for smart cities. IEEE Internet Things J. **1**(1), 22–32 (2014)
4. Al-Anbagi, I., Erol-Kantarci, M., Mouftah, H.T.: A survey on cross-layer quality-of-service approaches in WSNs for delay and reliability-aware applications. IEEE Commun. Sur. Tutorials **18**(1), 525–552 (2016)
5. Wang, T., Wu, Q., Wen, S., et al.: Propagation modeling and defending of a mobile sensor worm in wireless sensor and actuator networks. Sensors **17**(1), 139 (2017)
6. Wang, T., Li, Y., Wang, G., et al.: Sustainable and efficient data collection from WSNs to cloud. IEEE Trans. Sustain. Comput. **PP**(99), 1 (2017)

7. Zeng, J., Wang, T., Jia, W., et al.: A survey on sensor-cloud. J. Comput. Res. Dev. **54**(5), 925–939 (2017)
8. Ali, M., Khan, S.U., Vasilakos, A.V.: Security in cloud computing: opportunities and challenges. Inf. Sci. **305**, 357–383 (2015)
9. Botta, A., Donato, W.D., Persico, V., et al.: Integration of cloud computing and internet of things: a survey. Future Gener. Comput. Syst. **56**(C), 684–700 (2016)
10. Wang, T., Zeng, J., Bhuiyan, M.Z.A., et al.: Trajectory privacy preservation based on a fog structure in cloud location services. IEEE Access **PP**(99), 1 (2017)
11. Henze, M., Hummen, R., Matzutt, R., Wehrle, K.: A trust point-based security architecture for sensor data in the cloud. In: Krcmar, H., Reussner, R., Rumpe, B. (eds.) Trusted Cloud Computing, pp. 77–106. Springer, Cham (2014). https://doi.org/10.1007/978-3-319-12718-7_6
12. Sajid, A., Abbas, H., Saleem, K.: Cloud-assisted IoT-based SCADA systems security: a review of the state of the art and future challenges. IEEE Access **4**, 1375–1384 (2016)
13. Henze, M., Hermerschmidt, L., Kerpen, D., et al.: A comprehensive approach to privacy in the cloud-based Internet of things. Future Gener. Comput. Syst. **56**, 701–718 (2016)
14. Zhu, H., Liu, D., Zhang, S., et al.: Solving the many to many assignment problem by improving the Kuhn-Munkres algorithm with backtracking. Theor. Comput. Sci. **618**, 30–41 (2016)
15. Amponsah, S.K., Otoo, D., Salhi, S., et al.: Proposed heuristic method for solving assignment problems. Am. J. Oper. Res. **6**(06), 436 (2016)
16. Kuhn, H.W.: Statement for naval research logistics: "the Hungarian method for the assignment problem". J. R. Stat. Soc. **64**(4), 611–633 (2015)
17. Rodriguez, M.A., Buyya, R.: Deadline based resource provisioning and scheduling algorithm for scientific workflows on clouds. IEEE Trans. Cloud Comput. **2**(2), 222–235 (2014)
18. Bhoi, U., Ramanuj, P.N.: Enhanced max-min task scheduling algorithm in cloud computing. Int. J. Appl. Innov. Eng. Manag. (IJAIEM) **2**(4), 259–264 (2013)
19. Vizuete-Luciano, E., Merigó, J.M., Gil-Lafuente, A.M., et al.: Decision making in the assignment process by using the Hungarian algorithm with OWA operators. Technol. Econ. Dev. Econ. **21**(5), 684–704 (2015)
20. Kim, T., Dong, M.: An iterative Hungarian method to joint relay selection and resource allocation for D2D communications. IEEE Wirel. Commun. Lett. **3**(6), 625–628 (2014)

An On-demand Monitoring Approach
for Cloud Computing Systems

Zhenyue Long[1,2], Jijun Zeng[1,2], Hong Zou[1,2], and Yunkui Song[3(✉)]

[1] Information Center, Guangdong Power Grid Co. Ltd.,
Guangzhou 510000, China
{longzhenyue,zengjijun,zouhong}@gdxx.csg.cn
[2] CSG-Key Laboratory of Information Technology Testing,
Guangzhou 510000, China
[3] Institute of Software, Chinese Academy of Sciences, Beijing 100190, China
songyk@otcaix.iscas.ac.cn

Abstract. The number of virtual machines in cloud computing is constantly changing with business requirements, which raises a great challenge for monitoring dynamic objects. Traditional static monitoring methods set fixed monitoring cycles, but it is difficult to make a suitable tradeoff between monitoring timeliness and cost in cloud computing systems with a large number of virtual machines or container instances. To address the above issues, this paper proposes an on-demand monitoring approach for cloud computing. We introduce a variable cycle mechanism and an event driven mechanism in the interaction between agents and collectors to minimize network overhead and maximize monitoring efficiency. Finally, experimental results in TPC-W benchmark show that compared to the method with a fixed monitoring cycle, our approach has a lower monitoring overhead.

Keywords: On-demand monitoring · Monitoring cycle · Data transmission
Cloud computing · System maintenance

1 Introduction

Large-scale cloud computing platforms often need to manage thousands of service nodes, and monitoring such many resources often brings a great overhead on monitoring systems. On the other hand, monitoring systems often need to use some resources on cloud platforms, such as CPU, storage, network, so monitoring overhead inevitably decreases the efficiency of cloud computing platforms. Therefore, it is an important research topic on how to efficiently monitor large-scale cloud computing platforms and reduce the cost. The widespread periodic monitoring data transmission strategy is easy to use, but monitoring with a fixed cycle uses unnecessary network resources. Sundaresan [1, 2] introduced a resource consumption estimation model to dynamically adjust the length of monitoring cycles to reduce invalid network transmission, according to the estimated anomalous degrees. The event-driven transmission strategies stipulate that transmission is carried out, when a specific event occurs for a monitored object. Chung [3] presents three mechanisms for triggering events to balance

© Springer International Publishing AG 2017
G. Wang et al. (Eds.): SpaCCS 2017 Workshops, LNCS 10658, pp. 479–488, 2017.
https://doi.org/10.1007/978-3-319-72395-2_44

the monitoring efficiency and overhead. Work [4] combines two strategies to switch between two models based on the parameters set by users. We propose a communication model combining a variable monitoring cycle and an event driven mechanism, and dynamically adjust the threshold. The communication model maximizes the efficiency of collecting monitoring data on the basis of reducing network overhead. Finally, experimental results in TPC-W benchmark show that compared to the methods with a fixed monitoring cycle, our approach has lower monitoring cost.

2 On-demand Monitoring Approach

2.1 Model of Collecting Monitoring Data for Cloud

Host and VM nodes use a one-to-many mapping model, and we use a tree structure to organize performance data, because the tree can characterize layers and describe the relationship between hierarchy entities as shown in Fig. 1. The current monitoring data transmission strategy between physical servers and clients use a central physical server – master with a global data transmission strategy. For example, when a VM1 user obtains the monitoring information of the VM1 instance, the VM2 monitoring data will also be acquired. When VM3 users obtain the monitoring data of the VM3 instance, the VM4 monitoring data will also be obtained. This model leads to unnecessary network overhead. A virtual machine collects monitoring data with on-demand transmission to reduce unnecessary network transmission overhead, which transmits monitoring data according to the requirements of users. For example, users can only require the resource consumption information of VM1.

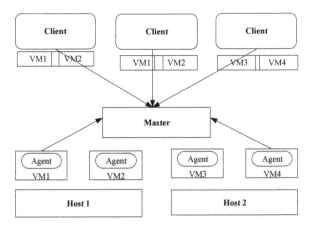

Fig. 1. Model of collecting monitoring data

As shown in Fig. 2, we use four components (i.e., Performance, VM, Usage and APP) to organize monitoring data. The above four elements are described as follows:

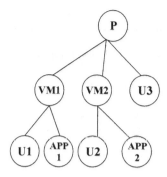

Fig. 2. Monitoring data organization

- Performance: represents performance data of physical servers;
- VM: is characterized by the VM = {ID} union {Functions}, where ID is the unique identifier of VM and represented by UUID;
- Usage: refers to the monitoring results of resource consumption. Both Host and VM focus on resources including CPU, Memory, Network and Disk;
- APP: is an application running on VM, which has properties including application ID, Type and sensitive resources. We describe APP as APP = {ID} union {Type} union {Resource}, where Type can be application server, database, and Resource can be CPU, memory, network, disk or their combination.

We optimize a query algorithm on physical servers with an index mechanism, and makes a global monitoring data template. The method quickly generates the copies of specified VM instances, and sends them to clients. We constrain the ID naming rules for Host and VM as ID = {IP, UUID}. We look at Host node as a special VM, and set the Host node UUID as DEFAUL, where a VM UUID running on a Host node can be described as an ID. Algorithm 1 shows that a hash constructs the mapping relationship between VMs (as the Host is a special VM) and its location.

Algorithm 1: Building mapping relationship
___
Input:hashTable ;
Output:CMD4C.
String ip = getIP (host) ;
hashTable.add(ID(ip,DEFAULT),host);
FOR VM vm in Children(host)
    String uuid = getUUID (vm) ;
    hashTable.add(ID(ip,uuid),vm);
END FOR

Then, when the client queries the monitoring data of a specified VM, a method of creating a replica implements the transmission of monitoring data from different clients. Algorithm 2 shows that, when the identity of a client request is the Host node, the replica instance of a Host node usage is constructed. When the identity of a client request is VM, a copy instance with the VM usage information is built.

Algorithm 2: Generating replication
___
Input: hashTable, Identification of Target Entity ID ;
Output: CMD4C.
Entity entity = hashTable.get(ID)
IF isHost(entity)
      CMD4C CMD4C = new CMD4C ();
      Children(CMD4C).add(entity.getUsage());
      Return CMD4C;
END IF
ELSEIF isVM(entity)
      CMD4C CMD4C = new CMD4C ();
      Children(CMD4C).add(entity)
      Return CMD4C;
END ELSEIF
ELSE
    This is an exception
END ELSE

2.2   Dynamic Adjustment for Monitoring Cycles

We discuss the on-demand transmission optimization between clients and physical servers. This sub-section discusses the communication mechanism between monitoring agents and monitoring collectors. Current cloud monitoring systems [5] interact with monitoring agents and collectors, and use a fixed cycle to monitor agents requesting data. When the number of virtual machines on the physical server exceeds 100, it takes up network resources, and the polling cycle is long. Communication mechanisms between monitoring agents and a monitoring collector can be classified as periodic and event-driven mechanisms. In general systems, the periodic communication is usually initiated by a collector to request data from the monitoring agent with a certain cycle. The event-driven communication is usually initiated by monitoring agents, which decide to collect data from a monitoring collector according to its own situation. The overhead of a periodic pull model is relatively stable, but the change of monitoring data can determine the pull cycle based on the current resource consumption situation. In this way, the monitoring efficiency cannot be compared with the event-driven push model. In the event-driven push model, although the efficiency is higher, it has higher overhead and lower efficiency, which is usually used to set the scene that the threshold conditions over the boundary to trigger a warning. Setting thresholds is the key to balance overhead and efficiency.

In general, the event-driven push model is more accurate with suitable thresholds. The periodic pull model has low consumption with appropriate cycles. Combining two strategies with coordinate parameters, it allows the server to adaptively select ways for each connection. Because virtual resources on cloud platforms have different permissions and access models, monitoring systems provides different efficiency and overhead for different resources. Therefore, the hybrid approach allows users to complete different requirements of efficiency and overhead with independent configurations, which makes monitoring cloud become more flexible and efficient. We present a model for combining periodic mechanism and event-driven interaction, operate a periodic type pulling algorithm in the monitoring collector, read data from the monitoring agent with polling cycles, and run the event driven calculation method in the monitoring agent. By calculating the mutation of monitoring data to determine whether a threshold is exceeded, we set a certain threshold, and send data to the monitoring collector. Huang [4] and Gang [6] have put forward similar methods in their work. However, both methods adopt fixed thresholds, but cannot detect the obvious changes of local data.

To complete efficiency and overhead, we define a parameter named as monitoring relative fault (MRER) in the scope of [0, 1], where the value 0 means that the representative fault of zero tolerance. Then, based on the historical monitoring data in the monitoring window, we decide to push or pull by checking whether the latest data relative to historical data exceed the tolerance of users. The algorithm is divided into two parts, where one part is an event driven pushing algorithm running in monitoring agents, and the other part is a variable cycle pulling algorithm running in a monitoring collector. The two algorithms together constitute the communication mechanism between agents and a collector.

2.2.1   Event-Driven Push

The algorithm is performed in a monitoring agent with a monitoring collector. It first gets the state information of current resources, puts monitoring information in the monitoring window, updates the window information, and calculates the threshold. It is derived from the product of the maximum difference between the data in the window and the MRER. We judge whether the difference between the state information of resources in the agent side and collector side is greater than the threshold, and judge whether the monitoring data is within the scope of alarms.

Algorithm 3: Determining push mechanism

Input: Difference between the highest and the lowest values in Window wd;
Monitoring Relative Fault Rate: mrer;
Output: Whether Push or Not isPush.
IF isPulled
    isPush = false;
END IF
ELSE
    Threshold = wd*mrer;
    IF abs(servernow-serverlast)>=Threshold
        isPush = true;
    END IF
    ELSE
        isPush = false;
    END ELSE
END ELSE

2.2.2 Pull with Variable Cycles

The algorithm first determines whether the monitoring agent pushes the data actively in the current cycle. The algorithm gets information about the current resource from the monitor agent, and puts it in the monitoring window. When updating the window information and calculating the new threshold, it decides whether the difference between the resources' monitoring information on the agent side and that on the collector side is greater than the threshold. This paper proposes the mechanism of slow increase and rapid decline to dynamically adjust the monitoring cycle. Assuming that the current monitoring cycle is t seconds, when the new calculated threshold is greater than the resource variation, we adjust the cycle as $t + t/2$, otherwise the cycle as $t/2$. The adjustment of monitoring cycles is allowed between tmax and tmin.

Algorithm 4: Determining cycles

Input: Maximum Monitoring Cycle tmax, Minimum Monitoring Cycle tmin;
Difference between the highest and the lowest values in Window wd;
Monitoring Relative Fault Rate mrer;
Output:Monitoring Cycle t.
Init I = 0
Threshold = wd*mrer;
IF abs(servernow-serverlast)<Threshold
     IF I>=N
          t=(t+t/2> tmax)? tmax :t+t/2;
     END IF
     ELSE
          I++;
     END ELSE
END IF
ELSE
     t=(t/2< tmin)? tmin:t/2;
     I=0;
END ELSE

2.2.3 MRER on Communication

In the operations of monitoring systems, whether the operations of event-driven push or variable cycle pull depends on the threshold in the algorithm, and the threshold depends on monitoring relative fault rate MRER. When the MRER value is smaller, it is easy to reach the threshold, according to the event-driven pushing algorithm, and even small changes in monitoring data can trigger the push operations. If the monitoring data are smooth, the variable cycle pulling algorithm determines to pull data periodically, continues to turn up the cycle until changes to the monitoring data exceed the threshold, and then turn down the cycle. When the MRER value is large, if the monitoring data have changed significantly, the threshold will not necessarily be reached, and the push operations occur less. The monitoring collector pulls monitoring data from agents according to the variable cycle pulling algorithm, and adjust the size of cycles to adjust the amplitude of monitoring data. When users only need to know the general information about the monitored objects, they can choose to set the MRER to a larger value. When the MRER value is moderate, times of the push and pull operations occur approximately.

3   Evaluation

3.1   Monitoring Overhead

Overhead without Injected Faults

This experiment does not inject faults and lasts 60 min. The experimental results in Fig. 3 show that the CPU utilization in our approach remains in a lower level, because the system is running in a stable condition and the abnormal degree is low. Furthermore, the monitoring system uses a larger monitoring cycle, and collects a fewer monitoring data. Figure 4 shows that the changes in a monitoring cycle affect network traffic. In the case of no injected faults, the network traffic in a fixed monitoring cycle is always maintained in a fixed range, and our approach adjusting monitoring cycles gradually adopts a large monitoring cycle due to the low degree of anomaly, so our approach has less overhead on collecting data.

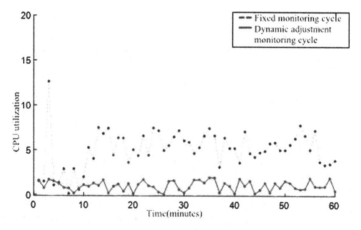

Fig. 3. CPU utilization with faults

Overhead with Injected Faults

Figure 5 shows the CPU utilization in different approaches. While faults last from 30 to 55th minute and from 90 to 115th minute, the CPU utilization in our approach is slightly higher than the methods with a fixed monitoring cycle. Because the system has the higher degree of abnormality in the two time quantums, our approach uses smaller cycles and performs more monitoring data. In other monitoring cycles, the system is much less abnormal, and the monitoring system uses a smaller monitoring cycle, so the CPU utilization of our approach is lower than that of the method with fixed monitoring

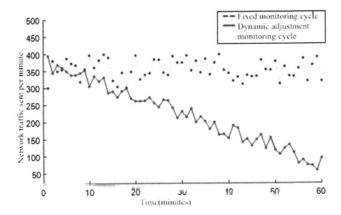

Fig. 4. Network throughput with faults

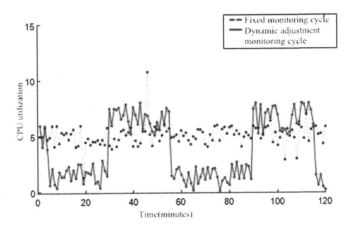

Fig. 5. CPU utilization without faults

cycles. During the experiment, the CPU utilization of our approach is lower than that of the method with fixed monitoring cycles. Figure 6 shows the comparative results in network traffics corresponding to different monitoring methods. After faults are injected, the anomaly degree becomes higher, and our approach informs monitoring systems to use smaller monitoring cycles, so network traffic sent per minute by our approach shows the tendency of fast growth. When the anomaly degree is lower, our approach makes the monitoring system use gradually larger monitoring cycle, so the network traffic has a decrease trend. During the whole experiment, the network traffic sent by our approach is lower than that sent by the method with fixed monitoring cycles.

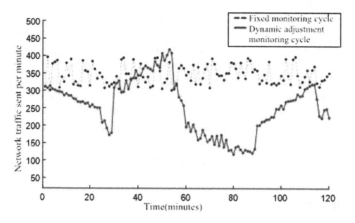

Fig. 6. Network throughput without faults

4   Related Work

The communication mechanism of cloud monitoring systems is the key that determines performance, and a reasonable communication mechanism can guarantee the efficiency of monitoring with less data transmission. The communication mechanism of monitoring agents can be classified as periodic and event driven mechanism.

The periodic communication mechanism refers to a regular interaction between monitoring servers and agents. A monitoring server periodically sends requests to agents collecting the technical specifications of monitored nodes, and the agents send performance data to the server when receiving requests from a server. Monitoring agents actively periodically send monitoring data to the monitoring server. The fixed cycle mechanism can improve the efficiency of monitoring by reducing communication cycles, which can lead to a large amount of additional overhead. Communication cost mainly includes overhead on network and computational resources. The fixed cycle communication can generate network consumption, while communication cycle can be adjusted through the real-time situation of monitored resources in dynamic cycle communication. Sundaresan [1, 2] put forward two kinds of cycle adjustment strategies for the typical applications of intermittent communication mechanism to guarantee monitoring efficiency on the basis of reducing invalid network transmission.

The event-driven communication mechanism is that data interaction happens, when monitoring agents find that the monitored object has a specific event. The occurrence time of event-driven communication is uncertain, and there is no specific rule related to the state of the system. Monitoring data transmission happens, when the change of the monitored object exceeds a certain threshold. Chung [3] presents three mechanisms of triggering events including migration sensitivity (OSM), time sensitivity (TSM) and hybrid (ACTC) to balance the monitoring efficiency and overhead. In OSM, when the resource change of the monitored node exceeds the threshold, the monitoring agent pushes the information to the monitoring server. OSM ignores useless updates, reduces the number of information transfers, and basically guarantees consistency. But when the threshold is large, most changes pushed on the server affect the monitoring efficiency. In TSM, when the monitoring cycle is greater than the time interval, the monitoring agent pushes the information to the monitoring server. TSM reduces the times of pushing data to a certain extent, but the changes in the monitoring cycle are missed. In a monitoring cycle, even if the load does not change, the pushed messages can increase the useless communication overhead. Work [4] combines two strategies and introduces tolerance parameters set by an administrator to decrease the times of data transmission, and to reduce the communication overhead. This strategy can guarantee high data consistency, but cannot ignore most of the unused updates, and then communication overhead has not been improved.

5   Conclusion

The number of virtual machines in cloud computing is constantly changing with business requirements, which raises a great challenge for monitoring dynamic objects. Traditional static monitoring methods set fixed monitoring cycles. It is difficult to make a suitable tradeoff between monitoring timeliness and cost in cloud computing systems with many virtual machines or container instances. To address the above issues, this paper proposes an on-demand monitoring method for cloud computing. We introduce a variable cycle mechanism and an event driven mechanism in the interaction between agents and collectors to minimize network overhead and maximize monitoring efficiency. Finally, experimental results in TPC-W benchmark show that compared to the method with a fixed monitoring cycle, our approach has a lower monitoring overhead.

References

1. Sundaresan, R., Kurc, T., Lauria, M., et al.: A slacker coherence protocol for pull-based monitoring of on-line data sources. In: Proceedings of 3rd IEEE/ACM International Symposium on Cluster Computing and the Grid, CCGrid 2003, pp. 250–257. IEEE (2003)
2. Sundaresan, R., Lauria, M., Kurc, T., et al.: Adaptive polling of grid resource monitors using a slacker coherence model. In: Proceedings of 12th IEEE International Symposium on High Performance Distributed Computing, pp. 260–269. IEEE (2003)
3. Chung, W.C., Chang, R.S.: A new mechanism for resource monitoring in Grid computing. Future Gener. Comput. Syst. **25**(1), 1–7 (2009)
4. Huang, H., Wang, L.: P&P: a combined push-pull model for resource monitoring in cloud computing environment. In: 2010 IEEE 3rd International Conference on Cloud Computing (CLOUD), pp. 260–267. IEEE (2010)
5. Bunch, C.: Automating VSphere: With VMware VCenter Orchestrator. Prentice Hall Press, Upper Saddle River (2012)
6. Gang, Y., Yu-lei, S.: Adaptive approach to monitor resource for cloud computing platform. Comput. Eng. Appl. **45**(29), 14–17 (2009)

Security on "A Lightweight Authentication Scheme with User Untraceability"

Niranchana Radhakrishnan[1], Marimuthu Karuppiah[1(✉)], Vijayakumar Pandi[2], and Md Zakirul Alam Bhuiyan[3]

[1] School of Computer Science and Engineering,
VIT University, Vellore 632014, Tamilnadu, India
mailtoniranch@gmail.com, marimuthume@gmail.com
[2] Department of Computer Science and Engineering,
University College of Engineering, Tindivanam 604001, Tamilnadu, India
vijibond2000@gmail.com
[3] Department of Computer and Information Sciences,
Fordham University, New York 10458, USA
zakirulalam@gmail.com

Abstract. Many smart cards based authentication schemes need been recommended in the writing. Recently, Yeh suggested a lightweight authentication scheme with user untraceability and claimed that his/her scheme is able to combat several attacks. Though, in this paper, we substantiate that Yeh's scheme will be still defenseless on different malicious attacks and also will be likewise unabated on give acceptable a few necessary security objectives.

Keywords: User anonymity · Smart cards
Offline password guessing attack · Authentication · Replay attack

1 Introduction

The increased advancement of distributed networks has led to growing exchange of resources and services among user devices. As a result, an escalation in transactions has been observed in this cyber-connected era.

Since distributed networks are open in nature, strong system security and effective privacy protection measures have become an implicit necessity for application systems. Therefore, user authentication is an important security measure that needs to be incorporated in such systems in order to differentiate legal users from attackers.

Till date, several literatures have proposed user authentication schemes using smart cards for preserving communication secrecy [1–11]. Recently, Chang et al. [12] proposed a user authentication scheme with user untraceability. Unfortunately, Yeh [13] claimed that Chang et al.'s scheme fails to offer the user untraceability property. In addition, Yeh proved that Chang et al.'s scheme is

© Springer International Publishing AG 2017
G. Wang et al. (Eds.): SpaCCS 2017 Workshops, LNCS 10658, pp. 489–496, 2017.
https://doi.org/10.1007/978-3-319-72395-2_45

insecure against various attacks. Then, Yeh presented an enhanced authentication scheme to fix the flaws of Chang et al.'s scheme. In this paper, first, we have shown that Yeh's scheme [13] does not meet the user anonymity property and there is no local password verification. Additionally, it is open to replay and offline password guessing attacks.

The rest of the paper is structured as follows. Section 2 review the Yeh's scheme. Section 3 explain the weaknesses of Yeh's scheme. Finally, Sect. 4 presents the conclusions.

2   Review of the Scheme in [13]

The authentication scheme in [13] comprises of three phases. registration phase, login and authentication phase, password update phase. They are explained as follows:

2.1   Notations

Table 1 defines the notations used throughout this paper.

Table 1. The notations

Notations	Descriptions
s_i	The server
u_i	The user
Pw_i	The password of u_i
x_s	s_i's secret key
Id_i	The identity of u_i
R_i	s_i's random number
p	Large prime number selected by s_i
y_s	The secret number of s_i
$h(\cdot)$	Secure one-way hash function
T, T_s	Timestamps
$\oplus$	The bitwise XOR operation
ΔT	Predefined legal transmission delay

2.2   Registration Phase

In this phase, u_i registers with s_i. u_i selects Id_i, Pw_i and two random numbers R_1, R_2 then sends $\{Id_i, Pw_i, R_1, R_2\}$ to s_i. On receiving the requisition for registration, s_i calculates $m_i = h(y_s||R_2) \oplus h(Pw_i||R_1)$ and $n_i = h(Id_i||x_s) \oplus h(Pw_i||R_1)$. Then, s_i stores $\{n_i, R_1, m_i, h(\cdot)\}$ in the smart card and send it to u_i through secure channel. Where as, s_i stores $h(h(y_s||R_2))$ instead of storing any information related to u_i, and maintains the cryptic value $h(h(y_s||R_2))$ as a random number in a predetermined table t such that s_i cannot retrieve any information related to u_i from $h(h(y_s||R_2))$.

2.3 Login and Authentication Phase

To login, u_i insets the smart card into device and then keys Id_i and Pw_i. Then the smart card perform the following steps:

1. u_i calculates,

$$a = m_i \oplus h(Pw_i||R_1) = h(y_s||R_2)$$
$$d = R_3 \oplus h(a)$$
$$b = n_i \oplus h(Pw_i||R_1) = h(Id_i||x_s)$$
$$n_i' = n_i \oplus h(h(a)||R_3)$$
$$CId_i = Id_i \oplus h(n_i||h(a)||R_3)$$
$$c = h(n_i||h(a)||b||R_3)$$

where R_3 is a random number choosen by u_i. Then, u_i sends $\{d, CId_i, n_i', c\}$ to s_i.

2. On receiving $\{d, CId_i, n_i', c\}$, s_i calculates

$$R_3^* = d \oplus h(h(y_s||R_2))^*$$
$$n_i^* = n_i' \oplus h(h(h(y_s||R_2))^*||R_3^*)$$
$$Id_i^* = CId_i \oplus h(n_i^*||h(h(y_s||R_2))^*||R_3^*)$$
$$b^* = h(Id_i^*||x_s)$$
$$c^* = h(n_i^*||h(h(y_s||R_2))^*||b^*||R_3^*)$$

and also verifies $c^* \overset{?}{=} c$. If the verification holds, then s_i authenticates u_i. Next, s_i computes $K = h(b^*||h(h(y_s||R_2))^*||R_4)$ where R_4 is a random number of s_i and s_i sends $\{K, R_4\}$ to u_i.

3. On receiving $\{K, R_4\}$, u_i calculates $K^* = h(b||h(a)||R_4)$ and verifies $K^* \overset{?}{=} K$. If the verification holds, then u_i authenticates s_i.

2.4 Password Update Phase

If the User u_i needs to change the password, then u_i uses the smart card and enters his Id_i, Pw_i and the new password $Pw_{i_{new}}$. After that the values of $m_{i_{new}} = m_i \oplus h(Pw_i||R_1) \oplus h(Pw_{i_{new}}||R_1)$ and $n_{i_{new}} = n_i \oplus h(Pw_i||R_1) \oplus h(Pw_{i_{new}}||R_1)$, is computed by the smart card. Then the values of $m_{i_{new}}$ and $n_{i_{new}}$ are saved in the smart card instead of m_i and n_i. If the maximum number of failed request is set to 3, then the failed number of requests exceeds the limit 3 the smart card will be locked and by the use of a specific user reverification procedure the smard card can be unlocked. This method is used to secure against an off-line password guessing attack because the number of instances of password guessing and testing is limited.

3   Cryptanalysis of Yeh's Scheme

We prove that the scheme of Yeh is vulnerable to several attacks in this section. Some of the suppositions are made about the efficiency of an attacker. Note that the following suppositions are somewhat practical and have also been made in recent schemes [14–17]. The assumptions are,

1. The attacker is able to tap, insert, block, alter or eliminate the messages which is sent through a public channel [18–23].
2. The attacker fetches or accidently picks the smart card of the authorized u_i then the secret values saved in the smart card is extracted by using side channel attacks [24,25].

3.1   Offline Password Guessing Attack

Suppose the values $\{n_i, R_1, m_i, h(\cdot)\}$ are stolen by the attacker from a lost smart card under the Assumption 2, and he intercepts the message $\{K, R_4\}$ under Assumption 1. Thus the attacker is able to involve in offline password guessing attack to discover the password Pw_i of u_i as follows,

1. The attacker guess the password Pw_i^*.
2. Computes $b^* = n_i \oplus h(Pw_i^*||R_1)$ and $a^* = m_i \oplus h(Pw_i^*||R_1)$.
3. Computes $K^* = h(b^*||h(a^*)||R_4)$.
4. Then verifies $K \overset{?}{=} K^*$. If it holds, then the password Pw_i^* guessed by the attacker is the correct one (i.e. $Pw_i = Pw_i^*$).
5. If the verification does not hold, then the attacker repeats the steps from (2)–(4) untill $Pw_i = Pw_i^*$.

Thus, the scheme [13] is open to off-line pasword guessing attack.

3.2   Absence of User Anonymity

As we discussed in Sect. 3.1, an intruder can discover Pw_i of u_i. In addition, he has $\{d, CId_i, n_i', c\}$ and $\{n_i, R_1, m_i, h(\cdot)\}$ in accordance with the Assumptions 1 and 2. thus, he can derive identity Id_i of u_i as follows

$$m_i \oplus h(Pw_i||R_1) = h(y_s||R_2) \oplus h(Pw_i||R_1) \oplus h(Pw_i||R_1)$$
$$= h(y_s||R_2)$$
$$= a$$
$$d \oplus h(a) = R_3 \oplus h(a) \oplus h(a)$$
$$= R_3$$
$$h(h(a)||R_3) \oplus n_i' = h(h(a)||R_3) \oplus n_i \oplus h(h(a)||R_3)$$
$$= n_i$$
$$CId \oplus h(n_i||h(a)||R_3) = Id_i \oplus h(n_i||h(a)||R_3) \oplus h(n_i||h(a)||R_3)$$
$$= Id_i$$

Thus, the scheme in [13] fails to preserve the user anonymity property.

3.3 Replay Attack

It is evident that there is an absence of a method for legitimate server to validate the uniqueness of the values in request $\{d, CId_i, n'_i, c\}$ of u_i. Thereby, an legitimate login request which is been already executed, can be utilized once again by the attacker to impersonate as an legitimate user, and also the server fails to find the suspicious behavior, will inturn acknowledge the attacker as expected. Thus, the scheme of Yeh [13] is vulnerable to replay attack.

3.4 Nonexistence of Local Password Checking

In the login phase, u_i inputs Id_i and Pw_i. The smart card does not check the correctness of Id_i and Pw_i. As a result, if u_i keys his/her Id_i and Pw_i or both wrongly the steps in authentication is been accomplished. From this we infer that the scheme is not able to detect the faulty inputs. Therefore, unneeded extra communication and computation overhead will happen.

3.5 Inefficient Password Change Phase

In the scheme [13], if u_i inputs the password wrongly, the smart card doesn't validate the exactness of password and executes the Sect. 2.4. Although u_i may input the password wrongly by mistake. This may lead to denial of service. So that u_i will no longer interconnect with server using the smart card. If u_i inputs Pw_i^* in its place of Pw_i and new password $Pw_{i_{new}}$ then the smart card executes the Sect. 2.4 as follows:

– The smart card computes $m_{i_{new}}$ and $n_{i_{new}}$ as follows

$$m_{i_{new}} = m_i \oplus h(Pw_i^* || R_1) \oplus h(Pw_{i_{new}} || R_1)$$
$$n_{i_{new}} = n_i \oplus h(Pw_i^* || R_1) \oplus h(Pw_{i_{new}} || R_1)$$

– Then the values of $m_{i_{new}}$ and $n_{i_{new}}$ are kept in the smart card instead of m_i and n_i

The password change phase succeeds, in case of entering wrong password. This may cause denial of service, which is clear from the following facts:

– During login and authentication phase, u_i inputs Id_i and $Pw_{i_{new}}$ (updated password).
– Then, u_i calculates,

$$a = m_{i_{new}} \oplus h(Pw_{i_{new}} || R_1)$$
$$= h(y_s || R_2) \oplus h(Pw_i || R_1) \oplus h(Pw_i^* || R_1) \oplus h(Pw_{i_{new}} || R_1) \oplus h(Pw_{i_{new}} || R_1)$$
$$= h(y_s || R_2) \oplus h(Pw_i || R_1) \oplus h(Pw_i^* || R_1)$$
$$\neq h(y_s || R_2)$$

- u_i selects a random number R_3 and computes the following values.

$$d = R_3 \oplus h(a)$$
$$\neq R_3 \oplus h(h(y_s||R_2))$$
$$b = n_{i_{new}} \oplus h(Pw_{i_{new}}||R_1)$$
$$\neq h(Id_i||x_s)$$
$$n_i' = n_{i_{new}} \oplus h(h(a)||R_3)$$
$$\neq h(Id_i||x_s) \oplus h(Pw_{i_{new}}||R_1) \oplus h(h(a)||R_3)$$
$$CId_i = Id_i \oplus h(n_{i_{new}}||h(a)||R_3)$$
$$c = h(n_{i_{new}}||h(a)||b||R_3)$$

- Next, u_i sends $\{d, CId_i, n_i', c\}$ to s_i.
- When receiving $\{d, CId_i, n_i', c\}$, s_i computes

$$R_3^* = d \oplus h(h(y_s||R_2))^*$$
$$= R_3 \oplus h(a) \oplus h(h(y_s||R_2))^*$$
$$\neq R_3$$

However, s_i is unable to derive the identity Id_i of u_i since $R_3^* \neq R_3$. Hence, u_i never pass the verification $c^* \overset{?}{=} c$ of s_i and s_i dismisses the session as login request message authentication fails. This shows that the method in [13] is open to denial of service attack.

4 Conclusion

We have analyzed authentication scheme of Yeh and demonstrated that his/her scheme doesn't achieve local password verification and anonymity of user. In addition, it is defenseless against off-line password guessing attack and replay attack. Hence, the scheme of Yeh is insecure for wireless network communication. Future works will be concentrated on strengthening the scheme of Yeh which can be competent to offer all the security requirements and goals.

References

1. Amin, R.: Cryptanalysis and an efficient secure ID-based remote user authentication using smart card. Int. J. Comput. Appl. **75**(13), 43–48 (2013)
2. Amin, R., Biswas, G.P.: Anonymity preserving secure hash function based authentication scheme for consumer USB mass storage device. In: 2015 Third International Conference on Computer, Communication, Control and Information Technology (C3IT), pp. 1–6. IEEE, February 2015
3. Giri, D., Maitra, T., Amin, R., Srivastava, P.D.: An efficient and robust RSA-based remote user authentication for telecare medical information systems. J. Med. Syst. **39**(1), 145 (2015)

4. He, D., Kumar, N., Chilamkurti, N.: A secure temporal-credentia-based mutual authentication and key agreement scheme with pseudo identity for wireless sensor networks. Inf. Sci. **321**, 263–277 (2015)
5. Islam, S.H.: Design and analysis of a three party password-based authenticated key exchange protocol using extended chaotic maps. Inf. Sci. **312**, 104–130 (2015)
6. Islam, S.H., Biswas, G.P., Choo, K.K.R.: Cryptanalysis of an improved smartcard-based remote password authentication scheme. Inf. Sci. Lett. **3**(1), 35 (2014)
7. Li, X., Niu, J., Karuppiah, M., Kumari, S., Wu, F.: Secure and efficient two-factor user authentication scheme with user anonymity for network based e-health care applications. J. Med. Syst. **40**(12), 268 (2016)
8. Karuppiah, M.: Remote user authentication scheme using smart card: a review. Int. J. Internet Protoc. Technol. **9**(2–3), 107–120 (2016)
9. Kumari, S., Karuppiah, M., Das, A.K., Li, X., Wu, F., Kumar, N.: A secure authentication scheme based on elliptic curve cryptography for IoT and cloud servers. J. Supercomput. 1–26 (2017). https://doi.org/10.1007/s11227-017-2048-0
10. Ali, R., Pal, A.K., Kumari, S., Karuppiah, M., Conti, M.: A secure user authentication and key-agreement scheme using wireless sensor networks for agriculture monitoring. Future Gen. Comput. Syst. (2017). https://doi.org/10.1016/j.future.2017.06.018
11. Guo, C., Luo, N., Jie, Y., Bhuiyan, M.Z.A., Chen, Y., Alam, M.: Key-aggregate authentication cryptosystem for data sharing in dynamic cloud storage. In: 14th International Symposium on Pervasive Systems, Algorithms, and Networks (I-SPAN 2017), Exeter, UK, 23–27 June 2017 (2017)
12. Chang, Y.F., Tai, W.L., Chang, H.C.: Untraceable dynamic-identity-based remote user authentication scheme with verifiable password update. Int. J. Commun Syst **27**(11), 3430–3440 (2014)
13. Yeh, K.H.: A lightweight authentication scheme with user untraceability. Front. Inf. Technol. Electron. Eng. **16**(4), 259–271 (2015)
14. Karuppiah, M., Kumari, S., Li, X., Wu, F., Das, A.K., Khan, M.K., Basu, S.: A dynamic ID-based generic framework for anonymous authentication scheme for roaming service in global mobility networks. Wirel. Pers. Commun. **93**(2), 383–407 (2017)
15. Kumari, S., Karuppiah, M., Li, X., Wu, F., Das, A.K., Odelu, V.: An enhanced and secure trust-extended authentication mechanism for vehicular ad-hoc networks. Secur. Commun. Netw. **9**(17), 4255–4271 (2016)
16. Karuppiah, M., Kumari, S., Das, A.K., Li, X., Wu, F., Basu, S.: A secure lightweight authentication scheme with user anonymity for roaming service in ubiquitous networks. Secur. Commun. Netw. **9**(17), 4192–4209 (2016)
17. Wu, F., Xu, L., Kumari, S., Li, X., Das, A.K., Khan, M.K., Karuppiah, M., Baliyan, R.: A novel and provably secure authentication and key agreement scheme with user anonymity for global mobility networks. Secur. Commun. Netw. **9**(16), 3527–3542 (2016)
18. Karuppiah, M., Saravanan, R.: A secure authentication scheme with user anonymity for roaming service in global mobility networks. Wirel. Pers. Commun. **84**(3), 2055–2078 (2015)
19. Wang, D., Ma, C.: On the (in)security of some smart-card-based password authentication schemes for WSN. IACR Cryptology ePrint Archive 2012:581 (2012)
20. Karuppiah, M., Saravanan, R.: A secure remote user mutual authentication scheme using smart cards. J. Inf. Secur. Appl. **19**(4–5), 257–320 (2014)

21. Wang, D., Wang, P., Liu, J.: Improved privacy-preserving authentication scheme for roaming service in mobile networks. In: IEEE Wireless Communications and Networking Conference (WCNC), Istanbul, Turkey, pp. 3136–3141. IEEE (2014)

22. Karuppiah, M., Saravanan, R.: Cryptanalysis and an improvement of new remote mutual authentication scheme using smart cards. J. Discrete Math. Sci. Cryptogr. **18**(5), 623–649 (2015)

23. Xu, J., Zhu, W.T., Feng, D.G.: An improved smart card based password authentication scheme with provable security. Comput. Stan. Interfaces **31**(4), 723–728 (2009)

24. Kocher, P., Jaffe, J., Jun, B.: Differential power analysis. In: Wiener, M. (ed.) CRYPTO 1999. LNCS, vol. 1666, pp. 388–397. Springer, Heidelberg (1999). https://doi.org/10.1007/3-540-48405-1_25

25. Messerges, T.S., Dabbish, E.A., Sloan, R.H.: Examining smart-card security under the threat of power analysis attacks. IEEE Trans. Comput. **51**(5), 541–552 (2002)

A Security Scheme of Big Data Identity for Cloud Environment

Rongxin Bao, Xu Yuan, Zhikui Chen$^{(\boxtimes)}$, and Yujie Zhang

School of Software Technology, Dalian University of Technology,
Dalian 116600, China
zkchen@dlut.edu.cn

Abstract. Nowadays, the security and privacy protection of Big Data have faced with severe challenges, especially on cloud environment with insecure channel. To address this issue, this paper proposes a security scheme of Big Data identity (SSBDI) for cloud environment, which can guarantee the security of Big Data transmission in the insecure channel. In SSBDI, firstly, linear congruential generator (LCG) based encryption matrixes and Vigenère cipher are employed to set the identity encryption by the client. After that, key bits are added to the end of cipher text in the encryption process. Finally, cipher texts are decrypted and computed in the cloud environment. Innovatively, each key bit can determine the encoding rule of one or more cipher text bits. Experimental results on National Institute of Standards and Technology (NIST) test show that the proposed scheme can meet the randomness of the security requirements. More important, with a very small amount of memory and CPU time cost, the scheme can encrypt massive data, which is particularly significant for Big Data identity encryption.

Keywords: Cloud environment · Vigenère cipher · Insecure channel
Big data ID · Security scheme

1 Introduction

Nowadays the development of social information and network leads to the explosive growth of data. Meanwhile, the increasing popularity and development of data mining technologies bring serious threat to the security of private information [1]. For example, Health Insurance data include personal medical and drug information [2]. Similarly, the data of Social Network contain individual's sensitive information such as address and contact information. The leaking of these sensitive data may lead to sharing of privacy information. Hence, the risk of security and privacy has been recognized as one of the key risks in Big Data [3, 4].

In fact, the meaning of Big Data security and privacy is more widely, and the threat is not limited to personal privacy leakage. As for other information, in the storage, processing, transmission and other processes Big Data are also facing various security risks. Particularly, the Big Data security issues in cloud computing over insecure channel are more challenging [5]. In the cloud computing, although the service provider controls the storage and operating environment of data, users still have some

© Springer International Publishing AG 2017
G. Wang et al. (Eds.): SpaCCS 2017 Workshops, LNCS 10658, pp. 497–506, 2017.
https://doi.org/10.1007/978-3-319-72395-2_46

ways to protect data security, such as utilizing cryptography to achieve data security or through a trusted computing environment to achieve safe operation [6, 7]. Therefore, a variety of effective schemes have been developed to track this problem. Specifically, existing security schemes can be categorized into two classes, namely weak-password and strong-password. The weak-password [8, 9] generally utilizes public-key cryptographic in which verifier tables are not required. Although weak-password schemes are convenient for user login, they lead heavy computational load and memory consumption. In contrast, due to the utilization of simple encryption methods, strong-password [10, 11] is feasible in computational load and memory consumption. However, strong-password schemes suffer from guessing attacks.

To address the aforementioned problems, this paper proposes a security scheme of Big Data identity for cloud environment over insecure channel. In practice, encryption is an effective way to deal with Big Data security and privacy issues. Hence, in our scheme, we first map identity into a target hex. After that, LCG-based encryption matrixes and Vigenère cipher are employed to set the identity encryption and decrypted in the cloud environment. Furthermore, key bits are added to the end of cipher text in the encryption process. Experimental results show that the cipher text generated by the proposed scheme have good statistical properties and random characteristics. Moreover, our scheme can improve the efficiency and reduce the consumption of space when encoding Big Data identity.

The contributions of the paper can be summarized as follows:

(1) By defining a mapping, the bit length of cipher text is reduced, yet, randomness and security of Big Data ID on cloud environment is greatly enhanced.

(2) By utilizing an innovation structure of adding the key bits to the encoding, SSBDI is not necessary to verify that the cipher text is repeated. Therefore, the CPU time cost is reduced effectively, which is particularly significant for Big Data encryption tasks.

(3) Different from previous security encryption schemes, which need data structure to store or ensure the non-repeatability of the temporary ID. This paper utilizes the combination of plaintext and key, so that it does not need to pre store the encrypted codes. Meanwhile it can achieve directly output encoding, saving memory consumption effectively.

2   Related Work

2.1   Vigenère Cipher

Vigenère cipher is proposed by Blaise de Vigenère. It uses the "one to many" corresponding rule, which means a plaintext letter can be substituted by multiple cipher text letters. Specifically, it is a polyalphabetic substitution based on the Vigenère tableau consisted of 26 Caesar tableaus. Different from other polyalphabetic ciphers, Vigenère key stream does not depend on the plaintext characters, yet it depends only on the position of character in the plaintext [12]. The cipher blocks and encryption equation are as follows:

Plaintext block: $P = p_0 p_1 p_2 \cdots p_{n-1}$;
Keyword block: $K = k_0 k_1 k_2 \ldots k_{n-1}$;
Cipher text block: $C = C_0 C_1 C_2 \ldots C_{n-1}$;

Encryption equation:

$$C_i = E(k_i, p_i) = (p_i + k_i) \bmod 26 \tag{1}$$

Decryption equation:

$$p_i = E^{-1}(C_i, k_i)(C_i - k_i) \bmod 26 \tag{2}$$

Substitution rules of mono alphabetic in plaintext make use of 26 Caesar Ciphers with shifts 0 to 25. The strength of such a cipher is that each of the characters in the plaintext corresponds to a plurality of cipher text characters, and each cipher letter uses a unique key character. Hence, the frequency information of the letter occurrence is hidden.

2.2 Encryption Method for Big Data

Recently, security of cloud environment has received much attention from academia [13]. Especially, Ding et al. [14] found that insider threats from cloud operators have become an important concern for Big Data security. Therefore, a variety of methods have been developed to track this problem. With regard to the problem of encryption method for Big Data identity, aforementioned studies can be summarized as four types, including the test selection method, extraction method, Linear Feedback Shift Register (LFSR) method and interpolation polynomial method.

Generally speaking, test selection method utilizes some traditional methods, including LCG, Hash function, ElGamal and so on. In the method, when two cipher texts are stored, there will be an exception, which ensures the cipher texts are not repeated. However, when half of the identities have been generated, the repetition rate of cipher texts will be higher and higher, and the time complexity of the algorithm increases exponentially. Similarity, the extraction method is proposed in [15]. The method requires that all encryption results are generated and stored in advance. Specifically, Peng [15] proposed a FWRF algorithm which makes each code extract a different probability. However, for multi-bit encryption tasks, regardless of the use of any optimization, optimized memory space is huge.

To encrypt the number on the basis of user's seed, Mashhadi and Dehkordi [16] proposed a LFSR based scheme, which encrypts a sequence of unique codes by continually shifting the register and inserting the value of the feedback function into the register. However, according to the test results in [17], the randomness of the encrypted sequence is not strong enough to meet the security requirement. Furthermore, for ease of verification, by constructing a Lagrange polynomial, the author in [18] makes it encrypt unique identity by passing given points and approximating a given curve.

According to the test results in [19], it takes more than 20 min to construct a 400°
interpolation polynomial.

To the best of our knowledge, no prior studies considered the Vigenère cipher
encryption scheme for identity of Big Data.

3 Security Scheme for Big Data Identity (SSBDI)

Assuming that n-bit cipher text needs to be generated, n bits are divided in i identity
bits and j key bits. Each key bit corresponds to a tableau of cipher, which can determine
the encoding rules of one to more bits in identity. In addition, the key bits are added to
the cipher text to ensure that all cipher texts do not repeat, which is an innovative and
bold method.

3.1 Framework for SSBDI

The basic idea of data encryption is the use of different forms of information to
camouflage sensitive information, so that unauthorized persons cannot understand the
protected data. SSBDI is based on Vigenère cipher, which can meet the security
requirements of data anonymity and insecure channel, and is lightweight for terminal
users.

The process of framework for SSBDI is shown in Fig. 1, which not only protects
the anonymity of the data identity but also allows the user to autonomously update the
key matrix. In the following sections of this chapter, we will describe how to encrypt
Big Data identity in details.

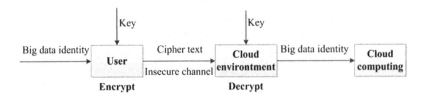

Fig. 1. The process of framework for SSBDI

3.2 Keyword Design

Assuming that each key bit has m possible values, and a key bit can be used to
determine the encoding rule for one or more bits of cipher text. Furthermore, the more
key bits there are, the more random the encrypted after the encryption, which is more in
line with the distribution fitting test and independence test.

If each bit of the key determines two bits in the cipher text bit, an encryption matrix
of m rows and 2 columns needs to be designed, and together they form matrixes A, B,
C, $D \in \mathbb{R}^{m \times 2}$. In the generation of the key bits, the elements of each column in the
encryption matrix are selected from the natural numbers 0 to $m-1$. Meanwhile, the
numbers in same column and row had better are not the same as far as possible, so as to

ensure the randomness of the generated codes. The encryption matrixes are shown as follows:

$$A = \begin{bmatrix} a_{0,0} & a_{0,1} \\ \vdots & \vdots \\ a_{m,0} & a_{m,1} \end{bmatrix} \quad B = \begin{bmatrix} b_{0,0} & b_{0,1} \\ \vdots & \vdots \\ b_{m,0} & b_{m,1} \end{bmatrix}$$

$$C = \begin{bmatrix} c_{0,0} & c_{0,1} \\ \vdots & \vdots \\ c_{m,0} & c_{m,1} \end{bmatrix} \quad D = \begin{bmatrix} d_{0,0} & d_{0,1} \\ \vdots & \vdots \\ d_{m,0} & d_{m,1} \end{bmatrix}$$

The key bits are generated by random functions in accordance with the above rules.

$$k_i = C_i = Random\,(m) \tag{3}$$

Random (m) denotes that generate a random positive integer less than m. Specifically, we use LCG to generate random numbers in keyword block. The general form of LCG is as follow:

$$Random\,(m) = (aC_{i-1} + b)\,mod\,m \tag{4}$$

where a and b are secret keys, which can be set or use compiler environment defaults. After giving the initial value C_0, the random number is generated according to this formula and further combined into a keyword block.

3.3 Big Data Identity Encryption Algorithm

We describe Big Data identity encryption algorithm for cloud environment in this part. To reduce computation load and avoid the revealing of Big Data ID, we use the Vigenère cipher technique to encrypt the identity in the client and then upload them to the cloud environment. In Vigenère cipher, it is better to have the cipher text bits of the same key bit not adjacent, which will appear to be more random. For example, the correspondence is defined as follows, k_i encrypts p_0 and p_2 as well as k_{i+1} encrypts p_1 and p_3 and so on. According to the key bits and Vigenère cipher encoding rules, the encryption process of Big Data identity is defined as:

$$C_j = E(P_j) = \begin{cases} (a_{k,j/2} + P_j)\,mod\,m & if\ \ j\,mod\,4 = 0 \\ (b_{k,\lfloor j/2 \rfloor} + P_j)\,mod\,m & if\ j\,mod\,4 = 1 \\ (c_{k,j/2} + P_j)\,mod\,m & if\ \ j\,mod\,4 = 2 \\ (d_{k,\lfloor j/2 \rfloor} + P_j)\,mod\,m & if\ \ j\,mod\,4 = 3 \end{cases} \tag{5}$$

where a, b, c, d denotes different encryption matrixes and P_j denotes bits of plaintext. Specifically, Eq. 5 is only for four key bits and four encryption matrixes situation. The ciphertext encryption scheme is outlined in Table 1.

Table 1. Big data identity encryption algorithm

SSBDI-ENCRYPTION (*amount*)▷amount is total number of Big Data

1 **for** $j \leftarrow 0$ **to** *amount*
2 **do** $p = Random(m)$
3 $q = Random(m)$
4 $l \leftarrow length[plaintext]$
5 **for** $i \leftarrow 0$ **to** l
6 **do if** I **mod** $2 = 0$ ▷ for two key bits situation
7 **then** $V[i] \leftarrow (plaintext [i]+matrix1[p, i /2])$ **mod** $(l-1)$
8 **else** $V[i] \leftarrow (plaintext[i] + matrix2[q, [i /2]])$ **mod** $(l-1)$
9 $V[i+1] \leftarrow p$
10 $V[i+2] \leftarrow q$
11 map all cipher texts in V to characters
12 **return** V

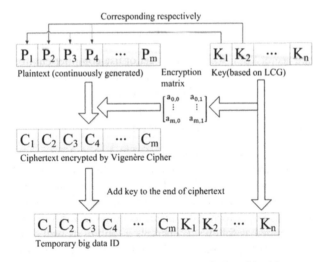

Fig. 2. The process of security scheme designed in this paper

As shown in Table 1, the plaintext is non-repetitive and key bits are added to the end of cipher text. In addition, different key bits correspond to different encryption matrix and plaintext ID is unique. Hence, the uniqueness of encrypted identity is easy to prove.

Figure 2 shows the flow chart of the encryption process in the scheme. The addition of the key bit guarantees the uniqueness of the temporary identity. The encryption process is reversible. Hence, when decrypting in the cloud environment, after obtaining the encryption matrix, it can be decrypted with the inverse operation of Eq. 6. The decryption process of Big Data identity is defined as:

$$P_j = E^{-1}(C_j) \qquad (6)$$

The existence of the security scheme is not forged. Even if the attackers cracked the encoding method and get the key bits, in the case of the encryption matrixes cannot be obtained, the original Big Data ID is still safe. Considering that attackers guess the encryption matrixes using the exhaustive method, matrixes require $g = 4 * (m * 2)^m$ guesses. If we set m is 36, g is about $2.92 * 10^{67}$, which is still a huge amount for computer. Therefore, the scheme proposed ensures the anonymity and security of Big Data identity.

4   Experiment Evaluation

In order to analyze the performance of the scheme proposed in this paper, three groups of experiments are conducted. In the first experiment, the randomness of the temporary ID encrypted is tested by NIST test in Ubuntu. The second experiment is conducted to evaluate the time consumption of SSBDI compared with two other security encryption methods in Ubuntu. Finally, in Windows OS, we evaluate the performance of SSBDI in terms of memory cost.

4.1   Stochastic Analysis

According to the random coding test method proposed by NIST 800-22, in this section, we have tested the encrypted codes of the proposed scheme comprehensively. After each test of the random binary subsequence, a P-value is generated, if the P-value is greater than the level of significance 0.01, then unique ID codes are determined by the test.

In order to ensure the randomness of sequences, we use a 4-bit plaintext with 4-bit keyword encoding rule in the test, and then generated codes is converted to binary subsequences. Since the converted binary subsequence lengths are not the same, we only intercept the last 25 bits of each binary subsequence, which is allowed in the NIST test. Afterwards, a total of 100000 random codes are generated in this experiment, which consisted of 2500000 binary subsequences. The test results are presented in Table 2.

It can be seen from Table 2 that the proposed method has a P-value greater than 0.01 in all 16 tests, better than the other two methods, which means that the method passes all NIST tests. Hence, SSBDI already has the randomness and unpredictability to meet the security requirements.

4.2   CPU Time Analysis

In the ID-based encrypted scheme, the main time cost is the stored procedure. As has been analyzed in related work, to encrypt Big Data, the feasibility of the extraction

Table 2. Results tested by NIST 800-22. Checkmark denotes the method pass the test. Cross mark denotes the method do not pass the test.

Statistical Test	P-value of SSBDI	SSBDI	LFSR	LCG
Frequency	0.860433	✓	✓	✓
Block frequency (m = 128)	0.953472	✓	✓	✓
Cusum-forward	0.687365	✓	✓	✓
Cusum-reverse	0.848333	✓	✓	✓
Runs	0.410956	✓	✓	✓
Long runs of ones	0.012516	✓	✗	✗
Rank	0.015008	✓	✓	✓
Spectual DFT	0.163646	✓	✓	✓
Non-overlapping templates (m = 9)	0.411217	✓	✗	✓
Overlapping templates (m = 9)	0.776836	✓	✗	✓
Universal	0.942632	✓	✗	✓
Approximate entropy (m = 10)	0.271404	✓	✗	✓
Random excursions	0.908587	✓	✗	✓
Random excursions variant	0.392215	✓	✗	✓
Linear complexity (M = 500)	0.330578	✓	✓	✓
Serial (m = 16)	0.227058	✓	✗	✓

method and interpolation polynomial method are very low. We take the selection method based on LCG, LFSR and SSBDI as an example, and test the time of encrypting fixed amount of Big Data identity. In the test, we use an 8-bit cipher text with 4-bit keyword encryption rule in SSBDI and the amount of cipher text is millions. Test results are shown in Fig. 3.

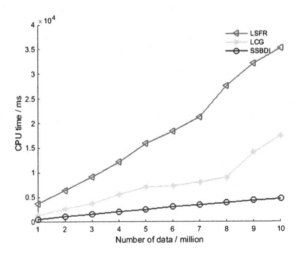

Fig. 3. CPU time analysis result

It can be seen from Fig. 3 that, in the millions of data encryption test, compared with LCG method and LFSR method, SSBDI can encrypt data in much less CPU time, which becomes more obvious as the number of data increases. The CPU time curve of our scheme is nearly linear.

4.3   Memory Analysis

In this section, we evaluate the performance of SSBDI in terms of memory cost. In the test, LCG and LFSR are chosen to compare with SSBDI. Specifically, the result of memory cost is based on Memory (dedicated working set) in Windows Task Manager.

First, we perform all three methods to encode 10 million 12-bits random codes. We choose 12-bit coding because it can ensure that the number of bits is enough and is conducive to the SSBDI key distribution. Afterwards, the methods are kept holding on for recording the memory cost. Finally, we close the methods and the Memory (dedicated working set) is initial memory cost of scheme.

Table 3 shows initial memory cost and the memory cost after running of SSBDI, LCG and LFSR. As shown in Table 3, the initial memory cost of the three methods is very close. However, after encrypting 10 million codes, our scheme SSBDI achieves lower memory cost than the others. Specially, it is about 20% lower than LFSR and 99% lower than LCG. Hence, our method can encrypt large amounts of data identity with only a small amount of memory.

Table 3. Memory cost (dedicated working set) of three schemes

Generator	Initial memory cost	10 million data memory cost
SSBDI	3396 KB	5528 KB
LCG	3432 KB	637692 KB
LFSR	3364 KB	6920 KB

5   Conclusion

Encryption is an effective way to deal with Big Data security and privacy issues. Therefore, in this paper, we proposed a security scheme of Big Data identity for cloud environment based on Vigenère cipher, namely, SSBDI, which addresses the problem that how to encrypt Big Data ID over an insecure channel safely and efficiently. In SSBDI, the encryption operations are performed by the client while cipher texts are decrypted in the cloud environment. Compared to some previous schemes, the proposed scheme is random enough and reached first place in CPU time and memory consumption. Due to the diversity of the rules in different regions, the scheme is scalable enough to adjust the coding structure according to the actual amount requirements. This allows us to apply the scheme to cloud environment with insecure channel. Our future work involves reducing system load and enhancing authentication security, so that the scheme can be applied to mobile devices.

Acknowledgements. This work was supported by the National Key Research and Development Program of China under Grant No. 2016YFD0800300.

References

1. Xu, L., Jiang, C., Wang, J., et al.: Information security in big data: privacy and data mining. IEEE Access **2**, 1149–1176 (2014)
2. Zhang, Q., Chen, Z., Yang, L.T.: A node scheduling model based on markov chain prediction for big data. Int. J. Commun. Syst. **28**(9), 1610–1619 (2015)
3. Mayer-Schönberger, V., Cukier, K.: Big data: a revolution that will transform how we live, work, and think. Houghton Mifflin Harcourt (2013)
4. Zhang, Q., et al.: PPHOPCM: privacy-preserving high-order possibilistic c-means algorithm for big data clustering with cloud computing. IEEE Trans. Big Data **PP**(99), 1 (2017)
5. Yi, M., Wang, L., Ma, Y.: Efficient security sequencing problem over insecure channel based on homomorphic encryption. China Commun. **13**(9), 195–202 (2016)
6. Zhang, Q., Chen, Z.: A distributed weighted possibilistic c-means algorithm for clustering incomplete big sensor data. Int. J. Distrib. Sens. Netw. **2**, 4 (2014)
7. Zhang, Q., Zhu, C., Yang, L.T., Chen, Z., Zhao, L., Li, P.: An incremental CFS algorithm for clustering large data in industrial internet of things. IEEE Trans. Industr. Inf. **13**(3), 1193–1201 (2017)
8. ElGamal, T.: A public key cryptosystem and a signature scheme based on discrete logarithms. IEEE Trans. Inf. Theory **31**(4), 469–472 (1985)
9. Hwang, M.S., Chang, C.C., Hwang, K.F.: An ElGamal-like cryptosystem for enciphering large messages. IEEE Trans. Knowl. Data Eng. **14**(2), 445–446 (2002)
10. Cao, T., Zhai, J.: Improved dynamic ID-based authentication scheme for telecare medical information systems. J. Med. Syst. **37**(2), 1–7 (2013)
11. Chaturvedi, A., Mishra, D., Mukhopadhyay, S.: An enhanced dynamic ID-based authentication scheme for telecare medical information systems. J. King Saud Univ.-Comput. Inf. Sci. (2015)
12. Bhateja, A., Kumar, S.: Genetic algorithm with elitism for cryptanalysis of vigenere cipher. In: 2014 International Conference on Issues and Challenges in Intelligent Computing Techniques (ICICT), pp. 373–377. IEEE (2014)
13. Zhang, Q., Chen, Z., Lv, A., Zhao, L., Liu, F., Zou, J.: A universal storage architecture for big data in cloud environment. In: IEEE International Conference on Internet of Things, pp. 476–480 (2013)
14. Ding, Y., Wang, H., Shi, P., Wu, Q., Dai, H., Fu, H.: Trusted cloud service. Chin. J. Comput. **38**(1), 133–149 (2015)
15. Peng, X.F.: Research of random numbers fetch algorithm based on windows. Comput. Eng. Des. **3**, 010 (2007)
16. Mashhadi, S., Dehkordi, M.H.: Two verifiable multi secret sharing schemes based on nonhomogeneous linear recursion and LFSR public-key cryptosystem. Inf. Sci. **294**, 31–40 (2015)
17. Lin, Y.T., Huang, Y.H., Hsiao, Y.H., et al.: An implementation of the efficient huge amount of pseudo-random unique numbers generator and the acceleration analysis of parallelization. In: International Conference on Data Science and Advanced Analytics, pp. 600–606. IEEE (2016)
18. Liu, Y.N., Ye, J., Cao, J.Y.: Verifiable random number based on interpolating polynomial over Fp. Sichuan Daxue Xuebao **42**(6), 105–108 (2010)
19. Zhou, J., Zou, S.D., Ming, L.I., et al.: A layered group key distribution scheme based on the lagrange interpolating polynomial. J. Xiamen Univ. (2007)

A Compact Construction for Non-monotonic Online/Offline CP-ABE Scheme

Junqi Zhang, Qingfeng Cheng[(✉)], Fushan Wei, and Xinglong Zhang

State Key Laboratory of Mathematical Engineering and Advanced Computing,
Zhengzhou 450001, China
qingfengc2008@sina.com

Abstract. Nowadays the mobile devices are becoming the necessities in our life, while they are generally resource-constrained, CP-ABE schemes designed for mobile devices should have the property of low computational complexity, therefore Online/Offline mechanism has prospect future in cryptographic mechanism. In this paper, we attempt to construct an unbounded Online/Offline CP-ABE scheme based on a non-monotonic access structure. During the offline phase, most of the computations for encryption are done; during the online phase, we transform the non-monotonic access structure with positive attribute sets into a monotonic access structure which is based on the LSSS access structure with positive and negative attribute sets, then it only needs a small amount of addition and multiplication operations for the rest components of encryption. Compared with the original non-monotonic CP-ABE scheme, our scheme remains the same on the public keys and the master secret keys, with only a small increase in computational complexity. The computational complexity during online phase is very small.

Keywords: Online/offline mechanism · Linear secret-sharing scheme
Bilinear maps · Non-monotonic access structure

1 Introduction

The concept of Attribute-Based Encryption (ABE) was introduced by Sahai and Waters [1] in EUROCRYPT 2005, it could improve the error-tolerance property of biometrics-based identity in IBE. In the ABE system we could encrypt the data for a group of receivers according to some policy, and the credentials are represented by a group of strings called "attributes", while the predicate is represented by a formula over these attributes. As the ABE system could support fine-grained access control, it could be widely used in cloud computing and big data. There are 2 main types of ABE system, Key-Policy ABE (KP-ABE) [2] and Ciphertext-Policy ABE (CP-ABE) [3]. In KP-ABE the key policy is associated with the access structure while the ciphertext is associated with a set of attributes, decryption is possible when the attribute set satisfies the key policy. Contrary to KP-ABE, in CP-ABE the private key is associated with the user's attribute set and the ciphertext policy is associated with the access structure.

We provide an example for ease of understanding: There are 3 students (A, B, C) in a laboratory, the attribute set of A is {Degree: postgraduate, Major: cryptography,

© Springer International Publishing AG 2017
G. Wang et al. (Eds.): SpaCCS 2017 Workshops, LNCS 10658, pp. 507–523, 2017.
https://doi.org/10.1007/978-3-319-72395-2_47

Name: Mandy}, B is {Degree: postgraduate, Major: cryptography, Name: Jack}, C is {Degree: doctor, Major: cryptography, Name: Jane}, A professor defined an access structure Π = {((Degree: postgraduate) $\wedge$ (Major: cryptography)}, and encrypted a project report based on an ABE scheme, then he disposed the access structure to the ciphertext. The professor stored the ciphertext in the cloud, all the students could download the ciphertext. However, only A and B satisfy the access structure and could decrypt normally. We could find that the ABE scheme has the fine grained access control property from the example above.

The ABE system with monotonic structure can express a wide class of access structures, however it still has limitations. To solve this problem, a possible solution [3] is to let the attribute space include attributes that express absence of attributes. While it is not convenient for practical applications due to the total number of attributes increases significantly. This problem was addressed by Ostrovsky et al. [4] in 2007. By introducing the idea of revocation mechanism to the ABE system, they proposed the first non-monotonic KP-ABE scheme. The scheme need not to increase the size of shares or the ciphertext and the access structure can deal with Boolean formula that includes AND gate, OR gate, and NOT gate. Several non-monotonic ABE schemes were constructed in [3, 5] subsequently. In 2014, Yamada et al. [6] firstly proposed unbounded CP-ABE and KP-ABE schemes with non-monotonic structure. While the scale of the ciphertexts and private keys are too large, which lead to high computational complexity. It provides us with a good idea to design an ABE scheme via a generic transformation.

In 2014 Hohenberger and Waters [7] applied the Online/Offline mechanism to an ABE scheme. The cost of key generation and encrypion mainly concentrated in offline phase, during online phase, the system needs little resources to generate the ciphertexts and keys.

In 2015 Rouselakis and Waters [8] proposed a large-universe CP-ABE scheme with multi-authorities, by allowing multiple authorities instead of one authority to control the key distribution, the system could achieve maximum versatility. However, the above schemes can not preserve access policies' privacy or sustain expensive computational cost during the encryption and decryption phases. In 2016 Chow et al. [9] proposed a framework for constructing multi-authority ABE schemes with attribute revocation and out-sourced decryption, from any pairing-based single-authority ABE scheme which satisfies a set of properties we identified.

In 2017, Shao et al. [10] proposed an Online/Offline and outsourced multi-authority ABE scheme with policy protection. The main idea is to alleviate the online computation overhead for owners by splitting the encryption algorithm to the online encryption and offline encryption. The scheme can lighten the computation burden for both owners and users and is quite appropriate for resource-limited devices in the multi-authority systems.

Our Contributions. In this paper, we applied the Online/Offline mechanism on a non-monotonic CP-ABE scheme. During conversion, we divide the encrypt phase into 2 parts: the online phase and the offline phase. During the offline phase, most of the computations for encryption are done; during the online phase, we transform the non-monotonic access structure with positive attribute sets into a monotonic access structure which is based on LSSS with positive and negative attribute sets, then it only needs a small amount of addition and multiplication operations for the rest components of encryption. Compared with the original non-monotonic CP-ABE scheme, our scheme remains the same on the public keys and the master secret keys, with small increase in computational complexity. However, the computational complexity during online phase is very small.

From literature [3] we could find that compared with the KP-ABE scheme, the CP-ABE scheme is conceptually closer to traditional access control methods. The disadvantage is the size of the private keys grows linearly with the scale of attribute sets.

2 Preliminaries

2.1 Definition of Online/Offline CP-ABE

Definition 1 (An Online/Offline CP-ABE scheme [7]): An Online/Offline CP-ABE scheme consists of the following algorithms: **Setup, Offline. Encrypt, Online. Encrypt, Extract, Decrypt.**

Setup $(\lambda, U) \rightarrow (Mpk, Msk)$**:** The setup algorithm takes as input a security parameter λ, the attribute scale U. Then it outputs a master public key Mpk and a master secret key Msk.

Offline. Encrypt $(Mpk) \rightarrow IT$**:** The Offline encrypt algorithm takes as input the master public key Mpk. Then it outputs an intermediate ciphertext IT.

Online. Encrypt $(M, Mpk, IT, \mathbb{A}) \rightarrow CT$**:** The **Online. Encrypt** algorithm takes as input the message M, the master public key Mpk, the intermediate ciphertext IT and the access structure $\mathbb{A}$, then it outputs the ciphertext CT.

Extract $(Mpk, Msk, S) \rightarrow sk$**:** The **Extract** algorithm takes as input the master public key Mpk, the master secret key Msk, and the attribute set S. Then it outputs a private key sk.

Decrypt $(sk, CT) \rightarrow M$**:** The decryption algorithm takes as input the private key sk, the ciphertext CT. If S satisfies the access structure $\mathbb{A}$, the algorithm will decrypt normally and return a message M.

Definition 2 (Security model for Online/Offline CP-ABE scheme [7]): For a polynomial time adversary $\mathcal{A}$, if the advantage of winning the following game is negligible, we say that the Online/Offline CP-ABE scheme is IND-CPA secure under the selective security model.

We simulate the following game between the adversary $\mathcal{A}$ and the challenger $\mathcal{B}$.

Init: $\mathcal{A}$ declares the access structure $\mathbb{A}$ as the target attack objects.

Setup: $\mathcal{B}$ chooses a security parameter and runs the **Setup** algorithm, then $\mathcal{B}$ gives the master public key Mpk to $\mathcal{A}$ and keeps the master secret key Msk.

Phase 1: $\mathcal{A}$ makes repeated private key generation queries with a restriction that none of the set of attributes in **Init** phase could satisfy the access structure $\mathbb{A}$, where $S \notin \mathbb{A}$. $\mathcal{B}$ runs the KeyGen algorithm and transmits sk to $\mathcal{A}$.

Challenge: $\mathcal{A}$ submits two equal length messages m_0, m_1 to $\mathcal{B}$. $\mathcal{B}$ flips a random coin $b \in \{0, 1\}$, and runs the Online. Encrypt(m_b, Mpk, Offline.Encrypt(Mpk)) algorithm. The ciphertext CT^* is given to the adversary $\mathcal{A}$.

Phase 2: Same as **Phase 1**.

Guess: The adversary $\mathcal{A}$ outputs a guess b'. The advantage of the adversary $\mathcal{A}$ in this game is defined as $Adv = |Pr[b' = b] - 1/2|$. If $Adv > \varepsilon$, we say that the adversary wins the game by the advantage of ε, otherwise we say that this scheme is indistinguishable under chosen plaintext attack.

2.2 Access Structures

Definition 3 (Monotonic Access Structure [11]): Let $\mathcal{P}$ be a set of parties, A collection $\mathbb{A}$ is said to be monotonic if, for all B, C, if $B \in \mathbb{A}$ and $B \subset C$, then $C \in \mathbb{A}$ holds. An access structure consists of several non-empty subsets. The sets in $\mathbb{A}$ are called the authorized sets, and the sets not in $\mathbb{A}$ are called the unauthorized sets.

For each access structure $\mathbb{A} \in \mathcal{AS}$, the set $\mathcal{P}$ of underlying parties consists of the following properties: the elements in $\mathcal{P}$ may have two types: either the element is non-negated (like x) or it is primed (like x^-), and if $x \in \mathcal{P}$ then $x^- \in \mathcal{P}$ and vice versa. Conceptually, prime attributes are associated with negation of non-negated attributes.

Definition 4 (Non-monotonic Access Structure [12]): For each access structure $\mathbb{A} \in \mathcal{AS}$ over a set of parties $\mathcal{P}$, one defines a possibly non-monotonic access structure $\tilde{\mathbb{A}} = NM(\mathbb{A})$ over the set $\tilde{\mathcal{P}}$ of all unprimed parties in $\mathcal{P}$. For each set $\tilde{\mathcal{S}} \subset \tilde{\mathcal{P}}, N(\tilde{\mathcal{S}})$ is defined as $N(\tilde{\mathcal{S}}) = \tilde{\mathcal{S}} \cup \{x' | x \in \tilde{\mathcal{P}} \backslash \tilde{\mathcal{S}}\}$. Then $NM(\mathbb{A})$ is defined by saying that $\tilde{\mathcal{S}}$ is authorized in $NM(\mathbb{A})$ if and only if $N(\tilde{\mathcal{S}})$ is authorized in $\mathbb{A}$. For each access set $X \in \tilde{\mathbb{A}}$, there is a set $N(X)$ in $\mathbb{A}$ containing the elements in X and primed elements for each party in $\tilde{\mathbb{A}} \backslash X$.

For example, let $\mathcal{P} = \{x_1, x_2, x_3, x_4, x_1^-, x_2^-, x_3^-, x_4^-\}$, then $\tilde{\mathcal{P}} = \{x_1, x_2, x_3, x_4\}$, one defines a non-monotonic access structure $\tilde{\mathbb{A}} = (x_1 \wedge x_2^- \wedge x_3)$ over the attribute set $\tilde{\mathcal{P}}$. We can get that only the set $X_1 = \{x_1, x_3\} \subset \tilde{\mathcal{P}}$ and $X_2 = \{x_1, x_3, x_4\} \subset \tilde{\mathcal{P}}$ are authorized in $\tilde{\mathbb{A}}$, and X_1 is associated with $N(X_1) = \{x_1, x_2^-, x_3, x_4^-\}$, X_2 is associated with $N(X_2) = \{x_1, x_2^-, x_3, x_4\}$. Thus we can get $(x_1 \wedge x_2^- \wedge x_3)$ is non-monotonic access structure in X_1 and X_2, but monotonic access structure in $N(X_1)$ and $N(X_2)$.

Definition 5 (Linear Secret-Sharing Schemes (LSSS) [11]): Given a set of parties $P = \{P_1, P_2, \cdots, P_n\}$, let (L, ρ) be the access structure $\mathbb{A}$, where L denotes a $l \times n$ matrix, each row in matrix L represents as a participant. LSSS consists of the following two algorithms:

Secret Sharing Algorithm: Let $s \in Z_p$ be the secret to be shared and randomly choose $r_2, r_3, \cdots, r_n \in Z_p$, we consider the column vector as $v = (s, r_2, r_3, \cdots, r_n)^T$, the secret shares $\lambda_i = L_i \cdot v$ belongs to the party $\rho(i)$, where L_i denotes the $i-th$ row of matrix L.

Secret Reconstruction Algorithm: Let S be any authorized access set, and let $I \subset \{1, 2, \cdots, l\}$ be defined as $I = \{i : \rho(i) \in S\}$. There exists constants $\{w_i\}_{i \in I}$ which can be computed in polynomial time such that, if λ_i are valid shares of any secret s, then we could recover the secret $\sum_{i \in I} \omega_i \lambda_i = s$.

2.3 Theoretic Assumption

Let G, G_T be two multiplicative cyclic groups of prime order p, g be a generator of G and e be an efficiently computable mapping $e : G \times G \to G_T$. For any $g, h \in G$, $a, b \in Z_p$, we have $e(g^a, h^b) = e(g, h)^{ab}$ and $e(g, g) \neq 1$. We say that e is a bilinear map if the group operation in G and e are both computable.

Assumption 1 $(m - (B)$ **assumption** [6]): The algorithm randomly picks $s, a, b_1, \cdots, b_m \in Z_p$, and defines

$$
\Psi = \{g, g^s,
$$
$$
g^{a^i}, g^{b_j}, g^{sb_j}, g^{sb_ib_j}, g^{a^ib_j}, g^{a^i/b_j^2} \quad \forall(i,j) \in [m,m]
$$
$$
g^{a^i/b_j} \quad \forall(i,j) \in [2m,m], i \neq m+1
$$
$$
g^{a^ib_j/b_{j'}^2} \quad \forall(i,j,j') \in [2m,m,m], j \neq j'
$$
$$
g^{sa^ib_j/b_{j'}}, g^{sa^ib_j/b_{j'}^2} \quad \forall(i,j,j') \in [m,m,m], j \neq j'
$$
$$
g^{sa^ib_jb_{j'}/b_{j''}^2} \quad \forall(i,j,j',j'') \in [m,m,m,m], j \neq j'', j' \neq j'' \}
$$

The adversary $\mathcal{A}$ runs in polynomial time and the advantage of $\mathcal{A}$ is $Adv(\mathcal{A}) = |\Pr[\mathcal{A}(\Psi, e(g,g)^{sa^{m+1}}) \to 0] - \Pr[\mathcal{A}(\Psi, T) \to 0]|$, where T is a random parameter in G_T. If $Adv(\mathcal{A}) \leq \varepsilon$, we say that the $m - (B)$ assumption holds.

3 The Bounded Online/Offline CP-ABE Scheme

We divide the Online/Offline mechanism into two phases: during Offline phase the system could carry on pre-encryption, and complete majority of the work to encrypt a message before it knows the message that will be used;during online phase the system needs little resources to generate the ciphertext when the specifics are known. In this paper we design a non-monotonic Online/Offline CP-ABE scheme, and prove the selective security of the scheme under $m - (B)$ assumption.

3.1 Main Construction

Our scheme is the first Online/Offline CP-ABE scheme with non-monotonic access structure, it is based on literature [6].

Setup (λ, U): The setup algorithm takes as input a security parameter $\lambda \in Z_p$ and sets the attribute set as U. It chooses groups G, G_T of prime order p with g a generator of G. Then it chooses random parameters $h, u, v, w \in G$, $b, \alpha \in Z_p$ and sets $v' = u^b$. The master public key is $Mpk = (g, h, u, v, v', w, e(g,g)^\alpha)$, the master secret key is $Msk = (\alpha, b)$.

KeyGen (Msk, S): The KeyGen algorithm takes as input Mpk, Msk. The attribute set is $S = (x_1, \cdots, x_k) \subset Z_p^k$, where $A_i \subset U$, it randomly picks $r, r_1, \cdots, r_k \in Z_p$ and $r'_1, \cdots, r'_k \in Z_p$ such that $r'_1 + \cdots + r'_k = r$. The algorithm computes the private keys as follows:

$$sk = \left(D_1 = g^\alpha w^r, D_2 = g^r, \left\{ \begin{array}{ll} K_{i,1} = v^{-r}(u^{x_i}h)^{r_i}, & K_{i,2} = g^{r_i} \\ K'_{i,1} = (u^{x_i}h)^{br'_i}, & K'_{i,2} = g^{br'_i} \end{array} \right\}_{i \in [k]} \right)$$

Offline. Encrypt (Mpk): The Offline. Encrypt algorithm takes as input Mpk and randomly picks $s \in Z_p$ and computes $key = e(g,g)^{\alpha s}$, $C_0 = g^s$, suppose that $l_{\max}$ be the maximum bound of rows in the access structure associated with the ciphertext, the algorithm randomly picks $\lambda'_i, a_i, t_i \in Z_p$ $(i \in [l_{\max}])$ and computes the ciphertexts as follows:

$$C_{i,1} = w^{\lambda'_i} v^{t_i}, C_{i,2} = (u^{a_i}h)^{-t_i}, C_{i,3} = g^{t_i}, C_{i,4} = w^{\lambda'_i}(v')^{t_i}$$

Then it outputs the intermediate ciphertext:

$$IT = (key, C_0, \{C_{i,1}, C_{i,2}, C_{i,3}, C_{i,4}\}_{i \in [l_{\max}]}).$$

Online. Encrypt $(Mpk, IT, (L, \rho))$: In Online. Encrypt phase, the algorithm takes as input IT, Mpk and M, and the non-monotonic access structure $\tilde{\mathbb{A}}$ constructed on $\mathcal{P}^+$. We can construct a monotonic access structure $\mathbb{A}$ based on $\mathcal{P}$, where $\tilde{\mathbb{A}} = NM(\mathbb{A})$. The access structure $\tilde{\mathbb{A}}$ is associated with (L, ρ), where L is an $l \times n$ matrix with $L = [L_1, L_2, \cdots, L_l]^T$ and $\{L_i\}_{i \in [l]}$ are row vectors of length n. The algorithm randomly chooses the vector $\bar{s} = (s, s_2, \cdots, s_n) \in Z_p^n$ and computes $\lambda_i = L_i \cdot \bar{s}(i = 1, \cdots, l)$, $\{\lambda_i\}_{i \in [l]}$ are shares of s, $\rho(i)$ is associated with λ_i and $\rho(i) = x_\tau$ (i.e. non-negative attribute) or $\rho(i) = x_\tau^-$ (negative attribute). The system computes the ciphertext $C = M \cdot key$ and $\{C_{i,5}, C_{i,6}\}_{i \in [l]}$, where $C_{i,5} = \lambda_i - \lambda'_i$, $C_{i,6} = t_i \cdot (x_\tau - a_i) \bmod p$, they are associated with the attribute set. Finally the system outputs the ciphertexts:

$$CT = (C, C_0, \{C_{i,1}, C_{i,2}, C_{i,3}, C_{i,4}, C_{i,5}, C_{i,6}\}_{i \in [l]}).$$

Decrypt (sk, CT): Decryption is possible when the attribute set S satisfies the access structure $\tilde{\mathbb{A}}$. The access structure $\tilde{\mathbb{A}} = NM(\mathbb{A})$ is associated with the secret sharing scheme (L, ρ), let $S' = N(S) \in \mathbb{A}$, $I = \{i \mid \rho(i) \in S'\}$. As S' is authorized in $\mathbb{A}$, there exists a set of coefficients $\{\mu_i\}_{i \in I}$ such that $\sum_{i \in I} \mu_i \lambda_i = s$. For any $i \in I$, it computes as follows:

$$\begin{cases} e(C_{i,1} \cdot w^{C_{i,5}}, D_2) \cdot e(C_{i,2} \cdot u^{-C_{i,6}}, K_{\tau,2}) \cdot e(C_{i,3}, K_{\tau,1}) = e(g,w)^{r\lambda_i} & \text{if } \rho(i) = x_\tau \\ e(C_{i,4} \cdot w^{C_{i,5}}, D_2) \cdot \prod_{j \in [k]} (e(C_{i,2} \cdot u^{-C_{i,6}}, K'_{j,2}) \cdot e(C_{i,3}, K'_{j,1}))^{\frac{1}{x_\tau - x_j}} = e(g,w)^{r\lambda_i} & \text{if } \rho(i) = x_\tau^- \end{cases}$$

In the case of $\rho(i) = x_i$, there exists an τ such that $\omega_\tau = \rho(i) = x_i$. Then it computes $e(C_0, D_1) \cdot \prod_{i \in I} \left(e(g,w)^{r\lambda_i}\right)^{-\mu_i} = e(g^s, g^\alpha w^r) \cdot e(g,w)^{-\sum_{i \in I} r\lambda_i \mu_i} = e(g,g)^{\alpha s}$.

Finally the algorithm recovers the message M.

3.2 Proof of Correctness

- In the case of $\rho(i) = x_\tau$, we compute as follows:

$$e\left(C_{i,1} \cdot w^{C_{i,5}}, D_2\right) \cdot e\left(C_{i,2} \cdot u^{-C_{i,6}}, K_{\tau,2}\right) \cdot e\left(C_{i,3}, K_{\tau,1}\right)$$
$$= e\left(w^{\lambda'_i} v^{t_i} \cdot w^{\lambda_i - \lambda'_i}, g^r\right) \cdot e\left((u^{a_i}h)^{-t_i} \cdot u^{-t_i \cdot (x_\tau - a_i)}, g^{r_\tau}\right) \cdot e(g^{t_i}, v^{-r}(u^{x_\tau}h)^{r_\tau})$$
$$= e(g,w)^{r\lambda_i} \cdot e(g,v)^{rt_i} \cdot e(u,g)^{-t_i \cdot x_\tau \cdot r_\tau} \cdot e(h,g)^{-t_i r_\tau} e(g,v)^{-rt_i} \cdot e(g,u)^{t_i x_\tau r_\tau} \cdot e(h,g)^{t_i r_\tau}$$
$$= e(g,w)^{r\lambda_i}$$

- In the case of $\rho(i) = x_\tau^-$, since $x_\tau - x_j \neq 0$, $j \in [k]$, we compute as follows:

$$e(C_{i,4} \cdot w^{C_{i,5}}, D_2) \cdot \prod_{j \in [k]} (e(C_{i,2} \cdot u^{-C_{i,6}}, K'_{j,2}) \cdot e(C_{i,3}, K'_{j,1}))^{\frac{1}{x_\tau - x_j}}$$
$$= e(w^{\lambda'_i}(v')^{t_i} \cdot w^{\lambda_i - \lambda'_i}, g^r) \cdot \prod_{j \in [k]} (e((u^{a_i}h)^{-t_i} \cdot u^{-t_i \cdot (x_\tau - a_i)}, g^{br'_j}) \cdot e(g^{t_i}, (u^{bx_j}h^b)^{r'_j}))^{\frac{1}{x_\tau - x_j}}$$
$$= e((v')^{t_i} \cdot w^{\lambda_i}, g^r) \cdot \prod_{j \in [k]} (e(g^{t_i}, u^{bx_j r'_j}) \cdot e(u^{-t_i x_\tau}, g^{br'_j}))^{\frac{1}{x_\tau - x_j}}$$
$$= e(g,w)^{r\lambda_i} e(g,v')^{t_i r} \cdot \prod_{j \in [k]} (e(g,u)^{t_i bx_j r'_j - t_i x_\tau br'_j})^{\frac{1}{x_\tau - x_j}}$$
$$= e(g,w)^{r\lambda_i} e(g,v')^{t_i r} \cdot \prod_{j \in [k]} e(g,u)^{-bt_i r'_j}$$
$$= e(g,w)^{r\lambda_i}$$

Since S' is authorized in $\mathbb{A}$, $\{\lambda_s\}_{s \in I}$ are valid shares of α, there exists constants $\{\mu_i\}_{i \in I}$ such that $\sum_{s \in I} \mu_s \lambda_s = \alpha$, so that normal decryption is possible.

3.3 Proof of Security

The scheme is based on Yamada's [6] unbounded CP-ABE scheme. We prove the security of the scheme under the $m - (B)$ assumption, where the $m - (B)$ assumption is variant version of the $q - 1$ assumption, the complexity of these two assumptions are equivalent.

Theorem 1. Suppose that the $m - (B)$ assumption holds, then no polynomial time adversary can selectively break our CP-ABE system by negligible advantage with a challenge matrix of size $l \times n$, where $l, n \leq m$.

Suppose we have an adversary $\mathcal{A}$ with non-negligible advantage, a simulator $\mathcal{B}$, We simulate the following game between the adversary $\mathcal{A}$ and the challenger $\mathcal{B}$, $\mathcal{B}$ guesses whether $T = e(g,g)^{a^{m+1}s}$.

Setup: $\mathcal{A}$ declares the non-monotonic access structure $\tilde{\mathbb{A}}^* = NM(\mathbb{A}^*)$ that it intends to attack, $\mathbb{A}^*$ is associated with the LSSS matrix (L^*, ρ^*). Where L^* is a $l \times n$ matrix, $l, n \leq m$. We divide $[l]$ into $posi$ and $nega$, where $posi = \{i| \rho^*(i) = x_v\}_{i \in [l]}$, $nega = \{i| \rho^*(i) = x_v^-\}_{i \in [l]}$, ($v \in [l]$). Therefore $posi$ is associated with the non-negative attribute, and $nega$ is associated with the negative attribute.

$\mathcal{B}$ randomly picks $\tilde{\alpha}, \tilde{u}, \tilde{v}, \tilde{h} \in Z_p$ and sets h, u, v, w as follows:

$$h = g^{\tilde{h}} \cdot \prod_{(j,k) \in [l,n]} (g^{a^k/b_j^2})^{-\rho^*(j)L_{j,k}^*}, \quad u = g^{\tilde{u}} \cdot \prod_{(j,k) \in [l,n]} (g^{a^k/b_j^2})^{L_{j,k}^*},$$

$$v = g^{\tilde{v}} \cdot \prod_{(j,k) \in posi \times [n]} (g^{a^k/b_j^2})^{L_{j,k}^*}, \quad w = g^a, \quad g = g.$$

During the computation phase, we consider the negative attributes in the index as elements of Z_p, for $A \in G$ and a negative attribute x_i^-, we define $A^{x_i^-} = A^{x_i}$.

Let $\alpha = \tilde{\alpha} + a^{m+1}$, we have $e(g,g)^{\alpha} = e(g,g)^{\tilde{\alpha}} \cdot e(g^a, g^{a^m})$, let $b = \sum_{i \in nega} b_i$, thus

$$v' = u^b = \left(g^{\tilde{u}} \cdot \prod_{(j,k) \in [l,n]} (g^{a^k/b_j^2})^{L_{j,k}^*} \right)^{\sum_{i \in nega} b_i}.$$

Then $\mathcal{B}$ sends the public parameters $mpk = (g, h, u, v, v', w, e(g,g)^{\alpha})$ to $\mathcal{A}$.

Phase1: $\mathcal{A}$ queries for the attribute set $S = \{x_1, \cdots, x_{|S|}\}$, if S is unauthorized $\mathcal{B}$ could generate the private key, otherwise $\mathcal{B}$ could not generate the private key. If S is unauthorized, $\mathcal{B}$ proceeds as follows:

As S is unauthorized in (L^*, ρ^*), $S \notin \tilde{\mathbb{A}}^*$, then $S' = N(S) \notin \mathbb{A}^*$. The vector $(1, 0, \cdots, 0)$ does not belong to the row vector of $L_{S'}^*$, then we could compute the vector $\bar{z} = (z_1, \cdots, z_n) \in Z_p^n$ so that $\bar{z} \cdot (1, 0, \cdots, 0) = -1$ and $\langle L_{S'}^*, \bar{z}^{\top} \rangle = 0$.

$\mathcal{B}$ randomly picks $\tilde{r} \in Z_p$ and sets $r = \tilde{r} - \sum_{i \in [n]} z_i a^{m+1-i}$, $\tilde{r}$ is randomly distributed since r is randomly distributed. We could compute D_1 and D_2 as follows:

$$D_1 = g^\alpha w^r = g^{a^{m+1}} g^{\tilde{\alpha}} g^{a\tilde{r}} \prod_{i \in [n]} g^{-z_i a^{m+2-i}}$$

$$D_2 = g^r = g^{\tilde{r}} \prod_{i \in [n]} g^{-z_i a^{m+2-i}}$$

To compute the private keys $\left\{ K_{i,1}, K_{i,2}, K'_{i,1}, K'_{i,2} \right\}_{i \in [|S|]}$. For convenience of description, we discuss in two parts:

① The system firstly computes $K_{\tau,1} = v^{-r}(u^{x_\tau}h)^{r_\tau}$ and $K_{\tau,2} = g^{r_\tau}$, where $\tau \in [|S|]$, we divide $K_{\tau,1}$ into v^{-r} and $(u^{x_\tau}h)^{r_\tau}$, then we could get:

$$v^{-r} = v^{-\left(\tilde{r} - \sum_{i \in [n]} z_i a^{m+1-i}\right)}$$

$$= v^{-\tilde{r}} \left(g^{\tilde{v}} \cdot \prod_{(j,k) \in posi \times [n]} (g^{a^k/b_j^2})^{L_{j,k}^*} \right)^{\sum_{i \in [n]} z_i a^{m+1-i}}$$

$$= v^{-\tilde{r}} \prod_{i \in [n]} g^{a^{m+1-i}\tilde{v}z_i} \prod_{(i,j,k) \in [n] \times posi \times [n]} (g^{a^k/b_j^2})^{L_{j,k}^* z_i a^{m+1-i}}$$

$$= v^{-\tilde{r}} \prod_{i \in [n]} g^{a^{m+1-i}\tilde{v}z_i} \prod_{\substack{(i,j,k) \in [n] \times posi \times [n] \\ i \neq k}} (g^{a^k/b_j^2})^{L_{j,k}^* z_i a^{m+1-i}} \prod_{(i,j) \in [n] \times posi} (g^{a^{m+1}/b_j^2})^{L_{j,k}^* z_i}$$

$$= v^{-\tilde{r}} \prod_{i \in [n]} g^{a^{n+1-i}\tilde{v}z_i} \prod_{\substack{(i,j,k) \in [n] \times posi \times [n] \\ i \neq k}} (g^{a^k/b_j^2})^{L_{j,k}^* z_i a^{m+1-i}} \prod_{j \in posi} (g^{\langle L_j^*, \bar{z} \rangle a^{m+1}/b_j^2})$$

$$= \underbrace{v^{-\tilde{r}} \prod_{i \in [n]} g^{a^{m+1-i}\tilde{v}z_i} \prod_{\substack{(i,j,k) \in [n] \times posi \times [n] \\ i \neq k}} (g^{a^k/b_j^2})^{L_{j,k}^* z_i a^{m+1-i}} \prod_{\substack{j \in posi \\ \rho(j) \notin S}} (g^{\langle L_j^*, \bar{z} \rangle a^{m+1}/b_j^2})}_{\Phi}$$

$$= \Phi \prod_{\substack{j \in posi \\ \rho(j) \notin S}} (g^{\langle L_j^*, \bar{z} \rangle a^{m+1}/b_j^2})$$

$\mathcal{B}$ sets $r_\tau = \tilde{r}_\tau - \sum_{\substack{(i, i') \in [n] \times posi \\ \rho^*(i') \notin S}} \frac{z_i b_{i'} a^{m+1-i}}{x_\tau - \rho^*(i')}$, r_τ distributes randomly since $\tilde{r} \in Z_p$.

$i' \in posi$ and $\rho^*(i) \notin S$, thus $x_\tau - \rho^*(i') \neq 0$. Then we compute $(u^{x_\tau}h)^{r_\tau}$:

$$(u^{x_\tau}h)^{r_\tau} = (u^{x_\tau}h)^{\tilde{r}_\tau} \prod_{\substack{(i,i')\in[n]\times posi \\ \rho^*(i')\notin S}} (u^{x_\tau}h)^{-\frac{z_i b_{i'} a^{m+1-i}}{x_\tau - \rho^*(i')}}$$

$$= (u^{x_\tau}h)^{\tilde{r}_\tau} \prod_{\substack{(i,i')\in[n]\times posi \\ \rho^*(i')\notin S}} \left(g^{\tilde{u}x_\tau} \cdot \prod_{(j,k)\in[l,n]} (g^{a^k}/b_j^2)^{L^*_{j,k}x_\tau} \cdot g^{\tilde{h}} \cdot \prod_{(j,k)\in[l,n]} (g^{a^k}/b_j^2)^{-\rho^*(j)L^*_{j,k}} \right)^{-\frac{z_i b_{i'} a^{m+1-i}}{x_\tau - \rho^*(i')}}$$

$$= (u^{x_\tau}h)^{\tilde{r}_\tau} \underbrace{\prod_{\substack{(i,i')\in[n]\times posi \\ \rho^*(i')\notin S}} \left(g^{\tilde{u}x_\tau+\tilde{h}} \right)^{-\frac{z_i b_{i'} a^{m+1-i}}{x_\tau - \rho^*(i')}} \prod_{\substack{(i',i,j,k)\in posi\times[n,l,n] \\ \rho^*(i')\notin S}} \left((g^{a^k}/b_j^2)^{L^*_{j,k}(x_\tau - \rho^*(j))} \right)^{-\frac{z_i b_{i'} a^{m+1-i}}{x_\tau - \rho^*(i')}}}_{\Phi_1}$$

$$= \Phi_1 \prod_{\substack{(i',i,j,k)\in posi\times[n,l,n] \\ \rho^*(i')\notin S,(i'\neq j)\vee(i\neq k)}} \left((g^{a^k}/b_j^2)^{L^*_{j,k}(x_\tau - \rho^*(j))} \right)^{-\frac{z_i b_{i'} a^{m+1-i}}{x_\tau - \rho^*(i')}} \prod_{\substack{(i',i,j,k)\in posi\times[n,l,n] \\ \rho^*(i')\notin S,(i'=j)\wedge(i=k)}} \left((g^{a^k}/b_j^2)^{L^*_{j,k}} \right)^{-z_k b j a^{m+1-k}}$$

$$= \Phi_1 \underbrace{\prod_{\substack{(i',i,j,k)\in posi\times[n,l,n] \\ \rho^*(i')\notin S,(i'\neq j)\vee(i\neq k)}} \left((g^{a^{m+1-i+k}}/b_j^2)^{L^*_{j,k}(x_\tau - \rho^*(j))} \right)^{-\frac{z_i b_{i'}}{x_\tau - \rho^*(i')}} \prod_{\substack{(j,k)\in posi\times[n] \\ \rho^*(i')\notin S}} (g^{a^{m+1}}/b_j)^{-z_k L^*_{j,k}}}_{\Phi_2}$$

$$= \Phi_1 \Phi_2 \prod_{\substack{j\in posi,\rho^*(j)\notin S}} (g^{a^{m+1}}/b_j)^{-\langle L^*_j,\vec{z}\rangle}$$

Finally we could get $K_{\tau,1} = v^{-r}(u^{x_\tau}h)^{r_\tau} = \Phi\Phi_1\Phi_2$, $\tau \in [|S|]$, Φ, Φ_1, Φ_2 could be effectively computed.

$$K_{\tau,2} = g^{r_\tau} = g^{\tilde{r}_\tau} \prod_{\substack{(i,i')\in[n]\times posi \\ \rho^*(i')\notin S}} g^{a^{m+1-i}b_{i'}z_i/(\rho^*(i')-x_\tau)}.$$

② We construct $K'_{\tau,1} = (u^{bx_\tau}h^b)^{r'_\tau}$ and $K'_{\tau,2} = g^{br'_\tau}$, where $\tau \in [|S|]$, $\sum_{\tau\in[|S|]} r'_\tau = r$. The scheme need to be updated during construction, $\mathcal{B}$ sets $K'_{i,1} = 1_G, K'_{i,2} = 1_G$, $i \in [|S|]$. There are two cases to discuss for $\tau \in nega$:

- In the case of $\upsilon \in [|S|]$, $\rho^*(\tau) = x^-_\upsilon$ and $x_\upsilon \in S$, at this time $\rho^*(\tau) \notin N(S)$. $\mathcal{B}$ updates $K'_{\upsilon,1}$ and $K'_{\upsilon,2}$, $K'_{\upsilon,1} \leftarrow K'_{\upsilon,1} \cdot (U^{x_\upsilon}H)^{b_\tau r}$, $K'_{\upsilon,2} \leftarrow K'_{\upsilon,2} \cdot g^{b_\tau r}$. Then $\mathcal{B}$ computes $(U^{\omega_\upsilon}H)^{b_\tau r}$ and $g^{b_\tau r}$.
  $(u^{x_\upsilon}h)^{b_\tau r}$ can be effectively calculated as follows:

$$(u^{x_v}h)^{b_\tau r} = (u^{\rho^*(\tau)}h)^{b_\tau r}$$

$$= (g^{b_\tau r})^{\rho^*(\tau)\tilde{u}+\tilde{h}} \cdot \Big(\prod_{(j,k)\in[l,n]} g^{(\rho^*(\tau)-\rho^*(j))L_{j,k}^* a^k / b_j^2} \Big)^{b_\tau(\tilde{r}-\sum_{i\in[m]} z_i a^{m+1-i})}$$

$$= (g^{b_\tau r})^{\rho^*(\tau)\tilde{u}+\tilde{h}} \cdot \prod_{(j,k)\in[l,n]} g^{(a^k b_\tau / b_j^2)(\rho^*(\tau)-\rho^*(j))\tilde{r} L_{j,k}^*}$$

$$\cdot \Big(\prod_{\substack{(i,j,k)\in[n,l,n] \\ j\neq\tau}} g^{(\rho^*(j)-\rho^*(\tau))L_{j,k}^* z_i a^{m+k+1-i} b_\tau / b_j^2} \Big)$$

Then we can get $g^{b_\tau r} = g^{b_\tau \tilde{r}} \prod_{i\in[n]} (g^{b_\tau a^{m+1-i}})^{-z_i}$.

In the above equation, when $\tau = j$, $g^{(\rho^*(j)-\rho^*(\tau))L_{j,k}^* z_i a^{m+k+1-i} b_\tau / b_j^2} = 1$, where $(i,k) \in [n,n] g^{a^{m+1}/b_\tau}$ does not exist.

- In the case of $\rho^*(\tau) = x_v^-$ and $x_v \notin S$, $\rho^*(\tau) \in N(S)$, $\mathcal{B}$ updates $K_{i,1}' \leftarrow K_{i,1}' \cdot (u^{x_1}h)^{b_\tau r}$, $K_{i,2}' \leftarrow K_{i,2}' \cdot g^{b_\tau r}$. Then $\mathcal{B}$ computes $(u^{x_1}h)^{b_\tau r}$ 和 $g^{b_\tau r}$, $g^{b_\tau r}$ could be effectively get.

$$(u^{x_1}h)^{b_\tau r} = (g^{b_\tau r})^{x_1\tilde{u}+\tilde{h}} \cdot \Big(\prod_{(j,k)\in[l,n]} g^{(x_1-\rho^*(j))L_{j,k}^* a^k / b_j^2} \Big)^{b_\tau(\tilde{r}-\sum_{i\in[n]} z_i a^{m+1-i})}$$

$$= \underbrace{(g^{b_\tau r})^{\rho^*(\tau)\tilde{u}+\tilde{h}} \cdot \prod_{(j,k)\in[l,n]} g^{(a^k b_\tau / b_j^2)(x_1-\rho^*(j))\tilde{r} L_{j,k}^*}}_{\Phi_1}$$

$$\cdot \underbrace{\prod_{(i,j,k)\in[n,l,n]} g^{(a^{m+k+1-i} b_\tau / b_j^2)(\rho^*(\tau)-x_1)L_{j,k}^* z_i}}$$

$$= \Phi_1 \cdot \underbrace{\prod_{\substack{(i,j,k)\in[n,l,n] \\ (k\neq i)\vee(j\neq\tau)}} g^{(a^{m+k+1-i} b_\tau / b_j^2)(\rho^*(j)-x_1)L_{j,k}^* z_i} \cdot \prod_{\substack{(i,j,k)\in[n,l,n] \\ (k=i)\wedge(j=\tau)}} g^{(a^{m+1}/b_\tau)(\rho^*(\tau)-x_1)L_{\tau,k}^* z_i}}_{\Phi_2}$$

$$= \Phi_1 \cdot \Phi_2 \cdot \prod_{\substack{(i,j,k)\in[n,l,n] \\ (k=i)\wedge(j=\tau)}} g^{(a^{m+1}/b_\tau)(\rho^*(\tau)-x_1)\langle L_\tau^*, \bar{z}\rangle} = \Phi_1 \cdot \Phi_2$$

As $\rho^*(\tau) \in N(S)$, $\langle L_\tau^*, \bar{z}\rangle = 0$, g^{a^{n+1}/b_τ} does not exist.

We can obtain $(K_{i,1}', K_{i,2}') = ((u^{x_1}h)^{\tilde{r}_i'}, g^{b\tilde{r}_i'})$ after updating, there exists $\tilde{r}_i' \in Z_p$ such that $\sum_{i\in[|S|]} \tilde{r}_i' = \sum_{\tau\in nega} b_\tau r = b$. Let $\tilde{r}_i' = \tilde{r}_i'/b$, $\sum_{i\in[|S|]} \tilde{r}_i' = r$, so that $(K_{i,1}', K_{i,2}') = ((u^{bx_i}h^b)^{\tilde{r}_i'}, g^{b\tilde{r}_i'})$.

As $\{\tilde{r}_i'\}_{i\in[|S|]}$ is associated with $\{b_i\}_{i\in nega}$, they are not completely randomized, we need to randomize $(K_{i,1}', K_{i,2}')$ so that $\{b_i\}_{i\in nega}$ are independent. $\mathcal{B}$ randomly picks

$\widehat{r}'_1, \cdots, \widehat{r}'_{|S|}$ so that $\widehat{r}'_1 + \cdots + \widehat{r}'_{|S|} = 0$. Then it updates $\{K'_{i,1}, K'_{i,2}\}_{i \in [|S|]}$ to $K'_{i,1} \leftarrow K'_{i,1} \cdot (u^{x_i} h)^{\widehat{r}'_i}$, $K'_{i,2} \leftarrow K'_{i,2} \cdot g^{\widehat{r}'_i}$.

$$(K'_{i,1}, K'_{i,2}) = ((u^{bx_i} h^b)^{r'_i}, g^{br'_i}), \text{ where } r'_i = \tilde{r}'_i + \widehat{r}'_i / b, \, i \in [|S|].$$

Finally $\mathcal{B}$ sends $sk = \left(D_1, D_2, \left\{K_{i,1}, K_{i,2}, K'_{i,1}, K'_{i,2}\right\}_{i \in [|S|]}\right)$ to $\mathcal{A}$.

Challenge: During challenge phase $\mathcal{B}$ construct the challenge ciphertext, the adversary $\mathcal{A}$ sends M_0, M_1 to the challenger $\mathcal{B}$, $\mathcal{B}$ randomly flap a coin $b \leftarrow \{0,1\}$ and construct the ciphertext as follows:

$\mathcal{B}$ firstly sets $C = M_b \cdot T \cdot e(g^s, g^{\tilde{a}})$, $C_0 = g^s$.

Then $\mathcal{B}$ randomly picks $\tilde{s}_2, \cdots, \tilde{s}_n \in Z_p$ and sets $\bar{s} = (s, sa + \tilde{s}_2, sa^2 + \tilde{s}_3, \cdots, sa^{n-1} + \tilde{s}_n)$.

$$\lambda_\tau = \langle L^*_\tau, \bar{s} \rangle = \sum_{i \in [n]} L^*_{\tau,i} sa^{i-1} + \sum_{i=2}^n L^*_{\tau,i} \tilde{s}_i = \sum_{i \in [n]} L^*_{\tau,i} sa^{i-1} + \tilde{\lambda}_\tau$$

$\tilde{\lambda}_\tau = \sum_{i=2}^n L^*_{\tau,i} \tilde{s}_i$ is known to $\mathcal{B}$, where $\tau \in [l]$, then $\mathcal{B}$ randomly picks $\tilde{t}_\tau$ and sets $t_\tau = -sb_\tau + \tilde{t}_\tau$ and computes the ciphertexts $\{C_{\tau,1}, C_{\tau,2}, C_{\tau,3}, C_{\tau,4}\}_{\tau \in [l]}$:

$$\begin{aligned}
C_{\tau,1} &= w^{\lambda_\tau} v^{t_\tau} = w^{\tilde{\lambda}_\tau} \cdot \prod_{i \in [n]} g^{L^*_{\tau,i} sa^i} \cdot v^{\tilde{t}_\tau} \cdot (g^{\tilde{v}} \cdot \prod_{(j,k) \in posi \times [n]} (g^{a^k / b_j})^{L^*_{j,k}})^{-sb_\tau} \\
&= w^{\tilde{\lambda}_\tau} \cdot v^{\tilde{t}_\tau} \cdot (g^{sb_\tau})^{-\tilde{v}} \cdot \prod_{i \in [n]} g^{L^*_{\tau,i}} \prod_{(j,k) \in posi \times [n]} (g^{-sa^k b_\tau / b_j})^{L^*_{j,k}} \\
&= w^{\tilde{\lambda}_\tau} \cdot v^{\tilde{t}_\tau} \cdot (g^{sb_\tau})^{-\tilde{v}} \cdot \prod_{i \in [n]} g^{L^*_{\tau,i} sa^i} \cdot \prod_{k \in [n]} g^{-L^*_{\tau,k} sa^k b_\tau / b_\tau} \cdot \prod_{(j,k) \in (posi \setminus \{\tau\}) \times [n]} (g^{-sa^k b_\tau / b_j})^{L^*_{j,k}} \\
&= w^{\tilde{\lambda}_\tau} \cdot v^{\tilde{t}_\tau} \cdot (g^{sb_\tau})^{-\tilde{v}} \cdot \prod_{(j,k) \in (posi \setminus \tau) \times [n]} (g^{-sa^k b_\tau / b_j})^{L^*_{j,k}}
\end{aligned}$$

$$\begin{aligned}
C_{\tau,2} &= (u^{\rho^*(\tau)} h)^{-t_\tau} = (g^{sb_\tau})^{\rho^*(\tau) \tilde{u} + \tilde{h}} \cdot (u^{\rho^*(\tau)} h)^{-\tilde{t}_\tau} \cdot \prod_{(j,k) \in [l,n]} (g^{(\rho^*(\tau) - \rho^*(j)) L^*_{j,k} a^k / b_j^2})^{sb_\tau} \\
&= (g^{sb_\tau})^{\rho^*(\tau) \tilde{u} + \tilde{h}} \cdot (u^{\rho^*(\tau)} h)^{-\tilde{t}_\tau} \cdot \prod_{\substack{(j,k) \in [l,n] \\ j \neq \tau}} (g^{sa^k b_\tau / b_j^2})^{L^*_{j,k}(\rho^*(\tau) - \rho^*(j))}
\end{aligned}$$

$$C_{\tau,3} = g^{-sb_\tau} g^{\tilde{t}_\tau}$$

$$C_{\tau,4} = w^{\lambda_\tau}(v')^{t_\tau} = w^{\lambda_\tau} u^{b t_\tau}$$

$$= w^{\tilde{\lambda}_\tau} \cdot g^{\sum_{i\in[n]} L^*_{\tau,i} s a^i} u^{b\tilde{t}_\tau} (g^{\tilde{u}} \prod_{(j,k)\in[l,n]} (g^{a^k/b_j^2})^{L^*_{j,k}})^{-s b_\tau \sum_{i\in nega} b_i}$$

$$= w^{\tilde{\lambda}_\tau} \prod_{i\in[n]} g^{L^*_{\tau,i} s a^i} (v')^{\tilde{t}_\tau} \cdot \left((\prod_{i\in nega} g^{b_i})^{\tilde{u}} (\prod_{\substack{(i,j,k)\in nega\times[l,n] \\ i\neq j}} g^{a^k b_i/b_j^2})^{L^*_{j,k}} (\prod_{(j,k)\in nega\times[n]} g^{a^k/b_j^2})^{L^*_{j,k}} \right)^{-s b_\tau}$$

$$= w^{\tilde{\lambda}_\tau} \cdot (v')^{\tilde{t}_\tau} (\prod_{i\in nega} g^{-s b_\tau b_i})^{\tilde{u}} \cdot (\prod_{\substack{(i,j,k)\in nega\times[l,n] \\ i\neq j}} g^{-s b_\tau a^k b_i/b_j^2})^{L^*_{j,k}} \cdot (\prod_{(j,k)\in nega\times[n]} g^{-s b_\tau a^k/b_j^2})^{L^*_{j,k}} \prod_{i\in[n]} g^{L^*_{\tau,i} s a^i}$$

$\mathcal{B}$ randomly picks two sets of values $\{z_\tau\}_{\tau\in[l]}, \{z'_\tau\}_{\tau\in[l]} \in Z_p$ and computes the ciphertext as follows:

$$C^*_{\tau,1} = C_{\tau,1} \cdot w^{-z_\tau}, \; C^*_{\tau,2} = C_{\tau,2} \cdot u^{-z'_\tau},$$
$$C^*_{\tau,3} = C_{\tau,3}, \; C^*_{\tau,4} = C_{\tau,4} \cdot w^{-z_\tau},$$
$$C^*_{\tau,5} = z_\tau, \; C^*_{\tau,6} = z'_\tau,$$

Finally $\mathcal{B}$ sends $CT = (C, C_0, \{C^*_{i,1}, C^*_{i,2}, C^*_{i,3}, C^*_{i,4}, C^*_{i,5}, C^*_{i,6}\}_{i\in[l]})$ to $\mathcal{A}$. $\{z_\tau\}_{\tau\in[l]}, \{z'_\tau\}_{\tau\in[l]} \in Z_p$ are randomly selected, however, we could find that the randomness does not affect the correctness and security of decryption.

Phase2: $\mathcal{A}, \mathcal{B}$ proceeds as in **Phase 1**.

Guess: $\mathcal{A}$ outputs a guess b' of b. If $b = b'$, $\mathcal{B}$ outputs 0 and guesses $T = e(g,g)^{s a^{m+1}}$. Otherwise outputs 1 and guesses T is a random parameter R in G_T. If $T = R$, $\mathcal{A}$ could not get any information about b, the advantage is 0. If $T = e(g,g)^{s a^{m+1}}$, suppose that the advantage of $\mathcal{A}$ is ε, we analyze the advantage of $\mathcal{B}$:

$$\Pr[b = b' \mid T = e(g,g)^{s a^{m+1}}] = \frac{1}{2} + \varepsilon$$

$$\Pr[b \neq b' \mid T = R] = \frac{1}{2}$$

The advantage of $\mathcal{B}$ is:

$$\frac{1}{2}\Pr[b = b'|T = e(g,g)^{s a^{m+1}}] + \frac{1}{2}\Pr[b \neq b'|T = R] - \frac{1}{2} = \frac{1}{2}(\frac{1}{2} + \varepsilon) + \frac{1}{2}\times\frac{1}{2} - \frac{1}{2} = \frac{\varepsilon}{2}$$

Therefore, if there exists a polynomial-time adversary $\mathcal{A}$ who can break the scheme by the advantage of ε, then there exists an algorithm that can solve the $m - (B)$ assumption by the advantage of $\varepsilon/2$. Therefore, the non-monotonic Online/Offline CP-ABE scheme is selective secure under the $m - (B)$ assumption.

$\square$

3.4   The Unbounded CP-ABE Scheme

In above section, we presented a system that imposed a bound of l_{max} attributes associated with any ciphertext. It can be regarded as bounded ABE scheme. Next we construct an unbounded CP-ABE scheme through certain conversion.

In **Setup** phase, the system only takes in the security parameter, the key gen phase is the same as above, the difference mainly centers on the intermediate ciphertext in offline encrypt phase.

The scheme introduces the "pooling" technique, during offline phase, the intermediate ciphertext consists of the main module IT_{main} and the attribute module IT_{att}, IT_{main} and IT_{att} are mutually independent during construction, they are stored in the pool. Suppose that L is a $l \times n$ matrix, the algorithm randomly picks in the pool. During online phase, LSSS scheme (L, ρ), a main module IT_{main} is associated with l attribute modules $\{IT_{att,i}\}_{i\in[l]}$. Any IT_{att} is associated with any IT_{main}. During online phase we can choose any modules needed, the modules left in the pool could be used to construct other ciphertexts.

During offline encryption phase, the system first picks a random $s \in Z_p$ and computes $key = e(g, g)^{\alpha s}$, $C_0 = g^s$, the main module is $IT_{main} = (key, C_0)$.

Then the system picks random $\lambda, a, t \in Z_p$ and computes $C_1 = w^\lambda v^t$, $C_2 = (u^a h)^{-t}$, $C_3 = g^t$, $C_4 = w^\lambda (v')^t$, the attribute module is $IT_{att} = (\lambda, a, t, C_1, C_2, C_3, C_4)$.

During online encryption phase, Since $\tilde{\mathbb{A}} = NM(\mathbb{A})$ is associated with a linear secret sharing scheme (L, ρ), suppose that L is a $l \times n$ matrix, the algorithm randomly picks a main module IT_{main} and l attribute modules $\{IT_{att,i}\}_{i\in[l]}$ in the pool, where $IT_{att,i} = (\lambda_i, a_i, t_i, C_{i,1}, C_{i,2}, C_{i,3}, C_{i,4})$, $C_{i,1} = g^{r_i}$, $C_{i,2} = (u^{a_i} h)^{-t_i}$, $C_{i,3} = g^{t_i}$, $C_{i,4} = w^{\lambda_i} (v')^{t_i}$. Then is Picks random $s_2, \cdots, s_n \in Z_p$ and sets the vector as $\bar{s} = (s, s_2, \cdots, s_n)^T$. $\{\lambda_i\}_{i\in[l]} = \{L_i \cdot \bar{s}\}_{i\in[l]}$, where $\{\lambda_i\}_{i\in[l]}$ are valid shares of s and $\rho(i)$ is associated with $\lambda_i \cdot \rho(i) = x_\tau$ (non-negative attribute) or $\rho(i) = x_\tau^-$ (negative attribute). Then it computes $\{C_{i,5}, C_{i,6}\}_{i\in[l]}$ as $C_{i,5} = \lambda_i - \lambda_i'$, $C_{i,6} = t_i \cdot (x_\tau - a_i) \bmod p$.

Finally the system outputs the ciphertext:

$CT = (C_0, C_1, \{C_{i,1}, C_{i,2}, C_{i,3}, C_{i,4}, C_{i,5}, C_{i,6}\}_{i\in[l]})$.

During online encryption phase, the main computation cost is modular multiplication with low computation, the decryption operation is the same as above.

During conversion, the 'Pooling' technique does not affect the structure of the ciphertext, the adversary attacks the final ciphertext during security proof, it does not affect the security of the scheme, thus we can prove the selective security of our scheme based on Sect. 3.3.

4 Comparisons

Performance Analysis:

In Table 1, we compare our scheme with the existing schemes of RW [13], YAH [6] and HW [7], the common point of these schemes is all of them are unbounded CP-ABE schemes, so that there is no restriction on the size of attribute sets and the number of allowed repetition of the same attributes which appear in an access policy. The difference is RW [13] and HW [7] support the monotonic access structure, whereas YAH [6] and our scheme could support the non-monotonic access structure. We assume E being the computation complexity of exponential operations, M being the computation complexity of multiplication, l being the rows of the LSSS matrix associated with the access structure and k being the number of the attributes.

Table 1. Comparisons of efficiency with other CP-ABE schemes

Schemes	Access structure	Offline. Encrypt	Online. Encrypt	Decryption (Paring)	Assumption
RW Section 4	Monotonic	$5lE + 2lM$		3	$q - 1$ assumption
YAH Section 7	Non-monotonic	$5lE + 2lM$		$2k + 1$	$m - (B)$ assumption
HW Section 4	Monotonic	$5lE + 2lM$	lM	3	$q - 1$ assumption
Our scheme	Non-monotonic	$7lE + 3lM$	lM	$2k + 1$	$m - (B)$ assumption

The scheme of RW [13] and YAH [6] has no Online/Offline mechanism, in order to facilitate the comparison of efficiency during encrypt phase, we merged their online. Encrypt and offline. encrypt tables together.

The **Offline. Encrypt** phase could be done before it knows the specific information of a message, during this phase the system could complete the majority of the work preparing to encrypt a message, therefore the cost of **Offline. Encrypt** does not degrade the efficiency of **Online, Encrypt** phase in the program. From Table 1 we can find that compared with other CP-ABE schemes, the computation complexity during **Online. Encrypt** phase is lower, and the scheme could support more expressive non-monotonic access structure. Finally, we proved the security of the scheme under $m - (B)$ assumption, the assumption is similar to $q - 1$ assumption introduced in RW [13], the difference is we have some additional terms in the problem instance.

5 Conclusions

We are exploring methods to make non-monotonic ABE scheme more expressive for practical application. To achieve this goal, we applied the Online/Offline mechanism to a non-monotonic CP-ABE scheme, it is the first unbounded non-monotonic ABE scheme that could support the Online/Offline mechanism. Then we prove the selective security under the $m - (B)$ assumption. Compared with the original scheme, the system could largely reduce the encryption complexity. We know that he outsourcing technique could reduce the decryption complexity, so we could combine the Online/Offline mechanism with outsourcing technique. These techniques could be performed on the resource constrained devices.

Acknowledgements. We would like to thank the anonymous reviewers for their invaluable comments on a previous version of this paper. Dr. Fushan Wei is supported by the National Natural Science Foundation of China (Grant No. 61772548).

References

1. Sahai, A., Waters, B.: Fuzzy identity-based encryption. In: Cramer, R. (ed.) EUROCRYPT 2005. LNCS, vol. 3494, pp. 457–473. Springer, Heidelberg (2005). https://doi.org/10.1007/11426639_27

2. Goyal, V., Pandey, O., Sahai, A., et al.: Attribute-based encryption for fine-grained access control of encrypted data. In: Proceedings of the 13th ACM Conference on Computer and Communications Security, pp. 89–98. ACM (2006)

3. Bethencourt, J., Sahai, A., Waters, B.: Ciphertext-policy attribute-based encryption. In: IEEE Symposium on Security and Privacy, SP 2007, pp. 321–334. IEEE (2007)

4. Ostrovsky, R., Sahai, A., Waters, B.: Attribute-based encryption with non-monotonic access structures. In: Proceedings of the 14th ACM Conference on Computer and Communications Security, pp. 195–203. ACM (2007)

5. Castiglione, A., De Santis, A., Masucci, B., et al.: Hierarchical and shared access control. IEEE Trans. Inf. Forensics Secur. **11**(4), 850–865 (2016)

6. Yamada, S., Attrapadung, N., Hanaoka, G., Kunihiro, N.: A framework and compact constructions for non-monotonic attribute-based encryption. In: Krawczyk, H. (ed.) PKC 2014. LNCS, vol. 8383, pp. 275–292. Springer, Heidelberg (2014). https://doi.org/10.1007/978-3-642-54631-0_16

7. Hohenberger, S., Waters, B.: Online/offline attribute-based encryption. In: Krawczyk, H. (ed.) PKC 2014. LNCS, vol. 8383, pp. 293–310. Springer, Heidelberg (2014). https://doi.org/10.1007/978-3-642-54631-0_17

8. Rouselakis, Y., Waters, B.: Efficient statically-secure large-universe multi-authority attribute-based encryption. In: Böhme, R., Okamoto, T. (eds.) FC 2015. LNCS, vol. 8975, pp. 315–332. Springer, Heidelberg (2015). https://doi.org/10.1007/978-3-662-47854-7_19

9. Chow, S.S.M.: A framework of multi-authority attribute-based encryption with outsourcing and revocation. in: Proceedings of the 21st ACM on Symposium on Access Control Models and Technologies, pp. 215–226. ACM (2016)

10. ShaoShao, J., Zhu, Y., Ji, Q.: Privacy-preserving online/offline and outsourced multi-authority attribute-based encryption. In: 2017 IEEE/ACIS 16th International Conference on Computer and Information Science (ICIS), pp. 285–291. IEEE (2017)

11. Waters, B.: Ciphertext-policy attribute-based encryption: an expressive, efficient, and provably secure realization. In: Catalano, D., Fazio, N., Gennaro, R., Nicolosi, A. (eds.) PKC 2011. LNCS, vol. 6571, pp. 53–70. Springer, Heidelberg (2011). https://doi.org/10.1007/978-3-642-19379-8_4

12. Attrapadung, N., Libert, B., de Panafieu, E.: Expressive key-policy attribute-based encryption with constant-size ciphertexts. In: Catalano, D., Fazio, N., Gennaro, R., Nicolosi, A. (eds.) PKC 2011. LNCS, vol. 6571, pp. 90–108. Springer, Heidelberg (2011). https://doi.org/10.1007/978-3-642-19379-8_6

13. Rouselakis, Y., Waters, B.: Practical constructions and new proof methods for large universe attribute-based encryption. In: Proceedings of the 2013 ACM SIGSAC Conference on Computer & Communications Security, pp. 463–474. ACM (2013)

14. Datta, P., Dutta, R., Mukhopadhyay, S.: Adaptively secure unrestricted attribute-based encryption with subset difference revocation in bilinear groups of prime order. In: Pointcheval, D., Nitaj, A., Rachidi, T. (eds.) AFRICACRYPT 2016. LNCS, vol. 9646, pp. 325–345. Springer, Cham (2016). https://doi.org/10.1007/978-3-319-31517-1_17

15. Brakerski, Z., Cash, D., Tsabary, R., Wee, H.: Targeted homomorphic attribute-based encryption. In: Hirt, M., Smith, A. (eds.) TCC 2016. LNCS, vol. 9986, pp. 330–360. Springer, Heidelberg (2016). https://doi.org/10.1007/978-3-662-53644-5_13

RPS-TSM: A Robot Perception System Based on Temporal Semantic Map

Haoyue Wang[1], Yangyang Zhang[1], Jianxin Li[1(✉)], Richong Zhang[1], and Md Zakirul Alam Bhuiyan[2]

[1] School of Computer Science and Engineering, Beihang University, Beijing, China
{wanghy11,zhangyy,lijx,zhangrc}@act.buaa.edu.cn
[2] Department of Computer and Information Sciences,
Fordham University, Bronx, NY, USA
zakirulalam@gmail.com

Abstract. Perception ability is important for robots to gain intelligence. From basic sensor data collection to environmental geometry construction, or further semantic information extraction, perception ability gets promoted with a better understanding of data. This paper proposed Temporal Semantic Map (TSM), which adds a temporal dimension on traditional semantic map. Robots can not only perceive the information of the current environment, but also understand the normal state and have a memory of the environment. We have built a Robot Perception System (RPS) which can construct the TSM, automatically infer the normal status of environment using TSM, detect environmental changes and possible anomalies without any hard-coded/human-written rules. We implement RPS on top of the well-known robot operating system (ROS) and evaluate it with a robot inspector application in real scenarios.

Keywords: Intelligent robot · Perception system
Semantic mapping · Anomaly detection · Sensor processing

1 Introduction

Perception, decision making, and execution are three core abilities of intelligent robots. Among them, perception is the basis of the others. Almost all decision making should rely on the perception of surroundings before driving the execution module to complete the task. Therefore, a powerful perception system will bring more intelligence to smart robots.

To help robots understand the environment, *semantic mapping* is proposed and becomes an important research area of robot perception, which extracts semantic info like scene, objects etc. from sensors and labels them on the geometry map. Current work on *semantic mapping* usually focuses on the algorithms of *scene recognition*, *objects detection* and *map segmentation*, etc. Moreover, such work only concerns about the semantic info extraction of current state of the

© Springer International Publishing AG 2017
G. Wang et al. (Eds.): SpaCCS 2017 Workshops, LNCS 10658, pp. 524–533, 2017.
https://doi.org/10.1007/978-3-319-72395-2_48

environment which, however, is usually insufficient for decision making in practical application due to lack of historical information. Take service robots as an example: if we need the robot to turn off the office light for us every night, we must write a rule for the task like "turn off light at 11:00 pm". What if we want the robots know when to turn off the light without human written rules? To automatically complete this task, the robots should not only extract semantic info from environment, but also have a memory of it and know what the environment should look like in normal, like a human. Then they will find the office brightness is always low at 11:00 pm and make a decision to turn off the light.

To deal with such challenges, in this paper, we propose Temporal Semantic Map (TSM) which adds a temporal dimension to the traditional semantic map, enabling robots to infer the normal status of the environment. We have also built a Robot Perception System (RPS) which can construct the TSM, automatically perceive environmental changes and detect possible anomalies without any hard-coded/human-written rules using TSM. With the normal status, robots know what the environment should look like in normal (the word normal here does not mean consistent, on the contrary, some frequently changed area may also be considered a kind of normal). Robots could understand the environment and know: (1) some parts of the surroundings are always consistent while others may change frequently. e.g. the desks in an office may be static but the chairs are often in different locations. (2) some status of the environment may be different in particular time. e.g. the office vision brightness is usually low at midnight, while high in the daytime. Our contributions include:

- A novel semantic map with temporal dimension, Temporal Semantic Map (TSM), is proposed. Using TSM, robots can infer normal status of the environment;
- A Robot Perception System (RPS) is designed and implemented that can construct the TSM, automatically perceive environmental changes and detect possible anomalies without any hard-coded/human-written rules;
- A robot inspector application is implemented to evaluate RPS in real scenarios.

In the rest of this paper, we discuss related work in Sect. 2, show RPS-TSM design and implementation in Sect. 3, evaluate RPS-TSM with an robot inspector application in Sect. 4 and concluded in Sect. 5.

2 Related Work

Recently, many works on robot perception have been proposed. A lot of works focused on the traditional *semantic mapping*, which usually includes *map segmentation*, *scene recognition* and *object detection*, etc. Friedman et al. [3] presented a Voronoi random fields (VRFs) method to segment the 2D occupancy grid map into room areas. Mozos et al. [7] employed hidden Markov models (HMM) to semantically infer about the nodes in the topological graph map.

Viswanathan et al. [13] proposed a solution to the visual place recognition problem by utilizing the LabelMe dataset [11]. Zhou et al. [15] used CNN to learn deep features for scene recognition tasks which got a great result. Then Sünderhauf et al. [12] implemented a semantic mapper using this CNN net and a series of one-vs-all classifiers to overcome the closed-set limitations. In addition, YOLO [8] and Faster R-CNN [9] focused on object recognition task which achieve a remarkable result. On the other hand, Beetz et al. [1] proposed Robosherlock for implementing perception systems. They also built a knowledge base named Open-Ease [2] for robot perception.

Our work provides a holistic system using TSM based on several works mentioned before. With RPS-TSM, robots can construct the geometry map of environment, segment the map into rooms, then label the rooms type using a scene recognizer. Moreover, a robot can record objects info and environmental info (e.g. temperature) with its location and a timestamp during daily work, have a sense of environment's normal status. With the normal status, the robot can perceive environmental changes without any hard-coded/human-written rules.

3   Design and Implementation

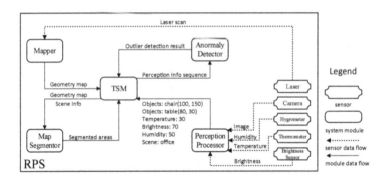

Fig. 1. RPS-TSM architecture

3.1   Overview

The system is built on top of the Robots Operating System (ROS), a widely adopted distributed message middleware for robot development, where ROS nodes communicate with each other by the publish-subscribe mechanism on topics or on-demand service mechanism. RPS-TSM follows the programming paradigm of ROS and its modules are implemented as ROS nodes. There are five modules (represented as rounded rectangles) in RPS and system architecture is shown in Fig. 1.

Logically, the TSM is a semantic map with memory of environment history. It is implemented as a map with corresponding database. The RPS is responsible for the construction of TSM. Then it will infer environmental normal status and detect anomalies using historical semantic info from TSM.

To construct the TSM, the Mapper module is responsible for generating a geometry map and sending it to TSM. Meanwhile, the Perception Processor module will send out scene recognition results and TSM module will record them in $\langle scene, localization\_info \rangle$ pairs. The Map Segmentor module will get the geometry map and scene info from TSM, segment the map into area blocks, label area blocks with scene tags and send them back to TSM. Now TSM has a traditional semantic map as shown in Fig. 3.

While robots moving around in the environment during their daily work, The Perception Processor will send image snapshots, object detection info and other sensors data to TSM with a timestamp and robot position. All the perception data will be recorded by TSM to form the temporal dimension of "temporal semantic map". Note that the temporal related data will update all the time during robots' daily work. The Anomaly Detector module is in charge of environmental normal status inference and anomalies detection using all the memorized perception information and semantic map from TSM.

The following sections will give the implementation detail of how to construct TSM, infer normal status and detect anomalies.

3.2   TSM Construction

The TSM construction includes geometry map building, scene recognition, object detection, environmental info perception, map segmentation and semantic labeling.

Map building: The map building task is accomplished by Mapper module which is implemented using Karto [5] (an open source 2D SLAM algorithm based on laser and odometry). It will generate a geometry occupancy map of the environment.

Scene recognition: The scene recognition task is executed by the Perception Processor module. While robot is constructing the environment's geometry map, the Perception Processor uses the CNN net in [15] which can predict scene type almost in real time on CPU, send scene type with corresponding location as $\langle scene, localization\_info \rangle$ pairs to TSM continuously.

Map segmentation and Semantic labeling: When map construction completed, the Map Segmentor reads geometry map from TSM and segments the map into area blocks according to the map's geometry structure [3]. Then it will count all scene recognition results in each area block and label them with the most frequent occurrence of scene type.

Object detection and Environmental info perception: Besides scene recognation, the Perception Processor is also in charge of object detection and environmental info perception. The Perception Processor is an extensible module that can deal with a variety of perception data, such as visual data and environmental data like temperature, humidity and brightness. For visual data, YOLO

[8] is adopted for object detection because of its high prediction performance on CPU devices (Carrying GPU devices on robots is usually impractical for weight, power supply etc. reasons). For other environmental data, the Perception Processor module just translates the raw data and transfers them to TSM. Certainly, many other perception data types like sound, WIFI signal intensity, etc. could be added to Perception Processor. All of the collected data will be used to form the environmental normal status.

TSM management: As shown in Fig. 1, TSM is the central module in RPS. The TSM stores the geometry map and scene labels as the traditional semantic map does, along with other types of temporal perception data, such as objects, temperatures, and so on. Each perception datum in TSM is a tuple of $\langle perception\_data, timestamp, location, data\_type \rangle$, as shown in Table 1. Other modules can look up any type of perception data in any past time point/range and location. e.g. The Anomaly Detector may want to get all historical objects data in a particular location of an office to detect if there is any anomaly, or get all brightness data at 11:00 PM in a particular location to see if the lights should be turned off. Most importantly, the temporal dimension enables the normal status inference & anomaly detection by historical perception data, making robots perceive the environment in a more intelligent way.

3.3   Normal Status Inference and Anomaly Detection

Another core module is the Anomaly Detector, which can infer the normal status of the environment and detect possible anomalies. It takes perception data e.g. temperature sequence or $\langle obj\_type, obj\_position \rangle$ sequence, treats the data as features in different dimension and detects outliers in the data sequence. The outlier points may be anomalies while the others represent the normal state of the environment.

Algorithm 1. Outlier Detection

   Input: $data\_list$: the perception data sequence
   Result: $outliers$: the detected outliers' index
1 $distances = GetDistanceMatrix(data\_list)$
2 $\rho = CalculateRho(distances)$
3 $\delta = CalculateDelta(distances, \rho)$
4 $\rho_{mid} = GetRhoMid(\rho)$
5 $\delta_{mid} = GetDeltaMid(\delta)$
6 **for** $i = 1;\ i \leq data\_list.size;\ i = i + 1$ **do**
7   **if** $\rho_i/\rho_{mid} \leq \rho\_ratio$ and $\delta_{mid}/\delta_i \leq \delta\_ratio$ **then**
8   add i to $outliers$
9   **end**
10 **end**
11 **return** $outliers$;

The proposed outlier detection method is inspired by the cluster algorithm [10]. The core idea of the original cluster algorithm is intuitive: the cluster centers are usually the points that have higher density, and far from other points whose density is higher than theirs. According to that paper, ρ represents a point's density and δ represents the minimal distance to other points whose density higher than it.

Using ρ and δ, we can define that a point i is an outlier if: $\begin{cases} \rho_i/\rho_{mid} < \rho\_ratio \\ \delta_{mid}/\delta_i < \delta\_ratio \end{cases}$

The reason is that the outliers are usually points far from the normal points in the feature space, so the ρ of outliers should be significantly lower and the δ should be relatively higher than normal points. Here ρ_{mid} is the median of all points' ρ and so as δ_{mid}. We use median rather than mean value to represent normal state here is because some points' delta may be INF which will be introduced in the following paragraph. ρ_ratio and δ_ratio are parameters to control the relative deviation degree to decide if a point is an outlier. These two parameters do not need to be adjusted carefully because outliers usually deviate obviously and the parameters just control the relative deviation. In practice, 0.2–0.5 works.

The ρ and δ of data point i are defined as:

$$\rho_i = \sum_j e^{-(\frac{d_{ij}}{d_c})^2} \qquad \delta_i = \min_{j:\rho_j>\rho_i}(d_{ij}) \qquad d_c = cut\_ratio \cdot max(d_{ij})$$

We use Gaussian kernel here for smoothness in contrast with the original cluster algorithm. d_c is used to decrease the points' contribution to density that too far from point i. We define the parameter cut_ratio to make d_c adaptive to the data shape in feature space. This parameter is usually set to 0.5, which means only the points whose distance less than a half of the max distance between points will be the main contributor to the density of point i.

The Algorithm 1 describes the proposed outlier detection method. Take the object perception data as an example. The object perception data is stored as $\langle robot\_location, obj\_list, timestamp \rangle$ where obj_list is a list of objects in the format of $\langle obj\_type, obj\_position \rangle$. We get all records of a specific object (e.g. desk) in the same $robot\_location$, so the input data to algorithm will be a list of desk positions e.g. [$[x_1, y_1]$, $[x_2, y_2]$, ... ,$[x_n, y_n]$] where the feature dimension here is two in this example. Considering a special case, if some records in the same $robot\_location$ do not contain the desk (which means the desk does not exist at that time), we simply set x_i and y_i to INF. This trick will automatically handle the situation that some objects appear or disappear because the INF points in feature space fit into our outlier definition naturally so that the algorithm will pick them out without any special logic. The algorithm will output outliers' index corresponding to the input data.

4   Application and Evaluation

4.1   Application

In order to evaluate the system, we have implemented a robot inspector application as shown in Fig. 2, which works automatically using RPS-TSM just like a human inspector. When the robot is placed in a new environment, it will automatically explore the environment and build a semantic map. After the semantic map is initialized, the robot will record all the perception info including objects' position and environmental data (e.g. temperature) along with the location and the timestamp to form the TSM during its daily work. When some anomalies are detected, the robot will record and report a warning message. This behavior is just like a human inspector walking around everywhere when he comes into a new place and memorizes the environment structure. After this, he will inspect the environment every day and memorizes what the surroundings should look like in mind. If there is any abnormal event, he will record and report it.

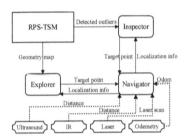

Fig. 2. The inspector application

Fig. 3. Generated TSM

The application has three ROS nodes besides RPS-TSM. The Explorer module takes geometry map from Mapper and localization info from Navigator, then selects the nearest frontier [14] point on map reachable for the robot, and send it as the next exploration goal to Navigator. The Explorer module will give a new goal to the Navigator when robot reached, failed to reach or timeout to reach. Our Navigator is implemented according to [6] and we added an escape mechanism based on the Artificial Potential Field [4] method, to reduce the possibility that robot may get stuck. The Inspector module responsible for the main inspection logic that sends target points to Navigator one by one, and collects anomaly info from RPS-TSM periodically. According to the described functionality of RPS-TSM, our evaluation can be split into TSM building and Anomaly detection in the following two sections.

4.2   Experiment of TSM Construction

A TSM consists of two parts: the semantic map and perception history. We run the inspector application in our office building to generate a corresponding TSM.

Table 1. An example of perception history corresponding to the map

Timestamp	Location	Type	Content
1499969045	A	Objects	tv_monitor: 160, 140; tv_monitor: 346, 165; cup: 148, 222; chair: 316, 249;
1499970274	A	Objects	tv_monitor: 301, 106; chair: 270, 197;
1499969045	A	Temperature	30
...	...	...	...

Initially, the robot had no map and started to explore in offices and the hall. After exploration and post processing, an occupancy grid map with scene labels is generated as shown in Fig. 3. There are two types of scene in the map: office and corridor. Note that there is a small area labeled falsely as a corridor in the office on the bottom of Fig. 3. The reasons may be: (1) this area is actually beside two walls in the office making the Perception Processor think it is a corridor, and (2) the wall caused the Map Segmentor module to segment the office into many small blocks falsely. After the semantic map construction, the robot started to inspect around and record all perception data with timestamp and location. An example objects perception history of location A in the semantic map can be referred to Table 1.

4.3   Experiment of Anomaly Detection

The Anomaly Detector uses the perception history to infer environmental normal status and detect anomalies. As shown in Fig. 4, these ten pictures are taken by the robot in the same location (point A in Fig. 3) while the view port of robot changes slightly due to the small localization error. It can be observed that except for the *chair* and the *cup*, the other parts of the scene remain as they are in the first nine pictures. In the 10th picture, a *tv_monitor* has been moved. The objects position in feature space for the Anomaly Detector can be viewed in Fig. 5. As a result, the robot reports abnormal information of *tv_monitor* #2

Fig. 4. The pictures taken by robot in the same location with objects info labeled on

in picture 10 and *chair* in picture 8. The *cup* in all ten pictures are not considered as anomalies because its position is always changing and disappearing sometimes. The *chair*'s position is also changing in all pictures but just disappearing once in picture 8. The position of *tv_monitor* #2 is consistent historically in the first nine pictures, so it deserved an anomaly in picture 10. This result demonstrates the effectiveness of Anomaly Detector and TSM module. Noting that our Anomaly Detector module can also handle other kinds of perception data sequence although we just show the object position case here due to space constraints.

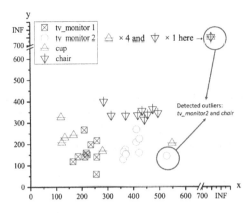

Fig. 5. The objects position in feature space

5   Conclusion

In this paper, we proposed the Temporal Semantic Map (TSM) which adds a temporal dimension to traditional semantic map and built a Robot Perception System (RPS) on it. The RPS-TSM can make robots understand the environment, infer normal status, perceive environmental changes and detect possible anomalies without any hard-coded/human-written rules. The preliminary experiments demonstrate the effectiveness of our system. Adding more modules which can increase robot perception ability, some performance optimization and experiments on long term execution in the real scenarios are left as future works.

Acknowledgments. This work is supported by NSFC program (No. 61472022, 61421003), SKLSDE-2016ZX-11, and the Beijing Advanced Innovation Center for Big Data and Brain Computing.

References

1. Beetz, M., Bálint-Benczédi, F., Blodow, N., Nyga, D., Wiedemeyer, T., Márton, Z.C.: Robosherlock: unstructured information processing for robot perception. In: 2015 IEEE International Conference on Robotics and Automation (ICRA), pp. 1549–1556. IEEE (2015)
2. Beetz, M., Tenorth, M., Winkler, J.: Open-ease. In: 2015 IEEE International Conference on Robotics and Automation (ICRA), pp. 1983–1990. IEEE (2015)
3. Friedman, S., Pasula, H., Fox, D.: Voronoi random fields: extracting topological structure of indoor environments via place labeling. In: IJCAI, vol. 7, pp. 2109–2114 (2007)
4. Khatib, O.: Real-time obstacle avoidance for manipulators and mobile robots. Int. J. Robot. Res. **5**(1), 90–98 (1986)
5. Konolige, K., Grisetti, G., Kümmerle, R., Burgard, W., Limketkai, B., Vincent, R.: Efficient sparse pose adjustment for 2D mapping. In: 2010 IEEE/RSJ International Conference on Intelligent Robots and Systems (IROS), pp. 22–29. IEEE (2010)
6. Marder-Eppstein, E., Berger, E., Foote, T., Gerkey, B., Konolige, K.: The office marathon: robust navigation in an indoor office environment. In: 2010 IEEE International Conference on Robotics and Automation (ICRA), pp. 300–307. IEEE (2010)
7. Mozos, O.M., Triebel, R., Jensfelt, P., Rottmann, A., Burgard, W.: Supervised semantic labeling of places using information extracted from sensor data. Robot. Auton. Syst. **55**(5), 391–402 (2007)
8. Redmon, J., Farhadi, A.: Yolo9000: better, faster, stronger. arXiv preprint arXiv:1612.08242 (2016)
9. Ren, S., He, K., Girshick, R., Sun, J.: Faster R-CNN: towards real-time object detection with region proposal networks. In: Advances in Neural Information Processing Systems, pp. 91–99 (2015)
10. Rodriguez, A., Laio, A.: Clustering by fast search and find of density peaks. Science **344**(6191), 1492–1496 (2014)
11. Russell, B.C., Torralba, A., Murphy, K.P., Freeman, W.T.: LabelMe: a database and web-based tool for image annotation. Int. J. Comput. Vis. **77**(1), 157–173 (2008)
12. Sünderhauf, N., Dayoub, F., McMahon, S., Talbot, B., Schulz, R., Corke, P., Wyeth, G., Upcroft, B., Milford, M.: Place categorization and semantic mapping on a mobile robot. In: 2016 IEEE International Conference on Robotics and Automation (ICRA), pp. 5729–5736. IEEE (2016)
13. Viswanathan, P., Southey, T., Little, J., Mackworth, A.: Place classification using visual object categorization and global information. In: 2011 Canadian Conference on Computer and Robot Vision (CRV), pp. 1–7. IEEE (2011)
14. Yamauchi, B.: A frontier-based approach for autonomous exploration. In: Proceedings of 1997 IEEE International Symposium on Computational Intelligence in Robotics and Automation, CIRA 1997, pp. 146–151. IEEE (1997)
15. Zhou, B., Lapedriza, A., Xiao, J., Torralba, A., Oliva, A.: Learning deep features for scene recognition using places database. In: Advances in Neural Information Processing Systems, pp. 487–495 (2014)

MediBchain: A Blockchain Based Privacy Preserving Platform for Healthcare Data

Abdullah Al Omar[1(✉)], Mohammad Shahriar Rahman[2(✉)], Anirban Basu[3], and Shinsaku Kiyomoto[3]

[1] University of Asia Pacific, Dhaka, Bangladesh
omar.cs@uap-bd.edu
[2] University of Liberal Arts Bangladesh, Dhaka, Bangladesh
shahriar.rahman@ulab.edu.bd
[3] KDDI Research Inc., Fujimino, Japan
{basu,kiyomoto}@kddi-research.jp

Abstract. Healthcare data are grabbing the interest of cyber attackers in recent years. Annihilating consequences of healthcare data could be alleviated through decentralization. A peer to peer (P2P) network enables the property of decentralization, where different parties can store and run computation while keeping the sensitive health data private. Blockchain technology leverages decentralized or distributed process, which ensures the accountability and integrity of its use. This paper presents a patient centric healthcare data management system by using Blockchain as storage to attain privacy. Pseudonymity is ensured by using the cryptographic functions to protect patient's data.

Keywords: Blockchain · Decentralization · Healthcare data
Pseudonymity · Privacy · Security

1 Introduction

Healthcare and Information Technology have recently attracted a lot of works in an amalgamated manner, which bring a lot of changes in healthcare. These changes not only affect treatment process of the patient but also require a careful data processing. With data processing data security and privacy issues arise simultaneously, as healthcare is completely dependent on data for treatment. Privacy of health data refers to the fact that the data of individual patient will be processed privately or authorization will be needed to access the data. And security refers to the fact of keeping sensitive data safe from eavesdroppers as well as from the intruders.

In the process of healthcare data preservation authenticated parties get the access to store it into and retrieve it from the system. Interaction between patient and the system needs to be in a secured way. In this interaction a patient could lose imperative data due to lack of security, as there are a lot of intruders in the network to access these valuable personal data. But losing healthcare data may

© Springer International Publishing AG 2017
G. Wang et al. (Eds.): SpaCCS 2017 Workshops, LNCS 10658, pp. 534–543, 2017.
https://doi.org/10.1007/978-3-319-72395-2_49

be proved very detrimental in some instances. By recent attacks on healthcare systems, different countries [2,3] had devastating data loss. These attacks could steal the sensitive personal health data successfully as those were kept in server without encryption. Cyber-attackers sometime intrude into the data preserving system and make personal private data insecure. Let's assume one scenario, where a patient keeps her data in any [1,4,5,14] electronic health record (EHR) system for preservation and also for further access. EHR systems help the patient to share personal data with the doctors or healthcare organizations. Suppose a patient is keeping her data in a system [1] where data being preserved with Blockchain. Personal data need to be shared with the system then the system will preserve it to the Blockchain. Accountability of data is system centric here. Sharing of the data with doctors or healthcare organizations will also be maintained by the systems, as a result the system will be responsible for patients personal data loss.

In our framework we resolve above discussed problems by storing the encrypted data in the system. If system loses control over the Blockchain the data will be safe as patient herself is accountable for it. Also data sharing is managed by the patient. By using cryptographic function with Blockchain technology our framework resolves the data preserving vulnerabilities. Our proposed framework addresses the aforementioned vulnerabilities related to data storage. However, data would be safe because our system will be holding the encrypted personal data and if the system gets attacked the stolen data will make no sense to the attackers as data would be encrypted. Such use of encryption will also help us to attain pseudonymity. Although there is no identifier for anonymized dataset [6] but it could be managed by encryption keys.

So **accountability**, **integrity**, **pseudonymity**, **security** and **privacy** of healthcare data must be maintained by the systems. Nowadays patients are loosing their interest in electronic health record systems as privacy and security are threatened in EHR systems. So integrity and accountability of EHR systems are also being questioned. Pseudonymity of patient is imperative as personal healthcare data are sensitive.

We briefly describe each of the security and privacy properties in the context of our system below.

- Pseudonymity: No entity will be able to identify any party of our system, even through data it will not be possible to identify any party.
- Privacy: Only registered parties will be able to interact with the system. Even Registered parties will not be able to get the private raw data of other party.
- Integrity: Only authenticated parties will be able to store private data.
- Accountability: Parties will hold their individual block-id without which no entity will be able to interact with that particular block.
- Security: Only encrypted data will be kept by the parties in the system which adds an extra level of security in our system.

1.1   Related Work

Some national level frameworks based on cloud for electronic medical system have been proposed in [4,5,9]. Patra et al. [9] proposed a model which is cloud-based dealing with patients private data. A system was built by Patra et al. to ensure cost effectiveness, and this national level information system was designed for rural areas where cost plays an immense role. Through the framework medical professionals and policy makers could serve the patients remotely with a cloud-based model which includes all the imperative data in a single cloud. The patients were encouraged to share their data in the cloud so that they could get the medical service from the professionals. Disease diagnosis and control could be possible by this remote treatment. Data collection and data delivery are the key points in symptom analysis. Rolim et al. [11] proposed a framework where the system processes data in the steps of data collection and data delivery. In this model sensors play the role of collector. The collector collects the data and sends directly to the system to store and work with this data further. Sensors are proposed to be attached with the medical equipment. These data would be accessed by the medical professionals. Yin et al. [15] introduced cloud based patient centric system. This model includes three layers: data collection layer, data management layer and data service layer. A Blockchain based access control manager for heath data for enhancing the interoperability was proposed in [7]. Their proposal involved the use of public Blockchain as an access control manager of health data which would be stored in off Blockchain mechanism.

Controllability and traceability are two key topics of privacy preserving systems. Xiao et al. [14] proposed a model which is based on Blockchain to help patients to own, control and share their personal data easily and securely with privacy preservation. This application based model also deals with Secure Multiparty Computing (MPC) and Indicator-Centric Schema (ICS). Simic et al. [12] showed a case study where the study concludes with the illustration of significant benefits of IoT and Blockchain in a combined manner. In their work the IoT devices are used as collectors of the private health data of the patient, and the real time data of patient could be saved in Blockchain. They also describe controllability and traceability capabilities of Blockchain. Scalability of the Blockchain in case of Big data has also been tested in their study. Ekblaw et al. [1] proposed a prototype named 'MedRec' which uses Blockchain as a backbone and tried to find the security issues solution for electronic health records (EHR). They tried to achieve integrity, authenticity, auditability and data sharing through Blockchain.

The backbone of our work is Blockchain. The pseudonymity of our secured mechanism lies on only cryptographic function that is to be used to encrypt the data. Blockchain technology is popular for its application in Bitcoin cryptocurrency [10], which is a public ledger to hold and maintain the transaction data and integrity [13]. One of the reasons for using Blockchain technology in cryptocurrency is its decentralized digital ledger property, which was presented by Nakamoto [8] in his Bitcoin cryptocurrency framework. Blockchain's data structure has been modeled by linearly sequenced blocks. Each block contains the cryptographic hashes corresponding to the previous and current block to ensure continuity and immutability of the chain. Chaining mechanism ensures integrity of this secured data structure.

1.2 Our Contribution

Our platform returns the control of the patients' private data to themselves. The main idea of this work is to keep the sensitive health data on the Blockchain to attain accountability, integrity and security. Patients will have the overall control over those blocks where their data will be kept. Present healthcare systems lack in pseudonymity but our platform gives the pseudonymity of patients. 'MediBchain' will regain the interest of patients in this vulnerable circumstance of EHR systems and will retain accountability, integrity, pseudonymity, security and privacy which are being lost in EHR systems. Analyses of these attributes are discussed in Sect. 3.

Organization of the paper: The remainder of the paper is organized as follows: Sect. 2 describes the protocol model. In Sect. 3, we analyze the protocol formally. We give some concluding remarks in Sect. 4.

2 MediBchain Protocol

In this section we present the architectural as well as the design view of our mechanism. Table 1 describes the Notations that is used in this section.

Table 1. Terminology table

Notation	Description
ID	ID of the User
PWD	Password of the user
U_D	Encrypted user data
U_{id}	Block number, where user data will be saved
ID_X	ID of the User X
PWD_X	Password of the user X
U_{DX}	User X's Encrypted data
U_{idX}	Block number, where user X's data is saved

2.1 Overview of Our Protocol

Figure 1 shows the high level view of our platform. The following entities and their roles are described briefly here.

Data sender is the patient, who will send her personal health data to the system. Data sender plays the vital role in case of data preservation. It must be ensured that the data that would be sent to the system are not wrong. However,

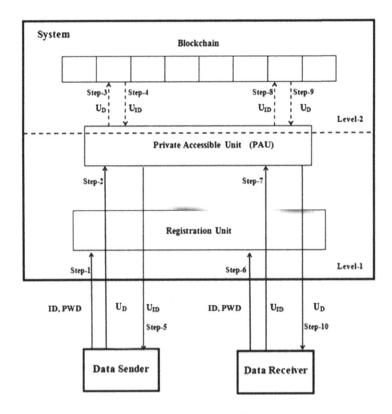

Fig. 1. High level view of this system.

our system will take the encrypted data from the user. Encryption of data will be done in user end.

Data receiver will request for the data after authenticating itself and accessing the system.

Registration Unit will act as an authenticator. When any party will come for the first time to take the service of the system; it will save their ID and PWD to be used further. Each party will have to register for once and need to preserve the ID and PWD. Further they just have to log in and access through secured channel for transaction of their private data.

Private Accessible Unit (PAU). Both the parties of the system will be able to interact with PAU after authentication. It needs a secured channel to interact with registration unit because through PAU they will send their data to the system. It is the intermediary unit of our system through which the element of one level could interact with the other.

Blockchain will hold the data of our users. Each transaction in the Blockchain will return an identifier. This transaction identifier will help the users to access the data further.

For better understanding our system is divided into two levels. Level-1 is Graphical User Interface (GUI). User will interact with our system through this level. Elements of level-1 are: Registration Unit and PAU. PAU is an important element of Level 1, as it interacts with both level 1 and 2. Level-2 is the backend of our system, which interacts with low level elements of this system through PAU. Element of level-2 is: Blockchain. Blockchain is being used as a repository of health data in our system. Our platform uses permissioned Blockchain which will require authentication to access.

Steps in the system: Steps of our system could be defined from Fig. 1.

Step-1: Data sender will request with the ID and PWD for accessing the system.

Step-2: Upon accessing the system in step-2, Data sender will send data to PAU for storing.

Step-3 & 4: Step 3 & 4 will take place in level-2 of our system, where PAU will send U_{ID} to Blockchain and it will return U_{ID} for future access to the Blockchain and also for finding the exact Block where the data were saved.

Step-5: In this step PAU will return the U_{ID} to the Data sender which was given by Blockchain.

Step-6: All the steps from this step onwards are related to Data receiver. As step-1, this step also requires sign in process. After this Data receiver can request for the data.

Step-7: In this step Data receiver will request for the data to PAU along with the U_{ID}. PAU will receive the U_{ID} for further use.

Step-8 & 9: Step 8 & 9 are same as step 3 & 4 but the data are not same for this steps. In step-8 PAU will request the Blockchain along with the U_{ID} and in Step-9 Blockchain returns it.

Step-10: This is the final step where PAU send the private data to the Data receiver.

2.2 Formal Description of Protocol

In this section we will define how Data sender, Data receiver, and our system work altogether in case of sending the data and receiving. For any kind of data transmission in our system, parties need to go through a step called registration. After confirmation of the Registration Unit that party can access the PAU.

Protocol Between Data Sender and System: Figure 2 shows the low level view of sending protocol. A patient will play the role of a data sender in this protocol. Data will be sent in encrypted form. These ciphertexts are generated from a function known as encryption function. $Enc(x,y)$ is the function for encryption. Below we will see how this function works,

$$Enc(key, Data) = U_{D} \tag{1}$$

By providing key and the health data to this function data sender will get U_D and will send it to the system. Public key encryption technique (e.g., Elliptic Curve Cryptography (ECC)) will be applied for encrypting private data.

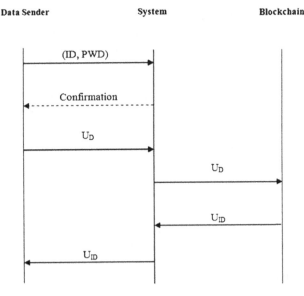

Fig. 2. Low level view of Sending Protocol

Suppose **X** is a Data sender of our system. At first X will request for getting into the system by providing the ID_X and PWD_X. Our system will send the confirmation to X if she provides the right ID and PWD. If X could sign in to the system properly and gets the confirmation then X will send U_{DX} to PAU through a secured channel. Secured channel will provide the security to X. In this stage PAU will interact with Blockchain. This interaction with the Blockchain will be done by the smart contract of our system.

Smart contract has been designed in such a way that Blockchain will return the number of the block. These block-ids will be used as U_{id} of a specific patient. Each time any patient will send a data through our system PAU will get the U_{id} for X it will be U_{idX}. PAU will send the U_{DX} to the Blockchain. Then Blockchain will return the special id for X that is U_{idX}. After that PAU will send the U_{idX} to X and end the protocol. X has to store this U_{idX} otherwise next time X will not be able to access personal data.

Getting the U_{idX} is the confirmation for Data sender X. Which means that the data has been kept to the system and then X could log out and end the secured channel transmission with the system.

Protocol Between Data Receiver and System: Receiving in our system will take two layers of authorization. Because after registering or signing into our system parties have to provide the U_{id} to get their data back through the secured channel. In the second phase if they fail to submit the U_{id} then they will not be able to access the data. U_{id} is the key to receive the actual data. It must be kept secured from sending phase. Figure 3 shows a low level view of receiving protocol.

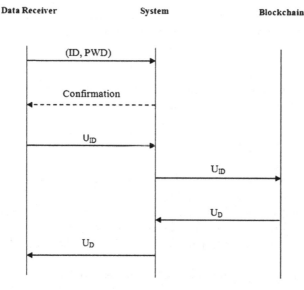

Fig. 3. Low level view of Receiving Protocol

Suppose user **X** wants to retrieve the data that has been kept in the system by X in the sending phase. As like sending phase this phase is also controlled by the authentication or Registration unit where X has to sign in first before accessing our system. This sign in required the ID and PWD of the user which was given in the registration phase. If X provides appropriate ID and PWD only then the system will send confirmation. After getting the confirmation X will be able to interact with the system through a secured channel. In this interaction with the system, X has to provide the U_{idX} that was given in sending phase. After getting the U_{idX} system will interact with Blockchain. This interaction will take place in level-2 of our system. Only PAU can interact with Blockchain, here the smart contract of our system will be the medium.

Smart contract will send the U_{idX} to Blockchain for retrieving the data of X from it. U_{idX} will be converted to the hash of that block in our designed smart contract. 256 bit hash of the corresponding block number will be checked in the smart contract, when the hash will be matched with any block then it will continue the process to retrieve the data. Otherwise this exception will be handled in our designed smart contract.

Suppose the hash of any block is,

0xe3b1c14298fc1c149afbf4c8196fb92427ae41e4649b934ca495991b7852b811

If the hash of U_{idX}'s corresponding block is same then X will be able to get data. For that purpose X needs to provide the correct U_{idX}. Blockchain will return the U_{DX} to X. By this returning function our system will end the session of data retrieval.

From the request X will have U_{DX} which has to be decrypted to get the actual data or plaintext. For decrypting user need to use $Dec(x,y)$ function.

$$Dec(key, U_D) = plaintext \tag{2}$$

X will use Eq. 2 with key and U_{DX} to get the actual data that was encrypted by X in sending phase. ECC will be applied for decrypting.

3   Protocol Analysis

o **Pseudonymity:** Only encrypted data will be kept by the parties in our system, which will provide pseudonymity to them.
o **Privacy:** Registration Unit of our system will ensure the privacy of parties, and encrypted data will provide the privacy too.
o **Integrity:** Only authentic party's interaction will be ensured by the Registration Unit.
o **Accountability:** By using the Blockchain technology we attain accountability.
o **Security:** If the block-id of user is somehow been leaked the attacker won't be able to get the raw data as the data would be encrypted.

4   Conclusion

This paper presents a privacy preserving mechanism for the health care data. By analysis of the protocol we showed the strengths of this platform. The overall intention of this paper is to develop a distributed system and divert the web platform in a distributed manner for the patients. The concern over anonymity has also been addressed in this paper. In our future research we will deploy this whole system.

References

1. Ekblaw, A., Azaria, A., Halamka, J.D.: A case study for blockchain in Healthcare: MedRec prototype for electronic health records and medical research data. In: IEEE Open & Big Data Conference (2016)
2. FoxNewsHealth. 'Ransomware' Cyberattack Cripples Hospitals Across England. Associated Press, May 2017
3. Glaser, A.: U.S. hospitals have been hit by the global ransomware attack - Recode (2017). https://www.recode.net/2017/6/27/15881666/global-eu-cyber-attack-us-hackers-nsa-hospitals
4. Gul, O., Al-Qutayri, M., Yeun, C.Y.: Framework of a national level electronic health record system. In: Cloud Computing (2012)
5. Hendrick, E., Schooley, B., Gao, C.: CloudHealth: developing a reliable cloud platform for healthcare applications. In: IEEE 10th Consumer Communications and Networking Conference (CCNC) (2013)

6. Kiyomoto, S., Rahman, M.S., Basu, A.: On blockchain-based anonymized dataset distribution platform. In: 2017 IEEE 15th International Conference on Software Engineering Research, Management and Applications (SERA) (2017)
7. Linn, L.A., Koo, M.B.: Blockchain for health data and its potential use in health it and health care related research. healthit.gov (2016)
8. Nakamoto, S.: Bitcoin: a peer-to-peer electronic cash system (2008)
9. Patra, M.R., Das, R.K., Padhy, R.P.: CRHIS: cloud based rural healthcare information system. In: Proceedings of the 6th International Conference on Theory and Practice of Electronic Governance (2012)
10. Raval, S.: Decentralized Applications: Harnessing Bitcoin's Blockchain Technology (2016)
11. Rolim, C.O., Koch, F.L., Westphall, C.B.: A cloud computing solution for patient's data collection in health care institutions. In: International Conference on eHealth, Telemedicine, and Social Medicine (2010)
12. Simic, M., Sladic, G., Milosavljević, B., et al.: A case study IoT and blockchain powered healthcare (2017)
13. Swan, M.: Blockchain: blueprint for a new economy (2015)
14. Yue, X., Wang, H., Jin, D., Li, M., Jiang, W.: Healthcare data gateways: found healthcare intelligence on blockchain with novel privacy risk control. J. Med. Syst. **40**(10), 218 (2016). https://doi.org/10.1007/s10916-016-0574-6. ISSN 1573-689X
15. Zhang, Y., Qiu, M., Tsai, C.W., Hassan, M.M., Alamri, A.: Health-CPS: healthcare cyber-physical system assisted by cloud and big data. IEEE Syst. J. **11**(1), 88–95 (2017). https://doi.org/10.1109/JSYST.2015.2460747. ISSN 1932-8184

The Art of Using Cross-Layer Design in Cognitive Radio Networks

Qusay Medhat Salih[1]([⊠]), Md. Arafatur Rahman[1,2],
Md. Zakirul Alam Bhuiyan[3], and Zafril Rizal M. Azmi[1]

[1] Faculty of Computer Systems and Software Engineering,
University Malaysia Pahang, Gambang, Malaysia
QusaySalih81@gmail.com, {arafatur,zafril}@ump.edu.my
[2] IBM Center of Excellence, UMP, Gambang, Malaysia
[3] Department of Computer and Information Sciences,
Fordham University, JMH 328A, Bronx, NY 10458, USA
mbhuiyan3@fordham.edu

Abstract. Cognitive Radio Networks (CRNs) have been obtained a significant focusing due to the ability of this technology to dissolve the issues of spectrum overcrowding and underutilization. In a CRNs, the secondary user (SU) is equipped to discover and use abandoned licensed channel, however, they must be desertion the channel if any interference is brought to the primary user (PU) who holds the channels. For that, the dynamic spectrum access (DSA) in CRNs is considered as an important application that allows for SU to use the licensed band in a dynamic way. Nevertheless, there are several challenges on CRNs such as interference, channel selection, routing, and etc. Cross-layer design can provide effective solutions in order to counteract these challenges. To this aim, in this paper, we have studied the existing related work about applying a cross-layer design in CRNs and how the upper layers and the lower layers parameters can optimize with the helping of a cross-layer. Finally, we have explained the implementation challenges of cross-layer design on CRNs.

Keywords: Cross-layer design · Cognitive radio network
Secondary users

1 Introduction

Radio spectrum is considered as precious resources for wireless communications. The spectrum resources, in ancient wireless networks, are used by a fixed spectrum policy that holds the licensed spectrum to the PU [1]. In recent decades, the request on the spectrum resource is being increased, and that called to change the policy of using the licensed spectrum [1,2]. Accordingly, the Federal Communication Committee (FCC) has enabled new rules for dynamically assigning the spectrum [3]. Subsequently, the CR employs to resolve spectrum limitation issues

© Springer International Publishing AG 2017
G. Wang et al. (Eds.): SpaCCS 2017 Workshops, LNCS 10658, pp. 544–556, 2017.
https://doi.org/10.1007/978-3-319-72395-2_50

through discovering the existence of spectrum holes and used it in a dynamic way [4]. However, CR is suffering from some challenges such as (interference, channel section, spectrum allocation, mobility, etc.) and that bearing on CR [5]. Hence, these challenges and problems can break down the performance of the CRNs [5,6].

Therefore, to make CR user can work efficiently, CRNs have to adopt a cross-layer style. For instance, to share the spectrum holes parameters with network layer, cross-layer will apply through combining getting spectrum sensing data which provide the physical layer and the spectrum schedule through a link-layer to the network layer. Combining these layers can help the network layer to discover the best routing path. For that, the cross-layer structure can provide different solutions for CR challenges and that it can help to optimize network performance.

Thus, this paper studies and discusses the previous related work about cross-layer design. In parallel, we explained how to apply the cross-layer methods in environments of CRNs, and how that can reflect positively on the CRNs and the layers performance. Also, we described the implementation challenges of cross-layer design on CRNs.

The rest of the paper is organized as follows: Sect. 2 explains why cross-layer design is considered as a solution for wireless and CR communication. Section 3 proposes different framework designs for the cross-layer. Section 4 describes how to apply the cross-layer in CR and how can that improve the performance it. Section 5 explains how we can develop the cross-layer framework to be more efficient with the environment of CR and how can benefit from the layer's parameters. Besides, it clarifies the challenges of cross-layer design and summarizes the way of sharing between five layers. Finally, Sect. 6 concludes the paper.

2   Why Cross-Layer Design

In an actual network, every layer in the network stack model has realized a different functional protocol that is interdependent with each other. It makes the process of interaction between these layers is complicated [8]. In spite of the network model drove up to dissolve the issues of designing the basic network functionalities, but it also creates restrictions on optimization of the network performance. From this point of view, the layered network structure has a major disadvantage by making it as a rigid network structure [8], which means the layers in the network stack just care about its functionality and its neighbor layers, and that makes the layers to disregard the interaction with other layers. For that, the ignore interaction between non-contiguous layers can lead to sub-optimal network performance [9]. For instance, it is difficult to enhance QoS and a management mobility in the layered structure due to that it needs to create the interaction between different layers. In reality, the network structure stack is suffering from the limitations and the non-interaction designing between the upper and lower layers. For that, this is called to break the constraints of the traditional network layer stack and optimize the network performance by using a cross-layer method.

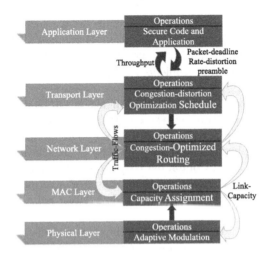

Fig. 1. Cross-layer design framework with information exchange between different layers [14].

In more details, Fig. 1 displays a design of a substitution of a cross-layer framework, where the data transfer between different layers. At link-layer, adaptive modulations are assigning to increase the rate of the link according to the channel conditions. This expands the achievable ability region of the network [10]. At every point of this operation, it refers to a potential giving of the various link-ability. According to the information state (facilities) of the link, MAC and the upper layer, choose from the capacity region at one point through applying the codes, time slots, or frequency bands for each of the links. Thus, the network layer operates together with the MAC layer to define the sequences of network flows that reduce the congestion.

Thus, solving for capability assignments and network flow are changed iteratively between two middle layers which represent a cross-layer framework (network and MAC layer). The process of congestion control and retransmission packet are defined at the transport layer. Lastly, the application layer establishes the most efficient encoding average.

3   A Proposition of Cross-Layer Design

The cross-layer style is a combine-style between upper and lower layers to improve many or all layers under assumed resource restriction. Cross-layer makes to use the cooperation between the protocol layers and evades unwanted interactions to amelioration the network performance in case of the designed is duly [11]. The cross-layer style will integrate data interchange between various layers (not necessarily neighbor layers), adaptivity at every layer to the existing data, and varieties into every layer to confirm it [12]. In generally speaking, this section will review different cross-layer design to boost the efficiency and performance of the network within a cross-layer style as shown in Fig. 2.

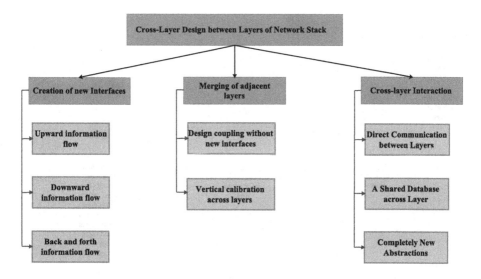

Fig. 2. A proposition of cross-layer design.

3.1   Motivation of Creates a New Interface

The new interfaces area is utilized for taking part among layers at run-time. The style of creating a new interface is a violation the network layer structure due to the traditional architecture is not supported that. We tend to distinguish this category into three sub-types according to [11].

Upward information flow. It refers to the case of following a layer protocol information in a lower layer to higher layers at the runtime according to create a new interface from the lower to a higher layer, as shown in Fig. 3(A). For instance, the loss of packet from the TCP receiver protocol to transport layer from the TCP sender can palpably converse the TCP transmitter to resend the packets if there is any damage in the packet.

Downward information flow. It refers to the case of following a layer protocol information in a higher layer to lower layers at the runtime according to create a new interface from the higher to a lower layer, as shown in Fig. 3(B). As shown, the link-layer will receive information from application layer regarding the delay requires. Also, the link-layer will then deal with packets from delay-sensitive at the applications with more importantly.

Back and forth information. In this class, there are two-layers employed at the same time to perform many functions, and this collaborate executes at the run-time. Usually, the iterative loop is obvious in between a couple of layers, with information flowing back and forth in between them as showcased in Fig. 3(C)

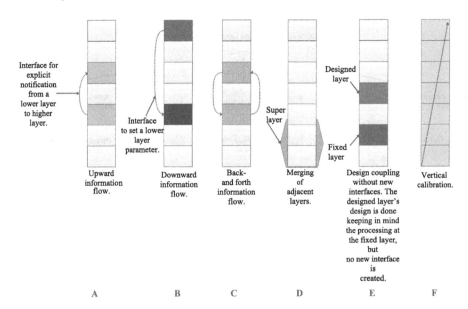

Fig. 3. Clarify the various kinds of cross-layer design suggestion. The rectangular boxes appear the protocol layers [11].

Obviously, the network structure, in this case, has included a couple of new interfaces.

3.2 Merging of Adjacent Layers

Another design of cross-layer is a meeting of adjoining layers. The amid this design, union of enterprises given by the principal layers is called a super-layer. This structure does not need to bother with any creation of new communication interfaces. They make a super-layer can connect with other parts of the stack through the use of interfaces that currently include the underlying stratified style, Fig. 3(D) shows the case of combined neighbor layers.

Design Coupling without New Interfaces. For this type, it includes the conjugation of two or a lot of layers while not building any additional the new interfaces at run-time. This category explains in Fig. 3(E) it's insufferable to switch one layer without creating a matching change to another layer.

Vertical Calibration across Layers. For this type, in light of the fact that the name proposes, the parameter that extends crosswise over layers at runtime is adapted, as represented in Fig. 3(F). The execution of utilization layers relies on the contribution of shifting parameters of the layers under it. It is supposed the mutual harmony that it can assist to acquire superior performance than the individual layer parameters.

3.3   Implementing Cross-Layer Interactions

Based on cross-layer interaction, and enforcement that it can be separated into three categories, as explained below.

Direct Communication between layers. The combine of runtime informa-tion enables the layers to be able to connect directly with each other, as came out in Fig. 4(a). In this case, the phenomenon of communication is transparent, and that making the parameters of one layer is available to another layer at runtime. Thus, there are a lot of methods that enable the layers to be able to connect with one another by protocol header or further information header.

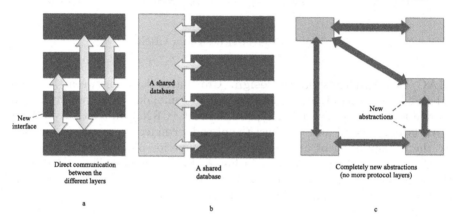

Fig. 4. Clarify the various kinds of cross-layer design suggestion. The rectangular boxes appear the protocol layers [11].

A Shared Database across Layers. As the name recommends, in this type, the database can reach it by every layer, as outlined in Fig. 4(b). The joint database is considered as a new layer that supplies the administration of capac-ity/recovery of information to/from every one of the layers. This class is appro-priate for the vertical building as specified in the previous area as mention it. However, this structure has a disadvantage due to this design requires creating new interfaces between the stack on the network layer and the database.

Completely New Abstractions. In this class, there is regularly a new abstraction with no more protocol layers, that we have explained it in schemati-cally organize as shown in Fig. 4(c). This class offers adaptability during run-time and design and that because of the wealthy interaction between the network lay-ers stack.

4   Cross-Layer Design for Cognitive Radio Networks

As illustrated in Fig. 5, this part describes the map of cross-layer design in CRNs and discuss some related works to explain why CRNs ought to implement the cross-layer design between these layers.

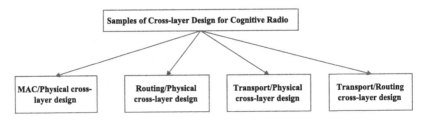

Fig. 5. Cross-layer design for CRNs

MAC/Physical cross-layer design. Cross-layer design between the physical and MAC generally used in CRNs due to combining these two layers contribute to the efficiency of this type of network (CRNs). In another word, the MAC layer has to be able to adjust the provider connection resources and modify the configuration of user mobility. The superior physical layer strategies, which include standard categories inclusive of a couple of coding and modulation schemes, superior antenna strategies, MIMO and OFDM technologies and extremely wide bandwidth, offer a terrific capacity of enhanced overall to reduce of delay, throughput and packet loss [12]. Overall, utilizing channel expertise at MAC layer enable to a utilization of the channel and outcomes overall in an efficient performance.

In [13], the author deal with combined of both the spectrum sensing at the physical layer and the cognitive protocol at the link layer to augment spectrum effectiveness whereas restricting the interference probability to PU. In [14], the author applied method of cross-layer style on pragmatic multi-channel MAC protocols, that incorporate between the physical layer for sensing process for spectrum at and the packet tabulation at MAC layer. In traditional CR protocols, the idle waiting for time-lots might involve a high average of the packet and loss, and poor quality of service outcomes for SU. To get over this drawback, in [15], The author proposed a cross-layer structure and applied the scheduling algorithm to reduce the rate of packet delay of the SU under restrictions on transferring rate power which sends by the SU and delay rate of the packet for the PU. Besides, the allocation algorithm for a useful resource is as well recommended to designate the SU channels at which the overall throughput of the CRNs increased.

In [16], the author recommended a cross-layer design as an arranging approach with reliable interference control at the link-layer for a couple of SU with a variety of QoS necessities. In CRNs, most vital elements are throughput enhancement and reduce power usage. Nevertheless, the conflicted case occurs while the throughput is increasing and the power decreasing where each other in a sensible state of affairs. To solve this problem, in [17], the author introduced a cross-layer strategy for combined link scheduling and power control in CRNs. Via this technique, the throughput, enhanced rate enables without extreme transmit powers.

Routing/Physical cross-layer design. The approach of cognitive radio provides a dynamic change of underlying radio community parameters of the physical layer. This dynamic control guarantees overall performance enhancement contrasted with traditional radios with static source assignment style. In [18], the author suggested a cross-layer promoting platform to collectively style the spectrum take part and flowing routing with interference challenges in CRNs. They can develop a promoting issue in the form of mixed-integer linear programming (MILP) to offer an intelligent routing.

Transport/Physical cross-layer design. For the multi-hop features in the wireless network, the ability of a link is time-various as an outcome of the elements which consist of interference, variable channel quality, then on. The phenomenon packet loss in wireless network appears for causes such as channel error, congestion, or node quality [19]. In order to enhance CR end-to-end procedure, the variable link capability ought to be taken into consideration.

For a long time, the artwork of combine between the physical layer and the transport layer for wireless networks has been investigated [19]. The bearing on strategies in the literature may be labeled towards a couple of classes. Within the primary class, the TCP protocol for congestion-control is confident to improve through the data that obtained from the physical layer into consideration. As an example, we can apply a significant information from the physical layer to distinguish the phenomenon of packet loss because of the congestion or bad link. However, rather than passively taking movement most efficiently in TCP, TCP and the physical layer can manipulate and enhanced collectively, these types of strategies belong to the second classification, which includes excess complex algorithms and additional sophisticated protocols, and achievements [18].

Many several parameters may be managed within the physical layer. It is tough and incorrect to possess by one management procedure to include the all of the optimization parameters. A useful method is to specialize in one parameter or two parameters within the procedures and suppose that alternative parameters are fastened. As an example, consideration facility management due to the significant method of harmonizing the physical-layer performance [20]. The routing direction is believed to be fastened in shared power control and congestion algorithmic. Once congestion appears, a technique attempts to avoid congestion and search a better routing path.

Transport/Routing cross-layer design. In CRNs, the transport layer also is suffering from congestion and low response issues in CRNs. However, there is a little bit of research that has been focused on transport-layer dilemmas in a cognitive radio setting [21]. In [22] the author revealed that the protocols within the transport layer are very slow to reply quickly. That means the protocol of transport-layer are not able to offer a powerful process, and not reliable to utilizing in CRNs. For this reason, the author diagnosed the necessities of protocols for the transport layer in CRNs and proposed a novel modular structure for supplementing the transport layer. In more details, by intending on using the cross-layer model through providing a new module to the existing layered community structure for incorporating cognitive capabilities between transport and network layer, and that will increase growth throughput for CR user. In including, this examine confirmed that during cognitive radio networks cut-up of the delivery layer from different layers is viable and protocols for the layered architecture can utilize available bandwidth correctly.

5   Develop Cross-Layer Approach and Challenges

A lot of research has been done to develop the prototype of communication in CRNs since 15 years [23]. However, CR user requests many complex operations to perform new features [23]. Precisely, for a CR is important to detect the surroundings and framework of functionality, distinguish the relevant attributes of this circumstance, make a decision founded on them, and eventually connect suitably. However, the issue in cross-layer design in CRNs that how to make an efficient cross-layer design and how integrated between the layers parameter in a manner consistent with requirements CRNs.

Meanwhile, a cross-layer design can develop through taking part a variety of protocol layer starting from the application layer and ended to physical layer [24]. For instance, the process of merging different layers in one layer that it can reduce the overhead in term of cross-layer information interchange [24]. However, to boost the network efficiency and increase the users interests, sharing between the layers of routing, MAC, physical, transport, and application become indispensable part, where the transport layer protocol is measured in the congestion control part, physical and MAC layers are identify in the arranging and sensing part, and routing is regarded in the fundamental interaction among congestion control and scheduling, and application layer is considered in QoS part [23].

As shown in Table 1, every layer in the network layer stack has a variety of parameters and features. For that, every layer can supply different information about the network environments [24]. In CRNs, there are new functions that have been added to the layers in network stacks due to the nature of dynamic spectrum access in CRNs [25,27]. For that, SU needs to discover the surrounding environment to be able to transfer the information with low-cost routing, and without making any interference with the PU [26,31]. In addition, to explore the unused spectrum in a reliability way [24,32]. Notwithstanding, the border of network layer stack has to violate to design a practical cross-layer model able to draw new horizons of managing the operations in CRNs.

The cross-layer violates the traditional layered structure through permitting for communication directly between layers or combine between distant layers [26], significantly for wireless networks. The cross-layer style provides a solution key to enhance network functionality [24]. Even so, the cross-layer style is

Table 1. Parameters and functions of the network layers stack

Layers	Parameters	Functionality of layers in CRNs
Application-Layer	Source coding rate, Buffer priority, Packet arrival rate	The principal function of Cognitive Radio Application Layer is to handle disputes between different applications when a new contact is created
Transport-Layer	Congestion control, Traffic patterns, Packet-loss,	The transport layer in cognitive radio employs to draw the way for QoS at the application layer and the and lower layers and also to initiate transport layer connection
Network-Layer	Network topology, End-to-End delay, Metric of routing, Packet size, Routing cost	The network layer in Cognitive Radio can supply two important services, namely Routing and Flow/admission control
Link-Layer (MAC)	Frame size, Medium Access Feedback, Control channel-related information	The link-layer in cognitive radio enable to saving the parameters and interfaces starting at link-layer radio to higher layers protocols of cognitive radio
Physical-Layer	Transmitter power, Spreading type, Channel state information, External interference and SINR, Operation mode, RSSI	Physical Layer in Cognitive Radio can supply two primary functions, namely the communication service and sensing services

debatable as a result of it violates traditional style principles of the network layer stack. In spite of being debatable in methods of the networking community, but it also has advantages of using a cross-layer style [30].

In other words, a cross-layer style proposals should be holistic [23]. As an example of developing a cross-layer design, In [24], the author proposed a new cross-layer design by using a planned to utility optimization drawback (GUOP) in CRAHNs with various restrictions of parts of the physical layer to the appliance layer. It is entirely different from the reverse cross-layer style. By calculative in an associate reiterative circle in between and all over layers with data flowing back and forth performing arts completely a variety of activities, the planned COVD is in a position to resolve the five-layers concerned networking drawback globally and optimally. For that, mix five-layer represent is made a replacement behavior for the cross-layer designs, and overcomes the challenges of participating between the layers stack.

From another perspective, the challenges of cross-layer implements in modularity design, protocol ability, system complexity, and compatibility between layers [23–25]. Once returning to the particular execution of the previous designs, the changes of protocols in multiple layers will affect on reusable of the software system, balancing protocol model and adaptability to different applications [27]. Through cross-layer fashion, the quality operating approach in the protocol stack is betterment [27]. Though, a wireless network with cross-layer style might also be contradictory with different platforms [29]. Therefore, inter-operation between totally different networks is tough to keep up. That it always requires noting that such problems typically do not exist in a very superimposed style theme [19]. To avoid these issues, exchange ought to be created amongst the functionality improvement via cross-layer style and profit loss of superimposed style [23,24].

The art of cross-layer design has rules to initiate the design through break the limitation of the network layer stack and create new interfaces to pass and integrate the information of every layer to other layers [28]. The features of cross-layer design have represented a solution for many challenges, especially in CRNs [14,24]. Nevertheless, the researchers in cross-layer design need to meet future challenges of design cross-layer pattern that must agree with the features and issues CRNs technology.

6   Conclusion

This paper studies and investigates the cross-layer design from various perspectives by relying on the revision of previous studies to clarify methods of designing cross-layer. Moreover, to explain how to apply cross-layer in CRNs, and to demonstrate the ability of these ways to solve the problems that face up the CRNs. However, the cross-layer design also has different challenges while implementation, therefore, it also discusses the challenges of implement a cross-layer in CRNs.

Acknowledgement. This work is partially supported by the RDU Grants (RDU1603129 and PGRS170333).

References

1. Cacciapuoti, A.S., Caleffi, M., Paura, L., Rahman, M.A.: Channel availability for mobile cognitive radio networks. J. Netw. Comput. Appl. **47**, 131–136 (2015)
2. Jing, T., Zhu, S., Li, H., Xing, X., Cheng, X., Huo, Y., Bie, R., Znati, T.: Cooperative relay selection in cognitive radio networks. IEEE Trans. Veh. Technol. **64**, 1872–1881 (2015)
3. Huang, X., Han, T., Ansari, N.: On green-energy-powered cognitive radio networks. IEEE Commun. Surv. Tutor. **17**, 827–842 (2015)
4. Saleem, Y., Rehmani, M.H., Zeadally, S.: Integration of cognitive radio technology with unmanned aerial vehicles: issues, opportunities, and future research challenges. J. Netw. Comput. Appl. **50**, 15–31 (2015)

5. Saleem, Y., Salim, F., Rehmani, M.H.: Routing and channel selection from cognitive radio network's perspective: a survey. Comput. Electr. Eng. **42**, 117–134 (2015)
6. Cai, Z., Duan, Y., Bourgeois, A.G.: Delay efficient opportunistic routing in asynchronous multi-channel cognitive radio networks. J. Comb. Optim. **29**, 815–835 (2015)
7. Bourdena, A., Mavromoustakis, C.X., Kormentzas, G., Pallis, E., Mastorakis, G., Yassein, M.B.: A resource intensive traffic-aware scheme using energy-aware routing in cognitive radio networks. Future Gener. Comput. Syst. **39**, 16–28 (2014)
8. Xue, D., Ekici, E.: Cross-layer scheduling for cooperative multi-hop cognitive radio networks. IEEE J. Sel. Areas Commun. **31**, 534–543 (2013)
9. Fu, B., Xiao, Y., Deng, H., Zeng, H.: A survey of cross-layer designs in wireless networks. IEEE Commun. Surv. Tutor. **16**, 110–126 (2014)
10. Edirisinghe, R., Zaslavsky, A.: Cross-layer contextual interactions in wireless networks. IEEE Commun. Surv. Tutor. **16**, 1114–1134 (2014)
11. Srivastava, V., Motani, M.: Cross-layer design: a survey and the road ahead. IEEE Commun. Mag. **43**, 112–119 (2005)
12. Liu, Y., Zhou, Q.: State of the art in cross-layer design for cognitive radio wireless networks. In: 2009 International Symposium on Intelligent Ubiquitous Computing and Education, pp. 366–369. IEEE (2009)
13. Zhao, Q., Tong, L., Swami, A., Chen, Y.: Cross-layer design of opportunistic spectrum access in the presence of sensing error. In: 2006 40th Annual Conference on Information Sciences and Systems, pp. 778–782. IEEE (2006)
14. Su, H., Zhang, X.: Cross-layer based opportunistic MAC protocols for QoS provisionings over cognitive radio wireless networks. IEEE J. Sel. Areas Commun. **26** (2008)
15. Saleh, G., El-Keyi, A., Nafie, M.: Cross-layer minimum-delay scheduling and maximum-throughput resource allocation for multiuser cognitive networks. IEEE Trans. Mob. Comput. **12**, 761–773 (2013)
16. Tian, C., Yuan, D.: Cross layer opportunistic scheduling for multiclass users in cognitive radio networks. In: 4th International Conference on Wireless Communications, Networking and Mobile Computing, WiCOM 2008, pp. 1–4. IEEE (2008)
17. Li, D., Dai, X., Zhang, H.: Cross-layer scheduling and power control in cognitive radio networks. In: 4th International Conference on Wireless Communications, Networking and Mobile Computing, WiCOM 2008, pp. 1–3. IEEE (2008)
18. Akyildiz, I.F., Lee, W.-Y., Vuran, M.C., Mohanty, S.: NeXt generation/dynamic spectrum access/cognitive radio wireless networks: a survey. Comput. Netw. **50**, 2127–2159 (2006)
19. Raisinghani, V.T., Iyer, S.: Cross-layer design optimizations in wireless protocol stacks. Comput. Commun. **27**, 720–724 (2004)
20. Chiang, M.: Balancing transport and physical layers in wireless multihop networks: jointly optimal congestion control and power control. IEEE J. Sel. Areas Commun. **23**, 104–116 (2005)
21. Rawat, P., Singh, K.D., Bonnin, J.M.: Cognitive radio for M2M and internet of things: a survey. Comput. Commun. **94**, 1–29 (2016)
22. Sarkar, D., Narayan, H.: Transport layer protocols for cognitive networks. In: INFOCOM IEEE Conference on Computer Communications Workshops, pp. 1–6. IEEE (2010)

23. Kliks, A., Triantafyllopoulou, D., De Nardis, L., Holland, O., Gavrilovska, L., Bantouna, A.: Cross-layer analysis in cognitive radio—context identification and decision making aspects. IEEE Trans. Cogn. Commun. Netw. **1**, 450–463 (2015)

24. Teng, Y., Song, M.: Cross-layer optimization and protocol analysis for cognitive ad hoc communications. IEEE Access **5**, 18692–18706 (2017)

25. Damljanović, Z.: Mobility management strategies in heterogeneous cognitive radio networks. J. Netw. Syst. Manag. **18**, 4–22 (2010)

26. Che-aron, Z., Abdalla, A.H., Abdullah, K., Hassan, W.H., Rahman, M.A.: A robust on-demand routing protocol for cognitive radio ad hoc networks. In: Kim, K.J., Wattanapongsakorn, N. (eds.) Mobile and Wireless Technology 2015. LNEE, vol. 310, pp. 33–43. Springer, Heidelberg (2015). https://doi.org/10.1007/978-3-662-47669-7_4

27. Rahman, M.A., Caleffi, M., Paura, L.: Joint path and spectrum diversity in cognitive radio ad-hoc networks. EURASIP J. Wirel. Commun. Netw. **2012**, 235 (2012)

28. Shakkottai, S., Rappaport, T.S., Karlsson, P.C.: Cross-layer design for wireless networks. IEEE Commun. Mag. **41**, 74–80 (2003)

29. Kawadia, V., Kumar, P.R.: A cautionary perspective on cross-layer design. IEEE Wirel. Commun. **12**, 3–11 (2005)

30. Conti, M., Maselli, G., Turi, G., Giordano, S.: Cross-layering in mobile ad hoc network design. Computer **37**, 48–51 (2004)

31. Che-Aron, Z., Abdalla, A.H., Abdullah, K., Hassan, W.H., Rahman, M.A.: RACARP: a robustness aware routing protocol for cognitive radio ad hoc networks. J. Theor. Appl. Inf. Technol. **76**, 12 (2015)

32. Rahman, A., Savoia, R., Uddin, M.M.: MCAST: mobility-aware channel-availability based channel selection technique. In: ICNS 2015, p. 93 (2015)

A Quality Model for Evaluating Encryption-as-a-Service

Jin Wu$^{(\boxtimes)}$, Zhiqiang Zhu, and Songhui Guo

Zhengzhou Information Science and Technology Institute,
Zhengzhou 450001, Henan, China
381892234@qq.com

Abstract. Cloud computing is a promising paradigm and seen as a trend on information and technology. However, it is a challenge to ensure the security of cloud computing. Compared with other security schemes, Encryption-as-a-Service (EaaS) not only avoids the risk of cloud, but also is more efficient. For commercial success of Encryption-as-a-Service, we present a quality model to evaluate the quality level of service. We define four quality characteristics of Encryption-as-a-Service, and propose the corresponding metrics based on practical experience and research. Moreover, we define LE_{EaaS} as a comprehensive metric for the quality level, and determine weighting coefficients utilizing CRITIC method, which will make the evaluation more practical.

Keywords: Cloud computing security · Encryption-as-a-Service
Quality model · CRIRIC method

1 Introduction

Being the latest computing paradigm, cloud computing is a promising service platform of the next-generation Internet for its feature, including resource-sharing, elastic scalable and dynamic-deploying. However, the security for the cloud computing is a challenge: Storing data at cloud increases the risk of data leakage and unauthorized access. In 2014, several Hollywood actresses' icloud accounts were attacked by hackers and resulted in lots of private photos stolen and leaked. Coincidentally, US cloud storage service Dropbox confirmed in 2016 that a data breach discovered and disclosed in 2012 was more serious than previously expected, which influenced nearly 69 million accounts. Cloud data centers are becoming the targets of attacks and intrusions [1]. Once the cloud data center is breached, or it is mismanaged by the cloud providers, some important information will be leaked, which will make a significant damage to customers. Thus, the security imposes restrictions on application of cloud computing.

Many security schemes have been proposed [2, 3], which most rely on encryption to ensure the confidentiality and integrity of customers' data. However, the server-side encryption in an untrustworthy environment like public cloud is too risky, while the client-side encryption can undermine the benefits of cloud since it is a time-consuming task for encryption and decryption [4]. Rahmani [5] develops a private cloud as an intermediary between the service cloud and customers, which is called Encryption-as-a-Service based on XaaS concept. Rahmani only presents the concept of

© Springer International Publishing AG 2017
G. Wang et al. (Eds.): SpaCCS 2017 Workshops, LNCS 10658, pp. 557–569, 2017.
https://doi.org/10.1007/978-3-319-72395-2_51

Encryption-as-a-Service, but do not specifically describe the architecture of EaaS. Nevertheless, thanks to the commercial benefit, many computer functions have move towards the cloud, and the idea of EaaS has been put into practice. AliCloud cooperates with Tass, the cryptographic technology and information security service provider, to launch the cryptographic service for cloud users. Another domestic cryptographic service provider Sansec as well as develops cloud cryptographic service. Both are with the same idea as EaaS, that is cryptograph computing cloudization. According to the idea of EaaS and the practical application environment, we propose the architecture of EaaS, as shown in Fig. 1.

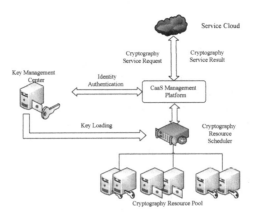

Fig. 1. Architecture of EaaS

The architecture of EaaS and its service mechanism is as follows:

a. When the customer requires an encryption service in general service cloud, the customer initiates the request to the EaaS management platform and sends his ID and password to it.
b. EaaS management platform completes the authentication through the key management center, and responds to the customer.
c. The resource scheduler gives the priority of virtual security machines (vSM) for sequence. According to the sequence, the first vSM is assigned to execute the customer's task.
d. The key corresponding to the customer and the data to be processed are loaded into the assigned vSM.
e. The vSM performs the task, and the results will be returned to the corresponding customer in service cloud.

Compared with other security schemes, there are three features of EaaS.

1. High efficient utilization of resources: EaaS utilizes large computing clusters to provide elastic service. Moreover, to some companies, EaaS can provide more dynamic cryptography service when it is booming on special situations.

2. High quality of service: Customers can acquire corresponding cryptography service depending on what they need. EaaS can provide higher quality service with a large computing cluster, which meets the customers' needs of high quality service in cloud computing environment.
3. Low cost: There is no need for customers to pay for extract charge, including cost for deploying cryptographic machines, administrators and routine maintenance.

As a novel commercial cryptography service pattern, EaaS also requires a comprehensive quality model to evaluate its service level like other service clouds. It is important and necessary to build the quality model for the cloud service, which can be explained from the organizations' view and the users'. For EaaS organizations, a quality model has three distinct advantages.

1. Service description. A quality model can be more intuitive in describing the functional performance of the system, which becomes an efficient external exhibition of the service.
2. Service monitoring. It is much more convenient and efficient for EaaS organization to monitor the service quality based on the model. The quality model allows adaption strategies to be triggered when undesired metrics are identified or when threshold values are reached.
3. Service adaptation. When the quality of the service is undesired, the system is necessary to be adapted. A set of potential alternative is generated, and it is necessary to estimate each alternative's impact on the system.

For users, a quality model is also necessary for service selection. Faced with several EaaS providers providing the identical service, the users tend to select the one with a higher quality based on the model.

Now many quality models have been presented. Jureta and Stéphane [6] propose a comprehensive quality model for service-oriented systems called QVDP. It evaluates the service quality in four sub-models and integrates the priority and dependency information within any quality model, but it is designed for a general service-oriented system and do not take the security into account. Lee [7] presents a quality model for evaluating Software-as-a-Service in cloud computing. It derives quality attributes from the key features of Software-as-a-Service (SaaS), and defines metrics for the quality attributes. But the metrics are too conceptive, which makes its practical application hard.

Most of the quality models are intended for general service, whereas EaaS provides cryptography service, and the security should be a crucial element, which most of the quality model do not research enough on.

Hence, the paper proposes a more specific quality model to evaluate the quality of cryptography service of EaaS. The rest of the paper is organized as follows. In Sect. 2, we will derive four quality characteristics of the model, and define the specific metrics. In Sect. 3, we will and utilize a method called Criteria Importance Through Intercriteria *Correlation* (CRITIC) [17] to define each weighting coefficient of the attribute, which makes it more simple to rank the services on their comprehensive service level.

2 Quality Model of Encryption-as-a-Service

2.1 Quality Characteristics of Encryption-as-a-Service

ISO/IEC 25010 [8] is intended to be used in conjunction with the other parts of the Systems and software Quality Requirements and Evaluation (SQuaRE) series of International Standards (ISO/IEC 25000 to ISO/IEC 25099). Currently there are three quality models in the SQuaRE series: the quality in use model, the product quality model and the data quality model. According to the concept of EaaS, it is a private cloud in essence. Hence, he product quality model which is intended for a system or a product can be applied to EaaS.

The product quality model properties are categorized into eight characteristics, and each characteristic is composed of a set of related subcharacteristics. The framework of the product quality model is shown in Fig. 2.

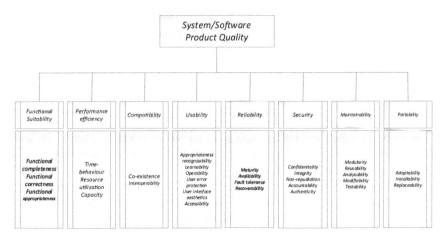

Fig. 2. Framework of the product quality model

The standard points out that it is not practically possible to specify or measure all subcharacteristics for all parts of a large computer system or software product. Therefore the model should be tailored depending on the objectives for the product.

Stalk and Hout [9] and Brockhoff et al. [10] investigate the features with which successful companies are in the competitive world markets. Their results indicated that the companies' success is related to the capability based upon three essential factors: time, cost, and quality. On the software system side, Frølund and Koistinen [11] present a set of practical dimensions for distributed object systems' reliability, performance and availability.

Based on previous studies and the practical experience, this paper defines the four following quality characteristics.

Efficiency: The efficiency of EaaS service measures the amount of relative resources used when providing the service and the performance under the stated conditions. In the paper, we define the subcharacteristics of it are *Time Behavior* and *Resource Utilization*.

The reason for defining the characteristic and its two subcharacteristics is that time and cost is crucial factors for service providers based on previous studies. It is the notion that *Time behavior* measures the degree to which the response and processing times and throughput rates when performing its functions. *Resource utilization* is from cloud providers' perspective. A large part of expense of cloud providers is concerned with the amount of resource. As a result, measurement of the resource utilization is imperative for measuring the cost of the system.

Reliability: The characteristic is the measurement for the ability of EaaS performs its functions under specified conditions for a specified period of time. Based on the research and practical need we tailor the model and define three subcharacteristics, that is *Availability*, *Fault tolerance* and *Recoverability*. The reason for retaining the characteristic and these three subcharacteristics is as follows.

Firstly, one of the factors of the successful companies should have in the service is quality, as some research concludes above, and it can be embodied by reliability to some extend.

Secondly, it is necessary for both providers and users to learn the reliability of the service, because EaaS provides cryptography service for various users, and once an unexpected fault occurs leading a system crash, it will bring great loss to the providers. What is worse, the failure will propagate to users who usage the service, making inestimable damage.

The three subcharacteristics can quantitatively describe the functional capability, which are helpful for providers to monitor and adjust their service and become one of the important reference indicators for users to select the service.

Security: We take the characteristic into the model depending on the nature of EaaS service. The EaaS providers and users should pay much more attention to the security of the system, because for the users, the main goal of using the EaaS service is to keep some sensitive and important data from leakage. If the security of the system is unknown, the quality model of EaaS is losing its significance to a great extent.

We define three subcharacteristics to measure the capability in more aspects. The three subcharacteristics are *Confidentiality*, *Integrity*, *Non-repudiation*. From the users view, these subcharacteristics can measure the quality of encryption service. *Confidentiality* measures the degree to which the system ensures that the data of users is accessible to those only authorized. *Integrity* evaluates the capacity of defending unauthorized modification to users' data, and *Non-Repudiation* measurement suggests the degree to which degree to actions or events can be proven to have taken place, preventing from being repudiated. The three subcharacteristics were necessarily required in evaluating the security of a system. Hence, we employ these subcharacteristics in our quality model.

Maintainability: A system can not be perfect in its initial launch and completely meet the users' need. Thus it should be modified and optimized periodically with the feedback of the users and improve its competitiveness, which is the reason for defining this characteristic.

We also define *Modularity* and *Reusability* as subcharacteristics for the characteristic. The rationale for defining *Modularity* is based on the Law of Demeter (LoD). The principle was put forward by Ian Holland in 1987 and says that an entity of the system should have least effect on the others. The principle is embodied by *Modularity* in system design nowadays. If the *Modularity* of the system is in a high degree, it indicates that it is easier to modify and maintain the system. *Reusability* measures the degree to which an asset can be used in more than one system. It can evaluate whether the system is modularized reasonably, which affects the efficiency in designing, modifying, maintaining the system, and furthermore, it is closely related to cost to EaaS providers. To commercial service providers, this subcharacteristic can not be overlooked.

In this section, we propose a quality model for EaaS, which is shown in Fig. 3. We will give more details on how these characteristics and subcharacteristics to be measured in next section, which makes the quality model more practical.

Fig. 3. Quality model of EaaS

2.2   Quality Metrics of Encryption-as-a-Service

For evaluating the degree of each attribute, we present metrics for each characteristics in this section and provide a description including formulas and relevant interpretations.

Efficiency: This paper measures efficiency by *Time Behavior* and *Resource Utilization*. Hence, *Efficiency* can be computes as:

$$E_{EaaS} = U_{serve} + U_{resource} \tag{1}$$

U_{serve} is ratio of execution time to total service time and $U_{resource}$ is *Resource Utilization*.

Total service time is composed of service waiting time T_{wait} and execution time T_{exe}, so U_{serve} is computed as:

$$U_{serve} = \frac{T_{exe}}{T_{wait} + T_{exe}} \tag{2}$$

Through the formula, it is clear that if waiting time is longer, value of T_{wait} is larger, which reduce the value of U_{serve}, indicating lower degree of *Time behavior*.

$U_{resource}$ measures the utilization of resources, including network bandwidth and other computing powers such as storage capacity, CPU and cipher machines. Hence, $U_{resource}$ can be computed as:

$$U_{resource} = U_{CPU} + U_{storage} + U_{network} \tag{3}$$

The components U_{CPU}, $U_{storage}$, $U_{network}$ represent computing resource utilization, storage resource utilization and network resource utilization.

We measure these utilizations following this formula:

$$U_{CPU/storage/network} = \frac{Resource_{allocated}}{Resource_{pre-defined}} \tag{4}$$

The denominator $Resource_{pre-defined}$ represents the amount of CPU/storage/network resource defined to provide the service, while the numerator $Resource_{allocated}$ is the actual amount of allocated resources. If the value of the metric is low, it is indicated that actual allocated resources are fewer than it is thought to be, which means that the system makes good resource usage.

Reliability: *Reliability* is composed of three subcharacteristics, and it can be computed as:

$$R_{EaaS} = A_{EaaS} + FT_{EaaS} + RC_{EaaS} \tag{5}$$

A_{EaaS}, FT_{EaaS}, RC_{EaaS} represent *Availability*, *Fault tolerance* and *Recoverability*.

Availability can be measured by this formula:

$$A_{EaaS} = \frac{Time_{available}}{Time_{total}} \tag{6}$$

where $Time_{total}$ is the total time operating EaaS service in a certain period of time, while $Time_{available}$ is the specific period of time to be available to invoke EaaS service. If the ratio is low, it means that little time is available for invoking the service, indicating the system is with a low operational and accessible degree when required for used.

Fault tolerance can be computed as [7]:

$$FT_{EaaS} = \frac{Num_{faults}}{Num_{totalfaults}} \tag{7}$$

where $Num_{totalfaults}$ is the total number of occurring faults identified in a certain period of time, while Num_{faults} represents the number of faults that do not cause failures of the system in the same period of time. The ratio reflects whether the system is stable enough regardless of some faults appearing. If the metric is high, it means the number of faults that do not cause failures are a large proportion, and it can be treated as the probability of the system getting into failure when a fault happens. The probability is a quantitative measurement for the fault tolerance capability.

Recoverability can be computed as [7]:

$$RC_{EaaS} = \frac{Num_{remedied}}{Num_{failures}} \tag{8}$$

where the denominator $Num_{failures}$ is the total number of failures in a certain period of time, while the numerator $Num_{remedied}$ is the number of failures remedied. In a period of time, if the metric is larger, it means that the number of the failures remedied get more, which reflects that the degree of failure recovery is higher.

Security: The measurement of the characteristic can be divided into three parts as:

$$Security = CD_{EaaS} + I_{EaaS} + NR_{EaaS} \tag{9}$$

The three parts of the formula are *Confidentiality*, *Integrity* and *Non-repudiation*.

To evaluate the security of the system, we can rely on some testing tools, such as oscanner, Mysqlweak. We put forward the evaluation for these subcharacteristics with the help of testing tools.

Confidentiality of data is usually measured by entropy. Thus, it can be computed as:

$$CD_{EaaS} = \frac{\sum (e_{before} - e_{after})}{\sum e} \tag{10}$$

$\sum e$ is the sum of entropy for data involved in the test, and $\sum (e_{before} - e_{after})$ means the sum of difference of the entropy for data involved between before and after the test. As we all know, the entropy is the measurement for uncertainty of information, and if the data is more uncertain, that means it is less impossible to be revealed, suggesting more confidential.

Integrity of data can be computed as:

$$I_{EaaS} = \frac{Num_{datachanged}}{Num_{data}} \tag{11}$$

where Num_{data} is the total number of data involved in the test, and $Num_{datachanged}$ is the number of the data which is tampered, deleted or inserted into other information. The ratio can be treated as the probability of data's integrity destroyed when it is attacked, which reflects the integrity protection degree of the system.

Non-reputation can be measured by the following formula:

$$NR_{EaaS} = \frac{\sum probability(i)}{Num_{file}} \tag{12}$$

The denominator Num_{data} represents the total number of files involved in the test, while the numerator $\sum probability(i)$ represents the sum of probability for every file, and more specifically, the probability that identifying the file holder from the others after tested. *probablity*(i) is the probability of ith file. The average of every file's identified probability actually reflects the probability that the users' events and actions be identified in EaaS system, which embodies the capability of the non-reputation for the system.

Maintainability: We define two subcharacteristics for the characteristic in previous section, and it can be measure as:

$$Maintainability = M_{EaaS} + RU_{EaaS} \tag{13}$$

M_{EaaS}, RU_{EaaS} represent the Modularity and *Reusability*.

According to the definition of modularity, we use the following formula to evaluate this subcharacteristic:

$$M_{EaaS} = \frac{\sum Coupling(i)}{Num_{module}} \tag{14}$$

The denominator Num_{module} represents the total number of module of the system, while the numerator represents the sum of coupling of every module. *Coupling*(i) represents the coupling degree of ith module.

In terms of software design, the coupling was usually applied as an important metric for *Modularity*. Hence, the average coupling of modules in system can reflect the *Modularity* of the system to some degree.

Reusability can be computed as:

$$RU_{EaaS} = \frac{\sum Num_{reqired\,mod}}{Num_{module}} \tag{15}$$

The denominator Num_{module} represents the total number of module of the system, while the numerator represents the sum of the number that each module is invoked. $Num_{required\,mod}$ represents the invoked number of ith module.

In order to more comprehensively compare the quality of a set of EaaS services we define the service level of aggregation LE_{EaaS}. The four characteristics are measured mutual independently, and have differential impact on the service quality in degree, but not in essence, and they are complementary linearly. Based on the feature of characteristics and relation between them, the paper combines them in addition model. Thus, LE_{EaaS} can be computed as:

$$LE_{EaaS} = \omega_1 \, Efficiency + \omega_2 \, Reliability + \omega_3 \, Security + \omega_4 \, Maintainability \tag{16}$$

$\omega_i(i = 1, 2, 3, 4)$ is weight coefficient, $0 \leq \omega_i \leq 1, \sum_{i=1}^{4} \omega_i = 1$. As mentioned above, the four quality characteristics have different degree impacts on the service level of aggregation LE_{EaaS}, which are quantitatively embodied in weighting coefficients. The value of each weighting coefficient illustrates that the importance of the attribute, which will greatly influences the evaluation result. Hence, it is crucial to determine each weighting coefficient with appropriate method. The paper will utilize *Criteria Importance Through Intercriteria Correlation* (CRITIC) to determine weighting coefficients in next section.

3 Evaluation for LE_{EaaS}

3.1 Determination of Weighting Coefficients

Methods of determining weighting coefficients can be divided into objective determination and the subjective. Objective determination is a method of determining the weighting coefficients by calculating the index value of each attributes, such as mean square deviation, principal component analysis (PCA), entropy value method and CRITIC, etc. [12–14, 17], whereas the subjective determines the weighting coefficients based on evaluators' experience, such as Delphi method, analytic hierarchy process (AHP), multivariate analysis, etc. [15, 16].

EaaS is a special cloud computing substantially, which is dynamic and changes real-timely, so it is unrealistic to use subjective method to determine the weightings. Thus, we determine the weighting coefficients utilizing objective method. The CRITIC method is an objective weighting method proposed by Diakoulak. The method takes the difference and correlation between each two characteristics into account, and measures them by two parameters, that is standard deviation and conflict, which the other objective method don't involve. Through the analysis of our quality characteristics, they are relative to some degree. For example, the system's reliability is also closely to its security, since if the security is weak, and it will lead bad reliability. Furthermore, CRITIC reflects the change of weighting coefficients with the fluctuate value of metrics, which meets the requirement for our dynamic system. As a result, we determine the weighting coefficients by CRITIC method.

Assume that the total number of tasks is n, and the number of characteristics is 4. The process of determining the weighting of each attribute is as follows:

Step 1: Standardization. It is necessary to standardize the four characteristics to eliminate the dimension difference between them. The data is first processed by the *Range Transformation*:

$$d_{ij} = \frac{x_{ij} - \min_{1 \le i \le n} x_{ij}}{\max_{1 \le i \le n} x_{ij} - \min_{1 \le i \le n} x_{ij}} \tag{17}$$

$$d_{ij} = \frac{\max_{1 \le i \le n} x_{ij} - x_{ij}}{\max_{1 \le i \le n} x_{ij} - \min_{1 \le i \le n} x_{ij}} \tag{18}$$

d_{ij} is the data which correspond to j attribute ($j = 1, 2, 3, 4$) of i task processed by the *Range Transformation* while x_{ij} is the raw data before processed.

The characteristics of the evaluation model can be divided into benefit-type ones and cost-type ones. The value of the benefit-type ones is thought to be as large as possible, while the value of the cost-type is as small as possible. If the characteristic is benefit-type, the standardized data is processed by formula (17), and if the attribute is the cost-type, it is processed by formula (18). In the above-mention evaluation model, the *Efficiency*, *Reliability* and *Maintainability* are the benefit-type ones, and the *Security* is cost-type.

Step 2: Calculating the standard deviation of each characteristic $\sigma_j (j = 1, 2, 3, 4)$:

$$\sigma_j = \sqrt{\frac{\sum\limits_{i=1}^{n} (d_{ij} - \bar{d}_{ij})^2}{n}} \tag{19}$$

Step 3: Calculating the correlation coefficient between each two attributes:

$$r_{tj} = \frac{\sum\limits_{i=1}^{n} (d_{it} - \bar{d}_{it})(d_{ij} - \bar{d}_{ij})}{\sqrt{\sum\limits_{i=1}^{n} (d_{it} - \bar{d}_{it})^2 \sum\limits_{i=1}^{n} (d_{ij} - \bar{d}_{ij})^2}} \quad (t \neq j) \tag{20}$$

$$r_{tj} = 1 \qquad (t = j) \tag{21}$$

where $t, j = 1, 2, 3, 4$, r_{tj} is the correlation coefficient between characteristic t and j.
Step 4: Calculating the corresponding weight of each attribute:

$$C_j = \sigma_j \sum_{t=1}^{4} (1 - r_{tj}) \tag{22}$$

$$\omega_j = \frac{C_j}{\sum\limits_{j=1}^{4} C_j} \tag{23}$$

C_j is the information included in j characteristic, and ω_j is the weighting of j characteristic.

The weighting coefficients can be determined through the process above, which can be plugged into the LE_{EaaS} computing formula to calculate LE_{EaaS} of different EaaS service for evaluating their service quality.

3.2 Example

We design five sets of services, and we have an evaluation on these services by applying the quality model. The data of the characteristics and result are shown in Table 1.

Table 1. Data of service and evaluation result

Service	Efficiency	Reliability	Security	Maintainability	LE_{EaaS}
1	0.8	0.8	0.6	0.9	0.9762
2	0.6	0.8	0.5	0.8	0.5948
3	0.4	0.5	0.6	0.7	0.3157
4	0.6	0.6	0.5	0.6	0.3906
5	0.4	0.6	0.5	0.8	0.4143

The result shows that by utilizing our model, the four characteristics are taken into account comprehensively, and embodied by the value of service level LE_{EaaS}. Thus, the quality of services rank as Service 1 > Service 2 > Service 5 > Service 4 > Service 3. The result also indicates that our quality model is practical for it takes the essential factors into account and is capable of discriminating between high quality services and the low ones.

4 Conclusion

Encryption-as-a-Service is proposed to meet the needs of cryptography service in cloud, and it is with higher efficient utilization of resources. Moreover it can provide higher quality of services with the low cost since the extract charge is cut down, including cost for deploying cryptography machines, administrators and routine maintenance. Evaluating the service quality of EaaS is an important activity for a successful EaaS management and providing a higher quality service.

In this paper, we present a comprehensive quality model for evaluating EaaS. The paper defines four quality characteristics of the service and gives the corresponding metrics and description. The paper also defines LE_{EaaS} as a comprehensive metric, and determines the weighting coefficients of each attribute by CRITIC method.

The quality model put forward in the paper can make up for the deficiency of some research, and effectively support the service description and application of EaaS.

References

1. Yan, Z., Deng, R.H., Varadharajan, V.: Cryptography and data security in cloud computing. Inf. Sci. **387**, 53–55 (2017)
2. Kamara, S., Lauter, K.: Cryptographic cloud storage. In: Sion, R., Curtmola, R., Dietrich, S., Kiayias, A., Miret, J.M., Sako, K., Sebé, F. (eds.) FC 2010. LNCS, vol. 6054, pp. 136–149. Springer, Heidelberg (2010). https://doi.org/10.1007/978-3-642-14992-4_13
3. Lifei, W., Haojin, Z., Zhenfu, C.: Security and privacy for storage and computation in cloud computing. Inf. Sci. **258**, 371–386 (2014)
4. Takabi, H., Joshi, J.B.D., Ahn, G.J., et al.: SecureCloud: towards a comprehensive security framework for cloud computing environments. In: Computer Software and Applications Conference Workshops, pp. 393–398. IEEE Computer Society (2010)

5. Rahmani, H., Sundararajan, E., Ali, Z.M.: Encryption as a Service (EaaS) as a solution for cryptography in cloud. Procedia Technol. **11**(1), 1202–1210 (2013)
6. Jureta, I.J., Herssens, C., Faulkner, S.: A comprehensive quality model for service-oriented systems. Softw. Qual. J. **17**(1), 65–98 (2009)
7. Lee, J.Y., Lee, J.W., Cheun, D.W.: A quality model for Evaluating Software-as-a-Service in cloud computing. In: ACIS International Conference on Software Engineering Research, Management and Applications, pp. 261–266. IEEE (2009)
8. ISO/IEC: Systems and software engineering – Systems and software Quality Requirements and Evaluation (SQuaRE) – System and software quality models (2011)
9. Stalk, G., Hout, T.M.: Competing against time: how time-based competition is reshaping global markets (1990)
10. Brockhoff, K.: Simplicity wins: how Germany's mid-sized industrial companies succeed. R&D Manag. **26**(2), 192–193 (2010)
11. Frølund, S., Koistinen, J.: Quality of services specification in distributed object systems design. Distrib. Syst. Eng. **5**(4), 179–202 (1998)
12. Zongjun, W.: Method of determining multi-target weighting coefficient and selection strategy. Syst. Eng. Electron. **15**(6), 35–41 (1993)
13. Yuda, H.: Practical Multi-target Optimization. Shanghai Scientific and Technical Publishers, Shanghai (1990)
14. Jiaji, X.: Multi-target Decision. Hunan Scientific and Technical Publishers, Changsha (1989)
15. Yuanyuan, W., Ye, T., Wengdong, W.: Index weight decision based on AHP for information retrieval on mobile device. In: International Proceedings of Computer Science & Information Tech (2012)
16. Zeyan, W., Xiaoxin, Y., Shenru, Z.: Weighting method and application based on ideal optimization schemes. Syst. Eng. **20**(2), 6–9 (2002)
17. Diakoulaki, D., Mavrotas, G., Papayannakis, L.: Determining objective weights in multiple criteria problems: the CRITIC method. Comput. Oper. Res. **22**(7), 763–770 (1995)

Forensic Detection for Image Operation Order: Resizing and Contrast Enhancement

Shangde Gao[1], Xin Liao[1(✉)], Sujin Guo[1], Xiong Li[2], and P. Vijayakumar[3]

[1] College of Computer Science and Electronic Engineering,
Hunan University, Changsha 410082, China
`xinliao@hnu.edu.cn`
[2] School of Computer Science and Engineering, Hunan University of Science
and Technology, Xiangtan 411201, China
[3] Department of Computer Science and Engineering, Anna University,
Chennai 600 025, Tamil Nadu, India

Abstract. Currently, many forensic techniques have been developed to determine which processing operations were used to tamper multimedia contents. Determining the order of these operations, however, remains an open challenge. It is important to detect image operation order, because we can obtain the complete processing history of multimedia content, and even identify who manipulated the multimedia content and when it was manipulated. In this paper, we investigate the detection for the order of contrast enhancement and resizing. Two new algorithms are proposed to detect contrast enhancement and resizing respectively. We use the SVM to extract fingerprint of digital images and then detect the image operation of resizing and contrast enhancement. Experimental results show that the average classification accuracy of the proposed method is 88.97%.

Keywords: Image forensics · Conditional fingerprints
Multimedia content · Resizing · Contrast enhancement

1 Introduction

Currently, with the rapid development of computer, smart phones, and other electronic devices, photos and other digital images have been the mainstream information carrier. In the field of digital forensics, digital images due to their great amount of information and intuitiveness are in favor. However, with the development of editing software and online tools, digital multimedia content can be easily manipulated and falsified [1]. As a result, it is difficult to identify the authenticity of multimedia content. However, since the multimedia content has been used as significant evidence to make decision or statement of the authorities, such as law enforcement, news agency, government, and hospital, it is critical to know whether the given multimedia content is trustful or maliciously tampered [2].

© Springer International Publishing AG 2017
G. Wang et al. (Eds.): SpaCCS 2017 Workshops, LNCS 10658, pp. 570–580, 2017.
https://doi.org/10.1007/978-3-319-72395-2_52

In order to respond to the serious problem of multimedia content security, many forensic techniques have been proposed. These techniques work by detecting the presence of fingerprint, left by different processing operations. Now we can use these techniques to identify the use of tamper operations, such as compression [2,3], contrast enhancement [4–7], resizing [8,9], median filtering [10], blurring [11,12], and so on [13].

However, due to the interplay of those operations, detecting the order in which these operations were applied to an image, remains an open challenge. Recently, in [14], Chu et al. proposed a new multiple hypotheses framework which can be used to forensically introduce the order in which manipulations were applied to a signal. The framework is used to verify the effectiveness of the proposed detection algorithm. However, the proposed algorithm has two major drawbacks. The selection of decision threshold can cause errors. In addition, when the operating intensity is unknown, it is difficult to extract the fingerprint.

In this paper, we propose a new approach that can be used to forensically determine the order of image resizing and contrast enhancement. First, we propose a new algorithm to detect the contrast enhancement and improve the resizing detection algorithm. By extracting sudden gaps and zeros in the histogram, we propose the new contrast enhancement algorithm. After adding an adaptive window clipping function, the detection efficiency of resizing is improved. Moreover, by extracting the fingerprint and conditional fingerprint, we obtain the best decision thresholds and use them to verify the effectiveness of the proposed distributed detection method. However, the distributed detection method can not classify mixed parameters. Finally, we propose to use the SVM method to determine the order of contrast enhancement and resizing. The five-fold cross-validation is used to identify parameters. Experimental results show the proposed methods can achieve a good performance.

2   The Proposed Contrast Enhancement and Resizing Detecting Algorithms

By extracting the impulsive gaps and zeros left in the histogram of digital images, we propose a new algorithm to detect the contrast enhancement. After adding an adaptive clipping function, we improve the detection efficiency of the resizing algorithm.

2.1   Contrast Enhancement Detection

Contrast enhancement works by applying a non-decreasing nonlinear mapping to the pixel values of an image. After nonlinear mapping, there will be sudden zeros or gaps in a contrast enhanced image's pixel value histogram. These impulsive zeros and gaps in the histogram are the standard fingerprint left by contrast enhancement. By classifying the normalized pixel value histogram, we propose a new contrast enhancement detection algorithm. Obviously, an unaltered image's pixel value histogram is typically smooth, so pixel values' number of one grayscale is nearly equal to that of its neighbor grayscale. By contrast, the contrast enhanced image's pixel value histogram will emerge impulsive gaps and zeros. Meanwhile, the pixel values' number of one grayscale is quietly different from that of its neighbor grayscale. We can use these features to extract the fingerprint left by contrast enhancement. The modified histogram $H(l)$ is obtained by performing the elementwise multiplication between $h(l)$ and a "pinch off" function $p(l)$ so that

$$H(l) = h(l)p(l), \tag{1}$$

where

$$p(l) = \begin{cases} 0.5 - 0.5cos(\pi l/N_p), & l \leq N_p \\ 0.5 + 0.5cos(\pi(l - 255 + N_p)/N_p)), & l \geq 255 - N_p \\ 1, & else \end{cases} \tag{2}$$

Next, a measure of the fingerprint of the modified histogram is computed using the formula

$$sum = \sum_{i=2}^{256} |H_i - H_{i-1}|. \tag{3}$$

Finally an image is classified as an unaltered or contrast enhanced using the decision rule

$$\delta_{ce} = \begin{cases} \text{the image is unaltered,} & if \quad sum < \tau_{ce} \\ \text{the image is contrast enhanced,} & if \quad sum \geqslant \tau_{ce} \end{cases} \tag{4}$$

where τ_{ce} is a decision threshold.

2.2 Resizing Detection

Kirchner et al. have developed an efficient approach to estimate p-map [9]. However, there remains low-frequency influencing the result of 2D DFT (Discrete Fourier Transform). We propose a new adaptive window cutoff function that can filter the low-frequency signal and then improve the effectiveness of the resizing algorithm. The detailed algorithm is as follows. In order to obtain the p-map, we first predict the value of each pixel using a predetermined linear filter

$$\alpha = \begin{bmatrix} -0.25 & 0.50 & -0.25 \\ 0.50 & 0 & 0.50 \\ -0.25 & 0.50 & -0.25 \end{bmatrix} \tag{5}$$

The prediction residual e is then determined by subtracting each predicted pixel value from the true value and used to calculate the p-map p according to the formula

$$p_{i,j} = \lambda exp(-\left|e_{i,j}^{\mu}\right|/\sigma), \tag{6}$$

where $\lambda, \mu > 1$, and $\sigma > 0$ are controlling parameters. If an image has been resampled, distinct spectral peaks will be present in the 2D DFT of the p-map.

Then we propose to use a new adaptive window cutoff function to filter low-frequency signal before detecting resizing, which is

$$F_{i,j} = \begin{cases} F_{i,j}, & \text{if} \quad (F_{i,j} \geq max(F_{i,j})/n) \\ 0 \,, & \text{else} \end{cases} \tag{7}$$

where $F_{i,j}$ is the result of 2D DFT of p, $max(F_{i,j})$ is the effective maximum and n is the input ratio. Resizing detection is performed by firstly using the 2D DFT of p to calculate the cumulative periodogram C of the p-map. Let

$$\rho = \max_{k_1, k_2} | \nabla C(k_1, k_2)|, \tag{8}$$

then resizing detection is performed by the following rules

$$\rho_{rs} = \begin{cases} \text{the image is unaltered,} & \text{if} \quad \rho < \tau_{rs} \\ \text{the image is resized,} & \text{if} \quad \rho \geq \tau_{rs} \end{cases} \tag{9}$$

where τ_{rs} is a decision threshold.

3   The Proposed Image Operation Order Detection Methods

In this section, we firstly introduce the conditional fingerprint, and then use the conditional fingerprint and fingerprint to detect the performances of the proposed distributed detection method and SVM detection method.

3.1   Conditional Fingerprint

If an image is contrast enhanced, all the pixel values in the histogram will be mapped from the low gray area to the high gray area. Therefore, sudden zeros and gaps emerged in the pixel values histogram. If an image is resized, the pixel value histogram is still smooth, and we can use p-map to detect resizing. After an image has undergone resizing followed by contrast enhancement, the 2D DFT of p-map is still periodic, which indicated the contrast enhancement has little influence on resizing. However, after an image has undergone contrast enhancement followed by resizing, the later operation may completely alter or disguise the fingerprint left by the earlier operation. As a result, those techniques applied to the detection of contrast enhancement or resizing won't be adequate for the detection of conditional fingerprint. While Gama intensity becomes smaller, after an image has undergone contrast enhancement followed by resizing, the region barely containing pixel values will be smaller. So we can extract the conditional fingerprint of contrast enhancement followed resizing by classifying the pixel value histogram of low grayscale regions.

$$sum = \sum_{i=1}^{n} |H_i| \,, \tag{10}$$

where n can determine the grayscale regions of the histogram.

3.2   The Distributed Detection Method

The distributed detection method uses the following multiple hypothesis to demonstrate the manipulation operation states [14]. When examining digital image ψ whose processing history is unknown, we know that ψ must exist in one of two states, i.e., ψ hasn't been manipulated by resizing or contrast enhancement or ψ is a manipulated version of another image ψ'.

$$H_0 : \psi \text{ is unaltered by resize or contrast enhancement;}$$
$$H_1 : \psi = rs(\psi');$$
$$H_2 : \psi = ce(\psi'); \qquad (11)$$
$$H_3 : \psi = rs(ce(\psi'));$$
$$H_4 : \psi = ce(rs(\psi'));$$

We then use the fingerprint and conditional fingerprint to differentiate between those states. The detailed steps of distributed algorithm are as follows, and the pseudo-code is given in Algorithm 1.

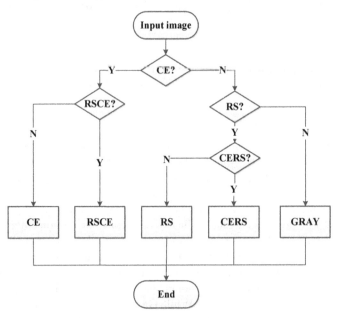

Fig. 1. Flow chart of the distributed detection

Step 1: According to the parameters shown in Table 1, create the testing image databases.
Step 2: Determine the best decision threshold of contrast enhancement, resizing and conditional fingerprint. After creating testing images $X = (x_1, x_2, \ldots, x_n)$, use (3), we obtain $sum = (s_1, s_2, \ldots, s_n)$ and then extract

Table 1. Operations used to create image database

Operation	Description
NULL	The images were not altered by any operations
CE	Contrast enhancement, where gamma correction $\gamma = 0.5, 0.7$
RS	Resizing, where scale factor $s = 1.25, 1.5$ ($B = 64$)
CERS	Contrast enhanced then resized, $\gamma = 0.5, 0.7; s = 1.25, 1.5$
RSCE	Resized then contrast enhanced, $\gamma = 0.5, 0.7; s = 1.25, 1.5$

Algorithm 1. The distributed detection algorithm

Input: the digital images: $x, sum, gmax, sum1$
Output: One of the five hypothesis testing states
1: **while** x **do**
2:     **if** $sum > \beta$ **then**
3:         **if** $gmax > \gamma$ **then**
4:             x is resized then contrast enhanced;
5:         **else**
6:             x is altered by contrast enhancement;
7:         **end if**
8:     **else**
9:         **if** $gmax > \gamma$ **then**
10:             **if** $sum1 > \delta$ **then**
11:                 x is is altered by resizing;
12:             **else**
13:                 x contrast enhanced then resized;
14:             **end if**
15:         **else**
16:             x is unaltered by contrast enhanced or resized;
17:         **end if**
18:     **end if**
19: **end while**

β from them. $\beta = (\beta_1, \beta_2, \ldots, \beta_t)$, where TPR $= 1$, NFR $= 0$. Similarly, as for resized images $Y = (y_1, y_2, \ldots, y_m)$, according to (8), we can calculate the max gradient of C, $gmax = (g_1, g_2, \ldots, g_m)$, and then extract $\gamma = (\gamma_1, \gamma_2, \ldots, \delta_k)$, where TPR $= 1$, NFR $= 0$. Finally, according to (10), we can obtain $sum1 = (s_1, s_2, \ldots, s_l)$, the best decision threshold of conditional fingerprint is, $\delta = (\delta_1, \delta_2, \ldots, \delta_s)$.

Step 3: Verify the effectiveness of the distributed detection algorithm according to Fig. 1.

3.3   The SVM Detection Method

According to the flow chart of distributed detection, we can achieve the image operation order. However, the distributed detection algorithm inevitably has two major drawbacks, it uses only a certain threshold to evaluate the algorithm, and there are multiple decision thresholds in actual process. The selection of decision threshold will cause the algorithm error. In addition, the distributed detection algorithm can not extract the mixed parameter characteristics. Therefore, we propose to use the SVM to extract the mixed parameters of the testing images and then detect the order of contrast enhancement and resizing. We use a radial basis function (RBF) to train and test images. The five-fold cross-validation was used to identify parameters determined by the detecting approaches. The detailed steps are as follows.

Step 1: Create the image databases. We use the five-fold cross-validation to identify parameters determined by the detecting approaches. Therefore, we random choose 20% of images in the image databases as training images and 80% of that as predicting images.

Step 2: Use the SVM to extract fingerprint in digital images. As for digital images $X = (x_1, x_2, \ldots, x_n)$, if they are contrast enhanced, use (3), we obtain $sum = (s_1, s_2, \ldots, s_n)$. When detecting resized images $Y = (y_1, y_2, \ldots, y_m)$, according to (6), (7) and (8), we can calculate the max gradient of C, $gmax = (g_1, g_2, \ldots, g_m)$. Finally, according to (10), we can obtain the integral of conditional fingerprint.

Step 3: Verify the effectiveness of the detection algorithm according to the SVM. The five-fold cross-validation is used to identify parameters determined by the detecting approaches.

4   Experimental Results

In this section, several experimental results are given to demonstrate the effectiveness of our proposed approaches for detecting the image operation order.

First we create a database of unaltered grayscale images from the 1338 images based on the UCID [15]. We then process the 1338 unaltered grayscale images using different settings for the gamma value, scale factor and the cross matching between gamma value and scale factor, as reported in Table 1.

We create five sets of images that had undergone with operations, i.e., NULL, CE, RS, CERS, RSCE, generated by manipulating images with contrast enhancement, resizing, receptively. This results a total 17394 images whose processing history matches with one of the forensic states. We classify each image as 'GRAY', 'RS', 'CE', 'CERS', and 'RSCE'.

4.1   Experimental Results of Distributed Detection

Following the distributed algorithm of Sect. 3, we can firstly obtain the best decision thresholds of contrast enhancement, resizing, and conditional fingerprint.

As for contrast enhancement, we randomly choose 100 images from the contrasted and gray images respectively. Use (3), we obtain $sum1 = (s_1, s_2, \ldots, s_{100})$ and $sum2 = (s_1, s_2, \ldots, s_{100})$. After classifying the discrete degree of $sum1$ and

Table 2. Contrast enhancement distinguishability accuracy

Actual class	Predicted class	
	GRAY	CE
GRAY	98.57	1.43
CE	0	100

$sum2$, we can find the decision threshold β to distinguish them, the detection result is as follows.

Via the confusion matrix of Table 2, we can determine β varies on the interval $[0.228, 0379]$, where the step size is 0.001, TPR $= 1$, NFR $= 0$. Similarly, following the proposed resizing detection and conditional fingerprint algorithm, we can obtain γ varies on the interval $[0.008, 0.117]$, δ varies on the interval $[0.007, 0.015]$.

In our experiments, the best decision threshold is set to be $\beta = 0.228$, $\gamma = 0.008$, and $\delta = 0.007$. Next, following the distributed flow chart shown in Fig. 1, we verify the effectiveness of our algorithm.

We test all the five sets of images, the results are shown in Tables 3, 4, 5 and 6.

As shown in Tables 3, 4, 5 and 6, the distributed algorithm can achieve a good performance. Specifically, in the case of constant gamma coefficient, the scaling factor has little impact on the efficiency of the algorithm. When the scaling

Table 3. Order distinguishability accuracy of $\gamma = 0.5$, $s = 1.5$

Actual class	Predicted class				
	CE	CERS	GRAY	RS	RSCE
CE	96.71	0	0	0	3.29
CERS	0	86.47	0	5.23	8.3
GRAY	1.42	0.30	95.89	2.39	0
RS	0	10.76	0	86.85	2.39
RSCE	0	0	0	0	100

Table 4. Order distinguishability accuracy of $\gamma = 0.5$, $s = 1.25$

Actual class	Predicted class				
	CE	CERS	GRAY	RS	RSCE
CE	96.71	0	0	0	3.29
CERS	0	84.38	0	8.45	7.17
GRAY	1.42	0.3	95.89	2.39	0
RS	0	8.82	0	88.79	2.39
RSCE	0	0	0	0	100

Table 5. Order distinguishability accuracy of $\gamma = 0.7$, $s = 1.25$

Actual class	Predicted class				
	CE	CERS	GRAY	RS	RSCE
CE	96.26	0	0.67	0	3.07
CERS	0	78.21	0	13.34	8.45
GRAY	1.42	0.3	95.89	2.39	0
RS	0	9.72	0	88.79	1.49
RSCE	0	0.15	0	0	99.85

Table 6. Order distinguishability accuracy of $\gamma = 0.7$, $s = 1.5$

Actual class	Predicted class				
	CE	CERS	GRAY	RS	RSCE
CE	96.26	0	0.67	0	3.07
CERS	0	76.76	0	14.65	8.59
GRAY	1.42	0.3	95.89	2.39	0
RS	0	9.8	0	88.71	1.49
RSCE	0	0.9	0	0	99.10

factor is constant, the higher the gamma coefficient, the lower the efficiency of
the algorithm. Additionally, the inevitable drawback based on the distributed
data detection is that it needs to determine the threshold in advance to detect
the algorithm. The experimental error depends on the selection of the decision
threshold, so we propose to verify the algorithm with SVM.

4.2 Experimental Results of SVM

In this experiment, we verify our detection algorithm based the mixed parameters
classifier. The five-fold cross-validation is used to identify parameters determined
by the detecting approaches. The detection procedures works as follow.

Table 7. Order distinguishability accuracy

Actual class	Predicted class				
	CE	CERS	GRAY	RS	RSCE
CE	100	0	0	0	0
CERS	0	78.3	1.375	19.075	1.25
GRAY	0	0	100	0	0
RS	0	19.88	1.5	78.62	0
RSCE	1.25	2.5	0	0	96.25

We randomly choose 800 images from each image database as train set and 200 images as test set. The experimental result is shown in Table 7.

Via the confusion matrix of Table 7, we can obtain that the average classification accuracy of the algorithm is 88.97%. Moreover, through the estimation of the mixed parameters, we can effectively solve the defects of distributed detection. Those experimental results can achieve a good performance.

5   Conclusions

In this paper, we propose to use the distributed detection method and SVM method to determine the order of contrast enhancement and resizing. In addition, we propose a new algorithm to detect the contrast enhancement and improve the algorithm of detecting resizing. Although the experimental results are well, we discover that the proposed distributed detection algorithm can not analyze mixed parameter. In order to solve this problem, we finally propose the SVM detection method. Experimental results show the average classification accuracy of the SVM method is 88.97%.

Acknowledgments. This work is supported by National Natural Science Foundation of China (Grant Nos. 61402162, 61472129, 61572182, 61370225, 61472131, 61272546), Hunan Provincial Natural Science Foundation of China (Grant No. 2017JJ3040), Opening Project of Shanghai Key Laboratory of Integrated Administration Technologies for Information Security (Grant No. AGK201605), Science and Technology Key Projects of Hunan Province (Grant Nos. 2015TP1004, 2016JC2012).

References

1. Stamm, M., Wu, M., Liu, K.: Information forensics: an overview of the first decade. IEEE Access **1**, 167–200 (2013)
2. Bianchi, T., Piva, A.: Reverse engineering of double JPEG compression in the presence of image resizing. In: IEEE International Workshop on Information Forensics and Security, Tenerife, Spain, pp. 127–132 (2012)
3. Huang, F., Huang, J., Shi, Y.: Detecting double JPEG compression with the same quantization matrix. IEEE Trans. Inf. Forensics Secur. **5**(4), 848–856 (2014)
4. Stamm, M., Liu, K.: Blind forensics of contrast enhancement in digital images. In: 15th IEEE International Conference on Image Processing, San Diego, CA, USA, pp. 3112–3115, October 2008
5. Stamm, M., Liu, K.: Forensic estimation and reconstruction of a contrast enhancement mapping. In: IEEE International Conference on Acoustics Speech and Signal Processing, Dallas, TX, USA, pp. 1698–1701, March 2010
6. Cao, G., Zhao, Y., Ni, R.: Forensic estimation of gamma correction in digital images. IN: 17th IEEE International Conference on Image Processing, Hong Kong, China, pp. 2097–2100, September 2010
7. Cao, G., Zhao, Y., Ni, R., et al.: Contrast enhancement-based forensics in digital images. IEEE Trans. Inf. Forensics Secur. **9**(3), 515–525 (2014)
8. Popescu, A., Farid, H.: Exposing digital forgeries by detecting traces of resampling. IEEE Trans. Sig. Process. **53**(2), 758–767 (2005)

9. Kirchner, M.: Fast and reliable resampling detection by spectral analysis of fixed linear predictor residue. In: 10th ACM Workshop on Multimedia and Security, Oxford, United Kingdom, pp. 11–20 (2008)

10. Kirchner, M., Fridrich, J.: On detection of median filtering in digital images. In: Media Forensics and Security II, February 2010

11. Su, B., Lu, S., Tan, C.: Blurred image region detection and classification. In: 19th ACM International Conference on Multimedia, Scottsdale, AZ, USA, pp. 1397–1400, November 2011

12. Cao, G., Zhao, Y., Ni, R.: Edge-based blur metric for tamper detection. J. Inf. Hiding Multimedia Sig. Process. 1(1), 20–27 (2010)

13. Ferrara, P., Bianchi, T., Rosa, A., et al.: Reverse engineering of double compressed images in the presence of contrast enhancement. In: 15th IEEE International Workshop on Multimedia Signal Processing, Pula, Italy, pp. 141–146 (2013)

14. Chu, X., Chen, Y., Liu, K.J.R.: Detectability of the order of operations: an information theoretic approach. IEEE Trans. Inf. Forensics Secur. 11, 823–856 (2016)

15. Schaefer, G.: UCID: an uncompressed color image database. Storage Retr. Methods Appl. Multimedia 5307, 472–480 (2004)

A Framework for Preventing the Exploitation of IoT Smart Toys for Reconnaissance and Exfiltration

Jeffrey Haynes, Maribette Ramirez, Thaier Hayajneh$^{(\boxtimes)}$,
and Md. Zakirul Alam Bhuiyan

Fordham Center for Cybersecurity, Fordham University, New York, NY, USA
{jhaynes,mramirez38,thayajneh,mbhuiyan3}@fordham.edu

Abstract. There are many concerns that come along with the Internet of Things that should be addressed because of its growing popularity. One major concern is the security issues related to connected devices. Connected toys are a category of IoT devices that are commonly overlooked when considering these issues, yet they are just as susceptible to attacks as any other device. This paper will look at recent incidents related to security issues involving connected toys and establish a framework with the intention of providing manufacturers with a set of standards that must be adhered to before a device can be marketed. The affected products in the discussed incidents are then tested against the proposed framework.

Keywords: Internet of Things (IoT) · Connected toys
Breach compromise · Framework

1 Introduction

The Internet of Things is gaining popularity and changing a big part of the world we live in today. Internet of Things devices are changing the way all people live their day to day life. These devices are defined as any object that contains a processing unit, memory, runs some form of software, and is in some way connected to the Internet to allow communication between devices [23]. Today's society is one where the idea of the Internet of Things appeals to many. It can, in many ways, make consumers' lives easier to navigate and simplify tedious tasks. However, with this knowledge needs to come the acceptance of the fact that any device, if connected to the Internet, is at risk of being attacked. This is a fact that is at many times overlooked or simply ignored.

One category of devices that consumers might not always think to classify as an Internet of Things device are children's toys. Unfortunately, this fact poses a huge security risk to the data stored on these devices and to those with whom the data concerns. These seemingly innocent devices can be weaponized and used in a manner for which they were not intended. This fact has recently been demonstrated a number of times with popular toy lines. In 2015 VTech,

© Springer International Publishing AG 2017
G. Wang et al. (Eds.): SpaCCS 2017 Workshops, LNCS 10658, pp. 581–592, 2017.
https://doi.org/10.1007/978-3-319-72395-2_53

a Hong Kong based company, was the victim of a data breach. This hack resulted in the attackers obtaining sensitive consumer information, such as mailing addresses and pictures to name a couple. Over 6 million children, along with over 4 million parents were affected in this data breach. VTech went on to change their Terms and Conditions to state that the consumer acknowledges and agrees "that any information you send or receive during your use of the site may not be secure and may be intercepted or later acquired by unauthorized parties [14]."

The goal of this paper is to develop a framework that toy manufacturers will follow to protect their data against possible security breaches. The proposed framework looks to provide clear guidance to manufacturers on the expectations for both the privacy and information security features of their products.

To provide a holistic view of the framework, this paper will accomplish the following: define pertinent terms used throughout the paper; discuss recent incidents related to security issues involving connected toys; present the proposed framework; test the previously-discussed affected products against the framework; discuss assessments made based on the test results; and outline future work to finalize and broaden the concepts of the framework.

2   Defined Terms

The Internet of Things (IoT) is changing the world we live in. IoT devices are defined as "... any device, regardless of size, use, or form factor, that contains a CPU and memory, runs software, and has a network interface which allows it to communicate to other devices, usually as a client, sometimes as a server." IoT devices do not always resemble what most would consider to be a traditional computer and they are often marketed as a single purpose device. They are built from "general purpose components" and use chipsets, firmware, and software that is found in other IoT devices [23].

The National Institute of Standards and Technology (NIST) is one of the oldest physical science laboratories in the U.S. that was established by Congress in 1901. It was formed in order to establish a system of measurement that would help America's competitiveness in the global industrial market. In 2013 President Obama issued an executive order that called NIST "to work with the private sector to identify existing voluntary consensus standards and industry best practices and build them into a Cybersecurity Framework." This lead to the creation of the NIST framework for cybersecurity [17].

The Advanced Encryption Standard (AES) is a symmetric block cipher that was chosen by the U.S. government to protect classified information. This standard is implemented in software and hardware throughout the world to encrypt sensitive data. NIST specified the new AES algorithm "must be a block cipher capable of handling 128 bit blocks, using keys sized at 128, 192, and 256 bits" [20].

The Children's Online Privacy Protection Act (COPPA) is an act that "imposes certain requirements on operators of websites or online services directed to children under 13 years of age, and on operators of other websites or online services that have actual knowledge that they are collecting personal information online from a child under 13 years of age." There is a six-step-by-step compliance plan to help operators determine if their company is covered by COPPA and how to adhere to the rules [10].

The Secure Hash Algorithm (SHA) is a set of algorithms published by NIST. SHA-1 is the second iteration of the algorithm, which was later found to not be as secure as other algorithms. These algorithms are a part of new encryption standards that are meant to keep data safe and prevent attacks [21].

3 Related Incidents

3.1 CloudPets Toys Breach

CloudPets, owned by Spiral Toys, are stuffed animals that allow users to record, send, and receive messages from anywhere in the world. CloudPets are connected to a mobile apps that allows parents and other loved ones to send messages to their children, which are later played through the stuffed animals. When a parent creates a CloudPets account they give it their child's name, email address, and a photo [27].

In February of 2017 an open database of links to over 2 million recorded voice messages was discovered. Troy Hunt, owner of data breach monitoring service Have I Been Pwned, brought the breach to the public's attention. In a statement, Spiral Toys said that to their best knowledge they could not detect any breach to their data being that all the leaked data was password encrypted [8].

Hunt found that over 820,000 user accounts were exposed. Personal information was stored within the database that was directly connected to the Internet, and required no username or password to access the information. This mistake left the database extremely vulnerable to a breach [8].

3.2 VTech Breach

In 2015, Hong Kong toy manufacturer, VTech, was victim of a security breach that resulted in the information of over 11.6 million users being compromised. VTech announced that their "Learning Lodge", an online store for VTech devices, database had been compromised. The Learning Lodge store allows users to download apps, music, games, books, and videos [11].

As a result of this hack the attackers were able to gain access to profile information, information on the adult registered users such as names, email addresses, and passwords. They were also able to acquire secret questions and their answers, IP addresses, mailing addresses, and users download history. The database also allowed access to children's names, gender, and date of birth. The data that was revealed could give the attackers a way of connecting the children to the parents through the information and therefore discovering the location of the children [11].

Another news site, Motherboard, reported that the attackers were able to obtain access to the photos of children and their chat logs. The attackers released the information to Motherboard and told them that the data was obtained through a SQL injection vulnerability [11].

VTech said that the majority of the accounts belonged to users in the U.S., of which 2.2 million were parents and 2.8 million were children. What makes this breach stand out about the rest is the fact that millions of children were affected by this incident. The profile information that was exposed revealed their names, gender, and date of birth [12].

VTech said that the images on their servers were encrypted using the 128-bit Advanced Encryption Standard algorithm. Audio files and chat logs were encrypted using AES 128, however, the decryption keys were not well protected. Considering AES is a secure algorithm it is not clear how the images were able to be decrypted [12].

3.3   Hello Kitty Breach

In 2015 Chris Vickery, a security researcher, revealed that he discovered a Sanrio database that had been leaked. This database contained over 3.3 million user accounts for a number of Sanrio owned websites, including hellokitty.com and mymelody.com. The data that was breached contained sensitive information such as users' full names, dates of birth, email addresses, and not only their encrypted passwords, but also reset questions and answers [24].

This breach was the second, within a month, to show the vulnerability of children falling victim to the same data security issues that usually only affect adults. The leaked passwords were said to be encrypted with SHA-1, however, they were not salted with random data. Sanrio went on to advise their users to change their passwords [24].

3.4   My Friend Cayla Vulnerabilities

The My Friend Cayla doll, made by Genesis Toys, is one of a number of devices that were found to be vulnerable. The doll was said to contain "a concealed surveillance device". For this reason, Germany banned the ownership and selling of the doll in February of 2017. The My Friend Cayla doll comes with a microphone and is connected to the Internet over Bluetooth. A complaint that was filed by the Electronic Privacy Information Center ("EPIC") with the U.S Federal Trade Commission ("FTC") stated that the doll, along with another toy called "i-Que", "violate consumer protection laws and 'subject young children to ongoing surveillance and are deployed in homes across the United States without any meaningful data protection standards'" [3].

The My Friend Cayla doll is advertised as a doll that can talk and interact with the user, play games, share photos, and read stories. When the doll is connected she can answer almost any question that is asked, and when the doll is not connected she can answer questions about herself. The doll works through the use of a third-party voice recognition software company, that enables it to use the microphone feature to have the conversations with the user and answer questions [3].

The Children's Online Privacy Protection Act has certain requirements set in place that vendors are required to follow. One is that companies who collect the personal information of children have to provide a direct notice of what is being collected and how that information is used. The company also has to be given "verifiable consent" from the children's parents before they begin collecting the data [3].

In the case of the My Friend Cayla doll, Genesis Toys did in fact disclose some information about what data is collected and how it is used in their Privacy Policy. The FTC complaint noted that the doll did not require any authentication procedure in order to pair with a phone. This means that any device with Bluetooth connection that is within a 50-foot range could potentially connect to the doll creating a huge security vulnerability [3].

3.5   Security Flaws in Smart Toy Bear and heroO Watch

In 2016, Rapid7 revealed security flaws that were found in Fisher-Price's Smart Toy Bear and the hereO GPS watch [22]. The Smart Toy is a teddy bear that connects to the Internet. It is described as "An interactive learning friend that talks, listens, and 'remembers' what your child says and even responds when spoken to." The Smart Toy also offers an app in which parents can customize it to know their children's name and age among other details. The app also gives free activities when the parent pairs the Smart Toy with the home network.

In February of 2016, manager of security advisory services at Rapid7, Mark Stanislav discovered a number of bugs that could be exploited. Rapid7 reported several API's that it found, which did not properly handle authorization. This fact put the children's profiles and the information they contained at risk. These were simple flaws that could have easily been avoided [22]. Since it is a children's toy it is easy to assume that the reason this happened in the first place was because it's security was not taken as seriously as it should have been.

The second device, hereO GPS watch, is a GPS tracking device that allows parent to track their child in real-time. The watch advertises that it features "breadcrumb trail logging, and smart location alerts", and allows parents to "track their children's whereabouts directly from the hereO Family smartphone companion app." In this case Stanislav found flaws that could allow authorization to be bypassed. He stated that this could potentially allow an attacker to add themselves to any family's group and that any notification of this could easily be worked to the attacker's benefit [22]. While it seems that this vulnerability was patched before any real damage could be done, it is extremely unsettling to know that it was ever a possibility.

3.6   Hello Barbie Vulnerabilities

In 2015, it was discovered that the Hello Barbie doll, Mattel's Wi-Fi enabled Barbie, could easily be hacked. The Hello Barbie doll comes with a microphone, and speaker that allows children to interact with the doll. If hacked the doll could be turned into a surveillance device that could spy on kids and listen to their conversations without their knowledge [4].

Matt Jakubowski, a U.S. security researcher, found that when the doll was connected to a Wi-Fi network it could be susceptible to hacking. The doll connects to the Internet through a Wi-Fi connection. The microphone allows the doll to record the children and then sends the information obtained to third-parties to process the speech before the doll responds [19].

Jakubowski was able to access the information system of the doll, obtain account information, the doll's stored audio files, and even more surprising direct access to the microphone [19]. Jakubowski found that once he had the location of the data, he could easily obtain other information. While the doll listens to conversation only when prompted and the audio is encrypted, once the hacker is in control of the doll they could simply override the privacy features [4].

4   Framework for Securing Connected Toys

The security controls outlined by The National Institute of Standards and Technology (NIST) were adopted and adapted to build the framework for securing internet connected toys.

As stated in its publication document, "the security and privacy controls in Special Publication 800-53, Revision 4, have been designed to be largely policy/technology-neutral to facilitate flexibility in implementation. The controls are well positioned to support the integration of information security and privacy into organizational processes including enterprise architecture, systems engineering, system development life cycle, and acquisition/procurement. Successful integration of security and privacy controls into ongoing organizational processes will demonstrate a greater maturity of security and privacy programs and provide a tighter coupling of security and privacy investments to core organizational missions and business functions [18]."

Using NIST Special Publication 800-53 (Rev. 4) Security Controls and Assessment Procedures for Federal Information Systems and Organizations, the following security criteria were established. A reference to the corresponding NIST control family is paired with each criterion.

- Proper and standardized notification on product packaging, specifically indicating that full access to all features of the product requires the creation of a personal online account. (AT-2: Security Awareness)
- Required strong end-to-end encryption implementation (HTTPS and AES 256). The product cannot locally store personal information in an insecure format, communicate over insecure channels, or communicate with unauthorized devices or servers. (SC-28: Cryptographic Protection; MP-4: Media Storage; SC-9: Transmission Confidentiality; SC-23: Session Authenticity)
- Manufacturers are required to facilitate and contribute to ongoing identification of vulnerabilities by communicating with the security community. (RA-3: Risk Assessment; RA-5: Vulnerability Scanning)

- Use of independent security audits to identify vulnerabilities before and during the lifecycle of the product. (AU-6: Audit Review, Analysis, and Reporting)
- Avoiding default passwords that are the same across same and differing products, and passwords that cannot be changed by users. (IA-3: Device Identification and Authentication)
- Access to a remote server is secure by enforcing physical and administrative restrictions, and implementing technical restrictions such as preventing unauthenticated software updates. (AC-17: Remote Access; CM-11: User-Installed Software).

A rating system was developed using these six framework criteria, and stylized into badges in an effort to make the security features of a product readily apparent and visible on its packaging to consumers.

A product that only adheres to two or fewer of the criteria earns a "C" rating, with a red badge to make the rating highly visible on packaging as a warning to buyers. Following three out of six criteria results in a "B" rating and a green badge; four out of six is a "B+"; five out of six is an "A" rating with a blue badge. Adhering to all six framework criteria earns the product the coveted "A+" rating. Simple star icons also adorn each badge, with the star count signifying the total number of criterion followed. Details of which criteria are followed can be outlined on the back of the product's package, or in finer print. Figure 1 displays the proposed ratings badges.

Fig. 1. Security badges to be displayed on product packaging.

5   Results and Analysis

A deeper analysis of the security flaws pertaining to each previously outlined breach allowed for mapping against the six proposed framework criteria. How each product line would have scored in this system was also calculated, and is depicted in Fig. 2.

5.1   CloudPets Toys Breach

The CloudPets Toys breach was shown to be the result of below standard password requirements for user accounts. This severely reduced the effort required by hackers to brute force, or "guess," the passwords of stored user accounts, despite the accounts being stored in secure environments. A tutorial video describing the setup process of the product officially recommended a password of "qwe" to users. While already short in length and the first three alpha characters on the American keyboard layout, the same three-character password was found to be the password of many user accounts [27].

Using the framework criteria, the CloudPets product was found to be lacking in five of the six categories and earned a C rating. There was notification of wireless connectivity and account creation requirements listed on the product packaging, but no other criteria were fulfilled.

5.2   VTech Breach

The breach of the VTech product was discovered to be a result of SQL injections to vulnerable company systems, leading to the compromise of millions of user accounts. While images and chat logs were encrypted using AES 128, the server housing the decryption keys was not well protected. Rather than correct these issues, VTech updated their terms of agreement to recuse themselves from liability for compromised user data [11].

Despite the issues revolving around its breach of data, VTech scored a B rating in this framework. Proper wireless connection requirements were posted on the product packaging, each device was issued with a unique password, and some firmware updates were pushed to connected devices.

5.3   Hello Kitty Breach

The Hello Kitty product breach was a result of a misconfigured MongoDB database installation, and resulted in the leaking of over three million user accounts. The MongoDB database required no credentials for access [24].

Hello Kitty's device was able to score a B rating in this framework. It also had significant internet connectivity notification on its packaging and configured new devices with unique passwords, while also regularly performing vulnerability assessments of its devices. However, Hello Kitty did not secure its own data centers, a flaw that likely would have been discovered had an independent security audit been performed.

5.4   My Friend Cayla Vulnerabilities

Many vulnerabilities were found in the My Friend Cayla line of dolls, including Bluetooth hacking capabilities, audio and still photo surveillance hacking, and insecure wireless transmissions. There is also no indication on the packaging of the wireless connectivity needs required to fully utilize the device. Genesis Toys likely marketed this product with little-to-no security assessment, causing it to be banned outright by Germany [3].

Against the proposed framework, My Friend Cayla scored a C. It did not adhere to any of the six criteria outlined in the framework.

5.5   Security Flaws in Smart Toy Bear and heroO Watch

Fisher-Price's Smart Toy Bear and heroO Watch products were found to be compromisable by an attacker taking advantage of weaknesses in the underlying software. In this case, there was improper handling of API calls resulting in the sender of messages not being appropriately verified. Data was also stored on the devices in an insecure format [22].

In the scale of the framework, the products earned a B+ rating. While the previously mentioned issues are of high concern, Fisher-Price adhered to four of the six criteria, including period device updating and ongoing vulnerability scanning. As was the case with Hello Kitty products, these issues would likely have been recognized via an independent audit of the product lines.

5.6   Hello Barbie Vulnerabilities

Mattel's Hello Barbie line of dolls were found to be vulnerable to hacking, giving attackers access to stored audio files and the built-in microphone of the doll. While the doll only records audio-encrypted conversations while a button on it is pressed, the device did not require secure and authorized connection by remote servers. If an attacker gets close enough to the doll to compromise it, the attacker can maintain remote access to the doll indefinitely, potentially recording conversations wherever the doll is taken.

Hello Barbie scored a B in the framework due to the lack of remote connectivity security and lack of independent auditing to discover such vulnerabilities. However, it does not ship with a default password across the product line, helping to boost its grade.

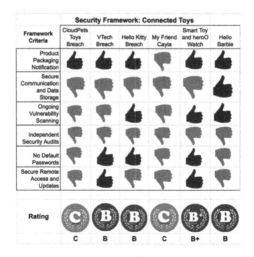

Fig. 2. Scoring each product.

6 Discussion

Looking at the security issues across product lines and brands, some assessments can be made.

- All six devices that were analyzed did not employ an independent security auditing system or vendor. The cost of hiring an independent contractor to assess the security vulnerabilities of these devices would impact the overall cost to the manufacturer, and raise the price of the product.
- Only one device, Hello Barbie, implemented secure data storage and communication into the products. All others relied on insecure connections to remote systems, and/or stored data locally in an insecure format. A need to keep manufacturing costs low can be attributed to this lack of strong security.
- All but one device, My Friend Cayla, had some form of signage on its packaging indicating the need to wirelessly connect the device to the internet and create a personal account with the manufacturer to fully utilize the capabilities of the product. Given the enormous backlash Genesis Toys received regarding the security issues of its device, competing manufacturers likely decided to add the language to its packaging to avoid a similar outcry.
- No device gained an A or A+ rating against the framework. Attribution can be given to the lack of standardized security framework for these device types, as well as manufacturing cost concerns.

7 Conclusion

The Internet of Things is a vast world of products and devices that is only continuing to grow its ubiquity and popularity. Due to the always-connected nature of these devices, it is paramount that a standard be established to rate the security implemented in each of these toys. This rating system should be placed visibly on the product packaging as a means of alerting consumers of the potential risks involved in purchasing the device, and subsequently connecting it to a home network. Without an established framework in place to put a security-related grade on these IoT devices, recent breaches have shown that connected toys can be compromised to be leveraged as a reconnaissance apparatus, or to expose sensitive personal data of parents and children. Subverting these tactics by nefarious actors is of utmost importance.

References

1. Dobbins, D.: Analysis of Security Concerns & Privacy Risks of Children's Smart Toys. Washington University in Saint Louis (2015). https://sever.wustl.edu/degreeprograms/cyber-security-management/SiteAssets/Dobbins%20-%20SmartToy_Security_Final%20Revised%209-28-15.pdf
2. Elgan, M.: This is Why Tech Toys Are Dangerous, 7 December 2015. http://www.computerworld.com/article/3012173/security/this-is-why-tech-toys-are-dangerous.html

3. Emery, D.: My Friend Cayla' Doll Records Children's Speech, Is Vulnerable to Hackers, 24 February 2017. http://www.snopes.com/2017/02/24/my-friend-cayla-doll-privacy-concerns/
4. Gibbs, S.: Hackers Can Hijack Wi-Fi Hello Barbie to Spy on Your Children, 26 November 2015. https://www.theguardian.com/technology/2015/nov/26/hackers-can-hijack-wi-fi-hello-barbie-to-spy-on-your-children
5. Gonsalves, A.: Baby Monitor Hack Highlights Manufacturers' Security Shortfalls, 15 August 2013. http://www.csoonline.com/article/2133852/privacy/baby-monitor-hack-highlights-manufacturers-security-shortfalls.html
6. Gray, S.: How Industry Can Protect Privacy in the Age of Connected Toys, 1 December 2016. https://iapp.org/news/a/how-industry-can-protect-privacy-in-the-age-of-connected-toys/
7. Greenburg, A.: This Hacked Kids' Toy Opens Garage Doors in Seconds, 4 June 2015. https://www.wired.com/2015/06/hacked-kids-toy-opens-garage-doors-seconds
8. Hern, A.: CloudPets Stuffed Toys Leak Details of Half a Million Users, 28 February 2017. https://www.theguardian.com/technology/2017/feb/28/cloudpets-data-breach-leaks-details-of-500000-children-and-adults
9. Holloway, D.: The internet of toys. Commun. Res. Pract. **2**(4), 506–519 (2016). http://www.tandfonline.com/doi/abs/10.1080/22041451.2016.1266124
10. Federal Trade Commission: Children's Online Privacy Protection Act of 1998. Children's Online Privacy Protection Rule. https://www.ftc.gov/enforcement/rules/rulemaking-regulatory-reform-proceedings/childrens-online-privacy-protection-rule
11. Kirk, J.: Data Breach at Toy Maker VTech Leaked Photos of Children, Parents, 30 November 2015. http://www.computerworld.com/article/3010513/security/data-breach-at-toy-maker-vtech-leaked-photos-of-children-parents.html
12. Kirk, J.: Toy Maker VTech Says Breach Hit 6.4 Million Kids' Accounts, 1 December 2015. http://www.computerworld.com/article/3011166/security/toy-maker-vtech-says-breach-hit-64-million-kids-accounts.html#tk.drr_mlt
13. Michael, K.: High-Tech Child's Play in the Cloud: be safe and aware of the difference between virtual and real. IEEE Consum. Electron. Mag. **5**(1), 123–128 (2015). http://ieeexplore.ieee.org/abstract/document/7353284/authors
14. Korolov, M.: VTech Not Backing Down on Terms Change After Data Breach, 19 February 2016. http://www.csoonline.com/article/3035021/security/vtech-not-backing-down-on-terms-change-after-data-breach.html
15. Larson, S.: Stuffed Toys Leak Millions of Voice Recordings From Kids and Parents, 27 February 2017. http://money.cnn.com/2017/02/27/technology/cloudpets-data-leak-voices-photos/index.html
16. Moini, C.: Protecting privacy in the era of smart toys: does hello barbie have a duty to report. Catholic Univ. J. Law Technol. **25**(2), 4 (2017). Article No. 4. http://scholarship.law.edu/cgi/viewcontent.cgi?article=1040&context=jlt&sei-redir=1&referer=https%3A%2F%2Fscholar.google.com%2Fscholar%3Fstart%3D20%26q%3Dhacked%2Bchildren%2527s%2Btoys%26hl%3Den%26as_sdt%3D0%2C33#search=%22hacked%20childrens%20toys%22
17. National Institute of Standards and Technologies, NIST. https://www.nist.gov/about-nist
18. NIST Special Publication 800-53 (Rev. 4). National Vulnerability Database. https://nvd.nist.gov/800-53/Rev4. Accessed 23 June 2017

19. Peterson, A.: Hello (hackable) Barbie, 4 December 2015. https://www.washingtonpost.com/news/the-switch/wp/2015/12/04/hello-hackable-barbie/?utm_term=.e774edd5573a
20. Rouse, M.: Advanced Encryption Standard (AES). http://searchsecurity.techtarget.com/definition/Advanced-Encryption-Standard
21. Secure Hash Algorithm (SHA). Techopedia.com. https://www.techopedia.com/definition/10328/secure-hash-algorithm-sha
22. Smith: Security Flaws Found in Fisher-Price Smart Teddy Bear and Kid's GPS Tracker Watch, 2 February 2016. http://www.networkworld.com/article/3028827/security/security-flaws-found-in-fisher-price-smart-teddy-bear-and-kids-gps-tracker-watch.html
23. Stanslav, M., Beardsley, T.: HACKING IoT: A Case Study on Baby Monitor Exposures and Vulnerabilities. Rapid7.com. https://www.rapid7.com/docs/Hacking-IoT-A-Case-Study-on-Baby-Monitor-Exposures-and-Vulnerabilities.pdf
24. Spring, T.: Hello Kitty Database of 3.3 Million Breached Credentials Surfaces, 9 January 2017. https://threatpost.com/hello-kitty-database-of-3-3-million-breached-credentials-surfaces/122932
25. Storm, D.: Hello Kitty Hack Exposes 3.3 Million Users, Joins Hello Barbie in Putting Kids at Risk, 22 December 2015. http://www.computerworld.com/article/3017974/security/hello-kitty-hack-exposes-3-3-million-users-joins-hello-barbie-in-putting-kids-at-risk.html#tk.drr_mlt
26. Unknown: Connected Dolls and Tell-Tale Teddy Bears: Why We Need to Manage the Internet of Toys, 23 March 2017. https://ec.europa.eu/jrc/en/news/why-we-need-manage-internet-toys
27. Unknown: Children's Messages in CloudPets Data Breach, 28 February 2017. http://www.bbc.com/news/technology-39115001
28. The White House: Cybersecurity-Executive Order 13636, 12 February 2013. https://obamawhitehouse.archives.gov/issues/foreign-policy/cybersecurity/eo-13636
29. Zunnurhain, K.: Vulnerabilities with internet of things. In: Proceedings of International Conference on Security and Management (SAM) (2016). http://search.proquest.com/docview/1806999232?pq-origsite=gscholar

Security and Attack Vector Analysis of IoT Devices

Marc Capellupo[1], Jimmy Liranzo[1], Md Zakirul Alam Bhuiyan[1(✉)],
Thaier Hayajneh[1], and Guojun Wang[2]

[1] Department of Computer and Information Sciences,
Fordham University, New York, NY 10458, USA
{mcapellupo1,jliranzo1,mbhuiyan3,thayajneh}@fordham.edu
[2] School of Computer Science and Educational Software,
Guangzhou University, Guangzhou 510006, China
csgjwang@gzhu.edu.cn

Abstract. The goal of this paper is to research and review through experimental testing the security of home automation devices. The methodology includes analysis and review of these home automation devices through traffic capture, device scanning, and wireless analysis. The devices that will be tested are the Amazon Echo, Osram Smart Lights, and TPLink power switch. We present a classification model to analyze the relation between potential risk and realized risk through potential vulnerabilities in these varying home automation devices. Possible security flaws that might be found include default configurations, easy to crack passwords, unencrypted traffic, responses to forged traffic, and full control of the device without any authentication. We also perform a review of their privacy exposure and outline the security vectors used to attack IoT devices, as well as the most recent malwares in control of over a million IoT devices.

Keywords: Component · IoT · Home automation · Security
Privacy · Malware

1 Introduction

Internet of Things (IoT) are a conglomerate of physical objects with capabilities to obtain an IP address and connect to the internet. These devices are spread across multiple industries and can be found in Manufacturing, Transportation, Utilities, Healthcare and Consumer's electronics. According to Garner [1] there are currently 8.4 billion IoT devices as of 2017, which represents a 31% increase from the past year. The unstoppable force driving this market are consumers with 5.2 billion IoT devices in their homes, a figure expected to triple within the next three years. These devices are built for a world of interconnectivity enabling each IoT device to communicate with each other. This enables the concept of Smart Homes, or homes with emended technologies that allows the automation of common task such as turning on a lightbulb with voice command,

© Springer International Publishing AG 2017
G. Wang et al. (Eds.): SpaCCS 2017 Workshops, LNCS 10658, pp. 593–606, 2017.
https://doi.org/10.1007/978-3-319-72395-2_54

automatically ordering items low on quantity within the refrigerator or asking you're the device to play a song or movie, all via voice commands or a mobile application. The most common IoT consumer's devices range from power outlets, lightbulbs, TV's, Amazon Echo "Alexa", and Google Home "Alexa competitor".

The history of IoT is a topic that seems like no one knows it's true origin, which makes them all right and wrong at the same time. Within its history, some go as far back as the Electromagnetic Telegraph invented in 1832, others start with the invention of the 2Way Wrist Radio in 1946. Although those technologies may play a role in the future of these devices, we believe that if the device was created prior the existence of the Internet and used a different protocol to communicate, it should not be considered an IoT device. The first known IoT device was a Toaster with capabilities to be turn on/off via Internet, it was developed in 1989 by Romkey [2].

In the 2008, there were more Internet of Things devices connected to the internet than people, according to Cisco. And it is estimated that by year 2020 there will be over 50 billion IoT devices. Consumer's account for nearly 62% of all IoT device and most can be found at home as can be displayed in figure one. People now have the capabilities to open their home door with an application instead of physical keys, their home can be embedded with automated sensors that recognize the owner's car approaching and automatically open the garage door. In a "Smart Home" nearly every device within the home has the capability to connect to the internet, the thermostats, or lights can be controlled remotely and you can even start your stove oven over the internet. It's like an object with a brain of its own which reminds you of your daily task and listen constantly for the magic wakeup command "Hey Alex, how's the weather?" all without having to touch a button.

In this paper, we analyze and review the privacy concerns, and attack vectors of home automation devices. Then we perform an experimental security testing against them. Our focus on privacy is based on the notion that consumers associate privacy risk have not been well study and all devices haven been thrown into the same category of IoT where in fact the device may be holding sensitive personal identifiable information that could be sued to profile an individual. The lack of oversight in these devices has enabled developers to capture more data than needed for device operability and consumers are not fully aware of all the type of data their devices are sending over the internet, often using connections not fully encrypted. Then comes the inability of these device to be able to self-protect against most common attacks. The spread of malwares from device to device and multiple attack vectors is due mostly because of careless product development where security does not play an important role.

In our experimental testing of home automation devices, we analyzed hardware we already owned and verify each software is uptodate. Then we concentrate on trying to expose the device Confidentiality, Integrity and Availability (CIA). We will outline possible danger of owning a vulnerable IoT device and which devices seem to have a well establish security mechanism in place and provides great security and privacy.

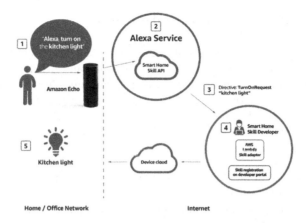

Fig. 1. Automated – smart home with amazon echo.

This paper is organized as follows. Section 2 introduces the existing work. Section 3 describe privacy in home automation IoT. Section 4 explains attack vectors and risk factors. Security Classification Model is given in Sect. 5 Lab setup and threats analysis are in Sect. 6. Experimental test and analysis is made in Sect. 7. Finally, Sect. 8 concerns the conclusions of this work.

2   Related Work

The heterogeneity in IoT devices has driven many researchers to study the privacy and security of these devices. However, their diversity, means of communication and lack of classification has spread the research across multiple industries without generating a clear consensus on which devices clearly protect their owner privacy and security regardless if it's an eHealth devices, manufacturing or consumer home device [16].

One of the main subjects being heavily analyzed is the mean of being able to verify the identity provided (username and password) and the type of access that such credentials are allowed [14,15]. Multiple researcher's [3–5] have propose different venues. for IoT. Some researchers focus on the lack of protection and risk associated with transmitting data and credentials in plain text [6–8]. Privacy research in IoT is mostly associated with security, and although they go handtohand, we believe there should be more concentrated privacy as a main domain. Studies surrounding privacy have been either too general [9] or too specific such as the Glucose Monitors [10]. One major factor contributing to the lack of privacy and security in these devices is the widespread of malwares [11] that currently affect these devices [12]. Thru the use of Honeypot researchers have been able to analyze how these devices are being attack, how they've been using them to conduct DDoS attacks and observing how the trend is on the rise on manufacturer are not even close to adopt a solution. Another area is the Home Automation IoT that constantly shares similarities and often refers to the Smart Home [13].

3   Privacy in Home Automation IoT

Consumer's home IoT devices are designed to collect information about user's behavior, daily routine activities, browsing history and other rich information that is used to personalize the device with the consumer lifestyle. The information generated by these devices could be used to identify or track all movement a person made in the day.

A study conducted in 2016 by TRUSTe and the National Cyber Security Alliance on U.S consumer privacy.

- 92% of those survey were worry about their online privacy, an increase of 45% from the previous year
- Only 31% understand how companies are sharing their personal information
- 89% will avoid a company that do not protect their privacy
- 74% have limit their online activity in the past year due to privacy concerns
- 19% felt forced to use a service/website they didn't trust because they had no other option.

Consumers no longer blindly trust companies to handle their personal information, some are due to the misuse and reselling of consumer's data and others just lost trust that any information stored online can be secure. The privacy damage done to consumers seem to have no ending, as all major industries have been affected by massive data breaches that has affected billion of consumer's personal identifiable information (PII) as well as their Patient Health Information (PHI). The inability to not have a choice where your data is store or be able to partially optout of a business agreement will greater hamper consumer's privacy.

The privacy risk with using the device is joint to the fact that IoT devices may collect more information than its required, and since consumers are unaware on it they may expose themselves to unwanted privacy risk. For example, the Amazon Echo, has a microphone constantly listening for anything within reach and waiting for the owner to say the magic word "Hey Alexa, do this...", but although Amazon claim they only record and send audio to the Cloud after the users queries the device others have reported the device turning on onitself and others are talking nearby. All that data could be used for targeted advertising, they can know what movie you watched, what music you're playing, and profile you based on your recent purchase. Recently there was a case involving an Amazon Echo and a murder case in Arkansas where police believe the device was a "witness to the crime". A request for the recording of the device was denied by Amazon, which leaves only speculations on what are they trying to protect.

3.1   Privacy Risk Associated with CloudBased Model

Due to the lack of space on the device, this information is stored on Cloud providers where consumers have no control of the location where the data is stored or who can access it and at times they may not even have a choice to select their own Cloud provider nor the IoT vendor provides details of the state of data security whether is encrypted or not. Although it is known that must IoT devices store their data on the cloud unencrypted, which could lead to a violation of the consumer privacy or an internal user affecting the integrity and confidentiality of the data.

Although the Cloudbased model is a key component in the evolution of these devices, it often leaves more questions than answer. For example, in the event that you can't choose your own provider what assurance do we have that such provider will remain in business, or that they will destroy all your data if you decide to cancel your contract. But what will happen in the event of a breach, does the company has any obligations to notify affected consumers? The answer to those questions will depend on the location of the Datacenter, as in the U.S.A business are required by law to notify affected consumers within a reason amount of time. But having your data stored within the U.S will not add extra privacy protection, instead you may find your data being released to the Government under the USA Patriot Act with a Subpoena or data older than 180 days could be released with an administrative request. The law limits the Cloud provider ability to notify affected consumes that their data has been released to Government, which could those affected will be unaware of a pending investigation. Then comes into place the value of the data uploaded that Cloud providers could be resell to third party businesses without user's knowledge.

4 Attack Vectors and Risk Factors

We first offer possible attach vectors. Then, we explain attack vectors and risk factors.

4.1 Attack Vectors

Consumers IoT devices not only face privacy risk, there are numerous security risk associated with owning one of these devices. They are susceptible to physical hardware attacks, network attacks, web attacks, attack against the Operating System and the application interacting with these devices. In fact, in part because most IoT developers have not pay much attention to security of IoT, in part due to uncertainty of whether the device will be accepted by consumers or not. These have led to a widespread of unsecure devices going in the market where security is an afterthought that if the devices is successful they will invest in securing the devices. But the challenge with this approach is that developers lack adequate measures for patch management.

The current solution of releasing the patch on the developer's website and expecting consumers to manually install it poses many flaws. First there is no way to notify all those affected, second most lack basic technical expertise to manually upgrade their device. Below we detail some of the most current attacks methods affecting IoT.

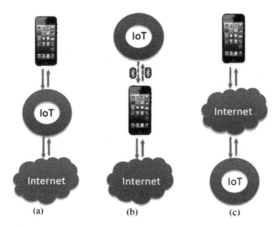

Fig. 2. IoT operational model: (a) direct, (b) transit, (c) external server.

In Fig. 2, we outline the operational model of how some of these devices operate. Some allow direct communication between the Mobile application and the IoT device, while others rely on the mobile application between the internet and the IoT devices, the mobile application as a gateway for the device and then there are those that all connections must go first via the internet and then to end user mobile application. This last behavior is irrelevant if the user is within the same private network.

4.2   Authentication and Authorization – Weak Security

The number one factor affecting the security of IoT devices if the lack of protection against the device authentication and authorization process. Since most of them do not employ an encryption algorithm the authentication exchange could be compromised by an attacker sniffing the wireless communication and intercepting the credentials in plaintext. Hackers have constantly challenge the authentication mechanism in part because developers often set hardcoded backdoor accounts that consumers are unable to change and an attacker could discover and use for mass exploitation of IoT. The lack of password policy management, enables an attacker to bruteforce the password of the device, because the device itself does not employ a firewall or other security measures to prevent to continuous request for authentication. Not enforcing a password policy is what allows consumers to set easily guessable password that most malware are attacking. On an investigation, we find the percentage of the most common password that are being exploited in millions of IoT devices where the average length is 6 characters long. With today's computing power, such password can be cracked in less than a minute. But unless consumers are made aware of it, they will continue to implement weak password.

IoT devices are designed to bypass home users internal NAT by default, exposing the device directly to the internet without the user having to configure their router manually. An innovative process, but a risky one when the connection is not properly secure. By opening a UDP or TCP unencrypted tunnel it enables an attacker to capture the direct link between the cloud and the home device and often allows an attacker to bypass of authorization and gain access to the device. Within the authorization process the device exchange its credentials which could be intercepted to gain authenticated access to the device. The main risk associated with bypassing authentication and authorization is that owners of these devices have no way of knowing if their device has been compromised nor have the ability to know if their device is affected by backdoor accounts.

4.3   Network Based Attacks

To extend the functionality of the device, they rely heavily on network connection. They end up connecting to a hub that connects to the home user router in order to provide internet access for the device. Given that it lacks enough memory and processing power, the connection is often sent using unsecure methods, where their main protection is obscurity as security. A method used to obfuscate the communication session but that could be easily deobfuscated by someone with knowledge of networking. It all depends on the vendor, if the device is from a reputable brand, it increases the likelihood of your device having greater security posture out of the box.

4.4   Malware Attacks

Cyber criminals are always looking for different ways to profit from the lack of security of any devices. In the IoT world, it is known that they are not systematically patched, this widen the opportunity for to exploit vulnerabilities within it, by creating malwares, "software" programmed to replicate and spread automatically from device to device. The main malware known to terrorize the IoT world is known as Bashlight, also known as Qbot, Torlus, Lizkebab and Gafgyt and was discover is mid2014. After its discovery, the source code was released in early 2015, since then over a dozen variant of the same malware have been infection IoT devices. Currently there are four main malwares infecting IoT devices; Bashlight, Mirai, BrickerBot and Hajime.

All of these malwares target IoT devices authentication and authorization. The last of the malwares in our section is the least destructive of all "YET" as of May 2017. The Hajime malware have been named the "Vigilante Botnet", because instead of using the device to conduct DDoS attacks or destroy it, it secures the device ports so it's unreachable by other malware trying the same vector attack. It currently has over 300,000 IoT devices within its C2 server and as of yet it has not been used for malicious purpose. Although it seems as a novel cause trying to protect the device, the malware has the same capabilities as the others and at the push of a button could turn from good to evil.

In Fig. 3, we outline the attack methodology being used to exploit IoT devices in the wild and then used the same methodology to conduct our experimental testing. As the first steps these malwares are taking after connecting to the

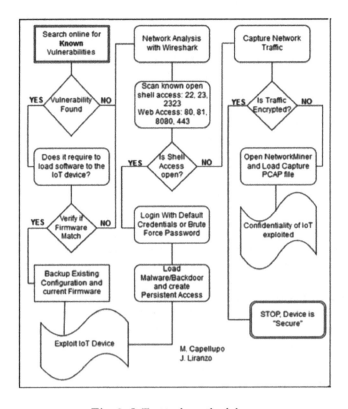

Fig. 3. IoT attack methodology.

device is to randomly downloading a list of 12 possible infected files and execute each one until one is proven to work. It displays that the attacker possible searched online for known vulnerabilities and its way of verifying if the devices is vulnerable is by downloading all scripts. If the device is not successful in gaining access with a backdoor account, it proceeds to bruteforce the password of the known users until successful. This is effective because IoT devices do not have account lockout mechanism in place to prevent the brute force attack. But in the event, that the devices are not vulnerable then we wanted to look at the privacy exposure of the device, which may expose sensitive information via unencrypted connection that we could use and expose the consumer confidentiality.

Hypothesis and Three main risk factors. Based on the security concerns presented above, we can identify the key characteristics with which we can create a general hypothesis about the current security posture of devices. Manufacturers in new, rapidly expanding markets like home automation products will push their products to market as fast as possible, often skipping over security measures in favor of fast development. The current market offerings of home automation IoT devices discuss little of their security protocols or development cycles. A number of devices have already been shown to have large security holes. Certain devices though already provide a number of security measures, such as the Amazon Echo which encrypts all end to end traffic. Based on these two examples, we can examine why certain devices are shipped with extensive security measures and others have little to no security at all. One proposed hypothesis for this model is that lowertiered devices in the model presented have a lower overall security posture than the highertiered devices. The key characteristics that come into play during the security posture analysis of the home automation devices can also provide a basis for this hypothesis and one with which we can build our classification model around.

In presenting this new classification model, we mold this around three different factors; connectivity, command input, and level of functionality. These three categories were determined by analyzing potential avenues an attacker may take to compromise a home automation IoT device. They also help distinguish how critical a device is by analyzing the potential consequences of a security compromise.

5   Security Classification Model

These multiple distinctions are factored into this final classification model. The Home Automation IoT Device Model Classification is structured as three separate classes.

5.1   Single Function Devices

These are ones that are limited in functionality to only a handful of features. This includes light bulbs, power switches, security cameras, and any type of external sensors. They are often used in unison with other devices, as part of a larger grouping in an attempt to create a "smart" home. If accessed individually, they are often issued instructions through a mobile phone app or from a smarter device that replicate the command instructions. For example, the Belkin WeMo smart plug can be powered on and off through the WeMo app, available on Android and iOS, as well as controlled remotely through voice commands issued to the Amazon Echo. The Osram Lightify Smart Bulbs can be accessed individually through the Lightify app but must be connected to the Lightify gateway adapter. These endpoint devices are most commonly configured by connecting to either the home WiFi network or wirelessly connected to a central gateway or hub, as is the case with the WeMo switch and Lightify bulbs.

5.2   Secondary Extended Functionality Devices

One line of devices that arguably started the smart home revolution are home utilities or furniture with the added functionality of a persistent network connection. The most notable example is smart televisions that connect to a network for features like streaming movies, music, and even a fullfledged browser. Although these devices could be considered to be outside the realm of home automation, it is included in this classification because they are still relevant in the analysis of the smart home security posture.

5.3   Control/Personal Assistant Devices

The highest tier, control/personal assistant devices, present the biggest security risk to home networks. These devices usually have dozens of functionalities, multiple input vectors, and can control and communicate with other devices throughout the smart home. Devices like the Amazon Echo, Google Home, and Logitech Harmony Home Control reside within this category.

6   Lab Setup and Threats

The methodology behind this experiment included analysis of review of home automation devices through traffic capture, device scanning, and wireless analysis. For our lab environment, we connected all over our devices to an Asus RTN12 wireless router. Our attack machine hosted the Kali operating system with two network interfaces, one to serve as a rogue access point for the IoT devices and one to observe wireless traffic. The internal wireless interface of the laptop was used for rogue access point, configured through Kali as "newhostk" and an external Alfa AWUS036NH wireless adapter was used to sniff wireless traffic. A number of home automation devices were used from different tiers of the classification model. We observed and analyzed the Osram Lightify Smart Bulbs, the TPLink Smart Plug, and the Amazon Echo Dot. There are a number of vulnerabilities we believe may be discovered during these tests. The first, most obvious vulnerability related to these devices is traffic interception.

Connectivity from these devices is important to recognize because wireless traffic can easily be intercepted from nearby parties. If traffic from the IoT device is not encrypted, private information about the network or the user can be leaked to anyone listening to the traffic. Rogue access points and man in the middle attacks present a similar attack vector because commands and even updates sent to the IoT device can be intercepted and tampered with. This could lead to malicious control and even full compromise of the device.

Manufacturers also need to be aware of authentication controls in the development of home automation devices. It is important to recognize what parties can and cannot interact with the device. Current security controls may allow any party to send commands to the device for interoperability purposes or because of forgone access controls. A device that responds to any command that is sent to it can easily be controlled by a malicious attacker. This extends even outside the network because phone apps and web interfaces used for device control present the same risk with default or credentials.

As with any network connected device, one potential vulnerability is the ability of an attack to pivot from one device in the network to another. Although compromise of a low functioning home automation device may have minimal immediate consequences, if an attacker is able to pivot to another machine on the network, this presents a major security vulnerability. Home automation devices that are susceptible to this pivoting will quickly become a focused target of malicious intruders.

7   Experimental Test Using Osram Lightify

The first unit we tested was the Osram Lightify Hub and Smart Bulbs. This device is shipped as a starter unit, with the hub and one smart bulb, then sold separately as individual bulbs. The first step of setting up the Osram Lightify environment is downloading the Android/iOS Lightify app that is required to correctly configure the devices. After creating account, the hub is plugged in and begins broadcasting its own WiFi connection. Before the app can be connected to the device, it is requiring a valid serial number to typed. This was tested by inputting serial numbers one character off from the correct serial number which failed authorization. Using the airodumpng tool on the Kali machine, we can see the Osram Lightify hub as SSID – Lightify7D**** and can see WPA2, CCMP, and PSK security mechanisms in place. The WiFi password, which is written on the back of the hub, is strong enough, with a mix of numbers, upper case, and lower case characters that we can confidently say that it will not be susceptible to a brute force attack. We manually connected to the device using the attack box's internal interface, testing as if we were able to crack the WiFi password. The device assigned our attack machine the IP address of 192.168.10.2 and a quick ping scan revealed only one live host (as expected) at 192.168.10.1, which we can assume is our Lightify hub.

A quick nmap scan revealed that only port 4000 is open on the device. Banner grabbing on the port did not reveal very much information but we believe this is the port the Lightify hub uses to send and receive commands. There is no web interface present or any other obvious sign of full device control so we continued the setup to find other attack vectors. We analyze sending crafted commands to devices in later steps.

We attempted to configure the hub to our rogue access point but was ultimately not able to connect to the outbound server and failed in later steps due to a "gateway error". This was verified to not be a problem with the access point set up. We continued the setup with the accessible WiFi to configure the smart bulbs. When plugging in the smart bulbs, which pulsed to identify they were in setup mode, they were not picked up by our wireless scanning. We believe this may be due to the lights using Zigbee or another wireless technology other than WiFi. We were not able to test for traffic encryption.

After two lights were connected to the Lightify hub, the last step was to reverse engineer the firmware to find ways to control the device. Because we considered that to be outside the scope of this project, we searched on Github for any repositories that might allow us to send commands the devices. We found multiple repositories and many of them worked successfully, allowing us to send on and off signals to all the lights in the network. The only requirement was to be on the same network as the Lightify hub.

7.1   TPLink Smart Plug

The TPLink Smart Plug involves a similar setup process to the Lightify bulbs with some key differences. The smart plug begins broadcasting its wireless connection as soon as it is plugged into a power source, with SSID TPLinkSmart Plugxxxx, the last four characters which are actually the last four of the MAC address of the device. Unlike the Lightify hub, the TPLink smart plug had an open WiFi connection with no authentication. We connected to the device and were assigned an IP 192.168.0.100. A ping sweep on the network showed the only live host to be 192.168.0.1. An nmap scan on the device revealed two ports to be open, port 80 and port 9999. Running the curl command against the 192.168.0.1 host returned only the code "...".

We found an exploit writeup for this exact device. After performing a similar analysis, the author reversed engineered the device firmware and revealed a number of substantial findings. The etc/shadow file was easily reversed to find the password of the "root" user as "media." Reverse engineering of the Kasa app, required to connect and control the device revealed the encryption method to be a simple XOR of a hardcoded value. The plug even stored the password for the WiFi network in plain text.

In addition, we accessed a Github repository of commands that we were able to send to the device. We were able to perform all the actions the device was capable of, including turning the device on and off, scanning for wireless access points, downloading firmware from a specified URL, flashing the firmware, even change the cloud server URL. Most interestingly, we were able to send a "get_sysinfo" command to the device that divulged just about every bit of information associated with the smart plug, including the model number, mac address, hardware and software version, and even the latitude and longitude geolocation information.

7.2   Amazon Echo Dot

The Amazon Echo Dot involves the same setup process as the other devices we tested but was much more closed off. The Amazon Echo had an open WiFi connection during setup but filtered any scan requests. Various voice commands were tested to reveal sensitive device-specific information but were unsuccessful. We connected the Echo Dot to our rogue access point but other than analyzing destination IP addresses that may define what service is being used, all the traffic to and from the device was encrypted. Ultimately, there was very little success with compromising the Amazon Echo.

8   Conclusion

In this paper, We have showed the home automation devices can present major security breaches to home networks and to the end user's privacy. The range of home automation IoT devices has expanded wildly over the past couple years and has extended functionality to just about every aspect of the consumer's house. From light bulbs to televisions to refrigerators, nearly every aspect of the living room can be connected to the network for remote control. We have demonstrated that with basic networking skills, a dedicated attacker can leverage these devices to inflict major damage. We were unable to exploit the microphone functionality of the Amazon Echo to listen in on a victim, observe its traffic, or exploit it in any other way. We were successful in controlling a majority of the functionality of the Osram Lightify lights while connected on the same network. Our experimentation of the TPLink power switch was a worrying revelation. Like the smart light bulbs, we were able to gain full device control, with the ability to turn the switch on and off as we pleased. We were also able to obtain a plethora of information, update most if not all of the settings, and obtain a plaintext string of the wireless network's password.

References

1. Gartner Says 8.4 Billion Connected. http://www.gartner.com/newsroom/id/3598917
2. Romkey, J.: Toast of the IoT: the 1990 interop internet toaster. IEEE Consum. Electron. Mag. **6**(1), 116–119 (2017)
3. Liu, J., Xiao, Y., Chen, C.L.P.: Authentication and access control in the Internet of Things. In: IEEE 32nd International Conference on Distributed Computing Systems Workshops. June 2012
4. Hummen, R., Shafagh, H., Raza, S., Voig, T., Wehrle, K.: Delegation-based authentication and authorization for the IPbased Internet of Things (2017)
5. Liu, J., Xiao, Y., Chen, C.P.: Authentication and access control in the Internet of Things. In: 2012 32nd International Conference on Distributed Computing Systems Workshops (2012)
6. Mohd, B.J., Hayajneh, T., Vasilakos, A.V.: A survey on lightweight block ciphers for low-resource devices: comparative study and open issues. J. Netw. Comput. App. **58**, 73–93 (2015)
7. Lee, J.Y., Lin, W.C., Huang, Y.H.: A lightweight authentication protocol for Internet of Things. In: 2014 International Symposium on NextGeneration Electronics (ISNE) (2014)
8. Yao, X., Chen, Z., Tian, Y.: A lightweight attribute-based encryption scheme for the Internet of Things. Future Gener. Comput. Syst. **49**, 104–112 (2015)
9. Ukil, A., Bandyopadhyay, S., Pal, A.: IoTPrivacy: to be private or not to be private. In: 2014 IEEE Conference on Computer Communications Workshops (INFOCOM WKSHPS) (2014)
10. Britton, K.E., Britton-Colonnese, J.D.: Privacy and security issues surrounding the protection of data generated by continuous glucose monitors. J. Diabetes Sci. Technol. **11**(2), 216–219 (2017)
11. Pa, Y.M.P., Suzuki, S., Yoshioka, K., Matsumoto, T., Kasama, T., Rossow, C.: IoTPOT: a novel honeypot for revealing current IoT threats. J. Inf. Process. **24**(3), 522–533 (2016)
12. Min, B., Varadharajan, V.: Design and evaluation of feature distributed malware attacks against the Internet of Things (IoT). In: 2015 20th International Conference on Engineering of Complex Computer Systems (ICECCS) (2015)

13. Bhide, V.H., Wagh, S.: ilearning IoT: an intelligent self learning system for home automation using IoT. In: 2015 International Conference on Communications and Signal Processing (ICCSP) (2015)

14. Islam, S.H., Arijit, K., Biswas, G., Bhuiyan, M.Z.A., Vijayakumar, P., Karuppiah, M.: Provably secure identity-based signcryption scheme for crowdsourced industrial Internet of Things environments. IEEE IoT J. (2017)

15. Alali, M., Almogren, A., Bhuiyan, M.Z.A.: Improving risk assessment model of cyber security using fuzzy logic inference system. Comput. Secur. (2017)

16. Luo, E., Bhuiyan, M.Z.A., Wang, G., Rahman, M., Wu, J., Atiquzzaman, M.: PrivacyProtector: privacyprotected patient data collection in IoT-based healthcare systems. IEEE Commun. Mag. (COMMAG) (2017)

Security Solution of RFID Card Through Cryptography

Md. Alam Hossain[1], Nazmul Hossain[1], Afridi Shahid[1],
and Shawon S. M. Rahman[2(✉)]

[1] Department of Computer Science and Engineering,
Jessore University of Science and Technology, Jessore 7408, Bangladesh
alamcse_iu@yahoo.com, nazmul.justcse@gmail.com,
afridi.justll@gmail.com
[2] Department of Computer Science and Engineering,
University of Hawaii-Hilo, Hilo, HI 96720, USA
SRahman@Hawaii.edu

Abstract. RFID was considered as an advanced technology for automatic identification of objects. RFID makes usage of radio alerts to discover, tune, kind and stumble on an expansion of items. Security prerequisite is necessary in most of the applications. User's Authentication at the end of the RFID technology creates one of the major attacks on the system. A crucial challenge in RFID technology research is to provide efficient protection for the systems against tag cloning and information modification. In this paper, we have proposed a system where the information has to be more secured than existing system. We have used an encrypt-decrypt tools which is used for encryption and decryption of the information by a decryption keywords. The encrypted information can be saved to the local database or online cloud storage. But the main advantage of our proposed system is that the whole operation has worked with windows OS. Besides we also analyze the runtime for our system for a particular data and get a relatively better consuming runtime. Safety requirement is critical this packages. Our framework can be used to minimize the unauthorized usage of RFID Card information and focus on the runtime.

Keywords: RFID · Security threats · CoolTerm · Cloud storage · Cloning
Information leakage · Read time

1 Introduction

RFID cards security is designed to provide facilitate, scalable entrance to applications, resources and services, and are fully handled by a security card provider. Security providers are giving their services according to the fundamental model. It is a wireless information system, with real-time visual display of activities, resulting in the improvement in efficiency with less human efforts in data entry [4]. It track and trace items automatically and consisting of three key elements: RFID tags, RFID readers, and a back-end database server to identify information. RFID is a rising generation that makes use of radio waves as the method to identify gadgets or objects. In order to analyze safety and privacy troubles, it is important to offer a quick introduction to the

© Springer International Publishing AG 2017
G. Wang et al. (Eds.): SpaCCS 2017 Workshops, LNCS 10658, pp. 607–616, 2017.
https://doi.org/10.1007/978-3-319-72395-2_55

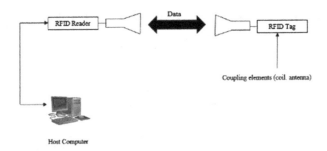

Fig. 1. RFID system

fundamental components of RFID systems. As shown in Fig. 1, a normal RFID system includes one or greater RFID tags, a reader, and a backend machine [10].

Every tag consists of an identical identity code [6]. A RFID reader transmits a low-stage radio frequency magnetic concern that energies the tag. The tag replay to the reader's query and make declaration of its presence through radio waves that transferring its precise identity records. This information is decoded through the reader and passed to the neighborhood software device through middleware. The middleware simulates as an interface between the tag reader and the RFID appliances tool. The device will then search the identification code with the records stored inside the host database or backend device. On this way, if it matches with the database information, the process will successful.

2 Existing System and Its Problem

In encryption area, current high-stop RFID structures are capable to encrypt and authenticate the information traffic with proprietary protocols. Encryption of reminiscence blocks may be realized at the software layer, that's transparent for the RFID tag. The specific Identifier (UID) is typically study-only and many RFID–transponders permit a permanent write lock of reminiscence blocks [9]. This will make sure of information integrity however, of course, now not message authentication and social engineering assaults including cloning, stealing records etc. Besides systems are not fully secured because the encrypted information are unprotected. As a result, warding off memory block encryption, we are trying to employing with data encryption-decryption method to establish extra safety the use of my encrypt-decrypt-tool allowing private key encryption method. In RFID area, some works also have done with fingerprint based method. It is considered as the latest technology. But it is not secured from virus infection. If it falls in infection of virus then all identifying data will hampered and must be saved repeatedly. Beside the whole system is too costly to process [8].

3   Related Work

The existing work [3] proposed a conceptual framework which can be integrated into the RFID Card to mitigate the unauthorized use of Card. The research aim was to integrate biometric authentication process into a clip able RFID Card. The processes are divided into three stages as shown in Fig. 2. **Stage 1: Design and Fabrication of Tag.** This stage comprises the design, calibration, simulation and fabrication of the tag antenna, and a controllable joint connected to a controller. **Stage 2: Fingerprint Matching and Storage.** This stage involves the process of acquiring, authenticating, securing and storage of the biometric authentication process, fingerprint in this case. **Stage 3: System Building and Testing.** This stage entails the integration of the various phases in a secured control unit and testing of the prototype. But the whole system is fully unprotected at the administration side. So existing systems has kept a major weakness for us. Analyzing this system, we have also seen that getting better runtime can be possible with more security.

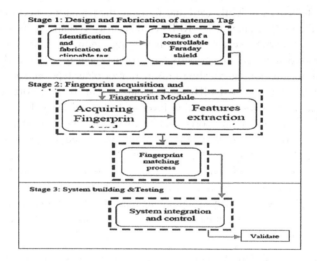

Fig. 2. Previous proposed RFID security system

4   Overview of the Proposed System

In this paper, we are trying to improve the extra security of the RFID card security system, which is provided by the security providers. This roadmap establishes security against some threats, such as information stealing from the administrator computer, card cloning through stealing information. Now a day, card cloning is a major threat all over the world. This threat increases unauthenticated access in a secure system. This proposed system especially works against some social engineering attacks those are neglected by the users and keep some weakness in the security system (Fig. 3).

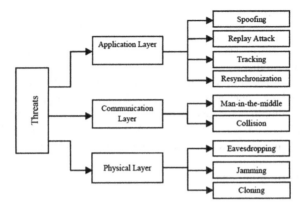

Fig. 3. Threats classification

Instrument of the Research Paper. The principal aim of this dissertation is to show the security challenges in RFID card and mitigate the primary concern of the system. Considering the major challenges in RFID card security system, we have designed and developed a client side encryption tool belongings more facilities for the security. As RFID card providers do not currently have robust security solutions that can secure the system from card cloning, Stealing information or other types of social engineering threats. The challenges in RFID card security can be categorized into three parts-Application layer, Communication layer and Physical layer. Figure 4 shows the threats classification [2]. The proposed architecture facilitates client side encryption [1] in the following advantageous ways to overcome some basic threats of RFID security. These include data stealing, card cloning, data loss etc. related social engineering attacks. Following on from this research, a roadmap will be developed that can be used to maintain the privacy and confidentiality of the information stored in the card. This roadmap will serve extra security as a guide against information stealing for cloning the card which is used by an unauthorized person. The process runtime is also better than existing [14].

Principle Operation of Our Proposed System. In this section, the methodology used in this research operation for solving the problem is stated below. At first the card is read by the reader. The read information is encrypted by our encrypted software and this information will save to the cloud memory. When the original information is needed, then only the administrator, who knows the decrypted private key can get the original information. As a result, the information of the card cannot be stolen through an unauthenticated person. Beside no one can clone the card and the authenticated card holder remains in security. It also helps the administrator that the information will save in the cloud memory with proper time. So administrator calculates the number of the uses of the card with proper time. The steps of methodology are depicted as follows.

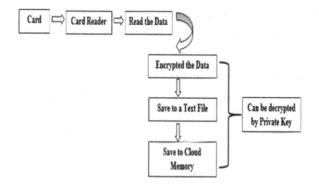

Fig. 4. The proposed system methodology

5 Performance Evaluation

Potential security properties are attainable within simple security proposed designs that are suitable for effectuation in RFID systems. In this research, we mentioned about the RFID, basis, application, advantages, using of RFID, how does it works etc. [7]. Protocol for anonymous identification simultaneously attains security against card cloning [5], information theft and skimming of the systems. For this reason we are trying to set up a new system of RFID system by encrypting the information. This works against some social engineering attacks. Release some weak points of the security system. And we make the system efficient because administrator of the system can identify, when the tag and how many times are used by the user. The system has some common characteristics. **Hardware.** The information's are read by the Arduino and radio frequency sensor. **Software.** Coolterm software for Arduino processing interface and encrypt-decrypt software for encryption and decryption. **Encryption Algorithm.** Since the software's raw code is written by c#, we use the built in encrypt and decrypt function and call them for encryption and decryption of data respectively. **Supported Providers.** To save the encrypted data almost all of the tools support OneDrive, Dropbox, Google Drive, SkyDrive etc. as Cloud Service Provider as well as local memory. **Supported Platforms.** Almost all of the support all types of windows platform likes Windows 7, Windows 8, Windows 8.1, Windows 10 and Linux. **Authentication.** The encrypt data can be decrypted by only authenticated person. **Offline Encryption.** Offline encryption is available. **Key management.** Key management is a common feature for all the tools consider in our discussion.

6 Result Analysis

6.1 Evaluation Table of Data Read Time

After installing the CoolTerm software, we took 256 KB, 512 KB, 1 MB, 2 MB, 3 MB and 5 MB sizes of data for reading them with the help of sensor as shown in Table 3. The average read time of CoolTerm is 5.06 s (from Table 1) (Fig. 5).

6.2   Graphical Representation of Data Read Time

A graphical representation of the data read time is given below.

6.3   Evaluation Table of Encryption Time

After installing the Encrypt Decrypt software, we took 256 KB, 512 KB, 1 MB, 2 MB, 3 MB and 5 MB sizes of data for encryption them with the help of Encrypt Decrypt software. The average encryption time of Encrypt decrypt is 4.18 s (from Table 2).

Table 1. Data read time.

Data size (KB)	Read time (sec)	Average data size (KB)	Average read time (sec)
256	1.7	1382.4	5.06
512	3		
1024	4.9		
2048	7.3		
3072	8.4		

6.4   Graphical Representation of Encryption Time

A graphical representation of the encryption time is given on Fig. 6.

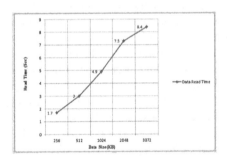
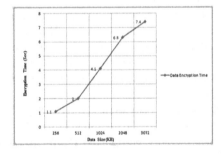

Fig. 5. Data read time for different data size

Fig. 6. Data encryption time for different data size.

6.5   Evaluation Table of Decryption Time

After installing the Encrypt Decrypt software, we took 256 KB, 512 KB, 1 MB, 2 MB, 3 MB and 5 MB sizes of data for decryption them with the help of Encrypt Decrypt software. The average decryption time of Encrypt decrypt is 4.18 s (from Table 2).

Table 2. Data encryption time

Data size (KB)	Read time (sec)	Average data size (KB)	Average read time (sec)
256	1.1	1382.4	4.18
512	2		
1024	4.1		
2048	6.3		
3072	7.4		

Table 3. Data decryption time.

Data size (KB)	Read time (sec)	Average data size (KB)	Average read time (sec)
256	1.3	1382.4	4.24
512	2.1		
1024	4		
2048	6.2		
3072	7.6		

7 Performance Analysis

7.1 User Efficiencies Performance

To drive the advantages of the, we have tried to analyze the advantages and disadvantages of different types of previous system. The analysis part is made on some important criteria like ways of ensuring reading data security, information leakage probability, complexity, cost of establishing and maintaining, user authentication, execution time etc. This system is mainly release the cloning and information stealing threats. From the following comparative analysis, we can see that system is user friendly, cost effective and ensures higher security than the available system in RFID card security system. **Disadvantages of the system:** (1) Tag collision occurs when many tags are present in a small area; but since the read time is very fast, it is easier for vendors to develop systems that ensure that tags respond one at a time. (2) The establishment of this system is quite expensive. (3) This system does not establish protection against application layer and communication layer threats. (4) For extra security the system always needs internet connection (Table 4).

7.2 Run Time Performance

Analyzing to the previous system, measuring read runtime we took 256 KB, 512 KB, 1 MB, 2 MB and 3 MB sizes of data for encryption and got 1.9, 3.2, 5.2, 8.2 and 9.2 (sec) respectively. Similarly, for encryption and decryption runtime we got 1.4, 2.2, 4.2, 6.4, 7.8 and 1.3, 2.1, 4.2, 6.2, 8 (sec) respectively. Comparing the previous and our proposed system it is seen to be that the proposed system is little bit faster than previous (Figs. 7 and 8).

Table 4. Performances.

Points of discussion	The system performance
Ensuring reading data	High
Information leakage probability	Small
Complexity	Small
Cost of establishing	Medium
User authentication	Medium
Execution time	Medium
Prevent card cloning	High
Prevent other social engineering attacks	Medium
Ensuring reading data	High
Information leakage probability	Small

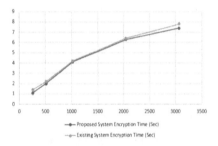

Fig. 7. Comparing encryption time.   **Fig. 8.** Comparing read time.

8   Future Work

We proposed a conceptual framework to alleviate the challenges facing RFID card; unauthorized usage of Card in particular. This conception will be fully implemented in application area in our future research, and will be evaluated in line with the various versed attacks and strategies. With our new concept, we use RFID card system. But this concept is also possible to add to the magnetic card system [18]. As a result, smart and credit cards system will be also secure through this research.

9   Conclusion

Many protection mechanisms have already been proposed to shield RFID structures in opposition to possible assaults. In this research, we identified the several challenges facing RFID Card. Especially we highlighted the different application field of the RFID technology as well as some feasible area of its application. We have established strong security based on encryption method. Besides we tried to keep better operation runtime. Comparing our proposed system with existing system, we have satisfied with both parameters such as system authentication security and operational runtime. In the case of security, the system is relatively secured for excluding the biometric system and for running the operation behind the windows. In the case of runtime, the system's required time is much better than the existing.

References

1. Juels, A.: Minimalist cryptography for low-cost RFID tags (extended abstract). In: Blundo, C., Cimato, S. (eds.) SCN 2004. LNCS, vol. 3352, pp. 149–164. Springer, Heidelberg (2005). https://doi.org/10.1007/978-3-540-30598-9_11
2. Kinoshita, S., Hoshino, F., Komuro, T., Fujimura, A., Ookubo, M.: Non identifiable anonymous-ID scheme for RFID privacy protection. 情報処理学会シンポジウム論文集 **2003**(15), 497–502 (2003)
3. Ikuesan, R.A., Norafida, B.I.: Users authentication and privacy control of RFID card. Department of Computer System and Communications, Faculty of Computer Science and Information Systems, Universiti Teknologi Malaysia, October 2012
4. Langheinrich, M.: RFID and privacy (Chap. 28). In: Petković, M., Jonker, W. (eds.) Security, Privacy, and Trust in Modern Data Management, pp. 433–450. Springer, Heidelberg (2017). https://doi.org/10.1007/978-3-540-69861-6_28
5. Mitrokotsa, A., Rieback, M.R., Tanenbaum, A.S.: Classification of RFID attacks. In: Proceedings of 2nd International Workshop on RFID Technology - Concepts, Applications, Challenges, Porto, Portugal, pp. 73–86, September 2008
6. Ohkubo, M., Suzuki, K., Kinoshita, S.: RFID privacy issues and technical challenges. Commun. ACM - ACM Digit. Libr. **48**(9), 66–71 (2005)
7. Yusof, M.K., Saman, M.Y.: The adoption and implementation of RFID: a literature survey. LIBRES **26**(1), 31–52 (2016)
8. Marci, M., King, J., Mulligan, D.K.: Security and privacy risks of embedded RFID in everyday things: the e-Passport and beyond. J. Commun. **2**(7), 36–48 (2007)
9. Chawla, K., Robins, G.: An RFID-based object localisation framework. Int. J. Radio Freq. Identif. Technol. Appl. **3**(1/2), 36–48 (2011)
10. Vollmer, B.C.: Biometrics, RFID technology, and the epassport: are Americans risking personal security in the face of terrorism?. Thesis, Master of Arts in Communication, Culture and Technology, Graduate School of Arts and Sciences, Georgetown University, Washington DC (2006)
11. Ravi, K.S., Varun, G.H., Vamsi, T., Pratyusha, P.: RFID based security system. Int. J. Innov. Technol. Explor. Eng. (IJITEE) **2**(5) (2013)
12. Wang, H.W.: Efficient DFSA algorithm in RFID systems for the internet of things. Mob. Inf. Syst. **2015** (2015)
13. Li, C., Qi, J.: A two-factor authentication design of fingerprint recognition system based on DSP and RF card. In: Proceedings of 2nd International Conference on Computer and Automation Engineering (ICCAE), Singapore, February 2010
14. Mitrokotsa, A., Rieback, M.R., Tanenbaum, A.S.: Classifying RFID attacks and defenses. Inf. Syst. Front. **12**(5), 446–453 (2010)
15. Qian, Q., Jia, Y.-L., Zhang, R.: A lightweight RFID security protocol based on elliptic curve cryptography. Int. J. Netw. Secur. **18**(2), 354–361 (2016)
16. Wang, S.P., Ma, Q.M., Zhang, Y.L., Li, Y.S.: An authentication protocol for RFID tag and its simulation. J. Netw. **18**(2), 446–453 (2011)
17. Nehete, P.R., Chaudhari, J.P., Pachpande, S.R., Rane, K.P.: Literature survey on door lock security systems. Int. J. Comput. Appl. **153**(2) (2016)

18. Banu Priya, R., Kavitha, P., Ashok, T., Logesh Kumar, N.C.M.: Smart ATM access and security system using RFID and GSM technology. Int. J. Innov. Technol. Explor. Eng. (IJITEE) **2**(5), 446–453 (2013)
19. Loukaka, A., Rahman, S.: Discovering new cyber protection approaches from a security professional prospective. Int. J. Comput. Netw. Commun. (IJCNC) **9**(4) (2017)
20. Al-Mamun, A., Rahman, S., et al.: Security analysis of AES and enhancing its security by modifying S-box with an additional byte. Int. J. Comput. Netw. Commun. (IJCNC) **9**(2) (2017)
21. Opala, O.J., Rahman, S., Alelaiwi, A.: The influence of information security on the adoption of cloud computing: an exploratory analysis. Int. J. Comput. Netw. Commun. (IJCNC) **7**(4) (2015)

Grouping Users for Quick Recommendations of Text Documents Based on Deep Neural Network

Rajendran Karthika[1]([⊠]), Lazarus Jegatha Deborah[1],
Pandi Vijayakumar[1], and Sivaraman Audithan[2]

[1] University College of Engineering Tindivanam,
Tindivanam 604001, Tamil Nadu, India
karti.rn@gmail.com, blessedjeny@gmail.com,
vijibond2000@gmail.com
[2] Sri Aravindar Engineering College, Villupuram 605109, Tamil Nadu, India
saudithan@gmail.com

Abstract. The use of Recommendation Systems in any domain plays a vital role in almost all information technology applications. The major focus of this research paper deals with users more preferably e-learners using the proposed Recommendation system. The major objective in developing any Recommendation system is based on many factors like accuracy, preciseness and fast measures. Recommendations given to each user is based on his/her domain interest was time consuming in the past. This research paper deals with the development of a recommendation system which is based on accuracy and fastness measures. One of the factors for developing a fast recommendation system can be obtained by developing efficient algorithms for grouping the existing and the new users quickly so that further domain recommendations might be easier. The proposed framework is based on deep neural network, which proved to be an efficient algorithm for high dimensional data training and testing. The accuracy of the algorithm is justified by the generation of semantic hash codes generated from the users' profile information and the subsequent hamming distance computation. The fast and the accuracy measures of the framework is justified and the experimental results are promising.

Keywords: Recommendation Systems · Users · Deep neural network
Semantic hash codes · Hamming distance

1 Introduction

Recommendation Systems (RS) play a vital role in e-commerce. RS recommends an item based on the users interest or preferences taken from the past rating history for the items. E-commerce sites make use of RS in order to retain the customers for purchasing their products, to cross-sell their products and to customize i.e. to adapt a product or an item to specific users. RS can be categorized into three types, namely collaborative filtering RS, content-based filtering RS and hybrid RS [1]. Content based filtering RS makes use of both the user profile information and the past history of purchasing items

© Springer International Publishing AG 2017
G. Wang et al. (Eds.): SpaCCS 2017 Workshops, LNCS 10658, pp. 617–626, 2017.
https://doi.org/10.1007/978-3-319-72395-2_56

or the items he liked the most. The items are compared to extract the features that are similar in those items. Based on this, the recommendation for an item is suggested to the user. Among the different types of RS, collaborative filtering RS ranks first in its popularity and implementation. Collaborative filtering RS compares the users with similar wavelength and recommends the item based on the items purchased by the other users who have the same taste. The users who have same wavelength in purchasing the items will come under a common group called a neighborhood. Hence a particular user will get a recommendation for an item, if the item is purchased or rated high for the users in his neighborhood. User profile information can be analyzed semantically to group them according to their interest. The time taken for grouping the users can be greatly minimized by converting the user profile information into semantic hash codes. The hash code can be compared with the codes available in the database using hamming distance measure and the user can be grouped easily. This grouping of users based on the profile information will help in recommending the text documents to the corresponding user fastly and accurately.

This paper focuses on categorizing the users based on the profile information given by them regarding their subject interest or the area of specialization to recommend the relevant documents very quickly according to their need. The profile information given by the user is stored in a database. Before processing the profile information, the relevant attributes from the user profile must be extracted to continue the further processing. To extract the relevant features, feature selection is done on the dataset to remove the irrelevant and redundant features [2]. This paper uses the booster algorithm [3] for selecting the subset of features that are strongly relevant with the help of a feature selection algorithm. After selecting the relevant attributes from the user profile, semantic hashing is done using the deep neural networks (DNN). Conventional information retrieval techniques, namely TF-IDF [4, 5], LSA [6] and LDA [7] have made many improvements for retrieving the relevant documents from the document corpus in a more efficient manner. Later, the semantic hashing technique has been proposed by [8] for retrieving the documents which converts the semantics of the document into a binary code. Semantic hashing uses a deep neural network for hashing the user profile vector to binary vector and to classify and label the users with the help of binary vectors. Semantic hashing is an information retrieval technique which converts high-dimensional user profile vector into low-dimensional binary vector. The main advantage of using semantic hashing is that the user profile information can be represented as a compact binary code which enables to classify the user according to their domain interest and the text documents can be recommended quickly and accurately to their respective groups.

The deep neural network consists of three layers of auto-encoder to implement semantic hashing for user profile information. Auto encoder [9] is an artificial neural network that belongs to unsupervised machine learning algorithm. Due to the absence of class labels in unsupervised learning, the network learns the features automatically from the unlabeled data. Auto-encoder as its name suggests, consists of both an encoder and a decoder. In the neural network [10], which consists of three layers, input layer to the hidden layer forms the encoder and hidden layer to the output layer forms the decoder. Softmax classifier is a supervised machine learning algorithm which is used to predict the class labels for the given user profile information.

The major objectives of the proposed framework is as follows.

- Feature selection on user profile dataset using booster algorithm.
- Converting the user profile vector to compact binary hash codes using deep neural network learning algorithm.
- Softmax classifier is used to predict the class label of user's profile for the training data.
- Hamming distance calculation between the test data and trained data hash codes in order to predict the class labels of test data.

This paper is structured as follows. Section 2 presents the survey of the related works. Section 3 describes about the proposed framework in a detailed manner. Section 4 gives the performance analysis of the proposed framework. Finally, we discuss the conclusion and future work in Sect. 5.

2 Related Works

Feature selection is the most preliminary step in the data mining process. The features can be discrete or continuous in nature [11]. If the features in the data set have continuous values, then before preprocessing the data in the dataset, firstly the continuous data values must be converted to discrete values. Extraction of relevant features from the high dimensional data set will be easier for the discrete data when compared to continuous data. Fast clustering based feature Selection algorithm (FAST) [12] is used to select the most relevant attributes by removing the irrelevant and redundant attributes from the dataset. FAST is the most recent feature selection algorithm found in the survey and it removes the redundant attributes with the help of minimum spanning tree construction. The FAST algorithm selects the best representative features and it also increases the classification accuracy.

Salakhutdinov and Hinton [8] developed a graphical model which performs the semantic hashing for lengthy documents based on the Restricted Boltzmann Machines (RBM). Instead of applying the TF-IDF directly to the document corpus, first apply the semantic hashing to the document corpus, which removes the unwanted documents and then perform TF_IDF to improve the accuracy. The drawback of RBM based semantic hashing is that, they are generative models and the training phase is more complicated and time consuming. Artificial neural networks can be trained with the help of backpropagation algorithm [13]. Backpropagation is a supervised learning algorithm which knows the desired output and it is compared with the output of the network to calculate the error. To minimize the errors, the weight and the bias values are adjusted and trained. Feng et al. [14] introduced the Deep Hash (DH) method which uses the both stacked RBM and Gaussian RBM (GRBM) for the pre training stage and supervised machine learning algorithm for the fine tuning stage to predict the class labels. The drawback of this approach is that it increases the training time and the evaluation time. Nguyen and Do [15] introduced a new method, namely Supervised Ranking-based Hashing (SRH) which represents the semantically similar neighbors of the converted binary hash codes effectively in the binary space.

Guan et al. [16] proposed a graph-based learning framework called Multi-type Interrelated Objects Embedding (MIOE). In this work, the author focused on social tagging data instead of user rating data to recommend the text documents. Habibi and Popescu-Belis [17] proposed to recommend the documents by getting the implicit queries based on the short conversations. Nagori and Aghila [18] proposed Latent Dirichlet Allocation topic modeling technique to recommend the documents to the e-learners based on their need.

The analysis of the review clearly shows that when a user profile is analyzed semantically and converted to binary hash codes, then grouping of users based on their interest or specialization can be done effectively. User profile feature selection is done with the help of the booster algorithm to select the strongly relevant features or attributes. Later the user profile vector is converted to binary hash codes with the help of deep neural network in the pre training stage followed by the class label prediction using the softmax classifier in the fine tuning stage. In the previous works, RBM performs semantic hashing, but it does not retrieve the abstract features and the complex correlations between the features.

3 Proposed Framework

The architecture of the proposed system is shown in Fig. 1. Large amounts of data gets accumulated and stored in the databases in day to day life that are high dimensional in nature. The data mining task is used to excavate the useful information from the high dimensional data. Data mining involves exploring the hidden and indeed valuable information from large data sets. Feature selection is the basic preprocessing step in high dimensional data. Feature selection removes the irrelevant and redundant feature from the data set [19]. The irrelevant feature must be removed from the data set because it decreases the accuracy of the classifier. The redundant feature should be eliminated since the same information is repeated in some other feature, and it does not contribute for classification or clustering. Learner profile information consists of his personal details such as name, age, address etc. as well as the area of interest or the specialization. Each and every user profile information consist of so many attributes and all user's profile information are stored in a database.

3.1 Profile Feature Selection

Booster [3] takes the feature selection algorithm, the dataset and the number of partitions as input. Booster uses the most recent feature selection algorithm called Fast clustering based feature Selection algorithm (FAST) [12]. This booster technique partition the data set based on the resampling technique. The feature selection algorithm is applied to each partitioned data set to obtain the subset of features. Finally the union of all feature subsets of the partitioned data set gives the most strongly relevant features. The algorithm is given below.

Algorithm: Booster

Input: Data set D, Feature Subset Selection algorithm f and the number of partitions m.

Output: Selected feature subset U*.

Step 1: Partition the data set D into m sets.

Step 2: Assign U* to NULL.

Step 3: For each partition do the following steps.

Step 4: Subract the partitioned set Dj from the original data set D.

Step 5: Apply the feature subset selection algorithm to the result of the previous step.

Step 6: The selected features are added to the set U* by union operation.

Step 7: Repeat steps 4 and 5 for all the partitions.

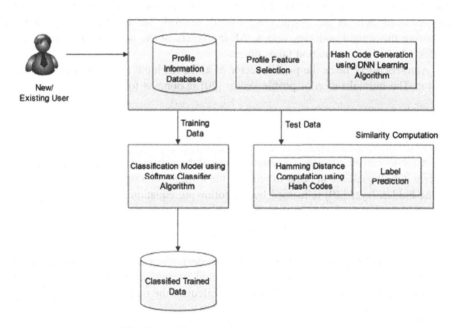

Fig. 1. Architecture of the proposed system.

From this algorithm, we come to know that by applying the feature subset selection algorithm f on the partitioned set, we get the relevant features from the subsets $U_1, \ldots, U_m$, where redundancies are removed, and hence U* will include more relevant features by eliminating redundancies from the set. So, U* will not contain a larger number of irrelevant features. For Booster to be effective, the number of partitions m plays an important role. If m is large, then it finds a large number of strongly relevant features. But the problem is that it will also have irrelevant features, which in turn will include more redundant features. The reason is that none of the feature selection algorithms can select every strongly relevant feature by discarding all irrelevant features and redundant features. Moreover, if m is too large, then it increases the computational complexity as well. But, if m is too small, then it may not include strongly relevant features for classification.

3.2   Hash Code Generation Using DNN Learning Algorithm

The deep neural network is an artificial neural network composed of several layers. Since the network has two or more hidden layers, the network is considered as deep neural network. Apart from the hidden layers, the network consists of an input layer and an output layer. The profile vector of a user is given as an input to the input layer and the hashed binary code is produced as output from the output layer.

Here we consider the deep neural network as a stacked three auto-encoders namely auto-encoder1, auto-encoder2 and auto-encoder3. The input layer and the hidden layer1 forms the auto-encoder1, the hidden layer1 and hidden layer2 forms the auto-encoder2, the hidden layer2 and output layer forms the auto-encoder3. Each and every auto-encoder acts as an independent neural network for training the features by adjusting the weight and bias values. All the layers in the network are composed of nodes where the computation takes place.

Auto-encoder1 takes the profile vector of a user as input and normalizes the input vector. The normalization of profile vector [20] is done as follows:

$$v_j = \frac{x_j}{\sum_{n=1}^{k} x_n} \tag{1}$$

After normalizing the input vector the sum of the values of all the nodes in the input layer will be equal to 1 in order to proceed the learning in a stable manner. The feature in the hidden layer [20] is learned by the following equation:

$$h_j = \propto (b_j + \sum_k w_{jk} v_k) \tag{2}$$

After completing the training of auto-encoder1, the output of the auto-encoder1, that is the hidden layer features is considered as the input to the auto-encoder2. Auto-encoder2 uses the sigmoid function to calculate the output value. $\propto$ is a sigmoid function [21], which is

$$y = \propto(x) = 1/(1 + e^{-x}) \tag{3}$$

The error is calculated to train the network through backpropagation algorithm and update the weight and bias values. The sum of squared error [20] is given as follows:

$$J = \frac{1}{2} \sum_i (o_i - v_i)^2 \tag{4}$$

Auto-encoder2 acts as a transition layer which performs the dimensionality reduction in order to reduce the features. If the number of hidden layers is increased in the deep neural network, it leads to the increase in cost and the complexity of training time. Auto-encoder3 is a denoising auto-encoder which takes the corrupted hidden feature as input and is learned through training to predict the original features from the input.

The deep neural network is used to convert the input user profile vector into hashed binary codes. Here threshold value is set to 0.5 to convert the output in terms of binary codes. The nodes in the output layer of the deep neural network will have the values such that if the output value is greater than 0.5 it is set to 1, otherwise it is set to 0.

3.3 Softmax Classifier Algorithm

In order to predict the class label of the learner, an activation function called a softmax classifier [20] is employed. It is a supervised machine learning algorithm which is used to predict the labels of unknown data. The output o_i for the node i is calculated as

$$o_i = \frac{\exp(a_i)}{\sum_{m=1}^{n} \exp(a_m)} \tag{5}$$

where $a_i = b_j + \sum_j w_{ij} h_j$. The softmax classifier is often used after the output layer of neural networks, which are applied to classification problems. Since it is a supervised learning algorithm, it can predict and assume the labels from the list of users. Further, the probability score is computed from the weight and bias values used in the back-propagation algorithm. Finally the label which has the highest score is denoted as the label of the particular user. Hence the training data can be assigned to the appropriate class label by training the user profile vector in the deep neural network followed by the softmax classifier as an activation function for classification.

3.4 Hamming Distance Computation for Hash Codes

The hamming distance measure is used to measure the similarity between two binary codes. The hamming distance is a number used to denote the difference between two binary strings. In this work, the training data are stored along with their class labels in the form of semantic hash codes. When test data is given to the deep neural network after the completion of the preprocessing, the DNN produces the semantic hash code. Now the test data semantic hash code is compared with the trained data hash code and it calculates the hamming distance between the hash codes to predict the class labels of the user for the given test data.

4 Performance Analysis

In the experimental analysis, we evaluate the performance of the preprocessed user profile information and the binary hash code generated by deep neural network learning algorithm. For the analysis we have taken 500 users as the total number of users out of which 350 users are used for training and 150 users are used for testing. The user profile feature selection and the hash code generation for user profile vector are done for both the training data and the test data. Later, the training data are trained using the supervised machine learning algorithm to predict the class labels for the binary hash codes of user profile and stored in a database. Now the binary hash code of the test data is compared with the hash codes stored in the database and hamming distance computation is done to predict the class label of the test data. The precision and recall [22] measure is given as follows.

$$Precision = \frac{number\ of\ relevant\ users\ who\ are\ correctly\ classified}{number\ of\ all\ retrieved\ users}$$

$$Recall = \frac{number\ of\ relevant\ users\ who\ are\ correctly\ classified}{number\ of\ all\ relevant\ users}$$

Here we compare the precision and recall value for the methods, RBM, DNN and P-DNN (proposed work) on grouping the users based on the semantic hash code generated from the profile information. RBM based semantic hashing produces the compact binary hash codes, but the training cost is high. DNN takes the user profile vector without performing the feature selection algorithm and converts to binary code. P-DNN performs the profile feature selection with the learner profile information and then converts the selected features into compact binary codes. P-DNN initially removes the irrelevant and redundant attributes from the learner profile information. Moreover, for the training data, it performs the conversion of user profile vector to binary hash codes in the pre training stage and assigns the corresponding label to hash code in the fine tuning stage using softmax classifier.

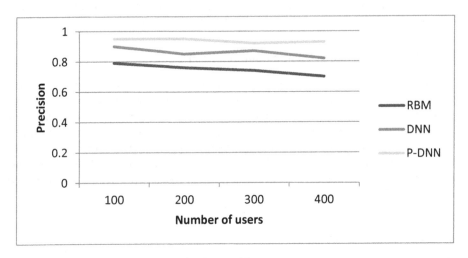

Fig. 2. Precision curve

Computation is greatly reduced for the test data because the hamming distance measure between the trained data and test data is used to predict the class labels of test data. Hence the precision and recall graph shown in Figs. 2 and 3 shows that P-DNN outperforms when compared to the RBM and DNN in grouping the users based on binary hash codes generated from the user profile vector.

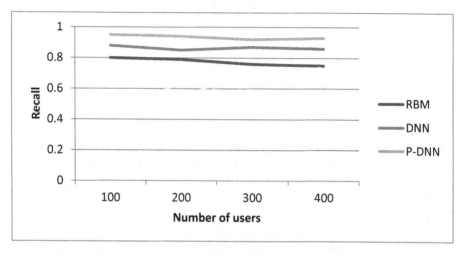

Fig. 3. Recall curve

5 Conclusion

In this research paper, we use the booster algorithm to select the strongly relevant features or attributes from the user profile. After performing the feature selection, the user profile vector is converted to binary hash codes using the deep neural network. Softmax classifier is used to predict the class labels of the binary hash codes for the training data. Moreover, the hamming distance computation of hashed binary code is done on the trained data and test data to predict the class label of the test data. This paper focuses on grouping the users based on their interest inferred from their profile information. Since the user profile information is represented as compact binary code, the grouping can be done effectively. Recommendation of text documents can be done accurately based on this grouping of users.

References

1. Devika, P., Jisha, R.C., Sajeev, G.P.: A novel approach for book recommendation systems. In: IEEE International Conference on Computational Intelligence and Computing Research (ICCIC), December 2016
2. Yu, L., Liu, H.: Efficient feature selection via analysis of relevance and redundancy. J. Mach. Learn. Res. **5**(2), 1205–1224 (2004)
3. Kim, H., Choi, B.S., Huh, M.Y.: Booster in high dimensional data classification. IEEE Trans. Knowl. Data Eng. **28**(1), 29–40 (2016)

4. Salton, G., Buckley, C.: Term-weighting approaches in automatic text retrieval. Inf. Process. Manag. **24**(5), 513–523 (1988)
5. Blei, D.M., Ng, A.Y., Jordan, M.I.: Latent Dirichlet allocation. J. Mach. Learn. Res. **3**, 993–1022 (2003)
6. Deerwester, S.C., Dumais, S.T., Landauer, T.K., Furnas, G.W., Harshman, R.A.: Indexing by latent semantic analysis. J. Am. Soc. Inf. Sci. **41**(6), 391–407 (1990)
7. Salton, G.: Developments in automatic text retrieval. Science **253**(5023), 974–980 (1991). http://www.jstor.org/stable/2878789
8. Salakhutdinov, R., Hinton, G.E.: Semantic hashing. Int. J. Approx. Reason. **50**(7), 969–978 (2009)
9. Bengio, Y.: Learning deep architectures for AI. Found. Trends Mach. Learn. **2**(1), 1–127 (2009)
10. Anderson, J.A., Davis, J.: An Introduction to Neural Networks. MIT Press, Cambridge (1995)
11. Hu, Q., Zhang, L., Zhang, D., Pan, W., An, S., Pedrycz, W.: Measuring relevance between discrete and continuous features based on neighborhood mutual information. Expert Syst. Appl. **38**(9), 10737–10750 (2011)
12. Song, Q., Ni, J., Wang, G.: A fast clustering-based feature subset selection algorithm for high-dimensional data. IEEE Trans. Knowl. Data Eng. **25**(1), 1–14 (2013)
13. Rumelhart, D.E., Hinton, G.E., Williams, R.J.: Learning representations by back-propagating errors. Nature **323**, 533–536 (1986)
14. Feng, W., Jia, B., Zhu, M.: Deep hash: semantic similarity preserved hash scheme. IET Electron. Lett. **50**, 1347–1349 (2014)
15. Nguyen, V.-A., Do, M.N.: Binary code learning with semantic ranking based supervision. In: IEEE International Conference on Acoustics, Speech and Signal Processing (ICASSP), May 2016
16. Guan, Z., Wang, C., Bu, J., Chen, C., Yang, K., Cai, D., He, X.: Document recommendation in social tagging services. In: Proceedings of 19th International Conference on World Wide Web, pp. 391–400, April 2010
17. Habibi, M., Popescu-Belis, A.: Keyword extraction and clustering for document recommendation in conversations. IEEE/ACM Trans. Audio Speech Lang. Process. **23**(4), 746–759 (2015)
18. Nagori, R., Aghila, G.: LDA based integrated document recommendation model for e-learning systems. In: International Conference on Emerging Trends in Networks and Computer Communications (ETNCC), pp. 230–233 (2011)
19. Guyon, I., Elisseeff, A.: An introduction to variable and feature selection. J. Mach. Learn. Res. **3**, 1157–1182 (2003)
20. Zheng, Yu., Wang, H., Lin, X., Wang, M.: Understanding short texts through semantic enrichment and hashing. IEEE Trans. Knowl. Data Eng. **28**(2), 566–579 (2016)
21. Han, J., Moraga, C.: The influence of the sigmoid function parameters on the speed of backpropagation learning. In: Proceedings of International Workshop Artificial Neural Computation: From Natural Artificial Neural Computation, pp. 195–201 (1995)
22. Manning, C.D., Raghavan, P., Sch€utze, H.: Introduction to Information Retrieval. Cambridge University, Cambridge (2008)

Module-Level Software Streaming Loading Model Based on Hypervisor

Lian Duan[1], Fang Qi[1], Guojun Wang[2], and Zhe Tang[1(✉)]

[1] School of Information Science and Engineering, Central South University,
Changsha 410083, China
tz@csu.edu.cn
[2] School of Computer Science and Educational Software, Guangzhou University,
Guangzhou 510006, China

Abstract. In the existing network computing system, the increasingly serious performance problems and endless security problems constantly troubled users and developers. Although the emergence of transparent computing, edge computing and fog computing alleviates this situation to some extent, they still do not fully utilize the collaborative computing power of server side and end-user. In order to address these problems, a new computing and loading model based on hypervisor, which is also called module-level software streaming loading model, will be introduced in this paper. Besides, Cleanroom Protocol and On-demand Prefetching Mechanism will be discussed in this paper. Based on this model, the system does not need to wait for OS or software data download completely when a device or a program to startup. It means the corresponding services can be immediately directly used or accessed by users. This solution can effectively reduce the waiting time for users and improve the user experience. Through a variety of comparative analyses, this model is proved to be an efficient and safe solution for the future computing and loading infrastructure.

Keywords: High-performance computing · Streaming loading
Hypervisor · Cleanroom Protocol · Prefetching

1 Introduction

In recent years, with the rapid developments in mobile Internet technology, the cloud computing, Internet of Things (IoT) and big data have become the main representative to network computing model. They utilize network as a transmission medium to expand the service capability of the end-users and achieve the purposes of on-demand service sharing.

However, due to intensive demands of computing, storage and network bandwidth resources from users, the current commonly used network computing model is easy to become a performance bottleneck. For example, cloud computing causes cloud server to be a performance bottleneck because of both computation and storage centralized in cloud side. Transparent computing uses the network to separate computing and storage, and allocates the calculations

© Springer International Publishing AG 2017
G. Wang et al. (Eds.): SpaCCS 2017 Workshops, LNCS 10658, pp. 627–636, 2017.
https://doi.org/10.1007/978-3-319-72395-2_57

to each terminal by block-level software streaming loading [1]. Although it can sharply reduce the cost of software management and greatly improve the performance, it requires higher network bandwidth to support its communication. Therefore, we need to research more efficient network computing model to make full use of the advantages of cloud computing and transparent computing and abandon its shortcomings to provide users with efficient service.

In the current network computing model, another big problem is that if the cloud server is damaged that will affect the user services on a large scale. Malicious attack and monitor from the cloud server can also lead to the risk of security and privacy in the user service process. In addition, users lack the ability to directly control the computing environment so that it is hard for users to trust the services provided in the network computing environment. To a certain extent, although current trust computing technology can ensure the safety and reliability when the computing resources start, the security of network computing environment is still difficult to be guaranteed when system is running.

In order to address these challenges, in this paper, we propose a new computing and loading model, which is named as module-level software streaming loading model based on hypervisor. The core idea of this model is to dynamically and safely provide services with software deployment, loading and implementation. And there is a novel protocol that called Cleanroom Protocol to be introduced. This protocol can effectively ensure the safety of entire system.

The rest of the paper is organized as follows. Section 2 discusses the related works. In Sect. 3, we introduce the module-level software streaming loading model, including hypervisor, Cleanroom Protocol, On-demand Prefetching Mechanism and the architecture of loading model. The performance analysis and security analysis are presented in the Sect. 4 and conclusion of this research is made in Sect. 5.

2 Related Work

In this context, we observed that whether the operating systems and application software can be quickly loaded and run smoothly becomes an important issue for software to deliver high-quality service operations. There is extensive research in this area.

Ming [2] has realized the operating system remotely loading on UEFI (Unified Extensible Firmware Interface), which defines the interface between the operating system and platform firmware and abstracts the underlying hardware platform. It has proposed that remote loading schemes of full virtualization, parts of virtualization and no virtualization for PCs' operating systems in the cable network environment. The OSes' boot time and I/O performance of these schemes are compared and analyzed in this document. Apart from this, the author also proposed the remote loading scheme of tablet PCs' (tablet personal computer) OSes in the wireless network environment.

The document [3] presents a distributed remote loading technology for operating system based on P2P technology. This technology can improve the server's overload problem when concurrent requests of loading OS. And it is different from other P2P network load technology which deployed on the operating system. In fact, it is a distributed operating system loading technology using BitTorrent-like protocol on the network bootloader that under the operating system. They deployed the download scheme based on iPXE, and then analyzed the loading time of different dynamic file size and different node numbers. Moreover, compared it with the existing loading protocols like TFTP, HTTP and come to the conclusion of P2P is superior to TFTP and HTTP. Accordingly, this scheme effectively improved the loading speed and addressed the server's overload problem. Although the two schemes mentioned above are solved the issue of loading operating system, the software applications remote loading is still a bottleneck.

Of course, there also have numerous studies on safe loading. Malware can escape the security monitoring programs by hiding their own behavior. Document [6] proposed an operating system hidden object association detection method based on virtual machine monitor. And the corresponding detection system are designed and implemented in this paper. Moreover, they set up the associated relationship of hidden objects to identify the complete attack path based on the operating system semantics. But this type of method needs to find the malicious behaviors by comparing the system semantics, so it is difficult to determine the equivalence relation between semantics and logic in the practical application.

The operating system vulnerabilities are often exploited by attackers, who then execute malicious code with kernel authority to steal user data. In order to build the memory-access-review mechanism of operating systems and applications, Ren et al. [7] came up with a low performance overhead and cannot be bypassed of memory page using information real-time tracking strategy. But this method cannot monitor the problem of malicious directly reading memory devices. In general, the current research schemes are still have many deficiencies such as the safety standards are difficult to develop, the complex deployment of security policies and the limited scope of the monitoring.

3 Module-Level Software Streaming Loading Model Based on Hypervisor

In this section, the hypervisor, the Cleanroom Protocol and the On-demand Prefetching Mechanism are introduced. And the brief architecture of the module-level software streaming loading model is presented.

3.1 Hypervisor

The goal of this research is to understand the remote loading of module-level software streaming based on the virtual machine environment. So it is designed based on hypervisor in this architecture, which is a virtual machine monitor. The hypervisor is an intermediate software layer that runs between the underlying physical server and the operating system. It allows multiple operating systems and applications to share hardware [22]. In the current situation, the hypervisor is mostly installed on the server, while in our architecture as shown in Fig. 1 it is used as a terminal rather than a server.

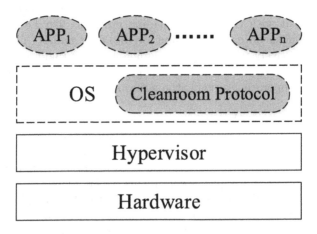

Fig. 1. The architecture of hypervisor

The hypervisor beneath the operating system, but it can startup, manage, and serve the operating systems and the application software. There are three basic features can be observed in the hypervisor. The first one is that it can offer choices of operating systems and load it to the client. Besides, it can load Cleanroom Protocol and it can also load desired software modules to users.

3.2 Cleanroom Protocol

In terms of security monitoring, there are still some safety problems which are difficult to be addressed. It is because of the limited scope of the monitoring, the complex deployment of security policies and other deficiencies.

Therefore, the Cleanroom Protocol, one of the novel protocols, is introduced to achieve the security of streaming computing and loading. It includes the system event intercept, the software feature extraction, the software feature analysis and other security monitoring technology. Both the server and the end-user construct the Cleanroom Protocol, the executable program and the prohibited program for users based on users' computing resources, which can effectively ensure the safety of the software streaming loading. Figure 2 lists the main steps involved in the software streaming monitor process.

As shown in this figure, when cloud server or the user terminal issues a request to start an application, the operating system will generate a user interrupt and switch the state from the user state to the kernel state. Map the addresses in

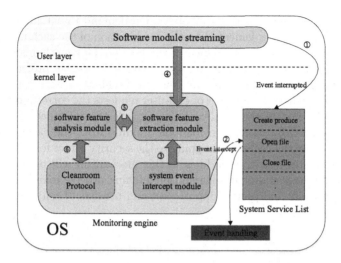

Fig. 2. The software module streaming monitor process

the system service list to the monitoring engine, such as SSDT (System Services Descriptor Table) in the Windows system and SCT (System Call Table) in the Linux system, then the system service access requests are monitored and filtered by monitoring engine. Specifically, at first, before the operating system kernel processes the startup requests of software, the system event intercept module resides in the monitoring engine is start the interceptor to capture the process information. And then, the process information is sent to the software feature extraction module to extract the features. Afterwards, the software feature extraction module extracts the signatures of activating application from the software module streaming according to the captured process information. The following is that send it to the software feature analysis module and compare it with the security policies of Cleanroom Protocol. Only the application software that conforms to the Cleanroom Protocol can run on the cloud server and the user terminal platform. Once the software runs while it isn't comply with the agreement, the system will terminate the running process of this software to eliminate the security risks of system.

3.3   On-demand Prefetching Mechanism

As stated previously, a flexible prefetching mechanism must be developed to improve the user experience and reduce network communication overheads. With the prefetching mechanism, the user can directly start the virtual machine in the client which has not cache any disk block, and does not need to wait for the virtual disk image to be completely transferred from the server to the client. At the same time, the prefetching mechanism can provide the virtual machine with better local operating performance.

To investigate the idea as stated above, On-demand Prefetching Mechanism, a mechanism mainly implemented by the combination of the caching process and the prefetching process, is developed in this model. This mechanism is different from any current prefetching mechanism such as block-level prefetching or file-level prefetching, since it is a module-level prefetching.

Specifically, when cloud server or end-user requests the corresponding services of this module, first in the local cache to retrieve the existence of module that currently required by user, then load the module from the cache if there is a desired module in the cache, or mapping to the security server for remote loading. Figure 3 illustrates how the modules in this mechanism will be loaded to end-user. This software module on-demand prefetching process mainly implemented by caching process and prefetching process and consists of ten main steps.

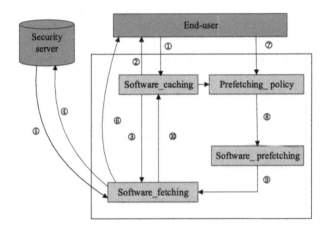

Fig. 3. Software module On-demand Prefetching process

The caching process:
① means inquire cache to request the desired software module.
② refers to the corresponding software module has been successfully queried and returned this module to end-user.
③④⑤⑥ refer to desired software module is not in the cache, then Software_fetching module retrieve the software module from the security server via internet to satisfy the needs of end-user.
⑩ writes the fetched software module to the cache.

The prefetching process:
⑦ means trigger prefetching mechanism when there is no require of software modules.
⑧ means prefetch the software modules according to the prefetching policy.
⑨④⑤⑩ write the prefetched software modules to cache.

3.4   Architecture

The objective of streaming loading is meeting user demands for any service, at any time and in anywhere. In addition, users do not need to install the software, just to use them directly, and the use experience has no difference with the native applications. The device can be a computer, a tablet or a mobile phone, and do not need to install the operating system that just a barely machine equipment. In such a model, basic system (including system kernel and basic application software), application software and Cleanroom Protocol are stored in the security server. The system does not need to wait for OS or software data download completely when a device and a program to startup. It means the corresponding services can be immediately directly used or accessed by users. The brief architecture of module-level software streaming loading model can be illustrated in Fig. 4.

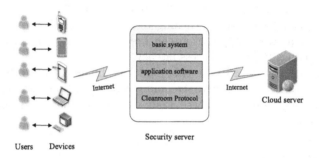

Fig. 4. The brief architecture of module-level software streaming loading model

This model actually refers to when the user terminal or cloud server request operating systems and applications, they are in the form of software module load to the client or cloud server. Besides, an On-demand Prefetching Mechanism consists of caching process and prefetching process will be implemented in this model. That is to say, what do you demand to load what, which is a good way to reduce the time overhead and memory usage. And all OSes and application software are filtered through the Cleanroom Protocol, all operations are performed under the Cleanroom Protocol to guarantee the safety of the loading process. These method can effectively reduce the waiting time of users to improve the user experience and enhance the security of the system.

4   Analysis of Model

Many types of models and frameworks for software streaming loading and computing can be found in the existing literatures and journals. However, these models can only load one of the operating systems and software so as to cause low performance. Besides, sometimes they cannot ensure the computer safety. The analysis of the performance and the security are discussed in this section.

4.1 Performance Analysis

Despite the adequate study in this area, the existing models do not offer dynamic and integral services for users. Hence, through a large number of comparative analyses, several advantages of the performance of this model are illustrated below compared with the traditional loading model.

Firstly, the system based on hypervisor is a virtual machine monitor. The current hypervisor runs on the server side while the hypervisor in this model runs on the terminal. It will change the traditional usage of hypervisor and make significant impact on software developer.

Furthermore, it can establish On-demand Prefetching Mechanism to predict future software module requests. This mechanism is mainly implemented by the combination of the caching and the prefetching process. What is more, the objective of the prefetching and caching is the module instead of the block. It can be observed that the cache hit rate increases from 24%–45% to 60%–70% and the user access latency reduces from 26% to 57% through the cooperation of the prefetching technology and the caching technology [14]. Thus, the prefetching technology in the cache application can break the limitation of cache hit rate and greatly reduce the users' access latency.

It should be mentioned that this model is different from other streaming loading models since the software streaming is based on software modules rather than software blocks or files. These analyses indicate that our proposed model is more efficient.

4.2 Security Analysis

The most novelty part is the Cleanroom Protocol in this research. Firstly, the Cleanroom Protocol works in the context of software streaming loading. The security server includes OSes and the application software, which are all certified for the safety. Only after the validation of security server, the application software can run properly. Therefore, the safety problems can be solved by creating this safe environment.

Besides, the process of security monitoring includes the system event intercept, the software feature extraction, the software feature analysis, and other security monitoring technology. During the system execution, the Cleanroom Protocol will kill the process once the abnormal process occurs. Thus, the higher level of security of this model can be proved.

5   Conclusion

This paper presents a module-level software streaming loading model based on hypervisor, which extends the traditional loading model from block-level to the module-level. In this model, the basic system, the application software and the Cleanroom Protocol are stored in the security server. Besides, the end-users can select and desire software services on demand from security servers. Additionally, it supports different types of equipment, such as the smart phone, the tablet PC, the laptop, the desktop computer and so on. The different types of operating systems, such as Windows, Linux, IOS, and Android, etc. can also valid. It should be emphasized that the device can be the bare metal or just have a small amount of memory. Of course, the model is extremely safe and flexible with the Cleanroom Protocol and the On-demand Prefetching Mechanism. Systems based on this model can be safer, less overhead and more user-friendly than the traditional one.

The research offers some new insights about the software streaming loading. It is presented as a holistic system which can support a border range of devices such as smart phones and tablet PC, etc., OSes such as Windows and IOS, etc. It also guarantees the computer safety to the greatest degree. Therefore, the core idea of this model is that the small terminal can solve complicated problems.

However, there are some limitations in this model. The streaming loading research was only based on virtualized environment while the non-virtualized environment was not taken into consideration. Furthermore, the model is temporarily in an ideal embryonic stage. It should be improved with future works that to instantiate this model and then to apply it to the reality.

To summarize, this model is considered helpful despite its limitation. On the other hand, it will be improved in the future and then be applied in the real life as soon as possible.

Acknowledgments. This work is supported in part by the Changsha Science and Technology Project of Changsha Science and Technology Bureau No. kq1701089, in part by the National Natural Science Foundation of China under Grants Nos. 61632009, 61772194 and 61472451, in part by the Guangdong Provincial Natural Science Foundation under Grant 2017A030308006 and High-Level Talents Program of Higher Education in Guangdong Province under Grant 2016ZJ01. The authors would like to thank the anonymous reviewers, guest editors and the participants of this project for their helpful comments.

References

1. Zhang, Y., Zhou, Y.: Transparent computing: spatio-temporal extension on Von Neumann architecture for cloud services. Tsinghua Sci. Technol. **18**(1), 10–21 (2013)
2. Ming, W.: Analysis and a case study of transparent computing implementation with UEFI. Int. J. Cloud Comput. **1**(4), 312–328 (2012)
3. Oliveros, W.V.A., Festin, C.A.M., Ocampo, R.M.: A P2P network booting scheme using a BitTorrent-like protocol. In: 2013 International Conference on IEEE (2013)
4. Liang, Z., Chunming, H., Tianyu, W., et al.: Prefetching mechanism for on-demand software streaming. J. Comput. Res. Dev. **48**(7), 1178–1189 (2011)
5. Zhang, Y.H., Li, Y.H., Zheng, W.M.: Cloudow: a SaaS runtime system based on the user-level virtualization technology. SCIENTIA SINICA Informationis **3**, 001 (2012)
6. Li, B., Wo, T.Y., Hu, C.M., et al.: Hidden OS objects correlated detection technology based on VMM. J. Softw. **24**(2), 405–420 (2013)

7. Ren, J.B., Qi, Y., Dai, Y.H., et al.: Transparent privacy protection based on virtual machine monitor. J. Softw. **26**(8), 2124–2137 (2015)

8. Dai, Y., Shi, Y., Qi, Y., et al.: Design and verification of a lightweight reliable virtual machine monitor for a many-core architecture. Front. Comput. Sci. **7**(1), 34–43 (2013)

9. Zhang, Y., Zhou, Y.: TransOS: a transparent computing-based operating system for the cloud. Int. J. Cloud Comput. **1**(4), 287–301 (2012)

10. Zhang, Y., Zhou, Y.: Transparent computing: a new paradigm for pervasive computing. In: Ma, J., Jin, H., Yang, L.T., Tsai, J.J.-P. (eds.) UIC 2006. LNCS, vol. 4159, pp. 1–11. Springer, Heidelberg (2006). https://doi.org/10.1007/11833529_1

11. Peng, T., Liu, Q., Wang, G.J.: A multilevel access control scheme for data security in transparent computing. Comput. Sci. Eng. **2**, PP (2016)

12. Zhang, F., Leach, K., Stavrou, A., et al.: Using hardware features for increased debugging transparency. In: 2015 IEEE Symposium on Security and Privacy (SP), pp. 55–69. IEEE (2015)

13. Chen, B., Xiao, N., Cai, Z., et al.: Prefetch mechanism for on-demand software deployment in virtual machine environments. J. Softw. **21**(12), 3186–3198 (2010)

14. Zhong, Y.Q.: Study on performance optimization based on web caching and prefetching technique. Jiangxi University of Science and Technology (2014)

15. Griffioen, J., Appleton, R.: Reducing file system latency using a predictive approach. In: USENIX Summer, pp. 197–207 (1994)

16. Chang, W., Zheng, H., Wu, J.: On the RSU-based secure distinguishability among vehicular flows. In: 2017 IEEE/ACM 25th International Symposium on Quality of Service (IWQoS), pp. 1–6. IEEE (2017)

17. Wei, C., Jie, W.: Progressive or conservative: rationally allocate cooperative work in mobile social networks. IEEE Trans. Parallel Distrib. Syst. **26**(7), 2020–2035 (2015)

18. Luo, E., Liu, Q., Abawajy, J.H., Wang, G.: Privacy-preserving multi-hop profile-matching protocol for proximity mobile social networks. Future Gener. Comput. Syst. **68**, 222–233 (2017)

19. Luo, E., Liu, Q., Wang, G.: Hierarchical multi-authority and attribute-based encryption friend discovery scheme in mobile social networks. IEEE Commun. Lett. **20**(9), 1772–1775 (2016)

20. Zhang, S., Choo, K.K.R., Liu, Q., Wang, G.: Enhancing privacy through uniform grid and caching in location-based services. Future Gener. Comput. Syst. (2017). https://doi.org/10.1016/j.future

21. Zhang, S., Wang, G., Liu, Q., Abawajy, J.H.: A trajectory privacy-preserving scheme based on query exchange in mobile social networks. Soft Comput. 1–13 (2017). https://doi.org/10.1007/s00500-017-2676-6

22. Hypervisor. https://zh.wikipedia.org/wiki/Hypervisor

The 3rd International Symposium on Sensor-Cloud Systems (SCS 2017)

SCS 2017 Organizing and Program Committees

1 General Chairs

Md. Zakirul Alam Bhuiyan	Fordham University, USA
Tian Wang	Huaqiao University, China

2 Program Chairs

Sheng Wen	Deakin University, Australia
Zhangbing Zhou	China University of Geosciences (Beijing), China & TELECOM SudParis, France

3 Program Committee

Bashar, A M A Elman	Plymouth State University, USA
Yonghong Chen	Huaqiao University, China
Siyao Cheng	Harbin Institute of Technology, China
Lin Cui	Jinan University (Guangzhou), China
Haipeng Dai	Nanjing University, China
Weiwei Fang	Beijing Jiaotong University, China
Zhitao Guan	North China Electric Power University, China
Xiali (Sharon) Hei	Delaware State University, USA
Qiangsheng Hua	Huazhong University of Science and Technology, China
Patrick Hung	University of Ontario Institute of Technology, Canada
Yongxuan Lai	Xiamen University, China
Feng Li	Shandong University, China
Guanghui Li	Jiangnan University, China
Jianxin Li	University of West Australia, Australia
Junbin Liang	Guangxi University, China
Wanyu Lin	University of Toronto, Canada
Zhen Ling	Southeast University, China
Anfeng Liu	Central South University, China
Chi (Harold) Liu	Beijing Institute of Technology, China
Kai Liu	Chongqing University, China
Liang Liu	Beijing University of Posts and Telecommunications, China
Peng Liu	Hangzhou Dianzi University, China
Xiao Liu	Deakin University, Australia

Xuxun Liu	South China University of Technology, China
Yang Liu	Beijing University of Posts and Telecommunications, China
Kai Peng	Huaqiao University, China
Zhen Peng	College of William and Mary, USA
Rajesh Prasad	Saint Anselm College, USA
Yiran Shen	Harbin Engineering University, China
Rui Tan	Nanyang Technological University, Singapore
Shaolei Teng	Howard University, USA
Jiliang Wang	Tsinghua University, China
Weigang Wu	Sun Yat-Sen University, China
Yong Xie	Xiamen University of Technology, China
Wenzheng Xu	Sichuan University, China
Guisong Yang	University of Shanghai for Science and Technology, China
Dongxiao Yu	Huazhong University of Science and Technology, China
Yong Yu	Shaanxi Normal University, China
Dong Yuan	Sydney University, Australia
Shigeng Zhang	Central South University, China
James Xi Zheng	Deakin University, Australia
Chunsheng Zhu	The University of British Columbia, Canada
Yanmin Zhu	Shanghai Jiao Tong University, China

4 Publicity Chairs

Zeyu Sun	Luoyang Institute of Science and Technology, China
Xiaofei Xing	Guangzhou University, China
Zenghua Zhao	Tianjin University, China

5 Steering Chair

Jiannong Cao	The Hong Kong Polytechnic University, Hong Kong

6 Steering Committee

Xiaojiang Chen	Northwest University, China
Kim-Kwang Raymond Choo	The University of Texas at San Antonio, USA
Mianxiong Dong	Muroran Institute of Technology, Japan

Wei Dong	Zhejiang University, China
Xiao-Jiang Du (James)	Temple University, USA
Guangjie Han	Hohai University, China
Weijia Jia	Shanghai Jiaotong University, China
Kuan-Ching Li	Providence University, Taiwan
Qing Li	City University of Hong Kong, Hong Kong
Limin Sun	Institute of Information Engineering, Chinese Academy of Sciences, China
Guojun Wang	Guangzhou University, China
Hongyi Wu	Old Dominion University (ODU), USA
Yang Xiao	The University of Alabama, USA

On-Street Car Parking Prediction in Smart City: A Multi-source Data Analysis in Sensor-Cloud Environment

Walaa Alajali[✉], Sheng Wen, and Wanlei Zhou

School of Information Technology, Centre of Cyber Security Research,
Deakin University, Geelong 3217, Australia
{wkalajal,wesheng,wanlei}@deakin.edu.au

Abstract. Smart car parking systems in smart cities aim to provide high-quality services to their users. The key to success for smart car parking systems is the ability to predict available car parking lots throughout the city at different times. Drivers can then select a suitable car parking location. However, the prediction process can be affected by many different factors in smart cities such as people mobility and car traffic. This study investigates the use of multi-source data (car parking data, pedestrian data, car traffic data) to predict available car parking in fifteen minute intervals. It explores the relationship between pedestrian volume and demand for car parking in specific areas. This data is then used to predict conditions on holidays and during special events, when the number of pedestrians dramatically increases. A Gradient Boosting Regression Trees (GBRT) is used for prediction. It is an ensemble method that can be more accurate than a single Regression Tree and Support Vector Regression. The probability of error for our model is 0.0291.

Keywords: Sensors · Ensemble · GBRT · Pedestrian · Car parking

1 Introduction

Recently, smart car parking has become an integral part of intelligent transportation systems, and it plays an important role in smart cities. Finding and providing appropriate parking for each user is the main purpose of the system [8]. However, the challenge of finding a parking area has increased due to increased vehicle volume in urban areas around the world. This phenomenon has had several environmental impacts. For example, in one small Los Angeles business district 47,000 gallons of gasoline were burned over the course of one year [19], and an estimated 30–40% increase in vehicle traffic has been generated by drivers looking for parking lots. This has increased air pollution and has had a negative effect on the environment [10]. However, despite the benefits of smart car parking systems, more research is required to achieve an effective and efficient system.

© Springer International Publishing AG 2017
G. Wang et al. (Eds.): SpaCCS 2017 Workshops, LNCS 10658, pp. 641–652, 2017.
https://doi.org/10.1007/978-3-319-72395-2_58

The performance of a system depends on the accuracy of information provided to users about the availability of parking lots. There are several models to solve car parking problems. The first kind focuses on driver behaviour to determine parking choices, the second one focuses on parking allocation and the last focuses on the impact of other transportation elements on parking events [24]. In smart cities, different types of traffic (car, pedestrian, etc.) interact with each other and that can impact the car parking conditions. Real-time information provided by on-street car parking systems about the availability of parking areas is not sufficient to provide efficient service because this information is useful only for drivers close to a parking area. This information is less useful for drivers who are further away, as it is likely to vary before they reach the destination. Therefore, providing accurate predictions for future parking availability will enhance parking services [17]. The problem of predicting parking availability has been investigated by several studies in recent years. However, none of these studies has considered information from other transportation elements in their predictions. To develop smart car parking solutions, multiple data sources are important. Pedestrian mobility data can influence prediction accuracy. The study in [7] addressed that a dramatic increase in pedestrian traffic in a specific place indicates an event in that area. This result was found by using the anomaly detection method on the pedestrian dataset in Melbourne.

Smart Transportation Systems for Smart cities are required a large number of the installed sensors in various locations. The generated data from the sensors is considered as a big data. Hence, this collected data requires functional resources for storage and processing purposes. Indeed, cloud services providers such as Amazon, Google cloud platform offer a flexible use of computing resources and storage services [2]. Therefore, in this paper we adopt the upload data from the sensors deployed in Melbourne CBD. As it will be a huge amount of data, it needs to be sorted in a cloud environment.

In this study we will investigate the prediction of available car parking lots in special days\events based on multi-source data and the following contributions are made:

- We used multi-source data in a smart city to enhance the prediction of car parking availability for each 15 min time interval.
- We investigated the relationship between pedestrian volume and the demand for parking lots, essential for avoiding prediction error on special days or events.
- We proposed GBRT (Gradient Boosted Regression Trees) as a prediction method According to the result reported in [1], GBRT is more accurate than a single regression tree. We evaluated our model with real data from the city of Melbourne.
- Using the car traffic data to indicate the demand for parking depends on location, the parking area on a street with high car traffic will experience high demand for parking lots. To the best of our knowledge, this is the first work that uses pedestrian traffic and car traffic data to predict available car parking lots on special days or events.

The rest of this paper is organized as follows: Sect. 2 related works, Sect. 3 includes important preliminaries, features selection, datasets and describe the used method. Result's discussion and evaluation are presented in Sect. 4. Finally, the conclusion in Sect. 5.

(a) Sensor Locations for Pedestrians

(b) Sensor Locations for Pedestrians and
Car Parking Streets

Fig. 1. Sensors map

2 Related Works

The problem of finding available car parking lots in smart cities has received significant attention from researchers in the last five years. Several studies have been introduced to address this. The developed solutions fall into two categories. First, several researchers focused on the reservation of parking lots in advance, which means that drivers must book parking lots before arriving at a lot. The work [11] introduced smart parking system called 'iPraker' to solve the availability of car parking lots by using the resource allocation concept to improve the reservations of car park lots. An intelligent parking space inventory control system has been discussed in [22] where a hybrid method from fuzzy logic and integer programming techniques used to determine the suitable response to the user request. In addition, [19] proposed a stochastic delay-tolerant method for improving the efficiency of assigning parking lots to incoming cars. Another work under the same umbrella [4] proposed a method for real-time predictions of available car parking areas for intelligent parking reservation (IPR) systems to reduce wait times. However, this system is sometimes inefficient because a reserved parking area cannot be used by other drivers during the time between the booking and the reservation.

The second category of methods proposed predicting available parking lots for a specific time interval, which allows drivers to plan their trips in advance. There have been several studies in this category. For example, a hybrid modelling approach for prediction is provided by combining agent-based and stochastic simulation to increase prediction accuracy [3]. In the work [9], the authors proposed a continuous-time Markov chain model to solve prediction problems. In this method, information about parking areas such as occupied lots, capacity and parking rate transfers into a car's navigation system through a vehicular network. The probability of available parking lots is computed by a navigation system based on the received data. The work [16] used the Poisson distribution to model the availability of parking lots. The estimation of available car parking lots is provided to the drivers when they arrive. The crowd-source system PocketParker was proposed in the work [15], and uses smart phones to detect arrivals and departures in parking areas by using an activity recognition algorithm. This data is then used to maintain area availability models. Similarly, ParkNet [13] uses smart phones to collect information about parking spaces. Each vehicle is supported by a GPS receiver and passenger-side ultrasonic range finder to identify the status of parking lots.

All listed methods were developed for off-street car parking. On-street parking problems differ from off-street car parking problems. Therefore, models based on probability distribution have been proposed with acceptable accuracy to adapt to on-street parking [17]. Some cities have used sensors to collect information from on-street parking areas such as San Francisco and Melbourne. A Multivariate auto-regression model has also been proposed in the work [25] using three prediction methods: neural networks, regression trees, and support vector regression on data collected from the cities of Melbourne and San Francisco. The results showed that regression trees had better accuracy. The authors used day of the week, time of day, and last previous observation to predict the availability of parking lots for a given time interval. A multivariate auto-regression model was proposed in the work [17] for on-street and off-street car parking predictions. In [23], a Neural Network was used for real time prediction. However, the computation was too time-consuming, and the authors divided the parking areas in the city to four areas of $1,800\,m^2$, $12,000\,m^2$, $3000\,m^2$, and $76,000\,m^2$. These were still large areas, and drivers spent much time identifying unused lots.

In this paper, we will focus on on-street car parking lots prediction in the city of Melbourne, Australia. We will aggregate the parking areas in each street rather than in large areas. Finally, we will consider other traffic factors in urban networks, such as pedestrian traffic and car traffic, near the car parking areas.

3   Method

This study involves sampling and analysing three datasets from different sources to predict available car parking lots for special days and events. The datasets were selected from the central business district (CBD) in Melbourne and have been collected from sensors installed on different streets as illustrated in Fig. 1. In the next section, important preliminaries description and problem definition are introduced.

3.1   Preliminaries

In this section we will first identify some preliminaries. Then we introduce the proposed method for prediction of car parking lots for spacial days or events.

1. Street lots is the number of car parking lots for specific street.
2. St. check_in(t), represents the number of cars entering a parking area.
3. St. check_out(t), is the number of cars leave the parking area, where $t = 15\,min$ time interval and working hours from 7 AM to 7 PM for all days in the week. St refers to a street name in Melbourne CBD. The data collected by sensors from three sources:
   a. Car parking dataset records

$$Cp = \{cp_1, cp_2, cp_3, \ldots, cp_N\}$$

   b. Pedestrians dataset records

$$Pd = \{pd_1, pd_2, pd_3, \ldots, pd_M\}$$

   c. Car traffic dataset records

$$Tr = \{tr_1, tr_2, tr_3, \ldots, tr_C\}$$

From CP we calculate the available car parking lots in time t as follow:

$$St.available(t)_i = St.available(t)_{i-1} - St.check\_in(t)_i \\ + St.check\_out(t)_i$$

Since this dataset has not included the streets latitude and longitude, we use the Geopy package in Python to assign the coordination for each street. The total number of lots have not been provided also, so we fixed it by scanning the parking events for each st in whole the year. The new dataset consists of arrival date, departure date, time, street name, street coordination, a total number of lots, bay id (sensor id which reports the arriving and departure events). Then we calculate the number of cars that are checked in and checked out for each street within each 15 min time interval, the two values will be used later to calculate the available lots in a 15-time interval. There are 28 sensors installed in strategic locations in the city of Melbourne to atomically record the number of pedestrian for 24 h a day for the whole week. The distance measure is used to find a pedestrian sensor within 200 m from parking location. The most important information is the sensor locations and the pedestrian volume.

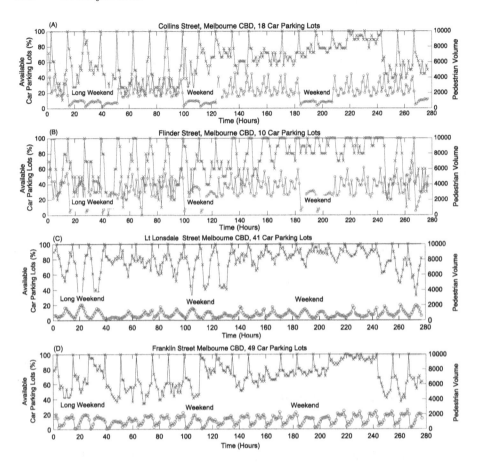

Fig. 2. Correlation between pedestrians and available car parking lots

3.2   Feature Selection and Correlation Analysis

1. Day in the week and time in the day

First, we explore the impact of day of week (weekday or weekend\holiday) on the value of available car parking lots. As demonstrated in Fig. 3, the demand on the car parking varies on weekday from the demand on weekends and also, at different time in a day. The average available car parking in all streets for one month data are: in the weekday for the times period (7 AM–10 AM) the average available car parking lots are 60%–90% and 55%–95% on the weekend. The second time interval is (11 AM–3 PM) and on weekdays the average available car parking lots is 40%–60%. On other hand, at the weekend the value is 50%. Finally, in the evening time 4 PM–6 PM, on weekdays 70%–80% and the weekend\holiday value is 70%–72%.

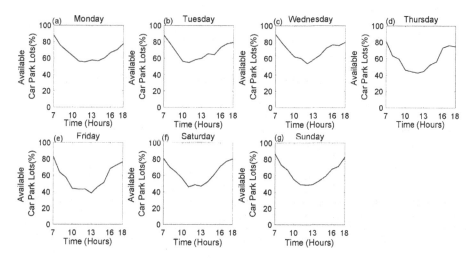

Fig. 3. Average available car parking lot in the week

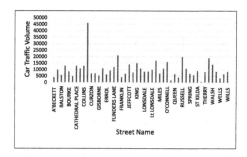

Fig. 4. Average daily car traffic in different streets

2. Pedestrians Volume

As can be seen in Fig. 2 there is a correlation between the available car parking lots and the pedestrians volume counted by sensors near car parking area. This correlation is significantly increased when the pedestrians volume has exceeded a defined threshold (Threshold = 4000). Therefore, we normalised the pedestrians volume by divide it by the value of threshold to get $\hat{P}$. In this case, the correlation increased when the $\hat{P}$ is more than 1. Different streets have different lots, therefore, we calculate the available car parking value as a part of a total number of lots on each street. Pedestrians volume is used as a feature in our model to reduce the prediction error for special days or events.

3. Car Traffic Volume

From the car traffic dataset we used the average daily car traffic for each street in the research region. This feature is used to classify the streets depend on the car traffic volume. As is clear from Fig. 4, that the average daily car traffic varies on different streets. We use the average daily car traffic because there is lack of an available dataset with hourly car traffic report.

Table 1. Datasets summary

Data source		Melbourne city
Time interval		1/1/2014 to 31/12/2014
Car parking data	# Streets	57
	# Sensors (Lots)	4,600
	# Records	13.5 Million
Pedestrians data	# Sensors	36
	# Records	278,326
Car traffic data	# Records	13,836 (57 records are selected in this study)

3.3 Dataset

We have used three datasets from different domains (on-street car parking data, pedestrian data, and car traffic data) from the city of Melbourne, Australia as shown in the Table 1. For the on-street car parking dataset, the data are collected by 4600 in-ground sensors installed in the different streets in the Melbourne CBD. These sensors report parking events in each lot such as arriving time and departure time and the parking duration. The dataset period used in this paper is from 1st of Jan 2014 to 31st Dec 2014. It consists of 13.5 million rows and 21 columns. The following attributes are selected from this dataset: Arrival time, Departure time, Area id, Area name, street id, street name, bay id [5]. The second dataset is the pedestrians dataset. The data are collected by 36 sensors out of 44 currently in use installed in the strategic streets in Melbourne CBD to monitor the pedestrians activities and analysis the change and development over time. The sensor hourly count the number of pedestrians who go by the installed location. It consists of 278,326 records, in our research we use this data to analysis the impact of pedestrians mobility on the car parking events. The data collected from 1st Jan 2014 to 31st Dec 2014. The format of the data is (Time, sensor id, sensor name, Hourly counts) [6]. Finally, car traffic data is used in our method. It includes the average daily vehicle volume in most streets in the Melbourne city published by VicRoad [18]. Street name, coordination and vehicles number are selected attributes from car traffic dataset.

3.4 Prediction Method

We proposed an ensemble learning Gradient Boosted Regression Trees (GBRT) as one of the most effective machine learning method for prediction implemented in Python [21]. Ensemble learning is defined in [14] as the use of several models generated by performing the learning method on the given problem. The integrating of these models will produce the final predictor. GBRT works to iterative integrate weak models to obtain a strong predictor. A sequence of regression trees are computed, each successive tree is used to build the next tree as explained by the following [12]: For a given training dataset $\{x_t, y_t\}, t = 1 \ldots n$ GBRT works as follow:

$$hi = argmin_h \sum_{l-1}^{n} S(y_t - H_{i-1}(x_t), h(x_t)) \qquad (1)$$

$$H_{i-1}(x) = \sum_{l=1}^{i-1} hl(x) \qquad (2)$$

where S represents the loss function, the m regression trees are combined to produce the final prediction $H(x) = h_1(x) + h_2(x) \ldots + h_m(x)$, where m is the number of generated trees.

4   Results Discussion and Evaluations

Throughout different experiments of this study, we come up with various observations and results using open source scikit-learn machine learning tools in Python [20]. In this section, we will display these results in details.

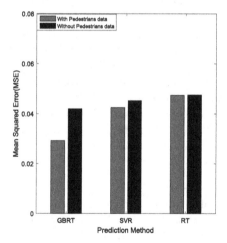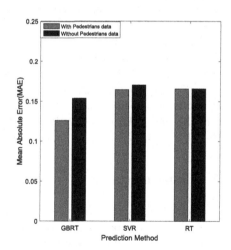

Fig. 5. Results evaluation

As illustrated in Fig. 5, the results are compared among three prediction methods GBRT (Gradient Boosting Regression Trees), RT (Regression Tree) and Support Vector Regression (SVR). Furthermore, another comparison is made between accuracy of prediction method when we consider pedestrians volume feature with the result when we ignore it. The results indicate that the GBRT ensemble method has higher accuracy compared to RT and SVR. Moreover, the integrated data from multiple sources such as pedestrians data and car parking data can increase the prediction method. This results in a prediction of the available car parking lots in seven streets in Melbourne city for 2000 steps, each step represents 15 min time interval. We used 7-fold cross validation to avoid over-fitting. Two metrics have been used: Mean Squared Error (MSE) and Mean Absolute Error (MAE) to evaluate the model accuracy.

1. MSE (Mean Squared Error)

$$MSE = \frac{1}{n} \sum_{t=1}^{n} (\hat{Y} - Y) \tag{3}$$

where $\hat{Y}$ is the predicted value and Y is the grand truth
2. MAE (Mean Absolute Error)

$$MAE = \frac{1}{n} \sum_{t=1}^{n} \frac{\sum_{i=1}^{m} |\hat{Y} - Y|}{m} \tag{4}$$

First, when we consider the pedestrians volume as a feature and use the GBRT method, we obtain MSE as 0.0291 and MAE as 0.1260 while when the feature is ignored, MSE and MAE become 0.0420 and 0.1537 respectively. This result reveals how considered pedestrians volume feature makes difference in MSE and MAE.

In order to evaluate adopted GBRT method, we compare it with other two different methods that are RT and SVR methods. Compared to RT method shows that the MSE with the pedestrian volume feature is 0.0474 and the MAE is 0.1655 but when we ignore pedestrians volume feature the MSE is 0.0475 and the MAE is 0.1658. Besides, considered SVR method outputs 0.0425 and 0.1646 for MSE and MAE respectively when the pedestrian data is included. Otherwise, the MSE is 0.0452 and the MAE is 0.1703 with ignoring the pedestrian data.

5   Conclusion

Previous studies reported the importance of a Smart Parking System as part of a Smart transportation system in Smart cities. However, there is a challenge regarding to providing accurate information about the availability of car parking lots to the users. Different studies have investigated this problem. The best solution is to predict the available car parking. Several pieces of research have conducted the prediction of available car parking. However, to the best of our knowledge, this is the first work has used multiple data sources to predicate the available car parking conditions in special days or events. An Ensemble Regression method (GBRT) has been used on an integrated data set from three sources (car parking, pedestrians, car traffic data) to predict available car parking for the on-street parking areas on the different streets in Melbourne city. The results show that using multi-source data and GBRT prediction method can reduce prediction error when there is an event or special day celebration near car parking area. For future work, a distributed Gradient boosting tree can be used with Apache Spark big data platform in the cloud to accelerate the proposed method.

References

1. Alazrai, R., Khalifeh, A., Alnuman, N., Alabed, D., Mowafi, Y.: An ensemble-based regression approach for continuous estimation of wrist and fingers movements from surface electromyography. In: 2016 IEEE 38th Annual International Conference of the Engineering in Medicine and Biology Society (EMBC), pp. 319–322. IEEE (2016)
2. Aydin, G., Hallac, I.R., Karakus, B.: Architecture and implementation of a scalable sensor data storage and analysis system using cloud computing and big data technologies. J. Sens. **2015**, 1–5 (2015)
3. Beheshti, R., Sukthankar, G.: A hybrid modeling approach for parking and traffic prediction in urban simulations. AI Soc. **30**(3), 333–344 (2015)
4. Caicedo, F., Blazquez, C., Miranda, P.: Prediction of parking space availability in real time. Expert Syst. Appl. **39**(8), 7281–7290 (2012)
5. Dataset1 (2017). https://data.melbourne.vic.gov.au/Transport-Movement/ Parking-bay-arrivals-and-departures-2014/mq3i-cbxd. Accessed Feb 2017
6. Dataset2 (2017). https://data.melbourne.vic.gov.au/Transport-Movement/ Pedestrian-traffic-hourly-count/cb85-mn2u. Accessed Feb 2017
7. Doan, M.T., Rajasegarar, S., Salehi, M., Moshtaghi, M., Leckie, C.: Profiling pedestrian distribution and anomaly detection in a dynamic environment. In: Proceedings of 24th ACM International on Conference on Information and Knowledge Management, pp. 1827–1830. ACM (2015)
8. Ji, Z., Ganchev, I., O'Droma, M., Zhang, X.: A cloud-based intelligent car parking services for smart cities. In: 2014 XXXIth URSI General Assembly and Scientific Symposium (URSI GASS), pp. 1–4. IEEE (2014)
9. Klappenecker, A., Lee, H., Welch, J.L.: Finding available parking spaces made easy. Ad Hoc Netw. **12**, 243–249 (2014)
10. Koster, A., Oliveira, A., Volpato, O., Delvequio, V., Koch, F.: Recognition and recommendation of parking places. In: Bazzan, A.L.C., Pichara, K. (eds.) IBERAMIA 2014. LNCS (LNAI), vol. 8864, pp. 675–685. Springer, Cham (2014). https://doi.org/10.1007/978-3-319-12027-0_54
11. Kotb, A.O., Shen, Y.-C., Zhu, X., Huang, Y.: iParker - a new smart car-parking system based on dynamic resource allocation and pricing. IEEE Trans. Intell. Transp. Syst. **17**(9), 2637–2647 (2016)
12. Li, Y., Zheng, Y., Zhang, H., Chen, L.: Traffic prediction in a bike-sharing system. In: Proceedings of 23rd SIGSPATIAL International Conference on Advances in Geographic Information Systems, p. 33. ACM (2015)
13. Mathur, S., Jin, T., Kasturirangan, N., Chandrasekaran, J., Xue, W., Gruteser, M., Trappe, W.: ParkNet: drive-by sensing of road-side parking statistics. In: Proceedings of 8th International Conference on Mobile Systems, Applications, and Services, pp. 123–136. ACM (2010)
14. Mendes-Moreira, J., Soares, C., Jorge, A.M., De Sousa, J.F.: Ensemble approaches for regression: a survey. ACM Comput. Surv. (CSUR) **45**(1), 10 (2012)

15. Nandugudi, A., Ki, T., Nuessle, C., Challen, G.: PocketParker: pocketsourcing parking lot availability. In: Proceedings of 2014 ACM International Joint Conference on Pervasive and Ubiquitous Computing, pp. 963–973. ACM (2014)
16. Pullola, S., Atrey, P.K., El Saddik, A.: Towards an intelligent GPS-based vehicle navigation system for finding street parking lots. In: IEEE International Conference on Signal Processing and Communications, ICSPC 2007, pp. 1251–1254. IEEE (2007)
17. Rajabioun, T., Ioannou, P.A.: On-street and off-street parking availability prediction using multivariate spatiotemporal models. IEEE Trans. Intell. Transp. Syst. **16**(5), 2913–2924 (2015)
18. Report (2017). https://www.lga.sa.gov.au/webdata/resources/project/Parking_Spaces_for_Urban_Places_-_final_abridged_report.pdf. Accessed Mar 2017
19. Schlote, A., King, C., Crisostomi, E., Shorten, R.: Delay-tolerant stochastic algorithms for parking space assignment. IEEE Trans. Intell. Transp. Syst. **15**(5), 1922–1935 (2014)
20. Scikit-learn (2017). http://scikit-learn.org/stable/index.html. Accessed Feb 2017
21. Sklean (2017). http://scikit-learn.org/stable/modules/ensemble.html. Accessed Mar 2017
22. Teodorović, D., Lučić, P.: Intelligent parking systems. Eur. J. Oper. Res. **175**(3), 1666–1681 (2006)
23. Vlahogianni, E.I., Kepaptsoglou, K., Tsetsos, V., Karlaftis, M.G.: A real-time parking prediction system for smart cities. J. Intell. Transp. Syst. **20**(2), 192–204 (2016)
24. Young, W., Thompson, R.G., Taylor, M.A.P.: A review of urban car parking models. Transp. Rev. **11**(1), 63–84 (1991)
25. Zheng, Y., Rajasegarar, S., Leckie, C.: Parking availability prediction for sensor-enabled car parks in smart cities. In: 2015 IEEE Tenth International Conference on Intelligent Sensors, Sensor Networks and Information Processing (ISSNIP), pp. 1–6. IEEE (2015)

A Weight-Bind-Based Safe Top-k Query Processing Scheme in Two-Tiered Sensor Networks

Xiaoyan Kui[1], Shigeng Zhang[1(✉)], Wei Li[2], Ping Zhong[1],
Xingpo Ma[3], and Huakun Du[1]

[1] School of Information Science and Engineering, Central South University,
Changsha 410083, China
sgzhang@csu.edu.cn
[2] Texas Southern University, Houston 77004, USA
liww@tsu.edu
[3] School of Computer and Information Technology,
Xinyang Normal University, Xinyang 464000, China

Abstract. Privacy and integrity are two important requirements in cyber security. Because of the limited computing capability and resources of sensor nodes, it is a great challenge to meet these two requirements at the same time for top-k queries in two-tiered sensor networks. In this paper, a weight-bind-based safe top-k query processing scheme named WBB-TQ (Weight-Bind-Based safe top-k Query processing scheme) is proposed to solve this problem. WBB-TQ combines the pair-wise-key encryption technique and the order-preserving symmetric encryption scheme (OPES) so that the storage nodes at the upper layer of the network can process top-k queries without knowing the exact values of either sensing data or their corresponding scores. Thus, the data privacy for top-k queries is preserved. To achieve the integrity of top-k query results, a novel weight-bind-based method is proposed in WBB-TQ to establish relationships among data items generated by each sensor node so that the Sink node can detect whether adversaries drop and/or tamper with part or all of the qualified top-k data items in the query results. Simulation results show that, WBB-TQ not only preserves data privacy and integrity of top-k query results, but also achieves a low cost of computation and communication on secure top-k query processing in two-tiered sensor networks.

Keywords: Two-tiered sensor networks · Top-k query · Weight · Security

1 Introduction

The wireless sensor network (WSN) has been an academic research focus in recent years; its development is diversified, and it has a variety of types, such as two-tiered sensor networks [1], multimedia sensor networks, and mobile sensor networks. Among them, the two-tiered sensor network is the emphasis of this paper. Two-tiered sensor networks can be divided into upper and lower layers. The lower layer is made of many sensor nodes with fewer resources, low computing power, and short communication

© Springer International Publishing AG 2017
G. Wang et al. (Eds.): SpaCCS 2017 Workshops, LNCS 10658, pp. 653–666, 2017.
https://doi.org/10.1007/978-3-319-72395-2_59

radius, which constitute the multi-hop ad hoc network; the upper layer is composed of data storage nodes, which constitute a wireless mesh network. The resources of the storage nodes are abundant, and their number is relatively fewer. The responsibilities of the storage nodes are to collect the sensing data from all sensor nodes and respond to query requests from users. Thus, the data storage nodes are considered to be the key nodes in a two-tiered sensor network.

In a hostile environment, these key nodes are more vulnerable to attack [1]. Once they are captured, the attacker can not only steal the data stored on them, but also use the captured nodes to drop and/or tamper with part or all of the qualified data items in the top-k query results, which will destroy the privacy and the integrity of top-k query results. In fact, privacy and integrity are two important requirements for cyber security. Thus, we must design secure query processing methods to ensure protection of the privacy and integrity of data in two-tiered sensor networks.

This paper discusses the security problem of the top-k query in two-tiered sensor networks, and the goal is to achieve data privacy and integrity protection in top-k queries. At present, limited research has been conducted in the field of safe top-k query in two-tiered sensor networks [1–8], and some deficiencies still exist in these research results. To resolve the difficulties in existing research into two-tiered sensor networks, a weight-bind-based safe top-k query processing scheme (WBB-TQ) is proposed. WBB-TQ can both achieve data privacy protection and realize data integrity verification in top-k queries. Moreover, WBB-TQ can reduce the communication overhead of sensor nodes in transmitting verification messages. WBB-TQ establishes data relationships among data items generated by each sensor node, which can realize data integrity verification in top-k query results. At the same time, the pair-wise-key encryption technique and the order-preserving symmetric encryption scheme (OPES) [4] are combined reasonably in WBB-TQ so that the data items and their corresponding score can be encrypted at the same time, which realizes the privacy protection of data items and their corresponding scores. Since the OPES encryption scheme can ensure that the order and size of one-dimensional data remains unchanged after encryption, WBB-TQ can guarantee that data storage nodes carry out top-k query processing successfully under the situation that data storage nodes do not decrypt the encrypted data items.

2   Related Work

2.1   Data Pivacy Protection Technology in Two-Tiered Sensor Networks

Currently, data privacy protection technology in two-tiered sensor networks can be mainly divided into three categories: data interference technique, data interval division technique (bucketing technique) [9] and data encryption technique. The data interference technique adds interfering data to the original data to confuse attackers; SafeTQ [5] is the typical algorithm using this technique to realize data privacy protection in top-k queries. SafeTQ must introduce an assistant computing node in each unit to cooperate with the data storage node to calculate the minimum threshold value from the first k data with the largest weight among all data items. This approach not only increases the cost of the network, but also incurs a security risk. When data storage nodes and assistant computing nodes are captured at the same time, the privacy of data is destroyed.

The data interval division technique (bucketing technique) is mainly used to support the safe range queries; the entire range of data is divided into many adjacent intervals, and each interval is assigned a unique ID number. The sensor nodes collect the sensing data and assign them to the corresponding data interval according to the size of the data; and then use a symmetric key between the interval and the external Sink node to encrypt the data belonging to the same interval. Then the encrypted interval data, together with the interval ID number, will be sent to a nearby data storage node. During range query, the minimum interval set that can cover the query range will first be determined based on the query range; and then these interval sets will be sent to the corresponding data storage nodes. When these interval sets are received, the data storage nodes will send the encrypted data in the corresponding interval to the Sink node. Many algorithms use the data interval division technique to achieve data privacy protection [8–13]; where the literature [9–13] only supports range queries, but it [8] can support both multidimensional range queries and multidimensional top-*k* queries. However, when using the data interval division technique to execute top-*k* queries, the data storage nodes will return all the data in the interval, but cannot return the top-*k* data accurately and incurs a large communication overhead. In addition, the query protocol proposed in [8] needs to reserve a key for every interval of each dimension data item on a sensor node; when the interval division is fine, the storage overhead of sensor nodes will be larger.

The data encryption technique is a secure data processing technology that uses a key encryption method to achieve data privacy protection. The order reserved encryption scheme OPES [4] is used in some privacy protection protocols, and it can ensure that the order and size of one-dimensional data remain unchanged after encryption. However, the OPES scheme only applies to one-dimensional data encryption; it cannot be used for multidimensional data encryption. Thus, the literature [4] can only achieve privacy protection for one-dimensional data.

2.2   Data Integrity Verification Technology for Top-*k* Query Results in Two-Tiered Sensor Networks

The existing data integrity verification technology for top-*k* query results in two-tiered sensor networks mostly uses the message authentication code (MAC) technique, although many methods exist for generating MAC. Literature [1] use the hash of the adjacent value of data items to generate MAC; the method of generating MACs in the literature [6] is complicated; and requires use of the stored symmetric key, node ID and weight value corresponding to the data items. Using MAC to verify the correctness of data items can achieve high accuracy, but often incurs greater communication costs. This is because, to improve the accuracy of verification, MAC needs to have a sufficiently long length in bits.

Two main data integrity verification technologies are used for top-*k* query results in two-tiered sensor networks: integrity verification technology based on data correlation and integrity verification technology based on a hash tree [8]. Integrity verification technology based on data correlation establishes a relationship by the size of adjacent data items generated by the same node to help verify the data integrity.

3   Network Model

The two-tiered sensor network model is shown in Fig. 1. The whole sensor network field is divided into η cells of the same size. Each cell has N sensor nodes and one storage node. Time is divided into epochs. Sensor nodes monitor the environment and send their sensing data to the corresponding storage nodes at the end of each epoch. Storage nodes can communicate with each other using a relatively longer link compared with the communication radius of the sensor nodes. Some of the storage nodes can communicate with the Sink node deployed nearby the sensor field using the on-demand wireless links [1], which are formed using a satellite. The storage nodes arnot only responsible for storing the data collected from the sensor nodes in their own cells, but also respond to queries sent from the Sink node. Generally, the storage nodes are the key nodes in such a two-tiered sensor network.

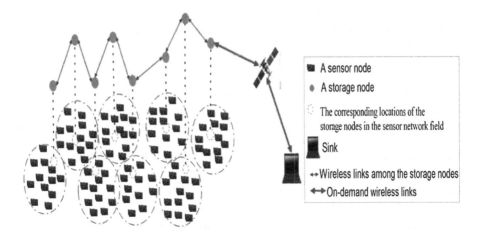

Fig. 1. A two-tiered sensor netwok model.

As in [1], we also assume a public scoring function $f(*)$ [14] which was loaded on each node before the nodes were deployed. Let $D_{i,j}$ denote the jth data item generated by sensor node S_i, and $d_{i,j}$ denote the score corresponding to $D_{i,j}$. Then, we have

$$d_{i,j} = f(D_{i,j}) \tag{1}$$

In addition, we also assume that data items generated in the same cell and the same epoch have different scores. For ease of presentation, a definition is given below.

Definition 1. Top-*k* data item: refers to the *k* data items which have the largest or smallest data scores among all the data items generated by the sensor nodes in the queried region and the queried epoch.

Other notations used in this paper are listed in Table 1.

Table 1. Notations used in this paper

Notation	Meaning
$Q_t=<C, t, k, QS>$	A top-*k* query primitive, where *C* is the identity of a cell, *t* is an epoch number, *k* is the number of the interested top data items, and *QS* is the set of sensor nodes located in the queried region in cell *C*.
R_t	The query result corresponding to Q_t.
M	The storage node in cell *C*.
$\{S_i\}_{i=1}^N$	The set of sensor nodes in cell *C*, where S_i denotes the sensor node with ID *i*, and *N* is the number of sensor node in cell *C*.
$\mu_{i,t}$	The number of data items generated by S_i in epoch *t*.
$D_{i,j}$	The jth data item generated by S_i in epoch *t*.
$d_{i,j}$	The data score corresponding to $D_{i,j}$
$\Phi_i=\{D_{i,j}\}_{j=1}^{\mu_{i,t}}$	The set of data items generated by S_i in epoch *t*.

As assumed in [5, 12], we also assume that the sensor nodes are secure. Although sensor nodes can be compromised, data items generated by a single sensor node have little effect on the final top-*k* query results. Compared with the sensor nodes, adversaries are more likely to compromise the storage nodes in the upper layer of two-tiered sensor networks, because the storage nodes are the key nodes in the networks. If the storage nodes are compromised, the adversary can launch several kinds of attacks, as follows:

- Privacy Attack: Adversaries undermine the privacy of the top-*k* query results by compromising the storage nodes and obtaining the data items stored on the nodes.
- Forgery Attack: Adversaries replace real data items generated by sensor nodes with false data items which are forged by the adversaries.
- Completeness-breaking Attack: Adversaries break the completeness of top-*k* query results by dropping some qualified data items, replacing qualified data items with unqualified data items, or using other tricks.

4 Design of WBB-TQ

WBB-TQ aims to protect the privacy, the authentication and the completeness of top-*k* query results in two-tiered sensor networks. To protect the privacy of the data items generated by the sensor nodes, two encryption schemes are used: One is OPES [4]; and the other is one of the good symmetric encryption schemes. The former is used to encrypt the scores of the data items; and the latter to encrypt the data items. Although symmetric encryption schemes are fit for sensor networks because of their light weight, we should not use only this kind of scheme to protect the privacy of data items for top-k queries. This is because the storage nodes cannot process top-k queries properly if sensor nodes encrypt both their data items and the scores of the data items using symmetric encryption schemes. Thus, we use another heavier encryption scheme, OPES, which can maintain the size order of the one-dimensional digits before and after they are encrypted, to encrypt the scores of the data items and to ensure that the storage nodes process top-k queries properly. The OPES scheme should not be used to encrypt the data items because they may be multi-dimensional.

To protect the authentication and completeness of top-k query results, a data-bound mechanism run on the sensor nodes is established to ensure binding relationships among the data items so that adversaries cannot easily to insert false data items and/or drop some real data items, and a verification algorithm is executed by the Sink node to verify the authentication and completeness of the top-k query results. WBB-TQ mainly consists of four stages, which are discussed below.

4.1 Nodes Deployment Stage

In the nodes deployment stage, materials that sensor nodes use to generate encryption keys should be loaded on the sensor nodes before they are deployed. Different kinds of materials should be loaded for the two different encryption techniques.

For symmetric encryption, an initial symmetric key and its corresponding ID should be loaded on each sensor node, and the Sink node should also have the initial symmetric keys loaded on the sensor nodes. In other words, each sensor node and the Sink node share one initial symmetric key. To improve the security of the network, the initial keys prepared for different sensor nodes should be different. Moreover, the symmetric keys kept by the sensor nodes and the Sink node should change synchronously as time passes. Let K_i^{t-1} and K_i^t denote the symmetric keys shared by the sensor node S_i and the Sink node during the $(t\text{-}1)^{\text{th}}$ and the tth epochs, respectively. Then, K_i^{t-1} and K_i^t have the following relationship:

$$K_i^t = \text{hash}(K_i^{t-1}) \tag{2}$$

where $hash(*)$ denotes a hashing operation using a one-way hash function.

For asymmetric encryption such as the OPES encryption scheme, which is used to encrypt the data scores in our scheme WBB-TQ, other materials should also be loaded on the sensor nodes and the Sink node. Because of the limitation of paper length, we do not describe this in detail. More details can be found in literature [4].

After all the needed materials are loaded on the sensor nodes and the Sink node, the sensor nodes are deployed randomly in the application area, and the storage nodes are also deployed in this area. To balance the load of the storage nodes, they should be deployed uniformly.

4.2   Data Report Stage

At the end of each epoch, each sensor node should send the data items generated in the current epoch along with information necessary for the authentication and completeness verification to the storage node in its own cell to be stored. In the following, we use the sensor node S_i in cell C as an example to elucidate this data report stage.

First, S_i computes the scores of the data items generated in the current epoch based on the public scoring function. Second, S_i orders the data items according to their own scores. Third, based on the order of the data items, S_i execute the encryption operations on the data items and the scores using both the symmetric encryption scheme and the asymmetric encryption scheme OPES. Finally, S_i sends the encrypted data items and the encrypted scores as well as the ID of the key shared by S_i and the Sink node to storage node M in cell C.

To ensure clarity, we describe the encryption procedure in greater detail. Suppose the data items generated by S_i in epoch t are ordered from big to small according to their scores; the ordered data sequence is as follows: $D_{i,1}$, $D_{i,2}$, $D_{i,3}$, ..., $D_{i,\mu_{i,t}}$.

Let $RPT_{S_i}^M$ denote the report sent from S_i to M at the end of the current epoch, $E_{K_i^t}\{*\}$ denote the encryption operation using symmetric key K_i^t, and ID_{key_i} denote the ID of the symmetric key shared by S_i and the Sink node. The content of $RPT_{S_i}^M$ can be expressed as follows:

- If $\mu_{i,t} = 0$, then we have

$$RPT_{S_i}^M = <ID_{key\_i}, t, E_{K_i^t}\{i\} > \tag{3}$$

In (3), the node ID i is encrypted to show that S_i has not generated any sensing data during the tth epoch.
- If $\mu_{i,t} \neq 0$, we use the symmetric key to encrypt each data item along with the score of its subsequent data item in the ordered data-item sequence. This operation is used to protect the privacy of the data items and prepare for the conservation of interity for the top-*k* query results. However, if no other information is included in the report, the storage node can not perform correct top-*k* query processing because it does not know the values of the data items in the report. Thus, we use OPES to encrypt the data scores and add the encrypted data scores to the report. Let $E_{OPES}\{*\}$ denote the encryption operation using OPES. Then, we have

$$RPT_{S_i}^M = <ID_{key\_i}, t, E_{K_i^t}\{i, d_{i,1}\}, E_{OPES}\{d_{i,1}\}, E_{K_i^t}\{D_{i,1}, d_{i,2}\}, E_{OPES}\{d_{i,2}\}, E_{K_i^t}\{D_{i,2}, d_{i,3}\},$$
$$......, E_{OPES}\{d_{i,\mu_{i,t}-1}\}, E_{K_i^t}\{D_{i,\mu_{i,t}-1}, d_{i,\mu_{i,t}}\}, E_{OPES}\{d_{i,\mu_{i,t}}\}, E_{K_i^t}\{D_{i,\mu_{i,t}}\} >$$
$$\tag{4}$$

4.3   Queries Processing Stage

The storage node M processes the top-*k* queries sent from the Sink node; and then sends the query results back to the Sink node.

Suppose M receives a top-k query $Q_t = <C, t, k, QS>$ from the Sink node. M first processes each data report in the tth epoch sent from each sensor node in QS. Then M puts the processing results of each report together to create the final top-k query result. Take S_i, which is supposed to be one of the sensor nodes in QS, as an example. We now show how the report sent from S_i is processed by M. Let RST_{S_i} denote the processing result of $RPT_{S_i}^M$ by M, and $n_{i,t}$ denote the number of qualified top-k data items in RST_{S_i}. Then, RST_{S_i} can be expressed as follows.

- If $n_{i,t} = \mu_{i,t} = 0$, we have

$$RST_{S_i} = <ID_{key\_i}, E_{K_i^t}\{i\} > \tag{5}$$

- if $n_{i,t} = 0, \mu_{i,t} > 0$, then

$$RST_{S_i} = <ID_{key\_i}, E_{K_i^t}\{i, d_{i,1}\} > \tag{6}$$

- if $0 \le n_{i,t} = \mu_{i,t} \le k$, we have

$$RST_{S_i} = <ID_{key\_i}, E_{K_i^t}\{i, d_{i,1}\}, E_{K_i^t}\{D_{i,1}, d_{i,2}\}, E_{K_i^t}\{D_{i,2}, d_{i,3}\}, \ldots\ldots,$$
$$E_{K_i^t}\{D_{i,\mu_{i,t}-1}, d_{i,\mu_{i,t}}\}, E_{K_i^t}\{D_{i,\mu_{i,t}}\} > \tag{7}$$

- if $0 < n_{i,t} \le k, \mu_{i,t} > n_{i,t}$, we have

$$RST_{S_i} = <ID_{key\_i}, E_{K_i^t}\{i, d_{i,1}\}, E_{K_i^t}\{D_{i,1}, d_{i,2}\}, E_{K_i^t}\{D_{i,2}, d_{i,3}\}, \ldots\ldots,$$
$$E_{K_i^t}\{D_{i,n_{i,t}-1}, d_{i,n_{i,t}}\}, E_{K_i^t}\{D_{i,n_{i,t}}, d_{i,n_{i,t}+1}\} > \tag{8}$$

As shown above, all the data scores encrypted using OPES and all the unqualified data items encrypted using the symmetric key along with the bound scores are removed from the top-k query result; because they are no longer of use.

4.4   Verification Stage

The Sink node verifies the authentication and completeness of the top-k query results using the algorithm proposed in this paper. Suppose the Sink node receives a top-k query result R_t; we elucidate the verification procedure of authentication and completeness, respectively, on R_t.

To verify the authentication of R_t, the Sink node first determines the symmetric key according to the key ID in R_t. Then, using this key, the Sink node decrypts all the encrypted data in R_t. After that, the Sink node checks whether R_t includes the score of each data item included in R_t. If R_t does not include the score of any data item included in R_t, R_t is considered inauthentic because some encrypted information must be dropped or replaced by adversaries and R_t should be suspicious. If R_t passes such a check, the Sink node recalculates the score of each data item in R_t, and compares the score worked out by the Sink node with the corresponding score included in R_t. If all the scores worked by the Sink node are equal to the corresponding scores in R_t, R_t is considered authentic. Otherwise, either false data are inserted in R_t; or encrypted data blocks including the qualified data items are dropped by adversaries before they are sent out from the storage node.

To verify the completeness of R_t, the Sink node should first verify the authentication of R_t. If R_t is not authentic, it must be incomplete; because there are equal to or less than k data items in R_t and the existence of false data in R_t means that one or more qualified top-k data item/items is/are dropped or replaced. If R_t is considered authentic and the score of each data item in R_t is also included in R_t, the following steps should be followed to continue verifying the completeness of R_t. Suppose Q_t aims to find k data items with the biggest scores in the query region and epoch. First, determine the smallest data score, which is denoted as d_{tail}, of the data items included in R_t; and the biggest data score, which is denoted as $d_{outline}$, among all the scores with no corresponding data items in R_t. The term $d_{outline}$ can also be considered as the biggest scores among all the data items generated by the sensor nodes in the queried region QS and the queried epoch. After that, compare d_{tail} with $d_{outline}$. If $d_{tail} \geq d_{outlin}$, R_t is considered compete. Otherwise, it is incomplete.

5 Simulation

We test the performance of WBB-TQ using OMNET++ as the simulator. To make a comparison, we implement WBB-TQ as well as Scheme 1 and Scheme 2 proposed in [1]. To ease presentation, we use Scheme 1 and Scheme 2 to refer to Scheme 1 and Scheme 2 proposed in [1], respectively.

Most of the parameters used in this paper are listed in Table 2; other parameters, such as the bit length of a data item, the bit length of a data score, and the bit length of a MAC, are the same as those in [1]. In Table 2, C_{size} denotes the area size of a cell, $|QS|$ denotes the number of sensor nodes in the queried region, and R denotes the communication radius of a sensor node. Like [1], we also assume that the energy consumed by sending a bit of data is the same as that of receiving a bit of data, and use the amount of data transmitted in the network to evaluate the energy consumption of the network.

Table 2. Parameters used in the simulation

Parameter	Value	Parameter	Value
C_{size}	400×400 m^2	N	500
R	50 m	$\mu_{i,t}$	20
$|QS|$	100		

The metrics used in this paper to evaluate the performance of WBB-TQ are the communication cost; inside a cell, the total communication cost is denoted as C_{in}; and the total communication cost outside a cell is denoted as C_{out}. Specifically, C_{in} refers to the total energy consumed by all the sensor nodes in a cell to send all the verification information generated by all the sensor nodes in the cell in an epoch to the storage node in the cell, and C_{out} refers to the energy consumed by the storage node to send the necessary verification information for a top-k query result to the Sink node so that the Sink node can verify the completeness and authenticity of the query result. According to the simulation results in [1], Scheme 1 performs better than Scheme 2 of C_{in} but worse than Scheme 2 of C_{out}. Thus, to evaluate the performance of WBB-TQ, we compare it with Scheme 1 of C_{in} and with Scheme 2 of C_{out}.

5.1   Performance of C_{in}

The simulation results of C_{in} are shown in Figs. 2 and 3. Specifically, Fig. 2 shows the results with $\mu_{i,t}$ taken as the variable. From Fig. 2, we can see that the performance of WBB-TQ on C_{in} is much better than that of Scheme 1. The value of C_{in} in WBB-TQ is smaller than that in Scheme 1, and the former also grows slower than the latter as the increase of $\mu_{i,t}$. The reason for such phenomenon can be described as follows. On the one side, in WBB-TQ, the bit length of the verification information corresponding to a data item is about twice that of a data score, which is much shorter in bit length than a data item. On the other side, the bit length of the verification information corresponding to a data item in Scheme 1 is about the length of a MAC, which is much longer than the bit length of a data item [1].

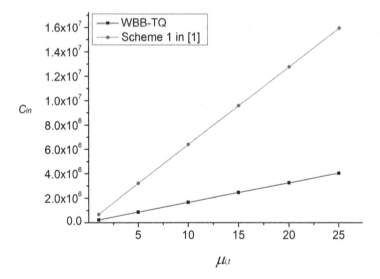

Fig. 2. Impact of internal communication cost C_{in} under parameter $\mu_{i,t}$

Figure 3 shows the simulation results of WBB-TQ and Scheme 1 on C_{in} with N taken as the variable. It is clear that the value of C_{in} in WBB-TQ is much smaller than that in Scheme 1, and the former also grows slower than the latter as the variable N increases. The verification information for a data item in WBB-TQ is much smaller than that in Scheme 1. Thus, the total communication cost of the total verification information in a cell in WBB-TQ is smaller than that in Scheme 1. In addition, as the

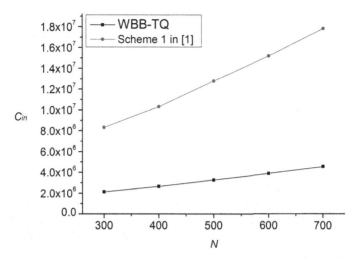

Fig. 3. Impact of internal communication cost C_{in} under parameter N

number of sensor nodes increases, the total number of data items generated by the sensor nodes in a cell also increases, and the increasing speed of the total amount of verification information in Scheme 1 is much faster than that in WBB-TQ because each data item needs a MAC in Scheme 1 while only a score, which is much shorter than a MAC, is needed in WBB-TQ.

5.2 Performance of C_{out}

The simulation results of C_{out} are shown in Figs. 4 and 5. Figure 4 shows the results of C_{out} in WBB-TQ and Scheme 2 when $\mu_{i,t}$ is taken as the variable. We can see that the values of C_{out} in WBB-TQ are much lower than those in Scheme 2. This means that the energy consumed by transmitting the verification information between the storage and the Sink node in WBB-TQ is much less than in Scheme 2. Also, C_{out} in WBB-TQ is much more stable than in Scheme 2. In fact, according to processing procedure in the Queries processing stage in WBB-TQ, the change of $\mu_{i,t}$ can not affect C_{out} too much.

Figure 5 illustrates the results for C_{out} in WBB-TQ and Scheme 2 when k is taken as the variable with other parameters kept the same. It is clear that C_{out} in WBB-TQ changes little while in Scheme 2 it increases significantly. The reason is as follows. Given a definite Δk which denotes the increased value of k, the increased bit length of the verification information sent out by the data storage node in WBB-TQ is just $\Delta k *$ l_{score}, where l_{score} denotes the bit length of a data score, while the increased bit length of the verification information sent out by the data storage node in Scheme 2 is at least $\Delta k * l_{MAC}$, where l_{MAC} denotes the bit length of a MAC. As mentioned in [1], l_{MAC} is much longer in bit length than l_{score}.

The results for C_{out} in WBB-TQ and Scheme 2 when $|QS|$, which denotes the number of sensor nodes in the queried region, is taken as the variable with other

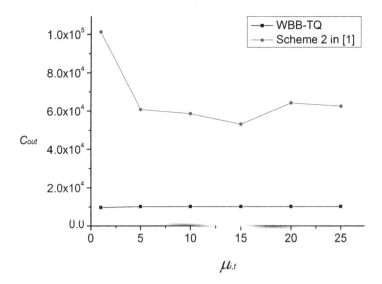

Fig. 4. Impact of external communication cost C_{out} under parameter $\mu_{i,t}$

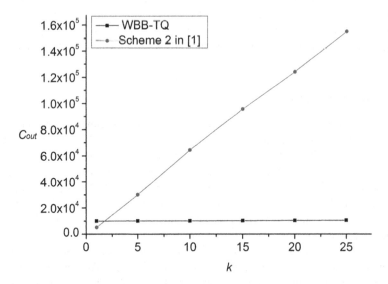

Fig. 5. Impact of external communication cost C_{out} under parameter k

parameters unchanged. It shows that C_{out} in WBB-TQ increases with the increase of $|QS|$. This is because a top-k result in WBB-TQ should include some verification generated by each sensor node in the queried region. The more queried sensor nodes, the more verification information should be included in the query result. However, the value change of C_{out} in Scheme 2 is not as great as that in WBB-TQ; because a top-k result in Scheme 2 only includes the verification information generated by the qualified top-*k* sensor nodes and the change of $|QS|$ affects the total amount of verification information generated by the top-*k* sensor nodes very little. Although C_{out} is more stable in Scheme 2 than in WBB-TQ, it is much lower in WBB-TQ than in Scheme 2.

6 Conclusion

Cyber security in two-tiered sensor networks has drawn more and more attention in the academic world. In two-tiered sensor networks, the security of top-*k* queries is facing threat. Thus, we proposed a secure top-*k* query processing scheme named WBB-TQ in this paper to prevent adversaries from undermining the authenticity and completeness of top-*k* query results. The security analysis in this paper also shows that the novel data-bound method and the verification algorithm proposed in the paper can ensure the completeness of the top-*k* query results. Moreover, the simulation results show that the energy efficiency of WBB-TQ is much higher than that of the state-of-the-art scheme proposed for securing top-*k* queries in two-tied sensor networks.

Acknowledgments. This work is supported in part by National Science Foundation (NSF) (Grant No. 1137732), the National Natural Science Foundation of China (Grant Nos. 61502540, 61562005, 61502057, 61572530, 61402542), the China Scholarship Council (Grant No. 2015 [3012]), the National Science Foundation of Hunan Province (Grant No. 2015JJ4077).

References

1. Zhang, R., Shi, J., Liu, Y., Zhang, Y.: Verifiable fine-grained top-k queries in tiered sensor networks. In: Proceedings of the 29th International Conference on Computer Communications (INFOCOM), San Diego, CA, USA, pp. 1–9 (2010)
2. Dai, H., Yang, G., Huang, H., et al.: Efficient verifiable top-k queries in two-tiered wireless sensor networks. Ksii Trans. Internet Inf. Syst. **9**(6), 2111–2131 (2015)
3. He, R., Dai, H., Yang, G., et al.: An efficient top-k query processing with result integrity verification in two-tiered wireless sensor networks. Math. Probl. Eng. **2015**, 1–8 (2015). Article ID 538482
4. Yao, Y., Ma, L., Liu, J.: Privacy-preserving top-k query in two-tiered wireless sensor networks. Int. J. Adv. Comput. Technol. **4**(6), 226–235 (2012)
5. Fan, Y., Chen, H.: Verifiable privacy-preserving top-k query protocol in two-tiered sensor networks. Chin. J. Comput. **35**(3), 423–433 (2012)
6. Liao, X.J., Li, J.Z.: Privacy-preserving and secure top-k query in two-tier wireless sensor network. In: Proceedings of IEEE Global Communications Conference (GLOBECOM), Anaheim, California, USA, pp. 335–341 (2012)
7. Ma, X., Song, H., Wang, J., et al.: A novel verification scheme for fine-grained top-k queries in two-tiered sensor networks. Wireless Pers. Commun. **75**(3), 1809–1826 (2014)
8. Yu, C.M., Tsou, Y.T., Lu, C.S., Kuo, S.Y.: Practical and secure multidimensional query framework in tiered sensor networks. IEEE Trans. Inf. Forencics Secur. **6**(2), 241–255 (2011)
9. Sheng, B., Li, Q.: Verifiable privacy-preserving sensor network storage for range query. IEEE Trans. Mob. Comput. **10**(9), 1312–1326 (2011)

10. Shi, J., Zhang, R., Zhang, Y.: Secure range queries in tiered sensor networks. In: Proceedings of the 28th International Conference on Computer Communications (INFOCOM), Rio de Janeiro, Brazil, pp. 945–953 (2009)
11. Zhang, R., Shi, J., Zhang, Y.: Secure multidimensional range queries in sensor networks. In: Proceedings of the 10th ACM International Symposium on Mobile AD Hoc Networking and Computing (MobiHoc), New Orleans, Louisiana, USA, pp. 197–206 (2009)
12. Chen, F., Liu, A.: SafeQ: secure and efficient query processing in sensor networks. In: Proceedings of the 29th International Conference on Computer Communications (INFOCOM), San Diego, CA, USA, pp. 2642–2650 (2010)
13. Shi, J., Zhang, R., Zhang, Y.: A spatiotemporal approach for secure range queries in tiered sensor networks. IEEE Trans. Wireless Commun. **10**(1), 264–273 (2011)
14. Das, G., Gunopulos, D., Koudas, N., Tsirogiannis, D.: Answering top-k queries using views. In: Proceedings of the 32nd International Conference on Very Large Data Bases (VLDB), Seoul, Korea, pp. 446–451 (2006)

A Floorplanning Algorithm for Partially Reconfigurable FPGA in Wireless Sensor Network

Jinyu Wang$^{(\boxtimes)}$ (iD), Weiguo Wu, Zhaonan Qin, and Dongfang Zhao

School of Electronic and Information Engineering, Xi'an Jiaotong University,
Xi'an 710049, China
wjyokok@gmail.com

Abstract. Floorplanning represents a critical step when dealing with Partially Reconfigurable (PR) designed Field Programmable Gate Array (FPGA) in Wireless Sensor Networks (WSNs). In the WSN, a task is always rejected by floorplanner when the free reconfigurable resources are enough but the shape is not matched, leading to high rejection rates and low utilization of resources. In this paper, we provide a novel algorithm named Best-Fit Duration and Transformation (BFDT) floorplanning to improve the performance of FPGA system. The main innovations of this paper are two folds. Firstly, to place tasks as many as possible and enhance the utilization of resources, we propose best-fit duration strategy based on the adhesion duration indicator, which keeps the positional relationship as long as possible between adjoining tasks. Secondly, we propose a task shape transformation method to allow some rejected tasks to be placed by changing their aspect ratio, therefore reduces the rejection rate. The BFDT performs very well in the simulation experiments with unknown task shapes and arriving times. Compared to the first-fit and best-fit algorithms, the BFDT reduces the rejection rate up to 22% and 13% in almost the same total execution time, which also holds a better resources utilization.

Keywords: Wireless Sensor Networks · Field Programmable Gate Array
Reconfigurable Computing · Floorplan · Computer Aided Design

1 Introduction

Due to the flexibility of wireless links, Wireless Sensor Networks (WSNs) are widely used in many fields (e.g., tracking objects in the battlefield, smart healthcare, industrial control and precision agriculture), a WSN is composed of multiple sensor nodes which consist of microprocessors and sensors, by processing data on the sensor node, and just transmitting the result, the onboard processing reduces the communication bandwidth and the power consumption of one sensor node [1]. Field Programmable Gate Array (FPGA) has received a considerable attention in recent years due to the high flexibility, low power consumption and desired computational power. In early days, the FPGA only supports static reconfiguration, within which all tasks cannot be interrupted until accomplished. With the development of hardware techniques, the FPGA allows part of resources to be reconfigured, which can dynamically change some tasks at runtime

© Springer International Publishing AG 2017
G. Wang et al. (Eds.): SpaCCS 2017 Workshops, LNCS 10658, pp. 667–679, 2017.
https://doi.org/10.1007/978-3-319-72395-2_60

while the rest of the system is not influenced. The Partial Reconfiguration (PR) [2] offers new opportunity to place more tasks at different time on the sensor device, thus PR has widely applied in the real-time application area, like WSNs.

The role of floorplanning in the WSN application is even more prominent to the offline application. In the latter, the required reconfigurable resources and the amount of tasks are determined before floorplanning; while in the former, since the quantity and the type of tasks enter into the system randomly [3, 4], resources in the device may be insufficient for placing the continually coming tasks. Therefore, the floorplanning of PR-based system directly affects the feasibility and the performance of the final solution. However, it is a quite complex and time-consuming activity, since the complex management of configurable resources [5] and shapes of tasks [6]. In this paper, we present a novel tasks floorplanning named Best-Fit Duration and Transformation (BFDT) algorithm for real-time applications. In conclusion, we summarize our contributions as follows.

1. We accurately model all of the hardware tasks in real-time applications.
2. We provide best-fit duration strategy based on the adhesion duration indicator, which keeps the positional relationship as long as possible between adjoining tasks. Therefore, the floorplanner can place more tasks and enhance the utilization of resources.
3. We propose a task shape transformation method to allow some rejected tasks to be placed by changing their aspect ratio, thus reduces the rejection rate.

The remainder of this paper is organized as follows: Sect. 2 discusses the related work on task scheduling and placement method. Section 3 presents a brief description of the task model and proposes two novel floorplanning algorithms. Section 4 discusses the obtained results. Section 5 concludes the paper and suggests future research.

2 Related Work

As discussed in Sect. 1, depending on the different application scenes, the mainstream floorplanning algorithm can be divided into two categories: online floorplanning [7] and offline floorplanning [8]. Several offline floorplanning algorithms have been proposed in the literature, the first class of algorithms focuses on the FPGA devices in which the resources are homogeneously distributed [9]. But heterogeneous resource is common in the state-of-the-art FPGA, one of the first floorplanner that considers the heterogeneity of FPGA resources has been presented in [10]. The Floorplacer in [11] cuts the device and tries to minimize the number of nets crossing two partitions based on a Nonlinear Integer Programming (NLP) bipartitioner. The method proposed in [6] consists of two main steps: firstly, a conflict graph model describes all of the possible conflicts among pairs of placements, in this step, the aspect ratio of a task can be altered to get a feasible solution; subsequently, each task defined by the required resources is placed on the device, this step uses a Genetic Algorithm (GA) based approach which satisfies the constraints of wire length within a task and between tasks. However, the trial-and-error process of GA may generate many candidate placements and the space of the solution is considerable, it will consume a significant amount of time. Different from offline placement which pursues high resource utilization, the target of online placement is to achieve the shortest execution time and the minimum rejection rate. Thus, the afore-mentioned methods cannot be applied directly to online floorplanning [12].

For online floorplanning, the first-fit and best-fit are two classical algorithms [12]. Based on these basic algorithms, the authors of [13] presented a placement algorithm named KAMER, while the resource manager of KAMER considers all maximal free rectangles, which reduces the rejection rate but result in a long resource management time. In [14], a multi-shape task implementation is proposed, the shape of a task can be altered and an abstract model is set up to evaluate the influence of different shapes, sizes and execution time for each task on the placement result. However, the number of candidate task shapes are limited and this work does not take the fine-grained task shape transformation into account, like the offline floorplanning do. In this paper, based on the abundant routing resources [6, 15], we proposed a task shape transformation strategy that enhances system performance through adjusting the aspect ratio of tasks.

The most recent floorplanner is [12], it is based on the best-fit algorithm and proposed an adhesion indicator to evaluate the merits of candidate resources, this indicator takes the positional relationship among tasks into consideration and lets tasks be placed closer, which also results in smaller fragmentation as well as lower rejection rate. However, the execution time of each task is different and this method does not consider the duration of adhesion among tasks. In this paper, an adhesion duration indicator is introduced, which considers both time length and positional relationship to fully use the reconfigurable resources.

3 The Proposed Approach

This section first provides a task description model and characterizes the FPGA device, and then, introduces the proposed floorplanning algorithm BFDT, because the BFDT is expanded from first-fit and best-fit algorithm, before detailing BFDT algorithm, a brief introduction of these two algorithms is introduced.

3.1 Characterization of FPGA and Task Model

The FPGA device can be characterized as a grid structure with the height of H and width of W, for example, the Xilinx Virtex-6 XC6VCX75T FPGA can be described using a grid with $H = 6$ (rows) and $W = 66$ (columns) [16]. Each point of the grid is described in a Cartesian integer coordinates with the position of (h, w), where h means the row and w is the column. The value of each point is initialized as 0, it is updated to the ID of a task (like: 1, 2, 3,..., N) when the task is placed on this point. Once a task is fulfilled, the corresponding point value is updated to 0 and can be placed again.

The hardware task is the minimal function unit we can control in a floorplanning process, in this paper, a task model is defined as (1).

$$T = \{a, e, d, h, w, s\} \tag{1}$$

$$Tlax_i = d_i - t \tag{2}$$

where a is the arriving time which means the time that a task comes into the prepared list and is ready to be executed, e is the execution time and d is the deadline which means that the task should be executed before this moment, or it will comes into the reject list and never be dispatched any more, $h * w$ is the amount of required reconfigurable resources for one task, s is a binary variable which 0 means the task has never be transformed. The laxity time of a task means the emergency degree and is defined in (2), t is the current time, with the passage of time, the laxity time is decreasing and the priority of the task is going high, until the $Tlax$ is less than zero which means the corresponding task is rejected. To reduce the complexity, some hypotheses should be satisfied as described in [12]: (i) All tasks are independent and there is no communications between them. (ii) The task schedule is the first come first service (FCFS) and the ready list is sorted by $Tlax$. (iii) The amount of reconfiguration resources beside CLB are abundant, like IO, BRAMs.

3.2   First-Fit Floorplanning Algorithm

The key idea of the first-fit algorithm is to scan the device grid from left to right, top to button, and it will stop when finding a solution for a task. Table 1 shows the pseudo code of the first-fit algorithm, *isEmpty()* function at line 1 checks whether all tasks have been estimated. Line 3 to line 4 judges whether the task could be placed in a certain time. Line 8 to line 9 means that if the time is too late to start a task, it will be rejected and be failure to execute. The floorplanning method in line 13 shows that if the task is placed successfully, *count* + 1. It is worth noting that after the executing tasks are finished, The function *updateDeviceInfo()* at line 17 releases corresponding resources and updates the value of points with respect to the device grid to 0. After finishing estimating all tasks, this algorithm outputs the total execution time T and the number of successfully placed tasks *count*.

The core function of the first-fit algorithm is *FirstFitPlacing()*, the point should satisfy constraint (3), where h_t and w_t are the height and the width of the need to schedule task, *value* (i, j) function represent the value of point (i, j). Thus, for each task, the time complexity of the first-fit algorithm is $O(H * W * h_t * w_t)$.

$$\sum_{i=h}^{h+h_t} \sum_{j=w}^{w+w_t} value(i,j) = 0 \tag{3}$$

3.3   Best-Fit Floorplanning Algorithm

In contrast to the first-fit algorithm which does not consider the fragmentation of free resources and the rejection rate of tasks, best-fit algorithm introduces an adhesion evaluation indicator to estimate the positional relation among tasks. The adhesion indicator can be calculated as the overlapped point counts of adjoining tasks. The larger

Table 1. Pseudo code of the first-fit algorithm

FirstFit():

Input: *task*; //one task information

prepared_list<task>; //all need to placed tasks information list

ready_list<task>; //tasks can be placed in a certain time

executing_list<task>; //executing tasks in a certain time

reject_list<task>; //failure to execute tasks list

Output: total execution time *T*, and successful placed tasks *count*;

BEGIN

1. **WHILE**(!*prepared_list*.isEmpty())

2.   **FOR**(*i*=0; *i<prepared_list.length*; *i*++)

3.   **IF**(*prepared_list*[*i*].getArriveTime()≤*T*)

4.   *ready_list*.add(*task*[*i*]); *prepared_list*.remove(*task*[*i*]);

5.   **END IF**;

6.   **END FOR**;

7.   **FOR**(*i*=0; *i< ready_list.length*; *i*++)

8.   **IF**(*ready_list*[*i*].getLatestStartTime()<*T*)

9.   *reject_list*.add(*task*[*i*]); *ready_list*.remove(*task*[*i*]);

10.   **ELSE**

11.   **END IF**;

12.   **IF**(FirstFitPlacing(*ready_list*.[*i*]))

13.   *count*=*count*+1;*executing_list*.add(*task*[*i*]); *ready_list*.remove(*task*[*i*]);

14.   **END IF**;

15.   **END FOR**;

16.   **FOR**(*i*=0; *i< executing_list.length*; *i*++)

17.   **IF**(*executing_list*[*i*].getRunnedTime()>=*executing_list*[*i*].getExecutedTime())

18.   updateDeviceInfo(*task*[*i*]); *executing_list*.remove(*task*[*i*]);

19.   **END IF**;

20.   **END FOR**;

21.   *ready_list*.updateTlax(*T*++);

22. **END WHILE**;

END

---

adhesion a task is, the closer to other placed tasks it will be. It is worth noting that the closer tasks often result in the smaller fragmentation and lower rejection rate.

The task schedule and the rejection judgment method are the same as the first-fit algorithm as described in Table 1, while the placing function at line 12 is much different, Table 2 presents the pseudo code of *BestFitPlacing()*, which is also the core method of this algorithm. Its process is as follows: finding all of the possible placing points for each candidate task; then counting the adhesion values of each solution; finally, placing the task to the point which has the maximum adhesion value. The *BestFitPlacing()* function can be implemented with a $O(H * W)$ time complexity, so using the best-fit algorithm to place a task, the time complexity is $O(H^2 * W^2 * h_t * w_t)$.

Table 2. Pseudo code of BestFitPlacing()

BestFitPlacing():
BEGIN
1. **FOR**(h=0; h<H; h++)
2. **FOR**(w=0; w<W; w++)
3.   **IF**(placing *task*[i] at point(h,w) success)
4.   Adhesion[i]=CountAdhesion(h,w);
5.   **END IF**;
6. **END FOR**;
7. **END FOR**;
8. placing *task*[i] at point(Max(Adhesion[i]));
END

The floorplanning process of seven tasks listed in Table 3 is shown in Fig. 1. The FPGA device grid is 5 * 8, task 1, task 2 and task 3 were placed at time 0 as depicted in Fig. 1(a). Figure 1(b) shows the placing result of task 4 using the first-fit algorithm at time 1, in this situation, task 4 becomes an obstacle for task 5 to be placed, thus, the floorplanner will reject task 5 at time 2. Figure 1(c) is the placing result of task 4 using best-fit algorithm, the adhesion indicator is 4 and it is the maximum value in this situation, and also, task 5 is able to be placed in the device.

Table 3. The information of seven example tasks

Task	Arrive time	Execute time	h	w
1	0	6	2	2
2	0	20	4	2
3	0	10	2	2
4	1	16	2	2
5	2	4	4	2
6	8	6	4	3
7	12	5	2	3

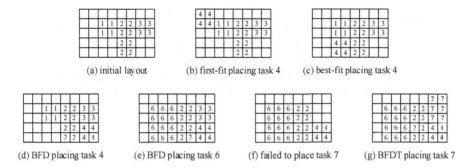

Fig. 1. The placing result of seven tasks using different algorithm

3.4 Best-Fit Duration (BFD) Floorplanning Algorithm

Best-fit is a basal floorplanning algorithm, however, it may produce external fragments if the execution time of a task is too short, leading to the low utilization of FPGA. In this section, the best-fit duration (BFD) floorplanning algorithm based on an **adhesion duration indicator** is proposed to enhance the utilization.

Back to Table 3, after task 1 and task 5 were finished and the corresponding resources are released, Fig. 1(c) is the device layout using the best-fit algorithm at time 6, in current situation, there are not enough resources for the upcoming task 6 and it will be rejected at time 8.

Figure 1(d) shows the placement of task 4 via BFD algorithm at time 1, although the adhesion of task 4 in Fig. 1(c) and (d) are the same, the time length of adhesion in this two results are different. At time 1, the remaining execution time of task 1, task 2 and task 3 are 3, 11 and 9, the adhesion duration indicator of task 4 in Fig. 1(d) are $2 \cdot 19 + 2 \cdot 9 = 56$ and it is larger than in Fig. 1(c): $2 \cdot 19 + 2 \cdot 5 = 48$, thus, we chose Fig. 1(d) as the feasible solution for task 4, in this scenario, task 4 can be bound with other tasks to save resource as long as they can, so task 6 can be placed successfully at time 8 and the layout is shown as Fig. 1(e). Because there are no more additional operations, the time complexity of BFD and best-fit are the same, O ($H^2 * W^2 * h_t * w_t$).

3.5 Best-Fit Duration and Transformation (BFDT) Floorplanning Algorithm

BFDT is an improvement of BFD algorithm. In order to obtain a lower rejection rate, we propose a **task shape transformation strategy**. The risk of changing aspect ratio of a task shape is the internal routing, but the abundant routing resources in state-of-the-art FPGA devices make it possible to transform the shape of a task in the FPGA floorplanning, the aspect ratio of a task is defined during the floorplanning process [7–11]. In this paper, two restrictions of the aspect ratio and the transformation strategy are also proposed in order to reduce the internal communications delay and the total execution time, the two restrictions below

(i) The change of aspect ratio for one task is restricted within a certain range to avoid extreme rectangular shapes. Because the greater the aspect ratio is, the farther the distance of points in the rectangle are, as well as the internal routing length, with the increase of internal routing length, the communications delay will increase. Constraint (4) is the definition of this restriction, where the required resources count is $h_t * w_t$, h_{t_temp} and w_{t_temp} are the candidate height and width of this task, the value of λ controls the limitation of the aspect ratio. It is worth noting that, if the original height or weight of a task is $1(h_t = 1$ or $w_t = 1)$, the lower limit value of λ is 1.

$$\forall t \in task, \forall \lambda \in N^*$$
$$2 \leq \lambda \leq h_t \cdot w_t \tag{4}$$
$$\frac{\lambda}{h_t \cdot w_t} \leq \frac{h_{t\_temp}}{w_{t\_temp}} \leq \frac{h_t \cdot w_t}{\lambda}$$

(ii) The task shape transformation strategy will be executed when a task is failure to be placed and the strategy runs only once for each task. Because the transformation process will consume a large amount of time, multiple executions of this strategy will increase the total execution time.

The detail pseudo code of this algorithm is shown in Table 4, when the BFD fail to place the original task which is never been processed, the added function $taskTrans()$ at line 13 is used to transform the task shape under restriction (i) and store all of the optional shapes. Once the candidate shape is placed successfully, the task's information will be updated (line 14 to line 19). After all candidate task shapes were processed, no matter what the result is, within the constraint (ii), the transformation strategy cannot run twice as shown in line 20. Function $taskTrans()$ is invoked $O(\log(h_t * w_t))$ times, so the BFDT algorithm has an overall time complexity of $O(H^2 * W^2 * h_t * w_t * \log(h_t * w_t))$.

Figure 1(f) shows the layout of FPGA device at time 12, the execution of task 3 was finished and released resources, task 7 failed to be placed because the shape of this task is 2 * 3 while the grid cannot match this kind of shape even though the count of free resources is enough. In this scenario, using the BFDT algorithm to transform the

Table 4. Pseudo code of the BFDT

BFDT:
… /*the same as the pseudo code in best-fit and algorithm from 1 to 11*/
12. **IF**(BFDPlacing(*ready_list*.[*i*]) *failure* **AND** *ready_list*.[*i*].getTransStatus==0)
13.   *tasktemp_list<task>* = taskTrans(*ready_list*.[*i*]);
14.   **FOR**(*j*=0; *j< tasktemp_list.length*; *j*++)
15.   **IF**(BFDPlacing(*tasktemp_list*.[*j*]))
16.   *count=count*+1; *executing_list*.add(*task*[*i*]); *ready_list*.remove(*task*[*i*]);
17.   **BREAK**;
18.   **END IF**;
19.   **END FOR**;
20. *ready_list*.[*i*].setTransStatus(1);
21. **END IF**;
…/*the same as the pseudo code in best-fit and first-fit algorithm from 15 to 22*/
END

shape of task 7 and the feasible placing solution is shown in Fig. 1(g), all of the seven tasks in Table 1 have been placed successfully and the rejection rate is 0%.

4   Experiments

The proposed floorplanning algorithm has been implemented in Java, all of the experiments have been performed on a 3.60 GHz Intel Core i7-4790 processor with 8 GB memory running a Windows operating system. The simulated FPGA device contains 10 000 CLBs, which the height and the width are both 100. This test suite in Table 5 consists of 5 sets with different area occupancy, arriving time and average execution time; in particular, with respect to intensity, there are three sets occupy 50 tasks and two sets consist of 100 tasks and the λ is 2, and to ensure the fairness, all of the experiment results are the average value of 20 replications of the test cases.

Table 5. Information of five task sets

TaskSet	Arrive time, Unit	Execute time, Unit	Height, CLB	Width, CLB	Quantity
Set1	[0, 50]	[10, 20]	[10, 30]	[10, 30]	50
Set2	[0, 100]	[10, 20]	[10, 30]	[10, 30]	100
Set3	[0, 50]	[10, 20]	[10, 20]	[10, 20]	100
Set4	[0, 50]	[10, 20]	[20, 30]	[20, 30]	50
Set5	[0, 50]	[5, 30]	[10, 30]	[10, 30]	50

In the first experimental session, we performed an extensive testing campaign considering a large set of test cases aimed at demonstrating that the proposed BFDT Floorplanning algorithm outperforms the other approaches. The evaluation indicators of this session are the rejection rate and the total execution time of each test suite, the rejection rate can be stated as (5)

$$\rho = \frac{N_{reject}}{N_{all}} = \frac{reject\_list.size}{prepared\_list.size} \tag{5}$$

where N_{reject} is the amount of rejected tasks which are not executed before the last begin time, in this paper, N_{reject} can be calculated by $reject\_list.size$ from Table 1. N_{all} is the number of tasks need to be placed and the value is $prepared\_list.size$. The total execution time represents the speed of the floorplanner and this indicator is calculated by variable T.

Figures 2 and 3 show the results of this first experimental session, in terms of rejection rate, BFDT is always able to find better solution than other algorithms, and the BFD algorithm follows, compared with first-fit, best-fit and BFD algorithm, the BFDT algorithm reduces the rejection rate up to 22%, 13% and 10%, respectively. The reason BFD has a better performance than first-fit and best-fit algorithm is that the proposed adhesion duration indicator not only considers the positional relation among tasks, but also takes the timeline into account, because the BFDT algorithm adjusts the

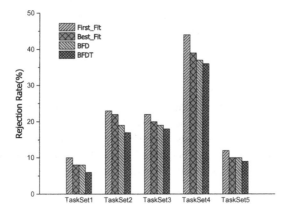

Fig. 2. Rejection rate comparison of five task sets

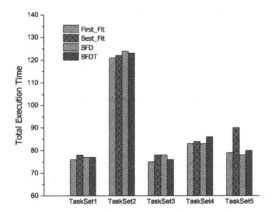

Fig. 3. Total execution time comparison of five task sets

aspect ratio of the shape when a task failed to be placed, thus, increasing the successful placement possibility further. It is worth noting that for the total execution time, the BFDT is not the most saving timing algorithm because the total executed tasks of BFDT is the highest, in particular, for taskset3, BFDT reduces the rejection rate of the first-fit algorithm by 18% while using the almost same amount of total execution time.

In the second session, we performed a more challenging comparison of BFDT against other algorithms, exploiting the fragmentation representation, in this paper fragmentation F is defined in (6) [2]

$$F = \begin{cases} (\frac{h-1}{A-1}) \cdot H \cdot W, & A > 1 \\ 0, & A = 1 \end{cases} \qquad (6)$$

where h is the quantity of partitions which only include continuous free CLB and A is the total number of free CLBs, H and W are the height and the width of a FPGA device grid, $H * W$ represents the amount of resources can provide. The smaller of F is, the more CLBs in one partition are, as well as the better performance of floorplanning algorithm will be.

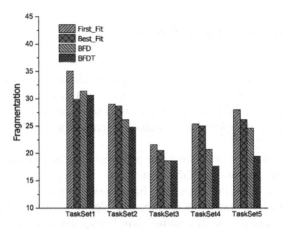

Fig. 4. Fragmentation comparison of five task sets

Figure 4 shows the fragmentation average value of five task sets in four algorithms, the first_fit algorithm has a highest fragmentation and the BFDT has the best performance. Figure 5 is the result of fragmentation changes with the update of each task in taskset5, it is worth noting that the fragmentation would be recorded when: (1) a task is placed successfully and the grid need to update, (2) a placed task is completed and the occupied CLBs are released, (3) a task is failure to be placed and added in the *rejected_list*, (4) a task is removed from the *rejected_list*. Thus, there are 100 variations occurred during the placement of taskset5 with 50 tasks. We can see from Fig. 5, the

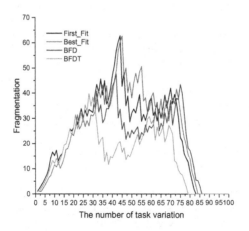

Fig. 5. Fragmentation variations of taskset5

fragmentation of BFTD is clearly smaller than that of the other three algorithms, especially from the variation range 35 to 60, for the first 31 times of variation, the BFD algorithm and the BFDT algorithm have the same fragmentation, it is because when the free CLBs are enough the placing method of this two algorithms are the same.

5   Conclusion and Future Works

This paper proposed a novel floorplanning algorithm for partial reconfigurable FPGAs in WSNs. The algorithm is based on the adhesion duration indicator and the task shape transformation strategy that allows more tasks in a sensor node to be executed. Experimental results demonstrated the effectiveness of the proposed BFDT algorithm with respect to other floorplanning algorithms in terms of the rejection rate and the total execution time.

As for future work, we will extend the proposed algorithm to take the task schedule into consideration, because in WSNs, some tasks have higher priority and these tasks need to be placed as much as possible, furthermore ongoing works are also investigating the possibility of extending the proposed algorithm to non-rectangle task which will reduce the rejection rate in a further step. Finally, the proposed algorithm will be combined with a prototyping platform for a WSN FPGA-based system.

Acknowledgements. This work was supported by National Natural Science Foundation of China under Grant Nos. 61672423 and Natural Science Foundation of Shaanxi Province of China 2016SF-428. We are also grateful to Xilinx, Inc. for their support in ISE 14.6 integrated development environment in auto placement and route.

References

1. Wang, T., Li, Y., Wang, G., et al.: Sustainable and efficient data collection from WSNs to cloud. IEEE Trans. Sustainable Comput. **pp**(99), 1 (2017)
2. Vivado Design Suite User Guide: Partial Reconfiguration. http://www.xilinx.com. Accessed 11 Aug 2017
3. Garcia, R., Gordon-Ross, A., George, A.D.: Exploiting partially reconfigurable FPGAs for situation-based reconfiguration in wireless sensor networks. In: 17th IEEE Symposium on FCCM, pp. 243–246. IEEE, New York (2009)
4. Wang, T., Li, Y., Chen, Y., et al.: Fog-based evaluation approach for trustworthy communication in sensor-cloud system. IEEE Commun. Lett. **pp**(99), 1 (2017)
5. Reardon, C., Holland, B., George, A.D., et al.: RCML: an environment for estimation modeling of reconfigurable computing systems. ACM Trans. Embedded Comput. Syst. **11** (S2), 43–64 (2012)
6. Rabozzi, M., Durelli, G.C., et al.: Floorplanning automation for partial-reconfigurable FPGAs via feasible placements generation. IEEE Trans. Very Large Scale Integr. Syst. **25** (1), 151–164 (2017)
7. Bsoul, M., Manjikian, N., et al.: Reliability-and process variation-aware placement for FPGAs. In: Design, Automation and Test in Europe Conference and Exhibition 2010, DATE, pp. 1809–1814. IEEE, New York (2010)

8. Belaid, I., Muller, F., Benjemaa, M.: Off-line placement of hardware tasks on FPGA. In: Proceedings of the Field Programmable Logic and Applications 2009, FPL, pp. 591–595. IEEE, New York (2009)
9. Montone, A., Santambrogio, M.D., Sciuto, D., et al.: Placement and floorplanning in dynamically reconfigurable FPGAs. ACM Trans. Reconfigurable Technol. Syst. **3**(4), 1–34 (2010)
10. Cheng, L., Wong, M.D.F.: Floorplan design for multi-million gate FPGAs. IEEE Trans. Comput.-Aided Des. Integr. Circuits Syst. **25**(12), 292–299 (2004)
11. Nguyen, T.D., Kumar, A.: Prfloor: an automatic floorplanner for partially reconfigurable FPGA systems. In: Proceedings of the 2016 ACM/SIGDA International Symposium on Field-Programmable Gate Arrays, FPGA, pp. 149–158. ACM, New York (2016)
12. Wang, C., Wu, W., Nie, S., et al.: BFT: a placement algorithm for non-rectangle task model in reconfigurable computing system. Iet Comput. Digit. Tech. **10**(3), 128–137 (2016)
13. Huang, M., Narayana, V.K., Simmler, H., et al.: Reconfiguration and communication-aware task scheduling for high-performance reconfigurable computing. ACM Trans. Reconfigurable Technol. Syst. **3**(4), 20:1–20:25 (2010)
14. Wassi, G., Benkhelifa, M.E.A., et al.: Multi-shape tasks scheduling for online multitasking on FPGAs. In: 2014 International Symposium Reconfigurable and Communication-Centric Systems-on-Chip, pp. 1–7. IEEE, New York (2014)
15. Rabozzi, M., Lillis, J., et al.: Floorplanning for partially-reconfigurable FPGA systems via mixed-integer linear programming. In: 2014 22nd Annual International Symposium Field-Programmable Custom Computing Machines, pp. 186–193. IEEE, New York (2014)
16. Xilinx Virtex-5 FPGA User Guide. https://china.xilinx.com/support/documentation/user_guides/ug190.pdf. Accessed 16 Jan 2017

CO-TDMA: A TDMA Protocol for Collecting Data and OAP at the Same Time

Hao He$^{(\boxtimes)}$ ⓘ, Weidong Yi, Ming Li, and Xiawei Jiang

School of Electronic, Electrical and Communication Engineering,
University of Chinese Academy of Sciences, Beijing, China
hehao_12@163.com

Abstract. Wireless reprogramming of wireless sensor networks (WSNs) usually requires switching to dedicated over-the-air programming (OAP) protocols,
and often needs to stop current work of data collection. This paper presents
CO-TDMA, a low power consumption TDMA protocol using adaptive beacons,
which provides a capability to both collect data and transmit OAP codes at the
same time. A CO-TDMA frame consists of several data slots, an access slot and
several beacon slots. The data slots are used to transmit collecting data, the
access slot is used to update network topology or other changes, and the beacon
slots are used to transmit data ACK beacon and optional OAP data. The major
contribution is the design of the adaptive beacon transmitted in beacon slots: in
data collection state, the beacon only carries the ACK information of collecting
data for every node in the network (Beacon-piggyback mechanism); when the
OAP transmissions are needed, the OAP codes will attach behind the ACK bytes
in the payload of a packet. The OAP information is encoded with rateless digital
fountain codes to close to 100% reliability if enough packets are received. By
multiplex use of beacon slots, we can transmit the OAP codes with very little
extra energy consumptions (0.113% RDC), without impacting the normal data
collection.

Keywords: WSN · TDMA · OAP · ACK · Beacon

1 Introduction

Since the ranges and positions of wireless sensor network (WSN) nodes deployments
may be vary due to different environments and applications, it is impractical to rely on
manual to reclaim and update the programs or configurations on nodes. Wireless
reprogramming becomes an important service for WSNs. Code updates are essential to
reconfigure the network, e.g., topology changes, fix software bugs, re-task or update
existing applications. It may cause a huge loss if the update failures occur, so an
over-the-air programming (OAP) service firstly needs to be fully reliable. Further, energy
consumption, scalability and update speed are the indicators that needed to optimize.

It is likely that several nodes will transmit at the same time, if no appropriate
countermeasures are taken, since there are many nodes in a certain WSN area. The
packets collisions may result in decreasing of the performance in both reprogramming
energy efficiency and time. Some existing methods [1], such as Deluge [2], usually rely

© Springer International Publishing AG 2017
G. Wang et al. (Eds.): SpaCCS 2017 Workshops, LNCS 10658, pp. 680–691, 2017.
https://doi.org/10.1007/978-3-319-72395-2_61

on a selective NACK-based ARQ approach. But it will bring the so-called NACK implosion problem when node density is increasing. By introducing soft TDMA MAC protocol and digital fountain code, SYNAPSE++ [3] is proved to be effective in terms of transmission overhead and recovery capability. Some new approaches [4, 5] introduce link quality perception to OAP. And there are papers [6] which focus on energy consumption place the WSN network in a Software-Defined Sensor Networks (SDSN) framework for discussion.

To our best knowledge, almost all OAP protocols are dedicated for OAP codes transmissions. The requirement for switching from original protocols impacts the performance of normal data collection. Therefore, we optimize a TDMA data collection networks, called CO-TDMA. By introducing an adaptive beacon based code distribution mechanism, the network has a capability to both collect data and transmit OAP codes at the same time. The basic idea is on demand to attach the OAP codes behind the adaptive beacon. The main contribution is the design of the adaptive beacon transmitted in beacon slots: in data collection application, the beacon carries the ACK information for collecting data; when the OAP transmissions are needed, the OAP codes will attach behind the ACK information in a packet. We encode the OAP codes with rateless digital fountain codes.

2 Related Work

This section is a brief introduction of several reprogramming approaches for WSNs.

2.1 Earlier Approaches

XNP [7] is the first network reprogramming protocol which works over single-hop networks and does not support image incremental updating. The multihop over-the-air protocol [8] (MOAP) extended to multihop networks and enhanced its data recovery ability through the NACK-based ARQ. However, MOAP may be inefficient in large multihop network, because a node has to receive the whole program before it starts disseminating it over the next hop.

2.2 Backbone-Based Approaches

The second solutions are based on the construction of a connected dominating set (CDS). It consists of core nodes and leaf nodes, and implements a two-phase dissemination of the data. Sprinkler [9] is the first protocol that used this approach. It assumes each node aware its location, which is used to construct a CDS. A packet-level pipelining scheme and a TDMA schedule are used for the transmissions between CDS nodes. GARUDA [10] is a further dissemination protocol based on CDS, which uses a distributed and lightweight algorithm to approximate the CDS. Besides, it uses availability bitmaps and a modified ARQ policy for error recovery. CORD [11] adopts a similar design. But by using coordinated sleep schedules at each node, it enhances the energy efficiency.

2.3 Contention-Based Approaches

The third solutions are contention-based approaches, whose nodes randomly compete for the channel. This solution has no need for the construction of a CDS and is more suitable for the dynamic network topologies. Deluge [2] is the first OAP system in this category. Through a three-way handshake mechanism based on advertisement (ADV), request (REQ) and actual code (CODE) transfer, Deluge jointly implements data transmission and NACK-based ARQ. The program image is transmitted page-by-page exploiting broadcast transmissions and pipelining. Pipelining and many techniques used in Deluge have been exploited by subsequent protocols.

Another protocol, MNP [12], also uses a special algorithm to reduce the problems caused by collisions and hidden terminals. Through a distributed priority assignment, at most one node sends the program image at any given time within a neighborhood. The sender election algorithm is greedy and distributed: the senders with a higher number of potential receivers are assigned a higher priority. MNP also uses sleep mode to reduce energy consumption.

Freshet [1] is based on Deluge, further optimizing the energy consumption during OAP. At the initial stage, some metadata (including the number of hops from the front wave where the code is currently being transmitted) is transferred to each sensor node. Using this information, the node estimates the time at which the program image will arrive vicinity and determines the time to enter sleeping period.

2.4 Rateless Codes Based Approaches

Another important approach is rateless codes, a more common technology used in deep space communications, which provides 100% reliability theoretically. Through a HARQ technique based on rateless codes on Galois fields of size 2^q with ($GF(2^8)$) (q = 8), an enhanced Deluge was presented, namely Rateless Deluge [13]. AdapCode [14] is an approach exploiting network coding on ($GF(2^5)$). In AdapCode, each node encodes the packet by a linear combination of coefficients randomly selected in the Galois field. SYNAPSE [15] also implements the HARQ mechanism, but uses the Fountain Codes with GF(2), which optimizes the hop-by-hop data dissemination. SYNAPSE++ [3] adds full support for pipelining through a joint design of MAC and fountain codes. It adopts the ADV-REQ-CODE paradigm and randomizes the transmission of ADVs to avoid collisions, and it optimizes pipelining and implements. Pando [16, 17], another method encoding data by Fountain Codes, avoids duplicate retransmissions and fully exploits the wireless broadcast effect in data dissemination.

Almost all of the above OAP protocols are dedicated for OAP codes transmissions. The requirement for switching from original data collecting protocols may impact the performance of normal data collection.

3 CO-TDMA Using Adaptive Beacons for Data Collection and Optional OAP

In this section, to provide a solution for transmitting both OAP codes and collecting data at the same time, we will present an OAP solution based on adaptive beacon and digital fountain used in TDMA data collection networks. The MAC layer adopts a

TDMA-based protocol to avoid packets collision, called CO-TDMA. A CO-TDMA frame consists of several data slots, an access slot and several beacon slots. We transmit the OAP codes by multiplex use of the beacon slots. The OAP codes are encoded with digital fountain codes.

3.1 CO-TDMA Frame Structure

A high efficiency way to transmit OAP codes is to use the TDMA protocols. We adopt a TDMA-based protocol to avoid packets collision in MAC layer, called CO-TDMA (collecting and optional OAP TDMA). As shown in Fig. 1, a C-TDMA frame consists of three parts: several data slots, an access slot and several beacon slots. The data slots are used to transmit collecting data from leaf nodes. The access slot is used to update network topology or other changes, which are mainly identified by network layer, and we don't discuss further. The beacon slots are used to transmit data ACK beacon and optional OAP data in a multiplexing way, which will be discussed later.

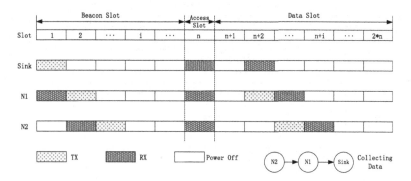

Fig. 1. A CO-TDMA frame structure

In Fig. 1, assuming there are n-1 nodes in the network, each node has a unique number i for the entire network. The preceding n-1 timeslots are beacon slots and the next n slots are data slots. According to number i, two sending slots of this node are allocated: a beacon slot with slot number (i) and a data slot with slot number ($n + i$). The receiving slots are then determined by its parent and children nodes. The slot with slot number (n) is access slot. All other slots are idle slots with radio powering off to save energy.

A typical communication process of CO-TDMA is also described in the diagram. Consider a route branch from node N2 via node N1 reach the Sink node, where slot allocation and communication activity for each node are shown in figure.

3.2 Adaptive Beacon Design

A typical DATA-ACK transceiver process is showed in Fig. 2. In the data slot of the previous frame, the child node sends data to the parent node; in the beacon slot of the next frame, the parent node sends a beacon carrying the ACK message to the child node (we call it Beacon-piggyback and discuss it in next paragraph). After the child node receives beacon, it analyzes the ACK information. If successful, continue to send the next packet, otherwise retransmission.

In the beacon slots, nodes broadcast beacons. Since there was no actual payload in a beacon packet besides the basic network information, we introduce a Beacon-piggyback mechanism whose one bit is corresponding with one node ACK (as shown in Fig. 3). To utilize the limited payload more efficiently, we use the Bit-Map data structure to store the ACK information. If the length of payload is L bytes, there are 8 * L bits, recorded as (0, 1, ..., 8 * L − 1). Each bit is corresponding with one node ACK information. 1 represents successfully receiving, and 0 indicates not received. The 0 bit indicates the ACK for the update, and the (1–8 * L − 1) bits represent the ACK for the collecting data.

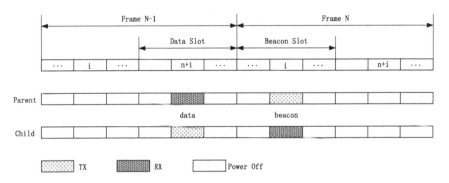

Fig. 2. A typical DATA-ACK transceiver process

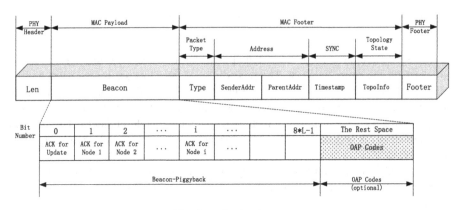

Fig. 3. Adaptive beacon

It is obvious that the length of beacon-piggyback is adaptive and is determined by the number of nodes in the entire network. An adaptive beacon carries ACK information and some basic network information. In this design, the rest space of MAC payload can be used to load OAP information on demand. In data collection state, the beacon only carries the ACK information of collecting data for every node in the network (Beacon-piggyback mechanism); when the OAP transmissions are needed, the OAP codes will attach behind the ACK bytes in the MAC payload of one packet.

The adaptive beacon carries Beacon-piggyback, optional OAP codes and some basic network information. It brings at least the following advantages:

(1) Without sending ACK packets individually, the energy consumption and complexity can be greatly saved.
(2) It is more efficient for all nodes sharing one beacon to carry their ACK information.
(3) Beacon slots are highly multiplexing used and provide a capability to transmit OAP codes.

3.3   Digital Fountain Codes

Assuming the transmission channels are erasure channels, each packet is either received without error or not received. To control the retransmission of erased packets, common methods for communicating over these channels employ a feedback channel from receiver to sender. If the erasure probability f is large, the number of feedback messages will be large and wasteful. Fountain Codes [18] is a useful method that requires no feedback or almost no feedback.

There are a number of variants of fountain codes. We don't discuss further details, and only introduce the LT codes that used in our method. A classic example to understand fountain codes is the balls and bins problem. If we throw many balls independently at random into K bins, the probability that one particular bin is empty after N balls have been thrown is:

$$\left(1 - \frac{1}{K}\right)^{N} \approx e^{-N/K} \tag{1}$$

In order for the probability that all K bins have at least one ball to be $1 - \delta$, we need $N \approx K \log_e(K/\delta)$ balls.

For balls number N, the expected number of empty bins is:

$$Ke^{-N/K} \tag{2}$$

This expected number is a small number δ (which roughly implies that the probability that all bins have a ball is $(1 - \delta)$) only if

$$N > K \log_e \frac{K}{\delta} \tag{3}$$

With the increasing number of balls, the probability that all bins have a ball is increasing. This basic idea can be used in digital fountain codes: if the number of receiving packets is larger than a certain number, the probability that all packets contain complete information is more than a certain value. If a node receives enough packets, the probability that contains complete information is close to 100%.

Encoding Process
Each encoded block tn is produced from the source file s1, s2, s3, ..., sK as follows:

(1) Choose the degree d_n of the block randomly from a degree distribution $\rho(d)$; the dn is actually a number between 1 and K; the appropriate choice of ρ depends on the source file size K, as we will discuss later.
(2) Uniformly at random choose d_n distinct input blocks, and set t_n equal to the bitwise sum, modulo 2, of those d_n blocks.

A simple example of fountain codes encoding and degree is shown in Fig. 4.

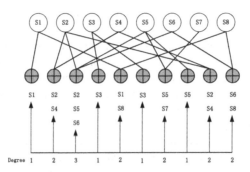

Fig. 4. Fountain codes encoding and degree example

Decoding Process
The decoder's task is to recover s from $t = sG$, where G is the pseudorandom matrix generated by encoding process. We will call the encoded blocks t_n check nodes. The decoding process is as follows:

(1) Find a check node t_n with 1 degree, which is connected to only one source block s_k (if there is no such check node, this decoding algorithm halts at this point, and fails to recover all the source blocks).
  (a) Set $s_k = t_n$.
  (b) For each source packet s_k, if it has been decoded, XOR s_k to all checks t'_n that are connected to s_k.
  (c) Remove all the edges connected to the source block s_k.
  (d) If there are at least 2 source blocks left in the source blocks list, add the encoded block to a holding area.
(2) Repeat (1) until all s_k are determined.

With fountain codes, it is possible to retrieve the original blocks through transmitting additional encoded blocks, until G is full rank at the receiver. The rate of the code can be extended on-the-fly depending on the number of blocks lost. This is the reason that why fountain codes are called "rateless" codes.

Degree Distribution

We mentioned above the degree distribution, the way we choose degree dn, the number of source blocks that each encoded block should consist of. Ideally, to avoid redundancy, we would like to generate a few encoded blocks that have just one source block, so decoding can get started, a majority of encoded blocks that depend on a few others. Such an ideal distribution exists, and it is called the ideal soliton distribution.

$$\rho(d) = \begin{cases} \frac{1}{K} & d = 1; \\ \frac{1}{d(d-1)} & d = 2, 3, \cdots K; \end{cases} \tag{4}$$

Unfortunately, due to random variations, it is possible that there will be source blocks that are never included in practice, or decoding process stalls when it runs out of known blocks. A variation on the ideal soliton distribution, called the robust soliton distribution, fixes these problems. It generates more blocks with very few source blocks, and also generates a few blocks that combine almost all of the source blocks, to facilitate decoding the last few source blocks.

By adding two extra parameters c and δ, the robust soliton distribution is designed to ensure that the expected number of degree-one checks is about:

$$s \equiv c \log_e(K/\delta)\sqrt{K} \tag{5}$$

rather than 1. The parameter c is a tunable factor usually less than 1, and δ is a bound on the probability that the decoding fails to run to completion after a certain number K' of blocks have been received. We define a function:

$$\tau(d) = \begin{cases} \frac{s}{K}\frac{1}{d} & d = 1, 2, 3, \cdots, (K/s) - 1 \\ \frac{s}{K} \log_e(s/\delta) & d = K/s \\ 0 & d > K/s \end{cases} \tag{6}$$

Then, we obtain the robust soliton distribution $\mu(d)$:

$$\mu(d) = \frac{\rho(d) + \tau(d)}{Z} \tag{7}$$

where

$$Z = \sum_d \rho(d) + \tau(d) \tag{8}$$

The number K' of encoded blocks required at the receiver to ensure that the decoding can run to completion, with a probability at least $1 - \delta$, is $K' = KZ$.

4   Experiments and Analyses

To evaluate the performance of method presented in this paper, we tested on Tmote sky platform (as shown in Fig. 5). The MCU is MSP430 and the radio is CC2420. The operating system is Contiki OS. There is a FT232BL chip on the node, which converts

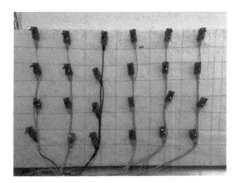

Fig. 5. Tmote sky platform testbed

USB to UART signal. We transmit the OAP codes to the sink node from computer by calling UART receiving interrupt service routines (ISR) function. We tested 24 nodes in the collecting network.

Since the most important attributes of the CO-TDMA are reliability and low power consumption, the simulations and experiments are carried out from these two aspects. Theoretically, the rateless fountain codes cannot guarantee completely 100% reliability, but the probabilities of decoding completion will infinitely close to 100% if receiving enough packets, which is enough for engineering. Therefore, we will analyze the relationship between successful decoding probabilities and the least receiving packets that are needed. Then, we will test the energy consumption of CO-TDMA in the different states.

We simulated the relationship between the probability of decoding completion $(1 - \delta)$ and the number of redundant receiving packets. The number of source packets is 1000 and each OAP payload within a packet is encoded into 50 bytes. Three groups of experiments with different parameter c are carried out. Figure 6 shows that the probabilities of decoding completion are rising when the redundant packets are increasing.

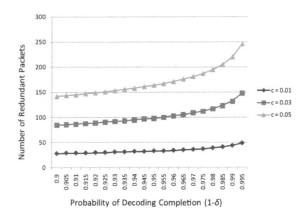

Fig. 6. The relationship between probability of decoding completion and redundant packets

The parameter c has great impact on the number of redundant receiving packets that are needed. The larger the c is, the more packets are needed.

Then, a simulation of the relationship between the parameter c and the number of redundant receiving packets is carried out (result shows in Fig. 7). With the same 1000 source packets and 50 bytes encoded OAP payload, three groups of experiments with different probabilities of failure δ are compared. The number of redundant packets that are needed is increasing when the parameter c is becoming larger. The lower the failure rate δ is, the more packets are needed.

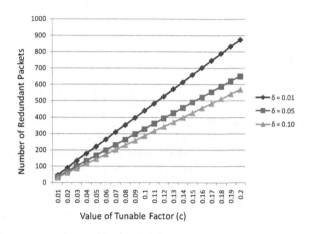

Fig. 7. The relationship between the parameter c and the number of redundant packets

The second issue we concern about is the energy consumption. Since the radio duty cycle (RDC) is a common way for WSN energy measurement, we have statistics on the different power consumption items under different network states (which can be used to calculate RDC). There are 24 nodes in the network and 50 slots in a CO-TDMA frame. The length of a slot is 20 ms and the guard time is set to 3 ms. The frequency of MSP430 MCU timer, TAR, is 32 kHz, which means it counts 32K in a second. We put 50 bytes OAP codes in an adaptive beacon payload. The Energest module in Contiki OS is used to help do the statistics. The average result of one frame of 1000 times is listed in Table 1.

When the network state switched from data collection to both data collection and OAP transmission, the RDC increased 0.113%. This means CO-TDMA achieves the OAP function by multiplexing use of beacon slots with very little extra energy consumption.

Table 1. The comparison of RDC in different network states

Network state	Average time (ticks)			RDC (%)
	Low power mode	Listen	Transmit	
Data collection	32657.3	136.1	37.5	0.528
Data collection and OAP	32633.8	137.2	73.6	0.641

In our design, a beacon payload is 80 bytes (the payload length can be extended in other application on demand). To verify the method, we used fixed 8 bytes for beacon-piggyback and 50 bytes for OAP codes in our example, and there is space (22 bytes) left in payload. The theoretical OAP transmission capability is over 4 Kbytes per minute in the example.

This method is suitable for the light weight network whose OAP application requires high energy efficiency and not particularly high for real-time performance. Some tunable characteristics can be used to achieve higher OAP transmission capability, such as extending payload in a packet or reducing the time spent of a slot. Further, using different channels to transmit OAP data will be also a reasonable direction.

5 Conclusion

This paper presents CO-TDMA, a low power consumption TDMA protocol using adaptive beacons, which provides a capability to both collect data and transmit over-the-air programming (OAP) codes at the same time. A CO-TDMA frame consists of several data slots, an access slot and several beacon slots. The data slots are used to transmit collecting data, the access slot is used to update network topology or other changes, and the beacon slots are used to transmit data ACK beacon and optional OAP data.

The major contribution is the design of the adaptive beacon transmitted in beacon slots: in data collection state, the beacon only carries the ACK information of collecting data for every node in the network (Beacon-piggyback mechanism); when the OAP transmissions are needed, the OAP codes will attach behind the ACK bytes in the payload of a packet. The OAP information is encoded with rateless digital fountain codes. By multiplex use of beacon slots, we can transmit the OAP codes with very little extra energy consumptions (0.113% RDC) and the radio on time spent, without impacting the normal data collection.

Through experiments, with enough encoded packets, the reliability is close to 100%. This method is suitable for the light weight network whose OAP application requires high energy efficiency and not particularly high for real-time performance. By adjusting of some tunable characteristics, CO-TDMA can achieve higher OAP transmission capability.

References

1. Krasniewski, M.D., Panta, R.K., Bagchi, S., Yang, C.-L., Chappell, W.J.: Energy-efficient, on-demand reprogramming of large-scale sensor networks. ACM Trans. Sens. Netw. **4**(1), 1–38 (2008)
2. Hui, J.W., Culler, D.: The dynamic behavior of a data dissemination protocol for network programming at scale. In: Proceedings of ACM SenSys, November 2004
3. Rossi, M., Zanca, G., Stabellini, L., Crepaldi, R., Harris III, A.F., Zorzi, M.: SYNAPSE ++: code dissemination in wireless sensor networks using fountain codes. IEEE Trans. Mob. Comput. **9**(12), 1749–1765 (2010)

4. Dong, W., Liu, Y., Zhao, Z., et al.: Link quality aware code dissemination in wireless sensor networks. IEEE Trans. Parallel Distrib. Syst. **25**(7), 1776–1786 (2014)
5. Zheng, X., Wang, J., Dong, W., et al.: Bulk data dissemination in wireless sensor networks: analysis, implications and improvement. IEEE Trans. Comput. **65**(5), 1428–1439 (2016)
6. Zeng, D., Li, P., Guo, S., et al.: Energy minimization in multi-task software-defined sensor networks. IEEE Trans. Comput. **64**(11), 3128–3139 (2015)
7. Jeong, J., Kim, S., Broad, A.: Network reprogramming, August 2003. http://www.tinyos.net/tinyos-1.x/doc
8. Stathopoulos, T., Heidemann, J., Estrin, D.: A remote code update mechanism for wireless sensor networks. California Univ Los Angeles Center for Embedded Networked Sensing (2003)
9. Naik, V., Arora, A., Sinha, P., Zhang, H.: Sprinkler: a reliable and energy efficient data dissemination service for wireless embedded devices. In: Proceedings of IEEE Real-Time Systems Symposium (RTSS), December 2005
10. Park, S.-J., Sivakumar, R., Akyildiz, I., Vedantham, R.: GARUDA: achieving effective reliability for downstream communication in wireless sensor networks. IEEE Trans. Mob. Comput. **7**(2), 214–230 (2008)
11. Huang, L., Setia, S.: CORD: energy-efficient reliable bulk data dissemination in sensor networks. In: Proceedings of IEEE INFOCOM, April 2008
12. Kulkarni, S.S., Wang, L.: MNP: multihop network reprogramming service for sensor networks. In: Proceedings of IEEE International Conference Distributed Computing Systems (ICDCS), June 2005
13. Hagedorn, A., Starobinski, D., Trachtenberg, A.: Rateless deluge: over-the-air programming of wireless sensor networks using random linear codes. In: Proceedings of IEEE International Conference Information Processing in Sensor Networks (IPSN), April 2008
14. Hou, I.-H., Tsai, Y.-E., Abdelzaher, T.F., Gupta, I.: AdapCode: adaptive network coding for code updates in wireless sensor networks. In: Proceedings of IEEE INFOCOM, April 2008
15. Rossi, M., Zanca, G., Stabellini, L., Crepaldi, R., Harris III, A.F., Zorzi, M.: SYNAPSE: a network reprogramming protocol for wireless sensor networks using fountain codes. In: Proceedings of IEEE Communications Society Conference Sensor, Mesh and Ad Hoc Communication and Networks (SECON), June 2008
16. Du, W., Liando, J.C., Zhang, H., et al.: Pando: fountain-enabled fast data dissemination with constructive interference. IEEE/ACM Trans. Netw. (TON) **25**(2), 820–833 (2017)
17. Du, W., Liando, J.C., Zhang, H., et al.: When pipelines meet fountain: fast data dissemination in wireless sensor networks. In: Proceedings of the 13th ACM Conference on Embedded Networked Sensor Systems, pp. 365–378. ACM (2015)
18. MacKay, D.J.C.: Fountain codes. IEE Proc.-Commun. **152**(6), 1062–1068 (2005)

Cloud-Assisted Data Storage and Query Processing at Vehicular Ad-Hoc Sensor Networks

Yongxuan Lai[1]([✉]), Lv Zheng[1], Tian Wang[2], Fang Yang[3], and Qifeng Zhou[3]

[1] Software School, Xiamen University, Xiamen 361005, China
laiyx@xmu.edu.cn, xmdxlz@stu.xmu.edu.cn
[2] College of Computer Science and Technology,
Huaqiao University, Xiamen 360000, China
wangtian@hqu.edu.cn
[3] Department of Automation, Xiamen University, Xiamen 361005, China
{yang,zhouqf}@xmu.edu.cn

Abstract. In this paper we propose an efficient cloud-assisted data storage and query processing scheme for VANETs. It integrates the cloud and vehicular networks to facilitate data storage and indexing, so queries could be processed and forwarded along different communication channels according to the cost and time bounds of the queries. Moreover, the cloud calculates a result forwarding strategy by solving a Linear Programming problem, where the query results choose the best path either through the 4G channel or through DSRC (Dedicated Short Range Communication). This research is the first step towards the integration of the cloud and the vehicular networks, as well as the 4G channel, to improve the effectiveness and speeding up of the query processing in VANETs. Extensive experiments demonstrate that up to 94% of the queries could be successfully processed in the proposed scheme, QRF much higher than existing query schemes, while at the same time with a relatively low querying cost.

Keywords: Cloud-assisted · Query result forwarding · Data storage
Query processing · VANETs

1 Introduction

One key and challenging issue in VANETs (Vehicular Ad-hoc Networks [1,2]) is the vehicular sensing and data gathering. On one hand, vehicular nodes are limited to road topology while moving, and under various road conditions and high moving speed the network usually suffers rapid topology and density changes [3]. The communications are usually fragmented and intermittent-connected. On the other hand, the vehicular sensed data are in large amount and characterized as continuous generation. The sensed data should be filtered and preprocessed before being shared or uploaded [4].

© Springer International Publishing AG 2017
G. Wang et al. (Eds.): SpaCCS 2017 Workshops, LNCS 10658, pp. 692–702, 2017.
https://doi.org/10.1007/978-3-319-72395-2_62

Generally speaking, a query could be diffused far away to retrieve remote data in VANETs. There are several steps in the query processing: (1) query requester diffuses the query to different data sources, either directly or by using multi-hop relaying techniques, (2) each node that receives the query computes a partial query result based on its local data, and (3) the nodes deliver the query result to the destination node. However, most of existing pull-based query schemes assume no fixed data server available in VANETs, and they only consider the resource of the in-network vehicular nodes [5–7]. Inevitably, those approaches incur relatively large query delays. Also, routing the query results back to the query originator is indeed a challenging problem because the query requester could be moving in the meanwhile, and routing the results based on simple geographic criteria among in-network nodes is not efficient.

To overcome this drawbacks of existing pull-based query processing, in this paper we propose an efficient scheme called CASQ (*Cloud-assisted Data Storage and Query Processing*) for the query processing in VANETs. The basic idea of our scheme is to integrate the cloud and vehicular networks to facilitate data storage and indexing, so queries could be processed and forwarded along different communication channels, including 4G and DSRC (Dedicated Short Range Communication [8]), according to the cost and time bounds of the queries. Extensive experiments demonstrate the effectiveness of the proposed algorithm in vehicular sensing applications. Up to 94% of the queries could be successfully processed in the proposed scheme, much higher than existing query schemes, while at the same time with a relatively low query cost. The rest of the paper is structured as follows: Sect. 2 describes the related work; Sect. 3 presents the detailed description of the CASQ algorithm; Sect. 4 describes the environmental setup and analyzes the simulation results; finally, Sect. 5 concludes the paper.

2 Related Work

Vehicles could be viewed as powerful mobile sensors, and numerous recent research works have addressed the problem of information gathering in vehicular networks. Palazzi et al. [9] proposed a delay-bounded vehicular data gathering approach, which exploits the time interval to harvest data from the region of interest satisfying specified time constraints, and properly alternates the data muling and multi-hop forwarding strategies. Yet the solution has to be integrated with a time-stable geo-cast protocol for the query propagation.

Besides, several works have addressed query processing in vehicular networks. Lee et al. [5] proposed the FleaNet scheme, a mobility assisted query dissemination where the node that submitted the query periodically advertises it only to its one-hop neighbors, which will see if they can provide some answers from information stored on their local storage. Similar to FleaNet, Roadcast [6] is a content sharing scheme for VANETs, it queries other vehicles that it encounters on the way. The keyword-based queries are submitted by the users and the scheme tries to return the most popular content relevant to the query. Differed with the proposed CASQ scheme, FleaNet and Roadcast only query from the one-hop neighbors, the problems of query and result routing do not arise. Xu et al. [10] considered the problem of searching documents in a vehicular network. They adapted the concept of Distributed Hash Table (DHT) [2] to a mobile environment and proposed a Hybrid Retrieval (HR) approach which chooses between a flooding scheme and a DHT scheme for indexing and searching based on the expected costs. Similar to [10], Delot et al. [7] proposed the GeoVanet scheme, which uses a DHT-based model that identifies a fixed geographical location where a mailbox is dedicated to the query to allow the user to retrieve his/her results in a bounded time.

Recently, there is also a research trend to integrate the cloud and vehicular networks. Eltoweissy et al. [11] for the first time coined the term of Autonomous Vehicular Clouds (AVC), where a group of largely autonomous vehicles whose corporate computing, sensing, communication, and physical resources can be coordinated and dynamically allocated to authorized users. The concept of VANET Cloud, however, is highly related to "edge computing" [12], which extends traditional cloud computing paradigm to the edge. The proposed scheme takes full advantage of resource at the cloud and the RSUs for the query processing at VANETs.

3   CASQ Framework

We assume each vehicle, v_i, monitors the road condition and surrounding environment through periodical sensing. It generates pieces of data and sends them to the roadside units (RSUs) through DSRC communications [13], which are one hop vehicle to infrastructure (V2I) or multi-hop vehicle to vehicle (V2V) transmissions. RSUs provide storage, and networking services between the vehicular nodes and the clouds. Also, vehicular nodes would route the metadata such as location, speed and etc. to RSUs when they are in contact, so RSUs are assumed to have full knowledge of the speed and traffic conditions near the roads within their covered areas. Queries are issued by vehicular nodes to get query results. A query is denoted by $query(s, f, t, a)$, where s is the source node that issues the query, f is a filter for the query, t is time bound for the query to return results, and a is the information attached by the source node to facilitate the query.

CASQ takes advantage of the cloud resource to cooperatively store and index the data so that queries could be processed efficiently and timely. The idea of the proposed scheme is straightforward, yet the main challenges lie in two aspects: (1) the data should be stored and indexed so that queries could be directed to the RSUs and access the query results quickly, and (2) query results should timely be forwarded back to the query requester, who is moving and expecting to fetch the query results on its way to destination. The ordinary nodes, RSUs and the cloud should cooperate with each other to process the query, and the forwarding mechanism of queries and results should be well designed. In the following subsections, we present the detailed description of the scheme.

3.1   Data Storage and Indexing

There are many data sources at the scenarios of VANETs, and large amount of data is injected into the network. The equipped devices of vehicles would generate the sensing data, and the electronic devices belonging to driver/passengers, e.g. phones, could also forward data to the on-board device through intra-vehicle communications.

When a piece of data is generated, the vehicular node would upload it to the nearest RSU through V2I communications, and an index entry of the data is uploaded to the cloud. Each piece of data is denoted by $data(id, sk, segs)$, where sk is a sketch describing the data, $segs$ is a list of data segments, which consists of data with large size. Each segment is denoted by $seg(sid, ssk, scon)$, which is of the similar form as $data$. Here sid is the segment id, ssk is the sketch of the segment, $scon$ is the detailed data of the segment. The sketches could be viewed as the metadata, which are generated and evolved as the data is processed and operated on, and the properties include the size, tag, locations, length, and etc. The sketch could be stored at the self-described format of Json or XML, which is fully supported by the mainstream search engines deployed at the cloud. The cloud is abundant of storage and computing resources, and we assume it is capable of storing and indexing the sensing data. For example, the Elasticsearch[1] search engine is a distributed, RESTful search and analytics engine capable that provides easy APIs to store and query the sketches.

3.2   Query Processing

A query is processed according to the surrounding environments of the vehicular nodes. If a node currently has no neighbors or is not in contact with an RSU, the query is sent to the cloud; if a node is within the coverage of an RSU or neighboring nodes, the query is first sent to the RSU or neighbors for query processing through V2V or V2I communications. If the query could be fully answered, the result is immediately returned and the query processing is finished. Yet there are cases when the query is not fully answered:

- the RSU has only part of the result, the query should be forwarded to the cloud for further processing. A *query_search* and a *result_forward* step are needed for the source node to get the results.
- the RSU has the whole data of query result, yet the node moves out of the coverage or there is not enough time receiving the result through the V2I or V2V communications. A *result_forward* step is needed to transfer and handle the query results properly.

Search Query Results. When a query is received by an RSU or the cloud, the receiver would search its data store and retrieve the result accordingly. For RSUs that receive the query, they just search their local data storage to extract query

---

[1] https://www.elastic.co/products/elasticsearch.

results. For the cloud we assume search engines are deployed, so the index of query result could be retrieved. Indexes indicate the location of the real data storage, so an "query_command" from the cloud could be forwarded to the dedicated RSU to extract the data of the query results. We denote $\mathbb{M} = \{m_1, m_2, ..., m_k\}$ as a set of RSUs where the query result $data$ is retrieved.

Forward Query Results. One main constraint of the query is the time budget, denoted by t, a bounded time for the query to be processed. A query is said to be successful only if the query result is returned to the requester within t; else the query is failed. So when the query result is acquired at an RSU, e.g. u_s, the result should be forwarded to the source node on time.

Basically there might exist three channels in the VANETs: DSRC (V2V, V2I), Wired (I2I) and 4G, and the time needed differs for different channels and forwarding strategies. We denote $\mathbb{D} = \{d_1, d_2, ..., d_l\}$ as a set of RSUs where the source node s would pass through to fetch the results, $x_{i,j}$ as the amount of data forwarded from m_i to d_j, and $x_{*,j}(= \sum_{i=1}^{k} x_{i,j})$ as the total amount of data received at d_j. In the proposed scheme, the query result could be forwarded along different channels or paths, and the time interval traveling the path could be estimated.

– $Path1$: Query result is uploaded to the cloud from the RSUs in $\mathbb{S}$, and the cloud forwards the result to the source node s through 4G. We denote the cloud by d_0, and denote the amount of data forwarded from m_i to the cloud by $x_{i,0}$. So the time needed for the transmission could be written as:

$$\varphi(x_{*,0}) = \eta_{4g} + \gamma_{x_{*,0}} + max(\frac{x_{*,0}}{BW_{u,4g}}, \frac{x_{*,0}}{BW_{d,4g}}) \tag{1}$$

where η_{4g} denotes the waiting time to establish the connection, $\gamma_{x_{*,0}}$ denotes the time needed for the data processing at the cloud and the RSUs, BW denotes the bandwidth of the channel, and the subscript u and d denotes the up and down link of the channel. Here function max implies the query results are uploaded to the cloud in parallel, and the data could be downloaded to the source node s at the same time.

– $Path2$: Query result is forwarded to the RSUs in $\mathbb{D}$ through I2I or V2V communications, and data is fetched when s moves through these RSUs. The time needed could be estimated by the travel time of s to visit the RSU in $\mathbb{D}$ one by one:

$$\rho = \frac{dis(u_s, d_1)}{v_{u_s,d_1}} + \sum_{j=1}^{l-1} \frac{dis(d_j, d_{j+1}) * \psi(j)}{v_{d_j,d_{j+1}}} \tag{2}$$

$$\psi(j) = \begin{cases} 1, & if \ \sum_{z=j+1}^{l} x_{*,z} > 0 \\ 0, & if \ \sum_{z=j+1}^{l} x_{*,z} = 0 \end{cases} \tag{3}$$

where $dis(a,b)$ is the distance between a and b, $\psi(j)$ is a function denoting whether d_j is the last RSU participating the forwarding, and $v_{a,b}$ is the average speed of node s moving from a to b. As mentioned at Sect. 3, we assume the speeds of vehicles could be estimated through periodic data exchange between vehicles and RSUs.

Data forwarding through path 1 is fast, yet with a much higher economic cost; and through $Path2$ it has a much lower economic cost, but there might be much larger delay. At extreme cases, all the data could be forwarded either along $Path1$ or $Path2$; yet at a more general case, the data could be forwarded through both paths to strike a balance between cost and time delay.

Solving the Query Result Forwarding Problem. The query result forwarding (QRF) could be defined as a linear programming problem:
    Objective:

$$min((x_{*,0} * (c_{u,4g} + c_{d,4g}) + \sum_{i=1}^{k}\sum_{j=l}^{l} x_{i,j} * c_{i,j} + \sum_{i=1}^{k}\sum_{j=1}^{l} x_{i,j} * c_{j,s}) \tag{4}$$

Subject to:

$$x_{i,j} >= 0 \tag{5}$$

$$(x_{*,j} + \sum_{i=1}^{k}\sum_{j=1}^{l} x_{i,j}) = |data| \tag{6}$$

$$\frac{x_{*,j}}{BW_{i2i}} <= \frac{dis(s,d_j) - R}{v_{s,d_j}} \tag{7}$$

$$\frac{x_{*,j}}{BW_{i2v}} <= \frac{2R}{v_{d_j}} \tag{8}$$

$$max\{\varphi(x_{*,0}), \rho\} <= t - \Delta \tag{9}$$

where $x_{i,j}$ is the amount of data forwarded from m_i to d_j, $c_{u,4g}, c_{d,4g}$ is the unit cost of the up and down channel of $4G$, $c_{i,j}$ is the unit cost of transmission from m_i to d_j. The cost c's are predefined parameters, and the target is to minimize the cost of the query result forwarding. Considering the $4G$ channel is expensive and might be overloaded by the large amount of vehicular nodes, $c_{u,4g}$ is set much larger than $c_{i,j}$, which makes a preference in the model for data to be forwarded through $Path2$.

Constraint 6 ensures all the data should be forwarded to the query source either through the cloud or through DSRC communications. In constraints 7 and 8, R is the radius of the coverage area of RSU, BW_{i2i} is the bandwidth of the RSU-to-RSU (I2I) communication channel, BW_{i2v} is the bandwidth of the RSU-to-Vehicle (I2V) channel, v_{s,d_j} is the average speed between node s and d_j, v_{d_j} is the average speed within the coverage area of d_j. Constraint 7 implies the data be prepared and received at d_j before s arrives the coverage area of d_j to fetch the data; constraint 8 implies there should be enough time for the node to fetch the data when it passes through the coverage area of d_j. At constraint 9, $\varphi(x_{*,0})$ and ρ are defined at Eqs. 1 and 2, t is the time bound for the query, Δ is the time elapsed before forwarding the query results. The constraint implies the forwarding time should be within the time bound of the query. Here we assume the query result are forwarded in parallel through different communication channels. The QRF problem is a linear programming problem, which could be solved efficiently in the worst case.

4 Experimental Study

4.1 Environment Setup

To verify the performance of the proposed algorithm, we conduct experiments on the ONE platform [14] with real-world road network. 120 RSUs are evenly deployed along the road of the city. A taxi trajectory data of Xiamen, China during July 2014 is used for the simulation. The whole data set contains about 5,000 taxis and the trajectory reporting frequency is 1–3 times per minute, yet for this simulation we extract 506 taxies and about 1/10 of the trajectories for performance evaluation. The speed of the vehicles ranges from 5 to 80 km/h, which differs according to road segments and time periods. The communication range of I2I or I2V used by the vehicles to exchange data is set to 60 m, yet the $4G$ channel does not have the limit of communication range. As defined at Eq. (1), the time needed for the data processing at the cloud or RSUs $\gamma_{x_*,0}$ is set around 1–5 s, and the waiting time to establish the connection η_{4g} is set 0.5 s.

The total simulation time is 16 h within a day, from 7:00 to 23:00. Every node senses a data sample every 60 s. The sampled data consists of pictures, which are selected in random from the Google Open Images dataset[2], which is of $\sim$9 million URLs to images that have been annotated with image-level labels and bounding boxes spanning thousands of classes. To simulate different sizes of sensing data, 1 to 5 images from the dataset are bundled together as one sample of the sensing. An query is defined as retrieving pictures given a label or tag. The time bound for the query follows a normal distribution: $t-N(600\,\text{s}, 40)$, and every node generates a query at an average rate of 0.1 query/minute. The Elasticsearch platform[3] is used as the storage and search engine at the cloud, and GLPK for Java[4] is used as a solver for the QRF problem.

A query is successful only when the whole result is returned to the requester before the bounded time. The bandwidth of the $4G$ channel is set 20 Mbps/5 Mbps for the down/up links, the bandwidth of the V2V or V2I channel is 500 Kbps/250 Kbps for the down/up links, and the bandwidth of the I2I channel is 124 Mbps. The cost of the channel $c_{u,4g}$ is set 10^{-2} \$/MB and $c_{i,j}$ is set 10^{-4} \$/MB. Besides CASQ, four other schemes are also implemented for the comparison:

---

[2] https://github.com/openimages.
[3] https://www.elastic.co/products/elasticsearch/.
[4] http://glpk-java.sourceforge.net/.

(1) Centralized: all the sensed data are uploaded to a centralized cloud server through 4G, and queries are processed on the cloud;

(2) Flooding: each vehicle receiving the query from one of its neighbors relays it, and the query result are flooded back to the query requester;

(3) FleaNet [5]: nodes that submit the query periodically advertises it only to its one-hop neighbors, which will see if they can provide some answers from information stored on their local storage;

(4) GeoVanet [7]: uses a DHT-based model that identifies a fixed geographical location (an RSU) where a mailbox is dedicated to the query to allow the user to retrieve his/her results in a bounded time.

4.2   Experimental Analysis

Overall Performance. Based on the trajectory dataset, about 485k samples are sensed and 48k queries are generated. Table 1 shows the overall performance of the compared schemes. The Centralized scheme uploads all the data through the 4G channel, and stores all the data at the cloud. So it has all the queries successfully processed, with a query radio of 100% and a very small query delay (2.85 s). Yet it also incurs the largest work load for the telephony network, whose unit cost is expensive (10^{-2} \$/MB). The total cost is about 2223.49 dollars for the data upload and query result download. In contrast, the Flooding, FleaNet and GeoVanet only depends on the in-network DSRC communications for the query processing. The total cost is less than 60 dollars, due to the small unit cost of V2V or I2V communications (10^{-4} \$/MB). However, the query ratio is much lower, which are less than 55% for all the three schemes. The query radio of FleaNet is about 9.01% and Flooding is about 34.25%. This is because in FleaNet the query is only forwarded to one-hop neighbors, while in Flooding scheme queries and results are flooded, where more nodes could receive the query and hence have more probability to answer the query and return the result. In GeoVant, queries are forwarded to fixed RSUs for storage, and the query results could be fetched by the query requester. So the scheme has relatively higher query radio, about 53.79% of the queries are successfully processed, and the cost is as low as about 29.15 dollars. Besides the Centralized scheme, the query delay are close to the time bound of the queries, which are about 600 s. Here the query who expires are not accounted for the delay calculation.

Table 1. Comparison of performance of the algorithms.

	Query ratio (%)	Query delay (s)	Cost (\$)
Centralized	100.00	2.85	2223.49
Flooding	34.25	549.23	55.18
FleaNet	9.01	591.34	12.13
GeoVanet	53.79	604.11	29.15
CASQ	**94.26**	**594.57**	**286.51**

The proposed CASQ scheme has a query radio as high as 94.26%. The cloud plays a vital role on the indexing of data, and helps to forward the queries to RSUs that have the query answers, which speeds up the query processing and avoids query expiration. Moreover, the 4G channel is adopted to forward the result to the query requester, which makes large number of queries be processed on time.

Flexibility of Queries. Pull-based model provides more flexibility in terms of queries. At this subsection, we study the impact of query parameters.

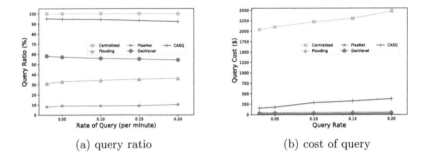

(a) query ratio   (b) cost of query

Fig. 1. Impact of query rate.

Figure 1(a) and (b) show the impact of query rate to the successful query ratio and query cost, where larger query rate generates larger number of queries. The main part of the Centralized scheme is to upload the sensed data to the cloud, where query results are extracted and routed back to the requester. So when the query rate grows, the cost of the query increases from 2038 dollars to 2471 dollars. This is because larger amount of query results should be download to the requesters. In the Flooding, FleeNet and GeoVanet schemes, the sensed data are stored within the network. The query ratios increase a little bit with the query rate, and the costs increase about 20–30% accordingly as more queries are to be forwarded to the encountered nodes. Yet the impact of query rate is relatively small on these schemes. For the CASQ scheme, the ratio of successful queries are almost not affected by the increased number of queries, yet the cost increases from 156.3 dollars to 379.1 dollars when the query rate grows from 0.05 to 0.20. This is because larger amount of query results should be forwarded to the requester. Yet due to limited bandwidth of the I2V channel, more data have to be routed through the 4G channel to the requester, which leads to an increase for the the overall cost.

5   Conclusions

In this paper, we have proposed an efficient cloud-assisted data storage and query processing scheme called CASQ in VANETs. Queries are firstly processed at the cloud and directed to RSUs to extract the query results. The cloud then computes a result forwarding strategy by solving the QRF problem, where the query results choose their best paths either through the 4G channel or through the DSRC communications. Query result are diffused to RSUs along the traveling path of the query requester, so the requester could fetch the result just before the query is outdated. Extensive experiments demonstrate the effectiveness of the proposed algorithm in vehicular sensing applications. Up to 94% of the queries could be successfully processed in the proposed scheme, much higher than existing query schemes, while at the same time with a relatively low querying cost. For the future work, we are going to investigate more types of queries within the framework of CASQ, and study the impact of traffic patterns to optimized the query processing procedures in VANETs.

Acknowledgements. This research is supported by the Natural Science Foundation of China (61672441), the State Scholarship Fund of China Scholarship Council (201706315020), the National Key Technology Support Program (2015BAH16FF01).

References

1. Al-Sultan, S., Al-Doori, M.M., Al-Bayatti, A.H., Zedan, H.: A comprehensive survey on vehicular ad hoc network. J. Netw. Comput. Appl. **37**, 380–392 (2014)
2. Dua, A., Kumar, N., Bawa, S.: A systematic review on routing protocols for vehicular ad hoc networks. Veh. Commun. **1**, 33–52 (2014). Elsevier
3. Zeng, J., Wang, T., Lai, Y., Liang, J., Chen, H.: Data delivery from WSNs to cloud based on a fog structure. In: Fourth IEEE International Conference on Advanced Cloud and Big Data, vol. 3, pp. 959–973 (2016)
4. Lai, Y., Xie, J., Lin, Z., Wang, T., Liao, M.: Adaptive data gathering in mobile sensor networks using speedy mobile elements. Sensors **15**(9), 23218–23248 (2015)
5. Lee, U., Lee, J., Park, J.S., Gerla, M.: FleaNet: a virtual market place on vehicular networks. IEEE Trans. Veh. Technol. **59**(1), 344–355 (2010)
6. Zhang, Y., Zhao, J., Cao, G.: Roadcast: a popularity aware content sharing scheme in VANETs. ACM SIGMOBILE Mob. Comput. Commun. Rev. **13**(4), 1–14 (2010)
7. Delot, T., Mitton, N., Ilarri, S., Hien, T.: GeoVanet: a routing protocol for query processing in vehicular networks. Mob. Inf. Syst. **7**(4), 329–359 (2011)
8. Xu, Q., Mak, T., Ko, J., Sengupta, R.: Vehicle-to-vehicle safety messaging in DSRC. In: 1st ACM International Workshop on Vehicular Ad Hoc networks, pp. 19–28. ACM (2004)
9. Palazzi, C.E., Pezzoni, F., Ruiz, P.M.: Delay-bounded data gathering in urban vehicular sensor networks. Pervasive Mob. Comput. **8**(2), 180–193 (2012)
10. Xu, Q., Shen, H.T., Chen, Z., Cui, B., Zhou, X., Dai, Y.: Hybrid retrieval mechanisms in vehicle-based P2P networks. In: Allen, G., Nabrzyski, J., Seidel, E., van Albada, G.D., Dongarra, J., Sloot, P.M.A. (eds.) ICCS 2009. LNCS, vol. 5544, pp. 303–314. Springer, Heidelberg (2009). https://doi.org/10.1007/978-3-642-01970-8_30
11. Eltoweissy, M., Olariu, S., Younis, M.: Towards autonomous vehicular clouds. In: Zheng, J., Simplot-Ryl, D., Leung, V.C.M. (eds.) ADHOCNETS 2010. LNICSSITE, vol. 49, pp. 1–16. Springer, Heidelberg (2010). https://doi.org/10.1007/978-3-642-17994-5_1

12. Hu, Y.C., Patel, M., Sabella, D., Sprecher, N., Young, V.: Mobile edge computing a key technology towards 5G. ETSI White Paper **11**(11), 1–16 (2015)
13. Kenney, J.B.: Dedicated short-range communications (DSRC) standards in the United States. Proc. IEEE **99**(7), 1162–1182 (2011)
14. Keränen, A., Ott, J., Kärkkäinen, T.: The ONE simulator for DTN protocol evaluation. In: Proceedings of the 2nd International Conference on Simulation Tools and Techniques, ICST, SIMUTools 2009, New York, NY, USA (2009)

EFAV-MERD: Expected Forwarding Area Volume and Residual Distance Mathematic Expectation Routing Protocol for UASNs

Haitao Yu[1], Qingwen Wang[2], Nianmin Yao[3(⊠)], Yan Chu[4],
Maojie Zhou[1], and Yingrui Ma[5]

[1] Tourism Department, Guilin University of Technology, Guilin 541004, China
[2] Xi'an Research Institute of High Technology, Xian 710000, China
[3] Computer Science and Technology Department,
Dalian University of Technology, Dalian 116024, China
Lucos@126.com
[4] Computer Science and Technology Department,
Harbin Engineering University, Harbin 150001, China
[5] Computer Science and Information Technology Department,
Daqing Normal University, Daqing 163712, China

Abstract. The design of routing protocols for Underwater Acoustic Sensor Networks (UASNs) has many challenges arising from long variable propagation delay, high mobility in 3D environments, limited bandwidth, energy-constraint, noise, multi-path and so on. In order to improve the reliability, reduce end-to-end delay and energy cost for UASNs, this paper presents a routing protocol based on expected forwarding area volume and mathematical expectation of residual distance to sink node, EFAV-MERD. In EFAV-MERD, next forwarding nodes are selected based on both the forwarding region volume and the expected residual distance mathematical expectation to improve transmission reliability and reduce transmission overhead. We conduct extensive simulations using NS-3 simulator to verify the effectiveness and the validity of EFAV-MERD.

Keywords: Underwater Acoustic Sensor Networks · Routing protocol
Mathematical expectation of residual distance · Forwarding area volume

1 Introduction

UASNs are widely used in coastline surveillance and protection, ocean disaster prevention, pollution monitoring, military defense, assisted navigation, marine aquatic environment monitoring, and resource exploration, etc. [1, 2]. In underwater environments, radio, cannot work well due to quick attenuation, resulting in short propagation distance. The acoustic signal is more suitable for underwater transmissions.

Due to underwater constraints and challenges, such as low propagation speed of acoustic signals, impaired underwater channels by multi-path effect, noise, path loss and Doppler spread, limited bandwidth [1], node mobility and limited energy, the routing protocols of terrestrial Ad hoc sensor networks cannot be applied in underwater environments directly. Therefore, designing a reliable, energy-efficient routing protocol

© Springer International Publishing AG 2017
G. Wang et al. (Eds.): SpaCCS 2017 Workshops, LNCS 10658, pp. 703–713, 2017.
https://doi.org/10.1007/978-3-319-72395-2_63

which can reduce the end-to-end delay as short as possible becomes one of the primary research issues in UASNs.

The currently existing routing protocols for terrestrial sensor networks can be classified into three types: proactive routing, reactive routing and location-based routing. However, the routing protocols designed for terrestrial sensor networks cannot work well in UASNs due to long propagation delay, high mobility, limited bandwidth, energy-constraint and high manufacture and deployment costs. On the one hand, proactive routing protocols, such as OLSR [3], provoke a large amount of signaling overheads in establishing routing tables for the first time and to update or maintain routing tables when network topology is modified because the latest topology information must be propagated to all over network [4]. On the other hand, reactive routing protocols, such as AODV [5], are more appropriate for dynamic environments but incur a higher latency and energy expenditure in underwater environments. Therefore, reactive routings are also unsuitable for UASNs due to the high latency in establishing paths, which is amplified by the slow propagation speed of acoustic signals, especially in large-scale or sparse underwater sensor networks [6]. Since location-based routing protocols for terrestrial sensor networks are based on the static node and 2D scenarios, they can not also be applied to UASNs directly.

Routing protocols for UASNs are broadly classified based on whether location information is needed: three-dimension location-based, depth-based, location- free routing. The three-dimension location-based routing includes FBR [7], DFR [8], VBF [9], HHVBF [10]. Depth-based routing includes DBR [11], hydro cast [12], VARP [13] and so on. Location-free routing is classified into clustering routing and beacon-based routing. H2-DAB [14], H2-DAB with Courier [15], 2H-ACK [16], E-PULRP [17], REBAR [18] and ERP^{2}R [19] are typical beacon-based routing protocols.

EFAV-MERD is different from the current three-dimension based underwater routing protocols. In EFAV-MERD, the nodes with the smaller mathematical expectation of residual distance to sink next hop have higher priority in forwarding packets, thus resulting in the lower end-to-end delay and the less hop number since the end-to-end delay mainly depends on the accumulative propagation distance from source to destination due to the low propagation speed of acoutic signals. The less hop number will reduce the packet transmission, thus improving energy efficiency since the energy consumption in underwater networks highly depends on the number of sending packets.

2   EFAV-MERD Routing Protocol

In this section, we present EFAV-MERD routing protocol in detail. For convenience, we define some symbols often used throughout this paper.

(1) Symbol R denotes the transmission radius of nodes if not specified.
(2) Symbol v_{sound} denotes the propagation speed of acoustic signals in the water.
(3) Symbol $\|\cdot\|$ denotes Euclidean norm.
(4) Symbol $sup(\cdot)$ denote the supremum function and $inf(\cdot)$ denote the infimum function.
(5) Symbol ρ denotes node density in networks.

Definition 1 (effective forwarding region, simply as EFR in the rest of this paper).
EFR of a packet is defined as follows: if node A forwards packet P received from node
S and node D is sink node, the effective forwarding region of P next hop is defined as
$\{t\|\overrightarrow{tF}\| \leq R \cap \|\overrightarrow{tS}\| > R \cap \|\overrightarrow{tD}\| < \|\overrightarrow{SD}\|\}$.

For example, as shown in Fig. 1, node F receives a packet forwarded or sent by
node S, the EFR of the packet next hop is the region represented by shape *abd*, the
region enclosed by blue curves.

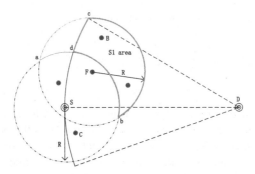

Fig. 1. Example for EFR.

2.1 Compute Holding Time

When node F receives a packet forwarded by node A, it will compute the holding time
of the packet if the packet is received for the first time. Nodes S and D are the source
node and destination node(sink node) of the packet. The holding time of the packet is
computed according to formula (1).

$$
\begin{aligned}
T_{holding} = (&\frac{V - inf(V)}{sup(V) - inf(V)} / \frac{ME - inf(ME)}{sup(ME) - inf(ME)})T_{Delay} \\
&+ (R - \|\overrightarrow{FA}\|)/v_{sound}
\end{aligned}
\tag{1}
$$

where V denotes the volume of EFR and ME denotes the mathematical expectation of
residual distance of next forwarding node to sink. T_{Delay} is expressed as formula (2),
namely the maximum propagation delay of one hop:

$$
T_{Delay} = R/v_{sound}
\tag{2}
$$

In order to reduce the calculation complexity, **Monte Carlo** [20] method is used to
calculate the volume of EFR since the computation of volume of irregular shapes
satisfied the application conditions of **Monte Carlo** methods.

Now, we compute **ME** in formula (1). As shown in Fig. 2, the mathematical
expectation of residual distance to sink is expressed as below:

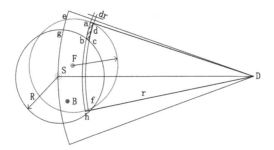

Fig. 2. Mathematical expectation of residual distance-I

$$E_{egf} = \int_{r_1}^{r_2} r \times \rho V_{abcd} / \rho V_{egf} \tag{3}$$

where $r2 = \left\| \overrightarrow{DS} \right\|$ and $r1 = \left\| \overrightarrow{DF} \right\| - R$. V_{egf} denotes the volume of the effective forwarding area, which can be computed using **Monte Carlo** method.

However, it is not easy to compute V_{abcd}. According to the position relationship between geometric graphics, it can be observed that a spherical crown can be obtained after the ball with the center of D and with the radius of r is segmented by the ball with the center of F and with the radius of R. Shape *abcd* can obtained after the spherical crown is segmented by the ball with the center of S and the radius of R. Shape *ijk* is a part of the spherical crown, which is the outer surface of shape abcd. Therefore, V_{abcd} can be computed as formula (4):

$$V_{abcd} = S_{ijk} dr \tag{4}$$

where S_{ijk} is the surface area of shape *ijk*, which can be easily computed using Calculus method (Fig. 3).

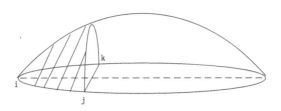

Fig. 3. Computing mathematical expectation of residual distance-II

2.2 Summary

Now we summarize the forwarding process of packets in EFAV-MERD. For the sake of simplicity, Table 1 summarizes the notations used in forwarding algorithm in EFAV-MERD.

The description of routing algorithm in EFAV-MERD is shown as Algorithm 1 in detail.

Algorithm 1 Algorithm for packet forwarding in EFAV-MERD

1: Node F receives **Pack** forwarded by node S

2: Get **PreCoord and PrevER** from **Pack**

3: Get *source ID*, *packet ID* from **Pack**

4: Get **CurCoord** using GPS system

5: IF < *source ID*, *packet ID* > is not in **AdjTable**

   Enqueue Pack to **PackQueue**

   Flag = False

   Add item (*source ID*, *packet ID*, **Flag**) into **AdjTable**

ELSE

   Drop **Pack** // receive a duplicated packet

   If $\left\|\overrightarrow{DS}\right\| < \left\|\overrightarrow{DF}\right\|$ // Pack has been forwarded by node with higher priority

   Flag = true;

   Dequeue **Pack** from **PackQueue**

   Endif

ENDIF

6: IF ||**DestCoord - PreCoord** || <R

   Drop **Pack**

   Remove **Pack** from **PackQueue**

   Flag = **True**

   ELSE if ||**DestCoord - curCoord** || <R

   $T_{holding}$ = 0

   Goto 10:

   ELSE Goto 9:

   ENDIF

7: Calculate **V** and **ME,** then calculate $T_{holding}$

8: set a **timer** with parameter $T_{holding}$

9：Update location information in **Pack** using **CurCoord**

10：IF **timer** expires

       Forward **Pack**

       Dequeue **Pack** from **PackQueue**

       Flag = True

           Wait for next packet

   ENDIF

Table 1. Notations used in forwarding algorithm.

Symbol	Meaning
Pack	Received packet
PreCoord	Coordinate of last hop forwarding node
CurCoord	Coordinate of the current node
DestCoord	Coordinate of the destination node
Tnow	Current time
R	Transmission range of nodes
Tholding	Holding time of Pack
AdjTable	Packet adjacent table for recording received packets
PackQueue	Packet priority queue
V	Volume of EFR
ME	Mathematical expectation of residual distance in EFR
Flag	The sign whether Pack has been processed

3   Simulation Results

3.1   Simulation Setup

In simulation, we use NS-3 simulation tool, a discrete event simulator, to evaluate the performance of EFAV-MERD. For simplicity, Table 2 summarizes the parameters used in the simulation.

Table 2. Parameter setup

Parameter	Value
Maximum transmission power	90 dB re μ Pa
Power threshold for receiving packet	10 dB re μ Pa
R	2 km
Data rate	16 kbps
Acoustic propagation speed	1500 m/s
Node number	200 ~ 500, randomly generate network topology
Deployment region	3D region of $(10 \text{ km})^3$
Movement model	RandomWalk 2D Mobility Model
Movement speed of nodes	2 m/s, change movement direction every 2 s
Source node	Randomly deploy at the depth of 10 km
Sink location	At the center of the surface
Payload of DATA	72 bytes
Running rounds	100
Packet generation model	Poisson distribution, one packet every 5 s
Simulation time for one round	1000 s

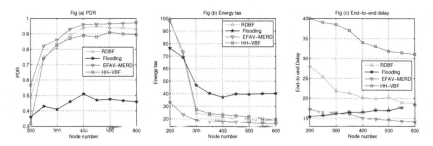

Fig. 4. Performance comparison among algorithms -I.

3.2   Performance Comparison and Analysis

Besides three common performance metrics: **PDR (packet delivery ratio)**, **end-to-end delay** and **energy tax**, we make statistics of three metrics: accumulated propagation distance (**APD**), forwarding time and hop number.

We evaluate EFAV-MERD routing algorithm against HH-VBF [10], RDBF [21], Flooding in terms of PDR, energy tax, average end-to-end delay, APD, hop number and forwarding time. In HH-VBF, the pipe radius is set to be 2000 m (the maximum transmission range). The comparison results in the simulation are shown in Fig. 4.

PDR Comparison

EFAV-MERD vs. Flooding. From Fig. 4(a), Flooding shows the far worse PDR than EFAV-MERD. It is due to the fact that in Flooding, after a packet is forwarded, all nodes receiving the packet will immediately forward it without suppressing duplicate packets. A lot of duplicate packets will increase the collision probability, thus reducing PDR correspondingly.

However, in EFAV-MERD, the nodes with large volume of expected forwarding area volume and small mathematical expectation of residual distance can become qualified for forwarding nodes. In this way, the number of forwarding nodes of packets every hop will be reduced correspondingly. In addition, in **EFAV-MERD**, duplicated packets are suppressed due to the holding time mechanism.

EFAV-MERD vs. RDBF. It can be seen from Fig. 4(a) that EFAV-MERD is $0.02 \sim 0.06$ higher in PDR than RDBF. One reason may be that RDBF only considers the residual distance to destination node in routing decision process. However, EFAV-MERD considers the volume of expected forwarding area. The larger the volume of expected forwarding area is, the higher the number of nodes with forwarding qualification is. So EFAV-MERD is higher than RDBF in PDR. In addition, EFAV-MERD assigns forwarding priorities to forwarding nodes according to the volume of expected forwarding area and the mathematical expectation of expected residual distance. Therefore, the forwarding priorities can be divided in fine granularity compared with RDBF. As a result, compared with RDBF, the number of the forwarding nodes can be reduced effectively in dense networks. The effect of collision probability on PDR will be reduced correspondingly.

EFAV-MERD vs. HH-VBF. EFAV-MERD is also obviously higher in PDR than HH-VBF. In EFAV-MERD, the nodes with larger forwarding area in the next hop become more qualified for forwarding packets. Therefore, the packet in the next hop will be received by more nodes, thus increasing the success probability of forwarding per hop. This is due to the fact that PDR of packets depends on the success probability per hop. In addition, in **EFAV-MERD,** the nodes with the smaller mathematical expectation of residual distance to sink have more qualified for forwarding packets. In this way, the hop number of packets will be reduced correspondingly.

Energy Tax Comparison

EFAV-MERD vs. Flooding. Among 4 algorithms, Flooding shows the worst performance in energy tax, about 20 J higher than the others on average. When ρ is below 400, Flooding shows the same tendency in energy tax with the others. However, after ρ is above 400, energy tax increases with the increase of node density. The main reason is that its collision probability sharply increases since it does not adopt any suppression mechanism of duplicated packets, thus resulting in the increase of energy tax in high network traffic. In addition, from Fig. 5(a) and (c), the forwarding time and the hop number of Flooding are far higher than **EFAV-MERD**. On the one hand, because the energies for transmissions account for most of energy consumption in UASNs according to the property of UASNs that the energy for transmission is about 30 times higher than that for receiving or idle state according to Table 2, the higher forwarding time results in the higher energy tax. On the other hand, in Flooding, hop number is far higher than **EFAV-MERD**.

EFAV-MERD vs. HH-VBF. From Fig. 4(b), In sparse networks, HH-VBF shows the similar energy tax. However, in the dense networks, Flooding shows the worst performance in energy tax. It is because the forwarding range of packets is confined within a routing pipe, which is larger than EFAV-MERD and RDBF. Therefore, the number of forwarding nodes in every hop will be more than that of the other two, thus increasing energy tax. With the increase of forwarding nodes per hop, the forwarding time per packets will increase correspondingly. According to the geometry property of transmission range of nodes (hemisphere shape), not all nodes in a hemisphere shape area overhear each other. Using the theories of geometry, it can be proven that a hemisphere shape can be three forwarding areas at least. In each forwarding area, each node can overhear each other. Figure 5(a) shows that HH-VBF has the highest forwarding time, which can account for the tendency of energy tax. In Fig. 5(c), HH-VBF is much higher in hop number than EFAV-MERD. Since the transmission power keep constant every hop, the higher hop number per packet will also lead to the larger energy tax.

EFAV-MERD vs. RDBF. The energy tax for EFAV-MERD is also lower than RDBF. It is due to the fact that EFAV-MERD considers two factors: the volume of expected forwarding area of next hop and the mathematical expectation of expected residual distance to sink while making routing decisions. RDBF only considers one factor, the current residual distance to sink. However, in EFAV-MERD, the forwarding priorities of nodes are divided in finer granularity. As a result, more nodes in RDBF have the same forwarding priority than EFAV-MERD in case of the same network setup. Since the nodes with the same priority still forward the same packet at the same time although they are within the reachable range of each other, the duplicate packets in RDBF will increase correspondingly, thus increasing energy tax, especially in dense networks. Same as HH-VBF, Fig. 5(a) and (c) also explain the phenomenon that EFAV-MERD is better in energy tax than RDBF.

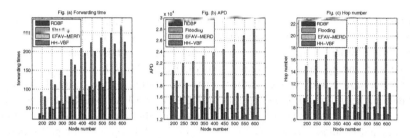

Fig. 5. Performance comparison among algorithms -II.

End-to-end Delay Comparison

EFAV-MERD vs. Flooding. Flooding is lower in end-to-end delay than EFAV-MERD when ρ is below 350. The reasons are follows. On the one hand, there is no holding time of packets in Flooding; on the other hand, the collision probability is low when ρ is below 350, thus packets can be delivered to destination node along shorter paths. However, after ρ is above 350, the effect of increase of propagation delay on end-to-end delay goes beyond the advantage of no holding time in Flooding. The advantage of no holding time is gradually weakened. Therefore, Flooding is higher in end-to-end delay than EFAV-MERD when ρ is above 350. In EFAV-MERD, the mathematical expectation of expected residual distance next hop is used as one factor for forwarding priority. It is capable of selecting the shorter path to forward packets from source node to sink. Figure 5(b) and (c) explain this phenomenon very well.

EFAV-MERD vs. HH-VBF. From Fig. 4(c), it can be observed that EFAV-MERD is 20 s lower than HH-VBF in end-to-end delay on average. The reasons are as follows: in HH-VBF, factor α in formula of holding time of packets is within [0,3] and α is mapped into the interval [0, 1.732] by means of square operation. However, the factor of T_{Delay} in EFAV-MERD is within the interval [0, 1]. In EFAV-MERD, the mathematical expectation of residual distance next hop and the volume of next hop forwarding area are considered as factors for determining holding time. However, HH-VBF considers the current advancement distance and the current projection distance on the center line of pipeline. That is to say, EFAV-MERD considers the current position and the position of next hop at the same time. In this way, EFAV-MERD more easily selects the best path than HH-VBF.

EFAV-MERD vs. RDBF. It can be seen from Fig. 4(c) that EFAV-MERD is about $5 \sim 12$ s lower than RDBF in end-to-end delay. It is due to the fact that RDBF only considers current residual distance to sink in routing decision process. However,

EFAV-MERD considers the mathematical expectation of residual distance of next hop in the process of selection of next hop forwarding nodes. As a result, EFAV-MERD can select the shorter propagation path than RDBF, shown as in Fig. 5(b).

4 Conclusions

Routing design of UASNs poses many great challenges: high dynamic of network topology, unreliable link, low transmission rate and propagation speed, energy- conversation. In order to improve the routing performance of UASNs, we presented a reliable and energy-efficient routing protocol, EFAV-MERD. EFAV-MERD makes routing decision based on the mathematical expectation of the residual distance to destination, the volume of next hop forwarding area. In EFAV-MERD, energy tax and end-to-end delay are reduced while guaranteeing the reliability of transmissions. Experimental simulation results show that EFAV-MERD improves the performance of networks in terms of data delivery ratio, energy tax, end-to-end latency, hop number, APD and forwarding time.

Acknowledgments. This work is supported by the National Natural Science Foundation of China under Grant No. 61073047, 61373027 and 61601475; Heilongjiang Scientific Research Foundation under Grant No. LC2015025 and F201128, Shanxi Province Natural Science Fund Young Talent Project under Grant 2014JQ8310; China Postdoctoral foundation General project under Grant 2013M542527; and the Fundamental Research Funds for Central University under grant No. HEUCFP 201753.

References

1. Akyildiz, I.F., Pompili, D., Melodia, T.: Underwater acoustic sensor networks: research challenges. Ad Hoc Netw. **3**(3), 257–279 (2005)
2. Akyildiz, I.F., Pompili, D., Melodia, T.: State-of-the-art in protocol research for underwater acoustic sensor networks. In: Proceedings of the 1st ACM International Workshop on Underwater Networks. ACM (2006)
3. Clausen, T., et al.: Optimized link state routing protocol (OLSR) (2003)
4. Al-Karaki, J.N., Kamal, A.E.: Routing techniques in wireless sensor networks: a survey. Wirel. Commun. IEEE **11**(6), 6–28 (2004)
5. Perkins, C.E., Royer, E.M.: Ad-hoc on-demand distance vector routing. In: Proceedings of Second IEEE Workshop on Mobile Computing Systems and Applications, WMCSA 1999. IEEE (1999)
6. Pompili, D., Akyildiz, I.F.: Overview of networking protocols for underwater wireless communications. Commun. Mag. IEEE **47**(1), 97–102 (2009)
7. Jornet, J.M., Stojanovic, M., Zorzi, M.: Focused beam routing protocol for underwater acoustic networks. In: Proceedings of the Third ACM International Workshop on Underwater Networks. ACM (2008)
8. Shin, D., Hwang, D., Kim, D.: DFR: an efficient directional flooding-based routing protocol in underwater sensor networks. Wirel. Commun. Mob. Comput. **12**(17), 1517–1527 (2012)

9. Xie, P., Cui, J.-H., Lao, L.: VBF: vector-based forwarding protocol for underwater sensor networks. In: Boavida, F., Plagemann, T., Stiller, B., Westphal, C., Monteiro, E. (eds.) NETWORKING 2006. LNCS, vol. 3976, pp. 1216–1221. Springer, Heidelberg (2006). https://doi.org/10.1007/11753810_111

10. Nicolaou, N., et al.: Improving the robustness of location-based routing for underwater sensor networks. In: Oceans 2007-Europe. IEEE (2007)

11. Yan, H., Shi, Z.J., Cui, J.-H.: DBR: depth-based routing for underwater sensor networks. In: Das, A., Pung, H.K., Lee, F.B.S., Wong, L.W.C. (eds.) NETWORKING 2008. LNCS, vol. 4982, pp. 72–86. Springer, Heidelberg (2008). https://doi.org/10.1007/978-3-540-79549-0_7

12. Noh, Y., Lee, U., Lee, S., et al.: Hydrocast: pressure routing for underwater sensor networks. IEEE Trans. Veh. Technol. **65**(1), 333–347 (2016)

13. Noh, Y., Lee, U., Wang, P., et al.: VAPR: void-aware pressure routing for underwater sensor networks. IEEE Trans. Mob. Comput. **12**(5), 895–908 (2013)

14. Ayaz, M., Abdullah, A.: Hop-by-hop dynamic addressing based (H2-DAB) routing protocol for underwater wireless sensor networks. In: International Conference on Information and Multimedia Technology, ICIMT 2009. IEEE (2009)

15. Ayaz, M., Abdullah, A., Faye, I., et al.: An efficient dynamic addressing based routing protocol for underwater wireless sensor networks. Comput. Commun. **35**(4), 475–486 (2012)

16. Ayaz, M., Abdullah, A., Faye, I.: Hop-by-hop reliable data deliveries for underwater wireless sensor networks. In: 2010 International Conference on Broadband, Wireless Computing, Communication and Applications (BWCCA). IEEE (2010)

17. Gopi, S., et al.: E-PULRP: energy optimized path unaware layered routing protocol for underwater sensor networks. IEEE Trans. Wirel. Commun. **9**(11), 3391–3401 (2010)

18. Chen, J., Wu, X., Chen, G.: REBAR: a reliable and energy balanced routing algorithm for UWSNs. In: Seventh International Conference on Grid and Cooperative Computing, GCC 2008. IEEE (2008)

19. Wahid, A., Lee, S., Kim, D.: An energy-efficient routing protocol for UWSNs using physical distance and residual energy. In: Oceans, IEEE-Spain. IEEE (2011)

20. Doucet, A., de Freitas, N., Gordon, N.: An introduction to sequential Monte Carlo methods. In: Doucet, A., de Freitas, N., Gordon, N. (eds.) Sequential Monte Carlo Methods in Practice, pp. 3–14. Springer, New York (2001). https://doi.org/10.1007/978-1-4757-3437-9_1

21. Li, Z., Yao, N., Gao, Q.: Relative distance based forwarding protocol for underwater wireless networks. Int. J. Distrib. Sens. Netw. **10**, 173089 (2014)

The 2nd International Workshop on Cloud Storage Service and Computing (WCSSC 2017)

WCSSC 2017 Organizing and Program Committees

1 Program Chairs

Yupeng Hu	Hunan University, China
Wenjia Li	New York Institute of Technology, USA

2 Program Committee

Habib Ammari	Department of Mathematics, ETH
Victor Chen	California State University, USA
Daniel Grosu	Wayne State University, USA
Tahar Kechadi	University College Dublin, Ireland
Vimal Kumar	University of Waikato, New Zealand
Rui Li	Hunan University, China
Xiaolong Li	Guilin University of Electronic Technology, China
Fang Liu	National University of Defense Technology, China
Yonghe Liu	UT-Arlington, USA
Alex X. Liu	Michigan State University, USA
Enzo Mingozzi	University of Pisa, Italy
Fei Peng	Hunan University, China
Zheng Qin	Hunan University, China
Danda Rawat	Georgia Southern University, USA
Xiaojun Ruan	West Chester University of Pennsylvania, USA
Houbing Song	West Virginia University, USA
Kewei Sha	University of Houston Clear Lake, USA
Nong Xiao	National University of Defense Technology, China
Quan Xu	City University London, UK
Lei Yang	Hunan University, China
Shu Yin	ShanghaiTech University, China
Jianping Yu	Hunan Normal University, China
Jiliang Zhang	Northeastern University, China
Sherali Zeadally	University of Kentucky, USA
Siwang Zhou	Hunan University, China

3 Publicity Chairs

Lei Chen	Georgia Southern University, USA
Sheng Xiao	Hunan University, China

4 Webmaster

Tianji Xu   Central South University, China

Fast Truss Decomposition in Memory

Yuxuan Xing[1(✉)], Nong Xiao[1], Yutong Lu[2], Ronghua Li[3],
Songping Yu[1], and Siqi Gao[1]

[1] State Key Laboratory of High Performance Computing,
National University of Defense Technology, Changsha, China
xingyuxuan_2012@nudt.edu.cn
[2] National Supercomputer Center in Guangzhou,
Sun Yat-sen University, Guangzhou, China
[3] Guangdong Province Key Laboratory of Popular High Performance
Computers, Shenzhen University, Shenzhen, China

Abstract. The k-truss is a type of cohesive subgraphs proposed for the analysis of massive network. Existing in-memory algorithms for computing k-truss are inefficient for searching and parallel. We propose a novel traversal algorithm for truss decomposition: it effectively reduces computation complexity, we fully exploit the parallelism thanks to the optimization, and overlap IO and computation for a better performance. Our experiments on real datasets verify that it is 2x–5x faster than the exiting fastest in-memory algorithm.

Keywords: Truss decomposition · Cohesive subgraphs · Triangle counting

1 Introduction

Graph mining is a popular research area with a plethora of practical applications, such as understanding and interpreting cooperative processes in social networks [1], analyzing complex networks [2], describing protein functions based on protein-protein networks [3] etc. Cohesive subgraph is an important vehicle for the analysis of massive graphs [4, 5, 23, 24].

K-core [2] and k-truss [6] are hierarchical subgraphs that represent the cores of a network at different levels of granularity. K-core requests each vertex has at least k neighbors and in k-truss, each edge must be involved in at least k − 2 triangles. Obviously, k-truss is more rigorous than k-core since it is based on triangles. In social networks, a triangle means two friends have a common friend that implies a strong tie among three friends. And k-truss requires all edges to be contained in at least k-2 triangles which also strengthens each edge connection in it by at least k − 2 strong ties. Figure 1(a) shows an example graph G and Fig. 1(b) is the 4-truss of G which also is the maximal truss. Given a graph G, the k-truss of G is the largest subgraph of G in which each edge has at least k − 2 triangles [6, 7]. The problem of truss decomposition is to find the k-truss of G for all k.

Truss decomposition is a well-studied topic in last few years. K-truss avoids the enumeration problem and can be detected in polynomial time. The majority of exiting

© Springer International Publishing AG 2017
G. Wang et al. (Eds.): SpaCCS 2017 Workshops, LNCS 10658, pp. 719–729, 2017.
https://doi.org/10.1007/978-3-319-72395-2_64

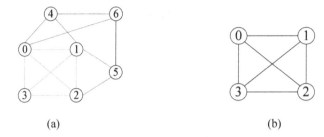

Fig. 1. (a) An example graph, G (b) the 4-truss of G (no 5-truss exits) (Color figure online)

approaches for truss decomposition are sequential and execute on a single machine [6, 8, 25]. Cohen [6] first introduced an in-memory algorithm for k-truss computation.

But it is very slow for handling large real-world graphs with power-law distribution. Wang [8] improved this algorithm through removing the bottleneck of processing high-degree vertices. Wang's solution is the fastest algorithm at present. However, both of them needs find triangles in initialization and decomposition stage. This seriously extends the execution time. Nowadays, it is very common that a server has several sockets and each socket owns multi-cores [26, 27]. Wang's solution can't take full advantage of the hardware resources because it is sequential execution both in truss initialization and computation phase. We propose a more efficient in-memory truss decomposition algorithm-pTD. It only needs find triangles in the initialization phase and stores useful information on the disks for truss computation. And we also make a detailed discussion about the parallelism of pTD and other optimization techniques.

In summary, we list our contributions in this work as follows.

- We design an efficient k-truss detection algorithm-pTD. It computes the k-classes iteratively bottom-up: start from 2-class to the kmax-class.
- pTD only needs once triangle counting that effectively reduce the truss decomposition time.
- We discuss the parallelism both in initialization phase and truss decomposition phase. And we overlap IO and computation for a better performance.
- We make detailed experiments on real graph datasets to verify the correctness and efficiency of pTD.

Organization: Sect. 2 describes some definitions of truss decomposition problem. We introduce the existing solutions and pTD in Sect. 3. The experimental results are presented in Sect. 4. We present some related work in Sect. 5. The last section conclude this paper and go through our future work.

2 Problem Definition

In this section, we formalize several core concepts related k-truss cohesive subgraph. Then we introduce the fastest in-memory truss decomposition algorithm raised by Wang [8] and our motivation.

2.1   Preliminaries

Given an undirected, unweighted graph G, V_g and E_g denote the vertex set and edge set, respectively. And we use n to represent the number of vertices and m represent the number of edges in G. We define NB_v as the set of neighbors of a vertex v, that is, $NB_v = \{u : (u, v) \in E_g\}$. And we define the degree of v as $DEG_v = |NB_v|$. We also assume each vertex in G is assigned a unique ID. Give any two vertices v and u, we use $v < u$ or $u > v$ to represent that v is ordered before u.

Let $v, u, w \in V_g$ be the three vertices on a cycle in G, we denote this triangle by $\triangle_{vuw}$. On basis of triangles, we define the support of an edge as follows.

Definition 1 (Support). The support of an edge $e = (v, u) \in E_g$, denoted by sup(e, G), is defined as the number of triangles that (v, u) is involved.

When G is obvious from content, we replace sup(e, G) by sup(e). And we proced to define the k-truss in G.

Definition 2 (K-Truss). A subgraph $G_s = \{(V_s, E_s) : V_s \subset V_g, and\ E_s \subset E_g\}$, if $\forall e = (v, u) \in E_s$, $sup(e, G_s) \geq k - 2$, then the subgraph G_s is a k-truss cohesive subgraph in G.

Obviously, the 2-truss is G itself. And the truss number of each edge is the maximum value it is contained in a subgraph, represent as $\emptyset e$. Thus, we define the k-class as follow.

Definition 3 (K-Class). The k-class of G, denoted by φ_k, is defined as $\{e : e \in E_G, \emptyset(e) = k\}$.

For a given graph G, truss decomposition computes the k-truss of G for $k \in [2, k_{max}]$. Figure 1(a) shows different types of edges in different colors. The black edge is 2-class, blue edges is 3-class and red edges is 4-class. Thus, the maximum truss of this graph is 4. Besides, we can see that the 2-truss is simply the graph itself. And the 3-truss is the union of 3-class and 4-class, the 4-class is the 4-truss. As a result, the k-trusses display the hierarchical structures of the graph at different levels of granularity.

2.2   Algorithm

We outline the algorithm of Wang for truss decomposition in Algorithm 1. It starts from an initialization that computes the support of each edge in G (steps 1–2). And in step 3, it sorts all edges in ascending order of their support and keep all sorted edges in an array A. The computation of supports can be done in $O(m^{1.5})$ time by the in-memory triangle counting algorithm [16]. And the sorting can be done in $O(m)$ time using bin sort [17]. In the truss computation phase, for each k starting from $k = 2$, the algorithm removes the first edge in the sorted edge array A iteratively and add it to φ_k since $sup(e) \leq (k - 2)$. Upon the removal of e, it also decreases the support of all other edges that form triangles with e, and update their new positions in the sorted edge array A meanwhile. This process continues until all edges with support no greater than $k - 2$ are removed. At last, it computes each k-class while all edges in G are removed. In the process of truss decomposition, finding the other edges in triangles with e takes most of the time. And this behavior is just like triangle counting in initialization phase.

Algorithm 1 Truss Decomposition

Input: G=(V_G, E_G)

Output: the k-class, φ_k for $2 \leq k \leq k_{max}$

/*initialization phase*/
1.   for each $e = (v, u) \in E_G$ do
2. $sup(e) = |NB(v) \cap NB(u)|$;
3.   sort all the edges in ascending order of their support

/*computation phase*/
4. $k \leftarrow 2$
5.   while(not all edges in G are removed)
6.   while($\exists e = (v, u)$ such that $sup(e) \leq (k - 2)$)
7.   let e be the edge with the lowest support;
8.   assume, w.l.o.g., $\deg(u) \leq \deg(v)$;
9.   for each $w \in NB(u)$ do
10.   if($(v, w) \in E_G$)
11. $sup(u, w) \leftarrow (sup(u, w) - 1)$;
12. $sup(v, w) \leftarrow (sup(v, w) - 1)$;
13.   reorder (u,w) and (v,w) according to their new support
14. $\varphi_k \leftarrow (\varphi_k \cup \{e\})$
15.   remove e from G

16. $k \leftarrow k + 1$

2.3 Motivation

Triangle counting is the foundation of truss decomposition and it takes most of the execution time. It needs almost find all triangles in G four times in Algorithm 1: one time in the support initialization and three times in the k-truss computation-it must find all triangles for each edge involved. The initialization for edge supports only need to know the number of triangles each edge involved. But in truss decomposition, the algorithm must get the other two edges' id constructed a triangle with e. Those two processing procedures are very similar and if we can reduce the number of triangle counting, we can speed up the k-truss computation.

Nowadays, it is common for a server with two or more sockets and each socket generally has multi-cores inside. It may have a better performance if we subtly parallel our algorithm. And it is obvious in Algorithm 1 that two parts can be parallel execution: triangle counting in steps 1–2 and truss computation in steps 9–12 only if replace the reorder process with traversing operation.

3 Parallel Truss Decomposition

In this section, we describe our truss decomposition algorithm and optimization strategy in detail.

Algorithm 2 pTD-parallel Truss Decomposition

Input: $G=(V_G, E_G)$

Output: the k-class, φ_k for $2 \leq k \leq k_{max}$

/*initialization phase*/

1.   parallel for each $e = (v, u) \in E_G$ do
2.   assume, w.l.o.g., $deg(u) \leq deg(v)$;
3.   for each $w \in NB(u)$ do
4. $pp = ID_{(u,w)}$;
5.   if $(v, w) \in E_G$
6. $qq = ID_{(v,w)}$;
7. $sup(ID_{(v,u)}) + +$;
8.   store pair<pp, qq> on disk;

/*computation phase*/

9. $k \leftarrow 2$, $q \leftarrow \emptyset$
10. while(not all edges in G are removed)
11.   while($\exists e = (v, u)$ such that $sup(e) = (k - 2)$)
12.   q.push(e);
13.   while(!q.empty)
14. $e = q.pop()$;
15.   for all stored edge pairs of e do
16.   sup(pair.first)--;
17.   if(sup(pair.first)==k-2)   q.push(sup(pair.first));
18.   sup(pair.second)--;
19.   if(sup(pair.second)==k-2)   q.push(sup(pair.second));
20. $\varphi_k \leftarrow (\varphi_k \cup \{e\})$
21.   remove e from G

22. $k \leftarrow k + 1$

The initialization in Algorithm 2 is a little different from 1. It finds all triangles for every edge e involved to initialize the support. Meanwhile, it stores edge pairs of each edge e on disk sequentially (steps 3–8). And in computation phase, it just reads the edge pairs from disk and decreases their supports due to the triangle missing (steps 15–19). This method contributes significantly to reducing the truss decomposition time. And we replace the sorted edge array A in Algorithm 1 with a FIFO queue q. For a new value of k, pTD puts all edges whose support equal to k-2 into q. During the computation, if any edge's support drops to k-2 and pTD just pushes it into the queue. This can avoid the sort operations introduced by the changes of edge supports.

Algorithm 2 only needs count all triangles in initialization phase, while it also has two challenges: triangle counting in initialization phase must count all triangles three times in order to store edge pairs together for each edge e; the size of edge pairs is so large that we can only store on disks result in serious I/O overhead. We discuss two optimization techniques as follows.

Optimization 1. It is obvious that steps 1–8 and steps 15–19 in pTD can be parallel execution and it is the same for steps 1–2 in Algorithm 1. We modify the source codes and launch N threads for computation: parallel initialize the support of each edge and parallel decrease edge pair's support for the same edge. (N = number of sockets × cores in one socket)

Optimization 2. The size of edge pairs is related to the number of triangles and is calculated as follows: S = T*3 * sizeof(edge pair), T is the number of triangles in G and it needs store three edge pairs for one triangle. It is difficult to keep all edge pairs in DRAM when the graph becomes larger and larger. And thanks to the continuous development of semiconductor technology, some storage-class memory [13–15] become mature gradually, such as PCM, ReRAM, 3D Xpoint, etc. They generally have compared performance with DRAM, but their capacity is much larger than DRAM. pTD stores all edge pairs on a NVMe SSD which is more friendly to random IO than HDD. To further reduce IO overhead, we can overlap the computation and read/write operation. In initialization phase, pTD partitions edges into chunks. When the supports of all edges in one chunk complete, it launches a series of write requests while continues computes the edge supports in next chunk. And for truss decomposition, pTD overlaps the read edge pairs operation and support decrease operation (steps 15–19) as above.

4   Experimental Evaluation

In this section, we evaluate the performance of pTD for truss decomposition. The experimental environment is described in the next subsection. We prove the performance of pTD and show the improvement of optimizations. And we verify the efficiency of pTD by comparing with Wang's solution which is the fastest existing in-memory algorithm.

4.1   Environment Setup

All experiments are conducted on a machine configured with two Xeon E5-2692 2.2 GHz CPU, 64 GB DRAM and running redhat 6.5 operating system. The datasets and intermediate data are stored on an Intel NVMe SSD.

We use five real datasets shown in Table 1. Wiki contains all the users and discussion from the inception of Wikipedia till January 2008. Skitter is an Internet topology graph and from traceroutes run daily in 2005. Orkut is a free on-line social network where users form friendship each other. LiveJournal is a free on-line community with almost 10 million members: a significant fraction of these members is highly active. Hollywood is one of the most popular undirected social graphs that vertices are actors and two actors are joined by an edge whenever they appeared in a movie together. The first five datasets except for Hollywood are from the Stanford Network Analysis Project [18] and the remaining one comes from the laboratory for Web Algorithmics (LAW) [19]. All of them are stored on SSD in binary format. And the number of vertices and undirected edges ($|V_G|$ and $|E_G|$), disk storage size (in bytes), maximum degree (d_{max}) and the largest k for any k-truss (k_{max}) are showed in Table 1. The edge pair size shows the data pTD needs store on disk.

Table 1. Graph datasets

Graph	$|V_G|$	$|E_G|$	Size	d_{max}	k_{max}	Edge pair size
Wiki	2.4 M	9.3 M	63.0 M	100029	53	0.21 G
Skitter	1.7 M	22.2 M	104.1 M	35455	68	0.64 G
LiveJournal	4.8 M	85.7 M	382.4 M	20333	362	6.39 G
Hollywood	2.1 M	229.0 M	896.2 M	13107	1298	158.12 G
Orkut	3.7 M	234.4 M	929.2 M	33313	78	14.03 G

4.2 Sequential vs Parallel

In this subsection, we parallel the edge support initialization both in Wang's algorithm and pTD. Figure 2 shows the results on Wiki and LiveJournal and other results is similar. We set the number of thread to 24 because our machine has 2 sockets and 6 cores on each of them. As can be seen, parallel the support initialization can achieve a better performance for both Wang's solution and pTD. Since pTD needs count every triangle three times while Wang's only once, it is interesting that Wang's solution is faster than pTD on LiveJournal while pTD behaves better on Wiki. This situation may be caused by the distribution of vertices degree and the implement of strategy for counting triangles. pTD counts all triangles for each edge sequentially with a binary search method that is also efficient for vertices with a large degree.

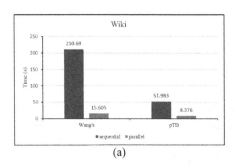
(a)

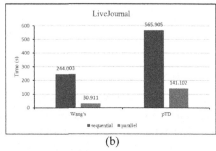
(b)

Fig. 2. Support initialization

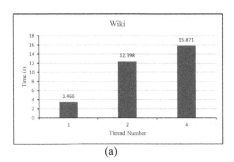
(a)

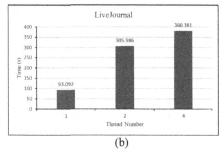
(b)

Fig. 3. Truss computation

We carry out the truss computation (steps 15–19 in Algorithm 2) with 1, 2 and 4 threads separately. The results are shown on Fig. 3. The execution time become longer as the number of threads increase. This may be caused by the bottleneck of the data exchange between CPU and DRAM. In the subsequent experiments, we just compare the optimized pTD and optimized Wang's solution.

4.3   Overlap Computation and IO

pTD needs write plenty of edge pairs on disk in initialization phase and read all edge pairs from disk file for truss computation. Figure 4 shows the effect of our computation and IO overlap technique. It has a good impact on both phases for write/read operations.

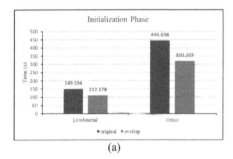
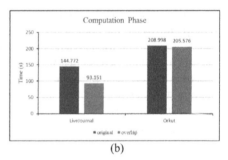

(a)   (b)

Fig. 4. IO optimization

4.4   Overall Performance

We have compared the performance of our pTD with optimized Wang's solution on five real datasets. Phase 1 is the edge support initialization phase and phase 2 is for the truss computation. As can be seen in Table 2, phase 2 of pTD is always faster than Wang's solution since pTD only needs read edge pairs from disks instead of finding triangles for each edge. Since the edge support initialization of pTD must find each triangle three times while Wang's just once, it is normal the initialization time for pTD

Table 2. Overall performance

Datasets	pTD (s)			Wang's (s)			Speed up
	Phase 1	Phase 2	Total	Phase 1	Phase 2	Total	
Wiki	7.35	3.47	10.82	15.61	18.48	34.09	3.15
Skitter	21.29	11.80	33.09	25.43	41.81	67.24	2.03
LiveJournal	109.16	93.09	202.25	30.91	369.74	400.65	1.98
Hollywood	1618.13	2024.61	3642.74	563.46	9609.66	10173.12	2.79
Orkut	313.69	206.90	520.59	133.12	2555.86	2688.98	5.17

is longer. Thanks to our "binary search", it seems our method sometimes is more efficient (on Wiki and Skitter datasets). Above all, pTD can achieve a 2-5 acceleration on our experiments.

5   Related Work

Triangle counting [20, 21] is a very important component in k-truss computation and always takes a large amount of computation time. The first in-memory algorithm for truss decomposition is proposed by Cohen [6]. But it is very slow for handling large real-world graphs. Wang [8] improved this algorithm by removing the bottleneck for processing vertices with high degree. It partly brings down the complexity of triangle counting for each edge in truss decomposition phase. In this paper, we propose a more efficient algorithm-pTD. pTD only needs count all triangles in G in support initialization phase that greatly reduce the whole truss decomposition time. Further, pTD adopts parallelism and IO/computation overlap techniques for a better performance.

Cohen also proposed a MapReduce-based truss decomposition algorithm [7, 10]. And Quick [22] introduced a parallel algorithm on Pregel-like graph processing systems [11, 12]. Both of them iteratively prune the graph based on the definition of k-truss via three sub-routines: enumerating all the triangles, counting the number of triangles for each edge, removing the edges with insufficient support until all edges dropped. Y. Shao raised triangle complete subgraph so that each computing node can find the local k-truss in parallel [9]. However, all of them suffer from high communication cost, large number of iterations to prune and distribution programming problems.

6   Conclusion

In this paper, we propose an efficient in-memory truss decomposition algorithm-pTD. It only needs once triangle counting in edge support initialization phase and stores the edge pairs involved in triangles for every edge on disks meanwhile. In the truss computation phase, pTD read the edge pairs of each edge from disk and decrease the corresponding edges' supports. To reduce the IO overhead, pTD overlap the computation and write/read operations in initialization/computation phase. Besides, pTD parallel the triangle counting for a further performance improvement. Above all, pTD is 2x–5x faster than Wang's solution according to our experiments on five real datasets.

Acknowledgments. We are grateful to our anonymous reviewers for their suggestions to improve this paper. This work is supported by the National High-Tech Research and Development Projects (863) and the National Natural Science Foundation of China under Grant Nos. 2015AA015305, 61232003, 61332003, 61202121.

References

1. Goltsev, A.V., Dorogovtsev, S.N., Mendes, J.: K-core percolation on complex networks: critical phenomena and nonlocal effects. Phys. Rev. E **73**(5), 056101 (2006)
2. Alvarez-Hamelin, J.I., Dall'Asta, L., Barrat A., Vespignani, A.: K-core decomposition of internet graphs: hierarchies, self-similarity and measurement biases. arXiv preprint cs/0511007 (2005)
3. Altaf-Ul-Amin, M., Shinbo, Y., Mihara, K., Kurokawa, K., Kanaya, S.: Development and implementation of an algorithm for detection of protein complexes in large interaction networks. BMC Bioinf. **7**(1), 207 (2006)
4. Wasserman, S., Faust, K.: Social Network Analysis: Methods and Applications. Cambridge University Press, Cambridge (1994)
5. Luce, R., Perry, A.: A method of matrix analysis of group structure. Psychometrika **14**(2), 95–116 (1949)
6. Cohen, J.: Trusses: cohesive subgraphs for social network analysis (2008)
7. Cohen, J.: Graph twiddling in a mapreduce world. Comput. Sci. Eng. **11**(4), 29–41 (2009)
8. Wang, J., Cheng, J.: Truss decomposition in massive networks. Proc. VLDB Endow. **5**(9), 812–823 (2012)
9. Shao, Y., Chen, L., Cui, B.: Efficient cohesive subgraphs detection in parallel. In: Proceedings of International Conference on Management of Data, Snowbird, UT, USA, 22–27 June (2014)
10. Dean, J., Ghemawat, S.: Mapreduce: simplified data processing on large clusters. In: OSDI (2004)
11. Malewicz, G., Austern, M.H., Bik, A.J., Dehnert, J.C., Horn, I., Leiser, N., Czajkowski, G.: Pregel: a system for large-scale graph processing. In: SIGMOD (2010)
12. Salihoglu, S., Widom, J.: GPS: a graph processing system. In: SSDBM (2013)
13. Seong, N.H., Woo, D.H., Lee, H.H.S.: Security refresh: prevent malicious wear-out and increase durability for phase-change memory with dynamically randomized address mapping. In: Proceedings of the 37th Annual International Symposium on Computer Architecture (ISCA), pp. 383–394, June 2010
14. Jung, M., Shalf, J., Kandemir, M.: Design of a large-scale storage-class RRAM system. In: Proceedings of the 27th International Conference on Supercomputing (ICS) (2013)
15. Intel, Micron: 3D Xpoint: Breakthrough Nonvolatile Memory Technology
16. Suri, S., Vassilvitskii, S.: Counting triangles and the curse of the last reducer. In: Proceedings of the 20th International Conference on World Wide Web, pp. 607–614. ACM (2011)
17. Batagelj, V., Zaversnik, M.: An O(m) algorithm for cores decomposition of networks. arXiv preprint cs/0310049 (2003)
18. https://snap.stanford.edu/data/index.html
19. http://law.di.unimi.it/datasets.php
20. Schank, T.: Algorithmic aspects of triangle-based network analysis. Ph.D. Dissertation, Universitat Karlsruhe, Fakultat fur Informatik (2007)
21. Latapy, M.: Main-memory triangle computations for very large (sparse (power-law)) graphs. Theor. Comput. Sci. **407**(1–3), 458–473 (2008)
22. Quick, L., Wilkinson, P., Hardcastle, D.: Using pregel-like large scale graph processing frameworks for social network analysis. In: ASONAM (2012)
23. Luce, R.D.: Connectivity and generalized cliques in sociometric group structure. Psychomertrika **15**(2), 169–190 (1950)
24. Mokken, R.J.: Cliques, clubs and clans. Qual. Quant. **13**(2), 161–173 (1979)

25. Zhao, F., Tung, A.K.H.: Large scale cohesive subgraphs discovery for social network visual analysis. In: PVLDB (2013)
26. Ou, Y., Xiao, N., Liu, F., et al.: Gemini: a novel hardware and software implementation of high-performance PCIe SSD. Int. J. Parallel Program. **45**(4), 923–945 (2017)
27. Yu, S., Xiao, N., Deng, M., Liu, F., Chen, W.: Redesign the memory allocator for non-volatile main memory. ACM J. Emerg. Technol. Comput. Syst. (JETC) **13**(3), 49 (2017)

Pyramid: Revisiting Memory Extension with Remote Accessible Non-Volatile Main Memory

Songping Yu[✉], Mingzhu Deng, Yuxuan Xing, Nong Xiao,
Fang Liu, and Wei Chen

State Key Laboratory of High Performance Computing,
National University of Defense Technology, Changsha, China
we.isly@163.com

Abstract. Remote Direct Memory Access (RDMA) provides the ability to direct access remote user space memory without remote CPU's involvement, shortening the network latency tremendously; in addition, a new generation of fast Non-Volatile Memory (NVM) technologies, such as 3D XPoint, is in production, and its property has the promise to access-speed like memory and durability-like storage. So, Remote access Non-Volatile Main Memory is reasonable. Traditional local memory extension is bounded by slow storage media (HDD/SSD). In this paper, first, we revisit local memory extension and propose a new memory extension model, Pyramid, extending memory with remote NVM; then, discussing the mechanism of remote data consistency, which can be delivered with RDMA operation of write-with-immediate in Pyramid; besides, we evaluate the performance of random access to remote NVM and manifest the performance opportunity brought by remote accessible NVM through comparing it with new technologies of storage-NVMe-SSD and PCM-based SSD. Finally, we argue that Pyramid promises memory scalability with good performance guarantee.

Keywords: Memory extension · RDMA · NVM · Data consistency
Data persistence

1 Introduction

For decades memory extension in single machine has been achieved through using a dedicated device for extending the virtual memory. The device is either HDD or SSD [1], by providing swap space for evicted page from DRAM. With the increasing pressure of data volume in big data applications, not only the financially-challenged performance of SSD/HDD but also the frequent page swapping will degrade system performance a lot [1]. Whereas, one simple and direct way of expanding memory capacity is to deploy large main memories, however, several factors make it exceedingly arduous to conduct: (1) large power energy consumption is triggered by the need of refreshing volatile DRAM cells, about 10%-30% of total system energy [2, 3]; (2) its density limitation to meet retention time requirements [4–6]; (3) its relative high cost

G. Wang et al. (Eds.): SpaCCS 2017 Workshops, LNCS 10658, pp. 730–743, 2017.
https://doi.org/10.1007/978-3-319-72395-2_65

compared with SSD and HDD. Bearing this in mind, the new emerging Non-Volatile Memories is considered to be the best replacements for DRAM by the computer system designers.

Non-Volatile Memory (NVM), such as Memristor, STTRAM, Phase Change Memory (PCM) [7] and 3D XPoint [8], incorporates a host of desirable features—access speeds comparable to DRAM, storage-like durability, low power consumption, and byte addressability. These new types of memory show the promise of being the candidate main memory with comparable performance and much higher capacity than DRAM. Especially, emerging NVM products are expected to hit the market in the next few years. As an example, 3D XPoint technology has been announced by Intel and Micron with an expected arrival time of 2016 [8]. However, every coin has two sides. There are some defects in NVMs, such as limited write endurance, asymmetric read and write performance. A recent study [9] has focused on the write endurance and performance for NVM-based memory extension, which harbored the idea that achieving memory extensions through treating NVM as a second-level memory, bypassing the file system and dedicating for extending the capacity of the main memory system, unlike the traditional swap system. Also, there are much research about using NVM as main memory has been done: profiling pages behavior and guiding the placement of pages to be in DRAM or NVM [10]; designing the memory allocator in regard to wear-leveling for NVM [11–13]; Mnemosyne [14], NV-heaps [15] concentrated on program model for NVM.

Currently, the data storage trend shifts from storage-centric to memory-centric for performance reasons. Traditional applications' data structures reside in memory on the same machine, which limits applications' scalability requirements for memory capacity; accordingly, RAMCloud [16] aggregates memories from thousands of servers to keep all information at all times with SSD/HDD as backups and every server manages its own memory, while FaRM [17] organizes distributed memory in a different way with exposing the memories of all machines in the cluster as a shared address space. The key to make distributed memory feasible is fast network technology-RDMA. RDMA provides reliable user-level reads and writes of remote memory. Compared to traditional network, it provides ultra-low latency and high throughput in view that is bypasses the kernel, avoids the overheads of complex protocol stacks, and performs remote memory accesses through the remote NIC without involving the remote CPU.

In this paper, we propose a memory extension model Pyramid, extending local memory with remote NVM, and scaling out NVM of one single machine (named NVM-requester) owning many cores for computing only with limited NVM capacity, and its typical applications are: key-value stores like MICA [18] and Memcached [19], Single-machine MapReduce system Pheonix [20], and graph processing as GraphChi [21], X-Stream [22], etc. In Pyramid, the machines providing NVMs are NVM-providers, which are the actual data locus. The NVM-requester is only used for applications' user interface and business logic; taking Key-Value store as an example, the operations of key-value pairs, such as Put, Get and Delete, are the business logic; the key-value pairs themselves are located in NVM providers separately. The benefits of remote memory extension comes from two main aspects: (1) the failure of NVM-requester does not cause data loss; (2) the ability of enormous memory spaces provision (memory capacity depends on the NVM-requester scale).

The remainder of this paper is organized as follows: Sect. 2 gives an overview of the background of our work. Section 3 presents remote memory extension-Pyramid. We present related work in Sect. 4 and conclude our work in Sect. 5.

2 Background

InfiniBand [23, 24] is an industry standard switched fabric that is designed for interconnecting nodes in High End Computing (HEC) clusters. One of the main features of InfiniBand is Remote Direct Memory Access (RDMA). This feature allows software to remotely read memory contents of another remote process without any software involvement at the remote side. This feature is extremely powerful and can be used to implement high performance communication protocols. In RDMA, actions are specified by verbs which convey requests to the network adapter. Each verb, such as post_send, is represented in the OFED API as a library function, ibv_post_send, with associated parameters and data structures. To initiate a transfer, ibv_post_send places a work request (WR) data structure describing the transfer onto a network adapter queue. Data transfers are all asynchronous: once a work request has been posted, control returns to the user-space application which must later use the ibv_poll_cq function to remove a work completion data structure from a network adapter's completion queue. This completion contains the status for the finished transfer and tells the application it can again safely access the virtual memory used in the transfer.

Userspace programs access RNICs (RDMA-able Network Interface Card) directly using functions called verbs. There are several types of verbs. Those most relevant to this work are RDMA read (READ), RDMA write (WRITE), SEND, and RECEIVE. Verbs are posted by applications to queues that are maintained inside the RNIC. Queues invariably exist in pairs: a send queue and a receive queue form a queue pair (QP). Each queue pair has an associated completion queue (CQ), which the RNIC fills in upon completion of verb execution. The verbs form a semantic definition of the interface provided by the RNIC. There are two types of verbs semantics: one-sided and two-sided.

One-sided verbs: The RDMA verbs (READ and WRITE) have memory semantics: they specify the remote memory address to operate upon. These verbs are one-sided: the responder's CPU is unaware of the operation. This lack of CPU overhead at the responder makes one-sided verbs attractive. Furthermore, they have the lowest latency and highest throughput among all verbs.
Two-sided verbs: SEND and RECEIVE (RECV) have channel semantics, i.e., the SEND's payload is written to a remote memory address that is specified by the responder in a pre-posted RECV. An analogy for this would be an unbuffered sockets implementation that required read to be called before the packet arrived. SEND and RECV are two-sided as the CPU at the responder needs to post a RECV in order for an incoming SEND to be processed.

Currently, there are three different selective transport modes when establishing a QP. Reliable Connection, Queue Pair is associated with only one other QP, messages transmitted by the send queue of one QP are reliably delivered to receive queue of the other QP, and packets are delivered in order; Unreliable Connection, a Queue Pair is associated with only one other QP, and the connection is not reliable so packets may be lost because the ACK is not sent by responder, messages with errors are not retried by the transport, and error handling must be provided by a higher level protocol; Unreliable Datagram, a Queue Pair may transmit and receive single-packet messages to/from any other UD QP, ordering and delivery are not guaranteed, and delivered packets may be dropped by the receiver, and multicast messages are supported (one to many). Operations available in each mode are shown in the Table 1 [32].

Table 1. Operations in UD, UC and RC mode

Operation	UD	UC	RC
Send (with immediate)	✓	✓	✓
Receive	✓	✓	✓
RDMA write (with immediate)		✓	✓
RDMA read			✓
Atomic: fetch and add/compare and swap			✓
Max message size	MTU	2 GB	2 GB

3 Remote Memory Extension

Traditional memory extension is achieved by page swap mechanism. Swapping is a process whereby a page of memory is copied to the preconfigured space on the hard disk, called swap space (a dedicated swap partition, a swap file, or a combination of swap partitions and swap files), if the system needs more memory resources and the RAM is full, inactive pages in memory are moved to the swap space to free up that page of memory. The total size of the physical memory and the swap space is the amount of virtual memory available.

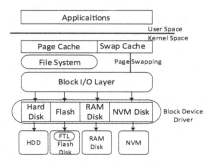

Fig. 1. Block device architecture

As depicted in Fig. 1, a swapped-out page passes through multiple layers in the VM hierarchy. The swap subsystem hands pages to the Block I/O Layer, which is responsible for the conversion of pages into block I/O requests, known as bio requests in Linux terminology [25].

These bio requests are queued by the I/O scheduler in Block I/O Layer. The I/O scheduler reorders, merges or delays a request before passing it to the device driver. A request is delayed to merge it with other contiguous requests that arrive in the near future. This delay can range from 5-6 ms [26] to minimize disk seek latencies while reading or writing. Lower in the stack, requests can be delayed or reordered again by the device driver. These additional software layers, which improve disk performance. However, flash devices do not suffer the same latencies as disks, so these delays can prove burdensome, let alone NVMs. Page swapping includes two kinds of page faults: soft page fault and hard page fault. A soft page fault need not copy data or access the I/O path; it adds a page back to the page table. In contrast, a hard page fault requires copying data from swap storage back into the memory and then adding it to the page table. According to the FlashVM [1], soft page-fault latency averages 5 µs, and the additional overhead associated with each hard page fault averages 181 µs; this overhead is nearly the same as the raw write latency of flash memory.

For NVM-based Disk, the implementation of PMBD [27] is similar to RAM Disk, which directly accesses NVM attached to the memory bus and exposes a logical block I/O interface to users; comparing to SSD, its maximum performance improvement of end-to-end application TPC-C [38] is only 5.7 times, while the write performance of raw NVM is several hundred times better than that of raw flash; that is to say, the software overhead impacts NVM more striking.

Therefore, the most effective and efficient way to reap the performance fruit of NVM is direct access from user space. However, the local NVM resources is limited due to the fact that NVMs, such as 3D XPoint, are expected to be deployed with just $4\times$ the capacity of DRAM in future systems [28]. As a result, NVM extension through network is imperative.

3.1 Overview of Pyramid

As mentioned above, Fig. 2 depicts the architecture of Pyramid. In Pyramid, NVM-providers offer NVM spaces to NVM-requester through RDMA, local DRAM or NVM of NVM-requester act as a cache layer (L4 cache) for remote NVM access. And remote memory operation must pass through L4 cache. Considering L4 cache is shared for remote NVM spaces, so efficient management of L4 cache is critical to performance improvement. Generally, Pyramid adopts traditional CPU cache mechanism expect that the cache-line unit is 4 KB–64 KB not 64B. Specifically, for remote memory write, if the component of L4 cache is DRAM, the write mechanism of L4 cache is "write-back" or "write-through", Pyramid assures that the data in L4 cache flushed to remote NVM explicitly with write-back schema; if the component of L4 cache is NVM, Pyramid set the write mechanism as write-back due to NVM is durable, data is reconstructed caused by system crashes, and Pyramid only flushes data to remote NVM implicitly at interval. As for remote memory read, the procedure in Pyramid is similar to traditional memory read process in local machine.

Basically, the two main aspects Pyramid concerns are remote data consistency and remote access performance, making remote NVM extension reasonable and attractive. In order to make these clear, on one hand, we illustrate remote data consistency from the RDMA transport semantics; on the other hand, we quantify the performance of remote NVM access comparing with that of NVMe-SSD and PCM-based SSD.

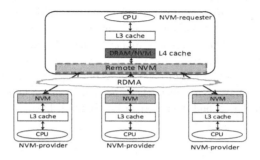

Fig. 2. Architecture of pyramid

3.2 Data Consistency of Remote Accessible NVM

Making data consistency to remote NVM is crucial, it guarantees that the stored data can survive system failure. Recent research [29–31] has adopted the sequence of {MFENCE,CLFLUSH,MFENCE} instruction to order memory writes in single machine: (1) MFENCE prevents memory operations from being reordered by CPU and (2) using the CLFLUSH instruction to write a cache line's contents to memory explicitly and manually flush CPU cache lines to make data persistent into NVM. Similarly, Remote accessible NVM also needs to guarantee data consistency remotely. On one hand, we illustrate the order rules in RDMA. The work request operation ordering is shown in Table 2, ordering semantics for WRs submitted to the Send Queue vary according to the operation type. Some operations can begin processing within the Channel Interface while other operations are still outstanding, potentially yielding out-of-order semantics for certain operation sequences (RDMA read and Atomic operation). In-order semantics can be guaranteed by setting the Fence Indicator for appropriate WRs. When the Fence Indicator is set for a given WR, WR cannot begin to be processed until all prior RDMA Read and Atomic operations on the same Send Queue have completed.

Table 2. Work request operation ordering

		Second operation			
		Send	RDMA write	RDMA read	Atomic operation
First operation	Send	#	#	#	#
	RDMA write	#	#	#	#
	RDMA read	F	F	#	F
	Atomic operation	F	F	#	F

#: order is always maintained.
F: order maintained only if send operation has Fence Indicator set.

According to the Table 2 [32], there are two possible consequences without or with setting Fence Indicator: (1) RDMA Read which followed by Sends, RDMA Writes, or Atomics - not setting Fence may lead to a case where the RDMA Read response will contain data that was modified by the second operation. Using Fence will make sure that the data that will be Read by the first operation will be the original (and expected) data. (2) RDMA Read or Atomic operations, which followed by Sends, RDMA Writes, or Atomics - not setting Fence may lead to a case that if the first operation complete in error on the initiator side (because its ACK fail to return, local protection error when writing the data or any other reason) and the second operation could still be observed by the target, and it may even cause data to be written in the target's memory. Using Fence will prevent the second operation to be observed by the target if the first one fails.

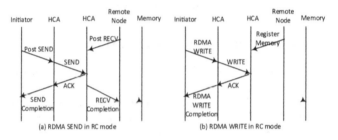

Fig. 3. RDMA SEND and WRITE procedure in RC mode

On the other hand, to deliver remote data persistence, in RDMA, this can be implemented in two schemas: (1) as depicted in Fig. 3(a), for two-sided transport semantics, initiator writes data is through SEND operation, which is sometimes referred to as a Push operation or as having channel semantics. Both terms refer to how the SW client of the transport service views the movement of data. With a SEND operation the initiator of the data transfer pushes data to the remote QP. The initiator does not know where the data is going on the remote node. It will receive an RDMA acknowledgement from remote node with RC transport mode. The remote node's Channel Adapter places the data into the next available receive NVM buffer for that QP. On an HCA, the receive buffer is pointed to by the WQE at the head of the QP's receive queue. Remote node polls the Completion Queue to check whether the data is persisted in NVM buffer or not. (2) For one-sided transport semantics, as presented in Fig. 3(b), RDMA WRITE operation, the remote node first allocates a memory range for access by the destination's QP (or group of QPs). A destination's channel adapter associates a 32-bit R_Key with this memory region. The remote node communicates the virtual address, length, and R_Key to any other node (initiator) it wishes to have access the memory region. The communication of address and R_Key is done by the client upper level protocol (TCP/UDP or SEND operation). Initiator writes data directly into the virtual memory space of the remote node. Also, remote node automatically sends an RDMA acknowledgement back to initiator in the context of RC transport mode. However, the fact of RDMA acknowledgement is that remote node guarantees that the data has been successfully received and accepted for execution by its HCA but does not make sure data has reach to the remote NVM. Typically, the fact that initiator receives the acknowledgement implies that the data has been almost (not all) written into the destination NVM buffer. Fortunately, based-on the semantics of RDMA WRITE with immediate data, immediate data is included in the last packet of an RDMA WRITE message. The Immediate data is not written to the target virtual address range, but is passed to the completion queue element in CQ after the last RDMA WRITE packet is successfully processed, which means data is persisted into NVM as remote node polls the completion queue element. Remote flush operation may be supported by RDMA in the future. Currently, strong data persistence needs the cooperation between initiator and remote node.

We evaluate the remote persistence performance. For persistence guarantee, initiator uses RDMA-write-with-immediate-data operation to write data remotely, remote node detects this operation and feedbacks with operation of RDMA-send-with-immediate-data; for comparison, the normal remote write is conducted with RDMA Write operation and they are all in Reliable Connection mode. In detail, using Lp stands for latency of persistence guarantee procedure and Ln presents for latency of normal remote write operation, the persistence cost ratio PCr is calculated according to the formula (1).

$$PC_r = (L_p - L_n)/L_p \tag{1}$$

Figure 4 shows that persistence cost ratio of correspond data size from 64B to 1 MB. On the whole, persistence cost declines gradually as the data size increases; for data size of 32 KB, this overhead accounts for about 10% of the total latency due to data transfer plays dominate role. Experimental results show that the persistence cost falls into the range of 1.5–2.5 µs, and the average persistence cost is circa 1.7 µs. This low latency is mainly due to CPU reads the immediate data from Last Level Cache, which the RNIC directly interacts with servicing the NIC's PCIe requests [32, 33].

In a nutshell, RDMA provides mechanisms to deliver remote memory consistency: (1) Work requests in the same Queue Pair executes in order with setting Fence indicators for RDMA Read or Atomic operations, system design just only cares about

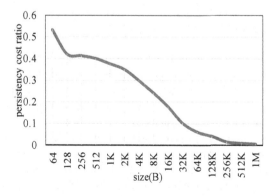

Fig. 4. Data persistence cost ratio from 64B to 1 MB

making memory operations between different QPs in order and this is guaranteed by concurrency mechanism; (2) remote data persistence is implemented with the cooperation between initiator and remote nodes, and its performance is acceptable.

3.3   Performance of Remote Accessible NVM

The cluster of Pyramid includes four machines, using one machine as NVM-requester and the other three machines are NVM-providers offering 4G DRAM (proxy for NVM).

First of all, we evaluate the performance of remote random write and sequential write with remote DRAM extension.

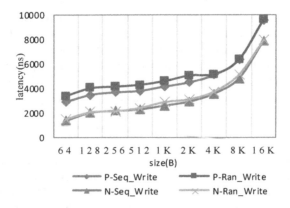

Fig. 5. Remote sequential and random write concerning data persistence: "P-Seq_Write" and "N-Seq_Write" stand for remote sequential write with and without persistence guarantee, respectively, "P-Ran_Write" and "P-Ran_Write" are remote random writes.

As revealed in Fig. 5, experimental results indicates that random remote write is about 5% longer than sequential remote write due to the RNIC on-chip-cache miss overhead for normal remote write situation; as for remote persistence write, random mode performance is almost the same with sequential mode when the data size is above 4096 bytes; and sequential remote write performs around 13.6% better than random remote write.

Secondly, for the sake of quantifying the performance of remote accessible NVM, we take PCM for illustration, its read latency is the same with DRAM ($\sim$ 70 ns access latency of Kingston DDR3 1600 MHz in our experiment) and write latency is set to 150 ns, this latency is emulated by inserting extra operations to poll the timestamp register (tsc), which is similar to Mnemosyne [14]. In light of long write latency of PCM and its read performance is comparable to that of DRAM, we simply evaluate remote NVM write performance and the write latency is injected in upper software layer at initiator side; since the max data payload supports by root complex is 128 bytes (The RDMA NIC in our experiment is Mellanox MT27500 ConnectX-3 HCA), so one latency of 150 ns is added every 128B data writes. Figure 6 shows one-way latency comparison between Remote Write DRAM and PCM of data size from 1B to 16 KB, Remote Write DRAM outperforms about an average of 52.5% over than Remote Write PCM; specifically, as the data size grows, the trend of performance degradation is more obvious. The reason of this is that PCM write performance dominates as the data size increases, specifically, when the data size goes up to 4 KB, the performance gap between remote PCM write and remote DRAM write approaches or exceeds that of local PCM write and DRAM write.

In view of RDMA Unreliable Connection semantics, remote write just takes one-way latency to complete, and latencies of random and sequential write are almost the same with data size of 4 KB or above. Therefore, the low latency of 4 KB remote PCM write operation is 5.79 µs, and the high latency will takes about 11.6 µs.

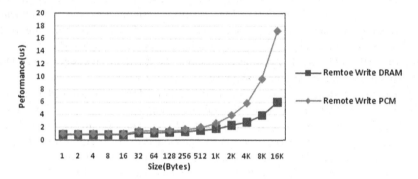

Fig. 6. One-way latency of remote write DRAM and PCM in RC mode

Finally, to manifest the performance opportunity brought by remote accessible NVM, we enumerate new technologies of storage-NVMe-SSD and PCM-based SSD for comparison. The recently announced Non-Volatile Memory Express (NVMe) drives represents the second major technology leap. NVMe is a software based standard [34, 35] that was specifically optimized for SSDs connected through the PCIe interface. Comparing with traditional-SSD, NVMe-SSD has the benefits of shorter hardware data path and simplified software stack, which provides better performance and scalability, according to experimental results [36] with benchmark FIO [37] of 4 KB random read operations: the total software overhead accounts for 7.3% with the total latency of 111 microseconds, while the ratio is 28% for SATA SSD. There are several previous studies regarding PCM-based SSD treat PCM as storage, in 2011, Onyx [39], based on Micron's first-generation P8P 16 MiB PCM chips (NP8P128 A13B1760E) drives many PCM chips concurrently, and provides 38 µs and 179 µs for 4 KiB read and write latencies, respectively; in 2012, a prototype PCM-based SSD built by Micron [40] uses the same PCM chip used in Onyx, and takes 20 µs and 250 µs for 4 KiB read and write, respectively, excluding software overhead; also, one recent study [41] shows that PCM-based SSD achieves an average read latency of 6.7 µs (the maximum is 194.9 µs) and write latency of 128.3 µs (the maximum is 378.2 µs) for 4 KB data request from the system perspective. Compared with

NVMe-SSD and PCM-based SSD, in our experience, 4 KB remote PCM write performs better, which elucidates remote NVM extension is promising in terms of not only memory capacity but also performance.

To sum up, for one thing, Pyramid provides the basic mechanism to achieve data consistency with RDMA; for another, although remote data persistence cost exists, remote NVM access still reveals good performance.

4 Related Work

This section places Pyramid in context with other research projects and systems:

Non-Volatile Main Memory: Recent years have seen increased interest in NVMM. Researchers have focused on NVMM-related problems, such as building NVMM file systems [42–45], hybrid DRAM/NVMM memory systems [46], memory allocators [11–13], memory management and paging mechanisms [47], and programming models [14, 15]. Mojim [48], one replicated and reliable system from NVMM to NVMM based-on PMFS [43]. While Pyramid is a remote NVM extension system with RDMA and delivers the data persistence guarantee.

In-memory system based-on RDMA: RAMCloud [16], a distributed in-memory key-value store, providing dozens of terabytes memory capacity with hundreds of commercial servers connected by InfiniBand. MICA [18], optimizing for multi-core architectures by enabling parallel access to partitioned data, speeding up data access with RDMA. At one-sided communication model, Pilaf [49] allowed its clients to directly read data from the server's memory through RDMA-read for GET requests. C-Hint [50] focused on cache efficiency with storage such as tracking data access history, making eviction decisions. FaRM [17], a distributed share memory system, used RDMA-read to perform its lock-free reads detecting inconsistent RDMA reads with concurrent CPU memory modifications with a self-verifying data structures. HERD [51] took combined Unreliable-Connection-based RDMA Write with Unreliable-Datagram-based Send for better performance for key-value service. Different from all these projects, Pyramid focuses on memory extension for single machine with remote NVM spaces, the memory extension machine is only used for applications' user interface and business logic and data is stored remotely.

5 Conclusion and Future Work

In this paper, we revisit the traditional memory extension through HDD/SSD or the emerging Non-Volatile Memory. Considering limitation of the memory scalability and the storage performance within a single machine, we propose a new memory extension model, memory extension with remote NVM spaces through RDMA and machine extending memory only cares about business logic. Then, we discuss the feasibility of remote NVM extension schema from the two main aspects of remote data consistency and access performance. The directions of future work include remote data consistency overhead and performance limitation in the context of specific applications, such as key-value stores, MapReduce or graph processing systems in single machine.

Acknowledgments. We are grateful to our anonymous reviewers for their suggestions to improve this paper. This work is supported by the National High-Tech Research and Development Projects (863) and the National Natural Science Foundation of China under Grant Nos. 2015AA015305, 61232003, 61332003, 61202121.

References

1. Saxena, M., Swift, M.M.: FlashVM: virtual memory management on flash. In: USENIX Annual Technical Conference (2010)
2. Charles, L., Karthick, R., Freeman, R., Wes, F., Michael, K., Keller, T.W.: Energy management for commercial servers. Computer **36**(12), 39–48 (2003)
3. Barroso, A.L., Clidaras, J., Hölzle, U.: The datacenter as a computer: an introduction to the design of warehouse-scale machines. Synth. Lect. Comput. Architect. **8**(3), 1–154 (2013)
4. Mandelman, J.A., Dennard, R.H., Bronner, G.B., DeBrosse, J.K., Divakaruni, R., Li, Y., Radens, C.J.: Challenges and future directions for the scaling of dynamic random-access memory (DRAM). IBM J. Res. Dev. **46**(2.3), 187–212 (2002)
5. Mueller, W., Aichmayr, G., Bergner, W., Erben, E., Hecht, T., Kapteyn, C., Kersch, A., Kudelka, S., Lau, F., Luetzen, J., Orth, A.: Challenges for the DRAM cell scaling to 40 nm. In: IEEE International Electron Devices Meeting, 2005. IEDM Technical Digest, December 2005
6. Nair, P.J., Kim, D.-H., Qureshi, M.K.: ArchShield: architectural framework for assisting DRAM scaling by tolerating high error rates. In: Proceedings of the 40th Annual International Symposium on Computer Architecture (ISCA), pp. 72–83 (2013)
7. Raoux, S., et al.: Phase-change random access memory: a scalable technology. IBM J. Res. Dev. **52**(4.5), 465–479 (2008)
8. Intel 3D XPoint. https://www.intel.com/content/www/us/en/architect-ure-and-technology/intel-optane-technology.html
9. Awad, A., Blagodurov, S., Solihin, Y.: Write-aware management of NVM-based memory extensions. In: Proceedings of the 2016 International Conference on Supercomputing. ACM (2016)
10. Ramos, L.E., Gorbatov, E., Bianchini, R.: Page placement in hybrid memory systems. In: Proceedings of the International Conference on Supercomputing (ICS), pp. 85–95. ACM (2011)
11. Moraru, I., Andersen, D.G., Kaminsky, M., Tolia, N., Ranganathan, P., Binkert, N.: Consistent, durable, and safe memory management for byte-addressable non-volatile main memory. In: Proceedings of the First ACM SIGOPS Conference on Timely Results in Operating Systems, p. 1. ACM, November 2013
12. Yu, S., Xiao, N., Deng, M., Xing, Y., Liu, F., Cai, Z., Chen, W.: WAlloc: an efficient wear-aware allocator for non-volatile main memory. In: 34th IEEE International Performance Computing and Communications Conference (IPCCC), 14th–16th December 2015, Nanjing, China, December 2015
13. Yu, S., Xiao, N., Deng, M., Liu, F., Chen, W.: Redesign the memory allocator for non-volatile main memory. J. Emerg. Technol. Comput. Syst. **13**(3), 26 p. (2017). Article no. 49
14. Haris, V., Tack, A.J., Swift, M.M.: Mnemosyne: lightweight persistent memory. ACM SIGPLAN Not. **46**(3), 91–104 (2011)
15. Coburn, J., Caulfield, A.M., Akel, A., Grupp, L.M., Gupta, R.K., Jhala, R., Swanson, S.: NV-Heaps: making persistent objects fast and safe with next-generation, non-volatile memories. In: ACM SIGARCH Computer Architecture News, vol. 39, no. 1, pp. 105–118. ACM, March 2011

16. Ousterhout, J., et al.: The case for RAMClouds: scalable high-performance storage entirely in DRAM. ACM SIGOPS Oper. Syst. Rev. **43**(4), 92–105 (2010)

17. Dragojević, A., Narayanan, D., Castro, M., Hodson, O.: FaRM: fast remote memory. In: 11th USENIX Symposium on Networked Systems Design and Implementation (NSDI 2014), pp. 401–414 (2014)

18. Lim, H., Han, D., Andersen, D.G., Kaminsky, M.: MICA: a holistic approach to fast in-memory key-value storage. In: 11th USENIX Symposium on Networked Systems Design and Implementation (NSDI 2014), pp. 429–444 (2014)

19. Jose, J., Subramoni, H., Luo, M., Zhang, M., Huang, J., Wasi-ur-Rahman, M., Islam, N.S., Ouyang, X., Wang, H., Sur, S., Panda, D.K.: Memcached design on high performance RDMA capable interconnects. In: 2011 International Conference on Parallel Processing (ICPP), pp. 743–752. IEEE (2011)

20. Yoo, R.M., Romano, A., Kozyrakis, C.: Phoenix rebirth: scalable MapReduce on a large-scale shared-memory system. In: IEEE International Symposium on Workload Characterization, IISWC 2009. IEEE (2009)

21. Kyrola, A., Blelloch, G.E., Guestrin, C.: GraphChi: large-scale graph computation on just a PC. In: OSDI, vol. 12 (2012)

22. Roy, A., Mihailovic, I., Zwaenepoel, W.: X-Stream: edge-centric graph processing using streaming partitions. In: Proceedings of the Twenty-Fourth ACM Symposium on Operating Systems Principles. ACM (2013)

23. Infiniband Trade Association. http://www.infinibandta.org

24. Top500 Supercomputing System. http://www.top500.org

25. Bovet, D.P., Cesati, M.: Understanding the Linux Kernel, 3rd edn. O'Reilly Media Inc, Sebastopol (2005)

26. Iyer, S., Druschel, P.: Anticipatory scheduling: a disk scheduling framework to overcome deceptive idleness in synchronous IO. In: SOSP (2001)

27. Chen, F., Mesnier, M.P., Hahn, S.: A protected block device for persistent memory. In: 2014 30th Symposium on Mass Storage Systems and Technologies (MSST), pp. 1–12. IEEE, June 2014

28. Crooke, R., Fazio, A.: Intel non-volatile memory inside. The speed of possibility outside. In: Intel Developer Forum (IDF) (2015)

29. Venkataraman, S., Tolia, N., Ranganathan, P., Campbell, R.H.: Consistent and durable data structures for non-volatile byte-addressable memory. In: FAST, vol. 11, pp. 61–75, February 2011

30. Yang, J., et al.: NV-Tree: reducing consistency cost for NVM-based single level systems. In: FAST, vol. 15 (2015)

31. Chen, S., Jin, Q.: Persistent b+-trees in non-volatile main memory. In: Proceedings of the VLDB Endowment, vol. 8, no. 7, pp. 786–797 (2015)

32. Infiniband architecture specification volume 1. https://cw.infinibandta.org/document/dl/7859

33. Kaminsky, A.K.M., Andersen, D.G.: Design guidelines for high performance RDMA systems. In: 2016 USENIX Annual Technical Conference (USENIX ATC 2016) (2016)

34. Huffman, A.: NVM Express Revision 1.1. (2012). http://www.nvmexpress.org/wp-content/uploads/NVM-Express-1_1.pdf

35. NVM-Express. NVM Express Explained (2012). http://nvmexpress.org/wp-content/uploads/2013/04/NVM_whitepaper.pdf

36. Xu, Q., et al.: Performance analysis of NVMe SSDs and their implication on real world databases. In: Proceedings of the 8th ACM International Systems and Storage Conference. ACM (2015)

37. Axboe, J.: FIO (2014). http://git.kernel.dk/?p=fio.git;a=summary

38. TPC. TPC-C Benchmark Standard Specification, Revision 5.11 (2010). http://www.tpc.org/tpcc/spec/tpcc_current.pdf
39. Akel, A., Caulfield, A.M., Mollov, T.I., Gupta, R.K., Swanson, S.: Onyx: a protoype phase change memory storage array. In: Proceedings of the 3rd USENIX Conference on Hot Topics in Storage and File Systems, Berkeley, CA, USA, HotStorage 2011. USENIX Association, p. 2 (2011)
40. Athanassoulis, M., Bhattacharjee, B., Canim, M., Ross, K.A.: Path processing using solid state storage. In: Proceedings of the 3rd International Workshop on Accelerating Data Management Systems Using Modern Processor and Storage Architectures (ADMS 2012) (2012)
41. Kim, H., et al.: Evaluating phase change memory for enterprise storage systems: a study of caching and tiering approaches. ACM Trans. Storage (TOS) **10**, 15 (2014)
42. Condit, J., Nightingale, E.B., Frost, C., Ipek, E., Burger, D., Lee, B.C., Coetzee, D.: Better I/O through byte-addressable, persistent memory. In: Proceedings of the 22nd ACM Symposium on Operating Systems Principles (SOSP 2009), Big Sky, Montana, October 2009
43. Dulloor, S.R., Kumar, S., Keshavamurthy, A., Lantz, P., Reddy, D., Sankaran, R., Jackson, J.: System software for persistent memory. In: Proceedings of the EuroSys Conference (EuroSys 2014), Amsterdam, The Netherlands, April 2014
44. Wu, X., Reddy, A.L.N.: SCMFS: a file system for storage class memory. In: International Conference for High Performance Computing, Networking, Storage and Analysis (SC 2011), November 2011
45. Islam, N.S., Wasi-ur-Rahman, M., Lu, X., Panda, D.K.: High performance design for HDFS with byte-addressability of NVM and RDMA. In: Proceedings of the 2016 International Conference on Supercomputing, p. 8. ACM (2016)
46. Mogul, J.C., Argollo, E., Shah, M., Faraboschi, P.: Operating system support for NVM +DRAM hybrid main memory. In: The Twelfth Workshop on Hot Topics in Operating Systems (HotOS XII), Monte Verita, Switzerland, May 2009
47. Bailey, K., Ceze, L., Gribble, S.D., Levy, H.M.: Operating system implications of fast, cheap, nonvolatile memory. In: Proceedings of the 13th USENIX Conference on Hot Topics in Operating Systems (HotOS 2013), Napa, California, May 2011
48. Zhang, Y., Yang, J., Memaripour, A., Swanson, S.: Mojim: a reliable and highly-available non-volatile memory system. ACM SIGPLAN Not. **50**(4), 3–18 (2015)
49. Mitchell, C., Geng, Y., Li, J.: Using one-sided RDMA reads to build a fast, CPU-efficient key-value store. In: USENIX Annual Technical Conference, pp. 103–114, June 2013
50. Wang, Y., Meng, X., Zhang, L., Tan, J.: C-hint: an effective and reliable cache management for RDMA-accelerated key-value stores. In: Proceedings of the ACM Symposium on Cloud Computing, pp. 1–13. ACM, November 2014
51. Kalia, A., Kaminsky, M., Andersen, D.G.: Using RDMA efficiently for key-value services. In: ACM SIGCOMM Computer Communication Review, vol. 44, no. 4, pp. 295–306. ACM, August 2014

Fully Decentralized Multi-Authority ABE Scheme in Data Sharing System

Xiehua Li[(✉)] and Ziyu Huang

College of Computer Science and Electronic Engineering, Hunan University,
Changsha 410082, China
beverly@hnu.edu.cn

Abstract. In this paper, we propose an attribute-based encryption (ABE) scheme that can be used in data sharing systems with multiple distrusted authorizes. Unlike prior multi-authority ABEs, this scheme can achieve secret key generation in a fully decentralized manner, which eliminates the security risk on central authority (CA) compromise. By separating the key generation process among authorities and data owners (DOs), our scheme is resilient to collusion between malicious authorities and users. This new fully Decentralized Multi-Authority ABE (f-DMA) scheme is derived from CP-ABE that is resilient to collusion between authorities and users. Our system distinguishes between DO principal and attribute authorities (AAs): DOs own the data but allows AAs to arbitrate access by providing attribute labels to users. The data is protected by access policy encryption over these attributes. Unlike prior systems, attributes generated by AAs are not user-specific, and neither is the system susceptible to collusion between users who try to escalate their access by sharing keys. We prove our scheme correct under the Decisional Bilinear Diffie-Hellman (DBDH) assumption; we also include a complete end-to-end implementation that demonstrates the practical efficacy of our technique.

Keywords: Multi-Authority ABE · Data sharing · Access control
Cloud storage

1 Introduction

Data sharing is commonly used in data outsourcing and cloud storage systems, especially in the scenarios that distrusted authorities collaborate on specific projects. For example, for fighting with disease like Ebola, hospitals and department of public health (DPH) need to collaborate. In this scenario, the data being shared is developed not only by the hospitals, but can originate from the DPH. The data originated from these authorities may maintain sensitive data about patient health record and should not be accessible by unauthorized user or authority. These types of scenarios are increasingly common, and require the ability to provide secure data access with fine-grained control. It is possible to provision such access using a trusted third party (TTP), such as a central authority (CA) that generates secret keys for specific data; however, TTP-based solutions are particularly problematic in multi-authority scenarios since they require distrusting principals to trust a single party.

© Springer International Publishing AG 2017
G. Wang et al. (Eds.): SpaCCS 2017 Workshops, LNCS 10658, pp. 744–756, 2017.
https://doi.org/10.1007/978-3-319-72395-2_66

In this paper, we introduce a fully decentralized fine-grained data sharing scheme to achieve access control among users of distrusting authorities and different DOs, without resorting to TTPs. Beyond authorities and the data owner, includes users who may not belong to any authority but need access to the data, and an untrusted third-party storage provider that hosts the data to be shared. Importantly, it does not require authorities to agree on a global identity for users: they may provide access attributes to users independently; the cryptographic mechanisms allow attributes from different authorities and DOs to combine to enable access to encrypted data and prevent collusion between authorities and users. Our scheme is based on CP-ABE (Ciphertext-Policy Attribute-Based Encryption) that is an attribute-based fine-grained access control and encryption method for secret data sharing. We extend the original CP-ABE into a multi-authority scenario and maintain its security and efficiency properties. The main contributions of this paper are as follows:

(1) We propose a fully decentralized scheme that can achieve secure data sharing among distrusting authorities, users and DOs. Our scheme is tolerant to DOs, authorities and users collusion attack.
(2) We propose a novel authentication and key generation protocol without revealing user's information, which is valuable for anonymous communication.
(3) We implement the f-DMA scheme based on cpabe library and measure its efficiency.

The remaining of this paper is organized as follows: We introduces a discussion of related work in Sect. 2. Then, we propose DMA scheme and security model in Sect. 3. Next, we analyze the performance of our scheme. We finally conclude this paper in Sect. 4.

2 Related WORK

ABE is a promising technique that enables fine-grained access control to encrypted data [2–6, 10], and is widely used in various applications [1, 7, 9, 11, 18–20]. In various ABE-based schemes, a trusted central authority (CA) is used to manage all the attributes and distribute keys. Once the CA gets compromised, there would be no privacy of the stored data. Hierarchy attribute-based encryption is an extension of original ABE system. Few researches have been done on this area. Gentry and Silverberg first proposed the notion of hierarchical encryption scheme [24].

With the commonly use of data sharing system, access control schemes that involves multiple authorities are proposed [8, 10, 25, 26]. Most of these schemes use CA as the TTP to generate public key and user secret keys. Chase firstly proposed a multi-authority ABE method [8] that introduced a global identifier (GID) for CA to generate user secret keys. Lewko and Waters *et al.* propose a multi-authority CP-ABE [12, 13] that uses CA only in the initialization phase. CA distributes the public parameters and verifies AAs according to the user's request. Yang *et al.* propose a DAC-MACS algorithm [14], CA is responsible for the generation of the global public key and private key and distribute a unique identity for the user and all the AAs. Later, they propose two multi-authority ABE access control schemes [15, 16] in which CA is responsible for authenticating all the AAs and users. In addition, CA also assigns GID for users and AID to each AA. In order to eliminate the security risk introduced by CA and protect user's identity, Taeho *et al.* proposed anonymous privilege control schemes [17, 22]. This scheme generalizes an access tree to a privilege tree. Several trees are required in every encrypted file to verify user's identity and to grant him a privilege accordingly.

3 Preliminaries and Definitions

We will first give the cryptographic background information of bilinear map and security model. Then, we will describe the access structure of our DMA scheme and give the security model.

3.1 Preliminaries

Let G_0 and G_1 be two multiplicative cyclic groups for prime order p and g be a generator of G_0. The bilinear map e is defined as, $e: G_0 \times G_0 \rightarrow G_1$. The bilinear map e has the following properties: (1) bilinearity: $\forall u, v \in G_0$, and $a, b \in \mathbb{Z}_P$, then $e(u^a, v^b) = e(u, v)^{ab}$. (2) Non-degeneracy: $e(g, g) \neq 1$. (3) Symmetry: $e(g^a, g^b) = e(g, g)^{ab} = e(g^b, g^a)$.

Definition. The Decisional Bilinear Diffie-Hellman (DBDH) assumption in a multiplicative cyclic group G_0 of prime order p with generator g is stated as: given g^a, g^b and g^c for uniformly and independently chosen $a, b, c \in \mathbb{Z}_P$, the following two distributions are computationally indistinguishable:

- G_0, g, g^a, g^b, g^{ab}
- G_0, g, g^a, g^b, g^c

The security of our scheme is based on the DBDH assumption which is widely used in security proof of various ABE schemes. The assumption is reasonable because discrete logarithm problems in large number field are widely considered to be intractable.

3.2 Threats Model

We assume that the data owners (DOs) and Cloud Storage Providers (CSPs) are semi-honest, which means they can implement the program properly but are willing to get illegal profits if given the opportunity. The Attributes Authorities (AAs) are assumed to be untrusted. In our scheme, the AAs calculate and distribute attributes and partial user specific secret keys to users. In general, AAs will follow the protocol, but they will try to collect all the secret key components and find more useful information to decrypt any ciphertext. They have the intention to collude with other entities like user, CSP, or other AAs to gain the information they want. Our assumption is based on the real application in data sharing and cloud storage systems.

Data users are untrusted entities. They are willing to collude with any entities in this system to collect useful information that they have no rights to access to.

3.3 Access Tree Definition in f-DMA

Let Γ be a tree representing an access structure. Every non-leaf node of the tree represents a threshold gate that is described by its children and a threshold value. If num_x is the number of children of a node x and k_x is its threshold value, then $0 < k_x \leq num_x$. If $k_x = 1$, the threshold gate is an 'OR' gate. If $k_x = num_x$, it is an 'AND' gate. Every leaf node x of the tree is described by an attribute and a threshold value $k_x = 1$. Attributes contained in the access tree can be issued by different authorities. The access tree in our scheme is defined as follows:

(1) Access tree is defined by DO. Leaf nodes represent attributes that are distributed by AAs.
(2) Each leaf node of the access tree is described as an attribute which is issued by its authority.
(3) If a user's attribute set S satisfies the access tree Γ, he/she can decrypt the data that are encrypted with this access tree.

4   System Architecture and Key Distribution

4.1   System Architecture

There are 4 entities involved in the DMA system: DO (Data Owner), AA (Attributes Authority), Cloud storage provider (CSP), and user. The system architecture of DMA is shown in Fig. 1. The entities are described as follows:

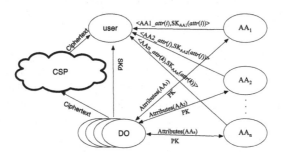

Fig. 1. f-DMA access control system architecture

1. DO (Data Owner). Data owner is responsible for calculating public key, defining access policy and encrypting data under the access policy. Furthermore, the data owner needs to upload the encrypted data to the remote cloud storage server. DO keeps the attribute update list (AUL) and user list (UL) to identify the authorized

user. For security purpose, DO computes part of users' private keys called user specific key **SK**d and sends it directly to the particular users via secure channels. The reason why DO generates and distributes **SK**d is for preventing authorities collusion attack.

2. AA (Attribute Authority). AA plays the role of attributes distribution and user authorization. It computes users' attributes based on the public parameters and distributes them to DO and users for access policy definition. Every AA can manage multiple attributes and has full control over those attributes. Moreover, AA computes attribute secret keys **SK**$_{AAi}(attr(i))$ and issues them to users via secure channel. AA$_i$ denotes the ith AA in our scheme, $attr(i)$ denotes an attribute issued by a an AA.

3. Cloud Server Provider (CSP). CSP is considered as a semi-trusted storage media that stores data. It is also responsible for updating the ciphertext when attribute revocation occurs. The CSP does not have the secret keys, so it can't decrypt the ciphertext. Based on the semi-trusted assumption, CSP can implement the algorithm honestly, but it will decrypt the ciphertext once it gets the key.

4. User. Ciphertext on the cloud server can be accessed freely by users. But only when the user's attributes satisfy the access policy that defined in the ciphertext, can he/she decrypt the ciphertext. User's attributes are distributed by a number of authorities according to the user privileges so that it can achieve cross-domain access control. In addition, DO prevents the collusion attacks between users by embedding a random number in the private property.

4.2 Key Distribution Protocol

In our scheme, we refactor the original CP-ABE and extend the key generation algorithm to a multiple authority scenario. In this system, user needs to first register in a set of AAs and get his secret key components from these AAs and DO. The registration and key distribution procedure involves two stages: (1) user registration and user specific secret key distribution stage, which is shown in Fig. 2(a). (2) attribute key distribution stage, which is shown in Fig. 2(b).

1. Users first register in an AA, and get a message with freshly generated nonce N_i and AA's signature over N_i. [sig$_{AAi}$; m] denotes the signature of AA$_i$ over message m. This message is used for verification and preventing replay attack. AA also generates partial user specific secret key **SK**$_{AAi} = g^{\alpha_i} * g^{\lambda_i}$. In our scheme, user is able to register to multiple DOs and AAs. Each time, registration and key distribution follows the same procedure.

2. User forwards N_i and AA's signature to DO. After verifying the user and AA, DO will generate part of user's specific key **SK**$d = g^{\alpha_d} * g^{\lambda_d}$ and send it to the user. User collects user specific secret key components from all registered AAs and DOs, and computes his own user specific secret key **SK**$u = g^{\sum \alpha_d + \sum \alpha_i} * g^{\sum \lambda_d + \sum \lambda_i}$.

3. For computing user attribute keys, AAs send DO the encrypted g^{λ_i} with DO's public key, along with this message a public parameter $e(g, g)^{\alpha_i}$ is also sent to DO for data encryption (see in Fig. 3(a)). Each DO collects g^{λ_i} from all AAs and

computes $g^{\sum \lambda_i}$ for attribute key calculation. Then, DO sends user a blinded parameter Pu as a partial attribute key. (see in Fig. 3(b))

$$Pu = A * g^{\sum \lambda_i} \tag{1}$$

where A is the blinder, such as g^x, $x \in \mathbb{Z}_p$ is a random number chosen by DO when generating user specific secret key. Here we can see that each user has a set of attribute keys that are in accordance with his/her user specific secret key. The reason to blind the partial attribute key $g^{\sum \lambda_i}$ is because whoever gets $g^{\sum \lambda_i}$ can generates whatever attribute keys he/she wants. We will describe this in details in the next section. Pu is encrypted with AA's public key, $[enc_{K\_AAi}; m]$ denotes encryption of message m over AAi's public key K_{AAi}.

4. User keeps his user specific secret key and forwards the encrypted Pu to AA. AA decrypts Pu. According to user's attributes, AA calculates blinded attribute keys and sends them along with user's attributes and AA's signature back to the user.

5. User forwards this message to DO. DO verifies AA, user's attributes and give back unblinded attribute keys back to the user. In Fig. 3(b). In addition, DO raises the unblinded attribute key from $g^{\sum \lambda_i} H(attr(i))^{r_i}$ to $g^{\sum \lambda_i} H(attr(i))^{r_i + r_s}$, so that user is not able to guess $g^{\sum \lambda_i}$ from Pu. Since r^i is a random number, the change of r^i won't affect decryption process.

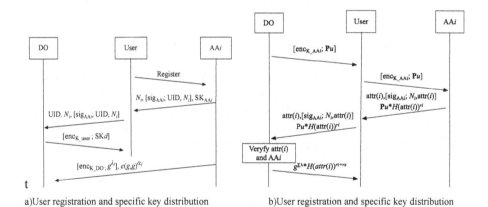

a)User registration and specific key distribution   b)User registration and specific key distribution

Fig. 2. User registration and key distribution protocol in f-DMA

4.3 f-DMA Access Control Scheme Construction

A. **Setup(PK, MK).** The setup procedure is used for generating public parameters. Any DO can run this procedure and broadcast **PK**. Other DOs and AAs will use this **PK** to generate keys in the future. Let g be the generator of a bilinear group of G, and the prime order of G is p, $e : G \times G \to G_T$ as the bilinear map. Let H :

$\{0,1\}^* \to G$ be the hash function which maps attributes to G. DO selects two random exponents $\alpha_d, \eta \in \mathbb{Z}_p$, and computes public key and master key as follows:

$$\textbf{PK} = \left(g, G, g^\eta, g^{1/\eta}, e(g,g)^{\alpha_d} \right) \tag{2}$$

$$\textbf{MSK} = (g^{\alpha_d}, \eta) \tag{3}$$

DO publishes **PK** all other principals in this system.

B. **KeyGen I.** In the f-DMA scheme, the KeyGen is divided into two phrases, KeyGen I and KeyGen II.

KeyGen I(MK) is run by all principals in this system. After registration, DO generates and issues $\textbf{SK}d = g^{\alpha_d} * g^{\lambda_d}$ to user. AA generates and issues $\textbf{SK}_{\text{AA}i} = g^{\alpha_i} * g^{\lambda_i}$ to user. User collects and combines these key components together to get his user specific secret key **SK**u.

$$\alpha = \sum \alpha_d + \sum \alpha_i, \quad \lambda = \sum \lambda_d + \sum \lambda_i \tag{4}$$

$$\textbf{SK}u = g^{(\alpha+\lambda)/\eta} \tag{5}$$

where $\alpha_i, \lambda_d, \lambda_i \in \mathbb{Z}_p$ are random numbers. λ_d, λ_i are unique for every user to prevent user collusion attack.

KeyGen II $((\textbf{PK}, \textbf{attr}(i)_{i\in\{1...n\}}))$ is run by multiple AAs to calculate attribute keys for users. AAs use the blinded parameter to calculate blinded attribute keys for user.

$$\textbf{BSK}_i = \left(\forall attr(i) \in S_{\text{AA}i}, V_i = A * g^\lambda * H(attr(i))^{r_i}, V_i' = g^{r_i} \right) \tag{6}$$

where $S_{\text{AA}j}$ denotes the set of attributes that AA$_j$ holds. $r_i \in \mathbb{Z}_p$ is a random number for each $attr(i) \in S_{\text{AA}i}$ chosen by AA$_j$. From Eq. (6) we can see that if g^λ is given to AA directly, any AA can forge arbitrary attribute keys since $attr(i)$ is a binary string and r_i is a random number. As shown in Fig. 4, DO will send user the final attribute keys by unblinding **BSK**$_i$. The final attribute keys is described as follows.

$$\textbf{SK}_i = \left(\forall attr(i) \in S_{\text{AA}i}, V_i = g^\lambda * H(attr(i))^{r_i}, V_i' = g^{r_i} \right) \tag{7}$$

C. **Encryption(PK, M, Γ).** DO encrypts the message M under public key and the access policy Γ. The encryption algorithm chooses a polynomial q_x for each node x in the access tree. For each node x in the tree, set the degree d_x of the polynomial q_x, $d_x = k_x - 1$, where k_x is the threshold value of the chosen node. The algorithm starts at the root node R, it chooses a random exponent $s \in Z_p$ and sets $q_R(0) = s$. Then, for any other node x, the algorithm randomly chooses other coefficients and set $q_{parent(x)}(index(x))$ such that $q_x(0) = q_{parent(x)}(index(x))$, is the index of node x's child nodes, and $parent(x)$ is node x's parent node.

Suppose Y is the set of leaf nodes in Γ, the ciphertext is constructed as follows:

$$CT = \begin{pmatrix} \Gamma, C' = M \cdot e(g,g)^{\alpha s}, \ C = g^{\eta s} \\ \forall y \in Y, \ C_y = H(att(y))^{q_y(0)}, \ C'_y = g^{q_y(0)} \end{pmatrix} \tag{8}$$

D. **Decrypt** $(CT, \mathbf{SK})$. Only when the user's attributes satisfy access policy defined in ciphertext, the user can decrypt the ciphertext. The decryption algorithm takes as inputs secret keys and ciphertext, where $\mathbf{SK} = (\mathbf{SK}_u \| \mathbf{SK}_1 \| \mathbf{SK}_2 \| \ldots \| \mathbf{SK}_n)$. "$\|$" is concatenation operation. We specify our decryption procedure as recursive algorithm. Let $i = attr(y)$, which $attr(y)$ represents the value of leaf node y, if the node x is a leaf node and $x \in S$, then computes

$$
\begin{aligned}
Decrypt(CT, SK, x) &= \frac{e\left(V_i, C'_x\right)}{e\left(V'_i, C_x\right)} = \frac{e\left(g^\lambda \cdot H(i)^{r_i}, g^{q_x(0)}\right)}{e\left(g^{r_i}, H(i)^{q_x(0)}\right)} \\
&= \frac{e\left(g^\lambda, g^{q_x(0)}\right) e\left(H(i)^{r_i}, g^{q_x(0)}\right)}{e\left(g^{r_i}, H(i)^{q_x(0)}\right)} \\
&= e(g,g)^{\lambda q_x(0)}
\end{aligned} \tag{9}
$$

If $i \notin S$, then we define $Decrypt(CT, SK, x) = \perp$.

When the node x is not a leaf node, for all the nodes z that are the children of x, the outputs is stored as F_z. Let S_x be an arbitrary k_x-sized set of child nodes. If no such set exists, the function will return $\perp$. The recursive computation is shown as follows:

$$
\begin{aligned}
F_x &= \prod_{z \in S_x} F_z^{\Delta_{i,S'_x}(0)}, \ where \begin{cases} i = index(z) \\ S'_x = (index(z) : z \in S_x) \end{cases} \\
&= \prod_{z \in S_x} \left(e(g,g)^{\lambda q_z(0)}\right)^{\Delta_{i,S'_x}(0)} \\
&= \prod_{z \in S_x} \left(e(g,g)^{\lambda q_{parent(z)}(index(z))}\right)^{\Delta_{i,S'_x}(0)} \\
&= \prod_{z \in S_x} \left(e(g,g)^{\lambda q_x(i)}\right)^{\Delta_{i,S'_x}(0)} = e(g,g)^{\lambda q_x(0)}
\end{aligned} \tag{10}
$$

The algorithm recalls the Lagrange polynomial interpolation to decrypt the ciphertext. If the set of attributes satisfy the access tree, we define $A = e(g,g)^{\lambda q_R(0)} = e(g,g)^{\lambda s}$. Then computes:

$$CT/(e(\mathbf{SK}u, C)/A) = CT/(e(g^{(\alpha+\lambda)/\eta}, g^{\eta s})/e(g,g)^{\lambda s}) = M \tag{11}$$

5 Security and Performance Analysis

5.1 Security Analysis

The Decisional Bilinear Diffie-Hellman (DBDH) problem [23] in group G of prime order p with generator g is defined as follows:

On input $g, g^a, g^b, g^c \in G$ and $e(g, g)^{abc} = e(g, g)^z \in G_T$, where $z = abc$, decide whether $z = abc$ or z is a random element.

Theorem 1: If Decisional Bilinear Diffie-Hellman assumption holds in group (G, G_T), then our scheme is chosen-plaintext secure in standard model.

Proof: Suppose there exists a probabilistic polynomial time adversary Adv can attack our scheme in the security model above with advantage ε. We prove that the following DBDH game can be solved with advantage $\varepsilon/2$. Let $e : G \times G \to G_T$ be a bilinear map, where G is a multiplicative cyclic group of prime order p and generator g. First the DBDH challenger flips a binary coin $\mu = \{0, 1\}$, if $\mu = 1$, he sets $(g, A, B, C, Z) = \left(g, g^a, g^b, g^c, e(g, g)^{abc}\right)$; otherwise he sets $(g, A, B, C, Z) = (g, g^a, g^b, g^c, e(g, g)^z)$, where $a, b, c \in Z_p$ are randomly selected. The challenger then gives the simulator $(g, A, B, C, Z) = \left(g, g^a, g^b, g^c, Z\right)$. The simulator Sim then plays the role of a challenger in the following DBDH game.

Init: The adversary Adv creates an access tree Γ^* which he wants to be challenged (Nodes inside the tree should be defined by Adv).

Setup: Sim sets the parameter $Y := e(A, B) = e(g, g)^{ab}$. For all $i \in S$, it will choose a random $d_i \in \mathbb{Z}_p$ and set $H(attr(i)) = g^{d_i}$. Otherwise it chooses a random number $\beta_i \in \mathbb{Z}_p$ and sets $H(attr(i)) = g^{b\beta_i} = B^{\beta_i}$. Then it will give this public parameters to Adv.

Phase 1: Adv queries for as many private keys, which correspond to attribute sets S_1, S_2, ... S_q, where none of them satisfy the Γ^*. After receiving the key queries, Sim computes the private key components to respond Adv's requests. Sim first defines a polynomial q_x for each node x of Γ^*. For each node x of Γ^*, we know q_x completely if x can be satisfied; if x is not satisfied, then at least $g^{q_x(0)}$ is known. Sim sets $q_R(0) = a$, for each node x of access tree, Sim defines the final polynomial $Q_x(\cdot) = b q_x(\cdot)$ and let $s = Q_R(0) = ab$. For all $i \in S_k$, he randomly picks $i \in S_k$, and compute $D = g^{(c+\lambda)/\eta}$, $V_i = g^{d_i r_i}$, $V_i' = g^{r_i}$, otherwise $V_i = g \cdot g^{b\beta_i r_i} = g \cdot B^{\beta_i r_i}$. Then, sim returns the created private key to Adv.

Challenge: The adversary Adv submits two equal length challenge messages M_0 and M_1 to the challenger. The challenger flips a binary coin γ, and returns the following ciphertext to Adv.

$$CT = \begin{pmatrix} \Gamma^*, \ C' = M_\gamma \cdot Z, \ C = g^{\eta s} \\ \forall y \in Y, \ C_y = B^{d_y q_y(0)}, \ C_y' = B^{q_y(0)} \end{pmatrix} \tag{12}$$

If $\mu = 1$, $Z = e(g,g)^{abc}$. Let $\alpha = ab$, $s = c$, then $Z = e(g,g)^{abc} = e(g,g)^{\alpha s}$. Therefore, CT is a valid ciphertext of the message m_γ. Otherwise, if $\mu = 0$, $Z = e(g,g)^z$, $C' = M_b e(g,g)^z$. Since $z \in Z_p$ is a random element, $C' \in G_T$ is a random element, therefore CT contains no information about m_γ.

Phase 2: Repeat Phase 1 adaptively.

Guess: Adv submits a guess γ' of γ. If $\gamma' = \gamma$, Sim outputs $\mu = 1$, indicating that it was given a valid DBDH-tuple, otherwise it outputs $\mu = 0$, indicating that he was given a random 5-element tuple.

When $\mu = 0$, the adversary Adv learns no information about γ, so we have $\Pr[\gamma \neq \gamma' | \mu = 0] = 1/2$. Since the challenger guesses $\mu' = 0$ when $\gamma' = \gamma$, we have $\Pr[\mu' = \mu | \mu = 0] = 1/2$. If $\mu = 1$, the adversary Adv gets a valid ciphertext of m_γ. $Adv's$ advantage in this situation is ε by definition, so we have $\Pr[\gamma = \gamma' | \mu = 1] = 1/2 + \varepsilon$. Since the challenger guesses $\mu' = 1$ when $\gamma' = \gamma$, we have $\Pr[\mu' = \mu | \mu = 0] = 1/2 + \varepsilon$. So the overall advantage of Sim in this DBDH game is:

$$\frac{1}{2}\Pr[\gamma = \gamma' | \mu = 1] + \frac{1}{2}\Pr[\gamma \neq \gamma' | \mu = 0] - \frac{1}{2}$$
$$= \frac{1}{2}\left(\frac{1}{2} + \varepsilon\right) + \frac{1}{2} \cdot \frac{1}{2} - \frac{1}{2} \tag{13}$$
$$= \frac{\varepsilon}{2}$$

Theorem 2: Our scheme is secure against collision attack between users and authorities.

In our scheme, in order to decrypt the ciphertext, the attacker must obtain bilinear pairing $e(g,g)^{\alpha s}$. In order to perform attack successfully, attacker must collect all valid attribute secret keys, but from the form of attribute secret key $\mathbf{SK}_i = \left(\forall attr(i) \in S_{AAj}, V_i = g^r * H(attr(i))^{r_i}, V_i' = g^{r_i}\right)$ we can see that $V_i = g^r * H(attr(i))^{r_i}$, where r is a random value chosen uniquely for each legitimate user. Based on Eqs. (7) to (10), decryption process can be implemented successfully iff $(e(\mathbf{SK}u, C) \cdot A) = e(g,g)^{\alpha s}$, which requires user specific secret key of the authorized users. Based on the security assumption in Sect. 3.2 authorized user will not participate in collusion attack.

In revocation, once the user is revoked, DO will re-encrypt the plaintext, generate new ciphertext $Me(g,g)^{\alpha' s}$ or $Me(g,g)^{\alpha s'}$ and new private key components $\mathbf{SK}'_u = g^{(\alpha_1 + r)/\eta}$ or $\mathbf{SK}'_{i'} = \left(V_{i'} = g^r * H(attr(i'))^{r_{i'}}, V_i' = g^{r_{i'}}\right)$, But the revoked users only has previous secret keys, so the revoked users can not decrypt. Our scheme can also resist collision attacks between attribute authorities. Attribute authority is only responsible for generating the attribute keys, even if multiple authorities collude, they will not obtain calculating factor g^r. Therefore, they can not get whole secret keys and decrypt the ciphertext.

5.2   Performance Evaluation

We present the performance evaluation based on our DMA implementation prototype. Our experiment is implemented on a Linux Ubuntu with Inter(R) Core(TM) i5-6500 @ 3.2 GHz and 2 GB RAM. The code is modified on original CP-ABE library [21]. The code uses the Pairing-Based Cryptography (PBC) library version 0.5.12 to implement the access control scheme. We will compare the computation efficiency of both encryption and decryption in two criteria: the number of authorities and the number of attributes per authority. In order to show the efficiency of our scheme, we implement other similar schemes that are propose in [8, 24–26] for comparison purpose.

Figure 3 shows the comparison of encryption and decryption time with different number of attributes. The encryption and decryption time are measured under file size 100 KB, attributes number varies from 2 to 20.

Figure 4 shows the comparison of encryption and decryption time with different file size. The number of attributes is set to be 20, the file size varies from 2 MB to 256 MB.

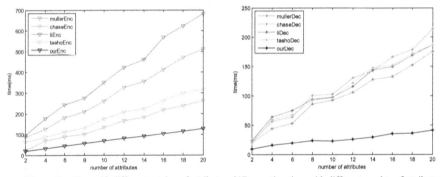

a)Encryption time with different number of attributes   b)Decryption time with different number of attributes

Fig. 3. Encryption and decryption time with different number of attributes

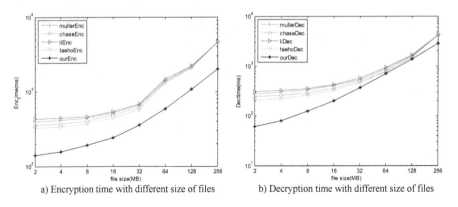

a) Encryption time with different size of files   b) Decryption time with different size of files

Fig. 4. Encryption and decryption time with different size of files

From the experiment results we find out that our scheme makes much improvement in key generation, encryption and decryption under different system set. The reason why our scheme is very efficient is that we refactor the original CP-ABE and extend it into multi-authority scenario.

6   Conclusion

Our scheme presents a fully decentralized Multi-authority ABE that allows multiple distrusting authorities achieve secure data sharing. We introduce a novel key generation and distribution protocol to prevent key forging and authority collusion attack. Theoretical analysis and experiment demonstrate that our scheme can not only achieve ciphertext access control, preventing collision attacks between users, DOs and authorities; but also improve the efficiency of ciphertext encryption and decryption. Therefore, the proposed method can be applied to multi-authority scenario in data sharing systems for efficient data encryption and decryption.

Acknowledgements. This work is supported by the National Natural Science Foundation of China under grant 61402160. Hunan Provincial Natural Science Foundation under grant 2016JJ3043. Open Funding for Universities in Hunan Province under grant 14K023.

References

1. Chow, R., Golle, P., Jakobsson, M., et al.: Controlling data in the cloud: outsourcing computation without outsourcing control. In: Proceedings of IEEE 3rd International Conference on Cloud Computing, pp. 85–90, July 2010
2. Shamir, A.: Identity-based cryptosystems and signature schemes. In: Blakley, G.R., Chaum, D. (eds.) CRYPTO 1984. LNCS, vol. 196, pp. 47–53. Springer, Heidelberg (1985). https://doi.org/10.1007/3-540-39568-7_5
3. Bethencourt, J., Sahai, A., Waters, B.: Ciphertext-policy attribute-based encryption. In: Proceedings of IEEE Symposium Security and Privacy, Berkeley, CA, pp. 321–334 (2007)
4. Waters, B.: Ciphertext-policy attribute-based encryption: an expressive, efficient, and provably secure realization. In: Proceedings of Public Key Cryptography (PKC 2011), pp. 53–70 (2011)
5. Wang, S., Zhou, J., Liu, J.K., et al.: An efficient file hierarchy attribute-based encryption scheme in cloud computing. IEEE Trans. Inf. Forensics Secur. **11**(6), 1265–1277 (2016)
6. Balu, A., Kuppusamy, K.: An expressive and provably secure ciphertext-policy attribute-based encryption. Inf. Sci. **276**, 354–362 (2014)
7. Kwon, H., Kim, D., Hahn, C., et al.: Security authentication using ciphertext policy attribute-based encryption in mobile multi-hop networks. Multimedia Tools Appl. **75**, 1–15 (2016)
8. Chase, M.: Multi-authority attribute based encryption. In: Vadhan, Salil P. (ed.) TCC 2007. LNCS, vol. 4392, pp. 515–534. Springer, Heidelberg (2007). https://doi.org/10.1007/978-3-540-70936-7_28
9. Liu, J., Huang, X., Liu, J.K.: Secure sharing of personal health records in cloud computing: ciphertext-policy attribute-based signcryption. Future Gener. Comput. Syst. **52**, 67–76 (2015)

10. Chase, M., Chow, S.S.M.: Improving privacy and security in multi-authority attribute-based encryption. In: Proceedings of 16th ACM Conference on Computer and Communications Security (CCS 2009), pp. 121–130 (2009)
11. Ahire, A., Jawalkar, P.: Secure system for data sharing using cipher-text policy attribute encryption with message authentication codes for data integrity. Int. Res. J. Eng. Technol. **22** (5), 1021–1027 (2015)
12. Lewko, A., Okamoto, T., Sahai, A., Takashima, K., Waters, B.: Fully secure functional encryption: attribute-based encryption and (hierarchical) inner product encryption. In: Gilbert, H. (ed.) EUROCRYPT 2010. LNCS, vol. 6110, pp. 62–91. Springer, Heidelberg (2010). https://doi.org/10.1007/978-3-642-13190-5_4
13. Lewko, A., Waters, B.: Decentralizing attribute-based encryption. In: Proceedings of International Conference on the Theory and Applications of Cryptographic Techniques, pp. 568–588 (2011)
14. Yang, K., Jia, X., Ren, K.: DAC-MACS: effective date access control for multi-authority cloud storage systems. IEEE Trans. Inf. Forensics Secur. **8**(11), 1790–1801 (2013)
15. Yang, K., Jia, X.: Attribute-based access control for multi-authority system in cloud storage. In: Proceedings of International Conference on Distributed Computing Systems (ICDCS), pp. 536–545 (2012)
16. Yang, K., Jia, X.: Expressive, efficient and revocable data access control for multi-authority cloud storage. IEEE Trans. Parallel Distrib. Syst. **25**(7), 1735–1744 (2013)
17. Taeho, J., Li, X., Wan, Z., et al.: Privacy preserving cloud data access with multi-authorities. In: Proceedings of IEEE INFOCOM, pp. 2625–2633 (2013)
18. Jahid, S., Mittal, P., Borisov, N.: Easier: encryption-based access control in social networks with efficient revocation. In: Proceedings of 6th ACM Symposium on Information, Computer and Communications Security, pp. 411–415 (2011)
19. Li, M., Yu, S., Zheng, Y., et al.: Scalable and secure sharing of personal health records in cloud computing using attribute-based encryption. IEEE Trans. Parallel Distrib. Syst. **24**(1), 131–143 (2012)
20. Hur, J., Kang, K.: Secure data retrieval for decentralized disruption-tolerant military networks. IEEE/ACM Trans. Netw. **22**(1), 16–26 (2014)
21. Bethencourt, J., Sahai, A., Waters, B.: The cpabe toolkit [OL]. http://acsc.csl.sri.com/cpabe/. 2007.3
22. Jung, T., Li, X., Wan, Z., et al.: Control cloud data access privilege and anonymity with fully anonymous attribute-based encryption. IEEE Trans. Inf. Forensics Secur. **10**(1), 190–199 (2015)
23. Canetti, R.: Decisional Diffie-Hellman assumption. In: van Tilborg, H.C.A. (ed.) Encyclopedia of Cryptography and Security, pp. 140–142. Springer, Heidelberg (2005). https://doi.org/10.1007/0-387-23483-7_99
24. Gentry, C., Silverberg, A.: Hierarchical ID-based cryptography. In: Zheng, Y. (ed.) ASIACRYPT 2002. LNCS, vol. 2501, pp. 548–566. Springer, Heidelberg (2002). https://doi.org/10.1007/3-540-36178-2_34
25. Muller, S., Katzenbeisser, S., Eckert, C.: On multi-authority ciphertext-policy attribute-based encryption. Bull. Korean Math. Soc. **46**(4), 803–819 (2009)
26. Li, J., Huang, Q., Chen, X., Chow, S.S., Wong, D.S., Xie, D.: Multiauthority ciphertext-policy attribute-based encryption with accountability. In: Proceedings of ACM Symposium on Information (ASIACCS), pp. 386–390 (2011)

Malware Variants Detection Using Density Based Spatial Clustering with Global Opcode Matrix

Zejun Niu, Zheng Qin, Jixin Zhang$^{(\boxtimes)}$, and Hui Yin

College of Computer Science and Electronic Engineering, Hunan University,
Changsha 410082, China
{zqin,zhangjixin}@hnu.edu.cn

Abstract. Over the past decades, the amount of malware has rapidly increased. Malware detection becomes one of most mission critical security problems as its threats spread from personal computers to cloud server. Some researchers have proposed machine learning methods which can detect malware variants by searching the similarities between malware and its variants. However, the large search space causes large time cost and memory space occupation. To reduce the search space while retaining the accuracy, we firstly propose to convert malware into global opcode matrix which is based on 2-tuple opcodes, and then cluster the opcode matrixes to patterns. We can easily recognize the malware variants by searching the similarities with the patterns. The experiments demonstrate that our approach is more efficient than the state-of-art approaches in time cost, memory space occupation and accuracy.

Keywords: Malware · Malware detection · Opcode matrix
Density based spatial clustering

1 Introduction

Malware (malicious software) is one of the major Internet security threat which damages cloud systems. Over the past decades, the amount of malware has rapidly increased. According to the survey [1], conducted by FireEye in June 2013, 47% of the organizations experienced malware security incidents/network breaches in 2013. In 2014, Symantec stated in its reports [2], the number of new malware variants grew by 317, 256, 956 in 2014 which represents a 26% increase compared with 2013. The main reason for this rapidly increase is that the malware variants can be produced easily using code obfuscation techniques. It is pertinent to note that 50% of new malware are obfuscated versions of existing known malware (malware variants).

With the increasement in readily available and sophisticated tools, the new generation cyber threats/attacks are becoming more targeted, persistent and unknown. Malware detection which is mostly based on traditional signature can hardly determine if the sample is indeed malicious. Traditional string signatures perform poorly when facing polymorphic malware variants. Because most of the new malware samples are variants of previously known samples, one way to ascertain the malware samples is to

© Springer International Publishing AG 2017
G. Wang et al. (Eds.): SpaCCS 2017 Workshops, LNCS 10658, pp. 757–766, 2017.
https://doi.org/10.1007/978-3-319-72395-2_67

inspect if the sample is sufficiently similar to any previously known malware programs. Some researchers have proposed machine learning methods which can detect malware variants by searching the similarities between malware and its variants. However, their computational complexity prevent them from being deployed in large scale or real-time detection required scenarios.

To reduce the search space dimension, some methods proposed to extract only a few local features for search space dimension reduction, but lose some useful information, the detection accuracy might be severely limited with the large detection data set [5]. So these approaches, such as Santos et al. cannot perform well when malwares are rapidly growing in volume facing the Internet today. To solve this problem, Zhang et al. [5, 6] proposed a method which converts the global opcode features into image to improve accuracy, but the feature dimension of the image is too large and the training time cost of their methods is too high for large scale data set.

In order to reduce the search space to improve the speed while retaining the accuracy, we propose a malware variant detection scheme which is based on global opcode matrix and density-based spatial clustering. Our approach is quite different from the above mentioned approaches. Unlike these approaches which need to compare the similarity with every training samples and extract only a few local opcode features. Our approach extracts global opcode features to retain the accuracy due to it do not lose any information, and clusters a few malware patterns which can represent a set of variants. We detect malware variants by searching the similarities with the malware patterns. We only check whether a malware sample is sufficiently similar to any patterns. Compared with the state-of-art approaches, the experiments demonstrate that our method can reduces the training/detection time cost on the basis of ensuring the accuracy rate.

The main contributions of our paper are summarized as follows. (1) We present a new malware variants detection approach, which is based on global opcode matrix and density based spatial clustering. (2) Our approach can reduce training/detection time cost and memory space occupation while retaining accuracy. (3) Compared with the state-of-art approaches, the experiments demonstrate that our approach could detect malware variants with higher accuracy rate, lower time cost overhead and lower memory space occupation.

The remainder of paper is organized as follows. In Sect. 2, we review related work; while in Sect. 3 we introduce the overview of our approach. In Sects. 4 and 5, we describe the details of our methodology. In Sect. 6, we represent experimental results and Sect. 7 shows the conclusion.

2   Related Works

In recent years, most of researchers have focused on detecting binary malware variants by using machine learning techniques to cover up the malware variants. Machine-learning-based approaches train classification algorithms that detect new malware, by means of datasets composed of several characteristic features of both malicious and benign software.

Santos et al. [3, 4] proposed a method based on the frequency of appearance of opcode-sequences and train several data-mining algorithms (Decision Trees, K-Nearest Neighbors, etc.) in order to detect unknown malware. Shang et al. [7] proposed a method that relies on static analysis of a program. Lee et al. [8] converted the API call sequence of the malware into a call graph. Then the call graph is reduced to a code graph used for semantic signatures of the proposed mechanism. Shabtai et al. [9] and Moskovitch et al. [10] used opcodes to examine the effectiveness of malware detection by using different N-gram size (N = 1–6) with various classifiers. Shabtai's findings showed that N = 2 performed best. However, the large detection delay is one of serious bottlenecks of these mentioned approaches when facing large scale or real-time detection required scenarios.

3 Overview of Approach

In order to reduce the malware detection time cost, memory space occupation on the basis of ensuring the accuracy rate, we propose a method which based on Density Based Spatial Clustering with Global Opcode Matrix. Our approach includes the following steps: (1) Global Opcodes matrix construction, (2) Malware opcode matrix patterns clustering, (3) Similarity searching with malware opcode matrix patterns.

Firstly, we decompile malware binaries and extract opcode sequences to construct opcode matrix which do not lose any information to ensure the detection accuracy rate. Then we cluster the malware opcode matrixes to malware patterns by using Density Based Spatial Clustering. Finally, when we detect a new instance, we search the similarities between the opcode matrix of the instance and the patterns. The new instance is malicious if it is sufficiently similar to one of the malware opcode matrix patterns. Our approach detects instances through comparing with only a few malware patterns, so it can reduce time cost and memory space occupation while retaining the detection accuracy rate.

4 Global Opcode Matrix of Construction

Our malware variant detection method extract global opcode features to construct opcode matrix which can ensure the detection accuracy rate. We decompile the malware instances to extract their opcode sequences, then we built 2-tuple opcodes according to these opcode sequences. The opcode matrixes are constructed by these 2-tuple opcodes and the element value of the opcode matrix is calculated by probabilities and information gains of the 2-tuple opcodes.

To represent malware instances by using opcode sequences, we have unpacked and decompiled a set of 2-tuple opcodes, and then built opcode profiles for each malware instance. Each profile contains a list of the 2-tuple opcodes and a frequency value that each 2-tuple opcodes appears. Since most of the operations which can represent malicious purposes require more than one opcode, long opcode sequences will introduce a high performance overhead, we select 2-tuple opcode for archiving both fast training/detection speed and high accuracy. Let opk be the operation codes (opcodes) which are decompiled from malware opcodes. Let osi be the operation code (opcode) sequences of length 2, osi = <opj, opk>. Assembly code snippet shown in Fig. 1, the following opcode sequences of length 2 can be generated as: os1 = < mov, call>, os2 = < call, push>, os3 = < push, jmp>, os4 = < jmp, move>, os5 = < move, call>.

move	ecx, 00449318
call	00426D1D
push	00401280
jmp	0040E520
move	ecx, 0044A8B0
call	0042B8C2

Fig. 1. Assembly code example.

The opcode matrixes are constructed by these 2-tuple opcodes with their probabilities and information gains. The opcode matrix is shown in Fig. 2, each 2-tuple opcode can be matched to one of the elements in the matrix according to $os_i = <op_j, op_k>$. Let $freq(os_i \mid x_j)$ be the frequency of os_i in x_j. Let $p(os_i \mid x_j)$ be the probability function of os_i in x_j, according to $freq(os_i \mid x_j)$. Let $w(os_i)$ be a the information gain function of os_i. Let $om(x_j)$ be an opcode matrix generated from x_j, according to $p(os_i \mid x_j)$ and $w(os_i)$. The element value $val(os_i \mid x_j)$ of the opcode matrix $om(x_j)$ is calculated by the probabilities $p(os_i \mid x_j)$ and the information gains $w(os_i)$ of os_i in the opcode x_j, as shown in Eq. (1).

$$val(os_i \mid x_j) = p(os_i \mid x_j) \, w(os_i) \qquad (1)$$

	op_1	op_2	...	op_k
op_1	$<op_1, op_1>$	$<op_1, op_2>$	...	$<op_1, op_k>$
op_2	$<op2, op_1>$	$<op2, op_2>$	...	$<op_2, op_k>$
...		... Matrix		
op_j	$<op_j, op_1>$	$<op_j, op_2>$	....	$<op_j, op_k>$
...		...		

Fig. 2. Opcode matrix.

The probabilities p(osi | xj) and information gains w(osi) are calculated by the frequencies freq(osi | xj) of the 2-tuple opcode, as shown in Eqs. (2) and (3), where p (osi | y1) be the probability of osi in the training malware opcode, p(osi) be the probability of osi in the whole training opcodes, and p(y1) be the probability of training malware opcodes.

$$p(os_i \mid x_j) = \frac{freq(os_i, x_j)}{\sum\limits_{os_i \in x_j} freq(os_i, x_j)} \qquad (2)$$

$$w(os_i) = p(os_i \mid y_1) \log\left(\frac{p(os_i \mid y_1)}{p(os_i)p(y_1)}\right) \qquad (3)$$

5 Global Opcode Matrix of Construction

Once we have generated the mentioned opcode matrix, we now discuss how to cluster malware instances by using these opcode matrixes and abstract several malware patterns from the clustered malware opcode matrixes for variant detection. A new instance is malicious instance if its opcode matrix is sufficiently similar to the existing malware patterns. Because we abstract only one pattern for representing each cluster of similar malware instances, we search the similarities between the opcode matrix of the new instance and the patterns, the search space can be reduced.

5.1 Malware Opcode Matrix Patterns Clustering

Clustering malware based on the 2-tuple opcodes which are mentioned in above section can be useful for automatically analyzing and detecting malware variant. New malware instances would be assigned to existing malware clusters, so we can recognize variations of known malware instances and merge them into one pattern for each cluster.

Before we cluster the similar malware instances, we need to represent the similarity between two malware instances. Let d(xi, xj) be the distance between the instance xi and the instance xj, according to the 2-tuple opcode, shown in Eq. (4). Let s(xi, xj) be the similarity between the instance xi and the instance xj, according to the distance, shown in Eq. (5). If s(xi, xj) is less than a value r, then the instance xi is similar to the instance xj, so we could cluster them into the same cluster.

$$d(x_i, x_j) = \sum_{m=1}^{row} \sum_{n=1}^{col} |val_{m,n}(x_i) - val_{m,n}(x_j)| \qquad (4)$$

$$s(x_i, x_j) = \frac{d(x_i, x_j)}{\sum\limits_{m=1}^{row} \sum\limits_{n=1}^{col} val_{m,n}(x_i)} \qquad (5)$$

We choose Density Based Spatial Clustering Algorithm, as shown in Fig. 3. Because it could cluster similar malware variants with less noise while comparing with Hirachical Clustering, K-Means, etc.

When we assign all of the malware instances into their clusters, the next we would merge the malware instances into one malware pattern for each cluster. We represent the malware pattern mpk by Eqs. (6) and (7), $N_{clusteri}$ represents the number of the cluster clusteri, xj is the malware instances clustered by clusteri. These patterns can be used for malware detection.

$$mp_{k<m,n>} = \frac{\sum\limits_{x_j \in cluster_i} val_{m,n}(x_j)}{N_{cluster_i}} \tag{6}$$

$$mp_k = \begin{bmatrix} mp_{k<0,0>} & mp_{k<0,1>} & \cdots & mp_{k<0,col>} \\ mp_{k<1,0>} & mp_{k<1,1>} & \cdots & mp_{k<1,col>} \\ \cdots & \cdots & \cdots & \cdots \\ mp_{k<row,0>} & mp_{k<row,1>} & \cdots & mp_{k<row,col>} \end{bmatrix} \tag{7}$$

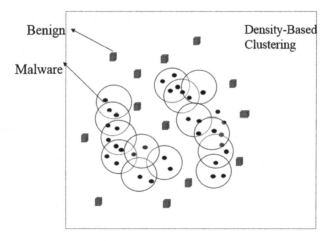

Fig. 3. Density-based spatial clustering.

5.2 Similarity Searching with Malware Opcode Matrix Patterns

When we need to detect a new instance x_i, we search the similarities between the opcode matrix of the new instance and the patterns. The new instance is malicious if it is sufficiently similar to one of the malware patterns. Let t be a threshold, if $s(x_i, mp_k) > t$, the instance x_i is sufficiently similar to the malware pattern mp_k.

6 Experiments

In this section, we present experiments to demonstrate the efficiency and the accuracy of our approach. Firstly, we introduce the experiment setup and the malware data set used in our experiments, then present several approaches for comparison. Finally, we present the time cost, memory space occupation and accuracy of our method comparing with several other approaches.

Experiment Setup. We implement our methodology on one PC. The version of its CPU is Intel(R) Xeon(R) E3-1226v3 @ 3.30 GHz, the RAM is 32.0 GB, the operation system is Windows 7. Our approach is developed on Visual Studio 2012 platform with C++ programming language.

Malware Data Set. In order to validate our approach, we used two different datasets to test our malware variant detection methodology: a malware dataset and a benign data set. We downloaded several malware samples from the VxHeavens [11] website to assemble a malware data set of *9168* about 7 GB malicious programs, including *10* large malware families which represent different types of malware such as Backdoor, Net-Worm, P2P-Worm, IRC-Worm, IM-Worm, Email-Worm, Worm Trojan Dropper, Trojan-GameThief, and Trojan Banker as shown in Table 1. These malwares had already been labelled with their family and variant names by the website. For the benign instances data set, we gathered *8654* legitimate executables (benign software) from our computers.

Table 1. The malware data set.

Malware family	number
Backdoor	3391
Net-Worm	904
P2P-Worm	360
IRC-Worm	159
IM-Worm	274
Email-Worm	113
Worm	795
Trojan-GameThief	742
Trojan Banker	1522
Total	9168

Cross Validation. In order to evaluate the time cost, memory space occupation and accuracy of the following algorithms, we use k-fold cross validation in the experiments. In this way, we select *9168* malware instances from the malware data set and select *8654* benign instances from our computers for machine learning and detecting. For each group of experiments, the malware data set was split for 10 times, and for each time it was split into two different sets, one for training, the other for detecting.

We implement our approach Malware variants Detection based Density Based Spatial Clustering (DBSCMD) and the opcode sequences for Data Mining based Malware variants Detection algorithm (DMMD) [3] and Malware variants Detection using Opcode Image Recognition(IRMD) [5] with real-life malware data sets.

Time Cost and Memory Space Occupation. To demonstrate that our approach could perform faster than the state-of-art methods with less memory space occupation, we present the training time cost the detecting time cost of our approach comparing with the DMMD approach and the IRMD approach. The training time cost and detecting time cost comparison results are shown in Fig. 4. The memory space over-head comparison results are shown in Table 2. Compared with DMMD algorithm, our approach (DBSCMD) achieves almost *131* speedup for detection and less than almost *2.9%* memory space. Compared with IRMD algorithm, our approach achieves almost *144* speedup for training and *5* speedup for detection. Because our approach detect malware instances through comparing with only a few patterns (listed in Table 3) while DMMD needs to detect all of the malware opcode matrixes in the training data which cost a large delay and occupy a large memory space.

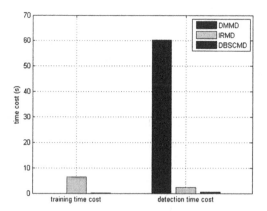

Fig. 4. The training and detection time comparison.

Table 2. The memory space overhead comparing DBSCMD with DMMD.

Data	DBSCMD	DMMD	IRMD
23/24 for detecting	1.12 MB	59.60 MB	0.014 MB
11/12 for detecting	2.08 MB	72.38 MB	0.014 MB
5/6 for detecting	3.04 MB	79.25 MB	0.014 MB
2/3 for detecting	5.08 MB	126.58 MB	0.014 MB

Table 3. The memory space overhead comparing DBSCMD with DMMD.

Data	Numbers of patterns
23/24 for detecting	78
11/12 for detecting	151
5/6 for detecting	233
2/3 for detecting	356

Accuracy Comparison. We implement our approach DBSCMD, IRMD and DMMD with same data sets. The accuracy comparison results are shown in Fig. 5. From the results, we could easily find that our approach can significantly improve the accuracy comparing with DMMD. Our approach achieves *91.4%* accuracy while the DMMD achieves *88.4%* accuracy. Compared with IRMD, the accuracy of our approach is not competitive, but our approach can significantly reduce the training and detection time cost. The true positive rate (TPR) and the true negative rate (TNR) comparison results are also shown in Fig. 5. We can find that our approach can also improve the TPR and TNR comparing with DMMD.

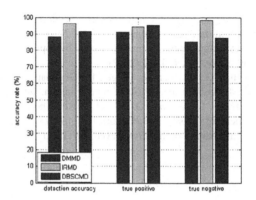

Fig. 5. The accuracy, true positive and true negative comparison

7   Conclusion

In this paper, we propose to convert malware into opcodes matrix which is based on 2-tuple opcodes, and then cluster the opcode matrixes to patterns. We can easily recognize the malware variants by comparing with the patterns. The experiments demonstrate that our approach is more efficient than the state-of-art approaches in time cost, memory space occupation and accuracy.

Acknowledgement. This work is partially supported by the National Science Foundation of China under Grant Nos. 61472131, 61272546, 61300218.

References

1. FireEye (2013). Information on http://www.inforisktoday.in/surveys/2013-incident-response-survey-s18
2. Symantec: internet security threat report, vol. 20 (2015)
3. Santos, I., et al.: Opcode sequences as representation of executables for data mining based malware variant detection. Inf. Sci. **231**(9), 64–82 (2011)
4. Santos, I., Devesa, J., Brezo, F., Nieves, J., Bringas, P.G.: OPEM: a static-dynamic approach for machine learning based malware detection. In: Herrero, Á., et al. (eds.) International Joint Conference CISIS 2012. Advances in Intelligent Systems and Computing, vol. 189, pp. 271–280. Springer, Heidelberg (2013). https://doi.org/10.1007/978-3-642-33018-6_28

5. Zhang, J., et al.: Malware variant detection using opcode image recognition with small training sets. In: 2016 25th International Conference on Computer Communication and Networks (ICCCN), pp. 1–9 (2016)

6. Zhang, J., Qin, Z., Yin, H., et al.: IRMD: malware variant detection using opcode image recognition. In: International Conference on Parallel and Distributed Systems, pp. 1175–1180. IEEE (2016)

7. Shang, S., et al.: Detecting malware variants via function-call graph similarity. In: 5th International Conference on Malicious and Unwanted Software, MALWARE, pp. 113–120 (2010)

8. Lee, J., et al.: Detecting metamorphic malwares using code graphs. In: Proceedings of the 2010 ACM Symposium on Applied Computing, SAC 2010, pp. 1970–1977 (2010)

9. Shabtai, A., et al.: Detecting unknown malicious code by applying classification techniques on opcode patterns. Secur. Inf. **1**, 1–22 (2012)

10. Moskovitch, R., Feher, C., Tzachar, N., Berger, E., Gitelman, M., Dolev, S., Elovici, Y.: Unknown malcode detection using OPCODE representation. In: Ortiz-Arroyo, D., Larsen, H.L., Zeng, D.D., Hicks, D., Wagner, G. (eds.) EuroIsI 2008. LNCS, vol. 5376, pp. 204–215. Springer, Heidelberg (2008). https://doi.org/10.1007/978-3-540-89900-6_21

11. Vxheaven (2017). Information on http://vxheaven.org/vl.php

Research on Graph Processing Systems on a Single Machine

Yuxuan Xing[(⊠)], Siqi Gao, Nong Xiao, Fang Liu, and Wei Chen

State Key Laboratory of High Performance Computing,
National University of Defense Technology, Changsha, China
xingyuxuan_2012@nudt.edu.cn

Abstract. With the rapid development of technologies such as cloud computing, the increasingly popularity of social network and other Internet applications, the data scale that human can access is growing at an unprecedented rate. Recently, technological changes associated with big data are hot in academy and industrial, and it's meaningful to dig out the potential information in massive data. Many real-world problems can be represented as graphs, such as supply chain analysis, genealogy, web graphs, etc. Large graphs demand efficiently processing technologies to derive valuable knowledge and many graph processing engines have been developed. This paper first introduces concepts of graphs and categories of graph processing engine on a single machine. Thereafter, it focuses on analyzing and summarizing current researches about key techniques on graph processing, including data structure, parallel programing, and partitioning strategies. Finally, current research work about graph processing engine on a single machine is summarized and further research directions are pointed out.

Keywords: Big data · Graph processing system · Single machine

1 Introduction

The increasing scale of real-world inter-connected data requires an efficient analysis engine for potential valuable information, and graph is the usual data structure to represent many problems, such as online social network, web link analysis, thesis references, etc. It's significant to obtain insights from the raw data. Therefore, developing an effective graph processing engine to analyze large graphs is beneficial for various areas to gain actionable knowledge.

Large-scale graph frameworks can be classified into two categories in total, distributed systems and systems on a single machine. Distributed systems make use of clusters to process large graphs. Pregel [1] is a distributed graph engine based on BSP model proposed by Google. One graph processing job is divided into multiple tasks to be executed parallel and iteratively, and communication is implemented by message passing. Another distributed graph processing system—PowerGraph [2] allows multiple machines to run a single vertex-program, and adopted a vertex-cut scheme to reduce communication overhead. GraphLab [3] is a notable framework developed by Carnegie Mellon University. It used global mapping table to record iterative

© Springer International Publishing AG 2017
G. Wang et al. (Eds.): SpaCCS 2017 Workshops, LNCS 10658, pp. 767–775, 2017.
https://doi.org/10.1007/978-3-319-72395-2_68

information. Many other distributed frameworks such as Giraph [4], Pegasus [5] can also process graph-parallel algorithms efficiently.

Current distributed graph processing engines deal with billions of edges by handing out tasks to different nodes. Meanwhile, they have many problems. First, many natural graphs have skewed power-law degree distribution, which easily result in work imbalance among cluster nodes. Second, it's difficult to partition natural graphs to minimize communication cost and keep data locality. Moreover, communication asymmetry, fault tolerance are all critical elements that influence distributed frameworks' performance. Besides, it's difficult for programmers to debug and optimize distributed algorithms.

For many large graph, single machine architecture is not only doable but strongly preferable [21–23]. Also in the context of reality product, aspects such as real-time recommendation and evaluation are as important as algorithms. Consequently, large-scale graph processing frameworks on a single machine have been developed. Some large-scale graphs own billions of edges, however, single-node platforms can be affordable because hundreds of GB to TBs RAM can be aggregated for providing sufficient memory [26, 27], and there's no need to divide graphs and communicate between multiple nodes. This paper researches on graph processing systems on a single node, analyzes key technologies applied in frameworks and provides guidance for future research directions.

The rest of the paper is organized as follows: Sect. 2 presents graph processing systems using CPU as computing resources on a single machine. Next, GPU-based frameworks are elaborated. Section 4 researches on hybrid systems using CPU and GPU as computing resources. Finally, difficulties about designing graph processing system on a single machine are discussed and further research directions are pointed out.

2   CPU-Based Graph Processing Systems on a Single Machine

GraphChi [6] is the first framework processing graphs with billions of edges on a single machine. It "thinks like a vertex" and adopts vertex-centric programming. As a disk-based system, and the main challenge is random data access. To address this problem, it proposed Parallel Sliding Windows (PSW). PSW processes the graph one sub-graph at a time and the whole graph is processed in one iteration. For processing large graph with limited resources, vertices are divided into several intervals and edges are divided into multiple shards. GraphChi first loads small shards into memory. Next, update-function is executed on interval's vertices. Finally, the data blocks are written back to disk. The processing procedure is descripted as Fig. 1. Parallel sliding writing algorithms makes processing large graphs on a single machine possible.

X-Stream [7] is the first edge-centric graph processing system using streaming partitions. Instead of standard vertex-centric scatter gather operations, X-Stream adopts edge-centric scatter gather scheme, such that system can sequential access to edge data and reduce data transfer time relatively. To eliminate random access to vertex set, X-Stream partitions graph into streaming partitions. Streaming partitions make a subset of vertices all in RAM and includes edges whose source vertex is in the vertex subset.

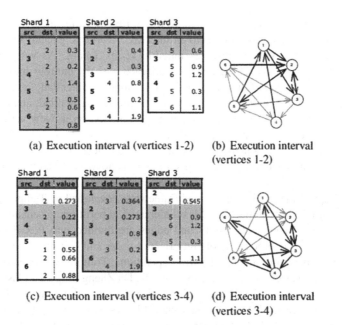

(a) Execution interval (vertices 1-2)   (b) Execution interval (vertices 1-2)

(c) Execution interval (vertices 3-4)   (d) Execution interval (vertices 3-4)

Fig. 1. Illustration of the operation of the PSW method on a Toy Graph [6]

However, as scatter and gather is based on edges, it is inevitable to generate commutative overhead during update phase. Besides, some important algorithms such as community detection are difficult to implement on X-Stream. To efficiently support various large-scale graph data mining applications, Huawei Noah's Ark Lab proposed VENUS [24]: a vertex-centric streamlined graph computation framework on a single PC, to analysis billions of magnitude log data and service for advertising and recommendation, etc. VENUS uses vertex-centric streamlined computing model, which efficiently reduces the disk I/O accesses and weakens the system bottleneck. The architecture is divided into two stages: offline preprocessing and online computation, depicted as Fig. 2.

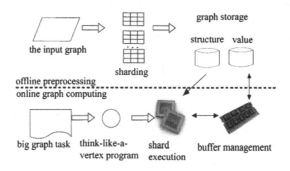

Fig. 2. The VENUS architecture [24]

Considering graph may not fit in RAM, VENUS splits the graph into several shards, and each shard corresponds to an interval of vertices. g-shard saves immutable graph structure and v-shard reserves mutable vertex values. As v-shards are much smaller than g-shards, VENUS always load each v-shard entirely into memory. To exploit large bandwidth of disk, each g-shard is scanned sequentially, and executing the update function in parallel is possible. Multiple threads are applied, and each thread is responsible for one sub-graph and executes computation on it. New vertex values are updated on vertices. When all g-shards and v-shards are processed, the iteration is completed. The storage scheme adopted in VENUS efficiently reduces the cost of I/O. Experiments conducted in [24] show that VENUS is up to $3\times$ faster than GraphChi and X-Stream.

GridGraph [8] is another disk-based framework developed by Tsinghua University. It employs grid representation and 2-level hierarchical partitioning scheme. Vertices are partitioned into P equalized chunks and edges are divided into P × P blocks. Grid-Graph accesses edge blocks in column-oriented order and just pass one time over the destination vertices for reducing the write operations. To improve system performance, GridGraph only selects active edges to schedule. Da Zheng proposed FlashGraph [9], a graph engine combining SSDs and RAM. The system is built up on top of a user-space SSD file system called SAFS (set-associated file system), which has high parallelism and high IOPS. And FlashGraph stores the vertices' state in memory and edge lists in SSD.

Ligra [10] is a lightweight graph processing system for shared memory on a single node. It programs parallel on a multicore machine using cilk plus grammar and only selects active vertices to execute. Also, the engine adopts CAS (Compare and Swap) scheme to avoid race conditions. Cassovary [11] and Galois [12] are also shared memory based single-node frameworks. Principally, communication overhead is much cheaper for shared memory system compared to distributed systems [13, 14]. However, the limited memory capacity of shared-memory systems restrict the capability to process big graphs. Main large scale graph processing systems merely take CPU as computing resource.

3   GPU-Based Graph Processing Frameworks

With the development of GPU, it is popular to handle computation on graphics processing units. The micro-architecture of GPU is different from CPU. GPU contains multiple streaming multiprocessors and each streaming multiprocessor consists of hundreds of cores. Thus, massive parallelism is available. Medusa [15] is the first GPU-based graph processing framework. Considering that graph processing algorithms can be executed parallel and thousands of GPUs cores run in parallel, Medusa provides a framework for graph processing on GPUs. And Edge-Message-Vertex (EMV) programming model is adopted in Medusa. The model interfaces hide the GPU programming details and makes developing graph processing algorithms much easier. The framework is presented in Fig. 3.

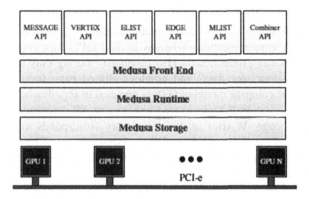

Fig. 3. Overview of Medusa [15]

To avoid grouping message, Medusa employs graph-aware buffer scheme to ensure messages sent to the same vertex consecutive. The sequential writing is achieved by reversing graph and insures each edge's reverse ID values with the common destination vertex are continuous.

To obtain high performance compared to low-level approaches, MapGraph [16] was proposed by Fu. It is a vertex-centric GAS abstraction. For a better system performance improvement, hybrid scheduling is applied according to the frontier size. When vertex degree is large, a vertex's computation tasks in the frontier are all assigned to cooperative thread array (CTA) and each thread of CTA handles one vertex neighbor. If vertex degree is greater than warp size but smaller than CTA size then scan based scattering is executed. Otherwise, warp-based scattering is performed to process the remaining vertices. Moreover, SOA (structure of array) is adopted to guarantee coalesced memory access. Besides, two-phase decomposition is explored by Map-Graph. To obtain better load balancing among threads, the scheme decomposes the scattering into schedule stage and computation stage. The schedule stage forms sets which have equal size adjacent edges. And in computation stage, each thread deals with equal size vertices and executes the same function.

Inspired by GraphChi [6], Khorasani designed Cusha [17]. Cusha is also a vertex-centric graph processing system on GPUs. To address irregular memory accesses, Cusha divides the graph into multiple shards and map them to GPU sub-components. And Cusha used CW (concatenated windows) for a higher GPU utilization. Experiments show that CuSha attains better performance compared with virtual warp centric method that uses CSR representation. Even though some graph processing frameworks can analysis graph data efficiently, it does not allow programmers to develop graph algorithms at a higher level. To address this problem, Gunrock [18] comes up with data-centric graph processing library on GPU and provides more simple and flexible APIs. Gunrock's operations include Advance, Filter and Computation. Both Advance and Filter are responsible for vertex generation and Compute procedure carries out update function for each element. Considering vertices' irregular neighbor list may cause load-imbalance, Gunrock employs per-thread fine-grained, warp cooperative and block-cooperative methods to deal with neighbor lists with different scales for load-balance. To ensure concurrent operations, different CPU threads with multiple GPU streams would control each individual GPU and hide computation with communication. Whereas limited GPU memory restricts the data scale that systems can process, GTS [19] proposed "storing only updatable attribute data and moving topology data" and employs slotted page format for out-of-core memory. The basic compute model of GTS is depicted in Fig. 4, where WA is short for read/write attribute vector, RA means read-only vector, SP represents small page while LP implies large page. WABuf in device memory corresponds to the data in main memory buffer and the same as others. When operations are to be executed, data are copied to device memory and after functions performed, updated buffer is synchronized to obtain latest data in main memory.

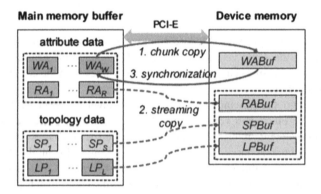

Fig. 4. Basic data flow of GTS [19]

Even though there are many optimizations adopted in GPU-based graph processing frameworks, it would be better to utilize all the computing resources in a single machine, namely, CPU and GPU, thus we can exploit memory and compute ability sufficiently.

4 Hybrid Graph Processing Systems

To make full use of computing resources on a single machine platform, Gharaibeh A designed TOTEM [20]. The paper gives a performance model estimating a hybrid system's performance and develops a hybrid graph processing framework on hybrid CPU and GPU systems. It also proposes degree centrality partitioning strategy. An illustration of TOTEM is described as Fig. 5. Because of natural graph's irregularity, TOTEM tries to fill more data into GPU to maximize the utilization of multiprocessors' cores. So TOTEM partitions graph according to vertices' degrees.

According to the experiments, it's better to assign vertices with highest degrees to CPU and left for GPUs. The scheme works due to natural graph's power-law distribution. Because GPU is good at regular computation tasks, many vertices with small

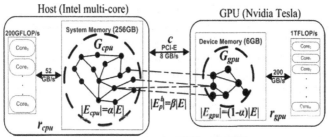

r_{cpu} r_{gpu} *Processing rates on the CPU and GPU*
c *Communication rate between the host and GPU*
α *Ratio of the graph edges that remain on the host*
β *Ratio of edges that cross the partition*

Fig. 5. Illustration of TOTEM [20]

degrees are assigned to GPUs so that thousands of threads can be executed parallel. However, CPU computation is the bottleneck of hybrid graph processing system on a single machine, and it's crucial to adopt appropriate data structure to cache more data in memory and handle much more data in GPU to improve systems' overall performance.

gGraph [25] is also a hybrid graph computation engine proposed by Shanghai Jiao Tong University. The system fully utilizes multi-core computing resources on a single machine, and it also comes up with an adaptive load-balancing method to boost the processing time. Furthermore, load and store unit is designed for data prefetching. The architecture of gGraph is described as Fig. 6.

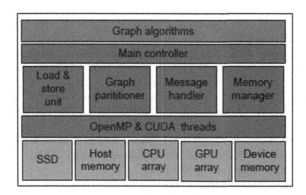

Fig. 6. gGraph architecture [25]

5   Conclusions and Future Work

This paper introduces graph processing systems on a single machine in detail, including CPU-based systems, GPU-based systems and hybrid systems. And we also introduce key techniques employed in graph processing frameworks, such as data structures, data partitioning, multi-core parallel programming, traversing patterns, programming models, and so on. CPU-based systems can utilize all host memories, but its cores are much less than GPUs. Though GPU-based systems could execute graphs quickly with their thousands of cores, their device memory is very limited. To explore a higher performance of a single machine, hybrid graph processing system may be a pretty solution. Data structure and data partitioning scheme could be the key factors influencing a hybrid system's performance.

Acknowledgments. We are grateful to our anonymous reviewers for their suggestions to improve this paper. This work is supported by the National High-Tech Research and Development Projects (863) and the National Natural Science Foundation of China under Grant Nos. 2015AA015305, 61232003, 61332003, 61202121.

References

1. Malewicz, G., Austern, M.H., Bik, A.J.C., et al.: Pregel: a system for large-scale graph processing. In: Proceedings of the 2010 ACM SIGMOD International Conference on Management of data, pp. 135–146. ACM (2010)
2. Gonzalez, J.E., Low, Y., Gu, H., et al.: PowerGraph: distributed graph-parallel computation on natural graphs. OSDI **12**(1), 2 (2012)
3. Low, Y., Bickson, D., Gonzalez, J., et al.: Distributed GraphLab: a framework for machine learning and data mining in the cloud. Proc. VLDB Endowment **5**(8), 716–727 (2012)
4. Avery, C.: Giraph: large-scale graph processing infrastructure on hadoop. Proc. Hadoop Summit **11**(3), 5–9 (2011). Santa Clara
5. Kang, U., Tsourakakis, C.E., Faloutsos, C.: Pegasus: a peta-scale graph mining system implementation and observations. In: Ninth IEEE International Conference on Data Mining, 2009. ICDM 2009. IEEE, pp. 229–238 (2009)
6. Kyrola, A., Blelloch, G.E., Guestrin, C.: GraphChi: large-scale graph computation on just a PC. OSDI **12**, 31–46 (2012)
7. Roy, A., Mihailovic, I., Zwaenepoel, W.: X-Stream: edge-centric graph processing using streaming partitions. In: Proceedings of the Twenty-Fourth ACM Symposium on Operating Systems Principles, pp. 472–488. ACM (2013)
8. Zhu, X., Han, W., Chen, W.: GridGraph: large-scale graph processing on a single machine using 2-level hierarchical partitioning. In: USENIX Annual Technical Conference, pp. 375–386 (2015)
9. Da Zheng, D.M., Burns, R., Vogelstein, J., et al.: Flashgraph: processing billion-node graphs on an array of commodity SSDs. In: Proceedings of the 13th USENIX Conference on File and Storage Technologies, pp. 45–58 (2015)
10. Shun, J., Blelloch, G.E.: Ligra: a lightweight graph processing framework for shared memory. ACM Sigplan Not. **48**(8), 135–146 (2013). ACM
11. https://github.com/twitter/cassovary
12. http://iss.ices.utexas.edu/?p=projects/galois
13. Zhang, K., Chen, R., Chen, H.: NUMA-aware graph-structured analytics. ACM SIGPLAN Not. **50**(8), 183–193 (2015). ACM
14. Prabhakaran, V., Wu, M., Weng, X., et al.: Managing large graphs on multi-cores with graph awareness. In: USENIX Annual Technical Conference, p. 12 (2012)
15. Zhong, J., He, B.: Medusa: simplified graph processing on GPUs. IEEE Trans. Parallel Distrib. Syst. **25**(6), 1543–1552 (2014)

16. Fu, Z., Personick, M., Thompson, B.: Mapgraph: a high level api for fast development of high performance graph analytics on GPUs. In: Proceedings of Workshop on Graph Data Management Experiences and Systems, pp. 1–6. ACM (2014)
17. Khorasani, F., Vora, K., Gupta, R., et al.: CuSha: vertex-centric graph processing on GPUs. In: Proceedings of the 23rd International Symposium on High-performance Parallel and Distributed Computing, pp. 239–252. ACM (2014)
18. Wang, Y., Davidson, A., Pan, Y., et al.: Gunrock: a high-performance graph processing library on the GPU. In: Proceedings of the 21st ACM SIGPLAN Symposium on Principles and Practice of Parallel Programming, p. 11. ACM (2016)
19. Kim, M.S., An, K., Park, H., et al.: GTS: a fast and scalable graph processing method based on streaming topology to GPUs. In: Proceedings of the 2016 International Conference on Management of Data, pp. 447–461. ACM (2016)
20. Gharaibeh, A., Reza, T., Santos-Neto, E., et al.: Efficient large-scale graph processing on hybrid CPU and GPU systems. arXiv preprint arXiv:1312.3018 (2013)
21. Han, W.S., Lee, S., Park, K., et al.: TurboGraph: a fast parallel graph engine handling billion-scale graphs in a single PC. In: Proceedings of the 19th ACM SIGKDD International Conference on Knowledge Discovery and Data Mining, pp. 77–85. ACM (2013)
22. Chi, Y., Dai, G., Wang, Y., et al.: NXgraph: an efficient graph processing system on a single machine. In: 2016 IEEE 32nd International Conference on Data Engineering (ICDE), pp. 409–420. IEEE (2016)
23. Yuan, P., Zhang, W., Xie, C., et al.: Fast iterative graph computation: a path centric approach. In: International Conference for High Performance Computing, Networking, Storage and Analysis, SC 2014, pp. 401–412 (2014)
24. Cheng, J., Liu, Q., Li, Z., et al.: VENUS: vertex-centric streamlined graph computation on a single PC. In: 2015 IEEE 31st International Conference on Data Engineering (ICDE), pp. 1131–1142. IEEE (2015)
25. Zhang, T., Zhang, J., Shu, W., et al.: Efficient graph computation on hybrid CPU and GPU systems. J. Supercomput. 71(4), 1563–1586 (2015)
26. Ou, Y., Xiao, N., Liu, F., et al.: Gemini: a novel hardware and software implementation of high-performance PCIe SSD. Int. J. Parallel Program. 45(4), 923–945 (2017)
27. Yu, S., Xiao, N., Deng, M., et al.: Redesign the memory allocator for non-volatile main memory. ACM J. Emerg. Technol. Comput. Syst. (JETC) 13(3), 49 (2017)

3D Model Reconstruction with Sequence Image of Aircraft

Huabo Sun[✉], Yang Jiao, Chun Wang, and Jingru Han

Institute of Aviation Safety, China Academy of Civil Aviation Science
and Technology, Beijing 100028, China
sunhb@mail.castc.org.cn

Abstract. In order to identify causes of civil aviation accidents, reconstruction and splice of wreckage is an important work for survey. This paper contributes to this research by proposing a wreckage 3D reconstruction method based on sequence image. According to the wreckage of fuselage and components, we respectively describe their reconstruction methods. Experiment results show that the algorithm can be well used to complete the mosaic reconstruction of aircraft wreckage and efficiency is greatly improved. The results show that, compared with physical splicing, the research result will help shortening the period and providing effective resolution to civil aviation accident investigation.

Keywords: Wreckage · Sequence image · Accident survey · Splice
3D model

1 Introduction

When a civil aviation accident occurs, an important procedure of the investigation is to reconstruct the wreckage of the aircraft. By stitching the wreckage, most of the damaged parts of the aircraft can be found. Then the flight shape and the speed before the crash could be speculated, which can help to identify the cause of the accident. However, the physical splicing is very difficult. With the development of technology, three dimensional aircraft splice can be realized by computer. For example, the French accident investigation bureau ever used computer technology to splice airplane wreckage [1, 2] of the Air France AF447 air crash. At present, there is no related research and software in domestic civil aviation field.

2 Conventional Data Acquisition and Processing Methods

At present, 3D modeling [3, 4] of reverse engineering mainly adopts 3D laser scanning technology. It obtains a large number of 3D point cloud data which is dense, uniform, high-precision. But this technology has some problems: ① High-precision scanner equipment is expensive, resulting in higher data acquisition costs. ② Because of the occlusion of aircraft, it is difficult to scan the entire 3D model of the aircraft. There are many omissions, such as the bottom of the wing, which is difficult to collect data. ③ Laser 3D scanning cannot obtain aircraft surface texture.

© Springer International Publishing AG 2017
G. Wang et al. (Eds.): SpaCCS 2017 Workshops, LNCS 10658, pp. 776–782, 2017.
https://doi.org/10.1007/978-3-319-72395-2_69

With the development of computer vision and photogrammetry theory in recent years, Image Based Modeling has been widely used. This modeling doesn't depend on any physical equipment and the acquisition of data is flexible. So it has been successfully applied to 3D digital city, cultural relics and so on.

Considering the existing problems of 3D laser scanning technology, this paper uses Image Based Modeling to build aircraft wreckage.

3 Modeling Based Image of Aircraft Wreck

Image Based modeling technology is a hotspot in the field of computer vision and photogrammetry. It obtains a 3D model by taking photos. With the development of Bundle Adjustment [5] and image dense matching algorithm [6], image based modeling has been greatly improved. In terms of modeling accuracy, image based modeling can even be comparable to 3D laser scanning [7].

This paper presents a model method based image for aircraft wreck. The subject obtains complete aircraft's images and groups the data. On this basis, the image model algorithm is used to build intensive 3D model [8] for each image group. Finally the model is spliced to build a complete 3D image of the aircraft (Fig. 1).

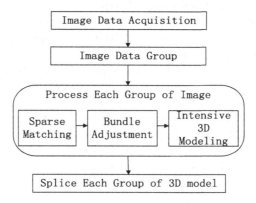

Fig. 1. Flow of wreckage model based image

3.1 Image Data Acquisition

The quality of image directly affects the accuracy and integrity of 3D modeling [9]. According to the principle of data processing, the requirements of data acquisition are as follows:

(1) As the surface of the aircraft is mostly white, aircraft surface reflection is strong. So in the shooting process, shading and other means can be used to avoid high light and inconsistent light on the image.

(2) In order to ensure complete shooting of the aircraft, the overlap between the two adjacent images is guaranteed to be above 70%, and the scale of the image is basically same.

(3) The scattered parts of the wreckage need to be placed on a flat ground for surrounding shots to collect data. The data acquisition of aircraft body requires subsection location. Wings and tail are photographed by encircling, and fuselage is photographed in parallel way.

3.2   Image Data Group

In order to raise the accuracy of model, we need to group the images. The principle of grouping is as follows:

(1) Wreckage images that were taken separately should be grouped separately.
(2) Aircraft body images should be divided into left wing, right wing, nose, left fuselage, right fuselage and tail. The data of each group will be processed separately.

3.3   Process of Each Image Group

The image data is grouped as described in 3.2. And then 3D model of each group is set up. Finally, all of the 3D models are spliced to build a complete 3D model. The procedure is divided into the following steps:

(1) **Sparse Matching of Each Image Group**
    Image data does not contain any coordinating information. The restore of the image need to the same point between the images. Therefore, the first step should be sparse matching of images.
    Sparse matching uses siftGPU algorithm for coarse matching. After coarse matching, the Ransac algorithm is used to eliminate the mismatching.
(2) **Bundle Adjustment of Each Image Group**
    The purpose of Bundle Adjustment is to restore 3D position and pose.
    Suppose the space target is T. O_S represents the center of camera projection. O_i is the main point. I represents imaging plane. The pixels which T projected on I is t. The projection relationship is as follows (Fig. 2):

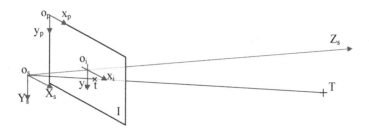

Fig. 2. Projection relation of space target point

The projection equation describes the geometric relationship of T, t and O_S

$$\tilde{m} = K \begin{bmatrix} R_{3\times3} & t_{3\times1} \\ 0^T & 1 \end{bmatrix} \tilde{M} \tag{1}$$

$\tilde{m}$ is the pixel coordinates which T projected on the image I. $\tilde{M}$ is the spatial 3D coordinate of T. $R_{3\times3}$, $t_{3\times1}$ represents the space position and pose of the camera's projection center at the moment of taking picture. K is the camera intrinsic matrix. When a sequence of images are continuously photographed for a space object, the surface points of this object are projected onto multiple images, as shown in Fig. 3:

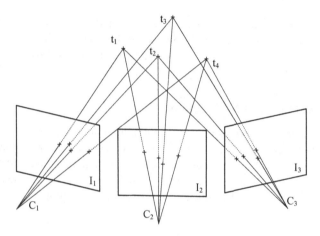

Fig. 3. Target projection image

The projective equations which derived by formula (1) describe the geometric relationship between the target surface points and the sequence image. The pixel coordinates of same point are used as the observation values of the projection equations. The relative position and pose of the sequence image can be calculated by bundle adjustment.

(3) **Intensive 3D Modeling of Each Image Group**

After relative spatial 3D position and pose are determined, each image group is taken for intensive matching in turn by SGM algorithm. Finally, an intensive 3D model of each grouping data is formed (Fig. 4).

The SGM algorithm uses scanline optimization of 16 directions. A cost aggregation of 16 directions is calculated for every pixel of each candidate match point. And then we added the results, as shown in Eq. (2):

$$S(p, d) = \sum_{r=1}^{16} L_r(p, d) \tag{2}$$

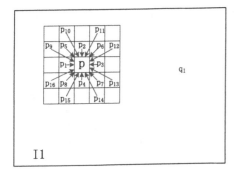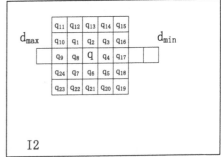

Fig. 4. SGM matching diagram

The extremum points are chosen as the best matching points in the parallax range. Thus, intensive image matching points can be obtained. The 3D coordinate of intensive matching points can be got by binocular stereo vision. Thus intensive 3D models of each image group are built.

3.4 3D Model Splice of Each Group

3D intensive models are spliced by using joint point. For each part of the aircraft body, two 3D models must share more than three same points before splicing. For the wreckage image, the 3D model does not have the same point as aircraft body, so it is necessary to select the connection points according to aircraft geometry. Finally, a complete 3D model is built by splicing 3D model of each group.

4   Experimental Results and Analysis

4.1   Data Acquisition

As shown in Fig. 5, 224 original images were collected by layered surrounding photography. Excluding blurred images and exposed abnormal images, there are 186 images. As the diagram show, the configuration of the aircraft is complex, and it is difficult to collect complete image data. The surface of aircraft is white bearing little texture, so high light appears on the image frequently. These are difficult factors for image processing.

4.2   Splicing Results and Analysis

According to the method described in this paper, the images are processed. After nearly 8 h, the aircraft's 3D model is built as Fig. 6.

As shown in Fig. 6, the image based model could build basic aircraft's 3D model. But due to the impact of texture, there are data missing in some areas of the model and it affects the integrity of the model.

Fig. 5. Experimental aircraft

Fig. 6. 3D model of experimental aircraft

5 Conclusion

There is a lack of research on the splicing and rebuilding aircraft wreckage model. So the author gives the solution and designs a detailed reconstruction algorithm. Then 3D model is reconstructed. The method has obvious advantages: simple collection, low cost, fast data processing. It is beneficial to shorten the investigation period of civil aviation accidents and provides technical support for the investigation of accidents.

Acknowledgments. The work presented in this paper is supported by Natural Science Foundation of China (ID: U1533102) and civil aviation safety project (ID: DFS20150125).

References

1. Gressin, A., Mallet, C., Demantke, J.: Towards 3D lidar point cloud registration improvement using optimal neighborhood knowledge [J]. J. Photogramm. Remote Sens. **79**, 240–251 (2013)

2. Lei, C., Gang, Z.: Research of virtual instrument simulation technology based on 3D terrain. J. Sichuan Univ. Sci. Eng. (Nat. Sci. Ed.) **23**(2), 178–180 (2010)

3. Jeong, Y., Nister, D., Steedly, D., Szeliski, R.: Pushing the envelope of modern methods for bundle adjustment. IEEE Trans. Pattern Anal. Mach. Intell. **34**(8), 1605–1617 (2012)

4. Liu, H., Sun, H., Luo, B., Yu, L.: Register aircraft point-clouds based point features. Appl. Mech. Mater. **556–562**, 5477–5481 (2014)

5. Zhao, L., Huang, S., Sun, Y., Yan, L., Dissanayake, G.: ParallaxBA: bundle adjustment using parallax angle feature parameterization. Int. J. Robot. Res. **34**(4–5), 493–516 (2015)

6. Sun, Y., Zhao, L., Huang, S., Yan, L., Dissanayake, G.: Line matching based on planar homography for stereo aerial images. ISPRS J. Photogramm. Remote Sens. **104**, 1–17 (2015)

7. Remondino, F., Spera, M.G., Nocerino, E., et al.: Dense image matching: comparisons and analyses. In: Digital Heritage International Congress, pp. 47–54. IEEE (2014)

8. Zhou, G., Zhou, X.: Seamless fusion of LiDAR and aerial imagery for building extraction. IEEE Trans. Geosci. Remote Sens. **52**(11), 7393–7407 (2014)

9. Kummerle, R., Grisetti, G., Strasdat, H., Konolige, K., Burgard, W.: A general framework for graph optimization. In: IEEE International Conference on Robotics and Automation, Shanghai, pp. 3607–3613 (2011)

Construction Research on Information Platform for Small and Medium-Sized Enterprises Based on Cloud Storage Technology

Shulan Yu, Yongzheng Tang[✉], and Chunfeng Wang

Yancheng Institute of Technology, Yancheng 224051, China
tyz@ycit.edu.cn

Abstract. With the rapid development of modern information technology, small and medium sized enterprises gradually show the trend of large-scale exchange and sharing of information, and the previous information architecture cannot meet the needs of the application. Based on the comprehensive analysis of business requirements and related technologies, a small and medium-sized enterprise information platform based on cloud storage technology is established, which makes the system have the advantages of loose coupling, powerful and easy to expand in this paper. The architecture includes cloud storage, a number of basic services and basic application support system. In this paper, the module design and data access design for these services and application systems are presented, which provides a theoretical reference for the development of the system.

Keywords: Cloud storage technology · Small and medium sized enterprises Information platform · Storage virtualization · Access equilibrium

1 Introduction

In today's Chinese economy, small and medium-sized enterprise and an important force to promote the growth of the national economy and maintain social stability, and their development prospects also greatly affect China's overall development prospects. However, small and medium-sized enterprises still have many shortcomings in management, which affect the development and growth of enterprises and can't improve their core competitiveness compared with mature state-owned enterprises.

In the construction process of the public service platform, through the introduction of cloud storage technology and cloud computing technology, small and medium-sized enterprises can realize the information management with low cost, data analysis and storage functions, and can improve the level of enterprise information and customized according to the characteristics of small and medium-sized enterprises [1]. Meanwhile, new characteristics of different systems are easily integrated in the cloud integration. These advantages of cloud services can enable SMEs to achieve a high level of information.

© Springer International Publishing AG 2017
G. Wang et al. (Eds.): SpaCCS 2017 Workshops, LNCS 10658, pp. 783–790, 2017.
https://doi.org/10.1007/978-3-319-72395-2_70

This paper designs the information platform of small and medium-sized enterprises mainly for information and data sharing in the process of information. The main purpose is to provide a fast and convenient information sharing and interaction platform for SMEs based on network technology and cloud storage mode.

2   Related Technologies

2.1   Cloud Storage

Cloud storage system refers to a system of external data storage and data service access function from the functional perspective. But unlike other storage systems, cloud storage system includes a large variety of the different types of network storage devices, and these storage devices are gathered together through the use of cluster, grid technology or application distributed file system.Therefore, cloud storage is not only a storage system, but can be regarded as a service.

2.2   Storage Virtualization

Storage virtualization refers to add a storage management of the middle layer in the middle of the physical storage device and the storage logic layer. The physical storage device is abstracted and the implementation details of the physical storage device are described. For applications, it only deals with the logical storage device allocated with itself, without regard to changes in physical storage devices [2]. The benefits of this can be a lot of scattered storage resources integration, so as to improve the overall utilization while reducing the cost of system management.

3   Frame Construction of Information Platform for Small and Medium-Sized Enterprises

The platform introduces cloud storage scheme to efficiently and reliably share and store the important data in the system. In this paper, we design an integrated framework of cloud storage and web framework, as shown in Fig. 1:

The following description of each layer:

Web layer: This layer mainly uses the Struts framework. The Web is subdivided into two layers, the first layer is the presentation layer, JSP is the main page for user interaction, transfer user request, display the processed data, the equivalent model of MVC Viewer; the second layer is the controller layer, the main business is the Action controller, the equivalent model of MVC Controller for forwarding processing service call layer processing user requests [3].

Service layer: This layer provides the business functions of the system or module and the DAO component is encapsulated and called. At the same time, the layer can directly handle the special data management requests issued by the smart client, including cloud storage, data analysis and decision making.

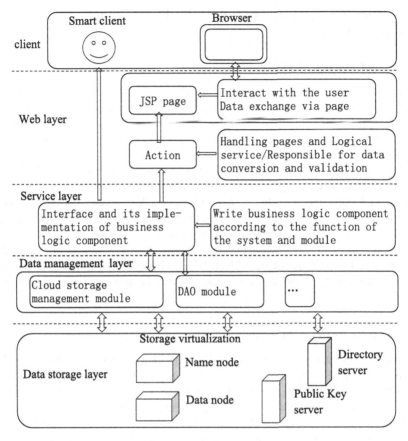

Fig. 1. Functional framework of platform

Data management layer: The DAO processing module in this layer encapsulates the Hibernate framework, mainly to provide data access, persistence, data storage layer interaction and other functions [4]. The cloud storage module logically manages the Name Node and Data Node of the data storage layer, and maintains the consistency of the data in the cloud storage environment.

Data storage layer: This layer classifies and manages the physical storage devices of the data and ensures the connectivity and reliability among various data servers. At the same time, the physical storage devices are abstracted by the storage virtualization technology.

From the above description, we design and implement the cloud storage architecture and the traditional website architecture. For users, cloud storage services can also be directly viewed as an application system in this design scheme.

4   Design and Implementation of the Key Modules in the Platform

4.1   Cloud Storage Module

The cloud storage module of this project use the HDFS structure. HDFS includes two types of nodes, one is the Name Node, and another is the Data Node. In general, the realization of the HDFS will be based on the structure of the cluster, that is configured with a Name Node and multiple Data Node, this project also uses such a configuration program.

The functions of Name Node include: (1) Map a data file to a block of data, and assign the data block to a different Data Node. (2) Cluster configuration management, manage and copy the data block. (3) Transaction log, record the generation and deletion of file, etc. (4) The effectiveness of the management of Data Node. Collect the overall operation of the system information by scanning each node.

The functions of Data Node include: (1) Data block is stored in the local file system, and the metadata of data block is stored for CRC check. (2) Response to requests from the data blocks and metadata. (3) Provide relevant information to Name Node.

4.2   Storage Virtualization Module

The platform construct the server virtualization cloud platform by "XenServer" and "CloudStack". The platform can manage the control node, use the route to control, and calculate the resource pool and the application/dynamic cluster through the management of the hardware, the network, storage in the physical environment.

Infrastructure cloud platform build a different virtual server by using "XenServer" and "CloudStack". The "CloudStack" can graphical manage the virtual server, and can adjust the hardware resources to improve the performance of the hardware according to the application of a virtual machine resources. At any time, the platform can meet the needs of the expansion of business applications. When the virtual server is not enough, the module can create a flexible template including a virtual server operating system and business applications within a few minutes.

4.3   Platform Cluster and Load Balance Module

We need to consider two aspects of load balancing for the entire platform. The first one is the load balancing of the query device, which can be realized effectively by the storage virtualization technology and the heuristic scheduling algorithm.

The second category is the platform access load balancing, which can be realized with the business application system deployed on different virtual machines [5]. The main idea is: to provide WEB services through TOMCAT. Apache will distribute the different business applications to the corresponding TOMCAT for processing, and each business will be as the APACHE distribution mark through the two domain name. Then, Apache automatically request according to the access.

4.4   Data Sharing and Exchange Module

The database design of the platform adopts the way of centralization and distribution, and construct the data center, data exchange and sharing mechanism. The database platform is responsible for the collection, storage and preservation of information resources, and continues to provide the basic data for the same variety of users and a variety of applications, while meeting the demand of government decision-making and enterprise information sharing. The architecture of data sharing and exchange platform is shown in the following Fig. 2

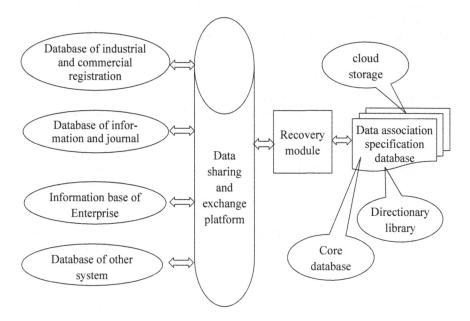

Fig. 2. The architecture of data sharing and exchange platform

The cloud storage module is used to store the data in the enterprise. The core database is used to save the data resources that are not suitable for the cloud storage module. The project uses three different forms to save these data resources, namely: database, directory server and file system.

(1) Database. The database system is used to save the business information, audit information and some important log information.
(2) Directory server. Use the directory server to store user profile information in the system. User profile information includes the user's name, system user name, password, and other information such as functional permissions. Use the directory server to save the user's file information, so as to support the single sign on function of the system.
(3) File system. Use the file system to save the log information, and help the user to manage the log files more simple. In addition, you can also use the file system to save some unstructured data, such as pictures, voice files, etc.

4.5   Integrated Service Center

The purposes of the establishment of enterprise information platform is to collect, and integrate the needs of enterprises, then finally to solve. In the construction of information platform in enterprise, because each enterprise data are in a "private" state, and generally are not shared. Therefore, when the web pages are released and combined when that are needed. That is not only inefficient, but also cannot analyze and deal with the demand [6].

In this project, due to the integration of cloud storage module, relevant data of the enterprise can be placed in the cloud, and the module can share information about configuration. The module can establish a cloud automatic processing as the core through the system knowledge base and automatic processing module.

4.6   Smart Client Module

Smart client is the bridge between the system and the end user, which is directly related to the user experience and application effect. The basic functions of the process are shown in the following Fig. 3

The smart client includes the following modules:

(1) Function module load manager. According to the different user permissions, the client will load with various functional modules. The function module load manager can load and manage these modules, manage their life cycle and maintain the communication between modules. These modules can access the system through a certain interface, and the user can also customize the module, and firstly upload the content to the system, then the administrator can be on line for other users to download and use. This is conducive to the dynamic and intelligent expansion of the system, and reduce the costs of maintenance and development.

(2) User behavior tracking and user feedback module. In order to be able to better cooperate with the development mode of the program, that is, the development of on-line mode, the system set up a user behavior tracking and user feedback module. This module has two functions: "behavior tracking" and "feedback" [7]. "Tracking" will record the user's keyboard and mouse events, and these events are transmitted to the server in order to further analyze the behavior of the user, so as to carry out the continuous improvement of user interface. The "feedback" module will use the implantable oriented technology, and embed the feedback interface to each functional interface. The user can submit the problems and suggestions when he uses the software. All of this information will be submitted to the server by the user behavior tracking and feedback module, which provides the basis for the improvement of the software.

(3) Network connection manager. The network connector is used to detect whether the server is a basic service component. It interacts with the network through the communication interface, and can help users improve the service experience according to the accessibility of the network, speed, and even the server busy degree. When the quality of the network is not good enough, the network connection manager will notify the relevant information to the "user interface main

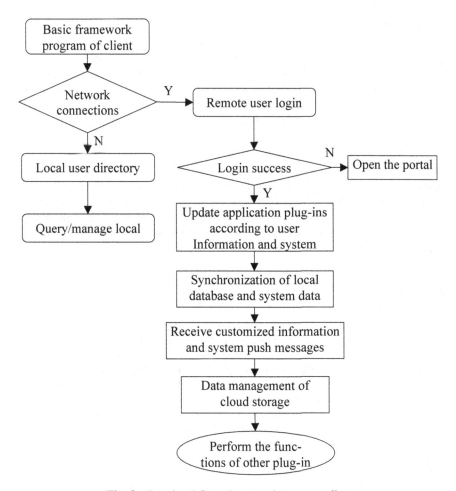

Fig. 3. Functional flow diagram of the smart client

frame", and the main framework can determine the application of some functional modules to switch to offline mode.

(4) Offline application virtual service. In order to make each function module in the relatively independent operation and simple environment, the offline application of virtual service will simulate an "online "service, and realize the remote part through the service interface. The server is matched with the local cache and persistent facilities [8]. After the network is unblocked, the user's offline data is automatically synchronized with the remote server.

(5) Automatic update mechanism. Client desktop automatically detects the client version of the server configuration, and found the new version, then automatically prompts to download and update according to customer needs.

5 Summary

According to the needs of information development for small and medium enterprises, a small and medium-sized enterprise information platform is designed and implemented, and the details of the implementation of the main modules are introduced in detail in this paper. The system can provide good information service for small and medium enterprises with the trial and improvement of the system and according to the feedback in the actual operation process.

The work and research contents of this paper are as follows: Firstly, based on the comprehensive analysis of business requirements and related technologies, a small and medium-sized enterprise information platform based on cloud storage technology is established, which makes the system have the advantages of loose coupling, powerful and easy to expand in this paper. Secondly, on the basis of the system storage virtualization, the module of service and application system are designed. And the paper has realized the seamless handover between multi-application systems.

References

1. Warnars, S.: Game information system. Int. J. Comput. Sci. Inf. Technol. **12**(6), 11–13 (2010)
2. Kivinen, T., Lammintakanen, J.: The success of a management information system in health care - a case study from Finland. Int. J. Med. Inform. **33**(6), 22–25 (2012)
3. Armbrust, M., Fox, A., Griffith, R., Joseph, A.D., Katz, R.H., Konwinski, A., Lee, G., Patterson, D.A., Rabkin, A., Stoica, I., Zaharia, M.: Above the clouds: a Berkeley view of cloud computing, pp. 1–6 (2016)
4. Kc, K., Anyanwu, K.: Scheduling Hadoop jobs to meet deadlines. In: IEEE 2nd International Conference Cloud Computing Technology and Science, pp. 388–392 (2010)
5. Dong, X.C., Wang, Y., Liao, H.M.: Scheduling mixed real-time and non-real-time applications in map reduce environment. In: 17th International Conference on Parallel and Distributed Systems. IEEE (2011)
6. Baker, J., Bond, C.: Megastore: providing scalable, highly available storage for interactive services. In: Proceedings of the 5th Biennial Conference on Innovative Data System Research, pp. 223–224 (2011)
7. Chang, F., De Dean, J., Ghemawat, S., et al.: Bigtable: a distributed storage system for structured data. In: Proceedings of the 7th USENIX Symposium on Operating Systems Design and Implementation, Seattle, USA, pp. 205–218 (2016)
8. Armbrust, M., Fox, A.: Above the clouds: a Berkeley view of cloud computing. Technical report no. UCB/EECS-2009–28, vol. 6, no. 2, pp. 3–5. University of California at Berkeley, USA (2009)

XoT: A Flexible Block I/O Data Transfer Protocol for Xen

Jin Zhang[1,2], Yuxuan Li[1,2], Chengjun Sun[1,2], Haoxiang Yang[1,2],
Jiacheng Wu[1,2], and Xiaoli Gong[1,2(✉)]

[1] College of Computer and Control Engineering,
Nankai University, Tianjin 300350, China
gongxiaoli@nankai.edu.cn
[2] State Key Laboratory of Computer Architecture,
Institute of Computing Technology, Chinese Academy of Sciences,
Beijing 100190, China

Abstract. The management of I/O resources is an important part
of virtualization. Although the traditional management is complex,
it becomes more challenging in virtualization. There has been many
researches on how to improve I/O performance or fairness on Linux using
extra semantic data, unfortunately many of them are not proper for virtualization. Because of the limitation of I/O protocol, such extra data
can not be transferred along with device data. This forms a semantic gap
between VM and hypervisor. In this paper, we proposed Xen on Turnout
(XoT), a flexible block I/O data transfer protocol for Xen. XoT makes
it possible to transfer extra important I/O data across the gap. We also
develop a prototype to prove the effectiveness of our protocol. Our result
shows that preferential effect are well achieved for user to manage block
I/O with the transferred extra data, with little performance lost.

Keywords: Virtualization · Virtual machine · Xen
Cloud computing · Block I/O

1 Introduction

I/O is one of the important aspects of virtualization, popular solutions such as
Xen and KVM have the ability that differentiated I/O services can be provided
across the VMs running on a physical machine. But this is not enough to satisfy
the growing variant requirements, for example providing a differentiated service
across applications running on different guests. There have been I/O schedulers
that are designed for I/O prioritization between applications such as Completely
Fair Queuing (CFQ) [1]. As well as many researches have worked on using semantic data such as priority and meta info to do the I/O control on linux. However
they don't consider the case of virtualization. Simply apply such methods to VM
or hypervisor will not work, because the virtualization I/O protocol cuts down
their data transfer path and forms a semantic gap.

© Springer International Publishing AG 2017
G. Wang et al. (Eds.): SpaCCS 2017 Workshops, LNCS 10658, pp. 791–800, 2017.
https://doi.org/10.1007/978-3-319-72395-2_71

In this paper, we discuss the limitation of the block I/O protocol on Xen. Through analysis and experiment, we determine the key points to solve the issue, including the block driver and the I/O data transfer protocol. After that we propose a solution called Xen on Turnout (XoT). This is a protocol based on the original Xen block transfer protocol. It is more flexible that allow user to transfer extra data along with device data. This provides the ability for I/O control mechanisms such as I/O scheduler to aware the condition of virtualization environment. So people such as system developers could easier tackle with the gap between hypervisor and VM and perform a unified I/O control experience like it used to be. We summarize our contributions as follows:

- We analyze and reveal the I/O transfer issue on Xen virtualization environment and find out the key to cope with it.
- We propose XoT protocol using *request stealing* and *sub protocol* techniques that provides a feasible and flexible way.
- We develop a linux kernel with Xen based prototype of the protocol mentioned above. The prototype uses an innovative I/O schedule framework called Split-AFQ [14] that has been modified to add support for protocol. Our results show the effectiveness of the protocol, while introducing little influence of the performance.

The remainder of this paper is organized as follows. At first we introduce the Xen block I/O architecture (Sect. 2). Then discuss the challenges of current design of Xen block protocol (Sect. 3). Then we show the design (Sect. 4) of XoT, a protocol to solve the semantic I/O gap issue. We implement a prototype and evaluate it (Sect. 5). Finally, we discuss related work (Sect. 6) and conclude (Sect. 7).

2 Background

2.1 Shared Memory Ring and blkif Protocol

Shared memory ring is a very important component in Xen. It is a shared memory page between hypervisor and VM, used as a ring buffer. The ring buffer is a fairly standard lockless data structure for producer-consumer communications. Each ring contains two kinds of data, a request and a response, updated by the two halves of the driver [3] (Fig. 1).

The blkif protocol is a unified block-device I/O interface for Xen guest OSes. It defines the blkif request and blkif response structures for requests and responses on the shared memory ring, respectively. It then defines the shared memory ring structures for requests and responses. Once the front end wants to do some I/O requests, it will construct a request with a specific request code, such as BLKIF_OP_READ, BLKIF_OP_WRITE. Up to now, the blkif code in latest stable kernel version(v4.12) has merely 7 types of request, all of which just for basic I/O purposes including READ/WRITE, BARRIER and DISCARD. After the ring has been flushed, the backend processes the requests and inserts responses into the ring.

2.2 Split Block Device Driver Model

Figure 2 shows a block I/O data flow under split driver model. The high level layer of VM's block I/O stack is similar to it used to be, working with a modified low level block device. A virtual block device, called *blkfront*, takes over the physical device's responsibility. The blockfront module handles all block I/O requests from VM application and retrieve segments from *bio* structs, which are included in the requests. Each segment contains a reference to a grant page. A grant page is shared memory page that is used to transfer data between frontend and backend. Finally these segments are sent with Xen blkif protocol to a shared I/O ring, then received by hypervisor on the other side of the ring to continue the travel. The receiver module on hypervisor side called *blkback*. It does a reverse work against blkfront, merging segments to bio structs and submitting them to form new requests to physical block device on host machine. After experiencing the I/O management and scheduling in hypervisor, VM's I/O requests finally touch the block device and reach the real end.

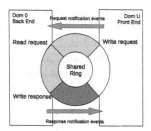

Fig. 1. The composition of a split device driver

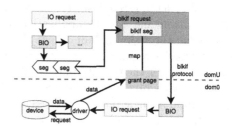

Fig. 2. I/O data flow

3 Motivation

There has been a long history of researches on linux I/O management. Classical ideas such as deadline scheduler and CFQ scheduler has already been used in the kernel. Nowadays, many novel I/O schedule methods tend to use semantic data and more complex strategies to handle I/O requests, such as SCS [4], split-level I/O scheduling [14] and request-centric I/O prioritization [9]. These methods using information from multiple parts or even whole of the I/O path for their strategies, rather than stay at single layer as pristine methods. But according to the background part, the whole I/O path in Xen is splitted into two separate parts. This makes it impossible to let methods mentioned above work on Xen as well. Meanwhile, Boutcher et al. has proved that in virtualization environment, one will not benefit from simply combination of classical schedulers on hypervisor and VM [2].

In this section, we are going to give a deep sight to the reason why methods mentioned above won't work and discuss the limitation of current Xen block I/O

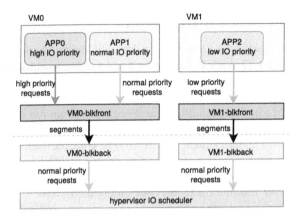

Fig. 3. Priority invert

protocol. In the first place, assuming that a hypervisor using priority driven I/O scheduler to let I/O requests be treated fairly according to the process's I/O priority. Meanwhile a VM's application set it's I/O priority to high, trying to obtain more throughput than others. AS scenario is illustrated in Fig. 3. When the high priority request comes to the blkfront module, the blkfront disassembles it and throws out the priority info, then just passes blkif read or write request to the hypervisor's blkback module. So finally the hypervisor only sees a batch of requests from a single blkback process, entangled with other processes' requests. Even if the method works well, unfortunately the high priority request is treated same as a request submitted by another blkback, which has normal I/O priority.

Now we take a look back to the blkif protocol. This simple protocol provides a relatively efficient way to transfer raw device data between VM and hypervisor, while cuts down the additional I/O information delivering way. On another side, many I/O control methods collect these information for their strategies. Without these information, the hypervisor could only do a macroscopic I/O control between VMs that may not meet the requirements sometimes.

As a summary of above, if we want to make the I/O transfer for Xen more feasible and take advantage of modern I/O schedule methods, extra I/O information must be able to be transferred to hypervisor as well. The critical point is at the I/O data transmission between VM and hypervisor, of which the core is the blkif protocol.

4   Protocol Design

In the following part, we will propose the XoT protocol. XoT provides a hook based interface for extra VM to hypervisor I/O data transfer. This protocol mainly powered by two features that we call them *request stealing* and *sub protocol*. The former make it possible to send standalone custom requests and responses on the blkif ring buffer instead of using a bypass, as well as the later provides the ability to deliver extra data with few modifications of blkif code.

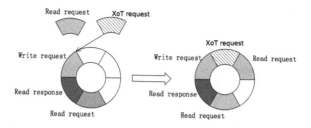

Fig. 4. Request stealing

Request Stealing. Request stealing is a little like the cycle stealing method used by DMA. When the blkif ring is almost idle, for example waiting for hypervisor's response or the VM having low system I/O workload, meanwhile the VM wants to send additional data to hypervisor, then XoT steals some request slots of blkif ring to send its own request. The hypervisor using a modified kernel that added support to this type of request would make response and send back it from the same path as well. Since the interrupt handler of block backend using a case statement to dispatch requests from the frontend, a hypervisor with unmodified kernel will just ignore this request simply, rather than throws exception or even crash.

Furthermore, if the VM needs to send request correlative data, XoT could just delays the original I/O request for one or more slots and steal these slots for itself, then puts the original I/O request in the slot next to the stolen slot, as Fig. 4 illustrates. This method build a relation between extra I/O data and I/O request naturally, regardless synchronizing.

Sub Protocol. XoT uses blkif protocol as a lower layer instead of re-implements the whole protocol, which borrows idea from network communication model. It means that using the request struct as a protocol transmit unit rather than what it used to be, shown as Fig. 5. The request struct has an array buffer, which stands for the *XoT protocol layer* payload on *blkif layer*. Variant I/O data then becomes different types of payload on XoT layer. The protocol request needs to be carefully constructed to fit the maximum size among the existed request structs, avoiding touching the *power of two barrier*.

The protocol frame is shown in Fig. 6. In figure the first XoT steals two request slots as a frame. The frame starts with a protocol header, following which are all the payload of protocol. The protocol header contains a magic number to differ from normal blkif data. One frame supports transfer multiple types of data at once. Each type of data has its own header. The data header has an 8 bits magic number at start to indicate type. Following the magic number is the header size and data size. Each data header has a pointer points to next header as well, to improve the searching complexity of specific type of data.

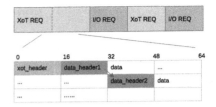

Fig. 5. XoT over Blkif   **Fig. 6.** XoT on ring and frame struct

Hook Interface. In XoT, there are two VM side sending hooks with a corresponding receiving hook on hypervisor side, providing one way data transfer from VM to hypervisor. A typical usage of hook interface should both register at least one VM hook and a hypervisor hook. One of the VM hooks will be called each time when there are I/O request handled by blkfront, giving the chance to send request related data. Another VM hook will be called when the system I/O load is low, giving the chance to send miscellaneous data that are not time sensitive or independent with I/O requests. Such data should be marked as discardable or delayable. If the system load becomes high, the protocol will discard the data if it is discardable, or delay the data sending until the system load return to low if it is delayable. A flag will be set to remind the discard or delay state of the last processed data.

Once the data has been received completely on hypervisor side, the receiving hook will soon be called. The receiver can retrieve specific data that it is interesting in. After that, a normal blkif success response will be sent automatically, similar as a response for normal blkif request.

5   Evaluation

5.1   Experiment Environment

In this section, we describe how we build a system implementing the solution mentioned above. The system is consisted with a specific VM storage configuration, a modified linux kernel and a modified I/O framework for test purpose. Because of the kernel requirement of the chosen framework, we don't use the latest version of kernel and Xen, but with kernel 3.2.51 shipping with Xen 4.1. We have reviewed the recent version of Xen and make sure it don't have great changes yet, so using an old version doesn't affect the effectiveness verifying at all. The code is open sourced on our website, http://mobisys.cc/pages/resource.html.

Hardware Setup. We use a PC as host machine, which has Intel Core i5-6500 CPU, 16 GB of memory. The host machine runs Xen 4.1 stable version as its hypervisor, and Ubuntu Server 12.04 as its operating system.

There are three VMs established on the testing server, each of them is allocated with 1 VCPU and 3 GB memory initially. All the VMs and the hypervisor

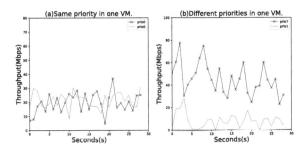

Fig. 7. Split-A test on single VM

uses a same modified kernel. The hypervisor is installed on a HDD(sda) while VMs are installed on another HDD(sdb).

5.2   Evaluation

Effectiveness. At first we test the control of VM application I/O to see whether the scheduler gains the ability to control application I/O in VM. We do the test with four workloads. Figure 7(a) shows reading performance for two threads in the same VM. Both of the threads are set to zero I/O priority, and do a 4 KB sequence reading on different random data files. The average throughputs of the two threads are 21.26 MB/s and 21.00 MB/s. This shows a fairness between the same priority. Figure 7(b) shows reading performance for two threads in the same VM that have different I/O priority. One thread is set to high priority (7) while another is set to low priority (1). The high priority thread has 42.55 MB/s throughput on average, as well as the low priority thread only gains 8.82 MB/s throughput on average. The result shows that read request from same VM respect priorities.

Then we test read performance from different VMs, Fig. 8(a) shows that the two same I/O priority threads in separate VMs are treated fairly. The average throughputs are 39.12 MB/s and 38.52 MB/s. Figure 8(b) shows that the thread who has a higher priority will be given more throughput. The thread with a higher priority (7) in VM1 has 57.40 MB/s throughput on average. Meanwhile the thread with a lower priority (1) in VM2 has 22.06 MB/s throughput on average.

CPU Usage. In this section we will test the influence of CPU usage after we applied the protocol. Figure 9a shows CPU usage comparison between original kernel and the modified one. The left group shows the result when system is idle. The VM and hypervisor CPU usage is 0.1% and 1.0% in original kernel, 0.2% and 1.5% in modified one. The right group shows the result when VM is busy on I/O. The VM and hypervisor CPU usage is 19% and 69% in original kernel, 24% and 73% in modified one. The result shows that the CPU usage slightly increases on heavy load due to extra data processing, while no remarkable extra cost when the system is idle.

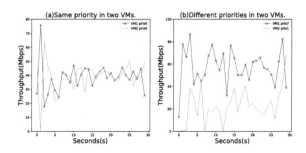

Fig. 8. Split-A test across two VMs

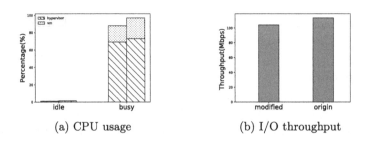

(a) CPU usage   (b) I/O throughput

Fig. 9. System costs

I/O Throughput. In this section we test the influence of I/O throughput after we applied the solution. Figure 9b shows a single thread continuously 1M sequence read test. The original kernel has 113.63 MB/s average throughput, while the modified one has 104.18 MB/s. This result shows that the throughput is lower than before because of the stolen requests, but not so much.

6   Related Work

6.1   I/O Protocol on Xen

The communication protocol based on shared memory ring has been discussed on XenSocket [15], XWAY [8] and V4VSockets [10]. They work on the interdomain network transport of VM. There has also been a discussion about Xen's blkif protocol in XenSocket, which is mainly focus on the performance and through-put. Wang et al. [12] work on the network I/O throughput of Xen, they mention about the blkif protocol as well but pays more attention to the VCPU scheduling mechanism.

6.2   Semantic Gap of Virtualization

Kim et al. [7] presents a task-aware virtual machine scheduling mechanism. It uses inference techniques to bridge the semantic gap and provides I/O-bound task scheduling. Virtusoso [5] aims to narrow the semantic gap in virtual machine introspection. As well as Xiong et al. [13] build a library called Libvmi to solve the semantic gap problem for virtual machine monitoring applications.

6.3 I/O Scheduler and Framework

There are many I/O schedulers and framework based on semantic data, such as SCS [4], split-level I/O scheduling [14] and request-centric I/O prioritization [9]. But none of them considers the semantic gap of virtualization. Tan et al. [11] proposed a disk I/O scheduling method for virtual machines called VMCD. It maintains independent V-Channel between backend driver and hypervisor native driver. With none modification of the I/O protocol, VMCD merely provides VM level I/O scheduling. PARDA [6] provides coarse-grained fairness to VMs, without assuming any support from the storage array itself. Because of the lack of information, it can not provide fine-grained control of I/O.

7   Conclusion

Even though the big data and artificial intelligence is so popular today, the footstone under them should never be ignored. Virtualization technology, the core of modern cloud computing architecture, are facing various challenges all the time. In this paper, we analyze the I/O control challenge from the gap between VM and hypervisor, as well as the limitation of current block I/O protocol of Xen. Then we propose XoT, a sub protocol over the existing I/O protocol, that provides a more flexible data transfer for block I/O of Xen. This make it possible for system developer to using novel I/O control strategies on virtualization environment. Through implementation and experiments in our prototype of Xen 4.1 and Split-AFQ, the protocol shows the effectiveness of our goal with little resource cost. Our future work is to work on the security and stability, as well as porting more existing I/O control methods to our protocol.

Acknowledgments. This work is supported by the Research Plan in Application Foundation and Advanced Technologies in Tianjin (14JCQNJC 00700), and the Open Project of the State Key Laboratory of Computer Architecture, Institute of Computing Technology, Chinese Academy of Sciences (CARCH201604).

References

1. CFQ (Complete Fairness Queueing). https://www.kernel.org/doc/Documentation/block/cfq-iosched.txt
2. Boutcher, D., Chandra, A.: Does virtualization make disk scheduling passé? SIGOPS Oper. Syst. Rev. **44**(1), 20–24 (2010)
3. Chisnall, D.: The Definitive Guide to the Xen Hypervisor. Pearson Education, London (2008)
4. Craciunas, S.S., Kirsch, C.M., Röck, H.: I/O resource management through system call scheduling. SIGOPS Oper. Syst. Rev. **42**(5), 44–54 (2008)

5. Dolan-Gavitt, B., Leek, T., Zhivich, M., Giffin, J., Lee, W.: Virtuoso: narrowing the semantic gap in virtual machine introspection. In: 2011 IEEE Symposium on Security and Privacy, pp. 297–312, May 2011

6. Gulati, A., Ahmad, I., Waldspurger, C.A., et al.: Parda: proportional allocation of resources for distributed storage access. In: FAST, vol. 9, pp. 85–98 (2009)

7. Kim, H., Lim, H., Jeong, J., Jo, H., Lee, J.: Task-aware virtual machine scheduling for I/O performance. In: Proceedings of the 2009 ACM SIGPLAN/SIGOPS International Conference on Virtual Execution Environments, pp. 101–110. ACM (2009)

8. Kim, K., Kim, C., Jung, S.I., Shin, H.S., Kim, J.S.: Inter-domain socket communications supporting high performance and full binary compatibility on Xen. In: Proceedings of the Fourth ACM SIGPLAN/SIGOPS International Conference on Virtual Execution Environments, pp. 11–20. ACM (2008)

9. Kim, S., Kim, H., Lee, J., Jeong, J.: Enlightening the I/O path: a holistic approach for application performance. In: FAST, pp. 345–358 (2017)

10. Nanos, A., Gerangelos, S., Alifieraki, I., Koziris, N.: V4VSockets: low-overhead intra-node communication in Xen. In: Proceedings of the 5th International Workshop on Cloud Data and Platforms, p. 1. ACM (2015)

11. Tan, H., Li, C., He, Z., Li, K., Hwang, K.: VMCD: a virtual multi-channel disk I/O scheduling method for virtual machines. IEEE Trans. Serv. Comput. 9(6), 982–995 (2016)

12. Wang, Y., Liu, M., Gao, B., Qin, C., Ma, C.: I/O congestion-aware computing resource assignment and scheduling in virtualized cloud environments. In: 2016 IEEE Trustcom/BigDataSE/ISPA, pp. 1280–1287. IEEE (2016)

13. Xiong, H., Liu, Z., Xu, W., Jiao, S.: Libvmi: a library for bridging the semantic gap between guest OS and VMM. In: 2012 IEEE 12th International Conference on Computer and Information Technology, pp. 549–556, October 2012

14. Yang, S., Harter, T., Agrawal, N., Kowsalya, S.S., Krishnamurthy, A., Al-Kiswany, S., Kaushik, R.T., Arpaci-Dusseau, A.C., Arpaci-Dusseau, R.H.: Split-level I/O scheduling. In: Proceedings of the 25th Symposium on Operating Systems Principles, SOSP 2015, pp. 474–489. ACM, New York (2015)

15. Zhang, X., McIntosh, S., Rohatgi, P., Griffin, J.L.: XenSocket: a high-throughput interdomain transport for virtual machines. In: Cerqueira, R., Campbell, R.H. (eds.) Middleware 2007. LNCS, vol. 4834, pp. 184–203. Springer, Heidelberg (2007). https://doi.org/10.1007/978-3-540-76778-7_10

The First International Symposium on Multimedia Security and Digital Forensics (MSDF 2017)

MSDF 2017 Organizing and Program Committees

1 General Chairs

Bharat Bhargava	Purdue University, USA
Sabu M. Thampi	IIITM-Kerala, India

2 Program Chairs

Mehmet Emin YUKSEL	Erciyes University, Turkey
Pradeep K. Atrey	University at Albany, State University of New York, USA
Zoran S. Bojkovic	University of Belgrade, Serbia

3 Program Committee

Ali Tekeoglu	SUNY Polytechnic Institute, USA
Babu Mehtre	IDRBT-Institute for Development and Research in Banking Technology, India
Boyang Zhou	Zhejiang University, China
Carlos Travieso	University of Las Palmas de Gran Canaria, Spain
Chang Wu Yu	Chung Hua University, Taiwan
Clement Nyirenda	University of Namibia, Namibia
Grienggrai Rajchakit	Maejo University, Thailand
Han Hu	Nanyang Technological University, Singapore
Harry Skianis	University of the Aegean, Greece
Jianping Fan	University of North Carolina, USA
Jozsef Vasarhelyi	University of Miskolc, Hungary
Kalaivani Chellappan	Universiti Kebangsaan Malaysia, Malaysia
Kalman Palagyi	University of Szeged, Hungary
Lisimachos Kondi	University of Ioannina, Greece
Mahbubur Syed	Minnesota State University, Mankato, USA
Mehmet Celenk	Ohio University, USA
Minh-Son Dao	Universiti Teknologi Brunei, Brunei Darussalam
Mohamad Zoinol Abidin Aziz	Universiti Teknikal Malaysia Melaka, Malaysia
Paolo Crippa	Università Politecnica delle Marche, Italy

Sunil Kumar Kopparapu	Tata Consultancy Services, India
Tammam Tillo	Xi'an Jiaotong-Liverpool University, China
Thomas Chen	City University London, UK (Great Britain)
Young Bin Kown	Chung-Ang University, Korea
Zoran Bojkovic	University of Belgrade, Serbia

4 Steering Committee Chair

| Sabu M. Thampi | IIITM-Kerala, India |

5 Publicity Chair

| Sabu M. Thampi | IIITM-Kerala, India |

Detecting Spliced Face Using Texture Analysis

Divya S. Vidyadharan[1,2(✉)] and Sabu M. Thampi[3]

[1] College of Engineering-Trivandrum, Thiruvananthapuram 695016, Kerala, India
[2] LBS Centre for Science and Technology, University of Kerala,
Thiruvananthapuram 695033, Kerala, India
divya.s.vidyadharan@ieee.org
[3] Indian Institute of Information Technology and Management-Kerala,
Thiruvananthapuram 695581, India
smthampi@ieee.org

Abstract. Images are widely accepted as evidence of events despite the fact that images can be easily altered with adverse intentions. It is difficult to identify image alteration carried out by a skilled criminal. Digital forensics investigators need sophisticated tools to prove the legitimacy of digital images. The proposed work focuses on detecting altered digital images containing human facial regions. The work presents a method for detecting spliced face among a number of faces in an image. The proposed method makes use of the inconsistencies in the illuminant texture present in image pixels. For each facial region extracted from the image, a texture descriptor is extracted from its illumination representation followed by a comparison of all the texture descriptors to identify the spliced face. Experimental results show that the proposed method achieved better detection results than existing methods.

Keywords: Illumination inconsistency · Image splicing detection
Texture analysis · Local Phase Quantization
Image forgery localization

1 Introduction

Image contents are considered as an authentic representation of events. Plenty of images are encountered in our day-to-day life as more and more hand-held devices are equipped with image capturing and image editing tools in addition to traditional digital still cameras. This substantiated with the handiness of a lot of image processing software led to the unlawful use of digital images. People started manipulating the image contents in accordance with illegitimate intentions. This has attracted researchers worldwide and a lot of image forensic techniques that reveal image alterations are being developed in recent times.

Different types of alterations include copy-pasting an image region from another image (image-splicing), copy-pasting an image region onto the same image (copy-move forgery). These kinds of forgeries have severe adverse effects

© Springer International Publishing AG 2017
G. Wang et al. (Eds.): SpaCCS 2017 Workshops, LNCS 10658, pp. 805–813, 2017.
https://doi.org/10.1007/978-3-319-72395-2_72

on social life, depending on the realm of the crime. For example, a forged photograph claiming an illicit circumstance with an innocent victim can cause unforeseen damage to the social reputation of the victim. Digital forensic investigators are constantly looking for tools to aid the investigation of digital crimes involving multimedia contents as evidence. Though a large number of publications in image forensics domain focus on image forgery detection [1,4,9,11], only a few works such as the techniques discussed in [2,3,5,7,10,13,14] have addressed the problem of locating spliced human facial region.

In the proposed work, image alteration involving copying a facial region from one image and pasting onto another image is considered. Consider a group photo, where a few persons were present originally, being altered to add one more facial region onto the photo, with a malicious intention of creating a forged evidence for a crime. Here, the problem is to detect the spliced photo by analyzing the image properties of all the faces. Usually, a copy-paste operation disrupts the original pattern of image properties. Therefore, image forgery detection techniques try to exploit these disruptions in image properties such as texture, scene illumination, and noise features. The proposed work presents a technique to identify spliced facial regions from an image containing a group of people by analyzing the texture in illumination representation of facial regions.

The rest of the paper is organized as follows. Related works are discussed in Sect. 2. The proposed method is explained in detail in Sect. 3. Experimental results obtained are discussed in Sect. 4. Finally, the conclusion is given in Sect. 5.

2   Related Work

Scene illuminant information is exploited as a forensics hint in a number of image forgery detection techniques. The related techniques where scene illuminants from human facial skin pixels are analyzed are discussed here [2,3,5,7,10,13,14].

Riess and Angelopoulou in 2010 introduced the concept of illuminant representation across an image [10]. Inconsistencies in this representation, if any, are visible as differently colored areas. Here, a manual examination of different facial regions is needed to detect the spliced person in an image. Carvalho et al. overcame the manual analysis of the illuminant representation by a machine learning technique that took into account the texture descriptors and edge descriptors for classifying an image as altered or original [3].

Francis et al. estimated the illuminant color from skin highlight region at the nose tip and detected the difference in illuminant color among different faces in an image [5]. The difference in the illuminant colors obtained from regions originally present in an image will be too low whereas the difference between illuminant colors between an original and spliced face will be noticeable. The closer illuminant color coordinates represent original faces and the face with largest illuminant color distance measure represents the spliced face.

Vidyadharan and Thampi detected the spliced face by analyzing the difference in the brightness distribution from the facial skin pixels [13]. The brightness distribution is obtained by taking the histogram of Value plane in

Hue-Saturation-Value colour space. Faces with closer brightness distribution are identified as original whereas face with a distant brightness distribution is identified as fake. The closeness of brightness distribution is measured using bin-by-bin and cross-bin histogram comparison methods.

Carvalho et al. improved the machine learning based image forgery detection technique in 2013 by using a large number of features and classifier fusion in 2014 [2]. In addition to forgery detection, Carvalho et al. addressed the problem of locating spliced face on images already marked as altered, using a machine learning approach and achieved a detection accuracy of 85% in locating spliced face.

Vidyadharan and Thampi proposed an unsupervised non-machine learning method for detecting spliced face from tampered images [14] in 2015. A Principal Component Analysis (PCA) is carried out directly on the gray level values of facial regions extracted from the illuminant representation to reveal the outlier spliced face. The method obtained an accuracy of 62% and 64% in Inverse Intensity-Chromaticity (IIC) based illuminant representation and Generalized Gray World (GGW) illuminant representation.

Mazumdar and Bora have proposed a spliced face detection method based on Dichromatic Reflection Model [7]. Here Dichromatic Plane Histogram (DPH) is extracted from each face and is used as a signature. These histograms are compared using correlation measure to analyze the similarities in the illumination among various faces in the image. The similarity score between faces are checked with a threshold to detect the spliced face among a group of faces in an image. The method obtains an accuracy of 91.2%, but omitted images containing different skin tones.

The proposed work is motivated by the fact that there will be inconsistencies in the texture pattern in the illuminant representation of an image, when image regions captured at different illumination conditions are spliced to form a forged image. Hence, we analyzed the variation in the texture pattern in the illumination representation across various facial regions in an image to locate spliced facial region.

3   The Proposed Method of Detecting Spliced Face

Different stages of the proposed system are shown in Fig. 1. The method proceeds by extracting texture features from all the faces from the illuminant representation followed by distance comparison between each pair of faces for detecting the spliced face.

The illuminant representation of facial regions captured at different lighting environment shows differences in the illumination pattern. Thus, the illuminant texture features extracted from the faces will be distinct for different faces in a spliced image. The proposed method detects spliced face by exploring the difference in the texture pattern as illustrated in Fig. 1. The different steps are detailed in the sub-sections. The algorithm of the proposed method is shown in Algorithm 1.

Fig. 1. Different phases of proposed system

Algorithm 1. Detecting spliced face from an image
_____
Input   : Image containing N facial regions.
Output : Identified Spliced Face.

1: Generate illuminant representation of the input image.
2: Extract the facial regions.
3: **for** i=1 **to** N **do**
4:     Generate the LPQ texture descriptor.
5: **end for**
6: **for** i=1 **to** N **do**
7:     **for** j=i+1 **to** N **do**
8:         **if** i >= j **then**
9:             $distMatrix(i,j) = Bhattacharya_{distance}(LPQ(i), LPQ(j))$
10:         **end if**
11:     **end for**
12: **end for**
13: **for** i=1 **to** N **do**
14:     $dist(i) = max(distMatrix(i,:))$
15: **end for**
16: Select the majority voted most distant faces as the spliced faces.
_____

3.1   Illuminant Representation and Facial Region Extraction

The facial regions are identified by specifying the bounding box enclosing each facial skin region from the input image. From the image, IIC and GGW

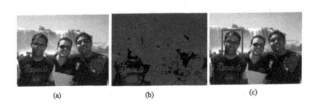

(a)   (b)   (c)

Fig. 2. (a) An input image (b) Illuminant representation (c) Detected copy-pasted face shown in the red box. (Color figure online)

illuminant representations are obtained by the method explained in Carvalho's techniques [3,10]. The IIC is based on the method proposed by Riess and Angelopoulou [10]. The GGW illuminant representation is obtained by applying the method proposed by Van De Weijer [12] on the image partitioned based on similar color [3]. From the illuminant representation, facial regions are extracted and converted to gray scale.

3.2   Extraction of Texture Features

The texture description of illumination pattern from each face is represented by Local Phase Quantization features proposed by Ojansivu and Heikkilä [8]. Here, the Fourier phase information is used. For each pixel in the input image, a neighborhood is considered and is represented in the frequency domain. In the frequency domain, the local frequency coefficients are taken at a set of frequencies. A threshold is used to get a binary representation of value at each of the frequency. The binary codes from the imaginary and real parts are combined to obtain an 8-bit binary code. This code is calculated for all the pixels in the image. The histogram generated from the codes of all pixels in the image is termed as the LPQ descriptor. The LPQ descriptor is generated from the facial illuminant representation of each face in the given image. Each descriptor is a 256 feature vector. For an image as shown in Figs. 2 and 3 LPQ features will be obtained.

3.3   Similarity Comparison and Detection of Copy-Pasted Face

Once the texture descriptors are extracted from the identified facial regions in an image, a similarity comparison is carried out. Since, the 256 bin LPQ can be considered as a distribution, we considered the Bhattacharya distance measure for comparing the similarity [6]. The descriptor obtained from each face will be compared with the descriptor of all the remaining faces. The most distant face from the current face is identified. This process is continued for all the faces and the majority voted distant face will be identified as the spliced face.

4   Experiments and Results

The proposed method is tested on images taken from DSO-I dataset in the tifs-database [3]. The tifs-database contains images in Portable Network Graphics (PNG) with a resolution of $2,048 \times 1536$ pixels. In images with two faces, it is impossible to discriminate the original and a spliced facial region by analyzing facial regions alone. Hence, images with three or more faces are selected resulting in a subset of 55 images, where each image contains at most one spliced facial region.

Performance is evaluated using Precision, Recall and F-Score as defined in Eqs. 1, 2 and 3 respectively,

$$\text{Precision} = \frac{N_{TP}}{N_{TP} + N_{FP}} * 100 \tag{1}$$

$$Recall = \frac{N_{TP}}{N_{TP} + N_{FN}} * 100 \qquad (2)$$

$$\text{F-Score} = 2 * \left(\frac{Precision * Recall}{Precision + Recall} \right) * 100 \qquad (3)$$

where N_{TP} represents the number of spliced faces located correctly, N_{FP} represents number of authentic faces detected as spliced, and N_{FN} represents the number of spliced faces detected as authentic.

Table 1. Experimental results on DSO-I dataset

Dataset	Illumination map	Precision	Recall	F-Score
DSO-I	IIC	61.02	65.45	63.16
	GGW	68.42	70.90	69.64

4.1 Experiments on DSO-I Dataset

For generating LPQ features, the source code provided by the authors [8] was used. The normalized LPQ feature histogram is computed with decorrelated LPQ with 3×3 window size. Gaussian derivative quadrature filter pair is used to compute the local frequency. Finally, the similarity among faces are examined using the Bhattacharya histogram distance measure [6]. When tested on 55 images from DSO-I dataset containing a spliced face, an F-Score of 69.64% is obtained in GGW map and 63.16% is obtained in IIC map as shown in Table 1.

4.2 Experiments with Spatial Pyramid Decomposition

We also evaluated the effectiveness of the proposed method with spatial pyramid decomposition of 1×3 and 2×2 subdivisions. In 1×3 spatial pyramid, the image is divided horizontally into three parts. Then, feature vector is extracted from each of the three parts and later combined to obtain the complete feature vector. In 2×2 spatial pyramid decomposition, the image is divided into 2 horizontal and 2 vertical blocks giving a total of 4 image parts. Feature vectors are extracted from all the sub-blocks and are concatenated to get the complete feature vector. The weights for the feature vector extracted from each sub-part for 1×3 and 2×2 spatial blocks are $1/3$ and $1/4$ respectively. Both 1×3 and 2×2 spatial pyramid decomposition is shown in Fig. 3.

When the whole image is considered without spatial pyramid decomposition we get a 256-bin LPQ descriptor representing the whole image. When 1×3 spatial decomposition is considered, each of the horizontal sub-block generates 256-bin LPQ descriptor and the final feature vector is a concatenation of these 3 feature vectors, resulting in a 768-bin feature vector. Similarly, for the 2×2 spatial decomposition, each of the 2×2 blocks generates a 256-bin LPQ descriptor and the final feature vector is a concatenation of 4 feature vectors, resulting in a 1024-bin feature vector.

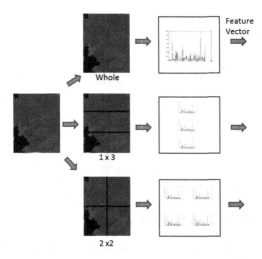

Fig. 3. The feature extraction steps involved in spatial pyramid decomposition.

Table 2 shows the results obtained with 1×3 and 2×2 spatial decomposition along with the results obtained when the feature descriptor from the whole image is used. Both the spatial pyramid decomposition with 1×3 sub-parts and 2×2 sub-parts showed better results in GGW map than in IIC map. However, the results reveal that LPQ descriptor exhibited the best F-Score when the facial region is treated as a whole without spatial decomposition.

While checking 1×3 spatial decomposition, we checked the effectiveness of comparing the facial region as a whole or as sub-parts such as the upper one-third, the middle region, and the lower one-third region. The results obtained for each region separately is shown in Table 3. The highest F-Score of 54.87% is obtained for the lower region from the IIC map. For GGW map, the highest F-Score of 60.72% is obtained for the middle region.

Table 2. Performance comparison of different spatial pyramid decomposition for IIC and GGW maps.

Spatial pyramid or whole	Dimensions	Illumination map	Precision	Recall	F-Score
1×3	708	IIC	61.40	63.63	62.5
		GGW	65.52	69.09	67.26
2×2	1024	IIC	44.83	58.18	50.64
		GGW	45	60	51
Whole	256	IIC	61.02	65.45	63.16
		GGW	**68.42**	**70.90**	**69.64**

Table 3. Performance evaluation for upper, middle, and lower blocks in 1×3 spatial pyramid decomposition is given here.

Illumination map	Block	Precision	Recall	F-Score
IIC	Upper	49.18	54.54	51.72
	Middle	47.46	50.91	49.12
	Lower	53.45	56.36	**54.87**
GGW	Upper	56.14	58.18	57.14
	Middle	59.65	61.82	**60.72**
	Lower	54.39	56.36	55.36

4.3   Comparison with Related Works

The F-Score of LPQ-based proposed method is compared with the existing non-machine learning approaches [13,14] tested on the same set of test images. The performance comparison shown in Table 4 shows that LPQ based proposed method performs better than PCA-based technique [14] and brightness distribution based methods [13].

Table 4. The performance comparison with existing techniques on the dataset DSO-I.

Method	Distance measure		F-Score
Brightness distribution [13]	Bin by bin	Minkowski-form	50
		Chi-square	53
		Bhattacharyya	63
	Cross-bin	Earth Movers Distance	39
		Match	39
		Kolmogorov-Smirnov	37
PCA based [14]	GGW		69
	IIC		64
Proposed method	GGW	Bhattacharyya	**69.64**
	IIC		63.16

5   Conclusion

The proposed spliced face detection technique is based on the texture differences between the spliced and original faces in the illumination representation. A comparison with the related works show that the proposed method performs better than the existing unsupervised approaches of spliced face detection. The method is useful during a digital crime investigation when the digital investigator has to figure out the spliced facial region in a suspect digital image. Another observation is that when analyzing facial regions for texture similarities from illuminant maps, it is good to process the image region as a whole without spatial pyramid decomposition. In the future, decision fusion techniques considering color descriptors along with texture descriptors need to be explored.

Acknowledgments. The authors would like to express their gratitude to Higher Education Department, Government of Kerala, for funding the research and College of Engineering, Trivandrum for providing the facilities.

References

1. Birajdar, G.K., Mankar, V.H.: Digital image forgery detection using passive techniques: a survey. Digital Invest. **10**(3), 226–245 (2013)
2. Carvalho, T., Faria, F.A., Pedrini, H., da Torres, R.S., Rocha, A.: Illuminant-based transformed spaces for image forensics. IEEE Trans. Inf. Forensics Secur. **11**(4), 720–733 (2016)
3. De Carvalho, T.J., Riess, C., Angelopoulou, E., Pedrini, H., de Rezende Rocha, A.: Exposing digital image forgeries by illumination color classification. IEEE Trans. Inf. Forensics Secur. **8**(7), 1182–1194 (2013)
4. Farid, H.: Image forgery detection. Sig. Process. Mag. IEEE **26**(2), 16–25 (2009)
5. Francis, K., Gholap, S., Bora, P.: Illuminant colour based image forensics using mismatch in human skin highlights. In: 2014 Twentieth National Conference on Communications (NCC), pp. 1–6. IEEE (2014)
6. Kailath, T.: The divergence and Bhattacharyya distance measures in signal selection. IEEE Trans. Commun. Technol. **15**(1), 52–60 (1967)
7. Mazumdar, A., Bora, P.K.: Exposing splicing forgeries in digital images through dichromatic plane histogram discrepancies. In: Proceedings of the Tenth Indian Conference on Computer Vision, Graphics and Image Processing, p. 62. ACM (2016)
8. Ojansivu, V., Heikkilä, J.: Blur insensitive texture classification using local phase quantization. In: Elmoataz, A., Lezoray, O., Nouboud, F., Mammass, D. (eds.) ICISP 2008. LNCS, vol. 5099, pp. 236–243. Springer, Heidelberg (2008). https://doi.org/10.1007/978-3-540-69905-7_27
9. Qureshi, M.A., Deriche, M.: A bibliography of pixel-based blind image forgery detection techniques. Sig. Process.: Image Commun. **39**, 46–74 (2015)
10. Riess, C., Angelopoulou, E.: Scene illumination as an indicator of image manipulation. In: Böhme, R., Fong, P.W.L., Safavi-Naini, R. (eds.) IH 2010. LNCS, vol. 6387, pp. 66–80. Springer, Heidelberg (2010). https://doi.org/10.1007/978-3-642-16435-4_6
11. Rocha, A., Scheirer, W., Boult, T., Goldenstein, S.: Vision of the unseen: current trends and challenges in digital image and video forensics. ACM Comput. Surv. (CSUR) **43**(4), 26 (2011)
12. Van De Weijer, J., Gevers, T., Gijsenij, A.: Edge-based color constancy. IEEE Trans. Image Process. **16**(9), 2207–2214 (2007)
13. Vidyadharan, D.S., Thampi, S.M.: Brightness distribution based image tampering detection. In: 2015 IEEE International Conference on Signal Processing, Informatics, Communication and Energy Systems (SPICES), pp. 1–5. IEEE (2015)
14. Vidyadharan, D.S., Thampi, S.M.: Detecting spliced face in a group photo using PCA. In: 2015 7th International Conference of Soft Computing and Pattern Recognition (SoCPaR), pp. 175–180. IEEE (2015)

Fine-Grained, Multi-key Search Control in Multi-user Searchable Encryption

Manju S. Nair[1,2(✉)], M. S. Rajasree[3], and Sabu M. Thampi[4]

[1] College of Engineering, Trivandrum, Thiruvananthapuram 695016, India
manjusnair8@gmail.com
[2] University of Kerala, Thiruvananthapuram 695034, Kerala, India
[3] Government Engineering College, Barton Hill, Thiruvananthapuram 695035, India
rajasree40@gmail.com
[4] Indian Institute of Information Technology and Management Kerala,
Kazhakkoottam 695581, India
sabu.thampi@iiitmk.ac.in

Abstract. Searchable encryption schemes support selective retrieval of encrypted data stored in the cloud storage. However, extending this scheme to support diverse set of users to selectively share and retrieve data from the cloud storage still remains as a challenge; it requires managing the access control policies of the users by a third party, the cloud provider. When multiple users are involved, the system needs to ensure that only controlled information is disclosed to a legitimate user and also a dishonest user colluding with the cloud provider cannot leak any thing beyond the granted privileges. The proposed model is designed to support fine grained search control on selected set of documents by authorized users. The system does not require shared keys or expensive trusted third parties. The search complexity is linear to the number of documents that can be accessed by an authorized user and is also secure against the possible leakage due to collusion attack. The security of the system is proved using rigorous security analysis.

Keywords: Searchable encryption · Search control · Keyword privacy
Bilinear pairing · Multi-key

1 Introduction

Technology advancement has made cloud computing a promising solution that supports high availability of data and resources from anywhere at any time using simple hand held devices. However the major challenge in outsourcing data to the cloud is security and privacy of the data as the data is with the third party, the cloud provider. Encryption ensures [10] security and privacy of outsourced data, but transforms the data so that no computation can be performed on it, including search. Searchable encryption protocols [2,5,6,8] support search on encrypted data without disclosing the search query or any other information about the sensitive data to the cloud provider.

© Springer International Publishing AG 2017
G. Wang et al. (Eds.): SpaCCS 2017 Workshops, LNCS 10658, pp. 814–825, 2017.
https://doi.org/10.1007/978-3-319-72395-2_73

Although several implementation schemes are there to support search on encrypted data, extending such a system to support multiple users to selectively retrieve data still remains a challenge. Providing search control in such a system allows a legitimate user to generate a trapdoor. The trapdoor should not reveal any information about the search query and should be secure against collusion attack. A trivial solution to the problem is to share secret keys to the authorized users. However, key sharing has several disadvantages. Firstly a user needs to keep several keys to access multiple users data. Secondly, secure channels are required for communicating secret keys. Thirdly it makes the user revocation expensive. Finally, the exposure of secret key by a malicious user can leak additional information such as the words searched by other users. Recent techniques like Attribute based encryption (ABE) can provide fine-grained search control. However, most of the ABE schemes require trusted third parties to generate the keys also these keys are lengthy.

2 Motivation

Popa and Zeldovich and Cui et al.'s work in this area sheds some light on the problem discussed above.

Popa and Zeldovich [12] put forward a new direction to address the problem allowing an authorized user to generate a single trapdoor for searching all permitted documents, which are encrypted using different secret keys by an owner. Each document is associated with some public information Δ_{ui} corresponding to each permitted user. The single trapdoor produced by the user is adjusted with Δ_{ui} to perform keyword search on the specific file. Adjusted trapdoor is compared with the encrypted keywords of each file for a match.

Cui et al. [7] in 2016, proposed a method for generating controlled trapdoors using a secret aggregate key. The owner generates an aggregate secret key for each user based on the subset of documents that can be accessed by each user. The aggregate key facilitates the generation of a single controlled trapdoor for searching all permitted documents by a user. The cloud provider using some public parameters converts this single trapdoor to multiple trapdoors for accessing the permitted set of data. However, the trapdoor is malleable, and so a curious adaptive adversary can convert a trapdoor generated by one user to a trapdoor for another user.

Motivated by the above two protocols the present study proposes a searchable encryption scheme supporting fine-grained search control by multiple users without using shared keys. We also analyzed the security threats pointed out in available literature against the above works and made our system secure against such attacks.

3 Problem Statement

In a multiuser environment the owner uploads the documents to the cloud and selectively authorizes other users to access the documents. The proposed system is designed to provide search capability to the right subset of documents and disclose only authorized documents as the search result to the legitimate users with out using shared keys. Providing such fine grained search control needs to address the following security requirements.

- *Query Privacy*: Trapdoor should not provide any information about the search keyword. The trapdoor should not be malleable and should be secure against dictionary attacks.
- *Query Unforgeability*: No other user including the cloud server should be able to generate a valid query on behalf of a legitimate user.
- *Controlled Information Disclosure to the Legitimate Users*: In a multi-user setting, the execution of a query by a legitimate user should return only those documents that are within the privilege level of the specified user even when the keyword is contained in several other documents.
- *Collusion Resistance*: As multiple users are involved, the protocol should ensure that the collusion of malicious users with each other or with the cloud provider leaks nothing beyond the privilege level.
- *User Enrollment and Revocation*: In multi-user settings, there should be efficient mechanisms for new user enrollment and user revocation. It should not affect other authorized users in the system. Moreover, a revoked user should no longer be able to access the data.

4   Related Work

Zhang et al.'s [13] system supports ranked multi-keyword search by multiple users without using shared keys. It employs a trusted administrative server responsible for re-encrypting the index and trapdoor. The granularity of search control is coarse-grained in the sense that an authorized user can search all the documents uploaded. The search complexity linearly varies with the number of documents and the trusted administrator is an expensive entity.

Bouabana-Tebibel and Kaci [4] uses Attribute based encryption (ABE) to encrypt the document-ids in the inverted index. ABE provides access to the right subset of document-ids to the users. A trusted attribute authority is employed to encrypt the index, generate user secret keys, and to provide trapdoors during searching.

Zhu et al. [14] proposes a system to support multi-keyword ranked queries in multi-user searchable encryption scheme without sharing secret keys among authorized users; this avoids the inherent disadvantages of sharing keys. The system provides query privacy to the users not only against the cloud provider but also against data owners by exploring the additive homomorphic encryption property of Paillier crypto system and proves the security. However, for each query the user needs to interact with the owner for the approval.

However most of the systems employed, either shared keys or trusted third parties to provide fine-grained search control. The proposed scheme is designed to support fine-grained search control without using shared keys or expensive trusted third parties.

5   Our Contribution

In this paper we provide a novel, secure and efficient protocol for providing fine-grained search control to a set of users without shared keys. The major contributions are

- Flexible and selective sharing of encrypted data without shared keys or trusted third parties.
- A user can generate a single trapdoor for searching all documents encrypted with different secret keys.

6   Complexity Assumption

Definition 1 (Bilinear Pairing). A bilinear pairing [3] is a map $e : G_1 \times G_2 \mapsto G_T$ with G_1, G_2 being cyclic groups of prime order P. g_1 and g_2 are the generators of G_1, G_2 respectively and the following conditions hold.

1. Bilinearity: $e(g_1{}^a, g_2{}^b) = e(g_1, g_2)^{ab} = e(g_1{}^b, g_2{}^a)\ \forall a, b \in \mathbb{Z}_p^*$.
2. Non-degeneracy: $e(g_1, g_2) \neq 1_{G_T}$ $i.e.,$ $e(g_1, g_2)$ generates G_T.
3. Computability: $e(P, Q)$ is efficiently computable.

Assumption 1 *(CDH Assumption). Given* $(g, g^a, g^b) \in G$ *as the challenge input, the Computational Diffie-Hellman problem is to compute a pair* $g^{ab} \in G$.

We say that the CDH problem is hard if the following probability

$$\epsilon = Pr[(g^{ab}) \leftarrow A(g, g^a, g^b)]$$

is negligible over a random choices of generator $g \in G$, and random choices of a and $b \in \mathbb{Z}_p$ for all adversaries A, who runs in polynomial time at most.

Assumption 2 *(q-SDH Assumption* [3]*). Given* $(g, g^s, g^{s^2}, \ldots, g^{s^q}) \in G$ *as the challenge input, the q-Strong Diffie-Hellman problem is to compute a pair* $(e, g^{\frac{1}{s+e}}) \in \mathbb{Z}_p \times G$ *for a random integer* $e \in \mathbb{Z}_p \setminus \{-s\}$.

We say that the q-SDH problem is hard if the following probability

$$\epsilon = Pr[(e, g^{\frac{1}{s+e}}) \leftarrow A(g, g^s, g^{s^2}, \ldots, g^{s^q})]$$

is negligible over random choices of $s \in \mathbb{Z}_p$ and $g \in G$ for all adversaries A, who runs in polynomial time at most.

7   The Proposed Method

7.1   Problem Definition

The system ensures fine-grained search control to a set of users. Any user in the group can upload encrypted files and authorize other users to perform keyword search on the right subset of permitted documents from the pool. A user can generate a single trapdoor for searching all documents encrypted with different secret keys. A legitimate user receives only those documents that are authorized to him even when the search keyword is present in several other documents. The system also ensures that a malicious user colluding with the cloud provider cannot leak any thing beyond the granted privilege level.

7.2   System Model

We consider a system model with four types of entities.

- Data owner: Encrypts all documents and generates encrypted index and necessary secret parameters to facilitate search by authorized users.
- Set of users: Each user generates a secret key using his private key and owner's public key which is used for producing trapdoors.
- Cloud provider: The cloud provider is assumed to be semi honest, means he will follow the protocol correctly but may try to infer as much information as possible, or may collude with some users and will try to extract more information.
- Documents: Each document is encrypted using unique secret key. An encrypted index is associated with each document to support searching.

Formally, our system consists of the following algorithms:

1. Setup (1^n): Executed by the cloud provider to generate the necessary global public parameter so that every user in the group can generate his own public/private key pair.
2. Keygen (1^n): Executed by the data owner to generate the master secret key, secret keys required to encrypt the documents and parameters to covert user generated trapdoor to document specific tokens.
3. Encrypt (msk, D_i): Executed by the owner to encrypt all documents and index. Keywords in each index file is encrypted using msk and a document specific key.
4. Search-Key-Gen(U_i): Each user U_i in the system generates his own secret key for searching, using his private key and owners public key following Elliptic curve DiffieHellman protocol.
5. Delegate(U): Algorithm executed by the owner of the documents to delegate access rights to the right subset of documents meant for the users.
6. Trapdoor (w, s_i): Executed by user to generate a trapdoor for searching.
7. Search (T_r, U_i): This algorithm is executed by the cloud provider. Using the trapdoor and the parameters provided, the cloud provider returns the documents that are accessible to the user containing the keyword.

8   Concrete Construction

The concrete construction of the frame work discussed above is as follows. Each user in the group generate his own public/private key pair from the public parameters provided.

1. Setup (1^n): We use Elliptic curve DiffieHellman protocol to generate public key /private key pairs. An asymertric Type 2 bilinear map groups is used in encrypting the keywords. The cloud server generates the following public parameters.
   - Public parameters for Elliptic curve DiffieHellman protocol.
   - Initialize a bilinear map group: Public parameters for bilinear mapping.
2. Keygen (1^n): A random $\gamma \in \mathbb{Z}_p$ is used as the msk.

$$msk = \gamma$$

   Also for each document D_i a secret key $d_i \in \mathbb{Z}_p$ and for each user U_i a secret key $u_i \in \mathbb{Z}_p$ is selected.
3. Encrypt (msk, D_i): Algorithm run by the owner to encrypt document D_i and to generate the index file for D_i. Takes k_i for encrypting the document and $t_i \in \mathbb{Z}_p$ as the searchable encryption key for D_i.
   - For each keyword w in the document D_i, outputs the cipher text as

$$c_w = e(H_1(w), g)^{t_i} e(g, g)^{\gamma t_i}$$

4. Search-Key-Gen(U_i): Let x and g^x denote the private/public key pair of owner and s_{u_i} and $g^{s_{u_i}}$ denote the private/public key pair of user U_i.

   User U_i computes $g^{x s_{u_i}}$ using his private key and owner's public key. This will be a point on the elliptic curve, the x coordinate and y coordinate are concatenated and hashed to a point in G_1 as $s_i = H(x||y)$ and is used as the secret key for generating the trapdoor.

$$s_i = H(x||y)$$

5. Delegate(U_i): Algorithm executed by the owner of the documents to delegate access rights to the subset of documents to user U_i.
   - For each user U_i owner computes

$$c = g^{(\gamma + u_i)}$$

   - An access control list is created for U_i. For each document D_i accessible to him an entry (D_i, Δ_i) is created in the list.

$$c_1 = g^{s_i \gamma} g^{(\gamma + u_i)(\gamma + d_i)}, c_2 = g^{(\gamma + d_i) t_i / s_i}, c_3 = g^{t_i / s_i}$$
$$\Delta_i = (c_1, c_2, c_3)$$

6. Trapdoor (w, s_i): The user generates the trapdoor for the keyword w using his private s_i

$$T_r = H_1(w)^{s_i}$$

7. Search (T_r, U_i): Cloud provider use the access control list of user U_i to perform search on the permitted set of documents. For each (D_i, Δ_i) in the list the provider computes $T_d = e(T_r.c1, c3)/e(c, c2)$ and compare it with the encrypted keywords for a match

$$c_w == T_d$$

if true it returns the document D_i to the user.

9   Security Analysis

The security of our system is analyzed in this section. In a multi-user environment the security notions concerning queries are controlled searching, query privacy and query unforgeability.

9.1   Controlled Searching

Entrusting controlled search to a legitimate user involves allowing a user to generate trapdoor to perform search only on the right subset of permitted documents. In the proposed scheme an access control list is provided which contains parameters to convert user generated trapdoor to a search token specific to the document by the cloud provider. The parameters are provided only for permitted documents. Hence cloud provider can produce search tokens only for the permitted set of documents.

Theorem 1. *The proposed scheme supports controlled search by a legitimate user.*

Proof. The cloud provider on receiving trapdoor Tr from the user U_i uses the access control list to determine the list of documents accessible to him. For each document D_i in the list, the cloud provider retrieves Δ_i and computes $e(Tr.c1, c3)/e(c, c2)$ and compares it with the encrypted keywords in the index for a match.

$$
\begin{aligned}
e(Tr.c1, c3)/e(c, c2) &= \frac{e(H_1(w)^{s_i} \cdot g^{s_i \gamma} g^{(\gamma+u_i)(\gamma+d_i)}, g^{t_i/s_i})}{e(g^{(\gamma+u_i)}, g^{(\gamma+d_i)t_i/s_i})} \\
&= \frac{e(H_1(w)^{s_i}, g^{t_i/s_i}) \cdot e(g^{s_i \gamma} g^{(\gamma+u_i)(\gamma+d_i)}, g^{t_i/s_i})}{e(g^{(\gamma+u_i)}, g^{(\gamma+d_i)t_i/s_i})} \\
&= \frac{e((H_1(w), g)^{t_i}) e(g^{s_i \gamma}, g^{t_i/s_i}) e(g^{(\gamma+u_i)(\gamma+d_i)}, g^{t_i/s_i})}{e(g^{(\gamma+u_i)}, g^{(\gamma+d_i)t_i/s_i})} \\
&= \frac{e((H_1(w), g)^{t_i}) e(g^{s_i \gamma}, g^{t_i/s_i}) e(g^{(\gamma+u_i)(\gamma+d_i)}, g^{t_i/s_i})}{e(g^{(\gamma+u_i)}, g^{(\gamma+d_i)t_i/s_i})} \\
&= \frac{e(H_1(w), g)^{t_i} e(g, g)^{\gamma t_i} e(g^{(\gamma+u_i)(\gamma+d_i)}, g^{t_i/s_i})}{e(g, g)^{(\gamma+u_i)(\gamma+d_i)t_i/s_i}}
\end{aligned}
$$

$$= \frac{e(H_1(w),g)^{t_i} e(g,g)^{\gamma t_i} e(g,g)^{(\gamma+u_i)(\gamma+d_i)t_i/s_i}}{e(g,g)^{(\gamma+u_i)(\gamma+d_i)t_i/s_i}}$$

$$= e(H_1(w),g)^{t_i} e(g,g)^{\gamma t_i}$$

$$\overset{?}{=} c_w$$

9.2 Query Privacy and Unforgeability

Query privacy refers to the amount of information leakage during query processing. Unforgeability ensures that no user other than a legitimate user can produce a valid trapdoor for searching.

Theorem 2. *Neither the cloud provider, nor any other user can generate a legitimate query on behalf of an authorized user and the query reveals nothing about the search keyword.*

Proof. A user encrypts the query word as $H_1(w)^{s_i}$, as s_i known only to the owner and the query generator; no one else can infer any data from the trapdoor. In addition, the trapdoor generated for the same keyword by different users are distinct which also ensures query privacy.

  Only user U_i and the owner can compute s_i. The owner of the document can compute $g^{s_{u_i}x}$ using his private key x and user U_i's public key $g^{s_{u_i}}$ as $(g^{s_{u_i}})^x$. Similarly the user U_i can compute $g^{s_{u_i}x}$ using his private key s_{u_i} and owner's public key g^x as $(g^x)^{s_{u_i}}$. By CDH Assumption 1 it is computationally hard for any other user to compute $g^{s_{u_i}x}$ and hence $s_i = H(x||y)$ where x is the x-coordinate and y is the y-coordinate of the point $g^{s_i x}$. Hence the query is unforgeable.

Theorem 3. *An attacker is unable to determine the keyword from the encrypted keywords and the parameters provided*

Proof. Cloud provider may try to infer some information about the keywords from the available parameters. The parameters are

$$c_w = e(H_1(w),g)^{t_i} e(g,g)^{\gamma t_i}$$

$$c = g^{(\gamma+u_i)}, c_1 = g^{s_i \gamma} g^{(\gamma+u_i)(\gamma+d_i)}, c_2 = g^{(\gamma+d_i)t_i/s_i}, c_3 = g^{t_i/s_i}$$

The cloud provider can launch an attack to identify a keyword if and only if he knows the values of t_i and γ. However, from the hardness of discrete logarithm problem, it is computationally hard to determine these values from the given parameters.

Theorem 4. *Collusion of a malicious user with the cloud provider can leak nothing beyond granted privilege level*

Proof. One or more malicious users can collude with the cloud provider and may try to learn information beyond their privilege level. Even though each user can generate the secret key for searching, the cloud provider can convert this trapdoor to a search token for D_i, if and only if the security parameter Δ_i is provided in the access control list by the data owner.

A colluding user can give his secret key s_i to the cloud provider. The parameters $c = g^{(\gamma+u_i)}, c_1 = g^{s_i\gamma}g^{(\gamma+u_i)(\gamma+d_i)}, c_2 = g^{(\gamma+d_i)t/s_i}, c_3 = g^{t_i/s_i}$ are chosen in such a way that it links a document specific secret key d_i to a user secret key u_i. As s_i is known to both U_i and owner, the owner generates his own secret key u_i for each user. Hence leaking s_i will not cause any security threat. Also with s_i the cloud provider is able to compute only g^{t_i} and $g^{(\gamma+d_i)t}$. By q-SDH Assumption 2. It is computationally hard to derive the values of u_i, d_i or γ from the given parameters.

9.3   New User Enrollment and User Revocation

Adding a new user, involves creating an access control list with parameters to support keyword search on the permitted set of documents by the owner. This will not affect any other user in the system. User revocation requires deleting the access control list corresponding to the revoked user, and also re-encrypting the index of all documents that are accessible to him. Re-encryption of index is required as the cloud provider can otherwise use the copy of previously stored parameters even after the access control list corresponding the user is deleted. In our scheme user revocation will not affect other users as it doesn't require redistribution of keys.

10   Experiments and Results

We used Pycharm community IDE and Charm Crypto 0.43 [1] framework, which facilitates rapid prototyping of crypto systems. In addition, we used the open source libraries OpenSSL-0.9, the Pairing-based cryptographic library [11] and GMP multiple precision arithmetic library gmp6.0 [9]. All experiments were performed on Ubuntu 12.04 with Intel core i7-3770 CPU @ 3.4 GHz and 8 GB RAM. We used NIST approved elliptic curve prime192v1 for public/private key generation by the users in the group.

10.1   Efficiency

The main objective of our system is to eliminate shared keys and expensive trusted third parties. Our system achieves constant size keyword cipher-text and a single trapdoor for searching all permitted set of documents by an authorized user. In the access control list, in addition to the document-id, we stored the public parameters c_1, c_2 and c_3 to facilitate search by the cloud provider. This increases the storage requirement only from n to $3n$ at most, where n is the total number of documents. Moreover, the search complexity of our scheme is linear to the number of documents that can be accessed by an authorized user.

Cui et al.'s [7] scheme generates user secret key based on the documents that can be accessed by a user and is given to the user for trapdoor generation.

Our scheme and [7] require two pairing operation for searching a document, but our scheme does not require long sequence of multiplications for computing document specific trapdoor for each document, that are accessible to a user.

Popa and Zeldovich [12] scheme user's secret key is assigned by the data owner and the scheme requires only one pairing operation for searching a single document, but the trade off is between security and efficiency as explained in Sect. 10.2.

10.2   Comparison with the Previous Works

Motivated by the works of Popa and Zeldovich [12] and Cui et al. [7], we developed the proposed system. We also addressed the security pitfalls pointed out in the literature while designing the new system.

In Popa and Zeldovich [12] the trapdoor generated $H(W)^{u_{k_1}}$ is transformed to document specific token using $\Delta = g_2^{(k_1/u_{k_1})}$. A malicious user colluding with the cloud provider can give his secret key u_{k_1} to the cloud provider and the provider can now recover $g_2^{k_1}$ from Δ. With $g_2^{k_1}$ he can compute $e(H(w), g_2^{k_1})$ for any keyword in that document, and can identify the keywords searched by other users. In effect the cloud provider can determine the keywords searched by other users in all the documents that are accessible to the colluding user. The problem is due to the fact that the transformation of trapdoor to document specific token depends only on u_{k_1} and document specific key k_i of which u_{k_1} is known to the user. In our construction, the transformation not only depends on user search key s_i and document specific key t_i but it also depend on the owners master key γ. Hence leaking of user's secret key will not cause the above security threat.

In Cui et al.'s [7] scheme the trapdoor is generated as a product $k_{agg}.H(w)$ and is malleable. A keyword is encrypted as $c_w = e(g, H(w))^t/e(g, g)^t$ in a document. When a keyword match occurs, an adaptive advisory can determine whether the two users are searching for the same keyword in a document, even though the keyword is not known. In such a case he is able to determine k_{agg_i}/k_{agg_j}. With this value he can covert a trapdoor generated by one user to a trapdoor for the same keyword by another user. So if there is collusion, the cloud provider can determine the aggregate keys of other users who had made at least a single query to any of the documents in the malicious user's permitted document list. In our work also the encryption of a keyword in the index is deterministic, but the trapdoor generated $H(w)^{s_i}$ is not malleable.

11   Conclusion

The proposed system supports fine-grained search control in multi-user searchable encryption. The system is flexible enough to support any user to upload encrypted documents to the cloud and permit other users to search, still holding the control of data with him. Each user in the group generates the secret key for search control, eliminating the need for secure channels to communicate secret keys.

The parameters for transforming user defined trapdoor to document specific search token, are derived in such a way that it is secure against collusion attack. A user can use a single trapdoor for searching all the documents encrypted with different secret keys uploaded by the same data owner. However, for accessing multiple user's data, the user has to generate a new secret key and use it for generating trapdoor to access the data. The search complexity is linear to the number of documents that can be accessed by a user.

Acknowledgments. The authors would like to thank College of Engineering Trivandrum for providing facilities to carry out the work and IHRD for sponsoring the research work.

References

1. Akinyele, J.A., Garman, C., Miers, I., Pagano, M.W., Rushanan, M., Green, M., Rubin, A.D.: Charm: a framework for rapidly prototyping cryptosystems. J. Cryptogr. Eng. **3**(2), 111–128 (2013)
2. Bao, F., Deng, R.H., Ding, X., Yang, Y.: Private query on encrypted data in multi-user settings. In: Chen, L., Mu, Y., Susilo, W. (eds.) ISPEC 2008. LNCS, vol. 4991, pp. 71–85. Springer, Heidelberg (2008). https://doi.org/10.1007/978-3-540-79104-1_6
3. Boneh, D., Franklin, M.: Identity-based encryption from the weil pairing. SIAM J. Comput. **32**(3), 586–615 (2003)
4. Bouabana-Tebibel, T., Kaci, A.: Parallel search over encrypted data under attribute based encryption on the cloud computing. Comput. Secur. **54**, 77–91 (2015)
5. Cash, D., Jaeger, J., Jarecki, S., Jutla, C., Krawczyk, H., Rosu, M.C., Steiner, M.: Dynamic searchable encryption in very-large databases: data structures and implementation. In: Network and Distributed System Security Symposium (NDSS 2014) (2014)
6. Chang, Y.-C., Mitzenmacher, M.: Privacy preserving keyword searches on remote encrypted data. In: Ioannidis, J., Keromytis, A., Yung, M. (eds.) ACNS 2005. LNCS, vol. 3531, pp. 442–455. Springer, Heidelberg (2005). https://doi.org/10.1007/11496137_30
7. Cui, B., Liu, Z., Wang, L.: Key-aggregate searchable encryption (KASE) for group data sharing via cloud storage. IEEE Trans. Comput. **65**(8), 2374–2385 (2016)
8. Curtmola, R., Garay, J., Kamara, S., Ostrovsky, R.: Searchable symmetric encryption: improved definitions and efficient constructions. In: Proceedings of the 13th ACM Conference on Computer and Communications Security, pp. 79–88. ACM (2006)
9. Granlund, T., et al.: GNU MP 6.0 Multiple Precision Arithmetic Library. Samurai Media Limited, Thames Ditton (2015)
10. Kamara, S., Lauter, K.: Cryptographic cloud storage. In: Sion, R., Curtmola, R., Dietrich, S., Kiayias, A., Miret, J.M., Sako, K., Sebé, F. (eds.) FC 2010. LNCS, vol. 6054, pp. 136–149. Springer, Heidelberg (2010). https://doi.org/10.1007/978-3-642-14992-4_13

11. Lynn, B.: PBC Library (2006). http://crypto.stanford.edu/pbc
12. Popa, R.A., Zeldovich, N.: Multi-key searchable encryption. IACR Cryptol. ePrint Arch. **2013**, 508 (2013)
13. Zhang, W., Lin, Y., Xiao, S., Wu, J., Zhou, S.: Privacy preserving ranked multi-keyword search for multiple data owners in cloud computing. IEEE Trans. Comput. **65**(5), 1566–1577 (2016)
14. Zhu, Y., Huang, Z., Takagi, T.: Secure and controllable k-NN query over encrypted cloud data with key confidentiality. J. Parallel Distrib. Comput. **89**, 1–12 (2016)

Overview of Performance Evaluation of Keyword Search Utilities in Forensic/E-Discovery Software

Adedayo M. Balogun[(⊠)] and Tranos Zuva

Vaal University of Technology, Vanderbijlpark 1911, South Africa
adedayob@vut.ac.za

Abstract. Digital forensics has been modeled into a number of stages, which include examination and analysis. Keyword search is a popular tactic used by investigators during evidence examination and analysis. However, the belief that the success of forensic analysis depends on the examiner's knowledge and experience has a strong hold in the digital forensic domain. It does imply the adequate awareness of the capabilities and limitations of the tools used by the examiner. Keyword search enables the examiner to quickly locate the existence of data items related to a case. This reduces investigation duration and eases the investigation process. This paper discusses the concepts of keyword search and the various keyword search techniques available. It highlights the algorithms on which they are based. In addition to the overview of, and argument for thorough understanding and evaluation of this technique in forensic utilities, this article also provides evaluation procedures to serve as direction for future evaluation/validation studies to ensure examiners know just how much to trust their software, as far as keyword searching is concerned.

Keywords: Computer Forensics · Electronic discovery · Keyword search
Digital evidence · Forensic software

1 Introduction

Over the years, the importunate obligation to cut cyber-misappropriations in a world teeming with automation has been difficult. The admirability of the dividends of information technology is equally threatened by the crimes associated. There is virtually no digital invention that cannot be abused [1]. The abundance of digital systems in the modern normal environment, as compared to the scarcity in the past, contributes to the exponential growth rate of cybercrime alongside its benefits [2].

Digital Forensics, the resultant process, is obliged to provide solutions to the cybercrime challenge. It is actually a technical component part of electronic discovery, which provides the complete framework for managing the technical, administrative and legal aspects of civil and criminal cases [3]. The Association of Chief Police Officers (ACPO) described it as the use of scientific and technical procedures to collect, examine, analyze and report digital evidences to establish facts about the e-crime under consideration [4]. The examination of a digital evidence is always a critical phase, as

© Springer International Publishing AG 2017
G. Wang et al. (Eds.): SpaCCS 2017 Workshops, LNCS 10658, pp. 826–836, 2017.
https://doi.org/10.1007/978-3-319-72395-2_74

though other phases, but also an intricate one. It usually involves a lot of activities, which certainly always include searching for incriminating data in the evidence [5, 6].

Keyword searching refers to seeking and reporting of all instances where a specified string occurs within a defined population of data [2]. Current investigation tools provide integrated search utilities for forensic examiners. These embedded search utilities are of different types and use various techniques. Ultimately, as every other automaton-based tool that is driven by algorithms, there are limitations in their performances [6]. Investigations may or may not require combination of search utilities for the maximum efficiency to be achieved [2, 7].

This paper has taken on the task to propose the comparison and evaluation of the performances of keyword search utilities that are embedded in popular forensic software. This would help to find out the strengths enjoyed and restrictions tolerated by examiners that use them. In the course of doing this, various keyword search techniques used by the forensic software are discussed. Insights are provided to the theories and applications of keyword search. The algorithms on which the techniques are to be based have also been highlighted. Subsequently, the procedures for analysis and interpretation of the evaluation results are highlighted.

The rest of this paper is organized as follows: Sect. 2 explains the need for undertaking this work. Section 3 provides brief overviews of search methodologies, levels, and strategies. It also describes the prevalent searching validation framework. Section 4 highlights the proposed validation procedures. Lastly, Sect. 5 presents the conclusions and future recommendations.

2 Background and Motivation

Digital evidence is usually a magnetic disk in its physical form, but investigators generally use software to translate the data in it to human-readable form during examination. The software translates the magnetic fields into sectors, and then arrange clusters of sectors as files and folders. Hence, the original layer has been bypassed by abstraction layers used by computer software. It is however a possibility that software developers do not completely understand the systems under consideration. In addition, the software may possess bugs. These shortcomings cause the imperfect interpretation of evidence by the software, and hence, inaccurate conclusions by the investigators [8].

Every electronic discovery process is done with the view of pursuing either a civil or criminal litigation. The legal courts are very particular about the reliability and authenticity of the facts being put forward by the evidence tendered. In response, various methodologies that incorporate the reliability standards are employed by investigators to ensure the admissibility of their evidences in the court. These standards suggest that the investigative tools and methodologies must: (1) be generally acceptable in the forensics field, (2) have been subjected to peer reviews and (3) have been tested scientifically [2].

The ACPO guide's principles and procedures stress the importance of displaying objectivity, continuity and integrity of evidence to the court, through preservation and documentation of investigation activities. This implies the necessity to explicitly demonstrate how the evidence was collected, examined and analyzed since digital evidence can be very easily altered even by the software tools used to process them [4].

In order to conduct a successful investigation, it is important that the examiner possess adequate knowledge about the capabilities, limitations and restrictions of the software employed. This would help to alleviate the interpretation deficiency that may otherwise make the examiner's evidence inadmissible [3].

Tests are being conducted by the Computer Forensic Tool Testing (CFTT) group, to validate certain features offered in forensic software. These tests are supposed to provide examiners with the basic knowledge required about their software. However, it is known that there exist an inexhaustive number of tools and capabilities that can possibly be tested [8]. There exists only a handful or no public tests on forensic software. Examiners are therefore, left with the option of carrying out validation tests on required features in software relied on by themselves [8].

Hence, it has been gathered that the courts require that evidence be properly preserved and documented for reliability and transparency purposes. Investigation methodologies have also yielded to the court's request by ensuring all investigation activities are documented. This includes their validation of the capabilities of the tools employed, in order to satisfy the court's requirements for admitting the evidence. It is also known that a research group has been testing certain features of forensic software, but is limited by the number of features, as well as software available. This has led to the necessity of individual validations for the required features of software by investigators. A validation of the keyword search feature across forensic software should therefore be useful for investigators who need to know the extent to which the keyword search feature of a software can assist in their investigations.

3   Overview

In order to test the functionalities of keyword search utilities, it is pertinent to understand what they do and how they do them. The scope, methodologies, and strategies of search utilities form the basis of how their validations are being carried out [8]. Hence, they have been briefly explained, as they form the basis of the performance evaluations this paper has set out to do.

3.1   Search Levels

The Search level basically refers to the scope of the search being performed. It explains the boundary within which a search on digital evidence is performed. These are the physical and logical levels. A search at the logical level would look through all data in the file system and partition table, while a search at the physical level would look through all data across the entire disk [2]. The physical level search works through every storage space on the disk, and as such, can find data in oblivious locations. Utilities that search at the physical level find patterns in host-protected areas, hidden partitions, unallocated clusters and marked clusters [7, 9]. It is also called the logical file search [5].

The logical level search is a somewhat higher level activity. It performs its searches within the logical structure of the disk, based on references of the master file table (mft). It is able to find data in deleted files, hidden and altered files, file slacks and unallocated spaces on the disk [7, 10]. Because of the way its search is based, it is known as the logical file system search [5]. The ways through which these theories are being exploited to suit forensic examinations would be highlighted in the next section.

3.2   Search Methodologies

The indexing and bit-wise methods are the known techniques for implementing keyword searches [1]. The bit-wise method is a traditional search technique in which the character patterns are compared to all the data on the disk every time [2]. It encompasses the slack spaces and unallocated spaces on the disk, and compares its search string with data in file fragments. This method ensures that the entirety of the storage space is checked. The drawback of the bit-wise methodology stems from carrying out a complete disk comparison every time a search is done [11]. Hence, its turnaround time is quite large, especially when large data is resident on the storage device. The other drawback is its inability to interpret files in native formats, as it reads data only in ASCII format [5]. Such data in files like PDF and XLS are thus omitted during string matching.

The indexing methodology is based on the use of indexes to compare specified search string. This methodology divides the search process into two stages – indexing and actual search. An index is "simply a list of offsets for occurrences of keywords" in the files on the storage device [12]. The indexing part is actually an automated process, and does not require user-intervention. Searches are then performed on examiner's request, by using the index to compare the offsets of the character patterns being sought [5]. The indexes are built from files, and are as such file-based. This allows a search that can compare contents of compressed and native files, which are accessible through the indexes. An undesirable feature of the indexing methodology is the lowly speed of creating its indexes. Searches performed after the initial indexing are quite fast, and make up for lost indexing time if lots of searches would be done eventually [2].

However, [5]'s opinion about the inapplicability of the indexing methodology to forensic purposes is debatable. Reference [5] cited the fact that indexing methodology is file-based and its high start-up index creation cost as the reasons. They mentioned that forensic examiners want to find their data at the physical level and cannot afford the several days of index creation. This has been nullified by the incorporation of both the bit-wise and indexing methodologies by forensic search utilities for more efficient results [11]. The search methodology used by the utility the examiner chooses, would produce different levels of efficiency. Hence, they should be taken note of, and be exploited for maximum results when possible.

3.3   Search Strategies and Features

Search utilities use a number of ways to find different type and forms of data. These ways are referred to as their strategies. Their abilities to use these strategies are known as their features. Certain features are mandatory for search utilities, while others would only enhance their effectiveness. It also helps to prove the thoroughness of examiners' investigations. A number of the strategies are highlighted thus:

Index Searching: This enables an utility to create the index of the entire data to be searched, and compare it with the string being searched for [8].

Boolean Logic Searching: An utility that uses this strategy employs the boolean operators – 'and', 'or', 'not' – to form compound search statements. This is particularly useful to save search time when all keywords are known [8].

Fuzzy Searching: The utility employs a proprietary algorithm to find occurrences of a mis-spelled string. Such utility would find 'Dictionary', even if the examiner spelled it as 'Dictionery', 'Decsionery', or 'Ditionnary' [8].

Character Set Searching: This allows a search to be conducted based on a certain set of characters. Utilities may further have variations to the character sets supported. Unicode and GREP are the most popular sets supported [8].

Wildcard Searching: This allows the utility to find matches of incompletely-specified strings. This occurs when an examiner is not sure about one or more characters in the supposed searched string. Such an utility would find 'proceed' when 'pro*' or 'pro????' is searched [8].

Concept Searching: Such utility can find words that translates in meaning to the string be searched. It is also known as synonym or thesaurus searching [8].

Phonic Searching: This enables the utility to find like-sounding matches of a string.

Proximity & Directed Proximity searching: An utility that uses this strategy can find matches that exist within a specified distance to the string being searched [6].

Numeric Range Searching: This enables the utility to find string matches only within a specified range of numbers.

Stemming/Truncation Searching: An utility that supports stemming or truncation would find words that are different to the specified string, but are formed from the same/similar word. This may help to find data that the examiner could have omitted. It would find 'clothing', 'cloth', 'clothier' and 'clothesline', when the examiner has specified 'clothe' [8].

Nested Searching: This enables an examiner to construct a compound search statement, as oppose a simple search string. Such statement may look like "Bill OR (Wendy AND Thomas)" [11].

Merge Searching: This allows a search utility to combine the results of more than one search operations, and return a result as if it were just a single search operation [11].

Regular Expression Searching: This allows the search utility to find strings specified in the natural language format, as opposed to the ASCII format. It then converts the expression to its ASCII equivalent before searching [8].

Metadata Searching: This requires an utility to find matches of specified strings in the metadata of files [8].

3.4   Prevalent Search Validations

The unavailability of uniformity and standards in the digital forensic field plays a central role to the problems facing tools' acceptability [1]. It is known that the calibration of digital forensic tools is impractical, unlike tools used in other scientific areas like DNA and Ballistics. This is attributable to the existence of indeterminate variables in digital evidences, which are always unique and different [8]. Reference [3] then suggested that the only way to measure the accuracy of digital forensic tools is to test them with known datasets.

Reference [13] suggested that the need to test digital forensic tools have arisen from the diversity of the tools available, and the adaptation of secondary tools for primary forensic tasks. They then stated that the setting aside of the tools' validation task for an acceptable authority would be a critical step at solving the current lack of tools' validations. This could be interpreted as encouraging the Computer Forensics Tool Testing (CFTT) unit of the National Institute of Standards & Technology (NIST) to be considered as the only or major validators and testers of tools, rather than individuals.

It had been explained earlier by [14], that individual investigators would be better off testing the specific features of the tools they needed. This was deemed as too expensive, technical and time-wasting by individual examiners [5]. However, [7, 8] explained the inevitable validations that examiners could perform at more conveniences.

Reference [8] suggested a number of validation techniques ranging from previewing data in a hex-viewer software to repeating an analysis procedure using another tool, in order to ensure tool reliability through obtained results. He also suggested the development of individual test data to check that a tool properly interprets them.

Reference [15] came up with a set of validation procedures for general keyword search utilities. It encompassed the opinion of [8], as it involved the development of known test data and design of search statements to reveal the capabilities and limitations of such keyword search tools.

Carrier's Forensic Tool Keyword Search Test. Reference [15], in his attempt to validate the features of searching utilities, designed a test image. He claimed the goal of his test was to simply establish the ability of a tool to identify several string types. Another search tool validation was conducted in a similar way to [15]'s, and offered similar test coverage [16].

As the image is supposed to be a known data set, he manipulated what was contained in the image. This meant that the location report of the search utility being tested would determine the success of such feature validation.

He placed certain files into specified sectors of the hard disk. He duplicated files and placed them in different other sectors. Reference [7] also fragmented some of the files, and split them into various sectors on the hard disk. Reference [7] also deleted some files on the hard disk, so as to create unallocated spaces on the disk. Reference [7] then added slack spaces to the sectors of some files. The detailed procedures of preparing the image are shown in Fig. 1. Reference [7] used the hex-viewer software to manipulate the data locations in the image.

```
# mkdosfs -s 1 fat-img.dd

Mount the image in loopback:

mount -o loop fat-img.dd /mnt

Copy file1.dat to /mnt (sector 271)
Copy file2.dat to /mnt (sector 272)
Copy file3.dat to /mnt (sectors 273 & 274)
Copy temp.dat as /mnt/file4.dat (sector 275)
Copy file5.dat to /mnt (sector 276)
Open /mnt/file4.dat in a hexeditor to manually extend it and make it fragmented. (sectors 275 & 277)
    o start file (sector 275, offset 0) with 'ck2'
    o end first sector (sector 275, offset 507) with '1frag'
    o start next sector (sector 277, offset 0) with 'ment1'
    o enter random values after 'ment1' to extend the file further.
Copy temp.dat as /mnt/file6.dat (sector 278)
Copy file7.dat to /mnt (sector 279)
Open /mnt/file6.dat in a hexeditor to manually extend it and make it fragmented. (sectors 278 and 280)
    o end the first sector (sector 278, offset 502) with '2fragment' (note the space)
    o begin the second sector (sector 280, offset 0) with 'sentence2'
    o enter random values after 'sentence2' to extend the file furter.
Copy second to /mnt (sector 281)
Delete /mnt/file5.dat (sector 276)
Unmount the image:

# umount /mnt/

Use 'fls' and 'istat' from The Sleuth Kit to identify the sectors that the following files have allocated:
    o file2.dat (272)
    o file3.dat (273, 274)
    o file4.dat (275, 277)
    o second (281)
Open the entire image in a hexeditor to add slack space strings.
Add 'ck1' to byte offset 400 of the sector that file2.dat allocated (272).
Add '1sla' to the final 4 bytes of the last sector that file3.dat allocated (274).
Add '3slack3' to anywhere after 288 bytes of the last sector for file4.dat (sector 277). (the file has a total size of 800 bytes)
Add '3cross3' so that it crosses any two sectors after the sector that 'second' allocated (281)
    o Add '3cro' to sector 283, offset 508
    o Add 'ss3' to sector 284, offset 0
Optional: The entire image is currently random values and therefore will not compress. To make it more portable, find a big area of the image that is
not being used and wipe it with zeros.
Test it.
```

Fig. 1. Search image development process [7].

Num	String	Sector	Offset	File	Note
1	first	271	167	file1.dat	in file
2	SECOND	272	288	file2.dat	in file
	SECOND	239	480	N/A	in dentry - file name
3	1cross1	271	508	file1.dat and file2.dat	crosses two allocated files
4	2cross2	273	508	file3.dat	crosses consecutive sectors in a file
5	3cross3	283	508	N/A	crosses in unalloc
6	1slack1	272	396	file2.dat and file2.dat slack	crosses a file into slack
7	2slack2	274	508	file3.dat slack and file4.dat	crosses slack into a file
8	3slack3	277	385	file4.dat slack	in slack
9	1fragment1	275	507	file4.dat	crosses fragmented sectors
10	2fragment sentence2	278	502	file6.dat	crosses fragmented sectors on ' '
11	deleted	276	230	file5.dat (deleted)	deleted file
12	a7b\c*d$e#f[g^	279	160	file7.dat	regexp values
13	FIrST			should find 'first'	
14	f[[:alpha:]]rst			should find 'first'	
15	f[a-z]r[0-9]?s[[:space:]]*t			should find 'first'	
16	d[a-z].?t.?d			should find 'deleted'	
17	[r-s][[:space:]]?[j-m][[:space:]]?[a-c]{2,2}[[:space:]]?[j-m]			should find '1slack1', '2slack2', '3slack'	
18	[1572943][[:space:]]?fr.{2,3}ent[[:space:]]?			should find '1fragment', '2fragment'	
19	a\??[a-c]\i*[a-c]**			should find a7b\c*	
20	[[:alpha:]]\??z\?y?Q?[a-c]\i*u*[a-c]**d\$[0-9]*e#			should find a7b\c*d$e#	

Fig. 2. Keyword search validation test results [7].

The approach shown in Fig. 1 was able to validate the ability of a search utility to support a number of features, using that image. Those features include: Stemming/Truncation, Nested searching, Merge searching, Wildcard searching, Regular expression searching, Case searching, and Metadata searching, amongst others. His test was also able to check the ability of a search utility to find data from deleted files, fragmented files and slack spaces. Figure 2 shows the strings that were searched to test for various functionalities of a search utility in forensic software.

4 Towards a Solution

4.1 Limitations of Carrier's Tests

The test image was designed to be used on unix systems. This was due to the fact that the tool he was trying to test – The Sleuth Kit (TSK) – is a Unix-based forensic software. Reference [7] is the developer of The Sleuth Kit. This is why he had decided to test his unix-based software rather than windows-based software which are more popular.

The size of the image developed for the validation was practically too small (25 mb), compared with what examiners need utilities to search through. Whereas, the complexities of large data size are known to affect the accuracy of searches [9]. Although, [7] admitted it was only designed for a mild test, rather than extensive one.

The test image was basically designed to only establish whether or not a feature is supported by the software, and not how efficient the tool's features are. The test did not use challenging search statements, which could reveal potential weaknesses a search tool may possess.

The validation involved only twenty different functionalities. There are however much more functionalities that could be tested for in a search utility.

4.2 Proposed Solution

In view of the limitations of [7]'s validation test for search utilities, the proposed work is planned to address the issues of operating system compatibility and test-data size. Hence this work would be an improvement on [7]'s Keyword Search Validation test for forensic search tools. At the same time, the forensic string searching tools testing framework provided by the Computer Forensics Tool Testing group would be adapted.

4.3 Methodology

The validation framework identified the components of a search tool validation to include: 'something to search with', 'someplace to search', 'something to search for', and 'search results' [17].

Something to search with, which is the interface between the examiner and the search utility, refers to the forensic software to be validated.

Someplace to search, within which the search utility performs its search activities, refers to the search image to be developed.

Something to search for, which would instruct the search utility about what to find, refers to the search statements to be designed.

Search results, which returns what the search utility finds, would reveal the capabilities and limitations of the search utility.

4.3.1   Tools and Procedures

The Forensic Software: The 'something to search with' to be used for the evaluation are the EnCase, Forensic ToolKit, ProDiscover, Oxygen, Helix, and SPADA software. The validations of the search utilities in the software would be done using the same test image and search statements. The search statements would be entered into the search query interfaces of these forensic software. Their results would then be compared, so as to interpret their performances.

The Harddisk Image: The 'someplace to search' would be prepared using the same process as [7] employed. A windows-based hexeditor software would be used to manipulate the sector locations, file contents, file sizes, file fragmentations, file availabilities on disk, and slack space availability on the image. The image would be manipulated to test for all of the strategies and features checked by [7] as well as all the strategies highlighted in the earlier section of this paper. The image would be made to the tune of 4 tb, unlike [7]'s 25 mb image. This would ensure that the results of the validations are fair and practical for examiners' considerations [18].

Search Statements: The 'something to search for' would be from two sources - Self-designed and Acquired search statements. They would be used to query the search utilities. The acquired search statements would be adapted from Carrier's search statements. The search statements would be constructed towards revealing the search levels, methodologies, strategies and features supported by the search utilities. There are no standard ways to design search statements [8]. Hence, the statements would be designed as deemed fit by the validator. The important motive is that the statements would request the search utility to return items available on the image.

Search Results: The results of the searches performed would be tabulated and used to draw inferences. These would reveal the fair extents of the capabilities and limitations of the search utilities embedded in the forensic software being compared.

4.3.2   Evaluation

The framework also stated that the requirements of the search utility being tested shall be classified into two:

Basic Requirements:

(1) the results returned by a search query is equal to the match set for the query.
(2) the tool shall perform its search using one or more specified character representations.

Other Requirements: All other functionalities and strategies that an examiner may require that a search utility perform and utilize respectively [17].

This means that any forensic software whose keyword search tool returns the exact number of hits expected, using a minimum of one character set may be passed good enough. However, the tools are likely to do more than the basic requirements. Their efficiencies would be ranked by the number of search features they are able to demonstrate successfully. This would be done after the search results for forensic software have been collected and interpreted.

5 Conclusion and Future Work

This paper has described the importance of keyword searches to forensic examiners' investigations. It also explained the necessity to demonstrate that the evidence is reliable for court admissibility. This included demonstrating that the tools used for the investigation worked as expected and did not alter the evidence. The existence of much more features and software than can be tested by a test group puts the onus on examiners to test their tools themselves. A validation test carried out by Brian Carrier was seen as a good attempt at testing search utilities. However, several limitations to his test are proposed to be addressed in future. This includes developing a larger test image, up to 4 tb. A windows-based hex-editor tool would be used to manipulate the structures, existence and locations of data in the image. The search statements would be made more complex to ensure the search tool's ability to employ the features classified as other requirements by the CFFT. Such future work is supposed to completely reveal the strengths and weaknesses of the keyword search utilities embedded in a minimum of 3 forensic software. It is aimed to give forensic examiners the accuracy ratings of the software they may want to consider for different cases.

References

1. Johnson, T.: Forensic Computer Crime Investigation. Taylor & Francis, Florida (2006)
2. Sheetz, M.: Computer Forensics: An Essential Guide for Accountants, Lawyers and Managers. Wiley, Florida (2007)
3. Casey, E.: Handbook of Digital Forensics and Investigations. Elsevier Academic Press, London (2009)
4. Association of Chief Police Officers: The Good Practice Guide for Computer-Based Electronic Evidence 4th version. http://www.7safe.com/electronic_evidence/ACPO_guidelines_computer_evidence_v4_web.pdf. Accessed 12 Sep 2017
5. Jee, H., Lee, J., Hong, D.: High speed bitwise search for digital forensic system. In: World Academy of Science, Engineering and Technology, vol. 32 (2007)
6. Lee, J.: Proposal for efficient searching and presentation in digital forensics. In: Proceedings of 3rd International Conference on Availability, Reliability and Security, pp. 1–5 (2008)
7. Carrier, B.: NTFS Keyword Search Test #1. Digital Forensic Tool Testing. http://dftt.sourceforge.net. Accessed 25 Aug 2017
8. Casey, E.: Handbook of Digital Forensics and Investigations. Elsevier Academic Press, London (2010)

9. Beebe, N.: Digital forensic research: the good, the bad and the unaddressed. In: Peterson, G., Shenoi, S. (eds.) DigitalForensics 2009. IAICT, vol. 306, pp. 17–36. Springer, Heidelberg (2009). https://doi.org/10.1007/978-3-642-04155-6_2

10. Pollitt, M., Shenoi, S. (eds.): Advances in Digital Forensics, vol. 194. Springer, Orlando (2005). https://doi.org/10.1007/0-387-31163-7

11. Guidance Software: EnCase Essentials: Forensic User Manual Version 8. http://www.guidancesoftware.com/products/ef_index.asp. Accessed 13 July 2017

12. Python Software Foundation: Keyword Searching and Indexing of Forensic Images. http://pyflag.sourceforge.net/Documentation/articles/indexing/index.html. Accessed 17 Aug 2017

13. Beckett, J., Slay, J.: Digital forensics: validation and verification in a dynamic work environment. In: Proceedings of the 40th Hawaii International Conference on System Sciences, pp. 1–10 (2007)

14. Casey, E.: Handbook of Computer Crime Investigation: Forensic Tools and Technology. Elsevier Academic Press, San Diego (2002)

15. Carrier, B.: File System Forensic Analysis. Addison-Wesley, Upper Saddle River (2005)

16. Craiger, P., Pollitt, M., Swauger, J.: Law enforcement and digital evidence. In: Bidgoli, H. (ed.) Handbook of Information Security. Wiley, New York (2005)

17. CFTT: Forensic String Searching Tool Requirements Specification Version 1.0. http://www.cftt.nist.gov/ss-req-sc-draft-v1_0.pdf. Accessed 5 June 2017

18. Garfinkel, S.: Digital forensics research: the next 10 years. Digit. Investig. **7**, S64–S73 (2010)

The 2017 International Symposium on Big Data and Machine Learning in Information Security, Privacy and Anonymity (SPBD 2017)

SPBD 2017 Organizing and Program Committees

1 Organizing Committee

Vasilis Katos	Bournemouth University, UK
Edward Apeh	Bournemouth University, UK
Neetesh Saxena	Bournemouth University, UK
Alexios Mylonas	Bournemouth University, UK

2 Programme Committee

Hongnian Yu	Bournemouth University, UK
Peter Bednar	University of Portsmouth, UK
Huseyin Dogan	Bournemouth University, UK
Paul Yoo	Cranfield University, UK

Distribution Network Topology Reconstruction Method Based on Lasso and Its Supplementary Criterions

Xiaoyu Li[1], Shufang Li[1(✉)], Wenqi Li[2], Shiming Tian[3], and Mingming Pan[3]

[1] Beijing Key Laboratory of Network System Architecture and Convergence, School of Information and Communication Engineering, Beijing University of Posts and Telecommunications, Beijing 100876, China
Lisf@bupt.edu.cn
[2] State Grid Henan Electric Power Company, Jinshui District, Zhengzhou 450052, China
[3] China Electric Power Research Institute, Haidian District, Beijing 100192, China

Abstract. In order to solve the problem of topology reconstruction in distribution network, a new data driven algorithm is proposed, which uses only the timing voltage to reconstruct the un-loopy and loopy distribution network topology without the prior knowledge. Firstly, the topology reconstruction problem is transformed into a convex optimization problem, and the Lasso regularization method is utilized to obtain a sparse correlation coefficient matrix (CCM), which represents the connectivity of the topology. Secondly, the "And" rule is employed to reduce the redundancy of CCM. And then the criterion of the voltage correlation analysis model is adopted as a supplemental criterion to reduce the error rate of CCM. Finally, the topology reconstruction of the distribution network is realized based on the accurate CCM. Simulation results show that the algorithm has high accuracy, universality and low computational complexity.

Keywords: Distribution network · Topology reconstruction · Lasso
"And" rule · Voltage correlation analysis

1 Introduction

With the development of Energy Internet, distribution network is not only power consumption terminal, but also the access carrier of distributed energy. Opportunities and challenges are brought with the rapid access of distributed energy. However, due to the frequent reconfiguration of the distribution network, the complicated routing, and the incomplete installation of the network sensing devices, it is difficult for the traditional method to reconstruct its topology [1–4].

At present, most of the researches on power system topology are limited to the fault identification of network topology transmission, that is, the topology information error caused by deviation of remote signal of switch. For instance, these methods are mainly

© Springer International Publishing AG 2017
G. Wang et al. (Eds.): SpaCCS 2017 Workshops, LNCS 10658, pp. 839–851, 2017.
https://doi.org/10.1007/978-3-319-72395-2_75

the innovation graph approaches [5, 6], the minimum information loss method [7], state estimation of branch current method [8], the load flow calculation method [10]. Since the inadequate distribution network measurement equipment, line parameters are not complete, the methods cannot be directly used for distribution network.

Fortunately, the voltage data of many parts of the distribution network can be monitored with the development of smart grid. In this case, the massive data provide the basis for the data-driven methods. The smart meters at households enable a new opportunity to utilize the timing data to reconstruct topology, which are previously unavailable in electric power industry [9]. One application of using these data is reconstructing the distribution grid topology based on the information theory and Chow-Liu algorithm, but it cannot reconstruct the loopy topology network. The reference [12] shows that neighborhood selection with the Lasso is a computationally attractive alternative method to obtain standard covariance selection for sparse high-dimensional graphs. Lasso algorithm theory and related rules are used to reconstruct the loopy topology, but it ignores the sufficient conditions of using Lasso algorithm, thus it needs more complex supplementary logic rules to improve the accuracy [13, 14].

After considering the physical model and operating mechanism of the distribution network, the Lasso algorithm and its simple and efficient supplementary criterion are firstly proposed for the reconstruction of the distribution network topology. The algorithm only needs the timing voltage of distribution network, which is easy to implement. Furthermore, the algorithm can reconstruct the topology of un-loopy or loopy distribution network topology with different complexity. The proposed algorithm has good accuracy and universality and low computational complexity.

The paper is organized as follows: Sect. 2 introduces the system model and the problem of data-driven topology reconstruction. Section 3 uses a proof to justify that the bus connectivity can be efficiently reconstructed by regularized linear regression, and a detailed algorithm is illustrated as well. The performance of the new method is evaluated in Sect. 4 and the summary is concluded in Sect. 5.

2 System Model

In order to solve the problem of topology reconstruction, we first need to describe the distribution network and its data. A distribution network is defined as a physical network with branches which connect different buses. To utilize the timing data collected by smart meters, for a S-bus system, we construct a graphical model $G = (N, S)$, where $N = \{1, 2, \cdots, p\}$ is the set of the vertices and $S = \{x_{ij}, i, j \in N\}$ represents the set of the unidirectional edges. In our graphical model, a node denotes a bus in the physical layer and is modeled as a random variable U. The edge which connects node i and k denotes the statistical dependence between the measurements collected at bus i and k. The physical network and the graphical model can be visualized in Fig. 1. At time t, the noiseless voltage measurement at bus τ is $v_\tau^t = |v_\tau^t| e^{j\theta_\tau^t} \in \mathbb{C}$, where $|v_\tau^t| \in \mathbb{R}$ expresses the voltage magnitude in per unit and $\theta_\tau^t \in \mathbb{R}$ denotes the voltage phase angle in degree. The measurements are in the steady state and all voltages are sinusoidal signals at the same frequency.

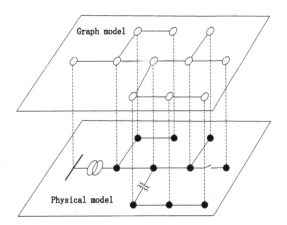

Fig. 1. A physical network with a graphical model layer.

3   Topology Reconstruction Algorithm

3.1   Conditional Independence Analysis

The structures of topology are divided into un-loopy and loopy type. The un-loopy network can be abstracted as a tree. Its topology is relatively easy to reconstruct because of the quantitative relationship between its edge and nodes. However, the loopy structure contains the bus in interconnection. Therefore, it is prone to the problem of incorrect connection between buses. Essentially, the problem of un-loopy reconstruction is a sub-problem of the loopy reconstruction problem. Wherefore, the problem of loopy topology reconstruction is analyzed directly.

In our graphical model, buses are modeled as random variables. Therefore, we use a joint probability distribution to represent the interdependency among buses:

$$P(U_N) = P\big(U_2, U_3, \ldots, U_p\big) = P(U_2)P(U_3|U_2)\ldots P\big(U_p|U_2, \ldots, U_{p-1}\big) \tag{1}$$

Bus 1 is the slack bus, which is a constant with unity magnitude and zero phase angle. Thus, it is omitted from the joint probability distribution above.

In a distribution grid, the correlation relationship between interconnected neighbor buses are higher than that between non-neighbor buses. Therefore, a reasonable approximation is:

$$P(U_N) \simeq \prod\nolimits_{\tau=2}^{p} P\big(U_\tau|U_{F(\tau)}\big) \tag{2}$$

where set $F(\tau)$ represents the neighbor set of bus τ.

Theorem 1. In a distribution grid, if the change of the current injection ΔI at each bus is approximately independent, the voltage changes of bus τ and the voltage changes of all other buses which are not connected with bus τ are conditionally independent, given the voltage changes of the neighbors of bus τ, i.e.:

$$U_\tau \perp \{U_n, n \in N\backslash\{F(\tau),\tau\}\}|U_{F(\tau)} \tag{3}$$

where expression $\backslash$ represents the logical operation of this expression display written as:

$$\mathcal{A}\backslash\mathcal{B} = \{i \in \mathcal{A}, i \notin \mathcal{B}\} \tag{4}$$

Proof: In this proof, we will firstly show the conditional independence for 8-bus system. Then, the conditional independence in generalized distribution networks will be proved in the following parts.

For the 8-bus graph model in Fig. 2, the circuit equation $YV = I$ is equivalent to:

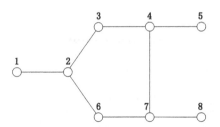

Fig. 2. Bus-8 distribute network system

$$\begin{bmatrix} y_{11} & -y_{12} & 0 & 0 & 0 & 0 & 0 & 0 \\ -y_{21} & y_{22} & -y_{23} & 0 & 0 & -y_{26} & 0 & 0 \\ 0 & -y_{32} & y_{33} & -y_{34} & 0 & 0 & 0 & 0 \\ 0 & 0 & -y_{43} & y_{44} & -y_{45} & 0 & -y_{47} & 0 \\ 0 & 0 & 0 & -y_{54} & y_{55} & 0 & 0 & 0 \\ 0 & -y_{62} & 0 & 0 & 0 & y_{66} & -y_{67} & 0 \\ 0 & 0 & 0 & -y_{74} & 0 & -y_{76} & y_{77} & -y_{78} \\ 0 & 0 & 0 & 0 & 0 & 0 & -y_{87} & y_{88} \end{bmatrix} \begin{bmatrix} V_1 \\ V_2 \\ V_3 \\ V_4 \\ V_5 \\ V_6 \\ V_7 \\ V_8 \end{bmatrix} = \begin{bmatrix} I_1 \\ I_2 \\ I_3 \\ I_4 \\ I_5 \\ I_6 \\ I_7 \\ I_8 \end{bmatrix} \tag{5}$$

where admittance matrix is Y, V is the voltage, and I represents the current. $y_{ij} = y_{ji}$ denotes the deterministic admittance between bus i and j, and the self-admittance is defined as $y_{ii} = \sum_{j=1,j\neq i}^{8} y_{ij}$. If $y_{ii} = 0$, there is no branch between bus i and j.

For bus 3, the neighbor set $N(3)$ is $\{2,4\}$. Given $V_2 = v_2$, $V_4 = v_4$, we have following equations:

$$I_1 + v_2 y_{12} = V_1 y_{11} \tag{6}$$

$$I_3 + v_2 y_{23} + v_4 y_{34} = V_3 y_{33} \tag{7}$$

$$I_5 + v_4 y_{45} = V_5 y_{55} \tag{8}$$

$$I_6 + v_2 y_{26} = V_6 y_{66} - V_7 y_{67} \tag{9}$$

$$I_7 + v_4 y_{47} = V_7 y_{77} - V_6 y_{67} - V_8 y_{78} \tag{10}$$

$$I_8 = V_8 y_{88} - V_7 y_{78} \tag{11}$$

For bus 1, due to the assumption of current injection independence $I_1 \perp I_3$, V_1 and V_3 are conditionally independent when V_2 and V_4 are given.

Let's extend the proof to a more general case. For a grid with N buses, the current and voltage relationship of bus s can be written as:

$$I_s + \sum_{i \in N(s)} V_i y_{si} = V_s y_{ss}. \tag{12}$$

Given $V_i = v_i$, for all bus $i \in N(s)$, the equation above can be written as:

$$I_s + \sum_{i \in N(s)} v_i y_{is} = V_s y_{ss} \tag{13}$$

If bus k, which is not connected with bus s, i.e., $k \in S \backslash \{N(s), s\}$, we have a similar equation:

$$I_k = V_k y_{kk} - \sum_{j \in N(k)} V_j y_{jk} \tag{14}$$

The relationship between the neighbor sets $N(s)$ and $N(k)$ can be divided into two scenarios.

(1) When $N(s) \cap N(k) = \emptyset$, Eq. (14) remains the same. Therefore, V_s and $\{V_k, V_{N(k)}\}$ are conditionally independent given $V_{N(s)}$.

(2) When $N(s) \cap N(k) \neq \emptyset$, Eq. (14) becomes Eq. (15):

$$I_k + \sum_{j \in N(s) \cap N(k)} v_j y_{kj} = V_k y_{kk} - \sum_{j \in N(k) \backslash N(s)} V_j y_{kj} \tag{15}$$

where V_s and $\{V_k, V_{N(k) \backslash N(s)}\}$ are conditionally independent given $V_{N(s)}$.

In conclusion, given $V_{N(s)}$, V_s and $\{V_k, V_{S \backslash \{N(s), s\}}\}$ are conditionally independent.

Based on the above analysis, it can be seen that the generators of Eq. (2) can be approximated by the assumption that the bus is only statistically relevant only with the adjacent bus. Therefore, Eq. (2) can be rewritten as:

$$P(U_N) = \prod_{\tau=2}^{p} P(U_\tau | U_{F(\tau)}) \tag{16}$$

Further, the core task of topology reconstruction is to find the neighbor set $F(\tau)$ of the bus τ, then, we need to select an efficient algorithm to find the neighbor set of each bus.

3.2   Lasso Algorithm + "And" Rule

Tt is assumed that U_N to follow a multivariate Gaussian distribution, the conditional distribution of $U_{N\setminus\{\tau\}}$ also follows a Gaussian distribution when the bus τ is given. Based on the Gaussian probability density function, Eq. (16) can be described by a linear equation based on $U_{N\setminus\{\tau\}}$ and $E_{N\setminus\{\tau\}}$, as shown below:

$$U_\tau = U_{N\setminus\{\tau\}}^T \beta^\tau + E_{N\setminus\{\tau\}} \tag{17}$$

where $U_{N\setminus\{\tau\}}$ represents the set of variables that do not contain bus τ, T denotes the transpose operator. In this linear equation, β^τ denotes the associated parameter vector of bus τ, $E_{N\setminus\{\tau\}}$ is the zero mean error term. The coefficients of nonzero in the vector β^τ indicate the degree of association between the associated nodes. Therefore, the problem of finding neighbor set of bus τ can be transformed into the correlation coefficient vector β^τ of bus τ.

A typical distribution grid is not fully connected. Therefore, the graph is sparse and many coefficients in β^τ are zero. A widely used constraint is L1 norm to ensure the sparsity because it leads to a convex optimization problem and can be solved efficiently. This type of problem is also known as Lasso [15]. It minimizes the sum of squared errors with a bound on the sum of the absolute values of parameters (L1 norm). With L1 norm penalty and N measurements, the linear regression in Eq. (17) is formulated as:

$$\widehat{\beta^\tau} = \underset{\beta^\tau(1)=0}{\arg\min}\{\sum_{t=1}^{N} (u_\tau^t - (\mathbf{u}_{N\setminus\{\tau\}}^t)^T \beta^\tau)^2 + \lambda \|\beta^\tau\|_1\} \tag{18}$$

where $\|\beta_1\|$ denotes L1 norm of β. $\lambda \geqslant 0$ is the regularization parameter.

The selection of the regularization parameter λ is critical because it affects the number of non-zero coefficients in β. When λ is small, the influence of penalty term is slight and feasible solution is close to the feasible solution of least squares method. When λ is large, the large number of β is zero, resulting in excessive sparse compression of the matrix. Therefore, finding the best regularization parameter λ is the key to solve the Lasso problem reasonably, and the optimal solution can be calculated as:

$$\lambda^\tau(\alpha) = \frac{2\widehat{\sigma_\tau}}{\sqrt{N}} \tilde{\phi}^{-1}(\frac{\alpha}{2p^2}) \tag{19}$$

where $\tilde{\phi} = 1 - \phi$ is the c.d.f. of $\mathcal{N}(0,1)$ and $\widehat{\sigma}_\tau^2$ is the empirical variance of timing voltage of bus τ. The probability of falsely joining two distinct connectivity components with the estimate of the edge set is bounded by the level α under the choice $\lambda = \lambda(\alpha)$ of the penalty parameter [12].

By solving the Lasso problem, we obtain the β^τ corresponding to the bus τ. The nonzero elements in β^τ indicate that the bus τ is connected to the bus of the corresponding element, and the sparse vector of each bus forms CCM.

Since the sparseness of CCM is not enough at this time, and it is an asymmetric problem, the relationship coefficients β_i^j and β_j^i between the bus i and j may not be zero at the same time. However, the direction of the distribution network topology is essentially non-directional, and the relationship between the bus i and j should only be unique. In this case, we chose to use the "And" rule to reduce the redundancy of CCM, as shown in the following equation:

$$e_i^j = \beta_i^j \wedge \beta_j^i \tag{20}$$

where the symbol $\wedge$ denotes logic and operation. If one of β_i^j and β_j^i is zero, then the correlation coefficient between bus i and bus j should be zero.

3.3 Supplementary Criterion

The "And" rule improves the accuracy of CCM in a certain level, but the Lasso algorithm satisfies the sufficient condition in solving the sparse matrix, otherwise it cannot optimize the convergence to the only feasible solution. Therefore, it is inherently possible to calculate erroneously CCM for Lasso algorithm [16–18].

Theorem 2. If β_τ is a feasible solution that obeys Eq. (21), then β_τ is the unique solution to both L0 and L1 minimization.

$$\|\beta_\tau\|_0 < \frac{1}{2}\left(1 + \frac{1}{\mu(\mathbf{A})}\right) \tag{21}$$

where $\|\beta_\tau\|_0$ denotes the number of neighbor set of bus τ.

For matrix $\mathbf{A} = \left[u_1, u_2, \cdots, u_p\right] \in \mathbb{C}^{p \times T}$, the mutual coherence of $\mathbf{A}$ is defined by:

$$\mu(\mathbf{A}) = \max_{1 \leq i,j \leq p, i \neq j} \frac{|u_i * u_j|}{\|u_i\|\|u_j\|} \tag{22}$$

where $\mu(\mathbf{A})$ represents the maximum cosine similarity between any bus voltage.

In conclusion, it can be seen from the expression of sufficient condition that the sufficient condition requires that the maximum cosine similarity between any buses should be lower when the number of neighbor set of any bus is raised. When the number of bus contained in the distribution network is larger, the neighbor set of the bus will be larger, and the sufficient condition of Lasso algorithm will be more difficult to meet. If the sufficient conditions cannot be met, the result of topology reconstruction will be wrong at some level. In this case, neighbor elements with multiple neighbors are incorrectly connected to adjacent nodes of adjacent nodes. Therefore, it is necessary for topology reconstruction to find more stringent supplemental criterions to ensure its correctness.

In order to further improve the accuracy of the algorithm, the criterion of the voltage correlation analysis model is employed as a supplemental criterion to extract the elements of the sparse CCM by satisfying the sufficient conditions of Lasso, so as to further improve the accuracy. The criterion $\mathbf{K}$ matrix is as follows:

$$K_{ij} = \begin{cases} > 0 & if\ i = j \\ < 0 & if\ i \sim j \\ > 0 & if\ \exists k \in V\ \ i \sim k\ and\ k \sim j \\ = 0 & otherwise \end{cases} \tag{23}$$

The $\mathbf{K}$ matrix is a symmetric matrix, where the connectivity element between bus i and j is K_i^j. If the bus i and j are directly connected, it can be obtained that $K_i^j < 0$. If bus i and j are separated by a connection or $i = j$, then it can be obtained that $K_i^j > 0$. In the other case, it can be obtained that $K_i^j = 0$.

The supplementary criterion requires that the logical connection relation detected by the element e_i^j of the "And" rule must be consistent with the logical connection relation described by the element K_i^j of the $\mathbf{K}$ matrix.

Let Λ be a positive semidefinite matrix. There exists a unique symmetric, positive semidefinite matrix $\mathbf{K} \in \mathbb{R}^{n \times n}$ such that:

$$\begin{cases} K\Lambda = I - 1_0 1^T \\ K1 = 0 \end{cases} \tag{24}$$

where Λ denotes the covariance matrix of the bus voltage, and I is the unit matrix, and 1_0 is the column vector whose first element is 1 and the remaining elements are zero, and 1 is the column vector of all 1. The calculation process is omitted due to space constraints, and can be found in the online extended version of the paper [11].

The relationship between the buses analyzed by the voltage correlation analysis model is more independent than the relationship computed by the Lasso algorithm because the branch elements are involved in the voltage correlation analysis model. Therefore, the voltage correlation analysis model is not sensitive to the size of the neighbor set of any bus, and does not reconstruct the wrong topology even though the neighbor set of any bus has more elements. In conclusion, $\mathbf{K}$ matrix criterion performance from voltage correlation analysis model can be better fit Lasso algorithm, as its supplementary conditions.

3.4   L&C Algorithm Summary

Through the above analysis, the core steps of topology reconstruction are summarized as L&C algorithm. The algorithm description and flow chart are as follows:

L&C Algorithm

Require: $|u_\tau^t|$ for $\tau = 2, 3, \cdots, p, \quad t = 1, 2, \cdots, T$

---

1. Normalize and standardize ΔVi such that it has a zero mean and a unity variance on real and imaginary parts.

2. **for** $\tau = 2, 3, \cdots, p$ **do**

   Solve the Lasso optimization problem for bus τ and find the parameter vector $\widehat{\beta^\tau}$

   end

3. Combine the relationship vector β of each bus to constitute CCM.

4. Upper triangular matrix and lower triangular matrix of CCM perform "and" operation to get **E** matrix

5. Calculate the covariance matrix of $|U_s|$ to solve the **K** matrix.

6. Use the **K** criterion to remove the error elements of the **E**.

7. The bus corresponding to non-zero elements of CCM are connected to reconstruct the distribution network topology.

---

4 Case Analysis

On the basis of the MATPOWER module of MATLAB, the 8-bus, 14-bus, 33-bus, 69-bus, 84-bus, 119-bus power distribution system is simulated [19]. In order to verify the universality and correctness of the algorithm to reconstruct the topology, the above-mentioned power distribution systems are equipped with an un-loopy and loopy type. In this paper, we set the active power (p_s^t) and reactive power (q_s^t) of the timing random variables to produce the timing voltage of each bus, and their ratio $(p_s^t/p_{init}, q_s^t/q_{init})$ with the initial value of the system (p_{init}, q_{init}), which are consistent with uniform distribution U(0.95, 1.05).

In order to unify the performance of the L&C algorithm in each model, we propose the error rate ER as follows:

$$ER = \left(\frac{\sum 1\left(s_{i,j} \notin S\right) + \sum 1\left(s_{i,j} \in \tilde{S}\right)}{|S|} \right) \tag{25}$$

in which, 1(expression) means that it will equal 1 if the expression holds. S represents the set of edges of the network, $\tilde{S}$ represents the set of edges of the non-network, $|S|$ represents total number of sides which do not connect to the transformer. ER is equal to the ratio of the total number of unconnected sides and wrong connected sides and the total number of the original topology sides.

For bus-33, the graph model is shown in Fig. 3. The density diagram of the CCM calculated by the L&C algorithm is shown in Fig. 4. Coefficients of CCM vary from small to large corresponding colors from white to dark orange. It can be seen from Fig. 4 that the correlation coefficients of the unconnected bus are zero, and the correlation coefficient of the connected bus is greater than zero, and the correlation coefficient is also increased with the increase of the correlation degree.

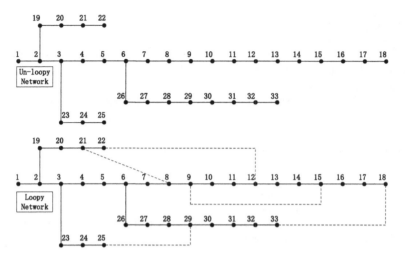

Fig. 3. Un-loopy and loopy 33-bus diagram model

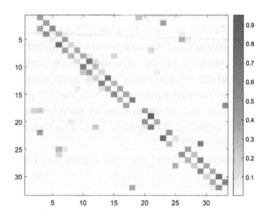

Fig. 4. Density diagram of CCM calculated by the L&C algorithm (Color figure online)

From the analysis of Table 1, it can be seen that the supplementary criterion added on the basis of the Lasso + "And" rule is valid. The supplemental criterion reduces the error rate and applies to both un-loopy and loopy networks.

In order to prove the universality and accuracy of the L&C algorithm and to consider the influence of the time sequence length of the input data on the algorithm, we test the contents of the design of Table 2 respectively. From the comparison and analysis of Table 2, we can see that the error rate of algorithm reconstruction is increasing with the increase of network complexity when the same time data is obtained, such as 720 time points. But with the time to acquire data becomes longer, the algorithm can guarantee the correct topology reconstruction. The essential reason is that in the reconstruction of complex networks, if the amount of input timing data is too small, the algorithm will be less than fit.

Table 1. Reconstruction of 33-bus topology error rate comparison table when each algorithm got same time (720 dots) voltage data

Algorithm name	Network type	
	33-bus un-loopy network	33-bus loopy network
Lasso + "and"	6.45%	15.79%
L&C	0.0%	0.0%

Table 2. Reconstruction of the error rate of each distribution network topology when the L&C algorithm obtains voltage data at different timing lengths

Network	Type					
	Un-loopy network			Loopy network		
	720	1440	4320	720	1440	4320
8-bus	0.0%	0.0%	0.0%	0.0%	0.0%	0.0%
14-bus	0.0%	0.0%	0.0%	0.0%	0.0%	0.0%
33-bus	0.0%	0.0%	0.0%	0.0%	0.0%	0.0%
69-bus	1.53%	0.0%	0.0%	1.33%	0.0%	0.0%
119-bus	6.14%	5.26%	0.0%	6.06%	5.30%	0.0%

From the perspective of the actual demand, the algorithm can reconstruct the topology by sliding window mode, and compare the reconstruction topology with the original topology to realize dynamic topology identification.

5 Summary

On the basis of the timing voltage data of the smart meters, firstly, the multi-dimensional Gaussian distribution model between the bus is established by analyzing the condition independence among the bus, and then the topology reconstruction problem of the distribution network is transformed into the linear regression problem between the buses. Then solve problems with Lasso algorithm to get the CCM of the distribution network. Contrary to the shortcoming of the Lasso algorithm for solving the linear regression problem, we propose supplemental criterion to correct CCM. Finally, the topology reconstruction of the distribution network is realized based on the accurate CCM. The proposed algorithm in this paper has the following characteristics:

(1) Easy to implement, without any prior conditions, the distribution network bus timing voltage data is used only to complete the topology reconstruction.
(2) High accuracy, the algorithm can converge to the optimal solution, and the accuracy of topology reconstruction is close to 100%.
(3) Universality, it can be reconstructed with different complexity of the distribution network, and distribution network topology can be either un-loopy or loopy type.
(4) Efficiency, the algorithm of the model is low in complexity, and can use the shorter time-series data to complete the topology reconstruction.

This paper is aimed at the reconstruction of single source distribution network, and it is necessary to study the reconstruction of multi-source distribution network on the basis of further improving L&C algorithm. Based on the new data-driven method, the topology reconstruction technology of distribution network is an important part of intelligent grid.

Acknowledgments. This work is supported by the Natural Science Foundation of China (Grant No. 61672292 and No. 61300162), and the State Grid Corporation 2016 science and technology project: Service information based business integration and data sharing service technology.

References

1. Ma, Z., Zhou, X., Shang, Y., Zhou, L.: Form and development trend of future distribution system. Proc. CSEE **35**(6), 1289–1298 (2015)
2. Wang, C., Li, P.: Development and challenges of distributed generation, micro - network and intelligent distribution network. Autom. Electr. Power Syst. **2**, 10–14 (2010)
3. Xu, S., de Lamare, R.C., Poor, H.V.: Dynamic topology adaptation for distributed estimation in smart grids. In: IEEE 5th International Workshop on Computational Advances in Multi-Sensor Adaptive Processing, CAMSAP 2013, pp. 420–423. IEEE (2013)
4. Clement-Nyns, K., Haesen, E., Driesen, J.: The impact of charging plug-in hybrid electric vehicles on a residential distribution grid. IEEE Trans. Power Syst. **25**(1), 371–380 (2010)
5. Zhou, S., Liu, Z.: An innovation graph approach to topology error identification. Autom. Electr. Power Syst. **24**(4), 23–27 (2000)
6. Zhou, S., Liu, Z.: Identification of multiple dynamic network structure changes by the innovation graph approach. Proc. CSEE **21**(10), 67–72 (2001)
7. Sun, H., Gao, F., Zhang, B., Yang, Y.: Application of minimum information loss based state estimation to topology error identification (2005)
8. Baran, M.E., Jung, J., McDermott, T.E.: Topology error identification using branch current state estimation for distribution systems. In: 2009 Transmission and Distribution Conference and Exposition, Asia and Pacific, pp. 1–4. IEEE (2009)
9. Weng, Y., Negi, R., Ilic, M.: Historical data-driven state estimation for electric power systems. In: IEEE International Conference on Smart Grid Communications, pp. 97–102, October 2013
10. Arghandeh, R., Gahr, M., von Meier, A., et al.: Topology detection in microgrids with micro-synchrophasors. In: 2015 IEEE Power and Energy Society General Meeting, pp. 1–5. IEEE (2015)
11. Bolognani, S., Bof, N., Michelotti, D., et al.: Identification of power distribution network topology via voltage correlation analysis. In: IEEE Conference on Decision and Control, pp. 1659–1664. IEEE (2013)
12. Meinshausen, N., Bühlmann, P.: High-dimensional graphs and variable selection with the Lasso. Ann. Stat. 1436–1462 (2006)
13. Liao, Y., Weng, Y., Rajagopal, R.: Urban distribution grid topology reconstruction via Lasso. In: Power and Energy Society General Meeting, pp. 1–5. IEEE (2016)
14. Liao, Y., Weng, Y., Liu, G., et al.: Urban distribution grid topology estimation via group Lasso (2016)
15. Jones, M.C., Pewsey, A.: Bayesian Lasso regression. Biometrika **96**(4), 835–845 (2009)
16. Donoho, D.L., Huo, X.: Uncertainty principles and ideal atomic decomposition. IEEE Trans. Inf. Theory **47**(7), 2845–2862 (2001)

17. Elad, M., Bruckstein, A.M.: A generalized uncertainty principle and sparse representation in pairs of bases. IEEE Trans. Inf. Theory **48**(9), 2558–2567 (2002)
18. Donoho, D.L., Elad, M.: Optimally sparse representation in general (nonorthogonal) dictionaries via $\ell 1$ minimization. Proc. Natl. Acad. Sci. **100**(5), 2197–2202 (2003)
19. Ahmadi, H.: Distribution test systems for reconfiguration. http://www.ece.ubc.ca/~hameda/downloads.htm. Accessed 24 June 2017

Author Index

Printed in the United States
By Bookmasters